D1285451

AMERICAN EDUCATION

Its Men,

Ideas,

and

Institutions

Advisory Editor

Lawrence A. Cremin
Frederick A. P. Barnard Professor of Education
Teachers College, Columbia University

AMERICAN EDUCATION: *Its Men, Ideas, and Institutions*
presents selected works of thought and scholarship that have
long been out of print or otherwise unavailable. Inevitably, such
works will include particular ideas and doctrines that have been
outmoded or superseded by more recent research. Nevertheless,
all retain their place in the literature, having influenced educational thought and practice in their own time and having provided
the basis for subsequent scholarship.

HISTORY

OF

THE PUBLIC SCHOOL SOCIETY

OF THE

CITY OF NEW YORK.

WITH

PORTRAITS OF THE PRESIDENTS OF THE SOCIETY.

BY

WM. OLAND BOURNE, A.M.

ARNO PRESS & THE NEW YORK TIMES
*New York * 1971*

Reprint Edition 1971 by Arno Press Inc.

Reprinted from a copy in
   The State Historical Society of Wisconsin Library

American Education:
   Its Men, Ideas, and Institutions - Series II
ISBN for complete set: 0-405-03600-0
See last pages of this volume for titles.

Manufactured in the United States of America

Library of Congress Cataloging in Publication Data

Bourne, William Oland.
   History of the Public School Society of the
City of New York.
   (American education: its men, ideas, and
institutions. Series II)
   1. Public School Society of New York.
2. New York (City)--Public schools. I. Title.
II. Series.
LA339.N5B68 1971   370.19'31   79-165733
ISBN 0-405-03601-9

HISTORY

OF

THE PUBLIC SCHOOL SOCIETY

OF THE

CITY OF NEW YORK.

DE WITT CLINTON.

HISTORY

OF

THE PUBLIC SCHOOL SOCIETY

OF THE

CITY OF NEW YORK.

WITH

PORTRAITS OF THE PRESIDENTS OF THE SOCIETY.

BY

WM. OLAND BOURNE, A.M.

———

NEW YORK:
WM. WOOD & CO., 61 WALKER STREET.
LONDON: SAMPSON LOW, SON & CO., 188 FLEET STREET.
BERLIN: STILKE & VON MUYDEN, LINDEN N°. 21.
PARIS: GUSTAVE ROSSANGE, 25 QUAI VOLTAIRE.
———
1870.

TO

George T. Trimble,

THE LAST PRESIDENT OF THE PUBLIC SCHOOL SOCIETY,

WHOSE SERVICES

DURING THE LONG PERIOD OF THIRTY-FIVE YEARS

WERE DEVOTED

TO THE INTERESTS OF POPULAR EDUCATION IN NEW YORK:

TO

The Trustees and Members of the Public School Society

AND TO

THE FRIENDS OF COMMON SCHOOL EDUCATION

INDEPENDENT OF SECTARIAN CONTROL,

THIS VOLUME

IS DEDICATED BY

THE AUTHOR.

PREFACE.

THE HISTORY OF THE PUBLIC SCHOOL SOCIETY OF THE CITY OF NEW YORK, presented in this volume, has been prepared in compliance with the request of the Society, and the repeatedly expressed wishes of numerous friends of the cause of public education. At the last meeting of the Society previous to its dissolution, held on July 22, 1853, a resolution was adopted authorizing " the President and Agent to place at the disposal of a competent writer such documents in possession of the Society as illustrate its rise, progress, and history." This resolution was not acted on until the close of 1854, when a very numerously attended meeting was held, at which a committee of five was appointed to superintend the work, and under whose revision it should be finally submitted to the public. This committee consisted of GEORGE T. TRIMBLE, the President, JOSEPH B. COLLINS, the Secretary, SAMUEL W. SETON, the Agent of the Society, Assistant Superintendent of Common Schools, HIRAM KETCHUM, and CHARLES E. PIERSON, M.D.

The committee elected a secretary for the performance of the work, whose fitness for the task was to be found more in the enthusiasm of his admiration for the Society, and his earnest sympathy with the cause of public instruction, than any other merit that he might possess. It is, perhaps, not impertinent to remark, that the author had for several years previously entertained the purpose of writing a History of the Society, while there were yet probabilities of its permanence as an educational establishment.

In the preparation of the History, the author has had the

assistance and recommendations of the Committee, and has had occasion to make use of the records of the Corporation of the city, the City Library, the Society Library, the Library of the Historical Society, the Journals of the Legislature, and the numerous records of the schools established by the Society. The acknowledgments of the author are made for the politeness and attention he has received from the Committee, to J. W. C. LEVERIDGE and W. P. COOLEDGE, late Trustees of the Society, and also to the Hon. WILLIAM B. MACLAY, the late DAVID T. VALENTINE, Clerk of the Common Council, GEORGE H. MOORE, LL. D., Librarian of the Historical Society, RICHARD FIELD, of the late Manumission Society, and to the late Clerk of the Board of Education, Hon. ALBERT GILBERT, and also his successor, THOMAS BOESÉ, Esq., together with the teachers of the several schools. Acknowledgments are also due to JAMES McMASTER, Esq., editor of the *Freeman's Journal*, and to the editors of the *Commercial Advertiser* and *Evening Post*, for the use of their files in collecting the materials for the work. The labor has been rendered less onerous by the courtesies and attentions which have been so uniformly extended during its progress.

The author will not anticipate criticism upon the style of the work. He lays no claim to *authorship* other than that of industrious compilation. His object has been simply to present a truthful and impartial history of the rise and progress of common school education in the city of New York, as furnished by the proceedings of the Public School Society, and the kindred institutions which became identified with it. It was not designed to give a general history of the Church or other private schools which preceded the organization of the Society. It has been a constant aim to compile and present those facts which would be interesting to the public, or of value for future reference.

While seeking to avoid too much detail, it has been the purpose to omit no fact which might be required to complete the record or to illustrate a principle.

The author makes no apology for the absence of ornamentation, dissertations, or criticisms. The various papers and reports of the Society contain all that need be said in its defence; while the speeches and debates of the learned controversialists, whose arguments are here collected, afford sufficient relief to the matter-of-fact style of the History. The large amount of material clamoring for preservation has excluded original discussion.

The plan of the work is simply chronological. The chapters are devoted to periods of longer or shorter duration, marked by some special event, which is made the occasion of a pause in the narrative. The controversy relative to the school fund, 1822-'25, the legislation and reorganization of the system in 1826, the Roman Catholic Orphan Asylum controversy in 1831, and the great school controversies of 1840-'42, are made the subjects of special chapters, in which the facts relative thereto are collected without disturbing the narrative of the text.

During nearly twenty-five years, the Public School Society was compelled to become the defendant in the various discussions relative to the sectarian distribution of the Common School Fund. Having been organized for the express purpose of establishing schools "*for the children of such parents as do not belong to, or are not provided for by, any religious society*," it bore the responsibility, in a special manner, of providing a *common school education* for the masses of the people. Hence, when the custodians of this broad trust witnessed the efforts made to obtain, for sectarian uses, the moneys secured by their agency, from a public which itself called upon the Legislature to be taxed for this special purpose, they felt that they would have been recreant to their duty, had they allowed these funds to be disturbed, without an emphatic protest. How earnestly and ably they carried on the defence, the pages of this volume will abundantly show.

In placing on record the several controversies, the author has preferred to preserve the memorials, speeches, and printed addresses in full, although some repetition thereby becomes unavoidable. He has chosen to do this, rather than by revisions

and abridgements to afford any reader grounds for surmise that
he had excluded important passages from a desire to conceal on
the one hand, or to magnify on the other. So far as the compass
of the volume would permit, everything is given complete. Not
one line has been omitted from a motive of partiality for the
Society, or of antagonism to its opponents.

It has been deemed proper to insert the various papers and
documents in their order in the text, rather than in the form of
lengthened notes, or an appendix. It is believed that this arrangement will be found the most convenient for the reader.

In the hope that this work will be found valuable in connection with the interests of popular education, it is committed to
the press.

W. O. B.

NOTE TO THE READER.

The reader of this volume may perhaps detect occasional errors in the
names of persons introduced in the history. They are requested to communicate all corrections to the author.

All persons having documents, facts, and personal recollections relative to
the Public School Society, or any of its officers in their official capacity, are
requested to communicate them to the author, care of the publishers. All
communications must be accompanied with the name and address of the writer.

CONTENTS.

CHAPTER I.

ORIGIN OF THE SOCIETY, AND PROGRESS TO THE YEAR 1817.

CHAPTER II.

HISTORY FROM 1817–1822.

CHAPTER III.

THE BETHEL BAPTIST CHURCH CONTROVERSY.

CHAPTER IV.

HISTORY FROM 1822–1826.

CHAPTER V.

HISTORY FROM 1826–1831.

CHAPTER VI.

THE ROMAN CATHOLIC ORPHAN ASYLUM AND METHODIST CHARITY SCHOOL.

CHAPTER VII.

HISTORY FROM 1831-1834.

CHAPTER VIII.

BISHOP DUBOIS AND PUBLIC SCHOOL NO. 5.—1834.

CHAPTER IX.

HISTORY CONTINUED.—1834-1839.

CHAPTER X.

THE ROMAN CATHOLIC SCHOOL QUESTION.—1840.

CHAPTER XI.

EXPURGATION OF SCHOOL BOOKS—1840–1841.

CHAPTER XII.

THE SCHOOL CONTROVERSY OF 1841–1842.

CHAPTER XIII.

THE SCHOOL QUESTION OF 1842.

CHAPTER XIV.

HISTORY FROM 1840–1853.

CHAPTER XV.

UNION OF THE PUBLIC SCHOOL SOCIETY AND THE BOARD OF EDU-
CATION—1853.

CHAPTER XVI.

ADMINISTRATION OF THE SOCIETY.

CHAPTER XVII.

NORMAL AND HIGH SCHOOLS.

CHAPTER XVIII.

INFANT SCHOOLS AND PRIMARY SCHOOLS.

CONTENTS.

CHAPTER XIX.

SCHOOLS FOR COLORED CHILDREN.

CHAPTER XX.

INTRODUCTION.

At an early period after the adoption of the Constitution of the State, the enlightened men of that time took measures to lay the foundation of a system of common school instruction, which was endowed by successive appropriations of public lands and revenues, until it has become one of the most important institutions in the State.

The local circumstances of cities and large towns made special organizations of the school systems expedient and necessary, and called for legislative action to meet the wants of the people. These modifications of the district system have all been found to justify the foresight of their projectors.

The system, however, had not become developed at the commencement of the present century to such an extent as to meet the wants of the city of New York, where the schools of private instructors, and the parochial schools, were the only institutions of an educational kind then in existence. The necessities of a large portion of the population called for some effort on the part of benevolent men, and the institution known as the Public School Society was the proud development of those early labors. The expansion of the system under the administration of the Society, until it should become the finest in the country, was fondly looked for by its friends; and their plans would doubtless have been realized under their control, had they not been anticipated by the organization of the Board of Education, in 1842.

The rise, progress, and termination of the Society afford a noble illustration of the voluntary system in our country, and presents an example of disinterested and faithful labor seldom, if ever, equalled. The long periods of service of many of the trustees are worthy of special notice, as an evidence of their self-denying and zealous labors. The following schedule shows the time of service of the gentlemen whose names are given:

Stephen Allen,	1824–'52	28
Leonard Bleecker,	1805–'30	25
Micah Baldwin,	1827–'45	18
James B. Brinsmade,	1827–'53	26
De Witt Clinton,	1805–'28	23
Benjamin Clark,	1814–'39	25
Robert C. Cornell,	1820–'45	25
William W. Chester,	1827–'51	24
Joseph B. Collins,	1828–'53	25
Lyman Cobb,	1834–'53	19
James F. Depeyster,	1824–'53	29
Mahlon Day,	1829–'53	24
John Groshon, Jr.,	1827–'38; '41–'53	23
John R. Hurd,	1821–'53	32
Timothy Hedges,	1828–'53	25
Lewis Halleck,	1831–'53	22
Hiram Ketchum,	1824–'50	26
Abraham R. Lawrence,	1834–'53	19
Lindley Murray,	1816–'45	29
Samuel F. Mott,	1826–'46	20
James McBrair,	1828–'49	21
William Mandeville,	1835–'53	18
Charles Oakley,	1829–'48	19
James Palmer,	1818–'47	29
George Pardow,	1828–'46	18
Samuel W. Seton,	1824–'53	29
Najah Taylor,	1816–'53	37
George T. Trimble,	1818–'53	35
Samuel Wood,	1818–'38	20
A. V. Williams,	1830–'53	23

It appears, from the above table, that thirty trustees gave seven hundred and seventy-six years of service to the public schools, being an average of nearly *twenty-five years*. In addition to the above, twenty-five other gentlemen served an average of fifteen years, among whom were Peter Cooper, Anson G. Phelps, J. O. Pond, M. D., Pelatiah Perit, Col. Henry Rutgers, and James I. Roosevelt, Jr. These facts are probably without a parallel. The objector to the Public School Society cannot urge, in this connection, that the men rendering the service were of an inferior grade, or that their services and duties were either of an indifferent character or indifferently performed. The list above given presents a rare collection of men distinguished alike for their moral and intellectual character, their philanthropy, their positions as business and professional men, and the stations which some of them have held in the State. The facts thus presented will ever be remarkable in the history of public education in New York.

One of the grandest features of the system was the opportunity it thus gave to philanthropic men to labor for the public, untrammelled by political influences and considerations. The officers were independent of the teachers, as they were of the intrigues of the political councils, and knew nothing of the political opinions of the teachers, or of their personal influence at the ballot-box. The Society was conducted—as a literary and philanthropic institution should ever be—entirely free from partisan interests and attachments.

Its organization and supervision in the higher sphere of morals and religion was not less catholic and conservative. Yet, in reference to the nature and extent of its religious teachings, it was compelled to pass through a severe ordeal of prejudice and antagonism. The principles and the practice of the Society in relation to this delicate duty are so fully exhibited in the pages of this work, that it would be superfluous to review them in this place. The author, however, avails himself of the opportunity afforded by this Introduction, to obtrude the only attempt at a presentation of his own views which is made in this volume.

Systems of education, however perfectly they may be adapted to develop the intellectual faculties, and to stimulate the inquisitiveness of the unfolding mind of youth, must, nevertheless, possess other powers and develop other elements of character, or they must necessarily fail of their true end. The education of man consists not in merely training the eye to see, or the mind to think, or the observation to seize upon its object of attention. It consists not in giving it a knowledge of handicrafts, or of professions—nor in imparting a knowledge of factors, of exponents and coefficients, of sines and co-sines, of logi-

B

cal processes or of metaphysical subtleties. It is not in imparting a knowledge of facts or principles, as though the mind of
man were a mere tablet of record, or a bundle of abstract ideas.
The highest province of education is that which it gains by its
RELATION—an intimate and inseparable relation to the moral cultivation of an immortal being, whose character is to be the subject of a final award.

There is a wide distinction between mere mental operations
and the moral activities of the soul. An educated man may be
a monster, viewed from the moral standpoint; but the converse
is not true, for a man whose life is the exhibition of a high
standard of morality must be more or less enlightened; for an
obedience to a pure moral law involves that acquaintance with
the higher principles of action which unites with it a good degree of intelligence and mental development. Education is of
two kinds: that of a highly advanced moral standard, which is
accompanied with spiritual refinement and elevation; and a
merely intellectual training, which assigns to the moral a subordinate rank.

Which of these two systems is best adapted to meet the
wants of the State?

The answer to this question has received, of late years, and
is still receiving, the profound attention of many of the master
minds of both the Old and the New Worlds. In our own country it is deepened by the imperative law of necessity growing
out of the structure of our political institutions, in which the
popular will governs through the silent and irresistible verdict
of the ballot-box. Old institutions, founded on a firmly compacted basis, which have been strengthened by hundreds of
years of custom and usage, and seem to be invested with a pre-
scriptive and " divine right," may be perpetuated and upheld by
the centralization of power in the hands of the few; but in the
young and swiftly-extending States of our great confederacy—a
power more fluctuating and without centralization—a power
divided among millions of citizens, and combined only by the
attractive force of opinions and sympathies—a power more capricious and mighty, which reverses its judgments without noise,
and executes its volitions without arms—a power which rolls
over the land with the tremendous pressure of an ocean swelling
on and overbearing every obstacle—in our land, such a power

must be controlled and guided, or its exercise will be the destruction of every thing dear to the citizen and the philanthropist.

If we look at the forces which are in action at the present time in our country, we shall find them to be somewhat different from those which operated at the foundation of our institutions. At that time there was a comparatively high degree of intelligence in certain classes, who were moved, however, not so much by intellectual convictions as by that sacred obligation of duty to man and to God, which led them on, "appealing to the Judge of all the earth for the rectitude of their intentions." At the present time, literary and scientific knowledge, or intelligence, is more popularly diffused ; but while the amount of intelligence is greater, the moral forces have not increased in proportion. This arises, in part, from the vast and rapid immigration of a population now reaching nearly five hundred thousand per annum, the most of whom have never enjoyed liberal provisions for their education, and have been brought up under the State establishments of the Old World. Yet the forces which act now belong to the same class as those which produced the Declaration of Independence and the Constitution of the United States, but they are of a lower order. They are not intellectual; they are moral. But while the founders of the Government acted from the very highest moral convictions, multitudes of our recognized citizens act from impulses, prejudices, and influences which belong to the lower grade of moral powers.

The foundation of character is laid in the moral nature. The heart is exercised while the mind is yet just unfolding its earliest power. The child loves before he reasons, and exhibits anger before he has learned to utter his first monosyllables. His moral powers are in action long before his judgment has begun to discriminate between right and wrong. It is only when the mind, by years of education and a force of character developed out of the moral nature, has learned to act in certain directions, that the man may be at all claimed as the subject of simply intellectual convictions. In truth, it may be asserted that no man has ever been a moral man simply by convictions gained from reasoning alone. When truth, honesty, love, temperance, and self-denial can be demonstrated by mathematical problems or purely metaphysical abstractions, we may hope to make men good men and upright citizens by intellectual training alone.

But the profoundest mental acquisitions have no such force. They fail of exerting a controlling influence in conduct and character. The crystal, no matter how smooth its planes, no matter how brilliant and transparent it may be, let it reflect never so much light, will never be softened and remoulded until the solvent shall have been applied. So the simply enlightened mind can never be made to crystallize into beautiful and harmonious proportions of character, unless it be united with the nobility and fervor of a pure moral nature. Education, while it develops one, must rest, for all its force in the individual and national life, upon the moulding and superior power of the other.

It is a common remark, that our free institutions depend for their perpetuity upon the intelligence and virtue of the people. This is true. But the permanence of a popular form of government in this country depends more upon the pure and elevated moral character of the people than upon its intelligence. Intellect is not enough. The diffusion of knowledge will not secure permanence and national honor. The only strong, sufficient, and reliable bond of union and guaranty of our national permanence is in the virtue of the nation—in virtue like that of the men who framed the Government, inspired by the same motives, controlled by the same sense, and weighed in the scales of the same solemn responsibility. Whatever is less than this, or substitutes any thing else for this, will fall short of the imperative demands of the national mind and heart.

Regarding the subject in this light, it must be evident that the moral training of the people becomes an act of self-preservation for the State. There is no danger to be apprehended to our civil institutions while every man is governed by a strict rule of obedience to the moral law. The danger is discernible, and magnified just in proportion as men violate and overturn this law in their daily practice.

Here naturally arises the question, how much and what moral instruction shall be given in schools supported by the State or towns at the public expense? There are some who maintain that secular schools—the common schools—are not designed to teach systems of morals or of theology, but simply to afford to the children of the State that amount of mental training which shall at least prepare them for entering upon the duties of citizenship, and be so far a safeguard against the social disasters and civil dangers which arise out of an ignorant and unrefined population. The province of the moral teacher, they contend, is at the fireside and the place of worship, where each parent and pastor can teach the moral and religious doctrines which they severally believe. This view is too narrow, if it is not impracticable. To divest our school literature of all that is moral, would be to destroy its best claims. It is safe to say it can hardly be done. The mere teaching of arithmetical rules, and the arts of reading and penmanship and grammar, will never be conducive to the highest purposes of education, while they may serve a lower. To reject all moral lessons, will be to proscribe, in one sense, every thing like the moral and religious principle in the minds of the rising generation. In tens of thousands of cases it will serve to deprive the young mind and heart of almost the only certain chance of obtaining moral teaching. There are many parents who are compelled to labor, often early and late, for a subsistence. Many are not qualified to instruct their children, and, if they were, are disinclined, being both indolent and vicious. As a consequence, the philanthropist, the patriot, the Christian, and the State itself, must step in and exert all their combined power to train up for good citizenship and for immortality the more than orphaned children who throng our thoroughfares.

There is a standard of moral teaching which can be reached, and easily so, without prejudicing the rights of conscience of any but those who positively ignore it altogether, and prefer the dangers of a helmless skepticism to the elevated obligations of duty. Morality all will agree in teaching, to a greater or less extent; but when a child is taught to love good and avoid evil, and the lessons of moral rectitude are pressed upon his mind, there is a step higher than this. Why should he do right? Now, unless the higher motives of Divine love or displeasure, and the obligations of the law of God, are written upon his heart, there is little reason for his doing right except that of interest, convenience, and policy. But selfish appeals to the moral sense of a child are about as powerful as they are to that of the convict who finds it inconvenient to be in a State prison— although, had not that condition befallen him, his blind vision would have persuaded him that it was for his interest to steal instead of work. Take away all religious motives for the observance of the moral law, and its requirements are made subordinate to a mere principle of selfishness—that very principle which is the root of all our evils.

We are forced, then, to choose one of two paths of action. We must either reject all moral and the fundamental religious truths together, or we must teach those principles of duty which will satisfy the wants of a moral being. To adopt the first course, would be disastrous to the welfare of society, and fatal to our civil institutions. To declare that moral lessons shall not be taught because they require and involve the sanctions of religion, would be to unhinge all the bonds which maintain social order and restraint. It would be a surrender of the highest rights of conscience and of the wants of the soul to a compromise with moral death.

However desirable it be that the moral and religious education of the young be conducted by parents, and their recognized religious instructors, universal moral and religious instruction will not soon be secured by those means. As already remarked, thousands of parents have neither the literary nor moral qualifications to fit them for this work, and the consequences are seen in the great disregard of law, order, and virtue on the part of hundreds of thousands of the youth of our land. These children are growing up like their parents, and will only propagate the seeds of moral ruin. If the State, then, to secure a system of common school education in which all shall harmoniously unite, emasculate the system by rejecting all that moral teaching which has any true power over the minds and hearts of the young, it will inaugurate the era of recklessness and corruption, by a withdrawal of the safeguards against it. There are tens of thousands kept away from school, not because of the *rights* of conscience, but because of *the blunting of conscience*, by the imperfect and wretched training under which their parents grew up. Thousands of parents are intemperate, vicious, thriftless, and improvident. They employ their children in begging, stealing, and imposture, in order to obtain the means for their miserable subsistence, and the unhappy growth of the young. This growth is more than a simply physical growth—it is accompanied by a development in moral deformity, a muscular depravity of heart and soul, which, Samsonlike, snaps the bonds of moral obligation like threads, and defies the control of the wise and good. It is well to talk of the rights of conscience, and to defend them to the last; but to speak of the rights of conscience in regard to a class of the people who know no conscience, is to degrade the question to the lowest level.

Higher ground than this must be taken. It must come to be received as the doctrine of public education, that morality shall be taught in all our common schools, if for no other reason than because it is essential to the safety of the State. It will be far better to teach morals to the young, than to teach and practise the laws of legal vengeance and expiation in the hardened criminal. It will be incomparably cheaper to the State to train up children in morality and industry at the public expense, than to pay five times the amount to punish and incarcerate one in fifty of the population over twelve years of age, for crimes against virtue, order, and human life. It will be a grander achievement of our institutions to see American youth growing up under the power of a pure moral code and religious inspiration, than to see them expert accountants, accomplished penmen, and moral deformities.

What is that amount of moral teaching which shall be given in our schools? is a question of the greatest importance, and it must sooner or later press itself upon the people of this country. The distinction must be fairly drawn between the fundamental truths of all religion, and those which are recognized by the professions of the several sects. All unite in the belief of a GOD superintending and sustaining all things by His power and goodness, and all unite in their estimate of the Holy Scriptures. Yet there are minor denominational questions which may, and always will, be excluded from every school. So long, then, as these fundamental principles are taught, there need be no danger that the rights of conscience will be invaded. It is only when pressing upon the fields of sectarian usages and peculiarities, that any one can justly complain of invasion of the rights of conscience. Around the cardinal truths all may unite, if they will. They who reject them, and refuse to learn these lessons, in common with their fellow-citizens, have no just ground of complaint.

It is not proposed to construct a national creed for our common school text-books. There is no danger to be apprehended from the teaching of the highest moral truths in our schools. The danger is in their exclusion. But when, beside their exclusion, private schools shall be established, to be supported by the public treasury, the danger will be largely increased. A common school creed cannot be established by law. Such a legal abortion would be a grand step toward an ecclesiastical establishment, and such an establishment would be the precursor of an era of despotism. A State creed is not necessary to entitle a nation to a specific religious character. Are Great Britain and France Christian nations because they have establishments, and the United States *not* a Christian nation because it has no establishment? Evidently not so. But if either of them is Christian above the others, then is that character due to our own country, because here the law of Christian liberty is more fully exhibited than anywhere else on the globe.

The Creator has endowed us with a class of faculties which are easily and naturally affected with the ideas of a God, and of His goodness, compassion, and power. Whether these ideas are or are not intuitions, which would spring up in the minds of an isolated and untaught individual or community, is not to the present purpose. It is enough to know that we are so circumstanced that these ideas become a part of our mental habit, and in some sense constitute our religious nature. It is this conviction which leads the mind to feel a shock at the words of the blasphemer, and shrinks from the chilling and negative propositions of the skeptic. It is this religious nature which must be cherished, fed, and developed, or the nation will become a nation of skeptics, and virtue almost a forgotten name.

These religious habitudes must be fully recognized in the settlement of this question. The moral nature of man must be weighed in the balance with all the other mighty considerations which cluster around it. Whatever the ultimate decision may be, it seems plain that no system of education can be productive of very durable advantages which shall entirely reject and exclude that amount of moral teaching which shall not only cooperate with the lessons of the Sunday school, the church, and the parent, but which shall aim to impart it where no such instruction is given.

This fact seems to be too much lost sight of in the discussion of this whole theme. Were all the children of the people under that wholesome moral discipline and religious training which is required to ensure, so far as such instrumentalities can ensure,

their becoming virtuous and God-fearing members of the com
munity, the common school could dispense with such lessons as a
prominent feature. Yet the history of the world will show that,
where the most scrupulous care has been taken of the moral
training of the young, the highest estimate has been attached to
its value in connection with literary culture. But while there
are many who jealously maintain the standard of moral training,
there are multitudes who are entirely reckless of these obligations.

The question, placed in its civil aspect, then, is, Can the
State be safe while hundreds of thousands of its youth are growing up without any moral education? If this question be answered in the negative, we have our justification for making
moral lessons an important part of our system. If, in order to
give the people of the country that education with which they
sympathize, and which they desire their children to enjoy, a few
objectors should be inconvenienced and disregarded, the demand
for rights of conscience on the part of a few should not be a bar
or an offset to the conscientious rights of the rest. There is
nothing taught in our systems of popular education, in any part
of the Union, to which any truly American mind and spirit
might object as a fatal or serious invasion of his rights. Freedom is ours, in obedience not to merely intellectual attainments,
but to the pressure of moral and religious obligation upon the
consciences of the noble men who constructed our civil edifice.
This same moral power is to be conservator of our institutions.
It must be so from their very nature. The delegation of political power to the hands of half a million or a million of voters
who shall have grown up without moral restraint or education,
will be placing the balance of power in the hands of men whose
ignorance and prejudices will lead them to vote blindly for measures which will precipitate disaster upon the nation. While an
equilibrium of power may exist between parties of cultivated
men acting under a conscientious regard to duty, the balance of
power, fearful and irresistible in its consequences, will be wielded by the ignorant and the vicious. Partial exhibitions of this
spirit have already been seen since the date of the confederation.
A jealous regard for the rights of conscience must be maintained; but the appeal to this element in our national character,
come from what sources it may, must not be allowed to blind us

to the consequences of too strict a construction of the meaning of the term. To exclude and override all moral teaching in our common schools, will be to give the ultimate control of our institutions to a mass of unthinking men, moved by their passions, and governed by the superior influence of designing but educated men, destitute of moral principle, and scorning the control of moral power. Such a state of things would soon see our happy Union become the prey of a social and civil despotism, in which the rights of conscience would be altogether obliterated, and the rule of might would make the rule of right.

The law of Massachusetts embodies a provision which covers the ground in a manner fully in harmony with the spirit of our institutions, and, at the same time, meets the wants of the State. It is as follows:

It shall be the duty of the president, professors, and trustees of the University at Cambridge, and of the several colleges, and of all preceptors and teachers of academies, and all other instructors of youth, to exert their best endeavors to impress on the minds of children and youth committed to their care and instruction the principles of PIETY, JUSTICE, and a SACRED REGARD TO TRUTH, LOVE TO THEIR COUNTRY, HUMANITY and UNIVERSAL BENEVOLENCE, SOBRIETY and FRUGALITY, CHARITY, MODERATION and TEMPERANCE, and those other virtues which are *the ornament of human society and the basis upon which a republican constitution is founded ;* and it shall be the duty of such instructors to endeavor to lead their pupils, as their ages and capacities will admit, into a clear understanding of the tendency of the above-mentioned virtues, *to preserve and perfect a republican constitution, and secure the blessings of liberty, as well as to promote their future happiness,* and also to point out to them the evil tendency of the opposite vices.

A common school system which does this, teaches religion in its practical relations to God, to man, and to the State—in its manifestations in the family circle, the highway, and the business of life—as a child and as a man—as a citizen and as a morally responsible being. It seizes and writes in deep lessons upon the minds and hearts of youth the principles of religious truth and conduct, without which no grouping of ideas or principles, in the form of any creed whatever, can be called in the least sense, *religion*. Divest religion of the principles comprehended in the above scheme, and its spirit and its practice are alike annihilated. Teach these, and the specific religious preferences or professions of the parents may be reserved, and properly so, for inculcation at the domestic or the church altar.

OFFICERS AND TRUSTEES

OF

THE PUBLIC SCHOOL SOCIETY, WITH THEIR TIME OF SERVICE.

TABLE showing the amount of moneys received and expended during each year of the existence of the Public School Society, with the Average Attendance of Scholars, the Annual Expenses, and the Cost per Scholar, exclusive of the Purchase of Real Estate, and Cost and Repairs of Buildings.

YEAR.	Receipts.	Expenditures.	Attendance.	Expenses.	Cost.
1807	$4,774.00	$1,163.09	70	$913.09	$13.04
1808	4,960.10	1,866.53	200	1,429.84	7.14
1809	1,858.01	2,516.52	250	1,637.11	6.54
1810	4,173.47	16,129.54	400	1,554.20	3.89
1811	15,557.68	8,082.45	550	2,639.91	4.54
1812	7,331.45	10,183.73	712	2,500.04	3.39
1813	4,511.00	2,788.13	950	2,788.13	2.93
1814	3,139.00	3,299.06	968	3,299.06	2.80
1815	6,250.95	4,193.61	958	4,193.61	4.21
1816	5,369.44	4,373.20	974	4,373.20	3.80
1817	6,075.08	4,347.36	1,218	4,347.36	3.57
1818	9,174.50	4,049.43	1,218	4,049.43	3.25
1819	10,659.74	19,344.26	1,449	7,376.02	4.75
1820	7,487.70	10,588.37	2,145	6,881.75	2.79
1821	10,025.08	16,128.07	2,811	6,769.55	2.15
1822	10,066.83	10,740.63	3,412	7,456.70	1.37
1823	10,222.82	17,341.45	4,090	7,364.45	1.80
1824	12,973.59	12,464.53	4,384	9,242.03	2.10
1825	16,477.33	14,266.07	4,059	10,266.07	2.52
1826	50,359.36	47,344.99	3,739	10,239.57	2.74
1827	63,969.97	64,724.79	4,564	18,645.68	4.08
1828	36,651.28	41,246.25	5,331	21,030.83	3.94
1829	61,975.60	61,611.18	6,150	22,004.80	3.57
1830	58,625.25	59,157.31	6,178	22,092.93	3.57
1831	117,645.19	117,232.88	6,323	21,938.39	3.47
1832	71,765.38	70,977.20	6,109	24,345.49	3.98
1833	91,792.93	89,650.84	7,826	25,101.95	3.34
1834	95,995.57	91,656.10	12,537	49,823.07	3.97
1835	108,354.83	115,518.95	17,318	63,749.79	3.68
1836	131,287.29	130,587.18	18,011	69,229.28	3.84
1837	127,224.74	128,342.47	17,932	72,845.69	4.06
1838	148,791.25	129,240.81	19,982	78,484.33	3.99
1839	112,713.25	130,572.95	21,206	100,485.24	4.73
1840	169,771.72	170,792.92	22,955	101,960.21	4.44
1841	155,815.20	156,857.45	23,654	105,398.13	4.45
1842	134,909.96	134,853.16	24,671	99,572.31	4.03
1843	123,352.98	122,297.22	20,136	94,384.24	4.68
1844*	277,313.12	219,264.33	20,236	168,394.62	8.32
1845	94,648.19	144,690.90	22,476	119,038.62	5.29
1846	158,558.12	158,375.51	23,392	121,817.47	5.20
1847	125,276.14	135,023.15	23,834	120,530.37	5.05
1848	137.963,46	137,963.46	24,226	119,057.85	4.91
1849	194,196.20	192,306.32	24,524	136,164.81	5.55
1850	153,054.17	154,300.56	24,290	128,086.83	5.26
1851	179,113.21	179,756.70	25,941	130,216.36	5.02
1852	177,543.02	177,543.02	24,320	141,906.67	5.83
....	$3,509,755.15	$3,525,754.63	488,589	....	4.29

NOTE.—There is an excess of expenditure over receipts of $15,999.48. The Treasurer's account for the first eight years could not be obtained complete.

* The financial year of the Board of Education commenced on the 1st of January—that of the Society on the 1st of May. To prevent the confusion consequent upon this difference the time was altered to correspond with that of the Board, and the statement for the year 1844 includes a period of twenty months. This gives the cost per scholar for twelve months $4.98, and $8.32 for the whole period.

THE

PUBLIC SCHOOL SOCIETY.

CHAPTER I.

ORIGIN OF THE SOCIETY, AND PROGRESS TO THE YEAR 1817.

Large Cities—Public Instruction of the Poor—City of New York in 1800—Parochial
Charity Schools—An Unoccupied Field—Proposition to Establish a New School—
The First Meeting—A Committee Appointed—Memorial to the Legislature—An
Act of Incorporation Passed—The Society Organized—The First Board of Trus-
tees—Address to the Public—Subscriptions—The Lancasterian System—The New
School Opened—Lot of Ground Presented by Col. Rutgers—Clothing for Poor
Children—Memorial to the Legislature—Application to the Common Council—
The School Fund—"The Free School Society"—New Apartments for the School
—Grant of Lots for a Building—New School House No. 1—Donations—Opening
of the School—De Witt Clinton's Address—The Law Amended—School No. 2—
Death of Benjamin D. Perkins—A School Library—Grant of Money by the Legis-
lature—Land Presented by Trinity Church—Opening of No. 2—Additional Trus-
tees—Moral and Religious Instruction.

THE population of the city of New York, at the commencement of the present century, was 60,489. The limits of the city
were marked on the north by the vicinity of Chambers street,
the population being located at the southern extremity of the
island. By that social gravitation which seems to have always
been inseparable from compacted communities, the metropolis
was not exempt from the characteristic feature of a substratum
of wretched, ignorant, and friendless children, who, even though
they had parents, grew up in a condition of moral and religious
orphanage, alike fatal to their temporal and spiritual advancement and elevation.

The influence of that spirit which is the outgrowth and the
evidence of true religious convictions, and a high sense of responsibility to the present as well as to the future, was not un-
felt in reference to this class of the population. Public economy, not less than religious duty—the merely commercial con-

1

siderations, not less than those that spring from the earnest belief of revelation—the social law of self-preservation, not less
than the higher law of duty—taught some of the best and most
honored men and women of that day the truth which half a century has elaborated into a mighty demonstration, that the literary and moral instruction of every child in the State is a prime
necessity. If the parent fails in this work, then the State must
assume the task, and provide for its performance. The answer
given to the question as then discussed, originated the institution, a record of whose labors, for nearly fifty years, is deemed
worthy of preservation.

There were several schools known as " Charity Schools " in
existence at the time, but they were under denominational or
other control; while a large class of children were practically
unsupplied with the means of instruction. An Association of
Ladies, members of the Society of Friends, organized for benevolent purposes, had established a Free School for girls, in 1802,
which was in successful operation in its peculiar sphere. This
school suggested the establishment of other schools on the same
plan and for the same class of children ; and the names of the
founders and friends of both institutions show the connection
and origin of the Society which afterward became so efficient in
the instruction of the youth of New York. To extend the
benefits of education to all who were excluded from the various
schools already established, became an object of earnest desire
with several philanthropic men who had observed the condition
of these children. At the request of Thomas Eddy and John
Murray, whose attention had been particularly directed to the
subject, a meeting was called of such persons as were likely to
unite in the effort. On the 19th of February, 1805, this meeting was held at the house of John Murray, in Pearl street.
Twelve persons were present, whose names are the following:
Samuel Osgood, Brockholst Livingston, John Murray, Jr., Samuel Miller, Joseph Constant, Thomas Eddy, Thomas Pearsall,
Thomas Franklin, Matthew Clarkson, Leonard Bleecker, Samuel
Russell, and William Edgar. After a full discussion of the
object for which they had been called together, they were unanimous in the opinion that the establishment of schools, for the
education of children not provided for by the parochial schools,
was a measure of high importance, not only to them, but to the

whole community, of which they formed so considerable a portion. At this meeting a committee was appointed to devise such plans as they might deem expedient, and report thereon at a subsequent meeting.

With a zeal and promptitude which were in harmony with the noble objects proposed, the Committee gave their immediate attention to the duty assigned them, and in a few days called a second meeting, at which they submitted their report.

Among the recommendations of that report was one to the effect that application be made to the Legislature of the State, then in session, for an act of incorporation. A memorial was accordingly prepared, which was signed by about one hundred of the most respectable men in the city, and was forwarded to the Legislature. It was as follows:

To the Representatives of the People of the State of New York, in Senate and Assembly convened :
The Memorial of the Subscribers, Citizens of New York,
RESPECTFULLY SHEWETH,

That, impressed with a solicitude for the general welfare of the community, they feel it their duty to address your Body on a subject which they regard as of deep concern.

Your memorialists have viewed with painful anxiety the multiplied evils which have accrued, and are daily accruing, to this city, from the neglected education of the children of the poor. They allude more particularly to that description of children who do not belong to, or are not provided for, by any religious society; and who, therefore, do not partake of the advantages arising from the different Charity Schools established by the various religious societies in this city. The condition of this class is deplorable indeed; reared up by parents who, from a variety of concurring circumstances, are become either indifferent to the best interests of their offspring, or, through intemperate lives, are rendered unable to defray the expense of their instruction, these miserable and almost friendless objects are ushered upon the stage of life, inheriting those vices which idleness and the bad example of their parents naturally produce. The consequences of this neglect of education are ignorance and vice, and all those manifold evils resulting from every species of immorality, by which public hospitals and almshouses are filled with objects of disease and poverty, and society burthened with taxes for their support. In addition to these melancholy facts, it is to be feared that the laboring class in the community is becoming less industrious, less moral, and less careful to lay up the fruit of their earnings. What can this alarming declension have arisen from, but the existence of an error which has ever been found to produce a similar effect—a want of a *virtuous education*, especially at that early period of life when the impressions that are made generally stamp the future character ?

The rich having ample means of educating their offspring, it must be apparent that the laboring poor—a class of citizens so evidently useful—have a superior claim to public support.

The enlightened and excellent Government under which we live is favorable to the general diffusion of knowledge; but the blessings of such a Government can be expected to be enjoyed no longer than while its citizens continue *virtuous*, and while the majority of the people, through the advantage of a proper early education, possess sufficient knowledge to enable them to understand and pursue their best interests. This sentiment, which must meet with universal assent, was emphatically urged to his countrymen by WASHINGTON, and has been recently enforced by our present Chief Magistrate in his address on the necessity of supporting schools, and promoting useful knowledge through the State.

Trusting that the necessity of providing suitable means for the prevention of the evils they have enumerated will be apparent to your honorable Body, your memorialists respectfuly request the patronage and assistance of the Legislature in establishing a free school, or schools, in this city, for the benevolent purpose of affording education to those unfortunate children who have no other mode of obtaining it.

The personal attention to be bestowed on these children for the improvement of their morals, and to assist their parents in procuring situations for them, where industry will be inculcated and good habits formed, as well as to give them the learning requisite for the proper discharge of the duties of life, it is confidently hoped will produce the most beneficial and lasting effects.

The more effectually to accomplish so desirable an object, your memorialists have agreed to form an association under the name of " The Society for Establishing a Free School in the City of New York." They therefore respectfully solicit the Legislature to sanction their undertaking by an Act of Incorporation, and to grant them such pecuniary aid or endowment as, in your wisdom, may be deemed proper for the promotion of the benevolent object of your memorialists.

All which is respectfully submitted.

NEW YORK, 25*th February*, 1805.

The nature and importance of the enterprise proposed by the petitioners were fully comprehended by the members of the Legislature, who sympathized with its objects, and promptly responded to the appeal thus made to their wisdom and patriotism. On the 9th of April following, an Act was passed, entitled, " An Act to incorporate the Society instituted in the City of New York, for the Establishment of a Free School for the Education of Poor Children who do not belong to, or are not provided for by, any religious society." The Act constituted De Witt Clinton, Samuel Osgood, Brockholst Livingston, John Murray, Jr.,

Jacob Morton, Samuel Miller, Joseph Constant, Thomas Eddy, Thomas Pearsall, Robert Bowne, Matthew Clarkson, Archibald Gracie, John M Vickar, Charles Wilkes, Henry Ten Brook, Gilbert Aspinwall, Valentine Seaman, William Johnson, William Coit, Matthew Franklin, Adrian Hegeman, Benjamin G. Minturn, Leonard Bleecker, Thomas Franklin, Samuel Russell, Samuel Doughty, Alexander Robertson, Samuel Forbes, John Withington, William Edgar, George Trumbull, Daniel D. Tompkins, William Boyd, Jacob Mott, Benjamin Egbert, Thomas Farmar, and Dr. Samuel L. Mitchill, a body corporate under the style of " *The Society for establishing a Free School in the City of New York, for the education of such poor children as do not belong to, or are not provided for, by any religious society.*"

The provisions of this Act were, that the yearly income of the Society should not exceed ten thousand dollars, and that on the first Monday in May in each year there should be elected thirteen Trustees to manage the affairs of the Society, who should be members of the said corporation, and actually residing in the city of New York; that the Trustees should meet regularly on the second Monday in every month, and that seven or more of them so convened should be a legal meeting of the Board: That any person who should contribute to the Society the sum of eight dollars, should be a member thereof; and that any person who should contribute the sum of twenty-five dollars, should be a member, and be further entitled, during the life of such contributor, to send one child to be educated at any school under the care of the Society; and whoever should contribute the sum of forty dollars, should be a member, and be entitled to send two children to be educated at any school under the direction of the said Society. The second section of the Act constituted the twelve gentlemen present at the original meeting, together with De Witt Clinton, the first Board of Trustees, who should hold office until the time fixed by the Act for the first election of officers.

The limitation of the income of the Society to the sum of ten thousand dollars is an indication of the rigid views of responsibility, as well as of economy, which controlled the founders and early patrons of the Society. Experience and philanthropy soon taught a more enlarged view of the necessities of the enterprise.

In conformity with the provisions of this Act, thirteen Trustees were elected at a meeting held on the 6th of May, 1805, and the Board thus elected was organized as follows :

De Witt Clinton, *President.*
John Murray, Jr., *Vice-President.*
Leonard Bleecker, *Treasurer.*
Benjamin D. Perkins, *Secretary.*

Gilbert Aspinwall,	Adrian Hegeman,
Thomas Eddy,	William Johnson,
Thomas Franklin,	Samuel Miller,
Matthew Franklin,	Benjamin G. Minturn,

Henry Ten Brook.

The Society had now assumed a responsible form, and the Trustees soon began to realize the magnitude of the enterprise which they had undertaken. With a labor of the utmost importance before them, a wide field and an organization perfected, they were now to provide means for carrying on their work. A building was required for the school, and funds were needed to pay the salary of the teachers and the other expenses incident to such an institution. Sensible of the necessity of the undertaking, and anxious that the friendless children whose welfare they had in view should begin to participate in the benefits designed to be bestowed upon them, the Trustees determined to make an immediate application to their fellow-citizens for pecuniary assistance. The following address was therefore published in the journals of the city :—

TO THE PUBLIC.

Address of the Trustees of the " Society for Establishing a Free School in the City of New York, for the Education of such Poor Children as do not Belong to, or are not Provided for by, any Religious Society."

" While the various religious and benevolent societies in this city, with a spirit of charity and zeal which the precepts and example of the Divine Author of our religion could alone inspire, amply provide for the education of such poor children as belong to their respective associations, there still remains a large number living in total neglect of religious and moral instruction, and unacquainted with the common rudiments of learning, essentially requisite for the due management of the ordinary business of life. This neglect may be imputed either to the extreme indigence of the parents of such children, their intemperance and vice ; or to a blind indifference to the best interests of their offspring. The consequences must be obvious to the most careless observer. Children thus brought up in ignorance, and amidst the contagion of bad example, are in imminent danger of ruin; and too many of them, it is to be feared, instead of being useful members of the community, will become the burden and pests of society. Early instruction and fixed habits of industry, decency, and order, are the surest safeguards of virtuous conduct; and when parents are either unable or unwilling to bestow the necessary attention on the education of their children, it becomes the duty of the public, and of individuals, who have the power, to assist them in the discharge of this important obligation. It is in vain that laws are made for the punishment of crimes, or that good men attempt to stem the torrent of irreligion and vice, if the evil is not checked at its source; and the means of prevention, by the salutary discipline of early education, seasonably applied. It is certainly in the power of the opulent and charitable, by a timely and judicious interposition of their influence and aid, if not wholly to prevent, at least to diminish, the pernicious effects resulting from the neglected education of the children of the poor.

Influenced by these considerations, and from a sense of the necessity of providing some remedy for an increasing and alarming evil, several individuals, actuated by similar motives, agree to form an association for the purpose of extending the means of education to such poor children as do not belong to, or are not provided for, by any religious society. After different meetings, numerously attended, a plan of association was framed, and a Memorial prepared and addressed to the Legislature, soliciting an Act of Incorporation, the better to enable them to carry into effect their benevolent design. Such a law the Legislature, at their last session, was pleased to pass; and at a meeting of the Society, under the Act of Incorporation, on the sixth instant, thirteen Trustees were elected for the ensuing year.

The particular plan of the school, and the rules for its discipline and management, will be made known previous to its commencement. Care will be exercised in the selection of teachers, and, besides the elements of learning usually taught in schools, strict attention will be bestowed on the morals of the children, and all suitable means be used to counteract the disadvantages resulting from the situation of their parents. It is proposed, also, to establish, on the first day of the week, a school, called a Sunday School, more particularly for such children as, from peculiar circumstances, are unable to attend on the other days of the week. In this, as in the Common School, it will be a primary object, without observing the peculiar forms of any religious Society, to inculcate the sublime truths of religion and morality contained in the Holy Scriptures.

This Society, as will appear from its name, interferes with no existing institution, since children already provided with the means of education, or attached to any other Society, will not come under its care. Humble gleaners in the wide field of benevolence, the members of this Association seek such objects only as are left by those who have gone before, or are fellow-laborers with them in the great work of charity. They, therefore, look with confidence for the encouragement and support of the affluent and charitable of every denomination of Christians; and when they consider that in no community is to be found a greater spirit of liberal and active benevolence than among the citizens of New York, they feel assured that adequate means for the prosecution of their plan will be easily obtained. In addition to the respectable list of original subscriptions, considerable funds will be requisite for the purchase or hire of a piece of ground, and the erection of a suitable building for the school to pay the teachers, and to defray other charges incident to the establishment. To accomplish this design, and to place the Institution on a solid and respectable foundation, the Society depend on the voluntary bounty of those who may be charitably disposed to contribute their aid in the promotion of an object of great and universal concern.

DE WITT CLINTON, *President.*
JOHN MURRAY, Jr., *Vice-President.*
LEONARD BLEECKER, *Treasurer.*
B. D. PERKINS, *Secretary.*

Gilbert Aspinwall,	Adrian Hegeman,
Thomas Eddy,	William Johnson,
Thomas Franklin,	Samuel Miller, D. D.,
Matthew Franklin,	Benjamin G. Minturn,

Henry Ten Brook.

NEW YORK, *May* (5th *Month*) 18, 1805.

After the appearance of this address, the labor of soliciting subscriptions was commenced, but, in consequence of adverse circumstances, among which was the occurrence of the yellow fever during the summer and autumn months, the progress made was slow ; and it was not until after numerous meetings, and great efforts on the part of the Trustees, during the ensuing twelve months, that the subscriptions amounted to a sum sufficient to warrant them in hiring a teacher and opening the school.

The subscription list, still preserved among the papers of the Society, bears at its head the honored name of DE WITT CLINTON, opposite to which is a donation of $200, followed by that of W. EDGAR, for $50, and MATTHEW CLARKSON, for $25, together with many of the most prominent and influential men of the time.

The enterprise, thus originated and endowed had reached, at the end of the year 1805, a position which led the Trustees to mature their plans for the opening of the school at as early a day as practicable. They had entered upon a work in which the adaptation of small means to produce the greatest result was a question of much importance. Diligent inquiry was accordingly made as to the best methods of instruction, and the systems adopted in other cities and countries in educating the same classes of children. Efficiency in operation, facility and simplicity, attractiveness and thoroughness, combined with economy, were eminently desirable, and care was taken to examine the merits of the various known systems of instruction. Among those which presented themselves prominently to the attention of the trustees, was that which had been for a few years successfully established in London by JOSEPH LANCASTER, and known as the LANCASTERIAN SYSTEM. This gentleman was then conducting his school in the British metropolis, with an average attendance of about one thousand pupils, and his extraordinary success and reputation as an instructor, together with the noticeable reform which had been effected in the moral and social condition of that class in the vicinity of his school, were such that the attention of the British public had not only been drawn toward the establishment, but it had received the notice of members on the floor of Parliament. The fame of the indefatigable founder had, moreover, become known in all parts of the world.

A system of instruction which had been so honorably endorsed and supported, could not fail to command the consideration of the trustees. Economy in expense, and facility in communicating instruction, were the characteristic features of this system. It comprehended reading, writing, and arithmetic. The pupils themselves were made the instruments of their own instruction. A school was divided into classes of ten or fifteen scholars, who were placed under the care of a monitor, while he was himself a scholar in a class of a superior grade.

The managers of the Society, after a careful consideration of the system devised by LANCASTER, with its apparatus and illustrations, did not long hesitate in regard to the propriety of an experimental test in their new school. In its introduction they derived essential aid from one of their own number, Benjamin D. Perkins, who had seen it in full operation in England, and who was acquainted with its regulations from a personal communication with its author. A teacher who appeared to be well qualified for the undertaking, William Smith, and who was employed by the Society for several years, was selected; and under his superintendence a school was opened on the 19th of May, 1806, in a small apartment in Bancker (now Madison) street. In a few days the attendance rose to forty-two, and the whole, together with those who were afterward added to the school, were under the direction of one teacher, the "monitors" rendering all the assistance in their power.

The Lancasterian system of instruction was, by the organization of this school, transplanted to the Western world, and for many years was almost universally adopted in large schools of even the higher classes of pay schools. The New York High School, which for a number of years held the first rank, under Daniel H. Barnes, Shepherd Johnson, John Griscom, and others, was conducted on the Lancasterian, or monitorial, system.

One clause in the act of incorporation, which regulated the meetings of the trustees, being productive of inconvenience, an act was passed by the Legislature on the 2d of April, 1806, providing that the trustees might hold their monthly meetings on any day of the week they might deem convenient. It was therefore immediately resolved, that their regular meetings should in future be held on the first Friday in every month.

In the same month, Col. Henry Rutgers, with characteristic liberality, presented to the Society a lot of ground in Henry street, for the purpose of erecting thereon a school-house, to meet the wants of the indigent in that populous part of the city. He afterward added an adjoining lot to this generous donation ; the estimated value of the whole being $2,500.

The labors of the instructor are either very much embarrassed or aided by the social condition of the pupils. The struggle for bread, and the physical necessities of children who suffer from cold, hunger, and wretchedness, are not only, from the very nature of the case, impediments to progress in education, but they serve to blunt the sensibilities, and make intellectual effort a toilsome and unwelcome task. Hunger and cold make their appeals very bitterly oftentimes, and efforts for self-preservation, or struggles against suffering, absorb the thoughts and energies, and become the chief care of beings thus situated. The moral, the intellectual, and the spiritual wants are far less keenly felt, or even perceived ; and the condition of dependence thus imposed upon thousands becomes a bequest in perpetuity, from which few rise to a higher level except by accident, or a native force of character which overcomes all obstacles by a resolute purpose to triumph. It was among this class that the Society laid its foundation ; and the trustees found, at the approach of the winter of 1806–7, that their labor of benevolence would fail very materially were they to neglect some of those humane offices which poverty demands at the hand of the philanthropist and the Christian. They therefore determined to examine into the personal wants of their beneficiaries, and they were not long in becoming convinced that clothing of every description would be required for their use. Efforts were accordingly made to supply these wants, and the trustees were gratified by the receipt of liberal donations of clothing, shoes, and hats, which, being distributed among the children, were sufficient to make them all comfortable for the winter. This continued to be the case for some years, but was finally abandoned when the schools increased in number and were more numerously attended.

In January, 1807, the trustees, not only encouraged with their success, but anxious to extend their labors, presented a memorial to the Legislature, containing a statement of what they had done, and soliciting pecuniary assistance to enable them to extend the operations of the association. The memorial met with a very favorable reception, and soon afterward the trustees were able to congratulate the friends of the institution on the passage of an act appropriating four thousand dollars toward building a house, and one thousand to be paid annually toward defraying the expenses of the school. These moneys were paid out of the moneys appropriated by the act entitled " An Act to lay a duty on strong liquors, and for regulating inns and taverns," to the payment of the contingent charges of the city of New York, the annuity to continue during the pleasure of the Legislature. The act was passed on the 27th of February, 1807, and was deemed of higher interest from the fact that this liberal appropriation received the unanimous consent of both branches of the Legislature.

While these proceedings were transpiring at the Capitol, the trustees made an application to the Corporation of the city for their assistance in promoting an enterprise which promised to be of incalculable benefit to the public. A committee from that body was accordingly appointed, who visited the institution, and soon afterward a building adjacent to the Almshouse was appropriated for the temporary accommodation of the school, with an additional appropriation of five hundred dollars to assist in putting it into a suitable condition for school purposes. As a consideration for these advantages, the Society agreed, on their part, to receive and educate fifty children belonging to the Almshouse. To this building the school was removed on the 28th of April, 1807, and before the close of the year it numbered one hundred and fifty pupils.

In the year 1808, the trustees had the pleasure of witnessing the growing utility of the institution, and the union of public and private exertions in their favor. The charter of the Society was deemed not to be sufficiently comprehensive, as it did not embrace all classes of poor children; and, desirous that the benefits of the establishment should not be restricted, they solicited and obtained from the Legislature an act, which was passed on the 1st of April, 1808, ordaining that the corporation should in future be denominated "The Free School Society of New York," and that its powers should extend to all children who should be the proper objects of a gratuitous education.

In order to provide effectually for the future wants of the school, on an enlarged plan, the trustees petitioned the Legislature, at the same session, for a liberal portion of the school fund of the State, whenever it should be deemed advisable to make a distribution. The preamble to the bill, by which the name of the Society was changed, recites, that, " Whereas, the trustees of the Society for establishing a free school in the city of New York, for the education of such poor children as do not belong to, or are not provided for by, any religious society, have, by their petition, represented to the Legislature, that the act incorporating that Society restrains them unnecessarily in the communication of the advantages of their establishment, by confining them to a certain description of poor children; and have also petitioned for a competent portion of the school fund applicable to the city of New York, in order to be the better enabled to proceed in the execution of their important duties; and, whereas, the said fund does not as yet amount to a sum sufficiently large to render an immediate distribution advisable, but as the Legislature are desirous of encouraging an institution so laudable and useful, by granting the petition of the said trustees in other respects," it was enacted that the name of the Society be changed to that of the " FREE-SCHOOL SOCIETY." This measure, although unaccompanied with any provision of moneys, was valuable in extending the sphere of the institution and increasing its claims upon the liberality of the public.

The tenement adjacent to the Almshouse in which the school was kept, could not accommodate more than two hundred and fifty children. This number was soon reached, and numerous demands for admission continued to be made far beyond the capacity of the house. The Almshouse was a long building of two stories in height, with a basement, and occupied the north end of the Park, parallel with Chambers street, extending from Broadway nearly to the line of what is now Centre street.

The demand for more ample accommodation pressed urgently upon the trustees, and as the most direct and certain source of aid, a further application for assistance was made to the Corporation in the autumn of 1808, and that body presented to the Society an extensive lot of ground in Chatham street, on which stood the State arsenal. This donation was made on condition that the Society should receive and educate gratuitously the children of the Almshouse, in the performance of which task it was eminently fulfilling both the letter and spirit of the design of its founders and friends. The value of the ground and the building upon it was estimated at ten thousand dollars. To this important donation the Corporation afterward added the sum of fifteen hundred dollars, to aid in preparing a new building for the reception of the school.

These handsome appropriations enabled the trustees to prosecute their work with a more hopeful confidence than they had yet entertained, and during the year 1809 they were principally occupied in the completion of the new building. A brick edifice was erected, one hundred and twenty feet in length and fifty feet in width, capable of accommodating in one room five hundred children. In the lower story there were apartments for the family of the teacher, for the meeting of the trustees, and for another school, which would accommodate one hundred and fifty pupils. In the adoption of their plan, the trustees had economy constantly in view ; but, at the same time, they were desirous that the style of architecture, and the external appearance of the building, should comport with the liberal patronage which the institution had received, and with the resources of a great and flourishing metropolis. Among the means of lessening the expenses of the establishment, they solicited and obtained, from several benevolent individuals, contributions of timber and other materials to the amount of one thousand dollars. They also negotiated with a master-mason and two master-carpenters, who generously superintended the work, and paid the laborers, without any pecuniary advantage to themselves. In the erection and completion of this extensive building, the Society expended more than thirteen thousand dollars.

The gentlemen to whose benevolence the Society was indebted for their contributions of building materials, and the superintendence of the construction of the edifice, are worthy of an honorable place among the early friends of the enterprise, and are as follows :

Abraham Russell,
William Tilton,
J. G. Pierson & Brothers,
Whitehead Hicks,
M. M. Titus,
Richard Titus,
Joseph Watkins,
B. W. Rogers & Co.,
Richard Speaight,
Abraham Bussing,
Daniel Beach,
P. Schermerhorn, Jr.,
Thomas Stevenson,
Thomas Smyth,
John McKie,
Wm. Wickham,

Isaac Sharples,
Jones & Clinch,
George Youle,
John Youle,
Forman Cheesman,
John Rooke,
George Lindsay,
Jonathan Dixon,
J. Sherred,
Alexander Campbell,
Wm. & G. Post,
Joel Davis,
Henry Hillman,
Ebenezer Basset,
Peter Fenton,
Wm. McKenny.

Liberal donations were also received from the public, amounting to about ten thousand dollars.

The building being completed, it was opened for school purposes, and dedicated by public exercises of an interesting character, on the 11th of December, 1809. The president, DE WITT CLINTON, delivered the following address :

DE WITT CLINTON'S ADDRESS.

On an occasion so interesting to this institution, when it is about to assume a more reputable shape, and to acquire a spacious and permanent habitation, it is no more than a becoming mark of attention to its patrons, benefactors, and friends, assembled for the first time in this place, to delineate its origin, its progress, and its present situation. The station which I occupy in this association, and the request of my much-respected colleagues, have devolved this task upon me—a task which I should perform with unmingled pleasure, if my avocations had afforded me time to execute it with fidelity; and I trust that the humble objects of your bounty, presented this day to your view, will not detract from the solemnity of the occasion—"that ambition will not mock our useful toil, nor grandeur hear with a disdainful smile the simple annals of the poor."

In casting a view over the civilized world, we find an universal accordance in opinion on the benefits of education, but the practical exposition of this opinion exhibits a deplorable contrast. While magnificent colleges and universities are erected and endowed and dedicated to literature, we behold few liberal appropriations for diffusing the blessings of knowledge among all descriptions of people. The fundamental error of Europe has been, to confine the light of knowledge to the wealthy and the great, while the humble and the depressed have been as sedulously excluded from its participation, as the wretched criminal, immured in a dungeon, is from the light of heaven. This cardinal mistake is not only to be found in the institutions of the Old World, and in the condition of its inhabitants, but it is to be seen in most of the books which have been written on the subject of education. The celebrated Locke, whose treatises on government and the human understanding have crowned him with immortal glory, devoted the powers of his mighty intellect to the elucidation of education; but in the very threshold of his book we discover this radical error: his treatise is professedly intended for the children of gentlemen. "If those of that rank (says he) are, by their education, once set right, they will quickly bring all the rest in order;" and he appears to consider the education of other children as of little importance. The consequence of this monstrous heresy has been, that ignorance, the prolific parent of every crime and vice, has predominated over the great body of the people, and a correspondent moral debasement has prevailed. "Man differs more from man than man from beast," says a writer,* once celebrated. This remark, however generally false, will certainly apply with great force to a man in a state of high mental cultivation, and man in a state of extreme ignorance.

This view of human nature is indeed calculated to excite the most painful feelings, and it entirely originates from a consideration of the predominating error which I have expressed. To this source must the crimes and the calamities of the Old World be principally imputed. Ignorance is the cause as well as the effect of bad governments, and without the cultivation of our rational powers, we can entertain no just ideas of the obligations of morality or the excellences of religion. Although England is justly renowned for its cultivation of the arts and sciences, and although the poor-rates of that country exceed five millions sterling per annum, yet (I adopt the words of an eminent British writer) "there is no Protestant country

---

* Montaigne's Essays.

where the education of the poor has been so grossly and infamously neglected as in England." * If one tenth part of that sum had been applied to the education of the poor, the blessings of order, knowledge, and innocence would have been diffused among them, the evil would have been attacked at the fountain-head, and a total revolution would have taken place in the habits and lives of the people, favorable to the cause of industry, good morals, good order, and rational religion.

More just and rational views have been entertained on this subject in the United States. Here, no privileged orders, no factitious distinctions in society, no hereditary nobility, no established religion, no royal prerogatives, exist to interpose barriers between the people, and to create distinct classifications in society. All men being considered as enjoying an equality of rights, the propriety and necessity of dispensing, without distinction, the blessings of education, followed of course. In New England, the greatest attention has been invariably given to this important object. In Connecticut, particularly, the schools are supported, at least three fourths of the year, by the interest of a very large fund created for that purpose, and a small tax on the people; the whole amounting to seventy-eight thousand dollars per annum. The result of this beneficial arrangement is obvious and striking. Our Eastern brethren are a well-informed and moral people. In those States it is as uncommon to find a poor man who cannot read and write, as it is rare to see one in Europe who can.

Pennsylvania has followed the noble example of New England. On the 4th of April last, a law was passed in that State, entitled " An Act to provide for the education of the poor, gratis." The expense of educating them is made a county charge, and the county commissioners are directed to carry the law into execution.

New York has proceeded in the same course, but on a different, and, perhaps, more eligible plan. For a few years back a fund has been accumulating with great celerity, solemnly appropriated to the support of Common Schools. This fund consists, at present, of nearly four hundred thousand dollars in bank-stock, mortgages, and bonds, and produces an annual interest of upwards of twenty-four thousand dollars. The capital will be augmented by the accumulating interest, and the sale of three hundred and thirty-six thousand acres of land. When the interest on the whole amounts to fifty thousand dollars, it will be in a state of distribution. It is highly probable that the whole fund will, in a few years, amount to twelve hundred and fifty thousand dollars, yielding a yearly income of seventy-five thousand dollars. If population is taken as the ratio of distribution, the quota of this city will amount to seven thousand five hundred dollars—a sum amply sufficient on the plan of our establishment, if judiciously applied, to accommodate all our poor with a gratuitous education.

On a comparison of the plan of this State with that of Pennsylvania, it will probably be found that we are entitled to the palm of superior excellence. Our capital is already created, and nothing more is requisite than a

* Edinburgh Review.

judicious distribution ; whereas the expense of school establishments in that State is to be satisfied by annual burdens.   The people of Pennsylvania are therefore interested against a faithful execution of the plan, because the less that is applied to education, the less they will have to pay in taxation. Abuses and perversions will of course arise and multiply in the administration of the public bounty.   And the laws of that State being liable to alteration or repeal, her system has not that permanency and stability to which ours can lay claim.   It is true that our Legislature may divert this fund ; but it would justly be considered a violation of public faith, and a measure of a very violent character.   As long as the public sentiment is correct in this respect, we have no reason to apprehend that any Legislature will be hardy enough to encounter the odium of their constituents and the indignation of posterity.   And we have every reason to believe that this great fund, established for sinking vice and ignorance, will never be diverted or destroyed, but that it will remain unimpaired and in full force and vigor to the latest posterity, as an illustrious establishment, erected by the benevolence of the State, for the propagation of knowledge and the diffusion of virtue among the people.

A number of benevolent persons had seen, with concern, the increasing vices of the city, arising, in a great degree, from the neglected education of the poor.   Great cities are, at all times, the nurseries and hot-beds of crimes. Bad men from all quarters repair to them, in order to obtain the benefit of concealment, and to enjoy in a superior degree the advantages of rapine and fraud.   And the dreadful examples of vice which are presented to youth, and the alluring forms in which it is arrayed, connected with a spirit of extravagance and luxury, the never-failing attendant of great wealth and extensive business, cannot fail of augmenting the mass of moral depravity. " In London," says a distinguished writer on its police, " above twenty thousand individuals rise every morning without knowing how, or by what means, they are to be supported through the passing day, and, in many instances, even where they are to lodge on the ensuing night." *   There can be no doubt that hundreds are in the same situation in this city, prowling about our streets for prey, the victims of intemperance, the slaves of idleness, and ready to fall into any vice, rather than to cultivate industry and good order.   How can it be expected that persons so careless of themselves, will pay any attention to their children ?   The mendicant parent bequeaths his squalid poverty to his offspring, and the hardened thief transmits a legacy of infamy to his unfortunate and depraved descendants.   Instances have occurred of little children, arraigned at the bar of our criminal courts, who have been derelict and abandoned, without a hand to protect, or a voice to guide them, through life.   When interrogated as to their connections, they have replied that they were without home and without friends.   In this state of turpitude and idleness, leading lives of roving mendicancy and petty depredation, they existed, a burden and a disgrace to the community. True it is that charity schools, entitled to eminent praise, were estab-

---

* Colquhoun on Police of London.

2

lished in this city; but they were attached to particular sects, and did not embrace children of different persuasions. Add to this that some denominations were not provided with these establishments, and that children the most in want of instruction were necessarily excluded, by the irreligion of their parents, from the benefit of education.

After a full view of the case, those persons of whom I have spoken agreed that the evil must be corrected at its source, and that education was the sovereign prescription. Under this impression they petitioned the Legislature, who, agreeably to their application, passed a law, on the 9th of April, 1805, entitled " An Act to incorporate the Society instituted in the city of New York, for the establishment of a free school for the education of poor children who do not belong to, or are not provided for by, any religious society." Thirteen trustees were elected under this act, on the first Monday of the ensuing May, with power to manage the affairs of the corporation. On convening together, they found that they had undertaken a great task and encountered an important responsibility; without funds, without teachers, without a house in which to instruct, and without a system of instruction; and that their only reliance must be on their own industry, on the liberality of the public, on the bounty of the constituted authorities, and the smiles of the Almighty Dispenser of all good.

In the year 1798, an obscure man of the name of Joseph Lancaster, possessed of an original genius and a most sagacious mind, and animated by a sublime benevolence, devoted himself to the education of the poor of Great Britain. Wherever he turned his eyes he saw the deplorable state to which they were reduced by the prevalence of ignorance and vice. He first planted his standard of charity in the city of London, where it was calculated that forty thousand children were left as destitute of instruction as the savages of the desert. And he proceeded, by degrees, to form and perfect a system which is, in education, what the neat finished machines for abridging labor and expense are in the mechanic arts.

It comprehends reading, writing, arithmetic, and the knowledge of the Holy Scriptures. It arrives at its object with the least possible trouble and at the least possible expense. Its distinguishing characters are economy, facility, and expedition, and its peculiar improvements are cheapness, activity, order, and emulation. It is impossible on this occasion to give a detailed view of the system. For this I refer you to a publication entitled " Improvements in Education, &c., by Joseph Lancaster; " and for its practical exposition I beg you to look at the operations of this seminary. Reading, in all its processes, from the alphabet upwards, is taught at the same time with writing, commencing with sand, proceeding to the slate, and from thence to the copy-book. And, to borrow a most just and striking remark, " the beauty of the system is, that nothing is trusted to the boy himself; he does not only *repeat* the lesson before a superior, but he *learns* before a superior." * Solitary study does not exist in the establishment. The children are taught in companies. Constant habits of attention and vigilance are

* Edinburgh Review.

formed, and an ardent spirit of emulation kept continually alive. Instruction is performed through the instrumentality of the scholars. The school is divided into classes of ten, and a chief, denominated a monitor, is appointed over each class, who exercises a didactic and supervisional authority. The discipline of the school is enforced by shame, rather than by the infliction of pain. The punishments are varied with circumstances; and a judicious distribution of rewards, calculated to engage the infant mind in the discharge of its duty, forms the key-stone which binds together the whole edifice."

Upon this system Lancaster superintended in person a school of one thousand scholars, at an annual expense of three hundred pounds sterling. In 1806, he proposed, by establishing twenty or thirty schools in different parts of the kingdom, to educate ten thousand poor children, at four shillings per annum each. This proposition has been carried into effect, and he has succeeded in establishing twenty schools in different parts of the kingdom, all of which are under the care of teachers educated by him, few of whom are more than eighteen years old. Several of the schools have each about 300 scholars; that at Manchester has 400. His great school in Borough Road, London, flourishes very much; it has sometimes 1,100 children—seldom less than 1,000.

When I perceive that many boys in our school have been taught to read and write in two months, who did not before know the alphabet, and that even one has accomplished it in three weeks—when I view all the bearings and tendencies of this system—when I contemplate the habits of order which it forms, the spirit of emulation which it excites, the rapid improvement which it produces, the purity of morals which it inculcates—when I behold the extraordinary union of celerity in instruction and economy of expense—and when I perceive one great assembly of a thousand children, under the eye of a single teacher, marching, with unexampled rapidity and with perfect discipline, to the goal of knowledge, I confess that I recognize in Lancaster the benefactor of the human race. I consider his system as creating a new era in education, as a blessing sent down from heaven to redeem the poor and distressed of this world from the power and dominion of ignorance.

Although the merits of this apostle of benevolence have been generally acknowledged in his own country, and he has received the countenance and protection of the first men of Great Britain, yet calumny has lifted up her voice against him, and attempts have been made to rob him of his laurels. Danger to the Established Church and to Government has been apprehended from his endeavors to pour light upon mankind. This insinuation has been abundantly repelled by the tenor of his life—his carefully steering clear, in his instructions, of any peculiar creed, and his confining himself to the general truths of Christianity. " I have," says Lancaster, " been eight years engaged in the benevolent work of superintending the education of the poor. I have had three thousand children, who owe their education to me, some of whom have left school, are apprenticed or in place, and are going on well. I have had great influence with both parents and children, among whom there is, nevertheless, no one instance of a convert to my religious profession." That knowledge is the parent of sedition and insurrection, and that, in proportion as the public mind is illuminated, the principles of anarchy are disseminated, is a proposition that can never admit of debate, at least in this country.

But Lancaster has also been accused of arrogating to himself surreptitious honors, and attempts have been made to transfer the entire merit of his great discovery to Dr. Bell. Whatever he borrowed from that gentleman he has candidly acknowledged. The use of sand, in teaching, undoubtedly came to him through that channel; but it has been practised for ages by the Brahmins. He may also be indebted to Bell for some other improvements, but the vital leading principles of his system are emphatically an original discovery.

The trustees of this institution, after due deliberation, did not hesitate to adopt the system of Lancaster; and, in carrying it into effect, they derived essential aid from one of their body who had seen it practised in England, and who had had personal communication with its author. A teacher was also selected who has fully answered every reasonable expectation. He has generally followed the prescribed plan. Wherever he has deviated, he has improved. A more numerous, a better governed school, affording equal facilities to improvement, is not to be found in the United States.

Provided thus with an excellent system and an able teacher, the school was opened on the 6th of May, 1806, in a small apartment in Bancker street. This was the first scion of the Lancaster stock in the United States; and from this humble beginning, in the course of little more than three years, you all observe the rapidity with which we have ascended.

One great desideratum still remained to be supplied. Without sufficient funds, nothing could be efficiently done. Animated appeals were made to the bounty of our citizens, and five thousand six hundred and forty-eight dollars were collected by subscription. Application was also made to the Legislature of this State for assistance, and on the 27th of February, 1807, a law was passed appropriating four thousand dollars, "for the purpose of erecting a suitable building, or buildings, for the instruction of poor children; and every year thereafter, the sum of one thousand dollars, for the purpose of promoting the benevolent objects of the Society." The preamble of this liberal act contains a legislative declaration of the excellence of the Lancaster system, in the following words: " *Whereas*, the Trustees of the Society for establishing a Free School in the City of New York for the education of such poor children as do not belong to, or are not provided for by, any religious society, have, by their memorial, solicited the aid of the Legislature; and whereas their plan of extending the benefits of education to poor children, and the excellent mode of instruction adopted by them, are highly deserving of the encouragement of Government."

Application was also made to the Corporation of the city for assistance; and the tenement in Bancker street being in all respects inadequate to the accommodation of the increasing establishment, that body appropriated a building adjacent to the Almshouse, for the temporary accommodation of the school, and the sum of five hundred dollars towards putting it in repair; the Society agreeing to receive and educate fifty children from the Almshouse. To this place the school was removed on the 1st of May, 1807, where it has continued until to-day.

The Corporation also presented the ground of this edifice, on which was an arsenal, to the Society, on condition of their educating the children of the Almshouse gratuitously; and also the sum of fifteen hundred dollars to aid in the completion of this building. The value of this lot and the old building, may be fairly estimated at ten thousand dollars; and the Society have expended above thirteen thousand dollars in the erection and completion of this edifice and the adjacent buildings. The income of the school during the last year has been about sixteen hundred dollars, and its expense did not differ much from that sum. This room will contain nearly six hundred scholars, and below there are apartments for the family of the teacher, for the meeting of the trustees, and for a female school, which may contain one hundred scholars, and may be considered as an useful adjunct to this institution. This seminary was established about twelve years ago by a number of young women belonging to, or professing with, the Society of Friends, who have, with meritorious zeal and exemplary industry, devoted much of their personal attention, and all their influence, to the education of poor girls in the elementary parts of education and needle-work. The signal success which attended this Free School animated the trustees with a desire to extend its usefulness, and to render it coëxtensive with the wants of the community and commensurate with the objects of public bounty. A statute was accordingly passed, on their application, on the 1st of April, 1808, altering the style of this corporation, denominating it "The Free-School Society of New York," and extending its powers to all children who are the objects of a gratuitous education.

From this elevation of prosperity and this position of philanthropy, the Society had the satisfaction of seeing that the wise and the good of this and the neighboring States had turned their attention to this establishment. A number of ladies of this city, distinguished for their consideration in society, and honored and respected for their undeviating cultivation of the charities of life, established a society for the very humane, charitable, and laudable purposes of protecting, relieving, and instructing orphan children. This institution was incorporated on the 7th of April, 1807, under the style of "The Orphan Asylum Society in the City of New York;" and at a subsequent period the Legislature, under a full conviction of its great merits and claims to public patronage, made a disposition in its favor, which will, in process of time, produce five thousand dollars.

A large building, fifty feet square and three stories high, has been erected for its accommodation, in the suburbs of the city, and it now contains seventy children, who are supported by the zeal and benevolence of its worthy members, and educated on the plan of this institution, at an annual expense of two thousand dollars.

An economical school, whose principal object is the instruction of the children of the refugees from the West Indies, was opened some time since in this city, where, in addition to the elementary parts of education, grammar, history, geography, and the French language are taught. It is conducted on the plan of Lancaster, with modifications and extensions, and is patronized and cherished by French and American gentlemen of great worth and respectability, who are entitled to every praise for their benevolence. Children of either sex are admitted, without distinction of nation, religion, or fortune. This seminary is in a flourishing condition, and contains two hundred scholars. There are two masters in this seminary, and two women who teach needle-work; and there is a printing-press, where such as have any talents in that way are taught that important art.

We have also the satisfaction of seeing the benefits of this system extended, either in whole or in part, to the charity schools of the Dutch, Episcopal, and Methodist Churches, and of the Presbyterian Church in Rutgers street; and also to the school founded by the Manumission Society, for the education of the people of color, which has, in consequence of this amelioration, been augmented from seventy to one hundred and thirty children.

In Philadelphia the same laudable spirit has been manifested. Two deputations from that city have visited us for the express purpose of examining our school. One of these made so favorable a report on their return, that a number of the more enterprising and benevolent citizens, composed of members belonging to the Society of Friends, immediately associated under the name of the "Adelphi Society," and raised, by private subscription, a sum sufficient to purchase a suitable lot of ground, to erect a handsome two-story brick building seventy-five feet in length and thirty-five in breadth, in which they formed two spacious rooms. The Adelphi school now contains two hundred children, under the care of one teacher, and is eminently prosperous. The other deputation made also a favorable report, and "The Philadelphia Free-School Society," an old and respectable institution, adopted, in consequence, our system, where it flourishes beyond expectation.

Two female schools, one called the "Aimwell School," in Philadelphia, and another in Burlington, N. J., have also embraced our plan with equal success.

I trust that I shall be pardoned for this detail. The origin and progress of beneficial discoveries cannot be too minutely specified; and when their diffusion can only be exceeded by their excellence, we have peculiar reason to congratulate the friends of humanity. This prompt and general encouragement is honorable to our national character, and shows conclusively that the habits, manners, and opinions of the American people are favorable to the reception of truth and the propagation of knowledge. And no earthly consideration could induce the benevolent man to whom we are indebted for what we see this day, to exchange his feelings, if from the obscure mansions of indigence, in which, in all human probability, he now is instilling comfort into the hearts and infusing knowledge into the minds of the poor, he could hear the voice of a great and enlightened people pronouncing his eulogium, and see this parent seminary, and the establishments which have sprung from its bosom, diffusing light, imparting joy, and dispensing virtue. His tree of knowledge is indeed transplanted to a more fertile soil and a more congenial clime. It has flourished with uncommon vigor and beauty; its luxuriant and wide-spreading branches afford shelter to all who require it; its ambrosial fragrance fills the land, and its head reaches the heavens!

Far be it from my intention to prevent future exertion. For, although much has been done, yet much remains to do, to carry into full effect the system. It would be improper to conceal from you, that, in order to finish this edifice, we have incurred a considerable debt, which our ordinary income cannot extinguish; and that, therefore, we must repose ourselves on the public beneficence. It has been usual to supply the more indigent children with necessaries, to protect them against the inclemencies of winter; for without this provision their attendance would be utterly impracticable. This has hitherto been accomplished by the bounty of individuals, and to no other source can we at present appeal with success.

The law from which we derive our corporate existence does not confine us to one seminary, but contemplates the establishment of schools. A restriction to a single institution would greatly impair our usefulness, and would effectually discourage those exertions which are necessary in order to spread knowledge among all the indigent.

Col. Henry Rutgers, with his characteristic benevolence, has made a donation of two lots in Henry street, worth at least twenty-five hundred dollars, to this corporation. By a condition contained in one of the deeds, it is necessary that we should erect a school-house by June, 1811; and it is highly proper, without any reference to the condition, that this should be accomplished as soon as possible, in order to meet the wants of the indigent in that populous part of the city. If some charitable and public-spirited citizen would follow up this beneficence, and make a similar conveyance on the opposite side of the city, and if the liberality of the public shall dispense the means of erecting the necessary buildings, then the exigencies of all our poor, with respect to education, would be amply supplied for a number of years.

After our youth are instructed in the elements of useful knowledge, it is indispensable to their future usefulness that some calling should be marked out for them. As most of them will undoubtedly be brought up in useful trades, pecuniary means to facilitate their progress to this object would, if properly applied, greatly redound to the benefit of the individual, as well as to the poor of the community.

In such an extensive and comprehensive establishment we are to expect, according to the course of human events, that children of extraordinary genius and merit will rise up, entitled to extraordinary patronage. To select such from the common mass—to watch over their future destiny—to advance them through all the stages of education and through all the grades of knowledge, and to settle them in useful and honorable professions, are duties of primary importance, and indispensable obligations. This, however, will require considerable funds; but of what estimation are pecuniary sacrifices, when put in the scale against the important benefits that may result? And if we could draw aside the veil of futurity, perhaps we might see in the off-spring of this establishment, so patronized and so encouraged, characters that will do honor to human nature—that will have it in their power

> The applause of listening senates to command,
>   The threats of pain and ruin to despise ;
> To scatter plenty o'er a smiling land,
>   And read their history in a nation's eyes.

The experience of the Society having made the expediency of an amendment of the law apparent, the trustees memorialized the Legislature accordingly, and on the 24th of March, 1810, an act was passed, directing that no person should be thereafter entitled to become a member of the Society unless he should contribute the sum of fifty dollars ; and that every member hereafter admitted should have the right to send one child to one of the schools of the Society ; but that nothing in the act should be deemed to affect the rights of those who were members at the time of the passage of the act.

It was also enacted, that at each first meeting of the trustees, after every annual election, it should be in their discretion to appoint, out of the members of the Society, an additional number of trustees, not exceeding five. In the same act the Legislature made a further appropriation of the sum of four thousand dollars for the Society.

The trustees deeming it advisable to establish, without loss of time, another school on the ground presented by Col. Henry Rutgers, subscriptions were opened early in the year 1810, for the purpose of enabling them to erect the contemplated building. The benevolence of the citizens of New York, great on all occasions, promptly responded to this effort ; and although the trustees had so recently collected the sum of ten thousand dollars, they obtained, on this occasion, an additional subscription of over thirteen thousand dollars.

In the autumn of the same year, the trustees were deprived of the services of one of their ablest coadjutors, by the death of their Secretary, BENJAMIN D. PERKINS. His labors in behalf of the Society had been of marked value, and a record was entered on the minutes expressive of their sense of the loss which had been sustained, and of their respect and esteem for the memory of their fellow-laborer.

A committee having been appointed to proceed with and

superintend the erection of the school-house in Henry street, and the necessary contracts having been completed, the corner-stone of the new building was laid on the 11th of November, 1810, by the benevolent donor of the site. The ceremony was witnessed by several members of the Corporation of the city, and other citizens.

In December of the same year, one hundred dollars were appropriated to the purchase of suitable books, to commence a circulating library for the school, additions to which were solicited from the members of the Society. During the same month a legacy of two hundred and fifty dollars was bequeathed to the Society by CHARLES LE ROUX, Esq.

The year 1811 was marked by the further extension of public patronage and assistance. The Legislature again testified their approbation of the institution, by the passage of an act, on the 30th of March, in which a grant of four thousand dollars was made to the Society for building purposes, and an additional annual sum of five hundred dollars, until the pleasure of the Legislature should otherwise determine.

Two eligible positions for schools having now been obtained, it appeared to the trustees that an additional school in the northwestern part of the city would enable them to extend the sphere of their usefulness with great benefit to that vicinity. The village of Greenwich at that time comprised a suburban population of considerable magnitude, presenting, in the character of a large class of its population, a ripe field for the labors of the Society. A large portion of the landed property belonged to the corporation of Trinity Church; and, inspired with some hope that the petition would be responded to, the trustees appealed to the vestry, in the spring of 1811, for a site for a new free school. The vestry promptly and generously granted to the Society two large lots of ground at the corner of Hudson and Grove streets, near the village of Greenwich. The estimated value of the lots was one thousand dollars.

The building in Henry street being completed, it was opened on the 13th of November, 1811, and known as School No. 2. The edifice was eighty feet in length and forty in width, and accommodated three hundred children; while in the lower story was an apartment suitable for the use of one hundred and fifty others. The building resembled that erected for No. 1, in Chatham street, although much smaller in size, and, like it, had accommodations for the family of the teacher. It was completed at an expense of about $11,000.

The increasing labor and responsibility devolving upon the trustees led them to desire a further addition to their working force by an increase of their number, and they applied to the Legislature for authority to make this election. In compliance with the request, that body passed an act, on the 28th of February, 1812, directing that the Society should thereafter elect six trustees in addition to those primarily authorized by law.

The system which had been commenced with so much solicitude and care had now reached a point in its history when it was regarded as being not only a permanent, but an expansive, institution. The responsibility of so organizing and maturing the system of instruction as to make it at once thorough in its operations and as faultless as possible in its details, in order that it should commend itself to the public favor and confidence, was deeply felt.

The original object of the Society having been to provide for the education of those children " who did not belong to, or were not provided for, by any religious society," the question would naturally present itself to the minds of all who were impressed with the importance of inculcating moral and religious truth, whether such a class of children, and so numerous as they appeared to be, should be left without such instruction. Pleasure and satisfaction were expressed by all acquainted with the schools at the results which had been reached in the literary training of the pupils, and the improvement in their conduct and intercourse, to which special attention was given. Yet there were some who thought that sufficient care had not been bestowed in the communication of specific religious instruction. A concern of such high importance had not, however, been overlooked by the trustees ; and they had pursued such measures in regard to it as they considered to be most expedient. The board was composed of persons of almost every religious denomination— men who were attached to their respective creeds, and who would not fail, on suitable occasions, to recommend them to the attention of others. But, in the schools under their care, they had studiously avoided the inculcation of the peculiar tenets of any one religious society or denomination. From the commencement of their effort, they had directed that the Holy Scriptures should be read daily in the schools ; and it was thought that the

minds of the children could not fail to be impressed with the
sublime precepts and the inspired teachings of the Sacred Volume. In order, however, to meet the wishes of all, it was
deemed expedient to suspend the exercises of the school on Tuesday afternoon of each week, and devote the time of the session
exclusively to the religious instruction of the children. An association of more than fifty ladies of the first position and character, and belonging to the different religious denominations in the
city, volunteered their services; and they accordingly met at the
schools to examine the children in their respective catechisms on
the day appointed for that purpose.

In addition to these labors, it was also determined that the
children should assemble at their respective schools on the morning
of every Sunday, and proceed, under the care of a monitor, to the
places of public worship to which they respectively belonged.

Thus far the schools had been organized for males only ; but
apartments were reserved in both the buildings for the use of
female schools, and in these rooms the FEMALE ASSOCIATION,
composed of ladies, members of the Society of Friends, conducted schools for girls. They adopted the Lancasterian plan of
instruction, similar to that of the male schools, and besides the
elementary parts of education, they taught needle-work and
other useful employments. The two schools were attended by
about three hundred girls, while the boys' schools numbered
about eight hundred pupils as the average attendance.

Nine years had now elapsed since the foundation of the Society, and the trustees had the satisfaction of seeing their efforts
not only crowned with success, but their enterprise placed on a
liberal and permanent basis, which exceeded all the anticipations
they had dared to entertain. They had introduced to this country a method of instruction well adapted to effect its objects,
comprehensive and economical. It had demonstrated its utility,
its simplicity, and its value, and had so stimulated the labors of
philanthropists in other cities and towns, that many similar institutions had sprung into existence, modelled after the parent society in New York. The benefits thus positively reaped were
multiplied, and an impetus was given to the work of popular
education, which could scarcely have been gained by any other
method, however good, which did not possess its novelty and its
characteristics.

CHAPTER II.

HISTORY FROM 1817-1822.

New Schools Proposed—Lancasterian Teacher from England—A Legacy—Instruction of Monitors—Economy—Discipline—School No. 3—School No. 4—School Libraries—Teachers Trained—Charles Picton—The Freemasons—Monitors and Apprentices—"Morning Schools"—New Regulations—Manual—Shepherd Johnson—Joseph Lancaster—Visit to New York—Finances—Memorial to the Legislature—Grant of $5,000—Address to the Parents and Guardians of Children—Sunday, and Sunday Schools—The Female Association—School No. 4 Opened—Death of John Murray—New Building for No. 3—Manual of Instruction—State of the Schools—Rev. J. N. Maffit's Address to the Schools—School No. 2—Catechism Adopted—Visit of a Committee of the Legislature—The Bethel Baptist Church—Special Privileges—School No. 5—Plans and Estimates for Extension of the System—A Man of Fortune, and a Man in Independent Circumstances—Lots for School No. 5 Purchased—The Bethel Baptist Church.

THE population in the eastern part of the city increased, and offered a growing field for the operations of the Society. In the early part of the year 1817, the propriety of erecting a school-house in a central location, between the Bowery and the East River, was discussed; and Thomas Eddy, James Palmer, Henry Eckford, Noah Brown, and Whitehead Hicks were appointed a committee to ascertain what amount of subscriptions could be obtained toward the purchase of lots and the erection of a building, and also to obtain plans and estimates. In consequence of the difficulty of procuring a proper site, the purchase was not made until 1818, when three lots were obtained in Rivington street, upon which the school known as No. 4 was afterward erected.

The employment of competent teachers for the schools suggested to the board the propriety of securing the services of an experienced teacher, well qualified to conduct a school on the Lancasterian system as taught in England. A committee of three was appointed to correspond with gentlemen in that country, who should select a teacher thus qualified.

During the year, a legacy of two hundred and fifty dollars was received from the estate of Mary McCrea, and another of five hundred dollars, bequeathed by John Van Blarcom, which were valuable contributions to the means of the Society.

The organization of a class of monitors, who should enjoy the benefits of a systematic training in advanced studies, formed an important measure in the work of the year.

The necessity of an economical administration of the affairs of the Society, which had always been of primary consideration with the trustees, was urged upon the attention of the board, and referred to a committee. The report embraced the following recommendations:

1st. That the office of assistants be abolished.

2d. That no rewards be given to the monitors in money, nor in any thing else, except on extraordinary occasions, and those of but small value.

3d. That one or two persons be appointed whose business it should be to purchase all supplies for the institution, on the lowest possible terms.

The first recommendation was promptly adopted, and a resolution was passed terminating the engagements of the assistant teachers at the expiration of the several terms for which they were employed. Jacob Lorillard and Lindley Murray were appointed supply committee; and the question in reference to monitors entered into the general plan of rewards and punishments, and the organization of the monitorial class.

The system of rewards and discipline occupied the special attention of the board during a part of the year, and the report of the committee to whom that subject had been assigned was submitted at the first meeting held in 1818.

During the latter part of the year, the residents in that section of the city known as Corlear's Hook presented a petition for the establishment of a free school in their vicinity; but the trustees were unable to comply with the application.

In the early part of 1818, information was communicated to the board that a room in the building on the corner of Hudson and Christopher streets could be procured from the Corporation of the city for school purposes; and Thomas C. Taylor, Najah Taylor, and John R. Murray were named as a committee to make application for the premises, if found suitable, and super-

intend their preparation for the reception of pupils. The committee reported, on the 1st of May, that the arrangements had
been made; and SHEPHERD JOHNSON, who had been trained in
Free School No. 1, was appointed teacher, at a salary of five
hundred dollars per annum. The school was opened on the 25th
of the same month, with 51 pupils, the number of which was
increased to 196 before the 5th of June.

The school increased in numbers with such rapidity, that, at
the meeting of the board held on the 23d of the same month,
the committee reported that 216 scholars had been admitted,
with a regular attendance of over 200. The room, however, not
being large enough to accommodate more than 164 scholars, a
recommendation was submitted that application be made to the
Corporation for the use of another apartment in the same building. This application was made and promptly granted.

At the meeting held on the 1st of May, the committee for
the purchase of lots in the eastern part of the city reported that
they had contracted with John R. Livingston for the purchase
of three lots of ground in Rivington street, between Ridge and
Pitt streets, for seven hundred dollars each. The action of the
committee was approved by the board, and they were authorized to make the purchase. The treasurer was directed to sell
sufficient stock held by the Society to meet the warrant of the
committee of purchase. The report of plans and estimates for
the building was submitted in September, and the sum of
$10,724.36 was named as the cost of the erection of the new
house, which became known as No. 4. The contract, however,
was made for $9,000.

At the close of the year, a committee on the "state of the
New York Free School" reported several measures of improvement, among which was the establishment of school libraries.
The resolution of the committee called for the expenditure of
fifty dollars for books for a library for each school, the use to be
limited to the best scholars, who should form a "class of
merit."

The same committee recommended that young men wishing
to qualify themselves for the profession of teaching on the system of Joseph Lancaster, should be allowed to visit the schools
and assist the teacher in the discharge of his duties, and, after a
period of six weeks spent in acquiring a knowledge of the sys-

tem, they should be furnished with a certificate to that effect, signed by the president and secretary.

The committee appointed to correspond with the secretary of the British and Foreign School Society, with reference to the selection of an experienced Lancasterian teacher, reported, early in June, that they had received a letter from that gentleman, communicating the fact that they had made choice of Mr. CHARLES PICTON, who was approved by the Society, and had been engaged on the terms offered by the committee, and that he would sail for New York in June. A resolution of thanks to the secretary was adopted, and the committee directed to receive Mr. Picton on his arrival.

At the meeting held on September 4, the chairman laid before the board a letter from the British and Foreign School Society, introducing Mr. Picton, the teacher, who had arrived, and awaited the action of the board. Mr. Picton was present and introduced to the trustees, and cordially welcomed to his new field of labor.

During the year 1810, an arrangement had been made between a committee of the Free-School Society and a committee acting on behalf of the Grand Lodge of Freemasons, for the education of fifty children of members of that Society, on the annual payment of three hundred dollars. The arrangement was approved by the board on the 4th of June, 1810, and was continued until the close of 1817, when the treasurer was notified that the Grand Lodge desired to terminate the agreement.

In January, 1818, a committee was appointed by the board to report upon the communication from the Grand Lodge; and in June the committee reported in favor of terminating the arrangement, and at the same time recommended that the children presented for admission by the Masons should enjoy all the advantages of the Free-School Society, without any discrimination. The report was unanimously adopted.

The committee on the classification and education of monitors, besides other recommendations, in October submitted a report, in which it was advised that monitors should be indentured as apprentices to the Society, to learn the art of teaching by a regular form, as in other pursuits. The matter was discussed at several meetings, and finally recommitted, as the power of the board to hold apprentices was doubtful. The committee was enlarged, and authorized to prepare a memorial to the Legislature, asking for the proper legal assistance in perfecting the measure, if deemed advisable.

The report on the general interests of the institution, which was presented by the committee in November, contained several propositions, which were adopted by the board. Among these were the following: Morning schools to be held from 6 to 8 o'clock, for the "apprentices," or monitors, and the more meritorious of the pupils in the higher classes; the ordering of an annual invoice of the quantity of supplies required in each of the schools for the year; a provision of $50 for a library for the several schools; and the permission to young men to practice teaching in the schools, and receive credentials accordingly.

A petition for the establishment of a school in the northeastern section of the city was received, and referred to a committee, consisting of James Palmer, Henry Eckford, Whitehead Hicks, John Withington, and Benjamin Marshall, who were directed to report on all questions relative to the enterprise.

A manual of the system of instruction adopted in the schools being deemed desirable, the preparation of the work was entrusted to Jeremiah Thompson, Rensselaer Havens, and Samuel Wood.

A resolution was adopted, on the 4th of December, in relation to the teacher of No. 3, as follows:

Resolved, That, on account of the increased size of SHEPHERD JOHNSON's school, and the satisfactory discharge of duty on his part, his salary be increased to eight hundred dollars, to date from the 1st of November last.

JOSEPH LANCASTER, the founder of the system of instruction known by his name, was at this time in the city of New York, on a visit in behalf of popular education. To afford him the opportunity of making his system known, as well as to receive the benefits of his suggestions and long experience, the board adopted a resolution, offered by the president, DE WITT CLINTON, permitting him to use the school-rooms of the Society at such hours as were not devoted to instruction, for the purpose of delivering lectures on the monitorial system.

The commencement of the year 1819 found the Society in a condition of active usefulness, but with insufficient means. The demands made upon its resources in order to keep the schools in operation, and to supply the books and other apparatus of instruction, were so considerable as to make an effort at retrenchment necessary, and almost imperative. The committee to whom the question of the financial condition of the Society had been referred, reported in January, and submitted the following facts :

The payments of the last quarter, exclusive of those on account of fitting up premises for No. 3, and building No. 4, amounted to $2,035.78, or $680 per month.

The expenses of the year, as estimated by the committee, amounted to $14,300 ; to provide for which there was a balance in the treasury of $2,235 ; probable collections in the Seventh Ward, $500 ; rents, &c., $100 ; total, $2,235 ; leaving a deficiency of $11,465.

The committee recommended that an application be made to the Legislature for pecuniary aid, and that temporary loans be secured until permanent relief should be afforded from other sources. The salaries of the teachers of Nos. 1 and 2 were also reduced to $800 per annum ; and it was also recommended that the regulations allowing board and clothing to the monitors general should be abolished, and an annual salary of $100 be allowed them. It was estimated that these retrenchments would save the Society about $1,000 yearly.

The committee also suggested that a statement of the financial condition of the Society should be made to the Female Association which had the charge of the schools for girls, and that they be informed that a payment of $500 a year as rental would be received in aid of the Society, but that the said communication should not be construed as a *demand*.

The report of the committee was adopted, and the several measures recommended were referred to appropriate special committees for their action.

On the 19th of January, the board held a meeting to consider the report of the committee to prepare a memorial to the Legislature, which was adopted, as follows :

To the Representatives of the People of the State of New York in Senate and Assembly convened :

The Memorial of the Free-School Society of New York,

RESPECTFULLY SHEWETH,

That, in the year 1805, your memorialists, under a deep conviction

3

that early and wholesome principles of education were of the first importance to the security, prosperity, and happiness of every community, united their exertions to establish the Free-School Society of New York.

Feeling the insufficiency of their efforts, unless sustained by public munificence, they have applied to the Legislature of the State at various times for aid and assistance, and met with an encouragement characteristic of the Representatives of an enlightened people.

Fostered by legislative bounty and private liberality, they have been enabled to persevere in the prosecution of their object, and to crown their original design with great success.

From the establishment of the Free-School Society to the present time, 7,541 children have been taught in the schools under its superintendence; and there are now in the schools 1,169 children who are daily instructed in the various branches of elementary education, so far as is requisite for the transaction of business in the ordinary concerns of life.

In extending these blessings, your memorialists have adopted the Lancasterian plan of instruction, which was introduced into the United States by them, and has been found preferable to all others. The experience of Europe, wherein its principles have been extensively adopted, sanctions its superior excellence; and in our own country, so far as it has been practised, it has received the most unqualified approbation. Its preference has been found in the saving of expense, when compared with the ordinary methods of school instruction, and in the ease and expedition with which children can be taught the requisite lessons. The expense of each pupil has been found to be less than four dollars annually, including teachers' salaries, stationery, and all other incidental charges; whereas, according to the former method, the annual expense was not less than sixteen dollars, in this city, for each scholar—a test that palpably evinces the superiority of the present mode of instruction.

The general influence of our schools has not been confined to the city of New York. In order to promote a more extended knowledge of the system, and the establishment of similar schools, they have been and are open, free of expense, to the inspection and attendance of persons from different parts of this and other States, a sufficient time to enable them to acquire the means and capacity of imparting instruction to others, on the Lancasterian plan, with ease and dispatch.

By direction of the trustees, Lancasterian lessons have been printed for the use of the Junior classes in country schools; and they are now engaged in preparing a manual of the system for the assistance of teachers in organizing and conducting their schools on the plan pursued in this city.

Public conviction bears a testimony that, your memorialists believe, has no exception to the happy results which have already been realized from these schools. Their salutary influence is everywhere acknowledged, and the condition of the poor finds a melioration that not only imparts present comfort and relief, but which will be felt by future generations.

Notwithstanding the liberality of former Legislatures, and the fruitful source of support which your memorialists have found in the contributions of individual charity, such has been the great increase of population, particularly by the influx of foreigners in the city of New York, and of the number of poor children whom the trustees of the Free-School Society have been impelled to provide for by the strongest dictates of duty and benevolence, that they have incurred recent expenses which their present resources are incompetent to discharge. During the past year they have established a third school at Greenwich, at an expense of about $1,200. They have also purchased lots, and are erecting a building to contain nearly 600 children, in the northeastern part of the city, the expense of which establishment will be about $13,000. This building is constructing in a quarter of our metropolis where the want of schools is extremely great, and where the blessings of elementary instruction among the lower orders were not enjoyed. Your memorialists could not, consistently with the noble plan of charity committed to their charge, hear the daily calls of this large portion of the community in vain, or behold the baneful triumph of increasing ignorance and vice, without an effort to remove the evil.

Trusting with confidence to the uniform liberality of an enlightened Legislature in diffusing the manifold blessings of education, and considering the State Government as the protecting parent, who has long nursed with parental regard this adopted child of her bounty, the New York Free-School Society, your memorialists, respectfully petition for a grant of ten thousand four hundred and sixty-five dollars, out of such funds as the wisdom of the Legislature shall designate, to enable them to complete their new improvements.

In respectfully soliciting this grant, and in congratulating the Legislature on the salutary effects of their former encouragement, your memorialists remark, that, as the city of New York rapidly increases in population, the number is multiplied of poor and suffering children, who must progress from the cradle to maturity, with no schools but those of profligacy and guilt, unless the hand of charity be extended to reclaim their steps. If we would prevent the vices and crimes of European cities from visiting our own; if we would prohibit the sanguinary penal codes of Europe from reaching our shores, we must look to early education and early habits, the fundamental springs of action and character in all communities, as the protecting resort; if we would perpetuate our civil institutions and our religious privileges, we must look to early education to guard and strengthen their foundation.

Believing these observations will be reciprocated by the public body to whom they address their memorial, they make their appeal with confidence, remembering it is to a body to whom your memorialists have never appealed in vain, when their object has been to extend the cheering light of education.

Let it be remembered, when the petition of your memorialists is considered, that nearly two thousand children will, the ensuing season, be under their care, and that it is on behalf of these, and many thousands more who will hereafter claim their charge, that your memorialists appeal to the Honorable Legislature.

The answer to this application was the passage of an act, on the 26th of March, making an appropriation of $5,000 for the use of the Society.

A committee having been appointed to prepare an address to the public on behalf of the Society, a draft thereof was offered for acceptance, recommitted, and at the meeting held on the 9th of April, it was adopted. This address contains a very clear expression of the views and motives which governed the Society and its friends, and is interesting not only as an embodiment of those views, but as an authentic avowal of the nature of the religious influences which at the time prevailed in the Society. Whatever differences of opinion may exist as to the theological character of the address, it may be safely assumed that men acting under such high convictions could not be unworthy of confidence in the delicate and responsible work of training the young and neglected members of society. The address is as follows :

AN ADDRESS

To the Parents and Guardians of the Children belonging to the Schools under the care of the New York Free-School Society.

SEC. 1. The New York Free Schools, for the instruction of such children as are the objects of a gratuitous education, have been established many years ; and the trustees have endeavored to render them useful and promotive of the moral and literary improvement of the scholars, and they still wish to do all in their power to advance the welfare of both children and parent.

SEC. 2. They wish to impress on your minds the importance of this establishment, that you may manifest an increasing concern for its prosperity, seeing that much depends on your coöperation in the support of an institution which is intended to promote not only the good of your children, but their happiness and yours, both here and hereafter.

SEC. 3. It is of great importance that the minds of your children should be early cultivated and moral instruction inculcated, and that, by example as well as precept, you should use all endeavors to preserve them in innocency.

SEC. 4. As a good education is calculated to lay the foundation of usefulness and respectability, both in civil and religious society, it is your duty to improve every opportunity to promote it.

SEC. 5. This institution holds out much encouragement, and you are bound by every moral obligation to avail yourselves of the advantages which your children may derive from a steady attendance at school, where they may acquire not only school learning to qualify them for business, but be improved in their morals and manners.

SEC. 6. Many of you have not been favored with the privileges your children now enjoy—that of a gratuitous education. Every parent who is solicitous for the welfare of his offspring, but whose circumstances may be such as not to be able to pay the expense, is invited to come forward and place them where they may be instructed in literature, in the paths of virtue, and in the road to happiness.

SEC. 7. The trustees may venture to say, that this institution may be productive of great good to you, and to your children especially, if, on your part, there is a disposition to promote it. We wish your children may be furnished with a good education, and early acquire good habits. As they grow in years, they should be impressed with the importance of industry and frugality. These are virtues necessary to form useful characters.

SEC. 8. You know that many evils grow out of idleness, and many more out of the improper use of spirituous liquors; that they are ruinous and destructive to morals, and debase the human character below the lowest of all created beings; we therefore earnestly desire you may be watchful and careful in this respect, otherwise in vain may we labor to promote the welfare of your children.

SEC. 9. In domestic life there are many virtues which are requisite in order to promote the comfort and welfare of families. Temperance and economy are indispensable, but without cleanliness, your enjoyments as well as your reputation will be impaired. It is promotive of health, and ought not to be neglected. Parents can, perhaps, scarcely give a greater proof of their care for their children, than by keeping them clean and decent, especially when they are sent to school, where it is expected they will appear with their hands, faces, and heads perfectly clean, and their clothing clean and in good order. The appearance of children exhibits to every observing mind the character of the mother.

SEC. 10. Among other moral and religious duties, that of a due observance of the first day of the week, commonly called Sunday, we consider of importance to yourselves and to your children. Public worship is a duty we owe to our Creator; it is of universal obligation, and you ought to be good examples therein, encouraging your families to the due observance thereof; and believing, as we do, that the establishment of what is called Sunday schools has been a blessing to many, and may prove so to many more, we are desirous you may unite in the support of a plan so well calculated to promote the religious duties of that day, which ought to be appropriated to public worship, retirement, and other duties connected with the improvement of the mind.

SEC. 11. Seeing, next to your own souls, your children and those placed under your care are, or ought to be, the immediate objects of your constant attention and diligent concern, you ought to omit no opportunity to instruct them early in the principles of the Christian religion, in order to bring them, in their youth, to a sense of the unspeakable love and infinite wisdom and power of their Almighty Creator; for good and early impressions on tender minds often prove a lasting means of preserving them in a religious life even to old age. May you, therefore, watch over them for good, and rule over them in the fear of GOD, maintaining your authority in love; and as very much depends on the care and exemplary conduct of parents, and the judicious management of children by tutors, we cannot too strongly recommend to their serious consideration the importance of the subject, as one deeply interesting to the welfare of the rising generation, and no less connected with the best interests of civil and religious society.

SEC. 12. As the Holy Scriptures, or Bible, with which you ought all to be furnished, contain a full account of things most surely to be believed and Divine commands most faithfully to be obeyed, and are said to make wise unto salvation through faith which is in Jesus Christ (2 Tim. iii. 15), it is the duty of every Christian to be frequent and diligent in the reading of them in their families, and in privately meditating on those sacred records.

SEC. 13. The trustees of the New York Free School, however desirous they may be to promote the improvement of the scholars in school learning, to qualify and fit them for the common duties of life, cannot view with an eye of indifference the more primary object of an education calculated to form habits of virtue and industry, and to inculcate the general principles of Christianity; for in proportion as you are established in a life of piety and virtue, you will be enabled to bring up your children in the nurture and admonition of the Lord, ever bearing in remembrance that example speaks a louder language than precept.

SEC. 14. It may not be improper to state to you, that the establishment of the New York Free School has been attended with much labor and personal exertions on the part of its friends and patrons; great expense has also accrued, and continues to be the case, where so many buildings are erected and so many teachers employed; and as all this is done in order to promote the good of your children, and to improve their condition, you cannot but feel a weight of obligation to the friends and patrons of so valuable an institution. In speaking of the teachers, it is due to them and their meritorious conduct to say, that they have manifested a zeal and concern for the welfare and impovement of the children placed under their care, and we wish they may be encouraged to persevere in the arduous service assigned them.

SCE. 15. There are divers other things which we could enumerate as connected with the subject of this address; but it cannot be expected, in a communication of this nature, we should embrace every duty or point out minutely every thing which might have a bearing on your religious and moral character; but, before we close, we think it necessary to subjoin the substance of such of the rules of the schools as may in part lay with the parents and guardians to notice and enforce. The trustees therefore call on you to see that these rules are strictly observed by your children:

1. Your children must be in school precisely at 9 o'clock in the morning and 2 o'clock in the afternoon.

2. They ought to be sent to school every day, both morning and afternoon; otherwise they may forget in one day what they learned the day before. Nothing but sickness, or some unavoidable circumstance, should induce you to keep your children at home one day. If they do not attend

school regularly, the teacher is to send to you to know the reason; and if they are absent from school six days in a month without sufficient reason, or if they frequently play truant, they are liable to be expelled, and you may find it very difficult to get them into school again. The trustees therefore earnestly hope that you will not, by keeping your children at home without cause, or by suffering them to be absent, counteract their endeavors to procure for them a good education.

3. It is necessary that you should see that your children go to school with clean faces and hands, their hair combed and in good order, and their clothes as clean and whole as possible; otherwise they are liable to be punished for your neglect.

4. A morning school is intended to be kept in the summer, to begin at 6 o'clock, and close at 8 o'clock.

5. A library of interesting and useful books has been provided for the use of those children who are forward in their learning; and as they may be indulged at times to take them home for awhile, they may prove a source of pleasure and improvement to both children and parents.

6. If your children behave well, and study their lessons at home, they will be rewarded with tickets; but if they behave badly, and will not study, they must be punished.

7. In order to get a child into the Free School, it is required that application be made at the school on the second day of the week, commonly called Monday, from the hours of 4 to 5 o'clock in the afternoon.

8. No child can be admitted under six years of age.

9. The children of parents who are able to pay for schooling cannot be admitted.

10. It is expected that parents see that their children regularly attend some place of worship.

DE WITT CLINTON, *President.*
JOHN MURRAY, Jr., *Vice-President.*
LEONARD BLEECKER, *Treasurer.*
LINDLEY MURRAY, *Secretary.*

John Adams,
Samuel Boyd,
Benjamin Clark,
Nathan Comstock,
Thomas Eddy,
Whitehead Hicks,
Jacob Lorillard,
Samuel Wood,
John R. Murray,
Thomas L. Ogden,
James Palmer,
Henry Rutgers,
Jeremiah Thompson,
Najah Taylor,
Thomas C. Taylor,
John Withington,
Rensselaer Havens,
Ezra Weeks,
Benjamin Marshall,
Francis Cooper,
Lyman Spalding,
Henry Eckford,
Charles Miller,
John Pintard,
Samuel James,
Isaac Collins,
William Cairns,
George T. Trimble,
William Perry,
George Suckley.

The committee to prepare a manual for the schools reported, during the month of April, adversely to the measure as being unnecessary. Their recommendation was laid upon the table, and, at the meeting in May, was taken up for consideration, and the committee was discharged. The original resolution was, however, referred to a new committee, consisting of George T. Trimble, Samuel Wood, and Lindley Murray, who were directed to prepare and submit a Lancasterian manual for the schools.

The great influence of a proper regard for the first day of the week on the moral habits and character of the young, has already been alluded to, and the estimate in which this influence was held has been fully shown in the address to parents and guardians. A committee on the general state of the institution made a special communication of the following facts : In School No. 1, out of 480 scholars on register, 397 attended church regularly ; in No. 2, of 437 on the register, 335 attended ; and in No. 3, of 333 on register, 312 were regular attendants at some place of worship. The trustees regarded this as an extraordinary and very gratifying circumstance.

At the annual election in May, in consequence of the desire of Leonard Bleecker to resign the office of treasurer of the Society, the duties of which he had discharged from the date of its organization, RENSSELAER HAVENS was elected in his place. This gentleman, however, declined to serve, and Mr. Bleecker was requested to discharge the duties until a new appointment could be made. At the meeting held on the 4th of June, GEORGE T. TRIMBLE was elected to fill the vacancy.

The committee to confer with the Female Association reported that the association, under a conviction that its funds would be reduced, and that their labors were only a department of the Free-School system, replied that it would be inexpedient for them to pay the sum designated as rental ; but, on a reconsideration of the matter, it was resolved to allow $400 per annum to the Society, which was accepted.

School No. 4, in Rivington street, was opened on the 1st of May, with 133 pupils on register, to which 223 others were added before the 24th of the same month, making, on that day, 356 ; of which 200 were boys and 156 were girls.

Charles Picton, the teacher sent out from England for the purpose, was appointed teacher of the new school ; and, to enable him to carry out the system on his own plan, he was authorized to conduct the school under such plans and regulations as seemed to him best calculated to perfect the objects of the institution. By a subsequent resolution, adopted in September, Mrs. Picton was appointed to the girls' school, which had been already opened on the 30th of August, with 182 girls.

During the month of August, the Society was bereaved of its vice-president, JOHN MURRAY, Jr., who died on the 4th of that month. He was chosen vice-president at the organization of the Society, and had held the office until his decease. With an enlightened mind, a devoted spirit of philanthropy, an earnest zeal, a spotless Christian character, and independent means, he had devoted the latter thirty years of his life to labors of public benevolence and reform. Thomas Eddy was elected as his successor in office, on the 1st of October.

The great increase in the number of pupils at School No. 3 rendered additional apartments necessary. A committee was appointed, and, in December, a report was submitted, recommending that a new building be erected on the lots granted by Trinity Church, at the corner of Hudson and Grove streets. At the same time, plans and estimates for the building were submitted, the cost of which was named at $8,500. The recommendations of the committee were adopted.

The tenure of the ground, as granted by the corporation of Trinity Church, did not secure it absolutely to the Society, and at the following meeting the matter was reconsidered, and a committee, consisting of John R. Murray, William Torrey, and Benjamin Clark, was appointed to consult with the vestry of Trinity Church, to obtain the privileges desired. The conference resulted in a proposition that, if the Society would release a certain portion of the property on Hudson street, the vestry would convey the title of the remainder in fee-simple to the Society. These terms were deemed favorable, and the committee were directed to complete the arrangement. The negotiation was terminated, however, by the payment of $1,250 on the part of the Society, as the purchase-money for the whole of the lots.

At the first meeting in 1820, the committee to prepare the manual reported that the British Lancasterian manual had been adopted as the basis of their own, and that such corrections and changes had been made as would adapt it to the use of the schools of the Society. The report of the committee was accepted, and the manual adopted and ordered to be printed. The work was accordingly done, and the first edition was published the same year. A part of the edition was furnished with samples of sewing by the girls, which were attached to pages of the book referred to in the text. The illustrated manuals bearing these samples were sold for $1.50 each, while those from which they were omitted were sold for 75 cents each. Charles C. Andrews, the teacher of the Colored School, having contemplated the publication of a manual, but having abandoned it in order to aid the committee, was awarded 75 copies as a complimentary consideration.

A committee was appointed early in the year to procure plans and estimates for a building in Hudson street; and after the subject had been fully considered, it was decided to erect a two-story building, 45 by 80 feet, with a cellar 7 feet in height, the expense not to exceed $6,500. William Torrey, Najah Taylor, and Samuel Boyd were appointed as the building committee.

The finance committee were authorized to borrow seven thousand dollars, secured by bond and mortgage on the property in Hudson street—an arrangement which was effected with the Mutual Insurance Company, at 7 per cent. At the close of the year, the building committee were able to report their task completed, with a charge for extra work of $217.50, which caused the total cost to exceed the estimates and appropriation only $109.94. The house was opened for the boys on the 15th of October, and for girls on the 23d of the same month. On the 2d of November, 279 girls had been entered on the register, under the care of Sarah F. Field, who had been appointed teacher.

At the close of 1820, a period of fifteen years from the foundation of the Society, the trustees were enabled to view their enterprise with high gratification; and at the date of the Sixteenth Annual Report, in May, 1821, the following statement of the schools in operation was published:

No. 1.	Lloyd D. Windsor, teacher,		480 boys.
2.	John Missing,	"	353 boys and girls.
3.	Shepherd Johnson,	"	540 boys.
	Sarah F. Field,	"	289 girls.
4.	Charles Picton,	"	527 boys.
	Eunice Dean,	"	400 girls.

The Society owned four commodious buildings, in which six schools were held, attended by 2,589 pupils. The treasury was in debt about $8,000.

At that time, Rev. John Newland Maffit, a young and very popular preacher of the Methodist Church, was attracting much attention by his remarkable oratory and powerful discourses. He expressed a desire to visit and address the children of the free schools; and information having been communicated to the board, an affirmative resolution was adopted, and Leonard Bleecker and Thomas Eddy were appointed to make the necessary arrangements. A young and talented preacher from England, Rev. GEORGE SUMMERFIELD, was also in the city, and the committee were authorized to make such appointments as they deemed proper. The 17th day of May was chosen for the occasion, and, to render a separate visit and address to each school unnecessary, they were collected in the Baptist Church in Mulberry street, near Chatham, known as the "Tabernacle," then under the care of Rev. ARCHIBALD MACLAY. Mr. Maffit was received by sixteen of the trustees at No. 1, and, accompanied by them, repaired to the place of assembly, where over 2,300 children were in readiness to join in the exercises of the day. The committee, in their report, remark as follows:

The minister commenced by reading the 10th chapter of Luke. He then engaged in prayer for the blessing of God upon the exercises of the day. After which he preached from Luke x. 42, "One thing is needful;" and the committee mention with much gratification that both the matter and manner of his address were peculiarly adapted to engage the attention and inform the minds of the children.

A similar privilege was soon after sought by Rev. THADDEUS OSGOOD, a travelling English missionary; but, in consequence of the very brief time which had passed' subsequent to Mr. Maffit's address, the suggestion was not adopted by the board. Several of the trustees, however, attended Mr. Osgood in his visits to Nos. 3 and 4, where he addressed the children in an appropriate manner.

The trustees, being desirous of reducing the expenses as much as possible, directed the treasurer to procure a loan at six per cent. on the property of No. 3, and pay off the mortgage to the Mutual Insurance Company, which was at 7 per cent. This was accomplished, and the first mortgage was cancelled.

The principal measure which occupied the attention of the board during the year 1821, was the division of No. 2, in Henry street, into two separate schools, male and female, the two sexes having been until that time admitted to the same school. This was effected during the year, extensive repairs and alterations being made, and on the 1st of November the girls' school was opened with 90 scholars, under the care of Rebecca Leggett.

Two thousand copies of the " Universal Catechism " were purchased for gratuitous distribution to the pupils belonging to the schools ; a stereotype edition of the " Scripture Lessons " was ordered to be prepared, and one thousand copies printed, for the use of the several schools.

At the close of November, a delegation of members of the Legislature visited several of the schools for the purpose of becoming more fully acquainted with the system of instruction adopted by the Society. These visits were very satisfactory to the delegates, who were cordial in their approbation of the method of instruction, the buildings, and the various arrangements of the institution. A committee, consisting of Benjamin Clark, John R. Hurd, and William T. Slocum, was subsequently appointed to draft a memorial to the Legislature, asking further aid in the erection of additional buildings. The paper was prepared and promptly submitted to the board, and Mr. Slocum was appointed delegate to visit Albany and lay it before the Legislature. The service was performed, but, in consequence of a great variety of other measures being pressed upon the attention of the Legislature, an adjournment took place before the object of the memorial was attained. It was deemed proper to enlarge the delegation, and James Palmer and Najah Taylor were selected for the purpose.

The trustees and agents of the Bethel Baptist Church were, at this period (1821–1822), making diligent efforts to extend their schools. As the bill which had been passed by the Legislature, upon the appeal of the trustees and friends of the Bethel Church, gave them special privileges not enjoyed by other religious denominations, of which they were evidently disposed to avail themselves to the fullest extent, by increasing the number of their schools, and their *pro rata* of the school moneys, the Free-School Society regarded the movement with much concern. The measures contemplated by the Bethel Society led the board to apprehend a collision upon ground which they had for some time regarded with interest as a good location for a school—that part of the city north of Walker street and between Broadway and the Bowery. A committee was accordingly appointed, in March, 1822, to select and negotiate for a site for a school building in the vicinity of the cathedral in Mott street.

The estimates, obtained by careful inquiries throughout the city, showed the unwelcome fact that many thousands of children were still vagrants, and unprovided with the means of instruction. This condition of things arose partly from the disabilities of the industrial classes in large cities, partially from the fact that the number of schools was small, and insufficient to accommodate the pupils ; while the great distances which many of the children were obliged to walk in order to reach them, offered a serious impediment to the attendance of the majority of younger pupils. A considerable addition to the number of schools was deemed, therefore, to be a prime necessity, and the board took into consideration the means by which this could be accomplished. At the meeting held on the 13th of March, propositions were submitted and discussed, which were substantially as follows :

To erect five new school-houses, at a cost of $10,000 each, would require an annual sum of $5,000 for ten years, and would provide for a new building every second year.

The population of the city at the time was 130,000, which, at four cents per capita, would yield a tax of $5,200.

The real estate at the assessed valuation of the year amounted to $50,619,720, the personal estate being assessed at $17,666,350, making a total of $68,285,070. The sum derived —$5,000—would be only $\frac{1}{13}$ of one per cent., or one cent on $136 of the taxable property of the city.

The amount of taxes for 1821 was $299,225, which would be increased only one sixtieth by the imposition of the proposed tax. In the words of the proposition :

A person that now pays $1 tax would pay in addition 1⅗ cents.
"   "   "   5   "   "   "   8   "
"   "   "   10   "   "   "   16   "
"   "   "   20   "   "   "   32   "

Or, assessed upon real and personal estate, as follows :

A person assessed as worth $100, in addition to his tax
                                    would pay only ¾ cents.
    "   "   "   1,000,   "   "   "   7½   "
In independent circumstances, 10,000,   "   "   "   75   "
A man of fortune, .   .   . 20,000,   "   " $1.50

The above estimates are interesting as historical facts in
reference to the city and its wealth, while the modest estimate of
$10,000 as making a man "independent," or ranking the owner
of $20,000 as a "man of fortune," is a genuine expression of the
social characteristics of that period.

To secure these additional resources, the following plans were
recommended : 1. To circulate petitions among the people, until
several thousand names should be obtained ; 2. When the petitions were signed, to apply to the Corporation for its influence
and aid before the Legislature ; 3. To vest the title of all purchases of property and school buildings erected by the Society in
the city, and to take a perpetual lease for the same ; 4. When
the mortgage upon the property of No. 3 should be paid by the
proceeds of the tax, to convey the title of the land to the city ;
5. That the Mayor, Recorder, and First Judge of the city and
county should be *ex-officio* members of the Society ; 6. That incorporated religious societies should not draw school moneys for
any other schools except those immediately connected with their
respective churches ; 7. That no religious society should establish a free school, except for the children of their respective
churches who were unable to pay for education.

Without adopting definitely the measures proposed, the
board appointed a committee to take the whole subject in
charge, and for that purpose selected Robert C. Cornell, John E.
Hyde, Rensselaer Havens, Benjamin Clark, John Adams, Najah
Taylor, and Lindley Murray.

The committee gave prompt attention to the measures referred to them, and had interviews with the Mayor and several
members of the Corporation. It was decided to postpone the
movement until a later period in the year, and the committee,
at their own request, were discharged, the secretary being directed, however, to lay the matter before the board two months previous to the next session of the Legislature.

The committee appointed to purchase lots for a new school
near the cathedral, reported that they had selected three lots in

Mott street, near Prince, 25 by 94 feet each, the price of which was $2,250, and interest from the 1st of January preceding. The lots were approved, and the necessary steps to have the deeds executed were ordered to be taken, and the treasurer directed to borrow the money for the payment.

At the meeting of the board held on the 5th of April, a letter was received from the trustees of the Bethel Baptist Church, complaining of the conduct of the Society in purchasing the property for the erection of a school-house in Mott street, and charging the board with an improper interference with their plans. The secretary was directed to reply to this communication, and furnish the complainants with a copy of the original resolution passed in 1821, appointing a committee to procure suitable lots for a school site, and also to inform them of the proceedings already taken by the board.

It was further resolved that a committee, consisting of John E. Hyde, James Collins, and Lindley Murray, be appointed to prepare a remonstrance to the Legislature on the subject of the law giving exclusive privileges to the Bethel Church in the distribution of the school fund.

The collision of interests which had been anticipated between these two boards had now assumed a positive form. The discussion gave rise to important subsequent legislation, and is made the subject of review in the following chapter.

CHAPTER III.

THE BETHEL BAPTIST CHURCH CONTROVERSY.

Sectarian Influence—Church Schools—The School Fund—The Bethel Baptist Church—Privileges Granted—School No. 5—Memorial to the Legislature—Memorial to the Corporation—Proceedings in the Legislature—Hiram Ketchum Elected a Trustee, and requested to proceed to Albany—Negotiations Between the Two Boards of Trustees—The Bill Laid Over by the Legislature—The Bethel Schools—The "Trustees of the Fire-Department Fund"—Certificate of Mr. Andrews—Certificate of Mr. Buyce—Certificate of Mr. Farden—New Church Schools—Proceedings in the Common Council—Memorial Adopted—New Memorials to the Legislature—Proceedings of the Legislature—Report of the Committee on Colleges, &c.—Adjournment of the Legislature—The Extra Session—The Bill Amended—The Common Council to Apportion the School Fund—The Bill Becomes a Law—The Controversy Closed.

THE Free-School Society had been in successful operation for fifteen years, and had encountered no other obstacles than those incident to the progress and development of a system of far-reaching benevolence and philanthropy. A movement of a disturbing character, however, arose from the rivalry and jealousy of other institutions, but particularly in the efforts made to obtain peculiar privileges for the benefit of the schools connected with the Bethel Baptist Church. The controversy and the legislation growing out of these attempts form an interesting feature in the records of the Society.

By the law of March 12, 1813, it was directed that the portion of the school fund received by the city and county of New York should be apportioned and paid to the trustees of the Free-School Society of New York, the trustees or treasurers of the Orphan Asylum Society, the Society of the Economical School, the African Free School, and of *such incorporated religious societies in the city as supported, or should establish, charity schools*, who might apply for the same. In 1822, the institutions which drew from the school fund in addition to the Free-School

Society, and those already named, were the Female Association, the Hamilton Free School, the Mechanics' Society, and the Roman Catholic Benevolent Society. By the sixth section of the law, the several societies therein named were prohibited from using the school fund for any other purpose than *the payment of teachers*.

The privilege of participating in the fund granted by the law to religious societies was peculiar to the city of New York, no religious society in any other part of the State being allowed such participation. This privilege was probably granted them at the time, because the number of schools under the charge of these societies was small, and, with a single exception, confined to the education of the poor of the respective churches to which they were attached.

The Lancasterian system of education having been successfully practised for a number of years in the schools of the Society, the number of pupils increased to such an extent, that the amount drawn from the common school fund' was more than sufficient for the payment of teachers employed. Application was therefore made to the Legislature, which, in 1817, passed an act containing, among other things, a provision allowing the Free-School Society to appropriate the surplus of the school fund, after the payment of teachers, to the erection of buildings for schools, the education of schoolmasters upon the Lancasterian plan, and to all the needful purposes of a common school education. This peculiar privilege was granted the Society because it was organized for the sole and exclusive purpose of educating the poor ; and, consequently, all the buildings which it should erect would forever be devoted to this object.

In 1820, the trustees of the Bethel Baptist Church in the city of New York opened a school in the basement of their church, in Delancey street, for the reception of poor children of every denomination ; and, the next year, received an apportionment from the common school fund, under the provision of the law of 1813, granting that privilege to religious societies. In 1822, the trustees of the Bethel Church obtained the passage of a law * granting them permission to appropriate the surplus

---

* An Act for the Relief of the Trustees of the Bethel Baptist Church, in the city of New York.

I. Be it enacted by the People of the State of New York, represented in Senate

4

money received from the school fund, after the payment of teachers, to the erection of buildings for schools, the education of schoolmasters, and all the other needful purposes of a common school education—a privilege nearly similar to that before granted to the Free-School Society. The passage of this law immediately excited the alarm of the board, and several religious societies in the city. It was perceived that it opened a wide door for the perversion of the fund, and that there would be a strong inducement offered to the church for the employment of teachers who would work cheap, that thus there might be a surplus to be used in the erection of buildings, which would not belong to the public, but to the church, and would probably come to be used for other purposes than the education of poor children.

It has already been stated, that the trustees of the Public-School Society, as early as 1821, had observed the want of a school in that part of the city bounded by Broadway and the Bowery, and Bleecker and Grand streets, and had made some inquiries for the purchase of lots for a school site, which had been unsuccessful, and the effort was abandoned for the time. The passage of the law above named revived their interest in this locality, which was stimulated by the efforts making on the part of Mr. Chase, the pastor of the church, to find a field for a

and Assembly, That it shall and may be lawful for the trustees of the Bethel Baptist Church, in the city of New York, or their successors in office, at any time hereafter to sell and dispose of two lots of ground, with the meeting-house thereon, now belonging to the said church, situate on the south side of Broome street, in the Eighth Ward of the said city, and to execute conveyances therefor in fee-simple to the purchaser or purchasers thereof.

II. And be it further enacted, That it shall and may be lawful for the said trustees, or their successors in office, to mortgage, in fee or otherwise, all those certain lots of ground, and the meeting-house thereon erected, belonging to the said church, situate at the corner of Delancey and Chrystie streets, in the said city, or any part or parcel thereof, for such sum or sums as the said trustees, or their successors in office, shall think proper; which mortgage or mortgages so made and executed shall be valid and effectual in the law.

III. And be it further enacted, That if any moneys be now remaining, or shall hereafter remain, in the hands of the said trustees, from the school moneys received by them for the support of the Bethel Free School, after a sufficient compensation to the teachers employed by them, it shall and may be lawful for them to apply such moneys to the instruction of schoolmasters, to the erection of buildings for schools, and to all other needful purposes of a common school education, but to no other purpose whatever.

new school under his supervision. A consideration of the matter was therefore had at a meeting on the 13th of March, 1822, when a resolution was adopted directing the purchase of lots in the vicinity of St. Patrick's cathedral, and appointing Isaac Collins, Rensselaer Havens, William T. Slocum, John L. Bowne, and James Palmer a committee to superintend the undertaking, and to procure estimates for the erection of a building.

At a meeting held on the 5th of April, a letter was received from the trustees of the Bethel Baptist Free School, stating that they had purchased lots in the vicinity of the Roman Catholic cathedral, and making a complaint that the purchase of lots in Mott street by the Free-School Society was an improper interference with their plans. A reply was directed to be sent to the complainants, and a committee of three, consisting of John E. Hyde, Isaac Collins, and Lindley Murray, was appointed to prepare a memorial and remonstrance to the Legislature on the subject of the late law.

On the 2d of August, the trustees adopted the following resolutions :

Resolved, That, in the opinion of this board, the last section of the act of the Legislature of this State, entitled "An Act for the Relief of the trustees of the Bethel Baptist Church in the city of New York," passed on the 8th day of February last past, is calculated to divert a large portion of the common school fund from the great and beneficial object for which it is established, and to apply the same for the promotion of private and sectarian interests; and, believing that the passing of said section was procured either from the want of information, or from some other cause not known to this board, they will use all the means in their power to procure a repeal of the last clause of said law.

Resolved, That the secretary send a copy of the preceding resolution to the trustees of the Bethel Free School.

At the following meeting of the board, a committee was appointed to confer with the Corporation, the commissioners of the school fund, and the directors of the various institutions entitled to participate in the school moneys, to secure their cooperation in procuring the repeal of the law, and to prepare a memorial to be presented to the Legislature. The committee consisted of Charles G. Haines, John E. Hyde, Isaac Collins, Gideon Lee, and Rensselaer Havens.

At the meeting held on the 6th of December, the committee

reported the following memorial, which was adopted, and ordered to be printed under the direction of the committee:

To the Honorable the Senate and Assembly of the State of New York:

The trustees of the Free-School Society of New York respectfully represent, that they consider the prosperity of the institution whose management is entrusted to their charge, as intimately connected with the moral condition of this metropolis. In all populous cities, there must be a great disparity in the pecuniary circumstances of the different classes of the community. A large portion of the people must be indigent and needy. Thousands of the rising generation must be emerging into active life, whose parents are unable to give them the rudiments of literary education, and whose minds have never been enlightened or restrained by the early inculcation of moral lessons and virtuous maxims. Unless some public establishment, or some voluntary association, embrace and relieve their condition, it must be evident that they will be exposed to temptations of the most pernicious kind, and contract habits of the most dangerous tendency. They will swell the list of crimes on the records of criminal courts, fill the penitentiaries with convicts, and subsist by committing depredations on the property of their fellow-citizens, and disturb the peace and safety of the whole community. They diminish the security of civil government, increase poverty and taxation, and promote the passage of severe and sanguinary laws.

To rescue such children from the dangers which naturally surround them, to shield them from temptation and early depravity, to direct their paths to future usefulness and respectability, is the grand object of the Free-School Society of New York.

When these free schools were established in 1806, there was a large number of poor children in the city of New York exposed to the most dangerous temptations, and whose minds were destitute of mental and moral cultivation. They were wandering in the streets in idleness, and daily falling into new and pernicious associations. They were growing up in a manner that prepared them for the almshouse, the hospital, the Bridewell, the penitentiary, and State prison. Since their commencement, more than fourteen thousand children have been admitted and entered on their registers, and but one solitary individual of this large number has been pointed out who has been arraigned in a criminal court.

The number daily instructed is now more than three thousand. It is almost unnecessary to dwell on the salutary effects of these schools. When we reflect that all free governments must rest on public opinion, and that, in proportion as public opinion is enlightened and the people rendered virtuous, popular institutions will be rendered more permanent and secure, the diffusion of elementary instruction, and the timely inculcation of correct principles of moral conduct, assume a consideration that must appeal to the feelings of every member of this community who regards his own happiness, the happiness of society generally, and the well-being of posterity.

No system of education has ever yet been devised that affords so many advantages as the Lancasterian plan. This was adopted by the Free-School Society of New York before it was embraced by any other State in the Union; and, whether we consider the economy of instruction, the facility with which children acquire the rudiments of education, or the excellency of the discipline which prevails, it stands without competition.

The free schools under our care are open to all religious denominations. No distinction of sect or name is known in admitting scholars. The government of the State, in a spirit of wisdom and munificence, has made a liberal annual allowance toward sustaining the expenses of their education; and if our income exceeds the expenditures, the surplus is appropriated toward erecting buildings for schools, which are the property of the public, for the perpetual reception of indigent children. Five houses have already been constructed, principally by the aid of private donations, in the different parts of the city of New York. They constitute a real estate which will be held in perpetuity for the benefit of the lower classes of the community, and which may be estimated at the value of sixty thousand dollars.

Your memorialists would further represent, that, with one exception, the different religious denominations of the city of New York who receive a portion of the common school fund, expend it in the education of poor children of their respective societies only.

Your memorialists are fully convinced of the wisdom of that provision of the general law regulating the expenditures of the common school fund, which limits the appropriation of said fund to the payment of teachers only; and they believe it inexpedient, and contrary to the original intention of the Legislature, that any part thereof should be applied to the erection of buildings, except in case of an institution expressly incorporated for purposes of educating poor children, and where real estate virtually becomes the property of the public.

But your memorialists regret to say, that a law was passed during the last session of the Legislature, which, they apprehend, may lead to incalculable evils, and produce consequences never contemplated at the period of its adoption. This statute is entitled, "An Act to relieve the Baptist Bethel Church in the city of New York," and it contains the following section : "And be it further enacted, That, if any moneys be now remaining, or shall hereafter remain, in the hands of the said trustees (naming the trustees of the said church) from the school moneys received by them for the support of the Bethel Free School, after a sufficient compensation to the teachers employed by them, it shall and may be lawful for them to apply such moneys to the instruction of schoolmasters, to the erection of buildings for schools, and to all other needful purposes of a common school education, but to no other purposes whatever." (Vide "Laws of New York," 1822, p. 22.)

As the sum drawn from the common school fund for each scholar is more than is requisite to pay the salaries of teachers on the Lancasterian plan of education, where the number of scholars is large, a very considerable surplus may remain. This surplus may, by said law, be devoted, in the opinion of your memorialists, to the purchase of real estate, or to the erection of buildings, which belong not to the public—not, in fact, to the poor of the city of New York, but to the Baptist Bethel Church. In this religious society the fee will permanently vest, and the estate and property thus created may be sold, and the fee conveyed to others. There is no limit to the number of scholars which may be instructed under the direction of this church, and the sum drawn from the commissioners of the school fund must conform to the returns made to them by this religious denomination. Teachers may be employed at low salaries, to increase this surplus, who are incompetent to the faithful discharge of their duty ; and there is nothing to prevent the conversion of the moneys drawn by the trustees of this church to the education of children who do not belong to that needy class of scholars who should be peculiar objects of instruction in the expenditure of the school fund in this city.

Your memorialists would respectfully ask, if this ever could have been the intention of the Legislature ? Why has a right been given to one religious society which is not imparted to another ? And why has a privilege been granted that not only vitiates the principles of equality, but perverts a part of the school fund intended—and wisely and humanely intended—to be expended to the last cent in the wholesome education of poor children ? When other religious denominations are compelled by law to exhaust all the funds which come into their hands for the purposes of instruction, is it politic, is it just, to select out one religious society, and give it an opportunity to dispose of the funds here spoken of, for other purposes than those connected with the early education of the poor ?

Your memorialists have but one object in view—the adoption of the most prudent and effectual means of educating the poor children of the city of New York. Whether this is done by this Free-School Society, or by other means, is not a matter of concern to them ; but when they see the existence of a law which, in their view, appears calculated to retard the great work of elementary instruction—which has a tendency to pervert a portion of the school fund from its proper object—which may diminish the number of poor children annually educated, and which may create a spirit of hostility heretofore unknown among the different religious denominations, and is unequal as well as pernicious, they conceive that a regard to their duty, and a sincere desire to increase the blessings of elementary instruction, dictates an appeal to the Legislature. Suppose that every Christian society in the city of New York was empowered to expend a portion of its dividend, drawn from the commissionerrs of the school fund, in objects different from that of educating poor children, would not the Legislature consider such an evil called for prompt and complete correction ? Why, then, shall the guardians of our public prosperity permit a law to exist which sets an example that may lead to such a grievance ? Have not the different religious denominations of this metropolis a perfect right to call on the Legislature for a law giving them authority to expend their surplus funds as they may think proper, or to erect buildings which may in time be converted into houses for sectarian uses, instead of being maintained as school edifices ?

Under these considerations, your memorialists respectfully request the Legislature to repeal the third section of the law which has been here referred to. They conceive that its being expunged from the Statute Book will seriously benefit the great interests of early education in the city of New York, and place the different religious societies on the broad basis of equality.

About three years ago, the Society for the Prevention of Pauperism in the City of New York made an annual report, in which it was stated, among other things, that there were about eight thousand poor children in this metropolis who were growing up destitute of instruction. This fact, and others of a similar nature, induced this Free-School Society to make bolder efforts to spread the lights of early knowledge. They have very recently erected two school-houses, in different sections of the city, in the midst of the most indigent portions of our population, capable of receiving one thousand scholars each, and by this means incurred a debt of sixteen thousand dollars.

Your memorialists deem it proper to state, that the Free-School Society of New York is composed of more than six hundred of the most respectable citizens, and that religious distinctions are unknown to their constitution. For fourteen years they have prosecuted the grand design of their institution with ardor and success. They have contracted debts and incurred heavy responsibilities on many occasions.

The Free-School Society of New York was created by the Legislature to exercise a wholesome supervision over the education of children who could look to no other certain source. This institution was the offspring of your honorable body, and to you it has to look for continuance and support. In seeking the repeal of a law which must have been passed without a comprehensive view of its effects and bearings, they trust that they shall not be accused of departing from that uniform desire to increase the blessings of a free and enlightened government which has ever controlled their action and guided their efforts.

Signed by order and on behalf of the Board of Trustees.

LEONARD BLEECKER, *Vice-President.*

LINDLEY MURRAY, *Secretary.*

NEW YORK, *January,* 1823.

The committee also reported the following memorial to the Corporation, which was adopted, and referred to the same committee to present to that body :

To his Honor the Mayor, Recorder, and Commonalty of the City of New York :

The trustees of the New York Free-School Society would respectfully represent, that they consider the diffusion of early education in the city of New York as intimately connected with the moral condition and future prosperity of this metropolis. If we would lessen taxes, by preventing pauperism—if we would lessen public burdens, by diminishing crimes and offences—if we would render the city more wealthy, by increasing individual exertion and enterprise—if we would give greater peace and security to our citizens, and render property more sacred—if we would give a broader basis and render firmer the foundation of our political and civil institutions, we shall encourage early education among the poor, inculcate virtuous maxims in the young mind as its powers are unfolded, and teach the principles of self-respect. Industry, sobriety, enterprise, and usefulness will follow.

History is the censor of ages. It teaches us that, in proportion as mankind assemble and reside in large bodies, that the distinctions of rich and poor are made more obvious—that they reciprocate baneful as well as virtuous sympathies. The poor, the depraved, and the desperate mingle together, and a standing corps of the base and the profligate will appear.

Idleness and want will stimulate the base propensities of our nature, and crimes and outrages will follow. Hence, whatever counteracts those evils which naturally arise in populous cities, should be embraced with ardor and cultivated with perseverance. And hence the necessity of a greater attention to the sources and causes of criminality and guilt.

Your memorialists would call the attention of your honorable body to what has already been effected by the Free-School Society of New York. They lay before you a memorial which has been prepared for the Legislature of this State, and also their last annual report. And, in doing this, they respectfully solicit your aid in obtaining the repeal of a law which they cannot but think is directly calculated to injure the interests of early education in this metropolis. In their view, the third section of the law to which they allude, and a copy of which is laid before your honorable board, tends to create irregularity among different religious denominations, to pervert a portion of the school fund to objects that may be foreign to the purposes of early education, and diminish the number of children which might be daily instructed.

Should these views be deemed correct by your honorable body, it is hoped that you will present such a memorial to the Legislature as will tend to produce a repeal of that portion of the statute to which reference has been made.

NEW YORK, *December*, 1822.

The memorials were adopted, and Charles G. Haines, Samuel Boyd, John E. Hyde, and Isaac Collins were appointed a committee to correspond with the Secretary of State as Commissioner of the school fund, and to confer with the New York city delegation to the Legislature, relative to the object contemplated in the memorial. It being deemed of importance that the members of the public bodies whose action was to decide the question should have the opportunity of inspecting the schools, the Committee were directed to invite the members of the Corporation and of the Legislature to visit the schools under the care of the Society.

On the 24th of January, 1823, a special meeting of the trustees was held, on the call of the Vice-President, to take into consideration a letter which had been received from Hon. J. B. Yates, relative to the memorial, in which he submitted his reasons for a stay of proceedings in the Legislature on the part of the Free-School Society. After some discussion on the communication, it was determined to press the matter upon the Legislature, and Isaac Collins and Israel Dean were appointed as a committee to proceed to Albany, to represent the interests of the Society before that body.

On the 18th of February following, another special meeting was called for the purpose of promoting the objects so earnestly desired, and to appoint another delegate from the board, who should proceed to Albany to advocate the repeal of the "third section." The committee on the memorial reported that the Corporation had, at their meeting on the evening previous, directed a memorial to be prepared and forwarded, praying for the same object.

The resignation of Thomas Gibbons as a member of the board was presented and accepted, and HIRAM KETCHUM, Esq., was unanimously elected as trustee to fill the vacancy. It was then resolved, that Hiram Ketchum be authorized and requested to proceed to Albany, to represent the interests of the institution before the Legislature.

At the meeting of the board on the 1st of March, a proposition to purchase the Baptist school-house was discussed and finally negatived, and the committee were directed to press the application at Albany, without reference to the contingencies which might arise in reference to the property held by the Bethel Baptist Church for school purposes.

Mr. Ketchum was, during this time, zealously engaged in Albany in the discharge of his duties; and on the 7th of March, a letter was received from him and laid before the board, communicating the fact that the committee to whom the question of the school law had been referred, had decided that, whereas a resolution had passed the House calling for information at the next session of the Legislature, relative to all the free schools in the city of New York, it was inexpedient to legislate further at that session on the subject of the Bethel Baptist schools. In consequence of this decision, the several committees on memorials and the delegates to Albany were discharged by a vote on the 4th of April.

In anticipation of the necessary action at the ensuing session of the Legislature, the Board of Trustees, at a meeting held on the 4th of July, appointed a new committee, consisting of Isaac Collins, Hiram Ketchum, Robert C. Cornell, and Lindley Murray, to prepare an address to the public, explaining the position assumed by the Free-School Society, which was subsequently submitted, approved, and ordered to be printed. At the meeting of the board on the 2d of January, 1824, a committee was appointed to draft a Bill, to be submitted to the Legislature, which should operate as a general law relative to the distribution of the school fund in the city of New York. The committee consisted of Benjamin Clark, Hiram Ketchum, Samuel Boyd, and Lindley Murray.

The pamphlet containing the address of the trustees to the public, with other matters, excited the attention of the trustees of the Bethel School, who solicited a conference between committees of the two boards. A committee was accordingly named, and, on the 6th of February, they reported the performance of the service assigned to them, and that several propositions had been suggested as the basis of an adjustment. The result of the interview with Mr. Chase, the pastor, was submitted, as follows: The trustees of the Bethel School were to close their No. 3, and transfer the children to Free School No. 3, the Society to take the new building from the Bethel Church on a long lease, they to continue their No. 1 only; the whole conditioned on the passage of the law repealing the "third section." B. Clark, R. C. Cornell, and Lindley Murray were empowered to make the proposed terms of adjustment as free from error as possible, and to complete the negotiation with the other institution. This committee subsequently reported that they had been entirely unable to effect any arrangement whatever.

Notwithstanding the unanimity of sentiment in favor of the repeal of the objectionable section of the law, and the numerous memorials which had been presented, the agents of the Bethel School had been able to exert a strong influence in the House, where, in consequence of the absence of facts and the lateness of the session, the subject, as already stated, was never reached. A resolution, however, had been adopted, calling for information from the several societies and asylums to which the money was distributed; and the compilation of these facts occupied a portion of the recess between the sessions.

The Bethel Baptist Church had, at the time, three schools in operation: one situated in Delancey street, in the basement of the church, one in Bleecker street, and one in Vandam street, in the basement of a Baptist church. The first of these schools, in Delancey street, was opened in 1820, and in the year 1821, the trustees of the church drew from the common school fund the sum of $1,545.39 for 686 scholars alleged to have been taught therein in the year preceding the 1st of May in the last-mentioned year; and on the 1st of May, 1822, the sum of $1,479.80 for 755 scholars; and in the year 1823, $1,986.04 for 1,211 scholars.

The nineteenth annual report of the Free-School Society presents an interesting review of the proceedings in the controversy up to the date of the report, which is substantially embodied in the following extracts:

After the passage of the law granting the peculiar privilege of applying the surplus to the erection of buildings, &c., the pastor of the Bethel Baptist Church, the Rev. Johnson Chase, applied to his trustees, requesting them to erect a building for a school in Elizabeth street. To this proposition the trustees were at first much opposed, it not comporting with their original design to have more than one school, which they thought they should be able to manage to advantage. Their pastor, however, was very earnest in his solicitations, and, to overcome all objections on account of the pecuniary embarrassments into which the erection of another building might involve the church, undertook to encounter all the expenses himself; accordingly, to gratify their pastor, and contrary to their own opinions of the propriety of the measure, they yielded their assent to it, and lots were purchased and a building commenced in the summer of 1822. The site of this building was in the immediate vicinity of the place where the trustees of the Free-School Society had for some time previously contemplated the erection of another school-house, and where they have since erected Free School No. 5 —a commodious building, and sufficiently ample to accommodate all the poor children in the part of the town where it is situated. Mr. Chase was advised of the intentions of the trustees of the Free-School Society as to the erection of this building, and the building itself was actually erected, though not finished, before he commenced his building in Elizabeth street; and, after he had commenced it, an individual member of the board of trustees offered to purchase his lots of ground, and remunerate him for all the expenses to which he had been subjected. This proposition was made, as it was conceived there would be no necessity for two free schools in the same neighborhood, and that the operations of the two, if established, must necessarily interfere with each other. The proposition was not, however, acceded to, and the building of the Bethel Baptist Church and Free-School No. 5 were prepared for the reception of scholars about the same time. One part of the building of the Bethel Baptist Church in Elizabeth street is now appropriated to a school-house, and the other part is used by a religious society as a place of worship. In the autumn of 1823, the trustees of the Bethel Baptist Church opened their school No. 3, in Vandam street, in the vicinity of Free-School No. 3. The immediate effect of this new school was to draw from Free-School No. 3 three hundred children. Many of the children thus withdrawn returned soon afterward to the school under the care of the Society.

The experience of the operations of the Bethel Baptist schools had fully justified the apprehensions formed of them by the board. From the document with which the trustees have been furnished, it appears that the teachers in these schools have been employed at low salaries, have labored under great disadvantages, and that the order and improvement of the schools have been by no means commendable.

On the 9th of March last, Jacob Drake, Esq., one of the commissioners of the school fund, and Jacob B. Taylor, Esq., one of the aldermen of the city, visited the schools of the Bethel Baptist Church, and a number of the free schools, with a view to ascertain their condition and comparative merits. The certificates of these gentlemen set forth that a want of cleanliness, order, and discipline in the Bethel schools was very manifest, together with the following extraordinary facts : There were on the register of School No. 3 of the Bethel Baptist Church, 450 scholars, when, in fact, 300 only could be seated in the school. It will be recollected that the trustees draw from the common school fund a certain amount per scholar, for the number of scholars *on register*. On the day when these gentlemen visited them, there were on register, in all the schools of the Bethel Baptist Church, 1,547 scholars, of whom were present only 886. Stephen Allen, Esq., and John Targee, Esq., consented to visit the schools on another day ; and they have been pleased to give their certificate. This certificate shows similar results as to the condition of the schools, the number of scholars on register and in attendance, as that of Mr. Drake and Alderman Taylor. The trustees also obtained a certificate from a committee of the Fire Department, as follows :

To the Trustees of the New York Free-School Society :

The undersigned, a committee from the " Trustees of the Fire Department Fund," in answer to the queries of some of your body relative to the Bethel schools in this city, reply : That there are now under our care over three hundred children, most of which are in the schools under your charge —the residue at the Bethel schools. At the *former*, they improve rapidly in learning, and give the strongest evidence of the good management of the institution. At the latter, it is the *reverse*. We are not, of course, satisfied with having children there, and shall consider it our duty to remove them, or discontinue our patronage, when parents refuse to do so. We have, therefore, no hesitation in expressing it as our opinion, that public good requires the discontinuance of the State grant to the Bethel schools, as the course pursued by their managers, in having teachers who are incompetent, and rendering their schools instruments for the furtherance of the views of a particular religious society, are calculated to subvert the intention of the State in the endowment of common schools.

Our opinions are formed from personal visits to *both* schools, and from the reports of our School Committee, who visit every three months and examine into the progess of the children claiming protection from our institution.

P. W. ENGS,
EDWARD ARROWSMITH,
JAMES M. TUTHILL,   } *Committee.*
WILLIAM VONCK,
J. M. HOYT,

NEW YORK, 16th *March*, 1824.

From the certificate of Mr. Andrews,* it appears that Mr. Chase has

---

* CERTIFICATE OF CHARLES C. ANDREWS.—I, Charles C. Andrews, of the city of New York, teacher, and late a trustee of the Bethel Free-School in said city, state as follows: That, when it was proposed by the Rev. Johnson Chase to establish a free school in the basement of the meeting-house of the Bethel Baptist Church in Delancey street, for the purpose of educating poor children connected with the congregation, and others in the neighborhood of the meeting-house, I readily assented to aid in so good a work, and offered my advice, as a teacher on the Lancasterian plan, in the promotion of a school to be conducted on that system. A board of trustees being appointed, and the rooms being fitted up, a school was opened accordingly, on the plan above named. Subsequently, Mr. Johnson Chase, having obtained a special act from the Legislature respecting the surplus funds of the said school, proposed to buy lots and erect a large school-house in Elizabeth street. This proposition was objected to by all the trustees as departing from the original plan, and as calculated to involve the church in difficulties which she was unable to sustain, and so greatly to increase the duties of the board, that a second school could not properly be attended to on their part. However, after several attempts to obtain the consent of the board, even with the offer of said Chase to build a school-house on his own account and credit, his proposals were accepted. A school-house was built and a school opened, contrary to my views and advice frequently expressed to Mr. Chase. My reasons were in accordance with those of each member of the board, which I had frequently an opportunity of hearing expressed by them individually; and I am under the impression that it was principally owing to the influence possessed by Mr. Chase, as pastor of the church, that his object in this respect was obtained.

The reasons for not agreeing to the establishing a second school on the part of the board have already been given; in addition to which, my own reasons were, that there would be no necessity for such school, as the Trustees of the Free-School Society contemplated building in the vicinity of the intended Bethel School, and I concluded that it would create a strife, far from being desirable or useful, between the two institutions; nor did I consider that the Bethel Board, from its infant state, possessed sufficient experience on such subjects to undertake a task so new and so arduous as a second school must necessarily impose; while, on the part of the New York Free-School Trustees, there existed all the requisite means and qualifications to carry into full effect the purposes designed by the establishment of such schools.

Within a few months, Mr. Chase proposed to the Bethel Board to open another been the active manager in the Board of Trustees of the Bethel Baptist Church; his conduct as a trustee of public funds will be shown by the following facts:

It appears that Mr. John Buyce was the first teacher employed in the Bethel Baptist Free-School in Delancey street; he was employed in 1820, and continued till 1821. At this time the trustees of the church were not

free school in Vandam street, in the neighborhood of a large school long established by the New York Free-School Society of this city. To this measure I also objected; nor was there a member of the board, to my knowledge, friendly to the measure; but the same partial feeling toward Mr. Chase, which, I conceive, brought the second school into existence, brought the third also, so far as it relates to the consent of the board. When it was proposed to employ the person having charge of the last-mentioned school as teacher, it never met my approbation, nor do I consider it a judicious appointment.

The Bethel Board, considering it necessary that much time should be spent in visiting their schools, and that their several occupations would preclude them from performing that duty, engaged me to pay weekly visits to the schools, and to superintend the literary concerns of the same; for which services the Board thought proper to compensate me; but from the views I have already expressed, and which I have had ever since the second school was established, together with a persuasion that the male teachers have never been so compensated as to induce them to maintain a reputation equal to other similar institutions, and knowing that men so situated merely remain in such employ to subsist while they are anxiously looking for more favorable opportunities, never can feel that energy which is absolutely necessary in teachers of well-conducted Lancasterian schools; finding, also, that this state of things was intended to continue notwithstanding the discouragement manifested by teachers, arising from their vain attempt to procure an increase of pay; and considering, also, that I was employed by gentlemen who viewed the operations of the Bethel Board in an unfavorable light, I considered it my duty to relinquish my membership with the said Bethel Board, and to resign the superintendentship of the schools under their care.

In relation to the comparative state of the Bethel Free Schools, and those under the care of the New York Free-School Society, it may be sufficient to remark, that the teachers of the Bethel Schools, Nos. 1 and 2, were both taught the Lancasterian system in the school under my care; and considering the shortness of the time in which they have been engaged on the plan, they have shown themselves worthy of encouragement; and if they had advantages similar to the teachers of the schools belonging to the Free-School Society, more good than now does, in my opinion, would result from their labors; but while the teacher of Bethel School No. 1 has to conduct a school on a system requiring uniformity in the various exercises, in a room in which it is not practicable to observe it, and the teacher of No. 2 has to contend with the pressure which an insufficient income occasions, evident disadvantages appear in these two schools, when contrasted with those of the New York Free-School Society.

The salaries of the Bethel School teachers are as follows:

School No. 1, A. R. Martin, teacher, . . . $500 per annum.
No. 2, Thos. Fardon, " . . . 400 "
No. 3, John Missing, " . . . 350 "

The teachers of other Lancasterian Schools in New York receive from $600 to $800 and $1,000 per annum.   CHARLES C. ANDREWS.

ALBANY, *March* 11, 1824.

permitted to draw from the school fund more than sufficient to pay the salary of their teacher; the privilege not having been granted them of appropriating the surplus. Mr. Chase asserts that Mr. Buyce was employed at a salary of $900 per annum; Mr. Buyce alleges that he was employed at a salary of $450 per annum; * and that, by the request of Johnson Chase, he took a draft on the treasury of the church for $900, with a private understanding with Mr. Chase that he was actually to receive only $450. It will be perceived that, by the operation resorted to by Mr. Chase, the vouchers of the treasurer would show that $900 of the public funds went to the payment of the teacher, when, in fact, one half of that sum remained in the treasury of the church. After the passage of the law allowing the church to use the school fund in the erection of buildings, Mr. Chase employed a teacher at $500 per annum. It also appears, by the certificate of Mr. Thomas Fardon,† a teacher of Bethel Free-School No. 2, that, previously to the departure of Mr. Chase for Albany, during the session of the Legislature of 1823, this gentleman proposed to Mr. Fardon to present a proposition to the board of trustees of the church to give him $600 salary, on condition that he should return $200 as a donation. The object of this certificate was, probably, to show that Mr. Chase did not employ teachers at low salaries, and, consequently, had no surplus for buildings.

The operation of the Bethel schools upon those of the Society were twofold. In the first place, they drew away pupils from the free schools, and diminished their revenue; and, in the second place, by absorbing so large a share of the school money, the balance to be distributed among the other institutions was

---

* CERTIFICATE OF JOHN BUYCE.—I, John Buyce, of the city of New York, do certify and declare, that I was employed by Johnson Chase as teacher of the Bethel Free-School No. 1, in the basement of the Baptist meeting-house at the corner of Delancey street and Chrystie street, for the years 1820 and 1821, at a salary of about 450 dollars per year. I further certify, that, at the request of the said Johnson Chase, I took a draft on the treasurer of said school for 900 dollars, with the private understanding between myself and said Johnson Chase that I was really to receive but about 450 dollars, and I believe said Johnson Chase knew I was paid but about 450 dollars.

JOHN BUYCE.

NEW YORK, *April 1st*, 1824.

† CERTIFICATE OF THOMAS FARDON.—I hereby certify, that, in consideration of frequent extra services rendered the Bethel Free-School establishment, Mr. Chase promised to present me 50 dollars in addition to my salary of 350. Also, that, previous to his departure to Albany at the last session of the Legislature, he desired to present a proposition to the board to give me 600 dollars per annum, on condition that I should return 200 as a donation, considering such a contract injudicious and unnecessary. However, being frequently entreated, and hoping to secure the 50 dollars (which, I feared, I should not receive as a present), I acceded, and proposed committing it to writing; thus it remains a verbal contract between Mr. Chase and myself.

THOMAS FARDON, *Teacher of Bethel Free School No. 2.*

NEW YORK, *March 27th*, 1824.

materially diminished. But other mischiefs were in the immediate future. Several religious denominations, observing the special privileges thus enjoyed by one of their number, manifested a disposition to follow the example, by enlarging their schools, and adapting them to the wants of the public by receiving children of all denominations. A school of this description was opened in Grace Church; another, for female children, by the Congregational Church in Chambers street; and a third, by the Dutch Reformed Church, in large rooms in Harmony Hall, at the corner of William and Duane streets.

The board of trustees of the Free-School Society, in view of these proceedings, deemed it their duty to apply to the Legislature, not only to repeal the section of the law granting peculiar privileges to the Bethel Baptist Church, but for such an amendment as would restrict the action of religious societies to the true intent of the common school law. The board, therefore, adopted the draft of a bill to be submitted to the Legislature.

Previous to making the application to the Legislature, the board thought proper to obtain the sanction and aid of the Common Council. They were induced to take this course not only because the petition of the constituted guardians of the city would have great influence with the Legislature, but because they were interested in the proper administration of the school interests of the city. The application of the trustees to the Common Council was referred to a very intelligent committee, who heard a full discussion of the question on the part of the Society, by several members of the board, and, on the opposition, by Rev. Messrs. Mathews and Wainwright. The committee reported fully and urgently in favor of the measures proposed by the Free-School Society, and recommended the adoption of a memorial to the Legislature. The memorial was unanimously adopted, as follows:

To the Honorable the Legislature of the State of New York, in Senate and Assembly convened :

The memorial and petition of the Mayor, Aldermen, and Commonalty of the city of New York, respectfully represent, that, as the constituted guardians of the institutions and general welfare of the city of New York, they think themselves called upon to apply to your honorable body for certain amendments in the laws relative to the distribution of the common school fund in said city.

By the act of March 12th, 1813, the portion of this fund for the city of New York, is directed to be distributed and paid to the trustees or treasurers of certain benevolent institutions in the act named, and such incorporated religious societies as then supported, or should thereafter support, charity schools within the said city, who might apply for the same; and such distribution is directed to be made to each school in proportion to the average number of children, between the ages of four and fifteen years, taught therein, free of expense.

By the fourth section, the religious societies in the city of New York are allowed to participate in the common school fund—a privilege peculiar to them, as it is not enjoyed by any religious society in the State out of said city.

Your memorialists respectfully conceive that, at the passage of the section last referred to, it was not contemplated by the Legislature that the respective religious societies provided for in the section would engage in the business of educating the children of poor people generally, but that, if any availed themselves of the privilege granted them, they would do so in the establishment of schools for the education of the poor of their respective congregations. This, however, is not the practical construction of the law, as some of the religious societies in the city are in the habit not only of receiving them in their schools, but of soliciting the attendance of poor children of every denomination and description, and drawing for them from the common school fund. It will readily be perceived that this course is dictated by the interest of every religious society which has established a school; for the greater the number of scholars, the larger will be the amount drawn from the fund. One religious society has already established three large schools upon the Lancasterian plan; and others, stimulated by this example, are exerting themselves to increase their schools already established, or have it in contemplation to establish new ones upon an extensive scale.

Your memorialists have witnessed, certainly with great pleasure, the zeal of the different religious societies in the city in so important a branch of Christian duty as the education of the poor; and if their exertions can be continued at the expense of private benevolence, they are worthy of all praise. But your memorialists think that large drafts from the common school fund, by the religious societies, would be attended with consequences much to be deprecated.

It will be seen, by reference to the act of 1813 above referred to, that a number of institutions supporting charity schools in the city of New York, besides religious societies, are authorized to draw from the common school fund. The principal among these institutions is the Free-School Society.

This Society has been in active operation for more than eighteen years, and your memorialists can bear testimony to the great extent of its utility. According to documents which have been made public, more than eighteen thousand poor and destitute children have been assisted in obtaining a common school education. There are now daily taught in these schools about four thousand children; and the good order and wise government of these

5

establishments are matters of public notoriety. Such is the organization of this Society, that it cannot, in the opinion of your memorialists, fail to be permanently useful. It enrolls among its members gentlemen of almost every religious sect known in this country; it is founded upon principles purely catholic, and is allied to no sect or party. Among the trustees who now manage its concerns, as well as those who have heretofore had charge of them, are numbered some of our most active, munificent, and public-spirited citizens, who are and have been willing to devote a portion of their time and talents to the single object for which the Society was organized—the education of the poor.

Such being the character of the Free-School Society, your memorialists think it permanently entitled to public patronage and support. The schools under the charge of the Society are, however, mainly dependent for the means necessary for their support upon the common school fund; the continuance and the future establishment of sectarian schools, for the purpose of general education, will have the effect to diminish the scholars in attendance upon the schools of the Society—many having already been induced to leave them—and thereby so diminish the amount drawn from the school fund as to render it insufficient for the support of the schools; they will, therefore, gradually decrease as the sectarian schools arise, and will finally be discontinued. This result the best interests of the poor of this metropolis, not only for the present but future generations, are, in the opinion of your memorialists, deeply concerned in preventing. Your memorialists do not deem it necessary to give, in this place, all the reasons which determine their minds to this opinion, but there are a few which they beg leave briefly to suggest.

The question for the determination of the Legislature at this time is presumed to be, whether the Free-School Society shall be suffered to continue its operations, and have the principal management of gratuitous education in the city of New York, or whether the religious societies shall take it out of their hands, and the poor be educated in sectarian schools?

The duties of religious societies are so numerous, that it is not believed that the business of educating the poor, if entrusted to them, would receive the attention it deserves, and might be expected, from a society organized for no other object. The success of large schools upon the Lancasterian plan cannot be entirely effected by competent teachers, but depends very much upon their being subjected to frequent visitations and examinations by persons of intelligence and standing in society. The happy effects of such visitations and examinations have been fully exemplified in the schools of the Free-School Society. These schools are visited semi-weekly by committees of the Board of Trustees, besides being occasionally visited by the whole board, consisting of thirty-six members.

If religious societies are to be the only participators of the school fund for the city of New York, a spirit of rivalry will, it is thought, be excited between different sects, which will go to disturb the harmony of society, and which will early infuse strong prejudices in the minds of children taught in the different schools. Moreover, your memorialists would suggest to your honorable body, whether the school fund of the State is not purely of a civil character, designed for a civil purpose; and whether, therefore, the entrusting of it to religious or ecclesiastical bodies is not a violation of an elementary principle in the politics of the State and country.

Your memorialists therefore pray, that the law relative to the distribution of the school fund in the city of New York be so amended as to prevent any religious society, entitled to a participation in the fund, from drawing for any other than the poor children of their respective congregations.

Your memorialists have prepared the draft of a bill containing this, among other amendments, upon which they have not deemed it necessary to offer any remarks in this place. They have been induced to make this application to your honorable body, not only by the deep interest which they feel in the establishing a system of gratuitous education which may be of permanent utility to the poor of this city, over which they have been called to preside, but because it is made their duty to raise, by a tax on the citizens, an amount for the purposes of education equal to that received by the city from the funds of the State.

And your memorialists, as in duty bound, will ever pray.

WILLIAM PAULDING, JR.,

Mayor of the City of New York.

[L. S.]   By the Common Council,

J. MORTON, *Clerk.*

The above memorial, and bill which it recommended, were unanimously adopted by the Corporation of the city of New York; but before the memorial was engrossed, a special meeting of the board was called, at the request of two highly respectable clergymen in the city of New York, to reconsider the subject. At this meeting the memorial and bill were again referred to a committee, consisting of Aldermen Burtsell, Mann, Taylor, Bolton, and Hone, who, after having fully investigated the subject, reported as follows. This report was adopted by the board without a dissenting voice:

IN COMMON COUNCIL, *February* 16*th*, 1824.

The committee on applications to the Legislature, to whom was referred for reconsideration the law and memorial relating to the free schools in this city, beg leave respectfully to report:

That they have taken into consideration the objections made to the said law, and have had the subject fully discussed before your committee by gentlemen of the highest standing as to character and intelligence, who were deeply interested therein; but, upon mature consideration, your committee are of opinion that it would be inexpedient to alter any of the provisions of the said law.

Your committee deem it inexpedient to repeat all the reasons which have induced them to recommend an application to the Legislature for the law in its present form, inasmuch as they presume it is a subject in a great degree familiar to the board, and as the memorial contains the principal reasons, to which they respectfully refer.

Your committee, however, consider it proper to state, that they believe this law to be of the utmost importance to the preservation of the New York Free-School Society, and, consequently, highly essential to the welfare of the community in general; and that, as this board may be considered the constituted guardians of the institutions and general prosperity of this city, it does seem, in the opinion of your committee, correct for them to interfere, and aid in the preservation of so benevolent and praiseworthy an institution.

The committee, therefore, respectfully recommend the adoption of the following resolution :

Resolved, That the draft of a law and memorial relating to common schools in the city of New York, as passed at a former meeting of this board, be approved of, and that his Honor the Mayor be requested to authenticate in the usual form, and forward the same to the Legislature.

Adopted by the Common Council.

J. MORTON, *Clerk.*

This emphatic approval of the course of the Society having been obtained, the committee continued its labors, in the expectation of being able to secure the desired amendments to the law at an early day in the then ensuing session. The following is the memorial adopted by the Society and presented to the Legislature during the regular session of 1824 :

To the Honorable the Senate and Assembly of the State of New York :
  The Memorial of the Trustees of the Free-School Society of New York,
RESPECTFULLY SHEWETH,

That, by the act of March 12th, 1813, the portion of the common school fund for the city of New York is directed to be distributed and paid to the trustees of the Free-School Society in the city of New York, and the trustees or treasurers of the Orphans' Asylum Society, the Society of the Economical School in the city of New York, the African Free-School, and of such incorporated religious societies in said city as now support, or hereafter shall establish, charity schools within the said city, who may apply for the same ; and such distribution shall be made to each school in proportion to the average number of children between the ages of four and sixteen years taught therein the year preceding such distribution, free of expense.

Your memorialists respectfully conceive that, at the passage of the act last referred to, it was not contemplated by the Legislature that any religious society would establish a charity school for the instruction of any other than the poor of their own congregation. But experience has proved that some religious societies in the city of New York do increase their charity schools, by receiving into them children who do not belong to their respective congregations, and thus draw from the common school fund a larger sum than they would otherwise be entitled to for the support of their schools. The operation of this proceeding is, to diminish the number of scholars in the schools under the charge of your memorialists, and, consequently, their proportion of the common school fund, upon which principally they are dependent for the support of their establishments.

Your memorialists would state, that the Society from which they derive their appointment is perfectly catholic in its principles, pledged to no sect or party; that it is composed of gentlemen of all religious denominations, and that there is nothing in the act incorporating it, or in the constitution by which it is governed, which prevents any respectable man from uniting himself with it, and having a choice in the selection of its officers and a voice in its proceedings; that the schools are open to the children of every denomination; and that, while the leading principles of the Christian faith are taught them, the points of collision between the different sects are carefully avoided.

Inasmuch as the law, in its present shape, has the effect to injure the establishments under the charge of your memorialists, they respectfully request that it may be so amended as to prohibit the religious societies in the city from drawing from the common school fund for any other than the poor children of the members of their own societies, or of those who statedly worship with them. Your memorialists believe that this amendment of the existing law is recommended by many considerations of sound policy; and, among these, not the least is, that the interests of the whole Christian community will be best promoted by encouraging the principle that each religious society is bound to provide for the education of their own poor children, and that, if they attempt to do more, they ought to do it at their own expense, and not to look to the funds of the State for assistance.

LEONARD BLEECKER, *Vice-President.* [L. S.]
LINDLEY MURRAY, *Secretary.*
January 27th, 1824.

We, the undersigned, unite with the trustees of the New York Free-School Society in their memorial to the Legislature, requesting that the respective religious societies in the city of New York be restricted, in drawing from the common school fund, to the poor children of their own congregation instructed by them.

In behalf of the trustees of the Methodist Episcopal Church in the city of New York.

JOSEPH SMITH, *President pro tem.* [L. S.]
GEORGE SUCKLEY, *Secretary.*
January 31st, 1824.

Certificates similar to the above, signed by the following persons, were placed in the hands of the Committee of Colleges, Academies, and Common Schools:

ARCHIBALD MACLAY, pastor of the Baptist Church in Mulberry street.
JOHN WILLIAMS, pastor of the Baptist Church in Oliver street.

WILLIAM MCMURRAY, president, and PETER NEEFUS, secretary. of the consistory of the Reformed Dutch Church in Market street.

THOMAS MCAULEY, pastor, S. WHEELER, President of the Board of Trustees of Rutgers street Church.

WARD STAFFORD, pastor of the Bowery Presbyterian Church. In behalf of the trustees, RICHARD COOK.

WILLIAM PATTON, pastor, REUBEN MUNSON, Chairman of the Board of Trustees of Central Presbyterian Church, Broome street.

PETER BONNET, president, STEPHEN LOCKWOOD, clerk, of the Board of Trustees of the Brick Presbyterian Church.

GARDINER SPRING, pastor of said church.

We, the undersigned, unite with the trustees of the New York Free-School Society in their memorial to the Legislature, requesting that the respective religious societies in the city of New York be restricted, in drawing from the common school fund, to the poor children of their own congregations instructed by them.

> PETER McCARTEE,
> JOHN JOHNSTON,
> JOHN McGREGOR, JR.,
> THOMAS SUFFERN,
> SAMUEL THOMPSON,

Trustees of the Presbyterian Church in Murray street, under the charge of the Rev. W. D. SNODGRASS.

January.

A number of respectable clergymen of the Methodist Episcopal Church, signed a certificate similar to the foregoing.

The Committee on Colleges, Academies, and Common Schools, to which the several memorials were referred, submitted a report and bill, which embodied the provisions of the bill drafted by the Society. The report is as follows:

REPORT OF THE COMMITTEE OF THE ASSEMBLY.

Mr. Gardiner, from the Committee on Colleges, Academies, and Common Schools, to whom was referred the memorial of the Mayor, Aldermen, and Commonalty of the city of New York, praying for an alteration in the law relative to the distribution of the common school fund in said city, together with the draft of an act prepared by the Corporation—also the memorial of the Free-School Society of said city—reported, that the act proposed by the Corporation of said city contains a revision of all the laws at present in force relative to the distribution of the common school fund in said city; that the only material alteration which it proposes in existing laws is, that each religious society in said city which now supports, or hereafter may establish, charity schools, may be restricted, in drawing from the common school fund, to the children of the parents or guardians who statedly worship with such society.

From the documents laid before your committee, it appears that the propriety of making the proposed alteration has been fully discussed by gentlemen of high standing in the city of New York, favorable to, and opposed to, the alteration, before an intelligent committee of the Corporation, who reported in favor of it, which report was unanimously adopted by the board.

It further appears, by the memorial of the Corporation, that the passage of the proposed act is considered by that body as necessary to the preservation of the Free-School Society of New York—an institution which, the memorialists represent, has been in operation more than eighteen years, and has assisted more than 18,000 poor and destitute children in obtaining a common school education ; that there are now daily taught, in the schools under the charge of the Society, more than 4,000 children, and that the good order and wise government of the establishments are matters of public notoriety. It is further stated in the memorial, that this institution is composed of gentlemen of all religious denominations ; that it is allied to no sect or party, but pursues its operations upon principles purely catholic. The Corporation further represent that the consequence of destroying this Society will be, that the poor children of New York will be educated in sectarian schools. It appears, by the last annual report of the Secretary of State, the acting superintendent of common schools, " that he is persuaded that some legislative remedy is necessary, to continue in full and vigorous operation this institution, which is certainly one of the noblest and most useful in the State—an institution which has certainly contributed more to the education of poor children, and the extirpation of vice and immorality, than any other of the numerous valuable ones which it contains."

The memorial of the trustees of the Free-School Society also prays, that the law be so amended as to limit the religious societies in said city, in drawing from the common school fund, to the poor children of the members of their own societies, or of those who statedly worship with them.

Certificates of concurrence in the prayer of the last-mentioned memorial, signed by the trustees of the Methodist Episcopal Church, two highly respectable pastors of Baptist Churches, the consistory of a Reformed Dutch Church, and the pastor and trustees of the Presbyterian Churches in said city, have also been laid before the committee.

These memorials were presented to the honorable the Assembly on the 24th day of February ultimo, but no remonstrance has as yet appeared ; and your committee have not deemed themselves justified in waiting any longer in expectation of such remonstrance, especially as it has been represented to them that the passage of the act the present session is a matter of great public importance.

Your committee have examined the several acts relative to the Free-School Society of New York, and find it to be a corporation limited to $10,000 income from its real and personal estate ; that the Mayor, Recorder, Aldermen, and Assistants of said city are *ex-officio* members of said corporation, and that it is made the duty of the trustees of said corporation to report annually to the general meeting of the said corporation, in May in each year, " a particular account of the state of the school, or schools, under their care, and of the moneys received and expended by them during the year, so as to exhibit a full and perfect statement of the properties, funds, and affairs of said corporation."

The committee are satisfied that the trustees of the Society have faithfully complied with this requisition of the act, and that the Society were the first to introduce in this country the Lancasterian system of education, and that they have brought this system to a high degree of perfection in their schools.

A number of reasons offered in favor of the passage of this act are, however, founded upon local peculiarities, with which a majority of your committee have not an intimate acquaintance; but it appears that these have been fully considered by the Corporation of the city of New York, who, from their particular knowledge of the interests and feelings of the city, are enabled to give them due weight, and who were obviously much interested in the question, as they are compelled by law to raise, by a tax on the citizens, an amount for the support of common schools equal to that received from the school fund of the State. Your committee, therefore, think that the decision of the Corporation on this subject is entitled to the respectful consideration of the Legislature.

There is, however, one general principle connected with this subject, of no ordinary magnitude, to which the committee would beg leave to call the attention of the House.

It appears that the city of New York is the only part of the State where the school fund is at all subject to the control of religious societies. This fund is considered, by your committee, purely of a civil character, and therefore it never ought, in their opinion, to pass into the hands of any corporation or set of men who are not diretly amenable to the constituted civil authorities of the Government, and bound to report their proceedings to the public. Your committee forbear, in this place, to enter fully into this branch of the subject; but they respectfully submit, whether it is not a violation of a fundamental principle of our legislation, to allow the funds of the State, raised by a tax on the citizens, designed for civil purposes, to be subject to the control of any religious corporation. It is not requested by the memorialists, however, that the religious corporations should be excluded entirely from a participation in the school fund; and perhaps it would not be expedient thus to exclude them at this time.

Your committee, therefore, ask leave to introduce a bill accordingly.

The Legislature adjourned without enacting any law affecting the interests of the Free-School Society. The questions involved, and the high respectability of the influence brought to bear in favor of a continuance of the privilege granted to the Bethel schools, made an immediate revision of the statute impracticable. Time was required for a full investigation of the whole matter, and the session closed without any other action than the reception of the memorials, the reports of committees, the discussions had in the Legislature, and the hearing of the opposing parties before the legislative committees.

The committee of the Society having the care of this important interest was continued, and, at the meeting of the trustees held on the 6th of August following, they submitted a brief report of their progress, which exhibits the liberality and the disinterested labors of the gentlemen named, in a manner worthy of record :

The Committee on the School Fund Law, in addition to what they have heretofore reported, state, that they have received from WILLIAM HOWARD, as a donation toward defraying the expenses of our agents at Albany, one hundred dollars, which, at his request, has been paid to Lindley Murray and Joseph Grinnell, in part of their expenses, who declined receiving any compensation out of the funds of the Society for their time, expenses, and laborious services during the last session of the Legislature.

They likewise mention, that the institution owes much to Mr. John Targee, for his ready and active exertions on their behalf during the above period, which were gratuitously rendered, from a thorough conviction that our application was made from the purest motives, and with the sole view to benefit the children of the lowest class of the community.

The committee recommend that John Targee be elected a member of this Society.

They further state, that they have appointed Rensselaer Havens, Joseph Grinnell, Lindley Murray, and Alderman Cowdrey, agents to attend the Legislature at the approaching session, to effect (if possible) the passage of the law which, for want of time, was laid over in April last.

On behalf of the committee,
LEONARD BLEECKER, *Chairman.*

NEW YORK, *July* 23, 1824.

During the interval between the sessions of the Legislature, overtures were made by the committee of the Society to secure an amicable adjustment with the Bethel Church, but without effecting the object. The extra session, therefore, found the case still open for settlement by the Legislature upon the merits of the question as it should come before that body.

The third meeting (an extra session) of the forty-seventh session of the Legislature commenced on the 2d of November; and, at an early day, the committee proceeded to Albany to protect and advocate the interests and claims of the Society. A number of gentlemen also appeared at the Capital in opposition to the bill, among whom were Rev. Drs. Milnor and Mathews,

Rev. Mr. Onderdonk, Rev. M. Hutton, who was connected with Dr. Mathews' congregation, Rev. Johnson Chase, and others.

At the instigation, it was generally understood, of Rev. Mr. Onderdonk, a motion was made in the Senate by Senator Livingston, that the Committee of the Whole be discharged from the further consideration of the bill, with a view to refer it again to a select committee. This motion prevailed, and the committee appointed consisted of Senators Livingston, Cramer, Ward, Burt, and Gardiner. This committee subsequently heard another full discussion of the subject by Hiram Ketchum, Esq., on the part of the Public School Society, and Messrs. Onderdonk and Chase in opposition, who, while they disagreed with each other as to the grounds of disaffection, were equally opposed to the bill. The committee were likewise divided in opinion upon the propriety of the passage of the bill as it came from the Assembly, and it was therefore agreed by the committee of the Senate that the bill should be so amended as to vest in the Corporation of the city the power of distributing the school money in such manner as they in their wisdom should think proper.

The committee of the Society, when consulted upon the amendment, replied, that they had no instructions from their constituents as to the acceptance of such a proposition ; but, upon consultation with the president of the Society (DE WITT CLINTON), it was deemed that they would not be warranted in an opposition which would embarrass the passage of the bill, and they accordingly gave their assent to the proposed amendment. The opponents of the bill waived their objections, and accepted the proposition as submitted by the committee, which, being modified by Senator Jordan, who was the author of the section making remuneration to the Bethel Church, was adopted by the Senate. The Assembly, without any discussion, unanimously accepted the amendment, and the bill was passed by that body, November 19, and, having received the signature of the Governor, it became a law.

The special provisions of the act which related to the questions immediately at issue were the following :

By section 3, the Corporation was directed to name the commissioners (one for each of the ten wards into which the city was then divided) in January, 1825, and once in every three years thereafter.

By section 4, the Corporation, in common council convened, was directed to designate, at least once in three years, the schools which should receive school moneys.

The act also recited a preamble, that, whereas " the trustees of the Bethel Baptist Church, in the city of New York, had expended moneys in erecting a commodious school-house in Elizabeth street," and which property, under the provisions of the act, might become in part useless to them, the Superintendent of Common Schools was authorized to appoint appraisers, who should estimate the damage to the trustees, and which should be repaid out of the school moneys, in four equal annual payments.

The exciting controversy being thus terminated, the trustees of the Bethel schools maintained them until the inexpediency of their longer continuance became too evident to be disregarded, and they were suspended.

The distribution of the school fund being thus committed by the new law to the hands of the Common Council, the trustees proceeded to mature a systematic plan for the enlargement and expansion of their scheme of instruction, and, at their meeting in December, 1824, entrusted the matter to a committee, consisting of Stephen Allen, Joseph Grinnell, Lindley Murray, Robert C. Cornell, Benjamin Clark, James Palmer, and Isaac Collins. The plans matured and submitted in this report of the committee comprehended an enlarged scheme for the reorganization of the system.

CHAPTER IV.

HISTORY FROM 1822 TO 1826.

The Annual Meeting—School-House No. 5—Annual Exhibit and Expenses for 1822—
Systematic Visitation—" Sections "—No. 5 Opened—Real Estate—Building Fund
—Corporal Punishment—Hiram Ketchum—New School Law—Application to the
Legislature—Committee of Ladies for Visiting Girls' Schools—School Sections
Appointed—School at Bellevue Hospital—No. 6—Visit of the Common Council
to the Schools—Resolutions—Pay System—The School Fund Controversy—The
Museum—Mrs. Scudder—Charles Picton Resigns, and Returns to England—Gen-
eral La Fayette—Visit to New York—Inspection of the Schools—The New
School Law—New Plans—The Pay System—The Common Council—Plans Ap-
proved—Proceedings in the Legislature—The New Law—Name of the Society
Changed—" The Public School Society "—Reorganization and Measures.

THE contest which opened with the year 1822 was the first
of the encounters with religious denominations which subsequently formed so prominent a feature in the proceedings of the
Society. The aim of the directors of the institution had always
been to respect and preserve the rights of all religious denominations, and to pay equal deference to the rights of conscience
of all portions of the community, at the same time that they
aimed to inculcate those fundamental ideas of religion and morals, without which civilized men present a condition which
differs from that of the savage merely in its artificial surround-
ings, and the tinsel and splendor of a more polished social life.
The pressure of sectarian influence, and the selfishness of sectarian acquisitiveness, led to the adoption of unworthy and reprehensible means in order to secure the public support of church
schools. The question, which had assumed a threatening appearance for some time, had finally taken a definite form in the discussion relative to the new school-site in Mott street, and the
rivalry on the part of the trustees of the Bethel Church to
secure all the advantages which had been granted them by the
act of the Legislature in their favor. This controversy has been
fully reviewed in the preceding chapter.

The month of May, which closed the seventeenth year of the existence of the Society, was marked by the usual annual meetings of the board, and the election of additional trustees. The special business which received attention, in connection with the working of the system, was that of approving the plans and estimates for the new school-building in Mott street, the purchase of the lots of ground, and other details essential to the carrying out of that measure.

The average number of pupils in attendance at all the schools, as appears by the exhibit of the trustees, was 3,412; and the expenses of the Society amounted, for the year, to $14,440. There was a debt of $6,000, secured by mortgage on school property, and a temporary loan of $2,500 on the obligations of the Society.

The advantage of a systematic visitation of the schools had been long apparent to the board; and as the number of schools was increasing, and a proper division of labor was requisite to prevent unnecessary confusion in the discharge of these duties, an amendment to the by-laws was proposed, by which a classification of the trustees should be made for the management of the schools. The proposition was referred to a committee, who reported a plan for the division of the members of the board into " sections," for the care of the respective schools. These " sections " were required to make monthly reports to the board. The recommendations of the report were substantially adopted.

The new school in Mott street, No. 5, was completed and ready for occupancy in the month of October, and on the 28th of that month it was opened, with 111 boys; the girls' school commencing on the 31st, with 49 scholars. JOSEPH BELDEN was appointed teacher in the boys' school, and MARY OTIS in the girls' school.

The erection of the building called for the expenditure of $9,591.09; to meet which, a loan of $10,000 had been obtained of Thomas Collins, at 6 per cent. per annum, and mortgages for $5,000 each had been given upon No. 4, in Rivington street, and No. 5, in Mott street.

This school affords one of the illustrations of the economy and integrity with which the contracts of the Society were executed, the cost of the building complete differing from the estimates only a trifling sum, including charges for " extra work."

The valuation of the real estate of the Society, at the close of 1822, was as follows:

School No. 1, and lots, ...		$20,000
No. 2,	. . .	10,000
No. 3,	. . . .	11,000
No. 4,	. . .	9,000
No. 5,	. . . .	12,000
Vacant lots in Hudson street,	. .	2,000
School furniture in No. 1,	. . .	1,000
" " No. 2, .	. .	800
" " No. 3,	. . .	1,100
" " No. 4, .	. .	1,100
" " No. 5,	. . .	1,000
Total, . . .		$68,000

From this amount, by deducting a mortgage of $6,000 on School No. 3, and $5,000 each on Nos. 4 and 5, making, in all, $16,000, we have the sum of $52,000 as the amount of property held by the Society beyond its liabilities.

In accordance with the direction of the board in the early part of the year, the proposition to raise a building fund, by special additional tax, was renewed, and on the 13th of December the subject was referred to a committee, consisting of Robert C. Cornell, Benjamin Clark, and Eleazer Lord.

At the meeting of the board held on the 10th of January, 1823, a resolution was adopted, ordering corporal punishment in the schools to be discontinued, prohibiting entirely the use of the rattan, and permitting only the use of a leather strap in extreme cases—the strap to be applied only to the hand of the refractory scholar. This was a step in a reform which became, at a later period, a marked feature in the administration of the schools.

The Legislature of the State was at this time in session, and active measures were diligently pressed forward to secure the repeal of the law granting special privileges to the Bethel school. The expediency of having a competent pleader and representative to present the views and interests of the Society to the Legislature was felt very sensibly; and, at the meeting of the board on the 18th of February, 1823, HIRAM KETCHUM, Esq., was elected a member, and immediately appointed to proceed to Albany to attend to the various measures which affected the institution, and obtain, if possible, the repeal of the obnoxious clause.

A committee was appointed, on the 7th of February, to report the draft of a new law relative to the distribution of the school fund—the committee being composed of Benjamin Clark, Robert C. Cornell, John R. Hurd, Joseph Grinnell, and Lindley Murray. This committee reported on the 18th of the same month, and their report was committed to Hiram Ketchum, Gideon Lee, John Rathbone, Jr., and Rensselaer Havens, to revise and lay before the Legislature. The committee first appointed reported also a brief memorial to that body, which, with other similar papers, form a part of the official action of the Society with regard to the distribution of the school moneys to sectarian and rival establishments. The memorial was adopted, as follows :

To the Honorable the Senate and Assembly of the State of New York :

Your memorialists, the trustees of the Free-School Society of New York, being deeply interested in the distribution of the common school fund in the city and county of New York, respectfully suggest that a revision of the existing laws on that subject for this city and county would, in their opinion, tend to promote the wise and benevolent intentions of the Legislature in making the liberal appropriations they have, for the education of poor children, and that the following regulations would be highly beneficial, viz. :

That each institution or society that receives of the common school fund shall receive in proportion to the average number of scholars that actually attend their schools each year, which number shall be ascertainable by the teachers keeping a record of the number of scholars that attend each school-time throughout the year, and the whole number of scholars thus recorded in a year shall be divided by the number of school-times, and this result shall be considered as the average number of scholars that have attended for a year.

That each institution or society (except the New York Free-School Society) who may receive of the common school fund shall expend the same in the payment of teachers, purchase of fuel and stationery, and for no other purpose whatever; and, should they have any balance unexpended at the close of a year, they shall pay it to the commissioners of the common school fund for the city and county of New York, to be added to the sum to be divided the ensuing year.

Your memorialists respectfully refer to the annexed bill on this subject, embracing the above provisions, and some others of importance, for the detail of their views; and, confiding in your wishes to extend the blessing of education to the greatest possible number, we earnestly request that you will take this subject into your wise consideration, and, if consistent with your views, adopt the annexed bill as a law, which, we sincerely believe, would greatly increase the benefit arising from the common school fund.

The delegates of the Society who visited Albany presented the memorial and draft of the proposed law, which were referred to the special committee on the matter of the repeal of the Bethel school privileges. The House adopted a resolution calling for information relative to schools in the city, and further action was accordingly postponed until the following session. The subsequent proceedings were so intimately involved with the Bethel school question, that they have been detailed in the preceding chapter.

The board deemed it essential to the success and discipline of the schools for girls, that they should receive the benefit of supervision on the part of intelligent and philanthropic women; and, after some care had been given to the selection of proper female visitors at the meeting of the board on the 4th of April (1823), the following resolution was adopted:

Resolved, That the secretary be requested to send a written invitation to the following ladies to visit the several female schools under the care of this board, for the purpose of inspecting those schools and the improvement of the girls, and to suggest quarterly, by a report to the trustees, their opinion of the state of those schools, and any change they may think advantageous in the exercises, &c.

COMMITTEE FOR No. 1: Mrs. John E. Hyde, Havens, Lucy Eddy, Grace Bleecker, Mary Bleecker, Mrs. Najah Taylor.

COMMITTEE FOR No. 2: Sarah Grinnell, Eliza Bowne, Hester Hussey, Sarah Bowne, Sarah Crocker, Mary Hicks, Anna Mott, Ann Comstock.

COMMITTEE FOR No. 3: Mrs. Wm. Torrey, Mrs. T. Whittemore, Mrs. Wm. Torrey, Jr., Mrs. Pringle, Mrs. Bayard, Miss Nichols, Mrs. Peters, Mrs. Weeks, Mrs. Oakley, Mrs. Van Buren, Mrs. Meigs.

COMMITTEE FOR No. 4: Mrs. Covell, Armenia Palmer.

COMITTEE FOR No. 5: Elizabeth Pearsall, Sarah Collins, Sarah Minturn, Mary Minturn, Jane Anthon, Louisa Anthon, Hannah Shotwell, Margaret Dudley, Martha Clarke.

In the month of June, after the annual election of officers for the year, the proposition to classify the trustees as special sections for the several schools was adopted, and the first classification was made, as follows:

SEC. No. 1 : Benjamin Clarke, John E. Hyde, Robert C. Cornell, Najah Taylor, Leonard Bleecker, Charles G. Haines.

SEC. No. 2 : John L. Bowne, Joseph Grinnell, Philetus Havens, Samuel Wood, David Lyon, Hiram Ketchum.

SEC. No. 3 : William Torrey, Eleazer Lord, Samuel Boyd, Ezra Weeks, Rensselaer Havens, William Howard, John Rathbone, Jr.

SEC. No. 4 : James Olmstead, James Palmer, Gideon Lee, George T. Trimble, Solomon Wheeler, John R. Hurd, Wm. T. Slocum.

SEC. No. 5 : John Slidell, Isaac Collins, Lindley Murray, Robert F. Mott, Israel Dean.

At the meeting at which the above classification was adopted, a proposition was offered and entertained relative to the organization of a school for the poor children at what was then known as the Bellevue Hospital. The proposition was referred to Isaac Collins and Rensselaer Havens, who reported at the next meeting that the Mayor, Commissioners, and Superintendent of the Almshouse unanimously regarded the enterprise with favor. A draft of a memorial relative to the proceeding was reported by the committee, adopted by the board, and Samuel Boyd being added to the committee, they were directed to lay it before the Common Council. On the 1st of August, the committee reported that the memorial had been received by the Corporation and referred to a committee, of which Samuel Cowdrey was Chairman, who strongly recommended the plan for a school at Bellevue. The commissioners were authorized to fit up appropriate apartments, and make the requisite arrangements for the new institution. The commissioners accordingly appropriated a spacious hall, 95 by 24 feet, on the second story of a large brick building attached to the Almshouse ; and the room having been furnished and fitted up for school purposes, the registry of pupils was proceeded with, and, on the 27th of October, School No. 6 was opened, with over 200 pupils, under the temporary charge of SHEPHERD JOHNSON, of No. 3, and several experienced monitors drafted from other schools for the purpose. Dr. Charles Belden was appointed teacher, and, on the 31st of the month, entered upon his duties. On the 4th of November, 270 pupils were present.

The attendance at all the schools, as appears by the annual exhibit for the year, was 4,090.

The Mayor and members of the Common Council having been invited to visit the schools of the Society and attend the

6

examinations and public exercises, those gentlemen on a number of occasions complied with the invitations, and the result of their visits was so satisfactory, that a resolution was introduced by Mr. Cowdrey, and unanimously adopted, in which a well-merited compliment was paid to the system. The extract from the proceedings of the Common Council is as follows :

IN COMMON COUNCIL, *October* 27, 1823.

Mr. COWDREY presented the following preamble and resolutions, which were unanimously adopted :

The Common Council, having attended the examination of the several free schools in the city, pursuant to the invitation of the Trustees of the New York Free-School Society, and having observed the great improvement made by the children in the different branches of useful knowledge, and, at the same time, the exemplary attention that is paid in these schools to neatness and cleanliness in the apartments, and regularity in the deportment and habits of the children, the zeal with which the teachers of both sexes perform their several duties, and the benevolence and public spirit of the trustees, by which they are prompted to bestow much of their time and to employ their best talents in so important a science to this interesting portion of the rising generation,

Resolved, That the thanks of this board, in behalf of the citizens and inhabitants of this city, are due, and are hereby tendered, to the said trustees and teachers, for their labors in this department of public duty, and the success which has so evidently attended their laudable exertions.

[Copy from the minutes.]

J. MORTON, *Clerk.*

At the meeting held in July, the question of establishing a rate of charges for tuition, to be paid by those who desired to do so, was pressed upon the attention of the board. It was stated that a considerable number of respectable citizens of the middle class would send their children to the schools of the Society, were it not for the fact that they were *free*, and therefore regarded only as charity schools for poor children. It was expected that a moderate rate of charge could be adopted without creating any unpleasant discrimination as to pay or charity scholars, and a committee was appointed to report upon the question. The gentlemen selected for the purpose were Isaac Collins, Hiram Ketchum, Robert F. Mott, R. C. Cornell, and John R. Hurd. The report was not presented for many months, and will be noticed in its appropriate place.

SAMUEL W. SETON was elected a trustee on the 3d of October, 1823.

The approaching session of the Legislature made it necessary that measures should be taken to present the interests of the institution on the general issue, but particularly in relation to the special legislation for the Bethel school. The memorials which had been presented to the Legislature at the previous session, with an address prepared and printed by a committee, under the direction of the board, were circulated, and copies forwarded to Albany for the members of the Legislature. Benjamin Clark, Hiram Ketchum, Samuel Boyd, and Lindley Murray were named as a committee to draft a bill to be submitted to the Legislature for their approval. The committee reported the draft of a law for the general purposes of the Society, and also a draft of a special law to limit the privileges of religious societies.

The year 1824 accordingly opened with an active renewal of the important controversy relative to the distribution of the school fund. The delegates to Albany were opposed by able and influential disputants, who closely contested the ground taken by the board. In February, however, a special meeting was held, at the call of the committee, when a proposition was submitted, in order to meet the objection which was so violently urged against the character of the Society, as being a " monopoly " and " a close corporation." By this scheme the property of the Society should be inalienably devoted to school purposes, and the schools should be under the supervision of the Common Council, and subject to their control. After a protracted discussion, the board adjourned, and reassembled the next day, when the following resolution was adopted :

Resolved, That this board will, on behalf of the Society, consent to the passage of a law that shall render the property of this institution inalienable, and sacredly pledged for the avowed objects of the institution, and place the schools under the general supervision of the Common Council; and they will most cheerfully unite with their fellow-citizens in any general plan for the extension of the monitorial system.

An interesting episode in school life was occasioned, in the spring of this year, by the liberality of Mrs. Scudder, the widow of John Scudder, the former proprietor of the American Museum, who generously presented four hundred tickets of admission to the Museum for distribution to the meritorious pupils of the schools. The schools were estimated, and an apportionment of one ticket to every forty-five scholars was decided upon, the time of admission being the Saturday afternoon of each week, when the successful scholars were accompanied by teachers, and visited the rooms of the Museum. This amusement served as a fine stimulus to the pupils, who industriously competed with each other for the prize.

On the 30th of April, CHARLES PICTON, the English teacher who had charge of No. 4, resigned his post in order to return to England. He had won a high reputation for his qualifications and character, and bore, on his return to his native land, the confidence and approbation of the board.

The average attendance had increased to 5,209, being a gain of 419 over the preceding year.

The months of August and September, 1824, were rendered important and interesting to the American people by the visit of General La Fayette to this country. His presence in New York created great enthusiasm, and a committee of the Common Council was appointed to make the arrangements for the civic reception and complimentary tributes of respect from the people. This committee conferred with a committee of the board, and preparations were made for an exhibition and review, in the Park, of the pupils of the free schools in the presence of the distinguished guest. General La Fayette was also invited to visit the schools, with which invitation he afterwards complied, including in his visits the colored school of the Manumission Society, subsequently incorporated with the free schools.

The 10th of September was appointed for the principal occasion, and, on the morning of that day, General La Fayette visited No. 3, where many of the officers and trustees were assembled to receive him. After exercises of the kind usual at an examination, an address was made by one of the pupils, and a certificate of membership was presented to him by the Vice-President, accompanied with some pertinent remarks.

At 2 o'clock [as is stated in the report of the committee], the children of the several schools (except No. 6) were collected in the Park, and arranged in two double lines around the walk next the fence, which was roped in for the occasion. The columns stood facing each other, with a space between them, through which the General was conducted by the committee and Mayor, and introduced to each of the teachers. The children, as he passed, expressed their feelings by the loud and continued clapping of hands. The General then took a stand in front of the City Hall, and the scholars were marched in review before him as they passed out of the Park. There were about five hundred boys and two hundred girls present at No. 3, and three thousand of both sexes in the Park. In conclusion, the committee have much pleasure in stating their belief that the proceedings of the day were witnessed by the General, and by thousands of our citizens, with peculiar interest, and that all were gratified by an exhibition of the state and magnitude of an institution whose moral and religious influence must be acknowledged, and whose political bearing is expressed in the motto on one of the banners used on this occasion—"Education is the Basis of Free Government."

The Legislature of the State having passed the bill to impose the duty of designating the institutions which should participate in the distribution of school moneys upon the Common Council of the city, the delegates to Albany reported the facts to the board in December, and a committee was appointed to report upon such plans for a reorganization of the system as would make it more efficient, popular, and useful. Messrs. Stephen Allen, Joseph Grinnell, Lindley Murray, Robert C. Cornell, Benjamin Clark, James Palmer, and Isaac Collins, were named for the purpose.

The committee promptly proceeded with their labors, and in January, 1825, made a long report, which was printed, and distributed among the trustees. It was made the subject of earnest discussion at regular and special meetings, and a committee was appointed to confer with the Law Committee of the Corporation; but as that committee declined to give any opinion without a specific proposition from the Society, the consideration of the report by the trustees was continued. The Law Committee having called a meeting of all interested in the schools participating in the school moneys, to be held on the 7th of March, the report was again taken from the table at the meeting on the 4th of that month, and adopted. It is valuable not merely for its facts, but because it became the basis of the subsequent reorganization of the Society, and is deemed worthy of republication.

REPORT OF A COMMITTEE OF THE TRUSTEES OF THE FREE-SCHOOL SOCIETY ON THE DISTRIBUTION OF THE COMMON SCHOOL FUND.

The committee to whom was referred the new law relative to the common school fund, respectfully report:

That they have given the subject that consideration which its importance seemed to demand, and were early led to believe that, as the portion of this fund for the city is placed by the new law at the disposition of the Common Council, it would be best to examine the whole system of common school education in this city, in order that a plan may be devised best calculated to economize and produce the greatest good from this noble fund.   In pursuing this examination, the committee have thought it right to extend their views beyond those who are considered the proper objects of gratuitous instruction, and to include those children who attend the minor and inferior pay schools.

Some of the defects in the present system of elementary education among the lower and poorer classes of society may be stated as follows :

1st.   *Of the private pay schools.*

Of the four hundred schools which have been ascertained to be in operation in this city, a large number are kept in small rooms, without sufficient light or ventilation, or a due regard to cleanliness—requisites so essential to the health and comfort of youth—and which schools are, in numerous instances, taught by persons without the necessary qualifications for the discharge of their important trusts, and, in some cases, even of doubtful morals.   On such teachers is the hard-earned money of our industrious citizens too often wasted, and—what is of much greater consequence—in such schools is the invaluable time of their offspring irretrievably lost.

The great variety of plans pursued in the different schools, and the various and dissimilar school-books used in them, retards the progress of, and increases the expense to, children removed from one to another.

The lower classes who attend pay schools, though taxed to raise a moiety of the school fund, derive no immediate benefit therefrom.

2d.   *Of the free and charity schools.*

The school fund, by being divided and distributed through so many channels, is rendered incapable of as economical management, and of producing so great an amount of good, as would be the case were it under the control and applied to its intended purposes by a single society having but the alone object in view of general education.

A fund designed for the civil education of the youth of this State is in part placed at the disposal of religious societies.

Most of the parents of children in the free and charity schools, though unable to pay for their instruction the prices usually charged in pay schools, could probably afford to make some compensation for the education of their children ; and, if so, the propriety of their entirely gratuitous instruction is questionable.

With respect to the objections under the first head, and which apply to a large portion of the lower-priced pay schools, your committee fully believe a remedy would be found in the establishment of Lancasterian pay schools, conducted by well-qualified and judicious teachers, or by increasing the number and opening the establishments of the Free-School Society for the reception of pay scholars.   It is well known that great complaints have been made by many of our citizens in the upper wards of the city, who are too poor to send their numerous children to good pay schools, and yet with feelings too independent to send them to free schools, that, notwithstanding they are taxed for the promotion of education, they do not derive any benefit from the school fund, as do citizens of all classes in every other county in the State.

In consequence of the poor condition of many of the minor pay schools, and of the very superior instruction and accommodation in our free schools, applications are sometimes made to the trustees of the latter for the admission of children of poor but industrious citizens, provided they may be allowed to pay a small sum annually for that which they are unwilling to receive as a gratuity. This is, however, inadmissible under our act of incorporation.

The superior advantages of the Lancasterian, or System of Mutual Instruction, so far as applied to an English elementary education, are too well established by the light of experience to admit of doubt or need discussion; and your committee therefore think the only question is, How shall schools of the description proposed be established, and under what auspices?

The committee believe that their usefulness would be much increased by their being subject to regular inspection and the control of trustees, and that the latter should be persons influenced by motives of benevolence and public good to undertake the important charge. Hence the propriety is inferred of the establishment of a public society for the purpose of promoting and superintending elementary instruction in this city. As the Free-School Society has had an experience of nineteen years, during which period it has educated more than twenty thousand of our poor children, your committee have been led to the inquiry, whether this Society could not with great advantage combine the proposed object with its present, and thus have the general superintendence of the education of all classes who may attend the public schools? This question is connected with the second division of our main inquiry—the state of our free and charity schools, and the best mode of applying the common school fund.

According to the United States census of 1820, the number of children in this city and county, of the age of 16 years and under, was 47,282 (and this number has probably increased subsequently to 53,000), of whom 27,000 may be computed to be between 5 and 15 years of age, and 20,000 are supposed to be receiving literary instruction in a greater or lesser degree; leaving 7,000 who do not attend any school. The number of children officially returned as having attended the free and charity schools of this city during the year ending April 30th, 1824, was 10,383. And the sum of $7,087 was drawn from the common school fund, to which a like sum raised by tax on our citizens was added, making the amount paid from the public funds that year, toward the support of those schools, $14,173. Of these 10,383 children, 6,976 were educated in the schools of the Free-School Society, the African Free School, the Female Association, the Mechanics' Society, the Hamilton Free School, the Orphan Asylum, and the Economical School, and the remaining 3,407 attended the various sectarian or church schools (including 1,616 reported as having been instructed in the Bethel Baptist schools). See the report of the Commissioners of School Moneys. There then was, and now is, ample room in our large and commodious school-houses to acommodate two thirds of these 3,407 children, and who could consequently, as no more teachers would be required in our schools, be therein educated at very little additional expense to us, and the amount annually paid (say $3,000 to $4,000) by the city for their instruction in church schools, might be appropriated to the erection of new school-houses in those sections of the city where they now are and may in future be want-ed, so as finally to provide sufficient accommodations to receive and instruct the 7,000 poor children now uneducated, and supposed to be roaming our streets, and many of them daily acquiring the most vicious habits.

It hence appears that the public moneys appropriated to schools would be more advantageously applied, and would produce a greater amount of good, by being confined to one channel. For a further development of this fact, your committee refer to the estimates and calculations appended to this report.

In reference to the impolicy of any part of the public funds being placed at the control of religious societies, your committee are unanimously and decidedly of the opinion that it is totally incompatible with our republican institutions, and a dangerous precedent in our free Government, to permit any part of such funds to be disbursed by the clergy or church trustees for the support or extension of sectarian education. The following remarks are extracted from your last annual report to the Society, and to that report we refer for a further illustration of this subject.

With respect to the school fund, it is purely of a civil character, being for a civil purpose; and the proposition that such a fund should never go into the hands of an ecclesiastical body or religious society, is presumed to be incontrovertible upon any political principle approved or established in this country. It is conceded that religion is essential to the preservation and prosperity of civil society; but then, the leading principle of all our legislation has ever been, to let religion support itself—let it draw all its resources from private benevolence; and any law that should impose a direct tax on our citizens for the support of religion, would assuredly meet the disapprobation of the whole community. And this feeling of the peo-ple does not arise from any disrespect for religion, but from a correct idea of her exalted character. It has been left to the experience of this country to show—what appears problematical in the eyes of Europe—that religion requires no aid from the civil arm; she needs no resources drawn from the treasury of the State, but her resources consist of the willing contributions of hearts subjected to her influence.

In this country we have our religious institutions. We have our clergy; they are, for the most part, well endowed and amply supported. The bene-ficial tendency of their influence upon society is acknowledged. But how are they supported? By private benevolence. And who would wish to have it otherwise? Nay, it may be asked, Whose heart would not be indig-nant at the proposition that the Government should tax the people for the support of these institutions and these clergy? And might it not be asked with equal propriety, If a religious society wish to educate the poor, and instill into their minds their own sectarian doctrines, is it not wrong that they should command the public funds for this purpose, but ought they not rather to do it—as all other religious instruction is afforded—at the expense of private benevolence? It is not believed that the funds of the State were ever designed to be used for sectarian purposes; and the trustees think it was a violation of sound political principle to allow religious societies originally any participation in the school fund.

The Committee of the Assembly on Colleges and Common Schools, to whose consideration the proposed law relative to the distribution of the school fund in the city was referred at the session of last winter, remark as follows:

There is, however, one general principle connected with this subject, of no ordinary magnitude, to which the committee would beg leave to call the attention of the House.

It appears that the city of New York is the only part of the State where the school fund is at all subject to the control of religious societies. This fund is considered by your committee purely of a civil character, and therefore it never ought, in their opinion, to pass into the hands of any corporation or set of men who are not directly amenable to the constituted civil authorities of the Government, and bound to report their proceedings to the public. Your committee forbear, in this place, to enter fully into this branch of the subject; but they respectfully submit whether it is not a violation of a fundamental principle of our legislation, to allow the funds of the State, raised by a tax on the citizens, designed for civil purposes, to be subject to the control of any religious corporation?

This important question was long agitated and ably argued in our sister State of Connecticut, as connected with their school fund, and it finally resulted, to the entire satisfaction of the citizens, by excluding the clergy and churches from having any control over it. Our own Legislature, at their last extra session, wisely erased from the statute-book the only law granting this privilege in this State; and your committee cannot believe the Corporation will ever engraft in the local code of the city a power which ought to be unknown in a republican State.

It is, therefore, much to be desired for the preceding reasons, and to prevent strife and jealousy and preserve that harmony which has heretofore so happily existed between the several religious societies in this place, that the honorable the Corporation would be induced, at an early day, to pass a resolution to this effect: "That it is inexpedient to permit any school established by, or under the care of, any religious society, to draw, in future, any part of the common school fund."

There is no reason to doubt but that most of the church schools would be continued and maintained out of their respective church treasuries, as was formerly the case before any distribution of the school fund was made, and as ever was, and still continues to be, the case with one religious society, who consider it their Christian duty to educate, with their own resources, all the children of their poor members, and of whom they have many. Should the church schools, however, be partially or wholly discontinued, your committee do not believe that any disadvantage to the public, or to the children attending them, will arise; as the means will be provided for educating them elsewhere, and probably in a more economical, and as well, if not in a superior manner.

Your committee now proceed to the inquiry, whether advantages would not arise from changing our free into pay schools, so far as to require from all the parents a small compensation—if it be only 12½ or 25 cents a quarter—for the instruction of their children. In this, the most important division of their report, the committee have availed themselves of the labors of a former committee who reported on the subject :

The primary object which the Free-School Society have in view, is the education of children of indigent parents in this metropolis. It is better that this object should be effected entirely at the public expense, or by private munificence, than that the children should go uneducated. There are, perhaps, in this city a number of charitable institutions, which, by holding out certain relief to the destitute, tend to relax those exertions which are necessary to the prevention of poverty, thereby increasing and perpetuating the very evils which they were humanely designed to remedy. Such institutions, it now requires no arguments to prove, do not promote the welfare of the community ; experience has furnished ample testimony, that the suffering ever attendant upon unmitigated poverty is a wholesome moral discipline, and that the dread of that suffering is powerfully influential in producing, on the part of individuals, those exertions and that providence by which, in most instances, the evil may be prevented. This reasoning, however, applies with mitigated force, if at all, to the charity of which the Free-School Society are the almoners. The direct effect of this charity is the intellectual and moral improvement of its recipients. Imparting to them, as it does, knowledge and virtue, they are thus supplied with the inducement and the means of all legitimate prosperity. If, however, the parents who send their children to the schools of the Society could be induced to render something in the way of compensation for their instruction, the committee are fully persuaded that the moral benefits resulting from these schools would be sensibly increased.

Small contributions from parents would not, probably, so diminish their means as to subject them to the least inconvenience, and would, moreover, go to foster a principle of most beneficial tendency, that every person is bound to render some return for services performed for him or his family : or, if he be under the necessity of receiving aid from the public, it must be in the way of coöperation with his own exertions.

The improvement of parents is not, however, the object for which the Society was organized : this object is the education of children. But if, in pursuing this main object, collateral advantages should accrue to parents, a consequence will be produced to which the Society can never be indifferent.

The principal advantages, however, resulting from the proposed measure will, in the opinion of the committee, be reaped by the children themselves. If parents pay for the education of their children, they will doubtless take a greater interest in it, and be more likely to require punctuality in their attendance upon the schools than under the existing system. That which costs nothing is generally regarded as of little worth ; the only standard of value for most things, with which the generality of mankind are acquainted, being the amount of money which they cost.

And here the committee would avail themselves of some valuable testimony on this subject contained in one of the reports of the Society for Promoting the Education of the Poor of Ireland—a Society which, we are informed in their Tenth Annual Report, afforded assistance to 513 schools, in which are instructed more than 40,000 children, and whose last annual expenditure was £14,282 9s. 9d. sterling. In some of the schools under their charge they have tried the experiment of receiving one penny weekly, amounting to 52 pence annually, from each child in attendance. It is not intimated that there was ever any difficulty in collecting that amount (except in one school, where many of the children became indebted for more than a year's dues). From an experience of the beneficial results of this requisition, the Society recommend to the schools under this charge, that in all cases the children should be required to pay a small sum weekly : by such means, they observe, the funds of the school will be augmented, the poor will set a higher value on the instruction imparted to them than they probably would if they were entirely indebted to the bounty of others for their education, and a habit of looking to their own exertions for their support will be cherished in their minds, which will prove of essential value to them throughout life. In a subsequent report, the practice is again strongly recommended, and the committee of the Society observe : "A greater value appears to be set upon the instruction received, where a payment, though small, is required. It induces parents to look more closely to the regular attendance of their children ; and it meets, besides, a feeling not uncommon in this country (Ireland), which ought, perhaps, to be rather encouraged than repressed—of repugnance to receiving education as a mere charitable boon, instead of obtaining through the means afforded by the exertion of honest industry.

In the eighteenth report of the British and Foreign School Society, the committee observe : " Experience has proved that the most effectual method of supporting local schools is the demand, in addition to the aid of the benevolent, of a small weekly sum from each scholar ; and the desire for instruction on the part of the industrious poor is generally so great, that, in most cases, nothing more is needed for the establishment of a school than the coöperation and activity of a few zealous persons, whose exertions can scarcely fail of being crowned with success." It is also stated, in the appendix to the report, that " in a populous part of Lambeth (a part of London), a school for the poor was erected on the plan of the British and Foreign School Society, intended to hold 300 children ; the building cost more than £1,000 ; subscriptions, though liberal, fell greatly short, and the trustees found themselves behind every year. The prospect being so dark, it was thought expedient to make the parents of the children pay something toward the education of them, and, ultimately, two pence per week was demanded. Some fear arose lest the attendance would be less. To obviate this, the master was instructed not to reject any child whose parents were unable to pay ; but only *one* such circumstance occurred. The experiment gave rise to an unexpected circumstance, too important to be overlooked, and promising a vast extension of the benefit of schools ; for the poor are so well pleased with the new plan, that the attendance has been increased, and the regularity of the attendance much improved. They feel a spirit of independence excited by paying for their children which deserves encouragement, and a hope is held out that the benevolent views of the friends to the education of the poor may meet a strong aid in the means thus afforded."

Thus much for the results of this experiment in England and Ireland. The committee would add another consideration on this subject. If the parents who now send their children to the free schools were in the habit of making some returns for the instruction furnished them, it would beget a feeling of respect and gratitude on the part of the children toward their parents ; they would feel under greater obligations to them, and thus be furnished with additional motives to the observance of that precept of the moral law which lies at the foundation of social order and good government —" Honor thy father and thy mother."

In addition to the preceding evidence from foreign countries, the committee are happy to have it in their power to lay before the board the testimony of some experience on the subject of inquiry in our own city.

The Female Association did for some time receive pay to the amount of one and two cents per week from each of their scholars. They found no difficulty in collecting this amount, nor was the attendance on their schools diminished, although, at the same time, the schools under the care of this board were open for the instruction of their scholars free of expense. The Association discontinued receiving pay, from the fear that they would otherwise debar themselves from participating in the common school fund.

The African School at one time received from the children in attendance an amount almost sufficient to pay the salary of the teacher.

With these results of experience before them, and reasoning from the knowledge in their possession of the dispositions and feelings of some of the poor of this city, and the pecuniary ability of most of them, your committee are decidedly in favor of the alteration above considered.

Having come to this result, the committee would now connect it with the considerations in the former part of this report relative to the minor pay schools, the economical management of the school fund, &c.

Any plan that can be devised to preserve harmony and good feeling among the various religious sects, by removing all grounds for jealousy and contention, to satisfy the just complaints of our worthy laboring citizens who contribute to the common school fund, to increase, and, at the same time, to economize the means we possess of enlightening, by literary, moral, and religious instruction, our numerous youth, to break up the many inferior pay schools, to promote an independent feeling, and unite all classes of our citizens, should—and, your committee cannot doubt, would—receive the cordial approbation of the Corporation, and of our citizens generally.

On a review of the whole subject, the conclusion to which the committee have arrived is the proposition that the *Free School Society* be changed into a *Public School Society*, and that children of all classes be admitted into the schools, paying therefor such compensation as may be within their pecuniary ability; and that, for the extension and support of these public schools, the whole of the common school fund be paid annually to said Society.

A few of the advantages that would result from the adoption of a general plan of public instruction are:

1st. A more general attention would be given by our citizens to the all-important subject of education.

2d. Harmony would be preserved among religious sects.

3d. All of our citizens would contribute, and all be entitled to a share of the benefits of the fund, in the cheap and good elementary education of their children.

4th. A great increase, by the small payments from the children, of the amount expended for public instruction.

5th. A uniform system in all the elementary schools of the city, which is very important, in consequence of the frequent removals of the middle and lower classes from one part of the city to another, and which uniformity cannot be expected in the different church schools and small pay schools.

6th. Feelings of independence, which it is highly important to cultivate, would be promoted among our poor and laboring classes.

Your committee now submit for the consideration of the board the following details of the proposed plan; and they do so with a full persuasion of its practicability, and the important benefits that would follow its adoption.

GENERAL PLAN.

Proposition 1*st*. The title of " The Free-School Society of New York " to be changed to that of " The New York Public School Society," and its charter to be so amended that children of all classes may be admitted into the schools, and required to pay for their instruction according to the branches they may learn, but not exceeding 50 cents per quarter; the trustees to have power to remit the charge in such cases as they may deem proper.

2*d*. Fifty trustees to be elected by the Society at their annual meeting; and the trustees so elected to have power to add to their number, provided the whole number of trustees shall not exceed one hundred.

3*d*. The Mayor and Recorder of the city to be *ex-officio* members of the Board of Trustees.

4*th*. One fourth of the whole number of trustees being present at any meeting of the board to constitute a quorum.

5*th*. Any person paying ten dollars to the treasury, for the benefit of the schools, to become, by virtue thereof, a member of the Society for life.

6*th*. The real estate belonging to the Free-School Society to be conveyed (subject to the incumbrances now on it) by said Society to the Corporation, and by the Corporation a lease thereof to be granted to the Public School Society in perpetuity, or so long as they shall use it for the sole purpose of promoting common school education in this city.

7*th*. The real estate of the African schools to be also conveyed to the Corporation, and leased, as above, to the Public School Society, and those schools to be immediately transferred to the charge of said Society.

8*th*. The schools of " The Female Association " to be taken under the care and control of the Public School Society, and that Association to increase the number of its members, and, in future, act as auxiliary to the Society in the care of all the female schools.

9*th*. The whole amount of the school fund to be paid annually to the New York Public School Society.

10*th*. The Society shall pay over to the Orphan Asylum and Mechanics School, $1.50 per scholar for all children gratuitously educated by them.

11*th*. To facilitate the operations of the Society, and to excite emulation among the trustees, the latter shall be divided into as many sections as there may be school-houses, and each section be attached to a particular school. The sectional boards to have the immediate care and management of the schools, but the general regulations for all the schools to be made by the meeting of all the sections.

The sectional boards to meet monthly at the school-rooms, to appoint school committees, and to attend to the concerns of their several schools.

The trustees generally to meet statedly once a quarter, and on special occasions, when deemed necessary.

At each stated meeting of the general board the several sections shall report on the state of their schools, and their reports shall contain a condensed view of their minutes, and those of the school committees.

A committee shall be appointed at each stated meeting of the trustees, to visit, during the succeeding quarter, all the schools under the care of the Society, and to report on their situation at the subsequent meeting.

The annual report of the trustees to the Society shall also be submitted to the Corporation and Legislature.

In the event of this plan being adopted by the board, and subsequently receiving the sanction of the Corporation, the only alteration necessary (though others may be convenient) in the late law relative to the school fund, is in that section requiring that the subjects of gratuitous instruction only be reported to the commissioners. It will be recollected that, although the Public School Society will be an independent body so far as it respects the management of the schools, they will always be subject to the Corporation, as their funds will be at the pleasure of that body. And the commissioners will be an intermediate body of general inspectors, independent of the Society, and reporting to the Corporation and Superintendent of Common Schools. The new interest which would be excited among our citizens by the proposed plan, and the reduction of the life subscription to so low a sum as $10, would probably induce a great number to become members of a Society which already counts upon its list about five hundred of our most respectable citizens.

By the Committee.

NEW YORK, *January 28th*, 1825.

Estimates of the revenue and expenses of the Public School Society, predicated on the whole of the school fund being paid to said Society annually, and on its schools becoming low-priced pay schools:

The simple calculation is, that each school will more than half support itself by the pay derived from the scholars, and that a considerable part of the school fund may therefore be annually applied to the purchase of lots and erection of new school-houses.

The school-houses now belonging to the Free-School Society will accommodate, according to the usual average attendance, ... 7,000 scholars,

And the two African school-houses, ... 1,000 "

_____

8,000 "

So that the Society, on the plan proposed, will have sufficient room immediately for all the children that may probably be transferred during the first year to its schools from others, in consequence of the proposed change, and can educate them at but little additional expense.

Suppose the Public School Society to have, during its first year, 8,000 scholars, including the colored children, and nearly all of them to be of the description of children now attending the free and charity schools:

The annual expense of all the
schools of the Society, with   5,209 scholars, was, last year, $10,000
Add the annual expense of the
African schools, . . .   843   "   say   1,800
Add the annual expense of the
Female Association, .   543   "   say   1,200
Add the annual expense for chil-
dren from other schools, .   1,405   "   say   500
                              ———
                              8,000   "
Which gives, for the expenses of the first year, ... $13,500
And the revenue of the Society during the same period will be :
From the school fund, ... $14,000
Less appropriation to the Orphan Asylum
and Mechanics' School, . . .   500
                              ———— $13,500
State annuity from city excise fund, ... 1,500
Lotteries, ... 1,500
Rents, &c., ... 500
                                    ———— $17,000

Leaving a balance in favor of the Society, without pay from
scholars, of $3,500
But the 8,000 children would probably pay, viz. :
1,000, ... $0,000
2,000, at 12½ cts. per quarter, per annum, . . 1,000
4,000, at 25 cts. 4,000
1,000, at 50 cts. 2,000
                                    ———— $7,000

Giving a balance of receipts over expenditures amounting to $10,500

As the receipts and expenses for the second year may be estimated the
same as those of the first, for the same schools, the whole of the balance of
the first year may be applied toward the purchase of lots and erection of a
new school-house.

In the new schools, a greater proportion of scholars will doubtless be
admitted, who are willing and able to pay.

The annual expense of each new school of 800 children will be :

For teachers, male, $900, and female, $350, and monitors, $150, $1,400
Stationery, fuel, &c., ... 300
                                              ————
                                              $1.700
And the receipts, viz. :
From 400 scholars, 25 cts. per quarter, . . . $400
From 400   "   50   "   . . . 800
                                        ———— 1,200
                                              ————
Balance against school, ... $500

In the new schools, the children will thus pay an amount equal to two thirds of the whole expenses.

From the preceding estimates, it appears that the Public School Society could, without resorting to loans or other sources of revenue, go on continually adding to the number of its school-houses. But probably not faster than the wants of the city will require; for it should be remembered that there are now 7,000 children not in a course of education, and that the population of New York is increasing very rapidly.

This report was widely read and approved.

The bill passed by the Legislature, November 19th, 1824, authorized the Common Council to appoint ten school commissioners, and to designate the schools which should participate in the school fund, and directed the first appointment to be made in January, 1825. Accordingly, the Mayor, Hon. Wm. Paulding, Jr., informed the Common Council of the requirements of the law; and, upon motion of Alderman Mason, at the session held on January 17th, the following-named gentlemen were appointed:

First Ward,	OLIVER H. HICKS.
Second "	JACOB DRAKE.
Third "	JOHN ADAMS.
Fourth "	HIRAM KETCHUM.
Fifth "	GIDEON TUCKER.
Sixth "	SAMUEL ACKERLY.
Seventh "	DAVID LYON.
Eighth "	PETER H. WENDOVER.
Ninth "	GEORGE S. DOUGHTY.
Tenth "	JOSEPH PIGGOTT.

The consideration of the fourth section of the law was referred to the Committee on Laws.* The general plans recommended in the printed report on reorganization being regarded with much favor by many prominent men of the city conversant with school interests, and the trustees being informed that the Law Committee were prepared to entertain the propositions, Isaac Collins, Robert C. Cornell, and Lindley Murray were appointed to confer with them on the whole question.

At the meeting of the Common Council held on May 4th, a letter from the secretary of the Free-School Society, on the subject of extending instruction to the poor children of the city who were not included in the charity schools of religious socie-

* See Appendix A.

COLONEL HENRY RUTGERS

ties, was read, accompanied with specimens of the penmanship of pupils. The papers were referred to the Law Committee. A brief report from that committee was submitted on May 11, approving and recommending the Free-School Society to the confidence and support of the public.

At the meeting of the Common Council held on April 25, Alderman Cowdrey moved that the law relative to the distribution of school moneys be taken up; but the motion was negatived, and the law was made the special order for the following Thursday. At the same meeting, a petition was presented from the trustees of St. Patrick's Cathedral and St. Peter's Church for an apportionment of school moneys, and laid on the table.

On Thursday, the 28th, on motion of Alderman Cowdrey, the special order was taken up for consideration. The petition of the trustees of the Roman Catholic churches was read, and the law reported by the committee was also read. The first section of the law was as follows:

Be it ordained, by the Mayor, Aldermen, and Commonalty of the city of New York, in common council convened, pursuant to the authority vested in them by the act of the Legislature of the State of New York, entitled "An Act relating to Common Schools in the City of New York," passed Nov. 19, 1824, that the institutions which shall be entitled to receive of the commissioners of the common school fund, payable to and raised in the said city, are hereby designated to be, the Free-School Society of New York, the Mechanics' Society, the Orphan Asylum Society, and the trustees of the African free schools.

Mr. Philip Hone, of the Board of Assistants, moved to amend, by adding, after the words "trustees of the African free schools," the following:

And the trustees of such incorporated religious societies in said city as support or shall establish charity schools, who may apply;

Provided, That the religious societies above named shall not be allowed to receive pay for any scholars except those whose parents or guardians are in the habit of attending their respective places of worship.

After some discussion, Mr. Hone called for a division of the question, and it resulted as follows:

Ayes—Aldermen Wyckoff and Reed, and Assistant Alderman Hone—3.

Nays—Richard Riker, Recorder, Aldermen King, Ireland,

7

Cowdrey, Webb, Mann, Taylor, and Ostrander, and Assistant Aldermen Bolton, St. John, Agnew, Burtsell, and Cox—13.

The board then passed to the consideration of the bill by paragraphs, and it was agreed to, signed, and passed, under the title of " A Law regulating the distribution of the Common School Fund in the City of New York."

On the 26th of September, the report of the Law Committee was called up, and made the special order at the next meeting of the board, October 10; at which time, after some discussion, it was made the order for the following meeting.

On the 24th, the special order was resumed, and, after debate and amendment, the recommendations of the committee were adopted, as follows:

In Common Council, *October* 24, 1825.

The Committee on Laws, to whom was referred the report of a committee of the Trustees of the Free-School Society on the distribution of the common school fund, proposing a change in the constitution of that Society, so as to admit children of all classes to their schools, for a compensation not exceeding one dollar per quarter, with power to remit the charge in proper cases; and to whom was also referred a communication from Aaron Ely, proposing the establishment of public schools in this city, report:

That the distribution of the common school fund in this city is at present confined to those only who are the subjects of a gratuitous education. The necessary operation of this limitation is the rejection from the free schools and other institutions participating in this fund, of the children of those who can pay for schooling, and the admission of such only as are unable to pay. The consequences are, that the children of poverty and want are left to form a community by themselves, and that the classes above them in point of circumstances, but whose parents or guardians are not of sufficient ability amply to provide for them, are omitted as objects of the public care and bounty in the invaluable objects of literary and elementary instruction.

To obviate these privations, so injurious in their nature and effects, by breaking down the distinctions that now divide these portions of the rising generation, and to promote their mutual benefit by instructing them together, as children of the poor citizens of an enlightened and growing republic, in the great and fundamental principles of knowledge and virtue, and thus fitting them for a course of future usefulness, is a task worthy the solicitude and exertions of our benevolent and public-spirited citizens.

The following are suggested as the outlines of a general plan for effecting this important object, viz.:

I. The title of the Free-School Society to be changed to that of " The New York Public School Society," and its charter to be so amended that children of all classes may be admitted to the schools, and required to pay for their instruction according to the branches they may learn, but not exceeding one dollar per quarter, in advance. The trustees to have power to remit the charge in such cases as they may deem proper.

II. Fifty trustees to be elected by the Society at their annual meeting; and the trustees so elected to have power to add to their number, provided the whole number of trustees shall not exceed one hundred.

III. The Mayor and Recorder of the city to be *ex-officio* members of the Board of Trustees.

IV. One fourth of the whole number of trustees being present at any meeting of the board to form a quorum.

V. Any person paying ten dollars to the treasury, for the benefit of the schools, to become, by virtue thereof, a member for life.

VI. The real estate of the Free-School Society, and of the African schools, to be conveyed, subject to the existing encumbrances, by the said societies to this corporation, and a lease thereof to be granted by them to the Public School Society, in perpetuity, or so long as they shall exist for the sole purpose of promoting common school education in this city.

VII. The whole amount of the school fund to be distributed to the said Public School Society, and such auxiliary institutions as shall be sanctioned by the Common Council.

The advantages which may be expected from the proposed alterations, in addition to those first suggested, are:

I. Experienced and well-qualified teachers, who shall be duly compensated for the employment of their time and talents.

II. Convenient, spacious, and well-accommodated school-houses, combining the advantages of cleanliness, light, and air.

III. Uniformity in the systems and modes, and in the books and subjects of instruction.

IV. In respect to the small payments which alone are to be allowed, and which are never to be required in cases of inability or inconvenience to make them, the expected advantages are: First, a great increase of the amount to be received and expended for public instruction. Second, the inculcation of the valuable principle, that every person is bound to render some return for services performed for himself or his family. Third, an increased interest on the part of the parents in the education of their children, and their due preparation for and their punctual attendance at school, connected with the encouragement of a laudable share of pride, emulation, and independence of character, in both parents and children. And fourth, from the consideration of the renewed obligation under which children will be placed to their parents, that they will be more practically instructed in the great commandment which says, " Honor thy father and thy mother."

V. A new impulse will be excited, and a more general attention be produced among our citizens at large, in favor of the all-important subject of elementary education.

VI. Harmony will be produced among religious sects, and, at last, all causes of disagreement will be removed, as all will be interested where all alike contribute to the great and common object.

In proof of the practicability of the plan now suggested, your commit
tee have ascertained that in Great Britain a similar method has been attended with success, as will be seen in the eighteenth report of the British and
Foreign School Society. And your committee have been furnished with a
letter from Mr. Charles R. Webster, dated Albany, 25th of April, 1825, to Mr.
Isaac Collins, of our city, from which they have his permission to make the
following extracts :

I have examined the minute-book of the Albany Lancaster school in
relation to the admission of pay scholars. We have but a single by-law on
the subject, which requires that all children, on admittance into the school,
shall pay in advance from twenty-five cents to one dollar and twenty-five
cents per quarter, according to the ability of their parents or guardians,
always excepting the children of such poor persons as are unable to pay ;
and those of this class have in all cases a preference, and are never refused
on any account whatever.

We have never met with any difficulty in the school in respect to the
scholars paying, or not paying. Each child has equal rights and privileges ;
and though the government of the school requires order and submission, it
is otherwise a perfect democracy. Each child rises or falls from his own
merit or demerit, and no regard is ever paid to the standing of the parent
or guardian. We have never found any difficulty on this subject.

Your committee, with the utmost brevity, remark in addition, that the
common school fund is appropriated in the other counties of the State with
the greatest advantage to the support of common or public schools ; and
the prosperity and unrivalled eminence of some of the Eastern States in
their elementary and public schools, and in the consequent dissemination of
useful knowledge among all classes of their citizens, are matters of notoriety and sources of gratification to themselves and their fellow-citizens.

And while, in other States, and in other parts of our own State, the
advantages of literary and scientific instruction are scattered as far and as
widely as possible, and the policy appears to be adopted that education
should be as diffusive as civil liberty—that it should be made to expand
with the increase of population as the surest guarantee of political happiness—and that, with the effort to extend the right of suffrage, and render it
universal, the influences of an education as salutary and as universal should
accompany this right as its correlative and best regulating power, your committee will respectfully suggest that the establishment of a similar policy as
applicable to our city is deserving the efforts of this board, of our liberal
institutions, and, indeed, of every citizen.

The committee therefore recommend to the board the following resolutions :

I. *Resolved*, That this board approves of the establishment of public
schools in this city on the principles above suggested, instead of free
schools.

II. *Resolved*, That this board recommend that a memorial be submitted
to the next Legislature by the said Free-School Society (as they propose),
for effecting the above object, and for securing the lands and buildings now
belonging to the Free-School Society and the African schools in this city as

public or common schools, and also for securing the proportion of the common school fund, to which this city is or shall be entitled, to the general purposes of education, and for the support of public or common schools, subject to any future alterations which the Legislature may deem proper; *Provided*, that the details be first considered by the committee of this board, the Commissioners of the School Fund, and the Trustees of the Free-School Society, and that they report such details for the consideration of the board.

Respectfully submitted,   S. COWDREY,
THOS. BOLTON,
E. W. KING.

On the 2d of November, the Board of Trustees appointed Isaac Collins, Benjamin Clark, James I. Roosevelt, Jr., Robert C. Cornell, and Lindley Murray a committee to prepare a memorial, a draft of a law, and a detailed plan of operations, to correspond with the new scheme, if enacted by the Legislature.

A special meeting of the Society was held on the 11th of November, to consider the measures proposed by the Board of Trustees, and resolutions were unanimously adopted in favor of their action, and directing that the board proceed with their appeal to the Legislature for a new charter. The committee acted with great diligence and intelligence in the matter, and all opposition being overcome, and the details of the law having been made complete, it was passed on the 28th of January, 1826. The law, being of unusual importance in the course of legislation on popular instruction in New York, is here inserted:

AN ACT

In relation to the Free-School Society of New York, passed January 28th, 1826.

Whereas the trustees of said Society have presented to the Legislature a memorial requesting certain alterations in their act of incorporation, Therefore,

Be it enacted by the people of the State of New York, represented in Senate and Assembly, that the said Society shall hereafter be known by the name of the PUBLIC SCHOOL SOCIETY of New York.

And be it further enacted, That it shall be the duty of said Society to provide, so far as their means may extend, for the education of all children in the city of New York not otherwise provided for, whether such children be or be not the proper objects of gratuitous education, and without regard to the religious sect or denomination to which such children or their parents may belong.

And be it further enacted, That it shall be lawful for the trustees to require of the pupils received into the schools under their charge a moderate compensation, adapted to the ability of the parents of such pupils, to be applied to the erection of school-houses, the payment of the teachers' salaries, and to the defraying of such other expenses as may be incident to the education of children; *Provided*, That such payment or compensation may be remitted by the trustees, in all cases in which they shall deem it proper to do so; and, *Provided, further*, That no child shall be denied the benefits of the said institution, merely on the ground of inability to pay for the same, but shall at all times be freely received and educated by the said trustees.

And be it further enacted, That nothing in this act contained shall be construed to deprive the said Society of any revenues, or of any rights to which they are now, or, if this act had not been passed, would have been by law entitled, and that the receipts of small payments from the scholars shall not preclude the trustees from drawing from the common school fund for all the children educated by them.

And be it further enacted, That the trustees shall have power from time to time to establish in the said city such additional schools as they may deem expedient.

And be it further enacted, That any person paying to the treasurer of said Society, for the use of said Society, the sum of ten dollars, shall become a member thereof for life.

And be it further enacted, That the annual meetings of the said Society shall hereafter be held on the second Monday in May in each year.

And be it further enacted, That the number of trustees to be chosen by the Society, at and after the next annual meeting, shall be increased to fifty, who at any legal meeting of the board may add to their number, but so as not in the whole to exceed one hundred, exclusive of the Mayor and Recorder of the city, who are hereby declared to be *ex-officio* members of the Board of Trustees.

And be it further enacted, That the stated meetings of the board shall be held quarterly, that is to say, on the first Fridays of February, May, August, and November in each year; *Provided*, That an extra stated meeting shall be held on the Friday next following the annual meeting in each year, for the purpose of organizing the new board, and transacting any other necessary business.

And be it further enacted, That one fourth of the whole number of trustees for the time being shall constitute a quorum for the transaction of business at any legal meeting of the board.

And be it further enacted, That the said Society is hereby authorized to convey their school edifices, and other real estate, to the Mayor, Aldermen, and Commonalty of the city of New York, upon such terms and conditions, and in such forms, as shall be agreed upon between the parties, taking back from the said Corporation a perpetual lease thereof, upon condition that the same shall be exclusively and perpetually applied to the purposes of education.

State of New York, }
Secretary's Office. }

I certify the preceding to be a true copy of an original act of the Legislature of this State, on file in this office.

ALBANY, *January* 28th, 1826.

    (Signed)   ARCHIBALD CAMPBELL, *Dep. Secretary.*

The announcement of the passage of the act was received with great satisfaction by the board, and the following resolutions were adopted :

Resolved, 1st. That the Committee on Public Schools be discharged, and that the thanks of the board be presented to Isaac Collins, one of their number, for his active and efficient agency at Albany in procuring the passage of the law amending our charter, and that the treasurer be directed to pay his bill of expenses.

2d. That the law be accepted, and that, in accordance therewith, this Society forthwith assume the name of the PUBLIC SCHOOL SOCIETY OF NEW YORK.

3d. That a committee of five be appointed to prepare and report a revised copy of by-laws founded on the new law, and with such alterations and additions as may appear expedient.

4th. That a committee of three be appointed to look out for suitable lots for two additional school-houses within the following districts, viz., in the rear of the Hospital, between Anthony and Reade streets, and near the junction of Spring and Macdougal streets.

5th. That a committee of three be appointed on the subject of the transfer of our real estate to the Corporation, and that they report their views of the terms on which a conveyance should be made.

6th. That, until after the next annual election, the board will continue to meet monthly, as heretofore, for the transaction of their usual business.

The committees were appointed to the several duties named in the resolutions, as follows :

To Revise the By-Laws—Lindley Murray, R. C. Cornell, J. E. Hyde, Isaac Collins, and James I. Roosevelt, Jr.

To Select Locations for New Schools—Robert C. Cornell, William W. Fox, and Isaac Collins.

On Transfer of Real Estate—James I. Roosevelt, Jr., Benjamin Clarke, and George T. Trimble.

The long-continued efforts of the Society to secure a just distribution of the school money, irrespective of sectarian institutions, and to reorganize the system, were thus rewarded with the seal of legislative approval and authority. The development of new plans and measures commence the history of a new year.

CHAPTER V.

HISTORY FROM 1826 TO 1831.

New Schools—No. 7 Opened—School No. 8—Schools at Harlem, Manhattanville, and Bloomingdale—School No. 9—Columbia College—New Locations—School No. 10 organized—School No. 11—Finances and Attendance—High School—The Pay System—Lotteries—Sunday Scholars—Infant Schools—Death of the President, DE WITT CLINTON—New Measures—Additional Tax—Address to the Public— Vagrancy—Visitor—Samuel W. Seton—Memorials—Power to Mortgage and Convey Property—The New Tax Obtained—The Schools of New York City—School No. 12—School No. 13—The School Fund—Application of the Roman Catholic Orphan Asylum.

THE important proceedings during the year 1825, relative to the reorganization of the system and the prosecution of the steps necessary to ensure the requisite legislation, did not divert the attention of the board from those measures which related to the healthful and immediate expansion of the sphere of labor of the Society, by the selection of additional sites for school buildings, and the erection of substantial and commodious edifices thereon. At the meeting of the board in May, a committee of five, consisting of J. I. Roosevelt, Jr., James F. Depeyster, George T. Trimble, R. C. Cornell, and Stephen Allen, was appointed, to select locations for schools, and to report on the expediency of hiring premises or erecting buildings, to meet the wants of the city. The committee, having examined several locations, reported, in September, in favor of establishing a school on the east side of Chrystie street, between Hester and Pump (afterward called Walker) streets, where three lots could be procured for fifteen hundred dollars each. A location in the rear of Trinity Church was also recommended, if the premises could be procured from the corporation of the church by a permanent lease, and, if possible, a purchase of the property. The committee reported resolutions authorizing the purchase of the lots in Chrystie street, and the appointment of a building committee to superintend the erection of a proper house. The resolutions were adopted, and William W. Fox, James Palmer, and Isaac Collins were selected as the Building Committee, who were directed to obtain plans and estimates for the erection of a school-house, which should be similar to No. 5, with the exception of a cellar instead of a basement.

On the 23d of September, the committee reported the plans and estimates for a house, which should be 40 by 80 feet, with furniture, fences, and other requisites, at a cost of $9,500. The report was adopted, and the committee directed to proceed with the erection of the building. The house was built, and opened as Public School No. 7, on the 1st of May, 1826, with eighty-seven pupils; under the care of STEPHEN R. KIRBY.

In April, the Committee on Locations reported in favor of purchasing three lots of ground in Grand street, between Wooster and Laurens streets, for $5,000. The board approved the recommendation of the committee, and appointed Isaac Collins, George T. Trimble, William W. Fox, and Robert C. Cornell to procure plans and estimates. They were submitted on the 29th of the same month, and approved; and Messrs. W. W. Fox, Isaac Collins, and James Palmer were appointed the Building Committee. The house was opened on the 1st of November, under the care of Mr. C. B. SHERMAN, Principal, and filled so rapidly, that, on the 1st of April following, there were 371 boys and 264 girls in attendance.

At the meeting of the board held in May, Messrs. Stephen Allen and James F. Depeyster stated that there were two or three school districts in Manhattanville, Harlem, and Bloomingdale, which were entitled by law to certain moneys—the proceeds of the sale of the Harlem Commons—and they suggested the propriety of a conference with the parties interested in those schools with reference to a scheme of transfer, by which they might be placed under the jurisdiction of the Society. Messrs. Stephen Allen, James F. Depeyster, and George T. Trimble were assigned the duty of making the requisite inquiries, and on the 12th of the same month they reported in general terms relative to the schools, but particularly with reference to that at Bloomingdale. They offered resolutions for the recognition of the school as one of those under the care of the Society, and providing for the selection and temporary appointment of a teacher, at a salary of thirty dollars a month. The resolutions were adopted, and the school, which had been under the care of the vestry of St. Michael's Church (Episcopal), became known as Public School No. 9. Jotham Wilson, a pupil who had for several years been a monitor-general, was selected as teacher.

The expenses of the Society for the fiscal year had been $47,344.99, leaving a balance in the treasury to the new account of $6,235.51. The annual exhibit showed the average attendance of pupils to be 5,170, of whom about three fifths were boys and two fifths were girls.

The Society having at that time no convenient place of meeting, an application was made to the Trustees of Columbia College, who courteously granted the use of their hall for the meetings of the Society.

The Committee on New Locations reported, on the 8th of September, in favor of purchasing three lots of ground in Wooster street, between Houston and Bleecker streets, and also three lots in Anthony, near Hudson street, and recommended the erection of a house on the lots in Anthony street. The resolutions to purchase land were adopted, but the recommendation to build was laid on the table. In November, the committee reported a new location in Church street, between Duane and Thomas streets, which, however, was not adopted. In January, 1827, they reported favorably upon a location in Duane street, near Hudson, the price for which would be $8,300, and a dower right of $50 per annum in favor of a lady then sixty-eight years of age. The location was approved, and the usual steps directed to be taken to complete the purchase; and the Building Committee was authorized to proceed with the preliminary measures to provide for the erection of an edifice. The house was completed, and opened as No. 10, on the 1st of November, 1827. Contracts were directed to be made for the building of No. 11, in Wooster street (which was completed and opened on the 15th of September, 1828), and the purchase of ground for No. 9, at Bloomingdale, and the erection of a frame house of two stories thereon. Four lots in Bloomingdale were purchased for $250, two of them being granted as a donation. These measures were severally prosecuted with promptitude and fidelity.

The annual report of the treasurer exhibited the fact that the expenditures of the Society had been $64,724.79, leaving a balance to new account of $5,480.69, with an average attendance of 5,030 pupils. Of the amount expended, about $26,000 were paid for buildings and lots of ground.

The close of the year 1826, and the early part of 1827, were partially devoted to the consideration of two important propositions : 1st, the establishment of a central high school, for the instruction of monitors and tutors, and as an advanced school for the reception of pupils from the public schools ; and, 2d, the question, whether the pay system had been the means of diminishing the attendance of poor children at the schools. The decrease in the number of scholars, as made apparent by the annual exhibit, presented a fact the very reverse of what had been anticipated. Instead of a considerable increase in numbers with the more extended facilities and new schools, there had been an actual diminution. The proceedings relative to these measures are presented in other pages of this volume.

The great evils of the system of gambling known as lotteries, had become manifest to the trustees, and they earnestly sought to have such a law enacted as would restrict, if not entirely prohibit, the traffic in lottery tickets. The Society received a considerable sum annually from the half of the license-tax paid by the dealers in lottery schemes ; but this did not blind their eyes to the fact that the system was pernicious, and should be discontinued. The annual report for the year 1827 makes the following allusion to this topic :

The subject of lotteries, in which, through the medium of moneys received for licenses to sell tickets, they are directly interested, has engaged much of the serious attention of the trustees. Fully convinced of, and deeply regretting, the great and increasing evils incident to this legalized mode of gambling, they have deemed it their incumbent duty to endeavor to moderate and lessen the mischiefs of this pernicious system, and accordingly directed a committee to prosecute offenders against the provisions of the old law, which prohibited the selling of tickets in foreign lotteries. They also presented a memorial to the Legislature, requesting, if they could not constitutionally abolish the whole system, that such further regulations might be adopted as appeared necessary for the limitation and curtailment of the evil. The board exceedingly regret that an act on this subject, which had passed both branches of the Legislature by large majorities, was negatived by the Executive on the ground of its being unconstitutional. Another bill was, however, subsequently introduced, passed, and has become a law, and which, it is hoped, will prove efficacious in preventing that branch of the evil arising from the sale of tickets in lotteries not authorized by this State.

The same report contains the following statement in regard
to the number of pupils attending school during the year, who
were also regular attendants at Sunday schools or churches :

> The trustees are aware of the importance of early religious instruction ;
> and although the nature of their association and its true interests require
> that none but such as is strictly and exclusively general and scriptural in its
> character should be introduced into the schools under their charge, they
> require from the teachers stated returns of the number of their scholars who
> attend at the various Sunday schools, or at places of worship, on the Sab-
> bath. The last reports for all schools, except No. 8, show that, on the 1st
> of April, of 3,925 children on the registers, 2,463 belonged to Sunday
> schools, and of the remainder, 1,142 were attenders at the various places of
> worship to which their parents were attached ; leaving but 326 unaccounted
> for, or who are negligent in this important duty.

During the month of May, a letter was received from Mrs.
Joanna Bethune, informing the board that an association of
ladies had been formed for the purpose of establishing an infant
school, and requesting the use of the basement of No. 8, in
Grand street, for the accommodation of the school. The Executive Committee were authorized to grant the use of such rooms
in the school buildings as were proper, and not otherwise appropriated. This measure laid the foundation of the very important change made in the system soon afterward, by which children of three years of age were taught with others in the infant
schools, which became known as Primary Schools or Departments. The Executive Committee took the whole plan into consideration, and referred the inquiries to a sub-committee, who
presented a report in favor of the system. On the 4th of February, 1828, this report was submitted to the board, by which
body it was adopted, and referred back to the Executive Committee, with full power to carry its several recommendations into
effect. This formed the distinguishing feature of the labors of
the board at the commencement of the year 1828.

The Society which had been so long favored with the valuable services of many of its original founders, and which still
retained some of the most honorable and useful in its board, was
at last called to mourn the loss of one of the most distinguished
and noble men of the State, who had rendered his name illustrious as well for his philanthropy as for his liberal and enlightened policy in all that serves to make the State preëminent for

its resources, its public works, and its literary institutions. His Excellency, DE WITT CLINTON, one of the social circle that originated the free-school system, who had been President of the Society from the time of its organization, and who was also Governor of the State, was called from the scenes of his earthly labors to his rest and his reward. His death occurred on the 11th of February, and was announced to the board at a special meeting held on the 15th of that month. Alderman Cowdrey offered the following preamble and resolutions, which were unanimously adopted :

The Trustees of the Public- School Society, being informed of the sudden decease of his Excellency, DE WITT CLINTON, who, among his other testimonials of public esteem and confidence, has held the office of President of this Society from its first organization,

Resolved, As the sense of this board, that, while it is our duty to bend with unmurmuring submission to the will of Divine Providence, we view this event as a signal calamity to our country, to the cause of science and public improvement, and the many useful institutions of which the deceased was a distinguished ornament and patron. That he occupied a large place in the affection and respect of his countrymen, as one of the most able and successful benefactors ; and that, as connected with this and similar associations, the cause of literature and benevolence has sustained in his death an unspeakable and irreparable loss.

This resolution was not one of mere eulogy, but was warranted by the great public services of the late President, to whose influence and labors the Society was largely indebted for its success, and the extension of its means and its sphere of labor. He was succeeded in the office of President by Col. HENRY RUTGERS, who was chosen at the annual election in the month of May following.

The increase in the population of the city, and the demand for more extensive facilities for instructing children not otherwise provided for, together with the fact that the pay system was found to disappoint the generous expectations of the board, combined to renew the anxiety of the Society for such an improvement and reorganization of the system as would meet all the requirements of the metropolis, and whose expansion should correspond with that of the city itself, until it should comprehend the children of every class, and thus promote a harmonious intermingling of the youth of the community, as a social and public benefaction.

The Executive Committee made these measures a subject of earnest consideration, and, at the February meeting, submitted a report to the board, together with an address to the public, relative thereto. The report recommended an additional tax of half a mill on a dollar on the real and personal estate in the city and county, which, at the valuation of that year, would have yielded about $50,000. This sum, with the income enjoyed by the Society at the time, it was estimated would be sufficient to add *three* new school-houses annually to the number in existence, and enable the Society to educate all classes free of expense, as well as to establish a high school and an academy, or classical seminary, for the preparation of teachers. The report is substantially incorporated, in its arguments and facts, in the address to the public which was submitted at the same time, and which was ordered to be printed and circulated. This address develops the germ of many of the plans and measures which have since that time been made a part of the system of popular education in the city, and is valuable as a presentation of the philanthropic and enlarged views which were realized years afterward in part by the Society, but more fully under the change of system in 1842, when the Board of Education was organized. For these reasons, as well as for its own interest, the address is here inserted :

ADDRESS TO THE PUBLIC.

The Trustees of the Public School Society feel constrained to appeal to their fellow-citizens upon the importance of enlarging the means of common education. A full knowledge of our condition cannot but produce a universal conviction that our present system of instruction is inadequate to our wants.

There is no part of our State which has the means of more ample endowments for public instruction, nor is there any part of it where the common welfare, not to say the common safety, so imperatively demands them ; and yet we are compelled to confess that there is not within the State a single district of any magnitude with which we could institute a favorable comparison.

It is an object of primary importance to ascertain, as nearly as may be, the number of our children within the proper ages for instruction, who are entirely destitute of it. It is impossible, with the data which we possess, to arrive at a precisely accurate result ; but it will be perceived by the following statement, that if we have fallen into an error, it is not that of exaggeration.

Provision is made by law for ascertaining, in all other parts of the State, the number of children between the ages of 5 and 15, and also the whole number annually instructed; and it is much to be regretted that it does not extend to this city. It appears, by the report of the Secretary of State for 1827, that, in other parts of the State, the ratio of scholars in the public and other schools to the whole population was 1 to 5, 1 to 4, and 1 to 3; and that these are about the average ratios which prevail throughout the State, with the exception of this city. In this city, this ratio is less than 1 to 7, supposing the population to have advanced with the same rapidity since 1825 as in the preceding five years.

If we adopt for our city the proportion furnished by the above report, and founded upon actual official returns, between the whole population and the children within the ages above mentioned, the result will be, that we had 45,300 of these children in 1825, when our population was but 166,000. If the increase of our population since 1825 has been in the same ratio as from 1820 to 1825, we must add to this number of children more than 7,000, making the whole number 52,300. About 10,000 children are taught at our public and charity schools. It was ascertained by a committee of teachers, about four or five years since, that we had 200 male schools. It is a liberal allowance to suppose the female schools equally numerous. If we add to these numbers 100 schools, and allow 35 scholars to each school—which we are persuaded is an over-estimate—we have 17,500 for the private schools.*

We have no means of ascertaining the number of Sunday scholars who go to no other schools; but it is evident that this number cannot be large, because the whole number of scholars in the Sunday schools does not exceed that in the public schools by more than 2,000, and because we know that a large proportion of Sunday scholars attend private schools.

From the best inquiries we have been able to make, the number of those scholars who attend no other schools does not exceed one in twenty, or 600 in the whole.

The result of these estimates is, that we have *twenty-four thousand two hundred* children, within the ages of 5 and 15, who attend no school whatever.

A large number of children, principally boys, are taken from school as soon as they arrive at 14, and some even at 12 years of age, to be bound out to service, and others are withdrawn even at 10 years of age, for other purposes. If we allow one half of the whole number above mentioned to have been withdrawn from school before the age of 15—though perhaps one third would be nearer the truth—the result will be as follows:

Whole number of children between 5 and 15 years of age,		52,300
" attending public schools, . . . 10,000		
" " private schools, . . 17,500		
" " Sunday schools not before included, 600		
" withdrawn before the age of 15, . . 12,100		
		40,200
Leaving		12,100

* This estimate corresponds with the opinions of those best acquainted with this subject.

TWELVE THOUSAND CHILDREN, between five and fifteen years of age, *entirely destitute of the means of instruction!*

This computation leaves out of view all those children of tenderer years who ought to be introduced into infant schools.

The diversity, magnitude, and character of our population give to this subject a deeper interest here than it can have elsewhere. The single fact that 20,000 emigrants arrived within our city during the past year, presents this subject in a sufficiently striking point of view.

Believing that the relative importance of our city in the State and national councils—that the security of our rights, of our property, nay, of our lives, depends upon the character of the people, and essentially upon their intelligence, the trustees cannot, under the present state of things, suppress their anxiety and alarm.

In many of our sister States, the deep interest of the people in common education may be traced back to the very fountain of their earliest institutions. They regarded the proposition, that our republican institutions rest upon the general intelligence and virtue of the people, as something more than a mere theory. In our own State, the towns in the several counties have been authorized to provide, by taxation, for the erection of school-houses, and " for fuel and appendages," and have also been empowered to levy, in the same way, a limited amount annually over and above the sum necessary, to secure a participation in the common school fund. In the city of New York there is no legal provision whatever for the support of common schools, except from the State fund ; and that is on the condition that the city shall raise an amount equal to that received.

It is time for us to pause, and inquire whether this subject has yet received the consideration to which it is entitled, and whether our public schools occupy their merited station among our political institutions.

It appears to the trustees that the due order of things has been inverted —that our common schools are not the proper objects of a parsimonious policy, but are entitled to an endowment not less munificent than the best of our institutions. Neither the sick nor the destitute have higher claims upon us than the ignorant. The want of knowledge is the most imperative of all wants, for it brings all others in its train. If education be regarded as a charity, it is the only one whose blessings are without alloy. It demands no jealous scrutiny as to the claims of its applicants, nor does it require to be so stinted as not to multiply their number. The obligations which rest upon us in regard to this great interest, both as men and Christians, are sufficiently obvious and imposing. To these are to be added the peculiar claims which are addressed to us as the citizens of a free country. If we would preserve our free institutions, the means of education must be coëxtensive with the right of suffrage.

Although the knowledge of an individual may not always be accompanied with corresponding virtue, yet we hold it to be certain that, politically considered, the community will always be more or less virtuous as they are more or less enlightened. All private interests harmonize in the public good ; and the more clearly this is perceived, the more will a single view to

PETER AUGUSTUS JAY.

the public welfare be regarded as the test of public spirit, and the just measure of popular favor.

If it be not true that the political power of the people is generally employed for what seems to them their own good, we must abandon all the theories of a republican government. If this power be thus employed, we need only enlighten the mind which directs it, and it is our fault if it be not found on the side of virtue and patriotism. Let it not be supposed that we would separate the power of knowledge from that of morals and religion. The remarks we have made we wish to be understood as applied to the people in their civil relations. But if we go further, and regard religion and morals as the highest objects of education, as they truly are, it certainly will not be denied that education furnishes the principal, and almost the sole means, of their diffusion.

On the other hand, let it be remembered that the uneducated and unenlightened must necessarily be the mere playthings and tools of political ambition. Those base men who pervert their station, or abuse the public confidence for private purposes, have nothing to fear but from just sentiment and enlightened opinion. Prejudice and ignorance are the very elements from which proceed all popular error, confusion, and violence. It is the business of education to purify this atmosphere and to drive out the pestilence. The hand which perchance may wield the public destinies, is nothing in itself; it is the terrible engine which it puts in motion which alone is to be dreaded.

It may not be without just cause that, in some other countries, it is considered a dangerous thing to enlighten the people. But with us, the question of their political power is settled—and, if they are true to themselves, it is settled forever. We wish to keep that power in their hands, and to enable them to exercise it with wisdom. The laboring classes have been justly called the backbone and sinews of the republic. It is not enough that they know how to read, write, and cast accounts. We wish to provide for them better excitements than they now have. We wish them to enjoy the pleasures, as well as other advantages, of intellectual occupation. We wish them to be able to understand and admire the beneficence of the Creator in the works of His hands. We wish them to feel that virtue is the first distinction among men, and knowledge the second, and to be themselves the great exemplar of these truths.

Entertaining these views, we hold that there is no object of greater magnitude within the whole range of legislation, no more imperative demand for public revenue, than the establishment of competent schools and seminaries of learning. We hold that, in the nature of things, nothing can be better entitled to a share of the public revenue than that from which private and public wealth derive all their value and security. In short, our schools are the very foundation upon which rest the peace, good order, and prosperity of society.

It is time to pass from this general view to a more particular consideration of the necessity and nature of the reform which is called for. We con-

8

ceive that our present establishments are altogether inadequate to the wants of the community.

The money expended upon public schools in Boston, in the year 1826, amounted to upwards of $54,000, exclusive of all expenses of building. From the best information we can obtain, the expenditures of that city for the same object, during the past year, amounted to $70,000.

The whole revenue of the Public School Society of New York, exclusive of about $4,400 received from pay scholars, for the year ending on the 1st of May last, was less than $20,000. This sum includes all the public moneys expended upon common schools, except $2,155.50 distributed to the Mechanics', the Orphan Asylum, and the Manumission Societies. It would be a waste of time to attempt to strengthen this statement by any comments we could make. We shall hereafter point out those particulars in which we conceive that our plan of public education needs to be enlarged.

We have already stated that our present system does not harmonize with the spirit of our political institutions. It is well known that the schools of the Society were formerly exclusively " free schools." It was thought that a reluctance naturally arising from a general spirit of independence to receive even instruction as a charity, would exclude many from the benefits of education.

The removal of this impediment, by receiving compensation from such as choose to make it, has doubtless been attended with very beneficial consequences. Public instruction has been, to a considerable extent, freed from its degrading associations with poverty and charity.

Still, these consequences have not been so extensive as was hoped. About two thirds only of the whole number admitted into our schools are pay scholars. It is not certain what portion of these would have been excluded if the old system had continued.

It is now in the power of the public to remedy this evil entirely, and to introduce a corresponding benefit, which the pay system was never competent, nor even designed, to produce.

We desire to see our public schools so endowed and provided, that they shall be equally desirable for all classes of society. To effect this, the means of instruction which are offered to the poor should be the very best which can be provided. They may not all be able to proceed so far in the path of learning as others in happier circumstances. But to the extent of their progress let them have all the helps which the present state of knowledge affords. This is no mere fanciful theory. The advantages of a free intercourse and competition between persons of all ranks and conditions in life, as exhibited in the Edinburgh High School, have been admirably illustrated by one of the first British orators of the age. He regarded such an institution as invaluable in a free State ; because, to use his own language, men of the highest and lowest rank in the community sent their children there, to be educated together. The practical beneficence of this system is attested by the noble institutions of a sister city. It is by such an union and intercourse that the real worth of outward distinctions is perceived—that the highest rewards of merit are felt to be equally offered to all—that the jealousies which are too apt to arise from difference of condition are melted away, and that the relations which subsist between the different classes of society are felt to be the relations of mutual advantage and dependence, and not those of hostility.

We are aware that it will be regarded by many as impracticable, that these advantages should ever be realized to the full extent we have contemplated, under the peculiar local circumstances of this city. This objection is not without foundation; but we are satisfied that it will be found to grow less and less the more our system of education is improved, and that it will be principally confined to the lower schools. But if it be admitted that an equal distribution of the blessings of education to all classes of society can never be realized, this surely does not lessen its importance to those who cannot receive it without our aid.

If we would make our schools what they ought to be, we must offer higher rewards for the qualifications of teachers. The dignity of the office of teacher has been too often measured by the subjects of instruction. It has been thought that those pursuits which are level to the capacities of boys do not require the talents which are called forth by the active competition of men. This estimate proceeds, in part, from the idea that education consists in teaching certain truths, as it were, by rote; whereas its highest office is to instil principles and call forth the powers—to instruct us how to think—to teach its pupils how to make that which they derive from other sources their own, not by the mere tenure of memory, but by incorporating it with the very substance and strength of their faculties.

We hasten to present to the public some changes in our system which we think necessary, and others which we hope to see adopted, sooner or later.

It is obvious, from what we have already said, that these schools should be supported from the public revenue, should be public property, and should be open to all, not as a charity, but as a matter of common right.

We propose that infant schools should be established throughout the city, to receive children from three to six years of age. The separation of these from older children is necessary, to prevent disorder, and to economize time and labor. The instruction of these children is peculiar; its expense is very trifling, and is much more than repaid by the great domestic economy which results from it. We need not enlarge upon its benefits. It is obvious that the receptacles of these children must be numerous, and be dispersed throughout the city, and that they should be under the charge of females.

The difficulty of sending very young children to places of instruction is among the principal obstacles which debar them from its benefits. The most important consideration respecting these schools is, that they appeal to parents before they have any apology, or even motive, for keeping their children at home, and that, when these children are once in the way of instruction, they are likely to be kept there.

In the next place, we would greatly enlarge the number of schools in which a common English education is taught. A very great majority of the scholars will leave these schools at the age of 15, or at an earlier period. These schools should be provided with such means of instruction as are best calculated to fit their pupils for the various departments of mechanic, mercantile, and agricultural industry. They should be amply provided with teachers of pure morals and sound learning—with men who are capable of inspiring and directing a just ambition.

The schools above mentioned form the basis of the plan which we propose; and until its foundations are firmly and amply laid, we would not proceed another step. Let these schools be increased and improved, until they shall be equal to the necessities of the community—until all the wants which are now felt, or which the people can be made to feel, shall be fully supplied—until, if possible, the 12,000 children who can now neither read nor write shall be gathered into their folds, and until our instruction shall correspond, both in kind and degree, with the capacities and opportunities of the people.

About minor points there will, of course, be differences of opinion. Whether those who may have the means of consulting their inclinations on this subject shall choose to send their children to the public schools, or not, is *comparatively* of no moment. But that ample means and inducements should be provided for all who would be otherwise destitute, is of the last importance; and we trust that, for this object, the opinions and efforts of all will be united.

Next in importance to this object is the establishment of one or more high schools, in which should be taught practical mathematics, natural philosophy, bookkeeping, and, in short, all those branches which are desirable for the active business of life in any of its departments, the learned professions excepted.

We would also recommend, if the means to be provided should be sufficient for that purpose, a classical school, in which the ancient and modern languages should be thoroughly taught.

To all these should be added a seminary for the education of at least such teachers as are required for common schools.

Thus we should present to the public establishments for education which would afford ample and permanent encouragement to all the talent of the community, instead of holding out a short-lived patronage, to be withdrawn when most needed—which would make that talent public property, and which would open to universal emulation the path to all public distinctions.

This plan is not without example, and is substantially, with the exception of a school for teachers, in successful practice in a neighboring city, to which we have before alluded.

To effect this object, the trustees would recommend a tax of half a mill upon the dollar on the amount of property in the city, according to its valuation in the present estimates of assessment. The fund thus to be raised should be forever kept separate from all other taxes, and sacred to the purposes for which it was created.

It is well known that the estimates just mentioned fall far short of the actual value of the property embraced in them, and that there is a vast amount of property which they do not touch. If no allowance were made for these circumstances, this tax would amount to 5 cents on $100—to 50 cents on $1,000—to $5 on $10,000. It is true that the poor man, who puts in 5 cents, has the same direct interest in the fund with the rich man, who contributes $50; but this difference is more than made up by the indirect advantages of the latter. We submit to the liberal consideration of the rich, whether their proportion of this money, expended for the purpose of disseminating wholesome knowledge and pure morals, would not be a profitable investment for their children; and whether their bonds and mortgages and public stocks are altogether beyond the reach of public opinion, and of that which must ultimately depend upon public opinion—the administration of the laws?

We may go still further, and say that, in so far as the expenditure proposed is necessary for the establishment of common or English schools, it is recommended by the principles of economy, in the strictest sense of that word. Those who are without education, must always be a degraded caste. Having no prospect of a material improvement in their condition, they are without the common incentives to industry, and hardly know what frugality means. Those who are unacquainted with the habits and pursuits of humble life, do not know how generally education is connected with independence, and the want of it with abject poverty. Add to this that the *caste* of which we are speaking—for such it unhappily is—is necessarily removed from all wholesome social influences, and that they are the natural prey of the cunning and profligate, and it will be perceived that, with regard to a great portion of them, and particularly the children of emigrants, we must choose between the expenses of their education and the cost of their maintenance in our almshouses and penitentiaries. It is proof enough of this, that, small as is the proportion of those who cannot read and write to our whole population, they constitute the majority of our convicts and paupers.

The more the community is enlightened, the more equally will its burdens be borne. It has not, perhaps, been sufficiently considered by political economists, that national wealth chiefly proceeds from the activity of mind, and must, therefore, be proportioned to the extent and universality of its development. There is a striking illustration of this truth in a lecture not long since delivered by Baron Dupin before one of the institutes of Paris. It appears by his statement, that, in some parts of France, those who are educated are $\frac{1}{10}$, in others, $\frac{1}{20}$, in others, only $\frac{1}{229}$ part of the whole population, and that the national revenue of these districts is nearly in corresponding ratios. Nay, more—that these proportions are not materially varied by the most striking superiority or inferiority of soil and climate.

It may be said that we have mistaken the effect for the cause. Wealth and education undoubtedly act and react upon each other. But it is certain that there would be little or no capital without education, and that capital derives its power of accumulation from education, which points out its uses, and creates a demand for it.

If it were necessary to add any thing to these considerations, the trustees might claim the support of all the middling and even wealthier classes of society, on the ground of private interest. The amount of their taxes would be repaid to them fourfold by the greater cheapness of education, even supposing they were to avail themselves only of the higher schools; and it will doubtless be an object of consideration to some individuals of these classes, that the cheaper education is, the more they can afford to purchase.

It would be impossible, without going too much into detail, to show how great a saving in the expenses of educating our children would result from large establishments under a proper superintendence. Suffice it to say, that, as far as experiments have been made, the results have been greater and more satisfactory than could have been expected.*

Is it necessary that the trustees should offer any further apology for proposing that a small portion of the public wealth should be devoted to the great objects of education? We perceive no evidence of a parsimonious spirit in our public councils in regard to the ordinary objects of public revenue. There is no lack of taxation for lighting and grading our streets—for our almshouse and penitentiaries. The expenditures for these objects, to say nothing of the enormous capital invested in these establishments, amounted, in the year 1826, to upward of $196,000. The expenditures for the same objects, during the past year, amounted to $221,000. We might refer to inferior objects for proofs of equal public liberality. In short, whenever revenue is wanted for any purpose deemed important to the comfort or character of the city, it is a matter of course to raise it by tax. We humbly suggest that a similar liberality ought to be shown toward an object inferior to no other.

We will not anticipate objections. It is impossible that there can be two parties in this community—one in favor of education, and one against it. We have none among us who are the avowed advocates of popular ignorance. The blessings of generations yet unborn await the success of our efforts. In their behalf, as well as our own, we make our solemn appeal to all classes, in the name of religion, of humanity, and of freedom. We would say to those who are in the most prosperous conditions of life, that the best security for their prosperity and their privileges is to be found in their greatest possible diffusion. To those who belong to its humbler ranks, we would suggest that no more honorable occasion was ever offered for the exercise of that political power which our free Constitution has given equally to all.

The address was printed, and five thousand copies were circulated among the citizens of New York, under the direction of Messrs. Heman Averill, Rensselaer Havens, and John R. Hurd.

---

* The expense of teaching 7,044 pupils in Boston, in 1826, in the public schools, was $54,417. The expense of 3,392 pupils, in private schools, was $97,395. Something ought, probably, to be allowed for there being a greater proportion of scholars in the private than in the public schools engaged in the higher paths of education.

The recommendation of the Executive Committee, that petitions be circulated among the people, was also adopted, and Messrs. Erastus Ellsworth, William Howard, and James B. Brinsmade were appointed a committee to obtain signatures.

The expenditures of the Society for the year amounted to $41,246.25, and the average attendance of pupils was 6,195.

The large number of vagrant and truant children, who spent their time in the streets and around the wharves of the city, indulging in idle and vicious habits, had constantly attracted the attention of the Society. As a mode of exerting a more direct and special influence upon these children and their parents, it was thought that the labors of an agent, who should devote a large share of his time to a personal visitation of the pupils and their parents, as well as to a canvassing of the city among those who did not attend the schools, would be productive of good results. The Executive Committee, therefore, made such an appointment, and, on the 1st of February, 1827, SAMUEL W. SETON entered upon his duties in that capacity. In May, he submitted a brief report, in which he stated that he had visited 1,700 families, numbering 3,700 scholars, of whom about 1,500 families sent their children to Sunday school.

The summer and autumn months of this year had been employed in ascertaining fully the sentiment of the citizens in regard to the Society, and the propositions embraced in the address relative to the new tax, and the remodelling of the system. The inquiry proved that great unanimity existed among the tax-payers in favor of the plans recommended, and the approach of a new session of the Legislature made the close of the year a fitting season to prosecute their claims before the public, and the authorities of the city and State. In December, the draft of a memorial was prepared and printed, and the trustees were districted into Ward Committees, to obtain signatures to the applications to the Corporation and Legislature. On the 26th of the month, these committees reported that 3,200 names of responsible citizens had been obtained, the number being subsequently increased to 4,000. They were referred to the committee having the subject of the new law under their consideration.

The Society having found it necessary, on several occasions, to raise money by loans secured by mortgage upon portions of the property of the Society, and the contingency of sales being likely to become expedient, the question of its legal power to make such transfers was fully discussed. To remove all doubt in reference to such a procedure, and to obtain the authority of the Legislature to act in the premises, application was made to that body, and, in January, 1829, a bill was passed and became a law, with the following features :

1. Whenever, by a resolution of a majority of the whole number of trustees of the Society, at any regular meeting of the trustees, duly convened, confirmed by a vote of any subsequent regular meeting after the said resolution shall have been published at least one month in one of the papers of the city, it shall be declared necessary to dispose of or mortgage any property of the Society, it shall be proper to grant, convey, or mortgage the said property.

2. That no mortgage or conveyance hitherto made shall be impeached or defeated by reason of any doubt as to the power of the Society.

The bill did not fully meet the desires of the trustees, but as it conferred the authority, the demand for which prompted the application, the board immediately resolved to mortgage school-houses Nos. 3 and 4, in order to raise a loan of $25,000.

The committee having in their care the application to the Legislature for an additional tax, discharged their duties with great zeal and efficiency, and, before that body adjourned, a bill was passed which received the signature of the Governor, authorizing the imposition of an additional tax equal to one eightieth of one per cent. of the value of the real and personal property in the city, for the purposes of common school education. This much-needed revenue was at last assured to the Society, and contributed to remove doubts and apprehensions in regard to the future capability of the institution to meet the demands upon its treasury.

The expenses of the system for the year ending May 1, 1829, were $62,256.72, the average number of pupils being 7,031.

In connection with the labors of the year, with reference to the action before the Common Council and the Legislature, an important step was taken to establish a comparison between the schools of the Society and the private schools of the city. The annual report for that year gives the following summary of the result :

Whilst the proposition for a special school tax was before the Corporation, two of the trustees were employed by their committee to take a census of the whole number of schools of every description in the city, their general character, number of scholars, &c. Much valuable information was thus collected, and a correct and very interesting view of the state of education in New York was obtained, and embodied in their report. From this document it appears that, about the 1st of February, the whole number of schools, of every class and quality (other than Sabbath), from Columbia College down to the most indifferent, was 463, under the charge of 484 principals and 311 assistant teachers, and containing 24,952 pupils. Of which numbers, our institution, in 11 buildings, counted 21 schools, with 21 principals and 24 assistant teachers (or monitors), and 6,007 children. Of the pupils in the private schools, about 11,000, or two thirds of their entire number, " are of nearly an equal grade as to advancement with those in the public schools. The cost of educating the children in our schools may be estimated at $2.75 each per annum, exclusive of interest on the buildings; and including the latter, it does not exceed $4, or $1 per quarter, which is less than is charged in the worst description of schools in the city, and is only about one third or one quarter of the price paid in a great many others, in which the course of instruction and branches taught are much the same as in the public schools. The system adopted and pursued in the latter is excellently adapted to promote habits of order, and to advance the children in their studies; and the trustees have no hesitation in asserting their belief that the pupils are better and more efficiently taught than in the great majority of the minor schools, and even in very many which are considered of a better class.

The annexed schedule presents the condition of the schools of the city in a condensed form :

| Number. | SCHOOLS. | Principal Teachers. | Assistants. | AGES. | | Above 15. | Attend Sunday Schools. | First Elements. | Geography, Grammar, and Arithmetic. | Higher Branches. | Mathematics. | Dead Languages. | Foreign Languages. | Males. | Females. | Whole Number of Pupils. |
				4 to 5.	5 to 15.											
430	Private......	432	259	1,013	13,631	676	4,489	6,907	7,214	1.869	492	442	850	7,922	7,398	15,320
3	Incorporated	6	23	33	1.008	40	168	220	841	270	52	48	141	633	448	1,081
19	Charity......	25	5	197	2,297	50	970	2,430	960	15	12	1	4	1,305	1,239	2,544
11	Public.......	21	24		6,007		3,808	6,007	475					3,112	2,895	6,007
463	Total........	484	311	1,243	22,943	766	9,435	15,564	9,490	2,154	556	491	995	12,972	11,980	24,952

Notwithstanding the very considerable provision made by the various establishments for the education of the youth of the city, an incontrovertible fact still remained to embarrass the friends of the system with the solution of the question of vagrancy. The report thus alludes to the facts :

The committee of the Common Council, from the result of the census of the schools and the estimated population of the city, draw the appalling inference that there are 20,000 children between the ages of 5 and 15 who attend no schools whatever; and if one third be deducted from this number, as having probably left school previous to the age of 15, and 3,000 more for any possible error in the data on which the calculation is founded, we have still the enormous number of 10,000 who are growing up in entire ignorance.

The year 1829 passed without any marked event other than the efforts made to develop the efficiency of the system of instruction, and the removal of all impediments to its greatest usefulness. The principal topics of inquiry were in relation to the infant schools, the system of rewards for the pupils, the practical results of the pay system of tuition, the manual for the schools, and a thorough revision of the by-laws. These several topics are treated under their appropriate sections, to which the reader is referred.

In February, 1830, a communication was received by the board from a committee appointed by a meeting of the residents in the vicinity of Eighth avenue and Twenty-first street, asking for the organization of a school in that part of the city. Hon. Gideon Lee presided at that meeting, and he addressed a letter to the Society, which accompanied the application, in which he offered a donation of $500 toward the erection of the building when contracted for. He also named a location near the Third avenue and Twenty-eighth street, to which he would contribute another sum of $500. The subject was referred to Messrs. Charles Oakley, James N. Wells, Robert C. Cornell, and Samuel F. Mott, as a committee to report upon the necessity for a school in those locations.

The committee promptly reported in favor of a school in the first-named vicinity, and another between No. 2 (in Henry street) and No. 4 (in Rivington street). The first of these schools was built as No. 12 and the second as No. 13, and located in Madison street. Four lots were selected in Seventeenth street, near the Eighth avenue, and the Property Committee were directed to proceed with the erection of a building thereon.

During the year, a neat building for No. 9, at Bloomingdale, was also constructed, and the school opened in August.

The new building for School No. 12, in Seventeenth street, was opened on the 17th of January, 1831, under very flattering auspices ; but the expectations of the board, and of the citizens, were very soon changed into feelings of regret and disappointment. The house had been occupied only five days, when, on the 22d of the same month, it was destroyed by fire. The report of the committee, which submitted the facts relative to the building, the opening exercises, &c., also gave official information of the loss. The building had been nearly covered by insurance, so that a loss of only about $3,000 was borne by the treasury. The Building Committee were directed to proceed immediately to rebuild the house, which was completed and opened on the 29th of August.

The necessity for an increase of funds for the use of the Society was pressing with greater urgency than ever upon the board, and measures were taken to call the attention of the Corporation to the wants of the Society. The Executive Committee appointed a sub-committee to draft a memorial to the Corporation, and that body approved the measure, but introduced a section into the law lodging the control of the additional tax of three eightieths of one per cent. exclusively in the hands of the Common Council. To this objection was made, and the Society remonstrated against the section, as being calculated to lead to pernicious results. The law was passed in accordance with their views, and the Society thereby placed in possession of a material increase to their resources.

The controversy respecting the distribution of the school fund was revived during this year (1831), by the applications from the Roman Catholic Orphan Asylum and the Methodist Charity School, the discussion of which made a special event in the labors of the year.

CHAPTER VI.

THE ROMAN CATHOLIC ORPHAN ASYLUM AND METHODIST CHARITY SCHOOL.

Application from the Asylum for a Portion of the School Moneys—Memorial and Remonstrance of the Society—Proceedings of the Common Council—Address of the Trustees, and Reasons for their Remonstrance—The Methodist Charity Free School—Report of the Law Committee—A Proposition—Report of.the Committee on Arts and Sciences of the Board of Assistants, on the Application of the Trustees of the Methodist School—Memorial of the Public School Society—Report of the Committee on Arts, Sciences, and Schools, of the Board of Aldermen—Decision Thereon.

THE law of 1824 relative to the distribution of the school fund, entrusted to the Common Council the duty of apportioning and distributing the school moneys of the city. Ten years had elapsed since the enactment of the law granting to the trustees of the Bethel Church the special privileges which gave rise to the spirited controversy which was terminated at the close of the year 1824 by the passage of the law, at the extra session of the Legislature, annulling these privileges, and restricting the trustees of the Bethel schools to the use of the public fund for the payment of teachers' salaries. The interval of seven years had witnessed the extinction of these schools, and the harmonious development of the public school system on a broad basis of liberality and union.

The directors and friends of the Roman Catholic Orphan Asylum, in Prince street, feeling the want of means to meet the large demands upon their resources by the increasing number of their pupils, and the accommodations requisite for their comfortable residence and instruction, determined to make application to the Common Council for a *pro rata* in the distribution of the school moneys, in order to test the liberality of the public authorities, as well as the sentiment of the community. Accordingly, on the 7th of March, 1831, an application was submitted to the Common Council, and referred to the Committee on Common Schools. The trustees of the Methodist Charity School, under the conviction that they had at least an equal right to the public fund, prepared and presented a petition, which was submitted to the Common Council on the 21st of the same month, and referred to the same committee.

The report was submitted on May 2, with the memorial and remonstrance of the Public School Society, which were laid on the table and ordered to be printed. The Executive Committee of the Society had taken the subject into consideration, and prepared a remonstrance, which was adopted at a meeting held on May 2, and ordered to be presented to the Common Council at the meeting to be held the same evening. The committee of the Society had already been heard in opposition to the proposed apportionment before the committee of the Corporation, which committee had concluded to report in favor of the Orphan Asylum. Alderman Lee, chairman of the committee, strongly urged that the trustees of the Society should withdraw their opposition, as they had resolved to report adverse to the Methodist, and all other church schools. The following is the memorial:

To the Common Council of the City of New York:

The memorial and remonstrance of the Trustees of the Public School Society of New York respectfully represents:

That the applications now before the Common Council from the Catholic Orphan Asylum and the Methodist Charity School, for a portion of the common school fund, are opposed to what your memorialists understand and believe to be a sound and well-settled principle in the distribution of this fund, as well as of all other moneys raised by general tax for the exclusive purpose of promoting literary education. That moneys so raised cannot constitutionally, consistently with the spirit of our free institutions, nor in accordance with good policy, be appropriated to the support of church schools, has, after mature deliberation, been so fully acknowledged by our city government, and the reverse now finds so few advocates in any quarter, that your memorialists refrain from remarks on that subject; and it is with no little regret they find themselves called upon, by the relation in which they stand to the deeply interesting subject of public education, to oppose the application from the Catholic Asylum. To the merits of this institution your memorialists willingly award the praise due to its object and mode of management; but believing, as they confidently do, that said application is liable to the objections heretofore successfully used against church schools, they feel bound to call the attention of the Common Council to the facts, that none but Catholics are permitted to participate in the management of the Asylum ; that the children attached to the institution are educated in the most rigid manner of the Church whose name it bears, and that any moneys devoted to its maintenance are and must be applied to the support and extension of the doctrines of that particular Church. That this is the case, will not be denied by those whose petition your memorialists respectfully and earnestly remonstrate against; and these facts mark in bold relief the strongly sectarian and exclusive character of this institution.

These objections are not deemed applicable to the Orphan Asylum at Greenwich, which is not sectarian, inasmuch as any female, of whatever or no religious name, may become a member of the Society by an annual subscription of the small sum of one and a half dollars, and entitled to vote for, and eligible to be elected, a member of its Board of Managers, and because this association, with its managers, has always and does now consist of members of various religious denominations.

It cannot be supposed that the rejection of church schools in the distribution of school moneys is owing to the single fact that they are connected with religious congregations, but because one of the objects aimed at in all such schools is to inculcate the peculiar doctrines and opinions of the sect having the management of them. It appears indisputable to your memorialists, that any institution having the same objects in view, and under the same exclusive control, is thereby rendered liable to the same objection, whether under the direct management of a religious society or not.

Your memorialists further contend, that, in asking to be taxed for the support of common schools, their fellow-citizens fully believed that the amount thereby raised would be devoted exclusively to the cause of literary education, and that no part would be given to institutions of a sectarian character.

Believing that the enlightened views of this community will be fully with them on this occasion, the Trustees of the Public School Society earnestly solicit that the applications from the Roman Catholic Benevolent Society and the Methodist Free School may not be granted.

So deeply interested do your memorialists feel in this important subject, and so intimately do they consider the result of these applications to involve the interests of common school education in this city, that they deem it their duty respectfully to request that a committee of their body may be heard before your honorable board before a decision be had thereon.

Witness the seal of the Public School Society, this 2d day of May, 1831.

The Executive Committee exercised a vigilant watchfulness in the case, and the consideration of the question before the Common Council having been postponed until the following Monday, they prepared an address to the public, giving their reasons for dissent. Very great and powerful efforts were constantly making to ensure the success of the joint application of the Roman Catholic Asylum and the Methodist Free School, and the Executive Committee, therefore, at a meeting of the trustees held on the 6th of May, submitted their address, which was adopted and ordered to be printed, as follows:

REASONS

Of the Trustees of the Public School Society for their Remonstrance against the Petition of the Roman Catholic Benevolent Society to be admitted to a Common Participation of the School Fund.

The "New York Roman Catholic Benevolent Society" having petitioned the Common Council for a participation in the common school money, the Trustees of the Public School Society have felt it to be their duty to present to the Corporation their solemn remonstrance against the said petition; and they now feel bound, by the urgency and importance of the occasion, to state more particularly the reasons on which their remonstrance is founded.

It appears that the committee of the Corporation, to whom this subject has been referred, have reported in favor of the petition. The committee have probably been in part led to this result by the great respectability of the petitioners, and by the humane character and excellent order of their institution. While this board acknowledges the weight of these recommendations, they cannot but regard the decision of the committee as a virtual abandonment of those "cardinal principles" which were established in 1825.

There are few, as we trust, who are willing to return to the dominion which was then cast off; but the first step in a retrograde course may render it impossible to stop short of the last. The petition of the Roman Catholic Benevolent Society ought, in the opinion of this board, to be rejected, because it is contrary to the fundamental principles of liberty and equal rights, to the Constitution of the State, and to a recent act of the Legislature.

It is not now to be denied in this country, that the power of taxing the whole community is given solely for the benefit of the whole community, and that, so far as it is practicable, the benefits procured at the expense of all should be participated by all. It is plain that the Corporation has no right to constitute a privileged class, however benevolent its character may be.

In order to test the case now under consideration, it is only necessary to ascertain whether the funds now proposed to be given to the Roman Catholic Benevolent Society would be so bestowed or employed as that all persons in the same circumstances would have an equal opportunity of enjoying them. In prosecuting this inquiry, we must look to probable practical results, and not to mere theoretical principles.

The Society in question is, to all intents, a close corporation. It may be true that the object of the Society is declared, by its constitution, to be "the support and education of destitute and unprotected orphans, without distinction of sex, country, or religious creed;" but it is proper to observe, that the constitution of the Society, so called, is necessarily merged in its charter, and that the objects of the Society, as there stated, are somewhat narrower. That barely recites, that certain persons had formed a Society for "the humane and benevolent purposes of assisting and relieving the poor, and of protecting and educating orphan children."

But let us suppose that the words of the constitution are as controlling as if in the charter; who are to select the orphans to be admitted into this asylum? The charter answers this question: "The said corporation"—that is, the persons who petitioned to be incorporated—"and their successors, have power to make all by-laws for the election or admission of new members," and these members choose the managers. All the managers of this institution are understood to belong to the communion whose name the Society bears; and it is not to be denied that it must always continue under the management of members of the Roman Catholic Church. The Society have not room for all orphans. Those of another faith are not formally excluded. But will it be pretended that the Roman Catholics, as a sect of Christians, disregard the injunction, "to do good unto all, especially to those who are of the household of faith"? Can it be pretended, then, that the benefits of the institution are equally open to all?

But there is another, and, perhaps, more serious objection to an equal enjoyment of these benefits by the whole community. It is believed that the system of education at this institution is so combined with religious instruction, that many persons having, as guardians or friends, an authority or interest in the disposition of orphan children, would be deterred from sending them there by preconceived opinions or conscientious scruples. And yet such persons may be compelled to contribute the very moneys which go to support this institution. But the objection to this principle extends much further; it embraces all, of every persuasion, who have conscientious scruples about paying their money for the support of any particular faith, or who, if they have not such scruples, derive no benefit from the expenditure, and regard it as an abuse.

In this point of view, how can this taxation be regarded as any better than the system of tithes? It is the same thing—compelling men to support an institution against their consciences, or of which they do not participate the benefits.

Let us now inquire why, if the petition of the Catholics is admitted, that of the Methodists, now before the Corporation, is to be rejected? or why any other church or any society within the fold of a church, may not set up similar claims?

Why were all the churches and religious societies deprived of a participation in the school fund in 1825?

There were many reasons why one harmonious system, under the inspection of the public and under the direction of one body of men, should be preferred to incongruous and irresponsible institutions; but it was none of these which procured the victory, then thought to be final, of liberal principles in education over sectarian views, and which brought about the revolution which then took place. That proceeded from the conviction that the school fund ought not to be diverted, in whole or part, to the purposes of sectarian instruction, but should be kept sacred to the great object, emphatically called COMMON EDUCATION.

The Roman Catholic Benevolent Society was placed among those excluded in 1825, because they were considered as clearly embraced in the same principle. The "Female Association" was excluded at the same time, though it received all children from every persuasion, and inculcated no particular tenets, because it was chiefly under the patronage of individuals connected with the Society of Friends. It will not be pretended that the orphanage of their pupils, however it may appeal to our hearts, can in this case affect our judgments.

Is an exception to be made in their favor, because they receive all of every sect ? Was it ever charged against either of the church schools that they refused to receive any children who came to them, whether heretics themselves, or the children of heretic parents ?

The committee of the Corporation say that neither equity nor sound policy can " warrant the continuance of the participation to the Greenwich Asylum, and at the same time withhold it from the Prince Street Asylum." The Greenwich Asylum was retained by the Corporation, in 1825, because it was not considered sectarian, and the Prince Street Asylum was rejected because it was sectarian. In other words, the schools of the one institution were regarded as, properly speaking, common schools, while those of the other were rejected as not such.

The Greenwich Asylum is not a close corporation. It is open to the membership of every female who chooses to pay $1.50. This board is perfectly satisfied with the decision which the Corporation then made; but if, upon investigation, it shall be found that this institution does, in consequence of its administration, come within the principle of exclusion, it is infinitely better that it should be excluded, than that the principle upon which all the honor and glory of the cause rests should itself be destroyed.

This board believes, with the committee above referred to, that the cardinal principle adopted by the Corporation in 1825 was so generally and strongly approved of by the community, that no deviation from it can now be advised. But this board cannot perceive that the principle was any other than that above stated.

Let us now look to the language of our State Constitution. It is thereby declared, " that the proceeds of certain public lands belonging to the State, together with ' The Fund denominated the Common School Fund,' shall be and remain a perpetual fund, the interest of which shall be inviolably appropriated to the support of *common schools* throughout the State."

It is well known that our common schools are supported by the joint funds derived from taxes and from the said school fund, so that no part of the money distributed by the Corporation can be diverted from the support of common schools without a violation of the Constitution.

What are common schools? This phrase cannot possibly mean any thing else than those schools which are commonly known by that name, and have been so called because they are common—that is, open to all. Those cannot be common schools which are the property of a particular corporation,

9

and from which all persons may be lawfully excluded who do not belong to a particular sect.

It seems unnecessary to go beyond the Constitution, which is the paramount law; but the act of the Legislature to which we have referred was passed under circumstances which clothe it with a peculiar authority in this discussion.

In the winter of 1828–'9, a petition to the Corporation was, at the instance of the board, circulated through the community, and very extensively subscribed, praying the Corporation to petition the Legislature for an increase of our taxes for the support of common schools. The sole and express objects of the petition were, that the means of "common education" might be extended, and that a fund might be set apart and kept sacred to that object. This board presented a memorial to the Corporation at the same time for the same object, and couched in nearly the same language.

The Corporation accordingly applied to the Legislature, and a law was passed, by which they were authorized to raise a certain sum "to be applied exclusively to the purposes of the *common schools* in the said city." See 2d vol. Rev. L., 240.

Can it be believed that the individuals who petitioned for the privilege of being taxed for common schools, or that the Legislature who granted that privilege, intended that the moneys thus to be raised should be applied to the support of any school not equally open to all? If the Roman Catholic Benevolent Society had asked that not they, but the city, should be taxed for the support of their school, would it have been granted?

The charity for which aid is now sought is of a most interesting character, but it ought, in the opinion of this board, to be supported by voluntary donations, and not by compulsory levies.

Whatever may be the result of our opposition to the present application, we trust it will be seen that it proceeds from no jealousy or prejudice in regard to the Catholic religion, but that, on the contrary, it has arisen from principles which are truly catholic, in the largest sense of that word, and upon the maintenance of which depend the vital interests of civil liberty.

ROBERT C. CORNELL, *Vice-President.*

LINDLEY MURRAY, *Secretary.*
NEW YORK, *May* 6, 1831.

At the special meeting held on May 12, after the organization of the new Board of Aldermen, the petition and report of May 2d, of the old committee, were referred to the Committee on Arts, Sciences, and Schools, consisting of Messrs. Dibblee, Meigs, and Hall.

While the committee had the matter under consideration, the Commissioners of School Money sent a communication to the Board of Assistants, presented July 11, stating that the time had arrived to designate the schools which should be entitled to participate in the distribution of the school moneys for the coming year. The communication was referred to the Committee on Arts and Sciences.

At the next meeting of the Board of Assistants, held July 18, Mr. Brush offered the following for adoption as an ordinance relative to common schools:

Be it ordained by the Mayor, Aldermen, and Commonalty of the city of New York, in common council convened, that a law regulating the distribution of the common school fund of the city of New York, passed July 14, 1828, and all other ordinances amendatory of the same, be, and the same are hereby, revived.

The statute of 1828 specified that "the institutions which shall be entitled to receive of the Commissioners of the School Fund, payable to and raised in the said city, are hereby designated to be the Public School Society of New York, the Mechanics' Society, the Orphan Asylum Society, and the Trustees of the African Free School in the city of New York."

The ordinance was sent to the Board of Aldermen for concurrence at its meeting on the 25th of the same month, on the reading of which Alderman Dibblee moved an amendment, to add to the societies or schools named in said law "The New York Catholic Benevolent Society."

A motion was made to lay the same on the table, which was lost. Considerable discussion followed, when it was moved to reconsider the vote last taken. The question being taken thereon, and a tie vote being had, the President gave his vote in the affirmative. The question being then reconsidered, it was moved that the matter be laid on the table, which was agreed to. On motion of Alderman Dibblee, it was made the special order at the next meeting.

The preliminary business of the meeting having been disposed of, at the session of the board held on August 3, Alderman Strong called up the special order of the day, and the ordinance was then read, as follows:

Be it ordained by the Mayor, Aldermen, and Commonalty of the city of New York, in common council convened:

That "A Law regulating the Distribution of the Common School Fund of the City of New York," passed July 14, 1828, and all other ordinances amendatory to the same, be, and the same are hereby, revived and reënacted.

The amendment proposed by Alderman Dibblee when the subject was previously under consideration, was also read, as follows :

To add to the number of societies or schools named in said law, the New York Catholic Benevolent Society ; which additional Society shall be entitled to a portion of the common school money for such orphan children as are, or shall be, taught in the school and maintained in the Orphan Asylum House in Prince street, at the expense of said Society ; and the said school be subject, moreover, to all the provisions, limitations, and restrictions recited and prescribed in and by said ordinance.

The ordinance and amendment occasioned—as they could not fail to do—a protracted discussion, in which many of the members took part. The question being at length called for, and a vote on Alderman Dibblee's amendment being had, it resulted as follows :

Affirmative—Aldermen Strong, Scott, Meigs, Dibblee, Hall, Woodruff—6.

Negative—Aldermen Sharpe, Van Wagenen, Lamb, Tucker, Jeremiah, Palmer—6.

The vote being thus equally divided, the President of the board, Alderman Cebra, gave his vote in the affirmative, and the amendment was adopted. The question being taken on the ordinance as amended, it was carried in the affirmative, and directed to be sent to the Board of Assistants for concurrence.

A special meeting of the Board of Assistants was held on the 5th of the same month, at which time the law, as amended, was submitted, and, on motion, was made the special order for the first Monday in September. At the appointed time (September 5) the special order was called up, on motion of Dr. Rhinelander, who moved a postponement for two weeks, in consequence of the absence of several of the members of the board. The motion was agreed to, but subsequently, on motion of Mr. Murray, the whole question was referred to the Law Committee.

The following petition from the Methodist Society was presented in the Board of Assistants on September 5, and referred to the School Commissioners :

To the Honorable the Board of Assistants :
The memorial of the Trustees of the Methodist Episcopal Church in the city of New York, RESPECTFULLY SHEWETH :
That your memorialists have supported for nearly forty years, in this

city, a school for the gratuitous instruction of male and female orphans, and the children of the poor and destitute. For a few years during this period, your memorialists, in common with the managers of other charitable institutions for the instruction of youth, annually received a portion of the school fund, which added to their ability in communicating instruction to those under their care, and assisted in furnishing articles of clothing to those orphan children who had no other dependence; many of whom, having received a suitable education, became useful and industrious citizens.

It is with deep regret your memorialists have to state that, in the year 1826, they were, by a decision of the Corporation, cut off entirely from receiving any further benefit from the school fund, and thrown altogether upon private charity for support, notwithstanding their school was in the same need of help and assistance as heretofore. In consequence of this sudden diminution of the means of support, many of the children under the care of your memorialists, and particularly the poor and destitute orphans, were deprived of many of the advantages they before enjoyed. The ordinary funds arising from the contributions of the benevolent being uncertain and insufficient for providing them with clothing in the season of the greatest need, whatever of clothing the orphan children have since received, has been the spontaneous bestowment of a few individuals.

Your memorialists would respectfully represent, that, while they continue their school operations as formerly, and freely admit every one who applies for admission whenever a vacancy occurs, whatever may be the religious profession of their parents or guardians, or to whatever religious community they belong, their resources, since the public school money has been withheld from them, are by no means sufficient for the pressing wants of the institution; and apprehensions are entertained that they will be unable to meet the expenses of the present year.

Your memorialists would therefore most respectfully entreat that your honorable board would take this their memorial into your most serious consideration, and grant them such an equitable proportion of the school fund as may enable them to provide, as formerly, for the comfort and instruction of the destitute children and helpless orphans now under their care, of which last-named there are more than fifty now in the school.

And your memorialists, as in duty bound, will ever pray, &c.

THE TRUSTEES OF THE METHODIST EPISCOPAL CHURCH
IN THE CITY OF NEW YORK.

By order of the board.

JOSEPH SMITH, *President.*

The report of the Law Committee * was submitted at the meeting held on September 19, as follows:

The Committee on Laws and Applications to the Legislature, to whom it was referred by a resolution of this board, to report on the constitution-

---

* Doc. No. XXI., Board of Assistants, September 19, 1831.

ality of the ordinance passed by the Board of Aldermen, appropriating the common school fund to the schools therein named, RESPECTFULLY REPORT:

That they entered upon the examination of the subject deeply impressed with its importance, and fully determined to give it a careful and dispassionate consideration.

The subject of education is at all times interesting, and particularly so in a country like ours, where the Government, in theory and practice, is purely one of public opinion—the stability of which depends solely on the virtue and intelligence of the people. The constituted authorities of this State, impressed with its consequence, took early measures to establish our primary seminaries of learning on a permanent basis, and munificently appropriated a large and liberal share of the public funds for the establishment and support of common schools, and for the diffusion of general information. The Constitution of 1821 provides, that "the interest of this fund shall be inviolably appropriated and applied to the support of common schools throughout this State."

Each county in the State is compelled to raise a sum equal in amount to that which is apportioned to such county out of this fund.

The city of New York now receives about ten thousand dollars from the State; which places twenty thousand dollars at the disposal of the Commissioners of the School Fund. The general act regulating school districts and the election of trustees and school commissioners, clearly points out what schools in the country are common schools; but as it was inconvenient, if not impracticable, to divide this city into school districts, the Legislature itself designated what schools should receive a portion of this fund prior to the year 1824.

This course frequently gave rise to difficulty and embarrassment, and opened a door for imposition, which was practised to no inconsiderable extent. By an act passed in that year, the Legislature imposed on the Common Council the duty of making such designation at least once in every three years. That act has been incorporated into the revised statutes, and this board is now called upon to exercise the discretionary power of distributing the interest of the school fund.

The first question which presents itself to the consideration of your committee is, What is meant by the term, Common Schools?

It is urged by many intelligent gentlemen, whose opinions are entitled to great respect, that every school and institution in which children are taught gratuitously is a common school. If the term be so broad and comprehensive, then every free school attached to the churches of the various religious denominations throughout this State is a common school. Such, however, could not have been the understanding of the early advocates of the establishment of a fund for the support of common schools, as no church schools have ever participated in this fund except those in this city.

A school, to be common, ought to be open to all; and those branches of education, and those only, ought to be taught in it, which tend to prepare a child for the ordinary business of life. If religion be taught in a school, it strips it of one of the characteristics of a common school, as all religious and sectarian studies have a direct reference to a future state, and are not necessary to prepare a child for the mechanical or any other business. No school can be common unless parents of all religious sects, Mohammedans and Jews as well as Christians, can send their children to it to receive the benefits of an education, without doing violence to their religious belief.

Your committee cannot, therefore, find a more correct and accurate definition of the term "common school," than to call it a school in which nothing but the rudiments of an English education are taught to all who are admitted into it, which is open to every child that applies for admission, and into which all can be admitted without doing violence to their religious opinions, or those of their parents or guardians.

Such, in the opinion of your committee, were the schools which the founders of our system of education intended to patronize and foster when they created the school fund. Such were the schools which the members of the Convention of 1821 had in view, when they adopted that article of the Constitution, by which the fund thus set apart by the bounty and munificence of the representatives of an enlightened and liberal people, was inviolably appropriated to the support of common schools.

The schools and institutions embraced in the ordinance referred to your committee, are the Trustees of the Harlem School, the Trustees of the Manhattanville School, the Trustees of the Hamilton School, the Trustees of the Yorkville School, the African Free School, the Public School Society of the city of New York, the Mechanics' Society, and the Orphan Asylum Society; and it is proposed, by the ordinance now under consideration, to add to the list the Roman Catholic Benevolent Society. Your committee, anxious only to arrive at a correct conclusion, feel constrained to examine particularly into the character of these schools and institutions, and ascertain what title they have to the appellation of common schools, as their claim to a portion of this fund depends solely on the decision of this question. Acting in their representative capacity, and discarding all private feeling and individual considerations, your committee will endeavor to test their claim to a participation in this fund by that Constitution which they have sworn to support.

The Harlem, Hamilton, Manhattanville, and Yorkville schools are incorporated institutions, located in the Twelfth Ward. They are free schools, to which parents of any religious denomination may send their children, and in which the ordinary branches of an English education are taught, disconnected with all sectarianism. If parents are desirous that their children should study any catechism in the Hamilton School, they are gratified in that respect; but it is not obligatory upon any one to study such catechism, nor is it introduced as a part of the system of instruction adopted by the trustees of the institution.

The African free schools were established for the special purpose of opening the avenues to a gratuitous education to the descendants of an injured race, who have a strong claim on the humanity and justice of our State.

It may be objected, that these schools are not open for the education and instruction of any except colored children. This, however, is not an insurmountable objection. The blacks are, by common consent, and by the Constitution of the United States, regarded as a distinct race, and the " partition wall " between them and us cannot be broken down, without doing violence to those feelings and prejudices which have become a part of our nature. These children must, then, be entirely shut out from all the means of obtaining an education necessary to make them good members of society, unless schools are established into which they can be admitted. Such institutions we find in the African free schools ; and it is due to the trustees of those schools to remark, that they have been eminently useful, and that they are prepared for the instruction of more scholars than now attend them.

Your committee are fully convinced that these five schools come within the meaning of the term " common schools."

The only remaining institution which, in their opinion, is entitled to a portion of this fund, is the Public School Society. This institution has been the most useful of all, as its operation is annually felt by more than six thousand of the rising generation, on whom will devolve the sacred duty of preserving and perpetuating our republican institutions.

This Society was incorporated in 1805, by the name of " The Society for Establishing a Free School in the City of New York, for the education of such poor children as do not belong to, or are not provided for by, any religious society."

In 1808, the power of the Society was extended to any children who are proper objects of gratuitous education, and its name changed to that of " The Free School Society of New York ; " and, in 1826, the name of this Society was changed to that by which it is now known, and its powers further extended so as to embrace children of all descriptions, whether the objects of gratuitous education or not, and without regard to the religious sect to which such children or their parents may belong. The public schools are open to all, the poor as well as the rich, and no particular religious creed is taught to the children who attend them. But a portion of the Scriptures is read in the morning by the teachers, without comment, in these as well as some of the other schools above named. The schools under the direction of the Trustees of the Public School Society may be emphatically called common schools, and have a just and legal claim to a portion of the school fund.

The original charter of the Mechanics' Society did not authorize the appropriation of any of their funds to the support of a school ; but, by an act passed January 26, 1821, the Legislature " empowered the Society to appropriate such part of their funds as may by them be deemed expedient, to the establishment and maintenance of a school for the education of the children of indigent or deceased members of said Society."

The Society, in conformity with the power vested in them, established a school ; and, by one of the school regulations, it is provided that " the legitimate subjects of it shall be children of the members of the Mechanics' Society, or the orphans of deceased members, and the children of respectable mechanics pursuing some trade or branch of mechanics in this city.

The children of other respectable citizens may be admitted by a special resolution of the School Committee." It was stated to your committee, by one of the trustees of said Society, that none except the children of members, or deceased members of the Society, were gratuitously educated in this school.

If your committee have been correct in the view which they have already taken as to the requisites of a common school, the Mechanics' School cannot receive a portion of the common school fund. It is exclusive in its character, and is calculated to divide society into classes and grades, contrary to the spirit of our Constitution and Government.

It has ever been a favorite maxim with American legislators, that " all mankind are born free and equal ; " and so closely is this principle connected with our political institutions, that, to make any discrimination between the different occupations of individuals, it would be considered as a departure from first principles, and a virtual violation of the Constitution. The division of society into grades, even for the purpose of education, would be productive of the most fatal consequences. An odious distinction will be early instilled into the minds of children, and the division lines of classes of society will be more strongly drawn than they ever have been under the most despotic governments of Europe. Children will then regard themselves as belonging to a particular rank in life, which will give rise to jealousies calculated to disturb the harmony and present arrangement of society. It was to obviate these difficulties that our system of common school education was adopted. The early associations of children make a deep and lasting impression ; and the intimacies formed between the children of the rich and poor at school will ripen into indissoluble friendship in maturer years.

It has been urged upon your committee, that, by the act of 1821, in relation to this Society, they have a perpetual vested right to a portion of the school fund. The second section of that act directs that the Commissioners of the School Money for the city of New York shall pay to the Mechanics' Society, in pursuance to the fourth section of the act entitled " An Act for the Establishment of Common Schools," passed March 12, 1813, a portion of the school money. The fourth section referred to merely designated what schools in the city of New York should receive a portion of the school fund. As the Mechanics' Society was, subsequently to the passage of that act, authorized to establish a school, in order to entitle them to receive a portion of the school fund, it was necessary that the Legislature should authorize the Commissioner of the School Fund to pay a portion of the money to said Society. It was for this purpose the second section above referred to was incorporated into the act of January 26, 1821. That section did not confer on the Mechanic's Society any other or greater right to the school fund than the fourth section of the act of 1813 did on all the other schools in the city of New York. The Legislature had the same power to repeal the one as the other, which power was exercised in 1824. Your committee, therefore, cannot avoid coming to the conclusion that the Mechanics' School is not entitled to a portion of the school fund.

The Orphan Asylum Society heretofore has received a portion of this fund, but it ought, in the opinion of your committee, to be placed on the same footing with the Roman Catholic Benevolent Society.

Your committee, however, individually take a deep interest in the welfare of these institutions, and are extremely solicitous for their continued prosperity and success in the work of benevolence. Although they have contributed in an eminent degree to alleviate the wants and miseries of a helpless class of individuals, who are thrown upon the world destitute and unprotected, and physically disqualified from procuring the means of assistance, yet they are very limited in their operations, and the schools attached to them are solely for the education of orphans who are supported by the bounty of these institutions.

The trustees of these institutions have assumed the station and responsibility of the natural guardians of the orphans received into them, and are bound to provide for their support and education. If the funds of these societies are insufficient to pay for the education of the children, they can be sent to the public schools, where they would be cheerfully received, and their education strictly and justly attended to.

As asylums, these institutions appeal to the sympathies of our nature and the best feelings of the human heart; and although they rank among the most laudable of the institutions which have sprung up in this age of benevolence, they want the most important characteristic of common schools, and are placed beyond the reach of legislative aid, so far as relates to this fund, which has been inviolably appropriated to a specific object.

It has been repeatedly charged that those institutions are sectarian. The information before your committee on this point is full and satisfactory. Any respectable female may become a member of the Orphan Asylum Society by paying a specific sum, and the door is open to all who wish to become members of the institution, without distinction of religion or country; but the recipients of their bounty are instructed in the Catechism of the Dutch Reformed Church, and are compelled to attend religious worship at a church of that denomination. This renders the Greenwich Asylum sectarian in its character.

The Roman Catholic Benevolent Society also has strong marks of sectarianism about it. None except Catholics can become regular members of the Society, although any person whose piety, dignity, and morality will reflect honor on the Society, may become honorary members. This feature in the organization of that institution will forever keep its government exclusively under the direction of that religious sect. And although it is open for the reception, support, and education of destitute and unprotected orphans, without distinction of sex, country, or religion, yet all who participate in its bounty are exclusively instructed in the doctrines of the Roman Catholic religion.

Here another objection presents itself, in which is involved a grave and serious constitutional question, a correct decision of which will save us from most of those religious struggles which have disturbed the peace and repose of Europe, and which have caused so much bloodshed throughout the world.

The question is this: Can we, without violating the Constitution, appropriate any of the public funds to the support of those schools or institutions in which children are taught the doctrines and tenets of religious sectarianism? The Constitution of this State declares that the .free exercise and enjoyment of religious professions and worship,'without discrimination or preference, shall forever be allowed in this State to all mankind. This article of the Constitution recognizes not only religious toleration, but perfect religious freedom, so long as that freedom is exercised in a manner not inconsistent with the peace and safety of the State. Each individual, in religious matters, is left to pursue the bent of his own inclination, and to follow the dictates of his own conscience.

If an effort should be made to raise a fund by taxation, for the support of a particular sect, or every sect of Christians, it would unhesitatingly be declared an infringement of the Constitution, and a violation of our chartered rights. Your committee cannot, however, perceive any marked difference in principle, whether a fund be raised for the support of a particular church, or whether it be raised for the support of a school in which the doctrines of that church are taught as a part of the system of education.

In the one case, an ordained and regularly constituted ministry are paid for delivering their lessons from the pulpit; and, in the other, a more humble, though not less useful class of teachers are paid for giving the same instructions in a different manner. Both tend to the same end, and both designedly promote the growth and extension of sectarianism. The one act will be as great a violation of the constitutional rights and conscientious scruples of the people as the other. Jews, Christians of every denomination, deists, and unbelievers of every description, contribute their due portion to the school fund, and it ought to be so distributed and disposed of that all may participate in the benefits flowing from it, without doing violence to their consciences. It would be but a poor consolation to an individual to know that he may entertain whatever religious opinions he pleases, and attend any church he may select, and at the time be legally compelled to contribute a portion of his property to the support of a school in which religious doctrines diametrically opposed to those he entertains are taught. Any legislation sanctioning such a principle would meet with the decided disapprobation of this community.

So thoroughly were the founders of our State convinced that religion in every shape should be untouched by legislative acts, that they urged and procured the adoption of an article of the Constitution disqualifying ministers of the gospel, and priests of every denomination, from holding any civil or military office or place within this State.

The duties of a spiritual guide and religious instructor were considered as incompatible with those of a civil or military station. It would be a virtual violation of this article of the Constitution to appropriate a fund, purely civil in its character and object, to the support of religious schools, and would not be sanctioned by a people ardently and devotedly attached to the maintenance of civil and religious liberty.

Your committee are of the opinion that, if the two asylums are admitted to accept a portion of the school fund, it will open the door for the admission of every school or institution in which children are taught gratuitously, notwithstanding it may be sectarian to the fullest extent.

Methodist, Episcopalian, Baptist, and every other sectarian school, must come in for a share of this fund. And the Common Council cannot stop here. If charity schools are founded in which the doctrines of an Owen and a Wright are taught, or in which the "Age of Reason" or the Khoran is adopted as a standard work, they will stand on the same footing as other religious schools. Should such a course be pursued, it will be a violation of the liberal principle established by the Common Council in 1825, of denying admission to all schools and institutions which were considered as sectarian. A departure from this salutary precedent will be productive of incalculable mischief. If all sectarian schools be admitted to the receipt of a portion of a fund sacredly appropriated to the support of common schools, it will give rise to a religious and anti-religious party, which will call into active exercise the passions and prejudices of men. A fierce and uncompromising hostility will ensue, which will pave the way for the predominance of religion in political contests. The unnatural union of Church and State will then be easily accomplished—a union destructive of human happiness and subversive of civil liberty.

It should ever be borne in mind, that ecclesiastical despotism is the worst and most oppressive species of tyranny; it is unnecessary to inquire why it is so. The fact is well attested by the history of every people who have lived under the government of monarchs and priests. Many of the miseries now endured by the laboring class in England are attributable to the accumulation of the immense revenues of the bishops and clergy, and to the odious and oppressive system of exacting tithes for the support of an established church. It would be an incipient step toward engrafting in our institutions a system not less odious and oppressive, not less fatal in its consequences to the liberties and happiness of our country, to place the interest of the school fund at the disposal of sectarians. It is to tax the people for the support of religion, contrary to the Constitution, and in violation of their conscientious scruples.

Your committee are of opinion that the ordinance referred to them is unconstitutional, so far as relates to the Mechanics' Society, the Orphan Asylum Society, and the Roman Catholic Benevolent Society, and therefore recommend that the same be amended so as to exclude those institutions from any participation in the school fund.

WILLIAM VAN WYCK,   ⎫
ERASTUS BARNES,   ⎬ *Law Committee.*
NEHEMIAH BRUSH,   ⎭

The report was read, and laid on the table.

At the meeting of the board on the 24th of October, Dr. Rhinelander moved that the school question be made the order for the day at the next meeting, which was agreed to. At the time designated, the board went into Committee of the Whole, Mr. Labagh in the chair. After considerable discussion the committee rose, reported, and asked leave to sit again, which was granted.

The Trustees of the Methodist Free School, while the matter was thus pending, sent a proposition to the Public School Society, which was laid before the Board of Trustees at their meeting on November 4th, in the following form :

NEW YORK, 4th November, 1831.

The subscribers, representing the Trustees of the Methodist Charity Free School in this city, respectfully offer to the New York Public School Society their school-house in Forsyth street, and 212 scholars attached thereto.

The premises are two lots of ground, under lease for twenty-four years unexpired, at the yearly rent of $100. The building thereon is a two-story frame building, 30 feet front by 85 feet deep. The whole upper part is occupied for the school-room, the lower part by the teacher, and for society meetings. The lower part is wished to be retained by the Trustees of the Methodist Episcopal Church until August next, and the school-rooms can be had immediately, upon an arrangement being made with the teachers, who are employed until May next.

GILBERT COUTANT,
Chairman of the Committee appointed by the Board of Trustees.

This proposition was referred to a committee, consisting of Najah Taylor, George T. Trimble, and Robert C. Cornell, who were appointed to confer with the committee of the Trustees of the Free School, and report their action thereon. The price demanded by the latter for their real estate—$3,500—was deemed to be too high, and at a meeting of the Trustees of the Public School Society, held on the 3d of February, 1832, the proposition was declined, and the committee authorized to continue the negotiation. No arrangement, however, was made between the parties.

The matter remained in this position until December 19, when Mr. Smith introduced the following resolution :

Resolved, That the Committee on Arts and Sciences, to whom was referred the petition of the Trustees of the Methodist Society, for a participation of the school money, be requested to report without delay.

The resolution accordingly went to the committee, who, however, did not report until May 7th of the following year—only one day previous to the expiration of its term of office, at which time the following report was made:

The Committee on Arts, Sciences, and Schools, to whom was referred the annexed memorial from the Trustees of the Methodist Episcopal Church, praying to be admitted to participate in the benefits of the common school fund, RESPECTFULLY REPORT:

That they have had the same under consideration, and have come to the following conclusion, viz.: That, inasmuch as the memorialists have stated in their petition—which your committee have every reason to believe to be true—that they at all times have admitted children of every denomination into their schools, and have, at the present time, about fifty orphans who are educated upon general principles, without reference to sectarianism, your committee are of opinion that they are of right and ought to be admitted to a participation of the fund, and would therefore beg leave to offer the following resolution, viz.:

Resolved, That the ordinance defining what societies shall be admitted to a participation of the common school fund be so amended as to embrace "The Trustees of the Methodist Episcopal Church in the City of New York."

Respectfully submitted by the committee,

NEHEMIAH BRUSH,
WILLIAM MANDEVILLE.

The order of time is anticipated by the insertion of the above report in this place; but as it gives the decision of the committee of the Board of Assistants, and permits a return to the proceedings in the Board of Aldermen, it is deemed proper to present it in this connection. No action was taken on the report.

The Trustees of the Methodist Free School had thus pressed their application upon the Common Council; but the conflicting opinions and interests which were brought to bear upon the members of both boards occasioned a protracted delay.

At the meeting of the Board of Trustees of the Public School Society, held on March 30th, the committee of the board submitted a memorial, which they stated had been referred to a committee, and had been printed, and made the special order for the day on the first Monday in April following.

To the Honorable the Corporation of the City of New York:

The memorial of the Trustees of the Public School Society HUMBLY SHEWETH:

That they have seen, with deep concern, that the application of the Methodist Episcopal Church for a participation in the fund raised for the support of common schools, has met with a favorable report by a committee appointed by the Board of Aldermen, and they feel constrained to present their respectful but plain and solemn remonstrance against the measure proposed. Your honorable bodies are not ignorant that the distribution of the school fund among the church schools of the city, prior to 1825, gave rise to multiplied abuses, which were arrested, and, it was hoped, terminated, by an ordinance of the Common Council, which was received with almost universal public approbation.

The reform which was thus established was followed immediately by an increased public interest in the schools; subsequently, by an accession to their funds; and recently, by a liberal and ample provision for that object.

Your memorialists, believing that the circumstances in which the increase of the school fund originated are worthy of great consideration, in reference to the measure now before the Board of Aldermen, beg leave to recall them to the memory of your honorable bodies.

In the year 1828, your memorialists made an earnest appeal to their fellow-citizens " upon the importance of enlarging the means of common education." Your memorialists soon after were instrumental in procuring the circulation, among the citizens generally, of a petition addressed to the Common Council in behalf of this great object. That petition was subscribed by several thousands of respectable individuals, and embraced a large proportion of our most wealthy citizens.

The object embraced in that petition is very plainly pointed out. The petitioners say they are desirous that the common schools of the city should be multiplied and improved, and, if possible, that others should be established for the introduction of certain of the higher grades of instruction. They propose an annual tax of not less than half a mill on the dollar upon the amount of assessed property in the city, " for the purpose of free and common education ; the fund thus to be raised to be kept separate from all others, and sacred to the purposes for which it is designed." And they pray the aid of the Corporation for the obtaining such a law as might be necessary for the purposes aforesaid.

If any further evidence be wanted as to the design of the petitioners above mentioned, your memorialists beg leave to state, from the best means of information, that great numbers of persons refused their signatures until they were assured that the funds to be raised were to be entirely protected from sectarian employment or control.

The petition above referred to was presented, together with a special memorial from your present memorialists, to the Common Council, early in 1829 ; and they were referred to a committee, who reported favorably thereto.

Application was accordingly made to the Legislature, substantially conforming in tenor, and exactly in spirit, with the petition and memorial aforesaid. The Legislature promptly passed a law, viz., on the 25th of April, 1829, by which the Corporation was authorized to collect, by tax, a sum of money equal to one eightieth of one per cent. upon the assessed property of the city, " to be applied exclusively to the purposes of common schools in the said city."

On the 13th of April, 1831, the Legislature passed a law increasing the amount to be raised to four eightieths of one per cent. for precisely the same objects.

Your memorialists cannot entertain a doubt that not a single cent of the fund thus raised by taxation ought to be under sectarian control, or applied to the exclusive benefit of any particular class of individuals.

Your memorialists presume that the present application has been encouraged by the success of that recently made by the Catholic Orphan Asylum.

Your memorialists feel bound to protest in this instance, as they did in that, on the ground that the admission of this school would be a violation of the Constitution and of the laws, and of good faith toward the public. They deem it also irreconcilable with the spirit of our republican institutions, inasmuch as it involves a compulsory support of religious instruction, without the ability to participate its benefits.

Your memorialists are compelled to differ with the respectable committee of the Board of Aldermen. The fact that " the school fund is raised equally," in their judgments, leads to the conclusion that it ought to be distributed equally.

In regard to the Methodist school (which alone is now under consideration), it appears that a preference as to admission is given to the children of parents of the same persuasion, provided they are sufficient to fill the school.

If, in such cases, no express preference or prohibition is given or enacted, the same result indirectly obtains from the sectarian character of the instruction or government of the schools.

A perfect equality in the distribution of school moneys characterizes every provision of the Legislature on this subject. It is alleged that they have not " shut out any school on account of its religious connections." If the omission of any prohibitory enactment furnishes an argument in favor of the present application, almost any claim that can be imagined may be established. But your memorialists, without further comment upon the great principles involved in the proposed measure, beg leave to state that the general principle of excluding the church schools, adopted in 1825, was not, as they have understood, intended to be given up or impaired by the admission of the Catholic Asylum School, but, on the contrary, this principle was expressly sanctioned and approved by the Common Council.

Your memorialists, in support of this assertion, refer to the report of the committee on the Catholic application, and which was signed by the chairman of the committee, who have now reported in favor of the Methodist school.

Your memorialists quote the language of that report:

It is known to the Common Council that few questions of public policy have caused so much excitement, as well in the government of the State as in the council of the city, as that of the distribution of school money. During several years prior to 1825, the agitation pervaded all classes of people, as well as most of our public institutions. The adjustment of the question, in the spring of 1825, was hailed with joy. The facts, arguments, and principles which guided the government and dictated the laws of distribution at that period, are too well understood by this Common Council to require to be recited in this report. The cardinal principles then adopted, the classes of societies and schools then admitted to a participation, and the classes of societies and schools then excluded, were so generally and strongly approved by the community, that no deviation from those principles can now be advised.

(Signed by)   G. LEE,
JOHN ROGERS,
DAVID BRYSON,
HENRY ARCULARIUS,
TYLER DIBBLEE.

The Methodist Church Charity School—the applicants now before you— was of the class and one of the number then excluded from participation in the school fund.

Your memorialists suppose that your honorable bodies considered the Catholic school as not coming within the rule applicable to sectarian schools, but, on the contrary, as entitled to a portion of the school fund, because the children of the Asylum would otherwise be deprived of the power of participating in it.

It is not difficult to perceive that, if the Methodist school is admitted, another, and the only remaining barrier to the admission of all the church schools, will be broken down. The children of the Catholic Asylum are all orphans. The Methodist school embraces " destitute children " also. If destitute children are to be admitted under the patronage of one persuasion, what fair and equitable distinction will your honorable bodies be able to fix, which will exclude any other persuasion? It is well known that the children of all the church schools were fairly embraced in the description of destitute children. The circumstance that the children in question receive other aid than that of instruction, creates, instead of removing, an objection, in the opinion of your memorialists. This distinction between the Methodist and other churches, if it now exists, will be shortly removed by sectarian zeal, and the schools of the Society represented by your memorialists will, of course, be subjected to a competition in which it is to be feared that their superior advantages will be outweighed by inducements of more than doubtful expediency. The bare suggestion of the subject in this view involves considerations on which your memorialists had supposed the public mind was made up.

If any thing more than what has been stated be necessary to show how the principle of " equal rights " would be affected by the measure now considered, let it be remembered that the moneys given to church schools are taken away from the public schools, and that there is a large portion of our fellow-citizens who belong to no religious society, and a great many who would refuse any instruction if encumbered with any ecclesiastical connection.

Your memorialists beg leave to add, that they feel confident that a return to the sectarian system will not ultimately be tolerated by public opinion. The public will not and ought not to consent to be taxed for sectarian education.

10

Your memorialists are therefore apprehensive, that, while the hopes held out to the churches by the success of the present application must prove ultimately fallacious; that the sources of the present revenues of the public schools would in that event be greatly diminished, and, in so far as the same depend on the aforesaid acts of the Legislature, would be withdrawn.

If the public confidence in the equal distribution of the school fund is ever lost, it is possible, not to say probable, that it will never be regained.

All which is respectfully submitted.

(Signed)   PETER AUGUSTUS JAY, *President.*

LINDLEY MURRAY, *Secretary.*

Dated this 24th day of March, 1832.

A long and earnest discussion took place upon the memorial, and it was deemed important that the members of the Board of Aldermen should be seen personally by committees on behalf of the Society, and they were accordingly appointed, as follows:

Alderman Cebra, to be seen by Messrs. J. I. Roosevelt, Jr., and James Heard.

"	Stevens,	"	Hiram Ketchum, Clark, and Richards.
"	Van Wagenen,	"	J. I. Roosevelt, Jr., and James Heard.
"	Lamb,	"	Ketchum, Clark, and Depeyster.
"	Tucker,	"	Oakley and Wells.
"	Meigs,	"	Mott and Peters.
"	Jeremiah,	"	Leveridge and Brinsmade.
"	Hall,	"	Swan and Depeyster.
"	Palmer,	"	Childs and Najah Taylor.
"	Woodruff,	"	Delamater and Wells.

The petition from the Methodist Society was presented in the Board of Aldermen on the same evening (September 5) on which it was laid before the Assistants, and was referred to the Committee on Arts, Sciences, and Schools. The report in favor of the application for school money was submitted on March 12, 1832, and was laid on the table, to be printed.

The remonstrance of the Public School Society against granting the application was laid before the board at the meeting held on March 26, and was referred to the Committee on Arts, Sciences, and Schools, and, with the other papers relative to the matter, was made the order of the day for the following meeting of the board. The committee reported on the remonstrance at the session held on April 2, in which the recommendations of the first report were reaffirmed, and their adoption strongly urged. The report was recommitted.

On May 2, the report, on motion of Alderman Palmer, was made the special order for the next meeting of the board, which was held on the 7th of the same month, when Mr. Palmer called up the special order relative to the school question. The report of the Committee on Arts and Sciences was then read, as follows:

The Committee on Public Schools, &c., to whom was referred the petition of the Methodist Episcopal Church, praying that a portion of the common school fund may be given to aid in the instruction of the destitute children and helpless orphans who are taught and assisted with clothing, &c., at the Methodist free school, ask leave to report:

That said committee have had the subject under their deliberation, and submit the following facts and resolutions:

That, for nearly forty years, the Methodist Episcopal Church have supported a school in this city for the gratuitous instruction of orphan children and the children of poor and destitute parents.

That they have received for several years a share of the common school fund, for all children taught in their school.

That, encouraged by this public munificence, and prompted by a laudable desire to render more extensive and desirable their free school institution, and during the time while they were admitted to participate in the school fund, the trustees took a lease, for twenty-one years, of two lots of ground in ———— street, and the Society erected thereon a school-house thirty by eighty feet, at the expense of about four thousand dollars.

That, in the year 1826, they were unexpectedly deprived of all participation in the common school fund, and they have since found great difficulty in sustaining their school.

That they have usually about two hundred scholars who are instructed at their school, among whom there are about fifty orphans, or children of parents entirely destitute.

That for shoes, clothing, &c., their poor children are dependent on private charity, the funds raised for the school being inadequate; and the petitioners therefore ask that the Corporation will grant to the said school an equitable proportion of the school fund.

It further appeared before your committee, that the concerns of said school were managed by fifteen trustees, chosen by the Methodist Episcopal Church.

That the fund which supports the said school is raised by contributions, and is kept distinct from the church fund.

That the teachers are of the Methodist religious denomination ; that the children of parents of any other religious denomination are admitted into the school when there are vacancies.

That the school-house is distant about fifty or sixty rods from Public School No. 7, in Chrystie street; that the trustees never encourage children to leave the public schools, but, on the contrary, refuse to receive such children.

After a full examination of facts, your committee have come to the unanimous conclusion that the prayer of the petitioners ought to be granted ; that they believe such a conclusion to be consistent with equity and justice, because the common school fund is raised equally. They believe it is consistent with the intention of the enlightened Legislature of the great State of New York, who, in their statutes which create and distribute their bounty to common schools, did not think proper to shut out any school on account of its religious connections.

Whether the Common Council would deem it expedient (should they adopt this report) to admit said school wholly, or only in part, to participate in the school fund without a more general enactment, your committee have no means of judging. They therefore submit the following resolution, which applies only to the destitute children in said school :

Resolved, That, in addition to the institutions in this city entitled to receive a portion of the common school fund, and the tax raised for the benefit of the public schools within the said city, the school of the Methodist Episcopal Church shall be entitled to receive its proportion for all the orphans and children of destitute parents who may be taught in said school, and who shall be duly returned, agreeably to the provisions of the revised statutes.   TYLER DIBBLEE,
                                                  CHARLES H. HALL,
                                                  HENRY MEIGS.

The memorial of the Trustees of the Methodist Society, and the remonstrance of the Public School Society, were also read. On motion, the board went into Committee of the Whole, Alderman Cebra in the chair. After some time spent in discussion, the committee rose, and the chairman reported that the Committee of the Whole had disagreed with the report of the Committee on Arts and Sciences.

The President then put the question, Will the board agree to the report of the Committee of the Whole ? and a decision being called, the question was decided in the affirmative, as follows :

Ayes—Aldermen Cebra, Van Wagenen, Sharpe, Lamb, Tucker, Jeremiah, Palmer, Woodruff—8.

Nays—Aldermen Meigs, Dibblee, and Hall—3.

The report of the Committee of the Whole being thus adopted, the agitation of the question ceased, and the Trustees of the Methodist Society abandoned their claim.

CHAPTER VII.

HISTORY FROM 1831 TO 1834.

Infant Schools—Primary Departments—Harlem School—Pay System Abolished—Lotteries—Deaf and Dumb Institution—Transfer of Property to the Corporation—New Plans—Delegation to Boston—Primary Schools—Female Teachers Employed—Vagrancy and Truantship—Ordinance of the Common Council—New Public Schools, Nos. 13 and 14—The Asiatic Cholera—Hospital School-Houses—Evening Schools—African Free Schools—Report on Reorganization—Manhattanville Free School—Samuel F. Mott—Public School No. 15—Opening of No. 14—Normal School—Salaries of Teachers—Evening Schools.

THE expansion of the school system, in order to enable it to keep pace with the wants of the metropolis, continually made new demands upon the labors of the Society. As the number of the schools increased, and the population in their respective districts became more dense, it was made apparent that a new order of facilities was required, and that a better classification of the scholars, as to age, proficiency, and qualification, would increase the efficiency of the system. An experiment had been made by an association of ladies for the establishment of infant schools, and the basement of School No. 8, in Grand street, had been granted for the purpose. A committee to examine this school and report upon the question, recommended the adoption of the plan which is fully detailed under its appropriate section, and also that a committee be appointed to examine into the expediency of a revision of the system of instruction in use for the "Junior Classes." This committee reported in July, 1830, and submitted a resolution that the 1st, 2d, 3d, and 4th classes be designated as the 3d or Junior Department, and that, where practicable, female teachers be employed for the care of the schools. The subject was subsequently referred to a new committee, who reported a manual and regulations for the Junior departments, which were to be called "Primary Departments;" and it was directed that application be made to the Legislature for authority to educate and draw money for children between two and sixteen years of age.

Overtures were made at this time by the Trustees of the Harlem School for the transfer of that school to the Society ; but as advantageous arrangements could not be made, and it appeared that, at most, only two of the residents at that part of the island could be induced to become members of the Society, and aid in the supervision of the school, it was deemed inexpedient to entertain the proposition.

Thus opened the year 1831.

An application having been made for a school at the Five Points, a committee was entrusted with the duty of examining the location, and reporting the facts in the case. Their recommendations were in the affirmative ; but the party with whom they supposed they had agreed relative to the terms of lease of the premises, subsequently refused to fulfil the contract except at a very considerable advance, and with restrictions which were deemed to be inimical to the objects of the Society, and the project was, for the time, abandoned.

The Society had now under its charge twenty-three schools and 7,383 pupils.

The practical as well as the financial results of the " pay system " were observed with much solicitude ; and when, at the beginning of the year 1832, the amount of tuition fees had been reduced to a comparatively trifling sum per quarter, the treasurer, Samuel F. Mott, in his quarterly report suggested that the charges for tuition be abandoned. Accordingly, on the 3d of February, on a consideration of the quarterly report of the treasurer, it was resolved, " THAT THE PAY SYSTEM BE ABOLISHED."

By the statute which had been in operation many years, and in obedience to which the Society had received considerable sums of money, the Society and the Institution for the Deaf and Dumb had been made the recipients of the tax upon lottery dealers. The directors of the latter institution informed the board, in February, that they had decided to apply to the Legislature for a grant of the whole amount so collected. The matter was referred to a committee, to consider and remonstrate ; but, on a conference with the Finance Committee of the Institution for Deaf-Mutes, they reported that it would be advisable to leave the disposition of the revenue to the Legislature, and a resolution was adopted declaring it inexpedient to interfere with the action of that body. This was substantially a surrender of the income, and was in harmony with the sentiments of the trustees, who had long borne their testimony against the lottery system, and felt unreconciled to receive the fruits of " that mode of legalized gambling," even that they might be expended in the cause of educating and reforming the children of those classes who suffered most by that vicious and seductive scheme.

The transfer of the property held by the Society to the Corporation of the city, which had been under consideration at various times, was again agitated at the beginning of the year 1832. The fact that the Society was in the annual receipt of a large amount of money from the public funds, part of which was expended in the purchase of grounds and the erection of valuable buildings, thus enabling the Society to become possessed of a constantly accumulating mass of real estate, was urged on every occasion by the advocates of opposing interests as a formidable objection to the institution. The pretext that the Society was " a close corporation," perpetuating itself by the choice of its own members and officers, was not weakened by the plea of its possession of so much real estate, which was obtained by the means of taxes upon " the people ; " and the trustees, ever anxious to promote the primary and noble object of the enterprise, and having no personal interests to subserve, were as desirous of lodging the title in the city as any of their opponents. Their desire was, however, just as strong that the property should not be diverted to other purposes, and that they should not be deprived of the power of carrying out the scheme of popular instruction whenever the wants of the city called for the purchase of additional locations and the erection of new buildings. At the meeting held on the 14th of February, the following preamble and resolutions were considered and laid on the table, and subsequently discussed, and the matter referred to a committee :

Whereas, By an act of the Legislature passed January 8, 1826, the Public School Society was authorized to convey their school edifices, and other real estate, to the Corporation of the city of New York, upon such terms and conditions, and in such form, as should be agreed upon between the parties, taking back from the said Corporation a perpetual lease thereof, upon condition that the same shall be exclusively and perpetually applied to the purposes of education; and, *whereas*, it is deemed expedient and proper that the authority given by the act of the Legislature above recited, except so far as relates to School No. 1, should now be exercised ; therefore,

Resolved, That a respectful communication be made to the honorable the Common Council, of the readiness of this board to make such conveyance to the city, and to accept from the city in return such lease as above mentioned, and that a committee of three trustees be appointed to arrange the terms and conditions of the transfer, and the form in which the same shall be made.

The transfer contemplated was not carried into effect, and the school property remained in the care of the Society until transferred to the Board of Education, in 1853. The Corporation did not deem it advisable or necessary to remove the property from the jurisdiction of the Society.

The State Superintendent had devoted a considerable portion of his annual report to the Legislature to a review of the school system of New York city, and had made important suggestions relative to the improvement of the schools. At the meeting of the board held on the 21st of the same month, the report was submitted, and, on consultation, a committee was appointed to report such plans as might be deemed calculated to meet the necessities of the schools. This committee was composed of Samuel F. Mott, James I. Roosevelt, Jr., Hiram Ketchum, R. Havens, J. B. Brinsmade, Lindley Murray, and R. Sedgwick.

The committee acted promptly upon the matters referred to them, and appointed Mr. Sedgwick and Samuel W. Seton as a sub-committee to visit Boston, for the purpose of inspecting the school system of that city. The deputation were deeply impressed with the flourishing state of the schools and the better-developed system of instruction in use in that city, as well as the more advantageous classification with regard to age and degree of attainments of the pupils. The committee, deeming a very material change of the whole system necessary, reported their views in part on the 4th of May, confining their recommendations to the introduction of " PRIMARY SCHOOLS " for young children who resided at too great distances from the schools already established. The recommendations were to the effect that ten primary schools be established, under the care of a " Committee on Primary Schools ; " that female teachers be employed, at a salary of $200 per annum, with an assistant, at a salary of $50 per annum ; that the ages be from four to ten years, and that, when scholars should reach the age of seven years, they should be transferred to the upper schools, if fitted to enter the sixth class.

The resolutions were adopted, and Messrs. S. W. Seton, G. T. Trimble, J. B. Brinsmade, J. H. Taylor, Mahlon Day, Heman Averill, and Samuel Demilt, were appointed as the Committee on Primary Schools. For specific information, the reader is referred to the chapter devoted to this grade of the schools. The growth of the city exhibited a corresponding increase in the multitude of its vagrant and untrained youth. The original object of the Society grew in importance with each year of its existence, and the adoption of remedial measures pressed upon the attention of the board with greater urgency than at any previous period.

The views entertained of this question may be inferred from the following passage, contained in the twenty-seventh annual report, adopted in the month of May:

The city of Boston, with a population more than two thirds less, expends annually nearly double the largest sum heretofore appropriated in a year to the purposes of education in New York. Their system should, of course, be much more complete and effectual than ours; and although, in some respects, it is so, yet it may be stated with confidence that the New York schools compare favorably with those of the same grades in Boston.

Truantship in that city is deemed a criminal offence in children, and those who cannot be reclaimed are taken from their parents, and placed in an institution called the "School of Reformation," corresponding, in many respects, with our House of Refuge, from which they are bound out by the competent authority, without again returning to their parents. As a necessary consequence, the percentage of absentees, or the difference between the number of children on register and the actual attendance, is less in the Boston public schools than those of New York. This subject has during the past, as in former years, received the attention of the trustees, and will probably be brought before the next board, in connection with the general subject of non-attendance at any school, which exists to such an alarming extent in this city. Efforts have been made by the present board to obtain, in some way, the active coöperation of the city government in applying a remedy to this extensive evil. Every political compact supposes a surrender of some individual rights for the general good. In a Government like ours, "founded on the principle that the only true sovereignty is the will of the people," universal education is acknowleged by all to be not only of the first importance, but necessary to the permanency of our free institutions. If, then, persons are found so reckless of the best interests of their children, and so indifferent to the public good, as to withhold from them that instruction without which they cannot beneficially discharge those civil and political duties which devolve on them in after life, it becomes a serious and important question whether so much of the natural right of controlling their children may not be alienated as is necessary to qualify them for usefulness, and render them safe and consistent members of the political body. The expediency of such a measure would be confined pretty much—perhaps entirely—to large seaport towns, and, in its practical operation, would be found to affect but a few native citizens. The number of families arriving in this city almost daily from Europe is so great as to require some measure of the kind; for the means heretofore used to induce the attendance of their children at the public schools have proved insufficient. The objectionable manner in which these children are employed, on their arrival here, needs no description; it cannot have escaped the notice of any observing citizen.

The subject having been brought to the notice of the city authorities, proceedings were had in the Common Council which resulted in the adoption of the resolutions which follow :

Resolved, That the Trustees of the Public School Society, and the Commissioners of the Almshouse, be requested to make it known to parents, and all persons, whether emigrants or otherwise, having children in charge capable to receive instruction, and being between the ages of five and twelve years, that, unless said parents and persons do or shall send such children to some public or other daily school, for such time in each year as the Trustees of the Public School Society may from time to time designate, that all such persons must consider themselves without the pale of public charities, and not entitled, in case of misfortune, to receive public favor.

Resolved, That the Trustees of the Public School Society, and the Commissioners of the Almshouse, are hereby authorized to take such steps as they may deem expedient, from time to time, to give the necessary publicity to the preceding resolution; and the commissioners are hereby requested to use such means as may be in their power and discretion to carry the same into effect.

Adopted by the Board of Aldermen, April 23, 1832.
Adopted by the Board of Assistants, May 7, 1832.
Approved by the Mayor, May 10, 1832.

Twenty thousand copies of these resolutions, in the form of a circular, were directed to be printed and distributed by the agent of the Society.

The Board of Trustees recommended Sunday-school teachers, the officers and agents of charitable institutions, and others, to urge constantly upon all their pupils or beneficiaries the importance of attending the public schools.

At the same meeting of the board, the Finance Committee submitted a statement, showing that the treasurer would have at his disposal, at the end of the fiscal year of the Society, a balance of about $37,000. This favorable state of the treasury led the board to adopt a resolution directing the appropriation of $10,000 toward the payment of the loan from the Savings Bank, and also another resolution to locate a school in the Eleventh Ward, and in the vicinity of Corlear's Hook. A Committee on Locations was appointed, consisting of Messrs. J. Heard, Benjamin L. Swan, Charles Oakley, Samuel F. Mott, William W. Fox, and R. C. Cornell. In November, the committee reported the purchase of four lots in Madison street, for No. 13, at a cost of $8,000; and, in December, the further purchase of four lots in Houston (then North) street, near Norfolk, for $6,000. The Building Committee proceeded promptly with their duties in reference to the erection of houses upon these locations.

The year 1832 is memorable in the sanitary history of the city, as the period of the first visitation to the New World of the Asiatic cholera. Its presence in the city, and its desolating sweep, arrested business, and impelled tens of thousands to leave their dwellings for a temporary residence in the country. Many also removed from one section of the city to another. Some of the school buildings were used as hospitals, and the schools generally were dismissed in advance of the usual season. The committee having the matter in charge made a report of the proceedings during the summer, from which the following facts are gleaned:

On the 6th of July, the committee were informed that the Board of Health intended to take possession of No. 4. They waited on the Mayor and the Board of Health, and remonstrated against using the school as a hospital, but to no purpose. The school was dismissed, the desks and furniture were taken out, and the building appropriated for the sick. On the 9th of July, No. 1 was closed. On the 15th, the Board of Health gave directions to close No. 2, in order that the building should be occupied as a hospital. On the 17th, Nos. 8 and 10 were closed; on the 18th, No. 11 was also closed; and on the 20th, No. 5 was dismissed. A large number of children having been sent to the "Sailors' Snug Harbor" from other portions of the city, a temporary school was opened during the season at that place, a building being granted for the purpose. The school was kept open from the 27th of July to the 31st of August, two sessions daily, seven days in the week, making a term of seven weeks of five days each, with an average of 104 pupils.

The epidemic passed away, and the schools resumed their sessions in the fall, at such times as were deemed expedient by the respective sections having them in charge.

The committee having in charge the recommendation to reorganize the system, made a partial report in November, specially with reference to evening schools. The committee reported a resolution declaring it inexpedient to establish evening schools, and a second resolution, offering accommodations to such persons or associations as would take the care of such schools under their own charge. The first resolution was laid on the table, and the second, after having been negatived, was reconsidered, and referred to James I. Roosevelt, Jr., to report upon the legal right of the Society to appropriate moneys to schools not under the charge of the board. The report was adverse to the appropriation, and the opinion was adopted in the form of a resolution, declaring it inexpedient to make a distribution of its funds to schools not under the management of the Society.

The Committee on Primary Schools reported that locations for five schools had been selected, these being the initiative of that branch of the system.

In November, the board received a communication from the Trustees of the African Free Schools, stating that they had appointed a committee to confer with a similar committee of the Society, relative to a union of the schools and a transfer of the colored schools to the Society. Messrs. Samuel Demilt, George T. Trimble, J. R. Hurd, S. F. Mott, and Lindley Murray, were selected for the purpose.

The committee on the improvement of the system, having been interrupted in their plans by the prevailing epidemic of the summer months, renewed their labors with increased zeal and earnestness in the fall, and, at the meeting in December, submitted a report, accompanied with a revised code of the bylaws, which formed the subject of protracted discussion, until they were finally adopted, after a long and careful examination. The general principles and measures recommended by the committee were the following ·

The extension of the system of primary schools, so as to embrace every portion of the city where the younger children were unable to attend the larger schools, as already contemplated and partially introduced.

The consequent improved classification of pupils in the upper schools.

The extension and advance of the grade of studies pursued in the public schools.

The establishing of a high school, or academy, where the higher branches should be taught.

The appointment of a larger number of qualified teachers, retaining, however, the monitorial system, which would be improved by this measure.

To accept the aid of gentlemen not connected with the board, in the care of the primary schools, the large number of which would call for the services of more committees, or "sections," than could be constituted from the board at that time.

To discontinue the system of rewards.

The appointment of a superintendent, or agent, in place of the "visitor," whose special attention should be given to the primary schools.

To regulate the depository and mode of distributing supplies.

The year being now at its close, the maturing of these plans became the prominent measure for 1833, during which year the system, materially improved and expanded, was placed in a position of increased strength and importance.

The operations of the year 1833 were opened in the board by the presentation of a memorial from the Trustees of the Manhattanville Free School, asking the Society to adopt it as a part of their system. The trustees had prepared a bill for enactment by the Legislature authorizing the transfer, which was afterward presented to that body; but, after some discussion, it failed to meet approval, and was lost. The transfer was, accordingly, not made at that time, although it was subsequently consummated under the authority of the Board of Education.

Pending the discussion of the new code of by-laws, the committee submitted a new chapter relative to evening schools, and a resolution was adopted declaring it to be expedient to establish evening schools under the care of the board.

The proposition from the Trustees of the African Free Schools for their transfer was reported upon favorably by the Committee of Conference ; but an impediment being discovered which made the authority of the Legislature necessary to secure the title to the property when transferred, further action was postponed.

In October, Samuel F. Mott, the Treasurer, tendered his resignation. The resignation was accepted, and George T. Trimble was elected as his successor.

An application for a school from a number of respectable citizens in that portion of the city near the Third avenue, between Fourteenth and Twenty-eighth streets, was presented to the board. The Mayor, Gideon Lee, united in the request, and a Committee on Locations was appointed to report thereon. Messrs. Charles Oakley, J. Heard, B. S. Collins, Benjamin L. Swan, and J. N. Wells, were selected for this purpose. The committee were directed to select a location in the vicinity of Avenue C and Seventh street.

On the 8th of November, School No. 14, in Houston street, was opened, on which occasion Peter A. Jay, the President of the Society, and Hon. Gideon Lee, the Mayor, delivered appropriate addresses. The school, at the following examination, met the expectations of the trustees—283 boys, 256 girls, and 261 in the primary department being present.

The report of the Committee on Locations was submitted at the meeting of the board in February, 1834, at which time they reported the purchase of four lots in Twenty-seventh street, between Second and Third avenues, at $800 per lot ; and the committee were authorized to select and purchase locations for six primary schools.

Communications were received at the same meeting from a committee, of which Gideon Lee was chairman, and T. Dwight, Jr., secretary, appointed by a public meeting of citizens to promote the formation of a school for the special instruction of common school teachers ; and from a joint meeting of conference of that committee, and a committee of the council of the University, of which Rev. Archibald Maclay, D.D., was chairman, inviting the appointment of a committee on behalf of the board to confer with them on the subject. A committee was accordingly appointed, consisting of Robert C. Cornell, Gulian C. Verplanck, and J. I. Roosevelt, Jr.

The board were enabled in their annual report, published in

May, 1834, to state that the number of pupils in the schools was 11,265; the receipts, including a balance of $15,000, were $100,056.31, and the expenditures were $91,656.10. The debt of the Society amounted to $40,000, due to the Bank for Savings, and secured by bond and mortgage on the property of the Society.

The salaries of the teachers had been raised during the year, so as to give the principals of the male departments $1,000, to principals of female departments, $400, and to assistant teachers in the female and primary departments, $160 to $250. The salary of monitors ranged from $25 to $200. There were then employed forty-nine teachers, twenty-eight assistant teachers, and seventy-five monitors, to whom $35,600 were annually paid for their services.

The experiment of evening schools for apprentices had been made during the winter of 1833–'34, four schools having been kept open for six months, from October to March. The result was satisfactory, although some difficulties had arisen which served to impair their usefulness.

The close of the twenty-ninth year of the existence of the Society, in view of the extent of the system which had been developed by its labors and the good which had been done, was an occasion of pleasure and congratulation. The promising condition of the schools, the practical value of the new measures, which had been fairly tried and found eminently useful, the liberal endowment from the public treasury, and the evidences of growing interest with which the institution was regarded by many of the prominent men of the city, as well as by distinguished strangers, were at once rewards and incentives of no small magnitude, and the board addressed itself to the labors of the future with confidence and hope.

CHAPTER VIII.

BISHOP DUBOIS AND PUBLIC SCHOOL No. 5.—1834.

Application of Bishop Dubois to the Trustees—Action of the Board—Committee
Appointed—Report of the Committee—Expurgation of School-Books.

THE reader will recollect that, in the year 1821, previous to
the controversy with the Trustees of the Bethel schools, the
Board of Trustees of the Public School Society had resolved to
occupy the ground below Bleecker street, and between Broadway and Bowery, by the erection of a commodious school-building. The location was chosen in Mott street, not far from St.
Patrick's Cathedral, on the spot which it still occupies. The condition of the children attracted the attention of Rev. Dr. Dubois, then Roman Catholic bishop of the diocese of New York,
and he was earnestly solicitous to improve the social and moral
condition of the multitudes of young persons of both sexes who
inhabited that portion of the city. No man professing the Christian faith, and a witness of the destitution, moral and intellectual, of hundreds who were either nominally or really professors
of the faith which he taught, could fail to be profoundly concerned at the spectacle. The benevolent bishop, moved as well
by his philanthropy as by his zeal to have the young instructed
in the doctrines of his Church, devised a plan for making available all the agencies and facilities which could be used in this
benevolent object. He therefore made an application to the
Board of Trustees in the following form, which was laid before
that body at a meeting held on the 1st of August, 1834:

The Roman Catholic Bishop, anxious to promote the education of the
children belonging to his persuasion around St. Patrick's, begs leave to
submit to the Board of Managers of the Public Schools the following requests, which he considers as sufficient to ensure the confidence of Catholic
parents, and remove the false excuses of those who cover their neglect under
the false pretext of religion, which they do not practice. He assures the

board that he is influenced by no sectarian motive, no views of proselytism, and that he is as much averse to encroach upon the conscience of others, as to see others encroach upon his. As his demands are grounded upon a long experience of the evils produced by the want of those regulations—abuses which it would require a long time to explain—he hopes the board will rely upon his candor in this case.

1st. That the board would permit him to present a Catholic teacher for that school, subject, of course, to the examination and approbation of the board, and also to the removal by the board, whenever they think it fit, according to the rules admitted for the other schools.

2d. That the use of the school shall be admitted to the Bishop, or clergyman appointed by him, with a society of young men employed by him, on Sundays, for the purpose of giving to the Roman Catholic children instructions in their religion ; and of keeping a Sunday school in the evening for poor apprentices and servants, who have no other time to devote to their education.

3d. That no books shall be received in the school but such as will have been submitted to the Bishop, as free from sectarian principles, or calumnies against his religion. And as many otherwise good books may require only that such passages should be expunged, or left out in binding, that on the recommendation of the Bishop, the board will order it to be done.

4th. That the bishop will be permitted to visit the school every now and then, and submit such observations to the board as he may think calculated to improve the system of education, but so that their final adoption may be left entirely to the judgment of the board.

5th. The bishop, moreover, begs leave to have evening instruction on religion given only to the Roman Catholic children by a clergyman appointed *ad hoc* by him after the school is broken up, any time between five and seven.

6th. As the School of the Sisters has been burnt in the late conflagration in Mulberry street, by which accident more than two hundred girls have been thrown out of education, if the upper part of the school could be conceded to them, with a different passage from that of the boys, until, at least, another school-house could be built on their own premises, this new favor would add to the gratitude of the bishop ; but, if found impracticable, may be dispensed with by the bishop having that school in the very inconvenient, unwholesome, and dark school-room under St. Patrick's.

Should the above requests be objectionable, could not one of the school-houses, which the bishop heard was for sale for want of sufficient scholars, be obtained on easy terms, and bought by the Trustees of St. Patrick's ?

The proposition was considered, and, after mature discussion, the following preamble and resolutions were adopted :

Whereas, The Constitution of the Public School Society offers and ensures to all classes and denominations of our fellow-citizens a free and equal participation in the advantages which it affords ; and, *whereas,* the religious

11

and moral instruction is given in the public schools entirely free from sectarianism, and it always has been and is now the design and endeavor of the trustees so to conduct them as that all sects may have their children educated therein, without fear of their peculiar religious views being interfered with; and, *whereas*, the propositions made by the Catholic bishop contain requirements of privileges from this Society, which have never been asked by, or granted to, any other, and which would be incompatible with the constitutiton : therefore,

Resolved, That it is both unconstitutional and inexpedient to accede to said propositions, but that it is deemed by the trustees highly desirable that the Catholic children generally should attend the public schools, and that the interest and coöperation of the bishop be requested in promoting this object.

Resolved, That a committee be appointed to wait on the bishop, furnish him with a copy of the preceding preamble and resolution, and give him such verbal explanations as may be proper; and particularly, that they inform him that the use of one of the rooms in each of the public school buildings is freely granted to any denomination of Christians for Sabbath-school instruction; and that, if there be in any of the school-books used in the schools, matter which can fairly be considered objectionable by any sect, the trustees would deem it a duty to have such matters erased, or the use of the book discontinued.

The committee to confer with Bishop Dubois was appointed, in accordance with the resolution to that effect, and consisted of Messrs. Lindley Murray, Charles Oakley, and James F. Depeyster. They discharged the duties assigned to them, and had an interesting and amicable interview with the venerable prelate. At the meeting of the board held on the 7th of November following, they submitted a report, which reads as follows :

The committee appointed to confer with the Roman Catholic bishop respectfully report :

That they have had a satisfactory interview with Bishop Dubois, furnished him with a copy of the resolutions adopted by the board, and gave such verbal explanations as appeared proper. The committee propose that a letter of the following import be addressed by the board to the bishop and trustees of the Catholic schools, viz :

To Bishop Dubois and the Trustees of the Roman Catholic Schools :

GENTLEMEN : The attention of the Trustees of the Public School Society having been recently called to the consideration of the expediency of some means being adopted to induce a more general attendance of the children of Catholics at the public schools, and Bishop Dubois having submitted several propositions which were deemed by the board inconsistent with the constitution of the Society, on account of their requiring certain privileges for one sect which had never been, nor could constitutionally be, granted to any, the trustees, impressed with a strong desire that the children of our Roman Catholic population should all attend the public schools as far as their education is not otherwise provided for, would respectfully invite such lay-members of the Catholic Church as feel an interest in this important subject, and are disposed to take an active part in the management of these schools, to become members of the Public School Society, and of its Board of Trustees.

The board have always desired, and do now decidedly wish, so to conduct the schools under their charge, as that all Christian sects shall feel entire freedom in sending their children to them. And if there be in the system of the schools, or in the books used in them, any matter which can reasonably be objected to by any denomination, they would gladly remove the same. And this invitation is given with the conviction that, if accepted, the gentlemen who may unite with us will have no difficulty in inducing such alterations, if any be needed, as will or should convince the members of your Church, that they may freely send their children to our schools, without fear of their peculiar views being in any degree interfered with.

By order and in behalf of the trustees.

The letter submitted by the committee was adopted, and ordered to be signed by the President and Secretary, and transmitted to Bishop Dubois and the trustees of the schools connected with that church. No reply was ever sent to the communication, and the matter was abandoned.

The proposition of the bishop relative to the expunging or erasing of certain offensive passages from the school-books was not then acted on; but on a revival of the school question, in 1841–'42, a revision was carefully executed *by order of the board.*

CHAPTER IX.

HISTORY CONTINUED.—1834 TO 1839.

Transfer of the African Schools to the Public School Society—The Manumission Society—School for Female Monitors—George T. Trimble—Transfer of Property to the Corporation—Library for Teachers—House of Refuge—School for Male Monitors—Public School No. 16—School for Colored Children—Music in No. 10—Death of Lloyd D. Windsor—School in Oak Street—Superintendent of Repairs—Workshop—Loan—Schools for German Children—Study of French—Public School No. 16 Opened—Surplus Revenue and the School Fund—Opening of Centre Street—Public School No. 1 Removed to William Street—African Schools—Trustees' Hall—Death of Joseph Lancaster—Vagrancy—Religious Instruction—Primary Schools—School for German Children—Lots for the Trustees' Hall Purchased.

The year 1834 was rendered specially interesting by the transfer of the schools for colored children, under the care of the Manumission Society, to the Public School Society, and the foundation of the Female Normal School, under the name of " School for Monitors."

The impediment which had affected the power of the Manumission Society to give a perfect title to the property proposed to be transferred, was subjected to a close investigation, and an application to the Legislature was found necessary. This application was made, and the authority having been granted, negotiations were immediately renewed, and on the 1st of August the Committee of Conference were enabled to report the completion of their labors. The property consisted of two lots of ground in Mulberry street, and the perpetual lease, for school purposes, of two lots in William street, both sites having brick buildings thereon. In addition to the real estate, the buildings contained fixtures, furniture, books, cabinets of specimens, &c., as also similar apparatus in seven hired rooms, where smaller schools were kept. The total appraised value of the property was $12,132.22. The number of scholars on register on the 1st of May was 1,608, with an average of 757. The school moneys in the possession of the Manumission Society, or to which it was entitled for the year, amounted to \$9,304.64, which sum was paid over to the Treasurer of the Public School Society.

Resolutions comprising the proceedings of the committee were adopted, and the following named gentlemen from the Manumission Society were elected members of the board: Messrs. Israel Corse, Thomas Bussing, Edmund Willetts, Henry Hinsdale, Charles Walker, Edmund Haviland, Thomas L. Jewett, William L. Stone, and Ira B. Underhill. These gentlemen, together with Samuel Wood and Mahlon Day, were appointed a "section," or committee, for the care of the colored schools. The title of No. 2, in Mulberry street, was changed to No. 1, and No. 1, in William street, was changed to a primary school.

Messrs. Samuel W. Seton, George T. Trimble, Samuel Demilt, Ira B. Underhill, and Thomas Bussing, were named as a committee to report on the system of instruction pursued in the schools, and recommend such changes as should make it conform to that of the schools for white children.

The Executive Committee, at the same meeting, submitted the report of a sub-committee on the expediency of establishing a school for female monitors, or normal school, which recommended the early organization of a school which should hold one session of five hours on Saturday of each week, in Public School No. 5, in Mott street. The report was referred back to the Executive Committee, to be carried into effect at the earliest day.

In November, George T. Trimble, the Treasurer, resigned his office, his predecessor, Samuel F. Mott, having returned from his visit to Europe. The latter gentleman, being nominated for the office, was unanimously elected to perform the duties which he had previously discharged with so much fidelity and ability.

The Board of Supervisors of the city and county held a meeting on the 15th of October, at which it was resolved that a special committee be appointed, to confer with the board of the Society relative to the transfer of the property to the city, taking back a perpetual lease of the same for school purposes. The proceedings were laid before the trustees at the quarterly meeting in November, and a committee of fifteen was appointed on behalf of the Society to negotiate the transfer.

In February, 1835, resolutions were adopted appointing a committee to procure a library for the trustees and teachers, and authorizing the expenditure of $100 the first year, and $50 annually thereafter, for works on education and science suitable for common schools, and such periodicals and other publications as related to popular instruction. Messrs. Gulian C. Verplanck, Hamilton Fish, and J. B. Collins were appointed as the committee.

A proposition submitted to the board by the managers of the House of Refuge, to adopt the school in that institution as one of their number, was subsequently reported upon adversely, and the measure was abandoned.

The necessity for a school in which instruction of a higher grade should be given, had been already frequently urged upon the board in various forms, and at the quarterly meeting in February, the board directed the Executive Committee to take the question of establishing such an institution into consideration. In November, the committee reported in favor of a school for male monitors, and the board authorized the organization of such a school, to be held every evening, except Saturday and Sunday of each week, from October to March, in No. 5, and the rest of the year on Saturdays, at school-house No. 7.

The Committee on Locations reported in favor of the purchase of four lots of ground in Fifth street, between Avenues C and D, and also two lots of ground in Laurens street, for a school for colored children ; both of which were confirmed by the board.

The number of pupils at this time in the schools was 17,318, and the expenses had been, for the year, about $115,000.

The year 1836 opened upon the Society with promises of increasing usefulness, which were at the time unclouded by any signs of adverse influences. The diligent care and faithfulness of the board had been guaranteed by its previous history, and they were cheerfully given with a singleness of purpose unsurpassed by that of any similar institution in the world.

A new proposition was now destined to awaken the interest of the board and of the schools. Mr. Darius E. Jones, a gentleman of cultivation and liberal views, who was a professional musician, had, for a period of six months, been giving lessons in vocal music in School No. 10 ; and the quarterly report from that section, presented at the February meeting of the board in 1836, proposed and recommended the introduction of vocal music as a branch of instruction in the schools. The scheme was referred to a committee, consisting of Messrs. Theodore Dwight, Jr., James I. Roosevelt, Jr., John Morrison, Samuel B. Childs, Samuel F. Mott, J. R. Hurd, and A. R. Lawrence. The committee reported six months afterward, without any declaration of policy other than that the matter should be left to the discretion of the several sections, and with the proviso that, where introduced, the Society should bear no expense in consequence, and that the lessons in music should not interfere with the regular course of school studies.

The Society and the cause of education met with a great loss, in the early part of the year 1836, by the death of LLOYD D. WINDSOR, Principal of No. 1, which position he had held for twenty years, with great honor to himself and advantage to the school. His loss was universally lamented, and he left behind him a hallowed memory and an unsullied name.

At the meeting of the board held in August, the Property Committee was authorized to erect a house on the lots in Fifth street, for No. 16.

The Committee on Locations had selected a piece of property on Roosevelt and Oak streets, near Pearl, and, acting under the powers vested in them, had negotiated for its purchase, at the price of $21,500. The board approved the selection of the committee, and in May, 1837, directed the President and Secretary to complete the purchase and affix the seal of the Society to the usual forms.

Peter A. Jay, Esq., the President of the Society, and Lindley Murray, Secretary, having declined a renomination, their offices were filled, at the annual election, by the choice of Robert C. Cornell as President, and Anthony P. Halsey as Secretary.

Considerations of economy, both in time and expense, suggested to the board the propriety of employing a Superintendent of Repairs, who should have the care of the carpenter's work, painting, glazing, &c., required upon the school-houses. The bills for carpenter's work alone averaged from seven to eight hundred dollars per month, and the remaining items of expenditure for other work made a considerable aggregate during the year. The Property Committee were therefore directed, early in the year, to examine the facts and make such recommendations as appeared to them necessary to meet the requirements of

the system.   A report from the committee, presented in August,
advised the erection of a workshop, and the appointment of a
competent foreman, at a salary not to exceed eight hundred dollars per annum.   The recommendations of the committee were
adopted, and the new feature thus introduced was successfully
and advantageously put into operation.   A workshop was erected on the rear of the lots belonging to the Society, known as No.
61 Thompson street, and Amnon McVey was appointed foreman,
at a salary of $750 a year.

At the close of the year, the board, in view of the demand
for additional means to purchase lots and erect buildings, ordered
a loan of $30,000, to be secured by bond and mortgage upon the
property of the Society.

The great increase in the number of children of emigrants
from Europe suggested the adaptation of the system to meet the
wants of that class of the population, as far as it could be done
consistently with the objects of the Society and the powers vested in them by the Legislature.   The rapid increase in the population speaking the German language, and the very large number of children who were professedly shut out of school in consequence of the absence of opportunities to speak or learn in
their own tongue, were made the subject of earnest consideration
by the board, at the meeting in November of this year (1837).
Several communications had been laid before the Executive
Committee at its session on the 2d of the month, and the matter
was referred to a sub-committee, consisting of Messrs. Lyman
Cobb, Joseph B. Collins, Lindley Murray, G. T. Trimble, and
A. P. Halsey.   This committee submitted a resolution to the
board, which was unanimously approved, and is introduced in
the following report to the Executive Committee.   As this question afterward became identified, in another form, with the name
of a gentleman who held a high position in the State, the proceedings in relation to this measure are entitled to a full detail,
independently of their own importance.   The report is as follows :

The committee to whom was referred the application of John Rudy and
Thomas Cook, for the establishment of schools for the benefit of German
children, have had that subject under consideration, and have given the
attention to it which its importance demands.   They are satisfied that a
necessity exists for affording to that class of our population opportunities

for receiving instruction which our present schools do not supply. Under this conviction, and knowing that the present by-laws do not invest the Executive Committee with power to establish schools of a different character from the present primaries, they presented to the trustees, at their meeting on the 17th of November, the following resolution, which was unanimously adopted :

Resolved, That the Primary School Committee be authorized, under the advice of the Executive Committee, to establish one or more primary schools for the instruction of German children in the English language ; and that the operation of existing by-laws be so far suspended as to allow the admission of children of that class to these schools from the ages of four to sixteen years ; also, to place the schools for boys under the care of male teachers, with such other modifications as may be necessary.

Believing that much good may be done to this class of emigrants by thus affording them the means of instruction, the committee recommend that an experiment be made with two schools for children of the ages contemplated in the above resolution ; and as the object is simply to prepare the children to pursue their education in the existing public schools, and thus to become identified with our native population, from doing which they are debarred by the causes stated in the applications, they further recommend that the term of attendance be limited to twelve months, and that it be particularly urged upon the sections, under whose care they may be placed, to give attention to this part of the subject, and to insist very rigidly on a compliance with this rule ; and in special cases where the removal to a public school may be beneficially made at an earlier period, to cause it to be done.

They therefore ask leave to introduce the following resolution :

Resolved, That the Primary School Committee be requested to open two schools for the instruction of German children in the English language, under such regulations as may be necessary, and in compliance with the general scope of the preceding remarks.

An effort was made to introduce another novelty into the schools, by the formation of classes for the study of French. The proceeding was altogether unofficial, and, the facts having been brought to the attention of the Executive Committee, the Committee on Teachers and Monitors investigated the matter, and made the following report :

The committee on teachers and monitors report on the subject of instruction in the French language, that they find on inquiry that a teacher of French offered his services some months since at Public School No. 10, previous to the present teacher of the male department taking charge thereof ; that with the implied, if not expressed, sanction of one or more of the section, he was permitted to attend one hour a day, three times a week, and to instruct all such of the scholars, male and female, as wished to attend, and were willing to pay one dollar per quarter, the hour appropriated to this object not being permitted or intended to interfere with the usual school hours.

The committee also find that tuition in French has been allowed in nearly all the other schools, on the same terms, precedent being assigned by the teachers as a ground of permission, and generally without the previous knowledge of the sections.

One or more of our teachers have become satisfied, from the experiment, of the impolicy of the measure, and it would probably be permitted to cease without any action of the trustees. But as none of the teachers appear to have thought there was any illegality in the plan, so long as it was not allowed to interfere with the usual school hours, your committee deem it proper to say, that although they do not consider the teachers much, if any, to blame for the past, as they have acted under an erroneous impression and from good motives, yet they think it requisite that in future our teachers should understand that the trustees are not willing that any person not in the employ of the Society be allowed to give instruction in any branch whatever, in our buildings, whether for pay or not, without the previous sanction of the Board or Executive Committee.

The committee recommend the adoption of the following resolutions :

1st. That the teachers be directed to put an end to the existing courses of instruction in French, so soon as agreements made with the French instructor will permit.

2d. That the teachers be directed not to permit instruction in any branch whatever to be given in our buildings, by any person not in the employ of the trustees, without the consent of the board.

The report and resolutions were adopted, and experiments of the kind were not again made, except under the proper authority and control of the several sections, or of the board.

The Property Committee, during the month of July, had made contracts for the erection of a building on the lots in Fifth street, between Avenues C and D, and the work was carried forward with all the promptitude which the case permitted. The house was completed and opened on the 27th of April, 1838, and this circumstance was the first marked occurrence of the new year, which was preceded, a few days before, by an order for the purchase of lots in Thirteenth street for a new school, No. 17, in order to relieve Nos. 3 and 12, which were overcrowded with pupils, the new location making a very appropriate site for a school.

The remarkable occurrences in our national and commercial history, which render the years 1834 to 1842 memorable as a development of grand economical laws, had matured in the first stage of their operation in a plethora in the national treasury, arising from the vast receipts from the revenue on imports and the sale of public lands. Under this state of things, a bill was passed in Congress and became a law, depositing the surplus revenue with the several States of the Union; and that portion which was deposited with the State of New York was, by a law passed at the session of the Legislature (1837–'38), appropriated for school purposes. This became a source of increased and very desirable revenue to the Public School Society, and, the facts being committed to the board by Hon. Gulian C. Verplanck, a committee on the subject was appointed, which reported a statement of the measure, with a copy of the law, and were thereupon discharged.

The Common Council had adopted resolutions and taken the preliminary steps for the opening of Centre street to Chatham, the Park at that time extending to an angle which made a circuitous route through Chambers street necessary for all other than pedestrians. The extension required the demolition and removal of No. 1, as that building occupied a position on the line of the opening. The school for colored children, known as No. 1, was located in William street, on lots leased from the city, but which had been vacated soon after the transfer to the Society in 1834, and a new house erected in Laurens, near Broome street. The building in William street was occupied, at the time of the extension, for public purposes, and, on its surrender to the Society, was replaced by a new and commodious house, the schools, in the interval, being accommodated in hired premises.

On the 4th of May, the name of the "African" schools was changed to that of "Colored."

The average attendance for the year ending May 1, 1838, as reported to the Commissioners of School Money, was 19,982, of which 1,441 were colored children.

The increase in the business of the Society by the multiplication of schools, the system of supplies, &c., made it expedient to secure sufficient apartments for the meetings of the board and its committees, as well as to provide for the preservation of the records, and a suitable depository. Only a part of these purposes were originally contemplated in a resolution by which a committee was appointed in November, 1837, to take such steps as might be deemed necessary to procure a hall for meetings of the board. The committee, in 1838, were directed, on their own recommendations, to apply to the Common Council for the use of an apartment in one of the public buildings, but the request was not granted. The committee reported in favor of making an appropriation of not over $1,500 a year for the purpose, which should be expended in rent, or in "interest on the cost," as the case might be. The recommendation was adopted, and the foundation laid for the "Trustees' Hall," now occupied by the Board of Education.

The new building for No. 1, erected on the lots occupied as a school for colored children, having been completed and prepared for the reception of pupils, the dedication exercises were held on the 16th of October. The scholars passed a creditable examination, and the audience were highly gratified at the condition of the school. Thirty of the trustees and a large number of visitors were present on the occasion.

During the month of October, the friends of education in New York were called to pay their tribute of respect to the memory of JOSEPH LANCASTER, the distinguished and indefatigable laborer in the cause of popular instruction, and the founder of the system known by his name, which had been so successfully adopted and improved by the Public School Society.

Mr. Lancaster took a great interest in the schools, and had commenced a series of visits for the purpose of inspection and counsel. On the 22d of October, an examination took place at No. 7, in Chrystie street, at the close of which he left the school. In crossing Grand street, he was thrown down by a horse and carriage, and very seriously injured. He was taken to the house of a friend, where his physicians attended him, but without avail. He was called to his rest on the 24th, two days afterward, and his remains were placed in the burying-ground of the Society of Friends, in Houston street, between the Bowery and Chrystie street.

On the announcement of the death of Mr. Lancaster in the Board of Trustees, Benjamin Clark, Lindley Murray, and Samuel F. Mott were appointed a committee to prepare a testimonial to his memory; which duty was performed, and the following "minute" was directed to be engrossed by a competent pupil of the public schools, and placed in the trustees' room :

JOSEPH LANCASTER,

THE AUTHOR OF THE MONITORIAL OR SYSTEM OF MUTUAL INSTRUCTION, ORIGINALLY KNOWN AS

THE LANCASTERIAN SYSTEM,

WAS BORN

NEAR LONDON ON THE 25TH OF SEPTEMBER, 1778,

AND DIED

AT WILLIAMSBURGH, IN THE STATE OF NEW YORK,

ON THE 24TH DAY OF OCTOBER, A.D. 1838.

HE TRAVELLED EXTENSIVELY IN BOTH HEMISPHERES, FOR THE PURPOSE OF
INTRODUCING AND PROMOTING HIS

Admirable System of Education:

A SYSTEM WHICH IS RAPIDLY AMELIORATING THE CONDITION OF MAN,

AND EXTENDING THE BLESSINGS OF

EDUCATION

TO MILLIONS WHO MIGHT OTHERWISE HAVE LIVED AND DIED IN THE DARKNESS OF

IGNORANCE.

IN THE PROSECUTION OF THIS NOBLE AND BENEVOLENT OBJECT

HE WAS ON A VISIT TO THE CITY OF NEW YORK, AND HAD JUST LEFT ONE OF THE

PUBLIC SCHOOLS,

WHEN HE MET WITH THE CASUALTY WHICH IN A FEW HOURS TERMINATED HIS MORTAL CAREER.

AS A

TRIBUTE OF RESPECT

TO HIS MEMORY,

THE TRUSTEES OF THE PUBLIC SCHOOL SOCIETY OF NEW YORK

HAVE CAUSED THIS SHEET TO BE EXECUTED BY A PUPIL OF PUBLIC SCHOOL NO. ——, IN THE
CITY OF NEW YORK.

Early in life, Mr. Lancaster had become impressed with the advantages of the system of mutual instruction, and resolved to develop his method at the most favorable opportunity. He opened a school in Southwark, in 1789, where he taught almost gratuitously. The success of his labors soon attracted attention to his system, and subscriptions began to pour in upon him to sustain him in his benevolent work, by which he was enabled not only to enlarge his own school, but to travel through the kingdom and introduce it in other cities. Numerous schools were established under his personal supervision. Dr. Bill now appeared as a rival, and claimed to be the originator of the monitorial system, and by his personal and professional influence he commanded so much attention, that Mr. Lancaster, who was a member of the Society of Friends, was overborne in the competition, and compelled to yield to the pressure of his more pretentious and successful rival. He visited the United States and Canada, the Legislature of which province made him an appropriation to assist him in developing the school system ; but, not deriving sufficient income from that source to complete his plans, he was again forced to retire from the active pursuit of his scheme, and sought a home in New York, with the expectation of giving some additional evidences of the perfection to which he had brought his system. He had submitted a proposition to the Executive Committee to make an experiment with forty children, and with the aid of ten others as monitors, to teach them in from four to six weeks to read and spell accurately. Mr. Lancaster was reluctant to communicate the details of his plan to the committee, or to permit them to be present at any of his exercises. The committee reported unfavorably upon the application, but recommended that he be allowed the use of a room for the purpose of teaching his classes. The report was accepted, laid on the table, and a resolution adopted declaring it to be inexpedient to grant the application.

Mr. Lancaster shared the fate of most pioneers in literature, science, and reform, for he never amassed any pecuniary rewards from his labors. A few friends had, however, purchased a small annuity for him, and he was devoting his time to general visitation and advisory examinations when his labors were terminated by his death.

The condition of the vagrant and unemployed children of the city was made again the subject of special consideration by the Executive Committee, and referred to a sub-committee to devise plans for correcting the evil. The committee reported a project, of which the leading features were:

1st. To appoint three visitors, who should visit certain sections of the city where such labors were most required, and urge upon children and parents the necessity and duty of improving the privileges offered them.

2d. To procure the passage of a law making it an offence in a minor to be found idle and uninstructed, and subject to commitment if reformation did not take place.

3d. The establishment of a Manual Labor Farm School, to which such children should be sent when arrested under the law.

Visits, printed addresses, handbills, and other means of securing the greatest publicity, were also recommended. The report was adopted, and a committee to prepare a memorial to the Corporation of the city submitted a draft of the paper they had prepared, in which similar views and plans were advocated. The memorial was adopted, and ordered to be properly signed, authenticated, and submitted to the Common Council. Nothing, however, resulted, except indirectly, from these efforts, as the plans were never matured, the board having failed to obtain the patronage or the sanction of either the city or the State.

At the meeting of the Executive Committee, November 26, a resolution was adopted appointing a committee, consisting of Joseph B. Collins, Samuel R. Childs, and William L. Stone, to inquire into the expediency of introducing into the schools suitable books setting forth " the principles of the Christian religion, free from all sectarian bias." A report was submitted, and an amendment of the by-laws was proposed, defining the position of the Society; but the agitation of the school question, which was then threatening the public mind, and which followed soon afterward, arrested any further action. The agent was directed to ascertain, by a new census of the schools, what proportion of the pupils attended Sunday schools.

A committee was appointed, in the early part of the year (1839), to examine and report upon the comparative advantages of the primary schools and primary departments. The first were the schools established in various localities, in order to place school privileges within the reach of the youngest children, many of whom would have been unprovided for, in consequence of the distance of the larger schools from their abodes. The result was much in favor of the departments of the large schools, but the discrepancy was easily understood and recognized, and the committee recommended such a revision of the manual as would not only develop the primary schools and make them more efficient, but would also remove the difficulties which apparently existed in regard to their cost and attendance. The committee were decided in their conviction that moral and physical education are far more important for children under six years of age than instruction in letters, and that frequent intermissions and varied exercises for children of that age are necessary, while the confinement of the scholars to a bench for hours in succession is injurious and improper. The recommendations of the committee were adopted.

The experiment of a school for the special instruction of German children had now been fairly tried, and the Primary School Committee was requested to submit a report thereon. They ascertained that, during the first year, 380 pupils had been admitted, of whom 328 entered the first class. Of these, 57 had learned to read, and, out of this number, 15 had removed to the country, and 27 had entered upon some business occupation. The object of the school—which was, to make it introductory to the public schools—had been lost sight of by the teacher, as no transfers had been made, in consequence of the reluctance of the scholars to leave the teacher and the school to which they had become attached, and the apprehension, which was strengthened by the declaration of many, that they would abandon school altogether if so transferred. The teacher desired that certain privileges in regard to advanced lessons might be granted, but the committee were unwilling to concur with the plan, except in a modified form. They recommended a school for German girls in the eastern section of the city, and two other schools, one for each sex, in any locality where they appeared to be required. The schools were to be strictly conducted as primary schools, except that the boys' schools might be under the care of a male teacher, and that minors of any age over four years might be admitted.

The committee, on obtaining a suitable place for the use of

ROBERT C CORNELL

the Society for its business departments, reported, in June, in favor of purchasing the property on the northwest corner of Grand and Elm streets, at a cost of $19,500, and the erection thereon of a suitable building. The recommendation was adopted, the appropriate committees were directed to prosecute the work with all the promptitude the case demanded, the plans were procured, and the building speedily put under contract.

Thus closed the year 1839.

12

CHAPTER X.

THE ROMAN CATHOLIC SCHOOL QUESTION.—1840.

Annual Message of Governor Seward—Petition of Roman Catholics to the Common
Council—Remonstrance of the Trustees of the Public School Society—Remonstrance of the Executive Committee—Commissioners of School Money—Communication from Rev. Felix Varela—School Books—Roman Catholic Association—
The Freeman's Journal Established—Public Meetings of Roman Catholics—Bishop
Hughes—Resolutions—Address to the Public—Rev. Dr. Pise—Catholic Memorial
to the Common Council—Board of Aldermen—Committee Appointed—Remon-
strance of Public School Society—Remonstrance of Methodists—Special Meeting
of Common Council to Hear the Petitioners and Remonstrants—Speech of Bishop
Hughes—Speech of Theodore Sedgwick—Speech of Hiram Ketchum—Rev. Dr.
Bond—Bishop Hughes—Samuel F. Mott—Second Session—Speech of Rev. Dr.
Bond—Speech of David M. Reese, M. D.—Speech of Rev. John Knox—Speech
of Rev. Dr. Bangs—Speech of Rev. Dr. Spring—Closing Speech of Bishop
Hughes—Rejoinder of Mr. Ketchum—Report of the Committee—Application of
Roman Catholics for School Fund Distribution Negatived.

THE repeated controversies in which the Society had been
engaged relative to the distribution of moneys raised for the purposes of common school education, and the legislation thereon,
had not yet put to rest the desire of a portion of the citizens for
a specific appropriation for the support of schools under a denominational control. The efforts of the several parties making
these appeals to the Common Council, the Legislature of the
State, and their fellow-citizens, were now renewed by a more
fully organized effort than had yet been made. This controversy
eventually influenced the action of the political parties in the
city, and threatened, were it not terminated, to override the
broader issues at large throughout the State, and become the
battle-ground for contending partisan interests. The beginning
of the year 1840 was the period chosen for the movement.

The Governor of the State, Hon. William H. Seward, in reviewing the condition of the common schools in his annual message, made the following recommendations, which, as they were

deemed by many to have been submitted with a reference to the pending controversy, are worthy of a place in this connection :

Although our system of public education is well endowed, and has been eminently successful, there is yet occasion for the benevolent and enlightened action of the Legislature. The advantages of education ought to be secured to many, especially in our large cities, whom orphanage, the depravity of parents, or some form of accident or misfortune seems to have doomed to hopeless poverty and ignorance. Their intellects are as susceptible of expansion, of improvement, of refinement, of elevation, and of direction, as those minds which, through the favor of Providence, are permitted to develop themselves under the influence of better fortunes. They inherit the common lot to struggle against temptations, necessities, and vices; they are to assume the same domestic, social, and political relations, and they are born to the same ultimate destiny.

The children of foreigners, found in great numbers in our populous cities and towns, and in the vicinity of our public works, are too often deprived of the advantages of our system of public education, in consequence of prejudices arising from difference of language or religion. It ought never to be forgotten that the public welfare is as deeply concerned in their education as in that of our own children. I do not hesitate, therefore, to recommend the establishment of schools, in which they may be instructed by teachers speaking the same language with themselves, and professing the same faith. There would be no inequality in such a measure, since it happens from the force of circumstances, if not from choice, that the responsibilities of education are in most instances confided by us to native citizens; and occasions seldom offer for a trial of our magnanimity by committing that trust to persons differing from ourselves in language or religion.

Since we have opened our country, and all its fulness, to the oppressed of every nation, we should evince wisdom equal to such generosity, by qualifying their children for the high responsibilities of citizenship.

The trustees of the Catholic schools prepared and submitted to the Common Council an application for a portion of the school moneys, which was transmitted to that body during the month of February, and printed on the 2d of March.

At a meeting of the Executive Committee of the Society, held on the 20th of the same month, for the purpose of considering what measures should be taken with reference to this application, it was deemed expedient to call a meeting of the Board of Trustees, to be convened on the 24th, that a carefully-advised course might be recommended. A committee, consisting of Samuel F. Mott, George T. Trimble, A. P. Halsey, Robert C. Cornell, Lindley Murray, Stephen Allen, and Peter Cooper, was appointed, to prepare a remonstrance against granting the application, and to adopt such other measures as they might deem necessary. The committee were also authorized to employ counsel, if the case demanded legal services.

At the meeting of the Board of Trustees held pursuant to the call of the Executive Committee, the following remonstrance was adopted, as a declaration from the trustees, to be followed by a more carefully prepared examination of the question by the Executive Committee.

To the Common Council:

The undersigned, in their associate capacity as Trustees of the Public School Society, and in their individual character as citizens, hereby respectfully but urgently remonstrate against the granting of a request presented by the trustees of the Catholic schools for a participation in the common school moneys.

Your remonstrants are opposed to this proposition, as being unconstitutional and inexpedient.

Unconstitutional—because in our State charter, and in our statute-book, the common school fund is appropriated to and for the benefit and support of *common* schools only and exclusively; and we deem it self-evident that no school can be so called, unless opened to all classes and descriptions of citizens, and conducted on a system to which none can reasonably object. Such is not the case with the Catholic schools. The peculiar sectarian tenets of that faith are part, and by them thought to be an essential part of the course of instruction; and hence all unbelievers in Catholic doctrines are unwilling, and may with good reason object, to send their children to such schools.

Unconstitutional—because it is utterly at variance with the letter and spirit of our chartered rights, and with the genius of our political institutions, that the community should be taxed to support an establishment in which sectarian dogmas are inculcated, whether that establishment be a school or a church.

Inexpedient—because the public schools, open to all without discrimination, and so conducted that no reasonable objection can be made by any to sending their children to them, are now in a very flourishing and satisfactory condition, and are annually increasing in numbers and usefulness; and which schools would, by the admission of church schools to participate in the school fund, be crippled, and probably destroyed.

Inexpedient—because the question was fully examined by the Common Council in 1822, and all the church schools, including the Catholic, which had previously drawn from the school fund, were cut off; and the great principle of non-sectarianism adopted as the basis for subsequent appropriations from this fund.

Inexpedient—because, by the concentration of the fund in one channel, a much greater amount of good is produced, than could be the case were it divided and subdivided among many; for in the public schools the same expense for teachers, &c., would be incurred in a school of 100 or 150, as in one of double the number.

Induced by these leading positions, which they consider fully tenable, and by others which brevity induces the omission of, your remonstrants urgently protest against the admission of the Catholic, or any other sectarian school, to a participation in the public moneys. And of such great import-ance do they consider the subject, that, unless the Common Council are pre-pared, on a mere statement of these objections, to deny the application, your remonstrants respectfully request that they may be heard, in defence of their positions, before a joint meeting of your two boards.

Our Executive Committee will prepare and present a remonstrance more in detail.

The committee appointed, as already stated, to act on behalf of the Society, prepared a remonstrance, which was promptly printed for general distribution, as well as for the use of the members of the Common Council. This paper was adopted by the Executive Committee, as follows :

To the Honorable the Common Council of the City of New York, the Remon-strance of the Public School Society, by their Executive Committee, RESPECT-FULLY SHEWETH :

That your remonstrants learn with regret and surprise, that the Trustees of the Catholic Schools, have petitioned for a portion of the school fund, to support the schools under their care. Nearly twenty years have elapsed since sectarian schools were excluded from a participation in this fund, and your remonstrants had indulged a hope, that the question was forever at rest.

The injustice of taxing the whole community for the support of sectarian schools is so manifest, and it is so glaringly incompatible with the genius of our political institutions, that the naked proposition would seem to carry with it its own refutation. The Constitution of this State declares, " that the proceeds of certain lands belonging to the State, together with the fund, denominated the common school fund, shall be, and remain a perpetual fund, the interest of which shall be inviolably appropriated to the support of *common schools* throughout the State."

So far as your memorialists are aware, there is not in any law regulating the *general* distribution of this fund, nor in either of the numerous circulars issued by the Secretary of State, in his capacity as Superintendent of Com-mon Schools, is there the most remote allusion to sectarian instruction in religion, except that on one occasion, after citing some ten or twelve class-books of a strictly literary and moral character, he refers to Sampson's " Beauties of the Bible," as a compilation well adapted to common schools ; but as if aware of the delicate ground on which he was treading, the secre-tary immediately remarks, " that the selection has been made without reference to any disputed points of doctrine ; and it is entirely free from all sectarian spirit ; " thus evincing his own view of the necessity of excluding sectarian instruction from the common school system of education.

Owing to the impracticability of apportioning the school moneys among the citizens of this city in the manner adopted for the districts, the Legislature was induced in 1813, to pass a law authorizing " such incorporated religious societies in the city of New York, as supported, or should establish charity schools," to participate in the income of the school fund. That income was then very small, and there was no direct tax on the city for school purposes, independent of the school fund tax. The amount thus drawn was so inconsiderable, that the subject did not attract much attention, until 1822, when it was discovered that one congregation, or rather its pastor, had embarked in the business of school-keeping as matter of speculation, and had established three charity schools.

By deceptive returns he managed to draw from the fund a greater sum than was required for the payment of teachers (to which its application was restricted by law). He then procured an enactment, authorizing him to apply the surplus to the erection of school-houses and all other purposes of education. Under a *liberal* construction of this clause, he ventured to build a church, with miserable accommodations for a school on the basement floor. These proceedings alarmed not only your memorialists, but the citizens generally, as well as several of the churches who had received and applied the public money in good faith, and they united in asking of the Legislature a remedy for these abuses. So important was the subject deemed, that the Corporation of the city, without a negative vote, joined in the application, which finally brought the whole question before the State government.

The committee charged with its consideration, after a patient investigation, during which, gross fraud and peculation were proved to have been practiced by the clergyman referred to, made a report in which the following language occurs :

There is, however, one general principle, of no ordinary magnitude, to which the committee would beg leave to call the attention of the house.

It appears that the city of New York is the only part of the State, where the school fund is at all subject to the control of religious societies. This fund is considered by your committee purely of a civil character, and therefore it never ought, in their opinion, to pass into the hands of any corporation, or set of men, who are not directly amenable to the constituted civil authorities of the government, and bound to report their proceedings to the public. Your committee forbear, in this place, to enter fully into this branch of the subject, but they respectfully submit whether it is not a violation of a fundamental principle of our legislation to allow the funds of the State, raised by a tax on the citizens, and designed for civil purposes, to be subject to the control of any religious corporation. [See page 70.]

The report was approved, and the only law of this State which ever authorized an ecclesiastical or religious association to use the " common school fund," was stricken from the statute book, and the right conferred on the corporation of this city, of designating the " societies and schools " to which the money should be given.

The conflict was thus transferred from Albany to New York, and the whole question was brought by the parties interested, before the municipal Government, and by them referred to a committee, whose report, after a patient and laborious investigation, is, perhaps, among the most impartial, able, and conclusive documents that ever was presented to your honorable body.

After a merited compliment to the respectable churches, and religious societies, who participated in the fund, and whose delegates had been fully heard, the committee concluded their report as follows: *—" but the weight of the argument, as urged before them, and which they have endeavored to condense in this report, and the established constitutional and political doctrines, which have a bearing on this question, and the habits and modes of thinking of the constituents at large of this board, require, in the opinion of your committee, that the common school fund should be distributed for civil purposes only, as contra-distinguished from those of a religious or sectarian description." The recommendation of the committee was approved by the Common Council, and all church schools were, and continue to be, excluded from participating in the fund.

Your memorialists were thus induced to prosecute the cause of general education with renewed vigor, but finding the sum derived from the school fund, and its equivalent local tax, very inadequate to the pressing wants of a rapidly increasing population, they procured the signatures of several thousands of our *largest tax-paying citizens*, to a petition to the Common Council, requesting that an application might be made to the Legislature, for authority to lay " an annual tax of not less than half a mill on the dollar, upon the amount of assessed property in the city, for the purpose of *free and common education;* the funds thus to be raised, to be kept separate from all others, and sacred to the purposes for which it is designated."

The whole tenor of this petition clearly shews, that it was in aid of " the common schools of the city," and of " free and common education," that the petitioners asked to be taxed. They declare that their object is " to provide for the security and permanency of our republican institutions by the general diffusion of knowledge."

Does any person believe that a sectarian education is necessary to the attainment of these objects? Or, that a diversion of the fund to ecclesiastical uses would not be a violation of the " purposes for which it was designed ? "

Your memorialists dwell with stress on this petition, because from it arose the present tax of four eightieths of one per cent, which is something more than three fifths of the entire sum devoted to the common school education in this city.

It is perhaps the only petition that ever was presented to a Legislative Body soliciting the *privilege* of being taxed. It was signed understandingly and on mature reflection, by thousands whose *immediate* pecuniary interest was adverse to the prayer : and hence, your memorialists respectfully urge,

* See Document, dated April 11, 1825, signed S. Cowdrey (Chairman), Thomas Polton, E. W. King. [See Appendix A.]

that a strict and sacred regard, in the distribution of its avails, should be had to the motives which influenced the petitioners.

With the greatly augmented means afforded by the proceeds of this tax, your memorialists were enabled not only largely to increase the number, but greatly to improve the quality of the public schools. At this time there are ninety-seven schools of the various grades, in the benefits of which, upward of twenty thousand children participated during the past year. The quality of these schools, it is believed, may safely challenge a comparison with those of the same grade, in this or any other country. The question is now submitted to the guardians of the city whether these schools shall be sustained or abandoned; and the funds created for their support, diverted to the support of ecclesiastical establishments.

Your memorialists feel warranted in presenting this issue, because the income of the "Public School Society" is scarcely sufficient to sustain the present public schools; and it cannot be doubted, that if the petition of the "Trustees of the Catholic Schools," is successful, similar applications will immediately be made by the numerous sects into which the Christian church is divided. And it is not perceived upon what ground they could under such circumstances be denied, nor why associations of unbelievers (of which there are a number in this city,) may not with equal, and in some respects greater propriety, demand and receive a portion of the fund.

The amount annually paid to teachers in the "public schools," is about $60,000. And it is a well-known feature of the system of education practised in the public schools, that a reduction of one half the number of pupils in each school (which is a probable consequence of the contingency referred to,) would not materially lessen the expense of tuition, without serious detriment to those remaining.

Should the school money be divided and subdivided among church schools, some of which would necessarily be very small, your memorialists entertain a confident belief, that the important cause of general education would receive a fatal check; for, besides the loss sustained in frittering away the fund among small schools, too numerous and diversified to undergo the healthy supervision of the commissioners, the managers of those schools, having what they might deem higher and more important objects in view, in the inculcation of religious creeds or dogmas, could scarcely fail to neglect the literary for the religious culture of the children's minds.

If it be urged that the Catholic schools are open to all without distinction, as to religious sect; your remonstrants reply, that this fact only enhances the objection to granting the prayer of their petition; which then virtually is, that they may be enabled to gain proselytes at the public expense; and that, too, in the most effectual way, by an influence exerted on the tender and susceptible minds of youth. Such an applicaton of public money is not, perhaps, inconsistent with purity of motive; but can it be done with justice to those who, with at least equal sincerity, entertain directly opposite views?

It is not understood that the Catholic clergy object to the public schools, on account of any religious doctrines taught in them, but because the peculiar doctrines of the Church of Rome are not taught therein : and they now ask for a portion of the public money in order that these doctrines may be taught, in connection with the kind of instruction for which alone these moneys were raised. And here it may be proper to state, that several interviews were formerly had with the Catholic bishop, for the purpose of removing any reasonable objections he might have to the system of instruction in the public schools, or to the books used in them ; and it was proposed to submit the books to his inspection, in order that they might, if found objectionable, undergo expurgation.

In selecting teachers for the public schools, no regard is had to the sectarian views of the candidates ; and since the application now under consideration, it has been ascertained that at least six of the teachers belong to the Roman Catholic Church.

Your memorialists disclaim all feeling of hostility to the respectable body against whose petition they remonstrate. Nor are they conscious of a want of sympathy for the oppressed of other lands, who seek an asylum in this ; on the contrary, they act under a firm conviction that the sooner such persons abandon any unfavorable prejudices with which they may arrive among us, and become familiar with our language, and reconciled to our institutions and habits, the better it will be for them, and for the country of their adoption. If this be true, the best interests of all will be alike promoted by having their children mingle with ours in the public seminaries of learning.

The theory and practice of our happy and equal form of government is, to protect every religious persuasion, and support none. It was supposed for ages, that religion could not flourish without aid from the strong arm of secular power ; and even now this delusion prevails extensively in the old world. The political compact by which these United States are governed, divorced the unholy alliance between Church and State. Yet, until within a recent period, the lingering remains of prejudice derived from pious but bigoted ancestors, retained one feature of the exploded system, in the code of a neighboring State ; but even there, those laws which taxed the people at large for the support of sectarian schools, have been abrogated ; and it remains to be seen whether the city of New York will take the first step in a retrograde course.

Your memorialists have no interest in the pending question, other than is common to the great mass of their fellow-citizens. But having devoted much time and gratuitous labor, in building up the present unrivalled public-school system, their feelings are more ardently embarked in the cause ; and they have greatly erred in estimating the tone of the public mind, if the views here expressed are not fully sustained by public opinion.

Powerful and pervading as the influence of party politics is known to be, it is believed that there are principles so dear, and so deeply rooted, that honest men, of every party, will lose sight of inferior objects, and unite in their support.

In conclusion, your remonstrants refer to the annexed communication and resolutions of the " Commissioners of School money," who derive their appointment from your honorable body, and whose duty it is to visit all schools that participate in the school fund, and report their condition to the Corporation of this city, and to the Superintendent of Common Schools at Albany. This document, it will be seen, fully sustains the reasoning and conclusions of your remonstrants.

All which is respectfully submtitted.

R. C. CORNELL, *President.*

A. P. HALSEY, *Secretary.*

NEW YORK, *Feb.* 29, 1840.

The trustees of the Society having sent communications relative to the application of the trustees of the Catholic schools to the Board of Commissioners of School Money, the subject came up before the board at their meeting on the 29th of February. The following extract from the minutes of that day was published by authority :

At a meeting of the Commissioners of School Money, held at the City Hall of New York, on the 29th day of February, 1840,

A communication having been received, at a former meeting, from the Trustees of the Public School Society of New York, referring to an application now pending before the Common Council, which prays that the schools in this city established and governed by one of the denominations of Christians, be admitted to a participation of the common school moneys ; and this board, deeming it their duty to consider and answer any communication connected with the interests of the schools subject to their visitation :

It is therefore unanimously *Resolved*, As the opinion of this board, that schools created and directed by any particular religious society should derive no aid from a fund designed for the common benefit of *all* the youth of this city, without religious distinction or preference.

That an appropriation of the school moneys to establishments controlled by any individual sect, would be unjust to all other denominations not similarly favored, and constitute a partiality irreconcilable with the spirit of our political institutions ; would narrow the liberal and expanded scheme of public education, for which the community at large, without religious discrimination, is taxed ; would make the common school money a source of intrigue, cupidity, and contention among the various portions of our citizens who are divided in tenets of faith ; and would, in its progressive results, render useless many of the commodious structures erected in this city at the general expense, which are now the thronged seats of public instruction ; and injure, perhaps fatally, the noble system of common school education that distinguishes our city and State.

Resolved, That a copy of these proceedings, signed by the Chairman and Secretary, in behalf of the Commissioners of School Money, be forwarded to the Trustees of the Public School Society of New York, with permission to make such use of it, in sustaining the common school system unfettered

by sectarian connections,.as, in their opinion, may best promote that object.   SAMUEL GILFORD, JR.,
                                Chairman of Common School Money.

M. B. EDGAR, *Secretary.*

The usual annual examinations of the several schools commenced on the 17th of March following, and on the 24th the examination of Public School No. 5, in Mott street, was held. After the exercises, the trustees retired to the recitation-room, and held a meeting for the consideration of important business. The Vice-President announced that Rev. Felix Varela, of the Roman Catholic Church, had sent a request to be furnished with a set of the reading-books used in the public schools. A committee was subsequently appointed, whose action gave rise to the expunging proceedings which became so prominent a topic of discussion ; and forming, as it does, an event of a peculiar character, the facts are presented in a succeeding chapter, embodying the report of the committee, in which a full statement of the case is detailed.

During the early part of the year 1840, the Roman Catholics organized an association to take such measures as might appear to be politic or necessary for the furtherance of their claims. The *Freeman's Journal,* a weekly newspaper, was also published, the first number appearing on the 4th of July, a prominent object of which was to press the claims of the school question with uninterrupted diligence upon the minds of the people.

The meetings of the Roman Catholics were held in the school-house attached to St. Patrick's Cathedral. On the 20th of July, a meeting was held, at which Rev. Dr. Power presided, when addresses were made by the Chairman, Dr. Sweeney, and Bishop Hughes. A committee was appointed to procure a more commodious place. The next meeting was held in the basement of St. James' Church, in James street, on the 27th of July, when THOMAS O'CONNOR, Esq., was called to the chair, and the bishop again addressed the assembly. At the close of his speech he submitted the following preamble and resolutions :

Whereas, The wisdom and liberality of the Legislature of this State did provide, at the public expense, for the education of the poor children of the State, without injury or detriment to the civil and religious rights vested in their parents or guardians by the laws of nature and of the land ; and, *whereas,* the administration of that system, as now conducted, is such that the parents or guardians of Catholic children cannot allow them to frequent such schools without doing violence to these rights of conscience which the Constitution secures equal and inviolable to all citizens, viz. : They cannot allow their children to be brought up under a system which proposes to shut the door against Christianity, under the pretext of excluding sectarianism, and which yet has not the merit of being true to its bad promise ;

And, *whereas*, Catholics who are the least wealthy, and most in need of the education intended by the bounty of the State, are those cut off from the benefit of funds to which they are obliged to contribute, and constrained either to contribute new funds for the purposes of education among themselves, or else to see their children brought up under a system of free-thinking and practical irreligion, or else to see them left in that ignorance which they dread, and which it was the benevolent and wise intention of the Legislature to remove ; therefore,

1. *Resolved*, That the operation of the common school system, as the same is now administered, is a violation of our civil and religious rights.

2. *Resolved*, That we should not be worthy of our proud distinction as Americans and American citizens, if we did not resist such invasion by every lawful means in our power.

3. *Resolved*, That in seeking the redress of our grievances, we have confidence in our rulers, more especially, as by granting that redress they will but carry out the principles of the Constitution, which secures equal civil and religious rights to all.

4. *Resolved*, That a committee of eight be appointed to prepare and report an address to the Catholic community and the public at large, on the injustice which is done to the Catholics, in their civil and religious right, by the present operation of the common school system.

5. *Resolved*, That a committee of three be appointed to prepare a report on the public moneys which have been expended by the bounty of this State for education, both in colleges and in common schools, to which Catholics have contributed their proportion of taxes, like other citizens, but from which they have never received any benefit.

James W. McKeon, Esq., seconded the resolutions, and the following committees were appointed :

On the Address—Right Rev. Bishop Hughes, James W. McKeon, Thomas O'Connor, Dr. Sweeney, James W. White, James Kelley, Gregory Dillon, H. O'Connor, and John McLoughlin.

On the School Moneys—C. F. Grim, James W. McKeon, and James W. White.

At the meeting held in the same place on the 10th of August, the committee to prepare the address presented their report, which was read by Bishop Hughes. After the reverend speaker had concluded, on motion of Mr. Shorthill, the address was adopted ; and, on motion of Mr. Gallagher, it was ordered that five thousand copies be printed for distribution. The address will be found in the chapter which treats of the " Expurgation of the School Books."

The meeting was further addressed by Rev. CONSTANTINE D. PISE, one of the Roman Catholic clergymen of the city, an accomplished scholar and an earnest and eloquent preacher, and JAMES W. WHITE, Esq.

On the 24th of August and the 7th of September, adjourned meetings were held, at which Bishop Hughes continued his remarks upon the exciting question of the time. On the 21st, the committee appointed to prepare the memorial to the Common Council submitted their report, which was read by Bishop Hughes, the Chairman, after which a committee of four gentle-men—Messrs. Thomas O'Connor, Dr. Hugh Sweeney, James W. McKeon, and J. Kelley—was appointed, to proceed with the same to the Board of Aldermen, then in session, and present it to that body. Rev. Dr. Power rose to address the meeting, when the committee retired from the hall, and presented the memorial to the Board of Aldermen, as follows :

PETITION

To the Honorable the Board of Aldermen of the City of New York:

The petition of the Catholics of New York RESPECTFULLY REPRESENTS :

That your petitioners yield to no class in their performance of, and disposition to perform, all the duties of citizens. They bear, and are willing to bear their portion of every common burden ; and feel themselves entitled to a participation in every common benefit.

This participation, they regret to say, has been denied them for years back, in reference to common school education in the city of New York, except on conditions with which their conscience, and, as they believe, their duty to God, did not, and does not, leave them at liberty to comply.

The rights of conscience in this country are held by both the Constitution and universal consent, to be sacred and inviolable. No stronger evidence of this need be adduced than the fact, that one class of citizens are exempted from the duty or obligation of defending their country against any invading foe, out of delicacy and deference to the rights of conscience which forbids them to take up arms for any purpose.

Your petitioners only claim the benefit of this principle, in regard to the public education of their children. They regard the public education, which the State has provided as a common benefit, in which they are most desirous, and feel that they are entitled, to participate ; and therefore they pray your honorable body that they may be permitted to do so, without violating their conscience.

But your petitioners do not ask that this prayer be granted, without assigning their reasons for preferring it.

In ordinary cases, men are not required to assign the motives of conscientious scruples in matters of this kind. But your petitioners are aware that a large, wealthy, and concentrated influence is directed against their claim by the corporation called the Public School Society. And that this influence, acting on a public opinion already but too much predisposed to judge unfavorably of the claims of your petitioners, requires to be met by facts which justify them in thus appealing to your honorable body, and which may, at the same time, convey a more correct impression to the public mind. Your petitioners adopt this course the more willingly, because the justice and impartiality which distinguish the decisions of public men in this country, inspire them with the confidence that your honorable body will maintain, in their regard, the principle of the rights of conscience, if it can be done without violating the rights of others; and on no other condition is the claim solicited.

It is not deemed necessary to trouble your honorable body with a detail of the circumstances by which the monopoly of the public education of children in the city of New York, and of the funds provided for that purpose, at the expense of the State, have passed into the hands of a private corporation, styled, in its act of charter, "The Public School Society of the City of New York." It is composed of men of different sects or denominations. But that denomination of Friends, which is believed to have the controlling influence, both by its numbers and otherwise, holds as a *sectarian principle*, that any formal or official teaching of religion is, at best, unprofitable. And your petitioners have discovered that such of *their* children as have attended the public schools are generally, and at an early age, imbued with the same principle—that they become untractable, disobedient, and even contemptuous toward their parents—unwilling to learn any thing of religion—as if they had become illuminated, and could receive all the knowledge of religion necessary for them by instinct or inspiration. Your petitioners do not pretend to assign the cause of this change in their children; they only attest the fact as resulting from their attendace at the public schools of the Public School Society.

This Society, however, is composed of gentlemen of various sects, including even one or two Catholics. But they profess to exclude all sectarianism from their schools. If they do not exclude sectarianism, they are avowedly no more entitled to the school funds than your petitioners, or any other denomination of professing Christians. If they do as they profess, exclude sectarianism, then your petitioners contend that they exclude Christianity, and leave to the advantage of infidelity the tendencies which are given to the minds of youth by the influence of this feature and pretension of their system. If they could accomplish what they profess, other denominations would join your petitioners in remonstrating against their schools. But they do not accomplish it. Your petitioners will show your honorable body that they do admit what Catholics call sectarianism (although others may call it only religion), in a great variety of ways.

In their twenty-second report, as far back as the year 1827, they tell us, p. 14, that they " are aware of the importance of early religious instruction," and that none but what is " exclusively general and scriptural in its character, should be introduced into the schools under their charge." Here, then, is their own testimony that they did introduce and authorize " religious instruction " in their schools. And that they solved, with the utmost composure, the difficult question on which the sects disagree by determining what kind of " religious instruction " is " exclusively general and scriptural in its character."

Neither could they impart this " early religious instruction " themselves. They must have left it to their teachers; and these, armed with official influence, could impress those " early religious instructions " on the susceptible minds of the children, with the authority of dictators.

The Public School Society, in their report for the year 1832, p. 10, describe the effects of these " early religious instructions," without, perhaps, intending to do so, but yet precisely as your petitioners have witnessed it in such of their children as attended those schools. " The age at which children are usually sent to school affords a much better opportunity to mould their minds to peculiar and exclusive forms of faith, than any subsequent period of life." In p. 11 of the same report, they protest against the injustice of supporting " religion in any shape " by public money—as if the early religious instruction, which they themselves authorized in their schools five years before, was not " religion in some shape," and was not supported by public taxation. They tell us again, in more guarded language, " The trustees are deeply impressed with the importance of imbuing the youthful mind with religious impressions; and they have endeavored to attain this object, as far as the nature of the institution will admit." Report of 1837, p. 7.

In their thirty-third annual report, they tell us that " they would not be understood as regarding religious impressions in early youth as unimportant. On the contrary, they desire to do all which may with propriety be done to give a right direction to the minds of the children entrusted to their care. Their schools are uniformly opened with the reading of the Scriptures, and the class-books are such as recognize and enforce the great and generally acknowledged principles of Christianity." Page 7.

In their thirty-fourth annual report, for the year 1839, they pay a high compliment to a deceased teacher for the " moral and religious influence exerted by her over the three hundred girls daily attending her school," and tell us that " it could not but have a lasting effect on many of their susceptible minds." Page 7. And yet in all these " early religious instructions— religious impressions, and religious influence," essentially anti-Catholic— your petitioners are to see nothing sectarian. But if, in giving the education which the State requires, they were to bring the same influences to bear on the " susceptible minds of their *own* children, in favor, and not against their *own* religion, then this Society contends that it would be sectarian ! "

Your petitioners regret there is no means of ascertaining to what extent the teachers in the schools of the Society carried out the views of their principals, on the importance of conveying " early religious instructions " to the susceptible minds of the children.   But they believe it is in their power to prove that, in some instances, the Scriptures have been explained, as well as read, to the pupils.

Even the reading of the Scriptures in those schools, your petitioners cannot regard otherwise than as sectarian ; because Protestants would certainly consider as such the intention of the Catholic Scriptures, which are different from theirs : and the Catholics have the same ground to objection when the Protestant version is made use of.   Your petitioners have to state further, as grounds of their conscientious objections to those schools, that many of the selections in their elementary reading-lessons contain matter prejudicial to the Catholic name and character.   The term " popery " is repeatedly found in them.   This term is known and employed as one of insult and contempt toward the Catholic religion, and it passes into the minds of children with the feelings of which it is the outward expression.   Both the historical and religious portions of the reading-lessons are selected from Protestant writers, whose prejudices against the Catholic religion render them unworthy of confidence in the mind of your petitioners, at least so far as their own childen are concerned.

The Public School Society have heretofore denied that their books contained any thing reasonably objectionable to Catholics.   Proofs of the contrary could be multiplied, but it is unnecessary, as they have recently retracted their denial, and discovered, after fifteen years' enjoyment of their monopoly, that their books do contain objectionable passages.   But they allege that they have proffered repeatedly to make such corrections as the Catholic clergy might require.   Your petitioners conceive that such a proposal could not be carried into effect by the Public School Society, without giving just grounds for exceptions to other denominations.   Neither can they see with what consistency that Society can insist, as it has done, on the perpetuation of its monopoly, when the trustees thus avow their incompetency to present unexceptionable books, without the aid of the Catholic or any other clergy.   They allege, indeed, that with the best intentions they have been unable to ascertain the passages which might be offensive to Catholics.   With their intentions, your. petitioners cannot enter into any question.   Nevertheless, they submit to your honorable body that this Society is eminently incompetent for the superintendence of public education, if they could not see that the following passage was unfit for the public schools, and especially unfit to be placed in the hands of Catholic children.

They will quote the passage as one instance, taken from " Putnam's Sequel," p. 296.

Huss, John, a zealous reformer from popery, who lived in Bohemia toward the close of the fourteenth, and the beginning of the fifteenth centuries.   He was bold and persevering ; but at length, trusting to the *deceitful Catholics*, he was by them brought to trial, condemned as heretic, and burnt at the stake.

The Public School Society may be excused for not knowing the historical inaccuracies of this passage ; but surely assistance of the Catholic clergy could not have been necessary to an understanding of the word " deceitful," as applied to all who profess the religion of your petitioners.

For these reasons, and others of the same kind, your petitioners cannot in conscience, and conscientiously with their sense of duty to God and to their offspring, intrust the Public School Society with the office of giving " a right direction to the minds of their children." And yet this Society claims that office, and claims for the discharge of it the common school funds to which your petitioners, in common with other citizens, are contributors. In so far as they are contributors, they are not only deprived of any benefit in return, but their money is employed to the damage and detriment of their religion, on the minds of their own children, and of the rising generation of the community at large. The contest is between the *guaranteed* rights, civil and religious, of the citizen on the one hand, and the pretensions of the Public School Society on the other; and whilst it has been silently going on for years, your petitioners would call the attention of your honorable body to its consequences on the class for whom the benefits of public education are most essential—the children of the poor.

This class (your petitioners speak only so far as relates to their own denomination), after a brief experience of the schools of the Public School Society, naturally and deservedly withdraw all confidence from it. Hence the establishment by your petitioners of schools for the education of the poor.

The expense necessary for this was a second taxation, required not by the laws of the land, but the no less imperious demands of their conscience.

They were reduced to the alternative of seeing their children growing up in entire ignorance, or else taxing themselves anew for private schools, whilst the funds provided for education, and contributed in part by themselves, were given over to the Public School Society, and by them employed as has been stated above.

Now your petitioners respectfully submit, that without this confidence, no body of men can discharge the duties of education as intended by the State and required by the people. The Public School Society are, and have been at all times, conscious that they had not the confidence of the poor. In their twenty-eighth report, they appeal to the ladies of New York to create or procure it by the " persuasive eloquence of female kindness," p. 5; and from this they pass on to the next page, to the more efficient eloquence of coercion under penalities and privations, to be visited on all persons, " whether emigrant or otherwise," who, being in the circumstances of poverty referred to, should not send their children to some " public or other daily school."

In their twenty-seventh report, pp. 15 and 16, they plead for the doctrine, and recommend it to public favor, by the circumstance that it will affect but " few natives." But why should it be necessary at all, if they possessed that confidence of the poor, without which they need never hope to succeed ? So well are they convinced of this, that no longer ago than last year, they gave up all hope of inspiring it, and loudly called for coercion by " *the strong arm of the civil power* " to supply its deficiency. Your petitioners will

13

close this part of their statement with the expression of their surprise, and regret that gentlemen, who are themselves indebted much to the respect which is properly cherished for the rights of conscience, should be so unmindful of the same rights in the case of your petitioners. Many of them are by religious principle so pacific, that they would not take up arms in the defence of the liberties of their country, though she should call them to her aid : and yet they do not hesitate to invoke the "strong arm of the civil power" for the purpose of abridging the private liberties of their fellow-citizens, who may feel equally conscientious.

Your petitioners have to deplore, as a consequence of this state of things, the ignorance and vice to which hundreds, nay thousands of their children are exposed. They have to regret, also, that the education which they can provide, under the disadvantages to which they have been subjected, is not as efficient as it should be. But should your honorable body be pleased to designate their schools as entitled to realize a just proportion of the public funds which belong to your petitioners in common with other citizens, their schools could be improved for those who attend, others now growing up in ignorance could be received, and the ends of the Legislature could be accomplished—a result which is manifestly hopeless under the present system.

Your petitioners will now invite the attention of your honorable body to the objections and misrepresentations that have been urged by the Public School Society, to granting the claim of your petitioners. It is urged by them that it would be appropriating money raised by general taxation to the support of the Catholic religion. Your petitioners join issue with them, and declare unhesitatingly, that if this objection can be established, the claim shall be forthwith abandoned. It is objected that though we are taxed as citizens, we apply for the benefits of education as "Catholics." Your petitioners, to remove this difficulty, beg to be considered in their application in the identical capacity in which they are taxed, viz., as citizens of the commonwealth. It has been contended by the Public School Society that the law disqualified schools which admit any profession of religion, from receiving any encouragement from the school fund. Your petitioners have two solutions for this pretended difficulty. 1. Your petitioners are unable to discover any such disqualification in the law, which merely delegates to your honorable body the authority and discretion of determining what schools or societies shall be entitled to its bounty. 2. Your petitioners are willing to fulfill the conditions of the law as far as religious teaching is prescribed, during school hours. In fine, your petitioners, to remove all objections, are willing that the material organization of their schools, and the disbursements of the funds allowed for them, should be conducted and made by persons unconnected with the religion of your petitioners, even the Public School Society, if it should please your honorable body to appoint them for that purpose. The public may then be assured that the money will not be applied to the support of the Catholic religion.

It is deemed necessary by your petitioners, to save the Public School Society the necessity of future misconception, thus to state the things which are not petitioned for. The members of that Society who have shown themselves so impressed with the importance of conveying *their* notions of "early religious instruction" to the "susceptible minds" of Catholic children, can have no objection that the parents of the children, and teachers in whom the parents have confidence, should do the same, provided no law is violated thereby, and no disposition evinced to bring the children of other denominations within its influence.

Your petitioners, therefore, pray that your honorable body will be pleased to designate as among the schools entitled to participate in the common school fund, upon complying with the requirements of the law and the ordinances of the Corporation of the city, or for such other relief as to your honorable body, shall seem meet—St. Patrick's school, St. Peter's school, St. Mary's school, St. Joseph's school, St. James' school, St. Nicholas' school, Transfiguration Church school, and St. John's school.

And your petitioners further request, in the event of your honorable body's determining to hear your petitioners on the subject of their petition that such time may be appointed as may be most agreeable to your honorable body; and that a full session of your honorable board be convened for that purpose.

And your petitioners, &c.

THOMAS O'CONNOR, *Chairman.*

GREGORY DILLON,
ANDREW CARRIGAN, } *Vice-Chairmen,*
PETER DUFFY,

Of a general meeting of the Catholics of the city of New York, convened in the school-room of St. James' Church, 21st of September, 1840.

B. O'CONNOR, J. KELLY, J. McLAUGHLIN, *Secretaries.*

When the petition was presented to the board, Alderman Chamberlain offered the following resolution:

Resolved, That it be referred to a special committee to inquire into the expediency of granting the prayer of the petitioners, to be heard before the board, and that they report to this board with all convenient dispatch, and that the petition be printed.

Alderman Graham rose, and moved a substitute for the resolution of Alderman Chamberlain, as follows:

Resolved, That the petitioners be heard before the full board on the subject of the petition, and that the next regular meeting of the board be assigned for that purpose.

A division being called for by Alderman Graham, the question was decided in the negative, as follows:

Ayes—Aldermen Balis and Graham—2.

Nays—The President (Elijah F. Purdy), Aldermen Rich, Chamberlain, Campbell, Hatfield, Jarvis, Smith, Nichols, Cooper, and Nash—10.

The question was then put, on the motion of Alderman Chamberlain, and it was unanimously adopted. The President then appointed Messrs. Chamberlain, Graham, and Jarvis, as the committee.

On the 5th and 19th of October, adjourned meetings of the Catholics were held, at which Bishop Hughes, and others, made vigorous appeals on behalf of their movement.

Remonstrances were prepared on the part of the Public School Society and the Methodist Episcopal Church, which are as follows :

To the Honorable the Board of Aldermen of the City of New York:
The memorial and remonstrance of the Trustees of the Public School Society of New York, RESPECTFULLY REPRESENTS :
That your memorialists learn that a petition from the Roman Catholics of this city is now before your honorable body, in which they again ask for a portion of the school money in aid of the schools under their charge. After the late unanimous decision of one branch of the municipal government, in which the other was supposed tacitly to unite, adverse to several petitions of the same kind from religious societies, it is unexpected to your remonstrants to be so soon placed in a position which, in their opinion, renders it necessary to oppose the application of a large and influential body of their fellow-citizens. But until the confidence which has been so long reposed in them by the city government, and the public generally, is withdrawn, they feel it to be an imperious though an unpleasant duty to remonstrate against what they deem a dangerous application of funds raised for the promotion of common and general education.

The subject has, however, been so fully elucidated and ably argued, in documents now among the public records, that your remonstrants cannot hope to shed any additional light upon it. They therefore beg leave to refer your honorable body to Document No. 80 of the late Board of Assistant Aldermen, as containing the reasons on which your remonstrants would rely, in opposing the applications of religious societies for a portion of the school fund. It is believed that no decision of the city government ever met with a more general and cordial response in the public mind. And as the Roman Catholics very recently issued an address to the people of this city and State, urging at large their reasons for a separate appropriation of school money, to which your remonstrants have replied, they now present copies of said documents, which they respectfully submit to your honorable body, as containing matter relevant to the question under consideration.

The petition of the Roman Catholics now pending presents, nevertheless, some points which your remonstrants feel called upon to notice.

By a misapprehension of the law in relation to persons who are conscientiously opposed to bearing arms, which is applicable to persons of every religious persuasion, they attempt to adduce an argument in favor of the prayer of their petition, and say, that they only claim the benefit of the same principle in regard to the education of their children. Now the facts are, that the law imposes a fine, or tax, as an equivalent for personal military service, and, in the event of there being no property on which to levy, subjects such persons to imprisonment, and numbers are every year actually confined in the jails of this State.

With the religious opinions of the denomination of Christians referred to, your remonstrants have nothing to do. In opposing the claims of the Roman Catholic, and several other churches, to the school money, they have confined their remarks to the broad general grounds alike applicable to all ; but the petitioners have seen fit to single out a religious society by name, and intimate, or indirectly assert, not only that their peculiar religious views lead to insubordination and contempt of parental authority, but that the trustees of the public schools who are of this denomination, by reason of their numbers, or the " controlling influence " they exert, have introduced the " same principle " into the public schools, and that their effects are manifested in the conduct of the Catholic children who have attended them. Your remonstrants feel bound, therefore, in reply, to state that, of the one hundred citizens who compose the Board of Trustees, there are only twelve of the denomination thus traduced ; and of these, six or seven accepted the situation by solicitation of the board, for the purpose of superintending the management of the colored schools, to which object they have almost exclusively confined themselves. Of the motive that induced this extraordinary portion of the petition, your remonstrants will not trust themselves to speak ; of so much of it as conveys an idea that the trustees who are of this religious persuasion introduce, or attempt to introduce, into the public schools their own peculiar opinions, they can only say, that no one of the numerous and serious charges brought against your remonstrants by the petitioners is more entirely destitute of foundation in fact. If a disposition existed in any quarter to give a sectarian bias to the minds of the children, it will readily be seen that the most successful method would be through the selection of teachers.

In one of the documents now submitted to your honorable body, it is stated that, in appointing teachers, no regard is had by the trustees to the religious profession of the candidates, and that six or seven of the present number are Roman Catholics. From an inquiry now made, it is found that only two of the teachers belong to the " Society of Friends."

It will thus be seen that the charge made in the petition of the Roman Catholics, that such of their children as have attended the public schools are generally, and at an early age, imbued with a principle which they impute to a portion of the trustees, falls to the ground, and is proved to be as unfounded as it is illiberal and ungenerous.

It is with regret that your remonstrants find themselves under the painful necessity of saying, that the petition of the Catholics contains garbled extracts and detached portions of some parts of their annual reports in relation to religious instruction, and so arranged and commented upon as to convey a meaning directly opposite to the one intended and clearly expressed in the original documents.

The same means are resorted to in quoting the language of the trustees, when urging the importance of using measures for inducing the poor to have their children educated. On different occasions, your remonstrants have suggested to the Common Council the expediency of requiring, by legal enactment, the attendance at some " public or other daily school" of the numerous " vagrant children who roam about our streets and wharves, begging and pilfering;" and this is tortured, in the Catholic petition, into a desire of " abridging the private liberties of their fellow-citizens," and an acknowledgment on the part of the trustees " that they had not the confidence of the poor."

The records of the schools will demonstrate that the industrious and respectable portions of the laboring classes repose entire confidence in the public school system and its managers.

The subject of objectionable matter in the books used in the public schools is so fully discussed in the papers now submitted to your honorable body, that little more would seem to be called for under this head. Finding their strenuous and long continued efforts to induce the Catholic clergy to unite in an expurgation of the books unavailing, the trustees commenced the work without them, and it is now nearly completed. If any thing remains to which the petitioners can take exception, no censure can by possibility attach to your remonstrants; and the trustees assert with confidence, that, if any has escaped them, there is now less matter objectionable to the Roman Catholics to be found in the books used in the public schools than in those of any other seminary of learning, either public or private, within this State.

In conclusion, your remonstrants would remark that they have not thought it expedient, on this occasion, to enter into a detailed defence of their conduct as regards all of the charges preferred by the Roman Catholics. Those charges are before your honorable body, and the trustees will cheerfully submit to any inquiry that you may see fit to institute in relation to them; and, even if it can be shown that your remonstrants are as " eminently incompetent to the superintendence of public education " as the petition of the Roman Catholics intimates, it would not, they respectfully suggest, furnish any apology for breaking down one of the most important bulwarks of the civil and religious liberties of the American people.

Should your honorable body decide to hear the petitioners before the collected board, your remonstrants respectfully ask to be heard on the same occasion, in reply.

ROBERT C. CORNELL, *President.*

A. P. HALSEY, *Secretary.*

NEW YORK, *October 3d,* 1840.

To the Honorable the Common Council of the City of New York:

The undersigned committee, appointed by the pastors of the Methodist

Episcopal Church in this city, on the part of said pastors and churches, do MOST RESPECTFULLY REPRESENT:

That they have heard with surprise and alarm that the Roman Catholics have renewed their application to the Common Council for an appropriation from the common school fund, for the support of the schools under their own direction, in which they teach, and propose still to teach, their own sectarian dogmas, not only to their own children, but to such Protestant children as they may find means to get into these schools.

Your memorialists had hoped that the clear, cogent, and unanswerable arguments by which the former application for this purpose was resisted, would have saved the Common Council from further importunity.

It was clearly shown, that the Council could not legally make any sectarian appropriation of the public funds; and it was as clearly shown that it would be utterly destructive of the whole scheme of public school instruction to do so, even if it could be legally done. But it seems that neither the Constitution of the State nor the public welfare are to be regarded, when they stand in the way of Roman Catholic sectarianism and exclusiveness.

It must be manifest to the Common Council, that, if the Roman Catholic claims are granted, all the other Christian denominations will urge their claims for a similar appropriation, and that the money raised for education by a general tax will be solely applied to the purposes of proselytism, through the medium of sectarian schools. But if this were done, would it be the price of peace? or would it not throw the apple of discord into the whole Christian community, should we agree in the division of the spoils? Would each sect be satisfied with the portion allotted to it? We venture to say that the sturdy claimants who now beset the Council would not be satisfied with much less than the lion's share; and we are sure that there are other Protestant denominations beside ourselves who would not patiently submit to the exaction. But, when all the Christian sects shall be satisfied with their individual share of the public fund, what is to become of those children whose parents belong to none of these sects, and who cannot conscientiously allow them to be educated in the peculiar dogmas of any one of them? The different committees who, on a former occasion, approached your honorable body, have shown that, to provide schools for these only, would require little less than is now expended; and it requires little arithmetic to show that, when the religious sects have taken all, nothing will remain for those who have not yet been able to decide which of the Christian denominations to prefer. It must be plain to every impartial observer, that the applicants are opposed to the whole system of public school instruction; and it will be found that the uncharitable exclusiveness of their creed must ever be opposed to all public instruction which is not under the direction of their own priesthood. They may be conscientious in all this; but, though it be no new claim on their part, we cannot yet allow them to guide and control the consciences of all the rest of the community. We are sorry that the reading of the Bible in the public schools, without note or commentary, is offensive to them; but we cannot allow the Holy Scriptures to be accompanied with *their* notes and commentaries, and to be put into the hands of the children who may hereafter be the rulers and legislators of our beloved country ; because, among other bad things taught in these commentaries, is to be found the lawfulness of murdering heretics, and the unqualified submission, in all matters of conscience, to the Roman Catholic Church.

But if the principle on which this application is based should be admitted, it must be carried far beyond the present purpose.

If all are to be released from taxation when they cannot conscientiously derive any benefit from the disbursement of the money collected, what will be done for the Society of Friends, and other sects who are opposed to war under all circumstances ? Many of these, besides the tax paid on all foreign goods thus consumed, pay direct duties at the Custom House, which go to the payment of the army and to purchase the munitions of war. And even when the Government finds it necessary to lay direct war taxes, these conscientious sects are compelled to pay their proportion, on the ground that the public defence requires it. So, it is believed, the public interest requires the education of the whole rising generation ; because it would be unsafe to commit the public liberty, and the perpetuation of our republican institutions, to those whose ignorance of their nature and value would render them careless of their preservation, or the easy dupes of artful innovators ; and hence every citizen is required to contribute in proportion to his means to the public purpose of universal education.

The Roman Catholics complain that books have been introduced into the public schools which are injurious to them as a body. It is allowed, however, that the passages in these books to which such reference is made are chiefly, if not entirely, historical ; and we put it to the candor of the Common Council to say, whether any history of Europe for the last ten centuries could be written which could either omit to mention the Roman Catholic Church, or mention it without recording historical facts unfavorable to that Church ? We assert, that if all the historical facts in which the Church of Rome has taken a prominent part could be taken from writers of her own communion only, the incidents might be made more objectionable to the complainants than any book to which they now object.

History itself, then, must be falsified for their accommodation ; and yet they complain that the system of education adopted in the public schools does not teach the sinfulness of lying ! They complain that no religion is taught in these schools, and declare that any, even the worst form of Christianity, would be better than none : and yet they object to the reading of the Holy Scriptures, which are the only foundation of all true religion. Is it not plain, then, that they will not be satisfied with any thing short of the total abandonment of public school instruction, or the appropriation of such portion of the public fund as they may claim to their own sectarian purposes.

But this is not all. They have been most complaisantly offered the censorship of the books to be used in the public schools. The committee to whom has been confided the management of these schools in this city offered to allow the Roman Catholic bishop to expurgate from these books any thing offensive to him.

But the offer was not accepted;—perhaps for the same reason that he declined to decide on the admissibility of a book of extracts from the Bible, which had been sanctioned by certain bishops in Ireland. An appeal, it seems, had gone to the pope on the subject, and nothing could be said or done in the matter until His Holiness had decided. The Common Council of New York will therefore find that, when they shall have conceded to the Roman Catholics of this city the selection of books for the use of the public schools, that these books must undergo the censorship of a foreign potentate. We hope the time is far distant when the citizens of this country will allow any foreign power to dictate to them in matters relating to either general or municipal law.

We cannot conclude this memorial without noticing one other ground on which the Roman Catholics, in their late appeal to their fellow-citizens, urged their sectarian claims, and excused their conscientious objections to the public schools. Their creed is dear to them, it seems, because some of their ancestors have been martyrs to their faith. This was an unfortunate allusion. Did not the Roman Catholics know that they addressed many of their fellow-citizens who could not recur to the memories of their own ancestors without being reminded of the revocation of the Edict of Nantes, the massacre of St. Bartholomew's day, the fires of Smithfield, or the crusade against the Waldenses? We would willingly cover these scenes with the mantle of charity, and hope that our Roman Catholic fellow-citizens will, in future, avoid whatever has a tendency to revive the painful remembrance.

Your memorialists had hoped that the intolerance and exclusiveness which had characterized the Roman Catholic Church in Europe had been greatly softened under the benign influences of our civil institutions. The pertinacity with which their sectarian interests are now urged has dissipated the illusion. We were content with their having excluded us, *ex cathedra*, from all claim to heaven, for we were sure they did not possess the keys, notwithstanding their confident pretension; nor did we complain that they would not allow us any participation in the benefits of purgatory, for it is a place they have made for themselves, and of which they may claim the exclusive property; but we do protest against any appropriation of the public school fund for their exclusive benefit, or for any other purposes whatever.

Assured that the Common Council will do what it is right to do in the premises, we are, gentlemen, with great respect,

Your most obedient servants,

N. BANGS,
THOMAS E. BOND,
GEORGE PECK.

On the 19th of October, the remonstrance of the Public School Society, and of the Methodists, were presented to the Board of Aldermen, and laid on the table until the report of the committee to whom the petition of the Catholics had been referred should be submitted to the board. When the reports of committees came up in the regular order of business, the special committee made a brief report, in which they recommended the following resolution :

Resolved, That the Board of Aldermen cheerfully grant the prayer of our Catholic fellow-citizens, to be allowed the privilege of being heard in support of their petition to have St. Patrick's school, St. Peter's school, St. Mary's school, St. Joseph's school, St. James' school, St. Nicholas' school, Transfiguration Church school, and St. John's school, designated as among the schools entitled to participate in the common school fund ; and that the President of the Board of Aldermen be requested to call a special meeting of the board on Friday evening next, at 4 o'clock P. M., and that he be requested to invite the members of the Board of Assistant Aldermen to hear the discussion, and that the privilege of discussing the same subject, in the same manner, be also extended to all other parties interested in it, either by counsel or otherwise.

The resolution was adopted, and the memorials and remonstrances were taken from the table, and referred to the committee.

The meeting was not held until Thursday, the 29th, when the Common Council assembled for the purpose of hearing the arguments by the petitioners and remonstrants, and a protracted debate ensued, the report of which was made for the *Freeman's Journal*. After the organization of the meeting and the reading of the preceding papers, the Right Rev. Bishop HUGHES rose to address the board in behalf of the Catholics, and spoke as follows :

Gentlemen of the Board of Aldermen :
Unaccustomed as I am to address a body of gentlemen such as I see here before me, I may not always be correct in the manner of my address; I hope, therefore, that any mistakes of mine may be imputed by this honorable board to my inexperience. I would also, on the threshold of the subject, observe, that in no part of the discussion on this question, so far as it has gone, am I conscious of having imputed to any gentleman who is opposed to the claim in which I have so deep an interest, any motive or design of a sinister character. I am sorry, therefore, that the Public School Society should have been pleased to refer to the language of our document as though imputation had thereby been cast upon their motives. I am sure, if they again review our documents, they will not find one solitary instance of any imputation dishonorable to them personally as gentlemen. We speak of their system apart from themselves ; and we speak of it with that free-

dom which it is the right of American citizens to speak of the public actions and public proceedings of public men; but again will I repeat, that in no instance to my knowledge has there been imputed to those gentlemen one solitary motive, one single purpose, unworthy of their high standing and their respectable character. They have alleged, in some of their documents, that we charge them with teaching infidelity; but we have not done so. We charge it as the result of their system—not that they are actively engaged in teaching infidelity; and not only do we not say this, but we interpose the declaration, that we do not believe such to be their intention, but that the system has gone beyond their intention. Yet, after this, they ascribe to themselves these imputations, and they cap their salvo by saying, that even the authors of the address shrink from a picture of their own coloring—a picture which they not only charge that we have drawn of them, but also of all other classes and denominations of our fellow-citizens. Now, I venture to repeat, that in no instance have we imputed to them motives which can reflect on them as honorable men. I make these observations in the commencement, simply to show how much has been written of the petitioners on assumptions which have no foundation on any thing that has been written or said by us. I know well the Public School Society is an institution highly popular in the city of New York; but I should be sorry to suppose that those gentlemen would permit themselves to interpose that popularity between them and the JUSTICE which we contend for when we seek that to which we believe we have a legal right. At the same time it is proper for me, at the commencement, to clear away another objection which an attempt has been made, in both the remonstrances that have been read, to oppose to the exceedingly simple principle for which we contend. The attempt has been made (and you will perceive the whole document, which issued as a report from the Board of Assistant Aldermen, as well as the remonstrances of the Public School Society and the Methodist Episcopal Church, is based on the same false assumption) to assume false premises in this matter; which are, that we want this money for the promotion of the ecclesiastical interests of our Church. Now, if these societies wish to enter their remonstrances against our petition, they should first read the language in which we have urged our claim; and if they had, they would have saved themselves the trouble, in my opinion, of reasoning on arguments which are but figments of their own creation, and no proposition of ours. Have not we distinctly stated not only what we want, but, to guard them against accusing us of what we do not want, have we not said that we do not want the public money to promote ecclesiastical interests?—for, to this money, for such a purpose, we have no right. And, also, have we not further stated, that, if it can be shown that we want the money for this purpose, that we will abandon our claim—that, if it can be shown that we want it for sectarian interests, we will relinquish it altogether? We have said, in the first place:

Your petitioners will now invite the attention of your honorable body to the objections and misrepresentations that have been urged by the Public School Society to granting the claim of your petitioners. It is urged by them that it would be appropriating money raised by general taxation to the support of the Catholic religion. Your petitioners join issue with them, and declare unhesitatingly that, if this objection can be established, the claim shall be forthwith abandoned. It is objected that, though we are taxed as citizens, we apply for the benefits of education as " Catholics." Your petitioners, to remove this difficulty, beg to be considered in their application in the identical capacity in which they are taxed—viz., as citizens of the commonwealth. It has been contended by the Public School Society, that the law disqualifies schools which admit any profession of religion from receiving any encouragements from the school fund. Your petitioners have two solutions for this pretended difficulty. First, your petitioners are unable to discover any such disqualification in law, which merely delegates to your honorable body the authority and discretion of determining what schools or societies shall be entitled to its bounty. Secondly, your petitioners are willing to fulfil the conditions of the law so far as religious teaching is proscribed during school hours. In fine, your petitioners, to remove all objections, are willing that the material organization of their schools, and the disbursements of the funds allowed for them, shall be conducted and made by persons unconnected with the religion of your petitioners, even the Public School Society, if it should please your honorable body to appoint them for that purpose. The public may then be assured that the money will not be applied to the support of the Catholic religion.

It is deemed necessary by your petitioners—to save the Public School Society the necessity of future misconception—thus to state the things which are *not* petitioned for.

Yet, notwithstanding this clear and simple language, you perceive both the remonstrances of the School Society and the Episcopal Methodists go on this false issue, that we want this money for sectarian and illegal purposes! Our language could not be plainer than it was on this point, and yet there has been uncharitableness enough in these societies to assert the contrary. I have deemed it necessary to make this explanation at the commencement, to impress your minds, gentlemen, with what it is we seek and what it is we seek not, because I know a deal may be done toward a proper elucidation of this subject by preserving its simplicity. The remonstrants warn you, gentlemen, against giving money for sectarian purposes. We join them in that admonition. We contend that we look in honesty and simplicity alone for the benefits of education; and, as members of the commonwealth, and as Catholics, we seek but that which we believe to be just, and legal, and right.

I shall now, gentlemen, review very briefly both the documents, because they submit to your honorable body the grounds on which that claim, which we believe to be just, is opposed. After the introduction of that from the Public School Society, we find, in the second paragraph, the following passages .

The subject has, however, been so fully elucidated and ably argued, in documents now among the public records, that your remonstrants cannot hope to shed any additional light upon it. They therefore beg leave to refer your honorable body to Document No. 80 of the Board of Assistant Aldermen, as containing the reasons on which your remonstrants would rely in opposing the applications of religious societies for a portion of the school fund. It is believed that no decision of the city government ever met with a more general and cordial response in the public mind.

Yes, it may well be so believed, for the reason that that whole document went on a *false issue*, and therefore it was thus believed. But if I prove— as I shall—that the premises had no foundation in reality, then the arguments founded thereon must fall to the ground, for they were but castles in the air. It proceeds:

As the Roman Catholics very recently issued an address to the people of this city and State, urging at large their reasons for a separate appropriation of school money, to which your remonstrants have replied, they now present copies of said documents, which they respectfully submit to your honorable body, as containing matter relevant to the question under consideration.

The petition of the Roman Catholics now pending presents, nevertheless, some points which your remonstrants feel called upon to notice.

By a misapprehension of the law in relation to persons who are conscientiously opposed to bearing arms, which is applicable to persons of every religious persuasion, they attempt to adduce an argument in favor of the prayer of their petition, and say that they only claim the benefit of the same principle in regard to the education of their children. Now, the facts are, that the law imposes a fine, or tax, as an equivalent for personal military services, and, in the event of there being no property on·which to levy, subjects such persons to imprisonment, and numbers are every year actually confined in the jails of this State.

Now I conceive the illustration there referred to was a strong one. The parents and guardians of tender offspring have a right connected with their nature by God himself in His wise providence, and they should be shown a strong reason for transferring it to others. And I adduced it as an illustration, and as a strong one—why? Because the defence of the country is a thing connected with self-existence and preservation; and yet, so tender is the genius of this happy country of the rights of conscience, it dispensed with all those who had religious scruples from a compliance with the law, and changed it into a small fine, whereby the right was shown, and also the disposition, to waive it.

With the religious opinions of the denomination of Christians referred to, your remonstrants have nothing to do. In opposing the claims of the Roman Catholic, and several other churches, to the school money, they have confined their remarks to broad general grounds alike applicable to all; but the petitioners have seen fit to single out a religious society by name, and intimate, or indirectly assert, not only that their peculiar religious views lead to insubordination and contempt of parental authority, but that the trustees of the public schools who are of this denomination, by their numbers, or the "controlling influence" they exert, have introduced the "same principle" into the public schools, and that their effects are manifested in the conduct of the Catholic children who have attended them.

Now, I am exceedingly surprised that those gentlemen should go so far from the text to draw reproach upon themselves. We said nothing to authorize this language. We simply stated the fact; we mentioned the circumstance of the controlling influence of those holding peculiar sectarian views; but we did not draw the conclusion whether the insubordination of the children of our poor people was the result of the principles taught in the schools, or of a want of domestic influence. And yet these gentlemen have gone on to draw upon themselves an imputation of which we respectfully disclaim the authorship. They proceed:

Your remonstrants feel bound, therefore, in reply, to state that of the one hundred citizens who compose the Board of Trustees, there are only twelve of the denomination thus traduced,——

Now, to this charge of traducing we beg to demur.

—— and of these, six or seven accepted the situation by solicitation of the board, for the purpose of superintending the management of the colored schools, to which object they have almost exclusively confined themselves.

Now I should be one of the last to detract from the merits of this denomination. Some of them I have known personally, and others by their history, and my opinion has always been of them that they are among the foremost in every benevolent act and social virtue, and to lend their arm to strengthen the weak and the oppressed; and therefore it is no reproach to them that they take the lead in this work of benevolence, for which I give them credit.

They go on to say:

Of the motive that induced this extraordinary portion of the petition, your remonstrants will not trust themselves to speak,——

It might be recollected, gentlemen, if there were a leaning that way, it was after the publication of the " Reply " to our " Address," which, though it has the name, is no *reply* to our arguments. It is not an answer; but in it they take the occasion to sneer at us, as I shall soon have occasion to show; yet I may here observe that it would have been better if they had addressed themselves to the principles of eternal justice on which we rest.

Of so much of it (they add) as conveys an idea, that the trustees who are of this religious persuasion, introduce, or attempt to introduce into the public schools, their own peculiar opinions——

We never charged that they did.

—— they can only say that no one of the numerous and serious charges brought against your remonstrants by the petitioners, is more entirely destitute of foundation in fact. If a disposition existed in any quarter to give a sectarian bias to the minds of the children, it will readily be seen that the most successful method would be through the selection of teachers.

Why there was no necessity for this vindication at all.

In one of the documents now submitted to your honorable body, it is stated, that in appointing teachers, no regard is had by the trustees to the religious profession of the candidates, and that six or seven of the present number are Roman Catholics.

I have seen this statement figure in almost every document of that Society, and yet I have not been able to find " six or seven of the present number who are Roman Catholics; " and I doubt if they can be found, except they are such Roman Catholics as we see our children become after they have been in these public schools—that is, Catholics who have no feelings in common with their Church—Catholics who are ashamed of the name, because in the school-books and from the teachers they hear of its professors only as " papists," and of the religion itself only as " popery." It is such as these, I fear, that pass as Catholics.   I only know of one who is worthy of the name.

From an inquiry now made it is found that only two of the teachers belong to the " Society of Friends."

And I don't suppose that better teachers could be obtained anywhere, when confined within the limits prescribed ; except they have the privilege to introduce religious instruction.   And without that it matters but little whether they are of the Society of Friends, or not.   They continue :

It is with regret that your remonstrants find themselves under the painful necessity of saying that the petition of the Catholics contains garbled extracts and detached portions of some parts of their annual reports in relation to religious instruction, and so arranged and commented upon, as to convey a meaning directly opposite to the one intended and clearly expressed in the original documents.

Now I will allow the reading of it, and if there are any garbled extracts there, I will be the first to correct it.   But I am surprised when we quote the words of their documents, that they should urge this charge.   Let the documents be read.   I have no dread on this subject.

The same means are resorted to in quoting the language of the trustees when urging the importance of using measures for inducing the poor to have their children educated.   On different occasions your remonstrants have suggested to the Common Council, the expediency of requiring, by legal enactment, the attendance at some " public or other daily school," of the numerous " vagrant children who roam about our streets and wharves, begging and pilfering," and this is tortured in the Catholic petition into a desire of " abridging the private liberties of their fellow-citizens," and an acknowledgment, on the part of the trustees, " that they had not the confidence of the poor."

Yet I should think, gentlemen, such a reluctance to attend their schools as to make it necessary to apply for a legal enactment to procure first the money, and then to compel an attendance, would show that they did want that confidence.   I know they have not the confidence of our body.   Yes, they have obtained two enactments from the Common Council, depriving the parents, in time of need—even when cold and starvation have set in upon them—of public relief, unless the children were sent to these or some other schools.   And I have seen them urging ladies in their public documents, to obtain their confidence by soothing words ; and I have seen them urging employers to make it the condition of employment.   Yet, after all this, they pretend that they have had the confidence of the poor.   I do not say that they have not merited it according to *their* views ; but I do not think they should expect all mankind to submit to their views of the matter, to the sacrifice of their own.

They say :

The records of the schools will demonstrate that the industrious and respectable portions of the laboring classes repose entire confidence in the public school system and its managers.

Then that portion in behalf of whom I stand here is not to be classed with " the industrious and respectable ! "

They then proceed to another point :

The subject of objectionable matter in the books used in the public schools, is so fully discussed in the papers now submitted to your honorable body, that little more would seem to be called for under this head. Finding their strenuous and long-continued efforts to induce the Catholic clergy to unite in an expurgation of the books unavailing, the trustees commenced the work without them, and it is now nearly completed. If any thing remains, to which the petitioners can take exception, no censure can, by possibility, attach to your remonstrants ; and the trustees assert with confidence, that if any has escaped them, there is now less matter objectionable to the Roman Catholics, to be found in the books used in the public schools, than in those of any other seminary of learning, either public or private, within this State.

Now they could not adopt a worse test, for I defy you to find a reading-book in either public or private seminary, that in respect to Catholics is not full of ignorance. Not a book. For if it were clear of this, it would not be popular ; and if they refer to this then, they refer to a standard which we repudiate. But it must be remembered those people can send their children to those schools or keep them at home. They are not TAXED for their support. But here we are. It is the public money which is here used to preserve the black blots which have been attempted to be fixed on the Catholic name. They say again (and it is an idea that will go exceedingly well with the public at large, for it will show how amiable and conciliating are these gentlemen)—that they have submitted the books to us as though we have nothing to do but to mark out a passage, and it will disappear. But are we to take the odium of erasing passages which they hold to be true ? Have they the right to make such an offer ? And if we spend the necessary time in reviewing the books to discover passages to be expurgated, have they given us a pledge that they will do it, or that they will not even then keep them in ? Have they given us a pledge that they will do it as far as their denomination is concerned ? And, then, after all the loss of time which it would require to review these books, they can either remove the objectionable passages, or preserve them, as they see fit. An individual cannot answer for a whole body. They may make a fine offer which may be calculated to impose on the public, but if we put the question if they are able and if they are willing, I should like to know whether they can, and will, pass a law to show us that they are sincere, and that the object can be carried out ? That would alter the case ; for we may correct one passage to-day, and another next week ; and then another body may come into power, and we may have to petition again and again. Could they, then, do it if they would ? And should they, if they could ?

They add :

In conclusion, your remonstrants would remark, that they have not thought it expedient, on this occasion, to enter into a detailed defence of their conduct as regards all of the charges preferred by the Roman Catholics. Those charges are before your honorable body, and the trustees will cheerfully submit to any inquiry that you may see fit to institute in relation to them ; and even if it can be shown that your remonstrants are as " eminently incompetent to the superintendence of public education " as the petition of the Roman Catholics intimates, it would not, they respectfully suggest, furnish any apology for breaking down one of the most important bulwarks of the civil and religious liberties of the American people.

This much, then, as regards this document, which, it will be perceived, goes on the false assumption that we want this money for a sectarian purpose, because it was so referred to in the report of the committee of the Board of Assistant Aldermen, which denied our claim; for, when I come to that, it will be found that every proposition in it goes on the assumption that we wish this money for religious purposes. If we did, it would be just to deny it to us. But I will now take up another document, and I regret that I cannot treat it with the respect I would otherwise wish to do. The document from the Public School Society, however it might have been led aside, and however feeble in its reasoning, contained nothing, I trust and believe, which was intended to be disrespectful to us. It was couched in language at which I cannot take offence. Though it was weak in its principles, its reasoning was decent. I cannot say as much for this, which is from

The undersigned committee, appointed by the pastors of the Methodist Episcopal Church in this city.

They commence by observing,

That they have heard with surprise and alarm——

They should have seen our petition, instead of taking "hearsay" for their authority.

—— that the Roman Catholics have renewed their application to the Common Council for an appropriation from the common school fund, for the support of the schools under their own direction, in which they teach, and propose still to teach, their own sectarian dogmas.

Where did they find that? Where did they find that statement? I should like to know, from the gentlemen who signed this remonstrance, where they have their authority for such an assertion? We disclaim it in the petition against which they remonstrate. It shows, then, how much trust can be placed in "hearsay," when they should and might have examined the petition against which they remonstrate, in which they can find no such thing.

In which they teach, and propose still to teach, their own sectarian dogmas: not only to their own children, but to such Protestant children as they may find means to get into these schools.

I ask these gentlemen again, what authority they have for such an assertion? I should like to see the argument which gives them their authority to use language and to make a statement so palpably false as this is.

Your memorialists had hoped that the clear, cogent, and unanswerable arguments by which the former application for this purpose was resisted, would have saved the Common Council from further importunity.

We shall see whether the arguments were so clear, cogent, and unanswerable, by and by.

14

It was clearly shown that the Council could not legally make any sectarian appropriation of the public funds; and it was clearly shown that it would be utterly destructive of the whole scheme of public school instruction to do so, even if it could be legally done. But it seems that neither the Constitution of the State nor the public welfare are to be regarded, when they stand in the way of Roman Catholic sectarianism and exclusiveness.

There is an inference for you!—and a very unfounded one it is, too.

It must be manifest to the Common Council, that, if the Roman Catholic claims are granted, all the other Christian denominations will urge their claims for a similar appropriation——

And, I say, they have the right to do it. I wish they would do it, for I believe it would be better for the future character of the city, and for its fame, when this generation shall have passed away. If they did claim it, and the claim was granted, then an effort would be made to raise good and pious and honest men.

—— and that the money raised for education by a general tax will be solely applied to the purposes of proselytism, through the medium of sectarian schools. But if this were done, would it be the price of peace? or would it not throw the apple of discord into the whole Christian community? Should we agree in the division of the spoils?

I am exceedingly sorry that the gentlemen who drew up the remonstrance had not more confidence in the power of their own religious principle, than to suppose that it would be necessary to contend violently for what they call the "spoils." We have submitted to be deprived of them for years, and we have not manifested such a disposition; and I am surprised that they, who understand so much of the power of religion, should attach so much value to the little money which is to be distributed, as to suppose that it would set Christians—professing Christians—together by the ears in its distribution.

Should we agree in the division of the spoils? Would each sect be satisfied with the portion allotted to it? We venture to say, that the sturdy claimants who now beset the Council would not be satisfied with much less than the lion's share; and we are sure that there are other Protestant denominations besides ourselves who would not patiently submit to the exaction.

After what they have said by authority as the grounds of their opposition, where, instead, they should have had history for their guide, I am not surprised that they should prophesy in the matter. I, too, may prophesy, and I will say that the "sturdy claimants" are as respectable as they are, and I trust it will never be attributable to us that we claim more than is our common right; and if that should be violated with respect to the Methodist Episcopal denomination, we shall be far from the ranks of those who may be the violators.

But, when all the Christian sects shall be satisfied with their individual share of the public fund, what is to become of those children whose parents belong to none of these sects, and who cannot conscientiously allow them to be educated in the peculiar dogmas of any one of them? The different committees who, on a former occasion, approached your honorable body, have shown that, to provide schools for these only, would require little less than is now expended; and it requires little arithmetic to show that, when the religious sects have taken all, nothing will remain for those who have not yet been able to decide which of the Christian denominations to prefer. It must be plain to every impartial observer, that the applicants are opposed to the whole system of public school instruction.

Have we said so? And on what authority have these gentlemen the right to say it, if we have not? Where are their data? And yet they come before this honorable body and make such assertions, with the sanction of their whole Church!

And it will be found that the uncharitable exclusiveness of their creed must ever be opposed to all public instruction which is not under the direction of their own priesthood. They may be conscientious in all this; but, though it be no new claim on their part, we cannot yet allow them to guide and control the consciences of all the rest of the community.

Why, it would be a silly and absurd thing, on our part, to look for it. But we never thought of it. It is a fiction of these gentlemen's own creation. I contend, we ask nothing for the community, but for ourselves, and I trust it will be granted if it is right; and if we can be shown that it is not right, we will abandon it cheerfully. But their assertion is wholly destitute of foundation.

We are sorry that the reading of the Bible in the public schools, without note or commentary, is offensive to them; but we cannot allow the Holy Scriptures to be accompanied with *their* notes and commentaries——

Have we asked such a thing?—or in any way solicited it?

—— and to be put into the hands of the children, who may hereafter be the rulers and legislators of our beloved country; because, among other bad things taught in these commentaries, is to be found the lawfulness of murdering heretics, and the unqualified submission, in all matters of conscience, to the Roman Catholic Church.

I have a feeling of respect for many of their denomination, but not for the head or the heart of those who drew this document up. Here it states an unqualified falsehood. Here it puts forth a false proposition, and that proposition has been introduced here as a slander. I can prove that it is so. And, depending on the confidence here reposed in me, I propose and pledge myself to forfeit a thousand dollars, to be appropriated in charities as this Council may direct, if those gentlemen can prove the truth of this allegation; provided they agree to the same forfeiture, to be appropriated in a similar manner, if they fail to establish its truth. If they can prove that the Catholic Church sanctions, or has made it lawful, to murder heretics, I will forfeit that sum. I feel indignant that we should be met, when we come with a plain and reasonable and honest request to submit to the proper authorities, with slanders such as that, and that in the name of religion, which is holy. I wish them to hear what I say. I know very well their books tell them so; but they should look at the original, and not at secondary authorities, when they assail our reputation and our rights.

But if the principle on which this application is based should be admitted, it must be carried far beyond the present purpose. If all are to be released from taxation when they cannot conscientiously derive any benefit from the disbursement of the money collected, what will be done for the Society of Friends, and other sects who are opposed to war under all circumstances?

With that I have nothing to do, and therefore I will pass on to another point.

The Roman Catholics complain that books have been introduced into the public schools which are injurious to them as a body. It is allowed, however, that the passages in these books, to which such reference is made, are chiefly, if not entirely, historical; and we put it to the candor of the Common Council to say whether any history of Europe, for the last ten centuries, could be written which could either omit to mention the Roman Catholic Church, or mention it without recording historical facts unfavorable to that Church.

And this is what the remonstrants call a strong issue. They assert that no history could be written which could either omit to mention the Roman Catholic Church, or mention it without recording historical facts unfavorable to the Catholic Church. If this be the case, I ask you whether, as citizens entitled to the rights of citizens, we are to be compelled to send our children to schools which *cannot* teach our children history without blackening us? But again they say:

We assert that, if all the historical facts in which the Church of Rome has taken a prominent part, could be taken from writers of her own communion only, the incidents might be made more objectionable to the complainants than any book to which they now object.

No doubt of it; and it only proves that Catholic historians have no interest to conceal what is the truth. But I contend that there are pages in Catholic history brighter than any in the history of Methodism; and that there are questions and passages enough for reading-lessons, without selecting such as will lead the mind of the Catholic child to be ashamed of his ancestors. The Methodist Episcopal Church is a respectable Church, and I am willing to treat it with becoming respect; but it is a young Church; it is not so old as the Catholic Church, and therefore has fewer crimes; but I contend, again, it has fewer virtues to boast of. And, in its career of a hundred years, it has done as little for mankind as any other denomination.

History itself, then, must be falsified for their accommodation; and yet they complain that the system of education adopted in the public schools does not teach the sinfulness of lying!

We shall come to that presently.

They complain that no religion is taught in these schools, and declare that any, even the worst form of Christianity, would be better than none; and yet they object to the reading of the Holy Scriptures, which are the only foundation of all true religion. Is it not plain, then, that they will not be satisfied with any thing short of the total abandonment of public school instruction, or the appropriation of such portion of the public fund as they may claim to their own sectarian purposes?

All the time they go on the false issue. They charge that which we disclaim, and they reason on a charge of their own invention, and which we never authorized. Now, as I have a word to say about the Holy Scriptures, I may as well say it at this as at any other time. Their assumption is, that, because the Scriptures are read, sufficient precaution is taken against infidelity. But I do not agree with them in that opinion, and I will give my reason. What is the reason that there is such a diversity of sects, all claiming the Holy Scriptures as the centre from whidh they draw their respective contradictory systems ?—that book which appears out of school, by the use made of it, to be the source of all dissension, when it does not come to the minds of children with such authority as to fix on their minds any definite principles. As regards us, while the Protestants say theirs is the true version, we say it is not so. We treat the Scriptures reverently ; but the Protestant version of the Scriptures is not a complete copy, and, as it has been altered and changed, we do not look upon it as giving the whole writings which were given by the inspiration of the Holy Spirit. We object not to the Holy Scriptures, but to the Protestant version without note or comment. We think it too much to ask Protestants to relinquish theirs, and take ours, for the use of the public schools. If we could ask you—if we could propose that you should take our book—if we should ask you to put out the Protestant Scriptures, and take ours, with our note and comment, do you think Protestants would agree to it ? Do you not think we should be arraigned as enemies of the word of God ?—for that is one charge made, when it is sought to denounce us. When we speak language of this kind, instead of understanding us according to our comprehension of the subject, they charge that we are enemies to the Holy Scriptures. But to object to their version is not to object to the Holy Scriptures ; and I am prepared to shów them that no denomination has done so much, in the true sense, for the Scriptures, as the Catholic Church.

The remonstrants add :

But this is not all. They have been most complaisantly offered the censorship of the books to be used in the public schools. The committee to whom has been confided the management of these schools in this city, offered to allow the Roman Catholic bishop to expurgate from these books any thing offensive to him.

And now they go out of their way to sneer at us, and you will observe the flippancy with which they do it :

But the offer was not accepted ;—perhaps for the same reason that he declined to decide on the admissibility of a book of extracts from the Bible, which had been sanctioned by certain Roman bishops in Ireland. An appeal, it seems, had gone to the pope on the subject, and nothing could be said or done in the matter until His Holiness had decided. The Common Council of New York will therefore find that, when they shall have conceded to the Roman Catholics of this city the selection of books for the use of the public schools, that these books must undergo the censorship of a foreign potentate. We hope the time is far distant when the citizens of this country will allow any foreign power to dictate to them in matters relating to either general or municipal law.

Prophets again—but not prophets of charity. I, sir, say, not prophets of good-will, for there is something more in their souls than the public welfare. There is something in their insinuation that is insulting, and a tone which does not show a mind enlightened and enlarged, and an appreciation of equal justice and equal rights. Just their way. They hear that an appeal has gone to the pope; and if we desired to appeal, also, we should claim the right to do it without asking permission from any one. Catholics all over the world do it when their consciences make it a duty, but not in matters of this kind. " These books must undergo the censorship of a foreign potentate ! " Now, we regard him only as supreme in our *Church*, and there's an end of it.

We cannot conclude this memorial without noticing one other ground on which the Roman Catholics, in their late appeal to their fellow-citizens, urged their sectarian claims, and excused their conscientious objections to the public schools. Their creed is dear to them, it seems, because some of their ancestors have been martyrs to their faith. This was an unfortunate allusion.

Some ! " Some of their ancestors have been martyrs to their faith." I speak of the Catholics of Great Britain and Ireland ; and when you reflect on the bigoted and unjust laws which Great Britain founded against all that were Catholics, by which their churches were wrested from them, and a bribe was offered as an inducement to the double crime of murder and of perjury—when it authorized any man to bring the head of a Catholic to the commissioner, and, if he would only swear it was the head of a priest, he got the same price as for the head of a wolf, no matter whose head it was— and. when legislation of that kind continued for centuries, this, you must agree with me, was being martyrs indeed. But when have the Methodists shown a sympathy for those contending for the rights of conscience ? When the dissenters of England claimed to be released from the operation of the " Test and Corporation " act, by which they were excluded from civil office, did the Methodist Episcopal Church assist them ? Not a solitary petition went from them for the enlargement of their freedom. And is it a wonder that we look to conscience, and admire those who had the firmness to suffer for conscience' sake ? By the penal laws against Catholics, the doors of Parliament were closed against us, if we had a conscience, for it required us to take an oath which we did not believe to be true, and therefore we could not swear it. There it is, sir ; it is because we have a conscience, because we respect it, that we have suffered ; and, while virtue is admired on earth, the fidelity of the people that are found standing by the right of conscience will command the admiration of the world. And yet, we are told, it was an unfortunate allusion !

Did not the Roman Catholics know that they addressed many of their fellow-citizens who could not recur to the memoirs of their ancestors without being reminded of the revocation of the Edict of Nantes——

They had nothing to do with it.

——the massacre of St. Bartholomew's day, the fires of Smithfield——

What is that to us ?   Are we the people that took part in that ?

——or the crusade against the Waldenses ?   We would willingly cover these scenes with the mantle of charity——

They had better not make the attempt, for their mantle is too narrow.

——and hope that our Roman Catholic fellow-citizens will in future avoid whatever has a tendency to revive the painful remembrance.

Let them enter upon that chapter, and discuss the charitableness of their religion, and I am prepared to prove—I speak it with confidence in the presence of this honorable assembly—that the Catholic religion is more charitable to those that depart from her pale than any other that ever was yoked in unholy alliance with civil power.

Your memorialists had hoped that the intolerance and exclusiveness which had characterized the Roman Catholic Church in Europe, had been greatly softened under the benign influences of our civil institutions.   The pertinacity with which their sectarian interests are now urged has dissipated the illusion.

Sectarian interests again, although we have disclaimed them !

We were content with their having excluded us, *ex cathedra*, from all claim to heaven, for we were sure they did not possess the keys, notwithstanding their confident pretensions ; ——

Why, they need not be uneasy about our excluding them from heaven, for their opinion is that they have no chance to enter if they have any thing to do with us ; and therefore our excluding them is of no avail.

——nor did we complain they would not allow us any participation in the benefits of purgatory——

Pray, what has that to do with common school education ?

——for it is a place they have made for themselves, and of which they may claim the exclusive property ;——

Well, it is no matter whether we believe in purgatory or not; it is no matter for the Common Council to decide.   But if they are not satisfied with our purgatory, and wish to go farther, they may prove the truth of the proverb, which says, " They may go farther and fare worse."

——but we do protest against any appropriation of the public school fund for their exclusive benefit, or for any other purposes whatever.   Assured that the Common Council will do what it is right to do in the premises, we are, gentlemen, with great respect, your most obedient servants,

N. BANGS,
THOMAS E. BOND,
GEORGE PECK.

And now I have gone through these two remonstrances, both of which, it will be seen, refer to the document of the Board of Assistant Aldermen, and rest their opposition on the same ground.   Of that document I will pass over the introduction; but I may observe that its authors, by what influence I am unable to say, have been made to rest their report upon an issue such as I have already described, and for which our petition furnishes no basis. I will first call your attention to the following observations :

The petitioners who appeared also contended that they contributed, in common with all other citizens who were taxed for the purpose, to the accumulation of the common school fund, and that they were therefore entitled to a participation in its advantages; that now they receive no benefit from the fund, inasmuch as the members of the Catholic churches could not conscientiously send their children to schools in which the religious doctrines of their fathers were exposed to ridicule or censure. The truth and justice of the first branch of this proposition——

That is, the payment of taxes.

——cannot be questioned. *The correctness of the latter part of the argument, so far as the same relates to books or exercises of any kind in the public schools reflecting on the Catholic Church*, WAS DENIED *by the School Society.*

Now, it is to be remembered that this denial of any thing objectionable in the books of the Public School Society was made at the period of the last application. I am persuaded those gentlemen, if they had known there was any thing objectionable to the Catholics, would not have denied it. I am sure they believed there was nothing, and from this circumstance I think I may fairly draw this inference, that they had not paid that attention to the books which they should have done, knowing the variety of denominations contributing to this fund and entitled to its benefits; or, knowing this, and the feelings and principles of Catholics, that they were incompetent for the proper discharge of their responsible duties. It is only on one of these two grounds that I can account for their *denial*. But since that time they have not only admitted that the objection was correct, but they have expunged passages from the books which, at the time of this denial, they said did not exist. I shall pass on, now, to the two questions on which the decision of the committee was made to rest. The first is :

Have the Common Council of this city, under the existing laws relative to common schools in the city of New York, a legal right to appropriate any portion of the school fund to religious corporations?

Whether they have, or not, one thing is clear and certain—that it is not as a "religious corporation" that we apply for it; and it seems to me that this should have struck the attention of the Public School Society, and the other gentlemen who have remonstrated. We do not apply as a religious body; we apply in the identical capacity in which we are taxed—as citizens of the commonwealth, without an encroachment on principle or the violation of any man's conscience. But, secondly, they ask :

Would the exercise of such power be in accordance with the spirit of the Constitution and the nature of our Government?

Certainly not. If the Constitution and Government have determined that no religious denomination shall receive any civil privilege, the exercise of such power will not be in conformity with the spirit of the Constitution and the nature of our Government. But there is throughout, and in all these documents, a squeamishness, a false delicacy, a persuasion that every thing which excludes religion abroad is right and liberal. It would be unnecessary for me to follow this report sentence by sentence, if there had not been so much reliance placed on it by those who have remonstrated; but as so much consequence has been attached to it, I will call your attention to some other passages. They go on to say:

Private associations and religious corporations were excluded from the management of the fund and the government of the schools. Private interest, under this system, could not appropriate the public treasure to private purposes, and religious zeal could not divert it to the purposes of proselytism.

Why, there is nothing of the kind intended. We have been driven, by the obligation of our consciences, and at our expense—which we are poorly able to bear—to provide schools; but they are not convenient, they are not well ventilated, and are not well calculated to give that development to your young citizens which they ought to have. Why argue, then, against religious corporations, and, in treating this question, bring prejudices into view which ought to have no existence in reality? They then go on to give the history and origin of the present law, and of the public school fund; and it seems that, for a period of time—and a long period—the Legislature designated the schools which might participate in this bounty. Each religious denomination provided for the instruction of its own poor; they had provided schools, and their exertions were honorable and laudable. The Legislature granted its aid, and the respective societies were encouraged to go on with the good work; and they did go on year after year, and then there was never heard that disputation which appears now to be so much dreaded. There was not then heard dissension between neighbors, or strife between societies; every thing went on peaceably—and why? Because the schools and the citizens were not then charged that religion was a *forbidden* subject. Nor should you now make it a forbidden part of education, because on religious principle alone can conscience find a resting-place. It should be made known that here conscience is supreme—that here all men are free to choose the views which their judgments, with a sense of their responsibility to an eternal weal or woe, shall offer for their adoption. It should be taught that here neighbors have the right to differ, and whatever is the right of one must be recognized as the right of the other; and the distribution of this fund will be better calculated to benefit the community than it can be by these public schools, where every thing seems to be at par except religion, and that is below par at an immense discount. They tell us, then, that

The law was imperative in its character, and the several religious societies of the city possessed a legal right to draw their respective portions of the fund from the public treasury, subject only to the restriction, that the money so received should be appropriated to the purposes of free and common education.

But that "*right to draw*" has been taken away; yet there is nothing in the act by which the right to draw is taken away which forbids their receiving it still, if, in the judgment of this honorable body, the circumstances of the case entitle them to it. It is not an impeachment; the Legislature had no intention to reflect on religious bodies—it had no intention to black-ball religion in the public schools; and yet that view has been taken of it. Such was not the case; but because circumstances had arisen—and what were they? Why, gross abuses had been practised by one of the religious societies, and

The funds received by the Church were applied to other purposes than those contemplated by the act.

Under some pretext, the favor to expend the school moneys had been conferred on that society in a way that distinguished it from all other Christian denominations and societies; and the other, seeing this privilege conferred on one, and not on the rest, ventured to remonstrate with the Legislature; they intimated that the partiality to that society of Baptists was an injustice to others, and they remonstrated against the law conferring exclusive privileges, and against no other thing whatever. And yet, by every document, and by this very document, it seems to be imagined that the Legislature did not revoke special favors granted to that society, but withdrew its aid from all Christian Churches; so that all the men who remonstrated against this partial legislation were found to have been themselves deprived of the privilege which they had enjoyed, and this on the strength of their own remonstrances for quite another thing. And the discretion which the Legislature had exercised to designate the schools which should receive this fund, was transferred to this honorable body, the Council of the city of New York. And why was it transferred? I cannot speak positively, but, while it seems to me that there were abuses shown to exist by the remonstrants, of which they made complaint, we may suppose the Legislature conceived it difficult for them to take cognizance of the matter, not being on the spot, but that the Common Council, being here, and being a body chosen by the people, in which, consequently, the public would have confidence, was the best and most fitting body to designate, from time to time, the institutions or schools which should be entitled to receive those school moneys. This must have been their intention, and yet this has been interpreted as repealing the law, in order to deprive those denominations of a legal right (for right they had, and they could come and demand the money), and not a mere transfer of the discretion to give this money, from the Legislature to the Common Council of New York. Now, all this, which is so plain and simple, has been construed by these gentlemen of the Public School Society as—what? As conferring a monopoly upon them—as a law disqualifying all religious denominations receiving it. So it has been interpreted. But, if it were so, we ask not for the money on the ground that we are a religious corporation, but of public utility, for the purpose of giving an education to a large and destitute class which otherwise will not have the means to procure it. We ask it to secure a public advantage; and if the objections anywhere exist to which I have directed your attention, they do not apply to our case. Gentlemen, I think it unnecessary to detain you any longer on this subject as referred to in this document, because, while the question is composed of one simple fact, they are arguing against dangers which do not threaten them. But then they go on to say :

To prevent, in our day and country, the recurrence of scenes so abhorrent to every principle of justice, humanity, and right, the Constitution of the United States, and of the several States, have declared, in some form or other, that there should be no establishment of religion by law ; that the affairs of the State should be kept entirely distinct from, and unconnected with, those of the Church ; that every human being should worship God according to the dictates of his own conscience ; that all churches and religions should be supported by voluntary contribution, and that no tax should ever be imposed for the benefit of any denomination of religion, for any cause, or under any pretence whatever.

All this is doctrine to which we subscribe most heartily. And while we seek to be relieved from the evils under which we suffer, we do not seek relief to the detriment of any other sect. What ! is this country independent of religion ? Is it a country of atheism, or of an established religion ? Neither the one nor the other ; but a country which makes no law for religion, but places the right of conscience above all other authority—granting equality to all, protection to all, preference to none. And while all these documents have gone on the presumption of preference, all we want is that we may be entitled to *protection* and not preference. We want that the public money shall not be employed to sap religion in the minds of our children—that they may have the advantages of education without the intermixture of religious views with their common knowledge, which goes to destroy that which we believe to be the true religion. There is another feature connected with this subject—which is the definition given of a public school, such as should be entitled to this money. " If the school money," say these gentlemen—and I must believe they are imposed on by a statement which is not correct. I believe if they had known the true statement, they would not have published in their report such a statement as this :

If the school money should be divided among the religious denominations generally, as some have proposed, there will be nothing left for the support of schools of a purely civil character ; and if there should be, in such a state of things, any citizen who could not, according to his opinions of right and wrong, conscientiously send his child to the school of an existing sect, there would be no public school in which he could be educated. This might, and probably would, be the case with hundreds of our citizens.

Now let me for a moment invite your attention to that part of the subject which I have now the honor to submit to you ; and it is that part on which all these documents go, that religious teaching would vitiate all claim to a participation in this public fund. A common education, then, as understood by the State, is a secular education ; and these documents contend that any religious teaching, no matter how slight, will vitiate all claim to a participation in this fund. Now the Public School Society, in their reports, have from time to time stated themselves, and, observe, with a consciousness that the jealous eye of the community is upon them—they state, still under this restriction, that they have imparted religion. Now if this doctrine be correct, they are no more entitled to the common school fund than others.

Or is the doctrine correct, and yet one must abide by it, and not another? Again, these gentlemen charge us with accusing them of teaching infidelity, when taking this tax they give that education, which, they state to us when we apply for a portion of this money, the State contemplates to give the scholar—that is, an education without religion. Now if the child be brought up without religion, what is he, if not an infidel? "Oh," they say, "we do not teach it." Is it necessary to teach infidelity? It does not require the *active* process. To make an infidel, what is it necessary to do? Cage him up in a room, give him a secular education from the age of five years to twenty-one, and I ask you what he will come out, if not an infidel? Whether he will know any thing about God? And yet they tell you that religious teaching is a disqualification. What will a child be, then, if you give him their education from his youth up to the age of twenty-one? Will he know any thing of God, and of a Divine Redeemer? of a Trinity, of the incarnation of the Saviour, and the redemption of the world by the atonement of Christ, or of any of those grand doctrines which are the basis and corner-stone of our Christianity? And because we object to a system of teaching which leads to practical infidelity, we are accused of charging the Public School Society with being infidels. They furnish the basis of the charge; we do not wish to do so. Now I ask you whether it was the intention of the Legislature of New York, or of the people of the State, that the public schools should be made precisely such as the infidels want? Permit me to say, when I use the term infidel, I mean no disrespect to those that are so. I would not be one; but I respect their right to be what they please. A few days ago, a gentleman who professes to be one of this class, and who would not allow his children to be scholars where religion is taught at all, said he could send them to the public school, for there the education suited him. What, then, is the consequence? That while the public education of New York is guarded in such a manner as to suit the infidel, the children become so. And is there any authority in this board, or of a legislative body at Albany, or is there any board in the Union, with power by the Constitution to exclude religion or to engraft it? Neither the one nor the other. The infidel says truly that there is no religion taught, and therefore he can send his children; and I should like to know why any member of a Christian Church should be forced to do violence to his convictions, and not be permitted to enjoy equal advantages? If the infidel can send his children to these schools, because no religion is taught there, and who, therefore, has to make no sacrifices of conscience, why cannot the Christian enjoy equal advantages? They say their instruction is not sectarianism; but it is; and of what kind? The sectarianism of infidelity in its every feature. But because it is of a negative kind, and they do not admit the doctrines of any particular denomination—because they do not profess to teach religion, therefore it is suited for all! As a test, therefore, of this principle, give this purely secular knowledge to a young man, keep him from intercourse with the rest of the world, give him nothing else, and what sort of a man would he be? What would be the state of his mind? A blank—a perfect blank as to religious impressions. But I contend that it is infidelity, and I hope the public school gentlemen hear what I say. But again, I do not charge it on their intention, and their assertion is purely gratuitous when they say that such an accusation is made against them. Here is the observation of the report on this subject :

If religious instruction is communicated, it is FOREIGN to the intentions of the school system, and should be *instantly abandoned.* Religious instruction is no part of a common school education.

Such, then, is the nature of that report which, I take leave to repeat, has been prepared by the gentlemen who drew it up as a committee, under the impression fixed on their minds that Catholics want this money to promote their religion, and that if it were granted to us, others would want it for their respective religions also ; and on this assumption they decided. But. against this false issue I protest, whether set forth in this report or in the two remonstrances before this Council—one from the Public School Society, and the other from the Methodist Episcopal Church. It is not my business to speak in relation to the Public School Society at large. Of its history I have taken pains to make myself sufficiently possessed to speak ; and I find that in its origin, so far from disclaiming all connection with religion, so far from conceiving religious teaching disadvantageous, it was originally incorporated for the purpose of supplying the wants of the destitute portion of the population, and their petition for a charter set forth

The benefits which would result to society from the education of such children, by implanting in their minds the principles of RELIGION and morality.

At this time every denomination taught its own, and received an equal portion of the fund from the public authorities to aid them in their good work, so that their children were provided for, and this Society came to gather in the neglected and the outcast—they came as gleaners, after the reapers had gone through the field, and a most benevolent purpose theirs was ; and their object, I repeat, when they applied to the Legislature, was set forth to be (for they did not conceal the advantages of a religious education), to produce benefits to society by the implanting in the minds of such children the principles of religion and morality. There were children belonging to no denomination ; and this Society, seeing the benefits which would result to society from the education of such children by implanting in their minds the principles of religion and morality, undertook this benevolent work, and covered themselves and the name of their Society with glory by that undertaking. But it is strange that what then was so advantageous to the community—the implanting in the minds of children the principles of religion and morality—should have ceased to be so now ; and that they or their successors should seek to make that very thing a disqualification, and to turn it against all denominations of Christians, and claim themselves to monopolize the fund and the teaching on the principle that no religion shall be imparted. Now has the Legislature seen fit to alter the charter, so as to make religious teaching a disqualification of all other sects ?

Was it for that purpose that this Society, step by step, obtained enlarged privileges, by which not only the neglected children of the community, but those of others, came under their care—that they obtained grants from the public treasury and the exchequer of the city, to an amount of many thousands of dollars, until the Society claims to be the true and only Society, though existing as a private corporation, electing its own body, fixing a tax for the privilege of membership, sometimes $10, at others $20, $25, and $50, any of which sums is too much for a poor man to pay ; and out of this organized body electing the trustees to carry on the work ?

I mention this, not to blame them—for they believe they are doing good —but to show that even with men who are honorable in every-day life, how much watchfulness and vigilance, how much tact and talent, is used to grasp more and more, till they absorb all, and completely deprive all others of any participation in the advantages of controlling this fund.

It is not my intention, as it is not my peculiar province, to enter into the legal part of the argument ; but I have to regret that the gentleman who did intend to treat it, and to whose department it belonged, has been unfortunately prevented by the bursting of a small blood-vessel. But, though my experience has not qualified me to enter into legal matters, yet, as a citizen, I might have the right to express my opinion on the monopoly which this Society claims ; and that opinion is contrary to the monopoly, and not only contrary to their monopoly simply regarded as a monopoly, but because I believe that a monopoly of this description should be regarded with double jealousy. Why ? Because this monopoly is of greater weight than in ordinary cases ; of great weight pecuniarily—for, last year, the fund amounted to $115,000—because the distribution of that money gives to them a patronage which, considering the weakness of human nature, is in danger of being used disadvantageously—because it gives to them privileges of infinitely higher importance than any that can be estimated by dollars and cents—the privilege of stamping their peculiar character on the minds of thousands and tens of thousands of our children. They ought to be men, to discharge the trust of such a monopoly, as pure as angels, and almost imbued with wisdom from above ; such men they should be, when they would venture to come and stand by the mother's side, and say, in effect, " Give me the darling which you have nourished at your breast —give it to me, a stranger, and I will direct its mind. True, you are its parent, but you are not fit to guide its youthful progress, and to implant true principles in its mind ; therefore give it to me, and give me also the means wherewith to instruct it." That is the position of that Society ; and they ought to be almost more than men for this—as doubtless they are honorable men in their proper places ; but of that we should have the most satisfactory evidence, that we may be well assured that they are fitted to discharge their duties. It is this consideration that brought me here, as the first pastor of a body of people large and numerous as they are known to be ; but, poor as many of them are, and exposed to many hardships, they have children with immortal souls, whose condition is involved in this question ; and if it is an impropriety in the clerical character, I would rather undergo the reproach, than neglect to advocate their rights, as far as I have the power, with my feeble ability.

The Catholics of the city of New York may be estimated as one fifth of the population; and when you take account of the class of children usually attending the public schools, and consider how many there are in this city who are in affluent circumstances, which enable them to give an education to their children, who do not therefore participate in the teaching of the public schools; and when you consider the numbers not attending any school at all—I say, of those people who, by their poverty, are the objects most usually composing the number that require the assistance of the common school fund, Catholics are one third, if not more. And when I see this one third excluded—respecting, as I do, their welfare in this life, as well as their welfare in a brighter world—then it is that I come forward thus publicly, and stand here to plead for them. I conceive we have our rights in question, and therefore, most respectfully, I demand them from this honorable board.

I am not surprised that there should be remonstrances against our claim; but I did hope, in an age as enlightened as this is, and among gentlemen of known liberality of feeling, that their opposition would not have been characterized as this has been. However, it is not to me a matter of surprise; for I believe if some of those gentlemen, who consider themselves now as eminent Christians, had lived at the period when Lazarus lay languishing at the gate of the rich man, petitioning for the crumbs that fell from the table, they would have sent their remonstrance against his petition.

When the Methodist Episcopal Church sent its petition for a portion of this fund, some eight years ago, then it was not unconstitutional! Yet, did the Catholics send in their remonstrance against it? When their theological seminaries obtained (and they still receive) the bounty of the State, did, or do, the Catholics complain? Has there been a single instance of illiberality on the part of Catholics, or a want of disposition to grant rights as universal as the nature of man may require? And I have been astonished only at this, that good men, with good intentions, should prefer to cling to a system, and to the money raised for its support by the public liberality—that they would sooner see tens of thousands of poor children contending with ignorance, and the companions of vice, than concede one iota of their monopoly in order that others may enjoy their rights. I say this because I am authorized to say it.

And what am I to infer, but that they prefer the means to the end? The end designed is, to convey knowledge to the minds of our children; the means, is the public fund; and, by refusing to cause the slightest variation in their system, they cling to the means, while they leave thousands of children without the benefit which the State intended to confer. They may pursue that course, but the experience of the past should have taught them that, while they maintain their present character, a large portion of their fellow-citizens have not—cannot have—confidence in them.

We have not had confidence in them for years past; and that we have endeavored to supply an education to our children ourselves, is sufficient proof that we shall endeavor to supply it for years to come, rather than suffer our children to be taught under a system which makes them ashamed of the religion their fathers profess.

But they have said, that, if a portion of this fund is given to Catholics, all other sects will want it. Then let them have it. But I do not see that that is probable; and my reason is this: They have sent in remonstrances against the claim of the Catholics, as you will see by a reference to Document No. 80, all of which go to prove that they are satisfied with the present public school system. And if they are satisfied, and their children derive benefit from it, let them continue to frequent the schools as they do now. The schools are no benefit to Catholics now; we have no confidence in them; there is no harmony of feeling between them and us. We have no confidence that those civil and religious rights that belong to us will be enjoyed while the Public School Society retains its present monopoly. We do not receive benefit from those schools; do not, then, take from Catholics their portion of the fund, by taxation, and hand it over to those who do not give them an equivalent in return. Let those who *can*, receive the advantages of these schools; but, as Catholics *cannot*, do not tie them to a system which is intended for the advantage of a class of society of which they form one third, but from which system they can receive no benefit.

There are many other topics connected with this subject to which I might advert; but I must apologize for the length of time that I have trespassed on your patience. I feel, unaccustomed as I am to address such a body, and hurried as was my preparation, that I have not been able to present the subject before you in that clear and lucid manner that would make it interesting; but it was not with that view that I claimed your attention in relation to it; it was with far higher motives; and I now, with confidence, submit it to your judgment.

THEODORE SEDGWICK, Esq. (with whom was Mr. Ketchum), as counsel for the Public School Society, then addressed the board, and said:

MR. PRESIDENT: I appear here, with my learned friend and associate, Mr. Ketchum, on behalf of the Trustees of the Public School Society; and I desire in the outset, for those whom I represent, as well as for myself, to reciprocate all that the reverend gentleman has said of the motives of the parties for whom we respectively appear. The trustees are animated by no feeling but a desire to promote what they conceive will be for the true interests and welfare of the city; in which they are as deeply interested as any men can be. They have no other interest than to maintain that which, in their judgment, is right in itself, and will be beneficial to the whole body. Impelled by these motives themselves, they are willing to believe that those who are opposed to them are animated by the same feeling. It is most especially desirable that, in a case like this, the petitioners should be heard, as they are being heard, in the most solemn manner the forms of the city government will permit. We have no doubt they will be fairly heard; we are convinced that the decision to which you may come, whether for or against them, will be righteously pronounced. The trustees, therefore, are most anxious that the case should be fully examined. What, sir, is the precise question before us? The petition, if I understand it, asks your honorable body for a civil ordinance—for an ordinance in regard to the application of money. I shall therefore waive all reply to that portion of the reverend gentleman's opening remarks which relates to the trustees themselves and the Methodist congregation. That part of his argument has nothing to do with the merits of the case; however pointed and piquant it may have been, it has nothing to do with the point which you have to decide. The trustees here sink into nothing; the petitioners also disappear from our view; and the real question remains, How is the intellectual condition of our children to be best promoted? On that question two great bodies are at issue, and it is especially consonant with our form of government, that both should be fairly heard; it is in consonance with that principle of our government, which bases it on harmony and compromise, with that respect which is due even to the opinions of the minority. The question is now being heard, as it only best can be heard; and all will rest content, no doubt, with the decision, whatever that decision may be.

If I understand this application correctly, it is an application to alter, to modify, or, at any rate, to affect the common school system of this State. Not only of the city, sir, for it has a more extensive bearing; it is to affect the whole system of the State of New York; and your honorable body cannot come to a proper decision of this matter, unless you bring your minds to the consideration of the origin of our system of education, its establishment, development, and extent. This system, sir, which you are this night called upon, in my humble judgment, not merely to modify, but to overthrow, had its foundation laid as far back as the year 1795. On the 9th of April, 1795, an act was passed "*for the encouragement of public schools;*" and it is well worth while to know what was the opinion of the Legislature which framed this act in regard to the kind of education to be communicated in the schools which were to receive its bounty. That act appropriated $20,000 annually for the support of those schools in the different counties of the State, in which the children should be "instructed in the English language, or be taught English grammar, arithmetic, mathematics, and such other branches of knowledge as are most useful and necessary to complete a good English education."

Such was the whole extent and aim of the system as it was originally founded. It was, to give a purely secular education. This act was the germ of our present system; but the question was not fully understood, nor its importance sufficiently appreciated; there was not sufficient genial heat in the body politic to develop it; it was not long acted under, and soon became obsolete.

In 1801, another act was passed, "*for the encouragement of literature,*" by which four lotteries were established, to aid in the accomplishment of the object—a pure object, deriving its support from a most impure source;

15

for the proceeds of these lotteries were to be applied to the support of the common school in such way as the Legislature might direct.

In 1805, the first step was taken to establish the system on a firm, permanent foundation, and then (2d April) the proceeds of the first 500,000 acres of the public lands which should be sold were set apart, to be invested as a permanent fund for the support of common schools for the education of the children of New York. This fund was afterward increased, during the years 1808, 1810, and 1811, by the receipt of the surplus fees of the Clerk of the Supreme Court, by the proceeds of certain stock in the Merchants' Bank in this city, and the sums then flowing from lotteries, lands, fees, and banks, were invested, from time to time, by the Comptroller, for the same object. In 1811, the fund was found to be of a considerable amount, and commissioners were appointed to report to the Legislature, at the next session, how this fund could be best appropriated, and also to prepare a system for the organization and establishment of common schools. They accordingly reported, and, in 1812 (10th June), the first general act was passed, which laid the foundation, broad and deep, of the present system.

That act directed, in general terms, that, as soon as the revenue from the school fund should amount to $50,000, it should be appropriated among the different counties of the State; commissioners and inspectors were to be elected by the towns, to expend the amount awarded to them; and trustees of the school districts were also chosen to carry out the scheme.

But in the first act a provision was inserted—and it is important in regard to the whole common school system to bear it in mind—that the towns and counties were not *compelled* to contribute to the expense of education at all. Such only as voluntarily accepted the system, and taxed themselves to a similar amount, were permitted to receive any portion of the fund. But if they chose to disregard the matter altogether, they were at liberty so to do. The next year this error—for so it seems the Legislature deemed it—was corrected. The towns and counties were compelled to adopt the system, and the supervisors were directed to tax the towns to the amount of the proportion allotted to them from the school fund. They did then what they had not before dared to do—they taxed the people directly for the purposes of education. That act was passed in 1814. The system thus established was, as your honors well know, incorporated in the Revised Statutes, which, in 1830, were made the code of our State; and that beautiful fabric still remains as it was then fashioned—so simple, and yet so beautiful, I should be loath to see a hand laid upon it.

The functions of the original Superintendent of Common Schools have been merged in the Secretary of State, but in other respects no alteration has been made. The annual revenue of the fund is divided among the counties, who are compelled to raise, by taxation, a sum equal to their respective shares; commissioners were elected, and by them the money is apportioned among the towns, and these again are subdivided into districts, and trustees elected to take charge of the school-houses, and to have the immediate supervision of the schools.

These trustees, at stated periods (once a year), make their report to the commissioners, the commissioners to the county clerks, and they to the superintendent, now Secretary of State; and thus is one harmonious system established throughout the State. In the last report, of 1840, it is stated that but one town in the State has not reported during the last year. At the establishment of the system, there was great diversity of opinion on the subject—there was great languor and indifference among the people, and it was long before the towns generally came to take an interest in it; it was long before the trustees made regular reports of the matters under their charge; but, as the last report of the superintendent shows, there has been a great progress of opinion; every town, except one, has made its report during the last year, showing the condition of its schools. In the year 1795, $20,000 were appropriated to the common school system; in 1845, it is calculated, by the report of the superintendent, that the capital of the common school fund will amount to *five millions of dollars.* These facts alone, then, show the certain progress made, not only in the means for the accomplishment of the object of the system, but in the minds and hearts of the people themselves. Five millions of dollars, then, will be the capital, and two millions will be annually expended for the education of the citizens of the State of New York! 10,766 districts have reported, and 557,229 children are actually under instruction in these schools! Now, I suppose, having reference to the magnitude of the State, and to its population and resources, it may most safely be affirmed, there is no such system for the education of the poorer classes of any country in the universe—no system of this grandeur, by which the people take care that the people shall be educated—made competent to discharge those duties, without which the form and fabric of our Government are a mockery. This is the general system throughout the State. Now let us examine more particularly those features which relate to this city, with which, at this time, we are more immediately concerned. In 1813, the first act to which I have alluded extended its provisions to this city; and it is somewhat remarkable that the Legislature then drew a line between the population of this city and of the country, and *required* the city to levy a tax for this object, before it required the country population to do so. In 1814, as I have already said, the system was applied to the entire State, and all counties were required to raise, by taxation, an amount equal to their portion of the fund. By that act, certain schools were specified as the recipients of this common school fund, and such other incorporated religious societies as then supported charity schools. In' 1824, this act was repealed, and the Common Council was authorized, once in three years, to designate the institutions and schools which should be entitled to receive the school moneys. After the passage of this act, a petition from a great portion of the property-owners of this city was presented to the Legislature, praying leave to raise, by taxation on this city and county, a further sum besides that already required of them, for the same purpose of educating the destitute poor. I claim no peculiar merit for them in so doing, but they are at least entitled to the credit, such as it is, of comprehending their own interest. They saw that the education of the poor was essential to their own welfare. Perhaps this is the only instance on record of citizens soliciting the favor of being taxed. It was granted, and the Corporation was then authorized to impose a special tax on this city for the support of schools. And what has since been the development of this system in this city ? In the year 1838, $34,000 were received from the school fund; $34,000, or an equal amount to that received, were raised under the compulsory clause of the school system acts, and $73,000 in addition were raised by this voluntary taxation; so that the annual revenue of the fund in controversy exceeds $140,000—no trifling sum, to be distributed by this municipal body. Now, if you please, what is the tendency of this system ?—its practical effect—its mode of tuition—the nature of its instruction ? In the first place, there is *no law* on the subject. The reverend gentleman has said that, if the prayer were granted, they would conform to the provisions of the law; he was willing that the body which he represents should apply the fund as the law directs. But the law makes no provision in the matter. If the Koran was taught in a common school, the law would not interfere—the law would not shut the school; it must be got at in some other way. This, the very essence of the matter, was left, and doubtless intentionally left, to the people of the State and to this honorable body. Throughout the State, the people elect their officers for the management of these schools; here it is done through this body, who are elected by the people. You, then, who are the representatives of the people, decide to whom this fund shall be distributed. Now, at the outset the question may arise—and a great portion of the remarks of the reverend gentleman compel a notice of it—whether the education of the people is a proper subject of governmental concern. If I understand the argument of the reverend gentleman, it tends to the negative of this proposition. When he says the trustees of our public schools " *take the children from their mother, deprive the parents of their offspring,*" I understand him to say—and it is not the first time, by any means, that this question has been mooted—that the State has no right to interfere; that the matter should be left to the parent; that the State should not interpose between the father and his child. If that argument is sound, then the whole system should be abolished; if the State ought not to interfere at all, taxation for this object must be done away with, and no further sums should be levied, and the school fund, guaranteed by the Constitution, should go back into the general coffers. But, right or wrong, such is not the understanding of the people of this State. They have said that there is a portion of every population that does not sufficiently appreciate the advantages of education voluntarily to secure them; they know, or think that they know, by experience, that such parents, unless compelled, will not properly attend to the interests of the child, and therefore the people of the State say, " We will interfere; no man shall come up to his majority, and claim the right of voting, without that education which shall prepare him, at least in part, to exercise that right. He shall have at least a portion of that instruction, without which he is a firebrand in the midst of a magazine." This matter, therefore, no longer admits of argument. The question to be argued here is, not whether the father and the mother are the best judges of the interests of the child in this point of view. If so, we are cast on the sea of abstract discussion. We must assume something—we must take something for granted. The postulate in this case is, "the State requires its children to have some kind of education." What kind, then, shall that be? Is the present system the best, or shall we have something new, and repudiate that which the experience of thirty years has sanctioned and approved? There are three kinds of education which the State might give. There is the purely secular education, such as the first act, to which I have referred, contemplates—such as the master gives to an apprentice. This secular education may be better or worse, more or less extensive. The child may be taught to read and write, and may be given what is called by the State "a purely English education." There is another kind of instruction the infant may be imbued with—those fundamental principles of morals about which there is no dispute, at least not in this country, nor in any part of Christendom—about which the body which the reverend gentleman represents and we Protestants all equally agree; as to the moral code of Christianity, there is no material difference of opinion among us. But, beyond that, there is still another branch of instruction which is properly called *religious*, and it is because those two phrases—"religious" and "moral"—have been used occasionally without an accurate apprehension of their signification, that the documents of the trustees have been misconstrued. But when the term "moral" education is used, it only means that education which instructs the children in those fundamental tenets of duty which are the basis of all religion; it does not mean that sectarian or dogmatic teaching which constitutes what is more properly termed a "*religious*" education. The common schools have meant from the beginning to teach the children the great moral precepts, "Thou shalt not steal, thou shalt not lie," and others; but they have not intended to teach either Episcopalianism or Methodism, Catholicism or Unitarianism, for from that controversial leaning they have intended—and if I understand the system, the Legislature intended—that the schools should keep aloof. It never can be imparted without involving the parents and the children in bitter disputes endless in their nature, whose inevitable effect would be to exasperate the minds of the parents toward each other, and be either useless, or positively injurious to the children. A religious education, properly so called, no man can undervalue. If a moral education is given, the other invaluable instruction must be superadded; but the State does not intend to give it. The State intends to give a "secular" and moral, but not a religious education; the State does not intend to give a sectarian education, and that is precisely what, if I apprehend correctly, the reverend gentleman does intend to give. Such as I have described is the character of the instruction in this State; and that of the city is in harmony with it. It is a system, I repeat, by which it is intended to confer a secular and moral education. It has been thought that, for the purposes of moral teaching, the Bible contains that in which all sects can agree—from which no sect can dissent. Now, what is the prayer of the petitioners? I suppose it is hardly necessary, in this age and in this country, to deny any feeling of hostility to

Catholics. If there is one feeling that has spread more than another throughout this country, it is one of religious toleration—it is, that this country was designed and was provided as an asylum for the oppressed of other countries. It has been so most fortunately for the Catholics of Ireland and the poor peasant of the Rhine. There is no feeling of hostility to the Catholic as such; still less to the foreigner as such. There was a time when Catholicism and Christianity went hand in hand—when their fellowship was broken by no jar nor schism—when all were Catholics. One of the best men who has ever adorned this country, was Bishop Cheverus, of Boston, one of the few who achieved a widespread reputation by mere acts of private benevolence. And while we can turn to such men as adorning the Catholic Church, it cannot be that there is any hostility to them as a sect; if there be, most assuredly I am not its mouthpiece; and while I repudiate all feeling of hostility to the petitioners, this I will further say, I would not for a moment lend my feeble aid to the public school system, if it were actuated or marked by intolerance or hostility to Catholics—if it did not maintain a perfect impartiality among all sects. I conceive that this is not a subject to argue as counsel, from a brief. Unless I were satisfied that the compliance with this petition would be dangerous to the whole system, as a lawyer I would not say a syllable in the matter. I would never, on such a subject, argue against my deliberate conviction as a counsel, for hire. The professional man must here be merged in the citizen, and it is only as such that I desire to be heard.

If this matter, however, is properly considered, there can be no pretence for making it hinge on Catholicism, or for awakening the violence of religious schisms. Although a portion of the Catholics, at this moment, are the most prominent petitioners of the most numerous body which demand a change of the system, yet, in point of fact, they are not more affected by it than others. The other denominations say, " We are satisfied with the present order of things, and with the education conferred; but, if you give a portion of these funds to one sect, to be administered by their hands, we shall claim our share also." So long as you give a secular education combined with moral instruction alone, and steer entirely clear of all doctrinal or sectarian principles, all are satisfied; but the moment an apprehension exists that a part of this great fund goes to increase the numbers and the power of *one* particular sect, that moment the others will eagerly strive to check what they believe a pernicious influence, and to check it in the same way. At present these sects tacitly consent to the system pursued by the trustees, because the common school is now literally a " *common school*," a neutral institution; but give a portion of this fund to promote the interests of that sect, and others will that instant press in, demanding their equal share. Those demands you will not be able to resist. I am not speaking of any speculative matter. You have, sir, petitions couched in these very terms; and if you answer the Catholic in the affirmative, you cannot give a negative to the other claimants. Consider, then, for a moment, the effect of this. After all the sects have divided the fund among themselves, what is to become of the children of that large class who are of no sect, or, at least, who wish no sectarian education to be given? Are they to be left utterly destitute? The conclusion is irresistible, that this is a direct attempt to subvert the whole common school system. The grounds taken by the petitioners are twofold. If I understand them correctly, they are totally at variance and incompatible with each other. One is, that the dogmas of religion, or religion properly so called, is not taught in these schools, but that what the reverend gentleman calls the sectarianism of infidelity is propagated in them. Another objection to the system is, that the children are made Protestants: in other words, that religion *is* taught to them. I leave it to the reverend gentleman to reconcile these propositions for the purposes of his argument; for the purposes of mine, it is sufficient that neither of them is tenable. One is false in point of reasoning, and the other in point of fact.

And now we approach the citadel, the centre of the discussion. Now, as to this matter, the petitioners ask your honors to pass a civil ordinance. The first question that suggests itself is, *Have your honors the power* to make the appropriation asked for? The committee of the Board of Assistants .have already intimated their opinion that no such power rests here—that this application, if made at all, should be presented to the Legislature. And the Board of Assistants have intimated the further opinion, that the Legislature has already passed upon this very question. That the Board of Assistants are right, there is, I venture to affirm, no doubt. The act of 1813, by which the Legislature undertook to direct how the school fund should be applied in this city, apportioned it among the Trustees of the Free-School Society—now the Public School Society—the Orphan Asylum Society, the Economical School, the African Free School, and *such incorporated religious societies as now support*, or thereafter shall establish, charity schools, or may apply for the same. That act, beyond any question, gave this body power to make the appropriation now asked for. The churches acted under it, and claimed their share of the school fund. On the 8th of February, 1822, an act was passed for the relief of the Bethel Baptist Church of the city of New York. That congregation went begging to Albany, as other congregations will go if this wretched system shall be introduced, and asked leave to apply that part of their share which was not wanted for teachers, to the erection of school-houses. The act was passed, and its natural consequences ensued. The teachers were underpaid, and false receipts were used in order to facilitate and conceal the increase of the property of the corporation. Here a gross fraud was perpetrated. That fraud was discovered, and it led to a change in the system. The nineteenth annual report of the School Society contains all the documents and proofs on the subject. It is sufficient for our present purpose that the fact of the deception was proved to the satisfaction of the Common Council of the city, and of the Legislature. The Common Council took the matter up, and addressed a memorial, signed by Mr. Paulding, then Mayor, to the Legislature, for the repeal of the act under which the fund was appropriated to religious societies in the city. They say:

The question for the determination of the Legislature, at this time, is

presumed to be, whether the Free-School Society shall be suffered to continue its operations and have the principal management of gratuitous education in the city of New York, or whether the religious societies shall take
it out of its hands, and the poor be educated in sectarian schools.

If religious societies are to be the only participators of the portion of
the school fund for the city of New York, a spirit of rivalry will, it is
thought, be excited between different sects, which will go to disturb the
harmony of society, and which will early infuse strong prejudices in the
minds of children taught in the different schools.   Moreover, your memorialists would suggest to your honorable body, whether the school fund of
the State is not purely of a civil character, designed for a civil purpose ;
and whether, therefore, the entrusting of it to religious or ecclesiastical
bodies is not a violation of an elementary principle in the politics of the
State and country.—*Nineteenth Report of Free-School Society.*

Upon that memorial a committee of the Assembly reported a bill to
repeal the act in question.   That report contains the following passage :

There is, however, one general principle connected with this subject, of
no ordinary magnitude, to which the committee would beg leave to call the
attention of the House.

It appears that the city of New York is the only part of the State where
the school fund is at all subject to the control of religious societies.   This
fund is considered by your committee purely of a civil character, and therefore it never ought, in their opinion, to pass into the hands of any corporation or set of men, who are not directly amenable to the constituted civil
authorities of the government, and bound to report their proceedings to the
public.   Your committee forbear, in this place, to enter fully into this branch
of the subject, but they respectfully submit whether it is not a violation of
a fundamental principle of our legislation, to allow funds of the State, raised
by a tax on the citizens, designed for civil purposes, to be subject to the
control of any religious corporation.—*Nineteenth Annual Report of Free-
School Society*, p. 51.

Upon that memorial and report, both holding this language, the act was
passed, under which your honors are now called upon to grant the claim of
the petitioners, on whose behalf the reverend gentleman has just addressed
you.   On the 19th of November, 1824, this law was enacted, entitled " An
act relating to Common Schools in the City of New York," by which it was
provided that

The institutions or schools which shall be entitled to receive the school
moneys, shall, from time to time, and at least once in three years, be designated by the Corporation of this city in Common Council convened.

Now I ask your honor, since statutes were first formed, was ever a church
designated in legal language as an " *institution* " or a " school ? "   That act,
then, coupled with that memorial and report on which it was based, compels
the conviction that it was the intention of the Legislature—if my mind is
not clouded by the views I have taken on the subject—it is as clear as the
sun at noon-day, that the Legislature intended that this fund should be
divided amongst " institutions and schools," and to be appropriated to the
purposes of education—of civil, secular education, not of religious, sectarian
instruction.   We are now, then, after the lapse of only fifteen years, arguing
before this honorable body the very question which was argued and decided
against these petitioners, and that not abstruse or complicated, but one of

the simplest in the very primer book of liberty. The only question which can by possibility be raised on this branch of the case is the change in the phraseology adopted in the Revised Statutes, vol. i. p. 483 (2d. ed.), where, instead of the words "institutions or schools," the words "*societies or schools*" are substituted. That, certainly, is not the language of the act of 1824—it is not as clear language as that used in the original act, but it is very apparent that the revisors changed the language without intending to changing the purport of the provision. Your honors are well aware that where any change of our statute law was considered necessary by the revisors, where an old enactment was altered, or a new provision was introduced, it is uniformly accompanied by a note to show the reason for the alteration. But there is no note nor comment whatever on this passage. Your honors are equally well aware that the revisors did, for the simplification, and, as they no doubt considered the improvement, of the law, sometimes change the phraseology of our statutes, to make it more elegant or precise; that is the reason why they here have substituted the word "societies" for "institutions." It is not to be supposed that they could deliberately revert to the exploded enactment, which existed prior to 1824, without note or comment, explanation or reason, to show why they had re-established a system once pronounced pernicious. As a matter of law, therefore, I affirm without hesitation this question has been passed upon by the Legislature, and that the sovereign power has removed from this honorable body the right or authority to apportion this fund among religious societies. If we are right in this part of the discussion, we might stop here. If this ground is well taken, the petition must unquestionably be rejected. Your honors cannot act for want of jurisdiction. But suppose us to be wrong—put out of view the act of 1824, and consider the question as it presents itself on general principles, as if we were to argue it before a committee of the Legislature. Have your honors acted on this subject already? The present disposition of the school fund is among the Public School Society, the Mechanics' Society, the Orphan Asylum, the Harlem School, the Manhattanville School, the Yorkville School, the Catholic Benevolent Society, the New York Institution for the Blind, the Half Orphan Asylum, the Association for the Benefit of Colored Orphans in New York. Of these the most prominent is the Public School Society, the utility and benefits of which it is impossible to extol too highly, but whose power the reverend gentleman most egregiously exaggerated. What are its powers? In 1805, this Society was incorporated by the Legislature under the name of "The Society for Establishing a Free School in the City of New York, for the education of such poor children as do not belong to, or are not provided for, by any religious society." In relation to the original petition on which the charter was granted, on which the reverend gentleman has commented, it is sufficient to observe, that at that time no school fund existed, and the petitioners might ask leave to give religious education, or any other species of education; whether wise or not, that petition has no connection with the application of the common school fund. In 1808, the power of that Society was extended to all children who were proper objects of gratuitous education, and the name was changed to "The Free School Society of New York." On the 8th of January, 1826, it was altered to "The Public School Society," by which name it is still known. The yearly income of this "magnificent incorporation," so "dangerous to the liberties of the people," is limited by its charter to $10,000 per annum. This Society has been called by the reverend gentleman, a "monopoly." I did not expect to receive to-night a lesson on the evils of monopolies.

That subject we pretty thoroughly discussed some years since, as you, Mr. President, no doubt well recollect. That discussion was carried on here by one of the most upright and boldest spirits that ever inhabited a mortal frame. It is foreign to this subject, but I shall never forego any opportunity of commemorating, with my faint praise, the name of William Leggett. But this Society, sir, is not one of those huge political engines which we were then taught to dread—a Society incorporated under a general statute, the privileges of which are open to all; the only object of which is to supply education to the poor; the annual income of which is limited to $10,000, is not, I need not assure your honors, such a "dangerous monopoly" as should exclude it from popular favor. It is just such a monopoly—just such a monster, if the reverend gentleman likes the phrase better—as any one of the churches which he represents. Some better ground of objection must be found than that this incorporation is a "monopoly." The argument of the reverend gentleman has certainly the merit of flexibility, but it stretches too far: he sets out with the proposition that this Society inculcates sectarianism, but when he found that would be turned against him, he goes on the other track, and charges them with infidelity. Not quite satisfied with either of these, he starts the certainly novel accusation that it is a monopoly, and finally he insists that the Society has not the confidence of the people. As to this matter, like most others, facts speak louder than words. A statement has been recently prepared in relation to the children taught in these schools, which shows the nature of their effects on the population of this city. The report not only gives the number of the children taught, but the occupation of the parents has been carefully set down, and a single glance at it will show what class of society is most interested in the support of this "dangerous monopoly." Of 16,000 children, no less than 1,488, or about one tenth, are the children of laborers; 1,461, or nearly another tenth, are the children of widows; 945 shoemakers; 502 cabinetmakers; 416 masons; 579 tailors; 493 blacksmiths; while of clergymen there are but 13; of doctors 44; lawyers 25; and the *gentlemen* figure in the list to the amount of 26. This is the proportion in which the children of the different classes enjoy the benefits of education from the Public School Society. The reverend gentleman's assertion that the Society has not the confidence of the public, is somewhat answered by this statement. But if it were otherwise, should it be thought strange, and would it be singular if the same eloquent voice which we have heard this night, is constantly raised to deter one large and important class of the people from entering those common schools, arousing the prejudices of the poorer part of our population as to the motives of the Society and the character of its instruction?

But it is not true. In point of fact they have the confidence of the people to a most remarkable extent.

This institution has organized 98 schools; expends annually about $130,000, and is, as I have said, the principal agent of the common school education in our city. This institution has, in its instruction, most sedulously confined itself to a secular and moral education, and most scrupulously eschewed every thing of a sectarian tendency. It is against this institution that these petitions are most especially aimed.

To come back to the other recipients of the school fund. The Harlem, Hamilton, Manhattanville, and Yorkville schools, as well as the African and Mechanics' Society, are, I believe, proper free schools, some of them devoted to particular classes of society, but all confining themselves to secular moral education—steering clear of sectarianism in every shape. The other institutions do, in some shape or other, convey religious instruction, and, as such, are exceptions to the general rule.

A report was not long since (I think in 1833) made by the Board of Assistants against the claims of these latter establishments, on the ground—the same we now urge—that this fund is intended for the purposes of secular education, and that those institutions, such as the Orphan Asylum, no matter how excellent they may be, no matter how much good they may effect, do not come within the pale of those educational establishments to which it was intended that this fund should be devoted. Unfortunately, the views of the report did not prevail. Your honors have already gone beyond the intention of the Legislature and the Constitution, and have already erroneously granted aid to institutions which do not strictly come within the original design of the common school system. But is this to be established as a precedent? I think not. The grants to these institutions, of small amount and little consequence, will hardly serve as a pretext for breaking up the system altogether. The application now before you is, that your honors will be pleased to designate, as among the schools entitled to participate in the common school fund, St. Patrick's school, St. Peter's school, St. Mary's school, St. Joseph's school, St. James' school, St. Nicholas' school, Transfiguration Church school, and St. John's school.

Now, if your honors please, what is the ground of this petition? First, that the Catholics who, as represented by the reverend gentleman, pay taxes equally with all other citizens, cannot enjoy the benefits of the schools, because their consciences will not permit them to send their children there. I am by no means disposed to underrate the force of this objection. If I oppose this application, it is with no desire to achieve a paltry triumph over the petitioners, or the reverend gentleman himself. Our object is that which actuates him: it is the wish, that the children of the poor be educated—to give them that which the petitioners say they are striving to obtain. If there is any thing in our system which, rightly considered, prevents their enjoyment of its advantages, the system is in that respect wrong. If a large body of our citizens cannot (in fact and for good reasons) participate in the advantages of our public free education, that education is on a wrong footing—is radically wrong. But the question is, after all, one of fact. Is the ground on which they prevent their children from going to these schools well taken ? What, then, is the reason which they assign ? As I have said, the objections resolve themselves into *two ;* and these two are totally incompatible and inconsistent with each other. One branch of the objection is, that the instruction is purely secular. This has been urged not only in the argument of the reverend gentleman, but the same view of the subject is presented in the documents presented to this board. It is there stated, in various forms, that religion is excluded—that religion is not taught—that the instruction is purely secular, and that the children grow up infidels in consequence. That is alleged to be the tendency of the schools. Such is the first objection. Now, what is the other, or the other head of this same objection ? That the Bible is used by the pupil *" without note or comment"* —that the schools are totally Protestant in their bearing, and tend to undermine the Catholic faith. One of these positions is, I suppose, with great respect, untenable : a child cannot well grow up a Protestant and an infidel at the same time. On which does the gentleman rely for the great responsibility he assumes in dissuading his parishioners from availing themselves of these schools—the Bible without *" note or comment"?* Is this the objection ? *Whose* " notes " or " *comments,*" I pray, does he intend to introduce into our common schools ? Is it possible that the Bible cannot, in this day and generation, be trusted in the hands of our American children ? If the whole Bible cannot be used, cannot such extracts from it be compiled as will satisfy all parties ? This has been the course actually adopted by the trustees. They habitually use a volume composed of selections from the Bible. Cannot these selections be made so as to satisfy all sects ? The real tendency of the reverend gentleman's reasoning in this matter cannot be appreciated, without recollecting the difference between the Catholic and Protestant Bible. I do not intend to draw any parallel between the texts of the translation which we use, and that of the Douay or the Catholic Bible. All our early associations are so interwoven with our own version, that it would be no easy matter to give the Catholic translation a fair and impartial judgment, as far as the richness, beauty, and force of style is concerned ; but on one point surely we of the Protestant faith cannot claim any superiority. In the *moral teaching* of the two versions there is no considerable difference ; in the doctrinal points there are, it is true, some important discrepancies. Where the word *repent* is used in our edition, in the Catholic it is, *do penance.* For the words *daily bread,* in the Catholic edition, are substituted, *supersubstantial bread.* But the great moral precepts (I speak now of the teaching of our Saviour) are the same. How can it be otherwise ? We are all Christians ; either Bible is the code of Christ ; but, as the reverend gentleman has said, it is the " notes and comments " which distinguish the Catholic from the Protestant edition ; it is to the edition without note or comment that the objection exists. This objection is a fundamental one in principle. The Catholic Bible is filled with marginal notes which inculcate dogmas proving, or seeking to prove, doctrinal points— transubstantiation, for instance, or the necessity of the fasts and penance. Now, for the purposes of this argument, the truth of these doctrines is not of the slightest importance. I do not care whether Protestant or Catholic be right. The question is not one of sectarian dogmas, but of education. The difference is not as to the justice or correctness of the " notes and comments," but as to the propriety of using any—whether our children shall be taught to love their neighbors, and not to lie and not to steal, or whether their young minds shall be occupied with the pros and cons of transubstantiation, penance, and fasts. Mankind has never disagreed as to the propriety of robbing, or cheating, or bearing false witness; but about these dogmas, these doctrines, the race has been cutting each other's throats for the last ten centuries. For the last four centuries these doctrines have dyed Europe with blood. It is these recollections, these reminiscences, which have dictated our legislation on this subject. It is these prodigious evils that American statesmen have striven to avoid. This is the evil which the trustees believe they see in the application now made, and in behalf of both Catholics and Protestants, they implore you to reject this petition. They have confined themselves, in the instruction given in these schools, to that which they believe is in conformity with the intentions of the State—a secular education—reading and writing, and the rules of arithmetic, with such instruction on the precepts of the Bible as they did suppose all persons calling themselves Christians could agree in. If this is wrong, the trustees are wrong altogether, and something else must be substituted. If a moral education is not of itself sufficient—if it is not the only proper education for our free schools, something else must be substituted. The religious, the doctrinal, the sectarian education, they have hitherto left to the fireside, to the parents, to the Sunday school. They do not pretend to give it; they do not pretend, by the use of the Bible, to teach more than that moral code which every class of Christians, whether Catholic or Protestant, they conceived would unite to give. In these matters it is worth while to look at the experience of other countries. The same controversy that has arisen here, has arisen also in Ireland; but there, in a country torn by religious schisms—and I state a fact well known to the reverend gentleman—both Protestants and Catholics have united in a selection of extracts to be used, some from our version, some from the Douay Bible. I do not say that this could be adopted here; but I do say, there is some neutral ground on which both parties can meet. I do not pretend that the scheme of the trustees is wholly unexceptionable; but I do say, that vastly greater defects must be discovered in it than have yet been pointed out, to justify its abandonment; and that with all its imperfections on its head, it is a thousandfold better than what is now proposed as its substitute. As to the other branch of this double-headed objection, that the books used in the schools are hostile to Catholics, and promote the Protestant interest: if they are so, they ought to be expurgated; and if they cannot be satisfactorily expurgated, the books themselves ought to be abandoned, and their places supplied by others. The trustees have viewed this matter in the same light; they have done all in their power to remove the Catholic objection, so far as it exists. I regret that the books are not here, that I might convince your honors how far they have gone to meet what they considered the well-founded remonstrances of the Catholics. They have expurgated whole passages of text from some books, and, in other instances, have pasted two leaves together, so as to annihilate completely the objectionable passages, until a new edition can be procured. This has been done, too, notwithstanding the refusal of the Catholic authorities to give the least aid; and surely it is not fair, when this has been done, to insist that these gentlemen were blamable for not discovering these passages sooner. I repeat, it is not common fairness.

They have offered to make the books unobjectionable to Catholics; they have asked the gentlemen who now complain, to lay their fingers on those passages which are objectionable, and they have promised that they should be struck out. But all coöperation and assistance has been refused.

There is one other branch of the question, as regards the conduct of the School Society, of no little importance. The schools, during the week, are under the control of the School Society, but on Sundays they have been used as Sunday schools by such religious societies as would pay for the fuel and take charge of the building. This privilege has been tendered to the Catholics. They have been told, "If you will avail yourselves, during the week-days, of the public schools, you may have the use of the buildings on Sundays, to give such religious education as you see fit, and you may use the Douay Bible or the Missal." Nothing, surely, can be fairer or more impartial than to place all the sects on an equality during the week, and, on Sundays, to use them as they choose for religious purposes. There is but one other branch of the reverend gentleman's remarks to which it will be necessary to refer; that is, as to the character of the schools for which a share of the fund is now demanded. The reverend gentleman insists that they will not be *sectarian schools*. But this must be so; they can be nothing else, from the nature of the case. The schools are attached to their churches; they are within the sound of the chant, almost within reach of the altar; and if sectarian schools are not to be established, what is the object of their establishment at all? If the objection to the existing schools is, that they convey no religious instruction, and these schools are intended to obviate such objections, what kind of education, I beg, will be given? What, to be sure, but the teaching of the Catholic faith? The very ground —the whole foundation—of their petition is, that the schools ought to convey religious education; and do they not, in the schools which they mean to establish, intend to convey religious instruction? And you need not be told by me that it will be a Catholic education—a purely Catholic, a sectarian education. If you, gentlemen, are prepared to lend your funds and your authority to such a scheme, you have only to say the word. The trustees of the public schools, and the gentlemen who compose the Public School Society, hope the result of this application will be such as will bring the children into the schools. Their object is, that the children shall be educated. If there is any thing in the objection made as to the character of the schools or the lessons taught therein, let a committee be appointed by your honors, from you own body, to investigate the subject. If any well-founded cause of complaint exists, it will doubtless be removed. But until it is established by better proof than we have here, that these schools are objectionable, and, by better argument than we have this night heard, that the public funds should be devoted to feed the fires of religious fanaticism, surely your honors will not abandon these long-established and excellent institutions.

HIRAM KETCHUM, Esq., spoke as follows :

MR. CHAIRMAN : This is an application on the part of the Roman Catholic Church, or of the schools under the direction of the Roman Catholic Church, to be permitted to participate in the school fund. I desire to say, this is not a controversy of Catholics with Methodists, or of the Catholics with the Society of Friends ; the question here is, whether the petitioners can, upon principles of public policy, be permitted to participate in the school fund. I may say, in advance, that I don't oppose the petition on behalf of the Public School Society because the petitioners are Catholics. Within the last eighteen years it has been my duty, on behalf of the School Society, to oppose many petitions for participation in this fund. Petitions have come from Episcopalian schools ; and those schools have been represented by a gentleman who is now one of the highest dignitaries in that Church in this State, and also by able counsel. Petitions have come from the Dutch Reformed Church, and they have been advocated with great ability. Petitions have come from the Methodist Church, and have likewise been advocated with great ability ; and from the Baptist Church, and they have been advocated with equal ability ; and from the Roman Catholic Church time and again ; and the prayers of these petitioners, when united as when separate, have, upon what were deemed sound public principles, been rejected by your predecessors. Now the petition comes from one society alone, and the question is, whether the same principle which excluded the Episcopalians, which excluded the Methodists, which excluded the Dutch Reformed Church, which excluded the Baptists, shall not now, as it has heretofore done, exclude the Roman Catholics also.

Mr. President, I regret that some things have been said on behalf of these petitioners that have been said. I regret that an attempt should have been made here to enlist prejudices against the Public School Society, because it is a corporation. The public schools of this city are managed upon the same principles on which the common schools throughout the State are conducted ; and if the public schools are wrong, the principles of the common schools throughout the whole State are equally erroneous ; and it seems to me that the question is not, whether the public schools are managed by a corporation or not, but whether, upon principles which have heretofore been discussed, there can be conceded to Catholics, or any other religious denomination, that which is now sought. If they be so fortunate as to prove that the public schools are on a wrong basis, still they have not gained their point—still they have not shown that Catholics, or any other religious denomination, are entitled to the fund. I may be permitted also to say, I regret that popular appeals have been made on this subject. I do not object to the trustees of that association coming here to petition ; but when I read accounts of popular appeals being made by a high dignitary of that Church to the people, to enlist the popular prejudice on this subject, I may be permitted to say that, at least, the course is a novel one. When I read accounts of the first pastor of that Church—when I read of a mitred gentleman being received by the people with " cheers "—when I read that he addressed them, and was " cheered " on, as we are accustomed to be in our public meetings, I must say there is something novel in the proceeding. The gentlemen composing this body, I conceive, are capable of reasoning on this subject; and it is hardly necessary that a mitred gentleman should descend into the arena, and appeal to the popular prejudice or passion to influence the judgment of this board. I am sure, sir, if I—and I speak it with all respect—if I, or any other man, had been passing St. James', at the times these meetings were held, we should have supposed that they were political meetings, and that possession of the hall was taken by either the " Whigs " or the " Democrats." It seems to me not becoming; it seems to me that it is not treating the question in a proper manner, to make these popular appeals, and then to come here *en masse* to ask your honors to grant the prayer of this petition, at the same time telling you that the Catholics are one fifth of our population. I care not how numerous they are. I know the Catholics, when joined by others on a former day, had their petition rejected; and I trust, when they come here alone, attended by the populace which they have excited, they will have no more nor any less conceded to them than is right, on sound principles of public policy.

There are two principles, or propositions, about which we shall not disagree. The first is, that the Legislature has power to direct that a public fund shall be provided for the education of every child in the State. There is no contradiction here of any sound principle. It is no violation of any sound public principle in the Legislature to enact that out of the public money raised by tax on all our citizens, every child in the State may be permitted to receive the rudiments of an education. There is one other principle which is equally in accordance with the well-established public policy in this State, namely, that not one cent, raised by public taxation, can go to support a religious institution—can go in payment for an education purely religious in its character. Now let us inquire, for a moment, the reasons on which these propositions rest. Why is it that the State can tax all the people for the education of our children? Because it is admitted that intelligence is necessary to enable every citizen to discharge his duty to the community—because our institutions rest upon the intelligence and virtue of the people; therefore it is right that the State should furnish that intelligence to every member; and it is no answer for any man, who is called to pay a tax for that legitimate purpose, to say, " I send my children to schools where I pay for their education. I do not wish to avail myself of the public fund. My children are educated at this or that classical school. I don't wish to participate, and therefore I won't pay the tax." This is an answer that the State would not admit for a moment. And it might be that the State adopted some system of education which might not suit all—the Lancasterian, for instance, as in this city. Now, some may say, " I dislike the Lancasterian system; I think it is calculated to impart a superficial education. I dislike it. I have a deep-rooted objection to that system." But will the State permit him to say, "I will withhold my tax. I cannot pay my tax, because I have an objection to the system which prevents my children participating in the fund; and therefore I ask the privilege of retaining my portion of the tax"? Would the State listen to such a plea? What, then, is the conclusion? Why, the State, having the right to educate the children, and having the right to tax the people for that purpose, must necessarily adopt some general system—it must follow some general rule; and whatever my scruples may be, whatever may be the scruples of any other individual here, or throughout the community, and however oppressive it may be to me, or to others, who cannot avail themselves of the system, they must submit. The great end which the State has in view—to impart intelligence to every citizen—must be accomplished, and on some principle adopted and established by the State itself. Well, what is the next principle and reason? We see that no tax can be laid for the support of religion. Why? Religion is the foundation of sound morals. That, no man will deny; we do not live in an age when any man denies it. Sound morals are essential to the preservation of the community; why, therefore, shall not the city be taxed for that which is essential to her preservation? Why shall she not be taxed for laying the foundation on which sound morals and sound political institutions rest? I will tell you why. We are divided into different sects, and, if we were taxed for the support of religion, it would happen—it could not be prevented—that a man would be taxed for the support of a religion in which he did not believe, and which he regarded as injurious. I should be taxed to support the Jewish religion; Dr. Brownlee would be taxed to support the Catholic religion, and the reverend gentleman who has addressed you here to-night would be taxed to support Dr. Brownlee's religion. And would they pay the tax? No; for it would be a violation of conscience. And you would then see the time arrive, if an attempt were made to collect such a tax, when men would march to the stake, as in years gone by. Right or wrong, you would see many Protestants go to the stake, before they would let a single dollar of their money go to teach the right reverend gentleman's religion. So, on the other hand, you would see thousands of Catholics suffer martyrdom, before they would contribute to a fund whereby they might, by chance, be contributing to the teaching of heresy. This is the reason why we cannot have a general tax for the support of religion. But again, we believe that religion is essential to sound morals. There is no gentleman here who will deny that the Christian religion is the great conservative principle of the community. And how is that best promoted and advanced? By being let alone; by giving every denomination a fair chance; by leaving religion to voluntary support. It is best for religion itself that it should be let alone to extend its own boundaries. Now, then, Mr. Chairman, to me it is most manifest that this community is bound to furnish the rudiments of a common education. The State is bound to do this, and to do it by some public system— by some ordinance, or by some law; the State is bound to make provision for furnishing this education. I do not say—I will not pretend to say—that

16

the State has a right to take the children from the arms of their mothers. I do not mean to say that the State has a right to force education on any body. That is not the principle. But I mean to say that the State ought to furnish a system which shall be open and acceptable to all. It ought to furnish bread, and say, Come and eat. I do not mean to inflict pains and penalties; I should think they would be hardly necessary. Let us go forth with persuasion. I am for using no force but the force of strong argument. Well, now, sir, if it is the duty of the State to furnish an education for the poor, and for all the children in the community, or for all that will avail themselves of it, the State must establish some system; and there is a system established in the city of New York upon what we supposed to be public principles—common schools in the common acceptation of that term.

Mr. Chairman, the idea that we are bound in our common schools to teach religion is a perfectly novel idea to an American mind. Who ever went to a common school to be taught religion? I am in the midst of Americans who have received their education in the common schools of this country, and I ask who ever went to a common school to receive religious instruction? I venture to say that the idea is perfectly novel. But do we mean to say that because no religion is taught in these schools, that they are irreligious? Far otherwise. Now the reverend gentleman has said—with all his professions of kindness he has said, that religion is below par in the public schools; at an immense discount. Now, is it so? He argues ingeniously, that if they are not taught the doctrines of some known sect, there is no religion. Why, sir, we have been taught sound morals in all our schools. I do not know any school in which they have not been taught. I do not know a mechanics' shop where the young American or Irishman goes to be instructed in the trade of a cabinet-maker or blacksmith, where he is not bound to be of sound morals. This obligation prevails everywhere—it is a thing which every body acknowledges. We are bound to teach it. " Thou shalt not lie; thou shalt not steal; thou shalt not bear false witness," are precepts which we teach in our schools. Who ever heard to the contrary? And if we are bound to teach them, we are at liberty to teach those general religious truths which give them sanction. I should like to know where there is a school in which the master is not at liberty to say, God's eye sees all you do; and if you steal, or lie, the retribution of eternal judgment will follow you. This is not teaching religion. This is morality, and an invoking of the common sanctions of that morality. Sir, it has been said of these schools that they do not teach this. Why, if the gentlemen had visited the schools—and I am afraid they have not—they would have seen, if their eyes had been properly directed, mottoes of this kind : " God sees and knows all our thoughts, words, and actions." " God sees all we do ; He hears all we say ; He knows all we do." " Son, reverence thy parent." And yet, gentlemen, we don't teach religion ; we don't teach purgatory ; we don't teach baptism or no baptism ; we don't teach any thing that is disputed among Christians. We have no right to do so : but we have the right to declare moral truths, and this community gives us that right—not the law, but, as my friend says, public sentiment.

And is there no common principle in which all agree? Is there not a principle to which all religious men refer? And have not we the right, thus far, to teach the sanctions of morality in these schools? And because we teach the principles which every body acknowledges, and no man disputes—which give offence to nobody, and ought not—are we to be told that these are religious schools? Why, in our common schools we have all been taught the common truths of religion, and yet no one ever went there to receive religious education.

Mr. Chairman, while in these common, established schools, we give the rudiments of an ordinary education—while we teach there to write and cypher, and read the newspaper, and discharge the duties of citizens—while this is done, there is another department in which religion is taught. We all know it—we all feel it; and while the Legislature can go to any extent to advance man in one department, that of common elementary learning, there is another, which is left to religion, where the pastor takes the children, where the Christian parent takes the children, where the benevolent Christian takes the children to his Sunday-school, or elsewhere, and brings them under the influence of religion. This department is supplied by voluntary contribution, and not one dollar can be paid by public tax. Now I do maintain, sir, that I speak of a line so clear, so broad, that every man who hears me, who has had the good fortune to receive an education in this country, will understand it; a broad, clear, and distinct line between secular and religious education. One is received under the influence of a religious teacher; that religious teacher gets his pay by the voluntary contribution of willing hearts; he dares not get it anywhere else; he does not want to get it in any other way. The other can draw on the State for any amount that the people, in their sovereign capacity, may determine.

We thus undertake in these public schools to furnish this secular education, embracing, as it does, not solely and exclusively the common rudiments of learning, but also a knowledge of good morals, and those common sanctions of religion which are acknowledged by every body. We have established such a system, and the question is, whether that system shall be destroyed and a new one established. That is the question. This system is known and understood; it has spread its schools all over our city; it is under one government; children removing from one ward to another find in each the same schools, are accommodated with the same books, meet with, and are instructed under the same uniform system. Now shall it be continued or not? Mr. Chairman, if the prayer of this petition be granted, it must be abandoned. I can show you this in a few minutes. Does the reverend gentleman suppose that he alone would be permitted to take this fund? Does he imagine that the various Protestant denominations will stand by, and look on, and see him draw ten, twelve, or fourteen dollars a child, for its education, and the making it—for it would be so; that would be the result after all—not only a fair scholar, but a good Catholic? Does he suppose he is going to have that business to himself, and that other reverend gentlemen are going to stand by, and build up no schools? It will not be as in former years, as the reverend gentleman conjectures; for then the bounty of the State was small, then only two dollars a head, or something of that sort, could be drawn, and the Lancasterian system was not introduced; then there was no inducement offered to the religious bodies; but with this large bounty the Presbyterians, the Episcopalians, the Baptists, and our friends, the Methodists, who are, it seems, such naughty people, will have their schools; and they will have them well filled, too; and not only filled with the children of their own disciples, but they will have an inducement to bring in others, because the more they draw in, the more money they will draw, and the consequence will be that the system of public schools will be broken up. Now, the consideration which I wish to bring to your mind is, whether the new system will be as good or better than the old. It is the common-sense way of acting, not to desert that which has done well, that which has done good service, unless we see that we are going to improve by the change. What is the charge brought against this system of public school instruction? What is the charge? What is the objection? What is the system established for? It is to furnish a good, common, ordinary literary education—a good literary and scientific education—to instruct our children in the rudiments of literature and science. Now there is no charge—and I want this body to look at this paper in reference to that—there is no charge against the School Society that it has not performed that duty—that it has not given what it was bound to give—the rudiments of a good literary education—that it has not enabled the children to read, and write, and cypher, and furnished them with the elements of geography, so as to fit them to go forth and discharge their duties as intelligent citizens. There is no charge against the Society that it has not performed this. What, then, is it? Why, it is this: that the Catholics, from conscientious scruples, cannot come in and participate in the advantages of the system. Their consciences forbid them to have their children educated in these schools. Now, Mr. Chairman, there is no man, I apprehend, that can have a higher respect for the rights of conscience, than he who now addresses you; but let us examine this matter, and with all respect for those whose claim we now discuss, I fairly and candidly ask, Can a Roman Catholic have conscientious scruples against my learning his son to read, to write, to cypher, and the common elements of geography? Can it be? Is it possible? Take a fair intelligent Protestant, and is it possible that any Roman Catholic could object to that man instructing his children to read, write, and cypher? Why, no; you might just as well say he has conscientious scruples against such a man learning his son "the art, trade, and mystery" of cabinet-making in a Protestant shop. You may just as well say that he has conscientious scruples against placing his son in the office of a Protestant lawyer to study law. Why, is it so in fact? Go into your fashionable schools, and I ask you if there are not there as many Catholics, as of other sects? I think I have in my eye those, among the petitioners themselves, who send their children to Madame this or that, who is a Protestant; and there are many Protestants here who send their children to the schools of Catholics; and in doing this, they consider themselves as compromising nothing, for there is no religion taught there. These considerations, which so press on the minds of these conscientious petitioners for the hardship endured by the parents who send their children to public schools now, are not appreciated in their own case when they send their sons to Columbia College, or to the schools of Protestant Mrs. Smith, or some other lady. Well, now, Mr. Chairman, if there be no conscientious scruples at all against employing Protestants to teach their children to read and write and cypher, on what can their conscientious scruples rest? It has been said (but I will not read the passage, because the commonly understood meaning of it has been disavowed) that the children that go to these schools do not reverence their parents, and that they feel a contempt for them, as though a special influence had been used by which they were led to do this. Now I supposed, until it was disclaimed so explicitly, that this had an application to the gentlemen of the Society of Friends. But the reverend gentleman has disavowed it; and he ought to do so, for I can tell that gentleman that the Friends never, perhaps in a single instance, sent or permitted children of theirs to go to these schools. They educate their own poor, and they ask the State for no participation. They do not send their children there, and I venture to affirm that, of the numerous children that go to those schools, not one attends the public ordinances of religion according to the mode established by the Society of Friends. And I will go farther and say, of those who are educated there, none are converted to their faith. Whatever may be intended here or elsewhere, it may be asserted, with perfect confidence, that those individuals make no proselytes; and also it may be said, that they have kept their people from being teachers, fearing such accusations as are made against them by the reverend gentleman.

And, Mr. President, if it is alleged—and I understand it now to be disclaimed—that the course of education begets irreverence to parents, I can only say they who affirm it speak of that which they do not understand. If they had gone to these schools, they would have seen what care is taken, what sound moral principles are inculcated, and they would then never have made this charge. But it is now disclaimed, and it is not for that reason, then, that they have conscientious scruples. But what else is there? It is affirmed that some of these books contain passages reflecting on Catholics. Now I submit to the candor of the gentleman, and of every one that hears me—because the books, containing numerous extracts from numerous authors, collected together for the use of these schools, contain a few passages which I may conceive reflect on me, or on my religion, or on my politics; is that a good reason why I should have conscientious scruples and objections against the entire system? Let us see where it would lead. Here is the Catholic, in turning over perhaps a thousand pages, finds some fifty lines that reflect on his religion. I venture to say the Calvinists, on turning over those pages, would find something reflecting on them. I have not made the experiment, but I have no doubt that would be the result. Then comes the high churchman, and if he does not find something there bearing on his peculiarities, I am mistaken. Then there are the Methodists, and if they do not find something there bearing on what people call their fanaticism, it is extraordinary. Then there is the politician, and there may be something extracted from Jefferson used in these schools, and to this a certain class of politicians may say, I cannot have my children taught Jeffersonianism. Well, then, there is my particular, worthy friend, Daniel Webster, who may have contributed something to the pages of these books, and a Democrat, who takes up the books, may say, I cannot go Webster any how ; I must have that expurgated. Now if all men must go on in this way, and conscientiously object to the system because in the reading-lessons they find some passages against their religious or political opinions, the whole of the books will be expunged. I do not mean to reflect on the conscientious scruples of any man, but I ask if we are not bound to take hold of this system in a fair and candid manner. We must have a public system ; and it is impossible to have a public system to which some man may not have scruples and objections. Well, sir, but what next ? Why, the Bible. I believe a chapter from the Bible, the Protestant translation, without note or comment, is read in some of these schools at their opening every day. Shall we give up this Bible, Mr. President ? It would be a very hard thing. I have no authority to say how far the trustees can go, or will go, in a spirit of compromise, with an earnest desire to get in these children, but I am here to say that it will be a great sacrifice to give up the Bible—to give up that translated Bible—containing, as we believe, and as I doubt not, a great part of Christendom believes, not only a fair translation, but a vast fund of pure English. It will be hard to give up that Bible, sir. It has furnished consolation in life, and hope in death, to many. The institutions of liberty and the altars of piety have sprung up in the path of that translated Bible ; and wherever that translated Bible has gone, popular institutions have risen. All those glorious principles, which here in this country are so conspicuous, have come from that Bible ; and wherever that translated Bible has been kept from the hands of the laity, there has been darkness and despotism.

We, sir, have a Declaration of Independence of which we are proud, because it contains those great principles of liberty which are found in the Bible. Yes, sir, there lies beyond that Declaration of Independence a book whose principles are a declaration of independence to man ; and wherever that book is read, man finds out his rights, and is willing to assert them.

Mr. President and gentlemen of the board, it is in your hands. It is at present in the hands of these trustees, but it is a very delicate trust. We are called upon to give up that Bible. I am not the man to say that it can be done, and I believe, if this is necessary to a compromise, we shall have to say, "No compromise." We cannot give up that Bible from our own hands, and the hands of the children of this republic. Mr. Chairman, we must go a little farther. Suppose we did now give up the Bible, and make a common selection from the two translations—the Catholic and our own ; suppose we made a common selection about which we all agree. Why, gentlemen, such a compromise was made across the water ; that compromise was agreed to by a majority of the Irish Catholic bishops, but the minority appealed to the pope. Now the gentleman is mistaken if he supposes I am capable of appealing to any prejudices improperly, but he has not denied this fact; and I expected it would have been denied, or somehow explained, how such an appeal was made from that country. Sir, such an appeal might be made in this country; and if so, in all candor I ask, whether it does not belong to a foreign potentate to say whether the Bible shall be read in our common schools? I ask if they can escape from that position? I want an answer to that question. And if there be a foreign power, spiritual or otherwise, to say that the Bible shall not be read, I ask if that power may not say that the Constitution and the Declaration of Independence shall not be read? I mean no reflection. This matter has come out in evidence here, and I draw from it what may be supposed to be legitimate conclusions. The gentlemen opposite may smile, but I ask if they can escape from these conclusions? I know there are many of the Catholic laity who are Americans by birth, and many by adoption, who would settle that question very soon. Though the mitre may be placed by a foreign power on the head of him that wears it, I know there is a feeling in the American bosom—be it Catholic or Protestant—that will not allow a foreign potentate, either directly or indirectly, to interfere. Now, Mr. President, I have got through all I propose to say on this subject, and again I put it to you, Shall we not have the privilege to learn our little fellow-citizens to read and write and cipher, and to teach them the common elements of geography and history? Shall we be prevented by a conscientious scruple? Mr. Chairman, I feel a strong desire that both Protestants and Catholics should be brought into the same schools, and I see in such a circumstance, great and wholesome and beneficial political results. When a stranger comes here from a foreign land, where he has been oppressed, I am willing to grant him an asylum, and to say that he shall have all the benefits of this land, and of our Constitution; and that if he has been oppressed, that he has come to a country where he shall be oppressed no more. All I ask is, that he shall give America his heart. If he comes with an Irish heart, let it become an American heart; let him stand by America, and by her children, enjoying the same rights as they enjoy, and growing up with them, amalgamate with them, and interchanging the same kind and benevolent feelings together. That is what I want. I want to see the country from which he came second in his regard to the land of his adoption, to the land of his children; and I want those children so brought up, that, when they become men, they shall have pure American feelings. I hope, sir, they will not be taught that we entertain the same feeling here that Orangemen and Protestants entertain in Ireland. We are not unfriendly to them; our children are not their enemies; let us, then, grow up and amalgamate together. I dislike any system that would cast off from American ground these children of foreign countries; and I ask the gentlemen if they cannot come in and place their children side by side with ours, and let them feel that in the schools there are no partialities, and that out of them they may go to their own Church and bow before their own altar? But for civil purposes, let all be brought up together.

Mr. Chairman, there is another very plausible argument presented here. They tell you, in their memorial, that they will engage to give as good an ordinary secular education as the public schools can give for the same money. They propose to allow their schools to be visited by the public authorities, or by the trustees themselves, and to place them under some general supervision. Now, there are two ways of insuring the fidelity of trustees, in directing the object of a public trust toward the end designed ; one is, by supervision, and the other is, by so creating the trust as to insure, by its organization, the requisite fidelity. The latter I prefer. Here is a religious society whose paramount purpose is religious instruction ; if to that be superadded a literary education, it will be subordinate to the other, as it ought ; its constant tendency will be, to neglect the literary education for the purpose of promoting the other, and therefore the object of the Legislature will most likely be neglected.

But here is the Public School Society, created for one single purpose, and that is, education. For that it is organized, and to that end all its operations tend. But if it had two objects in view, the paramount one would be that which would receive its chief attention ; the other and subordinate one would receive less. If you entrust this business of education to a religious society, religion will be paramount, and literature will be subordinate. Let that subordinate one be paid for by the State, and it would be in their case if they had no other object. But, gentlemen, the question is, Will you desert the Public School Society, and take up this new society ? It has been said that the Public School Society is a monopoly. In the country, the trustees are chosen by the people ; but in this city, owing to its peculiar organization, the matter is left to the superintendence of benevolent individuals, who are voluntary agents. They receive no compensation for their services, and experience has shown that the duties have been better discharged by that system than by any other. You may go to the schools in the State and examine the most favorable ones ; then visit the schools in this city, and the education in our schools will be found superior to that in the common schools elsewhere.

This Society is called a corporation ; but it is a corporation which is bound by law to report all its proceedings every year to this Council, and, at stated times, to the Legislature. It is a corporation of which the members of this board are *ex-officio* members. It is a corporation which has control of a great fund, and it has for its end the good of the State ; but it is willing that its real estate shall be transferred to this Corporation whenever the public good requires it, and to this end an offer has long since been made, and is now repeated. But if we are to have this common school system of education, I ask, if it is not better to have it under the supervision of men of business and of high character, who are willing to devote their leisure to its interests ? I wish to call your attention to another subject. This fund is a large one ; $73,000 is from the State and compulsory taxation. In the country, as explained by my associate, a certain sum is granted by the State, on condition that an equal sum is added to the school fund, by a tax laid on the people themselves who receive it. But, independent of that, our citizens came and asked to be taxed something more, and that amount is more than the other two. But it must be recollected, when this request to be permitted to tax themselves still farther was made, it was settled and determined that the churches should be excluded. When that was settled, and the schools were mainly under the supervision of the Common School Society, that Society got up petitions for this additional taxation; and because confidence was placed in that Society, the taxation was not opposed. Now, if we revert back to the common school system, this must come back too ; for I affirm, that the chief consideration which induced the petitioners —and they were men of great property among them—to sign the petition asking to be taxed for the purposes of education, was, that the School Society was to have the superintendence. The sum of $73,000 was thus raised, because confidence was reposed in the School Society, as antagonistic of those church societies.

Now, perhaps, the gentleman may ask, if the system is to be changed, that we should resort to the same course as is pursued in the country, where the people elect their own commissioners and trustees. But if we do, the schools must be governed on the same principles as these, and the only difference will be in the managers. And if it is to come to that, I am sure these trustees will be very willing ; for it is to them a source of great vexation to be compelled to carry on this controversy for such a period.

They are very unwilling to come here to meet their fellow-citizens in a somewhat hostile manner. They have nothing to gain, for the Society is no benefit to them; and they give days and weeks of their time, without recompense, to the discharge of the duties of their trust. They have nothing to gain, but they have arduous duties to discharge. Nor have they any thing to conceal. They report every thing to this Common Council, and therefore the public know all they do ; and if they are not found faithful to the trust—if, in the solemn judgment of this corporation, they do not answer the end proposed, elect others in their place ; and if the prayer of this petition be granted, it will be equivalent to their arraignment. I know not that I can add any thing more to my argument. It has been my fortune, during the last eighteen years, from time to time to argue this question before other boards, who came to a unanimous decision ; and at the very time when the question was referred to the Legislature, the petitioners were supported by a reverend gentleman of the highest respectability of that day, and by lay gentlemen of great talent. We had the discussion here until eleven and twelve o'clock at night, and the gentlemen of the Common Council—men of great respectability—denied the prayer of the petition, and the public sustained them in their decision. Our Roman Catholic friends come now with the same principle that was decided then, and I hope, sir, the prayer of the petitioners will not be granted.

The Rev. Dr. Bond then appeared as the representative of the Methodist Episcopal Church, but he gave way to the Right Rev. Bishop Hughes, who desired to make a brief reply to the two legal gentlemen who had addressed the board. He said :

I have a few remarks that I wish to make, partly in reference to myself and partly to my principles, and the views submitted with regard to those principles; but the debate has taken a range too wide and too legal for me to pretend to follow it throughout. I am not accustomed to the niceties of legislation, or the manner of interpreting statutes or acts of the Legislature; but, to sum up the whole of the two eloquent addresses made by the gentlemen who have just spoken, they amount to this: that either the consciences of Catholics must be crushed, and their objections resisted, or the Public School System must be destroyed. That is the pith of both their observations. They argue that there must be either one or the other of these two results, and those gentlemen are inclined to the course of compelling conscience to give way, they being the judge of our consciences, which they wish to overrule; so that the Public School Society—and I do not desire to detract from it as far as good intentions are concerned—shall continue to dispose of the public school fund, notwithstanding our objections and the reasoning on which they are based. The gentleman who last spoke appeared to imagine that I wished the exclusion of the Protestant Bible, and that, for the benefit of Catholics, I laid myself open to the charge of enmity to the Word of God; but I desired nothing of the sort. I would leave the Protestant Bible for those that reverence it; but, for myself, it has not my confidence. Another objection which he made was of a personal character to myself; but while that gentleman started with the beautiful rule of charity to others, and with a lecture on the propriety of retaining our station in life, and the impropriety of the public appeals of which he was pleased to speak, I regret that his practice was not in accordance with his precept; and that, while he was lecturing me on the subject, he himself should have gone beyond any thing which proper discussion called for. If I attended those meetings, it was because I felt the evil of the present system as regards us— not its evil as regards others; and we must be permitted to be the judge of our own duties, and to see for ourselves, while we accord to others the same right for themselves. I beg to disclaim any intention to overrule this community, or to bring any thing from Rome, except to those who believe in its spiritual authority. Consequently, all those remarks of that gentleman have been out of place; and for the rest I conceive the true point has not been touched. Not one of our objections or scruples of conscience has he undertaken to analyze, nor the grounds on which they exist. When I gave those reasons for our objections, I thought some argument would have been urged fairly against them, but the only end the gentleman appears to have in view, is the preservation of the School Society, and to maintain that they have a patent right to the office. That I know is his object; but I did not expect to hear any man construing the law as that its advantages cannot reach us unless we lay down and sacrifice our consciences at the threshold. I have spoken for myself, and I have disclaimed all high-handed objects; but the gentleman insists, notwithstanding the pledge which we have given, that, in spite of all, we shall teach our religion. I disclaim such intentions, and I do not think it fair in that gentleman to impute intentions which we disclaim. The gentleman has drawn a beautiful picture of society, if all could live in harmony (I would it could be reduced to practice), whether born in foreign parts or in this country. But if all could be brought up together—

if all could associate in such a state without prejudice to the public welfare, while the Protestants use such books as those to which we object, it could only be by the Catholic concealing his religion; for, if he owns it, he will be called a "papist." The gentleman says that one of the books to which we object is not a text-book used in the schools; but, if not, it is one of the books placed in the library—to which I do not say *we* contribute more than others, but it is supported at the public expense, to which Catholics contribute as well as others. I will read you one passage, and leave you to judge for yourselves what will be its effects on the minds of our children. The work is entitled "The Irish Heart," and the author, at p. 24, is describing an Irish Catholic, and he says: "As for Phelim Maghee, he was of no particular religion."

And how the gentlemen describe the public schools, but as schools of religion and no religion. They say they give religious instruction; but again they say, it is not religion, for it does not vitiate their claim.

As for old Phelim Maghee, he was of no particular religion.

When Phelim had laid up a good stock of sins, he now and then went over to Killarney, of a Sabbath morning, and got "*relaaf* by *confissing* them out o' the way," as he used to express it, and sealed up his soul with a *wafer*.

That is the term they apply to our doctrine of transubstantiation; and they want us to associate and to enjoy every thing in harmony, when they assail our religious right.

——and returned quite invigorated for the perpetration of new offences.

Now, suppose Catholic children hear this in the company of their Protestant associates! They will be subject to the ridicule of their companions, and the consequence will be, that their domestic and religious attachments will become weakened; they will become ashamed of their religion, and they will grow up *Nothingarians*.

But again, on p. 120, when speaking of intemperance, we find the following:

It is more probable, however, a part of the papal system.

And this, notwithstanding all that Father Matthew has done.

For when drunkenness shall have been done away, and, with it, that just relative proportion of all indolence, ignorance, crime, misery, and superstition, of which it is the putative parent, then truly a much smaller portion of mankind may be expected to follow the dark lantern of the Romish religion.

That religion is most likely to find professors among the frivolous and the wicked, which, by a species of ecclesiastical legerdemain, can persuade the sinner that he is going to heaven, when he is going directly to hell. By a refined and complicated system of Jesuitry and prelatical juggling, the papal see has obtained its present extensive influence through the world.

And, unless we send our children to imbibe these lessons, we are going to overturn the system! But is that the true conclusion to which the gentleman should come from our petition? Is that reasoning from facts and the evidence before their eyes? I have promised not to detain the board, and therefore I would merely say, if I have attended those meetings, it was not with the views the gentleman has imputed to me, nor to distinguish myself, as has been insinuated. I have taken good care to banish politics from those meetings ; and if I have mentioned the number of Catholics, or of their children, it was to show how far this system falls short of the end which the Legislature had in view. I disclaim utterly and entirely the intention imputed to me by the gentleman. But I will no longer detain the board.

Mr. Mott, one of the Public School Trustees, with the permission of the board, explained the manner in which the book which the right reverend prelate had last alluded to had found its way into the schools. It was one of a series of tales published by the Temperance Society ; and when a committee was appointed for filling the library, their attention was called to the first number of the series. They read two or three of them which had come from the press, and, as they appeared to be adapted to the reading of children, the committee admitted them, and by some mistake it was supposed that all the other volumes of the same series, and under the same title, were ordered too, and they were sent in as they issued from the press after that period, and in this way the book in question had crept in. But this being discovered by a Catholic trustee, it was withdrawn, and of this the gentlemen were fully apprised, and therefore he asked if it was generous or just to quote that book, under these circumstances, to strengthen the cause of the Catholics.

The Right Rev. Bishop Hughes assured the gentleman that he, until that moment, had not heard of the books having been withdrawn.

The Rev. Dr. Bond then again rose to address the board, as the representative of the Methodist Episcopal Church ; but as it was now 10 o'clock, it was proposed by one of the aldermen to take a recess until Friday afternoon, at 4 o'clock, which was agreed to, and the board adjourned.

SECOND DAY.

The board reassembled at 4 o'clock on Friday, the 30th of October, by adjournment from the previous day, but some time elapsed before the debate could be resumed, in consequence of the difficulty which the gentlemen who took part in the proceedings, found in gaining an entrance to the Council Chamber, through the greatly increased crowd of persons who were anxious and struggling to be present. After the room had been filled to overflowing, many hundreds were still excluded who desired admission; but the room was filled to its utmost capacity, even to standing room in the windows, and those still crowding round the entrance-door were obliged to endure the disappointment. DAVID GRAHAM, Esq., Alderman of the Fifteenth Ward, presided on this occasion as the *locum tenens* of the President, Mr. Alderman Purdy, who, however, was present, seated with the aldermen. There were also present many distinguished and reverend gentlemen of various denominations of this city, besides those who took part in the discussion. Dr. Brownlee was seated near Dr. Bond during that gentleman's speech, but he did not attempt to address the board.

The Rev. Dr. Pise, and other reverend gentlemen of the Catholic Church, were seated with the Right Rev. Bishop Hughes and the Very Rev. Dr. Power, and many preachers of the Methodist Episcopal Church were in the vicinity of the orator by whom they were represented.

When all the gentlemen were seated, the President called upon the Rev. Dr. Bond, of the Methodist Episcopal Church, to proceed with the debate on behalf of the remonstrants of that body.

The Rev. Dr. BOND spoke as follows:

MR. PRESIDENT AND GENTLEMEN OF THE COMMON COUNCIL: It may be necessary here, in the outset, that I should, on the part of those that I represent, disclaim all hostility to our fellow-citizens who have made their claim to this Council. To them we have no hostility—nay, we have no prejudice against them as a body; and of any hostility that may be found in the memorial which we have presented to this body, the address of the right reverend gentleman who opened this discussion last night will furnish us with a thorough explanation; for, when he adverted to that part of his memorial which related to the Society of Friends, he wished it to be expressly understood that he spoke of their creed apart from themselves. Now, this is the explanation we wish to make of our memorial which we have presented to this Council. We speak of the creed of the Roman Catholic Church apart from the Roman Catholics themselves. We are bound, not only by the obligations of social life, but by our common Christianity, to extend to them all the benevolence which we think ought to be exercised toward any other portion of our fellow-citizens. It may be asked why we adverted to their creed at all. Because it was wholly unavoidable. We could not do otherwise, because it was on its peculiarities that they rested their claim to a portion of this fund ; it was on their peculiar creed that they rested their scruples against sending their children to the public schools. We could, therefore, no otherwise resist their claim but by adverting to those peculiarities. And it is complained that we adverted to them with too little respect. Now, sir, we must be allowed to say, that whatever there is of disrespect to our Roman Catholic fellow-citizens in this memorial, they must allow something for the provocation. Sir, we had esteemed the public schools a common benefit, and we had made sacrifices to the system. We, too, should have been glad if we could have educated our children in our own way, and in our sectarian tenets, or prejudices, if you will ; but when we found the Legislature providing an education that should be universal, we brought all our sectarian feelings, and placed them on the altar of the public welfare. And when we found the public schools, which we esteemed so great a good, about to be destroyed by the sectarian prejudices of another denomination, we were alarmed, and we stated in our memorial that we were alarmed. And was there no cause for alarm ? Why, the public gatherings which were so feelingly alluded to last night were cause of alarm. Was there not cause for alarm, when, at a time of general excitement and political strife, there were these gatherings of the Catholics ? And was there not cause to fear that their object was to wrest from the Common Council by intimidation, what they had failed to obtain by reason and argument ? Such were our fears ; but really, sir, the complaint of want of respect in our memorial is wholly out of place. Why, the gentleman reminds me of a man who, while deliberately skinning a living eel, cursed the "varmint" because it would not hold still. Why, sir, this skinning is a serious matter. I hope, however, that we shall be allowed the apology which the right reverend gentleman made for himself and for those associated with him, when speaking of the Society of Friends and their creed——

The Right Rev. Bishop HUGHES interposed, and said he had not spoken of the *creed* of either the Society of Friends or of the Methodists. He did not suppose this body was sitting in judgment on creeds.

The Rev. Dr. BOND continued :

I admit that, when the reverend gentleman spoke of the Society of Friends, he did not speak of them by name. Well, but the right reverend gentleman says—and he contends it has an important bearing on this matter—that we have made a false issue ; that we charge that the applicants require a portion of this public money for sectarian purposes ; and this, he says, is "a false issue." If this be true, it will have an important bearing on the question. But we affirm that it is not a false issue : it is the true issue ; there can be no other issue. It will be remembered, sir, that we have only now to justify what we have alleged in our memorial. We are not going into the merits of the legal part of the question, for we are not of the legal profession ; and, after what we have heard from the legal gentlemen in this discussion, it cannot be expected. But we do affirm that the issue we, in common with the Trustees of the Public School Society, plead—that this money is applied for for sectarian purposes—is the true issue. How do we prove it? It has been one leading objection to the public schools, that no religion is taught in them. Well, it is also alleged that no religion can be taught there, unless we teach sectarianism. Now, if it be complained, on the part of our Roman Catholic fellow-citizens, that no religion is taught in these schools, surely they don't mean to keep schools in which they will teach no religion. We take them to be honest in what they say, and I hope that is not "a false issue." They allege that no religion is taught, and that none can be taught without teaching sectarianism. Now we take it for granted that they will not keep schools in which no religion is taught; or why do they object to the public schools? And if they teach religion, it must be sectarianism, for they themselves allege that no religion can be taught without teaching sectarianism; and if so, then will not the public money be used for sectarian purposes? There is only one way to escape from this position. What claim may be set up here, I know not; but else- where it is alleged that they teach the Roman Catholic religion, and that is not sectarianism, inasmuch as it is the only true religion.

This may be a salvo for them, but it is not for us. They will not expect that other denominations will admit that the Roman Catholic is the only true religion, and that it is not sectarianism. But if they do, and if they still say that theirs is the only true Church; and if they, only a branch of the common stock, only one of the many sects of our common Christianity, teach Catholicism there, they teach sectarianism as much as Methodists would do if they had one of these schools in which they taught Methodism. And if they teach Catholic sectarianism to their children, will not the money they claim, if allowed, be applied to sectarian purposes? This is all we said, sir; and is this "a false issue"? We say it is the true issue; there can be no other issue, for there can be no possible objection to this conclusion. So much for "the issue," sir.

But it was complained, sir, that we have said the arguments by which their application on a former occasion was resisted, were "clear, cogent, and unanswerable." We grant that this is a matter of opinion. We say, when we read them in the memorial of the trustees of the public schools, we thought them clear, cogent, and conclusive; but we accord to the gentle- man the right to form his own opinion; and can he complain if we claim the same privilege which we accord to him? But it was complained that we had alleged that "neither the Constitution of the State nor the public welfare are to be regarded, when they stand in the way of Roman Catholic sectarianism and exclusiveness." Why, is it not on the ground of sectarian exclusiveness that they make this claim? I take it for granted that, if they cannot conscientiously send their children to the public schools, their con- scientious objection is founded on their creed. There is something of pecu- liarity in their creed, for they alone, of all the denominations, have scruples on this subject; and we did not then intend to give offence by the term "sectarian exclusiveness." But again, it is complained that we alleged that

" it must be manifest to the Common Council, that, if the Roman Catholic claims are granted, all the other Christian denominations will urge their claims for a similar appropriation, and that the money raised for education by a general tax will be solely applied to the purposes of proselytism, through the medium of sectarian schools." And can any thing be clearer? Indeed, the gentleman does not take particular exception to this. " That the money raised for education by a general tax will be solely applied to the purposes of proselytism ! " Why, if they are honest in their prejudices for their form of worship, and if they believe their own religion the best, they will endeavor to impart their own views, and all the principles which they advocate, to those they take under their own care. And what is this but proselytism ? The word is not used offensively, for we only mean, by making proselytes, the making converts to their own faith. But we had said, " If this were done, would it be the price of peace ? or would it not throw the apple of discord into the whole Christian community ? Should we agree in the division of the spoils ? Would each sect be satisfied with the portion allotted to it ? " Is there any thing offensive in this question ? Might we not honestly differ respecting the amount appropriated to us severally ?

We venture to say, that the sturdy claimants who now beset the Council would not be satisfied with much less than the lion's share ; and we are sure that there are other Protestant denominations besides ourselves who would not patiently submit to the exaction.

And this has been spoken of, sir, by the right reverend gentleman, as though we had threatened a rebellion ! Is it necessary that we should stir up rebellion to carry out all we said ? We only said, " We are sure that there are other Protestant denominations besides ourselves who would not patiently submit to the exaction." Have the Catholics submitted patiently to what they consider a grievance ? Certainly not, for they have reiterated their claim again and again with a perseverance which, in a good cause, is praiseworthy. But we did not say we would rebel ; we said we would not "*patiently* submit ; " nor should we be patient, until we obtained a legal remedy. But we have said, " When all the Christian sects shall be satisfied with their individual share of the public fund, what is to become of those children whose parents belong to none of these sects, and who cannot conscientiously allow them to be educated in the peculiar dogmas of any one of them ? The different committees who, on a former occasion, approached your honorable body, have shown that, to provide schools for these only, would require little less than is now expended ; and it requires little arithmetic to show that, when the religious sects have taken all, nothing will remain for those who have not yet been able to decide which of the Christian denominations to prefer. It must be plain to every impartial observer, that the applicants are opposed to the whole system of public school instruction." Now, the gentleman admits it ; he says it is obviously true, that, when all is taken, nothing would remain. And would not the sects take all ? Who else would there be to take it ? And when they had taken all, nothing would remain. But we have alluded to a large body who would remain to be educated, when we have no money left for that purpose.

Our Roman Catholic brethren claim to be one fifth of the population. We shall not dispute this. But when the right reverend gentleman alluded to the statement that six Catholic teachers were employed in the public schools, he disputed five out of the six, and said that there was but one that deserved the name. Now, if you take these six teachers as a fair sample of this one fifth of the population which is nominally Catholic, how many would be left that are really Catholic? and how many would, on similar principles of calculation, really belong to any of the other sects who profess to belong to them? But again, allowing that all are Israel that are of Israel —that all are Christian that profess to be Christian—what portion of the city of New York is there that professes to belong to any sect at all? Not one half, I am sure. Well, what becomes of the children of those who belong to none of these sects? When the money is distributed among the sects, "what is to become of those children whose parents belong to none of these sects, and who cannot conscientiously allow them to be educated in the peculiar dogmas of any one of them?" Now, sir, the committees of the Public School Society expressly tell us, that it would require little less than the present appropriation to provide for these only. And why? Because the expense of tuition is not in proportion to the number taught. When you have provided what is necessary for a given number, a great addition may be made without augmenting the expense at all; and thus a great expense will be incurred for those who are of no denomination. But we shall advert to this hereafter. Sir, particular exception has been taken to our memorial, and the gentleman did us the honor to take it up *seriatim*, paragraph by paragraph; and therefore it may be requisite that I should thus follow him. I now, then, pass to another of the condemned passages which it contains:

We are sorry that the reading of the Bible in the public schools, without note or commentary, is offensive to them; but we cannot allow the Holy Scriptures to be accompanied with *their* notes and commentaries, and to be put into the hands of the children who may hereafter be the rulers and legislators of our beloved country; because, among other bad things taught in these commentaries, is to be found the lawfulness of murdering heretics, and the unqualified submission, in all matters of conscience, to the Roman Catholic Church.

Sir, we confess, if we march to our object, it must be by a plain road. We are a plain people, but we compromise nothing on the subject of religion. The right reverend gentleman denied that such are the contents of their books, and to confirm his opinion, he offers to bet me a thousand dollars. Sir, the right reverend gentleman must excuse me. He tells us our religion is a young religion. Be it so, sir; but our Church is old enough to teach us the sinfulness of betting. Sir, I have been taught, as one of the primary principles of morals, that it is sinful to take my neighbor's money without an equivalent. Now, should I accept the gentleman's offer, and cover his thousand dollars, he, or else I, should take the money of the other without an equivalent. It may be conformable with the creed of the right reverend gentleman, but he must allow me to have my " conscientious scruples," and I shall accord the same to him. But if I do not take up his bet,

17

I will try to do better. We have said in our memorial that their commentaries teach the lawfulness of murdering heretics. That is the first step. Now we are bound to sustain this; at least we are bound to show this Common Council on what authority we state this. We are bound to submit our authority to the Common Council, and then any gentleman will be able to make up his own mind on the subject. I hold in my hand, sir, what is called " The Rhemish New Testament," and it is proper that I should here say that we have not said, in our memorial, that these Catholic commentaries have received the sanction of the proper authorities of that Church. We said no such thing. We said Catholic commentaries—and I know of no commentaries among Protestants that have received the sanction of a Protestant Church; and yet do we not call them Protestant, in contradistinction to Catholic commentaries? All we have, then, to prove, is this, that this Rhemish New Testament is a Catholic New Testament, written and published by Roman Catholics, and with such sanctions as ordinarily obtain among the proper ministers of the Church. It may be alleged that it is necessary to have the sanction of His Holiness, or the council; but all I contend for is, that it has been circulated among Catholics, that it was translated for that purpose, and is therefore a Catholic commentary. That is all we contend for. We do not insist that the right reverend gentleman, or any Church council, or His Holiness himself countenances it. We could not summon His Holiness to testify on the subject; but in order to ascertain the weight of the historical record of that Church, we must take it as it is received by the Church itself. Now this book—the Rhemish New Testament—says:

The Douay Bible is usually so called, because, although the New Testament was first translated and published at Rheims, yet the Old Testament was printed some years after at Douay, the English Jesuits having removed their monastery from Rheims to Douay before their version of the Old Testament was completed. In the year 1816, an edition, including both the Douay Old and the Rhemish New Testament, was issued at Dublin, containing a large number of comments, replete with impiety, irreligion, and the most *fiery* persecution.

The Right Rev. Bishop Hughes. From what do you read ?
The Rev. Dr. Bond. I read from the second paragraph of the " Introductory Address to Protestants," of an edition of the Rhemish Testament, published in New York. It is attested by gentlemen of the highest reputation in this country—by men that will compare in character with any gentlemen, Protestant or Catholic, in any country; and they insist it is a true republication of that New Testament which was published at Rheims in 1582.

That edition was published under the direction of all the dignitaries of the Roman hierarchy in Ireland, and about three hundred others of the most influential subordinate priests. The notes which urged the hatred and murder of Protestants, attracted the attention of the British churches; and, to use the words of T. Hartwell Horne, that edition of the Rhemish Testament, printed at Dublin in 1816, " corrected and revised and approved by Dr. Troy, Roman Catholic Archbishop of Dublin, was reviewed by the

British Critic, vol viii., pp. 276–308, New Series; and its dangerous tenets, both civil and religious, were exposed.

This publication, with many others of a similar character, produced so great an excitement in Britain, that finally several of the most prominent of the Irish Roman prelates were called before the English Parliament to prove their own work. Then, and upon oath, with all official solemnity, they peremptorily disclaimed the volumes published by their own instigation, and under their own supervision and auspices, as books of no authority, because they had not been ratified by the pope and received by the whole papal Church.

Now have we made any mistake in calling this a Catholic commentary? It must be admitted we have some ground for it. And now for some of the "annotations," to show the ground we have for alleging that they do teach the lawfulness of murdering heretics.

And the servants said to him, Wilt thou we go and gather it up?

Mr. Alderman GRAHAM (Chairman). Will the speaker give the page?

The Rev. Dr. BOND. The 44th page, and the 28th verse of the thirteenth chapter of Matthew.

And he said, No; lest perhaps gathering up the cockle, you may root up the wheat also together with it.

Now for the commentary:

The good must tolerate the evil, when it is so strong that it cannot be redressed without danger and disturbance of the whole Church, and commit the matter to God's judgment in the latter day. Otherwise, where ill men, be they heretics or other malefactors, may be punished or suppressed without disturbance and hazard of the good, they may and ought by public authority, either spiritual or temporal, be chastised or executed.

I quote from the ninth chapter of St. Luke, p. 108:

And when his disciples James and John had seen it, they said, Lord, wilt thou we say that fire come down from heaven, and consume them? And turning, he rebuked them, saying, You know not of what spirit you are.

Now for the "annotation:"

Not justice nor all rigorous punishment of sinners is here forbidden, nor Elias' fact reprehended, nor the Church or Christian princes blamed for putting heretics to death: but that none of these should be done for desire of our particular revenge, or without discretion, and regard of their amendment, and example to others. Therefore Peter used his power upon Ananias and Saphira, when he struck them both down to death for defrauding the Church.

I quote from the 116th page, the 23d verse of the fourteenth chapter of St. Luke.

And the Lord said to the servant, Go forth into the ways and hedges, and compel them to enter, that my house may be filled.

Now for the commentary:

The vehement persuasion that God useth, both externally by force of His word and miracles, and internally by His grace, to bring us unto Him, is called compelling: not that He forceth any to come to Him against their wills, but that He can alter and mollify a hard heart, and make him willing that before would not. Augustine also referreth this compelling to the penal laws which Catholic princes do justly use against heretics and schismatics, proving that they who are by their former profession in baptism subject to the Catholic Church, and are departed from the same after sects, may and ought to be compelled into the unity and society of the universal Church again : and therefore, in this sense, by the two former parts of the parables, the Jews first, and secondly the Gentiles, that never believed before in Christ, were invited by fair, sweet means only : but by the third, such are invited as the Church of God hath power over, because they promised in baptism, and therefore are to be revoked, not only by gentle means, but by just punishment also.

I quote from the annotations of the 23d verse of the twentieth chapter of St. John :

The earthly princes, indeed, have also power to bind, but the bodies only : but that bond of priests which I speak of, toucheth the very soul itself, and reacheth even to the heavens : insomuch, that whatsoever the priests shall do beneath, the self-same God doth ratify above, and the sentence of the servants of the Lord doth confirm ; for, indeed, what else is this than that the power of all heavenly things is granted them of God ?

I quote from p. 214, verse 11, chap. xxv., of the Acts :

I appeal to Cæsar.

This is the annotation :

If Paul, both to save himself from whipping and from death sought by the Jews, doubted not to cry for honor of the Roman laws, and to appeal to Cæsar, the Prince of the Romans, not yet christened, how much more may we call for aid of Christian princes and their laws, for the punishment of heretics, and for the Church's defence against them.

I quote from annotations on the tenth chapter of Hebrews, 29th verse, on p. 373 :

Heresy and apostasy from the Catholic faith, punishable by death.

I will make but one more extract, and that is from the annotations on the Apocalypse, or the book of Revelations, seventeenth chapter, 6th verse, p. 430. It is in reference to the woman drunken with the blood of the saints :

It is plain that this woman signifieth the whole corps of all the persecutors that have and shall shed so much blood of the just : of the prophets, apostles, and other martyrs, from the beginning of the world to the end. The Protestants foolishly expound it of Rome, for that there they put heretics to death, and allow of their punishment in other countries. But their blood is not called the blood of the saints, no more than the blood of thieves, man-killers, and other malefactors—for the shedding of which, by order of justice, no commonwealth shall answer.

A friend suggests to me that I may also say the Rhemish New Testament is not found in the Prohibitory Index ; but I do not assert that this is in itself conclusive, for there are, I must admit, thousands of books that are not forbidden, for which Catholics are not responsible. All we contend for is this, that this book was published at Rheims by the Jesuits ; that they subsequently removed to and republished it at Douay ; since that it was republished in Ireland, under the sanction of the Catholic dignitaries, and of a large number of the priesthood of that Church. But when it was found that this work had created great alarm in England, and these very dignitaries were called before the British Parliament, they did not say it had not their sanction, but they alleged that, because it was not sanctioned by His Holiness, and had not received the sanction of the Church, but was only circulated among and sanctioned by a small portion of it, the Church was not responsible for it, as it was not of Catholic authority. We have not said, in our memorial, that it had the authority or was sanctioned by the Church. We know of no translation into any vulgar tongue which has received the sanction of pope or council. The Latin vulgate only has been so sanctioned. We only allege, then, that this is a Catholic publication, or that it is published by Catholics; and that these are Catholic commentaries. And we again affirm all we have said. We have, moreover, alleged that, "among other bad things taught in these commentaries, is to be found the absolute and unqualified submission, in all matters of conscience, to the Roman Catholic Church." But as it has been admitted that the Church has this authority with all who submit to that Church, it is unnecessary to prove that the commentaries teach it.

Sir, the next complaint was of the following paragraph :

The Roman Catholics complain that books have been introduced into the public schools which are injurious to them as a body. It is allowed, however, that the passages in these books to which such reference is made are chiefly, if not entirely, historical; and we put it to the candor of the Common Council to say, whether any history of Europe, for the last ten centuries, could be written which could either omit to mention the Roman Catholic Church, or mention it without recording historical facts unfavorable to that Church ? We assert that, if all the historical facts in which the Church of Rome has taken a prominent part could be taken from writers of her own communion only, the incidents might be made more objectionable to the complainants than any book to which they now object.

Sir, the gentleman did not deny this, for, as I recollect, he said it was true; he admitted " that, if all the historical facts in which the Church of Rome has taken a prominent part, could be taken from writers of her own communion only, the incidents might be made more objectionable," because they always write the truth. But then he alleges that they also record a great many good things. Certainly they have written " some good things," but it is not from these " good things " exclusively that history is to be written; it is not these " good things " that are to constitute history for the public schools. What is history ? History is " philosophy teaching by example ; " and could we be taught by example, if we only saw the bright side of the picture, and not the dark side too ? Could any such history be useful ? If we see but a partial record, how can we avoid error ? History is a beacon and a chart; but would it be so, would it be a proper directory if it contained only that which could be said in favor of any religious sect or denomination ? Such a record would be worthless as a history. The blessed Bible does not do so. Does any history contain a more particular record than this Book does, of the lapses and falls of the most eminent people of God ? Does not the faithful page of the sacred historian record the fall of David ? Yes, sir ; it records that that man, that holy Psalmist himself fell, being overcome by temptation, into the crimes of murder and adultery. Sir, it is a faithful history, and I would desire that all our histories should record all the good of Roman Catholics; but they must record the evil also, or they are not histories at all. But we have said, "History, then, must be falsified for their accommodation." And would it not be so, if only that which was good of them was recorded? "And yet they complain that the system of education adopted in the public schools does not teach the sinfulness of lying!" It may be painful to them, but are we to have no feeling? But the right reverend gentleman told us that the Methodist Episcopal Church is a young Church, and that this was the reason why there were not many very bad things said of us. He said our Church was only a hundred years old. Yet a great many bad things may be done in a hundred years. But we have not escaped unscathed, though, perhaps, the gentleman may not know it. Why, sir, Mr. O'Connell has published that our founder, Mr. Wesley, aided and abetted Lord George Gordon's mob! Yes, that, if Wesley did not originate, he aided and abetted it;—so that we have not escaped unscathed. But the reverend gentleman went further. He said we had done less good than any other denomination in Christendom. Why, we are not asking this Council any reward for what we have done; we make no pretensions. Whether we have done good, we leave others to decide. All we claim is, that we have stood in our lot. We believe the different sects and denominations in Christendom are permitted of God for wise purposes. We would not swallow them up if we could. We would not cross the street to make all other Protestants members of our Church. We have our work; we cannot do their work, they cannot do ours. We make no claim; but if we have not done a great deal of good, how can the gentleman with propriety profess so much respect for us? If we had done good, we should not have escaped, any more than our brethren so significantly and appropriately termed "Friends." They have done good, yet they have not escaped any more than ourselves. It is to them that the world owes the increasing disapproval of war; and though they have not been able to accomplish what they desire, and though they have been unresistingly oppressed, they have borne a patient testimony to their doctrine, and, with the revolutions of this world, the day will come when war will be no more. And have they not borne a holy testimony against slavery?—not a turbulent and an abusive testimony, but such as comports with the doctrines they teach; and yet they have not escaped, though they have confessedly done a great deal of good. It has been said that the Methodist Episcopal Church in England never favored the rights of conscience, nor aided in the enlargement of liberty. Why, there is no Methodist Episcopal Church in England at all. The Methodist Society in England claims only to be a society within the pale of the Church of England, as the Jesuits are a society within the pale of the Catholic Church. If it be alleged that the Methodist Society are not acknowledged by the Church of England, it will not be forgotten that the order of Jesuits have been suppressed by the pope. It seems, however, that the latter have been restored; and so our friends in England seem to be getting high in favor with the English establishment.

Yet, we owe them no allegiance; we send them no books to be sanctioned before we venture to use them in our schools; in short, we do not admit their right to dictate to us in any matter whatever. It is in this country only that there exists any Methodist Episcopal Church. But we are told that the Methodists in England have never taken any part, or given any aid, in the struggle for religious liberty. It is true, sir, that the Methodists in England, like the Methodists here, eschew all participation in political strife, as a society or Church. They do not think it any part of their vocation to call meetings in their churches, and address them on the political questions of the day, as some other Churches do. Perhaps they are too young a Church for this, and we hope it will be a long time before they get old enough to do so. But individually they act in these matters as others do ; and it is to the honor of the Methodist denomination in England, that their members generally gave their whole weight and influence to Mr. Wilberforce in all his benevolent efforts in favor of civil and religious liberty. During his long struggle against the slave trade, such was their attachment to him and his cause, that, in some parts of England, collections were made at the doors of their places of worship to aid in defraying the expenses of his election.

But we have said, " This is not all. They have been most complaisantly offered the censorship of the books to be used in the public schools. The committee to whom has been confided the management of these schools in this city, offered to allow the Roman Catholic bishop to expurgate from these books any thing offensive to him. But the offer was not accepted ; perhaps for the same reason that he declined to decide on the admissibility of a book of extracts from the Bible, which had been sanctioned by certain Roman bishops in Ireland. An appeal, it seems, had gone to the pope on the subject, and nothing could be said or done in the matter until His Holiness had decided. The Common Council of New York will therefore find that, when they shall have conceded to the Roman Catholics of this city the selection of books for the use of the public schools, that these books must undergo the censorship of a foreign potentate. We hope the time is far distant when the citizens of this country will allow any foreign power to dictate to them in matters relating to either general or municipal law." To this it is objected simply that the Roman Catholics of this country acknowledge the supremacy of the pope only in spiritual things ; that they do not acknowledge in him either political or civil, or any other than spiritual authority. Well, sir, we have not said they did, in our memorial. What, then, is the complaint ? We did not undertake to determine whether the submitting to His Holiness the question whether a book shall be used in our schools is a spiritual or temporal matter. But we really wish to know where temporal jurisdiction ends and spiritual jurisdiction begins. We should like to have some definite boundary, some line of demarcation drawn between temporal and spiritual authority. We did consider the public schools a secular matter altogether ; we did think it a temporal matter to decide what books should be used in our public schools, for professedly they do not intend to interfere with the peculiarities of any sect. But if this is really a spiritual matter, where will it end? What is it it cannot reach? What is it it will not reach? If it is a spiritual matter, then all that is necessary to carry out spiritual dominion must be granted; and' when was it that, to enforce spiritual dictation, temporal power was not resorted to if practicable? The time was when, to enforce this spiritual authority, a whole country was laid under interdict. Who does not know that the time was when the churches in England were all hung in black--when the dead were unburied—when the children were not baptized—and when nothing was done by the clergy which the community esteemed essential to their eternal interests, and subjects absolved from their allegiance because the king refused to submit to the pope of Rome? This power may not exist here; the pretension may have been abandoned; but if it has been, I should like to know it. I should like to know where the boundary is between temporal and spiritual power. I should like, for the first time, to be taught whether they consider the common interests of education a secular or a spiritual matter; and, if a secular, whether it is to be interfered with by this spiritual power. As yet it cannot be determined what books will be tolerated in the public schools by the Roman Catholic bishop, while an appeal has gone to the Roman pontiff; nothing can be done here until his answer is received! The gentleman did not deny this last night, when it was so alleged on the part of the Public School Society, and therefore he must pardon me if I believe it.

Sir, we did, in our memorial, regret that our Roman Catholic fellow-citizens, in their address, should have referred to the martyrs of their Church who suffered for opinion's sake, and we did say it was an unfortunate allusion. It was unfortunate because it was addressed to all classes of the community, and because, in this community, there are strangers from abroad, of all countries, among whom there are descendants of Protestants who suffered for their religion. We said it was an unfortunate allusion, and we said so because it would revive in the minds of many the memories of their ancestors, and they would thereby be reminded of the revocation of the Edict of Nantes, the massacre of St. Bartholomew's day, the fires of Smithfield, or the crusade against the Waldenses. Now, we did not mean to say that the right reverend gentleman has power to do these things now; we did not intend to insinuate that our Roman Catholic fellow-citizens would persecute now; but we said it was unfortunate. And was it not unfortunate to do any thing to revive the recollection of scenes so painful? But we said we were desirous to cover all these scenes with the mantle of charity, and the gentleman rebukes us. He tells us to attempt to do no such thing, for our mantle is too narrow. Well, I suppose he does not mean to practise this virtue himself, but to revive feelings in Protestants which we should wish not to recollect if it could be prevented. But he adverts to their sufferings for conscience' sake, and he went into details of the persecutions of Catholics in England. Now, sir, we are not here to justify persecution, nor to make excuse for it; we hate it, and we love to hate it; but we are here to say, and we must be allowed to say, that, whatever may be alleged against Protestants about persecution, that we are at liberty to be better than our fathers; we are at liberty to renounce both the practice and the tenets of our fathers, if they are found to be wrong. We say that, when Protestants persecuted Catholics, they were not half reformed—that they had brought much that was unchristian out of the Church from which they had come. But we have learned better now; we have abandoned those tenets and practices. Let the right reverend gentleman say as much for himself; let him say that, with them, it is not *semper eadem*, always the same. Let him say that the Roman Church has erred in matters of faith, or that she can err, and then the difficulty between Protestants and Catholics will cease from that moment. If the Catholics of the United States are at liberty to think for themselves on these subjects, and dissent from whatever they believe is not according to the Word of God—either their translation or the original—if they are at liberty to do this, the difficulty is at an end. But while they are bound by the decrees of an infallible Church—while they are not to determine any thing for themselves as a matter of faith—while they are not to believe that their Church can at any time be wrong in opinion, that she can never err—we have more cause to fear that Catholics will, if they get the power, persecute the Protestants, than they can have of persecution from Protestants. If they can say they do not believe as their fathers did, we may hope they will not do as their fathers have done; but while their motto continues to be "*Semper eadem*"—while they continue to declare that their Church is always and everywhere the same, we think, sir, we may not dismiss our fears. Let them renounce their infallibility, and we will be cured of our apprehensions. But again:

Your memorialists had hoped that the intolerance and exclusiveness which had characterized the Roman Catholic Church in Europe had been greatly softened under the benign influences of our civil institutions. The pertinacity with which their sectarian interests are now urged, has dissipated the illusion. We were content with their having excluded us, *ex cathedra*, from all claim to heaven, for we were sure they did not possess the keys, notwithstanding their confident pretension; nor did we complain that they would not allow us any participation in the benefits of purgatory, for it is a place they have made for themselves, and of which they may claim the exclusive property; but we do protest against any appropriation of the public school fund for their exclusive benefit, or for any other purposes whatever.

Now, the right reverend gentleman ought to have remarked here an error of the printer—the omission of the word "sectarian;" and, instead of "any other purpose whatever," it should have read, "any other *sectarian* purpose whatever."

Sir, the gentleman admits we are right—they do not exclude us from heaven; but then he alleges that we are as bad as we said they were, for we exclude Catholics. Now, if there are any that do not allow that good pious Roman Catholics are going to heaven, I do not know it. If there are any such in our denomination, it is unknown to me. I hold no such opinions, and I hope the gentleman himself will take it back again, when I assure him that the founder of Methodism, John Wesley, published the life of Baron De Rentz, and that he abridged and published "Kempis' Christian Pattern," both of which have been widely circulated amongst our people.

We do not deny that Roman Catholics may go to heaven, nor did we complain that we were denied any participation in the benefits of their purgatory; but the gentleman tells us to go farther and fare worse. Sir, we will take our chance for that—we will take our chance of faring worse, and of getting to heaven, too. But if the gentleman denies us the benefit of his purgatory in the next world, we hope he will allow us the benefits of this world. If he will allow our children the benefit of the public schools—of a place where they can learn to read God's Holy Word—if he will not persist in a measure which will destroy these schools, we will take our chance of going farther and faring worse. If he will allow our children a place where they can learn to read that Book which, as the great Mr. Locke says, has God for its author, salvation for its end, and truth without any mixture of error for its mattter, we will not complain of any other exclusion he may insist upon in the matter. But it is alleged that we are here to oppose Roman Catholics. Sir, we would oppose the Methodists if the same application was made by them. I would have stood here myself to oppose them, for I do not fear nor dodge any responsibility. We believe that all mankind are individually undergoing a moral and intellectual probation before God; and that we cannot, without incurring the Divine displeasure, substitute this probationary relation by one before any man, or any number of men, whether pope or Council, or the Methodist General Conference. None of these can release us from our obligations as probationers before God. "To our own master we stand or fall." If the Methodist Episcopal Church had issued her mandate to me not to appear before this body, and not to oppose this application, I would have set her authority at naught. We believe that these public schools are necessary to our form of government; that it is not safe to commit the preservation and perpetuation of the public liberty and of our civil institutions, to an ignorant, untaught multitude—to those who will be incapable of appreciating their value, or who may be made the dupes of better educated but more wicked men. We say, it is necessary to the perpetuation of public liberty that the community be educated—that all who exercise the elective franchise should be taught to value our civil institutions. But we say that no sectarian body can do this; it must be done by all together. If you were to give all this money to the sects, it could not be done. It can only be done by a common system; for, if all the sects had this money divided amongst them, there is one half of the community who would not suffer their children to be taught by them. What, then, is to become of these children? Our public liberties demand a public universal system of education, and this can only be effected by agents appointed by the State, and answerable to the State; it can never be done if the money be given to any denomination, or divided among all the sects. Sir, we allege this is the broad principle on which the common schools are established. Take this away, and you have no right to lay a tax at all; you could not lay a tax with any justice for this purpose. If the money is to be distributed among the different sects and denominations of Christians, and they are to use it as they think best, even for their own proselyting purposes—I speak of no particular denomination; all have their preferences and peculiar tenets, and all desire to make converts to their belief—I say, give the money to this end, and what follows? Why, that you ought to tax them severally according to what they receive. What right have you to tax Roman Catholics for the support of Methodist schools? or what right have you to tax Methodists for the support of Presbyterian schools? In short, what right have you to tax any sect for the support of the schools of rival sects? You have first to ascertain what each requires to support the schools under their care, and then to tax that denomination to the necessary amount. You have no right to tax me, as a Methodist, for the Roman Catholic schools, but only on the ground that education is necessary for the preservation of our public liberties, and for the public safety. Fall back upon the plan you formerly pursued, and you will again hear of complaints among the sects, that they do not receive from the public fund according to what they pay in. Now, the Methodists, perhaps, pay much less than some other denominations who are less numerous than themselves. We make it a part of our religion to pay our taxes if we are able; but we have very little to be taxed at all; and if we have but little to be taxed, we pay but little; and yet we could supply more children than some denominations who pay ten times more. Would they, then, have no right to complain if these schools were established on sectarian principles instead of public principles? Would not their complaint be just and proper? It is clear that you could not refute these complaints. And if you concede the prayer of these petitioners, if you grant their request, in order that you may remove their cause of complaint, you destroy the public school system, and you may take your leave of it from that very moment. The whole fabric will crumble into its original elements; it cannot stand.

But why should this system of public education be abandoned? Is it to appease the scrupulous consciences of the Catholics? The existence of public schools, or of the public school system, cannot affect their consciences, for they are not compelled to send *their* children to the public schools. Have they, then, any scruples of conscience about paying taxes for the support of this institution? The right reverend gentleman tells you himself they have not, for he tells you they have not complained, and do not intend to complain, of the appropriation by the Legislature of money raised by taxation to Protestant colleges. If, then, sir, you yield the claims of the Catholics, it will not be to their conscientious objections that you yield, but to the alleged injustice of compelling them to contribute to a public benefit from which they, as a sect, derive no advantage. You must, then, sir, go farther; you must release all from the payment of taxes who cannot conscientiously avail themselves of the advantages offered by the public schools, and this will include most of the large property-holders in the city; for these, being able to afford it, are bound by parental duty to afford their children a better education than can be given in the public schools. Yet these are not only willing to pay taxes for the support of public schools, but have petitioned the Legislature to tax them for this purpose, because they are aware that the education of the poor classes is necessary to the common welfare.

But, sir, I adverted to a foreign potentate; and I did say I desired to know where his spiritual authority ceased. And I am the more desirous of knowing this, because it is alleged—and the right reverend gentleman ought to know if it be true—that, by the oath taken by the dignitaries of that Church, they are bound to support a little more than the pope's spiritual authority. I will make no assertion, but I throw it out that the right reverend gentleman may say whether his oath of ordination does not bind him to a little more. Sir, I did say, and I emphatically repeat, that it is very desirable his fellow-citizens should know where that civil and spiritual authority terminate. I beg pardon for intruding so long upon your attention. I have gone through our memorial, and that is all we ask. At present I have nothing more to say.

The gentlemen who appeared as the representatives of the petitioners and the remonstrants having now been heard, the President inquired, What is the pleasure of the board?

An alderman moved that, if there were other gentlemen present who desired to be heard, that they be heard on sending their names to the President; which was agreed to.

Dr. Sweeney said that he appeared, with several other gentlemen, as a committee from the Catholics, but they withdrew their claim to be heard, as the Right Rev. Bishop Hughes was entitled to a reply.

Dr. David M. Reese, M.D. (a local preacher in the Methodist Episcopal Church), rose, and said:

Mr. President: I avail myself of the permission granted by the board to add a few observations on another branch of the subject, which is interesting to us all, to which I desire for a moment only to direct your attention. It appears to me, sir, that neither Romanism nor Protestantism is on trial here, and the question submitted to this honorable board is not whether the Roman Catholic Church shall have the exclusive control of any portion of the public treasure, collected, by public taxation, for the purpose of public education; it is not the question whether the Roman Catholic Church shall have it; but the great question in which we are interested, as a community, is, whether any denomination—whether any portion of this great community—shall have the exclusive control, though it be but of a single dollar, of the money raised by public taxation for the public benefit. I would hope, therefore, if I succeed in gaining your attention to the point— to the single point I submit to you—to call you for a moment from every consideration of a sectarian aspect. Indeed, I humbly conceive that religious creeds, that sectarian creeds of any kind whatever, are not at issue in the present controversy. If this application had come from Protestants as a body, from any political or religious sect, however numerous or powerful or popular they might be, the same objection would lie against the application, from whatever source it might come. I humbly submit, therefore, whether the right reverend gentleman to whom we had the pleasure to listen last night, would not have served the public more effectually by instructing his people that the opposition to this claim *is not an opposition to the Roman Catholics*, but to the principle of appropriating money raised by taxation for public purposes to any party whatever, for their exclusive control. I say, the reverend gentleman would have been serving the public, and would have been doing nothing unworthy of his highly honorable and sacred office, if he had applied himself to enlightening his people on this point—that the present opposition is not an opposition to *their* creed or to *their* Church, but that the same opposition would be against any other denomination equally as numerous and equally as respectable. Certainly, sir, this would have been more worthy of his sacred office than haranguing his people in their public assemblies for the purpose of exciting prejudices against the public schools. Before these prejudices were created, when these people had not yet been taught to look upon them as odious, the Roman Catholics sent their children to these schools, and availed themselves thankfully of their benefits. But now many of them have abstracted their children, merely because harangues of that kind have been made which are calculated to create disaffection amongst them. Sir, the opposition made to this memorial is neither sectarian nor religious; and, this being premised, it is impossible that it can involve a question of conscience at all. What is the question? It is complained that men, having taxed themselves and having paid that tax for a given purpose—the public benefit—have afterward voluntarily chosen, in the exercise of their freedom in this free country, to forego the benefits provided for the public indiscriminately. All are taxed for public education which is given by the public schools; but a portion of the citizens choose to relinquish the advantages of these schools. The question, then, resolves itself into this: Is it sound public policy to tax the citizens generally for a public purpose, when any portion on whom the tax is imposed, choose not to avail themselves of its advantages? You see, in this aspect, that it strikes at the whole public school system; for if the Roman Catholics are to be excused because they choose to forego the advantages provided, every other sect, whether for the sake of party politics or religion, might take the same attitude and plead the same conscience, and the result would be that there would be no provision made for public education, and the rising generation in multitudes would grow up like "the wild asses' colt."

Now, in this aspect, I humbly submit whether our fellow-citizens who are found peacefully enjoying their rights and liberties in this country, do not receive an equivalent for the taxes which they pay, in the proper exercise of the right of suffrage which is here secured; whether they ought not thus to contribute to the political advantages which this happy country furnishes; and whether they do not thus secure an ample equivalent for the taxes which they pay, even in cases where they voluntarily decline to avail themselves of the public schools? But, sir, I know a conscience may be created in this community by a bishop or other dignitary. Let them but turn their churches into bear-gardens, and agitate their congregations by exciting speeches, as has been done on this subject, and others will be taught to plead their newly-excited consciences beside Roman Catholics. And shall this great community be deprived of this system because such a conscience is created ? But if there can be no conscience in the matter in truth, the point is narrowed down to the question, Is it a hardship to pay a tax for a public benefit, when we thus forego the advantages ? Or ought every man who does not avail himself of the advantages which the system furnishes, to be exempted from taxation ? We know a disposition to avoid taxation exists in thousands; and if conscience is to be an excuse, conscience will easily be started to avoid the payment, and the result will be that no public education could be sustained, here or elsewhere.

As well might the petitioners ask for a separate almshouse or a separate hospital for their exclusive accommodation, and allege the hardship of paying a tax for the support of these public charities, while their consciences would not allow them to take shelter there in time of adversity; because, forsooth, a Protestant Bible is sometimes found there, and a Protestant chaplain sometimes reads a chapter there for the consolation of the sick and dying.

Sir, it is the enlightened public policy of our city, State, and nation, to provide and perpetuate the facilities for educating the entire population in the rudiments of secular learning, and to support these and other public institutions by public taxation. The provision is free for all, and all contribute to its maintenance. But if individuals among us choose to educate their own children, and refuse to avail themselves of the public schools, the act is their own, but in no wise furnishes them a pretext to complain. Especially when such individuals establish sectarian schools, in which, with the secular knowledge imparted, their own religious tenets are to be taught, is it not passing strange that they should wish to impose upon all other religions the tax of sustaining those schools in which their own religion is exclusively to be inculcated ? I care not whether such individuals be Roman Catholics or Protestants, they cannot by possibility possess any right of conscience which will give them a claim to impose upon any other man's conscience the burden of supporting their sectarian or exclusive schools. Nor can the money raised by public taxation to support public schools, be expended in any other schools than those of strictly public character, which denominational schools cannot be, in the nature of things.

The system of the New York Public School Society secures, confessedly, every desirable facility for secular learning, to an extent commensurate with the population. No religious test is required as a qualification for the office of teacher in these schools, and both trustees and teachers are promiscuously taken from all denominations, a number of Roman Catholics being engaged both as trustees and teachers. Great care, however, is taken to have none employed in these schools as teachers but persons of good moral character; and while all the peculiarities of doctrinal tenets which distinguish and separate Christian churches of every name are excluded, the purest morals in which all agree are taught among the lessons of each day, a chapter in the Bible being read at the opening of the school. The petitioners themselves do not allege any defect in the secular knowledge here taught, nor do they complain that any religious doctrines are inculcated in these schools. But they insist that their consciences will not allow them to sustain such schools, because NO religion is taught in them. And surely they would consent to none being taught, except their own religion, and hence it is for this purpose alone they have their own schools. It is idle, then, for the right reverend bishop to repeat his disclaimer of any intention to teach his own religion in his own schools; for in no other way can he make out his plea of conscience, nor can he in any other way make out a single plea against the present excellent system of public school instruction.

I do not design to prolong the discussion, but I feel impelled to say what I have said, for I have observed the excitement which exists, arising out of the false issue which the right reverend gentleman has created, and that hence all the publications on that side of the question in putting forth the claim of the Catholics, have treated it as though the opposition to it was an opposition to Roman Catholics. Sir, I disclaim it. I am not aware that any man in this community opposes it because it is the petition of Roman Catholics, but because it comes from a class of citizens, highly respectable and numerous, I admit, who ask for this money to be placed under *their own* control. I am sure those with whom I am associated do not oppose it merely because it comes from Roman Catholics. We believe the Public School Society confers on us, and on this community, an advantage by the secular instruction of the rising generation. We see, daily, multitudes in these schools of children who will soon be introduced on the stage as citizens of this republic, and it is vastly important that they should be educated and qualified for the discharge of the important duties of freemen. This public school system is preparing them for that purpose; it is attracting the attention of public men of other countries. These schools are regarded as the nurseries of intelligent freemen, who will hereafter have to take the guardianship of the liberties of this country. We are training up thousands of citizens, not only for New York, but for the West. New York contributes much to the population of this nation, and the power lies with this Board of Aldermen to direct their training so as to make them useful to their country. But there comes a petition, from a body highly respectable, I admit, who ask, " Let us have this money which is collected for a public purpose, and we will apply it to a private one." I know they disclaim sectarian views, if the money is obtained; but if their views are not sectarian, they can find no valid objection, nor make any improvement to the existing system of public schools. It is immeasurably important that the present system should be supported. The gentlemen to whom the schools are now intrusted have shown themselves amply qualified to discharge their duties, and I hope any attempt to destroy the present system will be frowned down, whether it be made by Catholic or Protestant, Christian or infidel.

The Rev. Dr. KNOX, of the Dutch Reformed Church, said:

MR. PRESIDENT: I should not have risen to claim your indulgence for a single moment, were it not to say that the Christian denomination with which I am connected, in their united sentiment are adverse to the prayer of the memorial now before you; and that they would unquestionably have been here with a counter memorial, if they had not cherished a confidence that, in the hands of this Corporation, the matter is perfectly safe. Sir, I regard the subject now before this honorable body as one of most momentous importance. The principle on which our Government is established is of a character to exclude all immediate connection, on the part of our Government, with religious things. All religion is fully tolerated, fully protected, and then it is left alone, and there I hope it will continue to be. It is not profaned by the contact of civil enactments. We have never heard of any "act of uniformity," to set a whole community by the cars. Sir, this principle, in this State, is guarded with most peculiar jealousy: there is not a minister of religion that can even be appointed as the superintendent of a common school, or be eligible to any civil office. Whether it is an innovation on our natural rights, I will not undertake to inquire; but with the existence of such enactments I feel perfectly satisfied. Let it so be. Interrupt this state of things, and whither will it lead? Who can foretell to what it may lead? The denomination with which it is my honor and happiness to be connected, was the first to introduce the gospel of salvation to these shores. Individuals of this communion laid the foundation of this city; they embraced a large portion of the population of the State, and bear a large part of its burdens; and I know that the feeling of this part of our population is unanimously in favor of leaving matters as they are. As a demonstration that they are disinterested, the particular Church which I serve has sustained a charity school more than a century; it sustains it still from the private charity of Christians; and they never received aid from the State, except, for a few years, a few dollars for each child, during the operation of the law referred to last evening.

Now, personally, in reference to our Roman Catholic friends, my feelings are entirely kind. I have not any other feeling. I am not a man of strife. But this matter would not be quietly submitted to. Were any denomination, existing among us, to put forth such a claim as is now before this board—were the Presbyterians to do it, we would not regard it as right. Were the Episcopalians, or the Methodists, to do it, we should not deem it right. In any case, we should not feel content to contribute to the general treasury of the State, if a portion of that treasury were to be taken hold upon by a particular denomination. Whilst the whole spirit of our Government, whether general or State, frowns upon any thing that looks like elevating one section of the Christian community in preference to another, it would not be kindly regarded if the prayer of this petition were complied with, and a distinction were conferred on one, and not on others. But, while I say that I feel kindness toward our Roman Catholic friends, candor would require me to go a little further than many have gone who have addressed you.

With reference to the system of religion by which they are distinguished, I cannot help regarding it as differing from others. They so regard it. It is exclusive; and they claim for it immutability and infallibility. Sir, can Protestants, believing as they do believe, consent to be directly instrumental in elevating to strength, and in cherishing, a system like this? I think not. I think the citizens of this State will say it ought not to be.

Mr. President, for myself, I wish our Catholic fellow-citizens to enjoy all the immunities that are enjoyed by any others; but with that I wish them to rest content. I have sought carefully, and according to my best ability, during this discussion and previously, to ascertain what is the precise ground of their dissatisfaction, and I confess I am not instructed yet. We are told that in these common schools religion is not taught; and in juxta-position we are told that the Bible is read. Now, with regard to the administration of those schools, we have had abundant testimony, both here and elsewhere, that they are conducted with extreme—with the very utmost care. Is disobedience to parents taught there? Are they taught to falsify the truth? or to do a wrong thing? On the contrary, are they not instruct-ed in the common fundamental principles of morals, while they are taught to read and write, and to discharge the duty of citizens when they arrive at maturity? The Bible is read, as it ought to be; and occasionally passages have been found in the books, admitted into the libraries, which are offen-sive to the feelings of Catholics. These have been expurgated as soon as detected, in every instance that I am aware of. But is this a sufficient reason for so great a change? Can you, or any gentleman who is in the habit of reading, for a single week or day, be perfectly sure that, even when reading works of a select kind you shall not find something that may not be conso-nant with your feelings? But let it be overlooked and passed by. Do these schools interfere with our religious instruction of our children? Do they take them away from the parent, or the pastor, or from the Sabbath school? Are they conducted by individuals of the same faith? I believe not. I am not able to find a just cause of complaint.

I have but a single remark more, for I have observed the great patience with which this honorable Council has sat to hear the remarks of gentlemen both yesterday and to-day, and I am unwilling to occupy more than another moment of their time on a single point. The gentleman who first addressed you yesterday afternoon, throughout the whole of his exceedingly able and eloquent address, labored this one point, to endeavor to produce an impres-sion on the minds of this Common Council that a false issue had been started —that they do not want the public money to aid them in communicating religious instruction. Why, Mr. President, it is strange that this single idea was not lost sight of during that long, able, and eloquent address of more than two hours' duration. But, sir, if they are willing to pledge themselves to give no religious instruction in their schools, why not allow their chil-dren to go to the common schools during school hours, and afterward give them religious education? I confess I do not know how this can be so. The only answer I can myself imagine is this: that, upon the whole, there is an influence exerted by a contact with the children in these schools ad-verse to feelings of reverence for Catholic peculiarities. That must be it. Well, now, is it so? Sir, my children are exposed, by mingling with the

18

community, to things which are adverse to their feelings—if you choose, their prejudices; they may at the same time meet with things which reflect on their family, and on their associations—their religious associations and their other associations too. Does that weaken their attachment to those associations? No, it strengthens them. They at once say, Those persons don't think as I do; they don't feel as I do. We may be taunted about our pastors or our faith; does that lessen our attachment to them? I think not. We think we are right and they are wrong, and we let it pass. Sir, I repeat, though I am not delegated to attend here to tell it, that these sentiments pervade the denomination which I represent, and with the expression of that fact I will retire, and not trouble the board any longer.

The Rev. Dr. BANGS, of the Methodist Episcopal Church, said:

SIR: I avail myself of the liberty which your resolution gives me, to make one or two remarks. It might be inferred by some, from the position we occupy here, that we appear here as a sect, to vindicate our sectarian principles and rights. Now, if such an impression should have existed, I wish to correct it. We appear here simply, with the rest of our fellow-citizens, for the purpose of opposing what we conceive to be an unjust application. We have nothing to ask for. We do not ask for a portion of the public money to enable us to educate our children. The time was when the Methodist Episcopal Church had a flourishing charity school, which they supported for upward of forty years without a cent from the public fund; but when the Legislature of the State concluded to distribute a portion in the city of New York among the charity schools, we received our proportion; and at the first, when a motion was made to take it out of the hands of charity schools, and give it to the public schools, we did remonstrate, with others. But we are very glad to say that, since we have seen the system in operation, and viewed its blessed effects on the minds of our children and the community, we joyfully acquiesce in the decision of the Common Council on that subject. There is one objection made to this system which somewhat surprised me. It was stated, if I did not misunderstand it, that, by taking these children and sending them to these schools, they are taken out of the hands of their parents and delivered over to the hands of the public officer of the State. Why, sir, this is very extraordinary. Suppose our brethren of the Roman Catholic Church established their schools—for they have them, I suppose—do they not take their children, during school hours, from the hands of their parents? Are they not, for the time being, taken out of the domestic circle, and delivered over to the hands of the public teacher? And does not every father and mother, when they resign their children to a school, an academy, or a college, deliver them out of their hands for the time being? But, sir, the sending of children to public schools in this city is not taking them out of the hands of the domestic government. The schools are established in the midst of us; we can send our children to them, and they are only absent from us about six hours, and the rest of the time they are with us. How, then, pray tell me, have these schools invaded the authority of the father and mother ? There is another point. If I did not misunderstand the senior pastor of the Roman Catholic Church, he told us that the instruction in these schools tended to infidelity. He disclaimed any intention to charge this upon the principles of the managers of that institution, but he said the system itself tended to infidelity. Now, sir, what is the great bulwark against infidelity ? Is it not the Bible, sir ? What are *all* the commentaries, what are all the dissertations that were ever written, even the most learned, in comparison with the Bible ? Are we to suppose that any human teaching in the Roman Catholic schools will be paramount to the Bible in checking the overflowings of infidelity ? Would I trust myself, or my denomination, in preference to the Bible ? No, sir. The Bible contains its own evidence of its own truth ; it reflects its own light, unobscured by the commentaries of feeble man ; and are we to be told that the Holy Scriptures, without note and comment, will lead to infidelity ? If I mistake not, one of the trustees told us that the Holy Scriptures were read every day, and that the children were taught that God made them, and that He saw their thoughts, words, and actions ; and these, we know, are the first principles of revealed religion, in opposition to sectarianism ; and, in all this, what testimony have we that these schools tend to infidelity ? For what shall we change the Bible, the Holy Book of God, which announces divine truths to man ? Shall we exchange this Bible for the teaching of the Roman Catholic schoolmaster ? Which is the best adapted to stem the flood of infidelity ? But they don't design to teach sectarianism ! What then ? I rejoice to be able to say here—and I believe the right reverend gentleman will join me in saying—that he believes in one God, in one Saviour, in the Holy Ghost, the forgiveness of sins, the regeneration of the heart by the Holy Spirit, justification by faith, and in a future day of judgment. I believe he will join with me, or any one else, in the belief of these truths. Are they not the truths of the Bible ? And may not these truths be taught our children ? Are they not taught in Roman Catholic schools ? What, then, do they desire to teach ? Why, the peculiarities of their system, and nothing else ; for all these leading truths are taught in the Bible. He wants something, I presume, that is not in the Bible ; for the Bible is taught there, and, if any thing else is to be taught that is not in the school, it must be something that is not in the Bible, and therefore it must be sectarian. Now, we have arrived at an age in our republic when we see the different sects and denominations, though they may not agree in all things, agreeing in all leading points. On these we can meet and unite, and strengthen each other's hands to do good in our day and generation. We therefore, as a denomination, unite with our brethren of other denominations, and those of no denomination—or, in other words, with the representatives of every society—to say, Let this fund be appropriated as it was intended to be, and let all share alike in the education of the rising generation. For myself, I could go still farther than has been gone, and say, that these little vagrants that are suffered to stroll about the streets and spend their time in idleness, I would compel to enter these schools ; and I believe it would be an act of humanity, if their parents were so indifferent to the welfare of their children that they allowed them to spend their time in idleness, or something worse. Let the State extend the hand of compassion, and take them out of the streets, to be taught where they will be saved from vicious indulgences; and I hope the time will yet come when it will be done.

The Rev. GARDINER SPRING, D.D. of the Presbyterian Church, said :

MR. PRESIDENT : As much time has been consumed, as this question has been abundantly discussed, and with great ability, especially by the learned counsel, had I not been urged to say a word on behalf of the Presbyterian Church, I should not have claimed your attention. I am not authorized by the Presbyterian Church, as a Church, to attend here; but if I had, I would have paid more particular attention to the subject than I have done. I can say, with my worthy brother of the Dutch Reformed Church, that the sentiment of the Church at large with which I am connected is one of entire unanimity of ardent and cordial opposition to the petition which is now before you from the Roman Catholic Church. I will state, sir, but a single fact, without recapitulating the valuable remarks of the other gentlemen, which has rested on my mind, and may have some weight in the bosom of some gentlemen with whom the decision rests. In the providence of God, sir, having been more than thirty years in this city, I have had opportunities of watching the progress of the Public School Society, and of knowing some of its history in that period of time. When it was separated from the Churches as such, and assumed its present shape, it was a solemn matter of compromise and contract on the part of the Corporation and the Public School Society. I do not say it was a contract in writing, but this was the understanding of all our Churches. We were solicited to give up our rights and denominational feelings, to which we were strongly attached, that this large scheme might go into operation and spread its influence over the community; and the alternative with us was, whether we should oppose that great scheme, and continue the pilfering which had been detected in one society, with its unpleasant attendant consequences, or aid the public school plan. And we sacrificed our feelings for the general good, on the sacred understanding that the system should be continued; and we shall consider it a violation of good faith if you grant this application. I can unite with some of my friends who have preceded me, in saying that, if this application had come from any other denomination, I would have opposed it. But I cannot say that I have no greater opposition to it because it comes from my Catholic friends. I do view it with more alarm on account of the source from which it comes. And any man who looks at the history of the Catholic Church, whether in or out of power, and finds she has ever been, and in those parts of Europe where she remains in power she continues to be, almost uniformly the enemy of liberty, will look upon this application with suspicion and fear. I do so not only as an American, but as a Christian, as a Protestant, and as a Presbyterian. The gentleman has sought to prove that the present system leads to infidelity. Now, sir, let no man think it strange that I should prefer even infidelity to Catholicism. Even a mind as acute as Voltaire's came to the conclusion that, if there was no alternative between infidelity and the dogmas of the Catholic Church, he should choose infidelity. I would choose, sir, in similar circumstances, to be an infidel to-morrow.

Mr. President, my worthy father—I would call him brother, for my hairs are almost as gray as his—has well said, that the great barrier to infidelity is the Bible. But, sir, the right reverend gentleman told us, yesterday, he had no confidence in the Protestant Bible; and yet you heard him, when he came to a community of Protestant citizens, ask for the bounty of the State to support such a system as his! With you, gentlemen, the power remains. I need not now, after what has been said—indeed, this would not be the proper place—urge any arguments at length on this subject, and therefore I will not further trespass on your time; nor need I scarcely ask pardon for detaining you so long, having been myself urged to say something on be-half of the Church with which I am connected.

The President said the closing remarks would be given to the petitioners.

Mr. KETCHUM observed that, if any new matter were intro-duced, he hoped he should have the opportunity to reply. The right reverend gentleman opened on the part of the petitioners; he had been replied to, and it was but right that he should have the right to reply to the other speakers; but if he urged new matter, either of fact or argument, he, on the part of the School Society, should claim the right to reply to that new matter.

The President called upon the Right Rev. Dr. Hughes to conclude the debate.

The Right Rev. Bishop HUGHES then rose, to reply to the arguments of all the gentlemen who had been heard on the sub-ject, and he spoke nearly as follows:

MR. PRESIDENT: It would require a mind of much greater capacity than mine to arrange and mature the topics, relevant or otherwise, that have been introduced into this discussion since I had the honor to address you yester-day. No less than seven or eight gentlemen of great ability have presented their respective views on the subject; and not only on the subject in regard to its intrinsic merits, but on subjects which they deemed at least collateral, but which I think quite irrelevant. The gentleman who last addressed you (Dr. Spring) is entitled to my acknowledgments for the candor with which he expressed his sentiments in reference to it—namely, that he was opposed to it more because it came from Catholics than if it had been presented by any other denomination. That gentleman is entitled to my acknowledg-ment, and I award it, if worthy of his acceptance. The subject—for it is exceedingly important that the subject should be kept in view—is one, as I stated before, that is very simple. We are a portion of this community; we desire to be nothing greater than any other portion; we are not content to be made less. There is nothing, sir, in that system of the Public School Society against which any of the gentlemen who have spoken, either in their individual capacity or as the representatives of bodies of people, have urged a single conscientious objection, and, of course, they have no right to complain; they are satisfied, and therefore I am willing that they should have the system; but I am not willing that they should press it upon me, and for good reason. And, sir, if this honorable body rejects the claim of your petitioners, what is the issue? That we are deprived of the benefits to which we are entitled, and that we are not one iota worse than we were before. That is our consolation. But the whole range of the argument of the gentleman who spoke last was, to show that this public school system was got up with the concurrence of public opinion, and that, having been so got up, it had worked beautifully, and that gentlemen who had never heard of conscientious objections to it, because it suits their views, deem it wonderful that we can have any conscience at all on the subject. That is the amount of it. What! no ground for conscientious objection, when you teach our children in those schools that "the *deceitful* Catholics" burned John Huss at the stake for conscience, when evidences are numerous before you of a more just and a more honorable character—when you might find on the page of history that, in Catholic Poland, every avenue to dignity in the State was opened to Protestants, by the concurrent vote of eight Catholic bishops, whilst the vote of any ONE of them, according to the constitution of the Polish Diet, of which they were members, could have prevented the law being passed;—and, what is more, when the first lesson of universal toleration and freedom of conscience the world was ever called to learn was set by the Catholics of Maryland. I speak in the presence of gentlemen who can contradict me if they know where to find the authority. And what was this but homage to the majesty of conscience by a Church which they wish to establish as a persecuting Church? That Church, sir, which the gentleman has come here to prove justifies the murdering of heretics, was the first to teach a lesson which Protestants have been slow to learn and imitate, but which the religion they profess should have taught them. But not these examples alone; there are hundreds more. At this day, in Belgium, where Protestants are in a minority of one to twelve, the State votes them an equal portion, and, where their clergy are married, a larger portion, and that with the concurrence of the Council and the Catholic bishops. The gentleman need not tell me of Catholicism—I know it well; and, what is more, I know Protestantism well; and I know the professions of goodwill of Protestants do not always correspond with their feelings. But I should like to know whether or not in Protestantism they find authority for persecuting to the knife not Catholics alone, but each other, even after they have proclaimed the right of every man to think for himself. With good reason, sir, do I contend for conscience; but they may think a Catholic has no right to have a conscience at all. They may think, because this system is beautiful in their view, that this pretension to conscience on the part of Catholics ought to be stifled as a thing not to be admitted at all. But that will not do. Man, in this country, has a right to the exercise of conscience, and the man that should raise himself up against it will find that he has raised himself up against a tremendous opponent. Now, what is it we ask? You have heard from beginning to end the arguments on this occasion; and, though I may not follow the wanderings of this discussion through all its minute parts, if I pass over any part, be assured it is not from any desire to avoid or any inability to refute what has been said against us. I may pass over many points, but I will not pass over any great principle; and you have no doubt given so much attention to the subject as to enable you, if I should not recapitulate the whole, to decide justly. It has been urged that, if you give Catholics that which they now ask, you will give them benefits which will elevate them above others; but I contend, most sincerely and most conscientiously, that we have no such idea; and when you shall have granted the portion we claim, if you should be pleased to grant it, I conceive then, and not before, shall we be in the enjoyment of the protection, and not privilege, to which we are entitled. That is my view of the subject; but I have been astonished to perceive the course of argument of the gentlemen who oppose our claim, generally speaking. What it is they contend for, I cannot determine; but it seems to be the preservation of the existing system. They were among the first to disclaim the doctrine that the end justifies the means; and if, in attaining their end, they find they cannot reach it without injustice, then, as conscientious and high-minded men, they should have paused by the way and have ascertained whether the means were worthy of them and of our glorious country. Yet, sir, they have generally overlooked this, and it is no new thing to find that they have labored to promote the benefit of their own Society at the sacrifice of the rights of others. Sir, it is the glory of this country that, when it is found that a wrong exists, there is a power, an irresistible power, to correct the wrong. They have represented us as contending to bring the Catholic Scriptures into the public schools. This is not true; but I shall have occasion to refer more particularly to this by and by. They have represented us as enemies to the Protestant Scriptures " without note and comment," and on this subject I know not whether their intention was to make an impression on your honorable body, or to elicit a sympathetic echo elsewhere; but, whatever their object was, they have represented that, even here, Catholics have not concealed their enmity to the Scriptures. Now, if I had asked this honorable board to exclude the Protestant Scriptures from the schools, then there might have been some coloring for the current calumny. But I have not done so. I say: Gentlemen of every denomination, keep the Scriptures you reverence, but do not force on me that which my conscience tells me is wrong. I may be wrong, as you may be; and as you exercise your judgment, be pleased to allow the same privilege to a fellow-being who must appear before our common God and answer for the exercise of it. I wish to do nothing like what is charged upon me; that is not the purpose for which we petition this honorable board in the name of the community to which I belong. I appear here for other objects; and if our petition be granted, our schools may be placed under the supervision of the public authorities, or even of commissioners to be appointed by the Public School Society. They may be put under the same supervision as the existing schools, to see that none of those phantoms, nor any grounds for those suspicions which are as uncharitable as unfounded, can have existence in reality. There is, then, but one simple question: Will you compel us to pay a tax from which we can receive no benefit, and to frequent schools which injure and destroy our religious rights in the minds of our children, and of which in our consciences we cannot approve? That is the simple question. Or will you appoint some other system, or will you leave the children of our denomination to grow up in that state of ignorance which the School Society has expressed its desire to save them from? Or shall the constable be employed, as one reverend gentleman seems to recommend (Dr. Bangs), or some public officer, to catch them and send them to school? For from this moment, in consequence of the language used, and the insulting passages which those books contain, Catholic parents will not send their children there, and any attempts to enforce attendance would meet with vigorous resistance from them. I have now presented what is in reality the simple issue; it is no matter whether we believe right or not, for neither the Catholic nor the Protestant religion is on trial here; and I repeat, therefore, that the gentleman who represents the Methodist Church has taken so much pains to distil through the minds of this meeting a mass of prejudice which it will take several hours, but, at the same time, very little beside, for me to refute and scatter to the winds. I shall, perhaps, not dwell long on that part, because I judge it is irrelevant to the case in hand, but still I shall feel authorized to trespass on the patience of the meeting a short time, though but a short time, to remove the improper prejudice which may have been created.

Now, I start again with a statement of the question, as I did the other day, and, notwithstanding all the learning—theological, legal, medical, and I know not what beside—which has been employed to oppose our position, and although I have had to meet so many able gentlemen who have been accustomed to public speaking, I rise in the proud consciousness that not a solitary principle laid down by me, or laid down in that petition, has been refuted. I see the question stand precisely where it did before the gentlemen began to speak, and I see the same false issue—and I challenge any gentleman to say that it is not a false issue—persevered in to this very hour; so that our argument has not been moved one iota. There must, therefore, be something powerful in our plain, unsophisticated, simple statement, when all the reasoning brought against it leaves it just where it was before.

I shall now take the gentlemen in order, and follow them according to the notes which I have taken and my recollection of their arguments, and I may possibly have some difficulty in avoiding a discursive reply. The first gentleman (Mr. Sedgwick) who spoke, took up this view: that, if this system is wrong, it ought to be overturned entirely. That I leave to the judgment of those with whom the confidence of the people has deposited the authority. He says that the people have a right to interfere, and to give to the children of the State an intellectual education; that this must be carried out in some form or other, and that this system is as little objectionable as any that could be presented. That may be; I do not dispute the possibility of it, because it is unimportant; but if he did mean to contend that that system which has been once sanctioned must continue to be sanctioned, although its sanction was merely by the tacit consent of the different denominations, and although it should become violative of the religious rights of any, then he goes beyond the limits which even the Constitution of the land has made sacred. I have been represented as endeavoring to create excitement on this subject. To that I shall refer immediately; but I may here refer to my objection to the existing system, on the ground that it has a tendency to infidelity, and may observe that I know clergymen of other denominations who are also opposed to it on the ground of its infidel tendency. There are many who have the conviction that it tends to infidelity, and who know that the preventive referred to is not equal to stem the tendency to infidelity which does exist.

The first gentleman who spoke, and he spoke with a frankness and sincerity for which I give him credit, contended—and, when I answer his objection, I wish to be understood as speaking to all that took up that objection —and it was urged more or less by the whole—that it was inconsistent to charge upon the system a tendency to infidelity, and then a teaching of religion, and that this teaching was anti-Catholic. Now, this would be inconsistent under some circumstances; but the gentleman left out the grounds on which that charge was made, and it will be proper, therefore, that I should state those grounds. In the document which emanated from the Board of Assistants last spring, they say that the smallest particle of religion is a disqualification, and that "religious instruction is no part of a common school education." Now, was it the intention of your honorable body to exclude all religion? Was it the intention of the State Legislature? Did any public authority require that the public school education should be winnowed, as corn on a barn-floor, and all religion driven out by the winds of heaven as chaff not worthy to be preserved? Was there such authority? Who made such a decision? And yet that very decision, I ask you, if we are not authorized to interpret as proof of the charge, that the system has a tendency to infidelity? For, banish religion, and infidelity alone remains. And, on the other hand, we find the gentlemen of the Public School Society themselves repeatedly stating that they inculcate religion, and give religious impressions, and I say it does them credit; for, as far as they can, they ought to teach religion. It would be better if they did for those who are satisfied with THEIR religious teaching. This explanation will set us right in the minds of your honorable body. It is first said, no religion is taught, and then it is admitted that religion is inculcated; and next, our petition is opposed because it is alleged that, if our prayer be granted, religion will be taught. What weight, then, is the objection of the Public School Society entitled to, if this be the fact? And where is our inconsistency? If there is a dilemma, to whom are we indebted for it but to the report of the Board of Assistants on the one hand, and to the testimony of the Public School Society on the other? Let us not, then, be charged with inconsistency.

Now, sir, I contend there is infidelity taught. I do not mean in its gross form; but I have found principles of inferiority in the books, and one that would pass current as a very amiable book—a religious lesson which I would not suffer a child to read over whom I had any influence. The lesson represents a father and his son going about, on Sunday morning, to the different churches, the little boy asking questions as they pass along from one to the other; at last the boy said to his father—I may not quote the words, but I shall be found right in substance: "What is the reason there are so many different sects? Why do not all people agree to go to the same place, and to worship God in the same way?" "And why should it not be so?" replied the father. "Why should they agree? Do not people differ in other things? Do they not differ in their taste and their dress?—some like their coats cut one way, and some another. And do they not differ in their appetites and food? and in the hours they keep, and in their diversion?" Now, I ask if there is no infidelity in that? I ask if it is a proper lesson to teach children, that, as they have a right to form their own tastes for dress and food, they have the right to judge for themselves in matters of religion? for—with deference to the Public School Society—children are too young to have such principles instilled into them. Let them grow up before they are left to exercise their judgment in such weighty matters—at least, do not teach Catholic children such a lesson at so early an age. And, in all I have said, I desire to be understood as abstaining most carefully from prescribing any rule, or method, or book, for any denomination with which I am not connected. But for Catholic children I speak, and I say, it is too early for them to judge for themselves. And is this all? No, sir; one other passage, and for that there may perhaps be something to be said as to its defence, because it is from the pen of an eminent Protestant divine, the Bishop of London. I presume the Bishop of London, when he wrote that passage, must have been writing on some subject connected with infidelity—he must have been writing against infidelity, and indulging in a range of argument which might be proper for such a subject, but out of place in the hands of common school children. What was that passage? Why, it is one which represents the Divine Redeemer as a *man of respectable talents.*

Mr. KETCHUM rose, and intimated his doubt of such a passage being in the books.

The right reverend prelate continued:

I have read it in their books, but the trustees have recalled them—I hope not for the purpose of depriving me of the opportunity of quoting the page. Such a lesson is now to be found in one of the books, which represents the Divine Redeemer as showing uncommon quickness of penetration and sagacity. I ask whether such a lesson is a proper one for children, and whether such is the instruction to be given to them of the Redeemer of the world? The gentleman who first spoke said it was not in reality religion that was taught, but mere morality that was inculcated—the propriety of telling the truth, and of fulfilling all moral duties. If this be true, it is still strange that the School Society should prefer the word "religious." He did not deny that it was a kind of religion, and that the precepts of the Decalogue were inculcated; and while the Public School Society admit that religion is inculcated, and the legal gentleman, their representative, does not disclaim it, so far as it forms the groundwork of a good moral character, it may be taken as admitted. And now, if they teach religion, let us know what it is to be. Let them not delegate to the teachers—some of whom may teach one religion, some another—the authority or permission to make "religious impressions," to give "religious instruction," to give a "right direction to the mind of youth," and all the other phrases which we find in their documents. Now, on the subject of religion and morals, would they teach morals without religion?—which, I conceive, will be found as visionary as castle-building in the air. Mr. Ketchum says they are taught not to lie; but, without religion, he furnishes no motive for not lying. If a man tells me not to lie, when it is my interest to lie, I, as a rational being, want a motive for telling the truth. My love of gain tells me, if I lie, and lie successfully, it will add to my fortune; and if I am told to abstain from lying at the risk of my fortune, let me have a reason. But if I am told there is a God to whom I am accountable, that is a motive, but then it is a teaching of religion. Yes, sir, when I am told there is a God, I am taught religion, and therefore I am astonished that the report which has gone forth from the other board should declare that the smallest teaching of religion vitiates the claim. You may as well think to build an edifice without a foundation, as to pretend to produce moral effects without religious belief.

There may not be the details of religion, but there must be the principle to a certain extent, otherwise you cannot lay the foundation of good morals for men. Now, sir, I will show you that Mr. Stephen Girard, of Philadelphia, who had no religious belief whatever, in his will, by which he bequeathed large sums of money for the purpose of procuring great and material benefits to society—but which has been looked upon by many Christians of every denomination in Philadelphia rather as a curse than a blessing— even he speaks of morality without religion nearly as the Public School Society does. He says:

Secondly, I enjoin and require that no ecclesiastic, missionary, or minister of any sect whatsoever, shall ever hold or exercise any station or duty whatsoever in the said college; nor shall any such person ever be admitted for any purpose, or as a visitor, within the premises appropriated to the purposes of the said college. On making this restriction, I do not mean to cast any reflection upon any sect or person whatsoever; but as there is such a multitude of sects, and such a diversity of opinion amongst them, I desire to keep the tender minds of the orphans, who are to derive advantage from this bequest, free from the excitement which clashing doctrines and sectarian controversy are so likely to produce. My desire is, that all the instructors and teachers in the college shall take pains to instil into the minds of the scholars the purest principles of morality, so that, on their entrance into active life, they may, from inclination and habit, evince benevolence toward their fellow-creatures, and a love of truth, sobriety, and industry; adopting, at the same time, such religious tenets as their matured reason may enable them to prefer.

That, sir, is the policy of Mr. Girard, who had no belief that was known to others. That was the policy of a man who, so far as was known, was as much a skeptic as Voltaire or Rousseau. He, by his bounty of two millions of dollars to the city of Philadelphia, provided that poor orphans should be brought up to respect infidelity. He did not say a word against religion, but he took care to stand by, not personally, but by his executors in his will, to prevent its precepts being inculcated in the minds of those who are the dependents on his bounty. They were to have the purest principles of morals instilled into their minds; but the attempt is vain when religion is not placed as the foundation of morals.

He, like the Public School Society, stands by to see that the potter shall give no form to the vase till the clay grows stiff and hardened. Then it will be too late.

The gentleman also made objections to our schools, because, he said, they were in our churches. The fact is, we were obliged to provide them where we could, and our means would permit; and there are some of them in the basement of our churches. And he conceived it impossible to keep them from sectarian influence, because the children would be within hearing of the chant of divine service;—as though sectarianism depended on geographical distances from church. But this could not have been a valid objection, because the Public School Society has had not only schools under churches, but in the session-rooms of churches.

I shall refer now to the learned gentleman who followed him (Mr. Ketchum); and I can only say that this gentleman, with a great deal of experience in this particular question, really seems to me to confirm all I say on the ground we have taken. I know he lectured me pretty roundly on the subject of attending the meetings held under St. James' Church. I know he did more for me than the pope: the pope "mitred" me but once, but he did so three or four times during the course of his address. He read me a homily on the duties of station; and he so far forgot his country and her principles as to call it a "descent" on my part when I mingled in a popular meeting of freemen. But it was no descent; and I hope the time will never come when it will be deemed a descent for a man in office to mingle with his fellow-citizens when convened for legitimate and honorable purposes.

But, from his speech, it would appear that his experience has been obtained by the discharge of the duty of standing advocate of denial; and yet, with all his experience and opportunities of research, his inability to overturn our grounds confirms me in the conviction that they are not to be removed, even by the aid of splendid talents; for that speech, like most others, went on the false issue that we want privileges. But we want no privilege. That speech, like the speech from the throne, might have been the speech of years past, and might have been stereotyped; for its only novelty, which proved to me that it was not all the work of antiquity, was the part which appertained to myself. And not only that, but I have to say that, when I came into this hall—and it is the first time I ever stood in an assembly of this description—I felt that I was thrown on the hospitality of the professional gentlemen; and I think, if I and that gentleman could have exchanged places, I should not have looked so hard at him as he did at me. In fact, throughout that speech he, with peculiar emphasis and a manner which he may perhaps have acquired in his practice in courts of law, fixed upon me a steady gaze—and he has no ordinary countenance—and addressed me so solemnly, that I really expected every moment he would forget himself, and say, " The prisoner at the bar." He did not, however. He passed that over; and, whilst I recognize and respect the " human face divine," because God made it to look upward, I may here observe, that it has no power to frighten me, even if it *would* be terrible; and therefore I was not at all disturbed by the hard looks which he gave me. The gentleman will pardon me, I hope, in this, for it is natural enough, after what has been said —though I know it was said in good humor—to claim the privilege to retort.

Well, sir, this was not all, but he told us something about going to the stake. He was sure, if any of the public money was voted to the denomination of a reverend gentleman whose name I will not mention, the Catholics would go to the stake. Now, sir, we have no intention to do so. We know the public money does go to the support of religion; it goes to the support of chaplaincies, theological seminaries, universities, and chaplains of institutions whose appointments are permanent; and be it remembered, that one of the first lectures delivered in one institution—the University of this city—which was aided from the public funds, was on the anti-republican tendency of popery. And yet we did not go to the stake for that; and why? Because, though our portion of taxation mingles with the rest, we have no objections to the use of it which the law prescribes, so long as no inalienable rights of our own are involved in the sacrifice.

But again, he said, if any of the money was appropriated to the Catholic religion, Protestants would go to the stake. I will not say whether Protestants are so exclusive. While we submit to taxation for Protestant purposes without going to the stake, whether, if we participate, they will go to the stake, is not for me to say.

Then he came to the Protestant Bible, "without note or comment;" and " it was hard for him to part with that translated Bible." He stood by it, and repeated that " it was hard to give up the Bible;" just as if I had said one word against it, and as if I was about to bring the pope to banish it out of the Protestant world, or wished to deprive any man who venerates it of any use he may think proper to make of it. And there, again, he looked so much as if he were in earnest, that, at one time, I thought he was actually about to rush to the "stake." But there was no stake there to go to, except that which he holds in the exchequer of the Public School Society. It is a most comfortable way of going to martyrdom.

Sir, the gentleman taunted me for having attended the public meetings of Catholics on this subject, and he imputed the prejudice which exists against the public school system to the observations I have made, as though it were of my creation. In answer to that, I may state—what has been the fact for years—that Catholics have been struggling to have schools, and to the extent of their means we have them; and what is the reason? Do you suppose that we should impose additional burdens upon ourselves, if we were satisfied with those public schools? Do you suppose we should have paid for our bread a second time, if that which these schools offered had not, in our opinion, been turned to a stone? No; the existence of our own schools proves that I have not excited the prejudice; but still it is at all times my duty to warn my people against that which is destructive or violative to the religion they profess; and if they abandon their religion, they are free; but so long as they are attached to our religion, it is my duty, as their pastor, as the faithful guardian of their principles and morals, to warn them when there is danger of imbibing poison instead of wholesome food. That is the reason; and I am sorry that he has not found a motive less unworthy of me than that he has been pleased to assign.

Then—and I may as well take up the question now as elsewhere—it has been said that it is conceived to be an inconsistency in our argument, that we object to the public schools because religion is taught in them; and yet, in the schools which we propose to establish, or, rather, which we have established, but for which we now plead, we profess to teach no sectarianism; and the question arises, "If you are opposed to religion in these schools because it is sectarianism, how can you teach religion in your schools, and yet your schools not be sectarian?" This is the position in which they place us; and, in answer, I have to state that, in the first place, we do not intend to teach religion. We shall be willing that they shall be placed under the same inspection that the public schools are now; and if it should be found that religion is taught, we will be willing that you shall cut them off. You shall be the judges. You may see that the law is complied with, and if we violate it, let us be deprived of the benefits for which the conditions were prescribed. But there is neutral ground on which our children may learn to read and cipher. If they read, it must be something that is written; words are signs of ideas, and, in the course of their instruction, they may be made so to shape their studies as to loathe Catholicism without learning any other religion. And this could be produced not alone in reference to Catholics, but Presbyterians, Methodists, Unitarians, or any other. They might find that their children disregard their own religion, while they are not taught any other. Suppose the Presbyterians, or any other denomination, were in the minority, and Catholics were numerically what Protestants are now, and therefore were able to decide what lessons their children should read in these schools, I ask you if the gentleman would not conceive he had reasonable objections, if they had forced upon them a system of education which teaches that their denomination, past, present, and to come, was deceitful? Now, take up these books, which teach all that is infamous in our history—which teach our children about the "execution of Cranmer," the burning of Huss, and "the character of Luther." If such a practice were reversed, what would he do?

Now, in our schools I would teach them—I would give our children lessons for exercise in reading that should teach them that, when the young tree of American liberty was planted, it was watered with Catholic blood, and that therefore we have as much right to every thing common in this country as others. I should teach them that Catholic bishops and Catholic barons at Runneymede wrung the charter of our liberties—the grandparent of all known liberty in the world—from the hands of a tyrant. I should teach them where to find the bright spots on our history, though the gentleman who represents the Methodists knew not where they were to be found. This I would do; and should I violate the law? If, instead of the burning of Huss, I gave them a chapter on the character of Charles Carroll of Carrollton as a reading-lesson, would that be teaching them of purgatory, and the doctrine of transubstantiation?

But if our circumstances were reversed, so that Catholics controlled the public schools, would not Presbyterians have a right to complain? And should not we be tyrants while we refused to listen to their complaints, if we spread before *their* children lessons on the burning of Servetus by Calvin, and on the hangings of members of the Society of Friends by those who held Calvin's doctrines? I should listen to their appeal in such a case with feelings far different from those manifested by them in regard to others. But I would do more, in order that those little vagrants of whom the gentleman speaks might come into school. Their parents themselves having by persecution been deprived, in many instances, of an education, do not fully appreciate its advantages, and if you seek to enforce the attendance of their children, they will resist; if you attempt to coerce them, you will not succeed. But if you put them in a way to be admitted without being dragged by force to the school, or without destroying their religious principles when they enter (which you have no right to do), then you will prepare good citizens, educated to the extent that will make them useful to their country. Then their parents, having confidence in their pastors, will send their children to schools approved of by them; and the children themselves may attend schools where they need not be ashamed of their creed, and where their companions will not call them "papists," and tell them that ignorance and vice are the accompaniments of their religion. That will be the result, and I conceive it will be beneficial.

Much has been said about the distinction between morality and religion, and about those certain broad principles on which it is thought all can agree. And yet our opponents contend, and I am surprised at the circumstance—gentlemen who are not only Christians themselves, but Christian ministers—contend all through for the rights of those who are not of the Christian religion, but are commonly called infidels. An attempt has been made to draw a distinction between morality and religion. I have already said—and there is not a gentleman here who will pretend to deny it—that morality must rest on religion for its basis. I refer you—and it is not an ordinary authority—to a man who passed through life with the most beautiful character and the most blameless reputation that ever fell to the lot of a public man; one who was distinguished almost above all other men; one of whom it would be profane to say that he was inspired, yet of whom history has not handed down one useless action, or one single idle word—a man who left to his country an inheritance of the brightest example and the fairest name that ever soldier or statesman bequeathed to a nation : that man was George Washington. Hear what he says, in his Farewell Address, on the attempt now being made to preserve morality, whilst religion is discarded from the public schools :

Of all the dispositions and habits which lead to political prosperity, religion and morality are indispensable supports. In vain would that man claim the tribute of patriotism, who should labor to subvert these great pillars of human happiness, these firmest props of the duties of men and citizens. The mere politician, equally with the pious man, ought to respect and to cherish them. A volume could not trace all their connections with private and public felicity. Let it be simply asked, Where is the security for property, for reputation, for life, if the sense of religious obligations desert the oaths which are the instruments of investigation in courts of justice ? And let us with caution indulge the supposition that morality can be maintained without religion. Whatever may be conceded to the influence of refined education on minds of peculiar structure, reason and experience both forbid us to expect that national morality can prevail in exclusion of religious principle.

'Tis substantially true, that virtue or morality is a necessary spring of popular government. The rule indeed extends with more or less force to every species of free government. Who that is a sincere friend to it can look with indifference upon attempts to shake the foundation of the fabric ?

Such is the warning, the solemn warning, of this great man. If you take away religion, on what foundation do you propose to rear the structure of morality ? No ; they stand to each other in the relation of parent and offspring ; or, rather, they are kindred principles from the same Divine source ; and what God has joined together let no man put asunder.

Now, with regard to all said by me against the Protestant Bible, I appeal to this honorable body whether I ever said one word hostile to that Bible ; and yet, from the address of the gentlemen on the other side, men abroad, who should read their speeches, would be led to believe that I not only entertained, but that I had uttered, sentiments of hostility to that work. And it is ever thus that our principles and our feelings are misrepresented, while gentlemen profess to be conscious of entertaining no prejudice against us as Catholics. One gentleman, however, avowed his hostility to us on this ground, and for his candor I tender my acknowledgment. The whole effort of some of the gentlemen—indeed, of all who have spoken on the subject— has been, to show that the system must be made so broad and liberal that *all* can agree in it. But I think they contend for too much, when they wish so to shape religion and balance it on its pedestal as to make it suit every body and every sect; for if infidels are to be suited, and it is made to reconcile them to the system, I want to know whether Catholics, or any other class, are not entitled to the right to have it made to suit them ? And if every body is to be made satisfied, why is it that Catholics and others are discontented and excluded ? Is it not manifest that what they profess to accomplish is beyond their reach ? Now, the infidels have found able advocates in the reverend gentlemen who have spoken in the course of this discussion—I mean the interests of infidelity ; and why is it, then, that the gentlemen who plead for that side of the question enter their protest against ours? I should like to know why there is this inconsistency. If the rule is to be general, why is it not general?

I pass, now, to the reasoning of one learned gentleman who spoke yesterday, and defended the Protestant Bible. Now, this was unnecessary in that gentleman; it was in him a work of supererogation to vindicate the Protestant Scriptures; it was useless to defend a point which had not been attacked. It was time lost; and yet, perhaps, not altogether lost, for, in some respects, it may have been profitable enough. In entering on its defence, he said it was the instrument of human liberty throughout the world; wherever it was, there was light and liberty; and where it was not, there was bondage and darkness; and he brought it round so that he almost asserts that our Declaration of Independence had been copied from the Bible. No doubt the just and righteous principles on which that Declaration has its foundation have their sanction in the Bible; but I deny their immediate connection, and on historical grounds, for it is known that its author looked upon St. Paul as an impostor; consequently their connection is not historically true. But while the gentleman referred to our notes (but which we disown and repudiate) as containing principles of persecution, how was it that, after the Protestant Bible, " without note and comment," came into use, every denomination of Protestants in *the whole world* that had the misfortune—for it must have been a misfortune—to be yoked to civil power, wielded the sword of persecution, and derived their authority for so doing from the *naked text?* Yes, in Scotland, in all her confessions of faith, in England—and I appeal to her penal laws against Catholics, and those acts by which the Puritans and Dissenters were pursued—men who had the misfortune, like ourselves, to have a conscience, were driven out, and all was done on the authority of the Bible, without note or comment, and for the public good, and the good of the Church. I do not say that the Bible sanctioned persecution, but I deny that the absence of notes is an adequate preventive. I refer to history. And almost to this day, though the Bible has been translated three hundred years, even in *liberal* governments, the iron heel of persecution has been placed on the dearest rights of Catholics. The gentleman to whom I allude said, no doubt, what he knew would be popular out of doors; for he seems, with others, to imagine that the world began at the period of the Reformation. He seems to think that every thing great originated at that period. But does he not know that eight hundred editions of the Bible had been printed before the Reformation? And does he not know that two hundred editions had been circulated in the common tongue, in the common language of the country? And has he yet to learn that the first prohibition to read the Bible came not from a Catholic, but from a Protestant—from Protestant Henry VIII. of " glorious memory "? He was the first to issue a prohibition; and it was not till Catholics saw the evil—not of the Bible, but the bad uses men were making of the Bible—that they placed its perusal under certain restrictions, and cautioned their people against hastily judging of it for themselves. All had been united and harmonious, but by the use, or abuse, which men made of the Bible, all

19

became doubt and speculation, and the positive revelation of Christ was shaken or destroyed. They saw this Bible, and what then? But, while these school gentlemen contend that it is a shield against infidelity, and that all sects here agree, how is it out of the schools? Why, no sects agree upon it. How is it that the Bible, which is given by the inspiration of God, the God of truth, is made use of, in this city even, to prove a Trinity and to disprove a Trinity? How is it that Trinitarians quote it to prove their doctrines, and Unitarians quote it to establish the opposite doctrines? How is it that, whilst one says from the Bible that God the Father is God alone, and that Christ is not equal to Him, for He says, "The Father is greater than I," another argues from the same Bible that the Father and Son are equal, because Christ says, "The Father and I are one"? And another comes with the Bible in his hand, and says, "I believe—and I can prove it from this Bible—that Christ *alone* is the Almighty God, and the Father and the Spirit are only attributes of the same person!" Why, this Bible, which they say is the foundation of all truth—and they say well, when it is truly understood; a grace which God can vouchsafe, and no doubt He does to many—this Bible is harmonious in its every doctrine. But this is not the point; the point is, the uses we see men make of it; and this is the sum of our reason that we wish our children not to be taught in the manner in which Protestant children are taught in reference to the Bible.

And then, again, if you teach that there is a hell, according to the Bible, others will contend that the Scriptures teach no such doctrine. And so I might pass on to other points to show you, whilst they thus contend for the Bible as the guide to truth, there is this disagreement among them, at least in this country, where human rights and liberties are understood, as allowing every man to judge for himself. Is there not, then, danger—is there not ground to apprehend that, when our children read this Bible, and find that all these different sects father all their contradictions on the Bible as their authority, they will derive their first notions of infidelity from these circumstances? But there is another ground on which it is manifest we cannot allow our children to be taught by them. Whilst we grant them the right to take, if they please, the Protestant Bible as the rule of their faith, and the individual right to judge of the Bible—and this great principle they proclaim as the peculiar and distinctive and most glorious trait in their religious character and history—and let them boast of it; there is no difficulty on the subject—they interpret the Bible by the standard of reason, and therefore, as there is no given standard of reason, as one has more and another less, they scarcely ever arrive at the same result; while the Bible, the eternal Word of God, remains the same. But this is not a Catholic principle. Catholics do not believe that God has vouchsafed the promise of the Holy Spirit to every individual, but that He has given His Spirit to teach the Church collectively, and to guide the Church, and therefore we do not receive as the Bible except what the Church guarantees; and wanting this guarantee, the Methodist gentleman failed to establish the book which he produced, with its notes, as a Catholic Bible. We do not take the Bible on the authority of a "king's printer" who is a speculating publisher, who publishes it but as a speculation. And why? Because, by the change of a single comma, that which is positive may be made negative, and *vice-versâ;* and then is it the Bible of the inspired writers? It is not. They proclaim, then, that theirs is a Christianity of reason; of this they boast;—and let them glory. Ours is a Christianity of faith; ours descends by the teaching of the Church. We are never authorized to introduce new doctrines, because we contend that no new doctrine is true from the time of the apostles, unless it has come from the mind of God by a special revelation; and, to us, that is not manifest among the reformers. We are satisfied to trust our eternal interests, for weal or woe, on the security of that Catholic Church and the veracity of the Divine promises. You perceive, therefore, that Protestants may agree in the system where this Bible is thus introduced; but it is not in accordance with the principles of Catholics that each one shall derive therefrom his own notions of Christianity. It is not the principle of Catholics, because they believe in the incompetence of individual reason in matters of such importance. It is from this self-sufficiency and imputed capacity that men derive such notions of self-confidence, which, owing to a want of power to control in some domestic circles, if taught to our children, lead to disobedience and disregard of the parental authority.

I have been obliged to enter into this, which is rather theological than otherwise, to put you in possession of the true ground. We do not take the Protestant Bible, but we do not wish others not to take it if they desire it. If conscience be stifled, you do not make us better men or better citizens; and therefore I say, gentlemen, respect conscience, even though you think it in error, provided it does not conflict with the public rights. I have sufficiently disposed of the addresses of the two legal gentlemen who have spoken. I will now call the attention of this honorable body to the remarks of the reverend gentleman who spoke in relation to the Rhemish Testament. I did use, sir, yesterday, an expression which I used with reluctance; but when we were charged before this honorable body—when the reverend gentleman who represents a numerous denomination charged us with teaching the lawfulness of murdering heretics, that expression came on me as a thunderbolt; because I thought that truth should proceed from the lips of age and a man of character. And, sir, I knew that position was not true, and that it was an easy matter to assert a thing, but not so easy to disprove it. I might take advantage of circumstances to charge a man with things that it would take weeks to disprove, and therefore I thought it necessary to nail that slanderous statement to the counter before it could have its designed influence here or elsewhere. That gentleman began with great humility, and with professions of being devoid of prejudice, and then he said that those meetings to which he referred, and which he called "public gatherings," had caused him to feel greatly alarmed about this question;—as if the stability of your republic was endangered, provided Catholic children received the benefits of a common school education! He said I had applied certain remarks to the creed of the Society of Friends; and though, perhaps, it was somewhat out of order, but wishing to set the gentleman right, I denied that I had done so. But since then the reporter has handed me the notes taken of what I did say, and from them also it appears that I said no such thing. He referred to the practice of teaching religion in the schools; but of that I have disposed already.

He then, while going through the introductory part of the remonstrance of the Methodist Episcopal Church, threw out constantly calumnious charges against the Catholic Church and the Catholic religion. He did not throw them out as assertions, but by inuendo, as "if it be true," and "I should like to know";—as if I am here for the purpose of supplying every thing he would "like to know." And how can I meet him, when insinuation is the form in which his charges are thrown out? Why, their very feebleness takes from an opponent the power of refutation. But when he comes to something tangible, then I can meet him. Having gone through a series of insinuations, he misrepresents our intentions. Notwithstanding we disclaim such an intention, he indulges in the gratuitous supposition that, if your honorable body should grant our petition, we shall secretly teach the Catholic religion. But if we do, is not the law as potent against us as against the public schools? If they teach religion, as they acknowledge, why may not we? We are not grasping to obtain power over others, but we desire in sincerity to benefit a portion of our own neglected children. I shall pass over, therefore, a great deal of what the gentleman "would like to know," for I do not know if it is of importance to the subject. He said this Rhemish Testament was published by authority; but he began by a retreat, and not by a direct charge. "He did not profess to say that our Church approved of it; but it was printed and published, and it was not on the *Index*"—as if every bad book in the world must be in the *Index;*—and, with this evidence of fact, he comes here and spreads before the American people the slander and calumny that the Catholics, by their notes and comments, teach the lawfulness of murdering heretics. Now, sir, I will take up that book, and the parts he read, with the notes giving an explanation, as though they came from Catholics. Do you know the history of that book, sir? If not, I can tell you. When Queen Elizabeth scourged the Catholics from their altars, and drove them into exile, these men held a common notion, which was natural and just, that England was their country, and that they were suffering unmerited persecution. The new religion, not satisfied with toleration for itself, grasped the substance of things—grasped the power of the State, seized all their temples, and, not even satisfied with this, scourged the Catholics from their home and country; and they did write these notes—and why? They wrote them in exile, smarting under the lash and the torture, and in connection, too, with a plan for the invasion of England by Philip II. of Spain. Their object was, to disseminate amongst Catholics of England disaffection to Queen Elizabeth, and thus dispose them to join the true Catholic and oppose the hereties, because the heretics were their enemies—were the enemies of their rights, and had crushed them. But when that book appeared in England, was there a single approval given it—a single Catholic that received it? Not one. When it was published for political ends—to aid the invasion of Philip—did the English Catholics receive it? Never. But the gentleman said it was published by the bishops of Ireland and with their approbation, and with the approbation of a great number of the Catholic clergy ; and this after his own admission that, insomuch as it had not been approved by the Holy See, the bishop of Rome, it was not of authority in the Catholic Church. Now, I shall take up both parts ; and first, I should like to know where is his authority that it was published by the bishops of Ireland ? I pause for a reply, and I shall not consider it an interruption.

Dr. BOND. Do you wish an answer ?

Bishop HUGHES. I do, sir ; I desire your authority.

Dr. BOND. Why, if we are to believe history, it is true ; it is stated in the *British Critic.*

Bishop HUGHES. Oh ! I am satisfied.

Dr. BOND. It could not have been reviewed if it did not exist.

Bishop HUGHES. Oh ! it is here, and that proves its existence without the *British Critic.* It was gone out of print again, and not a Catholic now heard of it, but your *liberal* Protestant clergymen of New York republished it. What for ? To bring infamy on the Catholic name. And it was from this Protestant edition, and not from Ireland, that the Methodist gentleman received it. I am now not surprised at his saying so often that he would " like to know," for a little more knowledge would be of great advantage to him. I need not read it.

Dr. BOND. Oh ! you had better.

Bishop HUGHES. Well, sir, any thing to accommodate you.

It is a remarkable fact, that, notwithstanding the Vulgate New Testament, as it was translated and expounded by the members of the Jesuit college at Rheims, in 1582, has been republished in a great number of editions, and their original annotations, either more or less extensively, have been added to the text ; yet, as soon as it is appealed to as an authority, the Roman priests admit both the value of the book and the obligation of the papists to believe its contents. We have a very striking modern instance to prove this deceitfulness.

Now, it must be recollected that this is a Protestant publication ; the Catholics did not circulate it, but the Protestant ministers did, to mislead their flocks, and to bring infamy on their Catholic fellow-citizens.

The Douay Bible is usually so called because, although the New Testament was first translated and published at Rheims, yet the Old Testament was printed, some years after, at Douay ; the English Jesuits having removed their monastery from Rheims to Douay before their version of the Old Testament was completed. In the year 1816, an edition, including both the Douay Old and the Rhemish New Testament, was issued at Dublin, containing a large number of comments replete with impiety, irreligion, and the most fiery persecution. That edition was published under the direction of all the dignitaries of the Roman hierarchy in Ireland, and about three hundred others of the most influential subordinate priests.

Now, I called for the gentleman's evidence for this, and the gentleman was found *minus habens*—he has it not to give. The prints said so, and he believed the prints ! Now, sir, this is a grave charge, and I am disposed to treat it gravely ; but I should not feel worthy of the name of a man—I

should feel myself unworthy of being a member of the American family, if
I had not risen and repelled such a charge as it deserved.

Dr. BOND. You have not read all I read.

Bishop HUGHES. I will read all the gentleman may wish, if he will not
keep me here reading all night.

The notes which urged the hatred and murder of Protestants attracted
the attention of the British Churches, and, to use the words of T. Hartwell
Horne, that edition of the ,Rhemish Testament printed at Dublin in 1816,
corrected and revised and approved by Dr. Troy, Roman Catholic archbishop of Dublin, was reviewed by the *British Critic*, vol viii., pp. 296–308,
New Series, and its dangerous tenets, both civil and religious, were exposed.

That is the testimony.

Dr. BOND. There is another paragraph.

Bishop HUGHES. Well, I will read the other.

This publication, with many others of a similar character, produced so
great an excitement in Britain, that, finally, several of the most prominent
of the Irish Roman prelates were called before the English Parliament to
prove their own work. Then, and upon oath, with all official solemnity,
they peremptorily disclaimed the volumes published by their own instigation and under their own supervision and auspices, as books of no authority, because they had not been ratified by the pope and received by the
whole papal Church.

Now, what authority have we for this charge of perjury against the Irish
bishops, better than the gentleman's own ? It is so stated here. What
authority is there for that ?

Dr. BOND. It was so stated before the British Parliament.

Bishop HUGHES. I should regret, on account of your age, if I used any
expression that might be deemed harsh.

Dr. BOND. Take the liberty to say what you please.

Bishop HUGHES. With regard to these notes, I have to observe, that
they were written in an age (1582) when the rights of conscience were but
little understood. Protestants in that age everywhere persecuted not only
Catholics, but each other. And, long after, the Puritans of New England,
with the Bible, and without notes, persecuted with torture, and even to
hanging, their fellow-Protestants. It was not wonderful, therefore, if, in
such an age, Catholics were found to entertain the opinions set forth in the
notes. But, bad as they are, it is remarkable that they do not sustain the
calumnious charge of the reverend gentleman, that they "teach the lawfulness of murdering heretics.

And now, sir, let me call your attention to the book itself.

In the thirteenth chapter of St. Matthew there is this text, at the 29th
verse. It occurs in the parable of the cockle (in the Protestant version
tares) and the wheat, in answer to Christ's disciples, who asked : " Wilt
thou that we gather it up ? And he said, No : lest, perhaps, gathering up
the cockles, you may root up the wheat also together with it." The annotation on this is :

Ver. 29. *Lest you pluck up also.* The good must tolerate the evil, when it is so strong that it cannot be redressed without danger and disturbance of the whole Church, and commit the matter to God's judgment in the latter day. Otherwise, where ill men, be they heretics or other malefactors, may be punished or suppressed without disturbance and hazard of the good, they may and ought by public authority, either spiritual or temporal, to be chastised or executed.

They may and ought "*by public authority!*" Why, the proposition of the gentleman was, that Catholics were taught to kill their Protestant neighbors. Now, there is not throughout the whole volume a proposition so absurd as the idea conveyed by him. Bad as the notes are, they require falsification to bear him out.

Again, Luke, ninth chapter, verses 54, 55 : "And when his disciples James and John had seen it, they said, Lord, wilt thou we say that fire come down from heaven, and consume them ? And turning, he rebuked them, saying, You know not of what spirit you are." Annotation :

Ver. 55. *He rebuked them.* Not justice nor all rigorous punishment of sinners is here forbidden, nor Elias' fact reprehended, nor the Church or Christian princes blamed for putting heretics to death. But none of these should be done for desire of our particular revenge, or without discretion, and regard of their amendment, and example to others. Therefore Peter used his power upon Ananias and Saphira, when he struck them both down to death for defrauding the Church.

I am afraid I shall fatigue this honorable body by going over these notes, nor is it necessary that I should follow the gentleman in all his discursive wanderings. There is nothing in this to authorize the murdering of heretics.

But again, Luke, fourteenth chapter, verse 23 : "And the Lord said to the servant, Go forth unto the ways and hedges, and compel them to enter, that my house may be filled." Annotation :

Compel them. The vehement persuasion that God useth, both externally by force of His word and miracles, and internally by His grace, to bring us unto Him, is called compelling. Not that He forceth any to come to Him against their wills, but that He can alter and mollify a hard heart, and make him willing that before would not. Augustine also referreth this compelling to the penal laws, which Catholic princes do justly use against heretics and schismatics, proving that they who are, by their former profession in baptism, subject to the Catholic Church, and are departed from the same after sects, may and ought to be compelled into the unity and society of the universal Church again : and therefore, in this sense, by the two former parts of the parable, the Jews first, and secondly the Gentiles, that never believed before in Christ, were invited by fair, sweet means only : but by the third, such are invited as the Church of God hath power over, because they promised in baptism, and therefore are to be revoked, not only by gentle means, but by just punishment also.

Sir, the punishment of spiritual offences, and the allusions here made to it, have their roots too deep and too widespreading to be entered into and discussed in the time that I could occupy this evening. It would be impossible to go over the historical grounds which suggest themselves in connection with the subject, to show the results to the state of society which grow unavoidably out of the breaking up of the Roman empire, and the incursion of new and uncivilized nations and tribes. Society had been dissolved, with all the order and laws of the ancient civilization. It was the slow work of the Church to reorganize the new and crude materials—to gather and arrange the fragments—to remodel society and social institutions as best she might. There was no other power that could digest the crude mass, the fierce infusions of other tongues and tribes and nations that had, during the chaos, become mixed up with the remains of ancient Roman civilization. She had to begin by religion, their conversion to Christianity being the first step, and the Catholic Church being the only one in existence. Hence, the laws of religion are the first with which those new populations became acquainted, and the only ones that could restrain them. Hence, too, what is called Canon Law went before, and Civil Law gradually followed, oftentimes mixed with and deriving its force from the older form of legislation. The actual state of society made it unavoidable that this should be the order of things. Civil governments oftentimes engrafted whole branches of the ecclesiastical law in their secular codes; and ecclesiastical judges were often the interpreters and administrators of both.

Canonical law and civil law, thus blended, became the codes of civil government, from the necessity of the case; and it is to this state of things that the authors of the notes make allusion in their text. But, as I have remarked, the subject is too deep to be properly discussed on this occasion, when time is so brief, and so many speakers to be replied to.

We now come to Acts, chapter twenty-five, verse 11 :

I appeal to Cæsar. If Paul, both to save himself from whipping and from death, sought by the Jews, doubted not to cry for honor of the Roman laws, and to appeal to Cæsar, the Prince of the Romans, not yet christened, how much more may we call for aid of Christian princes and their laws, for the punishment of heretics, and for the Church's defence against them. *August. Epist.* 50.

Here you see the working of human interest; and it is not the first time among Protestants and Catholics, nor will it be the last, that men have made the Word of God and sacred things a stepping-stone to promote temporal interests. They say there, " Heretics have banished us, and is it not naturally the interest of Catholics to join a Catholic prince to put down our stern persecutors? " As if they had said to their fellow-Catholics of England, A Catholic prince will soon make a descent on our country ; it will be your duty, as it is your interest, to join in putting down the heretic Elizabeth, who has driven us from our country.

I go now to Hebrews, chapter ten, verse 29 : " How much more, think you, doth he deserve worse punishments which hath trodden the Son of God under foot, and esteemed the blood of the Testament polluted wherein he is sanctified, and hath done contrarily to the spirit of grace ? " Annotation :

The blood of the Testament. Whosoever maketh no more account of the blood of Christ's sacrifice, either as shed upon the cross, or as in the chalice of the altar—for our Saviour calleth that also the blood of the New Testament—than he doth of the blood of calves and goats, or of other common drinks, is worthy of death, and God will in the next life, if it be not punished here, revenge it with grievous punishment.

" God will in the next life punish ! " Why, after all, bad as these notes are, objectionable and scorned and repudiated as they were by the Catholics of England—bad as they are, they do not sustain the gentleman—whose assertion has gone as far beyond the truth, as it is infinitely beyond charity. I do not find the notes from the Apocalypse, which would have gone to show, in like manner, that, bad as they were, they do not support the accusations made.

Dr. BOND. There are others as well.

Bishop HUGHES. Well, I will give you the rest.

The PRESIDENT. Perhaps it is not necessary. But, if they are, it is not necessary to interrupt the gentleman.

Bishop HUGHES. Such, then, sir, are the notes put by the Catholic translators of the New Testament at Rheims in 1582—smarting, as they were, under the lash of Elizabeth's persecution, and looking forward with hope to the result of the invasion by Philip II. They were repudiated indignantly by the Catholics of England and Ireland from the first ; and were out of print, until some Protestant ministers of New York had them published in order to mislead the people and to excite odium against 'the Catholic name.

But here, sir, is the acknowledged Testament of all Catholics who speak the English language. This is known and may be read by any one ; it is the fourteenth edition in this country ; it corresponds with those used in England and Ireland ; and if any such notes can be found in it, then believe Catholics to be what they have been falsely represented to be.

But the reverend gentleman disclaims originating the slander. He took it, we are told, from the *British Critic ;*—as if that which is false must become true from the moment it is put in type and printed. But, sir, he should have known that the article in the *British Critic* was refuted at the time, and has been since refuted in the *Dublin Review.* And it so happens that Dr. Troy, then Catholic Archbishop of Dublin, and who is here represented as having approved these notes, had to sustain a lawsuit with the Dublin publisher, who was also a Protestant—not for approving the work, but for DENOUNCING it, which destroyed the publisher's speculation, and involved a suit against the Archbishop for damages ! ! This is attested by Dr. Troy's letter, now before me, and by the legal proceedings, and in a speech made by Daniel O'Connell to the Catholic Board at the time (1817), we find the following :

From the Dublin Evening Post of the 6th of December, 1817.

CATHOLIC BOARD.—THE RHEMISH BIBLE.

A remarkably full meeting of the Catholic board took place on Thursday last, pursuant to adjournment ; Owen O'Conner, Esq., in the chair.

After some preliminary business, Mr. O'Connell rose to make his promised motion for the appointment of a committee to prepare a denunciation of the intolerant doctrines contained in the Rhemish notes.

Mr. O'Connell said that, on the last day of meeting, he gave notice that he would move for a committee to draw up a disavowal of the very dangerous and uncharitable doctrines contained in certain notes to the Rhemish Testament. He now rose to submit that motion to the consideration of the board. The late edition of the Rhemish Testament in this country gave rise to much observation. That work was denounced by Dr. Troy ; an action is now depending between him and a respectable bookseller in this city ; and it would be the duty of the board not to interfere, in the remotest degree, with the subject of that action ; but, on the other hand, the board could not let the present opportunity pass by of recording their sentiments of disapprobation and even of abhorrence of the bigoted and intolerant doctrines promulgated in that work. Their feelings of what was wise, consistent, and liberal, would suggest such a proceeding, even though the indecent calumnies of their enemies had not rendered it indispensible. A work called *The British Critic* had, no doubt, been read by some gentlemen who heard him. The circulation of the last number has been very extensive, and exceeded, almost beyond calculation, the circulation of any former number, in consequence of an article which appeared in it on the late edition of the Rhemish Testament. He (Mr. O'Connell) said he read that article ; it is extremely unfair and uncandid ; it gives, with audacious falsehood, passages, as if from the notes of the Rhemish Testament, which cannot be found in that work ; and, with mean cunning, it seeks to avoid detection by quoting, without giving either text or page. Throughout it is written in the true spirit of the inquisition ; it is violent, vindictive, and uncharitable. He was sorry to understand that it was written by ministers of the Established Church ; but he trusted that, when the charge of intemperance should be again brought forward against the Catholics, their accusers would cast their eyes on this coarse and illiberal attack—here they may find a specimen of real intemperance. But the very acceptable work of imputing principles to the Irish people which they never held, and which they abhor, was not confined to *The British Critic*. *The Courier*, a newspaper whose circulation is immense, lent its hand, and the provincial newspapers throughout England—those papers which are forever silent when any thing might be said favorable to Ireland, but are ever active to disseminate whatever may tend to her disgrace or dishonor. They have not hesitated to impute to the Catholics of this country the doctrines contained in those offensive notes— and it was their duty to disclaim them. Nothing was more remote from the true sentiments of the Irish people. These notes were of English growth ; they were written in agitated times, when the title of Elizabeth was questioned, on the grounds of legitimacy. Party spirit was then extremely violent ; politics mixed with religion, and, of course, disgraced it. Queen Mary, of Scotland, had active partisans, who thought it would forward their purposes to translate the Bible, and add to it those obnoxious notes. But, very shortly after the establishment of the college at Douay, this Rhemish edition was condemned by all the Doctors of that institution, who, at the same time, called for and received the aid of the Scotch and Irish colleges. The book was thus suppressed, and an edition of the Bible, with notes, was published at Douay, which has ever been since adopted by the Catholic Church ; so that they not only condemned and suppressed the Rhemish edition, but they published an edition with notes, to which no objection has, or could be, urged. From that period there have been but two editions of the Rhemish Testament ; the first had very little circulation ; the late one was published by a very ignorant printer in Cork, a man of the name of M'Namara, a person who was not capable of distinguishing between the Rhemish and any other edition of the Bible. He took up the matter merely as a speculation in trade. He meant to publish a Catholic Bible, and having put his hand upon the Rhemish edition, he commenced to print it in numbers. He subsequently became bankrupt, and his property in this transaction vested in Mr. Cumming, a respectable bookseller in this city, who is either a Protestant or Presbyterian ; but he carried on the work, like M'Namara, merely to make money of it, as a mercantile speculation ; and yet, said Mr. O'Connell, our enemies have taken it up with avidity ; they have asserted that the sentiments of those notes are cherished by the Catholics in this country. He would not be surprised to read of speeches in the next Parliament on the subject. It was a hundred to one but that some of our briefless barristers have already commenced composing their dull calumnies, and that we shall have speeches from them, for the edification of the Legislature and the protection of the Church. There was not a moment to be lost. The Catholics should, with one voice, disclaim those very odious doctrines. He was sure there was not a single Catholic in Ireland that did not feel as he did—abhorrence at the principles these notes contain. Illiberality has been attributed to the Irish people, but they are grossly wronged. He had often addressed the Catholic people of Ireland. He always found them applaud every sentiment of liberality, and the doctrine of perfect freedom of conscience—the right of every human being to have his religious creed, whatever that creed might be, unpolluted by the impious interference of bigotted or oppressive laws. Those sacred rights, and that generous sentiment, were never uttered at a Catholic aggregate meeting, without receiving at the instant the loud and the unanimous applause of the assembly.

It might be said that those meetings were composed of mere rabble. Well, be it so. For one he should concede that, for the sake of argument. But what followed ? Why, just this : that the Catholic rabble, without the advantages of education, or of the influence of polished society, were so well acquainted with the genuine principles of Christian charity, that they, the rabble, adopted and applauded sentiments of liberality and of religious freedom, which, unfortunately, met but little encouragement from the polished and educated of other sects.

(Then follows the passage which we have quoted in the preceding article.)

Mr. O'Connell's motion was put and carried, the words being amended thus :

That a committee be appointed to draw up an address on the occasion of the late publication of the Rhemish Testament, with a view to have the same submitted to an aggregate meeting.

Such, sir, are the history and the authority of the notes put to the Rhemish translation of the New Testament. The denunciation of Dr. Troy spoiled the sale of the work in Ireland, and the publishers sent the remaining copies for sale to this country ; but even this did not remunerate him, as his loss was estimated at £500 sterling. It must have been from one of these exiled copies that the Protestant edition published in this city, now produced, was taken. These being the facts of the case, if I were a Protestant I should feel ashamed of a clergyman of my church who, from either malice or ignorance, should take up such a book, with the unchristian view of blackening the character of any denomination of my fellow-citizens. But not only this, sir, but look at the array of the names of Protestant ministers in this city certifying, contrary to the fact, that this text and these notes are by the authority of the Catholic Church, and then say whether there is no prejudice against the Catholics ! I shall now dismiss the subject.

Sir, the Methodist gentleman, in the whole of his address, in which he made the charge I have now disposed of, and of which I wish him joy, slyly changed the nature and bearing of my language in the remarks I made last evening. For instance, respecting purgatory, of which I observed, if they were not satisfied with our purgatory, and wished to go farther, they might prove the truth of the proverb, which says they may " go farther and fare worse." He said I " *sent* " them farther. But that corresponds with the rest. I did not send them farther. I here disavow such feelings, in the name of human nature and of that venerable religion which I profess.

But he has seen that " betting," as he was pleased to call it, is a sin, because, forsooth, " he would get my money without an equivalent." Now, I think he suspected the contrary. But I did not propose betting. His calumny had taken me by surprise; but was it not fortunate, almost providential, that I had at hand a direct refutation ?—for, if his charge had gone abroad uncontradicted, the ignorant or bigotted would have taken it on his authority, and quoted it with as much assurance as he did on that of the *British Critic*—and for the same unholy purpose. He took me, I say, at an unfair moment, and then it was I stated that, if the gentleman could prove his charge—there were gentlemen here who had confidence in my word, and I said I would pledge myself to forfeit one thousand dollars, to be distributed in charities to the poor as this Council might direct, provided he would agree to the same forfeiture if he failed to prove it. This is not betting.

He says that his Church has taught him the sinfulness of betting. But this did not deserve that name. It was only an ordeal to test his confidence in the veracity of the slander contained in the Methodist remonstrance. I may not, indeed, have the same scruples about what he calls gambling that he has ; but I do remember—what he seems to have forgotten—that there *is* a precept of the Decalogue, a commandment of the living God, which says, " Thou shalt not bear false witness against thy neighbor."

I now pass to another portion of this gentleman's remarks. He contends that it is impossible to furnish reading-lessons from history for the last ten centuries, without producing what must be offensive to Catholics. The history of Catholics is so black, that the public schools could not, in his view, find a solitary bright page to refresh the eye of the Catholic children. This is set forth in the remonstrance of the Methodist Episcopal Church, and this the reverend gentleman undertook to support in his speech. He said that history must not be falsified for our accommodation ; that the black and insulting passages against us and our religion, placed in the hands of our children at the public schools, were not to be charged as a defect in the system, inasmuch as the trustees could find worse, but would be obliged to falsify history itself to find better. From this defence you can judge what confidence Catholics can place in this Society, or in the schools under their charge.

I contended that there existed portions of history eminently honorable to Catholics. But, says he, " history is philosophy, teaching by example ; the good and the bad must be taken together." Then how. does it happen that the bad alone is presented in the public schools ? Besides, if all the good and all the bad which history ascribes to Catholics must be presented, it would make a library rather large for a class-book in the public schools. Hence the necessity of a selection ; and how is it that, in the selection, the bad is brought out, and the good passed over in silence as if it did not exist? Why is the burning of Huss selected? why the burning of Cranmer? Why are our children taught, in the face of all sense and decency, that Martin Luther did more for learning than any other man "since the days of the apostles"? Why is "Phelim Maghee" represented as "sealing his soul with a wafer"—in contempt to the holiest mystery known to Catholics, the Sacred Eucharist? Why are intemperance and vice set forth as the necessary and natural effects of the Catholic religion? All this put in the hands of Catholic children by this Society, claiming to deserve the confidence of Catholic parents!

Now, the Methodist gentleman says that all this is right—that the trustees could not possibly, within the last ten centuries, find history which would not be offensive to Catholics; and that, to make it otherwise, it must be falsified. Now, sir, I should like to know whether it can be expected that we should have any confidence in schools, for the support of which we are taxed, in which our religious feelings are insulted, our children perverted, and whose advocates tell us gravely that we ought to be satisfied—that things cannot be otherwise, unless history is to be falsified for our convenience! To this we never shall consent. Religious intolerance has done much to degrade us, and its most dangerous instrument was depriving us of education.

The gentleman [Dr. Bond] has corrected some of my remarks of last evening on the Methodist Episcopal Church. The fact is, the style of remonstrance presented here as emanating from that Church, imposed on me the necessity of alluding to the history and principles of that denomination. It is unpleasant to me at any time to use language calculated to wound the feelings of any sect or class of my fellow-citizens. But they who offer the unprovoked insult must not complain of the retort. I stated that the Methodists in England had never done a solitary act to aid in the spread of civil and religious liberty in that country; that, whilst the Catholics aided the Dissenters in obtaining the repeal of the Test and Corporation acts, the Methodists never contributed to that measure by so much as one petition in its favor. But it appears I fell into a mistake, which the gentleman corrected with great precision and gravity. The "Methodist society" in England, he tells us, is something quite different from the "Methodist Episcopal Church" in the United States. The former consider themselves only as a society in the Established Church, just as the religious orders, the Dominicans, Jesuits, &c., are in the Catholic communion. Certainly it is new to me to learn that the Methodists and the Church of England are in such close and affectionate spiritual relationship. For, although the Methodists consider themselves a society within the pale of the Establishment, the members of the Established Church are quite of a different opinion, since it was only the other day that I read of a presbyter of that Church having been suspended by his bishop for having preached in a Methodist meeting-house! So that the affection of the Methodists for the Church of England does not appear to be very cordially reciprocated.

This gentleman tells us that the Methodists, who are only a "society" in England, are an "Episcopal Church in America." Yes, sir, Mr. Wesley, who was himself but a *priest*, actually consecrated a BISHOP for the United States! And hence the Methodist *Episcopal* Church—a new order of episcopacy, deriving their authority and character from Mr. John Wesley, a mere *priest*. But, with or without bishops, their whole history proves how much they imbibed of the intolerance of the Established Church of England, to which he tells us they are so intimately allied in that country, but which at all times spurns the connection. This same John Wesley held and wrote that no government ought to grant toleration to Catholics; because, forsooth, either from ignorance of Catholic doctrines, or bigotry against them, he was pleased to believe and assert falsely that they held it lawful to murder heretics. When the Government of Great Britain was about to mitigate the code of penal laws and persecution against the Catholics in 1780, who was more fervent and fanatical in opposition to the exercise of mercy than John Wesley? The great object of the Protestant Association, headed by Lord George Gordon, was to oppose the least mitigation of severity. Who was more active in the intellectual operations of that Society than Mr. John Wesley? Under the leadership of Lord George Gordon, they raised a rebellion in that year, and when the mob had plundered, destroyed, and burnt the houses and churches of the Catholics, spread consternation throughout the city of London, and caused human blood to flow in torrents, we have this same Wesley with sanctimonious gravity charging it all on the Catholics—the victims of its fury—and contending that it was a "popish plot." His services in that association had been acknowledged by a *unanimous vote of thanks*, dated February 17th of that very year. This was in 1780, when the mighty events which had occurred in this country taught the British Government the expediency of relaxing the penal laws against so large a portion of her subjects in England and Ireland. The rebound of those events had been felt throughout the world. They were the events created and accomplished by the great fathers of this republic, then struggling into existence; and whilst Catholics and Protestants fought bravely side by side in the ranks of independence—while a Catholic Carroll was signing its charter, and another Carroll, a priest and (tell it not in Gath) a Jesuit, was employed on an embassy to render the population of Canada friendly, or, at least, not hostile to our struggle—whilst a Catholic Commodore Barry was doing the office of a founder and father to our young and gallant navy—what was John Wesley doing? He was creeping to the British throne, to lay at the feet of His Majesty's Government the offer to raise a regiment, and put them at the disposal of the Crown, expressly to put down what he called the "American Rebellion"—to crush the rising liberties of your infant country!

Now, sir, I think I was authorized to state that the Methodists have done as little for the spread of human liberty, the rights and equality of mankind, as any other denomination, no matter how old or how young. If they have not done extensive mischief, of which the gentleman boasts, it is to be remembered that they never possessed supreme civil power, and that, in the order of time, they have been too insignificant, and are still too juvenile, to have done extensive evil. If they have done private good, as the gentleman contends, I confess it reminds me of Stephen Girard's charity. He was exceedingly rich, and, because he. was rich, people thought he was very wise. And inasmuch as he despised all external show of religion, it was inferred he was very charitable to the poor, without, however, making a display of it. If it was so, no man ever practised better the counsel of the gospel, " not to let the left hand know what the right hand doeth " in the matter. It was so private that no one ever could find it out. So is it with the Methodist Church with regard to any public benefit ever conferred on mankind—we have yet to hear of it.

I will now satisfy the gentleman on another subject which seems to trouble him, and on which he " should like to know." And as other gentlemen have alluded to it, I hope the same explanation will suffice in reply to them all.

Before the British Government released the Catholics from the penalties under which they labored, among which not the least was the exclusion of the schoolmaster, they called upon them to disavow principles which they knew Catholics did not entertain. But, in order to reconcile the prejudices of the English people, they had an investigation of those imputed principles before the Houses of Parliament; they called upon some distinguished Catholic citizens, and questioned them on several points, such as those the gentleman has so frequently referred to, among which was the spiritual authority of the pope. From the testimony which they took I now quote. It is part of the testimony of Dr. Doyle, Bishop of Kildare; but other bishops and public men were all examined on the same subject.

Question. According to the principles which govern the Roman Catholic Church in Ireland, has the pope any authority to issue commands, ordinances, or injunctions, general or special, without the consent of the king ? *Answer.* He has.

Question. If he should issue such orders, are the subjects of His Majesty, particularly the clergy, bound to obey them ? *Answer.* The orders that he has a right to issue must regard things that are of a spiritual nature; and when his commands regard such things, the clergy are bound to obey them; but were he to issue commands regarding things not spiritual, the clergy are not in any wise bound to obey them.

Consequently, if His Holiness, as the gentleman [Mr. Ketchum] said, should forbid the reading of the Declaration of Independence, it would not be of any authority.

Mr. KETCHUM. Does the book say so ?

Bishop HUGHES. I am authority myself in matters of my religion. Surely, sir, I am not here to betray it, and I am astonished that the gentleman is not better acquainted with history on the matter. He amused us, a little while ago, with the idea of what terrible consequences might ensue if the pope, a " foreign potentate," should forbid us to read the Declaration of Independence, or forbid the reading of the Bible in our common schools. He even apologized for his alarm with singular simplicity : " He meant no reflection. This matter had come out in evidence here." It was then, sir, I wondered at his not having read history, or having read it to so little advantage.

Did he not know that, long before the Declaration of Independence, Venice rose out of the sea, a Catholic State, with all her republican glory round about her ? And when the pope, in his capacity of " foreign potentate," attempted to invade her temporal rights, her Catholic sons did what they ought to have done—they unsheathed their swords and routed his troops. Did they thereby forfeit their allegiance to him as spiritual head of the Church on earth ? Not an iota of it. To a man who reads history and understands it, this fact alone points out the difference, in the creed of Catholics, between the pope and the potentate. The Venitians knew that the pope, in his spiritual capacity, belongs to a kingdom which is not of this world. And the allegiance of Catholics to him, out of his own small dominions, is due to him only in his spiritual capacity. Whatever temporal right was acquired over independent States by the popes in former ages, was owing to no principle of Catholic doctrine, but purely to the disorders of the times and the pusillanimity of weak rulers, who, in order to secure the pope's protection, made themselves his vassals. The popes, in such circumstances, would have been more or less than men, had they refused to embrace these opportunities of aggrandizement so placed within their reach and often pressed upon them. Now, every Catholic is familiar with this view of the subject, and yet, except a few of larger minds and better education, it has hardly penetrated the density of Protestant prejudice. Hence you hear them giving the most absurd construction to the duties of Catholics between the supposed conflicting claims of their country and the imputed principles of their religion. Permit me here to call your attention to the true and beautiful exposition of the case as set forth in the language of a gentleman who, though a Catholic, is acknowledged to be a man of as high honor, as lofty and patriotic principles, and as unblemished a character, as any man the nation can boast of : I mean Judge Gaston, of North Carolina. The State has no son of whom she is, or ought to be, prouder. And yet, up till within a few years, the laws of that State disqualified a Catholic from holding any, even the office of a constable. In a speech made by Judge Gaston in the convention for revising the State Constitution, in reference to this matter, he says :

But it has been objected, that the Catholic religion is unfavorable to freedom—nay, even incompatible with republican institutions. Ingenious speculations on such matters are worth little, and prove still less. Let me ask, Who obtained the great charter of English freedom, but the Catholic prelates and barons at Runnymede ? The oldest, the purest democracy on earth, is the little Catholic republic of St. Mavino, not a day's journey from Rome. It has existed now for fourteen hundred years, and is so jealous of arbitrary power, that the executive authority is divided between two governors, who are elected every three months. Was William Tell, the founder of Swiss liberty, a royalist ? Are the Catholics of the Swiss cantons in love with tyranny ? Are the Irish Catholics friends to passive obedience and non-resistance ? Was La Fayette, Pulaski, or Kosciusko, a foe to civil freedom ? Was Charles Carroll, of Carrollton, unwilling to jeopard fortune in the cause of liberty ? Let me give you, however, the testimony of George Washington. On his accession to the presidency, he was addressed by the American Catholics, who, adverting to the restrictions on their worship then existing in some of the States, expressed themselves thus : " The prospect of national prosperity is peculiarly pleasing to us on another account; because, while our country preserves her freedom and independence, we shall have well-founded title to claim from her justice the equal rights of citizenship as the price of our blood spilt under your eye, and of our common exertions for her defence under your auspicious conduct." This great man, who was utterly incapable of flattery and deceit, utters, in answer, the following sentiments, which I give in his own words: "As mankind become more liberal, they will be more apt to allow that all those who conduct themselves as worthy members of the community, are equally entitled to the protection of civil government. I hope ever to see America among the foremost nations in examples of justice and liberality; and I presume that your fellow-citizens will never forget the patriotic part which you took in the accomplishment of their revolution and the establishment of their Government, or the important assistance which they received from a nation in which the Roman Catholic faith is professed." By the by, sir, I would pause for a moment to call the attention of this committee to some of the names subscribed to this address. Among them are those of John Carroll, the first Roman Catholic bishop of the United States, Charles Carroll, of Carrollton, and Thomas Fitzsimmons. For the characters of these distinguished men, if they need vouchers, I would confidently call on the venerable President of this Convention. Bishop Carroll was one of the best men and most humble and devout of Christians. I shall never forget a tribute to his memory paid by the good and venerable Protestant Bishop White, when contrasting the piety with which the Christian Carroll met death, with the cold trifling that characterized the last moments of the skeptical David Hume. I know not whether the tribute was more honorable to the piety of the dead, or to the charity of the living prelate. Charles Carroll, of Carrollton, the last survivor of the signers of American Independence, at whose death both Houses of the Legislature of North Carolina unanimously testified their sorrow as at a national bereavement! Thomas Fitzsimmons, one of the illustrious convention that framed the Constitution of the United States, and for several years the Representative in Congress from the city of Philadelphia. Were these, and such as these, foes to freedom, and unfit for republicanism? Would it be dangerous to permit such men to be sheriffs and constables in the land? Read the funeral eulogium of Charles Carroll, delivered at Rome by Bishop England, one of the greatest ornaments of the American Catholic Church—a foreigner, indeed, by birth, but an American by adoption, and who, becoming an American, solemnly abjured all allegiance to every foreign king, prince, and potentate whatever—that eulogium which was so much carped at by English royalists and English tories —and I think you will find it democratic enough to suit the taste and find an echo in the heart of the sternest republican amongst us. Catholics are of all countries, of all governments, of all political creeds. In all, they are taught that the kingdom of Christ is not of this world, and that it is their duty to render unto Cæsar the things that are Cæsar's, and unto God the things that are God's.

I shall now proceed with the testimony of the Irish bishops in order, which was interrupted by the gentleman's question.

Here, sir, is the testimony of another bishop—Dr. Murray, the present Archbishop of Dublin, before a committee of the British Parliament:

Question. To what extent, and in what manner, does a Catholic profess to obey the pope?

Answer. Solely in spiritual matters, or in such mixed matters as come under his government—such as marriage, for instance, which we hold to be a sacrament as well as a civil contract; as it is a sacrament, it is a spiritual thing, and comes under the jurisdiction of the pope. Of course, he has

20

authority over that spiritual part of it; but this authority does not affect the civil rights of the individuals contracting.

Question. Does this obedience detract from what is due by a Catholic to the State under which he lives?

Answer. Not in the least; the powers are wholly distinct.

Question. Does it justify an objection that is made to Catholics, that their allegiance is divided?

Answer. Their allegiance in civil matters is completely undivided.

Question. Is the duty which the Catholic owes to the pope, and the duty which he owes to the king, really and substantially distinct?

Answer. Wholly distinct.

Question. How far is the claim that some popes have set up to temporal authority, opposed to Scripture and tradition?

Answer. As far as it may have been exercised as coming from a right granted to him by God, it appears to me to be contrary to Scripture and tradition; but as far as it may have been exercised in consequence of a right conferred on him by the different Christian powers, who looked up to him at one time as the great parent of Christendom, who appointed him as the arbitrator of their concerns, many of whom submitted their kingdoms to him and laid them at his feet, consenting to receive them back from him as fiefs, the case is different. The power that he exercised under that authority of course passed away when those temporal princes who granted it chose to withdraw it. His spiritual power does not allow him to dethrone kings, or to absolve their subjects from the allegiance due to them; and any attempt of that kind I would consider contrary to Scripture and tradition.

Question. Does the pope now dispose of temporal affairs within the kingdoms of any of the princes of the continent?

Answer. Not that I am aware of. I am sure he does not.

Question. Do the Catholic clergy admit that all the bulls of the pope are entitled to obedience?

Answer. They are entitled to a certain degree of reverence. If not contrary to our usages, or contrary to the law of God, of course they are entitled to obedience, as coming from a superior. We owe obedience to a parent, we owe obedience to the king, we owe it to the law; but if a parent, the king, or the law, were to order us to do any thing that is wrong, we would deem it a duty to say, as the apostles did on another occasion, " We ought to obey God rather than men."

Question. Are there circumstances under which the Catholic clergy would not obey a bull of the pope?

Answer. Most certainly.

Question. What is the true meaning of the following words in the creed of Pius IV.: " I promise and swear true obedience to the Roman bishop, the successor of St. Peter?"

Answer. Canonical obedience in the manner I have just described, within the sphere of his own authority.

Question. What do the principles of the Catholic religion teach in respect to the performance of civil duties?

Answer. They teach that the performance of civil duties is a conscientious obligation which the law of God imposes on us.

Question. Is the Divine law, then, quite clear as to the allegiance due by subjects to their prince?

Answer. Quite clear.

Question. In what books are to be found the most authentic exposition of the faith of the Catholic Church?

Answer. In that very creed that has been mentioned—the creed of Pius IV.; in the catechism which was published by the direction of the Council of Trent, called " The Roman Catechism," or " The Catechism of the Council of Trent; " " An Exposition of the Catholic Faith, by the Bishop of

Meaux, Bossuet;" "Verron's Rule of Faith;" "Holden's Analysis of Faith," and several others.

Such is the character and limitation of the pope's authority, attested under oath, by bishops and other Catholic dignitaries, before the British Parliament. The Catholics of Great Britain and Ireland had been bowed down to the earth by penal laws and persecution during three hundred years, with nothing between them and the enjoyment of all their rights but the solemnity of an oath. If their conscience had permitted them to swear what they did not believe, they might have entered on their political rights at any time; and yet, as martyrs to the sacredness of conscience, they resisted.

I have now, sir, supplied the reverend gentleman who presented the remonstrance from the Methodist Episcopal Church with all the information which the occasion permits on the subject of the pope's authority. But there is a good deal more to which, if time allowed, I might address myself. He became very logical, and insisted on the fact that the doctrines of the Catholic Church are always the same—immutable. He says that we boast of this; and we do so, most assuredly. From the hour when they were revealed and taught by Divine authority until the present, from the rising to the setting of the sun, the faith of the Catholic believer and the doctrines of the Catholic Church are everlastingly and universally the same. But then he concludes that, as Catholics in some instances in former times persecuted, so, their religion being always the same, they are still bound to persecute, or else disavow the doctrine, as Protestants do. Now, sir, we do disavow and despise the doctrine of persecution in all its essence and forms. But does it follow that, by this, we disavow any doctrine of the Catholic Church? By no means. And this proves that persecution never was any portion of the Catholic faith; for if it had been, the denial of it would cut us off from her communion. The Church we believe, by the promise and superintendence of Christ, her invisible Head and Founder, to be infallible. She received the deposit of the doctrines revealed by our Redeemer and His apostles; her office is to witness, teach, and preserve them. These alone constitute the religious creed and doctrines of the Catholic Church and her members. We believe in a Trinity, the incarnation of Christ, the redemption by His death, the divine institution of the Church. These, and whatever the Church holds as of Divine revelation, are the doctrines of our Catholic unity. And the individual who is now addressing you, and the Catholic martyr who is at this moment, perhaps, bleeding for his faith in China —for the Church has her martyrs still—hold and believe identically the same doctrines. But as there is unity in faith, so there is, in the Church, freedom of opinion on matters which are not determined by any specific revelation. Hence, we are republicans or monarchists according to individual preference, or the prevailing genius of the country we belong to. Hence, when the Catholic divines at Rheims were appending these notes to their edition of the New Testament, the Catholic bishops of Poland, with her twenty-two millions, were opening the doors of the Constitution to the fugitive Protestants of Germany, fleeing from the intolerance and persecution of their fellow-Protestants. The one act is as much a Catholic doctrine as the other, because, in both cases, the agents acted not by the authority of the Church, but in the exercise of that individual judgment for which their account stands to God.

But I must be brief. I cannot follow so many learned speakers through so much matter that is foreign to the subject ; for I agree with the medical gentleman, who said that neither the Catholic nor the Protestant religion was on trial here. It is not religious creeds that are to be tested by this Council. I have, however, given this explanation, and I trust it will be received, though it may have been tedious, as having its apology in the remarks which called it forth. I only wish that the gentleman who made the observation had made it one hour and a half sooner ; it would have saved all I have said on the subject.

But this speaker also (Dr. Reese) lectured me for attending certain meetings, as if it were a descent from my dignity to find myself in an assembly of freemen. I did not consider it as a descent. But really, when I came here in the simple character of a citizen, I did not think I should be vested with my official robes for the purpose of being attacked. Individuals as respectable as he attended those meetings, and I consider it no disgrace to have been there or here ; for even if this petition came not from Catholics, but from Methodists or any other Protestant denomination, whose consciences were violated by this system, I should be found in their midst supporting their claim. Let me add, too, that I would rather be so found, than, for all the exchequer of the Public School Society, exchange places with gentlemen, and have conscience and right for my opponents. He also contended that this want of confidence in Catholics was the result of my appeals, forgetting that the state of things which is now brought under public notice has existed for years, by efforts to provide a safe education for our children, long before those meetings were called, and before I attended them. And, besides, I conceive it is my bounden duty, if I saw principles inculcated which will sap the young minds of our children—and I have no doubt this honorable board will say it is my duty—to warn them, and to bring them within the pale of that authority which they acknowledge. I wonder if Presbyterian gentlemen would see Catholic books circulated amongst their children, and not warn their people against them ? I wonder, if these books contained reading-lessons about Calvin and the unhappy burning of Servetus, whether they would not warn their people ? I say, if they believe in their religion, they would be in the discharge of their duty. And, while on this subject, it occurs to me at this moment that, in the wide range of observation which has been taken, reference has been made to national education in Ireland. And we are told that, after books had been agreed upon, the bishops sent the question to Rome to be decided by the pope. What question ? Can they tell ? for I am sure I cannot. To this day I have never understood the exact nature of the reference to the pope. But, sir, this is no extraordinary thing. Under the jealous eye of the British Government, even in the darkest hour of her cruelty to Catholics, their intercourse with Rome was not interrupted. But, while that collection and compilation of Scripture lessons was agreed on in the more Catholic parts of the country where the population is divided between Protestants and Catholics, what is the fact? Why, in another part, the north of Ireland, where the Presbyterians are more numerous, they had conscientious objections to this selection of Scripture; they asserted their objections, and the British Government recognized them; and thus, while these lessons, by agreement, were in general use, an exception was made in favor of the Presbyterians, who had objections to the use of any thing but the naked word of God;—and I say, honor to those Presbyterians. The Catholics sent in no remonstrance. But if the rule applied to their case, by what authority will your honorable body determine that it shall not apply to ours? Oh! I perceive. The gentleman whose remarks I am reviewing, reasoned on, until he arrived at the conclusion that there were no conscientious grounds for our objection at all. True, we said we had; but he could not see what conscience had to do with a matter so plain. He said, here the community had built up a beautiful system; it was doing good. He asked, Shall we put it aside in deference to pretended scruples? Now, tell me when the despotism of intolerance ever said any thing else than this? Why, the Established Church of England said "we are doing good," "our doors are open to all," "the minister is at the desk, and the bread of life is distributed for the public good." What then? What business have these unhappy parents to find fault, for conscience' sake, and squeamishness? Now, sir, objections can exist to the slightest shade of violation to our conscience, and, therefore, I did not expect to hear this argument at this time of day. But the gentleman speaks of my addressing the public meetings to which he has alluded, as though my speaking there had been the cause instead of the consequence of the scruples of our people. Then it was I joined them to seek a remedy for our just complaint; but if, in your wisdom, this body shall think proper to deny it us, we must bear it.

He contended, again, that it would be turning the public money to private uses. That seems to me to have been fully answered. He also contended that it would be the giving of the money of the State to support religion. That I have disputed; for if so, I shall have no objections to join those gentlemen in their remonstrance. But at the same time it does appear strange to me, that the gentleman who pretends to have read the Scriptures with so much attention, should not have learned that principle—the most general, sir, and the most infallible of Christian principles for the guidance of our conduct—"Do unto others as ye would that others should do unto you." That is the principle; and is it not strange that such opposition should be made to us, when it is known that money raised by public tax goes to the support of literature under the supervision of the Methodist Episcopal Church? And why do not Catholics object to that? Because the tax does not belong to any particular sect; it is thrown into a common fund, and applied to such uses as the Legislature in its wisdom thinks proper. We, sir, however, ask for our own, and nothing else. But if you say that we shall be taxed for a system which is so organized that we cannot participate in it without detriment to the religious rights of our children, then I say that injustice is done even to our civil rights; for taxation is the basis of even civil rights. And I was not a little struck, in the course of the argument, that some gentleman should refer with so much emphasis as to a circumstance novel and unparalleled even in social life: that a certain class of gentlemen should petition for—what? The privilege of being taxed! They deemed it a *privilege;* and that was wonderful! and merit was ascribed to them for it. Yes, sir; but did it go to the extent only of their own pockets? Or did it not reach the pockets equally of those who did not petition? If to themselves only, it was all fair and proper, disinterested and patriotic: but great emphasis was laid on this class being most " intelligent" and "wealthy" and "respectable"—nobility almost; as though a question of this kind was intended for a particular class. But let me tell you, the honest man who occupies only a bed in a garret is also a taxpayer. Why give him a vote? Because he pays tax for the *space* he occupies. If he occupies a room and pays the tax, his rent is less; if the landlord pays, his rent is so much more. So, if he occupies a garret, or if he boards, it goes down to that; for the person who keeps the boarding-house pays the rent. If that tax is paid by the boarding-house keeper, the rent is so much less, than if the tax was paid by the landlord. If the boarding-house keeper pays the tax, he charges *more* for board. So that the boarder is a taxpayer, and it is so understood in our broad and excellent system of representation. The exclusive merit of this tax, then, is not to be given to any particular class, no matter how wealthy; and I was surprised that so much emphasis should be laid on it. I did not suppose that the interests of the poor were to be sacrificed to the respectability of the rich. The poor pay too, and it is a beautiful and admirable thing to see what a dignity this confers on human nature—what an interest this excites in the poor. I recollect passing along a street some time since, and I observed a little house, almost a shed or hovel, some fourteen or sixteen feet square, which was too small to be divided into two compartments. It had but one window, and this had originally had four panes of glass, but one having been broken, it was darkened. There had been some political party triumph; the boys in the streets had their drums out, and there appeared to be a popular rejoicing, and there I saw three lights burning in the window of this poor habitation. I was amused to see that a man living in so poor a hovel, and unable to buy a fourth pane of glass, should find means to light the other three. But, on further reflection, I said to myself, " There is philosophy there." What other nation can exhibit such a spectacle? This poor man, who must toil till the day he goes to his grave, participates in a political triumph. His bread has to be earned by daily toil; nevertheless, though the triumph, perhaps, will never benefit him, he exhibits a glorious spectacle to the world. He is a *man*—he feels it is recognized. It is a nation's homage offered to human nature. He is a *man* and a *citizen;* and, on reflection, I was delighted at a spectacle so glorious as this.

But, returning to the subject, they say all religion is left to voluntary contribution. Now, is this true in 'the sense in which it is here applied? Are not chaplains appointed to public institutions which are supported by the public money? And have you not given it to the Protestant Orphan Asylum, and the Half-Orphan Asylum? Have you not given it to the Catholic Benevolent Society? And do you suppose the Wesleyan Catechism is taught there? Do you suppose the Catholic Catechism is taught in the Protestant asylums? One gentleman argued that you had not power to do this. But if you have done it, does not that prove that you had the power? If you had power to do that, you have power equally to do this. I shall go further. I find, in the report of the regents of the University, that the Genesee Wesleyan Seminary—Theological Seminary, as I understand—has last year received $1,395.56 of the public money. This is not exclusively literary, as I understand it—

Dr. BANGS. Altogether literary.

Bishop HUGHES. I was under the impression that it was theological, and that religion was admitted. But those in this city furnish evidence that a religious profession does not disqualify.

I believe now, sir, I have gone through the substance at least, if not through every particular, of what has been said by the gentlemen who interpose their remonstrances and their arguments in opposition to our rightful claim. I will now read one authority, and I am the more willing because it is from the Public School Society itself. It is from the memorial which they presented to the Legislature in the session of 1823, in which they state, p. 7, "It will not be denied"—recollect, I do not quote this to show that our petition ought to be granted, but that, whatever opinion these gentlemen may *now* have of the unconstitutionality of granting this claim, they saw nothing unconstitutional in the practice then, and I know of nothing so far as the Constitution is concerned, neither of the State, nor of the United States—I know of no enactment which should change their opinion—" it will not be denied, in this enlightened age, that the education of the poor is enjoined by our holy religion, and is, therefore, one of the duties of a Christian Church. Nor is there any impropriety in committing the school fund to the hands of a religious society, so long as they are confined in the appropriation of it to an object not necessarily connected or intermingled with the other concerns of the church, as, for instance, to the payment of teachers; because the State is sure, in this case, that the benefits of the fund, in the way it designed to confer them, will be reaped by the poor. But the objection to the section sought to be repealed is, that the surplus moneys, after the payment of teachers, is vested in the hands of the trustees of a religious society, and mingled with its other funds, to be appropriated to the erection of buildings under the control of the trustees, which buildings may, and in all probability will, be used for other purposes than school-houses."

That is the statement of the Public School Society itself; and throughout this document—while the gentlemen here have been wielding against our petition the influence of respectable and wealthy classes—I find that, before the acquisition of their monopoly, they advocated the claims of the poor, who *cannot buy* education, sometimes scarcely bread. This is the class to whose welfare the eye of the enlightened, the patriotic, and the benevolent should be directed; this is the class that essentially requires education. Thus they say, " The school fund is designed for a civil purpose, for such is the *education of the poor.*"

Again, they say that the New York Free School (that was their own Society) has " one single object—*the education of the poor.*" Again, the Board of Trustees is annually chosen, &c., " for the education of the poor." And yet now I could point out thousands of our poor who are destitute of education, and who have no means to provide it. We do what we can, but we are too limited in means to raise, of ourselves, a sufficient fund. We have labored under great disadvantages; we have taught the catechism in our schools, because, while *we* supported them, we had the right to do so; but if you put them on the footing of the common schools, we shall be satisfied, and the State will secure the education of our children. You will secure them an education on the basis of morality; for they had better be brought up under the morality of our religion, though gentlemen object, than none at all. They say the objection to the present schools is, that there they are made Protestants. No, sir; it is because they are made *Nothingarians,* for we cannot tell what they are. I have now concluded, and if I have been obliged to trespass long upon your patience, recollect, as some extenuation, that I had a great deal to reply to in the arguments of gentlemen which were urged to overthrow the principles of our petition, but had no bearing on the petition at all. We do not ask for the elevation of the Catholics over others, but for the protection to which all are entitled. The question is exceedingly plain and simple. If it has or can be shown that we are claiming this money for sectarian purposes, then I should advise you to withhold it. But if, in honesty and truth and sincerity, it is a right belonging to us as citizens to receive our *pro rata,* then we appeal to you with confidence.

From the sentiments expressed here on behalf of the Public School Society, you can judge of the chance that Catholic children have in those schools to have their religious rights respected. It will be, as perhaps it has been, considered a great and a good work to detach them from a religion which is supposed " to teach the lawfulness of murdering heretics." Infidelity itself will be considered preferable to Catholicism in their regard, for one reverend gentleman has told you that, if there was no alternative, he would embrace the doctrines of Voltaire rather than the religion of a Cheverus or a Fenelon. If the Catholics have been obliged to keep their children from those schools in time past, you may imagine what effects these sentiments, this *animus* of the system, is likely to have on their minds for the time to come. But if it is our religious right to have a conscience at all, do not take pains to pervert it, for we shall not be better citizens afterward. Do not teach us to slight the admonitions of our conscience. Reverse our case and make it your own, and then you will be able to judge. Make it your own case, and suppose your children were in the case of those poor children for whom I plead; then suppose what your feelings would be if the blessings of education were provided bountifully by the State, and you were unable to participate in those blessings, unless you were willing to submit that your conscience should be trenched upon.

Here the right reverend prelate sat down, after having spoken for nearly three hours and a half.

Dr. BANGS. I wish simply to correct an error, into which the reverend gentleman has fallen, respecting an observation I made as to a matter of fact. I believe he understood me to say that it was my opinion the Legislature ought to take the children of Catholics and compel them to attend the schools. If so, he misunderstood me. I meant to say that those children that do not go to any schools ought to be compelled to go to the public schools.

A brief conversation ensued between the Right Rev. Bishop Hughes and Dr. Bond, in explanation of the charge made against John Wesley, that he had aided or excited Lord George Gordon's mob.

The Right Rev. Bishop HUGHES. Might I be allowed to read the passage from the chapter on " The Character of Christ," by the Bishop of London, to which reference has been had ? Speaking of Jesus Christ, it says :

His answers to the many insidious questions that were put to Him showed uncommon quickness of conception, soundness of judgment, and presence of mind, completely baffled all the artifices and malice of His enemies, and enabled Him to elude all the snares that were laid for Him.

Mr. KETCHUM rose, and said : I wish, sir, to say a few words in explanation. I do not wish to continue the theological discussion, but to make a few remarks on the precise issue before the board.

The CHAIRMAN. That has, I apprehend, been very fully debated.

Mr. KETCHUM. I desire to make a remark in reply to the gentleman on the other side, in reference to the publication of the Bishop of London. But first, sir, the reverend gentleman has endeavored, with great dexterity, to place this case upon the consciences of the Catholic society. He has represented the decision of this board against their petition as a violation of the rights of conscience. He well knows the favorable attitude in which they stand who appear to be persecuted for conscience' sake. Does the reverend gentleman mean to say here, he has conscientious scruples against these schools as public institutions ? Does he mean to affirm here that they have not performed all they promised—namely, to give a good secular education to the poor ? No ; that is not affirmed. Whatever he may have stated and whatever he may have contradicted, throughout the length of his address, he made no such declaration. But the Roman Catholics have conscientious scruples—they cannot send their children to these schools without sacrificing their right of conscience ! Now, the Friends cannot send their children to these schools, because they believe in their consciences that they ought to educate their own children ; but can the Friends say they are opposed upon conscientious grounds to these schools ? They are established by a public act of the State, for a public purpose, and they have accomplished their purpose—they have furnished all the education they promised. But now the reverend gentleman says his conscience, and the consciences of the Roman Catholic community, are violated, because they cannot send their children to these schools. Do they mean to say they have conscientious scruples against paying their portion of the tax for the support of these schools? It might well be that some denominations of Christians have conscientious scruples against sending their poor to be taken care of at the almshouse; but would they have the right to say that they would not therefore be taxed for the support of the poor? The conscientious scruple here is not against paying the tax, but against sending their children to these schools. Now, who compels them? Does the State interfere, and say they shall send their children to these schools? The State says that they, in common with others, shall pay the tax to support these institutions of learning. Have they alleged that their consciences are violated by paying this tax? Can they say so? No. Wherein, then, consists this pressure on their consciences?

Now, Mr. President, allow me to take another view of this conscientious objection. If I am taxed to support the religion of the Roman Catholics, my conscience is violated, because I am compelled to pay a tax to support that which I believe ought not to be supported. If you establish these sectarian schools through this community, and make Protestants pay for Catholic schools, then indeed you infringe the right of conscience, because you compel them to do that which is a violation of their consciences. But we do not compel them to attend these schools. We receive this public bounty, and we come here and account for the manner in which we use it. The gentleman does not object to this. He does not object to our doing good to the children that do come. That is not the objection; but he objects that he cannot send his children. He pays a tax for a necessary public purpose —admitted to be necessary—but, because he cannot come in and participate, he insists that this public fund shall be taken by the Roman Catholics, by the Methodists, by any and every other denomination, to support their religion. Grant this, and then indeed you will infringe the right of conscience. I do not mean that the reverend gentleman shall have the advantage here of standing on this right of conscience. The consciences of thousands and tens of thousands of this community will be violated, if they are to be compelled to pay a tax to the public treasury, and from thence to make religionists of a description that they oppose. I want this matter to be set right, not only in the estimation of this board, but of the public. I want them to see what this oppression of conscience is. If it is anywhere, it is on those who pay the tax of which they do not in their conscience approve; the pressure is not on the man that cannot send his children to participate in the fund. I cannot send my children to these schools. There are obstacles in the way as formidable as the gentleman's conscience. There are obstacles, perhaps, with tens of thousands who pay the tax but do not participate, and who cannot participate, because this obstacle exists. But have they the right to say they will withhold their tax? Would the State listen to such an objection? No; the State has established these public institutions for a necessary public purpose; every man must be taxed for their support; and if he does not avail himself of them, it must be his own fault, or his own peculiarities, perhaps. And now, what, after all, is the objection to these schools? Why, from the beginning to the end of this three hours' speech, we have heard that these books contain passages that reflect on Catholics.

The CHAIRMAN interposed.

Mr. KETCHUM continued. This is new matter, so far as I am concerned. From the beginning to the end of the gentleman's speech, we have heard that the books used in these public schools contain passages that reflect on Roman Catholics. Now, I submit to any fair, candid man, if this is the time of day to bring such a charge? The books have been placed in the hands of the reverend gentleman; he has been asked to put his finger on any objectionable passages, that the board might pass a resolution for its expurgation; and now the gentleman comes here, and lays great stress on and urges as an argument against the system, from the beginning to the end, the passages which the trustees offered to expunge. Sir, when the trustees offered to expunge the passages, in all fairness and candor, they were to be considered, for the true purposes of this argument, as expunged. And if they were expunged, what would become of three fourths of the gentleman's speech—all, indeed, except the theological part? And now, the next great topic is the Bible.

The PRESIDENT. The gentleman is not in order.

Mr. KETCHUM. I'll not press this matter, if it is disagreeable. I know the night is far advanced.

The CHAIRMAN. I must say the gentleman is out of order. The board agreed that the parties should be heard in the order in which their memorials were presented—that the petitioners should have the usual right to reply. They have been so heard, and the gentleman is therefore out of order, unless the board rescinds its resolution.

An alderman then observed, that there were some gentlemen that were desirous of putting in written legal opinions, and he moved that they have permission to do so at the next meeting of the board.

The PRESIDENT said that the next meeting of the board was Monday next, and therefore no order of the board was necessary for an adjournment on the subject.

It was, then, understood that legal opinions would be received at the next meeting of the board.

The debate was here brought to a close, and the Council adjourned a few minutes before 12 o'clock.

The protracted and exhaustive discussion being brought to a close, and the committee, having spent some time in visiting schools and making thorough examination of the facts involved in the question, prepared their report, which was submitted to the Board of Aldermen on January 11, 1841, asking to be discharged from the consideration of the subject. The report is subjoined :

REPORT OF THE SPECIAL COMMITTEE OF THE BOARD OF ALDERMEN.

BOARD OF ALDERMEN, *January* 11, 1841.

The Special Committee to whom was referred the petition of the Catholics for a portion of the school fund, together with the remonstrances against the same, presented the following report thereon, which was, on motion, accepted, and the committee discharged, on a division called by Alderman Graham, Jr. In the affirmative—The President, Aldermen Balis, Woodhull, Benson, Jones, Rich, Chamberlain, Campbell, Hatfield, Jarvis, Smith, Nichols, Graham, Cooper, and Nash—15. In the negative—Alderman Pentz—1. And one thousand copies thereof ordered printed, with the vote taken on the report.

SAMUEL J. WILLIS, *Clerk.*

———

Resolved, That all letters and papers touching and connected with the school fund question be referred to the Special Committee appointed for the purpose of investigating the subject.

By WILLIAM CHAMBERLAIN.

Resolved, That a committee of three be appointed, in conformity to the request of the Public School Society, and that a committee of the petitioners for a portion of the school fund, and also of the remonstrants, be invited to accompany them to examine the public schools, for the purpose of ascertaining what defects, if any, exist in their organization ; and that the said committee be instructed to report to this board whether any arrangement can be agreed upon which will be mutually satisfactory to the parties interested.

By WILLIAM CHAMBERLAIN.

———

The Special Committee to whom was referred the petition of the Catholics of New York relative to the distribution of the school fund, the several remonstrances and other documents connected with the subject, together with the above resolution of instructions, respectfully submit the following

REPORT.

In pursuance of the instructions contained in the resolution, they employed two entire days in visiting the public schools, accompanied by a committee of the petitioners, and also of the Public School Society, with a view to ascertain if any defects exist in their organization ; and after a thorough scrutiny, in which all parties participated, your committee not only failed to discover any thing strikingly defective in the system, but became strongly impressed with a conviction that the public schools, under their present organization, are admirably adapted to afford precisely the kind of instruction for which they were instituted. It is deemed essential to the welfare and security of our Government that the means of mental cultivation should be extended to every child in the community. The rising generation are destined to be the future rulers of the land, and their happiness can only be secured by such an education as will constitute them an intelligent community, prepare them to guard against the machinations of demagogues, and so to exercise the rights and franchises of citizens as not to deprive themselves of the invaluable privileges which are their birthright. That the public school system, as now organized, is calculated to effect these objects, your committee do not entertain a doubt; but, though they regard it as an incalculable public blessing, if they could be persuaded that it trespassed upon the conscientious rights of any portion of our citizens, they would begin to doubt the propriety of its continuance. They cannot, however, conceive that it is justly amenable to such a charge, so long as sectarian dogmas and peculiarities are excluded from the schools, and no pupils are either admitted into them, or excluded from them, against the consent of their natural or legal guardians. The system has grown up under the auspices of a voluntary association of individuals usually known as "The Public School Society," formed for the purpose of promoting education, and admitting to membership any citizen of good moral character who is not a clergyman, upon a contribution of ten dollars to its funds. This Society has watched with indefatigable vigilance and untiring assiduity over the rise and progress of the system, and by their unrequited labors it has been nurtured into maturity. In its present aspect, it is a monument of disinterestedness and public spirit, of which our city has reason to be proud. Your committee hereby acknowledge their indebtedness to the members of that Society for the prompt manner in which they responded to every call made upon them; and they cannot but hope that the spirit of candor which they have displayed, and which the petitioners in the same spirit acknowledge, will ultimately remove every barrier which, through misapprehension, as your committee believe, has hitherto retarded the entire success of their benevolent and patriotic exertions. It has been objected on the part of the petitioners, that the books used in the public schools contain passages that are calculated to prejudice the minds of children against the Catholic faith. This objection your committee discovered to be not wholly unfounded; but we are happy to have it in our power to add, that the School Society fully agree with us in the opinion that nothing in the books or usages of the schools should be continued that is calculated in the remotest degree to wound the feelings or prejudice the minds of children in favor of or against any religious sect whatever; that they have expunged such passages in the books as they have been able to discover in any way objectionable; that they desire to continue, and earnestly solicit the aid and coöperation of the petitioners, in the work of expurgation, until every really objectionable feature shall be entirely obliterated. The extreme difficulty of this undertaking is illustrated by the fact that some of the very same passages quoted by the petitioners as particularly objectionable, and which have been obliterated in the public school books, were found by your committee entirely unobscured in the books used in one of the Catholic schools. It is a melancholy fact that, in neighborhoods where Catholic children are numerous, the public schools number but few children whose parents profess the Catholic faith ; but after the arduous task of expurgation shall have been completed, and every well-grounded objection removed, your committee fondly hope that the school-houses will be filled with children, and that no parents or guardians, be their religious feelings what they may, will refuse to avail themselves of the benefits of the public schools for the education of their children, being fully persuaded that many years would elapse before any new system of instruction could be organized, with advantages equal to the one now equally available to every child in the community. If, with such a system, any portion of the children should be left uneducated, it cannot be justly chargeable to a want of comprehensiveness in the system, but is more fairly attributable to imperfections which human legislation cannot remedy. The general objections to sectarian public schools do not apply to cases where children are supported by charity, and necessarily confined to a particular locality, and not open to all children. Your committee think that all such establishments might enjoy the benefits of education at public expense, without an infringement of the principles contended for ; and, the rule being made general, their participation in the benefits of the school fund would not necessarily constitute a public recognition of their religious sectarian character. No school system can be perfect which does not place the means of education within the reach of every child who is capable of receiving instruction ; and such your committee believe to be the design and capacity of the system now in use in this city.

The public school buildings are constructed upon a uniform model. The books used are the same in all the schools, and the classes and departments in each are so similarly constituted and provided, that the removal of a pupil from one school to another will not interrupt his studies or retard his progress. Though religion constitutes no specific part of the system of instruction, yet the discipline of the schools, and the well-arranged and selected essays and maxims which abound in their reading-books, are well calculated to impress upon the minds of children a distinct idea of the value of religion, the importance of the domestic and social duties, the existence of God, the Creator of all things, the immortality of the soul, man's future accountability, present dependence upon a superintending providence, and other moral sentiments which do not conflict with sectarian views and peculiarities.

The different classes examined in several schools by your committee exhibited an astonishing progress in geography, astronomy, arithmetic, reading, writing, &c., and indicated a capacity in the system for imparting instruction far beyond our expectations ; and though the order and arrangement of each school would challenge comparison with a camp under a rigid disciplinarian, yet the accustomed buoyancy and cheerfulness of youth and childhood did not appear to be destroyed in any one of them. Such were the favorable impressions forced upon our minds by a careful examination of the public schools. It is due to the trustees to add, that not one of our visits was anticipated, and no opportunity was afforded to any of the teachers for even a momentary preparation. In the course of our investigations, we also visited three of the schools established by the petitioners, and for the benefit of which a portion of the school fund is solicited. We found them, as represented by the petitioners, lamentably deficient in accommodations and supplies of books and teachers. The rooms were all excessively crowded and poorly ventilated, the books much worn as well as deficient in numbers, and the teachers not sufficiently numerous. Yet, with all these disadvantages, though not able to compete successfully with the public schools, they exhibited a progress which was truly creditable; and, with the same means at their disposal, they would doubtless soon be able, under suitable direction, greatly to improve their condition. The object of the petitioners is to supply these deficiencies from the fund provided by the bounty of the State for the purposes of common school education. But, however strongly our sympathies may be excited in behalf of the poor children assembled in these schools, such is the state of the public mind on this subject, that, if one religious sect should obtain a portion of the school fund, every other one would present a similar claim, and it would be a signal for the total demolition of the system which has grown up under the guidance of many years of toilsome experience; attaining a greater degree of perfection than has perhaps ever before been achieved, and which is probably extending a greater amount of instruction, at smaller expense, than can possibly be imparted by any other school system that has been devised. This result of such a disposal of the school funds would most probably be followed by a counteraction in the public mind, which would lead to a revocation of the act by a succeeding Common Council, and the awakening of a spirit of intolerance, which in our country is, of all calamities, the one most to be dreaded. Political intolerance is an unmitigated evil; but the experience of past ages ought to admonish us to guard with unceasing vigilance against religious intolerance, as an evil greater in magnitude in proportion as eternal consequences exceed those of time. So long as Government refuses to recognize religious sectarian differences, no danger need be apprehended from this source; but when it begins to legislate with particular reference to any particular denomination of Christians, in any manner which recognizes their religious peculiarities, it oversteps a boundary which public opinion has established, violates a principle which breathes in all our constitutions, and opens a door to that unholy connection of politics with religion which has so often cursed and desolated Europe. Under these impressions of the impossibility of granting the prayer of the petitioners without producing the most fatal consequences, and impressed, at the same time, with an anxious desire to remove every obstacle out of the way of the public education of their children, if it could be done without sacrificing any fundamental principle, your committee invited the School Society and the petitioners to appoint delegates to meet them, with a view to effect a compromise, if possible. The invitation was promptly responded to, and several meetings were held, at which the subject was fully and very courteously discussed in all its bearings; and though we extremely regret to report that the conferences did not result as favorably as we had hoped, yet the spirit and tenor of the following propositions, submitted at our request by both the School Society and the petitioners, encourage a belief that our labor may not have been entirely in vain.

PROPOSITION ON THE PART OF THE PETITIONERS.

The schools represented by the undersigned, wherein children are instructed free of charge, shall be placed under the supervision of, conform to the system and discipline adopted by, the Public School Society, and consent that all the expenditures of the schools shall be made under the direction of that institution, to the purposes of common school education, and to no other purpose whatsoever, upon the following terms :

1st. That there shall be reserved to the managers, or trustees, of these schools respectively, the designation of the teachers to be appointed therein; who shall be subjected to the examination of a committee of the Public School Society, shall be fully qualified for the duties of their appointment, and of unexceptionable moral character ; or, in the event of the trustees or managers failing to present individuals for these situations of that description, then individuals having like qualifications, and of unexceptionable character, to be selected and appointed by the Public School Society, who shall be acceptable to the managers or trustees of the schools to which they shall be appointed ; but no person to be continued as a teacher in either of the schools referred to, against the wishes of the trustees or managers thereof.

2d. That the schools shall be open at all times to the inspection of any authorized agent or officer of the city or State government, with liberty to visit the same and examine the books used therein, or the teachers, touching the course and system of instruction pursued in the schools, or in relation to any matter connected therewith.

The undersigned are willing that, in the superintendence of their schools, every specified requirement of any and every law passed by the Legislature of the State, or the ordinances of the Common Council, to guard against abuse in the matter of common school education, shall be rigidly enforced and exacted by the competent public authorities.

They believe that the benevolent object of every such law is to bring the means of a plain education within the reach of the child of every poor man, without damaging their religion, whatever it may be, or the religious rights of any such child or parent.

It is in consequence of what they consider the damaging of their religion and their religious rights, in the schools of the Public School Society, that they have been obliged to withdraw their children from them. The facts which they have already submitted, and which have been more than sustained by the sentiments uttered on behalf of the Society, in the late discussion, prove that they were not mistaken.

As regards the organization of their schools, they are willing that they should be under the same police and regulation as those of the Public School Society; the same hours, the same order, the same exercises, even the same inspection.

LINDLEY MURRAY

But the books to be used for exercises in learning to read or spell, in history, geography, and all such elementary knowledge as could have a tendency to operate on their hearts and minds in reference to their religion, must be, so far as Catholic children are concerned, and no farther, such as they shall judge proper to put in their hands. But nothing of their dogmas, nothing against the creed of any other denomination, shall be introduced.

(Signed)   HUGH SWEENY,
                                                JAMES W. McKEON.

NEW YORK, *December* 19, 1840.

PROPOSITION ON BEHALF OF THE SCHOOL SOCIETY.

In compliance with the request of the committee of the Board of Aldermen, the undersigned committee of the New York Public School Society submit the following propositions as a basis of a compromise with their Roman Catholic fellow-citizens on the subject of the public schools; which propositions they are willing to support before the trustees of the Society, and which they believe will be sanctioned by that board.

The Trustees of the New York Public School Society will remove from the class-books in the schools all matters which may be pointed out as offensive to their Roman Catholic fellow-citizens, should any thing objectionable yet remain in them.

They will also exclude from the school libraries (the use of which is *permitted* to the pupils, but not *required* of them) every work written with a view to prejudice the mind of the reader against the tenets or practices of the Roman Catholic Church, or the general tendency of which is to produce the same effect.

They will receive and examine any books which may be recommended for the use of the schools; and should such books be adapted to their system of instruction, and void of any matter offensive to other denominations, they shall be introduced so soon as opportunity may be afforded by a call for new books.

Any suggestions in reference to alterations in the plan of instruction or course of studies, which may be offered, shall receive prompt consideration; and, if not inconsistent with the general system of instruction now prevailing in the schools, nor with the conscientious rights of other denominations, they shall be adopted.

The building situated in Mulberry street, now occupied by Roman Catholic schools, shall, if required for the use of the Public School Society, be purchased or hired, on equitable terms, by the trustees, should such an arrangement be desired.

Every effort will be made by the Trustees of the Public School Society to prevent any occurrence in the schools which might be calculated to wound the feelings of Roman Catholic children, or to impair their confidence in, or diminish their respect for, the religion of their parents.

Anxious to keep open every avenue to such an arrangement as will lead to a general attendance of the Roman Catholic children at the public

21

schools, and fully aware that some things may have escaped their observation which might be modified without violation of the conscientious rights of others, the undersigned wish it to be distinctly understood that, in offering the foregoing propositions as the basis of an arrangement, it is not intended to exclude other propositions which the Roman Catholics may make, provided they do not interfere with the principles by which the trustees feel themselves bound.

(Signed)   SAMUEL F. MOTT,
               A. P. HALSEY,   } *Committee.*
               J. SMYTH ROGERS,

NEW YORK, *December* 19, 1840.

Your committee deem it proper to remark, in vindication of the School Society, that they were only one of the numerous remonstrants against the prayer of the petitioners. Their views were represented in the late discussion before the board only by their legal advisers, Messrs. Sedgewick and Ketchum. The other gentlemen who participated in the discussion represented other bodies which are not in any manner connected with them. Sentiments were uttered by some of them which the School Society do not entertain, and for which they are not justly accountable. This explanation is deemed proper, in consequence of a remark in the above proposition of the petitioners which appears to be founded on an erroneous impression. The unwillingness of the petitioners to agree to any terms which did not recognize the distinctive character of their schools as Catholic schools, or which would exclude sectarian supervision from them entirely, was the obstacle to a compromise, which could not be overcome. However much we may lament the consequences, we are not disposed to question the right of our Catholic fellow-citizens to keep their children separated from intercourse with other children; but we do not believe the Common Council would be justified in *facilitating* such an object. They have an unquestionable right to pursue such a course, if the dictates of conscience demand it of them; and they have a just claim to be sustained by the Common Council in the exercise of that right; but they cannot justly claim public *aid* to carry out such intentions, unless they can show that the public good would be promoted by it, and that such public aid can be extended to them without trespassing upon the conscientious rights of others. But if any religious society or sect should be allowed the exclusive right to select the books, appoint or nominate the teachers, or introduce sectarian peculiarities of any kind into a public school, the exercise of such a right, in any one particular, would very clearly constitute such school a sectarian school, and its support at the public expense would, in the opinion of the committee, be a trespass upon the conscientious rights of every taxpayer who disapproved of the religion inculcated by the sect to which such school might be attached; because they would be paying taxes for the support of a religion which they disapproved. Your committee are, therefore, fully of the opinion that the granting of the prayer of the petitioners, or conforming to the terms of the proposals submitted by the committee who represented them, would render the school system liable to the charge of violating the rights of conscience —a charge which would be fatal to the system, because it would invalidate its just claim to public patronage.

The proposition of the committee who represent the Public School Society appears to us to have been conceived in a liberal spirit. Your committee think it goes as far as a due regard to the true objects of the institution would warrant, and seems to open an avenue which we would fain hope may yet lead to a satisfactory arrangement. Both propositions exhibit more liberality, probably, than either party had before given the other credit for; and we hope that result may prove to be an important step toward the accomplishment of an object which every patriot must desire with intense anxiety. Your committee respectfully ask to be discharged from the further consideration of the subject.

WILLIAM CHAMBERLAIN,
ROBERT JONES,
JOSIAH RICH.

The report of the committee being read, the question on its acceptance and adoption was put, and decided in the affirmative, as follows:

Ayes—The President (E. F. Purdy), Aldermen Balis, Wood-hull, Benson, Jones, Rich, Chamberlain, Campbell, Hatfield, Jarvis, Smith, Nichols, Graham, Cooper, and Nash—15.

Nay—Alderman Pentz—1.

The application of the Roman Catholics for the school moneys was thus negatived, and the committee were discharged.

The proceedings in the Board of Assistant Aldermen were interesting and important. The various petitions and remonstrances were referred to the Committee on Arts, Sciences, and Schools, whose report was submitted on the 27th of April. A brief statement of the facts, together with the report of the committee, will be found in the Appendix marked B.

CHAPTER XI.

EXPURGATION OF SCHOOL-BOOKS.—1840–1841.

Propositions of Bishop Dubois relative to School-Books—Rev. Felix Varela—Committee of Examination and Correspondence Appointed—Report of the Committee—Letter of Rev. Felix Varela—Letter to the *Freeman's Journal* by Rev. John Power, D.D.—Letter to Dr. Powers from the Committee—Address of the Roman Catholics—Reply of the Trustees of the Society—Letter to Bishop Hughes—Reply of Bishop Hughes—Letter of David Graham to the Society—Reply of the Committee—Expurgation of School-Books.

THE exciting discussion relative to the distribution of the school fund brought into requisition all the arguments and objections on both sides of the question, and, among the grounds of complaint, it was urged by the parties who advocated a change in the apportionment of the school money, that the text-books in use in the public schools contained passages which were not merely objectionable to Roman Catholics, but hostile to their faith, some of them being even " defamatory," and at the same time *false* in their statements of historical facts.

The trustees of the Society were anxious to remove every objection, and took measures to secure the fullest information upon the subject from the highest authorities in the Church, among laymen as well as the clergy, in order that the obnoxious passages might be detected and removed. This measure formed, at the time, the topic of animated discussion, and the facts are worthy of detail as an important event in the history of the school system.

The reader will have noticed, in the chapter devoted to the controversy of 1834, between Bishop Dubois and the trustees relative to Public School No. 5, in Mott street, that he submitted several propositions to the Board of Trustees, the third of which was as follows :

3d. That no books shall be received in the school but such as will have been submitted to the bishop as free from sectarian principles, or calumnies against his religion; and as many otherwise good books may require only that such passages should be expunged, or left out in binding, that, on the recommendation of the bishop, the board will order it to be done.

At that time no further action was taken in the matter, as the trustees could not concede the general proposition of the bishop, and no reply to their letter was ever received.

At a meeting of the trustees held at Public School No. 5, for the annual examination on March 24, 1840, the Vice-President stated that Rev. Felix Varela had made a request to be furnished with a set of the reading-books used in the schools, and the following resolution was immediately adopted:

Resolved, That the Secretary be requested to send a copy of each of said books to Mr. Varela for his inspection.

The following resolution was also unanimously adopted:

Resolved, That the board continues to entertain an anxious desire to remove every objection which the members of the Catholic Church may have to the books used or the studies pursued in the public schools, and that the Secretary be requested to renew the assurance given on a former occasion, that any suggestion or remarks which the Rev. Mr. Varela may deem it right to make, on his own behalf and that of his associates, after said books have been examined, shall receive the most serious and respectful consideration of this board.

The resolutions and books were ordered to be transmitted to Mr. Varela, and soon after the receipt he made a reply. At the meeting of the trustees held on the 1st of May, Mr. Varela's response was read, and the following resolution was adopted:

Resolved, That a committee of five be appointed to examine the books in use in the public schools, including those in the libraries, with a view to ascertain and report whether they contain any thing derogatory to the Roman Catholic Church or any of its religious tenets, with power to communicate with such persons of that Church as may be authorized to meet them in reference to such alterations.

The committee so appointed consisted of J. Smyth Rogers, M.D., Joseph B. Collins, Samuel F. Mott, James F. Depeyster, and Robert Hogan, M.D.

At the meeting of the Society held on the 25th of September, called for the consideration of the action of the committee, the following report was presented and adopted, and the recom-

mendation that the subject be referred to the Executive Com
mittee was adopted :

To the Trustees of the Public School Society :

The committee appointed on the 1st of May, 1840, to examine the school-
books, confer with the Roman Catholic clergy, &c., RESPECTFULLY REPORT :

That they have devoted much time in discharging to the best of their
ability, the important duty assigned them. Soon after their appointment,
the secretary placed in their hands a letter from the Rev. Dr. Varela, with a
few remarks regarding the school-books, copies of which had been placed in
his hand under the resolution of the board, passed on 24th of March. A
copy of Dr. Varela's letter is appended, marked A.

The committee early sought and obtained an interview with the Very
Rev. Dr. Power, Vicar-General of the Roman Catholic Diocese of New
York, during which he treated the subject with much apparent frankness
and candor, but gave very little encouragement to expect a satisfactory
arrangement of the points at issue. It resulted, however, in his requesting
a copy of the school-books, with an understanding that, when he had examined them, he would communicate with your committee. After a lapse
of several weeks, and when the committee were in daily expectation of a
communication from Dr. Power, a letter under his signature appeared in the
Freeman's Journal, a copy of which is in the appendix, marked C. This
unlooked-for course on the part of the reverend gentleman induced the
committee to address a letter to him, as per copy herewith, marked D, to
which the committee have not received any reply. About the middle of
August, the Roman Catholics of this city issued an " Address to the People
of the City and State of New York," urging their claims to a portion of the
school money ; see copy, marked E. The extraordinary character of portions of this address appeared to the committee to call for a prompt reply.
They accordingly prepared, and, with the sanction of the Executive Committee, issued a reply, a copy of which is annexed, marked F. Subsequent
to this, the committee had an informal interview with the Right Rev. Dr.
Hughes, Roman Catholic Bishop Coadjutor of New York, which resulted in
a request on his part to be furnished with copies of the school-books, and
as each member of the committee confidently supposed, for the purpose of
uniting with the committee in ascertaining objectionable passages. The
books were sent, and a letter was addressed to the bishop, a copy of which
is annexed herewith, marked G. The answer was received, marked H.

By referring to the report of the committee on " Arts and Sciences, and
Common Schools " of the Board of Assistant Aldermen, to whom was referred the petition of the Roman Catholics (p. 352 of Document No. 80), it
is stated that the committee had " been informed, by the officers of the
Public School Society, that no books are used in the schools which reflect in
any degree upon the Catholic Church." Your committee are unable to
account for this misapprehension on the part of the Board of Assistant
Aldermen. By reference to the annexed copy of a note addressed to David
Graham, Jr., Esq., chairman of that committee, in reply to one from him,

marked I, it will be perceived that your committee expressly acknowledged the existence of such passages. Their answer is subjoined, marked J.

From the foregoing statement, and the accompanying documents, it will be seen that your committee has been actuated throughout by the motives which influenced the Board of Trustees in creating it—that is, a sincere desire to remove, as far as may be done, without sacrificing the rights and feelings of others, every obstacle to the attendance of Catholic children at the public schools. It is now evident that the coöperation of the Catholic clergy in effecting an expurgation of the books cannot be relied on. The committee is fully aware of the importance of such aid in order to secure their influence in promoting the attendance of Catholic children, and, possibly, in preventing the necessity of a second revision. But it is believed that the time has arrived for the trustees to accomplish the work without them. If it does not have the effect so greatly desired, the trustees will have the satisfaction of reflecting that they have discharged their duty in the premises. Under a strong impression of the duty which devolves on the trustees to expunge words and passages clearly objectionable, your committee had made some progress in the work ; but a reference to the resolution appointing them showed that their powers do not extend beyond reporting the offensive parts. They have, therefore, asked for the present meeting, in order to lay before the board the parts adverted to, and obtain permission to continue the work.

In conclusion, the committee have to report that a petition is now before the Board of Aldermen, with a renewed request for aid to support the Roman Catholic schools. As the petition has not yet been printed, the committee is unable to furnish a copy. It is with feelings, more of sorrow than indignation, that this committee have to add that this petition—notwithstanding the repeated assurances made to the Roman Catholic clergy, that every obnoxious word should be expunged from the school-books, and that the trustees only await their aid in selecting them—contains some quotations, and again urges them, as a reason why they cannot permit their children to attend the public schools.

The committee respectfully suggest whether, under existing circumstances, it may not be expedient to refer further movements in opposing all applications for school money for schools connected with churches, to the Executive Committee, particularly as that committee will meet nearly every day for some time to come, in making the usual annual examinations of the schools.

All which is repectfully submitted,

JOSEPH B. COLLINS, *Chairman pro tem.*

NEW YORK, *September* 25, 1840.

———

A.

NEW YORK, *April* 8, 1840.

DEAR SIR : I received the books you had the kindness of sending to me, according to a resolution of the Board of Trustees of the Common Schools, in consequence of an information given by one of them as to my wish of examining said books. I thank the Board of Trustees for this mark of good feelings, and, in order to comply with their request, I will express my opinion on the subject.

The "Scripture Lessons" present, in the very title-page, an attack against the Catholic Church; for it is expressly stated that they are without *note* or *comment*, so as to call the attention of a child, and to tell him: "Your Church is wrong in giving the Bible always with notes; disregard her, and read the Scriptures without any note or comment, and find out a religion for yourself." This is to establish at once the Protestant fundamental principle, and to make the public schools completely sectarian.

In the Geography (p. 143), it is said that the Catholic clergy, who have vast influence, oppose the diffusion of general knowledge; and, in the very next page, it is said that Catholics pay great reverence to the priests. It is very easy to perceive that a child will think very little of such a reverence, and lose every regard for such a ministry.

There are also, in the description of Italy, some passages which evidently tend to diminish the consideration that a Catholic child has for the Catholic Church. I also noticed, in the "Reading-Book," the description of the character of Luther, with some expressions which, no doubt, will please the Protestants, but imply an attack against the Catholic Church.

By making these few observations, I do not allude to the question as to the petition made by the Catholics to obtain a part of the school funds, but I merely respond to the kindness of the Board of Trustees in sending me the books for examination.

With great respect, your obedient

FELIX VARELA.

To A. P. HALSEY, *Secretary of Public School Society.*

C.

To the Editor of the New York Freeman's Journal:

SIR: In compliance with your request, I must, in justice to myself, say that my duties are of so heterogeneous a nature as to leave me but little time to arrange my thoughts to my own satisfaction on any subject. Yet, as the education of Catholic children has been always to me a matter of deep interest, I claim familiarity with the subject, and can therefore approach it with less timidity and reluctance.

You, sir, are fully aware that the enemies of the Catholic priesthood say that we keep the people in ignorance, in order to promote our own interests. This charge has often been repeated, even in this enlightened community, by persons who cannot be ignorant of the efforts we are daily making to teach those under our care how to employ the faculties which God gave them to the best advantage.

Our sincere wish, sir, is to have instilled into their minds a clear notion of the compact and duties of society. We wish them to comprehend the comforts as well as the restraints of civilization, knowing that they are part of the materials which will form the edifice of the State, and which, by the simple process of a more graceful order and position, will contribute to its beauty and permanency.

The Catholic clergy glory in an association with the charms of literature. They consider education, next to the gospel—to be the best boon of Heaven to man. They know that it infuses a divinity into his spirit.

"Doctrina sed vim promovet insitam
Rectique cultus pectora roborant."

They know that nations have been rendered formidable by knowledge. They know that public liberty has never been injured by understanding its true meaning. They know that freedom has not been abused because society has learned to comprehend and obey the law. When, sir, I open the historic page, and learn that the bravest people whose history we can trace, loved and cultivated letters—when I see Sparta making the education of her sons the public care, and securing the culture of their minds by a public provision—with all this in view, sir, I should despise myself were I for one instant to place an obstacle in the way of public instruction, were it based on a proper foundation.

You, Mr. Editor, will agree with me, that the object of public instruction is to fit man for society. It is also an axiom, that man has various duties to fulfil, both of a public and private nature, toward the community. He has also, as a rational and accountable being, duties to perform toward his Maker. Now, without religion, what security have we that those duties will be punctually discharged? What guarantee have we that man will be honest in the dark, and without a witness? We have no pledge, sir, that the claims of society will be answered; and I therefore assert that a purely intellectual education will not fit a man for society. On this principle, sir, I am decidedly opposed to the education which is now given in our "public schools." It is not based, as in a Christian community it ought to be, on the Christian religion. Its tendency is to make deists.

There are, it is true, beautiful lessons in the class-books on the providence of God, the immortality of the soul, man's accountability, &c.; but these lessons do not constitute Christianity. We learn them from the light of reason alone, while the positive ordinances of the Christian religion are learned from revelation; and, as there is not the slightest allusion to these ordinances, we say that pure deism alone is taught in these schools.

My second exception is founded on the sectarian character of the public schools. The Holy Scriptures are read every day, with the restriction that no specific tenets are to be inculcated. Here, sir, we find the great demarcating principle between the Catholic Church and the sectaries introduced *silently*. The Catholic Church tells her children that they must be taught their religion by AUTHORITY. The sects say, Read the Bible, judge for yourselves. The Bible is read in the public schools, the children are allowed to judge for themselves. The Protestant principle is therefore acted upon, silently inculcated, and the schools are sectarian. It may be said that the Bible is introduced for the mere purpose of teaching its morality. But recollect, sir, that the morality of the Bible is founded on the law of nature, and is a clearer evolution or expression of that law; and as the motive for introducing the Bible into the schools is the inculcation of its morality only, a severe logic forces me to say, that the holy Book is made ancillary to pure deism.

There are libraries connected with our public schools, and it is notorious, that books which to Catholics must be exceptionable, as containing the most malevolent and foul attacks on their religion, were placed in the way of Catholic children, no doubt for the very laudable purpose of teaching them to abhor and despise that monster called popery.

How, then, sir, can we think of sending, under these circumstances, our children to those schools, in which every artifice is resorted to in order to seduce them from their religion?

One word to parents, before I close this hasty communication. If it be of acknowledged moment that parents should engage in those duties which concern the temporal welfare of their children, should not the most animated zeal be indulged in fixing and giving life to every moral and religious principle? In moral and religious acquirements consist the chief dignity and happiness of man. Deprive him these, and you leave him ignorant of the true grounds of rectitude and honor, and dry up the purest sources of human joy; you degrade him in the creation, and render him an improper object for the future reward of his Maker. Many parents, sir, by their inattention to this part of their duty, are the cause of ruin to those whom they professedly love, and, instead of being their best friends, become their worst enemies.

The objections to our claims for a due portion of the school fund are, I think, urged in bad faith. It is said that the State cannot lend itself to the support of sectarian principles. But recollect, sir, that this objection is urged by those whose conduct is truly sectarian, as far as regards the management of the public schools. This, I think, I have abundantly proved.

When the common school fund was created, it was not considered unconstitutional to extend it to the charity schools in connection with the incorporated religious societies in this city; and, if I am not much mistaken, the philanthropic and enlightened statesman with whom the measure originated, thought that the best application of the fund lay in giving it to those who would make a proper use of it, by giving that instruction which alone can save man from the tyranny of his passions, and make him a good member of society.

Would it not, Mr. Editor, be a libel on the memory of the founders of our glorious Constitution, to pervert that instrument to such an extent as to think that they, in disclaiming a *civil* preference for any form of Christianity, thereby intended that the public education of the country should not be founded on religion? In this respect I apprehend they did not depart from the rule of all wise legislators, and never contemplated that our charity schools should not participate in the fund set apart for public education, because the catechisms of the different religious societies of which this republic is composed would be taught in them.

I, sir, would be the last man to wish that the State would spend its means in supporting sectarianism; and the principle that induces me to make this avowal, bids me also to express my conviction that, unless public instruction be connected with religious instruction, there is no guarantee for the permanence of our civil institutions. I would, then, most respectfully say to our rulers, Let mental cultivation be general, but let it have religion for its basis. This will be the surest foundation not only for your internal improvement, but for the increase of your general prosperity. This will be the means by which your rank and consideration are to be raised into competition with the foremost of polished nations.

I am, sir, with great respect, your very humble servant,

JOHN POWER, *Vicar-General of the Diocese of New York.*

NEW YORK, *July 9,* 1840.

D.

NEW YORK, *August,* 1840.

The undersigned, on behalf of the committee appointed by the trustees of the Public School Society " to examine the books used in the public schools, including those in the libraries, with a view to ascertain and report whether they contain any thing derogatory to the Roman Catholic Church, or any of its religious tenets, with power to communicate with such persons of that Church as may be authorized to meet them in reference to such alterations," referring to the interview had with you on the evening of the 14th of May last, on the subject of their appointment, instruct me to inquire whether you have examined the books placed in your hands, agreeably to the request then made; and, if so, whether you will favor them with the result of your investigations. The committee has steadily prosecuted the objects indicated in the resolution appointing it, but does not feel prepared to report to the Board of Trustees until they have the benefit of those inquiries and objections which your feelings, and the duties of your station, must alike prompt. The committee is anxious to discharge the duty assigned it without delay. It is therefore very desirable to hear from you as early as your convenience will permit.

I am further instructed to say, that the committee cannot, in justice to themselves or to you, close this communication without expressing the regret and surprise caused by portions of a letter under your signature, which appeared in the *New York Freeman's Journal* of the 12th ult. A vivid recollection of the frankness with which you treated this deeply-interesting subject at the interview referred to, and the voluntary avowal then made of your entire satisfaction with the explanation given by the committee of the accidental introduction into the school libraries of a volume of the "Temperance Tales," in which there was one story justly obnoxious to Catholic censure, which, as you are aware, was withdrawn when discovered, and which, you remarked, might, under similar circumstances, have found its way into a Catholic library, still rests upon their minds.

These facts contrast so strongly with the imputations of base and dishonorable motives in which you have seen fit to indulge, and with the importance into which you attempt to magnify the single story referred to, that the committee will not venture to express the feelings which such a course on your part must necessarily give rise to. They would gladly find an adequate apology for this unmerited and unlooked-for attack in the "haste" with which you say it was written, and in the fact, as you allege, that your duties are of so "heterogeneous a nature as to leave you but little time to arrange your thoughts to your own satisfaction on any subject;" and they now submit to your more calm and deliberate consideration whether, pending an examination of the school-books, with a view to their expurgation, in which you promised coöperation, it would not have been more consonant with propriety and the generally acknowledged courtesies of life, if you had suspended your public denunciations of a large body of your fellow-citizens until they had furnished evidence of "bad faith," by refusing to expunge—as they assured you they would do—every thing in the school-books which might be pointed out as objectionable by yourselves and associates in religious faith.

On behalf of the committee.

E.

ADDRESS OF THE ROMAN CATHOLICS TO THEIR FELLOW-CITIZENS OF THE CITY AND STATE OF NEW YORK.

FELLOW-CITIZENS : We, the Roman Catholics of the city of New York, feeling that both our civil and religious rights are abridged and injuriously affected by the operation of the "common school system," and by the construction which the Common Council have lately put on the laws authorizing that system, beg leave to state our grievances, with the deep confidence in the justice of the American character that, if our complaints are well-founded, you will assist us in obtaining the redress to which we are entitled. If they are not well founded, we are ready to abandon them.

We are Americans and American citizens. If some of us are foreigners, it is only by the accident of birth. As citizens, our ambition is to be Americans ; and if we cannot be so by birth, we are so by choice and preference—which we deem an equal evidence of our affection and attachment to the laws and Constitution of the country. But our children, for whose rights as well as our own we contend in this matter, are Americans by nativity. So that we are, like yourselves, either natives of the soil, or like your fathers from the Eastern world, having become Americans under the sanction of the Constitution, by the birthright of selection and preference.

We hold, therefore, the same ideas of our rights that you hold of yours. We wish not to diminish yours, but only to secure and enjoy our own. Neither have we the slightest suspicion that you would wish us to be deprived of any privilege which you claim for yourselves. If, then, we have suffered by the operation of the " common school system " in the city of New York, it is to be imputed rather to our own supineness, than to any wish on your part that we should be aggrieved.

The intention of the Legislature of this State in appropriating public funds for the purposes of popular schools *must have been* (whatever construction the lawyers of the Common Council put upon it), to diffuse the blessings of education among the people, without encroachment on the civil and religious rights of the citizens. It was, *it must have been*, to have planted in the minds of youth principles of knowledge and virtue, which would secure to the State a future population of enlightened and virtuous, instead of ignorant and vicious members. This was certainly their general intention, and no other would have justified their bountiful appropriation of the public funds.

But, in carrying out the measure, this patriotic and wise intention has been lost sight of; and in the city of New York at least, under the late arbitrary determination of the present Common Council, such intention of the Legislature is not only disregarded, but the high public ends to which it was directed are manifestly being defeated.

Mere knowledge, according to the late decision, mere secular knowledge, is what we are to understand by education, in the sense of the Legislature of New York. But if you should allow the smallest ray of religion to enter the school-room—if you should teach the children that there is an eye which sees every wicked thought, that there is a God, a state of rewards and punishments beyond this life, then, according to the decision of the Common Council, you forfeit all claim to the bounty of the State, although your scholars should have become as learned as Newton or wise as Socrates! Is, then, we would ask you, fellow-citizens, a practical rejection of the Christian religion in all its forms, and without the substitution of any other, the basis on which you would form the principles and character of the future citizens of this great commonwealth ? Are the meek lessons of religion and virtue, which pass from the mother's lips into the heart of her child, to be chilled and frozen by icy contact with a system of education thus interpreted ?

Is enlightened villany so precious in the public eye, that science is to be cultivated, whilst virtue is neglected, and religion, its only adequate groundwork, is formally and authoritatively proscribed ? Is it your wish that vice should thus be elevated from its low and natural companionship with ignorance and be married to knowledge imparted at the public expense ?

We do not say that even the Common Council profess to require that the Christian religion should be excluded from the common schools. They only contend that the inculcation of each or any of its doctrines would be sectarianism ; and thus, lest sectarianism should be admitted, Christianity is substantially excluded. Christianity in this country is made up of the different creeds of the various denominations, and, since all these creeds are proscribed, the Christian religion necessarily is banished from the halls of public education.

The objections which we have thus far stated, fellow-citizens, ought to appear to you, in our opinion, as strong to you as they do to us. For, though we may differ in our definition of the religion of Christ, still we all generally profess to believe, to revere it, as the foundation of moral virtue and of social happiness. Now, we know of no fixed principle of infidelity except the *negation* of the Christian religion. The adherents of this principle may differ on other points of skepticism, but in rejecting Christianity they are united. Their confession of faith is a belief in the *negative* of Christianity, but they reject it *in toto ;* whilst the Common Council rejects it only in all its several parts, under the name of sectarianism.

It is manifest, therefore, that the public school system in the city of New York is entirely favorable to the sectarianism of infidelity, and opposed only to that of positive Christianity. And is it your wish, fellow-citizens—is it your wish more than ours, that infidelity should have a predominancy and advantages in the public schools which are denied to Christianity? Is it your wish that your children shall be brought up under a system of education, so called, which shall detach them from the Christian belief which you profess, whatever it may be, and prepare them, for initiation into the mysteries of Fanny Wrightism, or any other scheme of infidelity which may come in their way? Are you willing that your children, educated at your expense, shall be educated on a principle *antagonist* to the Christian religion? —that you shall have the toil and labor of cultivating the ground and sowing the seed, in order that infidelity may reap the harvest?

With us it is matter of surprise that conscientious persons, of all Christian denominations, have not been struck with this bad feature of the system as understood by the Common Council. A new sectarianism antagonist to all *Christian* sects has been generated in, not the common schools, as the State originally understood the term, but in the *public* schools of the Public School Society. This new sectarianism is adopted by the Common Council of this city, and is supported, *to the exclusion of all others*, at the public expense. Have the conscientious Methodists, Episcopalians, Baptists, Lutherans, and others, no scruples of conscience at seeing their children, and the children of their poor, brought up under this new sectarianism? It is not for us to say; but for ourselves we can speak : and we cannot be parties to such a system except by legal compulsion and against conscience.

Let us not be mistaken. We do not deny to infidels, for unbelief, any right to which any other citizen is entitled.

But we hold that the common school system, as it has been lately interpreted by the Common Council of the city, necessarily transfers to the interest of infidel sectarianism the advantages which are denied to Christian sectarianism of every kind.

Again, let us not be misunderstood. We are opposed to the admission of sectarianism of any and of every kind, whether Christian or anti-Christian, in the schools that are supported by the State.

But we hold, also, that, so far as the commonwealth is concerned in the character of her future citizens, even the least perfect religion of Christian sectarianism would be better than no religion at all. And we hold that, of all bad uses to which the public money can be perverted, among the worst would be the expending of it, in the shape of a bounty to education, for the spread and propagation of sectarian infidelity. Far be it from us to suppose that either the Legislature, Common Council, or School Commissioners ever intended such perversion. We hold, nevertheless, that the consequence which we have pointed out, and the apprehension of which is one of the reasons why we Roman Catholics cannot· conscientiously participate in the benefits of these schools, is necessary and inevitable. The education which each denomination might, under proper restraints and vigilance, give to its *own poor*, has passed and become a monopoly in the hands of " The Public School Society of New York." That corporation is in high and almost exclusive standing with the Common Council.*

* " The Public School Society " was originally incorporated for " the education of poor children who do not belong to, or are not provided for by, any religious society." The purpose was humane, patriotic, and benevolent. But, alas ! it has been most sadly departed from. One of the motives—indeed, the principal one—which they set forth in their petition for a charter from the people and Legislature of the State, was, in their own language, " the benefits which would result to society from the education of such children, BY IMPLANTING IN THEIR MINDS THE PRINCIPLES OF RELIGION AND MORALITY." This was in 1805. In 1808, they obtained a considerable appropriation of the public money, independent of the school fund ; and had themselves designated the " Free-School Society of New York," with an extension of their powers reaching

Now, the education which is imparted on the principle of the schools of that Society is, in our decided opinion, calculated, from its defectiveness, to disappoint the benevolent hope of legislative bounty, and to make bad and dangerous citizens. We all know that the belief of another world is, ultimately, at the base of all that is just and sacred in this. The love of God, the hope of future rewards, the dread of future punishment—one or all of these constitute and must be the foundation of conscience in the breast of every man. Where neither of them exists, conscience is but an idle word. Religion is but the development of these important truths, governing man by their internal influence on his passions and affections, regulating the order of his duties to God, to his country, to his neighbor and himself. If they have their full force, he will be a man of justice, probity, and truth. And in proportion as such men are numerous in the commonwealth, in the same proportion will the State enjoy security and happiness from within, honor and high estimation from without.

Now, holding these truths as indisputable, we ask you, fellow-citizens, to say whether this—not common, but public—school system, as it is now administered, under the interpretation of the Common Council, is calculated to raise up for your successors in the State men of this description; or, rather, whether it does not promise you men of a different and diametrically opposite character? The Common Council makes it a condition—an essential one of those schools—that religion shall not be taught, for this would be sectarianism. And thus the intellect is cultivated, if you please, but the

---

"all children who are proper objects of gratuitous education." In 1810, they obtained an act (for they never slumbered), putting the right of membership at a contribution of fifty dollars, and providing for them another extra appropriation. Thus they continued from year to year, until they finally got themselves denominated "The Public School Society of New York," and from that time labelled *their* schools, as if they belonged to the community at large, "Public Schools." They are not, certainly, in the ordinary sense of the terms, what they profess to be. They are merely *called* "public schools," but they belong to a private corporation, who have crept up into high favor with the powers that be, and have assumed the exclusive right of monopolizing the education of youth, and of receiving exclusively the public funds set apart for that benevolent and patriotic purpose.

But there is one circumstance which brands their exclusive pretension with the stamp of rare and peculiar arrogance. It is, that they claim the common school funds on the express ground of defeating the very end for which their charter was obtained, viz., "the benefits that would result to society from the education of (such) children, by implanting in their minds the principles of religion and morality." Now, in their apostasy from their first profession, they claim the merit of benefiting society by seeing that, in *their* schools, no principle of religion and morality shall be implanted! The same body, under different names, obtaining a charter and high pecuniary privileges in consideration of their doing a certain good work; and yet coming out openly to claim exclusively the bounty granted for that purpose, on the ground that they, and they alone, have taken the precaution that the good work shall not be performed in connection with education. Not only will they not perform it themselves, but they will not allow others to accomplish it. What would have been a benefit to society when they applied for a charter, would be a terrible injury now. And if, by chance, "the principles of religion and morality were implanted in the minds of children," there would result nothing but sectarianism, bickering, and religious wars, and, over and above, the equilibrium of the American Constitution would be awfully disturbed, the rights of conscience would be violated, and disasters innumerable would be the result. (VIDE the apprehensions of the lame and laboring report put forth, in April, on behalf of the public school system, as emanating from a committee of the Board of Assistant Aldermen, against the petitions of the Roman Catholics, Scotch Presbyterians, and others, who have the misfortune to believe still that society would be benefitted by having "principles of religion and morality implanted in the minds of children.")

heart and moral character are left to their natural depravity and wildness. This is not education ; and, above all, this is not *the* education calculated to make good citizens.

Education cultivates all the faculties of the human soul, the *will* as well as the understanding and memory.

The public school system not only does *not* cultivate the will (for this can hardly be done without the aid of religion), but it almost emancipates the will, even in the tender age of childhood, in reference to the subject of religion itself. We have found in the hands of our children lessons setting forth, in substance, that, after all, *humane* feelings and actions are about the best religion.

In these schools you give them knowledge without the moderating principle which will direct its use, or prevent its being applied to the worst of purposes. What principle do you inculcate that will check the lie that is rising to their lips, or cause confusion on their brow when they have uttered it ? None. Religion could accomplish this, but religion is excluded. If you tell them there is a God who will punish them, the atheist father, who thinks himself an honest man without God, and who thinks his own opinions good enough for his child, will appeal to the decision of the Common Council, and show that you violate the condition of the grant in favor of common schools, by speaking of God, or any thing sectarian. What principles of self-restraint are inculcated in this spurious system of education, which leaves the *will* of the pupil to riot in the fierceness of unrestrained lusts ? " Train up a child in the way in which he should walk, and when he is old he will not depart from it," is the maxim of one who judged of human nature with more than human penetration. But the Common Council has reversed it, and decided that the child will train up itself, provided you give it knowledge without religion.

Thus far, fellow-citizens, we have stated our objections to the present system of common school education, not as they affect us more than any other denomination of Christians.

We have stated them in view of the bearing which that sytem is likely to have on interests in which you are concerned as much as, or more than, ourselves, viz., religion, morals, individual and social happiness, and the welfare of the State.

We believe it was the warning voice of the illustrious Washington, among the most solemn words of *the* patriot, breathed into the ear of his beloved country, to *beware* of the man who would inculcate morality *without religion.*

We now come to the statement of grievances which affect us in our civil and religious rights as Roman Catholics.

Under the guarantee of liberty of conscience, we profess the religion which we believe to be true and pleasing to God.

We inherit it (many of us) from our persecuted fathers, for we are the sons of martyrs in the cause of religious freedom.

Our conscience obliges us to transmit it to our children.

A brief experience of the public school system in the city of New York convinced us that we could not discharge our conscientious duty to our offspring if we allowed them to be brought up under the influence of the irreligious principles on which these schools are conducted, and to some of which we have already alluded. But, besides these, there were other grounds of distrust and danger, which soon forced on us the conclusion that the benefits of public education were not for *us.* Besides the introduction of the Holy Scriptures without note or comment, with the prevailing theory that from these even children are to get their notions of religion, contrary to our principles, there were, in the class-books of those schools, false (as we believe) historical statements respecting the men and things of past times, calculated to fill the minds of our children with errors of fact, and at the same time to excite in them prejudice against the religion of their parents and guardians. These passages were not considered as sectarian, inasmuch as they had been selected as mere reading-lessons, and were not in *favor* of any particular sect, but merely *against* the Catholics. We feel it is unjust that such passages should be taught at all in schools to the support of which we are contributors as well as others. But that such books should be put into the hands of *our own* children, and that in part at our own expense, was, in our opinion, unjust, unnatural, and, at all events, to us intolerable. Accordingly, through very great additional sacrifices, we have been obliged to provide schools under our churches, and elsewhere, in which to educate our children as our conscientious duty required. This we have done to the number of some thousands for several years past, during all which time we have been obliged to pay taxes; and we feel it unjust and oppressive that, whilst we educate our children as well, we contend, as they would be at the public schools, we are denied our portion of the school fund, simply because we at the same time endeavor to train them up in principles of virtue and religion. This we feel to be unjust and unequal. For we pay taxes in proportion to our numbers, as other citizens. We are supposed to be from one hundred and fifty to two hundred thousand in the State.

And although most of us are poor, still the poorest man amongst us is obliged to pay taxes from the sweat of his brow, in the rent of his room or little tenement. Is it not, then, hard and unjust that such a man cannot have the benefit of education for his child without sacrificing the rights of his religion and conscience? He sends his child to a school under the protection of his Church, in which these rights will be secure. But he has to support this school also. In Ireland he was compelled to support a Church hostile to his religion; and here he is compelled to support schools in which his religion fares but little better, and to support his own school besides.

Is this state of things, fellow-citizens, and especially Americans, is this state of things worthy of *you*, worthy of your country, worthy of our just and glorious Constitution? Put yourselves in the poor man's place, and say whether you would not despise him, if he did not labor by every lawful means to emancipate himself from this bondage. He has to pay double taxation for the education of his child—one to the misinterpreted law of the land, and another to his conscience. He sees his child going to school with perhaps only the fragment of a worn-out book, thinly clad, and its bare feet on the frozen pavement; whereas, if he had his rights, he could improve the clothing, he could get better books, and have his child better taught, than it is possible in actual circumstances.

Nothing can be more false than some statements of our motives which have been put forth against us.

It has been asserted that we seek our share of the school fund for the support and advancement of our religion.

We beg to assure you, with respect, that we would scorn to support or advance our religion at any other than our own expense. But we are unwilling to pay taxes for the purpose of destroying our religion in the minds of our children. This points out the sole difference between what we seek and what some narrow-minded or misinformed journals have accused us of seeking.

If the public schools could have been constituted on a principle which would have secured a perfect *neutrality* of influence on the subject of religion, then we should have no reason to complain. But this has not been done, and we respectfully submit that it is impossible. The cold indifference with which it is required that all religions shall be treated in those schools—the Scriptures without note or comment—the selection of passages as reading-lessons from Protestant and prejudiced authors, on points in which our creed is supposed to be involved—the comments of the teacher, of which the commissioners cannot be cognizant—the school libraries, stuffed with sectarian works against us—form against our religion a combination of influences prejudicial, and to whose action it would be criminal in us to expose our children at such an age.

Such, fellow-citizens, is a statement of the reasons of our opposition to the public schools, and of the unjust and unequal grievances of which we complain.

You can judge of our rights by your own. You cannot be expected to know our religion; many of you have, no doubt, strong prejudices against it, which we are fain to ascribe precisely to the circumstance of your not having had an opportunity to know it.

But, notwithstanding your prejudices and your disapproval of our faith, we have confidence in your high principles of justice, under the sanction of our common Constitution, which secures equal religious and civil rights to all. Put yourselves in our situation, and say whether it is just, or equal, or constitutional, that, whereas we are contributors to the public funds, we shall be excluded from our share of benefit in their expenditure, unless we submit to the arbitrary and irreligious conditions of the Common Council, and thereby violate our rights of conscience?

Our religion is dear to us; for in the hearts of many of us it is connected with the history of our fathers' sufferings and our own. Education is dear to us, for the tyrants who wished to enslave our ancestors and us, made it criminal felony for the schoolmaster to come among us, unless he were the avowed enemy of our creed.

We seek for nothing but what we conceive to be our rights, and which can be granted without violating or abridging the privileges of any other denomination or individual breathing. They may be refused, as they have been. If they should, neither shall we yet suffer our children to receive the anti-religious education of the public schools, nor shall we kiss the hand that fixes a blot on the Constitution, by oppressively denying our just claims.

What do we contend for? Simply that our children shall be educated apart from these influences. *We contend for liberty of conscience and freedom of education.* We hold that the laws of nature, of religion, and the very Constitution of the country, secure to parents the right of superintending the education of their own children.

This right we contend for, but we have hitherto been obliged to exercise it under the unjust disadvantages of double taxation. If the State, considering our children as its own, grants money for their education, are we not entitled to our portion of it when we perform the services which are required?

It appears not, according to the decision of the Common Council, unless we send our children to schools in which our religious rights are to be violated, and our offspring qualified to pass over to the thickening ranks of infidelity. This shall not be. Much as we dread ignorance, we dread this much more.

If justice were done us, we could increase the number of our teachers to a proportion corresponding with the number of children. We could improve our means of teaching; we could bring our children out of the damp basements of our churches into pure air of better localities. In a word, give us our just proportion of the common school fund, and if we do not give as good an education *apart from religious instruction* as is given in the public schools, to one third a larger number of children, for the same money, we are willing to renounce our just claim. Let the proper authorities appoint any test of improvement that shall be general, and we shall abide by it. Neither do we desire that any children shall attend our schools except those

22

of our own communion—although, so far as *we* are concerned, they shall be open to all.

In a country like this, it is the interest of all to protect the guaranteed rights of each. Should the professors of some weak or unpopular religion be oppressed to-day, the experiment may be repeated to-morrow on some other. Every successful attempt in that way will embolden the spirit of encroachment and diminish the power of resistance; and, in such an event, the monopolizers of education, after having discharged the office of public tutor, may find it convenient to assume that of public preacher. The transition will not be found difficult or unnatural from the idea of a common school to that of a common religion, from which, of course, in order to make it popular, all Christian sectarianism will be carefully excluded.

" Resist the beginnings," is a wise maxim in the preservation of rights.

Should the American people ever stand by and tolerate the open and authoritative violation of their *Magna Charta*, then the republic will have seen the end of its days of glory.

The friends of liberty throughout the civilized world will fold their hands in grief and despair. The tyrants of the earth will point to the flag which your fathers planted, and cry, Ha! ha!

The nations from afar will gaze upon it, and behold with astonishment its bright stars faded, and its stripes turned into scorpions.

The above address was unanimously adopted at a general meeting of the Catholics of the city of New York, in the school-room of St. James' Church, August 10th, 1840, having been submitted by

† JOHN HUGHES, *Bishop of Basileopolis,*
    Coadjutor and Administrator of the
    Diocese of New York.
HUGH SWEENY,
THOMAS O'CONNOR,
JAMES W. McKEON,   } *Committee.*
GREGORY DILLON,
J. W. WHITE,
B. O'CONNOR,
JAMES KELLY,
JOHN McLOUGHLIN.

F.

REPLY

OF THE TRUSTEES OF THE PUBLIC SCHOOL SOCIETY TO THE ADDRESS OF
THE ROMAN CATHOLICS.

FELLOW-CITIZENS : The Roman Catholics of the city of New York, having appealed to you against a recent decision of the Common Council rejecting their petition for a portion of the school fund for the support of their church schools, and having seen fit to prefer charges of a gross and serious nature against the present system of public instruction in the city of New York, the trustees of the public schools feel it to be a duty which they owe to themselves, and to the community who have, for more than thirty years, in great measure confided to them the important subject of common education, to reply, and disabuse the public mind.

It is proper, at the threshold, to remove an important error which pervades almost every part of the address. It assumes that the plan of withholding the proceeds of the school fund and other school moneys from religious societies, is peculiar to the city of New York, and speaks of the late decision of the Common Council as something new; whereas neither the Constitution nor laws of the State contemplate any such use of the fund.

It never was so appropriated in any part of the State, except during a few years in the city of New York. This experiment resulted, inconsiderable as the amount then was, as it ever must result—in producing jealousies and abuses, which induced a repeal of the law nearly twenty years ago. The recent decision of the Common Council was, therefore, only in confirmation of a previous one, and was in strict accordance with the Constitution, the laws, and practice of the State. And it is worthy of special remark, as evidence of the soundness of the conclusion, that the vote was unanimous, every member being present.

With such portions of the address as relate to the general question, whether the school money shall or shall not be given to religious societies for the support of church schools, it is not proposed to detain you long. This question has been so conclusively settled by public opinion, and the consequent action of our legislative bodies, that, to enter upon a discussion of it now, might be considered an insult offered to the understanding of the people. There is, perhaps, no one axiom connected with our political institutions which is more strongly impressed on the mind of an American than this: "Religious establishments must not be supported by general taxation." In the primary question, the Trustees of the Public School Society have no interest that is not common to every citizen. In all that relates to the quality and management of the public schools, they feel a deep interest, and hold themselves strictly responsible to public opinion and the constituted authorities. It is proper, therefore, that the allegations contained in the address of the Roman Catholics be either admitted or refuted. They are of a grave and serious character, and such as should, if true, justly deprive the trustees of the confidence which has been so long reposed in them. But they are not true, nor is there even an attempt made in the address to sustain them by evidence. Bold assertion, vague generalizing, and mystical reasoning, are alone relied upon. It would be difficult, if not impossible, to follow the address through all the forms and windings it is made to assume, in endeavoring to fasten upon the public school system of education features the most odious to a moral and religious people. That document asserts that, according to the late decision of the Common Council, "if you should allow the smallest ray of religion to enter the school-room—if you should teach the children that there is an eye which sees every wicked thought, that there is a God, a state of rewards and punishments beyond this life, then you would forfeit all claim to the bounty of the State." It also avers that "the public school system in the city of New York is entirely favorable to the sectarianism of infidelity, and opposed only to that of positive Christianity;" that "it prepares the pupil for initiation into the mysteries of Fanny-Wrightism, or any other scheme of infidelity which may come in their way;" that "it is calculated to make bad and dangerous citizens; that no principle is inculcated that will check the lie that is rising to the pupil's lip, or cause confusion on their brow when they have uttered it;" that it "leaves the will of the pupil to riot in the fierceness of unrestrained lusts." But we forbear. These are, indeed, high and serious charges. Happily for the reputation of the city, and the welfare of the thousands who have received and are receiving their education in the public schools, they are as unfounded as they are monstrous. Even the authors of the address shrink from a picture of their own coloring, and declare that they do not mean to say "that either the Legislature, Common Council, or School Commissioners, ever intended such perversions."

What, then, fellow-citizens, do they mean? The answer is obvious. They claim to have discovered that the illustrious men who originated our admirable system of common school education, the framers of our State Constitution, and the successive legislative bodies who have enacted laws on the subject—in short, that the whole people of the State of New York, have been, for nearly thirty years, laboring under a gross and dangerous delusion;

and it follows, by necessary implication, that the authors of the address are the exclusive judges of what constitutes religion, and of the kind of education adapted to American citizens.

It is a most extraordinary feature of this address, that, with the school-books in their hands, not a quotation is made to sustain their charges; and the only book objected to by name is " The Holy Scriptures without note or comment."

Strange inconsistency! They charge us with teaching infidelity and a religion adverse to Christianity, and yet condemn us for using, unless accompanied by their own explanation, that which is the foundation of the Christian religion, and which believers and unbelievers unite in pronouncing the most perfect code of morals ever presented to the world.

The trustees of the public schools did suppose that, by introducing the Holy Scriptures into the schools, they would not only avoid the charge of teaching "infidelity and Fanny-Wrightism," but that, in using the impressive and sublime language of the inspired penmen, "without note or comment," they would disarm the jealousy and quiet the fears of all who believe in the Sacred Volume. Had they attempted to enforce the peculiar views of any who deduce their religious doctrines from the Scriptures, they would justly have incurred the charge of "sectarianism." But, says the address, religion is not taught in any form. It is true that religion is not taught in the sense that reading, writing, arithmetic, and geography are, nor was it ever intended that it should form a branch of public instruction. Our Constitution and laws have wisely omitted to provide for such instruction at the public expense, and have left it where it belongs—to the parent and pastor, and religious seminaries, supported by the voluntary contributions of its votaries.

The reading-books used in the public schools are the same as those used in private schools of a similar grade in which children of various religious persuasions, including those of our more wealthy fellow-citizens of the Roman Catholic Church, are educated.

Many of them contain the best, most sublime, and impressive essays on morals and religion that can be found in the English language, and are calculated to impress on the young mind a belief in the existence of God, the immortality of the soul, and a future state of rewards and punishments. They picture vice in its naked deformity, and present virtue in her most pleasing and attractive colors.

Let the records of our criminal courts, our prisons, and the receptacles for those who, by reason of "rioting in the fierceness of unrestrained lusts," have become a public charge, be examined with reference to the effect of our system of education on the mind and morals, as compared with any other system, and the result will be found highly favorable to the public schools.

Let the characters of the tens of thousands who have been educated at these schools be inquired into with a view to ascertain their value as citizens and their love of truth, as compared with those who have received their education by the opposite system, in this or any other country, and the friends of the "public schools in the city of New York" have nothing to fear from the result.

The address states that books have been found in the hands of Catholic children "setting forth in substance, that, after all, humane feelings and actions are about the best religion." The eminent prelate who read the address, and said that he was concerned in drafting it, on the same occasion read to the assembly, from one of the school-books, a story entitled " Sunday Morning." It is a dialogue between a father and son, and is evidently intended to convey a twofold moral: one, that worship is a work of the "mind and spirit," and that, when these are right, it will be acceptable in the Divine sight, however various in form and ceremony; and, by an accident which is made to happen to a poor man in the street, as the several congregations are retiring from their respective places of worship, it further aims to inculcate the doctrine that the Christian religion, in whatever form professed, leads to humane feelings and actions." The story occurs in the "American Popular Lessons," p. 124, and is certainly any thing but "sectarian." This is clearly the story referred to, and it assumes importance because it furnishes data whereby to estimate the charges against the public schools, and the books used in them, of which the address is so prolific.

There are portions of the address that it is difficult, if not impossible, to understand, or reconcile with other portions. One objection to the public school system is, that, in excluding the "different creeds of the various denominations," "the Christian religion necessarily is banished from the halls of public education." Yet it declares that "the Roman Catholics are opposed to the admission of sectarianism of any and every kind in the schools that are supported by the State." The questions then occur, Will they exclude religious instruction from the Catholic schools? and, if so, in what will they differ from the public schools? If they teach "science without religion," will it not, according to their own showing, produce "enlightened villany," and be liable to the awful consequences which they predicate of the system denounced? If, on the other hand, they mean—as they certainly must—to teach the Roman Catholic religion, how can they ask "to be supported by the State"?

They say that "they could not discharge their conscientious duty to their offspring, if they allowed them to be brought up under the irreligious principles on which the public schools are conducted;" and, while they ask of the State the means of supporting their schools, that they may train up their children "in principles of virtue and religion," they assure the public that they "would scorn to support or advance their religion at any other than their own expense."

A solution of some of these incongruities may, perhaps, be found in the fact that they do not class themselves among "sectarians," or "denominations of Christians," but claim to be emphatically "The Church." However sincerely and confidently they may entertain this view of the subject, can they, fellow-citizens, with propriety ask you to sustain the Legislature in giving it the high sanction of legal enactment? We think you will unite with us in saying, No!

That portion of the address which contains a statement of the grievances which are thought to affect the Roman Catholics in their "civil and religious rights," remains to be considered. And the trustees approach it with the seriousness which its importance demands.

The absence of a large portion of the Catholic children of this city from the public schools has been cause of deep and abiding regret to the trustees. At various times during the last ten years, efforts have been made to remove the obstacles to their attendance. Propositions have again and again been submitted to the Roman Catholic clergy to institute a joint examination of the books used in the public schools, with a view to their expurgation from every thing obnoxious to Catholic censure; but these overtures have not, the trustees regret to say, been met in the spirit in which they were made. Within the present year, a committee was appointed by the Board of Trustees to "examine the books in use in the public schools, including those in the libraries, with a view to ascertain and report whether they contain any thing derogatory to the Roman Catholic Church or any of its religious tenets, with power to communicate with such persons of that Church as may be authorized to meet them in reference to such alterations." An interview was accordingly procured with a dignitary of the Catholic Church, which, after a full and apparently a frank interchange of views, resulted in his consenting to receive a copy of each book used in the public schools, and an understanding that he would communicate with the committee when he had examined them.

Pending this effort to reconcile conflicting opinions and views, and before any communication is made to the committee, the Catholic press teems with misrepresentations of the public schools and abuse of the trustees, which are followed up by the address now under review; and that, too, after positive assurances had been given that every thing should be removed from the school-books to which they might see fit to object.

It is, therefore, evident that no expurgation—nothing of a mere negative character—will satisfy the Roman Catholic clergy. If the doctrines of their Church be not taught, nothing can be which they would not pronounce heretical, and "adverse to Christianity." Even the Holy Scriptures are sectarian and dangerous, "without note or comment;" and certainly no comments would be acceptable other than those of their own Church. The address does, indeed, declare, that "if the public schools could have been constituted on a principle which would have secured a perfect neutrality of influence on the subject of religion," then they would have no reason to complain; but in the same paragraph, they are careful to declare that such consummation is impossible. And why impossible? we would ask, unless one of the parties enters upon the undertaking with feelings of exclusiveness which forbid a compromise.

It is known that a large portion of the bishops and clergy of the Established and other Protestant Churches, and a majority of the Roman Catholic bishops of Ireland, have agreed upon a general system of education, and a collection of extracts from the Sacred Scriptures, for the national schools of that country. At the conference just referred to, the question was distinctly put, whether the objection of the Catholic clergy to the public schools, so far as regards reading the Scriptures without note or comment, would be removed by the use of these extracts in them? The answer was, that the dissenting bishops had appealed to the pope against the majority of their body, and, as His Holiness had not yet settled the question, he was not prepared to give an answer. The trustees very much regret that circumstances have placed them in a situation which renders this exposition necessary. But they could not do less, and discharge their duty to themselves and the public.

It now remains to speak of the real causes of complaint which the Roman Catholics have against the public schools. The books selected for the children have, from the first, been those used and most highly esteemed as school-books. The passages objected to, or nearly all of them, are historical, and relate to what is generally called the Reformation. The writers were Protestants, and took a view of the men and incidents of that excited and eventful period directly opposed to those entertained by the members of the Roman Catholic Church. These portions must, of course, be offensive to Catholics, and they furnish just cause of complaint. The books in all other respects are admirably adapted to the uses for which they were compiled. The objectionable passages are not numerous, but the books are not to be found without them. Had the overtures of the trustees for a joint examination been acceded to, expurgated editions would long ago have been prepared for the public schools.

The difficulty of procuring books entirely exempt from objection cannot, perhaps, be more forcibly illustrated than by the fact that one work, containing passages as liable to objection as almost any other, is now used as a class-book even in the Catholic schools. It is the intention of the trustees, nevertheless, to prosecute the work of expurgation until every just cause of complaint is removed. The use of one very excellent work has been recently suspended, until a few passages, objectionable on the ground alluded to, can be obliterated. The coöperation of the Catholic clergy is, however, very desirable, inasmuch as it is abundantly evident that the most careful and vigilant scrutiny on the part of the trustees may not enable them to detect every thing that the former would exclude.

At the same time that the trustees feel that, in yielding to the conscientious scruples of the Roman Catholics, they are bound to protect the feelings and interests of the Protestant Churches, they are even disposed to remove reading-matter to which they can see no objection, because it cannot be doubted that the fertile field of English literature will still furnish an ample supply.

A hope still lingers that every obstacle may be removed, and that their fellow-citizens of the Roman Catholic Church may be induced to permit their children to participate in the advantages which the public schools undeniably afford. For the attainment of this desirable end the trustees will make every sacrifice compatible with justice and propriety.

They remain ready and anxious to join with the Roman Catholics in efforts so to model the books and studies in the public schools as to obviate existing difficulties. They think that it may be done. But if—as was the case in the Irish national schools—an appeal to the pope should be necessary, they are free to confess, in the language of the address, that " a perfect neutrality of influence on the subject of religion " is indeed " impossible."

The trustees are strongly impressed with the importance of the religious culture of the minds of youth. The public schools are open for ordinary purposes only thirty hours in each week. Two entire days of each week may be devoted to instruction in the peculiar religious views of those whose inclination and sense of duty may prompt them to bestow the labor. Most of the public school buildings are now occupied on the Sabbath by Sunday schools. There is room for more, and the Roman Catholics have repeatedly been told that the school buildings were as open to them as to others.

Moreover, fellow-citizens, the trustees would observe that, if a portion of the school fund is given to the Roman Catholics for the support of their Church schools, it will be impossible to refuse the same boon to other Churches—in short, to all who may object, on conscientious grounds, to a general system of education. The effect would inevitably be, to destroy the present excellent establishment, and to introduce in its place innumerable small and inferior schools, in which, or in a part of them at least, the public money would be frittered away in efforts to establish in the minds of the rising generation the creeds and dogmas of each division and subdivision of the Christian Church.

In urging their rights of conscience, the Roman Catholics appear to have lost sight of the important fact, that a great proportion of their fellow-citizens would think their own rights of conscience violated in being taxed for the support of Catholic schools.

That *religion*, as a branch of study, should be excluded from the system of common school instruction, is the well-settled policy of the State; and even political men are agreed that it is scarcely of secondary importance that it should be exempted from the blighting influence of party politics. On both these points the trustees have, to the best of their ability, guarded the public school system.

In selecting teachers, no regard is had to the religious profession of the candidate. Moral character and qualifications for the important station are alone looked to. Those now employed embrace a variety of religious persuasions, including six or seven of the Roman Catholic faith.

In submitting the foregoing reply to the " Address of the Roman Catholics," the trustees of the public schools take occasion to say, that the duties they have assumed are as arduous as they are responsible. About one hundred of your fellow-citizens are engaged in this work, uniting in their number men of almost every religious persuasion and of every political party. Upon a faithful and judicious discharge of their duties depends, in no small degree, the future welfare of the city, and, to some extent, the continued prosperity of our beloved country. More than eleven thousand visits were made to the schools by the trustees during the past year. From these labors neither emolument nor honor are derived. Other and higher motives have induced the sacrifice.

Finally, the trustees invite the public, and the officers of Government, to institute a rigid examination of the present system. If a better can be devised, they will cheerfully surrender a trust which has afforded them no reward other than a consciousness of having done their duty. Without such examination, they feel assured that nothing will be done to disturb its operation.

An entire separation between Church and State is a prominent feature of our political compact. History is pregnant with the awful consequences of their union. Even in the arbitrary governments of Europe, slow as they are to correct abuses, the bands that unite them are becoming weaker and weaker; and it is confidently believed that the people of the State of New York are not prepared to take the first step in a retrograde course.

ROBERT C. CORNELL, *President*.

A. P. HALSEY, *Secretary*.

NEW YORK, *August* 27, 1840.

G.

September 15, 1840.

TO THE RIGHT REV. DR. HUGHES:

The committee of the Trustees of the Public School Society to whom has been assigned the duty of causing the school-books used in the public schools to be expurgated of the passages containing sentiments obnoxious to the Roman Catholic Church, have made some progress in their labors, and, having learned that the agent of the Board of Trustees placed in your hands, a short time since, at your request, copies of the various books used, for your examination, the committee are desirous of receiving from you, at your earliest convenience, a detailed specification of every passage by you deemed objectionable.

The committee are anxious to avoid the necessity of repeating the labor and expense of expurgation; and, being aware that many sentiments and opinions may be by you deemed exceptionable that would not strike the eye of a Protestant, however sincerely desirous of meeting your views, they feel the more in haste to be possessed of the result of your labors.

It is a source of regret to the committee that the Very Rev. Dr. Power, who was furnished, some months since, with copies of the books, has not communicated the result of his examination to them; and the committee will take the liberty of suggesting that your own labor may be diminished, if you should see fit to avail yourself of whatever progress he may have made in the work.

On behalf of the committee, very respectfully,

JOSEPH B. COLLINS.

H.

NEW YORK, *September* 15, 1840.

TO JOSEPH B. COLLINS, ESQ.:

DEAR SIR: I have just received your letter of this date, in relation to the expurgation of the books used in the public schools. I am at a loss to account for the supposition, on the part of your committee, that I was engaged in the special examination of objectionable passages, with a view to assist the committee in their laudable undertaking. This I should be most willing, however, to do, if my many and incessant duties left me sufficient leisure for the purpose.

I perceive, by the "Reply" of the trustees, that they are directing their attention to some of the principal passages. One of them, *unless my memory fails me*, I designated to one of your board more than eighteen months ago

—viz., the article about Huss, in "Putnam's Sequel;" and it has remained untouched up to this time.

With regard to the books which your agent had the kindness to send, I requested them through Dr. Hogan, without mentioning for what object, and never dreaming that the fact would have produced the impression that I was about to undertake the labor of a critical investigation of their contents. The committee, indeed, profess their willingness to reject whatever I shall find objectionable. But do they not promise too much? Now, the fact is, that I wished to have the books in order to see on what ground the trustees of the public schools could, consistently with facts, state, as they did before the Board of Assistant Aldermen, that the Catholics had no reason to object to the system so far as "relates to books or exercises of any kind in the public schools." This I should perhaps have stated, but the omission was purely accidental.

I have the honor to be, with great respect,

† JOHN HUGHES, *Bishop, &c.*

I.

Resolved, That it be referred to the Committee on Arts and Sciences, &c., to confer with the Commissioners of the Public Schools, and ascertain from them, and report to this board, whether any books of a sectarian character, or any books that contain any thing to the prejudice of any particular religious sect, either as to faith or church discipline, are permitted in the public schools.

NEW YORK, *May* 25, 1840.

DEAR SIR: By direction of the Committee on Arts and Sciences and Schools, of the Board of Aldermen, I have the honor to enclose to you (as above) a copy of a resolution offered by Alderman Chamberlain, and adopted at the last meeting of the Board, and to request that you will, at your earliest convenience, communicate to me, as chairman of the committee, a list of the books used in the schools established by the Public School Society.

Very respectfully yours,

DAVID GRAHAM, JR.,

Chairman of the Committee on Arts and Sciences and Schools, of the Board of Aldermen.

R. C. CORNELL,
    President of Public School Society.

J.

To DAVID GRAHAM, JR., ESQ., *Chairman of the Committee on Arts and Sciences and Schools, of the Board of Aldermen.*

The communication addressed to R. C. Cornell, President of the Public School Society of New York, under date of May 25, was laid before the Executive Committee of the Board of Trustees at its monthly meeting held on June 4, and then referred to a committee appointed at a previous meeting on the very subject referred to by you. This is mentioned in order to account for what might otherwise appear to be an unnecessary delay in responding to your note. I would premise that it has ever been the intention of the trustees of the public schools to divest them, as far as practicable, of every thing of a sectarian character; and we are not aware that any of the books used in them have been deemed objectionable by any Church or society of religious purposes except the Roman Catholics.

It has been known and lamented for years that the clergy of this Church have discouraged the attendance of the children of its members at the public schools; and in 1834, a committee was appointed to wait on Bishop Dubois for the purpose of removing any reasonable objection he might have to the course of studies pursued and the books used in the public schools, and to assure him of the wish of the trustees to alter or discontinue the use of any book against which a reasonable objection may lay, and at the same time to invite the coöperation in the management of the public schools of any lay member of the Catholic Church who feels an interest in the literary and moral culture of youth. This committee made a full report, embracing all the points insisted on by the bishop as necessary to induce him to recommend the attendance of Catholic children at the public schools. Your committee will be furnished with a copy of this report, if desired; but it may be sufficient to remark, that, to comply with all his propositions, would have been to divest the schools of their neutral character, and make them such as would necessarily have excluded the children of Protestant parents. To this, of course, the trustees could not assent.

Desirous of doing all they could to induce the attendance of Catholic children, a teacher professing that faith was employed as principal of school No. 5, which is located near the cathedral in Mott street. This experiment did not, however, answer the expectations of the trustees. The subject was again brought before the board by a verbal communication from the Rev. Mr. Varela, through one of the trustees. Whereupon the following proceedings were had, as appears by the minutes, from which the following are extracts:

"The Vice-President stated that the Rev. Mr. Varela, of the Roman Catholic Church, had sent a request to be furnished with a set of the reading-books used in the public schools; whereupon it was

"*Resolved*, That the secretary be requested to send a copy of each of said books to Mr. Varela, for his inspection. It was also unanimously *Resolved*, That this board continues to entertain an anxious desire to remove every objection which the members of the Catholic Church may have to the books used, or the studies pursued, in the public schools, and that the secretary be requested to renew the assurance given on a former occasion, that any suggestion or remarks which the Rev. Mr. Varela may deem it right to make on his own behalf, and that of his associates, after said books have been examined, shall receive the most serious and respectful consideration of this board.

"*Resolved*, further, That a copy of these resolutions be sent with the books referred to."

After a full opportunity to examine the books, a letter, of which the following is a copy, was received from the above-named gentleman:

NEW YORK, *April* 8, 1840.

DEAR SIR: I received the books you had the kindness of sending to me, according to a resolution of the Board of Trustees of the Common Schools, in consequence of an information given by one of them as to my wish of examining said books. I thank the Board of Trustees for this mark of good feeling, and, in order to comply with their request, I will express my opinion on the subject.

The "Scripture Lessons" present, in the very title-page, an attack against the Catholic Church; for it is expressly stated that they are *without note or comment*, so as to call the attention of a child, and to tell him, "Your Church is wrong in giving the Bible always with notes; disregard her, and read the Scriptures without any note or comment, and find out a religion for yourself." This is to establish at once the Protestant fundamental principle, and to make the public schools completely sectarian.

In the Geography (p. 143), it is said "that the Catholic clergy, who have vast influence, oppose the diffusion of general knowledge ; " and in the very next page it is said that " Catholics pay very great reverence to the priests." It is very easy to perceive that a child will think very little of such a reverence, and lose every regard for such a ministry.

There are also, in the description of Italy, some passages which evidently tend to diminish the consideration that a Catholic child has for the Catholic Church. I also noticed in the reading-book the description of the character of Luther, with some expressions which, no doubt, will please the Protestants, but imply an attack against the Catholic Church. By making these few observations, I do not allude to the question as to the petition made by the Catholics to obtain a part of the school funds, but I merely respond to the kindness of the Board of Trustees in sending me the books for examination.

With great respect, your obedient

FELIX VARELA.

To A. P. HALSEY, *Secretary, &c.*

Your committee will be enabled to estimate the importance he attempts to attach to the notes on the title-page of the " Scripture Lessons." We can only say that the trustees had not the most remote intention of conveying the ideas or suggestions intimated in Dr. Varela's letter.

The next objectionable passage occurs in Maltebrun's Geography, and it is certainly obnoxious to the charge made, as there is no way of removing this passage effectually, except by printing an edition expressly for the public schools ; and as this Geography is, in all other respects, much preferable to any other extant, the trustees have permitted the use of the present edition without having, in several years, thought of applying a remedy. By way of apology, or at least in extenuation of this neglect, it may not be improper to state that the same book, with the passage objected to, is now used in the Catholic schools in this city. As the remaining objections referred to by Dr. Varela are too general and indefinite to admit of a specific note here, we will proceed to state that the whole subject was again brought before the Board of Trustees at a meeting held last month, when the following proceedings took place :

" The secretary read a letter from the Rev. Dr. Varela, in reply to a communication made to him by order of the board, with a set of the books used in the schools, whereupon it was

" *Resolved*, That a committee of five be appointed, to examine the books in use in the public schools, including those in the libraries, with a view to ascertain and report whether they contain any thing derogatory to the Roman Catholic Church or any of its religious tenets, with power to communicate with such persons of that Church as may be authorized to meet them in reference to such alterations.

" Messrs. J. S. Rogers, Collins, Mott, J. F. Depeyster, and Hogan, were appointed as the committee."

At an early day after its appointment, the committee addressed a note to Dr. Power, the Vicar-General, requesting an interview with himself and others, for the purpose of discussing the subject referred to the committee. Such an interview took place on the 14th of last month, and resulted, after an open and frank interchange of views, in a request on the part of Dr. Power, that he might be furnished with a copy of each book used in the public schools. This request was promptly complied with.

The books are now undergoing the careful review of a well-qualified member of the committee ; but inasmuch as there are doubtless passages which might not appear objectionable to the committee, but which the jealous watchfulness and the religious duty of the Vicar-General would alike prompt him to detect, and as the committee is sincerely desirous of removing every obstacle to the attendance of Catholic children at the public schools, it was thought best to omit reporting to the board till ample time is afforded the objectors for investigation.

That the committee of the Common Council may be placed in possession of every fact and circumstance connected with this deeply interesting subject, it may be proper to add that, among the works passed upon and sanctioned by the Book Committee, the Executive Committee, and the Board of Trustees, as being suitable for the school library, was a collection of entertaining and highly moral stories entitled, " Temperance Tales." These tales proved so popular, that the publishers were induced to issue volume after volume; and the gentleman charged with the duty of procuring for the library all books ordered by the board, supposing that he was authorized to purchase the volumes issued subsequently to the date of the order, introduced into the library one volume which was afterward found to contain a story that is deemed objectionable by the Catholic clergy. This volume has been removed from all the school libraries.

In conclusion, the committee of the Board of Trustees take occasion to renew the assurance, that every thing in their power shall be done to divest the public schools of a sectarian character or bias.

The committee accompanied their report to the Board of Trustees with a specification of some of the passages which they deemed exceptionable. They are as follows :

New York Reader.—Page 205, erase last paragraph.

English Reader.—Page 51, strike out paragraph, " the Queen's bigoted zeal," &c., to " eternal welfare." Page 152, erase, " the most credulous monk in a Portuguese convent."

Sequel, Murray's.—The whole article, " Life of Luther." Pages 84 and 85, paste up " Execution of Cranmer." Page 279, erase, " and anon in penance, planning sins anew."

Putnam's Sequel.—Erase the article, " John Huss."

Maltebrun's Geography.—Page 111, erase first five lines. Page 123, erase last paragraph, chapter 134. Page 140, erase five lines from the top, " and there is no doubt the lower classes of Ireland are so." Page 145, erase, " inflict the most horrible tortures." Page 148, erase, " Italy to be submitted to the Catholic bishop." Page 155, erase, " from their religion," down to " ceremonies."

Hale's History of the United States.—Page 11, erase, " from the persecution of the Catholics," section 22.

Scripture Lessons.—Erase, in the title-page, the words, " without note or comment."

The revision and expurgation of the books was continued under the direction of the board, and all the objectionable passages were either stamped with ink from a wooden block, or the leaves pasted together or removed, or a volume discontinued as a text-book or library-book. This course, however, on the part of the trustees, was not satisfactory, and did not in the least abate the demands of the applicants for a separate provision to be made for their schools from the school fund, and the controversy subsequently became more animated than ever before. The mutilated volumes were gradually worn out and rendered unfit for use, and were replaced by new books, which were permitted to go into the schools without change or expurgation, and the discussion in reference to the text-books subsided. The action of the trustees was understood by a large portion of the public to have been in obedience to the direction and demands of the Catholic clergy; and at the meeting of the Society held November 6, 1840, the following declaration was submitted for adoption by the board:

In consequence of unfounded rumors prevalent in the city, the Trustees of the New York Public School Society deem it proper to state that the obliterations in the books used in the public schools have been made under their direction, from an earnest desire to remove, as far as possible, all obstacles to the coöperation of every portion of the community with them in the business of public education. They further deem it proper to state, that this matter of expurgation has been long a subject of consideration with them, and has only been delayed for the reasons set forth in their address now before the public.

After some discussion had upon this declaration, it was laid upon the table, where it was allowed to remain, and the agitation ceased.

CHAPTER XII.

THE SCHOOL CONTROVERSY OF 1841-1842.

Meeting of Roman Catholics at Washington Hall—Addresses by Rev. Dr. Power and Bishop Hughes—Central Committee Appointed—Ward Meetings and Committees —Petitions to the Legislature—Hon. John L. O'Sullivan's Bill—Action of the House of Assembly—Action in the Senate—Governor Seward's Message—Remonstrance from the City of New York—Hon. John C. Spencer—Report on the School Question—The Committee on Literature—Speech of Hiram Ketchum—Memorial and Remonstrance of the Public School Society—Proceedings in the Senate—Speech of Bishop Hughes—Public Meetings of Catholics—Election of Members of the Legislature—Roman Catholic Ticket Nominated. NOTE.—The *Journal of Commerce*—Review by one of its Contributors—Roman Catholic Excommunications—Bishop Hughes—Tristam Shandy.

THE proceedings before the Common Council relative to the claims of the Roman Catholics, were terminated by the vote adopting the report of the committee, submitted on the 11th of January, 1841. The result, although foreseen, was so decided in its character—only one member of the board having voted in the negative—that it gave little ground for expectation that the grievances complained of would be removed by that body. The committee of the Catholics, to whom the general care of the whole matter had been entrusted, accordingly called a meeting at Washington Hall, in Broadway, corner of Reade street, to be held on the 11th of February.

A crowded auditory assembled on the occasion, when THOMAS O'CONNOR, Esq., was called to the chair, Francis Cooper and Gregory Dillon were named as vice-presidents, and B. O'Connor and Edward Shortill, secretaries.

Rev. Dr. Power made the opening address, followed by Bishop Hughes, at the close of which, on motion of Dr. Hogan, it was

Resolved, That it is expedient to form a Central Committee, to be called " The Central Executive Committee on Common Schools."

James W. McKeon, Hugh Sweeney, M.D., Robert Hogan,

M.D., James W. White, and Thomas O'Connor, were named as the committee.

On motion of James W. White, it was

Resolved, That it is expedient to call meetings in each ward, for the purpose of giving public expression to our sentiments in disapprobation of the public school system as at present existing in New York.

On motion of T. L. Danaher, it was

Resolved, That the ward meetings be respectfully recommended to appoint committees in their respective wards, for the purpose of obtaining signatures to a memorial to the honorable the Legislature, praying for such modification in the school system of this city and county as will afford to persons of every denomination, without violation of their conscience, the advantages of the common school education provided by the bounty of the State.

On motion of Hugh Sweeney, M.D., it was

Resolved, That a committee of two shall be appointed by the meetings in each ward, whose duty it shall be to communicate with and to carry into effect in their respective wards the measures which may be recommended by the Central Executive Committee.

The resolutions were approved and adopted with great enthusiasm ; and a resolution tendering the thanks of the meeting to Alderman Pentz, for his " independent and honorable conduct in voting against the report of the committee," was received with the most lively and earnest demonstrations of applause.

The movement on the part of the Roman Catholics was thus fully organized, and the committees proceeded with great zeal and unanimity in the discharge of their several duties. Meetings were held, petitions were circulated, and signatures obtained to the number of about seven thousand. Mr. Joseph O'Connor, on behalf of the committee, proceeded to Albany, and placed the memorial in the hands of Hon. Gulian C. Verplanck, a member of the New York delegation in the Senate, who promised to present it to that body at the earliest day. Subsequent conferences between influential parties led to the adoption of another course, as the presentation of the memorials from Roman Catholics as a religious body was deemed inexpedient. They were returned to the committees of the Catholics, amended, and again placed in the hands of the Senator in the form of petitions from " CITIZENS OF NEW YORK."

On Saturday, March 13, Mr. John L. O'Sullivan, a member of the Assembly from New York, gave notice that he would, on some future day, ask leave to introduce a bill, entitled, "An Act to Extend.and Improve the Benefits of Common School Education in the City of New York." On Monday following, he asked and obtained leave to introduce his bill, which was read the first time, and, by unanimous consent, was read the second time. Mr. O'Sullivan then moved that the bill be referred to a select committee, consisting of the members of the House representing the city of New York. Mr. Bryson moved that it be referred to the Standing Committee on Colleges, Academies, and Schools; and, debate arising on the several motions, the subject was laid on the table under the rules.

On Saturday, the 20th of March, Mr. O'Sullivan called up the question, on the motion of Mr. Bryson, to refer his bill to the Committee on Colleges, &c., upon which some discussion was had, when the Speaker put the question whether the House would agree with the motion of Mr. Bryson, and it was decided in the affirmative, and the bill was accordingly referred. The committee consisted of William Duer, of Oswego, William B. Maclay, of New York, Levi Hubbell, of Tompkins, Isaac N. Stoddard, of Genesee, and Edmund Elmendorf, of Dutchess.

On Tuesday, March 30, Mr. O'Sullivan offered a resolution that the Standing Committee on Colleges, Academies, and Schools be discharged from the consideration of the bill relative to common schools in the city of New York, and that the same be referred to a select committee. Mr. Shaw moved to amend the resolution, by adding, at the end, the words, " consisting of the delegation attending this House from the city and county of New York." Mr. Culver moved to amend the amendment, by striking out all after the words " consisting of," and inserting the words, " the mover of this resolution." Mr. W. F. Brodhead moved to lay the whole question on the table, which was lost, and a long debate ensued, pending which the House adjourned.

On Thursday, April 1, Mr. O'Sullivan called up his resolution of reference to a select committee. The resolution was read, together with the amendments, when Mr. Culver withdrew his amendment, and the Speaker put the question on the amendment of Mr. Shaw, to refer to the members of the New York delegation, which was agreed to by the House.   The gentlemen comprising the delegation at that session were the following: William B. Maclay, Paul Grout, Norman Hickok, Edmund J. Porter, Cornelius H. Bryson, Solomon Townsend, George Weir, David R. Floyd Jones, Absalom A. Miller, Conrad Swackhamer, William McMurray, Abraham B. Davis, and John L. O'Sullivan.

On the 21st of the same month, the remonstrance of citizens of New York, against diverting the school fund from its legitimate objects was received from the Senate, and referred to the same committee.   The House adjourned without hearing any report on the matter, and the narrative of proceedings in the Senate will not be interrupted by the action of the Assembly.

After the organization of the Senate, the various topics of the message of Hon. William H. Seward, the Governor, were referred to appropriate committees, and so much as related to colleges, academies, and common schools, the school fund, the literature fund, and the United States deposit fund, was referred to the Committee on Literature.   This committee was composed of Erastus Root, of Delaware, John Hunter, of Westchester, and Gulian C. Verplanck, of New York.

Mr. Seward's recommendations are contained in the following extract from his message :

Previous to 1802, no foreigner could be naturalized until after a residence of fourteen years.   No one has better understood the tendency of republican institutions, or entertained more just views of the principles upon which they were founded, than the illustrious citizen who in that year recommended to Congress an amelioration of the naturalization laws.   " Considering the ordinary chances of human life," he observed, " a denial of citizenship under a residence of fourteen years is a denial to a great portion of those who ask it, and controls a policy pursued from their first settlement by many of the States, and still believed to be of consequence to their prosperity.   And shall we refuse the unhappy fugitives from distress that hospitality which the savages of the wilderness extended to our fathers arriving in this land ?   Shall oppressed humanity find no asylum on the globe ?   The Constitution has wisely provided that, for admission to certain offices of trust, a residence shall be required sufficient to develop character and design.   But might not the general character and capabilities of a citizen be safely communicated to every one manifesting a *bonâ-fide* purpose of embarking his life and fortunes with us ? "   In concurrence with these suggestions, Congress passed the act now in force concerning naturalization. Probably half a million of persons have, since that time, complied with its provisions, and secured to themselves the rights of citizenship ; and there

23

cannot now be less than half that number of electors of foreign birth in the United States. This class is largely increasing. The number of emigrants arriving at the port of New York, in 1828, was about twenty thousand. The number in 1840 was sixty-one thousand. Although the liberal and enlightened opinions of Jefferson have been the settled policy of the country for almost forty years, yet an issue is still maintained upon those opinions between a portion of our fellow-citizens and those to whom the law, passed in conformity with those sentiments, has given a full participation in our political rights and privileges. Hence arise mutual jealousies. The consequences of these jealousies are seen in the separation and alienation of classes having common interests; in the misfortunes of the weaker, in apprehensions of insecurity on the part of the stronger, and in the demoralization of portions of both; in frauds at elections, and fraudulent proceedings under the naturalization laws. The policy and measures which I have recommended have heretofore had for their object the elevation of the social condition of emigrants, and the assimilation of their habits, principles, and opinions with our own.

Not much, however, can be accomplished by legislation to affect the relations between masses of adult citizens, and the change desired in this respect must be left chiefly to time and the operation of our institutions. But it is not so in regard to the rising generation. The census of the United States is said to show that there are forty-three thousand eight hundred and seventy-one white persons in this State who have passed the age of twenty-one years without having learned to read and write. Let us make any allowance for any portion of adult foreigners, and there yet remains a large number of uneducated native citizens. The number of children now growing up in the same manner does not fall short of thirty thousand. These are the offspring, not of prosperity and affluence, but of poverty and misfortune. Knowing, from the records of our penitentiaries, that, of this neglected class, those are often most fortunate who, from precocity in vice, secure admission into the House of Refuge or the State Prison, through the ways of crime; and knowing, too, that almost every application for pardon is urged on the ground of neglected education, I have felt it an imperative duty to appeal to the Legislature to render our system of education as comprehensive as the purposes for which it was established. Of one thousand and fifty-eight children in the Almshouse of the city of New York, one sixth part is of American parentage, one sixth part was born abroad, and the remainder are the children of foreigners; and of two hundred and fifty children in the House of Refuge, more than one half were either born abroad, or of foreign parents. The poverty, misfortunes, accidents, and prejudices to which foreigners are exposed, satisfactorily account, to my mind, for the undue proportion of their children in the neglected class to which the attention of the Legislature was called. Although the excellent public schools in the city of New York are open to all, and have long afforded gratuitous instruction to all who seek it, nevertheless the evil there exists in its greatest magnitude. Obviously, therefore, something more is necessary to remove it than has yet been done, unless we assume that society consents to leave it without a remedy. These circumstances led me to the reflection, that possibly a portion of those whom other efforts had failed to reach might be brought within the nurture of the schools, by employing for their instruction teachers who, from their relations toward them, might be expected to secure their confidence. When the census of 1850 shall be taken, I trust it will show that, within the borders of the State of New York, there is no child of sufficient years who is unable to read and write. I am sure it will then be acknowledged, that when, ten years before, there were thirty thousand children growing up in ignorance and vice, a suggestion to seek them wherever found, and win them to the ways of knowledge and virtue by persuasion, sympathy, and kindness, was prompted by a sincere desire for the common good. I have no pride of opinion concerning the manner in which the education of those whom I have brought to your notice shall be secured, although I might derive satisfaction from the reflection that, amid abundant misrepresentations of the method suggested, no one has contended that it would be ineffectual, nor has any other plan been proposed. I observe, on the contrary, with deep regret, that the evil remains as before: and the question recurs, not merely how, or by whom, shall instruction be given, but whether it shall be given at all, or be altogether withheld. Others may be content with a system that erects free schools and offers gratuitous instruction; but I trust I shall be allowed to entertain the opinion, that no system is perfect which does not accomplish what it proposes; that our system, therefore, is deficient in comprehensiveness in the exact proportion of the children that it leaves uneducated; that knowledge, however acquired, is better than ignorance; and that neither error, accident, nor prejudice, ought to be permitted to deprive the State of the education of her citizens. Cherishing such opinions, I could not enjoy the consciousness of having discharged my duty, if any effort had been omitted which was calculated to bring within the schools all who are destined to exercise the rights of citizenship; nor shall I feel that the system is perfect, or liberty safe, until that object be accomplished. Not personally concerned about such misapprehensions as have arisen, but desirous to remove every obstacle to the accomplishment of so important an object, I verily declare that I seek the education of those whom I have brought before you, not to perpetuate any prejudices or distinctions which deprive them of instruction, but in disregard of all such distinctions and prejudices. I solicit their education less from sympathy, than because the welfare of the State demands it, and cannot dispense with it. As native citizens, they are born to the right of suffrage. I ask that they may at least be taught to read and write; and, in asking this, I require no more for them than I have diligently endeavored to secure to the inmates of our penitentiaries, who have forfeited that inestimable franchise by crime, and also to an unfortunate race which, having been plunged by us into degradation and ignorance, has been excluded from the franchise by an arbitrary property qualification incongruous with all our institutions. I have not recommended, nor do I seek, the education of any class in foreign languages or in particular creeds or faiths; but fully believing, with the author of the Declaration of Independence, that even error may be safely tolerated where reason is left free to combat it, and therefore indulging no apprehensions from the influence of any language or creed among an enlightened people. I desire the education of the entire rising generation in all the elements of knowledge we possess, and in that tongue which is the common language of our countrymen. To me, the most interesting of all our republican institutions is the common school. I seek not to disturb in any manner its peaceful and assiduous exercises, and, least of all, with contentions about faith or forms. I desire the education of all the children in the commonwealth in morality and virtue, leaving matters of conscience where, according to the principles of civil and religious liberty established by our Constitution and laws, they rightfully belong.

On February 24th, the President laid before the Senate a remonstrance from citizens of New York, against any diversion of the school fund from its legitimate objects, which was read, and laid on the table.

Petitions were put in circulation among the citizens of New York, by those favorable to an alteration of the school system, and, a respectable number of signatures having been obtained, the memorial was forwarded to Mr. Verplanck, who presented the same to the Senate, on the 29th of March. The paper was read, and referred to the Secretary of State, Hon. John C. Spencer, who was also at that time, by law, Superintendent of Common Schools.

The Secretary gave immediate attention to the important subject committed to his care, and, on April 26th, his report was laid before the Senate, read, and referred to the Committee on Literature. The following is the report:

IN SENATE, *April* 26, 1841.

REPORT

Of the Secretary of State upon Memorials from the City of New York, respecting the Distribution of the Common School Moneys in that City, referred to him by the Senate.

To the Honorable the Senate:

The Secretary of State, to whom have been referred by the Senate, during the last and present sessions, numerous petitions on the subject of the application of that portion of the public school moneys which is distributed in the city of New York, RESPECTFULLY REPORTS:

The memorials presented at the present session represent, that the legislative enactments on the subject of public instruction in the city of New York require a fundamental alteration to bring the benefits of common school education within the reach of all classes of the population; that the original intent of these enactments was to enable every school, which should comply with the law, to share in the common school fund; that this design has been defeated by the construction put upon the statutes by the Common Council of the city, in designating the Public School Society to receive nearly the whole amount of the fund belonging to the city; that this Society, being a corporation, has acquired the entire control of the system of public education; that the taxpayers, who contribute to the fund, have no voice in the selection of those who administer the system, or control over the application of the public moneys. They deprecate the influence of such a corporation, and consider it dangerous and detrimental to the public interests, while it is wanting in responsibility to the people. They complain also of injustice to those whose conscientious scruples they allege have been disregarded in the system of instruction adopted by that Society. They represent that there are other schools in the city equally entitled to partake in the bounty of the State, but which, with nearly eight thousand children, are excluded from any of its benefits under the present system. They pray that every school established by the taxable inhabitants of the city may be entitled to a distributive share of the public school moneys; and that the persons to control and administer the system of public instruction in the city may be appointed by the electors and taxable inhabitants.

At the last session, memorials of a similar character from a large number of Roman Catholic citizens of New York were referred to the undersigned, upon which he was unable, during that session, to report. Although these citizens have the same equal and common rights with all other citizens to submit their grievances to the Legislature and ask for redress, yet the circumstance of presenting themselves in the character of a religious denomination is, in itself, unfavorable to that impartial consideration of the subject which its importance demands. The hazard is incurred of giving to a question broad as the whole territory of our State, and comprehending all its inhabitants, an aspect of peculiarity, as if it concerned only those who presented their complaints. But great injustice would be done to the subject by this mode of considering it. It embraces interests vital to the well-being of the whole community; it involves the destiny of thousands upon thousands of the children of the republic, who are hereafter to take their share in the management of its affairs, and are to become good citizens or miserable outcasts—who are to sustain the laws and assist in the preservation of peace and good order, or to fill our dungeons and prisons, and occupy our scaffolds. In the contemplation of such results, the denominations and parties into which society is divided cannot be regarded, except so far as a just and well-ordered government is bound to protect, equally and impartially, the civil and political rights of all.

It is essential to the proper consideration of the subject, to understand the history of the legislation that has been had in reference to it; and particularly in relation to the Public School Society of the city of New York.

The first law relating to that portion of the school moneys apportioned to and raised in the city of New York, was passed in 1813, and will be found in the first volume of the Revised Laws of that year, at p. 267. It directed those moneys to be distributed " to the Trustees of the Free-School

Society, the Orphan Asylum Society, the Economical School, the African Free School, and the trustees of such incorporated religious societies in said city as now support, or hereafter shall establish, charity schools within the said city, who may apply for the same."

The act directed that the sum thus distributed should be applied to the payment of the wages of the teachers, and to no other purpose whatever. As these were all charity schools, it is obvious that the Legislature intended that the school moneys apportioned to the city, as well as those raised by tax, should be consecrated to the education exclusively of the indigent. Under this act, apportionments were annually made to the schools enumerated, and to those established by some eight or ten of the religious denominations, until the year 1824. By chapter 276 of the Session Laws of that year, the above-mentioned act was repealed, and the Common Council of the city was authorized to designate "the societies or schools which should be entitled to receive a share of the school moneys, and prescribe the rules and restrictions under which such moneys shall be received by such societies or schools respectively." Pursuant to this act, the Common Council have designated the schools of the Public School Society, and six or eight other schools, to which all the public moneys have, since 1826, been distributed, with some variations in different years as to the other schools. From the annual reports and other documents, a statement has been compiled, from which it appears that more than one million dollars has been paid to the trustees of the Society, under its different names, since 1813, out of the public moneys appropriated by the State, and raised by tax on the city for school purposes, and that $125,248.57, have been paid to the other schools before mentioned.

The Public School Society was originally incorporated in 1805, by chapter 108 of the laws of that session, which is entitled "An Act to Incorporate the Society instituted in the City of New York, for the establishment of a free school for the education of poor children who do not belong to, or are not provided for by, any religious society." In 1808, its name was changed to "The Free-School Society of New York," and its powers were extended "to all children who are the proper subject of a gratuitous education." By chapter 25 of the laws of 1826, its name was changed to "The Public School Society of New York," and the trustees were authorized to provide for the education of all children in the city of New York not otherwise provided for, "whether such children be or be not the proper subjects of gratuitous education;" and to require from those attending the schools a moderate compensation; but no child to be refused admission on account of inability to pay.

Thus, by the joint operation of the acts amending the charter of the Society, of the statutes in relation to the distribution of the school moneys, and of the ordinance of the Common Council, designating the schools of the Society as the principal recipients of those moneys, the control of the public education of the city of New York, and the disbursement of nine tenths of the public moneys raised and apportioned for schools were vested in this corporation. It is a perpetual corporation, and there is no power reserved by the Legislature to repeal or modify its charter. It consists of members who have contributed to the funds of the Society; and, according to the provisions of the last act, the payment of ten dollars constitutes the contributor a member for life. The members annually choose fifty trustees, who may add to their number fifty more.

In the last report of the Commissioners for School Money in the City and County of New York, dated in July, 1840, it is stated that " the number of schools subject to the visitation of the commissioners has increased to one hundred and fifteen; of these, ninety-eight are under the direction of the Public School Society." The same report states that the average number of scholars *on the registers* of these schools during the year was 22,955, and the average number of scholars *attending* them during the year was 13,189. This great disparity between the number registered and the number attending is accounted for by the absences and irregular attendance of the pupils.

Although the undersigned cannot find any provision by which the schools of the Society are placed under the visitation and supervision of the Superintendent of Common Schools, yet he would have undertaken a personal examination of them, if the pressure of his public duties and other circumstances beyond his control, would have permitted.

Several gentlemen of the city, eminently qualified, were, however, selected for that purpose; and they have diligently conducted a laborious inquiry, and submitted to the undersigned a mass of valuable information. The results of these examinations show very satisfactorily that commodious houses and good teachers are provided by the Public School Society; that the system of instruction is well devised and faithfully executed; that an efficient plan of visitation and inspection is prescribed by the trustees; and, although he has not positive information on the subject, he has no reason to doubt that such plan is carried into practical execution. Certain it is, that the trustees of the Society have exhibited the most praiseworthy zeal and devotion in the discharge of the great trust devolved on them; and many, if not all of them, have spared no exertions to bring into their schools the destitute children of the city.

The undersigned has supposed that, for the purpose of this report, this general view of the condition of the schools of that Society would be more useful than to encumber it with the large amount and great variety of details which have been collected. To the gentlemen who visited the schools and obtained the desired information, and to the officers of the Society, who have cheerfully rendered every assistance, he would take this occasion to express the obligations of the public, and his own.

Notwithstanding these favorable results of the efforts of the Public School Society, the memorials referred to the undersigned complain of the operation of a system which, in fact, devolves upon any private corporation the discharge of one of the most important functions of the government, without that responsibility to the people which is provided in all other cases. They allege that, in its administration, the conscientious opinions and feelings of large classes of citizens are disregarded; that other schools, maintained for the same objects and accomplishing the same benevolent results, are arbitrarily excluded from all participation in a common fund collected by the joint contributions of all; and that a fearfully large portion of the indigent children are not reached, or in any way benefited by the system of public education which now prevails. These are objections of the most weighty character, and cannot be overlooked by those whose duty and inclination alike prompt them to regard the greatest good of the greatest number. The merits of the Public School Society, the devotion and energy of its trustees, and the success of its schools, cannot and ought not to prevent an investigation to ascertain whether it is necessarily limited in its operation; whether it accomplishes the main purposes of its organization; or whether its continuance violates essential and fundamental principles, and thus presents a perpetual source of irritation and complaint. The question to be determined is far more broad and comprehensive than the merits of any particular society. It involves the inquiry whether the intentions of the Legislature have been fulfilled, to furnish the means of education "to all those who are destined to exercise the rights of citizenship."

There are numerous other schools in the city of New York, founded by voluntary associations, in which many thousands of the children of poverty and distress receive their education, imperfect and deficient as it may be in many instances. By a participation in the funds intended for the benefit of all, their means of extending the sphere of their usefulness will be augmented; and by extending to all who desire to exercise it, the right of participating in the same means, new schools may be established, and temples of education made as numerous as the nurseries of vice.

It can scarcely be necessary to say that the founders of these schools, and those who wish to establish others, have absolute rights to the benefits of a common burden; and that any system which deprives them of their just share in the application of a common and public fund, must be justified, if at all, by a necessity which demands the sacrifice of individual rights for the accomplishment of a social benefit of paramount importance.

It is presumed no such necessity can be urged in the present instance. On the contrary, the views which will be subsequently presented, afford strong ground for the belief that the education of a much larger number than now are, or under any circumstances may be expected to be, provided for by the Public School Society, or any one society, will be secured by inviting the coöperation and stimulating the exertions of all who are disposed to engage in the enterprise.

The complaint that, in the schools of the Public School Society, the conscientious opinions and feelings of large classes of our fellow-citizens are disregarded, may, at first, appear unreasonable. But when it is considered that the best of men adhere, with a tenacity proportioned to the strength and sincerity of their convictions, to those principles of religious faith upon which, in their estimation, their present and eternal welfare depends, and that they regard as the most sacred of duties the inculcation of those principles in the minds of their children, we ought not to be surprised at their anxiety to exclude all that is hostile to their views from the establishments to whose care they are invited to commit the education of their offspring. With many, the transmission of their own creeds to these objects of their affection is a part, and a most essential part, of their own religious professions; and any influences which interrupted it, would be deemed by such an invasion of their most sacred rights.

Some of the memorialists complain that the tendency of the instruction received in the schools of the Public School Society is unfavorable, if not hostile, to those principles of faith which they hold dearer than life itself; and they allege that, consistently with their views of religious duty to their children, they cannot send them to such schools.

On the other hand, those who oppose any change in the present system express their apprehensions that, by allowing to all schools a free and equal participation in the school moneys, the public funds will be applied indirectly, if not directly, to the inculcation of religious dogmas of all descriptions; and some are peculiarly apprehensive of the possible extension of certain doctrines which they deem erroneous and injurious. Thus the question of sectarian influences is mutually raised, with its usual aggravations. This is a question from the consideration of which some may feel disposed to shrink, from a vague and indefinite terror of the consequences of its discussion. But it is believed there is a mode of considering it without participating in the feelings of any side, but viewing all as having common and equal rights, and animated by the same spirit of beneficence, which will avoid conflict with every thing but prejudice, and conduct to safe and salutary conclusions.

According to the principles of our institutions, no one has the authority to determine whether the religious doctrines and sentiments of any class of our citizens be right or wrong. The immunity of the Constitution, and of an unequivocal public sentiment, is thrown around "the religious faith and profession" of all our citizens; and whether a particular creed is professed by a humble minority, or a powerful majority, can make no other difference than to excite, in the first case, the generous forbearance of those who may temporarily have the physical power to oppress, and to animate them to the strictest fidelity to their obligations. The only object which our fellow-citizens can have, is the education of all the children of the commonwealth, in literature, morality, and virtue. "No system is perfect, nor can liberty be safe, until all who are destined to exercise the rights of citizenship, are brought within the schools." "Knowledge, however acquired, is better than ignorance; and neither error, accident, nor prejudice, ought to be permitted to deprive the State of the education of her citizens."

These principles, recently promulgated by the highest executive authority in our State, have received the cordial approbation of our fellow-citizens. In approaching the subject in the same spirit which dictated them, and in endeavoring to reconcile prejudice, we must not ourselves commit the error of ascribing improper designs or erroneous principles to others. If there be error, let reason be enlightened to combat it; if there be prejudice, let the humanizing and liberalizing influences of education be brought to bear upon it. Let not error and prejudice be perpetuated, by being shut up and excluded from the light of science.

The object, then, being to procure education at all events—if not the best we could desire, at the first, yet to have education extended to all classes, in the assured hope of its continual improvement—we are to maintain the perfect equality of all our citizens in the enjoyment of their rights in determining the religious character of such instruction. Hence, the first inquiry to be made is, whether these rights can be maintained under a system which rests in any permanent body, or set of men, the control of the education of a city?

The great object to be attained is the education of the greatest number possible. If we cannot at once have that education in the most perfect form, or in the highest degree, still much is accomplished in having the good seed sown. It will not only fructify, ripen, and expand, but it will enrich the soil in which it is cast, and each successive harvest will be more rich and abundant than its predecessor. If the alternative be presented of having a limited number of schools, in which instruction of the highest grade is imparted, but from which one half the proper subjects of education are absent, or of having a large number of lower pretensions and less efficiency, but so organized and situated that all may attend, and affording strong grounds for the belief that nearly all will be gathered within them, it would seem that there ought to be no hesitation in the choice, and that the portals of knowledge ought to be at once thrown open as widely as possible, with the certainty that improvement will follow the very first elements of instruction.

It is very true that the Government has assumed only the intellectual education of the children of the State, and has left their moral and religious instruction to be given at the fireside, at the places of public worship, and at institutions which the piety of individuals may establish for the purpose. But it is believed that, in a country where the great body of our fellow-citizens recognize the fundamental truths of Christianity, public sentiment would be shocked by the attempt to exclude all instruction of a religious nature from the public schools; and that any plan or scheme of education, in which no reference whatever was had to moral principles founded on these truths, would be abandoned by all. In the next place, it is believed such an attempt would be wholly impracticable. No books can be found, no reading-lessons can be selected, which do not contain more or less of some principles of religious faith, either directly avowed or indirectly assumed. Religion and literature have become inseparably interwoven, and the expurgation of religious sentiments from the productions of orators, essayists, and poets, would leave them utterly barren.

Viewing the subject, then, practically, it may be regarded as a settled axiom in all schemes of education intended for the youth of this country, that there must be, of necessity, a very considerable amount of religious instruction. The trustees of the Public School Society have probably no more in their schools than could be well avoided, while they profess—and doubtless sincerely—their readiness to omit every thing that may be justly regarded as offensive, they yet maintain—and properly—that education is imperfect, without inculcating moral and religious principles; and hence they allow the reading of the Scriptures, or portions of them, and inculcate the leading principles of Christianity. But it is impossible to conceive how even those principles can be taught, so as to be of any value, without inculcating what is peculiar to some one or more denominations, and denied by others. For it unfortunately happens that, in the infinite diversity of opinion among those claiming to be Christians, there are but few articles of faith received by one denomination which are not rejected by another. Even the reading of the text of our common translation of the Scriptures is objected to by many, on account of its being, as they allege, erroneous and imperfect; while others deem its perusal by children, without explanation, positively injurious. Even the moderate degree of religious instruction which the Public School Society imparts must, therefore, be sectarian; that is, it must favor one set of opinions in opposition to another, or others; and it is believed that this always will be the result in any course of education that the wit of man can devise.

If these views are sound, this dilemma is produced: that, while some degree of religious instruction is indispensable, and will be had under all circumstances, it cannot be imparted without partaking, to some extent, of a sectarian character, and giving occasion for offence to those whose opinions are thus impugned. But, fortunately, there is a mode of escape from the difficulty. That mode will be found in a recurrence to the fundamental principles engrafted on our constitutions, by which no law can be passed "respecting an establishment of religion or prohibiting the free exercise thereof," and by which "the free exercise and enjoyment of religious profession and worship, without discrimination or preference, shall forever be allowed in this State, to all mankind." Those by whom our governments have hitherto been administered, have found that practical effect could be given to these principles only by scrupulously abstaining from all legislation whatever on those subjects which involved, or were in any way connected with, religious faith, profession, or instruction; and in this course of proceeding the people have found such a safeguard against oppression, such a security against the dissensions and animosities of intolerance and bigotry, and such a guarantee of peace and tranquillity, that it has been constantly, and under all vicissitudes, unanimously approved by them.

On this principle of what may be termed absolute non-intervention, may we rely to remove all the apparent difficulties which surround the subject under consideration. In the theory of the common school law which governs the whole State, except the city of New York, it is fully and entirely maintained; and in the administration of that law, it is sacredly observed. No officer, among the thousands having charge of our common schools, thinks of interposing by any authoritative direction, respecting the nature or extent of moral or religious instruction to be given in the schools. Its whole control is left to the free and unrestricted action of the people themselves, in their several districts. The law provides for the organization of districts, the election of officers, and the literary and moral qualification of teachers, and leaves all else to the regulation of those for whose benefit the system is devised. The practical consequence is, that each district suits itself, by having such religious instruction in its school as is congenial to the opinions of its inhabitants ; and the records of this department have been searched in vain for an instance of a complaint of any abuse of this authority, in any of the schools out of the city of New York. To those who will reflect on the multitude of denominations in our State widely differing from each other on subjects of such exciting interest, this result will not be more astonishing, than it will be convincing, of the wisdom of the principle of non-intervention by the State or its agents.

It is manifest that the great source of the difficulties in the city of New York arises from a violation of this principle. The practical operation of the school laws is to constitute the trustees of the Public School Society the officers and agents of the Government in the administration of the system of primary instruction in that city. That Society, in effect, engrosses the public education of the city ; and instead of operating on small masses, as in the interior, embraces the whole. In such a system the principle of non-intervention can be applied only by the total abandonment of all religious instruction. For, as is supposed to have been already shown, it is impossible to prescribe any amount of such instruction for a population of three hundred and thirteen thousand souls, without offending the religious principles of many. But if the degree and kind could be left to the choice of parents, in small masses, then the object would be obtained, with the concurrence of all, religious instruction would be imparted to the young, without encountering the feelings, prejudices, or conscientious views of any. The defect is one which, so far from being peculiar to the Public School Society, is necessarily inherent in every form of organization which places under one control large masses of discordant materials, which, from the nature of things, cannot submit to any control. If that Society had charge of the children of one denomination only, there would be no difficulty. It is because it embraces children of all denominations, and seeks to supply to them all a species of instruction which is adapted only to a part, and which, from its nature, cannot be moulded to suit the views of all, that it fails, and ever must fail, to give satisfaction on a subject of all others the most vital and the most exciting. If there is not entire fallacy in all these views—if the experience of twenty-five years, derived from the school districts of the interior, is not wholly worthless, then the remedy is plain, practical, and simple. It is by adopting the principle of the organization that prevails in the other parts of the State, which will leave such parents as desire to exercise any control over the amount and description of religious instruction which shall be given to their children, the opportunity of doing so. This can be effected by depriving the present system in New York of its character of universality and exclusiveness, and by opening it to the action of smaller masses, whose interests and opinions may be consulted in their schools, so that every denomination may freely enjoy its " religious profession " in the education of its youth.

To this plan objections have been made, that it would enable different religious denominations to establish schools of a sectarian character, and that thereby religious dissensions would be aggravated, if not generated. The first objection has already been partially considered. It is believed to have been satisfactorily shown, that there must be some degree of religious instruction, and that there can be none without partaking more or less of a sectarian character; and that even the Public School Society has not been able, and cannot expect to be able, to avoid the imputation. In this respect, then, matters cannot well be in a worse condition than they are at present. The objection itself proceeds on a sectarian principle, and assumes the power to control that which it is neither right nor practicable to submit to any denomination. Religious doctrines of vital interest will be inculcated, not as theological exercises, but incidentally, in the course of literary and scientific—and who will undertake to prohibit such instruction?

It is not perceived how religious dissensions will be aggravated. The objection supposes a particular school to belong to a particular denomination; of course, it will be in unison with it. The founders, teachers, and pupils of the different schools will act separately and independently in their respective spheres, and will not come in contact or collision with each other. A rivalry may, and probably will, be produced between them, to increase the number of pupils. As an essential means to such an object, there will be a constant effort to improve the schools in the mode and degree of instruction, and in the qualifications of the teachers. Thus, not only will the number of children brought into the schools be incalculably augmented, but the competition anticipated will produce its usual effect of providing the very best material to satisfy the public demand. These advantages will more than compensate for any possible evils that may be apprehended from having schools adapted to the feelings and views of the different denominations. The undersigned cannot but think those evils are magnified, and that the experience derived from the operation of the system in the other parts of the State effectually dispels all apprehensions of that nature. Besides, a peculiar remedy will be found, in the city of New York, from the proximity of the schools, and the opportunity thus afforded to become acquainted with any abuses by which the public moneys should be perverted to theological instruction, in place of those literary studies which should be pursued during the hours allotted to common school education. The watchfulness of those who apprehend the abuse may be relied on to detect it promptly, and to seek the needful remedy, by application to those having the power to apply it.

It is believed to be an error to suppose that the absence of all religious instruction, if it were practicable, is a mode of avoiding sectarianism. On the contrary, it would be in itself sectarian, because it would be consonant to the views of a particular class, and opposed to the views of other classes. Those who reject creeds, and resist all efforts to infuse them into the minds of the young before they have arrived at a maturity of judgment which may enable them to form their own opinions, would be gratified by a system which so fully accomplishes their purposes. But there are those who hold contrary opinions, and who insist on guarding the young against the influences of their own passions, and the contagion of vice, by implanting in their minds and hearts those elements of faith which are held by this class to be the indispensable foundations of moral principles. This description of persons regard neutrality and indifference as the most insidious forms of hostility. It is not the business of the undersigned to express any opinion on the merits of these views. His only purpose is, to show the mistake of those who suppose they may avoid sectarianism by avoiding all religious instruction.

But the schools and houses of the Public School Society ought not to be abandoned; and the inestimable benefits of its admirable arrangements and constant supervision should not be lost. Let them also be retained, and placed on the same footing with other organized schools, and allowed to participate in the public contributions in the same ratio. The character of their schools will secure them a preference with an intelligent public where no obstacles of a religious character interpose; and if all their houses cannot be filled, under teachers of their own selection, it cannot be doubted that the same benevolent spirit which has hitherto actuated the trustees, would induce them to permit their occupation by others, for a reasonable rent, or to transfer them to such associations as should desire to purchase them. The precious gems which now stud the city would thus be multiplied to an extent that can scarcely be calculated; all conscientious objections would be removed; the people themselves would become interested in the subjects of their own care and protection; a public spirit in the cause of primary education, and a desire for its improvement, would be excited and extended; a generous rivalry would be promoted; while the Public School Society would find ample scope for its benevolence in educating the children of those who approve its system, and in pursuing the original object of its institution—the gathering into its schools those who were not otherwise provided with the means of instruction.

Another prominent objection made by the memorials referred to by the undersigned is, that the existing system in New York devolves upon a private corporation the discharge of an important function of government, without a direct and immediate responsibility to the people. It is certainly an anomaly wholly unknown in any other department of the public service, that a private corporation, existing independently, not amenable in any form to the laws or to the Legislature, should be charged with what those laws regard as a part of the functions of the Government—the disbursement of the public moneys at its own will and pleasure, the selection of teachers, of whose qualification it is the sole judge, and the establishment and maintenance of a system of public education according to its own ideas of propriety. It is not subject to the supervision of the State authorities, to whom all other parts of the system of public instruction are committed. Education cannot be considered a subject of local interest in the city of New York more than in any other part of the State, although it has come to be so regarded by many, in consequence of the Legislature having devolved its own power upon the Common Council. But it is a public and common concern, of which the Government has taken cognizance, and which, for the common good of all, it is bound to see equally and fairly administered. The interest of the State is not only pecuniary, arising from the expenditure of more than $34,000, annually contributed from its own funds, but it is of a high social and political character; and every reason which should induce its guardianship and care over other portions of its territory, apply with equal force to the city of New York. Experience has shown the necessity for its interposition heretofore, without the application of the local authorities, to prevent the misapplication and waste of the school moneys.

The only species of control to which the Public School Society is subject, is that which may be found in the power of the Common Council to omit the designation of the schools of the Society to receive the funds raised for common school purposes. But, in the present condition of things, this power can, probably, never be exercised. That Society owns in fee, or has perpetual leases of, the numerous school-houses erected by means of the public school moneys, and the contributions, comparatively unimportant, of its members. If these houses should not be occupied, there would be a total want of the accommodations necessary for the public schools. The abuses must be flagrant, and wholly intolerable, which would justify the Common Council in driving into the streets the multitude of children who now occupy these houses, by withholding the public school moneys from the Society; and it may well be considered not the least among the evil consequences of the present system, that a private corporation should thus have acquired the title of what is substantially public funds and should be public property, and thus be enabled effectually to prevent the exercise of even the only semblance of control over its proceedings provided by law.

However acceptable the services of such a Society may have been in the first imperfect effort to establish common schools, however willing the people may have been to submit to an institution which promised immediate benefit, and however praiseworthy and successful may have been its efforts, yet it involves a principle so hostile to the whole spirit of our institutions, that it is impossible it should be long sustained amid the increased intelligence which its own exertions have contributed to produce, especially when other and more congenial means of attaining the same objects have been pointed out, and when, therefore, the necessity which called it into existence has ceased. The public attention is now roused to the subject, and many thousands of the citizens of New York demand the right of controlling, through responsible public agents, the education of their children, and the application of common funds to which they have contributed for a common object. We must forget that we live under a government of the people, before such a demand can be effectually resisted. Procrastination and delay will only increase its urgency, render it more exacting, and multiply the difficulties of satisfying it consistently with a just regard to the useful purposes to which the Public School Society may be applied. It must succeed, sooner or later; and it is the part of wisdom and duty to yield to that which is just in itself, promptly, and before agitation and excitement deprive acquiescence of all merit. We are not at liberty to say that our fellow-citizens who make this claim are incapable of performing the duty which they would undertake. Our constitutions admit their competency to manage all the affairs of government; and the foundation of our whole system must be overturned, before we can deny to them the capacity to determine on the mode, manner, and extent of instruction to be given to their offspring. Besides, the example of a sister city—Boston—where the managers of the public schools are, and for years have been, elected by the people in their respective wards—whose schools are equal, if not superior, to any others in our country—furnishes the most effectual answer to any apprehensions that might be indulged, from trusting the people with the selection of the agents to administer a system that so nearly concerns them. And yet in this, as in every other public business, the energies of the people require a system to regulate and conduct them to the best results. Such a system, emanating from agents of their own selection, and maintained, controlled, and superintended by them, will command the confidence and invite the coöperation of the constituents. This may be accomplished by the choice of commissioners of common schools in each ward of the city, who should form a board, to which some degree of permanency may be given by allowing the election of one third each year, which board should take the entire charge of the common schools of the city, receiving and disbursing the public funds, establishing schools and a system for their government and inspection, and providing the means of testing the qualifications of teachers. They might be aided by a city superintendent, with such compensation as should secure the best talent and the whole time of the incumbent; and then leave the schools to the management of trustees chosen by those who established them, and to the general laws of the State.

Considering the various feelings and interests that would be called into action by such a system, there can be little doubt that one of its immediate effects would be, to bring into the schools a large portion, if not the whole, of those who are now utterly destitute of instruction. With all the commendable and vigorous efforts of the trustees of the Public School Society, it cannot be denied that less than one half the children between 4 and 16 years of age, in the city of New York, are receiving the benefits of any education whatever. From the statements in the annual report of the Superintendent of Common Schools for the present year (Assembly Document No. 100), it appears that the whole number of white children in New York, in 1840, over 5 and under 16 years of age, was 62,952, and that 30,758 only are returned as attending some school, leaving 32,194 who were not in attendance on any school whatever. In a memorial of the Public School Society presented to the Legislature at its present session, it is stated that "multitudes are entirely destitute of the necessary means of acquiring the first rudiments of education, and must, unless specially provided for, grow up in gross ignorance." In the same memorial, it is alleged "that the whole extent of existing accommodations for the purpose of imparting school learning is sufficient for but about 35,000, as well in private as in public schools." The fact seems, then, undeniable, that the paramount obligation of imparting instruction to the mass of children has not been accomplished in the city of New York. That accommodations exist for a larger number than attend the schools, may be inferred from the fact already mentioned, that, while the Public School Society has registered on its books the names of children who have entered its schools to the number of 22,955, the average actual attendance of pupils amounts only to 13,189. The same inference may be drawn from the fact of the efforts made by the trustees to bring in a larger number of children than those who were registered—efforts which could not have been made if there were no room for their accommodation.

A comparison of the results obtained from statistical returns, between the numbers educated in New York and those instructed in the schools in the other parts of the State, will exhibit in a more striking manner the lamentable deficiency of the former. It appears, from the report of the Superintendent before referred to, that, while there are 592,000 children out of the city of New York between the ages of 5 and 16, there are 549,000 returned as attending the common schools. In the city of New York, the proportions were, as before stated, 62,952 children between the same ages, and 30,758 attending all schools, public as well as private. In that city, less than one tenth of the population are receiving the benefit of any instruction; while in the interior, more than one fourth of the whole population are returned as being in the public schools, without any enumeration of those placed in select schools. The like proportion must exist in the city and in the interior, of those who have already received all the education they or their parents desire, or who are engaged as apprentices, or in other employments preventing them from attending at any place of instruction. It is obvious, therefore, that the number not receiving education in the city cannot be accounted for in that manner. The probability is, that the number of those under 5 and over 16 who attend the schools, both in the city and out of it, is very nearly, if not quite, equal to the number between those ages who have received all the education they intend to attain.

With these facts before us, it must be admitted that the Public School Society has not accomplished the principal purpose of its organization, and for which the public funds have been so freely bestowed upon it—the education of the great body of the children of the city. From the remarks already made, it would seem to be manifest that the cause of this failure is not to be ascribed to the want of accommodations for the pupils; and there certainly has been no lack of exertion to induce their attendance. The trustees personally, and visitors appointed by them, have repeatedly traversed the city, to seek out the parents of the neglected children, and persuade them to avail themselves of the benefits of the schools. Tracts have been circulated, and handbills posted in every direction, for the same purpose. The city authorities have passed resolutions urging this imperative duty upon parents, and declaring that those who neglected to send their children to the schools at least some portion of the time, could not be considered proper objects of public charity. And yet the result is the same; the streets are infested with vagrant children, and "multitudes" of the youth are brought up in ignorance, and probably in vice. That there is a defect somewhere, is certain. In addition to the causes of dissatisfaction already mentioned, particularly that arising from religious feelings, it is believed that a

24

great obstacle to the efforts of the Society is to be found in the idea prevalent among the people, that an attempt is made to *coerce* them, directly or indirectly, to do something which others take a great interest in having done. They are not left, or called on, to act *spontaneously*—to *originate* any thing, or take any part in matters which they are told most deeply concern themselves. It is not a *voluntary system,* in the fullest and broadest meaning of the term. To illustrate the idea intended to be communicated, the present system may be compared to the religious establishments formed and supported by the governments of Europe, upon the plea that they are necessary to the moral instruction of the people; and that, without them, their subjects would degenerate into heathenism. It was reserved for the American people to prove the fallacy of this position. An experience of fifty years has shown that religious worship has been better provided for, and attendance upon it has been more general, by being left to the free and voluntary action of the people, without the aid of any legal establishment; in other words, without any attempt to coerce the support of religious institutions, or to compel any one to participate in their advantages. This remark is equally true of the city and of the country.

It is not intended to assert that the system of the Public School Society is like the religious establishments of Europe; but the comparison between those establishments and the practical operation of our principle of nonintervention, is instituted for the purpose of exhibiting clearly and distinctly the advantage of a voluntary system, particularly among a people governed by republican institutions. The plan of the Public School Society is, in some measure, antagonist to this system. It provides an educational establishment, and solicits the charge of children, to be placed under its exclusive control, without allowing to the parents of the pupil the direction of the course of studies, the management of the schools, or any voice in the selection of teachers; it calls for no action or coöperation on the part of those parents, other than the entire submission of their children to the government and guidance of others, probably strangers, and who are in no way accountable to these parents. Such a system is so foreign to the feelings, habits, and usages of our citizens, that its failure to enlist their confidence, and induce a desire to place their children under its control, ought not to excite surprise.

Since, then, the experiment which has been made for fifteen years, under such favorable auspices, has not accomplished its main purpose, of bringing under the control of any one private corporation the great mass of the indigent children of the city; and since it is obvious there are inherent difficulties, which will constantly accumulate, to prevent the success of such an experiment, is it not the dictate of wisdom, if not of duty, to vary the mode, and ascertain whether, by engaging the people themselves, actively and personally, in the care of the schools, a deeper and more extensive interest may not be awakened, and a larger number of children brought to the school-room? This, it is conceived, may be effected by the plan already suggested, of having schools organized, wherever required, under the jurisdiction of elected commissioners, authorized to participate in the public contributions in a just proportion. For reasons heretofore given by the undersigned, in his reports as Superintendent, he thinks these schools ought to be deemed public charities; and least of all should they have the character of a forced or compulsory charity. The same principle of apportionment which exists generally, may safely be applied to them, in proportion to the actual number of children between 5 and 16 years of age. As, in a city without regular territorial districts, that number could be ascertained only from the attendance at the schools, let such actual attendance form the basis of distribution. Let the schools be considered, like those of the State at large, as furnishing a just equivalent for moderate charges, adequate for the expense incurred beyond the public contributions; and apply the same principle which prevails in them, of authorizing the exemption from the expenses of the schools of those whose circumstances render it proper.

From the inquiries made by the gentlemen appointed for that purpose, the undersigned is satisfied that a large proportion—probably more than one half—of the pupils attending the schools of the Public School Society are children of those who are as able to pay for tuition as those persons who generally send to schools in the interior of the State. Mechanics, men who live by their daily labor, farmers, and others of very moderate property, constitute the great majority of those who pay the rate-bills for teachers' wages in the common schools. It may be justly urged as a cause of complaint, that, in the city of New York, the funds destined particularly for the benefit of the indigent are applied to the education of the children of those who are able to pay it themselves. The trustees of the Public School Society have made the effort to obtain from these persons payment of tuition charges. In the opinion of the undersigned, the principal reason for their failure is, that, with them, payment is an *exception* to the rule, instead of being the rule itself. Being declared to be free schools and charities, or being understood to be such, the individual called on for payment considers himself oppressed, in being singled out from others, whom he regards as equally bound to pay. It is probable, also, that an impression prevails that an adequate fund is provided by the State, and by city taxation, for the education of all. It is believed that, if the schools of the Society are placed on the footing already indicated, their superiority over most, if not all, of those that may be established by other associations, will enable the trustees to supply any diminution in the number of pupils caused by the establishment of other schools, from those classes of citizens who are able, and would prefer, to pay for the instruction of their children; and thus would the whole number of instructed children in the city be multiplied, and the funds of the Public School Society would, in all probability, be augmented, and rendered adequate to the highest grade and the most approved methods of instruction. If, however, contrary to those expectations, it should be found that the pay system cannot be relied on for the support of the schools, there can be no reason to doubt that the same liberal and enlightened spirit, which has heretofore induced the citizens of New York, and the Common Council, voluntarily to add to their public burdens for the great purposes of education, would continue to influence them, and would provide all the means necessary to render that city as distinguished for its care of the intellectual condition of its children, as for its wealth, enterprise, and benevolence.

The outlines of the plan submitted are as follows :

1. The election of a commissioner of common schools in each ward of the city.

2. The extension of the general school laws of the State to the city, with the modifications herein mentioned.

3. The commissioners to adopt and take under their charge the schools of the Public School Society, and the schools of the other associations and asylums now receiving the public money, as schools under their general jurisdiction, leaving the immediate government and management of them to their respective trustees and directors.

4. The commissioners to organize and establish schools in other parts of the city, wherever they can find a sufficient number of inhabitants to maintain them, as district schools, with the usual officers, to be chosen by such inhabitants, and with the usual power of districts, to hire school-rooms, provide teachers, and defray expenses by rate-bills.

5. The public school moneys to be paid directly to the commissioners by the Chamberlain of the city. Out of the amount, the compensation of a city superintendent, and of a clerk to the commissioners, and their necessary expenses, to be paid, the balance to be apportioned and distributed to the different schools under their jurisdiction, and to be applied exclusively to the payment of teachers' wages ; such apportionment to be made upon accurate lists, verified by oath, of the whole number of children between the ages of 5 and 16 actually attending the schools, to be ascertained by keeping an exact account of the number of pupils present the whole day, which, being added together and divided by 261—the number of school-days in a year, excluding Saturdays and Sundays—shall be deemed the average of attending scholars. The number of children exempted from paying tuition money and school expenses to be reported to the commissioners, with their average attendance, ascertained as before mentioned, and a sufficient sum to be apportioned in the first instance to the school in which they have attended, to make up to them respectively the amount of such exemption, if the funds be sufficient for that purpose ; and if not, then such funds to be apportioned wholly among the exempt pupils, in proportion to their attendance. If there be a surplus, then to apportion it among the remaining pupils not included in the first distribution. Provision to be made to detect and prevent improper exemptions; against which, however, an effectual safeguard will be found in the desire of the trustees to diminish the amount chargeable to pay scholars. If the public money appropriated in the first instance to the education of the indigent should not be adequate, there can be little doubt that the citizens of New York would consent to raise the additional sum required ; and, at all events, the paramount object of providing for the destitute to the greatest possible extent will have been attained.

If, after all that has been urged, the apprehension should still be indulged that any schools would be perverted to the purposes of a narrow and exclusive sectarianism during the hours allotted to instruction, instead of the proper subjects of a common school education, a remedy may be found by giving authority to the Board of Commissioners to investigate complaints of such an abuse, and, upon satisfactory evidence, dissolve the offending school, or withhold from it any share in the public school moneys.

The undersigned has thus endeavored to perform a duty unsought by him, and of which the difficulty and delicacy were fully appreciated. In its discharge, he is conscious of no other motive or object than the promotion, to the utmost possible extent, of that cause which, by official obligations as well as personal feeling, he is bound to promote. Much of time and anxious consideration have been bestowed, in the hope of presenting the subject in such a manner as should, at all events, place its prominent features in full view of the Legislature, and thus assist in arriving at such conclusions as may secure the rights of all, maintain existing institutions in all their vigor and usefulness, enlist the public feeling in the success of schools, and open them to the destitute of all classes.

All which is respectfully submitted.

JOHN C. SPENCER, *Secretary of State.*

ALBANY, *April* 26, 1841.

After the report had been referred to the Committee on Literature, Governor Seward and Mr. Spencer visited the city for the purpose of personal consultation with the trustees of the Public School Society, and their opponents, on the subject of the proposed alteration in the system. Several interviews were had, at which the bill was made the subject of earnest discussion.

The Committee on Literature, in the Senate, appointed a meeting for the purpose of hearing the contending parties, and affording them an opportunity to present their view. James W. McKeon and Wright Hawks appeared for the Catholics, and Hiram Ketchum for the Society, May 8th.

Mr. KETCHUM rose, and addressed the committee as follows:

MR. CHAIRMAN AND GENTLEMEN OF THE COMMITTEE: As a member of the Board of Public Schools of the city of New York, and in behalf of the Public School Society, I now appear here; and I will, by leave of the committee, make a few remarks upon the report which has been referred to it. The subject discussed in this report is one of great interest to the city of New York. It affects the cause of education, and especially of the education of the poor; and as the Public School Society has long had the principal charge of that matter, and as they believe that the statements, the inferences, and the reasoning contained in this report of the Secretary of State, are calculated to affect injuriously that cause, they have prayed that their views might be laid before the Senate, and sent in their memorial to that effect. The Senate having appointed a committee to hear the Public School

Society, I now appear to make such remarks as occur to me; premising that, probably, at no very late day, the Society, by way of memorial or remonstrance, will lay their objections to this report before the Senate and the public in a more permanent form, than they will now be presented to the committee.

In this report, drawn up with great ability, as every paper and document emanating from the Secretary of this State is drawn up—in this report, I say, there is contained a brief history of the legislation upon the subject of the distribution of the school moneys in the city of New York. As this passage occupies but a short space, I will take leave to read it. At page 2, the Secretary says:

It is essential to the proper consideration of the subject, to understand the history of the legislation that has been had in reference to it; and particularly in relation to the Public School Society of the city of New York.

The first law relating to that portion of the school moneys apportioned to and raised in the city of New York, was passed in 1813, and will be found in the first volume of the Revised Laws of that year, at page 267. It directed those moneys to be distributed " to the trustees of the Free-School Society, the Orphan Asylum Society, the Economical School, the African Free School, and the trustees of such incorporated religious societies in said city as now support, or hereafter shall establish, charity schools within the said city, who may apply for the same." The act directed that the sum thus distributed should be applied to the payment of the wages of the teachers, and to no other purposes whatever. As these were all charity schools, it is obvious that the Legislature intended that the school moneys apportioned to the city, as well as those raised by tax, should be consecrated to the education exclusively of the indigent. Under this act, apportionments were annually made to the schools enumerated, and to those established by some eight or ten of the different religious denominations, until the year 1824. By chapter 276 of the Session Laws of that year, the above-mentioned act was repealed, and the Common Council of the city was authorized to designate " the societies or schools which should be entitled to receive a share of the school moneys, and prescribe the rules and restrictions, under which such moneys shall be received by such societies or schools respectively." Pursuant to this act, the Common Council have designated the schools of the Public School Society, and six or eight other schools, to which all the public moneys have, since 1826, been distributed, with some variations in different years, as to the other schools. From the annual reports and other documents, a statement has been compiled, from which it appears that more than one million of dollars has been paid to the trustees of the Society, under its different names, since 1813, out of the public moneys appropriated by the State, and raised by tax on the city for school purposes, and that $125,248.57, have been paid to the other schools before mentioned.

The Public School Society was originally incorporated in 1805, by chapter 108 of the laws of that session, which is entitled, " An Act to Incorporate the Society instituted in the City of New York, for the establishment of a free school for the education of poor children, who do not belong to, or are not provided for by, any religious society." In 1808 its name was changed to " The Free School Society of New York," and its powers were extended " to all children who are the proper subjects of a gratuitous education." By chapter 25 of the laws of 1826, its name was changed to " The Public School Society of New York," and the trustees were authorized to provide for the education of all children of New York, not otherwise provided for, " whether such children be or be not the proper subjects of gratuitous education; and to require from those attending the schools, a moderate compensation; but no child to be refused admission on account of inability to pay."

This brief history of the distribution of the school moneys in the city of New York (continued Mr. Ketchum) is accurate so far as it goes; but the Secretary has left out some particulars which we deem of some importance in this discussion.

In the first place, these moneys were originally appropriated to the payment of teachers, and to no other purpose; but after the Lancasterian system of education had been introduced into the city of New York, and the Free-School Society had been established, it was found that, under the monitorial system, so great was the number of children attending these schools, that a larger amount of money was drawn from the public school fund than was necessary to pay the teachers; and in the year 1817, the surplus was permitted by the Legislature to be appropriated by the Public School Society for the purchase of books and stationery, and other incidental expenses attending the education of children; so that, from that time the Public School Society drew its quota, and applied it not only to the payment of teachers, but also to those other purposes which I have named. This privilege was at that time enjoyed exclusively by the Public School Society; and I suppose that the principle upon which the exclusive privilege was granted, was, that the Free-School Society—for so it was then called—was incorporated exclusively for the purposes of education, and of educating poor children; and there was, therefore, in the constitution of the Society itself, in the act of its incorporation, no inducement or motive for mal-application or misappropriation of the funds; and hence it was, I presume, that the Legislature, in its wisdom, saw no danger in trusting whatever funds were drawn by that institution, to be applied not only to the payment of teachers, but for the general purposes of education.

This, then, is one omission which the Secretary has made.

The second omission is, that the Secretary has not attempted to account (as I think he should have done) for the reason why the public school moneys in the city of New York were differently applied from those in the country. In the country, as the committee well know, the amount, as in the city, received from the common school fund is paid over to the proper officer in the county. The county has to raise by tax an amount equivalent to the sum thus received, and then it passes into the hands of commissioners chosen by the people in their respective districts. In the city of New York, however, no legislation of that description was provided. The money was paid over to the chamberlain, and the chamberlain was directed to pay it to certain designated societies—of which the School Society was one, and all religious societies maintaining charity schools; the Orphan Asylum and some others being specified.

Now, it seems to me that, in order to have presented the subject fairly and fully, the Secretary should have accounted for this difference. I will attempt to account for it now. In the country, that portion of the common school fund which goes to each county, is paid as a sort of premium, or *advance*, to induce the establishment and maintenance of common schools. The State says to the respective counties, We will give you so much; and this is given as an *advance*, or premium, or bonus, for the establishment and maintenance of these common schools throughout the country. In the country, the schools so established and so participating in this fund are the schools in which the children of the county—the children of the poor of the county—as well as the offspring of persons of property, generally receive their elementary education. The tax-paying part of the community —those who are called upon to raise this equivalent tax (in the first place, in order to receive the fund from the State, and, in the second place, to provide for the erection of school-houses in the respective school districts) —this tax-paying part of the community, I say, have, for the most part, their own sons and daughters educated in these very schools which are established and maintained by this money. Therefore, it will be plainly seen that this tax-paying community which, and which alone, elects the commissioners in towns—which alone elects the trustees in districts, have a direct personal interest in electing suitable persons; because those very persons are to take charge of the education of their children. There is probably very little danger that any thing like party politics will mingle up in the election of these officers; because these very officers are to perform a most important and interesting duty to the children of the very men who are called upon to pay the tax. Not so in the city of New York. There, by the law enacted in the year 1813, this fund was originally expressly appropriated to the education of the indigent—of the poor—of the children of those who do *not* pay tax—to those who are *the proper subjects of gratuitous education;* and none but charity schools, none but the children of the poor, none but the proper subjects of a gratuitous education, were to be benefitted at all by this portion of the fund so received from the State, and by the equivalent portion so raised by tax. To this the tax-payers in the city of New York consented; because, if the first objection to such a law had been made on the part of that city, it would not have passed in this form. This was undoubtedly a matter made to fall in or acquiesce with the wishes of the delegation from the city of New York; because the Legislature never would have undertaken, without such acquiescence, to have made that distinction; therefore I say, that the citizens of New York, through their representatives here, consented that the bread which the State had provided for their own children should be given to the poor; they voluntarily parted with it, and gave it to the indigent among them.

Thus, then, we see that the fund was given to the indigent by those who spoke for the people of the city of New York in the Legislature; and I have but this hour heard that a man, whose name is dear to us all—De Witt Clinton—was the man who principally represented the wishes of the city of New York at that time. It was De Witt Clinton that spoke in behalf of the city of New York—who made this provision.

And inasmuch as this was a gratuity, a charity for the poor people of that city, she chose that the money should pass through the hands of certain almoners of her own choice. She chose that the Free-School Society, the Orphan Asylum Society, the religious bodies which maintained schools there at that time, should be her almoners. Suppose, at that day, it had been proposed, as it is now proposed by the Secretary, that the people should choose commissioners—that the tax-paying portion of this people (because none others then were, or now are, entitled to vote on these matters in the country) should choose commissioners, there was lacking that powerful motive which would influence freeholders, and the tax-paying portion of the community, to elect proper men for the performance of this duty—the motive which was to be found in the fact that their own children were to be educated by these very persons. This probably may account very sensibly for the fact that, in the city of New York, the portion of the school fund allotted to her was to be distributed by those almoners of her charity whom her representatives thought proper to designate. Now, I ask, was there any thing inconsistent with sound principle in this? Is there any thing in it which violates the principle of the largest liberty and the purest democracy, of which we hear something in this report? In the city of New York, as I shall have occasion to show by and by—and more or less, I suppose, it is so in all the States of Christendom—there are voluntary associations, charitable associations, associations composed of men, incorporated or otherwise, who are willing to proffer their services to feed the hungry, to clothe the naked, to visit the destitute, and to see to the application of funds set apart for their relief. Such men are always to be found in large cities—men of fortune, men of leisure, men of benevolence, who are willing to associate together for benevolent objects, and who are usually made the almoners of the charity of others. Such is the case in the city of New York. That is the usual mode—(as I shall have occasion to show, though it can scarcely be necessary to do it before this intelligent committee)—that is the usual mode of distributing funds there, and experience has demonstrated that it has been attended with good and wholesome results. The city of New York chose, therefore, to adopt this mode of distributing her moneys; and this, probably, is one of the reasons why this distinction between the city and the country was incorporated in the act of 1813. Another reason undoubtedly was, that, in a city such as New York, there is more or less political excitement mingling in every public measure. All who have lived there know that, especially within a few years past, we have had a degree of political excitement which has been very inconvenient; and that at all times, in a close and dense population, more of that excitement and heat are felt than prevails amongst the more sparse population of the country, and, probably, possibly it entered into the consideration of the wise men (for, if they were like him whom I have named, they deserve that appellation in its highest sense) in the Legislature of that day, that, for the purpose of keeping this matter out of the vortex of party and political excitement, this money should be paid over to, and distributed under, the superintendence of agents consisting of these respective societies. This, then, it seems to me, is another omission in this report of the Secretary. I speak with deference. And the third omission is, that the Secretary has failed to tell us why the act of 1824 was passed, which gives the money provided by the State to the Common Council of the city of New York, to be distributed by them as they might think proper. I will supply the omission.

Anterior to the year 1824, the Legislature designated the institutions and schools which should participate in this fund. These were, the Free-School Society, and religious societies supporting charity schools, and some others. About the year 1822—(I would premise, however, that the religious societies, and all except the Public School Society, were restricted in the use of these funds to the payment of teachers)—about the year 1822, a society, called the Bethel Church of the City of New York, obtained a privilege similar to that which had been granted to the Public School Society, and applied the surplus, after the payment of teachers, to the purchase of stationery and the erection of buildings. The operation of that plan was this: inasmuch as that society, in common with all others, drew per head for the number of children taught in the schools, or, rather, for the number of children placed on the register of the schools, to be taught, this Bethel Church, under the direction of Johnson Chase, at that time their pastor, gave small presents and rewards, to induce children to come in. They came in, and their names were put on the register; and when the yearly account came to be made out, they drew for the number of children on the register, and the consequence was, that a large portion of the fund was appropriated to the erection of buildings belonging to the Bethel Church; thus using the common school fund of the city of New York, and the equivalent tax paid there, to the erection of religious temples to be used by a particular denomination of Christians. Before this law of 1822 was passed, and while the sum received was specifically appropriated to the payment of teachers, the Bethel Church, or, rather, their pastor, evaded the law in the following manner: The teacher was employed at a large salary; he received the salary with the understanding that, while he received it in one hand, with the other he should make over a portion to the church; so that the church received, after all, a portion of the funds paid to teachers.

This alarmed the Public School Society and the community of the city of New York, and the Society and the Corporation immediately sent a memorial up here, praying that the provision of the law giving peculiar privilege to the Bethel Baptist Church might be repealed. Hence ensued a contest which lasted two or three years before the Legislature, in which the people of the city of New York took great interest, and which was a very exciting contest even here, in the city of Albany. Here was seen to be an attempt made to take away the public school fund of the city of New York for the purposes of the Bethel Church; and the city authorities, and the associations participating in the fund, all became alarmed.

We came here and discussed this matter; and our proposition was, then, to restrict these religious societies to the poor children of parents statedly worshipping with those societies. This was thought to be a fair proposal. The subject was discussed on various successive occasions, until, at length, it was seen, by those who examined it, that this matter of paying the school fund to religious societies, whereby the doctrines of particular religious sects should be sustained and supported by this fund, was a violation of a great fundamental principle. It was the union of Church and State, which the laws and the institutions of this country abhor. It was taking the funds of the people—the tax received out of the pockets of the people—and applying it to the establishment and promotion of religious societies. Well, although it is a good thing to have these religious societies, yet it was seen that a vital principle was here violated. Hence, after many discussions in the Assembly chamber (discussions at which all the members were invited to attend—and almost all of them did attend, for we had generally a *quorum*, although it was before a committee night after night), the committee of the Assembly at length made a report favorable to the prayer of the memorial ; but suggesting, in that very report, whether even so much as was granted in the proposition referred to was not a violation of sound principle ; whether, in fact, religious societies ought to participate in the enjoyment of the fund at all, because, by such participation, the Jew might be made to support the doctrine of the Christian ; and, *vice-versâ*, the Christian that of the Jew, the Catholic of the Protestant, the Protestant of the Catholic, and so on. After much discussion, after the subject had been agitated before the Legislature week after week—(as a member of the Public School Society, I attended here six weeks)—after a great contest, in which we had to contend against the Bethel Church, the Episcopal Church, the Dutch Church, the Methodist Church, and the Roman Catholic Church, the bill came from the other House to the Senate, and there was discussed before a committee by the gentleman who is now Bishop of the State—Dr. Onderdonk— on the one side, and a member of the Board of Public Schools on the other. This was at the adjourned session of the Legislature, in the fall of 1824, the session having been continued over from the spring to the fall. In this fall session of 1824, I say, it was that this discussion was had. The committee of the Senate, seeing that the subject was involved in difficulties, and that it required a knowledge of local feelings which they did not, and could not, possess here in the Legislature, inserted an amendment in the bill of the House, declaring that they would refer the matter to the city of New York, and that the Corporation should dispose of the school fund apportioned to that city as they might please. And here I ask leave to say to the committee, that this power never had been asked for by the Corporation—that it never had been asked for by the Public School Society ; but that the committee of the Senate—(and a most intelligent committee it was : I do not recollect all the names at the moment, but I know that Mr. Suydam was one)—that committee decided that they were so ignorant of the peculiarities of the New York population with reference to this question, that they were incompetent to decide it rightly ; and they therefore, of their own motion, incorporated this section in the act, giving power to the Corporation of the city of New York to dispose of this fund as they thought best. Thus the power was granted. Now, the proposition of the Secretary in this report is, that the Legislature shall resume this power ; that that which the Legislature of 1824 thought proper to give of their own motion, as I have said— for in behalf of the Public School Society no such grant was asked ; and I felt great hesitation on the part of the Common Council whose memorial I bore, whether we should accept the grant—whether it would not be better to leave the disposition of the school fund here. We were fearful of local difficulty. We did not want the power vested in the Corporation; the Corporation did not want it; and I never gave my consent to it until after consultation with the President of the Free-School Society at that time, De Witt Clinton, then residing here, and who said it was more proper that the Corporation should exercise this power. It was then accepted. Now, I maintain, that if the proposition of the Secretary, that the Legislature should resume this power, is to be adopted, it is incumbent on him to show that the power thus delegated to the Corporation has been abused. I say, it is incumbent upon him to prove this fact. Here is the Legislature delegating a power—granting it to agents selected by the people, composed of the Common Council of the city of New York. Before this grant, the representatives of the people of the city of New York in this Legislature unquestionably had the sole power of indicating the course of legislation as to the disposition of the fund apportioned to that city. The Legislature never would have undertaken to say that these funds should be used in one way in the city of New York, and in another way in the country, except so far as they were authorized to say it by the consent of members representing the city and country respectively.

This is according to the usual course of legislation—local in its operation. " Well, then," said the committee of the Senate, in 1824, "instead of having this matter indicated to us by twelve or thirteen gentlemen who represent the city of New York in the Assembly, and one or two that may represent them in this body, we will say to the Common Council of that city, selected by the people—the chosen agents of the people—that they may distribute this fund as they think proper; and the question now is, Have these agents abused that power so as to make it requisite that the Legislature should resume it?" Sir, I submit, with great deference, whether, in this matter, the *onus* of proof does not lie upon those who ask the Legislature to resume it? I submit if the burden of showing that there has been an abuse of power—that the agent has been an unfaithful agent—does not devolve upon those who desire to take the power away? Now, has it been abused? I ask, has the Corporation abused the power thus voluntarily—without any request on their part—granted to them? That is a question which I now propose to discuss.

Immediately after the passage of this act, or as soon as, in the course of public business, it could be attended to—namely, on the 11th of April, 1825 (for it was anterior to that that the committee was appointed)—this matter was taken up by the Common Council of the city of New York, it was referred by them to the Law Committee, and this is the preamble to the report made on the day above mentioned :

The Committee on Laws, to whom were referred the 4th section of the act of the Legislature of this State relating to common schools in the city of New York, passed the 19th of November, 1824; the memorials of the trustees of the Charity School attached to the Reformed Protestant Dutch

Church of the city of New York; of the trustees of the First Protestant Episcopal Charity School in the city of New York, and of the trustees of the Methodist Episcopal Church, praying respectively for a participation in the common school fund; and also the report of a committee of the trustees of the Free-School Society, on the distribution of the said fund, proposing a change in the constitution of that Society, so as to admit children of all classes to their schools, for a compensation not exceeding fifty cents per quarter, with power to remit in proper cases, Report.

The committee consisted of Samuel Cowdrey, Elisha W. King, and Thomas Bolton, Esqs.

They patiently heard all parties (continued Mr. Ketchum). I believe the hearing occupied one or two evenings. The Methodists were represented, the Dutch were represented, the Episcopalians were represented, and the Public School Board was represented. The whole matter was fully and frankly discussed, and this principle: whether or not religious societies ought to participate in this fund, was fully gone into; and so far as the churches were represented, and so far as my learned associate was concerned (the Hon. Peter A. Jay), these various questions were discussed with great ability.

The report of the Law Committee is long; it sets forth the arguments on both sides, and the conclusion contains the following passage:

In the performance of this duty, they have felt all the importance and responsibility of the task assigned to them; and while they would willingly have retired from the appointment, and do each individually wish that the Legislature had passed the necessary law on this subject, on the recent application to them for that purpose, yet your committee cannot permit themselves to hesitate or falter in the course of public duty, when that course is plainly manifest to their understandings. Your committee will not conceal either their own private and personal wishes, at the commencement of their duties, that the well-organized churches and religious societies in our city might be permitted to continue in the reception of a part of this fund, as heretofore. But the weight of the argument as urged before them, and which they have endeavored to condense in this report, and the established constitutional and political doctrines which have a bearing on this question, and the habits and modes of thinking of the constituents at large of this board, require, in the opinion of your committee, that the common school fund should be distributed for civil purposes only, as contradistinguished from those of a religious or sectarian description.

This report was adopted by the Common Council with entire unanimity, it is believed.

That conclusion was ratified by their constituents; and I believe that every one of the religious societies, or nearly so, excepting the Roman Catholics, acquiesced in that decision. But that society, year after year, has come before the Common Council, and renewed their request for a separate portion of the school fund. With the best feelings for the applicants, in a spirit of kindness, with every disposition to do whatever could be done for them, year after year, and without respect to politics, whether the one party was in the ascendant or the other party was in the ascendant, the Common Council have, with almost entire unanimity, disallowed that request; and I believe that never, in either board, since the division of that body into two

boards, has there been but one dissenting voice raised against the ratifica-
tion of that decision. Now, if the committee please, who have complained?
The Roman Catholics. Our fellow-citizens, the Roman Catholics, are as
much entitled to be heard there, and here, as any other citizens; for, when
acting in a political capacity, we know no difference of religion. The request which was made and urged by them, conjoined with many powerful
Protestant sects and denominations of Christians, and which was refused to
them jointly, has been over and over again refused to them separately.

No disrespect was intended then. The Common Council, and every person engaged in the discussion of the question on behalf of the Common
School Society, took great care to say, " We do not reject you because you
are Roman Catholics; and, as evidence of this truth, we give you the fact
that we have rejected similar applications from powerful Protestants; but
we reject your request because we believe that a sound general principle will
not allow us to grant it."

I say, that the Corporation have been desirous, so far as that body possibly could, so far as they felt themselves at liberty, consistently with the
maintenance of a sound general principle, to accommodate these parties.
They have granted a privilege out of this fund to the Roman Catholic denomination, which has not been granted to any other. The Sisters of Charity, so called, under direction of the Roman Catholic Church, and connected
with it (I believe I am right; if not, I should be happy to be corrected),
established a most benevolent institution in the city of New York, called
the Orphan Asylum—the Roman Catholic Orphan Asylum. They took into
this institution poor and destitute orphans. They fed them and clothed
them most meritoriously, and they thus relieved the city of New York of
the maintenance of many who would otherwise, probably, have been a
charge upon it. After long discussion, and with some hesitancy, yet overcome by the desire to oblige, and aware of the limitation arising from the
very nature of that institution, the Corporation did permit the Catholic
Orphan Asylum to receive money from this fund; and, during the last year,
it received some $1,462 for the education of about one hundred and sixty-
five children—in common with the Institution for the Blind, and the Deaf
and Dumb, and those other benevolent and Christian institutions which are
altogether of a Catholic character, in the most comprehensive acceptation
of that term, as they are under no sectarian influence or government. Thus
this society, under the direction of the Sisters of Charity—ladies devoted
to the Roman Catholic Church, who are themselves Roman Catholics, and
given up to the service of that Church—this society, I say, has been permitted to draw this sum of $1,462 in one year. But when the question came,
" Shall their schools be permitted to draw from the fund?" the Corporation
had to say—and they have said, over and over again, though most reluctantly—" We cannot grant you that." Upon the last application made for
this purpose, the subject underwent thorough and prolonged discussion
before the Board of Aldermen, and the argument was conducted, on the
side of the Roman Catholics, with signal ability, by the Right Rev. Bishop
Hughes, of that Church. The hall of the Common Council was crowded

to overflowing; the avenues were crowded, and crowded, I believe I may say, without any intention of saying what is erroneous, by persons belonging to that denomination.

The subject, I repeat, underwent a very full and free discussion; and, after that had terminated, the Board of Aldermen gravely considered and discussed the subject, and at length, after some delay, came to the conclusion that they would go and visit the schools. Some of the members of the Board of Public Schools, feeling sensibly alive on the subject, expressed to me an apprehension that this was a mere evasion, and they feared that the question had now become mingled with politics. But I said, " Wait, gentlemen; let them go and see your schools; it is a natural desire. They ought to go. It is a great and delicate question, and they ought to be acquainted with it in all its details." They went and visited the public schools and the Roman Catholic schools, and they incorporated the result of their deliberations in a report which I have before me, and from which I shall quote by and by. It is drawn up with great ability, and the decision was, with but one dissenting voice, that the prayer of the petition should be rejected; and it was rejected. Who, then, complain of the operation of this system? Our fellow-citizens, the Roman Catholics. Failing to accomplish their purpose through the Common Council of the city of New York, they come and ask it here. Failing in their application to a body of representatives to whom they have applied year after year, and who represent a population in which is intermingled a greater mass of Roman Catholic voters than in any other district of the State of New York—failing to get, from the hands of a body thus constituted, the redress for the grievance which they complained of, they come here and ask it of you. I say, *they* come here, because I will presently show you, from their memorials, that none *but* they come here.

Now, I beg leave again to refer to the report of the Secretary. He says:

The memorials presented at the present session represent that the legislative enactments on the subject of public instruction, in the city of New York, require a fundamental alteration to bring the benefits of the common school education within the reach of all classes of the population; that the original intent of those enactments was to enable every school, which should comply with the law, to share in the common school fund; that this design has been defeated by the construction put upon the statutes by the Common Council of the city, in designating the Public School Society to receive nearly the whole amount of that fund belonging to the city; that this Society, being a corporation, has acquired the entire control of the system of public education; that the taxpayers who contribute to the fund have no voice in the selection of those who administer the system, or control over the application of the public moneys.

That is to say (continued Mr. Ketchum), that, at the last session, memorials were presented by the Roman Catholics, as such. The present, we are left to infer, are presented by citizens generally, not as Roman Catholics. Let us see how the truth of the matter stands. Here is the first memorial:

To the Honorable the Legislature of the State of New York :
The memorial of the undersigned, residents of the city of New York,

respectfully showeth: That your memorialists, being members of the Catholic Church, and connected with the several Catholic congregations in the city of New York, would respectfully represent to your honorable body, &c.

This (continued Mr. Ketchum) is from the first memorial presented by them as Catholics. It was presented in the session of 1840, and referred to the honorable Secretary last year. He did not think proper to make a report upon that; but then comes a second memorial from *citizens generally*, and on that he makes a report. The second is a memorial presented the 22d of February, 1841. It says:

That your memorialists are deeply interested in extending the advantages of education to every child in the commonwealth, regarding it as the best means of perpetuating the blessings of our republican institutions, and of correcting those evils in society which are beyond the sphere of legislation.
It is alleged by thousands of our population, that their conscientious scruples have been disregarded in the formation of the system of instruction adopted by the Public School Society. The confidence of this class of our citizens has been entirely withdrawn from the institution, and they complain of the severity of the oppression which compels them to submit to the decision and government of agents irresponsible to the public, and in whose appointment the electors are not permitted to participate, &c.

Among the first signatures to this memorial (remarked Mr. Ketchum) are those of Joseph O'Connor, James B. O'Donnell, Patrick Leach, and others. I never saw this memorial until this morning, but I perceive one name attached to it, as a sort of family name—PATRICK FARRELL—*three times* in succession; and, what is very singular, the handwriting seems to be very much alike. Be that as it may, I am satisfied, from what I have seen, that this is as much a memorial from Roman Catholics as the other was. The Secretary, in his report, in the passage which I have read, admits that the first memorial came in a shape not calculated, probably, to be very impressive. He says:

At the last session, memorials of a similar character from a large number of Roman Catholics, citizens of New York, were referred to the undersigned, upon which he was unable, during that session, to report. Although these petitioners have the same equal and common rights, with all other citizens, to submit their grievances to the Legislature and ask for redress, yet the circumstance of presenting themselves in a character of a religious denomination is, in itself, unfavorable to that impartial consideration of the subject which its importance demands.

Probably (continued Mr. Ketchum) that circumstance was discovered by the Secretary's sagacity, between 1840 and 1841; and this second memorial, therefore, is from *citizens* of New York. But I believe I may safely affirm that, if not exclusively, it is almost altogether signed by Roman Catholics. As the Secretary justly remarks, however, they have a right to apply here; they have a right to ask the Legislature to overrule the decision of the Corporation, although it may be supposed that in that Corporation they would have as fair a chance of being heard, and of having the merits of the controversy rightly adjudicated, as here; still, they have the right to come.

Now, what do they complain of? One of their complaints is, that the people are not represented in this Public School Society; that here is an agency used for a great public purpose which the people do not directly choose; and they complain of the Public School Society being a close corporation.

I suppose that, if the Corporation had granted the prayer of their memorial, to allow their societies—that is to say, St. Patrick's Church, and all such churches as belong to the Roman Catholic denomination in the city of New York—to participate in this fund, I suppose they would not have seen precisely that such great evils and dangers to liberty were to be apprehended from the distribution of the funds to these churches and the Public School Society. I think it fair to conjecture, that if their corporations, be they close or be they open, could have participated in that fund, we should not have heard any thing of their extreme regard for the liberties of the people. But, no matter whether we should or should not, they have a right to be heard, whatever their motives may be; no matter what might have deterred them from coming here, they have a right to be heard, and their arguments must be met and answered here, or else they must receive the action of the Legislature in their favor. All that I admit. But what is their complaint? As will appear by these memorials, and from the summary contained in the report of the Secretary, they complain that this money is paid to a close corporation—that the religious scruples of a large portion of our fellow-citizens are violated by this distribution of funds.

Now, I wish to call the attention of the committee to the fact now to be stated: there is no complaint in these memorials, nor will you hear any from any source, that the Public School Society does not furnish, to all the children who attend their schools, a good literary education; there is no complaint that, in these schools, children are not taught to read, write, and cipher; that they are not taught the elements of geography, astronomy, and of English grammar, as well as they could be taught. There is, I say, no complaint of that description; and, with the exception of complaints about the *tendencies* of the institution, there are no complaints against its actual operation; but the complaint is, that some of the citizens cannot, from conscientious scruples, send their children to these schools. Now, I invite the particular attention of the committee to this, which I deem most important: that, whatever may be said of the tendencies of these institutions, whatever may be said of the evil of the general principle contained in the alleged fact that these agents are not chosen directly by the people, nor responsible to them, yet, in the long lapse of thirty-five years of the operation of this Society, and from the year 1813 to the present time, during which these common school moneys have been received, there is no complaint *that they have ever failed to give a good education.* There is no complaint that the system has so far operated injuriously, excepting that such is the course of religious education, or, more properly speaking, the *want* of religious education, that the Roman Catholics cannot conscientiously send their children to our schools. But they *do* object that they cannot send their children to these schools; that those children, many of them eminent-

25

ly the subjects of a gratuitous education, cannot partake of the benefits of the fund on account of conscientious scruples.

Now, this is the very point which, year after year, has been discussed before the Common Council, and which, year after year, has been decided by that body. What is it? The Roman Catholics complain, in the first place, that they cannot conscientiously send their children to the public schools because we do not give religious instruction in a definite form and of a decided and definite character. They complain, in the second place, that the school-books in common use in the Society contain passages reflecting upon the Roman Catholic Church. And they complain, in the third place, that we use the Bible without note or comment; that the school is opened in the morning by calling the children to order and reading a chapter in the Bible—our common version. These are the three grounds on which they base their conscientious scruples. Now, I propose most respectfully to consider them. In the first place, our books contain occasional passages reflecting on the Roman Catholics. It is true that, in our ordinary school-books, the most approved of the day, there is an occasional passage which may be considered as reflecting injuriously on the Roman Catholic Church. We have all read, I suppose, as children—and I do not know but that this description may be one of those contained in these books—of the martyrdom of John Rogers, in the reign of Queen Mary. That reflects on the Roman Catholic Church; and there is an occasional passage which speaks of the Roman Catholic Church as Protestant divines, essayists, and orators sometimes allow themselves to speak of that Church. The Public School Society have offered, if the Catholics will point out these offensive passages, to erase them all from the books. They have said to the bishop of that Church, and to a committee of that Church, " We can find passages enough of good English for our reading-books without these; and if you will have the goodness to take these books and point out these offensive passages, we pledge ourselves to have them erased."

Now, all this matter was gone into by the intelligent committee of the Board of Aldermen to whose action I have referred—and I have their report before me. They called for a distinct and definite proposition from the Common School Society as to what they would do. I will read a few passages from the report:

PROPOSITION ON BEHALF OF THE SCHOOL SOCIETY.

In compliance with the request of the committee of the Board of Aldermen, the undersigned committee of the New York Public School Society submit the following propositions as a basis of a compromise with their Roman Catholic fellow-citizens on the subject of the public schools; which propositions they are willing to support before the trustees of the Society, and which they believe will be sanctioned by that board.

The Trustees of the New York Public School Society will remove from the class-books in the schools all matters which may be pointed out as offensive to their Roman Catholic fellow-citizens, should any thing objectionable yet remain in them.

They will also exclude from the school libraries (the use of which is *permitted* to the pupils, but not *required* of them) every work written with a view to prejudice the mind of the reader against the tenets or practices of the Roman Catholic Church, or the general tendency of which is to produce the same effect.

They will receive and examine any books which may be recommended for the use of the schools; and should such books be adapted to their system of instruction, and void of any matter offensive to other denominations, they shall be introduced so soon as opportunity may be afforded by a call for new books.

Any suggestions in reference to alterations in the plan of instruction or course of studies, which may be offered, shall receive prompt consideration; and, if not inconsistent with the general system of instruction now prevailing in the schools, nor with the conscientious rights of other denominations, they shall be adopted.

The building situated in Mulberry street, now occupied by Roman Catholic schools, shall, if required for the use of the Public School Society, be purchased or hired, on equitable terms, by the trustees, should such an arrangement be desired.

Every effort will be made by the Trustees of the Public School Society to prevent any occurrence in the schools which might be calculated to wound the feelings of Roman Catholic children, or to impair their confidence in, or diminish their respect for, the religion of their parents.

Anxious to keep open every avenue to such an arrangement as will lead to a general attendance of the Roman Catholic children at the public schools, and fully aware that some things may have escaped their observation which might be modified without violation of the conscientious rights of others, the undersigned wish it to be distinctly understood that, in offering the foregoing propositions as the basis of an arrangement, it is not intended to exclude other propositions which the Roman Catholics may make, provided they do not interfere with the principles by which the trustees feel themselves bound.

This portion of the report (said Mr. Ketchum), as will be seen, has reference to these offensive passages. Now, every body will say that is a fair offer—we will strike them out. But, gentlemen of the committee, I submit whether here, in this country, we must not, in matters of conflicting opinions, give and take a little? I have no doubt that I can find something in any public school-book, of much length, and containing much variety of matter, reflecting upon the Methodists—upon the heated zeal, probably, of John Wesley, and his followers; reflecting upon the Episcopalians, the Baptists, and Presbyterians. Occasional sentences will find their way into public discourses, which, if viewed critically, and regarded in a captious spirit, rather reflect upon the doctrines of all those churches.

Now, I submit, with great deference to the committee, whether this is a fair subject for conscientious scruples? As I have had occasion to illustrate heretofore, we find something in relation to politics, too, about which we may disagree. There are some very elegant passages from Thomas Jefferson's works which have found their way into our public school-books. Some man, imbued with strong prejudices against Thomas Jefferson, may say, "I cannot go Thomas Jefferson; my children shall never be instructed to read what Thomas Jefferson has said." On the other hand, there are many passages from the speeches of Mr. Webster which have found their way into school-books; and a Democrat may say, "I cannot go Mr. Webster; my children shall not be taught to admire him." And thus, if we are captious, we can find conscientious scruples enough. However, if it is *bonâ fide* a conscientious scruple, there is the end of it; we cannot reason with it. But, in the judgment of the Common Council, and as I think must be the case in the judgment of every man, the difficulty is got over by the proposition which has been made.

The next complaint is, that we do not give religious education enough. The memorials, all of which are public—and the speeches and documents which have been employed, and which, if necessary, can be furnished to the committee—all go conclusively to demonstrate that, in the judgment of those who spoke for the Roman Catholic Church, we ought to teach religion in our public schools—not generally, not vaguely, not the general truths of religion, but that specific religious instruction must be given. Now, I hardly suppose that this deficiency can be made the subject of conscientious objection.

The third and last complaint is, that our Catholic brethren cannot consent to have this Bible read in the hearing of their children. Now, on every one of these points the trustees have been disposed to go as far as they possibly could in the way of accommodation; but they never yet consented to give up the use of the Bible to the extent to which it is used in the schools. I say, the trustees have never yet consented to this surrender. But if they can have good authority for doing it, they will do it.

If this Legislature, by its own act, will direct that the Bible shall be excluded, I will guarantee that it shall be excluded. Thus much for these conscientious scruples; and, having these scruples, the Roman Catholics say they cannot come in. They, however, are in favor of this bill, the outline of which is given in the report of the Secretary. They are here, from the Catholic Board of Trustees, in strong force, to aid the passage of some bill founded on the Secretary's report. They will be satisfied with it; it will give them what they ask. Now, let us see *how*. There is no proposition contained in this report, that religious societies, as such, shall participate in this fund—none. It is too late in the day for any man to make *that* proposition. Anxious as the Secretary is to accommodate this matter, he does not say that religious societies shall participate in the fund. But what *does* he say? He says that the trustees of districts shall indicate what religion shall be taught in those schools. That is to say, that you shall have small masses; that these small masses shall elect their trustees; and as the majority of the people in those small masses may direct, so shall be the character of the religious instruction imparted. He assumes that there *must* be religious instruction in the schools; that, although the law makes no provision for it, yet that it is left practically with the people themselves, through their trustees, to indicate the religious instruction that shall be given. I will read what the Secretary says, at page 11 of his report:

It is by adopting the principle of the organization that prevails in the other parts of the State, which will leave such parents as desire to exercise any control over the amount and description of religious instruction which shall be given to their children, the opportunity of doing so.

Now (continued Mr. Ketchum), let us see how the argument stands. The complainants here are the Roman Catholics. They cannot conscientiously have their children taught in these schools, because religious instruction, in a definite form, is not given, and because the Bible is read. But when a school is formed in the Sixth Ward of the city of New York, in which ward (for the sake of the argument we will assume) the Roman Catholics have a majority in the district, they choose their trustees, and these trustees indicate that a specific form of religion—to wit, the Roman Catholic religion—shall be taught in that school; that mass shall be said there, and that the children shall cross themselves with holy water in the school, having the right to do so according to this report, the Catholics being in a majority there. Then, and not till then, can these Roman Catholics conscientiously send their children to school. That is to say, their objections to this system are to be overcome by having a school to which they can conscientiously send their children; and that school must be one in which religion is to be taught according to their particular views. Now, suppose that, in any given district, there should be about five hundred Roman Catholic children, and two hundred Protestant children. These Protestant children are compelled to worship according to the opinions of the majority; that is to say, they are compelled to be taught religion according to the doctrines of the Roman Catholic Church. I ask you, gentlemen, if *that* is not the tyranny of the majority? The Secretary admits that a majority of the people, in a given district, has a right to indicate what religion shall be taught in the district school; and to that religion, or that form, whatever it may be, the minority must submit. Thus, in a given district, the Protestant shall be taxed for the support of the Roman Catholic religion; or, on the other hand, the Roman Catholics shall be taxed for the support of definite Protestant religion; and thus, by abandoning the present system, we are to form and create a system which will overcome the difficulty. Is this reasoning like an American statesman?

I deny the Secretary's proposition. I affirm that it is false and erroneous from beginning to end. This school fund can never, under any circumstances, be made use of or employed in teaching the particular doctrines or particular dogmas of any religious denomination. If there were five hundred in one district, and but one man in that district that protested, he would have a clear right to do so. He has a right to say, " I will not pay my money to teach the Roman Catholic religion; I will not pay my money to teach the Protestant religion; I will not pay my money to teach the doctrines of Tom Paine; I will not pay my money to teach the doctrine of those who affirm that my Saviour was an impostor." Imagine a district in the city of New York where there is a majority of persons of this description, and where they shall teach their own doctrines (for, if the Secretary is right, these, being in the majority, have a right to teach what religion they please). I am supposing an extreme but possible case. Is this the scheme by which we are to get over the objections of those who alone complain of this system? No, sir. I affirm that the religion taught in the public schools is precisely that quantity of religion which we have a right to teach. It would be inconsistent with public sentiment to teach less; it would be illegal to teach more. And, on this point, I am happy to see that the Secretary has one passage in his report which expresses my views most fully, and which is couched in much better language than any which I could employ. He says:

It is very true that the Government has assumed only the intellectual education of the children of the State, and has left their moral and religious instruction to be given at the fireside, at the places of public worship, and at those institutions which the piety of individuals may establish for the purpose. But it is believed that, in a country where the great body of our fellow-citizens recognize the fundamental truths of Christianity, public sentiment would be shocked by the attempt to exclude all instruction of a religious nature from the public schools : and that any plan or scheme of education, in which no reference whatever was had to moral principles founded on these truths, would be abandoned by all. In the next place, it is believed such an attempt would be wholly impracticable. No books can be found, no reading-lessons can be selected, which do not contain more or less of some principles of religious faith, either directly avowed, or indirectly assumed. Religion and literature have become inseparably interwoven, and the expurgation of religious sentiments from the productions of orators, essayists, and poets, would leave them utterly barren.

Now (continued Mr. Ketchum), we have a right to say this. When the late head of this nation (so suddenly, under the providence of God, taken from us) declared, as others, his predecessors, had declared before him, that he bore his testimony in favor of the Christian religion as received in this land, he spoke as the representative of the American people. I am proud to say here, as an American, that there is no party in *that ;* that, whatever difference of opinion might have existed politically as to the merits of that distinguished man, the sentiment thus uttered by him was an American sentiment, which will be responded to by a vast majority of the people of this country—for, thank God, this is a Christian land.

We belong to different denominations ; indeed, we are Episcopalians, we are Roman Catholics, we are Baptists, we are Methodists ; but there are great truths of Christianity which, as a people, we coincide in. And although the law cannot point out precisely what those principles are, yet we can all feel them and judge of them. We have a right to teach our children, as we do teach them, that there is a God whose eye sees us—who penetrates the thoughts of our hearts—and that we are accountable beings. We have a right to inculcate these great religious principles, as the sanctions of that morality which we are bound to see enforced in these schools. The Legislature has nothing to do with religion specifically ; but so far as, by common consent, religion mingles itself with the approved literature of the country, and so far as it deals with great general principles from which morality derives its sanctions, the Legislature, and the schools, and every one under the patronage of this Government, has a right to recognize it.

Beyond that, no such right exists ; because, the moment you go beyond that, you trample upon the conscience of this or that man, whose conscience you are bound to respect. But these general principles, as properly stated here, must be recognized, and are recognized, in this land. In the schools we go thus far : we neither say nor do any thing to interfere with the pecu-

liar sentiments of any sect or denomination. Our trustees are, and always
have been, composed of persons of all denominations. We have had, in
our number, more than one excellent Roman Catholic, from time to time.
We have had Episcopalians, we have had Baptists, we have had Universal-
ists, we have had respectable men of all sects—men who are willing to devote themselves, without fee or reward, to the service of their fellow-men.
Precisely that amount of religion which would be approved and taught by
a board thus constituted—*that*, I say, and these general truths only, have we
a right to teach in institutions under the direction of the Legislature.

The next objection to this system, as a system—and this is not an objection to existing schools—is, that it does not reach all the children who are
the proper subjects of a gratuitous education. And here I will take leave
to read an extract from the report of the Secretary. He says:

Considering the various feelings and interests that would be called into
action by such a system, there can be little doubt that one of its immediate
effects would be, to bring into the schools a large portion, if not the whole,
of those who are now utterly destitute of instruction. With all the commendable and vigorous efforts of the trustees of the Public School Society,
it cannot be denied that less than one half the children between four and
sixteen years of age, in the city of New York, are receiving the benefits of
any education whatever. From the statements in the annual report of the
Superintendent of Common Schools for the present year (Assembly Document No. 100), it appears that the whole number of white children in New
York in 1840, over 5 and under 16 years of age, was 62,952, and that 30,758
only are returned as attending some school, leaving 32,194 who were not in
attendance on any school whatever.

Now (continued Mr. Ketchum), I grant most freely that, if there *is* this
number of children in the city of New York who do not attend the schools
on account of the defects in the system, the system ought to be either
amended or improved, or, if not susceptible of amendment, abolished, and a
new system substituted. But let us for a moment inquire into this matter.
There is some mistake in this census calculation. There must necessarily be
a mistake, because it makes out the number of 32,194 children who are not
in attendance on any school whatever. We report the number of children
on our books for the last year at 23,000; and it is stated by the Roman
Catholics that there are about 8,000 in their schools; making an aggregate
of 31,000 in the public and Roman Catholic schools. Deduct this from the
aggregate census number, and the number remaining is 31,952. From this
number no deduction is made for the children attending pay schools in the
city; this number is large in the ward in which I reside (7th). I have
heard a computation made, that there are over one thousand pay scholars in
this single ward; although this is more than the average in all the wards.
There must, therefore, be some mistake; the fact cannot be as it is here
represented. I doubt whether the persons who took the census were remarkably accurate or particular in obtaining information respecting the
attendance of children on schools.

Error there manifestly is, somewhere. Upon a given day many children
may not have been at school. There may have been a vast number of these

children actually attending school, and yet who were absent on that particular day.

The difference between the number of those who actually attend our schools and the number on the register, is twenty per cent.; that is to say, twenty children out of one hundred do not attend the schools daily. These children may be taken from school by their parents for various reasons: they may be wanted, in the season, to sell radishes, or for one operation or another, by which their parents can realize a little profit from their labor; and thus, at a given time, there may not be more than two-thirds of the twenty-three thousand children above named in actual attendance. If, then, the inquiry is made on a given day, What is the number of children who go to school to-day? the answer would be given in that form; and, therefore, you cannot thus arrive at just conclusions as to how many children are educated, and how many are left uneducated. The inquiry is supposed to be, How many children attend school? Many parents will not send their children when under six years; and, after that age, many of them are not kept at school more than three or four years. By the time they are ten or twelve years old, they will have acquired a knowledge of reading, writing, and ciphering, and other branches of education—which, their parents think, is all that is needed to prepare them for some employment. Therefore there may be many children between five and six not sent to school; and there are many between that age and the age of ten or twelve, who have received what is supposed by their friends to be a competent education; and a *vast* number between 12 and 16 are taken out, because, before the latter age, they can be made the instruments of profit to their parents. So that, in this calculation, you do not arrive at a result which shows you the number of children actually left uneducated. It is difficult to decide this point. The Public School Society made an investigation into the subject, with a view of making an application to the people for an additional tax: this, I think, was in the year 1829, when the population of the city of New York was about two hundred thousand. They made the investigation in the best manner they could, and arrived at the conclusion that there were about ten thousand children in the city who did not attend school.

The chairman of the committee here made the following inquiry:

In these 33,000 thus returned, are there any returns of children at select schools, or boarding-schools?

Mr. KETCHUM. Yes, sir.

The CHAIRMAN. The number, then, includes those who are returned from your Society, and are returned from other societies.

Question by Mr. VERPLANCK. In this 23,000 who are educated at the public schools in New York, are not children of ages between four and five years included?

Mr. KETCHUM. The city of New York limits the age of children to between four and sixteen.

Mr. VERPLANCK. Therefore there must be a number of children under five years not educated.

Mr. KETCHUM here stated that there was a gentleman present (Mr. Seton) who had in his possession all the statistical information requisite to answer any inquiries that might be put. That gentleman had long been a visitor engaged in the service of these schools. He was more intimately acquainted with all the details than he (Mr. Ketchum) could be, and would be happy to answer all inquiries. He had, indeed, come here for that purpose.

Mr. Ketchum then proceeded in his argument, as follows :

Well, now, here is shown to be a large non-attendance. There is no doubt of the fact; we cannot deny it, and we do not wish to deny it. But does this non-attendance result from this system ? I say not. There is no non-attendance, save from the children of our Roman Catholic fellow-citizens, that can be pointed out on account of prejudice against the schools. There is non-attendance, as you will be told by gentlemen of great practical knowledge on the subject, because parents will not send their children to school, or because the children will not go. There is a want of parental authority which leaves the children to say they will not go, and hence they grow up in idle and vagrant habits. They would not go to any other school sooner than to this. The objection is not to the school itself, but to the confinement. They will not go to school, and they cannot be made to go. What can we do ? The gentleman upon my left (Mr. Seton) was employed many years in visiting—in going round from house to house, for the purpose of inducing children to come in. We have now thirteen gentlemen employed to *visit* one day in each week, from house to house, to induce and persuade these children to come in—to overcome objections, and to get them in. That matter is under the charge of a committee of the board, and the result of their experience has been given. I believe that their exertions, during the last year, were the means of getting in about nine hundred children; but of this number, from the want of parental control, a small portion only remained more than a short time. Now, what system could bring in these children to a greater extent ? There is no prejudice against the schools : there cannot be any. No one who visits the schools, and who observes the cheerfulness and the happiness which there prevails, can fail to see that there is not any ground of prejudice. You cannot have more attractive schools than these. But the great difficulty is, that the children will not be persuaded to come. Nothing but legal provision can make them, and, probably, we are not prepared for a resort to force. But our Common Council have been very accommodating on this subject; they have gone hand in hand with the Public School Society; they have acted on the most friendly terms, and, on one occasion, they passed an ordinance (how long it remained in force I cannot say), providing that parents who did not send their children to some school should not receive bounty, in the winter season, from the Almshouse. That mode *has* been resorted to. There has been perfect coöperation between the two bodies; yet, notwithstanding this, and all other attempts, there are children whom we could accommodate, and who do not come; but I am bound to say, that our accommodations in some parts of the city are not such as will allow all to partake of the benefits of the schools. That is no fault in the system, but arises from the fact that the system itself is not carried out to the extent it ought to be. I believe that the trustees of the Society have asked the Legislature to help them to funds, to enable them to build additional school-houses. Our great difficulty arises from the cost of school-houses and the purchase of lots; for, as you, gentlemen, well know, there is a great difference between the cost of a lot of land in the city and a lot in the country.

The amount of money which would be required in the city of New York, for the purchase of a lot, or lots, of land proper for the erection of a building (to be three stories high, with a basement), which would accommodate our children under the Lancasterian system, and in which five or six hundred are educated, would be as much as all the school-houses in a single county, and the lots, too, would cost in the country. The great difficulty lies in getting the money. We have asked aid, and we shall undoubtedly have to ask aid again, to enable us to build school-houses. In this way we could accommodate more children, and could get more to attend. But this, gentlemen will at once perceive, is not the fault of the system, but results from the fact that we are not able to carry it out to the extent necessary. I have not considered this last point as fully as I could otherwise have wished, because the figures and statements of those who are personally acquainted with it will be at the service of the committee; and the committee will no doubt prefer to have the information directly from that source. I have thus considered the objections, not to the principle, but to the actual operation of this system.

I come, now, to consider the objections to the principles as set forth in these memorials. What are they? They represent, in the first place, that the original intention of the enactment which gave this fund to the Common Council, was, " to enable every school which should comply with the requirements of the statute to share in the common school fund."

That is an assertion from which, as a matter of fact, I dissent. I have said before, I was here at the time the act was passed. Gentlemen of the committee can only judge of the intention from the act itself; but I believe' I know pretty well what the intention of the Legislature was on the points that were mooted; and I am persuaded that the Legislature intended to give full power to the Corporation of the city of New York to distribute this money among such institutions as they should select. The Corporation had the right to adopt or reject any of these institutions.

The memorialists say that " it is dangerous and detrimental to the public interest to pour into the coffers of this institution the public money, or its influence and authority, while it is wanting in that high and requisite attribute of a public agent—responsibility to the people."

Now, I admit that, although no evils have yet, in practice, resulted from the operations of this Society; although the evil tendencies which are charged upon it have not, after a lapse of thirty years, developed themselves, yet, if the mode of employing the school fund contains within itself a principle which is unsound, which is inconsistent with our institutions, which is inconsistent with the spirit of the law and the Constitution under which we live, I admit that the Legislature is bound to correct that principle. It is stated here, that nearly the whole education of the poor of the city of New York is under the control of this Society. I refer to page 1 of the Secretary's report, where it is said (as part of the substance of the memorials) :

That this Society, being a corporation, has acquired the entire control of the system of public education ; that the taxpayers, who contribute to the fund, have no voice in the selection of those who administer the system, or control over the application of the public moneys.

And, at page 11, the Secretary says :

The practical operation of the school laws is, to constitute the trustees of the Public School Society the officers and agents of the Government in the administration of the system of primary instruction in that city. That Society, in effect, engrosses the public education of the city ; and, instead of operating on small masses, as in the interior, embraces the whole.

Now, let us consider these assertions. Is it true that, in the proper sense of the term, all education in the city of New York is under the control of the Public School Society ? How—from what source—does the Public School Society receive the funds by which alone they maintain these schools from day to day ? From the hands of the Corporation of the city of New York—from the hands of the representatives of the people chosen at the ballot-boxes. They have a right to indicate the institution and the schools that shall receive this fund, and to impose what restrictions they please. This Public School Society receives its daily sustenance from the representatives of the people ; and the moment that sustenance is withdrawn, it dies —it cannot carry on its operations for a day.

How is this matter guarded ? Here is a Corporation chosen by the people. The law provides that this Corporation shall appoint one school commissioner for each ward, upon whom it imposes the duty of visiting, examining, and inspecting every one of the schools participating in the school fund. It is made their duty, twice at least in a year, to visit the schools ; and it is also made their duty to report to the Corporation ; and the Society is bound yearly to report to the Corporation and to the Legislature. The members of the Corporation themselves are *ex-officio* members of the Society, and the Mayor and Recorder are *ex-officio* members of the Board of Trustees. This Society or corporation, called the Public School Society, is the almoner of this public bounty ; for although it was originally designed for those who were the proper subjects of a gratuitous education exclusively, yet it is not now thus restricted. But now, those who participate in this fund are mainly such as are the proper subjects of gratuitous education. These agents of the people—first, the Corporation, and, secondly, the School Commissioners — are to supervise and direct and control and give daily bread to the Public School Society, whom they make their almoners to do this work under their eye. Now, what sound principle is violated here ? What principle of republicanism dear to the heart of any man is violated by this ?

Here are agents of the people—men who, having a desire to serve mankind, associate together ; they offer to take the superintendence of particular works; they offer themselves to the public as agents to carry out certain benevolent purposes; and, instead of paying men for the labor, they volunteer to do it for you, " without money and without price," under your directions—to do it as your servants, and to give an account to you and an account to the Legislature. Again, then, I ask, what principle is violated? Mr. Chairman, voluntary public service is always more efficient than labor done by servants chosen in any other way. I resort to the experience of this Society, and to the experience of all other kindred societies, to demonstrate the truth of this assertion; and I say that all that experience *will* demonstrate, that public objects are better accomplished by these voluntary servants, than they are usually accomplished by persons chosen directly by the people; not, however, independent of the people—far otherwise; but agents acting as the voluntary servants of the people, under the direction of the people, for the accomplishment of objects dear to the people. The Secretary tells you that, since the year 1813, there has been expended the sum of one million of dollars. If the fact is so—and I have no doubt that the Secretary states it upon authority—he should have accompanied it with the information that, in the expenditure of this money, not a single cent has been found deficient. He ought to have stated—and would, I have no doubt, if it had occurred to him at the moment, when he paraded here, or stated here, this sum of one million dollars which the Society had expended since the year 1813—he ought, I say, to have added that, like faithful servants, the Society had accounted for every cent; because the reports on the files in his own office will show that such an account has been given. Now, Mr. Chairman, I submit that the real question which, as citizens, we ought to discuss, is, not what prejudice we shall appeal to on this side or that, but in what way will you have a great public duty performed in the best manner? Will you have it done by volunteers, who, from the experience of thirty years, have proved themselves faithful, honest, and efficient, and who, during the last year, according to a report now on the files, themselves visited the schools *eleven thousand times?* Point out to me your school commissioners who, receiving pay, have done such service. Again, I ask, is not the question really, how you will have this duty best performed? In sparse populations, most men are occupied, and cannot volunteer for a service of this kind; they have not the leisure; it is too troublesome; but in large cities—in this city, probably, and in the city of New York—there always will be a class of men having leisure, and full of benevolent feelings, who may not wish to mingle in the contests of politics or of public life, in any manner, but who desire to devote themselves to some good and benevolent object that may be effective, and in a quiet way accomplish something for the benefit of mankind. Will you, as wise men, say we shall avail ourselves of these voluntary services, or shall we mingle every thing in the turmoil of politics? Will you say, that every thing shall be discussed on party principles? and will you have the question discussed at the polls, whether this man or that man is a Whig or a Democrat, so that the trustees may be chosen according to their politics? It has not yet come to that here; but in Philadelphia, I am informed, party politics have reached the superintendents

of common schools; and, by and by, the politics of the teachers will be
inquired into before they can be elected. Do you desire to bring every
thing within this angry vortex? Is it wise? Is it judicious? Is it conscientious? Can we not let this "well enough" alone?

Why, I ask, when you can avail yourselves of such services—when there
are men who love to serve you in this way, why will you not accept their
services? Is there any danger to democratic principles in this? What is
your Hospital, but a corporation acting as almoners of charity? What is
your House of Refuge? I can speak understandingly about it, for I was
connected with, and of it, from the start. Benevolent men looked abroad
over that great city, and saw children taken up for crimes, associated with
felons, and there joined with the school of vice, to be made perfect in its
tortuous ways, without redemption or hope of redemption. Their hearts
bled over the spectacle, and they met together and consulted as to what
could be done. They held a public meeting and took up a subscription,
amounting, on that night only, to the sum of sixteen hundred dollars. In
less than three months, this sum of sixteen hundred dollars was increased,
by voluntary contributions, to the sum of sixteeen thousand. And then,
what did they say? · "We cannot get on with this matter; we cannot carry
out our benevolent object of taking these young culprits, who, if left to the
law, are certain to occupy our bridewells and our houses of correction; we
cannot do any thing for them without corporate powers; and we must,
therefore, ask the Legislature to give us a part of the sovereign power of
the State."

We came to the Legislature, and the Legislature gave us a part of the
sovereign power. They are now a corporation of which, if any of you were
in a foreign land, you would be proud and happy to boast. It is one of the
jewels of the country. It has gone on; it has received the bounty of this
Legislature; it has received from it its daily bread and support, and yet the
directors are not chosen by the people. They are chosen by their associates,
and experience proves that it is a good mode of carrying out the contemplated objects; and yet, if we are to have this doctrine all at once established, that nothing is consistent with republicanism or democracy that does
not come directly from the people, the House of Refuge must be destroyed;
we must next have the schoolmaster elected by the people. Sir, let us act
like men of sense. We must use the advantages we have, and keep our eye
steadily upon the great end we have in view—to wit, the amelioration of
society, the education of the children of the State; and it is surely wise to
employ the best means we have for the accomplishment of this object.

Look at the Institution for the Blind; look at the Institution for the
Deaf and Dumb. The name is legion of those associations and corporations, composed of philanthropic individuals, to which a part of the power
of the people is granted. I would not enter the arena here to declaim
against or to advocate corporations. I have nothing to say about moneyed
corporations; I have nothing to say as to the cry against those corporations,
whether it is right or wrong. That is not the question; but I am here to
contend that men have the right, and that it is their duty, to associate to-

gether, and that, if they cannot carry out the objects of their association without corporate powers, it is wise and proper that the Legislature should impart those powers. Your churches, your every thing which comforts, and heals, and blesses the land, are in this sense corporations, and the Public School Society is among the number.

But it is said that one million of dollars have been expended. Well, now, in speaking of the manner in which this money has been appropriated, the Secretary might have shown, if he had inquired or looked into the reports, that about three hundred thousand dollars of the amount is in property now held for the purposes of common school education, consisting of buildings and other property, in real and personal estate. It may be said that it is dangerous for a corporation like this to hold a large amount of property. If the committee please, this is a danger of which the Society has been sensible, and, years ago (as the record on their minutes will show), they offered to deed all this property to the Common Council, and to take a lease from them, to use it for special purposes of education. The Society is willing at this moment to execute such a deed ; but the Corporation of the city of New York have uniformly said : " Gentlemen, you manage your property better than we manage ours. We have business enough. Keep it." We have pressed the matter upon them. It is now an offer before them, which they can accept at any time. But the confidence which that Corporation, from year to year, and without respect to the politics of the members composing it, has had in this institution, has induced them not to accept the offer. And I am here on the part of the Society to say, that they are willing to submit to any legislation or restriction upon this subject which, upon consultation, shall be deemed wise and beneficial, and calculated to promote and secure the grand object of universal common school education. This is a matter about which there can be no difficulty ; and if the Secretary of State, or if this committee, will sit down with a committee of the board, and regulate this matter, it can be put in the same shape (whatever that may be—and I do not precisely know what it is) as the asylum for the blind, the asylum for the insane, or any other institution having buildings or property, toward the purchase or erection of which the State has contributed.

I do not know how the property of these institutions is fixed or held ; but any mode which the Legislature, or the Corporation of the city of New York, may designate, and which is applied to other institutions for kindred objects, will be acquiesced in by the Public School Society.

I have spoken of the fact that there have been no objections made to the schools ; but if there are dangers to be apprehended, it is wise in the Superintendent to discern them from afar. He stands as a sentinel on the watchtower, and it is his duty to look ahead and to see what dangers may come. I have spoken of the consequences which may possibly grow out of the system, but I repeat that, as yet, nothing of an injurious character has been discovered. There has been no complaint made of the actual operation of the schools, but something has been said in their favor ; and I propose now, by the leave of the committee, to submit from public documents some of those favorable things which have been said.

The School Commissioners are a body of men chosen one for each ward by the Corporation, whose business it is to visit these schools and report upon them. The law of 1824 makes it necessary that these school commissioners shall not belong to the Public School Society, the object being to have an impartial board. And I may say of the present school commissioners, that there are no gentlemen more respectable, and these gentlemen were competent to judge of such matters. They do visit the schools, and I will now read a short paragraph from their report of July 27th, 1840. They say:

The qualifications and efforts of the teachers employed, and the course of literary instruction in the schools, continue to deserve the approbation of the commissioners. Without intending to detract from the acknowledged merits of the many worthy individuals who devote themselves to the education of youth in the numerous pay schools scattered throughout the city, the commissioners may be allowed to express their belief that, generally, the schools supported from the school money will not, as regards the progress of the pupils in the several branches taught there, nor on the score of legitimate discipline, suffer by a comparison with any others in this metropolis.

I have mentioned that the committee of the Corporation of the city of New York, when they had this matter under investigation, thought it their duty, before they reported, to visit the schools; they did so, and this is what they say:

The different classes examined in several schools by your committee exhibited an astonishing progress in geography, astronomy, arithmetic, reading, writing, &c., and indicated a capacity in the system for imparting instruction far beyond our expectations; and, though the order and arrangement of each school would challenge comparison with a camp under a rigid disciplinarian, yet the accustomed buoyancy and cheerfulness of youth and childhood did not appear to be destroyed in any one of them. Such were the favorable impressions forced upon our minds by a careful examination of the public schools. It is due to the trustees to add, that not one of our visits was anticipated, and no opportunity was afforded to any of the teachers for even a momentary preparation.

Again:

The public school buildings are constructed upon a uniform model; the books used are the same in all the schools, and the classes and departments in each are so similarly constituted and provided, that the removal of a pupil from one school to another will not interrupt his studies or retard his progress.

Now here is an advantage which those who live in the city of New York understand and appreciate, and which a system contemplating the formation of schools by small masses, never can have. Here is a system suited to a migratory population. All the books, all the forms, all the lessons, are the same; and if a child removes from one ward to another, he can be put in the class coresponding to that which he left, and he stands upon the same footing. The blackboard is the same, the exercises are the same. Every one knows the advantage of continuing on the same course of education which has been begun, if it was judicious in the first instance. But what does this new system contemplate ? It contemplates the destruction of this peculiarity ; and this report of the Secretary goes on to speak of the advantages of the system pursued in the country. *Gentlemen, the poorest child in the city of New York has advantages in the way of education—of elementary education—which are denied to nine tenths of the sons and daughters of the farmers of the State of New York.*

I challenge an investigation on this point ; and I maintain that no committee of this, or of the other House, can act understandingly until they have visited these schools. They must do as the committee of the Common Council did—go and see for themselves. Why, then, should we change the system ?

But it is said—and said, too, in this report of the Secretary—that he proposes to retain these public schools. How retain them ? One of the features of the proposed new law is, that all school moneys shall be paid to the teachers. Under such a law we cannot live a day—not a day. We have to buy stationery and books; we have to build school-houses. We have large schools, and the surplus, after the payment of teachers, goes to the erection of school-houses, and the purchase of books and stationery. What do you think is the expense, in the city of New York, of educating a child ? —not alone the expense of which I have spoken, but of furnishing books, slates, and other stationery, and of fuel and repairs—not rent—but repairs of school-houses. The expense for one year is less than five dollars a scholar. For five dollars a whole year, this education, with all the necessary stationery, books, slates, and fuel, is furnished. I say, if we are only to receive pay for our teachers, we cannot exist a day.

There is another point. After the passage of the law of 1824, upon an investigation made at the time as to the condition of some of the destitute part of our population, a representation was made by the Public School Society, and, after the Corporation had excluded religious societies, the Public School Society exerted themselves in behalf of the cause of education, and induced a large number of the most considerable property-holders of the city of New York to petition to be taxed for the purpose of carrying out this system, and of extending it.

They petition the Corporation to be taxed. Sir, if ever there was a people borne down by taxes, it is the people of the city of New York who have property ; and yet, strange to say, men who paid from one hundred to two thousand dollars annual taxes, confiding in these trustees, and desirous of carrying out this system of education under the direction of these trustees, came forward at their instance, and prayed the Corporation to tax them more. A memorial for which I sought in vain with a view of bringing it here, but which could not be found, shows the names of these petitioners— names which will be familiar to some of the members of this committee. Here you have a perfect anomaly ! You can hardly produce a similar case in any country. The petitioners, I say, came forward and prayed to be taxed, at the instance of the Public School Society, for the purpose of carrying out the system—men who could not look to secure any person a benefit, because they did not send their own children to these schools. The consequence was, that the tax was laid, and it produced the sum of $72,000 annually. Only half that amount, however, was raised by our Common Council last year under that head.

Since (excepting in the year 1840, as above stated) this tax was imposed, it has yielded annually the sum aforesaid of $72,000. Now, if we are to adopt this plan of election by the people—if the system is to be so extended as to be made like that which prevails in the country, we must adopt the whole, and not a part only of that system; we must have all, if we have any of it; and this sum of thirty-six thousand dollars, thus raised by this tax, must be cut off. These petitioners have a right to say, " Gentlemen, the contract is violated; for although you may anticipate great evil in trusting this money to this Corporation, yet it was by reason of our reliance upon this Public School Society as our almoners, that we asked to be taxed. Now, off with the tax; let us have the system as it is in the country, and see what will become of the public schools."

The amount received from special tax was, during the last year, $36,075; and if we are to have the country system, that tax is relinquished, and then the money is to be given out to commissioners, for school districts in the small mass, to use the language of this report. For instance, we are to have commissioners elected in each ward; they are to partition the ward out into school districts. These districts are to elect trustees. If there is not money enough received from the State, and fund enough added to that which is laid by the general tax, then these small masses must be taxed to build up school-houses and to make up the deficiency. This I understand to be the operation of the system in the country. These trustees are to lay a tax (to make up the deficiency) upon the property-holders, and in this way we are to have small masses governed by these trustees. We are to have such religion as the majority may choose, and such books as the majority may choose, and the whole of this system, which has been so well tried, and has been productive of such good fruits, is to be exchanged for a new one. For I maintain that, unless there is some very special provision not contemplated on the face of this report, the public school system of the city of New York, as now constituted, cannot stand. You must either have the system as it is in the country, or our system as it exists at present in the city.

Now, is the committee prepared to report, and will the Senate be prepared to adopt such a report—one that shall cast off this system which has been tried and approved, and that we shall " fly to something that we know not of ?" Will they decide that the agents to whom the city of New York gave this power, some sixteen years ago, have been faithless to their trust, and that the power shall be restored to the Legislature ? Will they decide that they have now leisure to bestow more attention on this subject, and to look more into the details than their predecessors had ? It was an argument which forced itself strongly on the consideration of the Legislature of 1824 : " We cannot understand this matter; it is local; it is different, in some

26

respects, from any thing we have in the country. We cannot well judge of it, and we will leave you to settle it among yourselves." But if the Legislature of the present day has discovered a new mode of doing business, so that it can take upon itself a little more legislation for the city of New York, very well; I shall be glad to find that it is so. I shall be glad to find that this Legislature does not feel the same pressure of business that its predecessors felt in 1824, and that it can enter into these matters more minutely. We had no disposition to take the subject into our hands then, and we have no disposition that the Legislature should take it back now. The people in New York understand the subject, and the Roman Catholics cannot say that they will not be heard as well there as here. Why not leave the matter to us, the people of the city of New York? If you choose to have commissioners elected by the people, instead of being chosen by the Corporation, I say, "Amen; very well; enlarge their powers, if you choose; have the inspections and examinations more frequently if you choose, by the agents of the people, chosen by the direct votes of the people." But let us not disturb a system more healthful, and beautiful, and effective, as a system, than any other where the English language is spoken. There is nothing to be compared to it. If it shall be destroyed—if our Catholic brethren, of whom I wish to speak with great respect, have found so powerful an auxiliary in the honorable Secretary of State, that they shall be able to carry out their purposes here, and these schools should, in consequence, be destroyed, that officer will gain a renown which will go down through all time. But I should prefer the renown of him who fired the Ephesian dome to that renown.

Mr. Chairman, the Public School Society have come here once more to plead for the seminaries of elementary instruction under their charge. Sixteen years gone by they passed through one trying scene. They contest was long, arduous, and severe, and their hearts began to fail, and their hands to tire, but they succeeded then. Now, the contest is renewed, and the trustees engage in it with extreme reluctance; they have no personal interests to advance, and they are very unwilling to be put in hostile array against any of their fellow-citizens. They are men of peace; their ends and purposes are all peaceable; they desire, as servants of the people, to do some good to the rising generation, if permitted; they are willing to visit the schools, to foster them, to collect in them the destitute and the outcast, but they abhor controversy. If the Public School Society shall be permitted to go on, as in former years it has gone on, I cannot doubt there will always be found a class of citizens who, competent and efficient, are willing to volunteer their services in advancing the cause of education; and, under the careful and searching supervision of agents chosen by the people, I hope the trustees, and their successors, may be permitted, for ages to come, to continue their benevolent labors.

The committee proceeded with the consideration of the question, and, on the 11th of May, Mr. Root, the chairman, introduced a bill, which was passed by unanimous consent to its second reading, and ordered to the Committee of the Whole.

On Thursday, May 20th, Mr. Verplanck moved that the bill be made the special order for the next day, which was agreed to. The special order was not moved on Friday, but a remonstrance from the Public School Society, in reply to Mr. Spencer's report, was laid before the Senate. It is as follows:

In Senate, May 21, 1841.

MEMORIAL AND REMONSTRANCE

OF THE TRUSTEES OF THE PUBLIC SCHOOL SOCIETY OF THE CITY OF NEW YORK.

To the Senate of the State of New York:

The memorial and remonstrance of the trustees of the Public School Society of the city of New York, RESPECTFULLY REPRESENT:

That they have had under consideration the report of the Superintendent of Common Schools, in relation to public instruction in the city of New York, which was presented to your honorable body during the present session, and have given to it the careful and deliberate consideration which the high importance of the subject demands.

Having, during many years, devoted much time and labor in promoting and conducting public education in this city, your memorialists trust that it will not be considered obtrusive in them to present to the Senate the results of their observations and practical knowledge of the subject, as well as the facts and arguments on which they rely in justification of their remonstrance against the propositions contained in the report referred to. In doing so, your remonstrants feel relieved from the necessity of adducing any new or additional evidences of the quality and efficiency of the numerous schools under their charge. The annual returns of the Commissioners of School Money (a board of seventeen citizens, appointed by the Common Council), under whose supervision the schools are conducted, furnish decided evidence of their good quality; and, very recently, a special committee of the Board of Aldermen, after having visited and examined the schools, in company with a jealous and watchful delegation from the citizens, whose memorials gave rise to the report now under review, bore the most ample testimony to the excellency of the schools and efficiency of the system, and gave it as their opinion that, if " any portion of the children should be left uneducated, it cannot be justly chargeable to a want of comprehensiveness in the system, but is more fairly attributable to imperfections which human legislation cannot remedy." (See Document No. 40 of the Board of Aldermen, p. 560.)

During the past summer, the public schools were also inspected by a commission appointed for that purpose by the Superintendent, and your memorialists venture to appeal to their report to sustain the good character which is claimed for the schools The report now under review has, however, so fully and frankly assumed the correctness of this position, that comment on this head might, perhaps, have been spared. If, then, it be admitted that the system of public instruction which now exists in this city is good, and is acceptable to the municipal government and to the citizens generally, the question presents itself, Why should the Legislature of the State interpose its authority for the purpose of altering or changing that system ? The reasons assigned in the report of the Superintendent of Common Schools may be arranged under four principal heads :

1st. That public education in the city of New York is now chiefly under the control of a private corporation, which receives nearly all the money raised by a general and indiscriminate tax, and that those who pay the tax have no voice in the selection of those who administer the system, nor control over the application of the public moneys thus appropriated.

2d. That, in the management of the existing public schools, " the conscientious opinions and feelings of large classes of citizens are disregarded ; " that the system is " unfavorable, if not hostile, to those principles of religious faith," held by some of the memorialists " to be dearer than life itself ; " and that they " cannot, consistently with their views of religious duty to their children, send them to such schools."

3d. That " there are numerous other schools in the city of New York, founded by voluntary associations, in which many thousands of the children of poverty and distress receive their education," and that these schools are arbitrarily excluded from all participation in a common fund collected by the joint contributions of all.

4th. That the present system of public instruction has failed to accomplish the purpose for which it was organized.

The prominent objections urged in the report are here, it is believed, fully and fairly embraced ; and your remonstrants will proceed to consider them in the order in which they occur. In estimating the validity and force of the first objection, it is important to bring into view the probable motives that induced the Legislature to exempt the city of New York from laws applied to every other part of the State. The enlightened men who originated our general system of common school education must have seen, or thought that they saw, something so peculiar in the population of a large city, something so different from the more homogeneous and less changeable population of other parts of the State, as to demand special legislative provisions. When attention was directed to this city, it was found that several religious societies and churches supported charity schools for the education of the children of their indigent members, and that a number of philanthropic individuals had anticipated the action of the State, and had been for nearly ten years associated under a charter, for the purpose of educating those poor children who were not provided for in the Church schools. The Legislature, therefore, in 1813, when the first distribution was made, very naturally appropriated the amount apportioned to this city to these schools, in the ratio of the number of children taught in each. This mode of distribution continued until 1824, when the subject was again brought before the Legislature by the jealousies, disputes, and difficulties which had arisen amongst the recipients; and the conflicting parties presented themselves at Albany, for the purpose of sustaining their respective claims.

In the progress of the inquiries and discussion which ensued, it became manifest that moneys raised by a general and indiscriminate tax could not be given to any religious society or association, without a flagrant violation of one of the most prominent conditions of our political compact. That this obvious truth did not present itself to the notice of the Legislature, when provision was first made for the distribution in this city, can be accounted for only on the supposition that the small amount to be distributed, and the intrinsic difficulty of making suitable provision for a large, dense, and mixed population, induced a temporary resort to the readiest expedient that presented.

The report of the committee of the Assembly which was charged with the duty of assembling the claimants-referred to, contains the following passages:

It appears that the city of New York is the only part of the State where the school fund is at all subject to the control of religious societies.

Your committee forbear, in this place, to enter fully into this branch of the subject; but they respectfully submit, whether it is not a violation of a fundamental principle of our legislation to allow the funds of the State, raised by a tax on the citizens, and designed for civil purposes, to be subject to the control of any religious corporation.

Still, no plan adapted to the wants of the city was suggested. But the manifest propriety of referring the subject to the immediate, exclusive, and local representatives of its inhabitants, forced itself upon the Legislature. A belief that the municipal government would better understand the feelings and necessities of the local population, in its several parts and conditions as well as a whole, and be thereby better enabled to reconcile conflicting interests and opinions, doubtless induced the Legislature to delegate the power to the Common Council of the city.

Accordingly, in the session of 1824, as stated in the report of the Superintendent, a law was passed vesting in the Common Council the right to designate " the institutions and schools " which shall be entitled to receive a share of the school moneys, and prescribe the rules and restrictions under which such moneys should be received by such institutions or schools respectively.

It is here worthy of remark, that this act repealed the act of 1813, which expressly enumerated " religious societies " among the recipients; and yet, in transferring the power, no mention is made of such societies; but the parties designated as those among whom it might be divided was made to embrace all the other parties included in the act of 1813, viz., "institutions and schools."

If this may not be considered of binding obligation on the Common Council, it is certainly indicative—particularly when taken in connection with the language of the report of the committee of the Assembly, above quoted—of the feeling which prevailed on the subject of "religious societies," and at least lent the sanction of the Legislature to the continued use of private incorporations for purposes of common education. However this may be, the conflict was renewed in this city, and, after a patient hearing of the parties and a full investigation of the subject, religious societies were excluded; and your remonstrants were made, as stated in the report, the chief agents in disbursing the school money, and in carrying out the views of the Government in relation to common schools.

This duty they have continued to discharge with untiring industry and zeal from that time to the present; with what degree of abilty and success, will appear in the progress of this remonstrance.

After nearly forty years, the question is now for the first time raised in the Legislature, Shall a private corporation, the members of which are not elected by, nor directly responsible to, the people, be permitted, however successfully and judiciously, to disburse moneys raised by a general tax? It will readily be seen that, if a negative answer must be given upon the mere abstract proposition, and without regard to the checks and safeguards which may have been thrown around the trust, or to the length of time it has faithfully performed its functions and sustained a jealous and searching scrutiny, it will be a first step in a radical system of reform which, if carried out, can scarcely stop short of remodelling the organization of civil society. Our hospitals, our asylums for the insane, for the blind, for the mute, our dispensaries and houses of refuge, &c., must all fall before it, because all and each of these receive and disburse the people's money; and in none of them are the trustees or managers elected by, or immediately responsible to, the people. Indeed, the above institutions are in several respects more obnoxious to the objections urged in the Superintendent's report than is the institution now attacked. To several, if not all of them, the Legislature has secured the annual payment of large sums of public money, to be continued twenty, twenty-five, and thirty years, and without any direct or fixed system of supervision on the part of the people or their representatives. As regards the House of Refuge of Juvenile Delinquents—an institution which that eminent philanthropist and enlightened statesman, De Witt Clinton, declared to be "the best penitentiary institution ever devised by the wit and established by the beneficence of man"—the comparison does not stop here. This "private corporation" is not only entrusted with public money, but is permitted to exercise a "function which emphatically belongs to the Government"—that of carrying out the sentence of courts of criminal jurisprudence. Now, what are the circumstances under which your remonstrants are permitted to provide for public education?—a duty which some governments have never assumed, and which some of the most enlightened have, until very recently, entirely neglected.

They are under the supervision of a Board of Commissioners, consisting of seventeen citizens appointed by the immediate representatives of the people, and without whose certificate of approval they cannot draw a cent from the public purse. Should this Board neglect or refuse to discharge its duty, it is competent for the appointing power to strike your remonstrants from the list of recipients, and destroy at once their capacity for evil.

The Mayor and Recorder are *ex-officio* members of the Board of Trustees, and the board is required by law " to make a report, during the month of May in each year, to the Superintendent of Common Schools, and also to the Common Council of this city, containing a particular account of the state of their schools, and the moneys received and expended by them during the preceding year, so as to exhibit a full and perfect statement of the property, funds, and affairs of said Society." (See 4th section, Law of Common Council, March 7, 1834.)

In addition to these salutary provisions of law, the Superintendent of Common Schools, although he does not claim to be authorized, he very properly did, within a year, appoint a commission to visit and examine the schools under the charge of your remonstrants, and report their condition to him ; a duty which they performed, and the result is stated in his report to your honorable body, which is now under consideration.

These are facts accessible to all whose duty or inclination might prompt them to make the inquiry ; and yet, as your remonstrants perceive with surprise and regret, the Superintendent has overlooked them, and avers that the Public School Society is " an anomaly wholly unknown in any other department of the public service," and that it is " not amenable in any form to the laws, nor subject to any supervision by the government of its officers ; " and finally, that its existence " involves a principle so hostile to the whole spirit of our insitutions, that it is impossible it should be long sustained."

The strong and pointed terms in which the Superintendent deprecates the agency of persons who are not elected by the people in carrying out the intentions of government in relation to education, contrasts strangely with the facts that, at his suggestion, a law was passed, in 1839, authorizing him to appoint county visitors ; and in his last annual report he announces a material improvement in the discharge of duty on the part of commissioners and inspectors who are elected by the people, and attributes it chiefly to the diligence, advice, and stimulating example of the county visitors, who are not elected by, nor are they responsible to the people.

In a report made to the Legislature, in 1840, transmitting abstracts of the reports of the county visitors appointed by the Superintendent, it is stated that " they concur in representing the inspectors chosen at the town meetings as being generally not well qualified for that particular duty, and as being very remiss in its performance ; " " that the examinations of the inspectors are slight and superficial, and that no benefit is derived from them ; " and the Superintendent remarks : " It has already been shown to the Legislature from the official returns, that at least one half of all the schools in the State are not visited at all by the inspectors."

The practice of conferring on private corporations some of the functions of government, and entrusting them with public money, obtained in the earliest period of our existence as an independent nation, at a time and with a population as vigilant and as jealous of their own rights as can be justly claimed for those of the present day. Your remonstrants are fully aware that the trite political maxims which are arrayed against them in the report of the Superintendent of Common Schools exert a powerful influence on the public mind, and that those who would oppose their application, in any given instance, must encounter a strong current of popular prejudice. But it is respectfully submitted to your honorable body, whether the position in which the public schools of this city are placed by legal enactments does not render them as safe as other institutions incorporated for purposes of a kindred character, and afford as ample security against abuse ?

Your remonstrants will now preceed to consider the objections classed under the second head, viz. :

That, in the management of the existing public schools, the conscientious opinions and feelings of large classes of citizens are disregarded ; and that the system is unfavorable, if not hostile, to those principles of religious faith held by some of the memorialists to be dearer than life itself; and that they cannot, consistently with their views of religious duty to their children, send them to such schools.

These declarations, so far as the trustees have any agency or control, are entirely erroneous, and your remonstrants cannot withhold an expression of their surprise that the Superintendent of Common Schools should have been so inattentive an observer of events connected with the subject of education within this State, as not to be aware of their incorrectness ; and that he should, even indirectly, lend to them the high sanction of his official signature.

The first open attack upon the public schools of this city was commenced by those whose charges gave rise to this inquiry some years since, and they have been made to assume various and opposite forms. When disproved in one form, they have been revived in another.

At one time it was declared, " the public school system in the city of New York is entirely favorable to the sectarianism of infidelity, and opposed only to that of positive Christianity," that it " leaves the will of the pupil to riot in the fierceness of unrestrained lusts," and is " calculated to make bad and dangerous citizens."

Now, it is contended that the conscientious opinions and feelings of large classes of citizens are disregarded, and that the system is unfavorable, not to religion or morals, but to the "*principles* of religious faith " held by the complainants.

The former high and most extraordinary charges were promptly met and refuted. It now remains to show that the latter are equally destitute of foundation.

In the year 1834, an interview was had with the then acting Roman Catholic Bishop of this diocese, for the purpose of assuring him of the wish of your remonstrants to remove from the school-books every thing offensive to his Church, and to invite his active coöperation in attaining that end. More recently, the same overtures were made, verbally and in written communications, to dignitaries of various grades in the same Church. During the past year, a committee was appointed by the trustees of the Public School Society to examine the " books in use in the public schools, including those in the libraries, with a view to ascertain and report whether they contain any thing derogatory to the Roman Catholic Church, or any of its religious tenets, with power to communicate with such persons of that

Church as may be authorized to meet them in reference to such alterations."
Conferences were accordingly had with Catholic priests, and the school-
books were left with them for examination. These advances and proposals
of the trustees were not, however, met in the spirit in which they were
made. Those to whom the books were submitted, after detaining them
some time, declined uniting in any examination of their contents.

The trustees of the public schools nevertheless proceeded and completed
the work of expurgation without the aid of those who had complained so
vehemently of the injustice which had been done them. The evidences of
the truth of this statement are contained in numerous written and printed
documents; they are spread on the minutes of the proceedings of your
remonstrants; they are contained in the files of both departments of the
city Government, and have been widely circulated in printed statements,
both official and unofficial; and yet your honorable body is assured that the
conscientious opinions and feelings of large classes of citizens (meaning
Roman Catholics) have been disregarded.

In relation to the second and third branches of the charges included
under the second head, your remonstrants can only say that, so far as they
were able to discover, the exceptionable passages in the school-books were
such as occur in the histories commonly approved, or they were incidental
remarks of frequent occurrence. It is admitted that the objectors have the
exclusive right to judge, so far as regards the danger to their own offspring.
But in the progress of these negotiations and expurgations, your remonstrants were driven by the force of circumstances into the conclusion, that
the opposition to the public schools, and to the books used in them, had
some ulterior object in view. This may seem illiberal, but frankness demands
the avowal; and a single fact will serve to show that the conclusion is not
entirely without ground to rest upon.

During an examination of one of the Catholic schools, the committee of
the Board of Aldermen, in company with a delegation from your remonstrants, found in use, as a class-book, the identical work to which exception
had been taken, and the only one which, in the proceedings before that
Board, was quoted from as evidence that Catholic children could not be sent
to the public schools. Nor did the inconsistency of the affair stop here.
The exceptionable passage had long been erased from the copies in the public schools, while it remained unobscured in those attached to the Catholic
churches.

The propositions under the third head are: "That there are numerous
other schools founded by voluntary associations, in which many thousands
of the children of poverty and distress receive their education," and that
these schools, maintained for the same objects and accomplishing the same
beneficial results, are arbitrarily excluded from all participation in a common
fund collected by the joint contributions of all."

Without stopping to inquire whether the terms "voluntary associations"
may be properly applied to a board of trustees of a Church-school, your
remonstrants cannot withhold the remark that this part of the report would
have been more explicit and better understood if it had stated the fact that

the schools referred to are attached to, and are under the exclusive control of, Roman Catholic churches, viz.: "St. Peter's Church," "St. Mary's Roman Catholic Church," "St. Patrick's," "Transfiguration Church," "St. Joseph's," "St. James'," and "St. Nicholas' Church."

The citizens at large are not only shut out from the management of these schools by their organization, but the books used and the doctrines taught in them are so utterly exclusive and intolerant, as to forbid the attendance not only of the children of parents of every other religious sect, but of those of no sect.

They are not merely the incidental remarks of the historian, or extracts from the Holy Scriptures, "without note or comment," to which such strong exception has been taken in relation to the public schools, but they are such as ever have, and, in the opinion of your remonstrants, ever must tend, if sustained by tax imposed upon the anathematized portion of the community, to destroy public harmony; and such as would prove any thing rather than a "social benefit."

But your remonstrants deny that these schools are "maintained for the same object" as are the public schools; or, rather, they contend that objects are embraced in them, and are deemed of vital importance, which do not nor can they enter into the course of instruction in the public schools, because the conflicting opinions of the trustees do not admit of it. It is true that, when the glaring inconsistency of asking for public aid in support of schools so managed was urged upon the applicants, they proposed that no religious instruction should be given "during the usual school hours." But having in view the stringency with which the same party insisted on the necessity of religious in juxtaposition with secular education, and the warmth with which they denounced the public school system when they saw fit to charge it with excluding religion, and particularly when reference is had to their avowed dogma that there is no hope of salvation to those not of the Roman Catholic Church,—which dogma is now taught in their schools—it should not be cause of surprise that doubts were entertained of a full compliance with the condition; or, even if literally complied with, could it be considered such a separation of the two objects as the public might of right demand if taxed to support the schools?

The tenacity with which men adhere to "those principles of religious faith upon which, in their estimation, their present and eternal welfare depends," and which is so forcibly described in the report of the Superintendent, would seem to admonish legislators not to tax the whole community for the support of educational establishments which are controlled exclusively by those professing the same faith, lest the very sincerity which the report so justly attributes to persons of this class, should induce them to promote the religious at the expense of the literary education of the pupils; which certainly was not the intention of the Legislature in establishing the system of common school education.

Your remonstrants had supposed that the fact of the Public School Society being constituted of men professing every variety of religious faith, would neutralize sectarian tendencies and secure it against abuse. Whether a division of the city into small masses, under the immediate control of the people themselves, is better calculated to attain that end, will be considered in another place.

The fourth and last division of the objections to the existing system of education which are presented in the report of the Superintendent of Common Schools, remains to be considered, viz. :

That the present system of public instruction has failed to accomplish the purpose for which it was organized.

In order to sustain this hypothesis, it is stated, and certainly on what might be considered good authority, " that more than one half of the children between four and sixteen years of age, in the city of New York, are not receiving the benefit of any education whatever." That the number of such children is very great, cannot be denied ; but there can be no doubt— and your remonstrants assert with confidence—that it is greatly overrated in estimates founded upon the returns of the United States marshals, and for reasons which, on reflection, are entirely obvious. It is true, as stated in the report, that the trustees of the public schools drew the same conclusion from the data furnished in the census, in memorializing the Legislature for an appropriation of money for the erection of additional school-houses. The truth of the statement was questioned by some when the memorial was under consideration ; and subsequent reflection and inquiry have convinced all, that the actual number of uneducated children cannot be one third of that which is assumed in the report.

It is well known that very many parents will not send their children to school until they are six years of age ; and thousands refuse to continue them there after they are eleven or twelve, because they can then be placed in situations to support themselves, or can be made available in contributing to the support of the family. Pending the preparation of this remonstrance, an inquiry has been instituted for the purpose of ascertaining what proportion of the children who enter the public schools remain in them after twelve years of age ; and it is found, by returns received from ninety-one out of one hundred and two schools, that it is only seven and two thirds per cent. In a family of six children within the school age—say of the respective ages of five, seven, nine, eleven, thirteen, and fifteen—only half may be attending school ; and yet, none should be returned as being without the means of education, because the youngest may be kept at home in consequence of its age, and receive some instruction from the mother or older children, and the two oldest may have received as much education as the law contemplates or as the parents deem necessary. The youngest and the two oldest should, therefore, be excluded from the list of those who are not " receiving the benefits of any education whatever."

It is believed that the estimated number attending private schools is much too small, and the result of a partial inquiry made in a single ward (the Seventh) would appear to sustain this view. There are, moreover, a considerable number of children belonging to this city who are sent for education to the numerous colleges, academies, institutions, and boarding-schools located in this and the adjacent States, and the number cannot be very small who are taught at home under governesses and other private tutors. Both these classes should be included in the number attending private schools.

In connection with, and as having an intimate and most important bearing upon, this branch of the subject, your remonstrants ask attention to the facts derived from the report made by the Secretary of State to the Legislature during the present session (Document No. 277), by which it appears that the whole number of paupers supported at poor-houses in this State is 56,561; and that, of this number, 27,553, or nearly one half, are in the city of New York; or that the number of paupers in the counties, exclusive of New York, is as 1 to 42 and a fraction to the whole population, while the number in New York is as 1 to 11 and a fraction. The comparison between the out-door paupers, or those relieved at their own residences, shows a still greater disparity between the metropolis and other parts of the State. Of this class of persons there are in the State, exclusive of this city, 29,008; and in the city, 27,553; or the out-door paupers in the State, exclusive of the city, is as 1 in 73 of the whole population, and in the city as 1 to 12. But the great disproportion of paupers between the city and country is not fully made out by this method of estimating; for it is well known that, besides the thousands in the city who subsist by a practice but little known in the country (street-begging), there is a very large number who are indebted for permanent or temporary relief to private sympathy, and the benevolent institutions of which there are so many in the city. Could all these be added to the number contained in the official returns, it would be swelled greatly beyond the number in every other part of the State.

Your remonstrants have not the means at hand of presenting a comparative view of commitments and convictions for vagrancy and crime, but it is confidently believed that they would present results equally unfavorable to the city. Now, if the Superintendent of Common Schools can furnish reasons for these discrepancies, he will at the same time account for your remonstrants having failed to induce all the poor children in the city to attend the public schools.

This would seem a proper place to correct an error in the report, which states that there is not a "want of accommodation for pupils." The fact is far otherwise. The present school buildings are generally full, and some of them are crowded to a degree that is equally prejudicial to health and unfavorable to the acquisition of learning.

How the Superintendent was led into this error, is not perceived, unless he inferred it from the efforts used to induce the attendance of children; which is not improbable, from his adverting to those efforts in connection with the remark regarding accommodations. When a school is full, efforts in that vicinity are diminished, and they are directed to some other point. But the chief want of accommodation for pupils arises from the fact that there are portions of the city which have grown up within a few years, and in which there are no school-houses. This was explained in the memorial (referred to in the report) asking for an appropriation of money to erect additional school buildings.

Your remonstrants will now submit a few remarks in relation to the causes of the disparity between the registered number of children in the public schools and the average attendance to which reference is made in the report.

The irregular attendance of children who are entered on the registers of the public schools has ever been cause of serious regret to the trustees, and every thing has been done which ingenuity could suggest and zeal accomplish in order to lessen this acknowledged evil—an evil which is found to arise from various causes, many of which are justified by necessity, and many more have their origin in indifference, or the want of vigilance and firmness on the part of parents. All of them, it is confidently believed, are beyond the reach of any remedy proposed in the plan of the Superintendent of Common Schools. Among the justifiable causes, is the straitened circumstances of a large proportion of the parents whose children enter the public schools. In a numerous class of cases, the mother "goes out to work" one or two days in each week, and is under the necessity of retaining the oldest child at home to take care of the younger ones. Very many married women are thus employed for the purpose of contributing to the support of the family; and as there are more than one thousand four hundred widows whose children attend the public schools, it will be seen that this cause must embrace a large number; and it is a cause which, if it exists at all, can only be to a very limited extent in country districts.

Another most prolific cause of irregular attendance, ranging under this head, is the inability of many parents to furnish their children with suitable clothing, and particularly shoes, to encounter the cold and storms of winter. It is customary for the teachers to note, on the registers of daily attendance, unusual cold and storms, and such days will be found to diminish the attendance to the extent of one to two hundred in a single school-building; and yet it is not unusual to see numbers come to school with naked feet in moderately cold weather, and when there is ice in the streets. Another cause which exists to a considerable extent, but which may not, perhaps, be so clearly classed among those that are justifiable, and which cannot prevail in country districts, is the fact that many families rely for fuel, to a considerable extent, on such as children can pick up in shipyards, at buildings that are being torn down, &c.; and this is accordingly assigned by parents as a motive for keeping their children from school a part of each week. Another cause which many parents consider justifiable, and which does not operate in the country, is the frequent military and civic parades incident to the metropolis of this State.

Among the unjustifiable causes of irregular attendance, truancy deserves a prominent place; and it must be seen that this fruitful cause will prevail to a far greater extent in a large city than in country districts. In the former, there is an almost infinite variety of exciting circumstances which induce this vicious habit, and which are unknown in the latter. It can scarcely be necessary to enumerate them. The occurrence, or even the alarm, of fire leads to the absence of hundreds from school; and it is worthy of special remark that it can be indulged in with greater impunity in a large and mixed population like this city, than in the more scattered and uniform population of the country districts.

Having in view the fact that, if one hundred children are absent from school each twelve days during the year, it will reduce the average attendance twenty-four hundred, it should not be a matter of surprise, particularly when considered in connection with the causes and motives to absence which are peculiar to large cities, that the disparity is so great. It appears, from actual inquiry, to be even somewhat greater in Boston than in New York. It is estimated that the single fact that a large portion of the people whose children attend the public schools, move their places of residence in May of each year—a practice not known in any other city—causes the absence from school of one fourth of the children for two weeks. They are generally withdrawn several days before moving-day, and a greater number of days are lost afterward, before they enter another school. These and other reasons why the disparity between the registered number of children attending the public schools and the actual average attendance, is greater than in other parts of the State, are, to your remonstrants, so obvious, that they are surprised they did not occur to the acute and observing mind of the author of the report. And it is equally matter of wonder that, in calling attention to this difference, he did not advert to the very important fact that the public schools of this city are kept open all the year, while in far the greater part of the country districts they are kept open four, five, six, seven, eight, and nine months; even including the cities of Hudson, Albany, Troy, Schenectady, Utica, Rochester, and Buffalo, in which they are open the whole year. The district schools of the State (exclusive of the city of New York) are open an average period of less than eight months in each year; and in those which are strictly country districts, not including the cities, the average is found to be less. It will hence be seen that even those pupils whose actual attendance at the public schools in this city average eight months in a year, are, for all practical and beneficial purposes, obtaining an amount of school-learning fully equal to those who attend the country district schools; and when the great and acknowledged superiority of the public schools over the district schools generally is admitted into the estimate, it will be found that the balance is in favor of the public school system.

Your remonstrants feel assured, however, that the percentage of absentees in the district schools is altogether erroneous. From observation and inquiry made recently, it is evident that in some, and probably in a large part, of the district schools, means are not even used to arrive at any thing like accurate knowledge on this subject.

The report of the Superintendent of Common Schools supposes the continued existence of the public schools as part of his system; but in no part of the report is he more in error than in this. They could not endure a single year in connection with his system.

The mode of instruction in the public schools is a modification of that which originated with the late Joseph Lancaster, and is made to depend on a large number of pupils under few paid instructors. In lessening the number of pupils one half, the expense, as regards teachers, could not be diminished. The opening of the district schools could not fail to divert pupils from the public schools, and thereby reduce the claims of the trustees on the school fund, without reducing the pecuniary demands upon them. The present expense of tuition in the public schools is reduced to the lowest possible sum, and may safely challenge a comparison with that of equal quality in any other place, or even with that of the district schools of this State.

In the latter, as appears from the last annual report, the average cost per child for teachers' wages is $3.35 for less than eight months' tuition, one half of which is exclusively by females; while the average cost in the public schools of this city for twelve months' tuition, under teachers of a quality and grade unknown to the district schools, is $2.75.

The sum now at the disposal of the trustees is barely sufficient to sustain the schools as they are; any considerable reduction must close them.

The report does, indeed, provide for the reduced income, by supposing it will be made up in the tuition fees which the contemplated system involves. But this has been fairly tried, and was found to fail, for reasons which will be stated hereafter.

From an intimate knowledge of the subject, the trustees are persuaded that the public schools would be broken up by introducing the Superintendent's mixed system into the city, and that the district system of the State would, as a necessary consequence, supersede it.

The Superintendent himself evidently anticipates this result, and therefore suggests that such public school buildings as might not be wanted by the Society, under the new system, could be sold, or hired out.

In considering the plan submitted to the Senate, your remonstrants will, therefore, confine their remarks and reasoning to the district system of the State.

The objections to the introduction of this system into the city of New York may be ranged under the following heads:

1. Its tendency to associate itself with party politics;

2. Its want of uniformity; and

3. Its incapacity to remove the difficulties alleged to be inherent in the present system.

That it is obnoxious to the first objection, appears so evident, that it is matter of surprise that any intelligent person should entertain doubts upon the subject.

The place of district school teacher, provided competent persons are employed and the character of the public schools is sustained, must be, in a pecuniary point of view at least, as desirable as very many offices which are now sought for with so much avidity by political partisans, and which are so often bestowed with little regard to the qualifications of the applicant. It is not perceived why the appointment of teacher will not be subjected to the same practice.

If the practice has not obtained in the country districts, it is because the compensation does not hold out an inducement. Admit, then, that teachers will be selected with reference to their political attachments, and all will agree that consequences the most disastrous to the cause of public education must ensue.

A successful and judicious teacher of youth combines qualifications which are not, in very numerous instances, found in one person.

It has presented one of the greatest difficulties which your remonstrants have had to encounter, and induced them, some years since, to open two normal schools for the purpose of training, in connection with the monitorial plan of the public schools, young persons of both sexes to this important profession. These schools have been attended by more than three hundred pupils.

The practice of conferring office as a reward for political services, is cause of deep regret to reflecting men of all parties, and a hope was indulged that the system of common school education would be exempted from its deleterious and blighting influence.

To the second objection to the district system in this city, viz., "Its want of uniformity," the attention of the Senate is particularly solicited, because, of itself, it is deemed a fatal objection to the plan of the Superintendent of Common Schools. It is well known that a large proportion of the children who attend the public schools remove from one locality to another almost every year, and that many of them change more frequently. Under the present uniform system, these changes are attended by very little, if any, check to the progress of the pupil in his studies. On leaving one school, he is transferred, by certificate, to another, and enters a class of the same grade with the one he has just left, continues to use the same books, and is taught by the same method. The disadvantages which result to the pupil from frequent changes, where schools are under independent or adverse management, is too well known and universally admitted to require illustration. Much of the time of children so circumstanced, which is now devoted to the acquisition of learning, will then be thrown away in studying new methods of learning; and the brief period of time that the children of persons in low and moderate circumstances are permitted to devote to school learning, strongly admonishes those who provide the means, to study an efficient and economical use of that time.

Another and a most serious evil inseparable from the proposed system, is the diversity of books it renders necessary. The public schools of this city furnish books to their pupils without charge; while in the district schools of the State the pupil is left to provide them for himself. The consequence is, that the use of uniform books cannot be secured, and hence, when a child removes from one school to another, he may have to use books not used by other pupils in the same school, or the parent may, however poor, be compelled to procure new books as often as his child enters a new school. The expense would not, in very many instances, be submitted to, and confusion in the classes would be an inevitable consequence.

This has been frequently referred to by different superintendents, as a serious evil in the district schools in the country, where children seldom have occasion to leave one school for another; and it would, of necessity, be immeasurably enhanced under the same system in this city, where children so frequently change the place of residence.

The third and last objection to the district system, as applied to this city, is ".its incapacity to remove the difficulties alleged to be inherent in the present system ; " and if this proposition can be sustained, the principal motives for hazarding the abandonment of a long-tried and well-proved plan, for the purpose of introducing one of doubtful expediency, and which, it has been shown, is liable to other very serious objections, will cease to exist.

The report fully recognizes the propriety and necessity of " a very considerable amount of religious instruction," and very justly remarks, that " religion and literature have become inseparably interwoven."

It is evident, therefore, that an education strictly and exclusively literary and scientific is not contemplated. But it is contended that, in the public school system, the conscientious opinions and " feelings of large classes of citizens are disregarded." It has been shown that this charge is so far from the fact, that strenuous and long-continued efforts have been used to reconcile conflicting views, by subjecting the school-books to expurgation. If, however, the charge was as well as it is ill-founded, the questions present themselves, What is the remedy proposed ? and, What is its character and means of efficacy ?

The remedy is, a division of the city into school districts, or " small masses," under the general care and supervision of persons elected for the purpose in each ward, who are to be aided by a salaried superintendent ; but it leaves the " amount and description of religious instruction " to be determined by the parents inhabiting the district.

It will thus be seen that a cure is not even promised. The remedy can only scatter throughout the body a disease which is declared to be constitutional, and which now gives uneasiness to only one of the members.

It is not perceived that the scheme of the Superintendent sustains his own principles. The report very justly remarks, that, " according to the principle of our institutions, no one has the authority to determine whether the religious doctrines and sentiments of any class of our citizens be right or wrong," and certainly no such authority has ever been assumed by your remonstrants. But what must be the practical effect of the district system ? Every school district in this city would unquestionably contain persons professing a variety of religious opinions, and, as they are to determine the degree and kind of religious instruction to be given in the district school, it is inevitable that the majority will be enabled either to impose their own religious opinions and dogmas on the children of the minority, or to drive them into the street. What is there in the composition of small masses, or districts, that can be relied upon to reconcile conflicting " modes of faith," or overcome religious jealousies and bickerings ?

If men of enlightened and liberal minds—if those to whom the people look for advice and direction in spiritual matters, and whose decisions would not be appealed from, cannot agree upon religious reading which would silence sectarian jealousy, what can be expected of the " masses " of

27

which the school districts will be composed ? Or if—as would probably be the case in many districts—apathy and indifference to the subject should leave religious instruction to accident or the taste of the teacher, would not the spirit of proselytism, which induces the missionary to visit the " uttermost parts of the earth," step in and disturb what all would consider a dangerous harmony ? and, whatever might be the good effects of such interposition in stirring up the lukewarm, could it fail to produce fruits which would prove fatal to harmonious action in religious education ? These are grave questions, and demand—and, your remonstrants doubt not, will receive—mature and careful consideration. They did not escape the discerning mind of the Superintendent, but he contends that the apprehended consequences will not ensue, because the records of his department do not afford evidence of any difficulty in relation to religious instruction in the district schools of the State. As regards the fact, he is doubtless correct, but the inference he draws is inconclusive and unsafe. The cause of difficulty is found, in this city, to an extent that is unknown elsewhere, but will most assuredly be felt, sooner or later, wherever its influence can be made to reach. Already the books in the district school libraries, which have been officially approved by the Superintendent of Common Schools and his predecessors, are vehemently attacked, and for the reasons which are adduced against those used in the public schools of this city.

The report concedes that the power of determining the kind and degree of religious instruction which shall be given in public seminaries, must rest with the majority, and that the only hope of the minority is in the " generous forbearance of those who may temporarily have the physical power to oppress ; " and it is worthy of special observation, that this acknowledged principle is virtually, in substance if not in form, carried out in this city.

A vast majority of the people are well satisfied with the system of public education which now exists, as is abundantly evinced by the decided manner in which they sustain it through their immediate representatives, to which it has been subjected under every form of attack. The city, after all, is one large district, in which the majority prevails over the minority. It would be the same in the school districts : each would have its minority, who would be required to yield, and throw itself upon the " generous forbearance " of the majority.

No good reason occurs to show why a member of the minority in a small mass would be any better reconciled to his condition than if he belonged to the minority in the large mass. This difficulty is inseparable from any system of general education so long as religious opinions are blended with it, and people continue to reside together without regard to religious professions.

In relation to the generous forbearance adverted to in the report, your remonstrants will take occasion to say, in addition to what has been before submitted, that the exertions which have been used and the overtures which have been made to protect the rights of the minority, by those to whom the majority have seen fit, however indirectly, to intrust the subject, may safely challenge a comparison with any thing on record.

The trustees of the public schools yielded many points to the minority, and perhaps even more than public sentiment would have sustained them in.

In relation to the last effort to reconcile the minority to the public school system, the committee of the Board of Aldermen, under whose mediation it was done, say, in their report (Document No. 40, p. 568), that they are fully of the opinion that, to have yielded more, " would render the school system liable to the charge of violating the rights of conscience "—a charge which would be fatal to the system, because it would invalidate its just claims to public patronage.

The propositions of the committee who represent the Public School Society appear to us to have been conceived in a liberal spirit ; and your committee think they go as far as a due regard to the objects of the institution would warrant, and would seem to open an avenue which we would fain hope may yet lead to a satisfactory arrangement.

Among the reasons assigned in the Superintendent's report for the non-attendance of so many " vagrant children," is " an idea," said to be " prevalent among the people, that an attempt is made to *coerce* them, directly or indirectly, to do something which others take great interest in having done. They are not left or called upon to act *spontaneously*, to *originate* any thing, or take any part in matters which they are told most deeply concern themselves."

Of the existence of any such cause your remonstrants are entirely ignorant, nor do they believe any such feelings exist.

Is it probable that persons who are so utterly indifferent to the present and future welfare of their offspring, as to permit them to become vagrants, could be influenced by any such considerations ? Or, if it be possible that there are those who keep their children from school, and yet permit them to " infest " the streets as " vagrants," because they are not permitted to " take any part " in the management of the schools, what beneficial results could be hoped for from the " spontaneous " action of such persons, or from any plans or movements which might " originate " with them ? Your remonstrants confess that they are unable to perceive the force or propriety of this reasoning.

Having with frankness, and with the respectful freedom which our institutions secure to the citizen, noticed the most prominent parts of a public document which treats of a subject of deep and abiding interest to all, your remonstrants conceive that they cannot, in justice to themselves or the cause they have espoused, omit to notice some incidental parts of said document.

In alluding to the memorials presented at the present and last session of the Legislature, one is said to be from " Catholic citizens ; " thereby conveying the idea, or at least leaving it to be inferred, that the other was not.

It is not pretended that every signer of all these memorials was a Catho-·lic ; but nothing can be hazarded by asserting that each and every one of them was essentially, and in fact, a Catholic petition.

At no time since the decision of the Common Council in 1824, which excluded Church schools, has there been, either in this city or elsewhere, any other class of citizens who appeared in opposition to the public school system of instruction, under the control of your remonstrants. These citizens have, of course, the same rights that appertain to every other class; but it is of some importance that this fact should be correctly understood.

Your remonstrants are not aware of any error in the detailed history of the Public School Society which is given in the report; but they are unable to discover its object, or the bearing it has on the merits of the question under discussion. The report says, that more than one million of dollars has been paid to the trustees of the Society since 1813, while only $125,268.57 have been paid to other societies or schools. This statement is probably correct, but no attempt is made in the report to draw an inference of any kind from the premises. It is not pretended that the funds have been misapplied, or that the other societies, whose comparatively small share is thus presented to view, would have made a better use of the money. Your remonstrants must say, however, that this part of the report should, in their opinion, have been made to embrace other highly important facts which are intimately connected with it. One is, that, of the amount received by the Public School Society, more than one half was derived from a direct tax on this city, which was petitioned for at the instance of your remonstrants, by several thousands of the largest tax-paying citizens, with a full knowledge of the manner in which it was then disbursed, and, as your remonstrants have occasion to know, with a confident expectation that it would continue to be so disbursed, or that it would not, in any event, be devoted to the support of sectarian schools. It was also essential to a correct appreciation of the subject, to have stated, that more than one third of the amount paid to the trustees of the public schools was necessarily expended in the purchase of land and in the erection of school buildings; that this land and buildings are still in existence, and form, together, a proud monument of the liberality of our citizens. Documents referred to in the report state these facts; and in more than one of them it is announced that the fee of this property has been repeatedly tendered to the municipal government.

The surprise that no mention should be made of the investments in school-buildings is increased from observing that, in the report made by the Superintendent during the present session (Document No. 90), in answer to a call of the Senate, it is shown that the sum of $138,563.44 has been invested by your remonstrants in land and school buildings within the last five years.

In relation to the pay system which the report embraces, it is proper to state that it was practised during several years in the public schools of this city, and was found to be an unceasing source of deceptions, jealousies, and dissatisfactions. The mean-spirited and sordid would plead poverty without just cause; while the generous and noble-hearted would make great efforts and unreasonable sacrifices to sustain a commendable feeling of independence. In the city of New York, with its mixed and constantly moving population, it was impossible to discriminate, with even an approach to accuracy, between those who should pay and those who should be exempt; and every mistake caused deep and wide-spread discontent.

But a difficulty far more formidable had to be encountered, in carrying out the mixed plan of pay and exemption. It was found impossible to conceal the distinction from the children, and it consequently gave rise to a classification that disturbed the harmony of the schools, while it is eminently opposed to the genius of our political institutions. The amount received from pay scholars diminished each succeeding year, and the trustees were finally induced to place all the children upon that footing of equality which comports so entirely with the feeling which pervades the public mind. The consequence is, that the poorest citizen, instead of being required to solicit the admission of his children into the public schools on the free list, is enabled to demand their admission as a right, and on the same terms with those of his more prosperous neighbor.

The people of this city have seen fit to furnish the means of breaking down the odious distinction between the rich and the poor, and the question is respectfully submitted, Why should the State interpose to restore it ?

After the foregoing statements, remarks, and reasonings in relation to the report of the Superintendent of Common Schools were prepared, your remonstrants received a copy of Document No. 565, being "An Act to Extend the Benefits of Common School Education in the City of New York ; " and they are surprised to find that it does not bear even a remote resemblance to the plan proposed in the late report of the Superintendent.

Your remonstrants would be wanting in the open frankness due to the Senate of this State, and to the importance of the subject, if they should withhold an expression of the conviction forced upon them, that this act, if not framed with that view, will inevitably embrace the schools connected with the Roman Catholic churches in this city. The claims of these Church schools to a portion of the school money have been again and again refused to the parties on their direct application to the municipal government, and with a degree of unanimity scarce ever shown on any other occasion ; and yet this bill is so constructed, that it will accomplish that end by indirect means. It would, in the opinion of your remonstrants, be a serious error to suppose that Catholic citizens would be permitted to enjoy the benefits of this bill without opposition. Even a slight knowledge of the feeling which prevails among persons connected with our various religious denominations would serve to show that public education in this city would soon be thrown into utter confusion, by efforts to counteract what would be considered by many a dangerous means of influencing and moulding the tender minds of youth.

The bill appears to your remonstrants to be liable to the same objections which have been urged against the plan proposed in the report of the Superintendent, on account of its tendency to connect itself with party politics ; and to this may be added the danger, if not the necessity, of an alliance of politics with religion.

If, as will most assuredly happen, a struggle arises to plant schools with a view to sectarian influence, it must be seen that, in order to secure the favor of the commissioners, whose right it will be to determine between conflicting claimants, this process must be commenced at the ballot-boxes.

Besides the Catholic Church schools, there are a number of schools connected with other denominations of Christians, and all these will be immediately placed within the reach of this law. Can it be expected—is it reasonable to expect—that the people of this city, who have asked for and have cheerfully paid the special tax for the support of public schools, will be content to continue its payment when the proceeds are appropriated to the support of sectarian schools—schools in which the conscientious opinions and feelings of many must be daily and hourly violated? Is it a sufficient answer to this to say, that the field is open to all? Your remonstrants think not.

There are a number of small congregations to whom it may be inconvenient, or who may not choose, in consequence of the scattered manner in which their members reside, or who from other causes may decline opening schools of their own, and whose conscientious feelings are entitled to the same protection and consideration of those of the more numerous classes. There is also a very large class of citizens who, while they acknowledge the importance of religion in bridling the fierce and dangerous passions of the human heart, will view with jealous apprehension the first step toward an association of religion with politics. They cordially unite with the sentiment expressed in the report of the Superintendent of Common Schools, " that religious worship has been better provided for, and attendance upon it has been more general, by being left to the free and voluntary action of the people, without the aid of any legal establishment; " and they are well aware that, of all means for securing attachment to a particular form of religion, and a blind devotion to it through life, the most effectual is, to cultivate it in the tender and susceptible mind of youth; and hence they never can consent to be taxed for sectarian establishments of any kind, whether for adults or for children.

The municipal government has been most cordially sustained in its repeated rejection of plans which differ from the proposed law only in being more direct, and a confident belief is indulged that the Legislature of the State will not impose upon the city a measure to which it is so averse.

If the act under consideration is viewed entirely apart from the objections stated above, it will be found to conflict in important particulars with the theory and reasoning of the Superintendent of Common Schools to even a greater extent than the system which now prevails.

It is contended, in the report, that, to devolve upon a private corporation the discharge of an important function of government, to give to those who are not directly responsible to the people the right of disbursing public moneys, the selection of teachers of whose qualifications they are the sole judges, and the establishment and maintenance of a system of public education according to their own ideas of propriety, is an anomaly wholly unknown in any other department of the public service, and involves a principle so hostile to the whole spirit of our institutions, that it is impossible it should be long sustained, when other and more congenial means of obtaining the same objects have been pointed out.

These and other consequences, which have been shown to be fallacious, are predicated of the public school system in this city, and it now remains to consider how far they are obviated, if at all, by the project submitted to your honorable body. The act proposes the election of school commissioners by the people, in place of their being appointed by the Common Council, as is now done; a change which may be made, if thought expedient, without disturbing any other portion of the present public school plan. But the very next provision of the act is at open war with the principles laid down in the report as being of vital importance, and such as the spirit of the age will not endure to see disregarded. It provides, virtually, that any number of inhabitants of this city who shall desire to establish a school, may present an application to the commissioners, who are authorized, if they consider such persons adequate to the support of a school, and if a school be required in the place specified, to grant a certificate thereof; when all such associations shall "possess all the rights and powers conferred by law upon the inhabitants of school districts in any other parts of the State." In short, every such association, of *any number* of persons, is made a private corporation for the purposes specified, and is entitled to its ratable portion of the public money.

In the plan of the Superintendent of Common Schools, the commisssioners elected by the people were to organize and establish schools where they appeared necessary, as district schools, with the usual officers, *to be chosen by the inhabitants* of the *district*. The two plans, it will thus be seen, conflict directly with each other in a most essential particular.

While the Superintendent throws around his scheme those defences and safeguards which he says are called for by the spirit of the age and the nature of our institutions, the act now pending confers upon any number, however small, of persons who may associate for the purpose, and without being elected by, or, in any greater degree than your remonstrants are, amenable to the people, the duty of discharging what is declared to be one of the most important functions of the Government.

The report objects to the association represented by your remonstrants, on the ground of its "want of responsibility to the people," and yet the proposed law contemplates the creation of an indefinite number of associations for the same object, equally independent of the people, and it is not discovered but that each one will be as obnoxious to the principles laid down in the report as the Society to which such strong exceptions have been taken. It will be seen that the city will have to depend for the means of general education on accidental and capricious circumstances.

Some portions may be crowded with schools, while others may be left destitute; and inasmuch as the associations will be required to receive pay from those who can afford it, there is no little danger that portions of the city where schools are most needed will be left without them.

In short, it appears evident to your remonstrants that, under the proposed law, feelings and motives of the most discordant character will be brought into action in establishing and maintaining schools, and will be made to supersede those which have hitherto prevailed, and which, whatever else may be thought of them, have been directed to the one important object of promoting the moral and literary education of the youth of the city.

The act imposes upon teachers, trustees, and commissioners, duties so intricate and arduous that they never·will be performed. As regards the duties required of teachers, in addition to those attached to the profession, your remonstrants feel authorized, from a long-continued and intimate acquaintance with the subject, to say that they cannot be discharged without sacrificing far more pressing and important interests.

The report provides that the Board of Commissioners elected by the people shall establish schools and a system for their government and inspection, and for providing the means of testing the qualifications of teachers. But in the act under consideration, all these points are left to the discretion of any number of inhabitants of lawful age, and adequate to the support of a school, who may desire to establish one. It is not, perhaps, the province of your remonstrants to contrast the provisions of the projected law with the principles contended for in the report of the Superintendent; but it appeared to be so intimately connected with the deeply interesting subject of common schools that it could not be well omitted.

It will be seen that much of the reasoning which has been applied to the system in the report is applicable to that which is embraced in the act, and particularly such parts as refer to the importance of uniform schools throughout the city—a point which never can be abandoned without the most disastrous consequences. This objection will apply to the provisions of the act with increased force. To the existing public schools it would be equally if not more fatal than the system proposed in the report.

Its practical operation must, therefore, be viewed as embracing the whole city. Considered in this light, if the extra duties imposed upon teachers by this act are executed at all, it must be at the expense of the best interest of the pupils, or a supernumerary teacher must be employed to perform them.

This remonstrance has been extended far beyond the limits contemplated at the commencement; for which the only apologies that can be offered are the high importance of the subject of which it treats, and the deep and abiding interest which your remonstrants feel in that subject.

In conclusion, they would remark, that they have no private ends to answer, in opposing either the plan of the Superintendent of Common Schools, or the act presented, but not sanctioned, by the committee.

A careful examination of both has produced a clear and firm conviction that the former, however plausible it may appear, is not adapted to the peculiar circumstances of this city; and that the latter is ill-digested, and displays throughout an absence of that experimental knowledge of the matter which is indispensable to a successful result.

Your remonstrants are persuaded that the public schools of this city accomplish all that can be accomplished with the same pecuniary means; and that they are as free from any just cause of dissatisfaction to any class of citizens as human ingenuity can make them. Under these impressions, they feel bound to remonstrate against the proposed changes. But the same feelings and the same sense of duty which have led them to make no inconsiderable sacrifice of personal interest, comfort, and convenience, in sustaining the present system of public instruction, would cause them to yield cheerfully to any other system which the people and the constituted authorities of the State may see fit to substitute for it. If a better can be devised, they will, as far as they can, lend their aid in sustaining it.

ROBERT C. CORNELL, *President.*

A. P. HALSEY, *Secretary.*

NEW YORK, May 21, 1841.

The following are the names of the present Board of Trustees:

John T. Adams,
Stephen Allen,
Augustin Averill,
Micah Baldwin,
Caleb Bartlett,
Meigs D. Benjamin,
George W. Betts,
William Birdsall,
James B. Brinsmade,
James H. Blaisdell,
Thomas Bussing,
Abm. R. Lawrence,
Richard M. Lawrence,
James M'Brair,
William H. Macy,
William Mandeville,
Samuel F. Mott,
Lindley Murray,
Abner Mills,
John Morrison,
William D. Murphy,
Wm. W. Chester,
Samuel R. Childs,
Lyman Cobb,
Joseph B. Collins,
Peter Cooper,
I. T. Cornell,
Joseph Curtis,
Edward W. Cleaveland,
Albert Chrystie,
Mahlon Day,
Samuel Demilt,
Henry E. Davies,
Frederic De Peyster,
James F. De Peyster,
Charles Durfee,
Asahel A. Denman,
Benjamin Ellis,
Edward Ferris,
John Groshon,
Samuel Griffing,
Lewis Hallock,
Edmund Haviland,

Timothy Hedges,
Robert Hogan,
Jacob Harsen,
John R. Hurd,
John W. Howe,
John Jay,
Shephard Knapp,
Hiram Ketchum,
Charles Oakley,
George Pardow,
James Palmer,
Anson G. Phelps,
Pelatiah Perit,
Thompson Price,
Richard Paige,
Charles E. Pierson, M.D.,
George Pessinger,
James O. Pond,
William Rockwell, M.D.,
J. Smyth Rogers, M.D.,
James I. Roosevelt, Jr.,
Peter A. Schermerhorn,
Henry H. Schieffelin,
Henry M. Schieffelin,
Joseph Stuart, M.D.,
Samuel W. Seton,
Linus W. Stevens,
Willett Seaman,
Thomas L. Servoss,
Burritt Sherwood, M.D.,
Reuben Spencer,
William Smith,
James Stokes,
Najah Taylor,
George T. Trimble,
Isaac P. Trimble, M.D.,
Gulian C. Verplanck,
Joseph Washburn,
Benjamin R. Winthrop,
Edmund Willets,
Samuel Willets,
Abm. V. Williams M.D.

On Saturday, May 22d, Mr. Verplanck moved that all orders of business preceding the bill relative to common schools in New York be suspended, and that the Senate resolve itself into committee on the said bill. The motion was agreed to, and, after some time spent in debate and making amendments, the committee rose, and reported the same to the Senate. On motion of Mr. H. A. Livingston, the bill was laid on the table.

On Tuesday, the 25th, the Senate proceeded to the consideration of the report of the Committee of the Whole, when an interesting and animated debate ensued, which was terminated by a motion of Mr. Robert C. Nicholas, that the further consideration of the said report be postponed until the first Tuesday in January following.

The President put the question on agreeing with the said motion, and it was decided in the affirmative, by the following vote:

Ayes—Messrs. Denniston, Ely, Foster, Furman, Hull, Humphrey, Johnson, H. A. Livingston, Nicholas, Rhoades, Taylor—11.

Nays—Messrs. Dickinson, Hopkins, Hunt, Lee, Moseley, Paige, Scott, Sibley, Strong, Verplanck—10.

The defeat of the bill was unexpected by the advocates of change, and their disappointment and chagrin was not in any way concealed. Meetings were held, and Bishop Hughes made a very elaborate speech, reviewing the argument of Mr. Ketchum, which occupied the three evenings of June 16th, 17th, and 21st, in its delivery. The place selected was Carroll Hall, Thomas O'Connor, Esq., being appointed chairman, and Bernard O'Connor, secretary.

The Senate was then in session in the city of New York in its judicial organization as the Court of Errors, and the Hon. Luther Bradish, Lieutenant-Governor, and several of the senators, were present on the first evening.

Bishop Hughes spoke as follows:

Mr. Chairman and Gentlemen: The subject of education is one which at this time agitates, more or less, every civilized nation. If we look across the ocean, we find it the subject of discussion in France, in Prussia, in Holland, in Belgium, in Ireland, and even in Austria. It is not surprising, then, that this subject, which has but lately attracted the attention of governments and of nations, should become one of deep and absorbing interest.

But of all these nations there is, perhaps, not one which has placed education on that basis on which it is destined successfully, in the end, to repose.

In countries in which the inhabitants profess the same religion, whatever that religion may be, the subject is deprived of many of its difficulties. But in nations in which there is a variety of religious creeds, it has hitherto been found one of the most perplexing of all questions, to devise a system of education which should meet the approbation of all. This subject has engaged the attention of our own Government. In every State of the Union it has already been acted upon more or less fully. And in all these instances, whether we regard Europe, or regard this country, we find that there is not a solitary instance in which religion, or religious instruction in a course of education, has been proscribed, with the exception of the city of New York. And this proscription of religion in this city is not an act of public authority. There is no statute authorizing such an act; it has been the result rather of an erroneous construction put upon a statute, and which has been acquiesced in, rather than approved, for the last sixteen years. In the operation of that system, Catholics felt themselves virtually excluded from the benefits of education. Very shortly after that construction of the law was adopted, they felt themselves obliged to proceed in the best way that their poverty would allow for the education of their children. And, whilst they have been taxed with the other citizens, up to the present hour they have received no benefit from the system supported by that taxation; but, on the contrary, after having contributed what the law required, have been obliged to throw themselves back upon their own resources, and provide, as well as they might, the means of educating their children.

We have, from time to time, complained of this state of things. It has frequently been brought before the notice of the public. A Society—professedly the friend of education—having exercised supreme control over the whole question, we had no resource but to apply to that tribunal, which the law had authorized to use its discretion in distributing the money set apart for the purposes of education. We always insisted, in good faith, that the object—the benevolent object of this Government—was the education of the rising generation, and we never conceived that the question of religion, or no religion, had entered into the minds of those philanthropic public men who first established this system for the diffusion of knowledge. We applied, as I have remarked, at different times, to the tribunal to which allusion has been already made, and did so even till a very recent period, because, before we could apply to the Legislature of the State, it was requisite to comply with the forms prescribed, and that we should be first rejected by the Common Council of this city, to whom the State Legislature had delegated the discretionary power to be exercised in the premises. That course was regarded necessary, and we adopted it. The result was as *we* anticipated—denial of our request; and then it was that we applied to the Legislature of the State; submitted to them the grievances under which we labored, in the full confidence that there we should find a remedy.

Both before the Common Council and the Senate of this State, the means which have been taken to defeat the proper consideration of our claims have been such as we could not have anticipated in a country where the rights of conscience are recognized as supreme. The test has been put, not as to whether we were proper subjects for education, but whether we were Catholics! And in the course of the examination on which I am about to enter, I shall have occasion to show that, from the beginning to the end, the one object of the members of the Public School Society has been, to convince the public that we were Catholics; and they, it would appear, calculate as the consequence, that, if we were Catholics, then we had no right to obtain redress, or hope for justice.

In the course of my remarks I shall be obliged to refer to distinctions in religion, the introduction of which into the discussion of this question is ever to be much regretted. I shall have to speak of Catholics and of Protestants; and when I do so, let it be understood that I do not volunteer in that, but the course pursued by that Public School Society has imposed upon me the necessity to refer to these religious distinctions; and, in doing so, I trust I shall be found to speak of those who differ from me in matters of religion with becoming respect. I am not a man of narrow feelings. I am attached sincerely and conscientiously to the faith which I profess, but I judge no man for professing another. In the whole of my intercourse with Protestants, my conduct has been such, they will be ready to acknowledge, in Philadelphia and elsewhere, that I am the last man to be accused of bigotry. But I feel that I should be unworthy of that estimation—that the denomination to which I belong would be unworthy of sustaining that position which they are ambitious to occupy in the opinion of their fellow-citizens of other creeds, if they were to submit to the insult added to the injury inflicted on them by these men. I, for my own part, feel indignant at the recent attempt made to cast odium upon us and our cause; and it is because that turns entirely on the question of religion, that I shall be obliged to speak of Catholics and of Protestants, and refer to those distinctions which should never have been introduced.

Before taking up the report of the Secretary of State, I shall refer briefly to the conclusion of the discussion before the Common Council. There we had, as you will recollect, legal gentlemen and reverend gentlemen, advocates of the Public School Society, who had studied the question in all its bearings—volunteers and associates and colleagues on the same side; and, throughout that debate, the ground taken by them was, that, if our petition were granted, favors would be conferred on us as a religious denomination, tending to that against which all the friends of liberty should guard—a union of Church and State. So long as that idea was honestly entertained by these gentlemen, I could respect their zeal in opposing us. But that idea has disappeared, and yet their opposition has become more inveterate than ever.

The very last sentence of the speech of Mr. Ketchum before the Common Council of the city of New York was a declaration that this Society, so far from desiring a collision of this kind with us, were men of peace, to whom even the moral friction of the debate was quite a punishment; that, for them, it would be a relief if our system of education were assimilated, in its external aspect, to that of the State. I will read his own words:

Now, perhaps, the gentleman may ask, if the system is to be changed, that we should resort to the same course as is pursued in the country, where the people elect their own commissioners and trustees. But if we do, the schools must be governed on the same principles as these, and the only difference will be in the managers. And if it is to come to that, I am sure these trustees will be very willing, for it is to them a source of great vexation to be compelled to carry on this controversy for such a period.

They are very unwilling to come here to meet their fellow-citizens in a somewhat hostile manner. They have nothing to gain, for the Society is no benefit to them, and they give days and weeks of their time, without recompense, to the discharge of the duties of their trust.

I shall not now praise that Society. I have more than once given my full assent to eulogiums on their zeal and assiduity; but Mr. Ketchum praises them, and they praise themselves, and at this period of the controversy they are entitled to no praise from the thousands and thousands of the poor neglected children of New York, whom their narrow and bigoted views have excluded from the benefits and blessings of education.

I shall now, before proceeding farther, take up the report of the Secretary of State, and commence with that portion of it in which he gives a brief sketch of the origin of this Society:

The Public School Society was originally incorporated in 1805, by chapter 108 of the laws of that session, which is entitled, " An Act to Incorporate the Society instituted in the City of New York, for the establishment of a free school for the education of poor children who do not belong to, or are not provided for by, any religious society." In 1808, its name was altered to " The Free-School Society of New York," and its powers were extended " to all children who are the proper subjects of a gratuitous education." By chapter 25 of the Laws of 1826,·its name was changed to " The Public School Society of New York; " and the trustees were authorized to provide for the education of all children of New York not otherwise provided for, " whether such children be or be not the proper subjects of gratuitous education," and to require from those attending the schools a moderate compensation; but no child to be refused admission on account of inability to pay.

Thus, by the joint operation of the acts amending the charter of the Society, of the statutes in relation to the distribution of the school moneys, and of the ordinance of the Common Council designating the schools of the Society as the principal recipients of those moneys, the control of the public education of the city of New York, and the disbursement of nine tenths of the public moneys raised and apportioned for schools, were vested in this corporation. It is a perpetual corporation, and there is no power reserved by the Legislature to repeal or modify its charter. It consists of members who have contributed to the funds of the Society; and, according to the provisions of the last act, the payment of ten dollars constitutes the contributor a member for life. The members annually choose fifty trustees, who may add to their number fifty more.

He goes on to describe its different acts, by which its name and other attributes were changed, until, from being a Society to take charge of the children that were not provided for by any religious society, they came to have the control of the whole system of education in New York. The report informs us that the members of the Public School Society are so by virtue of a subscription of ten dollars; that they elect fifty trustees; that these fifty trustees have a right to appoint fifty others, and then the number is completed; that the city Council are members *ex-officio*. And this will, perhaps, go a great way in explaining the unwillingness of the Common Council to grant our petition.

The Society were so constituted, that, when we went before the Common Council, we virtually went before a committee of the Society.

In this state of things, the Governor of this State, with a patriotism and benevolence that entitle his name to the respect of every man that has regard for humane feeling and sound and liberal policy, declared for a system that would afford a good common education to every child. And, though I have never before spoken in public the name of that distinguished officer of the State, I do now, from my heart, award to him my warmest thanks, and those of the community to which I belong, for the stand he has taken on this subject. An attempt has been made to victimize him because he favored Catholics—because he dared to manifest a humane and liberal feeling toward foreigners. He survived that shock, however; and a recent excellent document from him, showing that he is not any longer a candidate for public favor, authorizes me to say, in this place, that every man who loves his country and the interests of his race, no matter what may be his politics, will cordially render the tribute of esteem and praise to that Governor—Seward.

Governor Seward knew too well the deep-seated prejudices of a large portion of the community not to feel that he had nothing to gain by being the advocate of justice to Catholics. But, whatever may be that distinguished statesman's future history, whatever his situation, however much thwarted and opposed, and perchance, for a moment, partially defeated by those who call themselves the friends of education, it will be glory enough for him to have inscribed upon his monument, that, whilst Governor of New York, he wished to have every child of that noble State endowed and adorned, in mind and intellect and morals, with the blessings of education.

When, therefore, we presented, as every oppressed portion of the community has a right to do, our grievances to the honorable Legislature of the State, these gentlemen, who are represented by Mr. Ketchum, through a speech of nine mortal columns, as the humble almoners of the public charity—these men, who are burdened with their load of official duty, which they are willing, Mr. Ketchum says, to put off—pursue us thither with unabated hostility. We supposed that the Public School Society would acquiesce in the justice of the plan of the Secretary. No! these humble men, all zeal for the cause of education, enter the halls of legislation with a determined spirit of opposition to us, which is, perhaps, unparalleled, considering the circumstances under which they acted.

One of the most difficult points in treating with these gentlemen is, to ascertain in what particular situation, and under what particular circumstances, their responsibility may be discovered. They are, it is said, but agents; they are wealthy and powerful—have every advantage in opposing humble petitioners as we are. And, with all these advantages, they presented themselves there, not to dispute the justice of our claims, nor the correctness of the ground on which the honorable Secretary placed the question before the Senate, but to appeal, even in the minds of senators, to whatever they might find there of prejudice against the Catholic religion, and the foreigner and the descendants of the foreigner.

One of the documents of which they made use was published in the *Journal of Commerce.* This question had been, in the Society, made the special order of the day for, I think, Friday, the 20th of May. In the *Journal of Commerce* of the previous day, there was published a most calumnious article, full of all those traditions against our religion which the minds of the uneducated portion of some of those denominations inherit ; and the agent of the Public School Society, sent, as we should understand, to represent justice and truth between citizens of the same country, is found distributing this paper all over the desks of the senators ! On that very day it was supposed that the vote on this very question would be taken, and the agent of the Public School Society is found supplying the senators—for I have a copy of the papers thus furnished, with the member's name written at the top, and the article referred to marked with black lines, so that there could be no overlooking it—with an article containing a mock excommunication, a burlesque invented by Sterne, and inserted in his " Tristram Shandy," but quoted by the Public School Society—for I hold it to be their act till they disclaim it—as a part of our creed, and made the ground of a sneer at the Secretary. " These are precious principles, to be preserved in the consciences of your petitioners ! " Religious prejudice will have its reign in the world. But it is a low feeling. Especially is it a low feeling in a country in the fundamental principles of whose government and laws the great father of our liberties insisted that conscience and religion should be ever free, and be regarded as above all law. There was to be no toleration, for that implied the power not to tolerate ; the word was therefore excluded from the language of American jurisprudence. And, that being the case, it was painful to find an honorable body of men, as the members of the Public School Society are regarded to be, employing such a means of approaching the Senate of New York—that Senate to which Justice, if she found not a resting-place upon the globe, like the dove to the ark, might return, and expect every hand to be stretched out to receive her.

If they deny that they approached the Senate with that document—too vile and filthy to be read in this audience; but if any gentleman has the curiosity to see it, here (holding up a volume of " Tristram Shandy ") he may read it word for word—let them call their agent to account. We will not let them rob us of our reputation. We stand ambitious to be considered worthy of membership in the great American family. Let them not, after depriving us of the benefit of our taxes, destroy our reputation.

I will now, after this introduction, take up the remonstrance of the Society. It is impossible for me not to feel indignant, when I think how these high-minded men have treated us—when I recollect how this same gentleman, who acted as their agent, and distributed that calumnious paper, was once a candidate for office, and gladly received the signatures of Catholics. And this was the recompense he offered.

I know not by whom this remonstrance was drawn up. I know not whether all the members of the Board of Trustees approved of it; but if they did, I trust there were no Catholics present. In page 3 of this remonstrance, which is signed by the President, "ROBERT C. CORNELL," we find the following declaration introductory to the subject:

The Legislature, therefore, in 1813, when the first distribution was made, very naturally appropriated the amount apportioned to this city to these schools, in the ratio of the number of children taught in each. This mode of distribution continued until 1824, when the subject was again brought before the Legislature by the jealousies, disputes, and difficulties which had arisen among the recipients, and the conflicting parties presented themselves at Albany for the purpose of sustaining their respective claims.

Now, in all the foregoing applications—in all the reports made by committees of the Common Council, you will find that there has not been one in which the subject of religion was not referred to as the ground of the refusal of our claims—in which it was not assumed that the laws were opposed to giving education-money—the public school fund, or any portion of it—to any religious denomination. This principle, it has been pretended, and the disputes among the sects, led to the alteration of the law, in 1824. But if we refer back to the memorial proceeding from this Society itself, we will find that no such thing existed at the time. We find that Mr. Leonard Bleecker sent a memorial at that very period—1824—in which he says:

It will not be denied, in this enlightened age, that the education of the poor is enjoined by our holy religion, and is, therefore, one of the duties of a Christian Church. Nor is there any impropriety in committing the school fund to the hands of a religious society, so long as they are confined, in the appropriation of it, to an object not necessarily connected or intermingled with the other concerns of the Church; as, for instance, to the payment of teachers, because the State is sure, in this case, that the benefits of the fund, in the way it designed to confer them, will be reaped by the poor. But the objection to the section sought to be repealed is, that the surplus moneys, after the payment of teachers, is vested in the hands of the trustees of a religious society, and mingled with its other funds, to be appropriated to the erection of buildings under the control of the trustees, which buildings may, and in all probability will, be used for other purposes than schoolhouses.

Here was the ground taken, and yet we hear these gentlemen, before the Common Council, say it was on account of constitutional difficulties and religious differences; whereas, it was simply because the money had been used for an improper purpose.

In page 5 of this remonstrance, this Society takes the ground, in opposition to the view of its being a monopoly and a close corporation—which it in fact is—that the same objection might be urged against hospitals, asylums for the blind, the insane, and the mute, dispensaries, and houses of refuge; and they institute a comparison between these institutions and the public schools.

Now, as to the fact that the Public School Society is a close corporation, they themselves do not deny that all citizens are excluded except those who can afford to pay ten dollars for membership. They do not deny that, but justify it on the ground that, inasmuch as these are corporations for the management of such institutions as I have named, the same reason exists for the constitution of a corporation for the direction of the public schools. And where, then, pray, are the rights with which nature, and nature's God, have invested the parents of these children? Pray, are they who are held competent to decide on the gravest questions affecting the interests of the nation, unworthy to have a voice in the education of their own children? And must they resign that to a corporation responsible neither to them nor to the public in any formal way? And, pray, are the people of New York lunatics, that they must have a corporation of keepers appointed over them? If the doctrine of this memorial be correct, they are to be so considered. But there is this difference: they pay taxes for education, and they have a right to a voice and a vote in the manner in which their money is to be expended. If the people are to be treated as lunatics, mutes, or inmates of the House of Refuge, then the argument of the Public School Society is a good one. I think the comparison instituted in the remonstrance utterly fails. I cannot dwell longer upon it.

I now come to a charge made against the petitioners:

At one time it was declared, "the public school system in the city of New York is entirely favorable to the sectarianism of infidelity, and opposed only to that of positive Christianity;" that "it leaves the will of the pupil to riot in the fierceness of unrestrained lusts," and is "calculated to make bad and dangerous citizens."

Now, it is true that we did view the Society as being opposed to religion. There can be no doubt of that. But, if that be true, it is equally true that the evidence on which we built that conclusion was furnished by themselves. And how? In every report of theirs it appears that, if any thing like a religious society presented itself, that character was enough to decide them in resisting its application. You will find this evidenced in their vindication and defence, both by Mr. Sedgwick and Mr. Ketchum. They contend that what they meant by religious instruction, was not religious instruction, and so it may be proper for me to enter a little into the examination of the meaning of these words.

When the trustees make the religious character of a Society the ground of denying them a portion of their funds, what is it that constitutes the objection? They do not decide against the infidel; for it seems, if the applicants had divested themselves of a religious character—if men of no religious profession, of no belief in a God or a future state, had presented themselves, no objection would be made, and, on their own premises, the trustees would be obliged to concede to their request. What, then, was the reason of the refusal, except the religious character of the applicants? And had we not fair ground here for inferring that they are opposed to religion? Examine their reports. Here is one: a report of the Committee on Arts, Sciences, and Schools, of the Board of Assistants, on appropriating a portion of the school money to religious societies for the support of schools. This is Document No. 80, and at page 389 we read as follows:

The amount of one hundred and seven thousand dollars, and upward,

28

as hereinbefore stated, has been raised by annual tax in this city, for purposes of a purely civil and secular character.

Well, if the education is to be purely "civil and secular," is religion mingled with it at all? And if religion is not to be mingled with it at all, then had we not a right to infer, from their own document, that they were opposed to religion, and brought up the children without any knowledge of their responsibility to God, or of a future life, or of any of those great principles of religion on which the very security of society depends? Were we not justified in this inference? They refused our application because we professed religion; and had we not a right to keep our children from the influence of a system of education that attempted to make a divorce between literature—that is, such literature as is suited for the infant mind—and religion, and to give instruction of a "purely civil and secular character," for which, we are told, $107,000 had been expended? How, I ask, can Mr. Cornell stand up and deny our charge, when such indisputable evidence of its truth is presented by their own documents?

Did Mr. Cornell, when they defeated us, find fault with the committee of the Assistants' Board, because they charged the Society with excluding religion from education? No! no! Enough it was that religious societies should be defeated, and that they should continue to wield their complex monopoly. No matter that they were charged with having no religion; no matter at all that their education was then described as "purely civil and secular."

This document goes on:

The appropriation of any part of that sum to the support of schools in which the religious tenets of any sect are taught to any extent——

Well, if you excluded the tenets of all sects, you excluded all religion, because there is no religion except what is included in the tenets of sects. I defy you to teach the first principles of religion without teaching the tenets of sectarianism. Then it was, on the faith of their own documents, that we charged on them the character which they had assumed, on the strength of which they had successfully opposed, one after another, all the denominations who reverence religion.

The document proceeds:

——would be a legal establishment of one denomination of religion over another; would conflict with all the principles and purposes of our free institutions, and would violate the very letter of that part of our Constitution which so emphatically declares that "the free exercise and enjoyment of religious profession and worship, without discrimination or preference, shall forever be allowed in this State to all mankind." By granting a portion of the school fund to one sect, to the exclusion of others, a "preference" is at once created, a "discrimination" is made, and the object of this great constitutional guarantee is defeated; taxes are imposed for the support of religion, and freedom of conscience, if not directly trammelled and confined, is not left in the perfect and unshackled state which our systems of government were intended to establish and perpetuate. No difference can be perceived in principle between the taxing of the people of England for the support of a Church establishment there, and the taxing of the people of New York for the support of schools in which the doctrines of religious denominations are taught.

And what are we to infer from this, except that they do not teach religion at all ? But they have changed their tactics. For they have, be it remembered, two strings to their bow : one for those who have religion, and one for those who have not ; and so we actually find that, whilst before the Common Council of New York they are destitute of religion, and give a "purely civil and secular education," at Albany they can be in favor of religion.

But there is still further evidence on this point. In page 18 of the report of the debate before the Common Council, we have the explanation of Mr. Ketchum, and it was one of the nicest managed points imaginable. Indeed, I could not but admire the sagacity of that gentleman and his associate, Mr. Sedgwick, in steering so adroitly between the teaching of religion and the not teaching of it, so that they taught it, but yet you must not call it religion. We put the gentlemen between the horns of a dilemma. We said, If you do not teach religion, then you are chargeable with making our common schools seminaries of infidelity ; if you do teach it, then you do exactly what you say excludes religious societies from a right to participate in the fund. But these gentlemen, with great skill and critical acumen, and a little sophistry, were able to steer, by a line invisible to my mind, between the horns of the dilemma.

In describing the different kinds of instruction, Mr. Sedgwick says :

But, beyond that, there is still another branch of instruction which is properly called religious ; and it is because those two phrases—"religious" and "moral"—have been used occasionally without an accurate apprehension of their signification, that the documents of the trustees have been misconstrued. But when the term "moral" education is used, it only means that education which instructs the children in those fundamental tenets of duty which are the basis of all religion.

That is to say, you build the roof before you lay the foundation. For whence, I ask, will men get their knowledge of duty, if not based on a substratum of religion ? But here, morality, so called, is made the basis of religion. Well, let us apply this to the schools, and see whether any Christian parent would submit to have his children placed under such a system.

There is a child at one of these schools. They tell him not to lie ; but children are inquisitive, and he asks, "Why should I not lie ?" You must answer, "Because God abominates a lie." There you teach religion. You explain the reason why the child should not lie—that religion requires and affords the reason of the performance of the duty ; not that the duty is the basis of religion. It is not enough to tell the child, "You are to speak the truth, and, when you know and fulfil your duty, then you may learn that there is a God to whom you are responsible." Washington himself, in his "Farewell Address," cautioned the nation against the man who would attempt to teach morality without religion. He says :

Of all the dispositions and habits which lead to political prosperity, religion and morality are indispensable supports. In vain would that man claim the tribute of patriotism, who should labor to subvert these great pillars of human happiness, these firmest props of the duties of men and citizens. The mere politician, equally with the pious man, ought to respect and to cherish them. A volume could not trace all their connections with private and public felicity. Let it be simply asked, Where is the security for property, for reputation, for life, if the sense of religious obligations desert the oaths which are the instruments of investigation in courts of justice ? And let us with caution indulge the supposition that morality can be maintained without religion. Whatever may be conceded to the influence of refined education on minds of peculiar structure, reason and experience both forbid us to expect that national morality can prevail in exclusion of religious principle.

Had we not, then, I would ask very respectfully, a right, when every petition had been rejected on the ground that the petitioners had a religious belief, to infer that religion formed no part of their system of education, and that the consequence which we charged upon them, and that Mr. Cornell repudiated with so much horror, inevitably and justly followed—namely, that the Public School Society was favorable to the sectarianism of infidelity ?

I now go on to show what the Public School Society boast of having done in our regard. They had offered, in reply to our objections to passages in their books—as, for instance, where it was stated that "John Huss was a zealous Reformer, but, trusting to the deceitful Catholics, he was taken by them and burned at the stake"—to expunge such objectionable passages when they were pointed out. They said, "Bishop, we submit our books to you, and if you will have the goodness to point out any objectionable passages, we will expunge them." Well, certainly there was something very plausible and apparently very liberal in this offer. But when the matter was pressed, it was found that all this was merely the expression of individuals; there was no guarantee that the books would be amended. Weeks, months, might be spent in examining the books, and then the approbation of the board was necessary in order to effect the alteration. Did they say that it should be given ? Never.

I pass now to another point; for, observe, I do not at all think myself called on to say one word in vindication of the able and eloquent and satisfactory report of the Secretary of State. That is not necessary. The language of that document will be its own vindication when the petty sophistries raised against it shall have been long forgotten ; for be assured, gentlemen, that, whatever may be the temporary opposition to any public measure, from the moment that there is discovered to be inherent in it—of its essence —a principle of justice and equality, its ultimate triumph is certain, and all the opposition which it encounters will have no more effect on it than that of the breeze which passes over the ocean, ruffling its surface, but destroying nothing of the mighty and majestic element which it seems to fret and disturb.

I take up this, then, not to vindicate the report, but rather in reference to the insulting attempt, as I will call it, to deprive Catholics of the free exercise of their own consciences, and the respect and esteem of their fellow-citizens. In reasoning on the subject, observe the course that is taken by

Mr. Cornell. He enters into a comparison between the schools of the Public School Society and ours—ours, supported in poverty, the humblest that may be, but still supported in a way sufficient to show our determination not to give up our rights or relinquish the maintenance and defence of a sound and patriotic principle. But this gentleman compares these our schools with theirs—on which more than a million of the public money has been expended, whilst we have been virtually shut out from all benefit from the public funds, not by any law of the State, but by a vicious interpretation of the law. He requires us to furnish as perfect a system as they do with the expenditure of a million of dollars! He is reasoning with the Secretary, telling him, in effect, that we are troublesome and designing people, and he says:

But having in view the stringency with which the same party insisted on the necessity of religious in juxtaposition with secular education, and the warmth with which they denounced the public school system when they saw fit to charge it with excluding religion, and particularly when reference is had to their avowed dogma, that there is no hope of salvation to those not of the Roman Catholic Church; which dogma is now taught in their schools.

I thank God that the Catholics—the long-oppressed of three hundred years, during which the ear of the world was poisoned with calumnies against them—have now liberty of speech, and ability to exercise it; and I call Mr. Cornell to account for what he has here written, and to which he has affixed his name. He says:

When reference is had to their avowed dogma, that there is no hope of salvation to those not of the Roman Catholic Church; which dogma is now taught in their schools.

The Catholics "avow" every dogma of their religion; but the two statements employed by Mr. Cornell are both false. It never was and never can be a dogma of ours, that there is "no hope of salvation to those not of the Roman Catholic Church." Neither is that dogma taught in our schools. This false statement must be accounted for by Mr. Cornell's ignorance of our doctrine on the one hand, and, on the other, his disposition to injure us. I call upon him—I arraign him before the people of New York, and the Senate whose confidence he has attempted to abuse, to prove his statement, or else to retract it.

And here it may be proper for me to explain something of this matter; for I know that, in the minds of Protestants, almost universally, there is that idea; and that, in the theological language of the Catholic Church, there is apparent ground for entertaining it. But, at the same time, I do know that that language, properly understood and fairly interpreted, does not imply the dogma imputed to us by Mr. Cornell.

It is very true that we believe that out of the true Church of Christ there is no salvation: first proposition.

It is true that we believe the Catholic Church to be the true Church of Christ: second proposition.

It is very true that, notwithstanding these propositions, there is no dogma of our creed which teaches that a Protestant may not hope to be saved, or may not go to heaven. Now, how is this explained ? In this way : When we speak of the Church, we mean the Church as Christ and His apostles did—in the sense that the ordinary means for the salvation of mankind are the doctrines and institutions which Jesus left on earth, which have all descended in the Church with our history and our name. This we believe ; but we do not believe that God has deprived himself, because He instituted these things, of the means of saving whom He will. We do not believe that, on this account, the power of the Almighty is abridged. Hence it is consistent with our dogmas to believe that God, who is a just Judge as well as a merciful Father, will not condemn any one for involuntary error. Their judgment will be individual. They were externally out of the Church ; but was it by their own will, or the accident of their birth and education in a false religion ? Did they believe that religion to be true in good faith, and in the simplicity of their hearts ? Were they ready to receive the light and grace of truth as God might offer it to them ? Then, in that case, though not belonging to the Catholic Church by external profession, they belonged to it by their internal disposition.

Consequently, we are not authorized to deny hope of salvation to those not of the Catholic Church, unless so far as the errors in which they have been involved have been voluntary and culpable on their part. And this is no new doctrine, as our opponents would have seen had they consulted the writings of the highest authorities in our Church. St. Thomas Aquinas, one of the greatest minds that ever contributed to enlighten the human race, as Protestants themselves acknowledge, writing in the eleventh or twelfth century, speaks of a man who is not even a Protestant, but a pagan, a man who has never heard of Christ or of Christianity ; and he, supposing that man to be moral, sincere, acting according to the best lights God has given him, tells us God would sooner send an angel to guide him to the way of salvation, than that such a one should perish. Such is the sentiment of St. Thomas Aquinas, expressed in his works ; and his works are approved of by our Church. How, then, can Mr. Cornell, or any other individual, say that we enter into judgment respecting those who die out of the pale of our Church ? I publicly call upon Mr. Cornell to retract or qualify his official statement.

Sentiments according with these I have quoted from St. Thomas Aquinas, I have myself preached in the cathedral of New York, and similar ones have been abundantly proclaimed by others ; and amongst them I would mention a very distinguished French bishop, then the Abbe Fressinous. In the third volume of his " Conferences," he has one special sermon on the subject of exclusive salvation, and he shows that, of all Christian denominations, there is no one more abounding in charity on this point than the Catholic Church. The same explanations are to be found in the writings of Bossuet, St. Francis of Sales, and St. Augustine.* With these facts well

---

* SALVATION OUT OF THE CHURCH.—In concluding this simple and brief view of

known, how did those gentlemen venture to take advantage of their and our relative situations, and calumniate us when we had no opportunity of repelling the unfair attack ?

Besides, Mr. Cornell says, " which is now taught in their schools." I deny the truth of that statement, and demand his authority.

But now, would it, think you, be improper on my part, considering that Mr. Cornell is not present, to imitate some of the liberties which he has taken with us in our absence ?

Throughout this document he has labored to prove that we are Catholics ; and not only that, but to show what our religion is ; though I am rather at a loss to imagine where he studied Catholic theology, in which, if he should persevere, I would suggest to him to consult better authorities than the *Journal of Commerce* and " Tristram Shandy."

Now, it never occurred to us to ask, Of what religion is Mr. Cornell and the Public School Society ? The whole ground assumed by them is, that they are not a " religious society." Well, what are they ? Are they an irreligious society ? Not at all. They are members of churches ; and I have taken the pains to ascertain that Mr. Cornell is a member of Dr. Spring's church ; and, if he lectures the Catholics, would it be very wrong in me to speak of the doctrines of his creed ? Let us look at the Westminster Confession of Faith, the rule of Presbyterian dogma, and see whether Mr. Cornell opens the gates of heaven to all religious denominations. I quote from the Westminster Confession as adopted and amended in the United States, and published by Towar and Hogan, Philadelphia, in 1827. In page 111 it is said :

The visible Church consists of all those throughout the world who profess the true religion.

So, to be a member of the visible Church, you must " profess " the true faith. " Together with their children." Happy children ! " And this is

the Catholic doctrine, it may be well to state here what is to be correctly understood of that Catholic sentiment, " Out of the Church there is no salvation."

" We do not pretend to deny (says Mr. Bergier) that there are numbers of men born in heresy, who, by reason of their little light, are in invincible ignorance, and, consequently, excusable before God. These, in the opinion of all judicious divines, ought not to be ranked with heretics." This is the very doctrine of St. Augustine (*Epis.* 43, *ad gloriam et alias. n.* 1.) St. Paul tells us, in his Epistle to Titus, chap. iii. : " A man that is a heretic, after the first and second admonition, avoid ; knowing that he that is such a one is subverted, and sinneth, being condemned by his own judgment." As to those who defend an opinion, either false or perverse, without obstinacy, and who have not invented it from a daring presumption, but received it from their parents after they were seduced and had fallen into error, if they diligently and industriously seek for the truth, and if they hold themselves ready to embrace it as soon as they shall have found it, such as these also are not to be classed with heretics." *L.* 1, *d. Bapt. contra Donat. c.* 4, *n.* 5.

" Those who fall with heretics without knowing it, believing it to be the Church of Jesus Christ, are in a different case from those who know that the Catholic Church is spread over the whole world." *L.* 4, *c.* 1, *n.* 1.

" The Church of Jesus Christ may have, through the power of her spouse, children and servants. If they grow not proud, they shall have part in his inheritance ; but if they are proud, they shall remain without." *Ibid. c.* 16, *n.* 23.

the kingdom of our Lord Jesus Christ, the house and family of God, out of which there is no ordinary possibility of salvation."

Here is another statement of Mr. Cornell:

They are not merely the incidental remarks of the historian, or extracts from the Holy Scriptures, "without note or comment," to which such strong exception has been taken in relation to the public schools, but they are such as ever have, and, in the opinion of your remonstrants, must ever tend, if sustained by tax imposed upon the anathematized portion of the community, to destroy public harmony; and such as would prove any thing rather than a "social benefit."

Now, by using the word "anathematized," he conveys the impression that all out of the pale of our Church are under our anathema. I demand the proof. I have studied our holy religion many a day, but never yet have I discovered any such anathema, and I defy Mr. Cornell to point it out.

Mr. Cornell goes on to say:

Your remonstrants had supposed that the fact of the Public School Society being composed of men professing every variety of religious faith, would neutralize sectarian tendencies and secure it against abuse.

Now, there is something exceedingly specious in this, but it is, indeed, a very spurious position. They refuse our application on the ground that we are a religious society; and when we then charge them with not being a religious society, they repudiate it as a stigma on their character. And what is their remedy? That they "will neutralize sectarian tendencies by the variety of the religions that they introduce." How is this? They are all members of churches, and that does them honor; but whenever they come within the magical circle of their official character, then, like negative and positive brought together in just proportions, they neutralize each other. Is this really the position that these gentlemen assume? How are the trustees chosen? In the most beautiful manner! One or two Catholics are taken, a Universalist, perchance, and so of other denominations, and then they say, "We are of all religions!" You will find that the mass of the Society belong to one sect, of which little or nothing is said, and that an odd one is taken from each of the other sects to sanctify their acts. There is a sufficient majority of one denomination. There is a tendency and aim which I am not unwilling to proclaim, a secret understanding—not so very secret, either—to the effect that, "as there is a large foreign population in New York, and mostly Catholic, our liberties would not be safe unless the interests of Catholics were not neutralized in their education." We reject that idea with scorn, that Catholics have to learn the principles of liberty from them. At a period when Protestantism was as little dreamed of as steam navigation, Catholics were the schoolmasters to the nations of the world in the principles of liberty. They were Catholics who wrung the great charter of English liberty from the hands of the tyrant. And was that their first effort in the cause of freedom? No. That was only the written recognition of their rights, which the encroachments of his predecessors had diminished; and, having thus secured their rights, they maintained them down to the period of the Reformation, when their high and honorable notions of liberty were trampled in the dust, and were never restored till the Revolution; and when that so boasted event in the history of England took place, it only recognized the rights lost at the period of the Reformation, which Catholics for centuries before had known and enjoyed. Let them not say, then, that our religion is inimical to liberty. That is a reproach which we spurn—which we abominate and abhor. We have nothing to learn from them of human liberty. Their part is to imitate us; not ours to imitate them.

If that is the principle referred to, we understand it perfectly well, and it is of no use for these gentlemen to moot it for the purpose of showing that our claim should be denied. Was that, indeed, their object? Not at all. But their object was, with hands that should have been better employed, to rake up that wretched remnant of prejudice against us, and pander to the vitiated taste that could relish it.

We see, then, that, so far as this remonstrance is concerned, there is not one solitary proposition which should for one moment have arrested the mind of the Legislature. The bill proposed by the honorable Secretary of State contemplated no special favor. Much as I honor that distinguished individual, I would not esteem him as I do, if he had, in his bill, proposed any thing which should have raised us above our fellow-citizens of other denominations. But the bill only places us on an equality with others; with that we are satisfied—with nothing less will we ever be satisfied.

But, hitherto, these gentlemen have assumed various shapes. They have viewed with self-complacency the beauty of their system; and as for their few schools—few, in comparison with the number of destitute and unprovided children—I have nothing to say against them. I proposed to place our schools under their direction, so far as regarded their police and management. But I would not permit them to teach our children that Catholics were deceitful—that Galileo was put into the Inquisition, and punished for the heresy that the earth revolved on its own axis around the sun. That, and similar statements of partisan writers, long and generally believed, begin to be better understood. Behind the anti-Catholic credulity in which they have hitherto been entrenched, there is now going on a deeper and sounder spirit of criticism, conducted by eminent Protestant as well as Catholic writers. At the very time of his trial, his doctrine was held and avowed by eminent cardinals and the pope himself declared, that, as a philosophical proposition, it was no heresy. His case is entirely misunderstood.

Galileo's crime was not teaching sound philosophy, but bad theology— wishing the Church to declare that his theory was in accordance with the Scriptures. For reasons like this, I would not allow them to mislead our children, but was willing to allow the gentlemen the external management of our schools. They, however, would have universal rule, or none at all.

What has been their panacea for all complaints? To invite the city Council to visit the schools. And, certainly, I presume it would be impossible to visit their schools without being satisfied with their appearance. But had I been able to have made my voice heard in the Senate of the State, when they made the proposition to visit their schools, I should have proposed something like an amendment. I would have prayed these senators, in the name of humanity and their country, of all the benevolence that beats in the human breast, to visit not the schools, but the lanes and alleys and obscure resorts of the poor neglected children of New York, and there see, not how much is done, but how much is left undone. These are the portions of the city that should be visited. It is utterly impossible, owing to their scattered condition, to learn the numbers of children in this city who are deprived by these gentlemen of the blessings of education. We who mingle with the people have the opportunity of learning their dislike of this system—that they would no more trust their children to it than to that tyrannical system of British misgovernment which their fathers knew so well, and from which they derived the sad legacy of ignorance and poverty. I refer to the laws which made education a crime in Ireland, and which have left the inhabitants of that country the degraded but unbroken people that they are this day, after a persecution of near three hundred years.

It is for these poor, neglected, uneducated children that I plead. Their parents will not send them to the public schools whilst constituted as at present, and I approve of their resolution. I trust that they never will send their children to schools managed by men who can send to the Senate of this State a burlesque upon our creed, and represent it as a genuine exhibition of our faith and principles. Rather will we trust to the kind and merciful providence of God, than voluntarily relinquish a principle by which we maintain the right implanted in the breast of every parent and secured by the laws, to have a voice in the education of his child. It is these children that should be visited. Then would these honorable senators, whom I know to be above all these petty prejudices which have been appealed to, do justice, and apply a remedy so far as the law would authorize them.

I must now soon conclude my remarks for this evening. I will merely refer to the objection of the Society to the bill of Mr. Spencer: its tendency to introduce party politics. Every thing is held, in this country, to be in the hands of the people; yet these gentlemen, after enjoying a monopoly for sixteen years, think it a great misfortune if the taxpayers should be allowed a voice at all in the selection of the teachers in the schools which they support, or any share whatever in their management.

The next objection to the bill is its want of uniformity. Because they happen to have school-houses exactly one like the other, and have a uniform style of books, the large and liberal and statesmanlike plan of the honorable Secretary should be given up; because, forsooth, these "humble almoners" pronounce it void of uniformity. "Humble almoners," who, after coiling their roots around the Common Council, and making them judges in the cause, go to Albany to defeat our claims. Well, they may call themselves "humble almoners," if they please; but they remind me very much of the beggar in Gil Blas; who, when he asked alms, always took good care to have his musket ready.

I have now gone briefly through this part of the subject, and I ask you whether we can have any confidence in men who can stoop to such artifices as I have exposed ? I call upon them to vindicate themselves from the dishonor of having circulated that document from " Tristram Shandy." It was done by one of their colleagues and their official agent, who, when charged with it, replied that he had done so under instructions. What instructions? Did they instruct him ? If not, let them say so by a public act. Until they do so, we justly charge them with being the traducers of our reputation. I charge them on the ground that they are responsible for the act of their agent; and they should have known better. Gentlemen claiming to be exclusively the judges of what is a proper system of education—who held that you are unworthy of having any thing to do with the schools of New York—should have known that that document was from " Tristram Shandy," written, I presume, for his amusement, by Mr. Sterne, who, though numbered amongst the clergy of the Church of England, was believed to be an infidel—a man who secretly scoffed at every thing sacred, and the working of whose rank imagination is too offensive for the eye of delicacy. Surely, then, these gentlemen should not have drawn weapons from such a source for the purpose of destroying the reputation of any class of their fellow-citizens.

This is not the first occasion on which we have been misrepresented ; and religious gentlemen, whose avowed purpose it is to preach the gospel of peace, have taken up the habit of abusing us, and have rung the changes on this topic, till, in some instances, some of their audiences, more liberal than they, have left the place disgusted. They remind me of a saying of this same Sterne, who, when quizzing the credulity of the people of England—for he was a great wag—said that, occasionally, he was straitened for the price of a dinner, but he could always manage to make a good meal of Cheshire cheese ; but it also happened that oftentimes he was in a similar strait in his official capacity, and was called on to preach when he had not a word of a sermon prepared, and then he took " a fling at popery." The people went away edified and delighted. For this reason, he says, I call popery my " Cheshire cheese." It seems to me that the occupants of half the pulpits of New York are nearly in the same predicament, and would die of inanimation, were it not that their stock of " Cheshire cheese " is still unexhausted.

I think I can safely say, that in none of our churches will you hear such abuse. We never touch upon secular affairs ; you will not even hear from our pulpits harangues about abolition. We explain and defend our creed, and, I trust, preach charity and peace and order. But it is not so with those who assail us as I have described, as I will have occasion to show when treating of Mr. Ketchum's speech, which I intend to do on to-morrow evening.

THURSDAY EVENING.

BISHOP HUGHES resumed his remarks, as follows :

The question, gentlemen, which has called us together, has had two stages of progress, which must be kept distinct in order to comprehend its present position. We have, from time to time, applied to the Common Council of this city for relief, which we knew they had the power to grant; and we had applied, as it were, in an isolated, and, if you please, as to appearance, in a somewhat sectarian character. The reasons of this will be easily understood, when you reflect that we had no intention to disturb the system of education so generally approved by our fellow-citizens. Our object was not to destroy that which was good for others, if they thought it so, but to find something that might be equally good for ourselves. Accordingly, we applied as Catholics, because it appeared that there were no other denominations whose consciences suffered under the operation of that system. And we did suppose that these considerations would have had some weight with the honorable Council. We might—as we are reproached with not having done—we might have interfered with the regulations of these schools—asked for a different order of books—required the erasure of such and such passages, and the insertion of others. They reproach us with not doing so; but if we had done so, it would, in the first place, have been pains thrown away; and, in the second place, we might thereby have disobliged many of our fellow-citizens of other denominations. Without our at all pressing the question upon them, farther than observing that even the reading of the Holy Scriptures, according to the Protestant version, was looked upon by us as an invasion of our conscientious rights, they took it up as an objection against the reading of the Scriptures at all, as if the presence of a Bible within the walls of a school was a thing we could not bear. It is needless to say how wrong that inference was; but we did not at all wish to disturb the Protestant's approbation of his version of the sacred volume, nor the order that seemed so generally approved; and that was the reason of the mode of our application.

In the course of my speech, therefore, you will understand that we did not so apply for relief because we wished to be apart, separate from the rest of the community—that it was not because we were exclusive or intolerant, as they have charged upon us, but because we supposed that they would not wish to have their children hear the Catholic version of the Bible read; and therefore they had no right to impose on our children the hearing of the Protestant version. If that be sectarianism, then we plead guilty to the charge; but, without feeling and acting so, we could not have our consciences simple, and, in their integrity, upright toward God.

When, however, after having gone through the ceremony—for it was nothing else—of appearing before the Common Council, and having been heard—and denied, as a matter of course—when we had gone through this ceremony required by the formulary of the law, then, indeed, we threw ourselves on our general rights as citizens, and appealed to that tribunal to which we must always look with confidence for the redress of every grievance that presses on us in our social condition. Nevertheless, our opponents followed us there, and fastened upon us the character, in which it had been the duty imposed on us by necessity, to appear before the Common Council.

We have had occasion already to point out some evidences of the use made of that in the remonstrance. You saw with what recklessness of truth, I am sorry to say, it was charged in that document that we were intolerant—that we taught there was no salvation out of the Catholic Church, and so forth. There are in that document of the Public School Society many other passages requiring examination ; but as the substance of them is contained in the speech of the learned gentleman who was their official organ before the Senate, I suppose that the refutation of the one will be the refutation of both, and therefore I deem it unnecessary to refer far-ther to that memorial.

They—that gentleman particularly—referred, in the course of the debate, to a proposition for accommodation, which was made on the part of the Society previous to the last decision of the public Council. They alleged that nothing could be fairer ; but when we had examined that, we found that of not a solitary grievance of which we had complained did it take notice—not the slightest notice. The whole proposal was, that they should correct the books, so far as their guardianship of the rights of conscience— for they are conscience-keepers for the several sects in this community !— would allow. · They would accommodate us by striking out passages insult-ing and offensive to our minds and injurious to our children. That was all the amount of the concession. Then, the second proposition was, that they would purchase from us—they can afford to do so—the only school-house which our humble means have enabled us to erect during the sixteen years of privation from the benefits of common school education. These were the only two features that distinguished that offer of accommodation. But Mr. Ketchum did not find it convenient to read the propositions that we submit-ted at the same time, and which, candor should have acknowledged, re-moved from us every imputation of being actuated by sectarian motives, or having in view the appropriation of the public money to the propagation of our religion.

I will now commence with the reading of but a small portion of that, sufficient, however, to show you that, on this ground, so far as information was concerned, they had it ; and if, with that in their possession, they con-cealed the truth, and suppressed it, on their heads be the responsibility that attaches to such conduct.

What is the great difficulty—the legal difficulty ? That public money cannot be applied to sectarian uses. Very well ; we met that. We said, Here are propositions that cover our whole ground :

That there shall be reserved to the managers or trustees of these schools respectively the designation of the teachers to be appointed, who shall be subjected to the examination of a committee of the Public School Society, shall be fully qualified for the duties of their appointment, and of unexcep-tionable moral character ; or, in the event of the trustees or managers fail-ing to present individuals for these situations of that description, then indi-viduals having like qualifications of unexceptionable character, to be select-ed and appointed by the Public School Society, who shall be acceptable to the managers or trustees of the schools to which they shall be appointed ; but no person to be continued as a teacher in either of the schools referred to against the wishes of the managers or trustees thereof.

That was the first proposition ; showing them that, so far as the teachers were concerned, all we wanted was, men in whom we could place confidence. The second proposition was :

That the schools shall be open at all times to the inspection of any authorized agent or officer of the city or State government, with liberty to visit the same, and examine the books used therein, or the teachers, touching the course and system of instruction pursued in the schools, or in relation to any matter connected therewith.

So that there was no concealment there, they themselves should be the inspectors ; and I will say it boldly, that, if they had been actuated by that deep feeling of humanity for which they claimed credit, they would have accepted that proposal to take our children under their care, affording to them the same means of gaining future happiness as they did to others.

The document goes on :

The undersigned are willing that, in the superintendence of their schools, every specified requirement of any and every law passed by the Legislature of the State, or the ordinances of the Common Council, to guard against abuse in the matter of common school education, shall be rigidly enforced and exacted by the competent public authorities.

They believe that the benevolent object of every such law is to bring the means of education within the reach of the child of every poor man, without damaging their religion, whatever it may be, or the religious rights of any such child or parent.

It is in consequence of what they consider the damaging of their religion and their religious rights, in the schools of the Public School Society, that they have been obliged to withdraw their children from them. The facts which they have already submitted, and which have been more than sustained by the sentiments uttered on behalf of the Society in the late discussion, prove that they were not mistaken.

As regards the organization of their schools, they are willing that they should be under the same police and regulations as those of the Public School Society—the same hours, the same order, the same exercises, even the same inspection.

But the books to be used for exercises in learning to read or spell, in history, geography, and all such elementary knowledge, as could have a tendency to operate on their hearts and minds in reference to their religion, must be, so far as Catholic children are concerned, and no farther, such as they shall judge proper to put in their hands. But none of their dogmas, nothing against the creed of any other denomination, shall be introduced.

Reference is here made to the sentiments uttered by the advocates of the Public School Society in their opposition to our claims before the Common Council. Many of my present audience were perhaps there, and they can remember what an array of individuals, otherwise distinguished by their character—what an arrray of bigotry and prejudice, and, we must say, of profound ignorance, was presented against us. One reverend gentleman came there, and said, in reference to our objection respecting the Protestant version of the Bible, that one of our comments taught " the lawfulness of murdering heretics." Before the Common Council I brought that gentleman to account, and I assure you that, considering his gray hairs, and the respect that is due to age and the sacred character of a minister of peace, I felt humbled at beholding the degraded position in which he found himself before I had done. He had, however, obtained a copy of an old version of the Scriptures, published by the Catholic refugees in the time of Queen Elizabeth, who, wishing to prepare the way for an invasion by the Spanish, wrote a series of notes on the Scriptures, which they thought would tend to effect that end. So soon, however, as these notes became known in England and Ireland, they were scouted with horror by all professing the Catholic name. A few copies of that version, however, remained lost and forgotten, and an ignorant publisher in Cork, thinking to make a profitable speculation, obtained one of them; and not knowing—as was afterward proved—the difference between it and the authorized version, he undertook to publish another edition of it. In the process of publication, however, the character of the work became known, and the Archbishop of Dublin forbade the publication. The publisher was ruined, and he commenced a suit for damages. The matter was referred to in committees of the House of Commons and of the House of Lords, and to all the particulars of the case was, of course, thus given the greatest possible publicity. Well, the publisher, being deprived of his anticipated sale in Ireland, where the Catholics would not purchase such a book, thought that, by sending some to this country, people as ignorant as himself might purchase them, and thus the work might not prove a dead loss. In this way a copy fell into the hands of one of these gentlemen; and what did they do? Why, about the very same period that "Maria Monk" was published—and I know not but from the same press—they emitted an edition of this Bible, in order to excite public odium against their Catholic fellow-citizens! It was then, with a copy of that in his hand, that that clergyman came forward to prove, by means of that forgery, that we taught the lawfulness of murdering heretics. Then, besides that, there was another gentleman, and he, in speaking on the subject of these very schools, and offering reasons why we should be denied the benefits of education, instituted a comparison—all the others had, with great professions of respect and benevolent feeling for us, said " it was not because we were Catholics " that they opposed us; oh! no; they always qualified it—but he instituted a comparison between the religion of Fenelon and Voltaire, and with marvellous candor, forgetting the preface, admitted that he opposed us because we were Catholics! This gentleman said, that, if he had no alternative, he would sooner be of the religion of Voltaire than of that of Fenelon. These are the sentiments to which I allude, and to which reference is here made, when we say that such sentiments are only calculated to strengthen the conviction that our Catholic children, from the prejudices against their parentage and religion, had no chance of justice in those schools. The committee to whom was referred an examination of the schools, make a report, and in that, after quoting the two propositions for an accommodation, they take occasion to say :

Your committee deem it proper to remark, in vindication of the School Society, that they were only one of the numerous remonstrants against the prayer of the petitioners. Their views were represented at the late discussion before the board only by their legal advisers, Messrs. Sedgwick and Ketchum. The other gentlemen who participated in the discussion represented other bodies, which are not in any manner connected with them. Sentiments were uttered by them which the School Society do not entertain, and for which they are not justly accountable.

So they say; but by whom? It would go abroad that this was a declaration from the whole body of the Public School Society. I do not believe that was the fact, and I have no reason to believe it. Because I do know that these gentlemen used, or at least admitted this sentiment—this bad sentiment of their associates—for the purpose of defeating us, and they were perfectly satisfied with the victory, without at all disclaiming the dishonorable means they had employed to secure it. But as easily could the English efface the stigma that rests upon them from their employment of the Indian's tomahawk during their warfare with America.

And I ask them, Is there on their records a disapproval of the declaration of Dr. Spring or of Dr. Bond?—the one, that we would murder heretics, and the other, that the religion of Voltaire was to be preferred to that of Fenelon. Have they, in any one official document, disavowed that? We challenge them to show that the question of a disclaimer has ever been mooted. On the contrary, we have reason to believe that they approved of these statements made by Drs. Spring and Bond, and that from their own document too, signed by their President and Secretary, which goes nearly as far. And yet these are the men to whom we are required to give the management of the education of our children! They have hedged education around with an impenetrable wall, beyond which no applicant from our body can be admitted, except on terms that violate our civil and religious rights. A state of ignorance and degradation is the destiny assigned to those who will not submit to their Procrustean system, to the dimensions of which all must submit to be adapted.

The Society acknowledge that Messrs. Ketchum and Sedgwick are their official organs. Well, we find Mr. Sedgwick, in the speech referred.to on last evening, absolutely disclaiming the teaching of religion. He said it was a mistake to suppose that what was called religious instruction meant any thing more than simple morality, which he stated to be the basis of all religion. And do these gentlemen intend to reverse the order of the Almighty, and, by giving this precedence to morality, to say that men must be good without a motive, and then they may learn religion? How, then, can they quarrel with us for saying that they attempted—what Mr. Spencer says well, is impossible—to divorce religion from education? It was on that ground that they appeared before the Common Council and defeated our claim; for, as you saw yesterday, and see to-day, the crime charged upon us, the disqualifying circumstance, was, that we belonged to a religious society, and the public money was not to be appropriated in any way except in the promotion of a "purely civil and secular education." When we told them that we supposed they were sincere in their declarations, and that, by divorcing religion from education, thus leaving the children without the necessary motive to virtue and morality, and wholly destitute of any principle to curb their rising passions, they seemed to exclaim, "Oh! what an impious set of men you suppose us to be—atheists!" No, not exactly; but I accuse you of being what you yourselves assume. You defeat all applications made by applicants professing religion. You contend that religion must not be any part of State education. Well, then, how can you be dissatisfied if we call you anti-religious, according to the principles you have yourselves assumed? The fact is, that, in order to conciliate those whose minds are haunted by a certain spectre of a union between Church and State, and in order to bring them to the support of the Society, they pretended to meet their views exactly; and then again, on the other hand, attempted to satisfy the scruples of conscientious parents by playing the several sects one against the other, and with so much adroitness, that the whole community came to the desired conclusion that the interests of education and morality were perfectly safe in the hands of the Society, and could not be safe in the hands of any other.

In taking up the speech of Mr. Ketchum, I must premise that he has divided it into two parts, and that, of the many columns by which it is supported, the first two or three are occupied with a detailed history of the legislation, so called, of the Common Council, on this question. Now, I understand the part of this gentleman—who has, perhaps, as deep a knowledge of the mystery of political wire-drawing as any other gentleman of his profession in the State—I understand his introduction of this matter entirely foreign to the subject. His object was, to impress the mind of the senators with the idea that, in New York, the question had been decided—that the Board of Aldermen had been changed—the position of parties changed—applications had been made from time to time, for sixteen years, and that, after the gravest reflection, under all possible variety of circumstances, the answer uniformly was, that it would be a violation of something that he calls "a great principle"—which, however, he does not think proper to define—if our claim were admitted. He wished to convey the idea that, if there had been any thing just or proper or true in our claims, it could not have escaped the notice of public officers in New York—the immediate representatives of the people; and that, consequently, the senators should approach the subject with minds already biased and prejudiced against us. The gentleman wished to lead the honorable legislators to say, "What! shall we, on the examination of one hour, at this distance from the city of New York, undertake to reverse the judgment sustained by the uniform concurrence of the various boards that have constituted the public councils of that city for sixteen years?" There was great generalship in all that on the part of the learned gentleman.

But I dispute the principle *in toto* which the gentleman assumes, and, before that honorable Senate, I would maintain that the gentleman has no foundation whatever for his assumption, and that this question should be viewed by them as if approached for the first time.

And what is my reason for assuming this position? You will mark, that the learned gentleman frequently styles the Common Council "the representatives of the people." My argument in reply, then, is, that, so far as regards this school question, they never were the "representatives of the people" for that question never was made one that could affect their election.

29

in the most remote degree. At least, so we thought. So far as we are concerned, we are right. True, whilst we were meeting to study this subject and bring it under public notice, these gentlemen of the Society were ever and anon charging us with political designs; and I recollect something of an amusing nature connected with that. It was my duty, on the day succeeding the debate before the Common Council, to proceed to Albany for the purpose of giving "confirmation." I went; preached three times on next day, Sunday. On Monday I drove to Troy, for the purpose of visiting the churches there; and on Tuesday I returned to this city. Well, what was the story?—of course, I do not say got up by these gentlemen, nor by the Public School Society—but it was said that I, having taken tea with the aldermen, a bargain was struck between us, and I was to go to Albany to get the Catholics to vote against the Governor, and then all would be right. That was a specimen of the stories that were circulated. But, while we were thus charged, they who brought the accusation were themselves not idle in that very department. The subject was introduced to their pulpits, and their congregations were lectured on it, and from that may be traced the attempt to defeat Governor Seward.

But we never made this a political question, and the Common Council have never acted on it " as the representatives of the people," because it never was applied as a test; but if the question were put between the Secretary's plan and the Public School Society, the latter would soon break down any board that would undertake to support them.

We were denied, it is true, by the Common Council; but we never looked on them as acting, in that matter, as the representatives of the people. We regarded them as independent judges. And, really, there is little ground for surprise at their decisions in the premises.

Now, I will suppose a case. Let us take that of a bank; for it is perhaps as good an illustration as I can furnish at the moment. A citizen has a controversy with the bank, and that controversy comes to a trial. The citizen complains that he is injured by the directors of the bank; he makes out his case, but, in the end, he finds, contrary to all his just anticipations and all his views of justice, that he is defeated, and judgment given against him. Well, he thinks this very hard. But he happens to learn that the judge before whom the case was tried, and the jury who rendered the verdict, are all directors of the bank, and his wonder at the result of the trial ceases. Do you see the application? These gentlemen, after having excluded all religious societies, made the word " religion " a kind of disqualification in a Christian community, in the year 1824; after that, with the subtlety which proves that they are wise in their generation, they got an act passed, by which the Common Council are made *ex-officio* members of the Public School Society, and thus constituted them parties and judges in the cause.

Let me not be misunderstood. I do not suppose for a moment that any gentleman of that Common Council would at any time knowingly deviate from the path of justice and duty on account of his official connection with that Society; but, at the same time, I do know that there is a powerful influence in association, against which the laws, with great wisdom, have guarded the judicial bench, when they declare that a judge should be of a single mind, elevated above all selfish considerations, and whose interests could never be affected by the result of any official act which he might be called on to execute, or any sentence which it might be his duty to pronounce. Here, then, were aldermen of different parties elected from time to time, and so made members—part and parcel—of this Society; and I ask, Would it have been a gracious thing in them, after having been so honored with a place in it, to become adverse to the interests of that body ? Let us bear in mind, too, that there is with most people a regard for consequences; and no alderman could imagine he would greatly benefit his interests by opposing a corporation that has acquired nearly the entire control of all the public money appropriated for the purpose of education in New York, and having its dependents spread from one end of the city to the other. I think it would require a strong and elevated mind, an unusual amount of moral courage, to enable any man so situated to oppose such a corporation.

I do not, then, admit the reasoning of Mr. Ketchum, for I deny his premises that the Common Council ever were " the representatives of the people " on this subject.

I will now commence my review of this speech. I read it carefully from beginning to end, and I was myself impressed with the idea that it scarcely required an answer. I was quite convinced of that, so far as the honorable senators were concerned, because I knew that, to the minds of men accustomed to reasoning, and to detect at a glance where the strength of a position rested, that speech must have appeared a thing altogether out of place. Nevertheless, it was hinted to me that the speech was not intended for senators alone, and the readiness with which Mr. Ketchum could furnish the report went considerably to strengthen that opinion. It was said that, though to me the speech might seem weak, yet to the generality of readers, particularly those unacquainted with the subject, it might seem very specious, and produce in their minds the very conclusions opposite to those which we would wish to see established. On that ground I have taken it up; and I must say that, with regard to Mr. Ketchum himself, I have the kindest possible feeling; and if, in the course of my remarks, I should happen to speak in a manner seemingly disrespectful, I beg that it may not be considered as having been so intended. Of the gentleman himself I cannot say any thing disrespectful; of his speech I hope I am permitted to say whatever the evidence may authorize. I mention his name with perfect freedom, because his name is attached to the speech, and because, principally, he is the official organ of that Society, and what he says is already endorsed by them.

After his introduction, Mr. Ketchum says:

This, probably, may account very sensibly for the fact that, in the city of New York, the portion of the school fund allotted to her was to be distributed by those almoners of her charity whom her representatives thought proper to designate. Now, I ask, was there any thing inconsistent with sound principle in this ? Is there any thing in it which violates the princi-

ple of the largest liberty and the purest democracy, of which we hear something in this report ?

Stop, Mr. Ketchum ! I tell you that there is not one word in that whole
report against such a state of things as that you represent to the minds of
the senators, by making a wrong application. What is represented as contrary to the principle of our Constitution, was the monopoly—the exclusive
system that has succeeded to the former ; and Mr. Ketchum is kind enough
to make an anterior reference to the period when all enjoyed the appropriation for the purposes of education. I stop him there, and say that he makes
a wrong application. He ought not to prejudice the minds of senators, or
the community, by pretending that the Secretary's report trenches on the
enjoyment of the largest liberty.

Mr. Ketchum goes on :

In the city of New York, as I shall have occasion to show by and by—
and more or less, I suppose, it is so in all the States of Christendom—there
are voluntary associations, charitable associations, associations composed of
men, incorporated or otherwise, who are willing to proffer their services to
feed the hungry, to clothe the naked, to visit the destitute, and to see to the
application of funds set apart for their relief. Such men are always to be
found in large cities—men of fortune, men of leisure, men of benevolence,
who are willing to associate together for benevolent objects, and who are
usually made the almoners of the charity of others.

Now, Mr. Ketchum, in the whole of this, is gliding imperceptibly to the
point he wishes to reach. And what is that point ? It is, to fix on the
minds of the senators that, as religious societies formerly took care of their
poor, and as other associations take care of other objects of benevolence, so
they were to look upon the Public School Society as taking care of education. In endeavoring to effect this conclusion, his reasoning glides imperceptibly, as on a colored surface which is black at one extremity and white
at the other, but in which the various shades are so nicely mingled that you
cannot ascertain the point where the change of color begins, so does the
progress of his sophistry elude observation. " Charitable associations ! "
Now, I will examine Mr. Ketchum's philosophy here. I consider that there
is here what may be called a rhetorical picture. He personifies the city of
New York, and calls it " she ; " then he takes her and places her on one
side, and places all the religious societies and benevolent societies, the Public School Society amongst the rest ; and, that being done, he says the city
of New York made them her " almoners." But when we take these societies away, where is " she ? " What becomes of her ? This is what I call a
rhetorical fiction. Mr. Ketchum need not pretend to say that the city of
New York made " almoners." They were self-created. When you take the
religious societies, each having its charity school, and this Society—which
we must not call irreligious, although it has always defeated its opponents
by saying that they profess religion—these constitute the people of New
York, and they received the money set apart for that specific purpose, and
in their sovereign power and wisdom they applied it as they thought proper. They managed it with perfect harmony, for I never heard of the occurrence of a dispute when each section of the community assumed the man-

agement of their own schools, and it was on account of a charge against one
society of misappropriating the public money that the controversy arose.

Afterward, referring to the Legislature by which that state of things
was changed to the present, he says :

Hence, after many discussions in the Assembly chamber (discussions at
which all the members were invited to attend—and almost all of them did
attend, for we had generally a *quorum*, although it was before a committee
night after night), the committee of the Assembly at length made a report
favorable to the prayer of the memorial ; but suggesting, in that very report,
whether even so much as was granted in the proposition referred to was not
a violation of sound principle ; whether, in fact, religious societies ought to
participate in the enjoyment of the fund at all, because, by such participation, the Jew might be made to support the doctrine of the Christian ; and,
vice-versâ, the Christian that of the Jew, the Catholic of the Protestant, the
Protestant of the Catholic, and so on.

What a splendid discovery ! The people hitherto living in perfect harmony, all enjoying that appropriation of public money—not, perhaps, expending it in the wisest manner, but, at all events, without disturbance or
dispute. But all at once it is discovered that, because they are religious
societies, it would be a violation of sound principle to allow them the public money. And why ? Because, in that case, the money paid by a Protestant might pass to the support of a Catholic school—or, if you please, to
the school of a Jew ; and that involved a violation of conscience. I confess, however, I cannot see that, nor do I think any reflecting man can see
it. But what is the fact respecting the turn of the legislation in relation to
the Public School Society, called, at that time, " The Free-School Society " ?
Simply that, because at that Bethel Baptist Church money had been improperly appropriated, occasion was taken to punish not the guilty party,
if there was guilt, but those who had memorialized against the abuse of
public money, and to disfranchise every man professing religion, because the
members of one particular Church had abused their trust ! And it is suspected that all this was not done without the secret instrumentality of that
very Free-School Society itself, which then, as at the present day, professed
to have no religion at all. So that, in this very Legislature—though I know
that another view of it is perfectly lawful—we see that the reasoning approved by Mr. Ketchum would go to brand a stigma on the sacredness of
religion ; it would lead to the inference that, because the adherents of one
religious sect have abused their trust in the employment of the public
money, that, therefore, all profession of religion should be an everlasting
disqualification ! But I pronounce such an inference unworthy the citizens
of a land in whose Constitution Christianity is recognized. And I ask,
Where was the usual penetration of Mr. Ketchum when he employed such
reasoning ? By the laws of this State, church property is exempted from
taxation ; and I am surprised that gentlemen of such tender apprehensions
can rest quietly at night, when they reflect that, possibly, Protestant money
is going to make up the deficiency in the revenues of the State caused by
the exemption from taxation granted to Catholic churches ! But I see no
harm at all in the state of things by which money is thus transferred. All

the churches are represented by all the people, and it matters not an iota if churches are exempted; the tax is paid by the members in another form.

So with the public school money. Although, in the manipulation of the money, it might happen that the identical dollar paid by a Protestant might pass into the treasury of a Catholic school, the Catholic dollar would go back to replace it in the Protestant school; it would be, in the end, all the same, for the question is not at all about the identity of the money. If the taxes could be kept separate, and the money paid by the Protestant go into the Protestant box, and the money paid by the Catholic go into the Catholic box, sure enough, they would get their own money; but it would be all the same if no such care had been taken. Here I would refer to the case of chaplains in our prisons, &c., not one of whom is a Catholic, but who have often received the contributions of Catholics; have they ever complained that that was a violation of the Constitution? Certainly not; and that practical view of the matter should have taught the gentleman the futility of his reasoning, that, if the money of one sect went into the hands of another, it was all the same; it was the money of the people, received from them in one form and returned to them in another, allowing them, in its employment, the noble and grand privilege—of which, I trust, they will not allow themselves to be deprived, no matter how they exercise it—of obeying the dictates of their own free consciences.

In the course of his speech, the gentleman makes a grand display of all the sects that were set aside by the Society. Then he asks the Senate, "Will this honorable body grant to Catholics what was denied to all these?" But there is a difference here; and what is it? There is not on record an instance of a complaint on the part of any of these sects that their rights of conscience were invaded. Episcopalians never made any such complaint, nor did Presbyterians, nor Methodists, nor did any of the other sects; but it happened that they had charity schools attached to their churches, and they thought, by giving such education as the State required, they were entitled to their share of the State bounty. But very different was the case of the Catholics. And now, suppose the circumstances of the case were reversed, and Catholics had the majority on which the Society depends, and would employ the power conferred by it in forcing on the whole community Catholic books and Catholic versions of the Bible, and give the children lessons about the burning of Servetus, and the ignorance of a whole nation in supposing the machine for winnowing corn to be an impious invention, and denouncing those employing it as guilty of a crime against the God who supplies the zephyrs and the breeze—suppose that case, and that the aggrieved minority complained and applied for redress, I trust that on the face of the earth there would not be found a Common Council of Catholics who would refuse to listen to so just a prayer.

Mr. Ketchum says farther, when speaking of the action of the Common Council on this application, that it had been referred to a Law Committee; and he quotes the decision of that committee. We, knowing the manner in which our former applications were disposed of, need not, of course, be surprised at the manner in which this report was expressed. To our last appli-

cation, made in the spring of 1840—when I was absent from this country—
to the Board of Assistant Aldermen, the usual negative was given; but then
it is to be observed, that the board was surrounded by the advocates of the
Society, and these things which we have stated, and which they have since
acknowledged, were denied by them; and on that denial was grounded the
refusal of our application. The advocates of the Society denied that there
were any passages in their books with which we could find fault; averred
that they contain nothing disrespectful to our religion. But, since then,
they have been obliged to retract that, and to acknowledge repeatedly that,
in making these assertions, they were not sustained by truth; that there
were passages in those books reflecting upon our faith; that these passages
had been taught to the children for years, and would have been retained till
this very day, had it not been for our detection and exposure. But it was
not at all surprising that, under the influence of a Society stretching its
gigantic branches over every quarter of the city, and hearing such assertions
from its advocates, the board should deny our claim. But let us glance at
the conclusion which Mr. Ketchum draws from such denial. He says:

That conclusion was ratified by their constituents; and I believe that
every one of the religious societies, or nearly so, excepting the Roman Catholics, acquiesced in that decision. But that society, year after year, has
come before the Common Council, and renewed their request for a separate
portion of the school fund. With the best feelings for the applicants, in a
spirit of kindness, with every disposition to do whatever could be done for
them, year after year, and without respect to politics, whether the one party
was in the ascendant or the other party was in the ascendant, the Common
Council have, with almost entire unanimity, disallowed that request; and I
believe that never, in either board, since the division of that body into two
boards, has there been but one dissenting voice raised against the ratifica-
tion of that decision. Now, if the committee please, who have complained?
The Roman Catholics.

I repeat, that I deny the philosophy of this reasoning. I deny that, in
any case, that portion at least of the community that has petitioned for a
reform of this system ever looked to the Common Council as their representatives on this question. And another argument against Mr. Ketchum's
position is, that this public Council were partisans in the case in which they
were called to deliver judgment. And I think that it would be well for
that Public School Society and the Common Council, if the latter, by their
election to office, are to be engrafted into the former, that the duty of judging between them and the community were delegated to disinterested parties. Mr. Ketchum goes on to say:

No disrespect was intended them. The Common Council, and every
person engaged in the discussion of the question on behalf of the Common
School Society, took great care to say, "We do not reject you because you
are Roman Catholics; and, as evidence of this truth, we give you the fact
that we have rejected similar applications from powerful Protestants; but
we reject your request because we believe that a sound general principle will
not allow us to grant it."

So there was always a precaution observed. Indeed, I myself remarked
that before the Common Council. They uniformly, with one exception, said
that they did not oppose us because we were Catholics. But Dr. Spring,

with great magnanimity and candor, neglected to take the hint, but declared that he was apprehensive of our faith gaining ground. He would oppose us, and preserve the Society as it was, even though the rights of the Catholics should be damaged, and that, for his part, he preferred the religion of Voltaire to that of Fenelon. The sentiment was indeed a black one, and it was rendered blacker by the brightness of the candor with which it was uttered.

Here again Mr. Ketchum states what is incorrect. He says:

We have rejected similar applications from powerful Protestants.

I deny that. I refer him to the records of the Common Council, and I will venture to affirm that he will not find there one "similar application." And why? Simply because there was no ground for any such application. For, although one denomination of Protestants may differ from another, and may carry their attachment to their respective dogmas to great length, yet there is one common ground on which they all, so far as I know, without exception, meet. What is it? That the Bible alone, as understood by each individual, is their rule of faith. They could, therefore, unite on their public school question so far as the Bible was concerned. But then they required that Catholic children, whose creed never admitted that principle, should be taught that doctrine. They had not the same reason that we had to go before the Common Council. We felt that we might as well at once give up to them our children, and allow them to educate them as they pleased, as to send them to their schools. I deny, then, the statement, that "similar applications" were made.

Mr. Ketchum proceeds:

I say, that the Corporation have been desirous, so far as that body possibly could, so far as they felt themselves at liberty, consistently with the maintenance of a sound general principle, to accommodate these parties. They have granted a privilege out of this fund to the Roman Catholic denomination, which has not been granted to any other. The Sisters of Charity, so called, under direction of the Roman Catholic Church, and connected with it (I believe I am right; if not, I should be happy to be corrected), established a most benevolent institution in the city of New York, called the Orphan Asylum—the Roman Catholic Orphan Asylum. They took into this institution poor and destitute orphans. They fed them and clothed them most meritoriously, and they thus relieved the city of New York of the maintenance of many who would otherwise, probably, have been a charge upon it. After long discussion, and with some hesitancy, yet overcome by the desire to oblige, and aware of the limitation arising from the very nature of that institution, the Corporation did permit the Catholic Orphan Asylum to receive money from this fund; and, during the last year, it received some $1,462 for the education of about one hundred and sixty-five children—in common with the Institution for the Blind, and the Deaf and Dumb, and those other benevolent and Christian institutions which are altogether of a Catholic character, in the most comprehensive acceptation of that term, as they are under no sectarian influence or government.

And pray, what sort of an institution is the Protestant Orphan Asylum? Is religion not taught there? And yet Mr. Ketchum singles out the Catholic Orphan Asylum, and speaks of the favor conferred upon it, in order to show the liberality of the Common Council. We are indeed grateful to that body for having placed ours on the same footing with other institutions of a kindred character. But the Common Council have granted money to the Protestant Half-Orphan Asylum, and denied an application of a similar grant to the Catholics. How can Mr. Ketchum assert that a "privilege" has been granted to us exclusively?

In reference to our last application, Mr. Ketchum proceeds:

The subject, I repeat, underwent a very full and free discussion; and, after that had terminated, the Board of Aldermen gravely considered and discussed the subject, and at length, after some delay, came to the conclusion that they would go and visit the schools. Some of the members of the Board of Public Schools, feeling sensibly alive on the subject, expressed to me an apprehension that this was a mere evasion, and they feared that the question had now become mingled with politics. But I said, "Wait, gentlemen; let them go and see your schools; it is a natural desire. They ought to go. It is a great and delicate question, and they ought to be acquainted with it in all its details." They went and visited the public schools and the Roman Catholic schools, and they incorporated the result of their deliberations in a report which I have before me, and from which I shall quote by and by. It is drawn up with great ability, and the decision was, with but one dissenting voice, that the prayer of the petition should be rejected; and it was rejected.

On this I remark, in reference to what I have, I believe, already referred to, that there has been always a panacea for every evil—the appointment of a committee to visit the schools. Why, this is one of the easiest things in the world! A little training, a little arrangement, a judicious wink to the teachers, will prepare every thing, so that it will be very hard if a pleasing exhibition could not be got up in any one of these schools for one hour, on any day out of the three hundred and sixty-five in the year.

But this has been the invariable remedy—no looking at the wounds which the system was from year to year, and from day to day, inflicting on less favored portions of the community; no visit to the back streets and miserable lanes of this city, in which so large a portion of its future inhabitants are grovelling in exposure to vice and degradation. Nothing of that was thought of. But the schools, enriched and adorned by the expenditure of more than a million of money, were inspected, and the gratified and approving visitors returned to the Common Council, to make their report that it was an excellent system, perfect in its details and admirable in its workings, and it was only the absurd bigotry and extreme ignorance of the Catholics that prevented them from reaping its benefits.

Then he compares, with all this, the state of our humble schools. Well, I will not pretend to say that the Catholic schools were in the best order. But here I remark, that, whilst at every stage and step of the progress of this question I have been obliged to controvert false statements, I can challenge them to point to a single instance in which they could dispute the truth of any of our documents. And now I will give a passing notice to that visit to the Catholic schools. Hear this statement. This committee say:

We also visited three of the schools established by the petitioners, and we found them as represented, lamentably deficient in accommodations, and supplies of books and teachers; the rooms were all excessively crowded and poorly ventilated; the books much worn, as well as deficient in numbers, and the teachers not sufficiently numerous; yet, with all these disadvantages, though not able to compete successfully with the public schools, they exhibited a progress which was truly creditable; and with the same means at their disposal, they would doubtless soon be able, under suitable direction, greatly to improve their condition.

Such is their testimony.

And now, shall I pass over this opportunity of making a comparison? When questioned before the Senate, the Society stated that they could not get the children to come; and here are our schools crowded to excess! I can show you, in a room not much larger than the square of the distance between two of the columns supporting the gallery of this building in which we are now assembled, upward of two hundred children crowded together. Yet the Public School Society are obliged to pay $1,000 a year of public money to visitors for the purpose of gathering children to their schools. For the fact came out, in the course of the investigation, that they paid that sum yearly to tract distributors for the purpose I have stated; whilst we, in our poverty, could not find room or books or teachers for the multitudes of children that thronged upon us, and whom this exclusive system consigns to degradation and ignorance and vice, unless something be done for them by others.

Such is the testimony of that very committee. And yet the decision to which they came is quoted by Mr. Ketchum as proof that a "great principle"—of which no definition known is given from the beginning to the end of his speech—prevented them from granting our petition. Well, I have called your attention already, and would do so again, to a point that shows as clear as noonday that this denial was not benevolent toward us, nor in accordance with equal-handed justice. They had opposed us as a sect—as being Catholics. The Secretary of State, however—a man whose integrity of character, legal knowledge, and profound and statesmanlike views have elevated him to the highest rank in the community—placed the question on entirely different grounds. Mr. Ketchum, in the last sentence of his speech before the Common Council, declared, that to the Public School Society the discharge of their duties was rather a burden, which nothing but the extreme benevolence of their nature had prompted them to assume; and, unless they were saved from this continued agitation, they would throw it off. Well, Mr. Spencer excludes all these objectionable features, and places the question on a broad basis, entirely removed from all sectarianism; and then, where are these benevolent gentlemen who are burdened with their charge—these "humble almoners" of the public bounty? At Albany, ready for a new fight! Not for their schools, but to oppose the Secretary; for Mr. Spencer only wishes to make education like the air we breathe, the land we live in—like other departments of human industry and enterprise—free! He would not hold the balances so as to afford the least advantage to any party, but would make all equal, and secure to them the enjoyment of the rights established by the Constitution of the country. And who opposed him? The Public School Society. Their interests were not invaded, but they could not admit the principle that we were to receive education consistently with the laws of the State. Why? You will find that, in the course of Mr. Ketchum's speech, he says the Public School Society could not stand one day if education were made free. If the monopoly which they have wielded for sixteen years should be touched by the little finger of free trade, they would perish. "They cannot live a day." And, gentlemen,·if they cannot live one day on the principles of justice and freedom, then I say that half a day's existence is quite enough for their exclusive system.

We have seen that Mr. Ketchum has introduced the committee to the schools, and now he comes to the point:

Who, then, complain of the operation of this system? Our fellow-citizens, the Roman Catholics.

Failing to get, from the hands of a body thus constituted, the redress for the grievance which they complained of, they come here and now ask it of you. I say, *they* come here, because I will presently show you, from their memorials, that none *but* they come here.

He has brought it round to that, and he thinks that, if that be established, the same prejudices, the same means, that were employed to defeat us in New York, would be equally efficacious at Albany. He says:

Failing to accomplish their purpose through the Common Council of the city of New York, they come and ask it here. Failing in their application to a body of representatives to whom they have applied year after year, and who represent a population in which is intermingled a greater mass of Roman Catholic voters than in any other district of the State of New York.

See the advantage that he takes of our known forbearance, and their activity. Because we, with honorable motives that should have been better appreciated, abstained from making this question a political one. But they did make it such a question, and endeavored to deter all public men from rendering justice to the oppressed Catholics.

Now, I am no politician; I belong to no party, and I can also, perhaps, speak with the greater freedom, because we have high-minded friends, and opponents too, amongst both political parties, and I can perhaps give a satisfactory answer to Mr. Ketchum's allusion to "voters."

After the election of the Governor, the papers in the views of this Society referred to it as a warning; and not only so, but individuals here wrote to the Governor in terms of reproach against the Catholics and the Irish, for not having been more grateful to him. They taunted him with it. And how is that to be answered? I should be sorry that ever the Irish should be ungrateful under any circumstances, or ever forget a friend: and especially at a time when the high and noble principles of justice and equality laid down by the fathers of this country seem to be passing rapidly into oblivion. If a public man stands up for the rights of even the humblest portion of the community, he is entitled to the gratitude and esteem of every man who loves his country. Not that the Governor conferred on us any peculiar favor. I disclaim that; he never asked any thing for us but what we conceived our right. But still he was taunted with references to

the ingratitude of the Irish. It was said, " There is what you got by advo-
cating the cause of the Irish ! " That shows whether we made our question
a political one; and I am glad, in one sense, that the Irish did not vary
from the principles in politics to which they had been in the habit of attach-
ing themselves; because that demonstrates that, whatever may be the opinion of calculating politicians respecting the Irish, that portion of this community have, perhaps, after all, an integrity of character and purity of principle which is not unfrequently found wanting amongst more elevated classes
of both political parties. It was discovered, then, that the Irish would not
abandon their principles from selfish motives. But now let me ask, What
was the case on the other side ? Many of them turned quietly round, abandoning all their old political associations and friends, in order to let Governor Seward know how much he had dared, when he declared for justice
and equal rights to all.

Such was the case, and our opponents cannot deny it. Mr. Ketchum,
then, is unfortunate in his allusion. He ought not—if he had what I shall
not now mention—if he had had presence of mind, I will say, he ought not
to have alluded to that matter at all, because it has brought up the proofs
of what was done by his own clients, whilst our vindication is triumphantly
effected.

We have thus been enabled to refute all the charges urged against us
from the pulpits and religious presses at the disposition of the Society, that
we made a political question of it, and so forth. They did, but we did not.

Gentlemen, I have dwelt longer on some topics than I intended, and
made less progress in my review of this speech than I anticipated. On to-
morrow evening I will proceed with my remarks.

On Friday evening a severe storm prevailed, and the meeting was adjourned to Monday, when Bishop HUGHES proceeded
as follows :

MONDAY EVENING.

BISHOP HUGHES rose, and proceeded as follows :

MR. CHAIRMAN AND GENTLEMEN : I have had occasion already to observe, that the question we are now discussing has passed, or, at least, is
now passing, through the second stage of its progress. In the first stage we
had to apply to the city authorities; and we were obliged, by the circumstances of the case, and for reasons that I have already mentioned, to apply
in a character which we did not desire, but which was forced upon us by
circumstances over which we had no control. The issue of that application
is known. Then we laid our grievances before the Legislature of the State ;
and the Secretary of State, to whom the question had been referred, placed
it upon grounds altogether different from those on which it had hitherto
been considered. Consequently, it was necessary for me, in reviewing Mr.
Ketchum's speech, to consider it under two heads. And hitherto my
remarks on it have applied to the question under the circumstances in

which it was previous to its reference to the Legislature of the State. We have now, however, to consider it on the ground on which it has been placed in the able and eloquent and liberal report of the Hon. Mr. Spencer. And I cannot avoid observing, in the first place, that, taking into account the principles of equality and of justice that pervade that document, I did conceive that the Public School Society could not have found any objections against it. For you will recollect that Mr. Spencer removes entirely the objections urged before the Common Council against the recognition of our claims. These objections were grounded on the principle that no sect or religious denomination had any thing to do with the money appropriated for the purpose of education. The Secretary has completely obviated that objection. He has regarded the petitioners in their civil capacity. He has exhibited the broad and general grounds on which every public institution in this country is conducted; but we find these gentlemen, nevertheless, as zealous, and their advocates as eloquent, against Mr. Secretary Spencer as they had been against us. There can be no charge, now, that a recognition of our claims would favor sectarianism—a union of Church and State. All that has disappeared, and with it, we had hoped, would have disappeared the opposition to our claims.

I will now follow Mr. Ketchum in his arguments before the Senate. And, first of all, I would direct your attention to the number of times in which he repeats that the petitioners are Catholics. He twists and turns that in a variety of ways, in order to convince the senators that, though we applied in the character of citizens, that advantage was to be taken away from us, and we were to be clothed before that honorable body with our religious character, by the hand of Mr. Ketchum. I should have less confidence in the stability of this Government, less affection for its constituted authorities, if I thought that such a circumstance could militate against us in the minds of those gentlemen who have been elected by the suffrages of the people to the guardianship of equal rights. I conceive, therefore, that Mr. Ketchum has mistaken the character of that assembly—that he has exerted himself in vain to fix on us the epithet of Roman Catholics, when we appeared in the character of citizens, and when our right to worship God according to the dictates of our conscience had been already, *à priori*, recognized by the Constitution of the country. And I ask, Is there any crime in being a Roman Catholic? Is there any advantage to be gained in bringing that against us? Is there any thing in the history of the country which could justify the hope of prejudicing the minds of senators by such an allusion? No. In the days when men stood side by side and shoulder to shoulder, and blood touched blood in the battle-strife, and with their brave swords they won the freedom of their country, was it asked, Who is a Catholic? or, Who is a Protestant? Had Mr. Ketchum forgotten the names and deeds of Kosciusko, of Pulaski, of La Fayette, and the Catholic soldiers of Catholic France? Was there any thing said against that religion by the fathers of our country, when they laid the foundation of the liberties we now enjoy? Was there any such charge against Charles Carroll, when he came and signed that glorious Declaration, risking more than all the other signers together ?   No.   Nor have we any cause to be ashamed of our religion, and God forbid we ever should!   I throw back, then, that manœuvre of Mr. Ketchum, and tell him, This is not the country whose Constitution makes apparent to the world that, to be a Roman Catholic, involves a deprivation of the rights and privileges of citizenship.

Last year, a petition was presented to the Senate, signed by Catholics alone ; this year, the petition had other signatures.   True, the petitioners were generally Catholics, but others signed it too ; and I hope and believe that they thought they asked but for justice.   However, Mr. Ketchum, in order to accomplish his purpose, takes up the petition presented last year, and taunts the Secretary, as if he were guilty of artifice in making it appear that the members of other religious denominations had joined in our petition.   He says :

Probably that circumstance was discovered by the Secretary's sagacity, between 1840 and 1841.

What does he mean by that allusion, except to remind the Secretary that it was by prejudicing the public mind by misrepresentations, that certain partisans succeeded in diminishing the vote for his Excellency the Governor ?   If Mr. Ketchum does not intend that by this delicate hint, I should like to know what he does mean.   He then affects to take up the objections :

One of their complaints is, that the people are not represented in this Public School Society ; that here is an agency used for a great public purpose which the people do not directly choose ; and they complain of the Public School Society being a close corporation.

Certainly, all these are grounds of complaint, and all these are so clearly set forth in the report of the Secretary, that you have but to read that document to see that Mr. Ketchum cannot shake one solitary position of that honorable gentleman.   Is not the Public School Society a close corporation ?   And is not Mr. Secretary Spencer's report calculated to place it on the same basis on which all our free public institutions are founded ?   Is the Secretary not a reformer, then, in reference to that Society ?   He does here precisely what Lord John Russell attempts to do in England, when he endeavors to break down the monopoly of the corn laws, and to make bread cheap ; Mr. Spencer wishes to break down the monopoly of education, and to make voting and education—the bread of knowledge—cheap.   That is to say, that the same people who are supposed to be capable of choosing a sheriff, or a governor, or a president, without paying for the privilege, should also have the right of choosing the teachers of their children without paying ten dollars for it.   Mr. Ketchum passes over that very lightly.   That is a point not to be seriously dwelt upon, and he glides into the old charge preferred before the Common Council, and takes up the old objections, although not one of them was presented in the petition before the Senate.   Keeping always before the mind of the senators that we are Catholics, he affects to take up these objections, and says :

Now, I wish to call the attention of the committee to the fact now to be stated : there is no complaint in these memorials, nor will you hear any from any source, that the Public School Society does not furnish, to all the children who attend their schools, a good literary education.

Let me caution Mr. Ketchum not to be so fast, and I will give him my reasons. From the manner in which the examinations are conducted, it is the easiest thing in the world to have all ready prepared for the day of visitation. When the examiners present themselves, pet classes are arranged, and in them pet pupils, who will perform their part admirably well. It is easy to have all this array, and so it is to be regarded rather as an exhibition than an examination. But if they desire their examinations to create universal confidence, let them have them as they are conducted in European universities, where the pupils stand forward, and any person who chooses examines them; when not the choice and prepared pupils are taken, but the subjects of examination are selected indiscriminately from the classes. Let such a method be adopted here, and I will venture to say that Mr. Ketchum will not have any thing to boast of over other schools. I do not, however, blame the visitors for not finding fault with the external management of these schools. I think it excellent; and the best proof of the sincerity of that opinion was afforded in our willingness to adopt and place the superintendence of our schools in the hands of these very gentlemen.

But Mr. Ketchum goes on:

The Roman Catholics complain, in the first place, that they cannot conscientiously send their children to the public schools because we do not give religious instruction in a definite form and of a decided and definite character. They complain, in the second place, that the school-books in common use in the Society contain passages reflecting upon the Roman Catholic Church. And they complain, in the third place, that we use the Bible without note or comment; that the school is opened in the morning by calling the children to order and reading a chapter in the Bible—our common version. These are the three grounds on which they base their conscientious scruples.

Now, it is a fact that we do not complain of any one of these things in our petition to the Senate. One of these complaints was expressed in the petition to the Common Council, and I have already explained the reasons of that presentation. But, in the petition to the Senate, we said, in general terms, that the conscientious scruples of a large portion of our fellow-citizens were violated by the system pursued in these schools. I will, however, take up these objections in order.

Mr. Ketchum says that we complain, in the first place, that we cannot send our children to the schools of the Public School Society "because religion is not there taught of a decided and definite character." Mr. Ketchum certainly has not stated the objection correctly, for I defy him to find such words in our petition. We complained in general against these schools, that, by divorcing religion and literature, they endangered the best interests of children who were to grow up to be men, and who, to be useful members of the community, should have their minds imbued with correct principles, and could not be so without being made acquainted with some religious principles. But we never complained that they did not give "definite religious instruction." Far from it; and when Mr. Ketchum asserted that we did, I am sorry to say that he asserted what he must or might have known to be untrue. And how do I prove it? In our propositions to the committee of the Common Council, when they had gone through with their ceremony of visiting the schools, and the Society had offered their propositions, the very last article of our proposal was in these words: "But nothing of their (*i. e.*, Catholic) dogmas, nothing against the creed of any other religious denomination, shall be introduced." Mr. Ketchum saw that; and I ask him, How could he undertake to make an argument by substituting language entirely different from ours, and presenting it as our objection? How could he say that we found fault with the Public School Society for not teaching religion in a "definite form," when they always disclaimed the right to teach it at all, and considered it a crime for any denomination to ask for it? This is what I call substitution—invention—a course unworthy of Mr. Ketchum, of his profession, and of that Society of which he was the organ.

I am well aware that, to a hasty reader, Mr. Ketchum's speech will appear very logical indeed. But I have, at the same time, to observe that, while he reasons logically, by drawing correct inferences from his premises, he has taken care previously to change the premises, and, instead of taking our principle as submitted by us, he gradually shifts it; preserving, however, enough to deceive a cursory reader, until he substitutes one entirely different, from which he reasons very logically, of course. Let us suppose Mr. Ketchum a professor of law in some university—for I have no doubt he could fill such a chair, and adorn it, too, if he would—and imagine him addressing a class of students. He says, "Gentlemen, one of the most important things in our profession is, to know how to conduct an argument, which you must always do with logical precision. And, to effect this, you are to follow this excellent rule: if your facts sustain your conclusions, well; if not, you must find other facts that will. The principle of this rule I call the principle of substitution, and an admirable principle it is; but you must be cautious how you use it, especially before a judge and jury. But if it is before a public, which reads fast—for there is a great deal to be read—you will find it work very well. Recollect, then, gentlemen, this great principle—'substitute' in your reasoning."

In such a way we might imagine Mr. Ketchum addressing his students. And you will find that few reason illogically. Even the inmates of the Lunatic Asylum reason very logically. One of them, perhaps, imagines himself a clock. He says, "Stand off! Don't shake me; I am obliged to keep time." That is logical reasoning. The only mistake is, that he "substitutes" a clock for a living creature; and, reasoning from this substitution, he draws the conclusion admirably. So it is with Mr. Ketchum.

We did not, I tell Mr. Ketchum, ask the Public School Society to teach religion in any definite form. We never complained of their not teaching it. We never did ask such an unreasonable thing from men who made it a crime for religious societies to have any thing to do with the public money.

He then states another objection: "that the books used in the schools contain passages reflecting on the Catholic Church." That is true; and he says, in the third place, that we object that "the Protestant version of the Bible is used, and that the schools are opened by calling the children to order and reading a passage from that Bible." Not a word of that in our petition. That is "substitution" again—removing the objections presented by us, and substituting others which might, as he supposed, lead to the denial of our claims, on the ground that we object unreasonably.

Mr. Ketchum takes up the objection, and, in order to show how unreasonable that was, he submits the proposition of the Public School Society, passing altogether over ours, which common justice required should have been also presented, as it would have discovered on our part a similar disposition, and have entirely undeceived the senators as to any alleged claim to have religion taught in a definite form.

There was no official declaration guarding against the possibility that, next year, another board might alter all these books to a worse state than ever ; and, consequently, their offer to expunge their books was altogether nugatory. Mr. Ketchum says, however :

This portion of the report, as will be seen, has reference to these offensive passages. Now, every body will say that is a fair offer—we will strike them out. But, gentlemen of the committee, I submit whether here, in this country, we must not, in matters of conflicting opinions, give and take a little ?

Well, I do not find the Public School Society, although very good at taking, at all disposed to give any thing.

I have no doubt that I can find something in any public school-book, of much length, and containing much variety of matter, reflecting upon the Methodists—upon the heated zeal, probably, of John Wesley, and his followers ; reflecting upon the Episcopalians, the Baptists, and Presbyterians. Occasional sentences will find their way into public discourses, which, if viewed critically, and regarded in a captious spirit, rather reflect upon the doctrines of all those churches.

In this way he gets over these passages, most insulting to us and our religion, which I pointed out to these gentlemen, after their having inculcated them in the minds of the children for sixteen years past. We have to add, however, that, in examining these books, we found no passages reflecting on those denominations.

Now, I will call your attention to Mr. Ketchum's views respecting conscience and conscientious scruples. We supposed that, when a man could not do a thing in conscience, the reason was, that he thought, by doing it, he would offend God. This is what we supposed to be a conscientious difficulty ; and therefore it was that we did not object (as he says, and as I shall have occasion to treat of presently) to the Protestants reading their version of the Bible ; because, believing it right, they could use it with a good conscience. But we Catholics did not approve of that version ; many other denominations do not approve of it—the Baptists and Unitarians, for instance ; and our objection was, that Mr. Ketchum and the Public School Society would force on us the reading of that version against which we had conscientious objections. We believe that, to yield to that, would damage the faith which we hold to be most pleasing to God. Suppose us to be in

30

error, if you please, but certainly the Public School Society have no right to rule that we are. They are not infallible, and, consequently, should recognize our right of conscience, as we recognize theirs.

But Mr. Ketchum has battled bravely against these principles, and, thinking it would be better for us to agree to offend our God and coincide with the Public School Society, wishes to beat down these scruples. And now, would you have his idea of a conscientious scruple? He institutes a comparison, in order to show how trifling such things are, and he says:

On the other hand, there are many passages from the speeches of Mr. Webster which have found their way into school-books; and a Democrat may say, "I cannot go Mr. Webster; my children shall not be taught to admire him." And thus, if we are captious, we can find conscientious scruples enough.

So that Mr. Webster's writings are placed, as it were, on a parallel with the Word of God himself; and a difficulty of which he is the subject is spoken of in the same way as if it were a difficulty in reference to God. And what is Mr. Ketchum's conclusion? That, whilst he would trample on our conscientious scruples about the deity, he bows with great deference to the scruple about Mr. Webster, and of this he goes on:

However, if it is *bonâ fide* a conscientious scruple, there is the end of it; we cannot reason with it. But, in the judgment of the Common Council, and as I think must be the case in the judgment of every man, the difficulty is got over by the proposition which has been made.

Well, now, just let him extend a little of that indulgence to us, in the case in which our account to our Creator and eternal Judge is involved. But not so. He next says:

The next complaint is, that we do not give religious education enough.

Where did Mr. Ketchum find that? That is "substitution" again. He has not found that in any thing from us. He proceeds:

The memorials, all of which are public—and the speeches and documents which have been employed, and which, if necessary, can be furnished to the committee—all go conclusively to demonstrate that, in the judgment of those who spoke for the Roman Catholic Church, we ought to teach religion in our public schools; not generally, not vaguely, not the general truths of religion, but that specific religious instruction must be given. Now, I hardly suppose that this deficiency can be made the subject of conscientious objection.

'But that is a false issue. On none of these points has he stated our objection. We never objected, as far as Catholic children were concerned, that they did not teach religion. We complained of a system from which religion was (according to them) excluded by law. But that, on the contrary, they did attempt surreptitiously to introduce such teaching, in a form that we did not recognize. What does he say then?

The third and last complaint is, that our Catholic brethren cannot consent to have this Bible read in the hearing of their children. Now, on every one of these points the trustees have been disposed to go as far as they possibly could in the way of accommodation; but they never yet consented to give up the use of the Bible to the extent to which it is used in the schools. I say, the trustees have never yet consented to this surrender. But if they can have good authority for doing it, they will do it.

If this Legislature, by its own act, will direct that the Bible shall be excluded, I will guarantee that it shall be excluded.

Now, perhaps one of the rarest talents of an orator is that which enables him to accommodate his discourse to the character of the audience whom he addresses. But, like all rare talents, it should be exercised with discretion. That the learned gentleman possesses it, however, is proved by the fact that the very declarations made by him before the Senate are contradicted by his statements before the Common Council, and *vice-versâ*. Before the Common Council, in the presence of a number of the clergy, he eloquently denounced the exclusion of the Bible from the schools. If a compromise depended on this, he must say, "No compromise!" Before the Senate, however, he is all obsequiousness. "Gentlemen, if you give us authority to exclude the Bible, I guarantee that it shall be so."

I recollect the beautiful period with which the gentleman wound up his sentiments before the Common Council. I remember him saying that "it would be hard to part with that translated Bible—hard, indeed; for it had been the consolation of many in death, the spring of hope in life, and wherever it had gone, there was liberty and there was freedom; and where it had not gone, there was darkness and there was despotism." But I must apologize for attempting to repeat, as I spoil the poetry of his eloquent language. At the time, however, I thought, What a beautiful piece of declamation that would be at a Bible Society meeting! for on such occasions, owing to the enthusiasm—the sincere enthusiasm—of the auditors, and the oftentimes artificial enthusiasm of the speakers, all history, philosophy, and common sense occasionally, are rendered quite superfluous. The most beautiful phrases, resting on no basis but fancy, may be strung together, and will produce the deepest impression. But I doubt much, when we come to examine the sober reality of the matter, whether the poetical beauties of Mr. Ketchum's picture will not be seen vanishing into thin air. I doubt much, indeed, whether the liberty whose origin and progress history has recorded, will be found to have sprung from "that translated Bible" in any sense, and especially in the sense of Mr. Ketchum. I, of course, yield to no man in profound veneration for the Book of God; but there is a point of exaggeration which does no credit, but injury, to that Holy Book.

Let us look at these translations of the Bible. The first was Tyndal's, then Coverdale's, and then the Bishops' Bible; these remained till the time of James I.; and during all that time—a period of about a century—if ever there was a period of degrading and slavish submission to tyrannical power in Engand, it was then, beyond all comparison. At the close of this period, a new translation was made, and dedicated to the king. It was discovered that the "only rule of faith and practice" during all this time was full of errors and corruption. Every one knows that James was one of the poorest of the poor race from whom he was descended. Yet, in their dedication,

the translators appointed to amend the "rule of faith" by a new translation, call him the "Sun in his strength," and that, from his many and extraordinary graces, he might be called "The Wonder of the World."

Now, during the succeeding sixty or eighty years, what were the doctrines of liberty in England ? It was then that the schoolmen of Oxford
and Cambridge taught from that translated Bible the dogma of "non-
resistance to the royal authority ;" that "passive obedience" was the duty
of subjects ; that no crime nor possible tyranny of the prince could authorize a subject to rebel. How could Mr. Ketchum forget all that ?

Let us examine the facts of the case, and ascertain how correct Mr.
Ketchum is, when he said that liberty had always followed the progress of
that translated Bible. You will find that, from the period of the Reformation down to the period of the Revolution, England was sunk to the lowest
degree of slavish submission to tyrannical authority. The spirit of old
English freedom had disappeared at the Reformation ; and it was only at
the Revolution that, like a ship recovering its equilibrium after having long
been capsized by the storm, that the old spirit righted itself again. But do
I speak poetry, like Mr. Ketchum ? Let me appeal to facts.

We find the fundamental principles of liberty as well understood by our
Catholic ancestors, centuries before the Reformation, as they are at the present day. They well understood the principles, that all civil authority is
derived from the people, and that those elected to exercise it are responsible
to those from whom they derive their power.

By one of the laws of Edward the Confessor, confirmed by the Conqueror, the duties of the king are defined ; and it is provided that, unless
he should properly discharge them, he should not be allowed even the name
of king as a title of courtesy, and this on the authority of a pope. The
coronation of Henry I. was based on as regular a contract as ever yet took
place in market-overt. By the coronation oaths of the several monarchs
between him and John, a similar contract was implied. By Magna Charta,
and its articles for keeping the peace between the king and the kingdom,
this implied contract was reduced to writing, and "signed, sealed, and
delivered by the parties thereto." In the reign of Henry III., Bracton, one
of his judges, tells us that, since the king "is God's minister and deputy,
he can do nothing else on earth but that only which he can do of right.
. . . Therefore, while he does justice, he is the deputy of the Eternal
King ; but the minister of the devil, when he turns to injustice. For he is
called king from governing well, and not from reigning ; because he is king
while he reigns well, but a tyrant when he violently oppresses the people
entrusted to him. . . . Let the king, therefore, allow to the law what the
law allows to him—dominion and power ; for he is not a king with whom
his will, and not the law, rules."—*Dublin Review.*

There was the language of a judge in the times before either the Reformation or James' translation of the Bible were dreamed of. I pass to another historical event—the crowning of John ; on which occasion Hubert,
the Archbishop of Canterbury, fearing that the monarch, from supposing
that his royal blood alone entitled him to receive the kingly office, should
throw the kingdom into confusion, reminded him that no one had such a
right to succeed another in the government unless chosen by the people.

That no one had a right by any precedent reason to succeed another in the sovereignty, unless he were unanimously chosen by the entire kingdom, and preëlected according to the eminency of his morals, after the example of Saul, the first anointed king, whom God had set over His people, though not a king's son or sprung of a royal race, that thus he who excelled all in ability, should preside over all with power and authority. But if any of a deceased king's family excelled the rest of the nation, to his election they should more readily assent. For these reasons they had chosen Count John, the brother of their deceased king, on account as well of his merits as of his royal blood. To this declaration John and the assembly assented.

I wonder whether an archbishop of Canterbury, now, with this translated Bible in his hands, would dare to utter such language in the presence of the monarch, when he was about to officiate at a coronation? Let us now turn to what occurred after this translation of the Bible. At the execution of the Earl of Monmouth, there were a number of Protestant divines who exhorted him to die like a "good Christian;" and the great point on which they insisted was, that the subject was bound to obey the prince with "passive obedience."

But the noble Earl, in whose breast there still burned something of the principles of the olden times of England, could not agree to that dogma, and then the divines, under the influence of this translated Bible, refused to pray for him. Their last words were:

Then, my lord, we can only recommend you to the mercy of God, but we cannot pray with that cheerfulness and encouragement as we should if you had made a particular acknowledgment.

The same doctrine was prevalent in the time of Tillotson, and he speaks of it not only as his own opinion, but as that of those for whom Mr. Ketchum claims the honor of being considered the apostles of English liberty. I quote from the *Dublin Review:*

Among those who importuned the unfortunate Lord Russell to make a similar acknowledgment, was Tillotson, who, by letter, told him that this doctrine of non-resistance "was the declared doctrine of all Protestant Churches, though some particular persons had thought otherwise," and expressed his concern "that you do not leave the world in a delusion and false hope to the hinderance of your eternal happiness," by doubting this saving article of faith. Within the same period, Bishop Sanderson delivered the doctrine in the following clear and explicit language. He declares that "to blaspheme the holy name of God, to sacrifice to idols," &c., &c., "to take up arms against a lawful sovereign, none of these, and sundry other things of the like nature, being all of them simple and, *de toto genere,* unlawful, may be done on any color or pretence whatsoever, the express command of God only excepted, as in the case of Abraham sacrificing his son, not for the avoiding of scandal, not at the instance of any friend, or command of any power on earth, not for the maintenance of the lives and liberties of ourselves or others, nor for the defence of religion, nor for the preservation of the Church and State; no, nor yet—if that could be imagined possible—for the salvation of a soul; no, not for the redemption of the whole world." This was considered a very orthodox effusion.

An article of faith that you dare not, under any circumstances, resist the kingly power.

Compare, then, the language of Protestant divines having this translated

Bible before them, with that of Catholic divines at a former period, and see the ground which Mr. Ketchum has found in England for his poetical assertion. But, perhaps, if we turn our attention to the Protestant governments on the continent of Europe, we may find his dream realized. Perhaps he may find it realized in Prussia. In that country there are two principal communions of Protestants, the Lutheran and the Calvinist. Now, the king calls his officers together, and tells them to draw up a liturgy—decrees that both will, and shall, and must believe or practice this liturgy. Or he may go to Norway, or Sweden, or Denmark, and the dark despotism of the North; perchance there he may find that liberty of which he speaks progressing with this translation. What kind of freedom, let me ask Mr. Ketchum, followed this "translated Bible" to Ireland—that everlasting monument of Catholic fidelity and Protestant shame?

But to come to this country: perhaps it was in New England, among the Puritans, that Mr. Ketchum's dream was realized. Ask the Quaker. Perhaps it was in Virginia. Ask the Presbyterian. Where was it? Let me tell you. It was in Maryland, among the Catholics. They knew enough of the rights of conscience to raise the first standard of religious liberty that ever floated on the breeze in America.

You may be told that Roger Williams, and his associates in Rhode Island, declared equal rights. Not at all; he excluded Roman Catholics from the exercising the elective franchise. But the Catholics did not exclude him. They may refer to Pennsylvania; the reference is equally unfortunate, for Penn wrote from England, remonstrating with Governor Logan, I believe, for permitting the scandal of Catholic worship in Philadelphia. Turn, now, look at the constellation of Catholic republics, before Protestantism was dreamed of as a future contingency. Look at Venice, Genoa, Florence, and that little republic not larger than a pin's head on the map—San Marino—which has preserved its independence for such a long course of centuries, lest the science of republicanism should be lost to the world. Look at Poland, when the Protestants were persecuting one another to the death in Germany: Poland opened her gates to the refugees, and made them equal with her own subjects; and in the Diet of Poland, at which the law was passed, there were eight Catholic bishops, and they must have sanctioned the law, for the liberism veto gave each the power to prevent it. I challenge Mr. Ketchum to point, in the whole history of the globe, to one instance of similar liberality on the part of Protestants toward Catholics.

Now, what becomes of that beautiful declaration of Mr. Ketchum, that, wherever that translation had gone, liberty had followed? I know, indeed, that in this country we all enjoy equal, civil rights; but I know also that it was not Protestant liberality that secured them. They grew out of necessity; and in the declaration of them there is no difference made between one religion and another. Catholics contended as valiantly as any other in the first ranks of the contest for liberty. And I fervently hope that it is too late in the day for any one to pretend that Catholics have been so blinded by their religion as to be unable to know what is liberty and what is not.

Be it understood, then, that not one of the objections which Mr. Ketchum has put into our mouths respecting the Bible was presented to the Senate by us.

Mr. Ketchum, after having thus disposed of our pretended objections, goes on to speak of the Secretary's report:

They will be satisfied with it; it will give them what they ask. Now, let us see *how*. There is no proposition contained in this report that religious societies, as such, shall participate in this fund—none.

Then, sir, I ask, What is your objection? In New York, before the Common Council, all your opposition was directed against "religious societies." Mr. Spencer has removed every ground for that, and I therefore ask, What is your objection? Your object is, to preserve the Public School Society in the possession of the monopoly, not only of the funds contributed by the citizens for the support of education, but also of the children. He says:

The trustees of districts shall indicate what religion shall be taught in those schools. That is to say, that you shall have small masses; that these small masses shall elect their trustees; and as the majority of the people in those small masses may direct, so shall be the character of the religious instruction imparted.

Mr. Spencer wishes to take from the Society that very feature which is objected to; that is to say, he wishes that religion shall neither be excluded nor enforced by law. And yet Mr. Ketchum, by his old principle of substitution, makes out quite a different proposition from the report, and infers that the trustees shall have the power to prescribe what religion shall be taught. I do not see that in the report at all. On the contrary, the Secretary leaves parents at liberty to act on that subject as they see proper. Mr. Ketchum supposes a case to illustrate his view of the matter, which, I must say, does not do him much credit. He says:

But when a school is formed in the Sixth Ward of the city of New York, in which ward (for the sake of the argument we will assume) the Roman Catholics have a majority in the district, they choose their trustees, and these trustees indicate that a specific form of religion—to wit, the Roman Catholic religion—shall be taught in that school; that mass shall be said there, and that the children shall cross themselves with holy water in the school, having the right to do so according to this report, the Catholics being in a majority there. Then, and not till then, can these Roman Catholics conscientiously send their children to school. That is to say, their objections to this system are to be overcome by having a school to which they can conscientiously send their children; and that school must be one in which religion is to be taught according to their particular views.

That is drawing an inference without the facts, for we never said so—never even furnished him with authority to say so; and although Mr. Ketchum has the authority of the Public School Society to speak, yet that does not enable him, when he states what is not the fact, to make it true. But I wish to know why he brought up that picture at all; why the Sixth Ward should have peculiar charms in his imagination; or why he should have introduced all that about the children crossing themselves with holy water. And pray, is it for Mr. Ketchum to find fault with what he supposes to be a religious error, and for which he is not at all accountable? He has not shown, nor has any man shown, that any such consequences would follow. It is impossible that the trustees could act so ridiculously as to permit such a thing; it was incredible that they, being responsible to the officers appointed by the State, and under the eye of such vigilant gentlemen as Mr. Ketchum and the Public School Society, could permit Mass to be celebrated in the school. Yet such is the picture presented by Mr. Ketchum—quite in accordance with his old course, and in order to excite popular prejudices, for which purpose this speech seems to have been so studiously prepared. For he well knew that, amongst a large portion of the Protestants, there is a vast amount of traditional prejudice against Catholics, which has, from being repeated incessantly and seldom contradicted, become fixed, occupying the place of truth and knowledge. Their case reminds me of what is related of Baron Munchausen. It is said that, when this celebrated traveller was old, he had a kind of consciousness that there was some former period of his life when he knew that all his stories were untrue; but he had repeated them so often, that now he actually believed them to be true.

It is to such persons as are under the influence of these prejudices and bigotries that Mr. Ketchum addresses his speech; and, if he utter the sentiments of the Public School Society, how, I ask, can we confide to their hands the training of the tender minds of our children?

But one of the most remarkable things in this speech is, that, after having beaten off in succession the different religious denominations, because, as he said, they would teach religion, having, in fact, played the one sect against the other, Mr. Ketchum turns round and affirms that the Society itself does teach religion. He says:

No, sir. I affirm that the religion taught in the public schools is precisely that quantity of religion which we have a right to teach. It would be inconsistent with public sentiment to teach less; it would be illegal to teach more.

The "exact quantity!" Apothecary's weight! Nothing about the quality, except that Mr. Ketchum, having made it an objection that we wished religion in a definite form, he will give it in an indefinite form—a fine religion; but, at all events, there is to be the "legal quantity." Well, now let us see something about the quality of this religion; and I wish to consider the subject seriously. And here let me refer to a beautiful sentiment expressed by the Secretary in his report. He says that religion and literature have become so blended, that the separation of the one from the other is impossible. A more true or appropriate declaration could not proceed from the lips of any man wishing the welfare of his country and his kind.

Now, whenever we made objections to that Society for pretending that religious subjects were excluded by law, it was on these grounds. We said, We refer you to the experience of public men—to that of the most celebrated statesmen in Europe, even the infidels of France, who have uniformly declared that society cannot exist except on the basis of religion. All of them, whether believing in religion or not, have admitted the necessity of having some kind of religion as a basis of the social edifice. But these gentlemen, in all their debates, have contended that the education to be given should be " purely civil and secular." That is their official language. And now, for the first time, Mr. Ketchum, before the Senate, declares that the Society does teach religion, and exactly the proper quantity.

Let me now call your attention to a passage in one of their reading-books, in order that we may see a specimen of this religion. I will now make a few comments on the passage, but I do conceive that there are persons of all those denominations who recognize the doctrine of the Divinity, who could not be induced to have the minds of their children inoculated with such sentiments as it contains. Referring to our blessed Redeemer, one of their school-books says :

His answers to the many insidious questions that were put to Him showed uncommon quickness of conception, soundness of judgment, and presence of mind, completely baffled all the artifices and malice of His enemies, and enabled Him to elude all the snares that were laid for Him.

Are these the ideas of the divine attributes of the Redeemer which the Christian portion of the community wish impressed on the minds of their children ? That such have been the sentiments taught by the Society for the last sixteen years, they cannot deny. And they may account for it as they please, but it has attracted the attention of many, that, for the last sixteen years, the progress of that young and daring blasphemy that trifles with all that is sacred has increased tenfold in this city. How do I account for it ? In two ways : first, because a large portion of the young are debarred from the benefits of education ; and, on the other hand, there is the attempt which has been made to divorce religion from literature. When such causes exist, you need not be surprised to find that infidelity thickens its ranks and raises on every side its bold and impious front.

I have presented you with a specimen of the quality of that religion which Mr. Ketchum says is dealt out with exact and legal measure.

Mr. Ketchum contends that it is religion of a decided character that we want. And pray, what are we to understand by a religion that is not decided ? A religion which is vague—a general religion ? What is the meaning of these terms ? I desire to have a definition of them.

If there is to be established by law a Public-School-Society-religion, I should like to have its confession of faith, and be informed of the number of its articles, and the nature of the doctrines contained in them. But it seems to me that Mr. Ketchum and this Public School Society resemble a body of men who are opposed to all physicians because they understand medicine ; and who, although themselves opposed to all practice of medicine, are yet disposed to administer to the patients of the regular practitioners. And the comparison holds good ; for, after all, children are born with a natural moral disease—want of knowledge and evil propensities, and education and religion are the remedial agents to counteract these evil tendencies and remove the natural infirmity. Then, we have the practitioners, as they may be termed, coming to see the patient, the whole community supplying the medicine-chest; and we have these men surrounding this chest, and exclaiming to the physicians, "Clear off! You are a Thomsonian, and you are a Broussaist, and you are a Homœopathic, and you are a regular practitioner, and you wish to prescribe remedies of a decided and definite character, which is contrary to 'a great principle;'" and, having thus banished all the physicians, they turn doctors themselves, and mix up their drugs into what they call a "general medicine," of which they administer what they call the legal quantity. But the gentlemen forget that neither the patient nor the medicine are theirs. Those who furnish the patient and supply the medicine-chest should have a voice in the selection of the doctors.

What do the gentlemen really intend? They object to religious societies, but, after they have got them pushed out of the house, they begin to teach religion themselves. Mr. Ketchum acknowledges that. He and Mr. Sedgwick, his associate, however, do not appear to have studied theology in the same school. One says that religion is the basis of all morality; the other, that morality is the basis of religion. And, after all, do men agree any more in their views of morality than religion? Certainly not. And yet you must give to the children, especially those of that class attending these schools—for it should be borne in mind that they, for the most part, do not enjoy the opportunity of parental or pastoral instruction—some supply of religious education. They are the offspring of parents who, unfortunately, cannot supply that deficiency; and if they are brought up in this way, with a kind of contempt for religion, or with the most vague idea of it, the most lamentable results must necessarily follow.

I now come to another point: the non-attendance of the children in the schools. Whilst our humble school-rooms are crowded to excess, the Society has been obliged to give $1,000 a year to persons for recruiting for children. In Grand street they have erected a splendid building, almost sufficient to accommodate the Senate of the State; and besides all that, we find that they are able to lavish public money in payment to agents to collect children. Mr. Seton, who has been a faithful agent of the Society, made that fact known, and stated that, by this means, eight hundred children were collected. And to whom was this money given? To tract distributors. A very good occupation, theirs, I have no doubt, but, at the same time, that was rather a singular appropriation by men so extremely scrupulous lest any portion of the public money should go to the support of any sect. But I suppose that was on the principle of what Mr. Ketchum calls "giving and taking;" that is, you give a tract and take a child.

Then, we have quite an effort, on the part of Mr. Ketchum, to prove that the trustees discharge their onerous duties much better than officers elected by the people. I will quote his remarks on that point:

This Public School Society receives its daily sustenance from the representatives of the people; and the moment that sustenance is withdrawn, it dies—it cannot carry on its operations for a day.

A most beautiful subversion of the actual order! For, so far from the Common Council patronizing the Society, it is the Society that patronizes

the Common Council, taking them into partnership the moment they are
elected; and, so far from being dependent on the Council, as was well remarked by a greater authority than I am on this subject, the Council are
dependent on the Society. The schools belong to the Society, just as much
as the Harlem Bridge does to the company who built it. What remedy is
there, then? The Society, self-constituted, a close corporation, takes into
partnership the Common Council, which then becomes part and parcel—
bone of the bone and flesh of the flesh—of the Society; and if any difference arises between the citizens and the Society, a committee of that very
Society adjudicates in the cause. Thus we have found that the Common
Council, after having denied our claim, and even when about to retire and
give place to their successors, followed us to Albany; and their last act, like
that of the retreating Parthian who flung his dart behind him, was, to lay
their remonstrance on the table of the tribunal to which we had appealed.
Mr. Ketchum says:

Here are agents of the people—men who, having a desire to serve mankind, associate together; they offer to take the superintendence of particular works; they offer themselves to the public as agents to carry out certain
benevolent purposes; and, instead of paying men for the labor, they volunteer to do it for you, " without money and without price," under your directions—to do it as your servants, and to give an account to you and an
account to the Legislature. Voluntary public service is always more efficient than labor done by servants chosen in any other way.

So that, because they serve gratuitously, they discharge their duties
much better than if elected by the people! Well, let us improve upon the
hint. Perhaps some of them may be kind enough to discharge the more
important functions of the Government for nothing. But if volunteers be
more efficient than officers chosen by the votes of the people, let us abolish
the farce of elections altogether. Not satisfied with this, Mr. Ketchum also
would seem to contend, that the volunteers ought not to be held responsible.

To establish his views on this point, Mr. Ketchum refers to charitable
and benevolent institutions. But where is the justice of the comparison?
The sick are incompetent to secure their own protection and recovery. The
inmates of the House of Refuge, on which Mr. Ketchum has a beautiful
apostrophe, referring to his own share in the erection of that one established
in this city, are likewise unable to take care of themselves. And here let
me say, in all sincerity, to Mr. Ketchum, that if he and the Public School
Society determine to perpetuate their system—if they continue to exclude
religion from education, and at the same time deprive four fifths of the children, as now, of any education at all, then he had better stretch his lines
and lay the foundations of houses of refuge, as the appropriate supplement
to the system. Neither does the comparison hold, as I have before shown,
in reference to lunatic asylums, &c.

Then Mr. Ketchum goes on to illustrate farther, and says:

But it is said—and said, too, in this report of the Secretary—that he
proposes to retain these public schools. How retain them? One of the

features of the proposed new law is, that all school moneys shall be paid to the teachers. Under such a law we cannot live a day—not a day.

What an acknowledgment is that!—that a law, which would make education free, giving equal rights to all, would be the death-warrant of the Public School Society!

There is another point on which Mr. Ketchum does not now dwell so emphatically. He says that there were a large number of taxpayers who—wonderful to relate!—asked for the privilege of being taxed—asked for that privilege for the purpose of supplying the Public School Society with money to carry out their benevolent purposes. Mr. Ketchum seems to consider that, at that time, there was a kind of covenant made between these petitioners to be taxed and the State authorities; that, when they petitioned and were taxed, the authorities of the State bound themselves to keep up this system *in perpetuum*. But did these persons ask to be taxed exclusively out of their own pockets? or did they ask for a system of taxation which should reach all the tax-paying citizens of New York? There is a fallacy in Mr. Ketchum's argument here. He supposes that, because these persons are large property-holders, that they are, therefore, *par excellence*, the payers of taxes. He forgets that it is a fact well understood in the science of political economy, that the consumer is, after all, the taxpayer; that it is the tenants occupying the property of those rich men, and returning them their large rents, who are actually the taxpayers. And what peculiar merit, then, can Mr. Ketchum claim for these owners of property, and petitioners, to have all the rest of the citizens taxed as well as themselves? But he insists there was an agreement—a covenant entered into between them and the State authorities; and if you interfere with its provisions, you must release these taxpayers from their obligations as such. With all my heart, I have no objection. All we want is, that there should be no unjust interference, no exclusive system, no extraneous authority interposed between the taxpayer and the purpose for which the tax is collected. But the fact that others, besides these petitioners, are equally involved in the burden, demolishes this argument of Mr. Ketchum.

In his conclusion, the learned gentleman insists that, unless the Society remain as it is, it cannot exist; and then goes on further—for it would be impossible for him to close his speech without again reminding the Senate that we are Roman Catholics. He says:

The people in New York understand the subject, and the Roman Catholics cannot say that they will not be heard as well there as here. Why not leave the matter to us, the people of the city of New York?

Thus Mr. Ketchum, after having first endeavored to impress the minds of the Senate that we had had all imaginable fair play—that other denominations had made applications similar to ours, which is not the fact—that our petition had uniformly been denied in the several boards representing the people of New York, whereas he knew that, in this question, the people of New York was never even represented by the Common Council—he goes on to say, at last: "Why not leave the matter to us, the people of the city of New-York?" I trust not, if a committee of the Public School Society, called the Common Council, are to be at once parties and judges. I hope that the question will not be referred back, although, for Mr. Ketchum's satisfaction, I may state that, if it were so referred, the Common Council would not, I will venture to say, now decide upon it by such a vote as they did before, when one man alone had the courage—whether he was right or wrong—to say "nay," when all said "yes." In consequence of that vote—as they have since taken care to tell us—this gentleman lost his election; but, what was of infinitely greater importance, he preserved his honor. Were the matter now before the Common Council, they would see a thousand and one reasons for hesitation before deciding as before. For when public men see that any measure is likely to be popular, they can find abundant reasons for taking a favorable view of the question. I will refer Mr. Ketchum to a sign from which he may learn what he pleases. Since the Common Council that denied our claims went out of office, their successors have had the matter before them; and when, in the Board of Assistants, it was proposed to pass a resolution requesting the Legislature to defer the consideration of the question, the motion was negatived by a tie vote.

Still, Mr. Ketchum will have the end of this speech something like the end of the last. Then he said that this was a most distressing topic to the gentlemen of the Public School Society—that they were men of peace. That I do not controvert; but certainly I must say that, in the course of this contest, they appear to have exhibited a spirit contrary to their natures. But so peaceful were they, Mr. Ketchum said, that, if any longer annoyed, they would throw up their office and retire. But, after all, they could send their agents to Albany to oppose us there: the one—Dr. Rockwell—to disseminate a burlesque on our faith, from "Tristram Shandy;" the other—Mr. Ketchum—to plead as zealously, but I think not as successfully, against the recognition of our claims. Mr. Ketchum says:

Now, the contest is renewed, and the trustees engage in it with extreme reluctance; they have no personal interests to advance, and they are very unwilling to be put in hostile array against any of their fellow-citizens.

Mr. Chairman, the lateness of the hour admonishes me that I have trespassed too much upon your patience. I have but one observation to make in conclusion.

These gentlemen have spoken much and laid great emphasis on the importance of morality; but, as I have already remarked, morality is not always judged of by the same criterion. Let me illustrate this. According to the morality which my religion teaches, if I rob a man, or injure him in his property, and desire to be reconciled to God, I must, first of all, if it be in my power, make reparation to the man whom I have injured. Again, if I should unfortunately rob my neighbor of his good name, of his reputation, either by accident or through malice, before I can hope for reconciliation with an offended God, I must repair the injury and restore my neighbor's good name. If I belied him, I must acknowledge the lie as publicly as it was uttered. That is Catholic morality. Well, now, these gentlemen have belied us; they have put forward and circulated a document which

existed only in the imagination of Sterne—a foul document—and represented it as a part of our creed. I do not say that they directly required this to
be done; but their agent did it, and he cannot deny it. I wonder now,
then, if they will have such a sense of morality as will impel them to endeavor to repair the injury thus done to our reputation, by any official declaration that that is a spurious document? I wonder if the conscientious
morality that presides over the *Journal of Commerce* will prompt its editors
to such a course? If it do not, then it is a morality different from ours.

I apprehend that no such reparation will be offered for the injury we
have sustained by the everlasting harangue of abuse and vituperation that
has been poured out against us for these few years past. Have we not been
assailed with a foul and infamous fiction, in the pages of a work called
" Maria Monk " ? And have its reverend authors ever stood forward to do
us justice, and acknowledge the untruth which, knowing it to be so, they
published ? Have they ever attempted to counteract that obscene poison
which they disseminated, corrupting the morals of youth throughout every
hamlet in the land ? Whilst denouncing, in their ecclesiastical assemblies,
the works of Byron and Bulwer, did they include in their denunciations the
filthy and enormous lie published under their auspices, the writings of
" Maria Monk " ?

What idea, then, must we form of their morality and religion ? And
here it would be unjust to omit mentioning that many Protestants, not
under the influence of blinded bigotry, have done us justice on this point.
In particular I refer to the conduct of one distinguished Protestant writer
who cannot be accused of great partiality for us, but who exposed and refuted the authors and abettors of this filthy libel to which I have referred.
I know that it would be incorrect and unjust to say that thousands of others, sincere Protestants, but high-minded, honorable men, have not taken
the same view of the subject. But I speak particularly of the morality of
the authors and publishers of these abominable slanders; and I regret that
the Public School Society, by their recent proceedings, should have allowed
themselves to sink to a kindred degradation.

Mr. Ketchum replied to the speech of Bishop Hughes briefly,
through the press, and several rejoinders followed from the pens
of the distinguished advocates of the opposing interests. The
question was constantly agitated, and became a very exciting
element in the election for members of the city delegation to the
Senate and House of Assembly, in the month of November.
An independent organization, and the nomination of a school
ticket, was determined upon by the Catholics, and measures
were adopted accordingly. Inquiry having been made among
the candidates of the " Democratic " and " Whig " parties, a
selection was made, and three new names were placed on the
school ticket, in default of gentlemen who did not respond satisfactorily to the wishes of the committee.

The *Freeman's Journal* of October 23 published a call for a meeting of " the friends of civil and religious freedom, in favor of extending the benefits of a common school education to the neglected and indigent children of this city," to be held on the following Tuesday, the 26th of the same month. The " Church Debt Association " held a meeting on Monday evening, at which Bishop Hughes was present, and made an address. He spoke at some length on the school question, and, in an earnest appeal to the audience, urged a full attendance the following evening.

On Tuesday evening, Carroll Hall, the place of meeting, was crowded at an early hour with an assemblage attracted by the promise of a speech from the bishop, as well as by the object of the meeting, which was to decide on a list of candidates to be voted for at the election then approaching. Bishop Hughes rose, and delivered a lengthy address, during which he presented a ticket for the support of the Catholics. A few passages will serve to show the spirit and enthusiasm which characterized the meeting. Said the reverend gentleman :

With political controversies and party questions I have nothing whatever to do. . . . It is impossible for me to say any thing personally of those whose names have been recommended to be placed on the list of candidates, and I would not for one moment urge that they should be placed there, had I not been assured, on the most positive evidence, and which I could not doubt, that they are friendly to an alteration in the present system of public education. . . . I will now request the Secretary to read the names placed on the ticket. Of that ticket I have approved. It presents the names of the only friends we could find already before the public, and those whom, not being so prominently before the public, we have found for ourselves.

The Secretary then read the following list :

SENATORS.

Thomas O'Connor,	J. G. Gottsberger.

ASSEMBLY.

Tighe Davey,	David R. Floyd Jones,
Daniel C. Pentz,	Solomon Townsend,
George Weir,	John L. O'Sullivan,
Paul Grout,	Auguste Davezac,
Conrad Swackhamer,	William McMurray,
William B. Maclay,	Michael Walsh,

Timothy Daly.

" Each name," says the report of the *Freeman's Journal*,

" was received with the most deafening and uproarious applause, and three terrific cheers were given at the close," on the subsidence of which the Bishop proceeded :

You have now, gentlemen, heard the names of men who are willing to risk themselves in support of your cause. Put these names out of view, and you cannot, in the lists of our political candidates, find that of one solitary public man who is not understood to be pledged against us. What, then, is your course ? You now, for the first time, find yourselves in the position to vote at least for yourselves. You have often voted for others, and they did not vote for you ; but now you are determined to uphold, with your own votes, your own rights. (Thunders of applause, which lasted several minutes.) Will you, then, stand by the rights of your offspring, who have for so long a period, and from generation to generation, suffered under the operation of this injurious system ? (Renewed cheering.) Will you adhere, to the nomination made ? (Loud cries of " We will ! we will ! " and vociferous applause.) Will you be united ? (Tremendous cheering—the whole immense assembly rising *en masse*, waving of hats, handkerchiefs, and every possible demonstration of applause.) Will you let all men see that you are worthy sons of that nation to which you belong ? (Cries of " Never fear—we will ! " " We will, till death ! " and terrific cheering.) Will you prove yourselves worthy of friends ? (Tremendous cheering.) Will none of you flinch ? (The scene that followed this emphatic query is indescribable, and exceeded all the enthusiastic and almost frenzied displays of passionate feeling we have sometimes witnessed at Irish meetings. The cheering, the shouting, the stamping of feet, waving of hats and handkerchiefs, beggared all powers of description.) Very well, then ; the tickets will be prepared and distributed amongst you, and, on the day of election, go, like freemen, with dignity and calmness, entertaining due respect for your fellow-citizens and their opinions, and deposit your votes. I ask, then, once for all, and with the answer let the meeting close, Will this meeting pledge its honor, as the representative of that oppressed portion of the community for whom I have so often pleaded, here as well as elsewhere—will it pledge its honor that it will stand by these candidates, whose names have been read, and that no man composing this vast audience will ever vote for any one pledged to oppose our just claims and incontrovertible rights ? (Terrific cheering and thunders of applause, which continued for several minutes, amid which Bishop Hughes resumed his seat.)

The ticket was adopted by acclamation, and the meeting adjourned.

A letter of inquiry was addressed to the candidates before the public, by a committee selected for the purpose, in which they were requested to state their views on the school question, and whether they were favorable to the Public School Society,

GEORGE T. TRIMBLE

or to a change of system. Those of the candidates then in the city replied to the inquiry, and a card also appeared, signed by Messrs. Solomon Townsend, D. R. Floyd Jones, George Weir, Paul Grout, Conrad Swackhamer, Auguste Davezac, William McMurray, George G. Glazier, David Dudley Field, and Edward Sandford, in which they declared that they "discountenance altogether the schemes and the objects of the present Governor of the State," who, as they charged, had originated all the difficulties of the school question.

The election for members of Assembly resulted as follows:

Solomon Townsend,	18,374
D. R. Floyd Jones,	18,349
William B. Maclay,	18,268
George Weir,	18,231
Paul Grout,	18,195
C. Swackhamer,	18,092
A. Davezac,	18,060
William McMurray,	17,970
John L. O'Sullivan,	17,644
Daniel C. Pentz,	16,889
Joseph Tucker,	16,336
William Jones,	16,312
Nathaniel G. Bradford,	16,308

The last three names in the above list are those of candidates not on "the regular ticket" of the party supposed to be most favorable to the objects of the Carroll Hall party. The three names voted for by the Catholics, as recommended by Bishop Hughes, with the number of votes they received, are the following: Michael Walsh, 2,330; Tighe Davey, 2,172; Timothy Daly, 2,163.

The vote for Senators resulted as follows: Thomas O'Connor, 2,202; J. G. Gottsberger, 2,175.

This demonstration at the ballot-box of a religious body, under the leadership of its most popular and prominent dignitary, occupying the chair of bishop of the diocese, was universally regarded by the people at large, and especially by the members of other communions, as highly offensive and dangerous as a precedent, and antagonistic to the spirit of our republican institutions. It created a profound impression, which, however, was sensibly relieved when the canvas had been completed, and the strength of the Carroll Hall party was ascertained by the test vote on the last three candidates. The comparatively small number of votes of all parties who were willing to make the sectarianism of our schools a special issue, dissipated the apprehensions of many who feared that a powerful organization would be created for further movements. It was the last effort made, as the occasion for a distinct issue was removed by the action of the Legislature in 1842. The proceedings during that session, and the change introduced, are made the subject of the next chapter.

The reader of the speech of Bishop Hughes will have noticed several allusions to "TRISTRAM SHANDY," LAURENCE STERNE, and the *Journal of Commerce*. The record will not be intelligible without an explanation of the facts.

After Mr. Spencer's report appeared, the session of the Legislature being far advanced, the indications of success on the part of the Catholics threatened the friends of the Society with the decay of their system. One of them wrote a reply to the report of the Secretary, which was published in the columns of the *Journal of Commerce* at the last moment. The bill had been made the special order for Friday, May 21st. On Thursday, the 20th, the article appeared, and a number of copies were sent by a gentleman in New York to a friend in Albany, by whom they were marked, and placed on the tables of the senators, so that they would attract immediate attention. It was as follows:

From the Journal of Commerce of May 20, 1841.

REPORT OF THE SECRETARY OF STATE BRIEFLY EXAMINED.

MR. EDITOR: The report of the Secretary of State on the subject of school education in the city of New York, having been before the public for several days, and feeling, as I do, a deep interest in the cause, I am constrained to make a few suggestions in reply to it, in the hope that I may contribute a little to a full understanding of this interesting question.

The importance of universality in the systems of education adopted by the people has not been overdrawn, and cannot be too much appreciated. No one should be left without the opportunity of making some progress in those studies, the acquisition of which will qualify him for a high and honorable and useful station in society—at least, to prepare him to exercise the responsible privilege of deciding, by the right of suffrage, the course of legislation under which he would prefer to live. This is the principal feature of the report; this is its professed object. Regarding it as an essential principle, that, as all have civil equality, they should also enjoy an equality in the means of education, the Secretary has proposed the destruction of one system and the substitution of another. If the figures he presents were consistent with facts, and the new system were not open to powerful objections, his report would meet with even more general approbation than it receives at present.

The statistics which he furnishes respecting the number of children in and out of school, show that 32,194 did not attend any school, while less than that number, or 30,758, were registered on the books of schools, of whom 22,955 were embraced in the public schools—the average attendance being 13,189.

The disparity between the attendants upon the means of instruction, and those children not attending, is far less than, by this statement, would appear to be the case.

1. The public schools in this city are open to the reception of children and youth between four and sixteen years of age, but the proportion of those *over twelve or thirteen* is but as one to twenty-five or thirty. Hence, a very large reduction in the number of non-attendants must be made. I have no data by which I can give the number of children between twelve and sixteen, but there is doubtless at least one third of the whole number, making a consequent reduction of 15,000 or 20,000; leaving the number of non-attendants at 15,000 to 17,000, instead of 32,194.

2. A large number of children are foreigners, who do not speak our language, who are unacquainted with the schools, do not feel their importance or understand the system, and who will not be enticed into school. For these, another proportion must be deducted.

3. Many of the poorer class of the population find it necessary to avail themselves of the services of their children for their own support, and they are consequently put out to work, in factories and other places, at an early age. Many occupations are performed principally by children eight and ten years of age, and no doubt several thousands are thus engaged. For these, another reduction must be made.

In this manner, by an appeal to facts which may be apparent to every one who will look at the subject, we reduce the number of non-attendants to about 8, 10, or 12,000. I might add another item: many of the children of wealthy parents are not sent to school, but are placed under the care of private teachers and governesses. Thus we leave the number of children who may be justly called non-attendants, at about the number of those who are prevented from attending these schools by their parents and priestly censors, whose jealous anxiety is so watchful lest the children might receive any sectarian bias "hostile to their views."

The next deficiency to be accounted for is the great difference between the registered and actual attendance at the schools; and this is no more difficult than the other.

1. Many of the children are kept from school by their parents for the sake of their services.

2. Children are mortals as well as ourselves, who are but "children of larger growth," and often are sick, or feign sickness, as the case may be.

3. Many of the parents, being poor, are obliged to resort to daily labor for support, leaving their children at home, or in the neighborhood. Being thus left without restraint or counsel for the day, and not feeling a desire for books (few children of poor people do), they amuse themselves by play, or whatever may suit their tastes or convenience.

Other details might be given, but these will serve as a clue to some of the causes of non-attendance; and although any one might be considered unimportant in itself, all of them combined present an aggregate of no inconsiderable amount. Hence the inference on this point, that something is defective, which needs the stimulus of sectarian influence to correct it, falls to the ground.

The Secretary then compares the attendance at country schools with that in the city, and argues that, because there is a larger proportion in the former, the citizens of New York should adopt the district system. Let us see whether this will stand the test. He says, " the like proportion must exist in the city and in the interior, of those who have already received all the education they or their parents desire, or who are engaged as apprentices, or in employments preventing them from attendance at any place of instruction."

As we have before shown, the children leave school at about twelve years of age in the city; but in the country, where it is expected that the children will assist on the farms, &c., during the busy seasons of agricultural life, they attend principally in the winter, or not much more than half the year; and, to supply this absence, they attend school until they are sixteen or eighteen years of age. Here we have, in the same fact, two causes which make a material difference, viz. : Does the average attendance equal that of the city ? and do not the children attend school until a period later in life by three, four, or five years ?

The presumed insufficiency of the Public School Society, therefore, in not educating all the children not in private schools, has been shown to be altogether exaggerated; causes over which neither legislation nor school can have control, existing in the community, and conspiring to prevent the attendance of children.

These causes, as will be inferred from what I have above presented, are of a social rather than a civil nature—poverty, for instance, which makes its imperious demands on the labor of the young; wide difference of language; and, doubtless, to some extent, prejudice against our policy. Hence, if we wish to see all our children in school, under proper training and guidance, we must seek to improve the domestic condition of the families; we must give the parents the means of supporting themselves and their children. Who will do it ?

Let us pass on to notice a few of the Secretary's arguments :

1. He thinks that the district school system is eminently fitted to prevent sectarian influence; "and the records of this department have been searched in vain for an instance of abuse of the system to sectarian biases." Can any be furnished from the records of the Public School Society ?

2. If this is the case in the district schools, why does he say, in the same

sentence, that each district has that kind of "religious instruction most congenial to the opinions of the inhabitants"? If the population is Presbyterian, it will be a Presbyterian school; and Baptists and Episcopalians and Romanists will feel that they are doing wrong to send their children to places where principles "hostile to their views" are taught. If the population (a majority) decide on having a Catholic school, or any other, is there not an abuse of privilege? So far, however, as I am acquainted with the country schools, there is just the same amount of religious instruction given in them as in the public schools of New York—the reading of the Scriptures. My earliest instructions were received in a district school in Westchester county.

3. The Secretary considers it an axiom that, in all schemes of education, there must of necessity be some religious instruction; "and that it must therefore be sectarian—that is, it must favor one set of opinions in opposition to another." Hence all must be banished, or we must have schools "congenial to the spirit and opinions of the inhabitants." The great argument is *equality*. Very well; if a Mohammedan should come to this country and send his children to the public schools, and become dissatisfied because the reading-books contain sketches of the impostures of the Prophet, he sets up the claim of *equality*, and demands that every book containing any thing derogatory to the character of Mohammed should be submitted to his examination, while he publishes an "*Index Expurgatorius*," and insists that every volume in the schools throughout the city should be blotted and mutilated to please his views. This is granted, but he demands more: that the Public School Society be broken up, and some system established by which he may be formed into a "district," and receive money enough to educate his children according to his creed, "for its transmission is a part of his religious profession!" and, with commendable pertinacity, so effectually plies his "equality" arguments as to conquer a whole community. My own opinion is, that when the majority are on an equality, the people, in democratic construction, are on an equality; and the term does not necessarily involve the harassing and perplexing of a whole community at the dictate of a few.

4. This cry of equality has been raised by the memorialists because they think it will touch a tender chord in the hearts of the American people. It has; but they will find it does not vibrate in unison with theirs on this question; for none are more exclusive than these self-same sticklers for equality, none more bigoted, none more arrogant.

5. But the Secretary says, knowing "that they regard as the most sacred of duties the inculcation of those principles in the minds of their children, we ought not to be surprised at their anxiety to exclude all that is hostile to their views," "for the transmission of their creed is a most essential part of their religious profession." What are these principles, the transmission of which is so essential? I happen to take the following:

EXCOMMUNICATION OF MR. HOGAN, PASTOR OF ST. MARY'S CHURCH, PHILADELPHIA.—By the authority of God Almighty, the Father, Son, and

Holy Ghost, and the undefiled Virgin Mary, mother and patroness of our Saviour, and of all celestial virtues, angels, archangels, thrones, dominions, powers, cherubims and seraphims, patriarchs, apostles, prophets, evangelists, &c., may he, Mr. Hogan, be damned ! . . . May the holy choir of the holy virgins, who, for the honor of Christ, have despised the things of this world, damn him ! May all the saints, from the beginning of the world to everlasting ages, who are found to be beloved of God, damn him ! . . . May he be damned wherever he be, whether in the house, or in the stable, the garden, or the field, or the highway ; or in the woods, or in the water, or in the Church ; may he be cursed in living and dying ! . . . May he be cursed in his brains, in his vitals, his temples, his eyebrows, his cheeks, his jawbones, his nostrils, his teeth and grinders, his lips, his throat, his shoulders, his arms, his fingers, his veins, his thighs, his genitals, his hips, his knees, his legs, and feet, and toe-nails ! . . . May the Son of the living God, with all the glory of His majesty, curse him ! And may heaven, with all the powers that move therein, rise up against him, and curse and damn him, unless he repent and make satisfaction. Amen. So be it. Be it so. Amen.

Are not these principles very essential, and their transmission indispensable ?

6. If these memorialists find it necessary to teach their religious creeds to their children, why do they not do it in the domestic circle, at the fireside ? The knowledge which they acquire at school will make them more intelligent, and enable them better to receive parental instruction. There is a good reason. The light which they enjoy there is calculated to break the superstitious spell of saints, confessing to the priest, relics, absolution, penance, and give to them notions of God himself, in His Word and works, which would conflict with the value of holy water, and dead men's bones, and prayers measured out by chains of beads.

7. I have before referred to the principle of giving to districts " the power of appointing their religious instruction most congenial to the feelings of the population." This is the whole object of the report—to adopt a system by which any district may have any religious sentiments inculcated which they desire. If this is not sought by the report, there is no object to be gained by any change of system.

But the Secretary says, in closing : " If . . . any schools would be perverted to the purposes of a narrow and exclusive sectarianism, a remedy might be found by giving authority to the Board of Commissioners to investigate complaints, and to dissolve offending schools, or withhold its share of the school money." If no religious reading of the Scriptures can be had without sectarian influence, according to his own principle, will the Scriptures be banished from the schools ? If, as is an axiom in his language, " all schemes of education must convey some religious instruction," which, he says, must necessarily be sectarian in its tendency, will he remove the influence by removing the religious instruction, which can be done only by shutting our schools altogether ? There is an inconsistency here.

8. As the memorialists depend so much on equality, so let us throw ourselves back on our democratic principle of the majority ; and as the great mass of our citizens are in favor of the old system, let us retain it.

9. The Secretary has attempted to excite the jealousy of the Legislature and the people, by saying that the Public School Society is "subject to no control," except that the Common Council can omit designating their schools as recipients of the public bounty; that they are not accountable to any authority—a perpetual corporation; that the people have no choice of trustees, &c. This is as unjust to the trustees as it is unwise in its tendency. There has been but little or no fault found with these indefatigable public servants, but by the Roman Catholics, who do it on sectarian grounds, and the aspersion contained in it is not in harmony with the just tribute of commendation primarily given by him. Further, it is involving the people in a new subject of discussion and contest. We have enough opposition and collision without adding more.

10. The Secretary recommends the new system because it will be "voluntary." This has struck me as being a peculiarly happy feature in the Public School Society. One hundred intelligent citizens devoting a great deal of their time, voluntarily and gratuitously, to the education of the youth of this city, is a consideration of no small moment, and a Society which is more efficient can seldom be found. Of all the different classes of effort made by men for the accomplishment of any enterprise, the voluntary exertion claims the highest place. It is more efficient because it is more energetic; it is more noble because it is more disinterested; and it is more valuable because it reaps a richer reward. Who, then, is in favor of changing this system for one founded on the election of commissioners and trustees elected by the people? Are not the body of intelligent men now acting in that capacity just as intelligent as if they had their mental scale guaranteed by the ballots of the people?

11. The Secretary admits that it is an objectionable feature in this measure that it originated with a sect. This certainly is a powerful argument against it. It is done at the dictation of a minority of the citizens; this minority always combined a religious body, and commenced on professedly sectarian grounds. Let us, if we value our liberty—if we value the harmony of the community—if we place a just estimate on the perpetuity of our institutions—let us be very watchful against the march of sectarian privilege. This will be a first step—a great one. Make this compromise, set this precedent, loosen the restraint which has hitherto existed, and threat will follow demand, and discord will follow non-compliance, and rupture will terminate in the granting of the boon sought for—a privileged Church establishment.

12. The Secretary suggests that the system he recommends will, by exciting emulation in the different sects, bring into the school all children not attending any. If this is a state of society which will promote the harmony and union of the whole, human nature will have undergone some change. This emulation between sects, in so large and thickly populated a city, embracing numerous denominations, will lead to unfair means for obtaining scholars. Each school receiving a proportion of the fund depending on the number of scholars, one teacher will make one offer, another will give a greater inducement to the children, and thus sectarian feuds, religious squabbles, school and church quarrels, would agitate the community.

13. But, could this be avoided, he promises us something as much to be deprecated. "The watchfulness of those who apprehend abuse may be relied upon to detect it promptly, and to seek the needful remedy." Now, it may be said in this case, as has been said of party spirit, "Never was the country so likely to be destroyed as when party spirit was prevalent throughout the land"—a remark founded on an acquaintance with human nature.

Cabals, parties, and divisions destroyed the Roman government, and may, in turn, destroy ours; and any thing which might promote envyings, jealousies, heart-burnings, captiousness, and the rancor of party spirit, should be crushed rather than encouraged. The vigilance of those who watch for abuse is very apt to be itself, in its morbid vision, the creator of the objects it pretends to see; and often the character of individuals and associations is destroyed by the combination of parties and cliques. As this vigilance sees through a very questionable medium, it is better to establish a system not depending on the accusations of opponents, but on the confidence of the people; and as the former kind of care and watchfulness is seldom regarded by those who have the power in their hands, its exercise would be not only perplexing, but worse than useless.

14. Proscription would follow from both of these causes. Instead of an argument, I will present a fact which will be its own commentator. At Paisléy, in Scotland, the schools were conducted on this principle, and the consequence was, that the enmity became so great that one set of people would not trade with another; a third would not speak to the fourth, and thus the social ties between townsmen were rudely snapped asunder by this execrable spirit.

15. The trustees, being elected by the people, will add another item to the political capital of electioneers. Parties will test their strength, and the successful candidates will, of course, appoint teachers whose opinions are not "hostile to their views," and the consequence will be, that the school-house will become a politico-religious nursery, as changeable as the sentiments and population of the several districts. If this transmission is desirable, let the people speak for themselves.

AMERICUS.

On Tuesday evening, June 1st, a meeting of the Catholics was held at Washington Hall, in New York City, at which addresses were made by James W. McKeon and Bishop Hughes. In the course of his remarks, Mr. McKeon said:

The temporary defeat of the bill might be ascribed to the efforts of the School Society, which had its agents watching every step of its progress with argus eyes. The conduct displayed he was indignant to name. It was the meekness of the dove without its innocence, the cunning of the serpent without its wisdom. Ay, they pushed their exertions to an extremity at which they recoiled upon themselves; for, though the dishonorable means resorted to effected the object, it has pulled down upon them a load of obloquy from which their institution could not rise unstained through series of years of its existence. *A vile, loathsome, and revolting attack upon the faith of a large portion of the petitioners* was placed, by a functionary high in the confidence of the Society, in the hands of senators *on the morning it was supposed the vote would be taken on the bill.*

In reference to the same matter, Bishop Hughes used the following language :

I do not say that the trustees of the School Society were themselves personally the distributors of these slanders ; but, to give you a specimen of what was done, their agent, or one of their agents, at Albany, was detected placing on the desks of the senators, what think you ? Why, *an absurd and abominable malediction*, which they put forth as the Catholic form of excommunication, but which, in fact and in truth, was nothing more than a pure fabrication of STERNE, written for his own amusement, in his book called "TRISTRAM SHANDY." And these high literary gentlemen, these self-constituted, peculiar, exclusive dispensers of light and knowledge and education, were either so ignorant as not to know the true character and origin of the document which they so industriously circulated, or, knowing its character, they were so bigoted, and careless of honor and truth and justice and good principle, in their anxiety to forward a bad cause, that they did not hesitate to give the falsehood currency. . . . That Society, which has so perseveringly opposed every effort which we have made for redress, has abundantly earned for itself that epithet, which has been often applied to it, of a soulless corporation, and has used every artifice and means in its power to vilify and defame us and our principles. Yes, *defamation* is the term. I do not say they have done it knowingly. That is not a point for me to determine. But they have *defamed* us. I aver it, and insist upon it—they have *defamed us* with their extracts from "Tristram Shandy," and other documents of an equally high literary character, creditable to the liberality and the pretensions to learning and knowledge of a body so ambitious to be the sole instructors of the youth of the city. And I challenge them to meet me and prove that what they have laid to our charge has any foundation in truth, or is any thing else but *defamation*.

After the delivery of the great speech by Bishop Hughes, the anonymous author of the " Brief Review " above given, published, also anonymously, the first part of a " Review of the School Question," in which the following passage occurs :

In the opinion of the writer, too much importance has been attached to the simple extract which has called forth so much remark. It was given as a fact to show the nature of the principles which would be supported by sectarian schools, at least in part, and but a solitary remark was offered, for the arguments and statistics were the objects of attention ; but as it has been made so prominent a topic ever since the defeat of the bill, and the pretext for calumniating the Public School Society, I am constrained to submit the proofs.

I am accused of *defaming* their faith. Now, defamation may be true or false in its terms, but I believe it is not measured so much by these, as by the injury effected to the reputation of any individual or cause. If I am charged with being a libeller in the latter sense—that of injuring their cause—I plead *guilty;* but if in the first—that of uttering falsehood—I plead emphatically *not guilty.*

What was the conduct of the Bishop ? Did he confront me with evidence that the form had not been used ? Did he deny that any such person as Mr. Hogan had been a pastor of one of their churches ? Did he produce evidence that it had not been pronounced in this simple instance, if in no other ? No, none of these ; but he pronounces it to be an INVENTION of Sterne's, a libel, a defamation.

As nothing has been said heretofore in relation to the case of Mr. Hogan, I shall not stop to furnish evidence which would be gratuitous, as it has not been denied. If Bishop Hughes, however, thinks it important, and will make his wishes known, *it shall be produced.*

Instead of presenting the details of the above case, I introduce an extract from the *London Quarterly Review,* for March, 1841, pp. 303, 304 (Mason's American reprint), which will exhibit the similarity of the curse used in Ireland with the one referred to above. " The examination was taken down in order to be laid before a committee of the House of Lords, *on oath.*"

Q. Were you in the chapel on the day of the cursing ?
A. I was.
Q. Did you hear it ?
A. I did.
Q. What did the priest say ?
A. I'll be bound he cursed her well. . . . [The next witness came, promising to tell all about it, to oblige Mr. ———, but evincing the greatest dislike to be known to have done so.]
Q. Were you in ——— Chapel the day the woman was cursed ?
A. I was.
Q. Did you hear it ?
A. I did.
Q. At what Mass ?
A. At second Mass.
Q. Did the priest give a reason for cursing the woman ?
A. He said it was " going here and there."
Q. What did he mean by that ?
A. Because, he said, she was to and fro, going sometimes to mass and sometimes to church.
Q. What did he say to her ?
A. He said enough, I'll be bound.
Q. What *did* he say ?
A. He cursed every inch of her carcass.
Q. Did he bid the people not to speak to her ?
A. He desired them not to speak to her, or deal with her, or have any thing to do with her.
Q. Did he curse her child ? [the poor creature was pregnant at the time.]

A. He cursed every thing that would spring from her.

Q. Did he say any thing about the child she was carrying—did he curse the fruit of her womb ?

A. I did not hear him say *that ;* he cursed every thing that would spring from her.

Q. How was he dressed ?

A. He threw off the clothes he had on, and put on a black dress.

Q. Did he do any thing with candles ?

A. 'Tis the way ; the clerk quenched all the candles but one, and himself put out that, and said, " so the light of heaven was quenched upon her soul ; " and he shut a book, and said the gates of heaven were shut upon her that day.

Q. What do you mean by saying "he cursed every inch of her carcass"?

A. He cursed her eyes, and her ears, and her legs, and so on—every bit of her.

. . . The neighbors of the poor woman withdrew from intercourse with her. Shopkeepers refused to sell even bread to her. Her own children were included in the curse, except one, who was in the service of a Roman Catholic lady, and was prohibited from speaking to his mother. The poor woman with whom they lodged was so tormented by the neighbors that they were obliged to quit the house, and must have perished in the street, had they not been received into the house of a Protestant ; and when the poor creature's confinement approached, a Roman Catholic lady prohibited the usual person from attending her, under threat of losing her support ; and no one could be found to attend until the wife of the clergyman of the parish (from whom we heard this ourselves) interested herself to obtain from the priest a reluctant permission.

The above is modern excommunication. I will now carry the reader back to a more remote period, and show the character of the formulæ used in other days, as well as to prove that the very form so strongly objected to was known and in use *more than six hundred years before the birth of Sterne.*

In a work entitled the *Protestant Journal,* for 1831, pp. 536–539, I find the following historical narrative, taken from the *Historiæ Ecclesiæ Evangelicæ in Hungaria,* pp. 153–156 :

At a congregation of Protestant ministers, members of the presbytery of the thirteen towns in Hungary which were at that time subject to the dominion of Poland, held at Filcau, November 13, 1630, Barbara Von Grottendorf, wife of Lewis Szgedi, of Varallia, complained that she was deserted by her husband, who had avoided her society for years, and had been guilty of violation of the laws of marriage, and prayed for divorce. Forty-five days were allowed to Szgedi to make his appearance before this ecclesiastical court. Notice to this effect was given him, not only by affixing his name to the church-doors at Varallia, but he was further summoned by name every Sunday for six weeks, at the conclusion of divine service. As the defendant did not make his appearance at the end of this time, permission was given to Barbara Von Grottendorf to marry another husband, John Krebell, a goldsmith of Varallia. These circumstances being communicated to Ladislaus Hoszszuthoty, president of the chapter of Czepus, the latter prohibited John Pilemann, the Protestant pastor of Varallia, from uniting them in marriage. As, however, Pilemann proceeded to solemnize the marriage, Hoszszuthoty fortified himself with the authority of the cardinal, Peter Pazmann, archbishop of Strigonum, and primate of Hungary, and twice summoned Peter Zabler, superintendent of the presbtery, John Serpilius, one of the elders, and Pilemann himself, to appear before the archiepiscopal consistory.

They were charged with contumacy, and the president told them that they were worthy of excommunication. The narrative proceeds:

He then procured an interdict, issued by Cardinal Pazmann against the twenty-four pastors of the presbytery generally, and against Zabler, Serpilius, and Pilemann, individually; and further, that the sentence of excommunication which follows this historical notice should be publicly read at the cathedral, on the 19th, 22d, and 27th days of December, 1632. Knowing the inveterate hatred of the Romish clergy, and dismayed at the effects which they too well knew would follow from this excommunication, the Protestants had recourse to Prince Lubemiski, chancellor of the kingdom of Hungary, and to other persons of distinguished rank. At length, after many negotiations and the most humiliating concessions, the intolerant provost consented to take off the excommunication on condition of one hundred and thirty dollars being paid. Additional fruitless attempts were made to propitiate him; but finally the advocates of the Protestants succeeded in pacifying him, by paying him fifty gold crowns, on the 23d of March, 1633.

Here follows the form of excommunication, which is different from that first given, by its being more virulent and persecuting, cursing even their conception, though it is nearly the same in its outlines. I make only one short extract:

I adjure thee, O Lucifer! with all thy imps, also with the Father and the Son, and with the Holy Spirit, and with the human nature and nativity of the Lord, and with the virtue of all the saints, that thou rest not night and day until thou hast brought them to destruction, whether they be drowned in rivers, or be hung, or be devoured by beasts, or be burnt, or be slain by enemies; let them be hated by every person living, or even their ghosts.

A cardinal in the true Church, standing up at the altar *and praying to the devil*, as superior to the Lord of Hosts, and blasphemously uniting Lucifer, the prince of hell, in his invocations and imprecations, with the King of saints! This is the last extremity, certainly; but probably the cardinal had the best reason for invoking Lucifer and his imps, on account of his more familiar acquaintance with them. It will be recollected that Sterne was born in 1713, and that these things occurred *eighty years anterior to the birth of Sterne*, and about one hundred and thirty years before the publication of "Tristram Shandy."

This testimony, however, being merely historical, and the actors in it having been long since numbered with the dead, it may be questioned with the greatest coolness by any one who wishes to dispute it. I therefore pass on to my last proof that Sterne did not *invent* the form of excommunication attributed to him.

I have on the table before me a book entitled "*Glossarium Archæologicum:* continens Latino Barbara, Peregrina, Obsoleta, et Novatæ Significationis Vocabula, &c. Authore HENRICO SPELMANNO, Equite, Anglo-Britanno, Londini, MDCLXXXVII." On pp. 205—206 of this book, I find the following formula, which, as will be seen at the close, Spelman obtained from a manuscript volume compiled during the reign of William the Conqueror, who occupied the throne of England from the time of the Norman conquest, decided by the battle of Hastings in 1066, until 1087, nearly *seven centuries prior to the publication of "Tristram Shandy."*

EXCOMMUNICATIO.—Ex auctoritate Dei omnipotentis, Patris, et Filii, et Spiritus Sancti; et sanctum canonum, sanctæque et intemeratæ virginis Dei genetricis Mariæ, atque omnium celestium virtutum, angelorum, archangelorum, thronorum, dominationum, potestatum, cherubin, ac seraphin, et sanctorum patriarcharum, prophetarum, et omnium apostolorum et evangelistarum, et sanctorum innocentium qui in conspectu agni soli digni inventi sunt canticum cantare novum, et sanctorum martyrum, et sanctorum confessorum, et sanctarum virginum, atque omnium simul sanctorum et electorum Dei, Excommunicamus et anathematizamus hunc furem, vel hunc malefactorem N., et a liminibus sanctæ Dei ecclesiæ sequestramus, ut æterni suppliciis cruciandus mancipetur cum Dathan et Abiron, et cum his qui dixerunt Domino Deo, "*Recede a nobis, scientiam viarum tuarum nolumus,*" et sicut aqua ignis extinguitur, sic extinguitur lucerna ejus in secula seculorum, nisi resipuerit, et ad satisfactionem venerit. Amen.

Maledicat illum Deus Pater qui hominem creavit. Maledicat illum Dei Filius, qui pro homine passus est. Maledicat illum Spiritus Sanctus, qui in baptismo effusus est. Maledicat illum sancta crux, quam Christus pro nostra salute hostem triumphans ascendit. Maledicat illum sancta Dei genetrix et perpetua virgo Maria. Maledicat illum sanctus Michael animarum susceptor sacrarum. Maledicat illum omnes angeli, et archangeli, principatus, et potestates, omnisque militia celestis exercitus. Maledicat illum patriarcharum et prophetarum laudabilis numerus. Maledicat illum sanctus Johannes, precursor et Baptista Christi prœcipuus. Maledicat illum sanctus Petrus, et sanctus Paulus, et sanctus Andreas, omnesque Christi Apostoli simul et ceteri discipuli; quatuor quoque evangelistæ qui sua predicatione mundum universum converterunt. Maledicat illum cuneus martyrum et confessorum mirificus qui Deo bonis operibus placitus, inventus est. Maledicant illum sacrarum virginum chori, quæ mundi vana causa honoris Christi respuenda contempserunt. Maledicant illum omnes sancti, qui ab initio mundi usque in finem seculi Deo dilecti inveniuntur. Maledicant illum cœli et terra, et omnia sancta in eis manentia!

Maledictus sit ubicumque fuerit, sive in domo, sive in agro, sive in via, sive in semita, sive in silva, sive in aqua, sive in ecclesia.

Maledictus sit vivendo, moriendo, manducando, bibendo, esuriendo, sitiendo, jejunando, dormitando, dormiendo, vigilando, ambulando, stando, sedendo, jacendo, operando, quiescendo, mingendo, cacando, flebotomando.

Maledictus sit in totis viribus corporis. Maledictus sit intus et exterius. Maledictus sit in capillis. Maledictus sit in cerebro. Maledictus sit in vertice, in temporibus, in fronte, in auriculis, in superciliis, in oculis, in genis, in maxilis, in naribus, in dentibus, in mordacibus, in labris, in gutture, in humeris, in harmis, in brachiis, in manibus, in digitis, in pectore, in corde, et in omnibus interioribus stomacho tenus, in renibus, in inguinibus, in femore, in genitalibus, in coxis, in genibus, in cruribus, in pedibus, in articulis et in unguibus. Maledictus sit in totis compaginibus membrorum; a vertice capitis usque ad plantam pedis, non sit in eo sanitas.

Maledicat illum Christus filius Dei vivi toto suæ majestatis imperio; et insurgat adversus eum cœlum cum omnibus virtutibus, quæ in eo moventur, ad damnandum eum nisi pœnituerit, et ad satisfactionem venerit. Amen. Fiat. Fiat. Amen.

EXCOMMUNICATIO.—Auctoritate Dei Patris omnipotentis, et Filii, et Spiritus Sancti, et beatæ Dei genetricis Mariæ, omniumque sanctorum, et sanctorum canonum. *Excommunicamus, anathematizamus,* et a liminibus sanctæ matris Ecclesiæ sequestramus illos malefactores N. consentaneos quoque vel participes, et nisi resipuerint, et ad satisfactionem venerint; sic extinguatur lucerna eorum ante viventem, in secula seculorum. Fiat. Fiat. Amen.

Hæ Excommunicationum formulæ sequuntur Emendationes legum, quas Gulielmus Conquestor edidit, in libro vocato *Textus Roffensis*, MS. et videntur sub eo ipso ævo conditæ; quia in superioribus nusquam, quod scio, reperitur beatæ virginis Mariæ invocatio.

In Gorton's " Biographical Dictionary," vol. ii., in a notice of Sir Henry Spelman, I find the following language: " He printed a specimen in 1621, and in 1626 appeared the first part, entitled, ' *Archæologicus in modum Glossarii ad rem antiquam posteriorum folio.*' The sale of this valuable work was so unpromising, that the second part was not published till after the death of the author." " His death took place in 1641, and his body was interred in Westminster Abbey."

See also Hale's " Analysis of Chronology," 4 vols. 8vo., London, 1830, at p. 341 of vol. iii., where reference is made to Boxhornius' " History of the Low Countries," and Brandt's " Abridgment," vol. i. p. 6, where the said form may be found.

Here, then, we have the grand point decided. Bishop Hughes alleges that the form first quoted was a fabrication of Sterne's. Now, books can be referred to which were published eighty-seven years before the birth of Sterne, and one hundred and twenty or one hundred and thirty years prior to the publication of " Tristram Shandy; " and the volume on the table before me is of the *third edition*, which was printed *twenty-four years before Sterne was born.*

In the scenes above narrated, personages of more importance than Yorick, Obadiah, Captain Shandy, and My Uncle Toby, played their parts, before any of them had even the ideal existence which Sterne gives them. I know not how Bishop Hughes can set aside such proof, except on the principle that " coming events cast their shadows before," and, in this case, casting an unusually long one.

It will be seen, by the extract from his speech, that he charges the Public School Society with circulating and approving the " Brief Review," because *they do not disclaim it.*

Because they do not officiously disclaim and condemn the murder of Thomas á Becket, they must be held responsible! Because they do not disavow the murder of Queen Anne, they must be held responsible for the conduct of Henry VIII.! Because they do not condemn the burning of the Alexandrian library by Caliph Omar, it is their act till they disclaim it—or, at least, they approve of it! And, on the same principle, *until the Roman Catholic Church disclaims the curses above given we hold them responsible!* A *politic* denial by Bishop Hughes is not sufficient; it must come from popes, cardinals, bishops, and priests; for those dignitaries authorized and sanctioned them. The reverend speaker must admit my application of his argument, or retract his unwarrantable abuse of the Public School Society in relation to this matter.

If he persists in denying the truth of my evidence, as I have proved *my* side of the question, if he thinks it desirable, *he* must produce the excommunication *which was used in the case of Mr. Hogan.* This is the alternative; and, in the mean time, I shall not be overawed by the legal, literary, and ecclesiastical array of gentlemen whose research can pierce no farther into the gloom of antiquity than the " Life and Character of Tristram Shandy."

AMERICUS.

[For the convenience of the reader the following translation of the form of excommunication as given by Sir Henry Spelman is inserted.]

EXCOMMUNICATION.

By the authority of God Almighty, the Father, the Son, and the Holy Ghost, and of the holy canons, and of the pure and holy Virgin Mary, the Mother of God, and of all heavenly intelligences, angels, and archangels, thrones, dominions, and powers, cherubim, and seraphim, and of the holy patriarchs, prophets, and all apostles and evangelists, and holy innocents, who in the sight of the Lamb have been found worthy to sing the new song; and of the holy martyrs and holy confessors, and holy virgins, and of all the holy and elect of God together, we do excommunicate and anathematize this thief, the malefactor N., and do separate him from the threshold of the holy Church of God, that he may be given over to be tormented with everlasting punishments, with Dathan and Abiram, and with those who said unto the Lord God, "Depart from us, we desire not the knowledge of thy ways;" and as fire is extinguished by water, so let his lamp be extinguished, world without end, unless he shall repent and make satisfaction. Amen.

Curse him, God the Father, who created man. Curse him, the Son of God, who suffered for man. Curse him, the Holy Spirit, who is poured forth in baptism. Curse him, the holy cross, which Christ ascended for our salvation, triumphing over the enemy. Curse him, the holy mother of God, and perpetual virgin, Mary. Curse him, St. Michael, the receiver of holy souls. Curse him, all angels and archangels, principalities and powers, and all the host of the heavenly army. Curse him, the worthy multitude of patriarchs and prophets. Curse him, St. John, the forerunner, and particularly the baptizer of Christ. Curse him, St. Peter, and St. Paul, and St. Andrew, and all the apostles and disciples of Christ, together with the four evangelists, who by their preaching converted the whole world. Curse him, the wondrous company of martyrs and confessors, that have been found acceptable unto God by their good works. Curse him, the bands of holy virgins, who for the sake of the honor of Christ have counted worthless the vanities of the world. Curse him, all saints, who from the beginning of the world unto the end of time, are found beloved of God. Curse him, heaven and earth, and all holy things abiding therein.

Cursed be he wheresoever he shall be, whether in the house, or in the field, or in the way, or in the footpath, or in the wood, or in the water, or in the church.

Cursed be he in living, in dying, in eating, in drinking, in hungering, in thirsting, in fasting, in slumbering, in sleeping, in watching, in walking, in standing, in sitting, in lying down, in working, in resting, [in the calls of nature,] and in blood-letting.

Cursed be he in all the powers of his body. Cursed be he inwardly and outwardly. Cursed be he in his hair. Cursed be he in his brain. Cursed be he in the crown of his head, in his temples, in his forehead, in his ears, in his eyebrows, in his eyes, in his cheeks, in his jaws, in his nostrils, in his teeth, in his gums, in his lips, in his throat, in his shoulders, in his arms, in his wrists, in his hands, in his fingers, in his breast, in his heart, and in all the inner parts of his body to his stomach; in his veins, in his groin, in his thighs, in his genitals, in his hips, in his knees, in his legs, in his feet, in his joints, and in his toes. Cursed be he in all the structures of his limbs; from the crown of his head to the sole of his foot; let there be no soundness in him.

Curse him, Christ, the Son of the living God, in all the authority of his majesty; and let heaven, with all the intelligences that abide therein, rise up against him for his damnation, unless he shall repent and make satisfaction. Amen. So be it. Be it so. Amen.

EXCOMMUNICATION.—By the authority of God the Father Almighty, and of the Son, and of the Holy Ghost, and of the blessed Mary, mother of God, and of all the saints, and of the holy Canon: We excommunicate, we anathematize, and we separate from the threshold of the holy mother Church, these malefactors, N., and those who sympathize and participate with them; and unless they shall repent and render satisfaction, let their lamps be put out before the living, for ever and ever. Be it so. So be it. Amen.

These forms of excommunication follow the emendations of laws, approved by William the Conqueror, in a manuscript volume called the *Textus Roffensis*, and appear to have originated at that very period, because nowhere in earlier times, so far as I know, is found the invocation of the Virgin Mary.

CHAPTER XIII.

THE SCHOOL QUESTION OF 1842.

Hon. John C. Spencer—The Legislature of 1842—Appointment of Committees—Committee on Colleges, Academies, and Common Schools—Hon. William B. Maclay—Hon. John I. Dix—Governor Seward's Message—Report on the School Question—Proceedings of the Legislature—Mr. Maclay's Bill Passed.

THE disappointment of the advocates of Mr. Spencer's school bill was very great. Mr. Spencer, with the perseverance which formed a prominent feature of his character, had sought to win support to the measure by the elaborate report presented to the Legislature in April. He was charged by opponents with having "coquetted with the New York delegation all winter, to obtain their aid in its passage." He had appeared, on one occasion, before that delegation, to whom he submitted and advocated his plan, Dr. William Rockwell, Joseph B. Collins, and Theodore Sedgwick being present on behalf of the Public School Society.

The postponement of the question by the Senate until January, 1842, caused the election of the members of the Legislature for that year to be regarded, as already stated, with more than usual interest by all parties. The candidates of the Whig, as well as those of the Democratic party in the city of New York, were respectively addressed by the friends of the Public School Society in a series of interrogatories. Their support was withheld from any candidate in favor of any change in the existing system of public instruction, and a refusal to reply to the questions proposed was deemed as favoring such change.

The excitement in respect to the "school question" was very great, and the election of the successful candidates turned upon that issue. Upon the assembling of the Legislature in January following, and *before the organization* of the two Houses, the question engaged the thoughts, and was the topic of constant conversation among leading Democrats at the Capitol. As a party, they had much to lose by the continued agitation of the question ; and yet, having a majority in both branches, they had also to incur the responsibility of its settlement. With this view, and anticipating that the subject would be laid before the Legislature by Governor SEWARD, in his message, more than usual care was taken in the organization of the Committee on Colleges, Academies, and Common Schools, to which that portion of the message was referred. In the House of Assembly, as soon as the new Speaker (Levi S. Chatfield) had been chosen, he announced among his political friends his determination of appointing William B. Maclay, of New York, as chairman of the Committee on Schools. Horatio Seymour (afterward Governor of the State), and other leading men, were then members of the body. Mr. Maclay had already served in the House during the sessions of 1840 and 1841. At the preceding session, the House of Assembly had chosen, by ballot, three of its members as a committee to investigate the affairs of the New York and Erie Railroad Company. Mr. Maclay was a member of this committee, and was absent from the city of New York in the prosecution of the duties assigned him during the election of the past autumn, and had been elected without any pledge or committal to any of the parties. The presumption was, that, under his direction, a full and dispassionate inquiry would be made in relation to the public schools in the city of New York. He at first declined to act as chairman of the Committee on Schools, and urged that Gen. JOHN I. DIX, then a representative from the county of Albany, should be appointed, alleging that his capacity and integrity would inspire confidence, among those who were either unwilling or unable to examine for themselves, in the conclusions at which he should arrive, while the committee would have the advantage derived from his past experience as superintendent of the schools of the State. This view was acquiesced in, but, on consultation with General Dix, he declined to accept the position, and the programme of the committee remained as originally proposed by the Speaker, with the advice of Michael Hoffman, and other experienced members of the party to which he belonged.

As had been anticipated, Governor Seward devoted a considerable portion of his message to a discussion of the subject of public instruction in the city of New York. The recommenda-

32

tions thus presented are given in full in the following extract
from the message :

It was among my earliest duties to bring to the notice of the Legislature
the neglected condition of many thousand children, including a very large
proportion of those of immigrant parentage in our great commercial city—
a misfortune then supposed to result from groundless prejudices and omis-
sions of parental duty. Especially desirous, at the same time, not to disturb
in any manner the public schools, which seemed to be efficiently conducted,
although so many for whom they were established seemed to be unwilling
to receive their instructions, I suggested, as I thought, in a spirit not inhar-
monious with our civil and religious institutions, that, if necessary, it might
be expedient to bring those so excluded from such privileges into schools
rendered especially attractive by the sympathies of those to whom the task
of instruction should be confided. It has since been discovered that the
magnitude of the evil was not fully known, and that its causes were very
imperfectly understood. It will be shown to you, in the proper report, that
twenty thousand children in the city of New York, of suitable age, are not
at all instructed in any of the public schools ; while the whole number in
all the residue of the State, not taught in common schools, does not exceed
nine thousand. What had been regarded as individual, occasional, and
accidental prejudices, have proved to be opinions pervading a large mass,
including at least one religious communion equally with all others entitled
to civil tolerance—opinions cherished through a period of sixteen years, and
ripened into a permanent conscientious distrust of the impartiality of the
education given in the public schools. This distrust has been rendered still
deeper and more alienating by a subversion of precious civil rights of those
whose consciences are thus offended.

Happily, in this as in other instances, the evil is discovered to have had
its origin no deeper than in a departure from the equality of general laws.
In our general system of common schools, trustees chosen by tax-paying citizens levy taxes, build school-houses, employ and pay teachers, and govern
schools which are subject to visitation by similarly elected inspectors, who
certify the qualifications of teachers ; and all schools thus constituted participate in just proportion in the public moneys, which are conveyed to them
by commissioners also elected by the people. Such schools are found distributed in average spaces of two and a half square miles throughout the
inhabited portions of the State, and yet neither popular discontent, nor
political strife, nor sectarian discord, has ever disturbed their peaceful instructions nor impaired their eminent usefulness. In the public school system of the city, one hundred persons are trustees and inspectors, and, by
continued consent of the Common Council, are the dispensers of an annual
average sum of $35,000, received from the common school fund of the State,
and a sum equal to $95,000, derived from an indiscriminating tax upon the
real and personal estates of the city. They build school-houses chiefly from
the public funds, they appoint and remove teachers, fix their compensation,
and prescribe the moral, intellectual, and religious instruction which one

eighth of the rising generation of the State shall be required to receive. Their powers, more effective and far-reaching than are exercised by the municipality of the city, are not derived from the community whose children are educated and whose property is taxed, nor even from the State, which is so great an almoner, and whose welfare is so deeply concerned, but from an incorporated and perpetual association, which grants, upon pecuniary subscription, the privileges even of life-membership, and yet holds in fee-simple the public school edifices, valued at eight hundred thousand dollars. Lest there might be too much responsibility, even to the association, that body can elect only one half of the trustees, and those thus selected appoint their fifty associates.

The philanthropy and patriotism of the present managers of the public schools, and their efficiency in imparting instruction, are cheerfully and gratefully admitted. Nor is it necessary to maintain that agents thus selected will become unfaithful, or that a system that so jealously excludes popular interference must necessarily be unequal in its operation. It is only insisted that the institution, after a fair and sufficient trial, has failed to gain that broad confidence reposed in the general system of the State, and indispensable to every scheme of universal education. No plan for that purpose can be defended, except on the ground that public instruction is one of the responsibilities of the Government. It is, therefore, a manifest legislative duty to correct errors and defects in whatever system is established. In the present case, the failure amounts virtually to an exclusion of all the children thus withheld. I cannot overcome my regret that every suggestion of amendment encounters so much opposition from those who defend the public school system of the metropolis, as to show that, in their judgment, it can admit of no modification, either from tenderness to the consciences or regard to the civil rights of those aggrieved, or even for the reclamation of those for whose culture the State has so munificently provided; as if society must conform itself to the public schools, instead of the public schools adapting themselves to the exigencies of society. The late eminent Superintendent, after exposing the greatness of this public misfortune, and tracing it to the discrepancy between the local and general systems, suggested a remedy, which, although it is not urged to the exclusion of any other, seems to deserve dispassionate consideration. I submit, therefore, with entire willingness, to approve whatever adequate remedy you may propose, the expediency of restoring to the people of the city of New York—what I am sure the people of no other part of the State would, upon any consideration, relinquish—the education of their children. For this purpose, it is only necessary to vest the control of the common schools in a board, to be composed of commissioners elected by the people; which board shall apportion the school moneys among all the schools, including those now existing, which shall be organized and conducted in conformity to its general regulations and the laws of the State, in the proportion of the number of pupils instructed. It is not left doubtful that the restoration to the common schools of the city of this simple and equal feature of the common schools of the State would remove every complaint, and bring into the seminaries the offspring of want and misfortune, presented by a grand jury, on a recent occasion, as neglected children of both sexes, who are found in hordes upon the wharves and in corners of the streets, surrounded by evil associations, disturbing the public peace, committing petty depredations, and going from bad to worse, until their course terminates in high crimes and infamy.

This proposition to gather the young from the streets and wharves into the nurseries which the State, solicitous for her security against ignorance, has prepared for them, has sometimes been treated as a device to appropriate the school fund to the endowment of seminaries for teaching languages and faiths, thus to perpetuate the prejudices it seeks to remove; sometimes as a scheme for dividing that precious fund among a hundred jarring sects, and thus increasing the religious animosities it strives to heal; sometimes as a plan to subvert the prevailing religion, and introduce one repugnant to the consciences of our fellow-citizens; while, in truth, it simply proposes, by enlightening equally the minds of all, to enable them to detect error wherever it may exist, and to reduce uncongenial masses into one intelligent, virtuous, harmonious, and happy people. Being now relieved from all such misconceptions, it presents the questions whether it is wiser and more humane to educate the offspring of the poor, than to leave them to grow up in ignorance and vice; whether juvenile vice is more easily eradicated by the Court of Sessions than by common schools; whether parents have a right to be heard concerning the instruction and instructors of their children, and taxpayers in relation to the expenditure of public funds; whether, in a republican government, it is necessary to interpose an independent corporation between the people and the schoolmaster; and whether it is wise and just to disfranchise an entire community of all control over public education, rather than suffer a part to be represented in proportion to its numbers and contributions. Since such considerations are now involved, what has hitherto been discussed as a question of benevolence and of universal education, has become one of equal civil rights, religious tolerance, and liberty of conscience. We could bear with us, in our retirement from public service, no recollection more worthy of being cherished through life, than that of having met such a question in the generous and confiding spirit of our institutions, and decided it upon the immutable principles on which they are based.

This portion of the Message of the Governor was referred to the Committee on Colleges and Schools. Some time having elapsed, and no report having been made by the committee on the subject, a resolution was offered in the Assembly by Hon. John L. O'Sullivan, one of the New York city delegation, asking that the Standing Committee on Colleges, &c., be discharged from the further consideration of the subject of common schools in the city of New York, and that the same be referred to a select committee. This motion was resisted by Mr. Maclay, who placed his opposition on two grounds: 1st. That he was unwilling that any one should suppose that he had been indifferent to the subject which had been referred to the Standing Committee, or afraid to act upon it ; 2d. That the Secretary of State, as would appear by a reference to his annual report, had promised a distinct report upon the subject of common schools in the city of New York, which had not yet been communicated to the House, and which the committee, as a matter both of use and propriety, desired to wait for. The motion of Mr. O'Sullivan was lost.

There was an evident disposition, on the part of the dominant party in the Legislature, to leave the subject with the committee to which it had been referred. On the 13th of January, Senator A. B. Dickinson introduced, in the Senate, a bill, which was substantially that of Mr. Spencer, but failed to obtain its reference to a select committee. On the 14th of February, Mr. Maclay submitted to the House the following report, accompanied by a bill, which was subsequently amended and enacted :

IN ASSEMBLY, *February* 14, 1842.

REPORT

Of the Committee on Colleges, Academies, and Common Schools, on so much of the Governor's Message as relates to the Common Schools in the City of New York.

Mr. Maclay, from the Committee on Colleges, Academies, and Common Schools, to whom was referred that portion of the Governor's Message which relates to the common schools in the city of New York, together with sundry petitions praying for an alteration of the existing system of common schools in said city, and a bill entitled "An Act to Extend and Improve the Benefits of Common School Instruction in the City of New York," REPORTS :

That the matters referred involved important inquiries, which have been diligently made by the committee, with the view of presenting to the House such conclusions as might, if adopted, tend to correct existing evils in the system of common school instruction in the city of New York, and at the same time extend its benefits.

The importance of universal education in a republic is so manifest, that, while it has continually engaged the care of the Legislature, every one who has been elevated to the Executive chair of the State has pressed it with zealous earnestness upon the representatives of the people. Even while the revolutionary war was still unfinished, that revered patriot, George Clinton, in his annual speech of 1782, thus addressed the Legislature :

In the present respite from the more severe calamities and distresses of the war, I cannot forbear suggesting to you a work which, I conceive, ought not to be deferred as the business of peace : the promotion and encouragement of learning. Besides the general advantages arising to society from liberal science, as restraining those rude passions which tend to vice and disorder, it is the peculiar duty of the government of a free State, where the highest employments are open to citizens of every rank, to endeavor, by the establishment of schools and seminaries, to diffuse that degree of literature which is necessary to the due discharge of public trusts.

The same revered Executive, in 1798, in his last message, felt it his duty to call the attention of the Legislature to the fact, that the benefits arising from the establishment and endowment of academies were principally confined to the children of the opulent, and to recommend the foundation of common schools throughout the State, as happily adapted to remedy this inconvenience, and to dispense the blessings of knowledge to the whole community.

His successor, John Jay, concurring entirely in the views of his predecessor, recommended universal education as the most effective means of multiplying the blessings of social order, and diffusing the influence of moral obligation.

The communications of the illustrious and patriotic Tompkins bear ample testimony to his adherence to the liberal and statesmanlike views of his predecessors.

In his address to the Legislature in 1816, he reminds them that, as guardians of the property, liberty, and morals of the State, they were required, by every injunction of patriotism and wisdom, to endow, to the utmost of the resources of the State, schools and seminaries of learning. From that period until now, the constitutional duty of the Executive to suggest for the consideration of the Legislature such matters as are in his judgment expedient, has not been deemed to have been fully discharged, without similar manifestations of enlightened zeal for the general diffusion of the benefits of education among all classes of the community. The unanimity of the long line of honored statesmen who have presided over the interests of the State in regard to this subject, while it is among the most delightful themes of contemplation, affords the most conclusive evidence that the policy is firmly established in the affections of the people. However they may have differed upon other measures of importance to the public weal, on this subject there has existed no contrariety of opinion.

The powerful arguments used by successive Executives in defence of this system, and the cheerfulness with which the people have submitted to additional burdens to sustain and extend it, would seem to render unnecessary any observations of your committee in favor of public education; but they cannot refrain from noticing a suggestion, that the difficulties in regard to the education of the young in the city of New York resulted from its being adopted among the responsibilities of Government, and that the Legislature ought not to extend encouragement to this great object, but leave it, like religion, to the voluntary and unregulated action of the people.

This suggestion proceeds upon an erroneous supposition, that the performance of acts of utility and beneficence to others, in the affairs of this transitory life, is considered as of equal obligation upon the consciences of men as the observance of those religious rites and duties which relate to their own eternal happiness in the life to come.

But experience is an instructive teacher on this as on every other subject. There are States in this Union which consent, and States which refuse, to establish a system of common schools; while deplorable ignorance prevails in the latter, knowledge and morality are found in the former, and just in proportion to the efficiency and universality of their system of public instruction. Even in the city of New York, containing within its bounds so great an amount of wealth and liberality, experience has fully shown the danger of trusting to any visionary hope that adequate provision for the instruction of the poor could be obtained by voluntary contributions alone. The Public School Society is only sustained by moneys derived from the common school fund, and taxes levied upon the people by law. Our statute-book bears concurrent testimony with the codes of other civilized countries, that the force of law must concur with the injunctions of religion, to clothe the naked, feed the hungry, relieve distress, and educate the offspring of the poor.

All that appertains to public instruction in the city and county of New York, is substantially under the control of an incorporated institution known as "The Public School Society." The extraordinary powers of this Society have been ably and elaborately set forth in two reports which were made to the Legislature at its last session. This Society was incorporated in 1805. The late Superintendent of Common Schools, after recapitulating the different laws which have been passed in relation to it from that period to the present time, thus concludes the summary:

Thus, by the joint operation of the acts amending the charter of the Society, of the statutes in relation to the distribution of the school moneys, and of the ordinance of the Common Council, designating the schools of the Society as the principal recipients of those moneys, the control of the public education of the city of New York, and the 'disbursement of nine tenths of the public moneys raised and apportioned for schools, were vested in this corporation. It is a perpetual corporation, and there is no power reserved by the Legislature to repeal or modify its charter. It consists of members who have contributed to the funds of the Society; and, according to the provisions of the last act, the payment of ten dollars constitutes the contributor a member for life. The members annually choose fifty trustees, who may add to their number fifty more.

From the petitions of many thousand inhabitants of New York, it appears that objections are widely prevalent against this organization of public schools in that metropolis, and that the system so far fails to obtain the general confidence, that a very large number of children are left destitute of instruction. By the report of the acting Superintendent of Common Schools, made at the present session of the Legislature (Assembly Document No. 12), it appears that the whole number of children in the State (exclusive of the city of New York) between the ages of five and sixteen, is 583,347; and of that number, 562,198, being more than ninety-six hundredths, attend the common schools; while in the city of New York, out of the number of 65,571 children between the same ages, the whole number reported by the commissioners of that city as attending the schools was only 41,385, being less than sixty hundredths of the number, although the share of common school moneys distributed by the State and expended in the city, amounting to $35,415.10, was equally large in proportion with that expended in other counties of the State. But in addition to that sum, an equal amount of $35,415.10, together with the additional sum of $60,000, was raised by the Common Council, swelling the total amount entrusted with the Public School Society, for the purpose of education in one year, to the sum of $130,830.20; while the whole sum expended in all the rest of the State, and by means of which 562,198 scholars are taught, is only $581,555.75; making the expense in the city of New York more than $3.15 for the instruction of each scholar, while in the other parts of the State it is less than $1.04 for each scholar. In other words, the expense of instruction under the public school system in New York is more than three times the expense of instruction under the district school system.

The comparison between the number of children attending school in the country and the city is still more favorable to the former, if the supposition of the acting Superintendent of Common Schools be correct. There are, he says, upon an average, about fifty-five children instructed in each of the districts reporting; and assuming an equal average number to be under instruction in each of the 239 districts from which no reports have been received, the aggregate number of children between five and sixteen, exclusive of the city of New York, not taught in any district school, would amount to only about 8,000.

Apart from these considerations, it can no longer be concealed or denied that the failure of the public schools to accomplish the objects contemplated by the establishment, results, in a great degree, from a disinclination on the part of many parents to entrust these schools with the education of their children. The fact is, indeed, abundantly shown in the number of petitions now before the Legislature for a change in the present system, that it requires no additional proof. During the last sixteen years, the Public School Society, as it appears from its own admissions, has had to defend its monopoly against the struggles of discontented masses of the population. Evidence more conclusive and affecting is seen in the multitudes of children in the streets and on the wharves of the city, growing up to the rights and responsibilities of citizens, but strangers to the simplest elements of learning, and acquiring only the education of vice. The rule of universal experience is, that people in the country are less zealous for the diffusion of education, and submit with less willingness to the burdens imposed for its maintenance, than those residing in cities.

But here the rule is reversed. The statistics of the school system throughout the State show that ignorance is clearing off, like a thick fog, from the agricultural districts, and settling with ominous portent over the emporium of the State.

Now, those who oppose any change of the system, have attempted to account for so extraordinary a result by explanations ingenious and plausible. But, so long as facts are facts, it will strike every man of ordinary reflection, that there is a deeper cause than any they have felt at liberty to assign or admit. That cause is complex, not simple.

In the first place, there is something exceedingly incongruous with our republican habits of thinking, in the idea of taking the children of a population approaching half a million of souls, taxing them at the same time for the support and maintenance of the schools, and, when both the children and taxes are furnished, withdrawing both out of the hands of guardians and taxpayers, and handing them over to the management of an irresponsible private chartered company. Such a concentration of power into mammoth machinery of any description is odious to the feelings, and sometimes dangerous to the rights, of freemen. The genius of our institutions is, to distribute power where it can be done, and, where it cannot, to define and restrict it. 'When thus distributed, it may not be capable of producing the same amount of good, but then its capacity for evil will be diminished in the same ratio; and, if it go wrong, the remedy is always more simple, apparent, and easy of attainment.

In the next place, the population of the city of New York is by no means homogeneous; on the contrary, it is the object of education to make it so. Any system based upon the supposition that that homogeneousness now exists, and all will therefore absolutely conform, or can be obliged to conform, assumes the end to be attained, and overlooks the means of its accomplishment.

The error is the same which lies at the basis of established churches; and the failure of the public schools, however assiduous or efficient these schools may be, arises from the very cause which prevents, in this country, the existence or toleration of an established system of religion.

The Public School Society have alleged that they are not more a monopoly than the different boards for hospitals and other charters in the city of New York. But there is this manifest difference in the two cases, which strips the argument of any force or pertinency: the inmates of these charitable institutions are cast upon the State, and she must find guardians for them. Not so the children of the city. They are surrounded by their parents, guardians, and friends, who have opinions which demand respect and rights which cannot be disregarded.

The committee, after mature reflection, are unable to accord their assent to the inference which the advocates of the Public School Society derive from this argument. In the first place, supposing—which is untrue—that the constitution of the Public School Society, and its peculiar and overshadowing powers and privileges, were analogous to the other institutions referred to, the abuses or important objections of the one could not be disproved or corrected by admitting that the others were monopolies. Many contend that the banking institutions of the State are satisfactorily conducted, and accomplish the purposes of their establishment; but what should we think of their understanding, should they advance this as an argument to prove that the actions of many of these institutions had not resulted in disgrace and calamity? When confined within narrow boundaries, possessing limited powers, affecting few interests, and conducted with devoted assiduity and energy, a corporation may, and often does, accomplish much public good. But the concentration of vast powers, the enlargement of the sphere of operation, and the disregard or violation of popular rights, or even popular sentiment, will render any corporation intolerable.

It is too late to argue that private chartered corporations, with extraordinary powers and privileges, are more suitable or efficient agents for public objects than the community acting under general laws. But the question is not upon the merits or defects of other institutions; it is, whether the Public School Society has or has not failed to accomplish the great object of its establishment—the universal education of the children of the city of New York. That it has signally failed, has been shown by the statistics of the schools; and there is, moreover, incontrovertible proof in the fact that nearly one half of the citizens of the metropolis protest against the system, and demand its modification.

The withholding of public confidence has been felt by the Public School Society itself, and they have endeavored humanely, but fruitlessly, to remove it. They heretofore employed benevolent females to induce the poor to send their children to the schools. They next obtained from the Common Council an ordinance of a compulsory nature; and they have now public agents, at salaries, who are engaged in the labor of recruiting for the schools; but all in vain.

Such, then, is the evil to be corrected. But what is the remedy ? The committee confess that this, as in every similar instance, is the most difficult question. Nevertheless, it is apparent that the evil began with a departure from the confessedly equal and just system of common school education which prevails in all the other parts of the State; and it can only be effectually and satisfactorily corrected by bringing home the education of the young of the city to the business and bosoms of their parents. The common school system of the State successfully and admirably accomplishes that object; and the committee therefore recommend that the system shall, as far as it is practicable, be extended to the city and county of New York.

In accordance with these views, they submit a bill, providing that, hereafter, there shall be elected, in each ward of the city, three commissioners and two inspectors of common schools, and extending to the city so much of the general law of the State as relates to the powers and duties of these officers. This change, in harmony with the general system, contemplates the division of the city into a convenient number of school districts, and directs that the people shall elect trustees, who shall, in regard to common schools therein erected, establish, maintain, and regulate common schools in such districts, subject to the general regulation of the school commissioners, who are to apportion the public moneys among the several schools in the ratio of persons interested therein.

In this recommendation the committee unanimously concur.

In accordance with the foregoing views and recommendations, your committee have instructed their chairman to introduce a bill.

The following review of the report of Mr. Maclay appeared in the *New York Evangelist* of March 3d. After quoting the material portions of the report, the review continues:

It is not our purpose to enter into a protracted discussion of the principles which should characterize any system of public education, and the measures requisite to accomplish this object of fondest pursuit with every citizen who values the progressive development of the powers of human society under a free government, and who regards as the most important lever in the overturning of all systems of despotism, and abodes of crime, the intellectual and moral cultivation of the people. We wish to present a few facts in relation to that point to which the committee has attached the greatest importance : Has the Public School Society fulfilled its trust ? And we here remark, that the report of the committee contains many palpable errors, which are calculated to give a very unfavorable character to the existing system of public schools in this city, which we feel it our duty and privilege to correct.

I. The report of the committee represents that the number of children in the State, exclusive of this city, of the school age, between five and sixteen, is 583,347 ; attending school, 562,198, or ninety-six per cent. In the city, there are 65,571, while the number represented as attending school was 41,385—less than sixty per cent.

In the first place, we contend the accuracy of these returns, and for several reasons. The carelessness and negligence of inspectors, the desire to make the largest returns, for the purpose of obtaining larger rates from the comptroller, not from fraud, but circumstances favoring these returns—and their acknowledged incorrectness. In proof of these positions, we copy, from the report of the Commissioners of Common Schools of this city for 1841, the following curious facts. See also report of Superintendent of Common Schools, Schedule F, in full.

In 1824, the number of children residing in the districts was 383,500 ; number under instruction, 402,940 ; being an excess of children taught over those residing in the districts of 19,440 !

In 1825, children in the districts, 395,586 ; children under instruction, 425,586 ; excess, 30,000 !

In 1827, children in the districts, 419,216 ; children taught, 441,826 ; excess of pupils over children in the districts, 22,640 !

In 1839, in twenty-seven counties in the State, there was an excess of more than 25,000 children reported as receiving instruction over the children of the legal age in the districts !

It would be arguing but little for the good sense of our readers, were we to comment upon such gross errors as these, and to attempt to convince them that the returns of last year are as liable to be full of errors as those of preceding years. But what an overpowering argument in favor of the district system ! It actually educates from twenty to thirty thousand children more than reside in the State !

II. Upon the report, then, which we may fairly presume to be incorrect, the committee enter into a comparison between the State and this city, and represent that, of 65,571 children of the legal age, only 41,385, or a little less than sixty per cent., receive instruction, making a consequent deficiency of 24,186.

The limit prescribed by law to the school age is from five to sixteen years of age. Now, it is a fact so evident that it is almost superfluous to present our corrected statement, that, in the country, children are engaged at agricultural labors during the summer, and attend school in winter the full time allowed by law ; while, in the city, that mass of the people who take advantage of the public schools are poor, and require the pecuniary assistance of the children to obtain their own subsistence. Hence, they are withdrawn from school at about twelve years of age ; and it is a recorded and well-known fact, that only seven per cent. of the children in the public schools are over twelve years of age. If, then, we regard the school age as consisting of eleven years—from five to sixteen—we must deduct four elevenths from the duration of pupilage among the city population, it being here but seven years. This will reduce the deficiency 23,844, and leave less than 500 unprovided for. But three elevenths will be more nearly correct, the number over twelve years making nearly this difference ; and we have but 6,383 uninstructed—about one fourth of the number stated by the committee.

In addition to the fact thus shown, the children instructed in private schools will leave but few of the juvenile part of our population who receive the " education of vice " spoken of by the committee, because the doors of the Public School Society are shut against them. And when it is recollected that many of these children are poor, we can easily see the social and domestic causes which tend, more or less, throughout the Union, to make the actual attendance at school much less than the number on register.

But this is not all. We have presented some of the ridiculous errors which crowd the returns of the district system in the country ; we will now take a single specimen from the towns of the State, and bring forward our neighboring city of Brooklyn, which enjoys that system, to show the relative percentage of attendance—assuming that the returns from cities are more correct than those from among scattered portions of the population.

The report of the Commissioners of Common Schools for 1836 exhibited the following state of the schools :

In the First District, there were 1,651 children ; under instruction, 210— or twelve and three fourths per cent.

In the Fourth District, 215 children ; under instruction, 55—a fraction over twenty-five per cent.

In the Sixth District, 300 children ; under instruction, 51—a fraction over one sixth, or sixteen per cent.

Lest we should appear to select a very unfavorable year by which to make the comparison, we again refer to the report of the Superintendent of Common Schools for 1840 and 1841, by which it appears that, in 1840, there were 6,206 children, of whom 2,120, or thirty-four and one sixth per cent., were under instruction. In 1841, there were 7,966 children in the districts, of whom 2,274—only twenty-eight and four sevenths per cent.—were under instruction.

If these things are done in Brooklyn, what might we not assume of parts of the country where the population is distributed over wide districts ?

III. The district system is more expensive than that which now exists in this city, and we are obliged in this respect also to differ from the report of the committee. They report that the expenses of instruction in this city is $3.15 for each child, while in the districts it is less than $1.04 per scholar. How such statements can be placed before an intelligent Legislature, is somewhat remarkable ; but they must be corrected.

1. The amount of money paid by the State, out of its treasury, is $1.04, while no mention is made of the amount raised by the inhabitants of the districts themselves. See §§ 61, 62, 63, 65, 68, 78, 79, 85, 86, and others, of Article Fifth, Title I., chapter xv., part 1, of the Revised Statutes, in relation to district schools. The money paid by the State is the deficit in the necessary expenses of the district, and is not the entire expense of the schools.

2. The money paid by the State to the Public School Society is $35,415.10 ; number of children reported, 41,385 ; the expense to the State being less than one dollar. The balance raised by the Common Council corresponds in nature to that raised by the districts ; the city being regarded as one vast district, and the commissioners the acting trustees of the school moneys.

3. The number of children in the schools of this city being received as reported, we have the total expenses of these schools, $115,799.42, divided among 41,385 children, on the whole charge about $2.70 ; while the full expenses under the district system, in funds raised by the districts and by the State, is $3.15—the cost of our public schools, as erroneously stated by the committee.

4. We refer again to the Brooklyn commissioners for another fact.

In the Second District, 38 children were instructed, and the money paid by the commissioners was $114.81—or $3.02 and a fraction.

In the Sixth District, 51 children instructed ; $196.75 paid from school fund—or a few cents less than four dollars.

The total expenditure, however, from the public fund, for 1,197 children, was $1,604.26—or $1.34 and a fraction for each child—considerably more than the sum stated by the committee, independent of the sum raised by the respective districts.

IV. It will be seen at a glance, by any one who appreciates the necessity of fairness in making comparisons between different localities and between different classes of the population, that inferences drawn from data so incongruous as those furnished by thinly-settled and densely populated districts, must be defective and hazardous when great changes in public policy are predicated upon them. A brief comparison between New York and cities and towns where the district system exists, is, therefore, the only true method for determining the relative efficiency and value of the two systems under discussion.

To avoid tediousness in these comparisons, we will take the aggregate of several towns—Albany, Brooklyn, Hudson, Troy, Utica, Schenectady, Rochester, and Buffalo. In 1840, the number of children was 28,125 ; under instruction, 12,182—or 3,761 children less than one half, or forty-three and one third per cent.

In 1841, children residing in the same towns, 29,908; under instruction, 13,195—or only forty-four and one ninth per cent.

From these facts, gleaned from the public records of the State, we may learn that the district system in the towns is less favorable to the intellect-ual growth of the young than the Public School Society of this city; and when we keep in view the numerous chances of error as displayed by the returns before given from the country districts, we hazard nothing in saying that the closest scrutiny only makes more apparent the great superiority of our present excellent schools.

The report of the committee states that the population (according to their erroneous manner of extending the school age in this city to sixteen years, instead of confining it to twelve, as we have shown is the proper limit) of children instructed in the public schools, is sixty per cent.; while the last comparison just given shows that, in the thickly-populated towns under the district system, the proportion is only from forty-three to forty-five per cent.—a difference of twenty-five per cent. in favor of our existing institutions. The mean percentage for several years is about thirty in Brooklyn, under the district system, and sixty in New York, under the pub-lic schools; we have a difference of one hundred per cent. in favor of the Public School Society. In Williamsburgh, only fourteen and one third per cent. are returned as under instruction!

V. It is folly to expect efficiency in any system which is not under the administration of competent and faithful directors; and the important fea-ture of supervision and visitation speaks incomparably for the praise of the zealous and worthy trustees of our Public School Society, when contrasted with the maladministration and paralysis which characterize the district system. The last report of the trustees states that they had made 14,142 visits to the schools under their charge during the previous year; averaging 130 visits to each school! In Brooklyn, which we prefer to quote as an example, on account of its contiguity, eight schools had been visited three times, or one visit to three schools during a whole year!

With such incontestable facts before us, we are astonished that any one can for a moment attack an institution of such decided superiority; and much more, that a committee of the Legislature should present such a mass of *ex parte* and perverted statements to the consideration of that body.

VI. The report states $130,000 were paid to the Public School Society during one year. Now, this is the amount of the money distributed to all the institutions for common school instruction, of which the Society re-ceived $120,271; making a difference of about eight per cent. in this state-ment also, in favor of the Society. We see no reason why exaggeration should mark every step of this report, in even the slightest particulars.

We might multiply facts *ad infinitum* almost, but the foregoing are suffi-cient to demonstrate the erroneous and palpable absurdities which have crept into the report of the committee, and which we must correct in order to counteract the tendency it would otherwise have to injure our public institution in the estimation of our fellow-citizens throughout the State and the country at large.

VII. But, while these facts are before us, we cannot omit to bring forward the testimony of the Commissioners of Common Schools of Brooklyn, in favor of our public school system, and which is worthy of most serious consideration from the fact that they wish to be relieved from the incubus of the district system. They remark as follows:

We may be proud of the beauty and healthfulness of our local position, contrasted with our elder and sister city, New York; but in our public school system we are far, very far behind her, in all its essential elements. Having visited many of the schools under the charge of the Public School Society in that city, with a view of obtaining information which might be of service in conducting our own, we deem it but a just tribute to say, that we regard them as admirable models of imitation, and think, if she has any institutions of which she may boast, those public schools are entitled to the foremost rank.

That the defective condition of our schools results mainly from their being conducted on the isolated district system, we entertain no doubt; nor is this a hasty conclusion. This conviction, long since entertained, has been deepened by time and investigation; for, however well adapted that system may be to a country or village population, our own experience, and that of other cities in our State, have fully evinced that it is not adapted to the exigencies of a city population. We therefore hope that the attention of your board will be early directed to obtain from the Legislature of our State an act for the organization of a Board of Education for our entire city; and, in making this suggestion, we feel assured that we embody a sentiment prevailing to a wide extent in our community. Indeed, we may summarily say, that the reasons which would so obviously forbid an attempt to conduct the municipal administration of our city, by nine distinct corporations, acting without concert, are equally applicable in conducting a system of popular education for our youth.

Our population is proverbially floating in its habits, and the wave that lands a class of it, peculiarly needing common school instruction, in one district to-day, to-morrow conveys them to another. If the parent finds no permanent resting-place, the children should be able to find their level on the floor and in the healthful atmosphere of a well-conducted school-room; and this would be realized had we such a system as has been suggested.

In view of these facts, which crowd upon us at every step of our examination, we are more forcibly impressed with the belief that the district system would be a destructive blow to the cause of education in our city. And if we are to regard the unimpeachable evidence contained in the archives of the State, we must resist every step which is taken to impose it upon us, for we are firmly convinced that it is incompetent to promote the great purposes of education in our city.

VIII. The advantage of having a general board, in preference to leaving this cause to the action of the popular will, is denied by the committee, and is scornfully treated as an anti-democratic principle, which is, in the words of Mr. Spencer, "entirely hostile to the spirit of our institutions." We would not be understood as impeaching the capacity of the people to manage the education of their own children, but we must record the deplorable truth, that the almost universal experience of the country system shows it to be incapable of inspiring that interest in its operations which, the committee apprehend, will be its inevitable tendency. We hazard no unwarrantable assertions, but appeal again to the *experimentum crucis* of fact and recorded testimony to bear us out, and present a comparative statement which will be its own commentator.

We have before repudiated the idea of comparing a densely-populated and commercial seaport like New York with thinly-settled agricultural districts, and preferred to compare cities and towns under the district system with this city. Brooklyn being, in part, a commercial city, with a considerable shipping interest, and the citizens being linked to New York by social and business ties which make it a part of this city, in one sense, because many reside in one who do business in the other, is the most pertinent instance which can be adduced. What, then, are the facts as before stated in relation to these towns, and particularly Brooklyn? According to the report of the Superintendent of Common Schools for 1840 and 1841, about forty-four per cent. of the children were under instruction; while in Brooklyn (taken as a single instance), which more nearly resembles New York than any other city in the State, by the report of the commissioners for 1836, 1,197 children, out of a population of 4,756, or twenty-five and one fifth per cent., received instruction in these schools. Now, if the system is calculated to bring out the action of the people in favor of the schools, it would be manifested by the number of children sent, the prosperity of the schools, the number of times visited, and the progress made by the scholars; while all of these data prove beyond dispute that very little regard is paid to the schools by parents or instructors, and the popular rights of parents to educate their own children is disregarded by them, and the young are abandoned to the withering influence of apathy and ignorance.

We regard the whole of this movement, therefore, in appealing to the democratic feelings of the people and of the Legislature, as an insidious effort to carry this proposed change to its consummation, in order to accomplish indirectly what the intelligence and patriotism of the whole community shrank from with dread and amazement—the favoring of a large and politically powerful sect, who know their strength and are determined to use it to the utmost advantage. The tendency of opening the administration of the schools as proposed, will inevitably be, to make them the subject of political influences in the election of commissioners and inspectors, and of sectarian cupidity in the exercise and operations of the schools. To deny this, would be to deny the history of mankind, the universal experience of the human race, and to argue in opposition to that predominant principle of the soul which is the main-spring of its action, *self-love*, whether it be private or public, individual or collective, confined to persons or guiding the policy of nations. This controlling principle will lead to measures having party and sectarian aggrandizement for their object, which will disregard the sacredness of the public weal, or the unfettered and unbiassed character and objects of public expenditures.

Facts, too positive to admit of a shadow of denial, come again to our aid.

At our last election for members of the Legislature, a religious sect, upon whose united strength at the ballot-box depends the decision of every election, made the alteration of our public school system a matter of conscientious scruples, and, accordingly, could not give their vote to any man who would not favor their demands for a change. Thus, "fearing to offend God" by neglecting facilities, as citizens, to produce this change, they prepared and voted upon a ticket of their own choice; and it is a fact eminently worthy of notice and serious consideration, that ten members of the New York Legislature were placed in their seats by the votes of this sect who unite to place their religious preferences and claims in contact with the ballot-box—the chairman of the committee himself being one of them; a sect which has thoroughly identified itself with this change, and whose journals declare that their course is regarded with anxiety and encouragement by the members of the same faith in the Old World. With this glaring fact before us, will any presume to doubt that repetitions of this conduct will be continually recurring whenever opportunities present themselves? Here, then, is this principle of self-love illustrated beyond dispute, in the effort at sectarian aggrandizement at the ballot-box.

It may be objected, that the bill does not contemplate any sectarian appropriation. But we ask, Will the committee, or will any one, deny to "the people" the free exercise of a right which they are so zealous in thrusting into their hands? Will they interfere in the free choice of "the people" in educating their children as they will, after they have opened the course to them?

Another feature in this movement is to be much deprecated: the operation of the law will be to place in the hands of one sect the disposal of six or eight hundred per cent. more of the school fund than belongs to them by virtue of their tax-paying ratio. We hope we shall not subject ourselves to the imputation of harshness or meanness in making the following comparison, but we think it is pertinent and forcible. We take this illustration because it is the strongest, and will exhibit the principle in its true light.

That part of the population which has originated and strenuously carried on this contest against the present system, and whose immediate benefit is contemplated by it—the Roman Catholic—is, according to their own authenticated statements, about one tenth of the population of the State. Grant that they number one seventh in the city, we would therefore have a population of 45,000 Roman Catholics. We will allow one half as males (which is too much), we have 22,500; one half of these regarded as adults, would give 11,250 persons of an age qualified to hold property by law. Now, if we assume that one tenth of these are holders of real or personal taxable property to the amount of $5,000 each, we have, as the aggregate amount held by this class of the population, $6,250,000, or two and a half per cent. of the real and personal taxable estate of the city. Taking this standard as being nearly correct, two and a half per cent. of the school fund would be a little over $3,000 as their *pro rata* proportion of the public money, if shared in the ratio of taxes paid.

In the absence of data which exhibit the relative amount paid to the Comptroller by different denominations, such exhibits not coming within the provisions of a democratic people in the public records, we think we have been liberal in estimating, first, the number of property-holders as one

33

tenth; and second, when we bear in mind that a large part of this denomination are poor emigrants, we do not hazard much in saying that their aggregate property is not over that above estimated.

Now, although they amount to one seventh of the population, we will assume that only one twentieth of the children of the public schools are Roman Catholic, which will be about 2,000; and these, at the cost of their education, receive the benefit of nearly twice the amount paid by their parents to the public fund.

We would not have entered into such a comparison, especially where we are obliged to make estimates, because it may be regarded as invidious, but the frequent appeals about "taxpayers' rights" have induced us to do it in order to show that the rights of a large proportion of taxpayers who dissent from them will be invaded, by taking from them and their children a large annual sum, and appropriating it to the support of religious principles and doctrines to which they can never subscribe. Lest we should be accused of proceeding on false assumptions, we introduce the testimony of Bishop Hughes, who is better acquainted with the condition of his people than ourselves. On page 24 of his speech at Carroll Hall, he remarks:

They (the Public School Society) proposed to purchase the only schoolhouse our humble means have enabled us to erect during sixteen years.

In a speech at Washington Hall he spoke of

The poor, the degraded, and indigent children, who were deprived of education by the Public School Society.

On page 11 of the address of the Roman Catholics, we find the following language:

Although most of us are poor, still the poorest man amongst us is obliged to pay taxes from the sweat of his brow, in the rent of his room or little tenement.

We hope we shall give no offence to any; but when a great and serious charge is enforced by arguments based upon pretensions of which these extracts are the real truth, we are obliged by our duty as citizens, if we regard no higher incentive, to bring out and submit to the consideration of our fellow-citizens and the Legislature, every thing which may tend to the equitable and righteous adjustment of this dispute.

Having shown that they cannot, according to their own statements in reference to their "humble means"—which are made the ground of appeal to the action of their fellow-citizens—pay a larger proportion of the taxes than we have estimated, we deprecate any measure which will throw into a determinate sectarian channel any portion of the public fund, as it would be dangerous in precedent, hazardous in adoption, and destructive in its operations.

We also submit, in this place, another fact: the Roman Catholic Orphan Asylum has been receiving, for a number of years, an annual appropriation from the common school fund, which last year amounted to $1,525.46, in addition to the advantages of the public schools. Hence, this appropriation, and any additional sum, diverted from its public use, would be an unconstitutional and unjust taxation of all sects for the sectarian schools of one denomination. In other words, they would receive the largest appropriation, because they would have the largest number of public school pupils, while they pay only a trifling percentage of the taxes. The injustice of this need only be shown to be felt by all.

We have predicated upon pretty good premises that they pay two and a half per cent. of the taxes, while they are one seventh of the population. According to the report of the committee, there are 65,571 children of the legal age in the city; one seventh of the children would be 9,368, who would receive the appropriation. In other words, one class of the population, who pay one fortieth, or two and a half per cent. of taxes, would receive one seventh, or fourteen and two sevenths per cent. of the public fund. Stated in dollars and cents, it would be one seventh, $18,000, instead of one fortieth, or $3,000. If our citizens are willing to be taxed according to their religious belief, and receive back again in the same ratio, so let it be; but we do not wish to see the people pay taxes as citizens, receive money as citizens, and expend it as sectarians.

The operation of this principle will more or less affect every denomination according to their wealth or numbers, while the richest, who have no children at the public school, will not receive their proportion at all.

The foregoing estimates are not given as being strictly correct. But as an alteration in one item will require a corresponding change in its correlative estimates, the result will not be found to vary much from that above advanced. We have attained a proximate truth sufficiently correct for all practical purposes.

The argument that they are taxpayers because consumers, is no stronger than the other; for if we take the relative amount of property held, we may easily form an opinion of the relative amount of consumption, the property, in general, being regarded as the index to the capability and social rank of its possessors.

The Constitution of this State, section 3 article 2, provides that

The free exercise and enjoyment of religious professions and worship, without discrimination or preference, shall forever be allowed in this State to all mankind.

Here we have freedom of opinion guaranteed, and the laws of the land will extend that protection which all must receive; but there is a wide difference between protection and patronage. This is a distinction it will be well to observe, for protection is not intended to encourage a demand for patronage, which would violate the constitutional rights of others, by taking from one class of citizens the taxes which "belong to them," and appropriating them to the support of another. It would not better the law to make it applicable to all, for then all sects would receive a patronage from the Government for the education of their children, which would be but the incipient step to encroachments of a more alarming character. But while the distribution of the public fund is regulated as contemplated by the act, a direct patronage would be extended to the poorest sect, which, as an inevitable necessity, would receive the largest share of the public money, because it has the largest number of children who would become its recipients.

But what would be done, in the midst of this sectarian squabble, with those who do not belong to any religious denomination? Are they to have no consideration? Are their rights to be disregarded, and their children be obliged to attend sectarian institutions, or grow up without instruction? These are questions which merit some thought, at least when we know that a very large part of the community are not actual professors of any religious belief.   *   *   *   *   *   *

An important statement made by the committee is, that the people have lost confidence in the Public School Society, and desire a change. Now, they must be unacquainted with the views and feelings of the people of this city, or they would not have hazarded such an assertion. So far as our observation tends to convince us, and the almost unanimous voice of the intelligent, virtuous, and high-minded portion of the community may be regarded as expressive of their feelings, we fearlessly assert that the Public School Society does enjoy the confidence of the higher classes of the people; while the following items, taken from a large number of others, contained in a document of the highest authority, will show whether the confidence of the poor and laboring classes has been withdrawn from the public schools:

Of the parents of children who attend these schools, there are, blacksmiths, 493; bakers, 148; butchers, 224; carpenters, 323; cartmen, 943; cabinetmakers, 502; laborers, 1,477; masons, 416; printers, 158; shoemakers, 945; seamen, 248; tailors, 579; widows, 1,461; washerwomen, 253; weavers, 200; ship-carpenters, 176.

In drawing to a conclusion, we recur to the question with which we started: Has the Public School Society fulfilled its trust? and we answer, If facts, and evidences, and records, and the testimony of its opponents themselves, are to be regarded, we can emphatically say, *It has.*

The committee regard as an important effect of education, its tendency to make society as equal and homogeneous as possible; and they might well have added, that the institutions for education must themselves possess this feature, which is one of the most valuable of the characteristics of the public schools of our city. A family of children residing in the Third Ward may remove to the Seventeenth, and enter the same class and pursue the same lessons which they left in the other school. Thus a uniform and perfectly homogeneous system of education diffuses its light and benign influence over the whole city, and says to all, " *Venias!* Come, without money and without price!" It is impossible for us to conceive how the district system, with its local dissimilarity, and different methods of operation and instruction and books, and conflicting sentiments, can be any other than the most discordant and heterogeneous.

Mr. Barker moved that the bill be recommitted, with instructions to add to it a section providing for a reference of the subject to the electors of the city of New York at the next charter election, and after the same shall have passed the Legislature, and that it should not become a law unless a majority of the electors voting gave their votes in its favor.

Mr. Barker supported his proposition by stating that it was not usual for him to interfere in the concerns of other counties. But the members from New York, Herkimer, and Genesee (Messrs. Maclay, Loomis, and Smith) would at least deem the proposition a democratic one. The matter was local. There was as much propriety in submitting the question to the people as in the case of the Croton Water Works Bill.

Mr. Weir, of New York, continued the debate, and concluded by asking the mover to withdraw his resolution. Mr. Barker declined, saying that he was too much of a Democrat to do so.

Mr. Maclay said he trusted that the good sense of the House would reject the proposition, whatever the mover might think of it. It was true, as a general remark, that in this State, where elections occurred at brief intervals, where public measures of the least importance were discussed with great freedom, and where any man of ordinary observation might anticipate, with a reasonable degree of certainty, the course of public opinion, these appeals to the people were entirely unnecessary, except on very important and rare occasions. He did not deem this to be one of those occasions.

In saying so, he desired to be understood as yielding to none in a sincere wish, neither to go below nor beyond the wishes of his constituents, but to reflect, as truly as he was able, their sentiments and opinions. In this connection, however, it was worthy of remark, that the people of the city, neither by petition nor through the press, had asked that this matter be referred to them for a decision. He had taken some pains, during that and the preceding session, to inform himself on this subject, and he could state that he had never heard an individual express a desire for such a reference as was proposed. The public mind had settled down upon the conviction that the common school system of the city of New York was in contravention of the liberal spirit of our free institutions, and not calculated to diffuse the benefit of education as widely as was desirable and essential. The time for action had now come, and he besought his political friends in the House not to commit so great an error as to suffer this question to be mingled with important political questions which were to come up at a future election. He appealed to such as regarded the education of the masses as one of the great securities of free government, to contrast the condition of the city and county as presented in the reports from the public officers, and especially in the fact that, in New York alone, there were nearly three times as many (twenty thousand) children who attended no school whatever, as in the whole State beside. It was in the power of the Legislature to apply the correction, not by procrastination, but by a law which would bring these children within the public schools without infringing the conscientious rights or opinions of any of our fellow-citizens.

The debate was continued by Messrs. Davezac, Powell, Smith, Warren, Humphrey, Loomis, Grout, Swackhamer, Barker, R. G. Baldwin, and D. R. F. Jones. The result was the rejection of all amendments, and the reference of the bill to the Committee of the Whole.

Late on the evening of the 12th of March, the bill was taken up for discussion. Mr. McKee moved that the House adjourn, which was lost by a tie vote. Mr. Mead expressed the hope that the bill would be postponed, owing to the lateness of. the hour and the fewness of the members present. Mr. Baldwin, of New York, and others, opposed the passage of the bill, to whom Mr. Maclay replied, stating that there were two classes or divisions of persons in New York as related to this subject. One class was composed of those who were satisfied with the present school system, and the other of those who desired a change. To the former, the bill proposes to leave the schools as they were; to the latter, it gave schools regulated as common schools were in every other part of the State. It was as fair a proposition, as considerate to existing interests, as could be presented, and he trusted the House would act upon it with as little delay as practicable. Upon a division, it was found that a quorum did not vote, and the House adjourned.

On the 21st of March, the bill coming up on its third reading, Mr. E. G. Baldwin addressed the House in opposition to its passage, and concluded by moving to postpone the final question until the next day.

Mr. Maclay expressed a hope that the motion would not prevail, and moved that it be laid upon the table, which was carried. Mr. D. S. Wright then moved that the bill be recommitted to the Committee on Colleges, &c., with instructions to add a provision submitting the question to the decision of the people of the city of New York at an election. The motion was lost by a vote of twenty-one in the affirmative and fifty-six in the negative.

Mr. Lawrence moved the reference of the bill to the Committee on Colleges, with instructions to report the following amendments as an additional section :

And the said supervisors shall, in the apportionment of the moneys appropriated and raised for the support and encouragement of common or district schools in the city of New York, apportion and divide the same to and among the several wards, according and in proportion to the average number of children over 5 and under 16 years of age, who shall have actually attended the common or district schools therein the preceding year, which shall have been kept open at least nine months in the said year.

Mr. Baldwin, of New York, moved to amend the amendment, by adding thereto the words, " and that no religious doctrine or tenet shall in any manner be taught, inculcated, or practised, in any of the common or district schools in the city of New York."

Mr. Maclay resisted the amendment of Mr. Baldwin, on the ground that it was not contained in the general school law of the State, and was a stigma sought to be fastened upon the friends of the measure then under discussion, as well as upon people of the section of the State which he in part represented, and who were as worthy of being trusted without any such enactment as the inhabitants of any other portion of the State.

The amendment of Mr. Baldwin was, however, adopted by a majority of five ; but when the question recurred, and was taken on the original motion of Mr. Lawrence as thus amended, it was lost. The bill was finally passed in the Assembly, by a vote of sixty-four in the affirmative and sixteen in the negative.

After the Speaker had declared the bill passed, a suggestion was made, that it required a vote of two thirds of all the members on altering the powers of the Corporation of New York, and an appeal was taken from the decision of the chair.

Mr. Maclay had anticipated this objection, and had referred the chairman of the Committee on Two Thirds Bills to the fol-

lowing precedents, to show that acts in relation to Supervisors
had been modified by subsequent general acts: The People
ex rel. Phœnix *vs.* The Supervisors of the City and County of
New York, 1 Hill's· Reports, 362–368 ; The People *ex rel.* Up-
ham *vs.* Whiteside, 22 Wendell's Reports, 14, 15 ; Warner and
Ray *vs.* Beers, 22 Wendell's Reports, 103–189 (in Error), with
opinion of Bradish in this case.   Mr. Humphrey, of Tompkins
county, chairman of the Committee on Two Thirds Bills, rose in
his place, and stated that it was the opinion of the committee,
and his own, that the bill before the House was a majority bill.
The appeal was then withdrawn, and the bill sent to the Senate,
and in that body referred to the Committee on Colleges, &c.,
consisting of Mr. H. K. Foster, of Oneida, John Hunter, of
Westchester, and Erastus Root, of Delaware.

The vote in the House can scarcely be regarded as the
strength of the opposition to the measure.   That opposition was
reserved for the Senate.   In that body, all of the senators from
what then constituted the First Senate District, composed of
New York, Richmond, and Kings counties, Messrs. Furman,
Franklin, Varian, and Scott, were opposed to any change in the
school system of New York.   Mr. Foster, the chairman of the
Senate committee, called upon Mr. Maclay, and stated that,
while he himself approved of the bill, it was not usual to attempt to carry a local bill through the Senate in opposition to
the wishes of the representatives from the district to be affected
by it.   In this dilemma, Mr. Maclay stated that the defeat of the
bill at the present time, as was well known, would enure to the
benefit of their political opponents, and that, aside altogether
from the merits of the question, it was not uncharitable to suppose that this consideration had its weight with Messrs. Furman
and Franklin.   The case was different with Messrs. Scott and
Varian, the Democratic senators.   If they could show any objection to the bill on the score of public good, it was entitled to be
considered and received.   For this purpose, Mr. Maclay proposed that a meeting should be called at the room of Senator
Hunter, and that he and Mr. Foster, Messrs. Varian and Scott,
and himself, should be present, when the whole matter could be
discussed more freely and dispassionately than in the Senate.
The meeting was accordingly held, all the parties just named
being present.   Mr. Maclay proposed that the bill should be

read section by section, and that any objection to any portion of it should be made; and, were none made, the sections not objected to should be deemed to be approved. This was accordingly the course adopted. Mr. Varian objected to the whole bill, and was opposed to any change whatever in the then existing laws. Mr. Scott stated that he was fearful that, if the election for school officers and trustees took place at the same time as the other elections in the city of New York, that the streets of New York would be drenched in blood, and he therefore proposed that, if the bill was to be pressed to a vote in the Senate, a provision should be added to it by which the officers to govern the schools should be elected in the month of June in each year. In reply, Mr. Maclay expressed his own preference for a separate election of school officers, but that he had omitted it in the bill, under an apprehension precisely the reverse of those entertained by Judge Scott. So far from believing that any such uncommon interest or excitement would attend the election of these officers, he feared that the people, as a general thing, would neglect the duty of voting, and that, on this account, he had provided the election should take place at the same time as that for other officers. He would, however, cheerfully yield his opinion on this point. He accordingly drew a section providing for the election of school officers in the month of June following, and this was approved by Mr. Foster, and subsequently added to the bill, which was passed April 9th, and received the signature of the Governor. It is as follows:

AN ACT

To Extend to the City and County of New York the Provisions of the General Act in Relation to Common Schools.

The people of the State of New York, represented in Senate and Assembly, do enact as follows:

SEC. 1. There shall be elected in each of the wards of the city and county of New York, two commissioners, two inspectors, and five trustees of common schools, who shall be elected by ballot, at a special election to be held on the first Monday of June in each year, by the persons qualified to vote for charter officers in the said wards, and to be conducted in the same manner, by the same inspectors, at the same ward districts, and subject to the same laws, rules, and regulations as now govern the charter elections in said city.

The commissioners of common schools so elected shall constitute a Board of Education for the city of New York, a majority of whom shall constitute a quorum; they shall elect one of their number president of said board, who shall preside at the meetings thereof, which shall be held at least as often as once in three months; and they may appoint a clerk, whose compensation shall be fixed and paid by the supervisors of said city and county.

The commissioners so elected in each ward shall be the commissioners of schools thereof, with the like powers and duties of commissioners of common schools in the several towns in this State, except as hereinafter provided.

The said inspectors of common schools so elected in the several wards shall have the like powers and be subject to the same duties with the inspectors of common schools of the several towns of this State, except as hereinafter provided.

The trustees of common schools so elected in their respective wards shall be the trustees of the school districts which may be formed and organized therein, with the like powers and duties as the trustees of school districts in the several towns in this State, except as hereinafter provided.

SEC. 2. All such provisions of the third, fourth, fifth, and sixth articles of Title Two, chapter fifteen, part first, of the Revised Statutes, and of the several acts amending and in addition to, and relating to the same, not inconsistent with the provisions in this act contained, shall be, and the same are hereby, declared applicable to the city and county of New York.

SEC. 3. For all the purposes of this act, each of the several wards into which the said city and county of New York now is, or may be hereafter, divided, shall be considered as a separate town, and liable to all the duties imposed; and entitled to all the powers, privileges, immunities, and advantages granted by the said third, fourth, fifth, and sixth articles of Title Two, chapter fifteen, part first, of the Revised Statutes, to the several towns in this State, so far as the same are consistent with this act.

SEC. 4. The forty-fourth section of the act entitled "An Act to Amend the Second Title of the Fifteenth Chapter of the First Part of the Revised Statutes, Relating to Common Schools," passed May 26, 1841, is hereby repealed; and all the other sections of the said act not inconsistent with the provisions of this act, are hereby declared applicable to the city and county of New York.

SEC. 5. No compensation shall be allowed to the commissioners, inspectors, or trustees of common schools for any services performed by them; but the commissioners and inspectors shall receive their actual and reasonable expenses while attending to the duties of their office, to be audited and allowed by the supervisors of said city and county.

SEC. 6. The said commissioners of common schools of each ward are hereby authorized to appoint a club, whose compensation shall be settled and paid by the Board of Supervisors.

SEC. 7. Whenever the trustees elected in any ward shall certify in writing to the commissioners and inspectors of common schools thereof, that it is necessary to organize one or more schools in said ward, in addition to the schools mentioned in the thirteenth section of this act, it shall be the duty of said commissioners and inspectors to meet together and examine into the facts and circumstances of the case; and if they shall be satisfied of such necessity, they shall certify the same under their hands, to the said Board of Education, and shall then proceed to organize one or more school districts therein, and shall procure a school-house, and all things necessary to organize a school in such district, the expense of which shall be levied and raised pursuant to the provisions of section nine of this act; and the title to all lands purchased by virtue of this act, with the buildings thereon, shall be vested in the city and county of New York.

SEC. 8. Whenever the clerk of the city and county of New York shall receive notice from the Superintendent of Common Schools of the amount of moneys apportioned to the city and county of New York, for the support and encouragement of common schools therein, he shall immediately lay the same before the supervisors of the city and county aforesaid.

SEC. 9. The said supervisors shall annually raise and collect by tax, upon the inhabitants of said city and county, a sum of money equal to the sum specified in such notice, at the same time and in the same manner as the contingent charges of the said city and county are levied and collected; also, a sum of money equal to one twentieth of one per cent. of the value of real and personal property in the said city, liable to be assessed therein, to be applied exclusively to the purposes of common schools in said city; and such farther sum as may be necessary for the support and benefit of common schools in said city and county, to be raised, levied, and collected in like manner, and which shall be in lieu of all taxes and assessments, to the support of common schools for said city and county.

SEC. 10. The said supervisors shall, on or before the first day of May in every year, direct that a sum of money equal to the amount last received by the chamberlain of said city and county, from the common school fund, be deposited by him, together with the sum so received from the school fund, in one of the incorporated banks of the said city and county (each bank to be designated by the said supervisors), to the credit of the commissioners of common schools in each of the said several wards, in the proportion to which they shall respectively be entitled, and subject only to the drafts of the said commissioners respectively; who shall pay the amount apportioned to the several schools enumerated in the thirteenth section of this act, to the treasurer of the societies or schools entitled thereto, or to some person duly authorized by the trustees of such societies or schools to receive the same.

SEC. 11. So much of the seventh article of Title Second, chapter fifteen, part first, of the Revised Statutes, and the several acts amending and in addition to, and relating to the said article, as is specially applicable to the city and county of New York, and all other acts, and all provisions therein providing for, or directing, or concerning the disbursing or appropriation of the funds created for or applicable to common school education in the city and county of New York, and all and every provision for raising any fund, or for the imposition of any tax therefor, so far as the same are inconsistent with this act, are hereby repealed.

SEC. 12. All children between the ages of four and sixteen, residing in said city and county, shall be entitled to attend any of the common schools therein; and the parents, guardians, or other persons having the custody of care of such children shall not be liable to any tax, assessment, or imposition for the tuition of any such children, other than is hereinbefore provided.

SEC. 13. The schools of the Public School Society, the New York Orphan Asylum School, the Roman Catholic Orphan Asylum School, the schools of the two Half-Orphan Asylums, the school of the Mechanics' School Society, the Harlem School, the Yorkville Public School, the Manhattanville Free School, the Hamilton Free School, the Institution for the Blind, the school connected with the Almshouse of the said city, and the school of the association for the benefit of Colored Orphans, shall be subject to the general jurisdiction of the said commissioners of the respective wards in which any of the said schools now are, or hereafter may be, located, subject to the direction of the Board of Education, but under the immediate government and management of their respective trustees, managers, and directors, in the same manner and to the same extent as herein provided in respect to the district schools herein first before mentioned in said city and county; and, so far as relates to the distribution of the common school moneys, each of the said schools shall be district schools of the said city.

SEC. 14. No school above mentioned, or which shall be organized under this act, in which any religious sectarian doctrine or tenet shall be taught, inculcated, or practised, shall receive any portion of the school moneys to be distributed by this act, as hereinafter provided; and it shall be the duty of the trustees, inspectors, and commissioners of schools in each ward, and of the deputy Superintendent of Schools, from time to time, and as frequently as need be, to examine and ascertain and report to the said Board of Education whether any religious sectarian doctrine or tenet shall have been taught, inculcated, or practised in any of the schools in their respective wards; and it shall be the duty of the commissioners of schools in the several wards to transmit to the Board of Education all reports made to them by the trustees and inspectors of their respective wards. The Board of Education, and any member thereof, may at any time visit and examine any school subject to the provisions of this act, and individual commissioners shall report to the board the result of their examinations.

SEC. 15. It shall be the duty of the said Board of Education to apply for the use of the several districts such moneys as shall be raised to erect, purchase, or lease school-houses, or to procure the sites therefor; and also to apportion among the several schools and districts provided for by this act, the school money to be paid over to the commissioners of schools in each ward, by virtue of the tenth section of this act, and shall file with the chamberlain of said city and county, on or before the fifteenth day of April in each year, a copy of such apportionment, and stating the amount thereof to be paid to the commissioners of each ward; which apportionment shall be made among the said several schools and districts according to the average number of children over four and under sixteen years of age, who shall have actually attended such school the preceding year. But no such school shall be entitled to a portion of such moneys that has not been kept open at least nine months in the year, or in which any religious sectarian doctrine or tenet shall have been taught, inculcated, or practised, or which shall refuse to permit the visits and examinations provided for by this act.

SEC. 16. The commissioners of schools of the respective wards, when they have received from the chamberlain of said city and county the money apportioned to the several schools and districts in their several wards, shall apply the same to the use of the schools and districts in their several wards, according to the apportionment thereof so made by the said Board of Education.

SEC. 17. The said commissioners of each ward shall, within fifteen days after their election, execute and deliver to the supervisors aforesaid a bond, with such sureties as said supervisors shall approve, in the penalty of double the amount of public money appropriated to the use of the common schools of their respective wards, conditional for the faithful performance of the duties of their office, and the proper application of all moneys coming in their hands for common school purposes; such bond shall be filed by the said supervisors in the office of the County Clerk.

SEC. 18. This act shall take effect immediately.

CHAPTER XIV.

HISTORY FROM 1840 TO 1853.

Position of the Society—Views of the Board of Trustees—Policy of the Board—Trustees' Hall Completed—Annual Exhibit—Powers of the Society under the Law of 1842—Erection of New Buildings—Amendments to the Law—High School—School for Italians—Change of Official Year—Public Schools Nos. 17 and 18—Josiah Holbrook—Natural History—Text-Books—Uniformity of System—Committee on Condition of the Schools—Corporal Punishment—Female Association—Death of Robert C. Cornell, President of the Society—Proceedings of the Society—Public School No. 18—Board of Education and Normal Schools—Controversy of the Board of Education with the Society, relative to New Buildings—Proceedings of both Boards—Speeches of Hiram Ketchum, John L. Mason, and Joseph S. Bosworth, Esqs.—Law of March 4, 1848—Death of Lindley Murray, President of the Society—Sale of Property in Oak Street—Deficiency—Application to the Board of Education—Transfer of Property Proposed—Amendments to the School Law—Union of the Board of Education and the Society Proposed—Loan—Sale of Property in Twenty-Fifth Street—Sale of Public School No. 10.

THE importance of the controversy relative to the school fund, and the uncertainty which hung over the result, served as an obstacle to any marked change in the system, while the demand upon its resources had already reached a point at which the Society found itself encumbered with about $103,000 of indebtedness. The long-cherished plans of the trustees were therefore compelled to await the issue of the contest before any further considerable outlay could be made for the expansion and elevation of the system.

The decision was, however, obtained in 1842, by the passage of the act creating the Board of Education, and the alternative, which had been impending so long, had fallen upon the Society. It was, to wait patiently until the structure they had reared should become remodelled and made to harmonize with the new scheme, or to continue under the restrictions it imposed, as long as might be, and then surrender its trust to the city. The light in which the new law was regarded may be seen from the following observations contained in the annual report for 1842 :

After a successful career of thirty-seven years, during which it has been their lot, under the blessing of Divine Providence, to be the humble instruments of conveying the benefits of moral and literary instruction to many, very many thousands of the children of their fellow-citizens, both native-born and of foreign origin, it has pleased the Legislature of our State to enact a statute which, the trustees fear, will result in subjecting their noble institution to the blighting influence of party strife and sectarian animosity.

The glory of their system—its uniformity, its equality of privilege and action, its freedom from all that could justly offend, its peculiar adaptation to a floating population embracing an immense operative mass, unable, from their circumstances, to devote many years to educational pursuits—is dimmed, they fear, forever.

The boast of our city, that in her public schools the children of the rich and the poor, of the American and the foreigner, all mingled as a band of brothers, imbibing feelings and acquiring sentiments of an equality of rights and privileges, both as citizens of this great republic and children of our common Father, in whose sight all the people of the earth are as one, is overthrown.

How far and how long the board may be able to continue their schools under the intricate provisions of the " act," they are, at this time, unable to ascertain. It may be sufficient to say, that the simple, comprehensive, and compact system matured through so many years of assiduous examination and careful adaptation to its object, is about to be impaired, if not destroyed, by the introduction of another of complex character—a system which, if not impracticable, is, in their judgment, ill-suited to a city population.

Some of the fears entertained by the trustees were not long after realized, by the changes gradually introduced, and the impediments which arose in the way of their success. The history of the " district system " in New York City has yet to be written, and its progress and development will exhibit the operation of one of the grandest educational experiments ever made.

The trustees of the Public School Society, although prevented, by a prudent caution, from entering upon any plans for increasing the number of their schools, or advancing the grade of studies, improved the time by a jealous and careful scrutiny of the schools, and the endeavor to remove every thing that could impair their usefulness, or diminish the confidence of the community in the system. It was their constant aim to preserve, in all its integrity, a scheme of popular education rendered eminently honorable by the names of distinguished men who had been interested in it from its inception, and to hand it down to their successors in a form massive and enduring, and as faultless as practical wisdom, enlightened philanthropy, and liberal endowment could make it.

During the year 1840, the building erected for the use of the Society as a Trustees' Hall was completed, and furnished in a plain but appropriate style. Apartments were assigned for the offices, depository, and two primary schools. A portion of the building was also adapted for the use of a clerk, who had charge of the house, and assisted in the general business of the Society.

In 1842, Samuel F. Mott resigned his office as treasurer, and, at a meeting of the Board held July 14th, Anthony P. Halsey, the secretary, was elected to fill the vacancy; and, at the same meeting, Joseph B. Collins was chosen to fill the post vacated by Mr. Halsey.

The average number of pupils in the schools, as appears by the annual exhibit, was 24,671, of which 1,329 were colored children.

The question of power soon arose as to the right of the Society to erect new buildings under the law of 1842, and to appropriate moneys for certain purposes which were specially provided for under the supervision of the Board of Education. The system had been brought to such uniformity and harmony, that a scholar could leave one school and go into a class in another, and there continue the same lessons, in the same books, as though he had only changed the teacher; but the new law entrusted the schools to the independent government of the local boards of school officers of the wards. The trustees were anxious to prevent this system from becoming established, and authorized the Executive Committee to secure, if possible, the repeal of the law, or, at least, such declaratory amendments as should continue the power of the Society to erect buildings, and to do all the other acts contemplated by its charter. The committee pressed the matter upon the attention of the Legislature, and that body, at its next session, adopted such amendments as seemed to meet the wants of the Society.

One of the measures which had long been contemplated by the trustees, was the establishment of a High School, or Normal School, of elevated character, for the preparation of teachers; and, during the year 1843, the proposition was renewed, and received the attention of the board.

In the early part of the same year, a proposition was made

for the establishment of schools for Italians, to be conducted on principles similar to those of the schools for Germans. The matter was referred to the Primary School Committee, who submitted to the Executive Committee, on July 6th of that year, the following report:

The Primary School Committee, to whom was referred the subject of opening a school to educate exclusively Italian children of this city, RESPECTFULLY REPORT:

1. The desired object can be better attained by the attendance of the Italian children at our primary schools; for experience proves that a foreign language can be more readily acquired by a person in attending a school where his own language is unknown, "necessity" being the most speedy and thorough teacher.

2. In educating children in our schools, it is intended to give them habits and feelings adapted to our institutions and Government; and when a foreigner adopts our country as his home, it is expected that he should subscribe to our forms, and particularly to our system of education, which is intimately and inseparably connected with our forms of government.

3. When foreigners are in the habit of congregating together, they retain their peculiar national customs, prejudices, and feelings; they therefore remain much longer unsettled, and are not as good members of society as they would otherwise be. This is apparent to all who are acquainted with our German school. Children attending that school, as is well known, retain their national costume, manners, and feelings; while those German children who mingle promiscuously in other schools, lose all trace of nationality.

4. Children, like adults, are clannish. It is difficult to conduct a school composed of foreigners, with a foreign teacher, without exciting continual prejudices between it and our other schools.

Finally, information has been obtained which induces the committee to believe that the more intelligent class of Italians do not desire such a school, and that, like most of the better class of Germans, they would prefer that those of their countrymen who come here with good intentions should be Americanized as speedily as possible. This result, in the opinion of this committee, will be most easily and promptly attained by the attendance of their children at our primary schools.

The report was accepted and adopted, and the committee discharged from the further consideration of the subject.

Inconvenience had arisen from the fact that the annual meetings of the Society, and the close of its fiscal year, occurred during the month of May, while those of the Board of Education corresponded with the other public departments of the city, and dated from the 1st of January. Application having been made

34

to the Legislature, the time was changed by a law passed on the 23d of March, 1844. The time of the stated meetings of the trustees was also specified to be the first Fridays of January, April, July, and October.

During the year 1843, Public School No. 17, in Thirteenth street, near the Seventh avenue, was built upon the ground purchased some time previously ; and, in 1844, No. 18 was established by the hiring of premises for the two upper departments.

A new and very attractive feature was introduced into the schools in the summer of this year. Mr. JOSIAH HOLBROOK, who was zealously devoted to the introduction of scientific lessons, had, for several years, resided the greater part of his time in the city, laboring to promote a taste for the natural sciences among the children of the various schools and institutions. After having given undoubted proofs of the success of his method of teaching and illustration, the subject was formally recognized by the board, and one hour a week was appropriated to the preparation of maps, drawings, specimens of minerals, geometrical solids, diagrams, &c., for exchange with the pupils of schools in other cities and towns, thus stimulating a system of artistic and scientific exchange, which called out the sympathies and the enthusiasm of the pupils. The annual report for 1845 makes the following record of the new studies thus introduced :

At the suggestion of Mr. J. HOLBROOK, to whose untiring exertions the cause of education is largely indebted, the board has authorized the school sections to permit a limited portion of time to be occupied by the pupils in preparing specimens of writing, mapping, and drawing, with a view to the exchange of such specimens for those of other schools in this and the other States. It was thought that such an interchange of the results of mental and artistical labor on the part of the children would excite a healthful rivalry, and produce a more rapid and full development of their faculties. Through the above-named gentleman, numerous specimens of the kind referred to were forwarded to the "Department of Common Schools," in the office of the Secretary of State at Albany ; and, in acknowledging the receipt, Mr. Randall, the General Deputy Secretary, has paid a high but well-merited compliment to the pupils of the public schools. In his letter to Mr. Holbrook, this enlightened, practical, and most indefatigable officer says :

The young gentlemen and ladies who have furnished these neat and beautiful specimens are entitled to the approbation not only of the department, but of every enlightened friend of education. They will be carefully preserved for the examination and inspection of the members of the Legislature, and others upon whom the interests of elementary instruction are dependent for encouragement and support. And I beg to assure the young ladies and gentlemen engaged in these interesting and improving pursuits, that their progress and attainments will be watched with the utmost anxiety and solicitude by this department, and by those having in charge the numerous public schools throughout the State; that the specimens they have already furnished, and may hereafter furnish, will be laid before the general convention of superintendents at Syracuse, in April next, and compared with similar specimens from other parts of the State; and that in this, as in every other branch of intellectual science, they must be careful above all things to bear in mind that, whatever attainments they may make are to be regarded only as a successive series of means for the improvement of their mental and moral being, their advancement in sound knowledge, and their progress in wisdom and goodness.

In consequence of the condition of the treasury of the Society, and a question as to how far the full development of this system would involve the board in expenditure, were a grand central school-exchange to be established, the plan of Mr. Holbrook was encouraged by the grant of certain facilities, and a room for his collections of specimens, but no considerable expense was incurred. Mr. Holbrook continued his labors with great success, so far as his means enabled him, and visited other cities and localities. He continued his explorations and collections from time to time until the year 1851, when his useful and honorable career was closed by a fatal accident, while he was alone upon a geological tour. On a visit to Virginia, near Lynchburg, he went out in the pursuit of his favorite objects, and was not again seen until his body was found at the river's side, at the foot of the cliff. It was supposed that he went too near the edge of the precipice, and fell from the brink upon the rocks beneath. His death was much lamented by thousands who had been stimulated to intellectual activity by his lessons and his plans.

The new system of ward schools having been in operation about two years and a half, some of its defects had become apparent, and, among others, the want of uniformity in the text-books, instruction, and classification. The report of January, 1845, contains the following remarks upon this dissimilarity:

Convinced, by every year's experience, of the great importance to the rising generation in the humble walks of life, of uniformity in the books used in the schools, and in the course of instruction adopted in them, it is a matter of regret to the board that a similar uniformity does not prevail in all other schools for that class of our city. Limited, by their circumstances, to a comparatively short period for the acquisition of school learning, and being eminently migratory in their character, the trustees have ever found great economy in time and mental labor by maintaining a system which furnished the same books and the same method of instruction throughout their widely-spread establishment. With the industrious poor man, time is emphatically money; with his children, so far as education is concerned, it is more than money. Not only the individual welfare of the future citizen calls loudly for the profitable occupation of the brief period allotted to education, but it is vitally essential to the best interests of our common country.

At a special meeting of the board, held September 12, 1843, a committee of " one from each section, chosen by the section," was appointed, to examine and report upon the condition of the schools. This committee was continued from year to year, and presented reports and recommendations upon the various topics which were suggested by their investigations. In the early part of 1845, they submitted reports, one of which related to corporal punishment in the schools. The following resolution was adopted on the recommendation of the committee :

Hereafter no corporal punishment, by blows or otherwise, shall be inflicted on any pupil or pupils in presence of the school, or during school hours, but after the school is dismissed, and then in the presence of the assistant or monitors, or both, with such number of large scholars as may be necessary for witnesses in case of complaint of any aggrieved party ; and in no case shall such punishment be inflicted until after proper admonition, parental in its character, be given, with a view of convincing the delinquents of the impropriety of their conduct, and the necessity of reformation ; and no stripes or blows to be applied to the head, or any part of the body other than the back, near the shoulders.

A proposition to give a pecuniary reward to the teacher who should successfully conduct his or her school without corporal punishment, was rejected ; but a resolution granting a certificate for the disuse of the rod twelve months, was adopted.

In March, 1845, the " FEMALE ASSOCIATION " communicated to the board that they were prepared to surrender the rooms in No. 5 which they had occupied for their school, and to discontinue it. The section of No. 5, and the Property Committee, were authorized to attend to the transfer, and the principal sum devised by Col. Henry Rutgers, on which the Society had paid $45 annual interest, became the property of the Society.

During the month of May, the Society was again bereaved of its presiding officer, ROBERT C. CORNELL being called to rest from his earthly labors. Appropriate resolutions were passed by the board, and the following "minute" was entered upon the record:

It becomes the painful duty of the board to record oh their minutes a notice of their late president, ROBERT C. CORNELL.

On Tuesday, May 20, 1845, Mr. Cornell went to his office apparently in good health, resumed his official duties with his accustomed assiduity, and was constantly occupied in the discharge of those duties until half-past 2 P. M., when he became suddenly indisposed, was assisted to a carriage, and conveyed to his residence, where, in the bosom of his family, he departed this life at about half-past 7 o'clock of the same day. Thus it may be said of him, with almost literal accuracy, that, like the grass, he passed away. " In the morning they are like grass which groweth up. In the morning it flourisheth, and groweth up; in the evening it is cut down, and withereth."

He was educated in this city to mercantile pursuits, and, by a diligent attention to them for a number of years, acquired what he deemed a competent fortune, and was influenced to retire from business, not for the purpose of self-indulgence, or to wear out a life then in its prime in indolence, under the name of repose, but in order to devote his time, his talents, and his laborious exertions to the cause of benevolence.

In this laudable occupation he had been almost entirely engaged for a number of years, when, at the earnest solicitation of this board, he became its presiding officer.

It is not our purpose to record the eulogy of his character as a citizen or a philanthropist; other institutions, and the community in which he lived, and which he adorned, will not fail, in grateful remembrance of his services, to perform this service. But the board unanimously and cheerfully bear testimony that, in their intercourse with their late president, they have found him, in personal disposition and bearing, amiable, courteous, obliging, and gentlemanly; as a " man of business," clear-headed, sagacious, and intelligent, possessing habits of exact punctuality, accuracy, industry, and never-tiring perseverance. Every piece of business in which he engaged seemed to claim his undivided attention until it was acomplished; and he never left any business for to-morrow which could be done to-day; and, above all, he was a man of truth and integrity, and perfectly fearless in the discharge of his duties.

At a meeting of the board in May, 1844, Mr. John R. Hurd called attention to the fact that an important location for a school remained unoccupied, in the vicinity of Forty-second street and the Sixth avenue. Messrs. Peter Cooper, John R. Hurd, and William Dusenberry were appointed a committee to select a location. Messrs. J. S. Howe, H. S. Benedict, and William Dusenberry were named as a " section " to take charge of the school when it should be opened. In May, 1845, the Committee on Locations reported in favor of four lots in Forty-seventh street, between the Eighth and Ninth avenues, which were directed to be purchased, at the price of $1,900. The erection of a building was referred to the Executive Committee. The house was built, and known as No. 18.

At the annual meeting of the Society, January 12, 1846, the office of president, which had been filled by George T. Trimble *pro tempore*, was assigned to LINDLEY MURRAY, who discharged the duties of presiding officer only two years.

In April, a communication was received from the Board of Education, in which it was stated that certain teachers of the Fourteenth Ward schools were refused admission to the Normal Schools of the Society, although they were entitled to the privilege by the recent amendments to the school law. Messrs. A. P. Halsey, John T. Adams, John R. Hurd, James N. Cobb, Peter Cooper, and Joseph B. Collins, were appointed a committee to confer with the representatives of the Board of Education. The following resolution was referred to the same committee:

Whereas, By the act of the Legislature of New York passed the 18th day of April, 1843, power is granted to the New York Public School Society to establish Normal Schools; and,

Whereas, By the act of said Legislature, passed the 7th day of May, 1844, said power is distinctly recognized, and said Normal Schools are included among the number entitled to draw money from the public treasury for their support, on condition of such schools affording instructions to all such pupils as may be intended for teachers in any schools established under the acts aforesaid; therefore,

Resolved, That it is expedient and proper for this board to proceed forthwith to establish such Normal School or schools as may be suited to the purposes named in said "act" of May 7, 1844, to be kept open five days in each week, and to be placed under such supervision, and to be conducted under such rules and regulations, as this board may from time to time direct.

The Normal Schools were freely opened to the teachers of the ward schools, and so continued until the adoption of the system by the Board of Education, when they were much extended and improved.

A controversy arose, in the month of February of this year, between the Society and the Board of Education, as to the power of the Society to erect new buildings and open new schools, under the provisions of the amended law of 1844. The question originated in the Board of Education, by a preamble and resolution, offered on the 11th of February, by Mr. Henry Nicoll, commissioner of the First Ward, as follows :

Whereas, It is expedient for this board to have more particular information in relation to several matters than is contained in the report of the Public School Society, made on the 11th instant ; be it therefore

Resolved, That the trustees of the Public School Society be, and they are hereby, requested to report to this board the number of new school-houses erected by the said Society since the 7th day of May, 1844, as well as those now in the course of erection, with all grounds purchased for school purposes, with the character, location, and cost of the same ; and that they also report to this board whether the title to any of the said school-houses or grounds has been vested in the Mayor, Aldermen, and Commonalty of the city of New York.

Mr. Thomas Addis Emmet, one of the commissioners for the Twelfth Ward, offered the following resolution, which was likewise adopted :

Resolved, That the Public School Society be also requested to furnish this board with the date of organization and location of schools under their care, established since the 31st of January, 1845.

On the 8th of April, the reply of the Society was transmitted to the board by Joseph B. Collins, the secretary, which was laid on the table for further consideration ; and, on June 10th, the subject being renewed, it was referred to a special committee, consisting of Messrs. Robert F. Winslow, of the Eleventh Ward, John M. Seaman, of the Seventeenth Ward, and John L. Mason, of the Fifteenth Ward. On the 20th of January, 1847, the committee submitted their report adverse to the right of the Public School Society to " establish any new school " under the amended law of May 7, 1844. The facts and reasonings of the report came up subsequently on the adoption of the report, and were presented by able counsel for both parties, whose arguments are given below. The recommendations of the committee were the following :

1. *Resolved*, That, in the opinion of the Board of Education, the Public School Society has no right, since the passage of the act entitled " An Act more Effectually to Provide for Common School Education in the City and County of New York," passed May 7, 1844, to establish any new school ; and that, if any such schools have been or may be established, they are not entitled to participate in the apportionment of the school moneys.

2. *Resolved,* That the Public School Society be required to specify, in their annual returns of scholars to be made to this board, for the apportionment of the school moneys, the number of scholars who have attended and are connected with any schools established by them since May 7, 1844.

3. *Resolved,* That the said trustees be required, in their annual reports of moneys received and disbursed by them for the support of their schools, to specify how much has been expended for the support of any schools established by them since May 7, 1844, including in such expenses not only the salaries of their teachers, but also the prices, if any, paid for the rent of buildings or lots, or in the purchase of lots and erection of buildings, or in the payment of interest on moneys expended for that purpose.

The report was laid on the table, and ordered to be printed; and, on the 10th of March, the president laid before the Board of Education a communication from the president of the Public School Society, asking an opportunity to be heard before the board before any action should be had on the report of the Special Committee. On the reading of this communication, Mr. Nicoll offered a resolution ordering a special meeting of the board on the following Wednesday, March 17, for the purpose of hearing the Public School Society by their committee. The board accordingly met, and HIRAM KETCHUM, Esq., on behalf of the Society, made the following remarks:

MR. PRESIDENT AND GENTLEMEN OF THE BOARD OF EDUCATION: By a report of a committee of your board, dated January 20, 1847, the following resolution is recommended to your adoption:

Resolved, That, in the opinion of the Board of Education, the Public School Society has no right, since the passage of the act entitled " An Act more Effectually to Provide for Common School Education in the City and County of New York," passed May 7, 1844, to establish any new school; and that, if any such schools have been or may be established, they are not entitled to a participation in the apportionment of the school moneys.

It is quite natural that the Public School Society should feel a deep interest in the deliberations and final action of your board upon this resolution. The Society has, therefore, respectfully requested your board to allow an expression of their views, which request has been kindly and promptly granted; and therefore, on behalf of the Society, I now appear to solicit your attention for a few moments.

The Board of Education is entrusted with the school fund, for distribution in the mode pointed out by law. The Public School Society is entitled to a portion of this fund, and the great practical question is, By what rule shall the amount be ascertained which the Society is entitled to receive? Shall the Society draw from this fund according to the number of children over four and under sixteen years of age, who shall have actually attended the schools of the Society the preceding year without charge? or shall it draw only for the children of the above description taught in such of those schools as were established on or before the 7th day of May, 1844—the date of the act—and were in existence at that time ? Confessedly there have been schools opened and established by the Society since the passage of the act, in which children have been gratuitously educated. Are these schools entitled to a participation in the fund ?

The answer to these questions must be looked for in the law itself. That law contains the declaration of trust under which the Board of Education receives the money. The law provides the rule of duty as well for this board as for the Public School Society.

To the law, then, let us look. The 12th section of the act of 1844 says : "It shall be the duty of the Board of Education to apportion all the school moneys, except so much as shall have been raised for the purpose of establishing and organizing new schools, to each of the several schools provided for by this act and the acts mentioned in the preceding section, according to the number of children over four and under sixteen years of age, who shall have actually attended such school without charge the preceding year."

Among the schools provided for by the act are those of the Public School Society. The exception quoted, of so much money "as shall have been raised for the establishing and organizing new schools," refers to the money raised under the act for the special purpose of building schoolhouses, which is a distinct fund from the school fund proper. The 12th section further provides for any school that shall have been organized since the last annual apportionment. The provision is for *any* school. Then comes the exception : "But no school shall be entitled to the portion of the school moneys in which the doctrine or tenets of any Christian sect shall be taught," &c.

Now, the Legislature have prescribed who shall not receive from the school fund ; and, according to every sound rule of construction, it is not competent for any persons acting under the law to add to the negative exception. The general words of the law embrace all children taught in the schools within the prescribed ages. The exception excludes children taught in schools where sectarian doctrines are inculcated. None others can be excluded. Therefore, children educated in the schools opened since the passage of the act of May, 1844, cannot be excluded.

But how shall the Board of Education be informed of the number of scholars taught in the schools of the Public School Society ? The 36th section of the act provides for the transmission of this information. "The trustees shall, on or before the 15th day of February in every year, make and transmit a report in writing to the Board of Education." What information shall it contain ? The same section furnishes the answer.

1. The whole number of schools within the jurisdiction of the Society—specially designating the schools for colored children.

This certainly means, within the jurisdiction at the time of the report, and not at the date of the passage of the act.

2. The length of time each school shall have been kept open.

3. The whole number of scholars over four and under sixteen years of

age, which shall have been taught free of expense to such scholars in their schools during the year preceding the 1st day of February.

4. The average number that has actually attended their schools.

5. The amount of moneys received during the last year from the commissioners of school money, or from the chamberlain of the city, and the purposes for and the manner in which the same shall have been expended.

6. A particular account of the state of the schools, and of the property and affairs of each school under the care of the Society.

Now, it will be seen that the trustees of each ward, and the trustees of the Public School Society, are alike bound to report the number of schools within their jurisdiction, and the condition of the schools at the time of making their reports.

Then, if the schools of the Public School Society, opened and established since the passage of the act of 1844, are within the jurisdiction of the Society, it would seem to follow, conclusively, that these schools are entitled to participate in the school moneys. If they are not within such jurisdiction, it follows not only that they are not entitled to participate, but that the trustees of the Society, in reporting the new schools and claiming a portion of the school fund, have subjected themselves to a penalty under section 37.

The next inquiry is, whether the schools established by the Public School Society since the 7th of May, 1844, are within the jurisdiction of the Society. If they are not, the Society has no legal title to them or control over them. Those who deny this jurisdiction, deny it on the ground that the Society has no right to establish such schools. Let us look at the question of right.

What is now the Public School Society, was, originally, incorporated as " The Society for Establishing a Free School in the City of New York, for the education of such poor children as do not belong to, or are not provided for by, any religious society." By the 2d section of this act, passed April 9, 1805, the trustees of the corporation were authorized to establish two or more free schools in the city of New York, whenever the Society might judge it expedient. Here, then, we have a purely benevolent Society organized and incorporated. Here is the Society, disconnected from any grant of money, from the school fund, or any other public fund, operating actively with the means supplied by its members and private contributions.

Thus existing, it had a right by law—the law of its creation—to build as many school-houses and open as many schools as it pleased. Now, with great respect, I inquire, When was this original corporate right ever taken from the Society ? While I am on this original act, allow me to make another suggestion. The Public School Society is called, in the report of the committee, " a close corporation." The 6th section of the original act enacts that the Mayor, Recorder, Aldermen, and Assistants of the city of New York shall and may be *ex-officio* members of said corporation, and that any person who shall subscribe and contribute to the benefit of the said Society the sum of eight dollars, shall, by virtue of such contribution, be a member of the said corporation. Is that a close corporation? Show me one more open.

By an "Act for the Encouragement of Free Schools in the City of New York," passed July 27, 1807, there was granted by the Legislature to this Society the sum of $4,000, for the purpose of erecting a certain building or buildings for the instruction of poor children; and every year thereafter, until the pleasure of the Legislature should be otherwise expressed, an annuity of $1,000 was granted to the Society, "for promoting the benevolent objects of said corporation."

In 1808, the title of the corporation was changed to that of the "Free-School Society of New York," and its powers were extended "to all children the proper objects of a gratuitous education."

Farther grants to the Society, for the purpose of erecting suitable accommodations for the instruction of poor children, were afterward made by the Legislature. So that the Legislature not only gave the power to build, but the means to execute the power. One of the grants of means is contained in the 2d section of the act of 5th April, 1817, which allows the Society to appropriate any surplus school money, after the payment of teachers, &c., to the erection of buildings for schools. By the act of 28th April, 1826, the title of the Society is again altered to that of "The Public School Society of the City of New York," and the power is again conferred on the trustees "from time to time to establish in said city such additional schools as they may deem expedient."

From this recital, it will be seen that the power to build school-houses and establish additional schools was always possessed by the Public School Society, and is still possessed, unless the power is taken away, as contended, by the act of 1844.

Here let it be remembered, that this right is a chartered right, originally granted, and subsequently confirmed. For the means to purchase ground and build school-houses, the Society is, and ever has been, dependent upon private or public bounty. The exercise of the right to build assumes the possession of the means to do so. Now, supposing the means are in hand, cannot the Society employ those means in the erection of new school-houses?

It will be observed that I am not now upon the question whether or not the Legislature has furnished the means to build—that will be considered in another place—but whether this body has taken away the power to build? Has not the Society the same power in this respect that it had when the original act was passed?

It is admitted, in the report of the committee, that the section of the act of 1826, authorizing the Society to establish such additional schools as it might deem expedient, is now in full force, unless it is repealed by the 50th section of the act of 1844. This same admission might also be extended to the 2d section of the original charter, which, as we have seen, gives the trustees power to establish two or more free schools in the city of New York. The "50th section of the act of 1844 repeals the acts of 1842 and 1843," and all other acts specially applicable to public or common schools in the city and county of New York, as far as the same are inconsistent with the provisions of this act.

The argument is, that the power to establish new schools, in the Public School Society, is inconsistent with the act of 1844, and is, therefore, repealed. Admitting, for the present, that the Legislature could, in this manner, without the notice required by the statute, divest a corporation of a chartered right, the first question is, Did the Legislature regard the power to establish new schools as inconsistent with the act of 1844 ?

The committee say it appears to them, " from an examination of the act of 1844, in connection with the act of 1842, that the Legislature intended to vest the power of establishing new schools exclusively in the school officers named in these acts."

" The first section of the act of 1842," say the committee, " provides for the election of commissioners, inspectors, and trustees of schools in the several wards of the city, and declares that these officers respectively shall have the like powers, and be subject to the same duties, with the commissioners and inspectors of common schools, and the trustees of school districts in the several towns of the State, except as thereinafter provided.

" Now, by reference to the powers and duties of commissioners, inspectors, and trustees of common schools in the several towns of the State, it will be seen that the whole power of establishing common schools, and the whole charge of them, is vested in these officers, and in them exclusively."

That is to say, the common school system of the State takes in all the children, in every district. Therefore, when that system is extended to the city of New York, as it was by the act of 1842, it is equally comprehensive here—it embraces all the children of the city. I mean to state the argument correctly.

Now, I wonder that the learned committee did not see that their argument proved too much. For, if this argument be sound, the very existence of the Public School Society, all its chartered rights, are inconsistent with the new system, upon the reasoning employed. But did the Legislature so regard it ? No; for this very act of 1842 puts the schools of the Public School Society " under the jurisdiction of the commissioners of the respective wards in which any of the said schools now are, or hereafter may be, located, subject to the direction of the Board of Education, but under the immediate government and management of their respective trustees, managers, and directors, in the same manner and to the same extent as herein provided in respect to the district schools herein first before mentioned, in said city and county," &c. Here, then, the act of 1842 expressly provides for schools of the Public School Society thereafter to be located. Such new erections were not at that time regarded as inconsistent with the extension of the common school system of the State to the city of New York.

The 7th section of this act provides for the organization of schools under the new system, and provides that none such shall be organized unless it can be certified " that it is necessary to organize one or more schools in said ward, in addition to the schools mentioned in the 13th section ; " that is, in addition to the schools of the Public School Society then or thereafter to be located in the respective wards. The act, however, did not, in express terms, provide any means for the erection of any new buildings by the Public School Society. This omission was evidently undesigned; for, in the amendment of the act, in 1843, it is provided that "the trustees of the Public School Society may appropriate all moneys received by them by virtue of the act, to any of the purposes of common school instruction, including the support of normal schools," which they were authorized by law to do before the passage of this act; provided always, that the fee of all real estate purchased under the act "shall vest in the city and county of New York."

Consequently, then, the new system introduced by the act of 1842 was not deemed by the Legislature inconsistent with the establishment of new schools by the Public School Society. Nor was it so deemed when the amended act of 1843 was passed.

Did the Legislature of 1844 mean to say the establishment of new schools by the Public School Society was inconsistent with the provisions of the act passed by that body? It is said this power was granted exclusively to the school officers named in the act. By the 8th section of this act, before the organization of any new ward school, it must appear that an additional school is necessary; that is, additional to the schools already organized. If there are a sufficient number of public schools in the neighborhood of the contemplated organization, then no additional school shall be organized. The power, then, of the Public School Society to open new schools, is not inconsistent with the power of the ward officers to organize additional schools. If it were true, as a fact, that the new system must necessarily occupy the whole ground of common school education, then, of course, the power to build new school-houses must be exclusive; but this is not true as a fact; the new system occupies not the whole, but additional ground. Now, the question comes, Additional to what? I answer, Additional to the schools, among others, of the Public School Society—a corporation having schools, and possessing a chartered right to establish new schools.

But the committee describe the mode pointed out by the 8th section of the act of 1844 for the organization of a new school, and say: "In order, then, to establish a new school, a majority of the school officers of the ward must, in the first instance, determine that it is needed; and then they must apply to the Board of Education, stating the reasons of their application; and the Board of Education must investigate the matter, and grant or deny the application, as they may deem best."

"Surely," say the committee, "such careful provisions in regard to the establishment of new schools is entirely inconsistent with the idea that the same power is concurrently given to a close corporation, with no responsibility as to the manner of its exercise."

Why are these careful provisions prescribed in the act? Because the money is to be raised by a special tax, imposed upon all the property of the city, for the express purpose of buying the land and erecting the school-house. This tax is imposed, in effect, by the very men who make the scrutiny. The formalities, therefore, are required to determine the question, Is the high and extremely delicate function of government, the imposition of a tax, to be exercised? But if the Public School Society have the money, derived from private or public bounty, what objection can the Legislature have to its appropriation in the organization of a new school? especially as such organization may prevent the necessity of laying a tax to erect an additional school. Such appropriation is not, certainly, inconsistent with the power vested by law in the ward officers to organize additional schools.

That the intention was to provide for the establishment of additional schools only, is obvious enough from the reading of the statute; but, beyond this, the contemporaneous history of the school controversy exemplifies the same truth. The schools of the Public School Society were always the favorites of the commissioners of school money, of the Corporation of the city, of the Legislature of the State, and of the public at large.

There were never any complaints made against this Society for infidelity in the expenditure of the many thousands of dollars entrusted to it. There were never any allegations that it did not furnish a good and an economical education to the many thousand children instructed in its schools. Every investigation made—and there were many—showed that the management, order, and discipline of the public schools in the city were far preferable to those of country schools. The Legislature never meant to say or do any thing indicating an unfriendly feeling to the Public School Society. There were no facts to authorize such feelings; but it did come out, in the investigations made by the Legislature, that there were many children in the city of New York who, from prejudice or some other cause, did not receive the advantages which the Society proffered. The new system was therefore enacted, not to destroy the old schools or retard the operations of the Society, but to provide additional schools, which should take up the scholars whom the Society could not or did not reach.

Thus the two systems were intended—and wisely so—to operate side by side, under the supervision of this board.

And now let us ask, Does not experience show that the two systems mutually stimulate each other, to the great advantage of the pupils instructed in the schools? I am informed that the public schools were never better attended, and were never more useful; and it will, I am sure, be admitted, that the ward schools have been greatly aided by the example of the public schools.

It is thus apparent that the Legislature did not intend to repeal the clear chartered right of the Society to multiply the number of its schools.

Having shown that the Legislature never regarded the right of the Public School Society to open new schools as inconsistent with the provisions of the act of May, 1844, and therefore that there never was an intention to repeal the portions of the charter conferring this right, the next question is, Could the Legislature, if it had been so disposed, repeal the charter?

The report of the committee, in discussing this point, refers to the case of McLaren *vs.* Pennington, 1 Paige's Reports, 107.

The following is a part of the marginal note in this case:

The privileges and franchises granted to a private corporation are vested rights, and cannot be divested or altered, except with the consent of the corporation, or by a forfeiture declared by a proper tribunal.

A State cannot pass any law which alters or amends the charter of a private corporation, without the consent of such corporation.

" Yet," the committee say, " it is a principle equally well settled, that public corporations, or those whose powers are a public trust, to be executed for the common weal, are entirely within the control of the Legislature; that these powers are not vested rights as against the State, but that they may be abrogated as well by a general law affecting the whole State, as by a special act altering the powers of the corporation." In support of this principle, reference is made to the case of The People *vs.* Morris, 13 Wend., 325, 331.

This was a case of alleged interference with rights granted in the charter to the village of Ogdensburgh, St. Lawrence county. The defendant was indicted for selling spirituous liquors and permitting the same to be drunk in his grocery store, without having obtained a license as a tavern-keeper. He admitted the sale of liquor, &c., but justified, under a license from the trustees of the village, to "keep a grocery and victualling house in the village, in which to sell fruit, victuals, and liquor." The act of incorporation of the village authorized the trustees " to regulate and license grocers and keepers of victualling-houses and ordinaries, where fruit, victuals, and liquor shall be sold to be eaten or drunk in such houses or groceries." Under this authority, a license was granted to defendant, and paid for by him.

The Supreme Court did not sustain the justification of the defendant under the village license, and they put themselves upon the ground that political power, conferred by the Legislature, could not become a vested right as against the Government, in any individual or body of men.

Then the question is, Is the right to educate children, granted by the act of 1805 and confirmed by the act of 1826, political power, within the sense of this decision ? If it be, it would seem to follow that the powers of our colleges and universities, granted by charter, which are powers to educate, are political powers, and not the subjects of private right. Yet we see that a very different doctrine was held by the Supreme Court of the United States, in the great case of Dartmouth College *vs.* Woodward, 4 Wheaton, 518. In that case, there was a charter granted by the British crown to the trustees of Dartmouth College. An act of the Legislature of New Hampshire was passed, altering the charter in a material respect, without the consent of the corporation. This act was declared to be unconstitutional and void. This case, I contend, is analogous to the one now under consideration. The powers granted to the Public School Society are not political powers.

I have considered this point because I have been called to it by the position taken by the committee, and have thus been led to the discussion of the legal rights of the Society ; not that I suppose the time will ever come when there will be a disposition to exercise these rights in opposition to the will of the Legislature.   The Society would probably shrink from a conflict with the Legislature.

It is thus manifest that the Public School Society has a chartered right to build school-houses and open schools ; that it was never the intention of the Legislature to take away or interfere with that right ; and that it had no right to take away such chartered right without the consent of the Society—which consent has never been given.

Then the proposition of the committee, that the Public School Society, since the act of May 7, 1844, has no right to establish any new school, is untrue.   As an abstract proposition, it is confessedly untrue.

The next proposition of the committee is, that, if any such schools have been or may be established, that they are not entitled to participate in the apportionment of the school moneys.

This, too, is untrue ; for the Society has a legal right, as has been shown, to draw for all scholars, between the ages of four and sixteen years, educated free of expense in the schools within its jurisdiction.   The schools opened since May 7, 1844, are confessedly within the jurisdiction of the Society, so that there is no longer room for argument.

But the great practical question, after all, is, Whence can the Society obtain the means of opening new schools ?

1st. It can borrow money and mortgage its property for the payment thereof, under the act of 1829.   Of this there can be no doubt in the mind of any man who will look at that act.   The money so legally borrowed is the property of the Society ; and, having means, it can establish new schools.

2d. The Society can participate in the apportionment of the school moneys, in the same manner and to the same extent as the ward schools. The manner is pointed out in section 6 of the act of 1844.   The extent is defined in section 12 :

It shall be the duty of the Board of Education to apportion all the school moneys, except so much as shall have been raised for the purpose of organizing and establishing new schools, to each of the several schools provided for by this act, according to the number of children, over four and under sixteen years of age, who shall have actually attended such school without charge the preceding year.

The Society's schools and the ward schools alike draw from the fund, according to the number of children taught ; they participate *per capita.* There is, then, no doubt as to the rule by which the money shall be received. For what purposes can it be used ?   Section 12 provides that, if the money apportioned agreeably to that section shall exceed the necessary and legal expenses of either of the schools or societies provided for in the act, the balance shall be paid into the city treasury.

Then the Public School Society can use the money it receives to pay its necessary and legal expenses.   What are these ?   The necessary expenses of a school for supplying gratuitous education to all children whom it can accommodate and instruct, are easily indicated.   There must be one or more teachers ; there must be fuel, school furniture, stationery, and a house.   All these must be paid for, and the expenses therefor are necessary expenses. They are legal expenses, too, if the objects named are within the scope of the purposes for which the fund was originally created by law. Now, what are these purposes ? Section 5 of the act of 1844 defines them ; they are, purposes of common schools in the city of New York. This section provides that there shall be raised by tax a sum equal to that received from the school fund, and also one twentieth of one per cent. on all assessable property in the city of New York, and to be applied exclusively to the purposes of common schools in said city. Then, if salaries of teachers, fuel, school furniture, stationery, and a house—objects all of which are necessary to the existence and operations of common schools—are comprehended in the purposes of common schools, the expenses necessary to procure them are both necessary and legal expenses, under section 12 already referred to.

What objects were included in the purposes of common schools in the city of New York, before the passage of the act of May, 1844 ?

I first notice the act entitled "An Act Relating to Common Schools in the City of New York," passed November 19, 1824. The provisions of this act require that an equal amount received from the school fund shall be raised by tax ; and the aggregate amount shall be deposited in a bank, to the credit of commissioners of the school fund. The act farther provides, that the institutions or schools entitled to receive said school moneys shall. once in three years, be designated by the Corporation of the city of New York, who shall have power to prescribe the limitations and restrictions under which said moneys shall be received by said institutions or schools, or any of them.

Under this law, the Corporation of the city of New York, by ordinance, designated the institutions and schools which should participate in the fund ; and they provided that every other institution and school, besides the Public School Society, should receive only a sufficient amount to pay teachers employed, but that this Society was authorized to apply any surplus, after paying the salaries of teachers, to the erection of buildings for schools, and to all the useful purposes of a common school education. By the judgment, then, of the Corporation, the school fund, without any special designation thereto by the Legislature, could be appropriated to the erection of buildings, and all the needful purposes of education in common schools. By an act passed April 25, 1829, the Corporation of the city of New York is authorized annually to raise and collect by tax a sum equal to one eightieth of one per cent. of the value of the real and personal property in the city liable to assessment, to be applied exclusively to the purposes of common schools in the said city.

By another act, passed April 13, 1831, the Corporation is authorized to lay an additional amount, to be applied exclusively to the purposes of common schools in said city.

Thus the Legislature authorized the funds to be raised, defining the object to be, generally, for the purposes of common schools, but not specifying what particular objects were comprehended within those purposes. The Corporation could prescribe the limitations and restrictions under which

35

each society or school should receive the fund, but it could not enlarge the purposes for which the fund was created. With this power only, the Corporation settled, by ordinance, that building school-houses, purchasing stationery, &c., were purposes of common schools, as well as the payment of teachers. Under this practical construction of the law, before the act of 1842, the school moneys for this city were distributed, for nearly twenty years, without objection or complaint, either from the Superintendent of Common Schools or the Legislature, who were annually informed of the mode of distribution.

The same language, to designate the object of the fund, is employed in section 5 of the act of 1844, as was previously employed in the acts of 1829 and 1831. Does it not, then, follow, that this fund can be now used for like purposes—that the fund, similarly created and described, had been used with manifest approbation?

If there were no other enactment in the act of 1844 for raising money by tax, then, beyond all controversy, this question must be answered in the affirmative. The words, "the purposes of common schools," in the 5th section, would embrace all the purposes of common schools; and "the necessary and legal expenses" of the Public School Society would be those expenses to which it was subjected in accomplishing any or all of these purposes.

But it is said the act of 1844, besides the fund composed of the school moneys, and the equivalent tax raised in the city, and the farther tax of one eightieth of one per cent., to be applied exclusively to the purposes of common schools, provides a mode, in the same section 5, for raising and collecting an additional sum for erecting, purchasing, or leasing school-houses, and procuring sites therefor, and the fitting up thereof. Now, because the objects last specified are specially provided for in the act, it is said they cannot be embraced in the provisions for creating the other fund, although the terms of those provisions are sufficiently comprehensive to embrace the same objects. With great respect, I deny this conclusion; it is unsound and illogical. The additional provision for raising money for some of the purposes of common schools, shows that, in the judgment of the Legislature, more funds were required for these purposes; but it by no means proves that the same purposes were not comprehended under the general expression, "purposes of common schools." The new system required new houses, and it demanded more aid for this purpose than could be supplied by the fund as formerly constituted. To supply houses, therefore, for this new system, required an additional source of revenue; but the opening of that source did not change the character of the old fountain of supply; that remains as before.

Under the act of 1844, then, the Board of Education receives the school money; it apportions it among the schools and societies mentioned in the act, to be by them applied to the purposes of common schools in the city of New York. The purposes of common schools have been defined by established usage. What these purposes are, is settled by approved custom. Among others, they are, the payment of teachers' salaries, the purchase of stationery, fuel, and school furniture, the hiring of rooms, and the erection of buildings for schools.

Although the erection of buildings for schools is clearly one of the purposes of common schools, yet, in the apportionment of school money for a single year, as this board is bound to apportion, it might, perhaps, admit of a doubt whether a purpose so permanent, looking forward to many years in the future, could properly be provided for in such annual apportionment. I say, it might admit of a doubt, unless the board can find evidence, in the act itself, that such erections were contemplated by the Legislature. Is there such evidence in the act of 1844 ? The last sentence in the 11th section of this act is in these words :

Titles to all school property, real and personal, hereafter purchased from all moneys derived from the distribution of the school fund, or raised by taxation in the city of New York, shall be vested in the Mayor, Aldermen, and Commonalty of said city.

This sentence contemplates that real estate might be purchased with money derived from the distribution of the school fund. How could there be any such money, unless there happened to be a surplus after the payment of teachers, &c. ? This surplus had generally been found in the schools of the Public School Society. If the surplus could not be used in the erection of school-houses, it would have to go back to the city treasury. If—as seems to be contemplated in the sentence quoted—it could be used for the purchase of real estate, the title to that estate was made to vest in the Corporation. To me it seems that the words quoted are entirely insensible, unless they recognize the fact that, as in all former times since 1817 had been the practice, the Public School Society should have the right to vest the surplus in real estate. It will be remembered that section 11 makes provision for the schools of the Public School Society, and other corporate schools, and it was not necessary to use the sentence quoted, in order to vest the title to the real estate purchased for ward schools in the Corporation ; that had been done before, at the end of section 9. Connect these considerations with the fact that, in the amendatory act of 1843, the power to use the school fund for the purchase of real estate was clearly given to the Public School Society, and the title to such estate was made to vest in the Corporation, and it seems to me the intention of the Legislature cannot be doubted.

Yet still I confess that intention has not been as clearly expressed as I could desire ; and if this board entertain a serious doubt as to its right to allow the Public School Society to use the school moneys for the erection of school-houses, although the title should be vested in the Corporation, then I would respectfully suggest that it unite with the Public School Society in an application to the Legislature, now in session, to pass a short declaratory act, making that clear which now seems obscure.

In such an act I am willing that there should be inserted a provision that the Public School Society should not erect a new building, unless the location were approved by this board.

It will be readily seen that, under the increased expenses of the Society, growing out of the new order of things, there will probably be very little surplus moneys remaining in its hands; yet I respectfully suggest that the same right to use that surplus, heretofore enjoyed, should be still retained.

With these remarks, the whole subject is respectfully submitted.

At the conclusion of Mr. Ketchum's speech, Mr. Mason offered a resolution, being an amended form of the first recommendation of the committee, as follows:

Resolved, That, in the opinion of the Board of Education, the Public School Society has no right, since the passage of the act entitled "An Act more Effectually to Provide for Common School Education in the City and County of New York," passed May 7, 1844, to establish any new schools entitled to participate in the apportionment of the school moneys.

Mr. Mason sustained his resolution in a reply to Mr. Ketchum, as follows:

Mr. President: Before proceeding to the discussion of the resolution which has just been read, I beg leave to submit one or two preliminary remarks.

In the first place, I am happy that this discussion has taken place, and that this board so promptly acceded to the request of the Public School Society, to allow them to be heard on the subject of this resolution by their committee. Such a course was due to that Society, composed as it is of so many of our most respectable citizens, and exercising so important an influence upon the public education of the city. It was due also to this board, that, before deciding on a step so important as that involved in the resolution, it should patiently hear and examine both sides of the question.

In the next place, the impression has been made in some quarters that the resolution and the report of the committee on which it is founded, proceeds from a feeling of hostility on the part of the board toward the Public School Society, and that a desire exists to injure and weaken the Society. For myself, I utterly disclaim any such feeling. The Public School Society is, in my judgment, entitled to the warmest gratitude of this community. For a number of years the common school education of the city was, for the most part, committed to this Society; and it has, with great ability and fidelity, discharged the high trust confided to it; and I would resist to the utmost of my power any attempt to interfere in the least degree with any of the powers conferred upon it with regard to those schools which existed at the time of the passage of the act of 1844; and these I believe to be the sentiments of the board.

But the question is a naked question of law, involving the interpretation of the statute under which we are constituted, and one which it is absolutely necessary for us to settle, in order properly to fulfil the duties we have to perform.

I have listened, this evening, to the able argument of the learned advocate of the Public School Society in opposition to the resolution and report of the committee now under consideration, but he has failed to convince me that the position taken by the committee is erroneous. On the contrary, I have no doubt that the construction given by the committee to the act of May 7, 1844, is the true one.

Let us clearly understand the question involved; for, with great respect, I think the learned gentleman has somewhat obscured it.

The question before us, then, is, not whether the Public School Society has or has not faithfully discharged the trust confided to it. I should have no hesitation in answering this question in the affirmative. Nor is it whether, by the law of 1844, the schools of the Society are merged in the ward schools; such a position has never been advanced, much less contended for.* Nor is it whether the Society have or have not a corporate right to establish free schools, to be supported by the private contributions of the members of the Society. But the question is, whether the Society has a right to establish new common schools, which will be entitled, under the act of 1844, to participate in the school moneys, and a right to use their surplus funds, derived from the school moneys, in building or renting school-houses for such new schools.

This was the question discussed in the report of the committee. The term " schools " was indeed used in that report without any other designation or qualification, because it was only with common schools that this board has any thing to do.

In order the more clearly to understand the subject, I will briefly advert to the course of legislation in relation to common schools.

The Legislature, many years since, established the common school system, extending to every part of the State, except the city and county of New York.

By the provisions of that system, as is well known, different officers are elected in the various towns of the State, each having their distinct and appropriate duties: commissioners, to receive the school moneys apportioned from the revenue of the common school fund, and to distribute them, with a like amount raised by tax, among the school districts; inspectors, to examine into the qualifications of persons proposed as teachers; and trustees of districts, to take charge of the school-houses, pay the teachers, &c.

These officers, it is also well known, have exclusive jurisdiction in these matters. They alone have power to establish common schools in their respective towns, and no other schools but common schools thus established, and managed by the school officers of the town and district in which they are situated, have a right to participate in the school moneys.

---

* Allusion is here made to some of Mr. Ketchum's remarks which do not appear in the printed report published by the Society. These remarks, as they appear in print, are somewhat modified from their original shape. The reply now presented immediately followed the remarks, and were founded on a few notes, many of which were taken while Mr. Ketchum was speaking, and have since been reduced to writing at the request of the Board of Education.

This common school system, I have said, did not originally, nor until a very late period, extend to this city.

The various religious societies in the city had, for the most part, schools belonging to their respective denominations; and, in the year 1805, the Free-School Society, now the Public School Society, was established for the instruction of poor children who did not belong to, or were not provided for by, any religious society. The schools which it formed, according to the original plan of the Society, were to be supported by private contributions, and it was, in every respect, a private eleemosynary institution.

In the year 1826, however, the character of this Society was essentially changed. The first section of the act of January 28, 1826, entitled "An Act in Relation to the Public School Society of New York," altered its name to that of "The Public School Society of New York;" and the second section made it the duty of said Society to provide, so far as their means might extend, for the education of all children in the city of New York not otherwise provided for, whether such children were or were not the proper subjects of gratuitous education, and without regard to the religious sect or denomination to which such children or their parents might belong.

Thus an important public trust was committed to the Society; the common school education of the city was placed under its control; the duties and powers of commissioners, trustees, and inspectors in the county, were vested in its officers; they became the executive officers of the Government for this important branch of public service; new and distinct powers were grafted upon their original charter; and, by a subsequent section of the same act, their right to draw upon the school fund was expressly recognized.

But, in the year 1842, the Legislature saw fit to extend the common school system, which prevailed throughout the State, to the city of New York, with some modifications.

The act of 1842 provided for the appointment of commissioners, inspectors, and trustees, with the like powers and duties with the commissioners and inspectors of common schools, and the trustees of school districts in the several towns of the State, "except as thereinafter provided."

Now, if the powers and duties of those officers in the several towns in the State were to be exercised by them, and by them alone, and were exclusive in their very nature, they must be equally so in the city, excepting in so far as they are modified by the act itself; and this position by no means proves, as the learned gentleman insisted, that the schools of the Public School Society are merged in the ward schools, and all the powers of the Society destroyed, if, as we know to be the case, the exception provides for its schools.

The 13th section of the act of 1842 expressly recognizes the schools of the Public School Society then in existence, protects them in the enjoyment of all their rights, and secures to them, in a manner that never was done before, their full share of the school moneys.

But, as to all matters not embraced within the exception, the powers and duties of the commissioners, inspectors, and trustees, are and must be exclusive, or the act has no meaning. If this is not so, but the Public School Society could go on establishing new schools as before, it is incumbent upon it to show that power to do so is reserved to it in the act.

The learned advocate of the Society has invoked the 7th section of the act of 1842 to his aid. It provides that, " whenever the trustees elected in any ward shall certify in writing, to the commissioners and inspectors of common schools thereof, that it is necessary to organize one or more schools in said ward, in addition to the schools mentioned in the 13th section of this act (in which section the schools of the Society are expressly named), it shall be the duty of the said commissioners and inspectors to meet together and examine into the facts and circumstances of the case; and, if they shall be satisfied of such necessity, they shall certify the same, under their hands, to the Board of Education, and then shall proceed to organize one or more school districts therein, and shall procure a school-house," &c. The provision of the act of 1844 is the same in substance, although more general in its terms. The 8th section provides that, whenever the commissioners, &c., shall certify to the Board of Education that it is necessary to organize one or more additional schools in said ward, &c. It is obvious that the same construction must be given to these words "in addition," in the act of 1844, as was given to the words of like import in the 7th section of the act of 1842, just referred to.

It is strange that this section should have been adverted to by the learned gentleman. If it means any thing, it means that the power of erecting schools in addition to those then established, is vested in the ward officers. There are, say the Legislature, certain schools established by the Public School Society; with these schools we do not wish to interfere, but whenever schools are needed in any ward, in addition to those already established, you, the commissioners, inspectors, &c., must judge of that, and establish them, if found necessary.

To insist, as was done in the argument of the counsel, that these words, " in addition," mean in addition to the schools thereafter to be established by the Society, is begging the question.

The 13th section of the act of 1842 was next referred to, which puts the schools of the Public School Scoiety under " the general jurisdiction of the commissioners of the respective wards in which any of the said schools now are or may hereafter be located;" and it was insisted that the act provides for schools thereafter to be located or established. So far from it, the act merely defines under whose jurisdiction the existing schools of the Society shall be, in case of a division, or alteration of the bounds, of any of the wards; that they shall be subject to the jurisdiction of the officers in whose bounds they then were, or, upon a division of the wards, they might happen to be.

The question then arises, Had the Legislature the right to take away this power from the Public School Society of establishing new common schools?

It is contended that they had not, because it was a chartered right.

The learned counsel has spent much time in endeavoring to show that the Society has a chartered right to establish free schools, to be supported by private munificence, and that this right is not taken away. I might safely concede this position, and the argument would not be advanced a step; any more than it would be if he had proved—what no one denies—that any individual has a right to educate as many children as he pleases, free of expense. But that would not prove that such an individual has a right to use the public moneys to aid him; nor that, if the law has once given him some aid, he has a vested right in it for all time to come.

The distinction is between the corporate right to establish free schools at the Society's expense, and the right and duty of establishing common schools to be supported at the public expense.

The one we do not interfere with; the other is, and always, from the nature of the case, must be, subject to legislative control.

The established doctrine on this subject is well expressed in the case of the People vs. Morris, 13th Wend., 323, 341, in which the court say that "public corporations, or those whose powers are a public trust, to be executed for the common weal, are entirely within the control of the Legislature; that these powers are not vested rights as against the State, but that they may be abrogated as well by a general law affecting the whole State, as by a special act altering the powers of the corporation."

The learned gentleman has been at some pains, in examining the particular facts of that case, to show that the power exercised by the defendant in that case, of selling spirituous liquors, was a political power; and he contended that the right to educate children is not a political power. I would ask, What is a political power? What is the meaning of political? It is defined to be something which relates to public affairs—affairs in which the whole public are interested. And are we to be gravely told that the regulation and licensing of grocers and victualling-houses in a village (which was the power referred to in the case quoted from Wendell) is a political power, in which the whole public are interested, and which the Government can regulate as they please; but that the education of all the children of our city is a matter of private concern, with which the public have nothing to do—which the Legislature cannot regulate or control; and that, having once delegated certain duties relative to it to a private corporation, they have placed the matter forever out of their reach?

The case of Dartmouth College vs. Woodward, 5 Wheaton, 518, cited by the counsel, does not in the least conflict with that of The People vs. Morris. The decision in that case was put expressly on the ground that the college was a private eleemosynary, and not a public corporation, and so the gentleman himself read from the case, and felt bound to insist that the Public School Society was a private, and not a public, corporation. If so, let it confine itself to those private rights originally granted to it, and not claim to exercise the powers conferred upon it as the agent of the Government, and there is then no question on which we are at issue. But let it not insist upon a perpetual grant of public and political powers and duties, because its charter gives it certain private rights.

There is, then, no constitutional objection to the establishment of the new system. It is no violation of the chartered rights of the Society. It is only a withdrawal of a public trust confided to it, and vesting it in other hands.

But again. The exercise by the Public School Society of the right to establish new schools, is entirely inconsistent with the exercise of the same right by this board. It would be in the power of the Society to prevent this board from ever establishing any new schools.

Our proceedings are public, and necessarily slow. The ward officers must first determine that a school is necessary; they must then apply to this board, which meets ordinarily but once a month; the matter is referred to a committee, who may report at the expiration of one month, perhaps two. The site for a building must then be purchased, and appropriations made, which generally take another month. In the meanwhile, before the ward officers have fairly commenced operations, the Public School Society, whose deliberations are more secret, may have purchased ground and erected a building in the very neighborhood of the one proposed to be established by this board, and render the establishment of a school by the ward officers entirely unnecessary and inexpedient. I do not mean to say that the Society would take such a course. I do not believe they would. I merely state the case by way of illustration, to show what could be done, and thus test the accuracy of the position taken by us on this subject. It cannot be that the Legislature meant that this power should be exercised simultaneously by both bodies.

The soundness of the position taken by the committee will further appear by the course of legislation with regard to the school moneys.

The words "school moneys" are used throughout the act of May, 1844. The term is a technical one, and is defined, in 1 R. S., 196, 1st ed. § 2, to mean the revenues of the common school fund which are annually distributed for the support and encouragement of common schools.

These moneys are paid into the hands of the commissioners for schools in the several towns of the State, and, together with the moneys raised by tax in the towns, are apportioned by the commissioners among the several school districts, and paid to the trustees (1 R. S., 470, 1st ed. §§ 5–6), who are required to appropriate them to the payment of teachers' wages (ib. 481, §§ 8–9); and the moneys received from both these sources are designated by the general term of "school moneys."

The sums necessary for purchasing the sites for school-houses, for building, hiring, or purchasing school-houses, keeping them in repair, furnishing them with necessary fuel and appendages, are provided for by additional tax imposed upon the inhabitants at a school-district meeting (ib. 478, § 61, sub. 5).

By an act passed April 17, 1838 (Laws, 1838, p. 220), the sum of one hundred and ten thousand dollars of the income of the United States deposit fund is directed to be annually distributed to the support of common schools, in like manner and upon the like conditions as the school moneys are or may be distributed.

There are also various other acts to be found in the statute-book, showing how sacredly the school moneys are appropriated to the teachers' wages as, for instance, a law passed in 1837 (Laws, 1837, p, 232), authorizing the inhabitants of school districts to levy a tax for the purchase of a book to record the proceedings of the trustees; and another law, in 1841 (Laws, 1841, p. 236), authorizing a special tax, not exceeding $20 in any one year, to purchase maps, globes, black-boards, and other school apparatus—all showing that the "school moneys," so called, could not be used in these ways, but that they are sacredly appropriated to the support of teachers.

The Public School Society would have had no right at any time to appropriate the school moneys received by it to any other purpose, but for the permission given in the act of April 5, 1817, referred to by the counsel.

The act of May 7, 1844, makes the same distinction between "school moneys," properly so called, and the sums necessary for establishing and organizing new schools.

The 5th section provides that the supervisors shall annually raise, by tax, a sum of money equal to the city's share of the school moneys received from the general fund, and also one twentieth of one per cent. of the real and personal estate in the city, to be applied exclusively to the purposes of common schools in said city.

That these purposes are not erecting, or leasing, or purchasing sites for school-houses, or school-houses themselves, is manifest from what follows in the same section, which provides that the Corporation shall raise by tax such further sum as may be necessary for these last-mentioned objects, and also for fitting up of the school-houses.

The sums first designated in section 5 are, by the 6th section, directed to be deposited to the credit of the commissioners of common schools in the several wards, and of the societies and schools enumerated in the 11th section (including the Public School Society), in the proportion to which they shall respectively be entitled.

By the 7th section, the balance of the funds to be raised, pursuant to section 5, for the erection, purchase, or leasing of school-houses, and procuring the sites therefor, and fitting up thereof, are placed at the disposal of the Board of Education, by appropriation, for the establishment and organization of schools, as provided in the 8th section.

The 8th section provides for the establishment of new schools by the Board of Education, and by none other; and these schools are denominated by the 3d section, "ward schools."

Here, then, are two distinct funds, both placed under the control of the Board of Education: the first consisting of the funds annually raised for the support of common schools, and denominated "school moneys" throughout the act. In these moneys the Public School Society participates according to the number of its scholars, in common with the ward schools, and the other schools and societies mentioned in the act.

The second fund is a special one, to be raised from time to time, for establishing and organizing new ward schools, and them alone.

Now, if we turn to the 11th section, we shall find that the schools of the Public School Society, with the other schools mentioned in the section, "participate in the apportionment of the 'school moneys' in the same manner and to the same extent" as are provided with regard to the ward schools.

The next section (12th) shows in what manner and to what extent the ward schools, and, of course the schools of the Public School Society, are entitled to participate in the school moneys which may be apportioned to them.

If, by reason of peculiar circumstances, any of the newly-organized schools are entitled to a larger sum than they will receive under the apportionment, then the Board of Education are required to make for them such further allowance out of the said school moneys as may be just and proper. But "if the school moneys apportioned agreeably to this section shall exceed the necessary and legal expenses of either of the schools or societies provided for in this act, the board shall authorize the payment only of such necessary and legal expenses; any balance remaining in deposit at the end of each year shall be paid by the Board of Education into the city treasury, and any deficiency to meet the necessary and legal expenses of either of the said schools or societies shall be supplied by the Common Council, in anticipation of the annual tax for the support of common schools, as provided by section 5 of this act."

Now, what are these "necessary and legal expenses" to which the school moneys are to be applied?

The words must have the same meaning in their application to the Public School Society and the ward schools, because the Society participates in these moneys only in the same manner and to the same extent as the ward schools.

The learned gentleman contends that the Public School Society has the right, under the term "necessary and legal expenses," to build new schoolhouses whenever it shall deem proper. If this is so, and if the building of new school-houses is a necessary and legal expense, within the meaning of the act, then, if the cost of erection of a new school-house should exceed the sum apportioned to the Society, the Board of Education would be bound to certify the fact to the Common Council, and the Common Council would be bound to provide for the deficiency by tax, and the way is clear for the Society to extend their schools when and where they please.

By parity of reasoning, the officers of the ward schools have a right to establish new schools of their own motion, without the interference of the Board of Education, because the ward schools and the Public School Society stand on the same footing precisely with regard to these school moneys. If the building of new school-houses is, upon a just construction of the act, one of the "necessary and legal expenses" of the Public School Society, it must be also one of the necessary and legal expenses of the ward schools; and we are thus driven to a conclusion entirely at variance with the whole scope and tenor of the act, and with many of its positive provisions.

No person who reads the act can doubt for a moment what are the "necessary and legal expenses" of the ward schools, to which the school moneys may be applied. They are, upon the most liberal construction, the annual expenses required to keep up the school—payment of teachers, fuel, ordinary repairs, stationery, &c. ; and they cannot be applied to building or hiring school-houses for new schools, because the power of establishing new schools, and raising the requisite funds for that purpose, is placed in the Board of Education.

If, then, the ward schools have no power to expend the school moneys annually apportioned to them in the establishment of new schools, how can the Public School Society make such an application of the school moneys apportioned to them, when they participate in these moneys only in the same manner and to the same extent with the ward schools ?

Let the Society point out the clause or section in the act of 1844 which gives them this power.

An express authority was given them thus to use the school moneys by the act of April 5, 1817—the act of 1842 was supposed to take it away ; the 13th section of that act declaring that, so far as related to the distribution of the school moneys, the schools of the Public School Society should be considered as district schools of the city.

This power was restored by the 13th section of the act of 1843, which authorized the trustees of the Public School Society to appropriate all moneys received by them by virtue of that act " to any of the purposes of common school instruction, including the support of normal schools, which they were authorized by law to do before the passage of that act : *Provided*, however, that the fee of all real estate purchased under that act shall vest in the city and county of New York."

The 11th section of the act of 1844, corresponding to the 13th section of the act of 1843, omits this power altogether, except as it regards the normal schools. Its language is as follows :

And said schools (*i. e.*, the schools of the Public School Society, with others) shall participate in the apportionment of the school moneys in the same manner and to the same extent as herein provided, in respect to such schools as may be organized under this act, or which shall have been organized under the act passed April 11, 1842, or the amended act passed April 18, 1843, and including the support of normal schools of the Public School Society for the education of teachers employed, or to be employed, in any of the schools, subject to the provisions of this act. Titles to all school property, real or personal, hereafter purchased from moneys derived from the distribution of the school fund, or raised by taxation in the city of New York, shall be vested in the Mayor, Aldermen, and Commonalty of said city.

Now, why was this power, to the Public School Society so expressly given in the act of 1843, stricken out of the act of 1844 ?

Because, as we have been told, the act of 1844 is sufficiently clear without it.

Is it so ? Was it, then, stricken out at the instance, or with the sanction or concurrence, of the friends of the Public School Society, because the act of 1844, in its other provisions and clauses, was so clear in support of the claims of the Society as to render this clause unnecessary ?

Where are those other clauses and provisions ? The learned counsel has referred us to but one, but that one he has considered conclusive. It is the last sentence of the 11th section, just quoted, with regard to the titles of school property; and the question has been asked with an air of triumph, Why provide for the manner in which the titles to real estate, thereafter purchased from moneys to be derived from the distribution of the school fund, shall be vested, if no real estate whatever can be purchased from those moneys?

To this I answer:

1. That, if the power is given by this clause, it is only given by implication. It is inferred from the phraseology that the Legislature intended to give the power; it is not given in express terms.

Now, it is a rule that you cannot, from a single clause or a few words in a statute, imply a power or authority, when there are other clauses or sections in the statute which expressly prohibit it. The law or statute must be so construed, if possible, as to be consistent with itself.

You cannot infer, from the provisions about the title to property to be purchased with the school moneys, that the Society had a right to expend their surplus moneys in the establishment of new schools, when the very next section requires all these surplus moneys, after defraying their "necessary and legal expenses," which, we have seen, means the ordinary current expenses, to be paid into the public treasury. You cannot, I say, infer this, if there is any other construction which will make the two sections harmonize.

2. If we look at the 13th section of the act of 1843, we shall see, I think, the true reason of the section in question, and the explanation of the difficulty.

That section provided that the fee of all real estate purchased under that act should vest in the city and county of New York. The act of 1844 was passed on the 7th of May, and repealed the act of 1843, or, at least, this section of it. On the 1st of May, 1844, the amount apportioned to the Public School Society, with others, had been paid. It was paid under the act of 1843, and the Society had a right to employ it in the manner authorized by that act. The act of 1844 was prospective, and applied only to moneys thereafter to be received. It might have been a question whether, if a purchase of real estate were made by the Public School Society after the 7th of May, 1844, out of moneys received on the 1st of May, 1844, it would have been obliged to vest the title in the Corporation, the act of 1843 having been repealed; and, to obviate any doubt on this point, the section in the law of 1844 was doubtless passed.

If it were necessary to adduce any authority in support of the views I have taken of this whole subject, it is at hand—and authority which ought to be, with the Public School Society, perfectly decisive. It is that of their own recorded opinions, expressed not once, or twice, or casually, or inadvertently, but frequently and deliberately, from year to year.

The position now taken by its learned advocate is, that the acts of 1842 and 1844 have not taken away any of the powers which the Society formerly possessed, and were not framed with that intent, but that the right of the Public School Society to establish new schools with the public moneys, and to have those schools supported at the public expense, still exists in full vigor; that the only object of the new system was to supply the wants which the Society could not satisfy; in fine, that the new system only came in aid of the Society, and that the two systems were intended, and wisely intended, to operate side by side, I think the expression was.

Now, let us look at the published documents of the Society.

In the thirty-seventh annual report, for 1842, published shortly after the act of April, 1842, they say, in reference to that act:

It has pleased the Legislature of our State to enact a statute which, the trustees fear, will result in subjecting their noble institution to the blighting influence of party strife and sectarian animosity. The glory of their system, its uniformity, its equality of privilege and action, its freedom from all that could justly offend, its peculiar adaptation to a floating population, embracing an immense operative mass, unable, from their circumstances, to devote many years to educational pursuits, is dimmed, they fear, forever.

How can this be, if the doctrine now contended for be true? If this Society has the same power now which it formerly possessed, of extending its schools *ad libitum*, how is the glory of the system dimmed in the least degree? Is it because the officers elected by the people can establish common schools without the intervention of the Society, and that the exclusive right of the Society is taken away, or because the power of establishing new schools was considered as altogether lost?

But to this same report is appended a sketch of the rise and progress of the Public School Society—an extremely interesting document, which ought to be read by all who wish to become acquainted with the history of common school education in this city.

On page 37 we read as follows:

In April, 1842, by hasty legislation, an act was passed, materially altering the existing arrangement and supervision of the schools and the distribution of the school moneys, &c., and contravening the special statutes under which this Society had hitherto acted.

How are we to understand this, if all the powers of the Society are in full force, and the new system is only auxiliary to the old? The admission of new schools to participate in the school moneys is no contravention of any special statutes under which the Society had acted, for new schools had before been admitted to a participation of those moneys without a murmur from the Society. Besides, they had as much money under the new law as under the old. How, then, did the new law contravene the old, except by taking away some of the powers of the Society? and what powers were taken away, but those of extending their schools indefinitely?

Let us now turn to the thirty-eighth annual report, for 1843, published shortly after the act of April, 1843. In that report they say:

At the time of their last report, the trustees were under painful apprehensions as to the future prospects of the institution, induced by the then recent enactment of the law of April, 1842, the operation of which, they much feared, would paralyze the public school system, and probably result in the dissolution of the Society. They have now the satisfaction of stating that, on their application, the Legislature passed an amendatory act, which, although not granting all that was asked for, has rendered the law alluded to more clear and less objectionable, by the adoption of one very essential and other important features. Under the act as it now stands, the board hope to be able not only to continue their present schools, but also to make gradual additions to them; for they feel assured that the eminent advantages they derive from long experience, especially in their economical arrangements, will enable the Public School Society to enlarge their school accommodations out of an appropriation that would scarcely sustain them upon any other foundation.

We can be at no loss to divine what that one very essential feature was which the Legislature had inserted in the law of 1843; for the trustees expressly say that, by virtue of it, they would be able to make gradual additions to their schools out of their appropriation. It was the clause in the 13th section, before alluded to, authorizing them to "appropriate all moneys received by them by virtue of that act, to any of the purposes of common school instruction, including the support of normal schools, which they were authorized by law to do before the passage of that act."

Here, then, we have again the deliberate opinion of the trustees, expressed in no equivocal terms, that this clause of the act of 1843 restored to them the power of adding to the number of their schools, which had been taken away by the act of 1842.

But this is not all. Their next annual report was dated January 1, 1845. In that report they say:

By the provision of the act of April, 1843, sufficient means having been placed at the disposal of the board, they availed themselves of it, and have erected a new public school on Thirteenth street, and also several new primary schools in desirable locations.

Thus reiterating the fact that their power to increase the number of their schools was derived from the provision of the act of 1843, which placed sufficient means at their disposal.

They then add as follows:

By the provisions of the act of April, 1844, it is understood the board are prohibited from the further erection of buildings; and it is even doubted whether they are authorized to pay rent on school premises, or the interest on the large debt, which, in the absence of an adequate tax, they were induced to incur by mortgaging several of the school-buildings from time to time during a series of years past, in order to meet, as far as practicable, the pressing wants of a rapidly-increasing population. Should application be made to the Legislature, at its next session, for relief in the premises, it can hardly be doubted that it will be granted.

Thus it will be seen that the trustees of the Public School Society took, from the very beginning, the same view of the law which the committee have done, and that they thought it so clear, that they did not hesitate to publish it from year to year to the world as the only true interpretation. They had not then, nor until a comparatively recent period, discovered that the new system was only an auxiliary to the old, designed to provide additional schools for those whom the Society could not or did not reach; and it ought not to be a matter of surprise or disappointment to them if this board should, on examination, entertain the same opinions as to the meaning of the law which the trustees of the Society themselves have so frequently and deliberately expressed.

The construction for which the committee have contended, is one which will not interfere with the schools of the Public School Society established before the act of 1844. It leaves them, as the law of that year left them, in the enjoyment of all their privileges, and with a fund amply sufficient for all their necessary and legal expenses.

The trustees of that Society now have under their care eighteen public schools, in which were instructed, during the last year, 14,103 children, and fifty-six primaries, or schools for small children, having 8,108 children, and two public and six primary schools for colored children, in which 1,181 pupils were taught; making an aggregate of 23,392 * pupils taught in eighty-two schools under their jurisdiction during the last year.

The school moneys apportioned to the several schools and societies in the city of New York, for the year 1846, amounted to $189,107.17; of which sum the Public School Society received, for their twenty public and sixty-two primaries, $122,184.99, or two thirds of the whole; while the ward schools, under the immediate care of the ward officers, received for their nineteen ward schools and primaries the sum of $55,356.08; the difference between these two sums and the whole amount apportioned being distributed to the orphan asylums and other corporate schools provided for by law.

The resolution now before you will not, it is believed, affect any of the schools of the Public School Society, except two or three primaries established since the passage of the act of May, 1844, nor deprive the Society of any part of the moneys which may be necessary to enable them to sustain their schools on the most liberal scale; but I respectfully submit and insist that this board are bound to see that the public moneys under their control are not appropriated in a manner or for purposes contravening the provisions of the law which we are called upon to execute, and therefore hope that the resolution proposed by the committee will be adopted.

At the close of Mr. Mason's remarks, the Board of Education adjourned to the following Wednesday, the 24th of March, at which meeting Hon. JOSEPH L. BOSWORTH continued the reply to Mr. Ketchum, and spoke as follows:

MR. PRESIDENT: I should not have entered into this discussion with such formal preparation as the papers before me would seem to indicate, but for a single consideration. The able argument which was made before this board at its last meeting, in behalf of the Public School Society, has since been repeated to the people, by the publication of it in pamphlet form. This indicates that the Public School Society has great confidence in the soundness of its positions, and regards the questions under discussion—and

* See the Fortieth Annual Report of the Public School Society, for 1847, for these particulars.

justly so, I concede—as questions of important public concern. Entertaining very different views from those presented in behalf of that Society, I have deemed it due to the questions before the board, and to the interest which the people of this city have in the decision of these questions, to not only examine them with care, but to reduce my views to form, that I might reëxamine them before attempting to present them here, and thus be the better able to judge of their accuracy. This is my apology, if any be necessary, for departing, on this occasion, from the usual manner of discussing questions before the board.

The practical questions for the Board of Education to decide are these:

To what extent has the Public School Society a right to participate in the " school moneys," since the passage of the act of May 7th, 1844, entitled " An Act more Effectually to Provide for Common School Education in the City and County of New York "?

What portion of those moneys can this board " authorize " to be paid annually to that Society?

These questions should be determined accurately. This board has a duty to perform in apportioning these moneys, and its members desire to know what that duty is, and to discharge it faithfully and firmly. Their business is to execute the law as they find it, and not to pervert it, or enlarge or restrict the clear meaning of its provisions by construction or inference.

By the act of May 7th, 1844, certain moneys which this board must apportion are designated as " school moneys, or moneys for the purposes of common schools; " as contradistinguished from moneys to be raised by taxation " for the erecting, purchasing, or leasing of school-houses, and procuring the sites therefor, and the fitting up thereof." Secs. 5 and 12; and 1 R. S., 183, sec. 2.

The moneys usually denominated " school moneys " consist of the amount annually received for the use of the common schools of this city from the common school fund of the State, an equal sum to be raised by taxation, and also a further sum " equal to one twentieth of one per cent. of the value of the real and personal property in the said city, liable to be assessed therein."

The act says (sec. 5) that these school moneys shall " be applied exclusively to the purposes of common schools in the said city."

By section 12, it is declared to " be the duty of the Board of Education to apportion all the school moneys, except so much as shall have been raised for the purpose of establishing and organizing new schools, to each of the several schools provided for by this act, and the acts mentioned in the preceding section, according to the number of children over four and under sixteen years of age, who shall have actually attended such school without charge the preceding year."

By section 14, the board is required to " file with the chamberlain of said city and county, on or before the first Monday of April in each year, a copy of their apportionment, stating the amount thereof to be paid to the commissioners of each ward, and to the trustees, managers, or directors of

36

the several schools enumerated in the 11th section of this act." The chamberlain may pay on the drafts of the commissioners or of the trustees the sums severally "apportioned" to them, "but no such drafts shall be paid unless countersigned by the president and clerk for the time being of the Board of Education."

Section 6 declares that "the said Common Council shall, on application of the Board of Education, and at such monthly or quarterly periods subsequent to the 1st of May in each year as they may determine, direct that a sum or sums of money equal in the aggregate to the amount last received by the chamberlain of said city and county from the common school fund, together with the sum so received from the school fund, and also one twentieth of one per cent., as provided in the preceding section, be deposited by him in one of the incorporated banks of the said city," to the credit of the commissioners of the ward schools, and of the schools and societies mentioned in the 11th section of the act, subject to the drafts of such commissioners, and of some person duly authorized by such societies to draw for them; "the said drafts to be countersigned" by the president and clerk of this board, as provided by section 14.

Such are the moneys to be apportioned, and such is the process by which the money is to be drawn when apportioned.

First, the board apportions the moneys; next, files with the chamberlain a copy of the apportionment; and lastly, applies to the Common Council, and, on such application, the Common Council directs the chamberlain to deposit those moneys in bank to the credit of the commissioners, societies, and schools entitled to draw them; but, when so deposited, they are to be drawn by authority of drafts made by such commissioners, and the authorized agents or officers of the schools or societies, and countersigned by the president and clerk of the board.

The provisions already cited contemplate not only an apportionment of all the "school moneys," but the deposit of all of them, and the receipt of all of them by the commissioners, societies, and schools enumerated in the 11th section of the act. But there are other provisions which limit and restrict the operation of those above cited.

The 11th section provides that "the schools of the Public School Society," and also other schools enumerated in that section, "shall participate in the apportionment of the school moneys, in the same manner and to the same extent as herein provided in respect to such schools as may be organized under this act, or which shall have been organized under the act passed April 11th, 1842; or the amended act, passed April 18th, 1843."

The question, then, is: To what extent is it herein provided that the schools organized under the three acts last named may participate in the apportionment of the school moneys?

They cannot participate in the school moneys to such an extent that they or their officers can use a dollar of such moneys to purchase a lot, erect, or hire a school-house.

All moneys needed for such purposes are raised under a special power contained in section 5; and, when raised, can, by section 7, be only drawn by authority of a "special appropriation by the said Board of Education; and all drafts upon said funds shall be made by the president of the board, countersigned by the clerk, and made payable to the order of the persons to whom the same shall be paid."

If the Public School Society can participate in these "school moneys" to an extent which will enable it to use any portion of them to erect or hire buildings, or purchase lots, then it can participate in them to a greater extent than the ward schools can, and to an extent which will enable it to apply them to uses to which the ward schools are prohibited from applying them.

But the 11th section says this Society "shall participate in the same manner and to the same extent."

The 12th section further provides, that "if the school moneys apportioned agreeably to this section shall exceed the necessary and legal expenses of either of the schools or societies provided for in this act, the board shall authorize the payment only of such necessary and legal expenses; any balance remaining in deposit shall be paid by the Board of Education into the city treasury."

The board, then, has a duty to perform beyond the act of apportioning, filing a copy of an apportionment made according to the number of scholars taught, and applying to the Common Council to direct a deposit of the moneys thus apportioned.

If, on making such apportionment, the board ascertains from the report of this Society that the moneys thus apportioned exceed the amount of the actual annual expenses of the Society in conducting the schools for which the Society is entitled to draw, the board is expressly prohibited from authorizing the payment of only such actual expenses. When I say *actual* expenses, I assume none to have been incurred except such as will be "necessary and legal." The necessary and legal expenses of an honest and intelligent agent will not exceed the actual expenses of his agency.

"The Board of Education shall authorize the payment only of such necessary and legal expenses;" and "the Board of Education shall pay any balance remaining in deposit at the end of each year" "into the city treasury."

It is the duty of the board, then, to keep all of the moneys "apportioned," beyond the amounts sufficient to defray "the necessary and legal expenses" of the several schools and societies within its control, until the end of the year; and, at the end of each year, to pay any balance remaining in deposit into the city treasury.

In this very provision is contained a clear prohibition against the Public School Society using any of the "school moneys" to establish new schools. It is a clear answer to their claim, to have all the moneys "apportioned" to scholars according to numbers paid over to them absolutely. If the Legislature intended to allow them to use surplus "school moneys" to erect new buildings and purchase new lots, why prohibit the board from authorizing the payment to them of all the moneys to which they would be entitled by an "apportionment" according to the number of scholars taught? Why declare that the board shall authorize " the payment only of such necessary and legal expenses " ?

If the act be construed to prohibit the Society from establishing any new " common schools," this provision is intelligible and easily executed. But if the power be conceded to the Society to establish as many new schools as it may deem expedient, and the right be also conceded to it to use surplus " school moneys," to purchase new lots, erect new buildings, and organize new schools, then this provision is unintelligible, as this board can never conjecture what its legal expenses for any current year will be ; and may assume to withhold moneys to which the Society has an absolute right, and full power to expend, when received, as may suit its pleasure.

The argument in behalf of the Public School Society proves too much. If its construction of its powers be correct, it can establish as many new schools as it may deem expedient, and will be entitled to participate in the school moneys for instructing children in such new schools. If this be so, then its powers and rights are immeasurably greater under the act of May 7, 1844, than they were before the act was passed. The 12th section of that act provides that " any deficiency to meet the necessary legal expenses of either of the said schools or societies shall be supplied by the Common Council of the said city, in anticipation of the annual tax for the support of common schools, as provided in section 5 of this act. The Board of Education shall, in all cases, certify to the Common Council the cause of such deficiency, and that the same was unavoidable ; and unless such certificate be made, the said Common Council may refuse to raise the sum required to meet such deficiency."

It is clearly the duty of the Common Council to supply any deficiency to meet the necessary legal expenses of the Society in conducting each and all of its schools which are entitled to participate in the apportionment of the school moneys. If, then, the Society may establish an indefinite number of new schools, by mortgaging their property to raise money to erect new buildings, may supply those new schools with teachers, books, and stationery—if such acts are legal—if such new schools may participate in the school moneys, then it is the duty of the Common Council to raise any amount which may be required, in addition to the school moneys apportioned to the Society, to defray the necessary expenses of conducting such new schools.

On such a construction, the Public School Society has an unlimited and unregulated power and discretion to establish as many schools as it may deem expedient, and the Common Council must raise the requisite means to pay the expenses of conducting them. That Society, instead of being restricted to a right (so far as relates to its right to claim and apply public funds) to use only its surplus of school moneys in erecting new buildings, after amply compensating its teachers (as it was restricted by the act of April 5, 1817), has now the right to ask for, and be furnished with, the means to defray the necessary and legal expenses of any number of new schools which it may see fit to establish. A construction which leads to such conclusions is absurd.

The act of May 7, 1844, abrogated the power of the Society to establish new schools for the purpose of merely increasing the number of common schools, and, for all practical purposes, to establish any new school. That point I will consider presently. I state the proposition here merely for the purpose of observing that, on such a construction of the act, there is no conflict in its provisions, and that each and all of them are intelligible.

Under such a construction, the board can easily determine what sum to authorize to be paid to this Society. The Society can, if it has kept its accounts properly, report to the board how much it paid, for the year ending at the date of its last report, for teachers, books, stationery, and fuel, for the schools established prior to May 7, 1844 ; what amount it paid for rent of buildings, or for interest on mortgages of the buildings in which such schools were kept. The board will authorize the payment of a sufficient amount of the school moneys to defray the like amount of expenses for the current year. If, from any "unavoidable" cause, they prove insufficient to defray the necessary and legal expenses of the current year, the board will give the necessary certificate to make it compulsory on the Common Council to supply the deficiency. In that way the Society is certain of receiving ample means to sustain and conduct efficiently all the schools established when this act was passed. If they determine to establish more schools, then it will be because they are determined to execute the duties which the officers elected under this act were elected to perform. It is made the duty of the officers elected under this act to organize new schools whenever and wherever they are necessary. Suppose these officers pass upon an application for a new school, and decide that one is not necessary in the place designated. The officers of the Public School Society, in their greater experience and sounder discretion, determine it expedient to establish, and do establish, one there. The moneys apportioned to the Society, after paying its other expenses, are insufficient to defray any part of the necessary and legal expenses of this new school. How can this board certify that such expenses were unavoidable ? Unless this board does so certify, the Society has no certainty of obtaining money to meet the deficiency. And yet, if its powers are such as it has urged here, it is the duty of the Common Council to supply that deficiency.

The only construction which can be given to the act which will render its provisions harmonious, is this : The Public School Society is deprived of the power to increase the number of its schools. This board shall authorize the payment to it of only sufficient moneys to defray the necessary and legal expenses of "the schools" which had been established by it on the 7th of May, 1844 ; and if all the moneys "apportioned" to it are insufficient to defray those expenses, the deficiencies shall be supplied. By that rule, it will participate "in the same manner and to the same extent" as the ward schools. By any other rule, it will participate in a different manner and to a different extent.

The Society cannot strengthen its claim by invoking that provision which declares that the moneys appropriated shall "be applied exclusively to the purposes of common schools."

The erection of school-houses, the purchase or hiring of lots, is not a "purpose" to which the ward schools or their officers can apply this money. It is not a use to which it can be applied under the common school law of the State. There is nothing in the act to tolerate the position that such a class of expenditures is legitimately for common school purposes, when the acts of that Society are in question, and that the same kind of expenditures would not be for common school purposes when the acts of the ward officers and of this board were in question.

Neither can that Society strengthen its claim by that part of the 12th section which provides that, "if any school shall have been 'organized' since the last annual apportionment, 'it shall be entitled to draw for the scholars taught in it.'"

That clause clearly refers to schools organized by the ward officers and this board. The 3d section declares that the schools organized under this act shall be designated "ward schools." The 8th, 9th, and 10th sections provide how these schools shall be organized. The 11th section provides that the various schools enumerated in it shall participate in the school moneys in the same manner and to the same extent as herein provided in respect to such schools as may be organized under this act.

Section 12 provides for the apportionment of all the school moneys, "except so much as shall have been raised for the purpose of establishing and organizing new schools." Then comes the provision that, "if any school shall have been organized since the last apportionment," &c.

Thus this clause incontestably refers to "any school organized under this act." The great object for which this act was passed was to organize new schools. The possibility of the Public School Society organizing a new school is not alluded to throughout the act.

Nothing can be found to support the claim of the Public School Society in the 36th section of the act, which requires them to report annually "the whole number of schools within their jurisdiction." To make an argument out of that provision, it must be assumed that this act contemplates that the number of their schools will or may be increased. I shall undertake to show that the act contemplates that the number of their schools may, and probably will, be diminished; that some subsequent report will show a diminished number of schools within their jurisdiction, and that, too, though they perform their full and whole duty to the public, and do it well.

The New York Orphan Asylum School, the Roman Catholic Orphan Asylum School, the school of the Mechanics' Society, the Harlem School, the Yorkville Public School, the Manhattanville Free School, the Hamilton Free School, the Institution for the Blind, the school of the Leake and Watts Orphan House, the school connected with the Almshouse, and the school of the association for the benefit of the Colored Orphans, also have the right, as well as "the schools of the Public School Society," to participate in the school moneys in the same manner and to the same extent as the ward schools. The trustees or managers of these various schools and societies are also required, by section 36, to report annually and severally "the whole number of schools within their jurisdiction." And yet, by section

11, it is only " the school," the single and solitary school of each of them, that can participate in the school moneys. Either of those societies can make as strong an argument on section 36, in favor of the right of a " new school " of theirs to participate in the school moneys, as the Public School Society.

That Society cannot strengthen its claim by appealing to the concluding clause of section 11, which provides that " titles to all school property, real or personal, hereafter purchased from all moneys derived from the distribution of the school fund, or raised by taxation in the city of New York, shall be vested in the Mayor, Aldermen, and Commonalty of the city and county of New York."

Before the act of May 7, 1844, was passed, that Society held a large amount of moneys derived ·from the " distribution of the school fund," and raised by taxation in the city of New York, which, by the act of April 18, 1843, that Society was authorized to expend in purchasing lots and erecting buildings. But the latter act required the title to all school property purchased with such moneys to be vested in the city Corporation.

Those moneys had not been wholly expended when the act of May 7, 1844, was passed. The act of April 18, 1843, was repealed by the act of May 7, 1844.

Hence, the latter act required the Society, if it used that balance to purchase school property, to vest the title to all property, which they should thereafter purchase with those moneys, in the Corporation. The title to all they had previously bought with it had been already so vested, if the officers of that Society did their duty. The Legislature did not intend, by repealing the act of 1843, to give that surplus to the Society. That body intended that, though real or personal estate should be purchased after the repeal of the act of 1843, with that money, that the title to such real or personal estate should be vested in the Corporation.

This view answers the whole argument made in behalf of the Public School Society, so far as it was based on the terms and provisions of the act of 1844.

The 50th section of this act repeals the acts of April 11, 1842, April 18, 1843, and all other acts specially applicable to public or common schools in this city and county, so far as the same are inconsistent with the provisions of this act.

The act of 1842 was unlike the act of 1844. The 13th section provided that " the schools of the Public School Society " " shall be subject to the general jurisdiction of the said commissioners of the respective wards in which any of the said schools now are or hereafter may be located." The act of 1843 had the same provision. This clearly contemplated the establishment of new schools by the Society. There is no such provision in the act of 1844.

The 15th section of the act of 1842 made it the duty of the board to apportion the school moneys among all the schools in proportion to the number taught ; and section 16 made it the duty of the ward commissioners, when they received this money, to apply it at once to the use of these schools according to the apportionment. The act of 1843 had the same provisions.

By the act of 1844, the money which goes to this Society is not paid to the ward commissioners, but is so far placed under the control of this board, that the board is prohibited from authorizing the payment of only enough of the moneys apportioned, to defray the necessary and legal expenses of the Society in conducting the schools entitled to participate in these moneys.

Why could not that Society, after it had received an apportionment under the act of 1843, use those moneys to establish new schools? The reasons are these: the 11th section of that act repealed all acts " and all provisions therein providing for, or directing, or concerning the disbursing or appropriation of the funds created or applicable to common school education in the city and county of New York," so far as the same were inconsistent with the provisions of that act.

That act made two funds : one, to organize new schools, which was placed under the exclusive control of the ward officers ; the other, to defray the expenses of schools fully organized. Hence, although the Society had more money apportioned to it, and received more money, than was required to defray the expenses of its established schools, it could not use the surplus to establish new schools. Section 9 of that act, like section 5 of the act of 1844, directed that the school moneys thus apportioned should be applied exclusively to the purposes " of common schools in said city."

The general act in relation to the common schools of the State, which, by the act of 1842, was extended to this city, did not provide for using such moneys to purchase lots, or hire or erect school-houses, but, on the contrary, prohibited such use of them. It was, then, inconsistent with the provisions of the act of 1842 for the Public School Society to use those moneys for any such purpose. In 1843, the Legislature authorized them to use the school moneys which they received for " any of the purposes of common school instruction, which they were authorized by law to do," before the passage of the act of April 11, 1842. This amendment gave authority to do that which the act of 1842 did not allow to be done.

There is no such authority contained in the act of 1844. The latter act only gives the right to " participate in the same manner and to the same extent " as the ward schools. The extent to which the ward schools can participate, is such as will defray the expense of schools fully organized and established. Neither the ward officers nor this board can employ these moneys to establish new schools.

The Public School Society, in their annual report for 1845, declared that they understood such to be the fair meaning and force of the act of 1844. At page 4 of that report, the Society expressed its own deliberate judgment of its powers under the act of May 7, 1844, in these words :

By the provisions of the act of April, 1844 (meaning May 7, 1844, as that is the date of the passage of this act), it is understood the board are prohibited from the further erection of buildings ; and it is even doubted whether they are authorized to pay rent on school premises, or interest on the large debt, which, in the absence of an adequate tax, they were induced to incur by mortgaging several of the school-buildings, from time to time, during a series of years past, in order to meet, as far as practicable, the pressing wants of a rapidly-increasing population.

The Society now claim not only that such opinion was erroneous, but that they have the power, under that act, to establish as many schools and erect as many buildings as they please ; that such schools will be entitled to participate in the "school moneys," and that such moneys may be applied to defray the expense of erecting such new buildings. The view of the law which the Society expressed in their annual report for 1845, was undoubtedly correct ; but that view the Society now repudiate.

The last and main ground on which the Public School Society rests its claims, is the power given by the act incorporating it. Its learned advocate contended that this Society "had a right by law—the law of its creation— to build as many school-houses and open as many schools as it pleased ; " that this right was indestructible, and that the Legislature could not abrogate it.

To the first proposition, in the broad terms in which it is expressed, I cannot subscribe.

The Society, in its origin, was an eleemosynary institution—it was a charity school. The objects of its bounty were precisely defined. The act of incorporation (passed April 9, 1805) recites "that De Witt Clinton, and others, have associated themselves for the laudable purpose of establishing a free school in the city of New York, for the education of the children of persons in indigent circumstances, and who do not belong to, or are not provided for by, any religious society."

The 2d section of that act gave power to the trustees, for the time being, to establish two or more free schools, when a majority of the members of the Corporation, at a general meeting, by a majority of all of them, "shall judge it expedient, for the more fully extending the benefits of education to poor children, agreeably to the benevolent design of the said association."

The act of April 1, 1808, extended "the powers" of the Society "to all children who are the proper objects of a gratuitous education," and changed its name to that of "The Free School Society of New York."

This was the whole extent of its powers down to January 28, 1826. I deny that the Society had the right to establish more schools than could be employed to teach children who were "the proper objects of a gratuitous education." Its powers, conferred by the law of its creation, had this extent, and no more.

Conceding these powers to be irrepealable, and the argument in behalf of the Society establishes an abstract right, which, practically, is a mere abstraction, and nothing else. It can have no occasion to increase the number of its schools to instruct children of this description. A tithe of its established schools will accommodate all the indigent children who are the proper objects of a gratuitous education. If by that phrase is meant such children as cannot acquire a common school education without the exercise of the bounty of the benevolent members of this Society, then it may be answered that this city contains now no such children. If there are not schools enough to accommodate all children, whether their parents are rich or poor, or do or do not belong to any religious society, then it is the duty of the ward officers, and of this board, to supply the deficiency. We have no pauper scholars in this city. None need go a-begging for admission to a common school. All are provided for. The power of the Society to provide schools for pauper children has been reduced to a skeleton abstraction, by the intelligence, liberality, and humanity of our citizens. They have provided a system under which all can be educated on common terms, with common rights, and without any one having the power to point to any other as a beneficiary. Each can feel the consciousness of a common independence, of equality of privileges and rights.

In 1826, an act was passed by which this Society was made the agent or instrument of the public in disseminating common school education. That act made it its duty to "provide for the education of all children in the city not otherwise provided for, to the extent of its means." By that act, the same agency was entrusted to that Society which, by the act of May 7, 1844, is entrusted to the officers elected under the latter, but with this striking difference : the latter officers are not limited in the amount of duty by "the extent of their means." They are required to supply all needed accommodations, and draw on their constituents for the means to defray the expense. It is as much within the power of the Legislature to repeal the act of 1826, as the act of 1844. The latter act has repealed the former. The officers elected under the act of 1844 are charged with doing the whole duty which the act of 1826 charged that Society to perform, so far as its means might extend.

The act of January 20, 1829, gave power to that Society, on complying with certain formalities, and on the resolution of a majority of the whole number of trustees at a regular meeting, confirmed by a vote of any subsequent regular meeting, declaring it "necessary and proper" so to do, to mortgage any of its property "for the purpose of carrying into effect the objects of the said Society, as the same are set forth and expressed in any of the acts of the Legislature relating thereto."

So far as they are authorized to mortgage, to carry into effect the objects expressed in the act of 1826, the power is clearly repealable, and has been repealed. The Society has no power to mortgage their property, to run a race of competition with a public body which is charged with the duty of providing for the entire common school education in the city. Although the Society may have the abstract right to mortgage, to raise means to erect buildings and open new schools to instruct poor children, who are the proper objects of a gratuitous education, we must do the Legislature the justice to suppose they could not have contemplated that the Society would resolve it to be "necessary and proper" so to do, after ample means had been provided for the education of all children in the city.

The 50th section of the act of 1844 repeals all laws inconsistent with its own provisions, especially relating to the public or common schools. It repeals the act of 1826, which made that Society the agent of the public to educate all children, and created a class of officers to perform that sacred duty, and no other.

It repealed the power of the Society to mortgage their property for any such purpose. It repealed their power to establish " common schools," properly so called.

It repealed, as the act of 1842 in effect did, the law of February 27, 1807, which gave the Society $1,000 annually out of the excise duties.

It repealed the act of March 30, 1811, which gave the Society annually an additional $500 out of the excise duties, " to promote the benevolent objects of the said corporation." The act of 1844 makes the taxation which it authorizes a substitute for, and declares it to be the extent of, all assessments for common school education.

It repeals all laws authorizing the Public School Society to receive any more of the school moneys than may be required to defray the necessary and legal expenses of the schools in existence when that act was passed, and prohibits this board from authorizing the payment to it of more than such expenses.

All such provisions are clearly inconsistent with the act of May 7, 1844.

Under this construction of the act, the schools of this Society may, and probably will, decrease in number. So far as they are established in leased buildings, they will terminate with the expiration of the leases. When they are terminated, if a new school is needed, the ward officers and this board must establish one. In that event, the Society will have occasion to report a decreased number of schools " within their jurisdiction." They may not resolve it to be necessary and proper to mortgage their property to supply its place, when they consider that the people have elected officers, made it their duty to supply the desired accommodations, and given them power to command the means to defray the necessary expense.

These considerations show, as I think, conclusively, that the Society has no power to establish new " common schools," properly so called, nor any right to mortgage its property for any such purpose. Its original power to establish free schools for the education of poor children is at best but a mere abstract right, without there being practically any such objects to call for its exercise. Its present schools will more than accommodate all of that description which in legal contemplation can exist, while there is a body of officers existing under an act which imposes the duty and furnishes the means of providing for the education of all children in the city.

It is not, perhaps, unnatural that the Society should regret that its present powers will confine its new operations to the benevolent and charitable designs of its founders. A laudable ambition may have disposed its members not only to desire the education of the indigent, but also of the children of those parents who may feel competent to construct a system adapted to their wants, and which the public may so fully approve, that they will feel both pride and pleasure in sustaining it.

They certainly cannot regret the substitution of a new agency for managing public instruction, unless they are conscious that they can perform the same high duty with more economy, and more in conformity with the public wants. The passage of the act of 1844 is no reflection upon the intelligence, patriotism, or fidelity of their officers. The public sense of the value of their services is evinced by the provision, which supplies ample means to continue their established schools with success and efficiency.

It is not unnatural that the people should desire the election by themselves of officers who have the power of subjecting them to taxation, and the expenditure of their money for public purposes. It would seem all fit and proper that it should be so. Public attention is evidently sufficiently observing of the action of the school officers to indicate that, if they fail to meet public expectation, successors will be elected to fill their places, who will bring to the discharge of their duties increased intelligence and efficiency.

The possession of power by the Public School Society, equal to that of the ward officers, to organize new schools, can only be desired for the patriotic purpose of proving the Society to be a better public agent than the officers elected under the act of 1844. Two agents equally good, when either one can do the whole duty, would seem to be unnecessary. Unless the Public School Society can serve the public better than their officers, the exercise of the same powers concurrently by both would not promise any practical utility. As the law now is, I am forced to the conclusion that the Society has not the power which it claims, and which, for the purpose of removing doubts, it generously invites this board to unite with it in an application to the Legislature to grant to it. That is a matter which, I think, properly belongs to the people, by whom the members of this board were elected. The application, when made, should be made by them, and not by their officers, who were elected to execute the law as it is.

The board cannot properly devote itself officially to any thing else than a full and efficient discharge of the trust confided to it, and to an impartial and firm execution of the law which defines its powers and prescribes the rule of its action. I think that the Board of Education is expressly prohibited by that law from authorizing the payment to the Public School Society of any greater amount of the school moneys than shall be sufficient to defray the necessary and legal expenses of "the schools" established and within its jurisdiction at the time that act was passed.

At the close of Mr. Bosworth's remarks, the question was taken on the adoption of Mr. Mason's amendment, and it was decided in the affirmative.

When the resolution was reported to the trustees of the Society, the subject was referred to the Executive Committee, with directions to memorialize the Legislature for a declaratory act, defining the powers of the Society. This course was accordingly taken, and on the 4th of March, 1848, the following bill was passed, and became a law:

The People of the State of New York, represented in Senate and Assembly, do enact as follows :

Sec. 1. Any schools which have been established by the Public School Society of the city of New York, since the passage of the act entitled "An Act more ,Effectually to Provide for Common School Education in the City of New York," passed May 7, 1844, may be continued and supported, and may be allowed to participate in the public money apportioned to said Society, in the same manner as if they had been established before the passage of said act ; but the said Public School Society shall not establish any new school without the consent of the Board of Education.

Sec. 2. The said Public School Society have power to purchase, erect, or, hire óther buildings in place of those now occupied by their schools, whenever it shall become necessary for the purpose of said schools now existing.

Sec. 3. This act shall take effect immediately.

This definition of the powers of the Society set the question at rest, and the trustees saw that they had reached the limits of their sphere of labor, and that thenceforth their energies were to be employed in imparting the highest efficiency to the schools then under their care.

The annual meeting of the board was held on the 11th of January, 1847, at which time GEORGE T. TRIMBLE was elected President, which office he held up to the day on which the Society terminated its existence.

LINDLEY MURRAY, the late President, was, at the time, on a visit to the island of Madeira, whither he had sailed in the pursuit of health. But the long life of usefulness which he had spent was drawing to its close, and, on his return voyage, he was called to sleep in peace, in the hope of a glorious immortality.

In May, 1849, A. P. HALSEY, the Treasurer, tendered his resignation, and JOSHUA S. UNDERHILL was elected as his successor.

It being deemed expedient to close the primary school in Oak street, and dispose of the property, an opportunity was presented of selling it at the price of $8,000, which the Society accepted, and it was transferred to its new owners.

The demands made upon the treasury became so much greater than its resources, that the trustees found themselves obliged to appeal to the Board of Education for special appropriations to meet deficiencies. These deficiencies were usually provided for, in whole or in part, until 1850, when an application was made for $50,140.10, the deficit existing at that time. The Board of

Education granted $35,000, leaving $15,000 unprovided for, as liable to objection under the provisions of the law relative to expenditures for property, the title of which had not been vested in the city. In 1851, the application was urged anew, and referred to the Finance Committee of the Board of Education, who submitted a report adverse to the appropriation. When the result was communicated to the trustees of the Society, a resolution was immediately presented, in the following form :

Resolved, That, in the opinion of the Board of Trustees of the Public School Society, it is expedient to repeat a tender of the transfer of the property held by the Society to the Common Council of New York, in accordance with the sanction of the final clause of the act of January 28, 1826, relating thereto.

The resolution was laid on the table, and the committee having charge of the matter were directed to visit Albany, to take such steps as might be found necessary to protect the rights and privileges of the Society, a bill being then under consideration relative to the school systems of the city. The committee discharged the duty assigned them, and reported that a section had been introduced into the bill, which had become a law, which contained the following proviso :

But nothing in this act shall take away from the Public School Society any right which they have heretofore enjoyed ; and the Board of Education are authorized to provide the Public School Society with all necessary moneys to make all proper repairs, alterations, and improvements in the various school-premises occupied by them.

The year 1852 brought, at its commencement, a formal communication from the Board of Education relative to an event which had already been freely discussed as impending, and likely to be consummated at a not distant period—the union of the two systems, and the harmonizing of the whole scheme of common schools in the city under one Central Board. At the meeting of the trustees, January 26th, a communication was laid before them, in which it was stated that the Board of Education had appointed a committee to confer with a committee on behalf of the Society relative to a plan of union. Messrs. George T. Trimble, Peter Cooper, and Joseph B. Collins were named as the Committee of Conference, to which Messrs. Charles E. Pierson and James F. Depeyster were subsequently added.

In May, the board decided to borrow $40,000 on bond and mortgage of their property, that amount being necessary to meet the expenses of the schools, and the Treasurer and Finance Committee were directed to take the usual course for obtaining that amount.

In November, the trustees resolved to sell the primary school in Twenty-fifth street, between Madison and Fourth avenues; and in January, 1853, information being given that Duane street would be widened by the addition of twenty-five feet from the north side of the street, and that the property known as No. 10 could be sold for a considerable sum, Messrs. Linus W. Stevens, William H. Neilson, James F. Depeyster, and George T. Trimble were appointed to report on the expediency of the sale. This measure became more necessary from the fact that the building would be reduced to so small a size as to be practically valueless, and also that a large ward school, under the care of the Board of Education, had been erected in the vicinity, at the corner of North Moore and Varick streets. The committee were directed to take only preliminary steps toward the sale of the property, so that the decision of the Legislature upon the bill for the consolidation of the two systems should be known. In the event of the failure of the bill, the property should be sold. The bill failed at the regular session, and the property was sold to Thomas Hope, for $39,900. The proceeds were to be appropriated to the payment of the floating debt of the Society. In accordance with the terms of the sale, the school was closed on the 30th of June, and the premises which had so long been occupied for the education of youth in the paths of knowledge, virtue, and religion (the building was long occupied for a Sunday school), was diverted to very different purposes.

CHAPTER XV.

UNION OF THE PUBLIC SCHOOL SOCIETY AND THE BOARD OF EDUCATION.—1853.

Corporate and Popular Boards of School Officers—Resources—Importance of a Uniform System—Proceedings of the Board of Education—Committee of Conference Appointed—Basis of Union Adopted—Proposed School Bill—Proceedings of the Society—Legislative Compromises—Extra Session—Bill Passed—Commissioners and Trustees Appointed by the Society—Transfer of Property to the Corporation —Report of the Committee—Address of Peter Cooper—Meeting of the Board of Education—Reception of the Members appointed by the Society—Resolutions of Hon. Erastus C. Benedict, President of the Board—Remarks of William D. Murphy, Esq.

THE influence of the popular sentiment, combined with the embarrassments growing out of the dissimilarities of the system of the Public School Society and that established by the law of 1842, became more apparent every year. How far the educational scheme of a great metropolis is likely to be affected, in its partisan relations, where the school officers are chosen at a general election, longer experience in the city of New York will probably demonstrate. But the Board of Education having been in existence about ten years, and being composed of members chosen by the popular suffrage, it was calculated to attract the sympathies of the majority of the population. The Board of Education exercised a control over the common school moneys, which were, in the early years of the board, carefully guarded. The revenue of the Public School Society was found to be insufficient for its expenditures, and a more frequent and urgent resort was had to obtaining moneys either by the sale of property, or on bond and mortgage. The applications made on several occasions to the Board of Education for the amount of certain deficiencies, were always warmly contested in that body, and, on several occasions, were granted only in part, and even in opposition to the recommendations of the Finance Committee, who reported adversely on the question of the appropriations.

The rights and privileges of the Society had been clearly defined, as was supposed, by the amendments of 1843 and 1844; but, notwithstanding the special provisions of "the declaratory act," much importance was attached to the issue raised, that the Society had no right to open new schools and erect new buildings—the expansive power of the school administration being deemed to lie only in the Central Board, which had the power to grant or refuse the application of the boards of school officers of the several wards of the city.

The ample means placed by law at the disposal of the board were partially expended in the erection of substantial school-houses, the first of which were somewhat similar to those of the Society, with the difference that the basement-story, instead of being sunk four or five feet below the level of the street, was built above ground, thus giving improved light and ventilation. A competition, however, soon arose between the wards in regard to the size, character, and appointments of the school edifices, until the whole system of large and noble buildings became discussed both as an economical and educational necessity and advantage. The contrast thus drawn between the imposing structures of the ward schools and those of the Society was more marked every year. The transfer of pupils from the old to the new schools was constant, and yet the Society was steadily increasing the number of its pupils from the thousands of residents who were annually swelling the mighty tide of population at a rate scarcely known in the history of the world. These and other causes had at last evidently fixed the limits of the sphere of usefulness in which the Society should labor. Its long-urged purpose of establishing daily normal schools of a high and commanding character, and a high school or academy for collegiate education, were placed altogether beyond its grasp. In ten years, the schools of the new system had already outnumbered those of the Society. A noble institution had been founded, and a building erected, at a cost of about $50,000, for the "Free Academy," and the financial power, very far exceeding in amount the fondest hopes of the Society, had been exercised in the rapid development and execution of plans which they had cherished for a quarter of a century.

An objection had long been urged against the Society. By its charter, it was an "association" of voluntary members. The

37

trustees and Executive, elected by the body itself, were responsible to the Society, and the elections were therefore only calculated to make the governing power perpetuate itself. The popular sympathies in favor of an unrestricted system, as opposed to a " close corporation," were easily excited, and the advocates of change, innovation, or of denominational pretensions, were loud and persistent in their condemnation of this feature in the constitution of the Society. On a number of occasions, from the time of the controversy with the Baptists, in 1822, down to the successful contest maintained against it, from 1840 to 1842, the climax which gave the highest force to argument, statistics, and appeals, was the fact that the Society was a " close corporation." Neither the labors, the discipline, the system, nor the character of the Society could be impeached, except upon sectarian appeals for a portion of the school fund, or by men who were willing to make it subserve a temporary purpose for political exaltation and preferment. The character of its officers and members, their positions in business and social circles, their integrity and conscientiousness, their prudence and economy, exercised even to the disadvantage of the schools from necessity, were beyond reproach or attack. Never, probably, in the history of the world, has an institution of such extent, and authorized to expend so much public money annually, been conducted with such scrupulous care in regard to its expenditures; and none has ever surpassed it in the results of its labors with the same amount of means.

The most liberal and enlightened friends of education in the city could not remain insensible to the fact, that the prejudices which had been aroused could not soon be overcome, and that, however perfect a corporate system of public instruction might be made, were its resources sufficient, the day had passed for a full development of the scheme of the Public School Society. It became apparent that the interests of public education in the city demanded a uniform system, under the care of one Central Board, which should combine, if possible, a conservative character with that of the popular prestige. The decision of this proposition left no alternative—the Public School Society must become a part of the new system, and surrender its independent trust. How far these considerations may have induced members of the Board of Education to restrict the revenue of the Society in order to expedite the consummation, is a fair ground of conjecture, and is left for the judgment of the reader.

A resolution was offered by Wm. Hibbard, M.D., one of the commissioners for the Seventeenth Ward, in the Board of Education, on the 21st of January, 1852, and submitted to the Society at an adjourned meeting held on the 26th of the same month, in the following communication :

To GEORGE T. TRIMBLE, *President of the Public School Society :*

SIR : At a meeting of the Board of Education, held on Wednesday evening last, the following resolution was adopted, viz. :

Resolved, That a committee of three members of this board be appointed to confer with a committee of the trustees of the Public School Society, for the purpose of effecting a union of the two systems.

Whereupon William Hibbard, of the Seventeenth Ward, Samuel A. Crapo, of the Sixteenth Ward, and Edward L. Beadle, of the Fifteenth Ward, were appointed as said committee.

Will you, sir, be pleased to lay this subject before the body over whom you preside, and signify to them the hope, on our part, that a similar committee will be appointed on their part, and advise us of the result at your earliest convenience.

Very respectfully, your obedient servant,

WILLIAM HIBBARD, *Chairman.*

Saturday, January 24, 1852.

After a long discussion upon this important proposition, George T. Trimble, Peter Cooper, and Joseph B. Collins were appointed as the committee on behalf of the Society. On the 9th of April, Dr. Charles E. Pierson and James F. Depeyster were added to the number.

The joint committees thus appointed held numerous sessions, and at length submitted several propositions on behalf of both parties, and, on the 1st of October, they were presented to the Board of Trustees. A special meeting for their consideration was called for the 15th of the same month, at which time they were read, as follows :

The Public School Society to transfer to the city all the real and personal estate now held by said Society, subject to all the debts, liens, and encumbrances thereon, the payment of which shall be assumed by the city ; the property so conveyed to be forever devoted to the purposes of public education.

And said Society also to surrender and discontinue its organization and existence.

Previous to the dissolution of said Society, it may select and appoint fifteen of its trustees to be commissioners at large of common schools, and members of the Board of Education, who shall serve as such during the continuance in office of the present members of the Board of Education.

And thereafter there shall be, in addition to the present number of commissioners, one member of the Board of Education from each ward, who shall be appointed by the school officers of each ward.

The said Society to appoint, previous to its dissolution, for each of the wards in which one or more schools of the said Society are now established, three of its members, to be trustees of common schools for the wards, who shall be so classed that one shall serve until January 1st, 1855, one until January 1st, 1856, and one until January 1st, 1857, who shall possess the same powers and rights with, and be liable to the same duties as, the present ward school trustees.

Vacancies among the trustees so appointed to be filled in the same manner as vacancies among the ward trustees are now filled.

And, after the 1st of January, 185–, there shall be eight ward trustees to serve four years, two of whom shall be elected each year.

The foregoing propositions to be presented to both boards. If it passes them, then both shall unite in an application to the Legislature for the passage of a law consummating the union upon the basis of this programme.

A long and earnest debate arose upon this report, after which the following resolution was adopted :

Resolved, That the report of the Committee of Conference just submitted be adopted, as a general basis for legislative action, by the Board of Trustees of the Public School Society ; *Provided*, that the trustees to be chosen under the proposed plan shall not be required to reside in the wards for which they are appointed to serve ; and *provided*, further, that the Committee of Conference of this Society shall unite with a committee of the Board of Education in drafting a law to carry into effect such report, and for such other modifications of existing laws in relation to schools in this city as may be deemed advisable ; such proposed law to be submitted first for the approval of the Society (at a meeting to be called for the purpose) and of the Board of Education, and then for adoption by the Legislature.

The ayes and nays were called, upon taking the question, and the gentlemen voting are recorded as follows :

Ayes—Messrs. G. T. Trimble, Peter Cooper, J. B. Collins, H. H. Barrow, F. W. Downer, J. F. Depeyster, John Davenport, Benjamin Ellis, W. Mandeville, A. Merwin, W. H. Neilson, R. G. Perkins, M.D., C. E. Pierson, M.D., Israel Russell, H. M. Schieffelin, S. W. Seton, L. W. Stevens, I. W. Underhill, W. Underhill, J. B. Varnum, L. B. Ward—21.

Nays—I. S. Underhill, J. T. Adams, W. P. Cooledge, J.

B. Brinsmade, J. R. Hurd, J. W. C. Leveridge, W. R. Vermilye—7.

The committee of the Board of Education submitted their report to that body, and, on the 10th of November, a committee, consisting of William D. Murphy, E. L. Beadle, Charles D. Field, Charles H. Smith, and J. E. Cary, were appointed to prepare the draft of a bill to be presented to the Legislature. This committee reported on the 8th of December, and the report was ordered to be printed. The trustees considered the same report at their meeting on the 17th of the same month, and, with such amendments as appeared proper, was approved, and ordered to be returned to the Board of Education as accepted. The Board of Education submitted a copy as amended at a regular meeting of that body, and, with two slight alterations, it was directed to be returned, with the approbation of the trustees.

These suggestions were happily met by the Board of Education, and on the 14th of January, 1853, the trustees received official information of the action of the board. There remained now no point of difference between the two bodies, and the measure was recommended for adoption by the Society. A special meeting was called, to be held on the 19th, at the Trustees' Hall, at which time Peter Cooper was called to the chair.

The bill, as adopted by both boards, was read, and, after a full discussion, the following preamble and resolution were adopted:

Whereas, The Legislature of the State of New York, in the year 1805, granted an act for incorporating an institution denominated "The Free-School Society," for the purpose of founding schools for educating a class of children not otherwise provided for, which was sustained mainly by the voluntary contributions of their fellow-citizens; and

Whereas, The said schools having been, for many years, conducted in a manner satisfactory to all parties interested therein, on the solicitations of the Board of Trustees of said schools, the wealthy and other citizens of this city petitioned for a tax to be levied on the property of its citizens, to be devoted to sustaining said schools, to be expended through the agency of said trustees, the name thereof having been also changed to that of "The Public School Society," at the same time; said Society were required to provide the means of education for all children, as far as their means permitted, and which they continued to do for a series of years with energy, economy, and usefulness; and

Whereas, The Legislature of the State did, in the year 1842, establish another system of common school education, modelled after that established for the State at large; and

Whereas, By the terms of said act, and the various amendments thereto, it was required that the Public School Society should thereafter draw its funds for the support of its schools, through the agency of the trustees, denominated " The Board of Education," created by the act aforesaid; and

Whereas, In consequence of adverse construction being put upon the terms of said act, the trustees of the Public School Society, in order to avoid a clashing of jurisdiction, did surrender their independent right to establish new schools; and

Whereas, The said trustees did, in the year 1851, procure from the Legislature an amendment to the school act, which, in the judgment so expressed by members of the said Board of Education, would enable the said trustees to obtain all the necessary funds for carrying on and improving the schools then under their charge; and

Whereas, The said Board of Education have refused to furnish the Public School Society with the necessary funds when solicited to do so; and

Whereas, The Board of Education did, by resolution, invite the trustees of the Public School Society to confer in relation to a proposition for the union of the two systems of education, which invitation was met by corresponding action on the part of the trustees of the Public School Society; and

Whereas, Pursuant to such proposition and the corresponding conference and action of both bodies, viz., the " Board of Education " and the Board of Trustees of the Public School Society, a form of union has been agreed upon, as set forth in the proposed act accompanying this paper; and

Whereas, Notwithstanding the Public School Society have, during a period of nearly half a century, conducted, with eminent success, energy, and economy, a great educational institution, in which hundreds of thousands of children have received instruction, yet yielding to the necessity of the case as above stated, and not from a conviction of their best judgment, and also hoping that a weighty sense of its importance will lead to the management of our common schools being committed to the hands of worthy citizens who will consult the public weal exclusively; therefore

Resolved, By the Public School Society, now duly convened pursuant to several days' notice in five of the public newspapers in the city of New York, that our Board of Trustees be, and they are hereby, authorized to take all necessary measures for procuring the enactment of the act herein referred to, with such alterations and amendments as may seem to them wise and proper in this matter, and hereby confirming whatsoever our said Board of Trustees have done and may do in the premises as fully as if done by ourselves.

The projects of union having thus been concurred in by both bodies, the several committees took the necessary steps for the enactment of the bill by the Legislature. On the 17th of February, Messrs. Peter Cooper, John Ely, William Mandeville, H. M. Schieffelin, and S. W. Seton, were appointed a committee to visit Albany, and take such measures as might be deemed proper to have the interests of the Society fully represented and recognized.

The bill became the subject of considerable controversy, and the conflicting opinions and views had a fair field of encounter on so important an issue as the surrender of the charter of a great public institution, which had done so much for the city and the nation at large. Compromises and concessions were, however, made by all parties, in order to consummate the plan of union. Its failure would have resulted in a loss of strength on the part of the Society from the fact of such steps having been taken, and a virtual surrender of its independence in all that pertains to the dignity and immunities of an establishment of high character would have been almost inevitable. It would, moreover, have placed the Board of Education in a position of delicacy and responsibility which would have been irksome to every man of fine feeling, while it would have given the antagonists of the Society a position of power to embarrass it which would have been full of unpleasant reminiscences. Notwithstanding all the influence brought to bear upon the measure, the differences were not reconciled at a sufficiently early day, and the Legislature adjourned without the final vote, the bill lying on the docket so closely in order that one or two days more would have disposed of it in the regular course of business.

An extra session of the Legislature having been convened, the bill was called up at an early day, and passed June 4th, and became a law. The first six sections are as follows:

AN ACT

RELATIVE TO COMMON SCHOOLS IN THE CITY OF NEW YORK.

The People of the State of New York, represented in Senate and Assembly, do enact as follows:

SEC. 1. The Public School Society of the city of New York shall, on or before the first day of September, eighteen hundred and fifty-three, convey and transfer, according to this act, by deed to be approved by the Counsel to the Corporation of said city, all their corporate property to the Mayor, Aldermen, and Commonalty of the city of New York, subject to all the liens and encumbrances thereon, and the debts of said Society; and thereupon the said property shall belong to the said Mayor, Aldermen, and Commonalty in the same manner as the school property now used and occupied by the ward schools belongs to the said Mayor, Aldermen, and Commonalty; and the schools of the Public School Society shall be ward schools, subject to the same control, and enjoy the same rights and privileges as if originally organized as ward schools; but such portions of the property aforesaid as have been granted to the Public School Society, subject to the trust that the same shall be devoted to the purposes of common schools, shall be held subject to such trust; and the premises now known as Trustees' Hall, situated at the corner of Grand and Elm streets, shall be used and occupied by the Board of Education as long as they may think advisable, for the meetings and business thereof, and for such educational purposes as said board may direct; and the residue of the property aforesaid shall be conveyed, for the purposes of common schools, in the same manner as the property purchased by the authority of the Board of Education, for the purposes aforesaid.

SEC. 2. The Public School Society shall, at the time of such conveyance, make a detailed statement of all their property, real and personal, and of all their debts of every description existing at the time of such conveyance, which shall be certified as a full, just, and true statement of all such property and debts, by their president, treasurer, and secretary, and shall deliver one copy thereof, so certified, to the Comptroller of the city of New York, and the other copy, so certified, to the clerk of the city and county of New York, for the use of the Board of Supervisors of the city and county of New York; and the said Board of Supervisors shall thereupon proceed to audit and determine the amount of all the debts of the said Society, and shall cause the same to be certified and filed with the said Comptroller.

SEC. 3. Upon the amount of the debts of the said Society being so certified and filed, it shall be lawful for the Mayor, Aldermen, and Commonalty of the city of New York, and it shall be their duty, to raise by loan a sum not exceeding the amount of the debt so certified and filed, by the creation of a public fund or stock, to be called "The Public Education Stock of the City of New York of the Year One Thousand Eight Hundred and Fifty-Three," which shall bear an interest of five per cent. per annum, and which shall be redeemable at a period of time not more than twenty years from the passage of this act. The said Mayor, Aldermen, and Commonalty shall determine of what number of shares the said stock shall consist; and the said stock shall be disposed of by public competition, under the direction of the Commissioners of the Sinking Fund of the city of New York. The moneys raised by virtue of this act shall be applied for the purpose of paying and discharging all the said debts; any deficiency, by reason of interest accruing on the said debts, after the same are so certified and filed, shall be paid by the said Mayor, Aldermen, and Commonalty out of the city treasury; and any excess, by reason of the said stock being disposed of at a premium, shall be held as a part of the sinking fund hereinafter provided.

SEC. 4. The Board of Supervisors shall, yearly and every year, until the said stock shall be wholly redeemed and paid off, order and cause to be raised by tax on the estate, real and personal, of the freeholders and inhabitants of and situated within the said city and county, and to be collected according to law, a sum of money sufficient to pay the interest on the said stock as the same falls due, and to pay and discharge the principal by the time the same shall be payable. All of which moneys so to be raised shall be under the management and control of the Commissioners of the Sinking Fund of the city of New York; and all such moneys so to be raised are hereby inviolably pledged to pay the interest and redeem the principal of the said stock.

SEC. 5. The Public School Society may, immediately after so conveying all their corporate property, appoint fifteen from the then trustees of said Society to be commissioners of common schools for the city of New York, and members of the Board of Education, designating the ward for which each person is appointed, and not more than one for any one ward, who shall hold their offices till the first day of January, one thousand eight hundred and fifty-five; and the said Public School Society may also, at the same time, appoint from among their own trustees three trustees of common schools for each ward of said city in which one or more of the schools of said Society are now established, designating the ward for which each person is appointed; and the said trustees so appointed shall be so designated in the certificate of appointment that one shall serve until January first, eighteen hundred and fifty-five, one till January first, eighteen hundred and fifty-six, and one until January first, eighteen hundred and fifty-seven. The said appointments shall be made by a certificate signed by the officers of said Society, and filed with the clerk of the Board of Education; and the said commissioners and trustees so appointed shall have the same rights and powers, and be subject to the same liabilities and duties, as other commissioners and trustees of common schools in said city, except that they need not reside in the wards for which they are appointed. Any vacancy occurring in the office of any such commissioner or trustee, shall be filled in the same manner as vacancies in school offices are now filled.

SEC. 6. As soon as the said Public School Society shall have conveyed all their corporate property, and made and filed the statements, and made and filed appointments of commissioners and trustees, provided for in the previous sections of this act, the corporate powers and existence of the said Public School Society shall cease, and their schools be merged in the system of public instruction provided by the act entitled "An Act to Amend, Consolidate, and Reduce to One Act the Various Acts Relative to the Common Schools of the City of New York," passed July third, eighteen hundred and fifty-one, so as to be and remain, pursuant to the provisions of this act, an integral portion thereof, and then and thereby the said Society shall be dissolved, and then and from thenceforth the common schools in the city of New York shall be numbered consecutively by the Board of Education.

On the passage of the bill, a special meeting of the Society was called, at which a resolution was adopted extending an invitation to the Board of Education to hold its meetings in the

Trustees' Hall, and another resolution, " that the board surrender their schools to the Board of Education, and convey their property to the Mayor, Aldermen, and Commonalty of the city of New York, on the 1st day of August next, agreeably with the act of June 4, 1853."

A committee of five trustees was appointed to make the preliminary arrangements necessary to carry the law into effect, and Messrs. J. W. C. Leveridge, L. W. Stevens, Joseph Curtis, W. P. Cooledge, and John Davenport, were selected for that duty.

At a meeting held on the 1st of July, the Board of Trustees proceeded to nominate and elect the fifteen commissioners required by the law, and the following gentlemen were declared to be chosen: C. E. Pierson, M.D., J. W. C. Leveridge, John T. Adams, Israel Russell, Thomas B. Stillman, Joseph Curtis, H. H. Barrow, Joseph B. Collins, L. W. Stevens, J. F. Depeyster, B. R. Winthrop, Peter Cooper, John Davenport, William H. Neilson, William P. Cooledge.

The following gentlemen were chosen as trustees:

First Ward.—George E. Cock, Pelatiah Perit.

Fourth Ward.—Robert R. Crosby, Justus S. Redfield.

Fifth Ward.—Ebenezer Platt, Timothy Hedges, Joseph W. Kellogg.

Sixth Ward.—Willett Seaman, James Marsh, Roe Lockwood.

Seventh Ward.—James B. Brinsmade, Joseph R. Skidmore, John Gray.

Eighth Ward.—Orlando D. McClain, Wyllis Blackstone, Joseph Potter.

Ninth Ward.—William Mandeville, Charles C. Leigh, Washington R. Vermilye.

Tenth Ward.—Thompson Price.

Eleventh Ward.—Nehemiah Miller, Abner Mills, S. P. Patterson.

Twelfth Ward.—Ebenezer H. Brown, Daniel F. Tiemann, Thomas Richmond.

Thirteenth Ward.—Richard Reed, Benjamin B. Atterbury, Samuel W. Seton.

Fourteenth Ward.—John Ely, Lewis C. Hallock, Jacob Harsen.

Fifteenth Ward.—Eli Goodwin, Joseph B. Varnum, Caleb Swan.

Sixteenth Ward.—John W. Howe, B. C. Wandell, L. A. Rosenmüller.

Seventeenth Ward.—J. D. B. Stillman, Isaac Ward.

Eighteenth Ward.—Augustin Averill, Roger G. Perkins, James Stokes.

Twenty-first Ward.—William P. Lee, Henry M. Schieffelin, F. W. Downer.

Twenty-second Ward.—Lebbeus B. Ward, J. C. Hepburn, M. H. Mott.

On the 22d of July, at a special meeting called by the Committee of Transfer, a verbal report was made, and the action of the committee was approved. It was also

Resolved, That the several sections of the Public School Society invite the ward officers of their district to meet with them previous to the 1st day of August, with the view of placing the schools in their hands, during the vacation, for the purpose of repairs, cleaning, &c.

On the adoption of this resolution, the Board of Trustees adjourned, *sine die.*

The Society then held a meeting for the transaction of some formal business, among which was the reading of the deed of conveyance of the property to the city. Complimentary resolutions, returning thanks to the President, GEORGE T. TRIMBLE, and the Secretary, JOSEPH B. COLLINS, were passed, and the Society adjourned, to meet on the following Friday.

On the day appointed, being the 29th of July, the Society held a meeting, at which the Committee of Transfer submitted their final report, as follows :

To the New York Public School Society :

The committee appointed to make the necessary arrangements for terminating the " existence of the Public School Society," in conformity with the act of June 4th, 1853, RESPECTFULLY REPORT :

That they have completed the service assigned, in all respects, and now propose to lay before the Society a statement of the manner in which it has been done, and the results which have been severally attained.

It may not be deemed out of place for them to allude to the fact, that they have acted in all that pertains hereto from a sense of duty, and not from choice. They have fully felt the ungracious nature of the task allotted to them, but their best services have been held hitherto subject to the behest of the Public School Society in its days of noble usefulness, and hence it was not for them to shrink, when, in a grave posture of its affairs, it has become necessary to bring its concerns to a close, and expunge its name from among active and benevolent public institutions.

Since it must be so, to fully carry out the law which merges it in the Board of Education has been their constant care, and they trust that it will be found that nothing to this end has been left unaccomplished.

In order that the schools should be fully supplied with all necessary articles of use before their surrender, especially since, in the change at hand, and the possible confusion which may result at first from it, they may be for a time unprovided with indispensable supplies, the committee, at an early moment after their appointment, caused the following notice to be sent to the teachers generally, viz. :

Any authorized supplies for your school that may be required prior to the vacation in August next, will be delivered, if previously drawn for, during the first week in July, say from the 1st to the 7th. No further supplies will be furnished by the Public School Society, except at the time now specified.

To obtain the supplies needed, your pass-book, with all the due bills which you may have on hand, must be sent to the depository on or before June 27th.

It will be perceived that an early day was fixed in this notice for delivering the supplies to be drawn for. This was done in order that they might be easily placed in the schools before the time assigned for making a complete inventory of the property.

While the foregoing measure was in progress, the committee caused blank forms of inventory to be prepared, divided into three classes : first, a list of supplies in all their variety—books, slates, paper, pens, maps, &c. ; second, a list of books in the several libraries ; and third, a blank sheet, upon which to describe such philosophical apparatus, minerals, curiosities, &c., as might be found in a portion of the schools.

To the first, a properly-drawn certificate was attached, which the principal of every school was directed to sign ; and to the second a similar attestation of the correctness of the return was added, for the signature of the first assistant or librarian of the boys' department of the public schools ; but to the third, as it was expected to embrace such matters only as were considered the special property of the school in which they might be found, the Society having no claim upon them as not having originally provided them, no certificate was attached.

The calls for supplies were promptly made, and from every school, in greater or less quantity, with scarcely an exception. The delivery of these begun early in July, and it was completed before the 15th instant. So general had been the call, that goods to the value of about $2,750 were distributed on this single occasion. In this stage of the matter, and consistent with the plan originally laid down, the following notice was printed for circulation, viz. :

You are hereby required to furnish a detailed statement, by filling the blanks in the accompanying list of articles, of all the personal property or supplies in the school under your charge, adding thereto any other items that you may find on the premises, the names of which are omitted in said blanks.

To enable you to do this effectually, you will require the pupils to return all books and other supplies that may be in their possession, including library-books, on or before the 15th of July, after which date no books or supplies are to be taken from the school.

You will furnish the agent at the depository with four fair copies of said detailed statement by Wednesday, 20th of July, attested by your signature.

This notice, together with the blank forms of inventory of the personal property, was distributed by the agent in person, who accompanied them with such verbal explanation as would enable the parties concerned to return the papers in suitable condition for use on or before July 20th. Beside the agent, one of the committee visited the schools generally, that an assurance might be felt that all would be correctly and seasonably done.

Pending the arrangement of these matters, a sub-committee waited upon the treasurer, and received from him the various deeds, leases, &c., in his possession, and placed them in the hands of the counsel of the Society, to make by their aid the necessary deed of transfer and assignment of the leases, to the Mayor, Aldermen, and Commonalty of the city, as the law for the merging aforesaid requires.

So carefully had every step been taken, that, when the committee met, as it did on the 20th ultimo, they found every paper complete, and all in a satisfactory form. That these were receivable from one hundred and ten principal teachers and twenty librarians, the exceeding promptness with which the returns were made is both remarkable and commendable.

The following list comprises all the papers submitted to the committee on the occasion referred to :

Inventories from boys', girls', and primary departments of Public Schools Nos. 1 to 18, and Nos. 1 and 2, colored.

Inventories of libraries in boys' departments

Inventories from Primary Schools Nos. 1 to 55, and Nos. 3, 4, and 6, colored.

Inventories from male, female, and colored normal schools.

Inventory of supplies, &c., at the depository.

Inventory of property at the workshop.

List of articles delivered from Public School No. 10, by order of the board, to Ward Schools Nos. 14 and 29.

List of stoves, &c., from Public School No. 10, on storage with J. L. Mott.

These papers the committee had ordered to be prepared in quadruplicate, and, being so received, they were assorted, making four similar volumes, which were directed to be suitably bound in time for the meeting of the board, called for the 22d instant. For two of these four volumes the law had already provided an owner ; a third, it was resolved, should be presented to the Board of Education, and a fourth to the Society, for such disposition as it might see fit to make of it.

At the same meeting of the committee, a deed of transfer was presented, with an assignment of the leases aforesaid, also, which were carefully compared with a correct list of the property, and then, with some revisions, were ordered to be engrossed.

The following exhibits the property, the fee-simple of which is in the Public School Society, the same now conveyed in the deed aforesaid :

Public Schools Nos. 3, 4, 5, 7, 8, 9, 11, 12, 13, 14, 15, 16, 18, and, colored, Nos. 1 and 2.

Public School No. 2, on three lots, one held in trust.

Primary Schools Nos. 3 and 44, 5 and 20, 10 and 29, 14 and 40, 25 and 26, 27 and 28, 35 and 55, 38 and 39, 41 and 51, 42 and 43, 45 and 46.

Carpenter's shop, 94 Crosby street, and Trustees' Hall.

The above furnishing accommodations for sixty-nine schools.

The following shows the property held by lease, the same being expressly assigned to the authority before named in the lease aforesaid :

Primary Schools Nos. 2 and 13, 19 and 37, 33 and 34, 53 and 54.

The same furnishing premises for eight schools.

In addition to the property owned or leased by the Public School Society, the following premises are hired from year to year, at the sums annexed below, all being used for primary school purposes :

Primary School No. 1, Orchard street, .	.	$200
" " 4, Chrystie street,	. .	200
" " 6, Suffolk street,	. .	130
" " 7, Sixth street, .	. .	200
" " 8, King street,	. .	200
" " 9, corner Amos and Bleecker streets,		200
" " 11, Pearl street,	. .	200
" " 12, corner Broome and Ridge streets,		200
" " 15, Stanton street, .	. .	150
" " 18, Cannon street,	. .	200
" " 21, Twentieth street,	. .	175
" " 23, Avenue C and Fourth street,		200
" " 24, cor. Bleecker and Downing streets,		200
" " 30, Centre street,	. .	300
" " 36, Forty-third street,	. .	200
" " 48, Houston street,	. .	150
" " 49 and 50, Eleventh street,	.	300
" colored, 4 and 6, Second street,	.	350
" " 3, Fifteenth street, rent paid to 1856.		

The same providing for twenty-one schools.

The title to the ground on which the following schools stand, is already in the city :

Public Schools Nos. 1, 6, 17 ; Primary Schools Nos. 31, 32 (three rooms), and 52 ; affording accommodations for twelve schools.

The whole number of schools under the charge of the Public School Society is therefore as follows, viz. :

In houses belonging to the Society, held in fee, .	. .	69
" " " the ground held by lease,		8
" " " " owned by the city,		12
In houses rented for the purpose, .	. . .	21

Total, ... 110*

* For the location of these schools, see pages 594, 595.

The schools generally having prepared a fifth copy of the inventory of personal property, one of the committee, with the agent, was detailed to visit the several schools, and insert it in the visitors' book. They were also directed to insert in the book of the public or upper schools, copies of the record of the March examinations, and the reports of the committee on stoves and fuel lately printed, and in the book of the primary schools the record of the June examination, with the printed reports just named. These papers, being secured in the books, will furnish, in permanent form, important statistics to our successors, show the care and accuracy with which our affairs, or a part of them, have been managed, and exhibit also at a glance, to their several future supervisors, the grade and standing of our various schools and departments, giving, as they do, honor, qualified praise, or censure, where they have proved to be due.

The committee, viewing it as a matter of considerable importance, have attempted a valuation of the property now about to be surrendered by the Public School Society to the city, and with the following result :

Value of real estate, ...	$495,300.00
Value of personal property, ...	109,520.46
	$604,820.46

There are mortgages upon the real estate, with accruing interest, as follows :

One due Chambers street Bank for Savings, .	$75,000	
" Bowery Savings Bank, . .	35,000	
" New York Mutual Life Insurance Co.,	40,000	
" on lot in Forty-seventh street (Public School No. 18) at time of purchase, .	800	
		150,800.00

Leaving the value of property unencumbered, .	$454,020.46
Add to which the balance of the treasurer's account,	401.39
Making the value of the property transferred to the city,	$454,421.85

For the information of those who are desirous of knowing the various items of which this aggregate is made, a schedule of the property, with the valuation in detail, is appended to this report.

The committee is informed that all the floating debt of the Society has been paid, inclusive of rents, to August 1st, 1853. That section of the law which provides for a certificate of the amount of this debt to the Board of Supervisors is therefore inoperative.

The striking fact that the Public School Society is about to close its existence, and transfer so large an amount of unencumbered estate to the city of New York, excites in the minds of the committee an honest exultation, as it must in those of all the well-wishers of the Society; because upon grave occasions, and in public bodies, those who should have been and who might have been better informed, have declared it an insolvent and rotten concern, which was seeking to conceal its real condition by urging a union with a healthy and living institution. This calumny, at least, is now forever silenced. In this connection it may be added, that, in its disbursements of public money to the amount of millions of dollars, the first instance is yet to be shown where it has diverted a single dollar from its legitimate channel of service. The committee would even go so far as to add, that few institutions, here or elsewhere, of like or shorter duration, can exhibit a similar fact. In view of this statement alone, who shall say that the Public School Society has not acquired fame enough ?

In referring to the payment of the floating debt, the committee feel that the Society is under many obligations to some in the community who have been its creditors, for their very great forbearance during its pecuniary embarrassments. Though it has done the best it could under the circumstances, as it trusts they have believed, yet such has been its keen sense of the justice and pressing nature of their claims, and such its desire to meet them, that a less considerate course on their part would have rendered its position at times intolerable. To cancel all its obligations to its creditors itself, has been its principal wish, the gratification of which has, it seems, not been denied to it.

Among the many subjects of inquiry which presented themselves to the committee, that relative to the probable number of children which has received instruction in its schools since the Society's organization in 1805, has claimed and received a good deal of attention, and the committee finds little ground of doubt that the whole number is six hundred thousand. To have educated this great number of youth, is to have been the dispenser of incalculable good to the community at large ; a fact which, while it is a source of sincere congratulation to the active participants in the labor, may console them for the sacrifices of time and effort which they have made in the discharge of their constant and arduous duties. Moreover, since the opening of the normal schools, more than one thousand two hundred teachers have been educated and fitted for service, a large proportion of whom are now actively discharging the responsible duties of their vocation in the schools of this city, securing, by this means, to a period still remote, the blessings of judicious education to the children of this commercial metropolis. Not a few of the whole number are also diffusing the moral lessons and intelligence, acquired in our schools, among the children of the neighboring cities and towns, or in the more distant parts of the Union, who have found it, we trust, no mean passport to the confidence and good offices of their new supervisors that they have graduated in the schools of the Public School Society.

It may be interesting, as a matter of history, to state, that the personal and real property of the Public School Society has been twice already tendered to the city authorities. The offer was made to satisfy a popular objection ; it having been argued that so much public property should not be controlled by a corporation, because it might, sooner or later, become corrupt, and squander it in the advancement of private objects, or in the furtherance of ends not contemplated by the law. It is, perhaps, honorable to both parties, that the tender was as often rejected, and the Society asked to hold steadily on its course.

On this day, the schools of the Public School Society have closed for the summer vacation; when they open again, their Alma Mater will have ceased to be. New auspices, new school officers to a large extent, and a new system of government and responsibility, will have supervened the ancient order of things. All the public schools of the city will then own one common head. The active, and, we trust, generous rivalry of systems which has grown up of later times, will no longer continue. Rivalry, if any there be, must be felt among members of the same household, or, at least, between one municipal division of the city and another, or between individual schools. What is to be the result of the change, it is not for us to say—whether for the better in relation to the common good, or for the worse. If we fear the latter, the sequel may disappoint us; if we were confident of the former, we could lay down our corporate trust with cheerfulness, and with an abiding hope in the future. The result is with the almighty Disposer of events.

The books containing an inventory of our personal property, with a certificate of the correctness of the return, to be signed by the officers of the Society, together with the deed of transfer, assignment of leases, &c., are presented herewith, and, when properly signed and legally executed, may be delivered to the recipients named in the law, who, the committee are informed, are in attendance for the purpose. This done, the Society may proceed to confirm the nomination of its commissioners and trustees, and thereupon its existence will cease.

As a conclusion to their labors, the committee offer the following resolution:

Resolved, That the books of minutes of the Society, of the Board of Trustees, of the Executive Committee, and of other standing committees, together with all the reports, documents, and treasurer's vouchers, and a copy of the inventory of personal property, &c., be deposited with the New York Historical Society.

(Signed)   L. W. STEVENS, *Chairman.*
                             JOSEPH CURTIS,
                             WILLIAM P. COOLEDGE,
                             JOHN DAVENPORT,
                             J. W. C. LEVERIDGE.

NEW YORK, *July* 29, 1853.

38

ESTIMATED VALUE OF REAL ESTATE AND PERSONAL PROPERTY BELONGING TO THE NEW YORK PUBLIC SCHOOL SOCIETY, JULY, 1853.

SCHOOLS.	LOCATION.	TITLE IN.	NO. OF LOTS.	GROUND.	HOUSE.	FURNITURE.	SUPPLIES.	TOTAL.
Pub. Schools.								
No. 1........	William st.	City.......	3	....	$12,000	$2,800	$1,200 00	$16,000 00
" 2........	Henry st.	2 in Socie-ety & 1 in Rutgers Church.	3	$8,000	10,000	3,000	1,250 00	22,250 00
" 3........	Hudson st.	P. S. Soc...	65 × 130	20,000	14,000	3,400	1,480 00	38,880 00
" 4........	Rivington st....	"	{ 75 × 100 20 × 65	12,000	4,000	2,000	1,015 00	19,015 00
" 5........	Mott st..........	"	3	10,000	8,000	2,200	1,075 00	21.275 00
" 6........	Randall's Island.	City.........	....	....	....	3,000	1,000 00	4,000 00
" 7........	Chrystie st......	P. S. Soc.	3	12,000	8,000	2,200	880 00	23,080 00
" 8........	Grand st........	"	3	12,000	12,000	2,800	1,040 00	27,840 00
" 9........	82d st...........	"	4	2,500	4,000	800	500 00	7,800 00
" 11........	Wooster st......	"	3	12,000	10,000	2,600	1,105 00	25,705 00
" 12........	17th st..........	"	4	12,000	11,000	3,000	1,310 00	27,310 00
" 13........	Madison st......	"	4	11,000	11,000	3,000	1,115 00	26,115 00
" 14........	Houston st......	"	4	11,000	11,000	3,000	1,190 00	26,190 00
" 15........	27th st..........	"	4	11,000	14,000	3,600	1,285 00	29,885 00
" 16........	5th st...........	"	4	11,000	12,000	3,000	1,300 00	27,300 00
" 17........	13th st..........	City.......	4	....	12,000	3,000	1,085 00	16,085 00
" 18........	47th st..........	P. S. Soc...	4	5,000	16,000	3,600	1,240 00	25,840 00
Colored, 1....	Mulberry st......	"	2	6,000	3,000	1,800	500 00	11,300 00
" 2....	Laurens st......	"	50 × 98	5,000	6,000	2,000	500 00	13,500 00
Trustees' Hall	Grand st........	"	2	20,000	20,000	2,500	3,460 00	45,960 00
Work Shop...	Crosby st.......	"	1	4,000	2,000	2,500	....	8,500 00
Primary Schools.								
No. 1........	Orchard st.:....	Rented....	....	....	....	400	140 00	540 00
" 2 & 13..	Bayard st.......	P. S. Soc...	1	Leased	4,800	800	305 00	5,905 00
" 3 & 44..	Cannon st.......	"	1	2,500	3,800	600	230 00	7,130 00
" 4........	Chrystie st......	Rented....	....	....	....	400	145 00	545 00
" 5 & 20..	Cherry st.......	P. S. Soc.	{ 21 × 86 1	2,500	3,600	500	205 00	6,805 00
" 6........	Suffolk st.......	Rented....	....	....	....	300	140 00	440 00
" 7........	Sixth st.........	"	....	....	....	400	140 00	540 00
" 8........	King st..........	"	....	....	....	400	175 00	575 00
" 9........	corner Amos & Bleecker......	"	....	....	....	400	170 00	570 00
" 10 & 29..	Amos st.........	P. S. Soc.	{ 25 × 95 1	4,000	4,800	400	275 00	9,475 00
" 11........	Pearl st.........	Rented....	....	....	....	400	140 00	540 00
" 12........	Ridge st.........	"	....	....	....	400	145 00	545 00
" 14 & 40..	Chrystie st......	P. S. Soc.	{ on rear 25 × 50 1	2,000	4,000	600	230 00	6,830 00
" 15........	Stanton st......	Rented....	....	....	....	400	155 00	555 00
" 17 & 47..	Trustees' Hall...	P. S. Soc..	....	....	....	300	225 00	525 00
" 18........	Cannon st.......	Rented....	....	....	....	300	195 00	495 00
" 19 & 37..	Greenwich st....	P. S. Soc..	1	Leased	4,800	800	270 00	5,870 00
" 21........	Twentieth st....	Rented....	....	....	....	300	130 00	430 00
" 22........	Av. C & 4th st..	"	....	....	....	250	125 00	375 00
" 23........	Rivington st....	Basement of P. S. No. 4.	....	....	....	100	215 00	315 00
" 24........	corner Bleeker & Downing......	Rented....	....	....	....	400	180 00	580 00
" 25 & 26..	Thompson st....	P. S. Soc...	1	3,500	4,800	600	220 00	9,120 00
" 27 & 28..	Seventeenth st..	"	{ 25 × 95 1	3,000	5,000	800	325 00	9,125 00
" 30........	Centre st........	Rented....	....	....	....	400	180 00	580 00
" 31 & 32..	Stone st.........	City.......	1	....	6,000	1,000	560 00	7,560 00
" 33 & 34..	Barrow st.......	P. S. Soc..	{ 24 × 100 1	Leased	4,800	800	270 00	5,870 00
" 35 & 55..	25th st..........	"	1	4,000	4,800	800	275 00	9,875 00
" 36........	43d st...........	Rented....	....	....	....	400	150 00	550 00
" 38 & 39..	Factory st.......	P. S. Soc..	{ 50 × 66 2	5,000	6,000	900	265 00	12,165 00
" 41 & 51..	West 18th st....	"	1	3,600	4,800	800	285 00	8,885 00
				$214,500	$262,000	$71,150	$29,995 00	$575,145 00

ESTIMATED VALUE OF REAL ESTATE AND PERSONAL PROPERTY (Continued.)

SCHOOLS.	LOCATION.	TITLE IN.	NO. OF LOTS.	GROUND.	HOUSE.	FURNITURE.	SUPPLIES.	TOTAL.
				$214,500	$262,000	$71,150	$29.995 00	$575,145 00
No. 42 & 43..	Clinton st.......	P. S. Soc.. { on rear 40 × 50 1		$2,500	$3,000	$600	$250 00	$6,350 00
" 45 & 46..	Rivington st.....	" { 36 × 100 2		4,000	5,000	800	250 00	10,050 00
" 48........	Houston st......	Rented....		....	....	300	200 00	500 00
" 49 & 50..	Eleventh st.....	"		....	....	600	210 00	810 00
" 52........	Horatio st.......	City........		....	....	3 10	160 00	460 00
" 53 & 54..	Greenwich st....	P. S. Soc....	1	Leased	4,800	800	265 00	5,865 00
Colored:								
No. 3........	West 15th st.....	Rented.....		....	....	200	125 00	325 00
" 4 & 6....	Second st........	"		....	....	400	215 00	615 00
School Libraries..................					....	....	2,000 00	2,000 00
Stoves at J. L. Mott's................					....	....	151 20	151 20
Furniture and supplies delivered at W. S. No. 14..					....	84	....	84 00
" " " " 29..					....	30	5 00	35 00
Stereotype plates at Depository............					....	....	205 26	205 26
Fuel on hand in the Schools............					....	....	225 00	225 00
Treasurer's balance, cash in hand............					....	....	....	401 39
Total.........................				$220,500	$274,800	$75,264	$34,256 46	$605,221 85

The report was adopted, and, the President having announced in a few words that the Society had closed its official career, and had executed its last official trust, nothing now remained but to exchange their last salutations as trustees and members of the Society.

PETER COOPER then rose, and addressed the Society as follows :

MR. PRESIDENT AND GENTLEMEN : With your indulgence, I will venture a few remarks that I have penned, on an occasion that commands our deepest consideration. We are now, Mr. President, about to resign our stewardship over an institution that has exerted an influence over hundreds of thousands of the young of our city, who are now, in their turn, spreading that influence far and wide over our common country. Let us, then, Mr. President, each one of us, try in all sincerity to adopt the language of the poet, where he says,

> " 'Tis greatly wise to talk with our past hours,
> And ask them what report they bore to heaven ;
> And how they might have borne more welcome news ; "

where the responsibilities of our stewardship will be found impressed indelibly on every heart, causing us to rejoice in every triumph of virtue, and to sorrow over all the errors we have made. How important, then, it is to listen to the knell of the departed hours—yes ! as if an angel spoke. They call upon us to gather wisdom by reflection on the experience of the past, and to apply that wisdom to the discharge of the duties that are now before us. The stewardship that we are now about to resign is not a reprieve from the responsibility of the future. On the contrary, Mr. President, that stewardship should have prepared us better to perform those duties that are now about to devolve upon us. These duties are of unmeasured importance, not only to the children of this community, but to the cause of suffering humanity throughout the world. When we cast our minds over the struggling nations of the earth, and look on the fierce encounter now waging between the friends of freedom and progress, and those despots who are now striving by every means in their power to uproot and destroy the véry foundations of liberal government; when I see, Mr. President, those monarchs of Europe hanging their armies, like an incubus, about their peoples' necks, eating out their substance, degrading their morals, and making them their ignorant slaves, to perpetuate the pride and selfishness of their oppressors; when I think, Mr. President, of the bare possibility that tyranny may again triumph over the continent of Europe; when I look at the history of the past, and judge of what is possible for the future; when I recollect those frightful monuments of former grandeur and lost greatness—monuments now standing as beacons in the pathway of nations, warning us of danger, and telling us, with silent eloquence, beware, lest a worse thing come upon us; when I reflect on the exalted privileges that now elevate us among the nations of the earth—privileges that other nations are sighing and suffering in vain to obtain; when I look on all this, I ask myself, *Can it be* that these dear-bought, inalienable rights—the rights to worship God according to the dictates of our own consciences, and to form and carry on a government of our own choice—I ask myself, Can it be that rights and privileges like these *can* ever be given up and lost?

I tremble for the answer, when I see the combined influences of pride, of selfishness, of bigotry, and superstition, all uniting to undermine the virtues and misdirect the energy and intelligence of our people. Our mission, Mr. President, has been, and will continue to be, one of no ordinary responsibility and importance. It is one that claims from us our united and continued effort to spread far and wide the science of just, necessary, and useful knowledge, until all shall know, from the least to the greatest, those things that make for their peace. And now, Mr. President, as we are about to enter on a new and most important field of labor, under different circumstances, and with new associates, who, I trust, we shall find as truly and earnestly devoted to the great cause of human improvement as we are or ever have been —and although they may have adopted different means to attain the same end, it will be our duty to be slow to find fault or condemn what may at first appear less desirable than the customary rules and practices that have prevailed within our own Society. It will better become us to look to those motes that may by possibility float unperceived in our own eyes, that we may more clearly perceive those difficulties that will encumber our own path, and that of our associates, with whom, I trust, we shall ever act with a pure desire to carry forward a system of public and general education that, I hope, will maintain the confidence of the community, and prove a blessing to the world.

The Board of Education was at the same time holding a special session in another part of the building, called for the purpose of effecting the union; and on motion of Dr. J. Weldon Fell, commissioner for the Eighth Ward, a committee was appointed to inform the new members that the Board of Education was ready to receive the commissioners nominated by the Society. The President, Hon. ERASTUS C. BENEDICT, appointed Dr. Fell, Hon. James W. Beekman, and Charles Vulté as the committee, in whose company the new members soon entered the hall.

As they entered the room, the board rose, and the President offered the following preamble and resolutions:

Whereas, On the joint application of this board and the Public School Society, the said Society was authorized by law to convey their property to the city Corporation, and to transfer their schools to the care of this board, and, after appointing certain of their own trustees to remain as school officers of the wards, including fifteen to be members of this board, to dissolve their corporate existence; and

Whereas, Said Society has completed said arrangements, and has ceased to exist as a separate institution; therefore,

Resolved, That the Public School Society is entitled to the lasting gratitude of the people of this city, and of the friends of education generally, for their unremitted and successful efforts, continued through nearly half a century, in disseminating the blessings of education and virtue among thousands who otherwise would have been allowed to grow up in ignorance and vice.

Resolved, That we cordially welcome to their seats in this board, Thomas B. Stillman, Linus W. Stevens, Peter Cooper, William H. Neilson, John T. Adams, Israel Russell, Joseph B. Collins, John Davenport, James F. Depeyster, Benjamin R. Winthrop, Charles E. Pierson, M.D., William P. Cooledge, Henry H. Barrow, Joseph Curtis, and John W. C. Leveridge, who have been so selected as members thereof, and that we rejoice in the confident hope that the cause of public education will be strengthened by the union now completed, and will receive at their hands the same faithful, intelligent, and disinterested service which it has hitherto received from their enlightened philanthropy and patriotism.

WILLIAM D. MURPHY, Esq., commissioner from the Seventh Ward, seconded the resolutions of Mr. Benedict, and said:

MR. PRESIDENT: The present is an occasion upon which I cannot restrain an expression of the feelings which press upon me for utterance. The cause of education, in view of its influence upon the moral and social welfare of man, is the greatest of all those enterprises which can claim or receive our attention. It decides whether man shall be a savage or a civilized being, and gives rise to the distinctions between savage and civilized society. The years are comparatively but few since we had in our State, and, indeed, in our country, no system of public education. The Society which, by law, has now expired, and a portion of whose members are now coming into this board, was the pioneer in evolving and building up the great system of popular education in our city, in the State of New York, and in the Union. The members of that Society have nobly won the lasting gratitude of the people of the State, and particularly of this city, for their faithful, untiring, and persevering labors in the enlightenment and training of so many of the people of our land. Many of those faithful men have gone through a life of honor and usefulness, and, after a life of labor, have gone home to the reward of righteousness. The gentlemen who have constituted the Public School Society have been more like fathers than trustees, for they have cherished the schools under their charge, and the great interests of public education with an affectionate care.

Mr. President, we often hear of institutes, colleges, and universities which boast of their alumni, their graduates, and their labors. We hear of institutions which boast of the senators, the governors, and the honorable men who have been indebted to them as their Alma Mater. But here we have an institution which boasts, not of its tens or its hundreds, but may proudly boast of the thousands and hundreds of thousands who have enjoyed the blessings of education under its fostering care—thousands who adorn society, and labor honorably all over the country. The Public School Society has done much toward moulding the State of New York, and it has moulded and improved and elevated the educational system of the whole Union. It has enlightened thousands of minds, cheered thousands of hearts, and quickened the fires of patriotism now burning in every State of the Union. Even in the West Indies, this Society aided to kindle the fires of liberty before the act of emancipation which made freemen of hundreds of thousands of slaves. Where are the men who have done these things? Many of them are not here. But their successors are here. You cannot find a philanthropic institution in the city of New York where the members of the Public School Society do not perform a large share of the duty. Now, sir, we are told of the age of chivalry, when men hazarded their all, and achieved heroic deeds in behalf of their wives, their children, or their fellow-men. But if those men were entitled to praise, what shall we say of the men who, for half a century, moulded the impressible minds of hundreds of thousands of children, leading them to usefulness and honor, and added a bright lustre to the beauty and glory of our free institutions? They have discharged their duties without faltering, swerving, or defalcation. There is no one of them who

" Weighed his virtue in the well-poised scale,
  And took the yellow bribe."

I confess, sir, language fails me to bear a fitting testimony to the services of these laborious and faithful men. I know not how to find words to express the honor due to them.

Mr. President, I very cordially approve all that is said in the resolutions. I venerate those men, whose hearts were warm, whose doctrines were pure, and whose lives have demonstrated, and now demonstrate, that their hearts, their labor, and their time were consecrated to the high and sacred cause of public education.

Mr. Murphy was warmly responded to by the members of the Board of Education, who expressed their sympathy with the speaker by a spontaneous applause, and the new members were formally qualified for their office.

Thus terminated, forty-eight years after its inception, the career of the Public School Society, leaving its progress and its labors intimately associated with the advancement of all the great institutions of learning and of benevolence which were contemporaneous with its own existence, not less than of the city of which it was an ornament, and upon which it conferred benefits as great as they were invaluable and enduring.

CHAPTER XVI.

THE ADMINISTRATION OF THE SOCIETY.

The Lancasterian System—Social Problems—Elevation of the Masses—Educational Systems—Progress and Development—The Public School Society—Visitation and Division of Labor—Economy—Teachers and Salaries—Monitors—Depository—Workshop—Rewards and Libraries—Evening Schools—Vagrancy, Agent, and Visitors—How Shall the Poor be Reached?—Compulsory Measures—The Social Problems Unsolved—The Free and Pay Systems—Pay System Abandoned—Lotteries—Corporal Punishment—Moral Power of the Teacher—Extract from the Manual—Music Introduced, but Discontinued—Moral and Religious Instruction—Sectarianism—The Position of the Society—Sunday Schools and their Influence—Religious and Moral Education Essential to the Welfare of Society—Concluding Observations.

THE system of instruction adopted by the Society at its origin, was that which had been introduced to the notice of the British public by Joseph Lancaster, and which became known by his name, although, as a characteristic style, it was also called the Monitorial System of Instruction. The Lancasterian method was the basis, but was modified and improved materially in the schools of the Society. It was based upon two fundamental propositions—emulation and economy. It aimed to excite the mental and moral activities, by the distinction it bestowed upon the more industrious and advanced pupils, by their appointment as monitors; while the economy of this kind of service was obvious, where a moderate cost was an essential element in the prosperity of a school, especially for the poor. There is a class of duties not very high, nor requiring a great degree of literary attainment, which may be performed by the higher grade of pupils, which, while the exercise of instruction becomes a decided benefit to themselves in many respects, renders unnecessary the employment of adult and experienced teachers. Children learn easily from one another; and the alphabet, simple spelling, the primary rules of arithmetic, and other lessons are quickly taught and as well learned by the children as though they were pointed out by the finger of the philosopher. The dignity of the office of monitor, filled by rotation, in the several duties of the school-room, was an incentive to those old enough, while it seemed to invest the monitors with that degree of authority which made the discipline of a class of ten or twelve pupils as easy to them as to an adult teacher.

To the ignorant, any progress whatever in the acquisition of knowledge is valuable, and hence the teachings of advanced pupils were of as much consequence to the learners as though they were under more competent control. Although it was an economical system, it did not *cheapen* knowledge, in an obnoxious sense; it merely gave, in its least expensive presentation, and through the hands of equals, those first draughts from the fountains of knowledge which otherwise had been denied to the masses of the lowly.

Although the questions of the social and moral elevation of the masses have engaged the attention of the most profound thinkers of the civilized world during the present century, it is a no less conspicuous fact that the condition of millions seems to serve as a barrier to their advancement. Notwithstanding all the expenditures made in this direction for asylums, schools, and gymnasiums, the underlying mass of the community suffers from intellectual darkness and moral death.

There is a tendency in many institutions, after having passed through their early stage, and endowments increase, to enter upon a transition period, which carries them beyond the sphere for which they were originally designed. The ragged school becomes a school for children well clothed, and of the middle class. The rooms in which the poor learned their alphabets, become filled with the children of parents who desire them to read history, grammar, and algebra, if not higher branches. The teacher who first gathered his group of unwashed and reckless urchins, gives place to the tutor who has his maps, his atlases, and his lexicons. This advance is not simply progress; it is substitution. One class of pupils is replaced by another, and a new order of charities is required for the benefit of the humbler classes. This transition has taken place, to a large extent, in the city of New York. The schools of the Society, which were founded for the instruction of those " poor children who did not belong to, or were not provided for by, any religious society," and were consequently not provided for by any parochial school, after the lapse of about twenty years, became so numerous and respectable as to excite the attention of the public at large, as institutions for general instruction. It became an object of earnest care with the Society to elevate the character of the schools in all their aspects. They were known as schools for "poor children," and many parents did not desire to send their children to schools which were distinctively for that class. To remove these disadvantages, the system was developed by a long and careful process. Additional endowments were secured, experienced teachers took the place of many of the monitors, more costly apparatus was purchased, the grade of instruction was advanced, and the schools were offered to the public as institutions where the children of all classes might meet on common ground, and engage in the strife for honor and reward.

But social laws cannot always be overborne, even by the most enlightened and philanthropic adaptations. In proportion as the comfortably-clad and cleanly and polished pupil makes his appearance, the opposite class shrink from the contact. Social affinities are too strong, and social distinctions are too marked. Contrasts are too plainly seen. Although theories of popular commingling may be very pretty exercises for the sycophant or the demagogue, facts and truths of a stern and impressive significance often laugh them to scorn, and the self-consciousness of the poor, the abject, and the desponding, lead them to avoid associations where the silent but not less powerful invidiousness of social contrasts is so clearly displayed.

The progress of substitution, of which mention has been made, has taken place to a large extent in the school system of New York. Instead of confining itself to the instruction of the children of the poor, the advances made raised them, in a measure, above the level of thousands who are too unfortunate and too dependent, while the means which would support several schools of lower grades were expended upon a single school. The necessity of securing a system by which children of all classes might meet on common ground, rendered it inevitable that the schools should be advanced to such a rank as very soon removed them beyond the level of thousands. The private pay schools became fewer in number in proportion to the population, and the number of uneducated children of the poor kept steadily increasing with the population. The statistics which were viewed with so much interest and anxiety in 1825, when about ten thousand children were estimated to be without instruction, lost none of their significance in 1835, when it was reported that there were *twenty thousand* untaught wanderers to be found in the streets. Yet this mass grew, in the next decade, to thirty thousand, and, in 1855, the estimates reported to the Board of Education made the number of vagrant and uneducated children reach the appalling figure of *sixty thousand*, in a resident population of less than seven hundred and fifty thousand.

While this vast increase was going on with the steady accretion of thousands annually added to the ranks of the children of the school age, the system rolled up the amount of its expenditures from the sum of $125,000, distributed by the Society, to the $300,000 apportioned under the care of the Board of Education ; and even this liberal fund was increased so rapidly, that the last-named census of children who were non-attendants at schools was contemporaneous with an outlay of over *eight hundred thousand dollars* for the schools under the care of the Board of Education. The modest and yet substantial houses of the Public School Society were superseded by imposing edifices erected at great cost, as well for the buildings as for their appointments. The grade of instruction had been so far advanced, that, in place of the elementary training of early years, the course comprised music, French, algebra, history, and other studies, in the grammar schools, with a collegiate course in the Free Academy, and schools for girls, in which select branches are taught which had hitherto been reserved for the higher class of institutes for young ladies. The system had been developed into a noble educational scheme, but it had changed its channel, and the stream flowed over a new bed, while it left a rapidly augmenting number of the poor stranded on the further shore, or drifting down to be lost in the eddies of ignorance and vice.

As the outgrowth of circumstances which could not fail to arrest the attention of the civilian and the reformer, a new order of schools grew up, inspired by the same motives and covering substantially the same ground as that so nobly occupied by the founder of the Lancasterian system. They added, however, a more liberal supply of material aid, together with an industrial organization and scheme, which proved of eminent advantage.

" Industrial Schools " have become the nursery where benevolent women of the first rank in society, as well as men of philanthropy, fortune, and learning, delight to devote much of their time in rescuing the poor and uneducated children from their almost hopeless condition. Fifty years of development had resulted in a more imperative demand for a simpler and better-adapted system of education for the children of the extreme poor. The original work of the Society was similar to that of the Industrial Schools of the present decade.

In the month of May, 1817, the treasurer of the Society acknowledged the receipt of two hundred and fifty dollars from the executor of Mrs. Mary McCrea, *to be expended for the clothing of the children.* The schools, during their early operation, often suffered in attendance from the fact that the children were not able to find garments suitable for the season, and donations of clothing, shoes, hats, &c., were received by the trustees, for distribution among the pupils. The ladies who assisted in the care of the girls, taught sewing and needlework, and much labor of a useful kind was performed by the pupils in repairing the clothing sent as donations, or making up the goods contributed for the purpose. In 1823, a regulation was adopted assigning three afternoons in the week to sewing exercises.

ADMINISTRATION.

The system early adopted by the trustees, and continued with a fidelity and diligence which were remarkable, called for a constant supervision of the schools in all the departments of instruction, discipline, and economy. When the number of schools had become sufficiently numerous, the committees on schools were changed in their organization, and the trustees were divided into " sections," who had the special care of their respective schools during the year for which they were appointed. The records attest the uniform fidelity with which this duty was performed. The visits of the trustees to their several charges were made at all hours, and without any notice whatever to the teachers. The industry with which this part of the labor was performed may be estimated from the fact that, during the year ending May 1, 1840, the trustees made 11,844 visits to their schools, and, during the following year, no less than 14,112 visits were recorded on the books. The controlling principle in the minds of these faithful officers, next to a sense of their duty as " men who must give an account," was a consciousness that they were invested with a grave and momentous trust, which made them responsible to their fellow-citizens for the performance of an honorable stewardship. The men who composed the Society, with few, if any, exceptions, were not those who would abandon their post of duty for trifling considerations, or yield passively to the storms of prejudice or of opposition which might be raised around them for the overthrow of their institution. With a high appreciation of the position they held as the founders of a system of popular instruction designed for the tens of thousands of youth of a great metropolis, their endeavor was, with a single purpose, to extend, advance, and ennoble it with each passing year, in the hope that it would be rendered more massive and more enduring by successive labors, until it should rest upon a basis as broad as humanity and as lasting as time.

ECONOMY.

A characteristic feature of the administration of the Society was the strict economy practised in all the expenditures, whether for teachers, buildings, fuel, or supplies. There is an economy which is often a misnomer, and a blind and pernicious system of penurious calculation may often be productive of more evil than a too liberal outlay. The law universally applied to all the disbursements of the institution was that of a jealous caution over the expenditures. The question invariably asked was, how to secure the greatest result from a given amount of means, and how the benefits should be the most equally and widely distributed. Limited in resources, and with a pressure of demand from every part of the city for the opportunities and facilities of obtaining instruction, the closest calculation was necessary ; and, fortunately for the public interests, the school moneys were destined to pass through the hands of men who felt that they were under a high obligation to use them with as much prudence as they would their own. No ambitious pretensions in order to gain popular clamor in their favor, were needed ; no contracts to be given to favorites who could exert a political influence ; no relatives or friends who could submit estimates which were to benefit the officers who superintended the work, ever seemed to offer inducements to the trustees to overstep the prudence of men who knew how to conduct their own affairs—many of whom, while they were enriching the city with their labors in the department of public instruction, were also quietly building their own fortunes by the very virtues and habits which enabled them to mould and develop the system which they adorned.

TEACHERS.

In reviewing the history of the Society, the policy pursued toward its teachers may be condemned by many who do not sufficiently reflect upon its position and its resources. The grade, also, of the schools may, perhaps, be overlooked. Yet it will be seen that, when the resources permitted, the trustees were not insensible to the claims which competent teachers had upon their consideration. The qualifications of teachers, and their duties, are inevitably to be regarded, and a teacher of minor qualifications cannot reasonably expect the same compensation as one who finds all his scholarship and talent called into requisition for the training of advanced pupils. A salary of $600 or $800, and rent, advanced to $800 or $900, or $1,000, was not by any means a contemptible sum, compared even with the larger salaries of the principals of Boston and New York schools at the present time. The amount ordered to be guaranteed to "a teacher from England completely competent to teach on the Lancasterian plan," was $800, his expenses to this country to be paid by the Society. Shepherd Johnson, a former monitor, was appointed teacher of No. 3, at its opening in 1818, at a salary of $500, which was increased, during the same year, to $800. In 1820 and 1821, the teachers of the schools made application for an advance of their rate of compensation, which was denied; but, "in order to equalize the same, the salary of Shepherd Johnson was raised to $900." In 1822, Charles Picton, the English teacher who was duly accredited by the Society in England, and who had, by several years of faithful service, earned the respect and confidence of the Society and the public, had an allowance of $950. A committee on the question of salaries reported a scheme, at the same time, based upon the attendance, so that the compensation should be partly dependent upon the industry and efficiency of the teachers themselves. The plan proposed that $2 per scholar should be paid for two hundred scholars or less; over two hundred and under six hundred, $1.50 in addition; over six hundred, $1 in addition. By this scale, a school of three hundred pupils would give the teacher a compensation of $550; five hundred pupils, $850, &c. The schools were thus rated:

No. 1, 500 pupils, ... $850 salary.
  " 2, 400 " . . . . 700 "
  " 3, 600 " . . . . 1,000 "
  " 4, 600 " . . . . 1,000 "

The salary of Eunice Dean, one of the female teachers, was raised from $250 to $300 per annum.

In 1827, the by-laws were altered so as to limit the salaries to the following rates:

Male teachers, per annum, ... $800
  " monitors general, per annum, . . . 200
  " assistants, " . . . 100
Female teachers, " . . . 350
  " monitors general, " . . . 100
  " assistants, " . . . 50

The office of assistant teacher had been abolished in 1817. The system was very materially changed and improved under the important law of 1832. Assistant teachers were to be appointed, and two sections were adopted as a part of the new code of by-laws, fixing the rates of salaries as follows:

The salary of the principal teacher in the boys' schools shall not exceed $1,000; that of the assistant teacher shall not exceed $600; that of the monitor general shall not exceed $200; that of the assistant monitor general shall not exceed $100.

The salary of the mistress in the female school shall not exceed $400; that of the assistant shall not exceed $250; that of the monitors general shall not exceed $100; that of the assistant monitors general shall not exceed $50.

The maximum for the assistant teachers was adopted at $500, but, in 1835, the teachers applied for an increase to $600, and it was made discretionary with the Executive Committee to increase the salary of assistants to that sum in cases where they deemed it was deserved.

In 1836, the following tariff was adopted:

Principal teachers, male department, not to exceed	$1,000
Assistants,	700
Passed monitor,	400
First "	200
Second "	100
Teachers in the female departments not to exceed	450
Assistants,	300
First monitor,	125
Second "	100
Teachers of primary departments not to exceed	275
Assistants,	160
First monitor,	100
Second "	75
Teachers of primary schools not to exceed	200
and $2.50 for each child over *sixty*, but the additional number so allowed for not to exceed *thirty*.	
First monitors of primary schools not to exceed	100

In 1842, the Board of Education was established, and the trustees of the ward schools were enabled to pay salaries much larger than those paid by the Society. This not only induced a spirit of competition and jealousy between the wards themselves, but between the teachers employed by the Society and those in the ward schools. It also tended materially to injure the public schools by the frequent withdrawal of long-experienced teachers from the service of the Society, attracted by the increased emoluments offered by the ward officers. This evil became so prominent, that, in 1851, a committee was appointed to report upon the whole subject, and Messrs. G. T. Trimble, A. P. Halsey, C. E. Pierson, L. W. Stevens, B. Ellis, W. R. Vermilye, W. H. Neilson, J. B. Collins, and John Davenport, were entrusted with the consideration of all questions relating to the salaries of teachers. The committee reported a scale substantially the same, but providing that, after two years of acceptable service, the assistant male teachers should receive $750 per annum. The other recommendations of the report were of the same character, making a period of faithful service of two or three years the basis of an increase of compensation. This scale of salaries was continued during the existence of the Society.

Etch'd by H B Hall N 3, 1870

SAMUEL W. SETON.

MONITORS.

The success of the Lancasterian system being dependent, in a very great degree, upon the ability and character of the several monitors, who formed an indispensable part of the scheme, attention was early given to the training and preparation of the most promising of the pupils, in order to prepare them for the special work of teaching according to the most approved methods of the plan of mutual instruction. While there was but one school in existence, the number of monitors was too small to warrant any specified classification for that purpose. But when the number was increased, and a considerable body of monitors was employed in the schools, arrangements were made for their instruction. Monitors had been indentured as "apprentices" to the Society, in all practicable cases, and were expected to remain until they were twenty-one years of age, and then to receive a certificate of qualification which should secure them positions in any city in the Union.

The trustees of the Society believed that they were introducing to the people of the United States a system of great value, specially adapted to the necessities of the underlying masses of society. Whatever, therefore, could increase its efficiency and multiply its powers, was adopted as fast as circumstances or means allowed.

The course adopted for the training of monitors is treated of in the chapter devoted to the high school and normal school, and only a brief summary will here be given of the general regulations adopted for their employment and supervision.

The house in which the school was originally established having become unfit for longer use, a commodious building was erected on Tryon Row, at the east side of the Park, since changed by the extension of Centre street. The school was opened for the reception of scholars on the 12th of December, 1809, soon after which William McAlpin and Shepherd Johnson, who subsequently distinguished himself as the first teacher of No. 3, and more recently as a teacher of the New York High School, were indentured to the Society. This usage was continued in every practicable case.

In 1818, a Committee on Monitors reported a form of indenture, which would probably have been adopted by the Society,

39

but a question arising as to the power of the board to hold apprentices, the subject was recommitted, with power to memorialize the Legislature to grant the requisite authority. The monitors general had been boarded and clothed by the Society, being, at the time of their apprenticeship, inmates of the family of the teacher of the school in which they were employed. During the year 1819, a committee upon retrenchment recommended that the monitors be allowed a compensation of $100 a year, and reside with their parents—a recommendation which was adopted by the board. Some objection arose against the change, and it was waived; but, in 1820, a resolution was adopted reducing the allowance to the teachers for the board of the monitors general to $2.50 per week. The expenses of each of these lads amounting to about $200 per annum, it was deemed a measure of economy to reduce the cost of such assistance, and, in 1821, resolutions were adopted reducing the salary to $100 during the time of their service, and that steps be taken to secure positions for them as teachers of Lancasterian schools, the Secretary being directed to advertise in one newspaper in New York City, and one in Albany, that three such teachers were prepared to enter upon their duties. The School Committees were directed to expend fifty cents per week in securing the services of proper monitors.

In 1826, Jotham Wilson, the monitor general of No. 5, applied for an increase of $100 to his salary. A committee was appointed to consider the general subject of salaries of monitors, who reported in favor of allowing $50 for the first year, and an annual addition of $50, until it should reach a maximum of $200 for males; and $25 a year, with the annual addition of $25, until the maximum of $100 for female monitors should be reached. The Executive Committee were charged with discretionary exercise of power in the case.

The Society had, however, been making material advances both in its own organization, its resources, and its system. Its schools were larger, and eight capacious buildings were the evidences of its labors and its prosperity. In order to keep pace with these advantages, it was necessary to adopt a more enlarged and liberal policy with the monitors general, who had become of prime importance to the system. This was very fully perceived by the Executive Committee, who applied, in May, 1827, for authority to appoint two monitors general in each school at a maximum of $300 for males, and $200 for females, to which proposition the Board of Trustees gave an unanimous consent. In October of the same year, the by-laws were amended so as to limit the maximum to $200 for males, and $100 for females.

The grades of salaries paid subsequently to this time have been already presented in the preceding sections.

An increase of salaries of teachers and monitors naturally followed the improvements made in the schools and the system of instruction. The experience and improvement of the monitors particularly, as they continued at their posts and became more mature in age, all presented additional incentives to the trustees to retain them in their own schools, and thus appropriate the scholarship and experience acquired by the young teachers to the institution in which they had been trained. The advantages of this system were exhibited in many instances in which monitors subsequently attained high rank as teachers, some of whom have held, or now hold, honorable positions as professional and business men. The discipline submitted to by the pupil was developed in the proficiency of the monitor, whose habits and principles thus formed, became the basis of exalted and enduring character.

THE DEPOSITORY.

One of the measures adopted by the board, having in view the scrupulous and careful appropriation of the resources of the Society, was that of establishing a depository for the systematic supply of the schools with the text-books, stationery, and apparatus which they severally required. A system of supplies had been for many years in use, under the direction of the Supply Committee, but, in 1832, at the time of the remodelling of the school system, by-laws were adopted for the regular distribution of the supplies to the schools. The depository was kept at Public School No. 5, in Mott street, the purchases being made by the Supply Committee, and distributed on the proper warrant by the agent. The depository was removed to the "Trustees' Hall" on the completion of that building, and the same system was adopted on a much enlarged scale by the Board of Education after the union of the two systems.

THE WORKSHOP.

In 1837, the number of schools had increased to seventeen, including two schools for colored children, beside a large number of primary schools, many of which occupied hired premises. The amount of work and materials annually required to keep these buildings in repair, and to supply them with appropriate apparatus, was very considerable, and suggested, as a measure of economy not less than convenience, the employment of a master workman, who should be known as the Superintendent of Repairs, and who should keep a shop for the special work of the schools. The measure was recommended by Samuel F. Mott, Treasurer, who introduced a resolution at a meeting of the board, February 3, 1837, referring the matter to the Property Committee. A report approving the plan was submitted at the August meeting following, and the committee were authorized to have a workshop erected on the rear of the school lot in Thompson street, and the Executive Committee was empowered to employ a competent foreman, who should be nominated by the Property Committee. AMNON McVEY was chosen to fill the position thus created, and the excellence of the appointment has been fully proved by the faithful service of thirty years, during which an extraordinary amount of work has been done under his direction. Mr. McVey is the architect of the Hall of the Board of Education, and of many of the largest and most substantially built school-houses in the city.

REWARDS, LIBRARIES, ETC.

The influence of proper incentives upon the minds of the scholars was early recognized by the teachers and trustees of the Society, and systems of reward were adopted calculated to stimulate the pupils to diligence and punctuality. Tickets, to be distributed to the deserving, and returned when forfeited by misdemeanor, were furnished to the teachers, who kept records of the merits and demerits, and at the end of the week the account was balanced, and the credit carried to the quarterly account of the pupil. At the end of the quarter, premiums were distributed to those who were entitled to receive them. These premiums consisted of books, knives, thimbles, scissors, balls, tops, marbles, or other articles suitable to the tastes or wants of the children. Difficulties attended the system, however, and it was partially dispensed with and removed, and subsequently modified into a system of credits which entitled the pupils to receive premium certificates, which were redeemed at certain periods by books proportioned to the number and merit of the certificates.

It was deemed to be of great importance to the schools to provide the children with a suitable class of books for reading at home, not only for the general effect which such books would have upon the children and the families they represented, but as a higher and more estimable reward for good character as pupils. As early as 1818, a committee on the state of the schools submitted a report, recommending, among others, the following resolution :

Resolved, That a committee be appointed to purchase and otherwise procure suitable books of voyages, travels, history, &c., to the amount of fifty dollars for each school, for the purpose of forming libraries for the use of the scholars. That the committee prepare rules for the regulation of the libraries, and that such boys as may be selected by the master and approved by the School Committee on account of their progress in learning and good behavior, shall be admitted as members of the library, shall form a " CLASS OF MERIT," and wear a badge. The number of this class in each school shall not exceed fifty. All catechisms, or other books on religion that contain sectarian principles, shall be excluded from the libraries, but such other religious books as may be approved by the Board of Trustees shall be admitted.

Nathan Comstock, Benjamin Marshall, and John R. Murray were appointed a Committee on Libraries, and they proceeded promptly with the discharge of their duties. Each school was provided with a library, and the several public schools subsequently established by the Society were provided with libraries as a necessary part of their apparatus.

Measures were adopted, in 1837, to establish a teachers' library, but, from the absence of interest on the part of the teachers, it never became sufficiently extended or valuable to take rank as an auxiliary in the system.

EVENING SCHOOLS.

One of the agencies which were devised for the purpose of reaching the large class of children and youth who are debarred from the opportunities of instruction in the day schools, was that of evening schools. The first mention of these schools, under the supervision of the Society, appears in the records for the year 1823, at which time a resolution was adopted, permitting the teachers to hold evening schools in their respective buildings, on condition of furnishing their own fuel and lights, and that they should repair whatever injuries might occur to the buildings or furniture, and with the proviso that the insurance would not thereby be rendered invalid. But this plan contemplated a compensation for instruction, which was a perquisite to the teacher. The evening school system is intended to benefit the industrial, and not the vagrant classes, although many have attended the evening schools who should have been members of day schools. An evening school for colored pupils had been established many years before by the Manumission Society.

In 1832, an association of gentlemen, composed of W. D. Coit, J. H. Taylor, and others, applied for the use of School No. 10, in Duane street, for a free evening school. Shortly afterward, Floyd Smith and others applied for permission to use School No. 3 for similar purposes. Messrs. Joseph Brewster, John H. Smith, Charles Durfee, and others applied for No. 5, and J. H. Taylor for a room in No. 8, for gratuitous instruction in the evening. These applications were granted, subject to the supervision of the several "sections" having the charge of those schools.

At the close of 1832, a committee on a reorganization of the system reported a chapter to be incorporated in the new by-laws, providing for the establishment of evening schools. The plan was adopted in January, 1833, as a part of the new system, and a resolution was passed relative to teachers and monitors, as follows:

Resolved, That, in future engagements with the male teachers, assistants, and monitors, it be made a condition that their time and services, if required by the Executive Committee, in attending the evening schools, shall be given without additional pay.

The schools thus made a part of the scheme of instruction were opened in October, 1833, and continued until March of the following year. The number of pupils who attended the four schools was 1,245. The annual report states that, although they occasioned some inconvenience, and were more expensive than the day schools, the good effects were such as to give promise of permanent utility. The result of the labors of the year following was less encouraging, and, after an experiment of three or four years, they were abandoned. The Board of Education subsequently adopted the system, under the care of an active committee, and the result was neither doubtful nor insignificant. The failure of the attempt made by the Society was in consequence of the unwillingness of the teachers to work five months in the year, and sacrifice their evening repose, without extra compensation ; although the terms of agreement with the teachers and monitors required them to perform these duties.

VAGRANCY.—VISITOR AND AGENT.

Reference has been already made to the original object of the Free-School Society, which was, to provide instruction for the children of the poor, who either had no connection with any religious persuasion, or disregarded it where it existed. The tendency among the members of this portion of the community is to recklessness, vice, and indolence. Vagrancy, beggary, and unlawful means of procuring a barely animal subsistence, form the summit of the low plane of their mental or moral sphere. To raise them from this condition is a work of humanity, as well as of Christianity, and the means by which it can be effected are ever worthy of consideration and experiment.

Observation and inquiry exhibited the fact that thousands of children of the school age were vagrants, untaught and uncared-for by their parents, who exhibited no concern for the attendance of their offspring, and neglected to send them to school. To supply this want in part, and to exert a direct and leading influence upon this class of the population, it was deemed advisable to employ a gentleman who should fill the post of " visitor." Acting in this capacity, his duties were, to visit the children and parents at their homes, and use all the influence which could be brought to bear upon them to secure their attendance and advancement. He was also to visit the families whose children were allowed to become vagrants, and induce the parents to send them to school. To this position, in the month of May, 1827, Mr. SAMUEL WADDINGTON SETON was appointed, who continued in the discharge of the same, or other responsible duties, during the existence of the Society, and was afterward appointed, by the Board of Education, Assistant Superintendent of Common Schools. No more fitting selection could have been made, the temperament, sympathies, and habits of the gentleman chosen being eminently calculated to make him useful in that sphere. How well his duties were discharged, and with what lasting power over thousands who personally knew him, no written records will ever fully testify; but they are inscribed in imperishable influences which have made bright and honorable many a son and daughter of destitution, who, but for him, would have trodden a dangerous and darkened path to the grave.

In 1833, the office of "visitor" was abolished, and the duties of Mr. Seton were defined by a new title, in which capacity he had a general business supervision as "agent," being chiefly the receipt and distribution of supplies. Mr. Seton was elected a trustee in the year 1823, and was called to fill the post assigned him, in consequence of his zeal, intelligence, and peculiar fitness for the work. He continued to hold his office as trustee during the existence of the Society.

The efforts made to counteract the evils of vagrancy and truancy, proved however, at that time, as they have since, in a large degree abortive. These evils are not to be eradicated in a community like that of New York, even if the work be possible, by any other than the boldest and most persistent as well as far-reaching means. In the twenty-fourth annual report (for 1829) it is remarked that

The committee of the Common Council, from the result of the census of the schools, and the estimated population of the city, draw the appalling inference that there are 20,000 children between the ages of five and fifteen who attend no school whatever; and if one third be deducted from this number as having probably left school previous to the age of fifteen, and 3,000 more for any possible error in the data on which the calculation is founded, we have still the enormous number of 10,000 who are growing up in entire ignorance.

The twenty-seventh annual report (1832), making a reference to the fact that a committee had been sent to Boston to visit the schools of that city, alludes to vagrant children in the following language:

Truantship in that city is deemed a criminal offence in children, and those who cannot be reclaimed are taken from their parents by the police, and placed in an institution called the "School of Reformation," corresponding, in many respects, with our House of Refuge; from which they are bound out by the competent authority, without again returning to their parents. As a necessary consequence, the percentage of absentees, or the difference between the number of children on register and the actual attendance, is less in the Boston public schools than those of New York. This subject has, during the past as in former years, received the attention of the trustees, and will probably be brought before the next board, in connection with the general subject of non-attendance at any school, which exists to such an alarming extent in this city. Efforts have been made by the present board to obtain, in some way, the active coöperation of the city government in applying a remedy to this extensive evil. Every political compact supposes a surrender of some individual rights for the general good. In a Government like ours, "founded on the principle that the only true sovereignty is the will of the people," universal education is acknowledged by all to be, not only of the first importance, but necessary to the permanency of our free institutions. If, then, persons are found so reckless of the best interests of their children, and so indifferent to the public good, as to withhold from them that instruction without which they cannot beneficially discharge those civil and political duties which devolve on them in after-life, it becomes a serious and important question whether so much of the natural right of controlling their children may not be alienated as is necessary to qualify them for usefulness, and render them safe and consistent members of the political body. The expediency of such a measure would be confined pretty much—perhaps entirely—to large seaport towns, and, in its practical operation, would be found to affect but few native citizens.

The Executive Committee held the questions of vagrancy reform under discussion during the year 1831, and, in November, a proposition was submitted from that committee, to the effect that application be made to the Corporation, and also to benevolent societies, that, in dispensing charities to the poor, it be made a condition of such relief that their children be sent to school. The proposition was referred back to the committee, with power. A memorial was accordingly addressed to the Common Council, inviting the attention of that body to the condition of the vagrant children, and praying for the passage of some regulations which might abate the evil. The Common Council took the subject into consideration, and passed the following resolutions :

Resolved, That the trustees of the Public School Society and the Commissioners of the Almshouse be requested to make it known to parents and all persons, whether emigrants or otherwise, having children in charge capable of receiving instruction, and being between the ages of five and twelve years, that, unless said parents and persons do or shall send such children to some public or other daily school, for such time in each year as the trustees of the Public School Society may from time to time designate, that all such persons must consider themselves without the pale of public charities, and not entitled, in case of misfortune, to receive public favor.

Resolved, That the trustees of the Public School Society and the Commissioners of the Almshouse are hereby authorized to take such steps as they may deem expedient, from time to time, to give the necessary publicity to the preceding resolution; and the Commissioners of the Almshouse are hereby requested to use such means as may be in their power and discretion to carry the same into effect.

Adopted by the Board of Aldermen, April 23, 1832.

Adopted by the Board of Assistants, May 7, 1832.

J. MORTON, Clerk.

These resolutions were laid before the trustees, and, on motion, twenty thousand copies, in a suitable handbill form, were ordered to be printed and circulated.

In June, 1838, Joseph B. Collins offered the following resolution for adoption by the Executive Committee:

Resolved, That a committee be appointed to prepare and submit to this committee a project of a plan which may lead, through the aid of our Common Council and Legislature, to a more general attendance of the children of the poor and laboring classes at school, and prevent the multitudes now roaming through our streets from the continuance of a habit so destructive to good morals.

The resolution was laid on the table, but, in September, was taken up and adopted, and Joseph B. Collins, Charles Oakley, Gulian C. Verplanck, Samuel F. Mott, S. Allen, and Robert C. Cornell, were appointed to report upon the objects named.

In December following, the propositions of the committee were laid before the board. The report is as follows:

In contemplating the subject assigned to them, the committee early became sensible of the manifold difficulties of various character by which it is surrounded. So great, indeed, did they appear, as almost to preclude the hope of ever accomplishing any essential reform of the existing deplorable evils. Still they cannot but earnestly desire that the few and scanty lights their labors may throw upon the subject may lead, in time, through the continuous efforts of the Public School Society, to the fulfilment of the design contemplated by the resolution. The chief obstacles to be overcome would seem to be of two classes—moral and physical. The moral embrace indifference and viciousness of both parents and children; the first arising, in part at least, to the parents, from themselves never having enjoyed the benefits of education ; the latter, from their intemperance and indolence.

Among children, a disinclination to go to school grows out of a dislike of control on the one hand, and, on the other, from the allurements of places of amusement of various descriptions—theatres, circuses, gambling-houses, and dram-shops.

The physical impediments result from the extreme poverty of parents, who, for want of means, are unable to provide suitable clothing for their children to attend school in, or need, or conceive they need, their assistance in procuring a livelihood for the family.

These impediments must be surmounted, before we can hope to attain the end in view.

From the high character long enjoyed by the States of Connecticut and Massachusetts in regard to the universality of education among their citizens, the committee were naturally led to seek in the school systems and statistics of those States the object of their inquiry. They therefore opened a correspondence with a gentleman in each, of great practical experience, a thorough knowledge of the subject, and of untiring zeal in the cause of education and of moral improvement among the people. From Connecticut, the committee learned the existence of a statutory provision, applicable in a degree to our wants, but, at the same time, were informed that it is rarely enforced in practice. An abstract (a) is annexed. Could enactments of a similar character be acted upon in our community, doubtless great good would result ; but the committee are not sanguine in the belief that the morbidly excitable sensitiveness of our laboring classes would permit a scrutiny of so inquisitorial a character.

An approximation to it may, however, arise under the arrangements the committee may propose, connected with the establishment of a Farm or Manual Labor School, under the management of a society to be especially organized for this object.

In closing the report the committee submitted the following plans :

1st. A committee of five members, to be designated the Committee on Neglected, Vagrant, and Unfortunate Children, shall be appointed by the Executive Committee, whose duty it shall be to examine and nominate to the Executive Committee three persons or more, to act as district visitors ; to instruct and receive reports from such visitors ; and, in general, to have a supervision of all matters arising under such visitations. The visitors shall receive a salary not exceeding $—— per annum.

The general duty of such visitors shall be to visit the districts around Public Schools No. 8, 1, 5, and 10, and the primaries connected therewith, look out for pupils, and encourage parents to enforce a more regular and general attendance of their children at school. The visitors may also be required to examine and ascertain what neighborhoods are now most in need of additional primary schools, which, with any other useful and relevant matters, they shall report to said committee, to be, in their discretion, brought before the Executive Committee.

2d. The Public School Society shall endeavor to procure the aid of our city government in the following measures, viz. :

1. A renewal and frequent publication, by handbills and otherwise, of a resolution of the Common Council in 1832 (b).

2. The passage of a resolution calling upon all benevolent societies receiving aid from our city treasury, to use efficient means to promote the sending to school of all the children of families assisted by them, and requiring a report of the means used, and extent of their efforts.

To procure the enactment of a modification of the laws respecting education now existing in Connecticut, subjecting the stubborn and vicious minor to his being committed to a manual labor school or asylum, for moral reformation, to be established; and, finally,

The founding, under their own management, or that of a society to be organized for that purpose, of a manual labor school, in an insular situation, to which refractory children may be sent at the request of their parents, or under the law the passage of which they now ask for.

The committee are aware that, among the class of children they hope to reach, there are not a few who are kept from school by insufficiency of suitable clothing; they trust, however, that, on the report of such cases by our visitors, means may be found, through our city authorities and benevolent societies, to remove this impediment (c).

The ability of even young children to contribute in some degree to the support of the family, impresses upon the committee the belief that the establishment of departments in our primary schools to which infants of a very early age, say two and a half to three years, might be admitted, would be highly beneficial, and would meet with less objection than any other from the most indifferent parent, since, at so young a period, they may be said to be only a burden to their parents, incapable of earning or picking up any thing; and, on the other hand, they are yet in more controllable moral condition than even at a comparatively but little farther advanced period of life. Parents would soon participate in the benefits of the discipline of our schools in the improved docility of their children. . . .

(a.) *Laws of Connecticut.*—Parents and guardians required by statute to have their children taught to read, write, and cipher as far as the four rules of arithmetic. Selectmen shall inspect the conduct of the heads of families, and, if any neglect compliance with the above, may admonish them; which, if they neglect, they shall take charge of, and bind out, children of such parents. When children, minors, are stubborn, and refuse to obey the requisition of their parents, they may be committed to the county jail for thirty days.

(b.) See resolutions of Common Council, *ante*, page 618.

(c.) *Revised Statutes of New York.* BEGGARS AND VAGRANTS.—Any child found begging may, on proof, be committed to any place provided for the support of the poor; there to be detained, employed, and instructed in useful labor, until discharged by the Superintendent of the Poor, or bound out by the Commissioners of the Almshouse.

The report was adopted, and referred to the Executive Committee for their action and the memorial to the Common Council was ordered to be engrossed and transmitted to that body. Owing to the overshadowing importance of the controversies which arose soon afterward, and the comprehensiveness of the plans themselves, the committee were prevented from the accomplishment of any material work as contemplated by the scheme, and it is therefore unnecessary to prolong the review of the proceedings in this important project any further than to give the language of the thirty-fifth annual report (1840), in which the result is thus presented :

Originally instituted for the exclusive benefit of the neglected poor, it has ever been a subject of prominent interest with the Board of Trustees to promote, by such means as lay within their power, the attendance of the children of that class at their schools. In the early years of the institution, the duty of visiting parents was occasionally enjoined upon the trustees ; subsequently, it was more especially performed by a competent and faithful agent, who devoted almost his entire time to this object. The rapid increase of the schools since their being thrown open to all classes having required the daily attention of the agent, the duty of visiting parents has ceased to be a distinct portion of his engagements. It was hoped that the great increase in the number, and the notoriety of the schools, would sufficiently attract the attention of parents, and render a special visitation any longer unnecessary. It soon, however, became evident that the criminal indifference of many parents to the welfare of their children was such, that some extraordinary effort was necessary to bring their offspring within our walls. Various expedients were devised, with very limited success. Personal application, aided by kind entreaty, and accompanied by a judicious and well-timed explanation of the benefits of early culture, offering the most promising means of accomplishing the object aimed at, the trustees, at the commencement of the past year, engaged the services of several intelligent and faithful visitors for that purpose ; and it is gratifying to the board to be able to state that, although the success of the visitors has fallen short of the desired results, yet that they have probably been the means of inducing some hundreds of children to attend our schools, who, but for their agency, would have remained mere vagrants in our streets. The trustees have felt so far encouraged by the trial, as to reëngage the services of the visitors, as well as to add to their number.

The trustees regret that their applications to the Corporation for compulsory enactments, which might convert the poor vagrant children who throng our streets and wharves into happy public school scholars, have been

unsuccessful ; but they indulge a hope that though, at first view, such measures may appear to be adverse to our political institutions, an examination
of the subject will show that the good of the community requires that exercise of authority, and that it will yet be deemed expedient.

Whatever of partial and temporary advantage may have
arisen from the measures adopted by the Society, the fact still
remained evident, at the close of every year, that the number of
neglected and uninstructed children was augmenting in a ratio
equal to that of the population of the city, if, indeed, it did not
exceed it. In the face of certain social laws and proclivities,
embarrassing and difficult to the philosopher, and alarming to
the philanthropist and the civilian, all compulsory and reforma-
tory measures seem to be defied by this progression in juvenile
delinquency and immorality. It must be left for perhaps another age to develop the effective remedy.

In addition to the labors of the agent and visitor of the Society, the trustees called into requisition the aid of the visitors of
the American Tract Society, whose regular monthly visits, in the
distribution of tracts, were calculated to exert a valuable influence. Many parents were, by these friendly advisors, made
acquainted with the character of the schools ; and although the
results fell far short of the necessities of the case, many pupils
were added to the rolls.

FREE AND PAY SYSTEMS.

Great systems of popular education require long periods for
their development, and the lapse of time and variations of circumstances call for experiments which are sometimes followed
by important results. The establishment of free schools in the
city of New York was itself experimental, and the benefits
which were successively reaped every year strengthened the zeal
and hopes of its friends. Progress, therefore, became early the
aim of the Society, and it was never lost or forgotten.

The schools grew so much in the public esteem, and, their
numbers having increased by the addition of several large and
substantial buildings, it became an object of desire with many
respectable citizens that their children should enjoy the advantages of these institutions. But an impediment existed in the
fact that they were " free " or " charity " schools—a distinction

that implied a condition of dependence and necessity on the part of those who were instructed in them. This was obnoxious to many who were satisfied with the schools, yet felt that there was a caste classification which would, in a measure, degrade their social position. To remove this difficulty, it was proposed that such regulations should be made as would secure the admission of both pay and free scholars. The subject was first introduced at a meeting of the Board of Trustees held July 4, 1823. The following minute records the action in reference to this change of system :

It being stated that some dissatisfaction exists among the middle classes of our citizens on account of their not partaking of the benefit of the common school fund, and on a suggestion that advantage would arise from our opening our schools for the children of all ranks, and receiving a small compensation for their education, the subject was referred to the consideration of Isaac Collins, H. Ketchum, Robert F. Mott, R. C. Cornell, and John R. Hurd.

The committee submitted a report in January following, but the change proposed was deemed of so much importance, that it was laid on the table, to be considered after a month's notice to that effect. At the same time, the exciting questions growing out of the proceedings relative to the Baptist schools were pending, and the attention of the Society was called to the legislation necessary to remedy the evils of the law giving special privileges to those schools. That law having been amended, and a powerful and successful appeal having been made to the Legislature and Corporation of the city, the amplified resources placed at the disposal of the Society enabled them to project great improvements, as well as an expansion of their system.

The committee to which the consideration and protection of the interests of the Society had been committed in reference to the said law, were also instructed to report a plan for a reorganization of the system ; and, after a careful examination, a report was submitted which covered the whole ground. It was adopted, and its recommendations were, with little modification, embraced in the new scheme ; and, being an exposition of practical plans and results, as well as the groundwork for the experiment of the pay system, the reader is referred to Chapter IV., where it may be found.

On the passage of the law of 1826, a committee of five was

appointed to revise the by-laws of the Society, in conformity with the recent enactment. The committee made a report, in which they recommended a scale of tuition fees, as follows : For tuition in the 1st, 2d, and 3d classes, 25 cents per quarter ; for the 4th, 5th, and 6th classes, 50 cents per quarter ; for the 7th, 8th, and 9th classes, $1 per quarter ; and for the higher studies, $2 per quarter. Grouped by the studies pursued in the schools, the first class were taught the alphabet, spelling, and writing on slates, 25 cents ; the second grade continued these, with reading and arithmetical tables ; the third grade continued the latter studies, with writing on paper, and definitions ; while the fourth, or highest grade, continued these, with the addition of grammar, geography, and the use of maps and globes. In November of the same year, Alderman Cowdrey introduced a resolution for the appointment of a committee to ascertain whether any reduction in the number of scholars had taken place since the introduction of the pay system, and, if so, the causes and the best means for their removal. Najah Taylor, Joseph Grinnell, and Samuel Cowdrey were appointed as that committee.

The report was submitted in February, 1827, from which it appeared that a considerable decrease had taken place in the number of pupils at the various schools. On April 30, 1826, the number of pupils was 3,457, and on the 1st of November, 2,999, making a decrease of 458. This difference was becoming greater at the time of the report. The tuition fee was assigned as an important cause of the decline, which, together with the fact that several large church schools were in operation, which opened their doors to all classes, without distinction, on the free system, had a tendency to withdraw scholars from the Society. The figures are given as follows :

School.	April 30. No. of Pupils.	November 1. Pay Scholars.	Free.	Total.
No. 1,	415	452	40	492
No. 2, Boys,	396	245	116	361
Girls,	319	210	95	395
No. 3, Boys,	515	293	114	407
Girls,	320	187	97	284
No. 4, Boys,	423	176	128	304
Girls,	324	177	112	289
No. 5, Boys,	506	320	59	379
Girls,	239	123	55	178
	3,457	2,183	816	2,999

This result exhibited a loss of 458 in six months.

Another reason assigned by the committee was the introduction of the advanced studies, at $2 per quarter, which were pursued by only a few in each school. In the girls' department of No. 3, only one pupil was entered at $2 per quarter. The system of separate classification for these pupils acted as a drawback on the other portions of the schools, and the fees received by no means met the expenses. The result, as stated in the report, showed that there was a great decrease in the number of high-grade scholars, and that, during the first quarter, one hundred and seven had paid $2; during the second quarter, thirty-nine; and during the third quarter, only thirteen remained in all the schools at that price. The report observes:

Your committee believe that the true and legitimate system of our public schools would be, to open our doors to all classes of children, free of any expense; and the only branches that should be taught in them, should be such as have before been designated, viz.: reading, spelling, writing, and arithmetic.

The committee recommended that the maximum of the tuition fees be reduced to $1 per quarter, and that the higher branches be considered as the reward of merit in those cases where taught.

The several recommendations of the committee were considered from time to time, and then laid on the table for the action of the new Board of Trustees. But no action was had upon the matter, and the system, as originated, was destined to have a longer experiment.

During the following year (1828), the subject was renewed, upon a report being made from the Executive Committee, in which it was strongly urged that the schools should be made free to all classes, and be so far advanced in their grade as to invite children of the more favored ranks in society, and, by an addition to the revenues of the common school system, the Society would be warranted in the expenditures which such an expansion would require. The committee recommended the publication of an address to the people, and the circulation of petitions for the assessment of half a mill on the dollar for common school purposes. The resolutions were adopted, and Robert Sedgwick, Joseph B. Collins, and James I. Roosevelt, Jr., were appointed

40

the committee. At a subsequent meeting, R. C. Cornell, S. Cowdrey, and Lindley Murray were added to the number.

In November, 1828, the returns from the several schools having shown a very great decrease in the amount of tuition fees, the Finance Committee was directed to report upon the facts.

In August, 1829, the committee submitted a report setting forth the operation of the system. Many parents paid, at first, as an entrance fee, but without intending to continue. Others insisted.on being recorded as pay scholars, promising to pay at some future time, but neglected to fulfil the engagement. Many were unable, and a large class insisted on the fact that the schools were supported by the public, and that they had a right to the advantages without charge, even when they were able. The committee recommended a strict adherence to the by-laws in reference to the tuition fees. The report was laid on the table.

In 1831, the Treasurer, Samuel F. Mott, called the attention of the board to the diminution in the fees from pupils, and the matter was referred to the Executive Committee. The report which was made by the committee in the month of May, confirmed the previous experience, and exhibited the fact that parents would enter their children as pay scholars, and, having fallen in arrears for two or three quarters, would send their children to other schools, to repeat the same process. The report recommended a maximum of $1 per quarter, and the payment to be entirely optional with the parents. The by-laws were altered in accordance with the suggestions of the committee, and an experiment of the voluntary system of payment was entered upon. The result is seen in the report of the Treasurer for the quarter ending February 1st, 1832, in which the amount received for tuition fees was stated to be $103.91. The recent enactments of the Legislature, by which the income of the Society was much increased, together with the fact that the pay system was deemed by some to be a compulsory method of making the people pay twice for their schools, combined with the pittance from that source, induced the Society to adopt the recommendation of the Treasurer, and it was abolished by a resolution of the board on the 3d of February, 1832, after a trial of five years, during which every effort had been made to remove objection, hold out inducements, and make the system contribute to inspire self-respect and self-reliance in the minds of those who were chiefly benefitted by the schools. The numerous cases of deception, and the excuses of every kind which were resorted to in order to evade payment, and the expedients to obtain a place on the register as pay pupils, without any intention of complying with the rules, were very mortifying to the Society, who found so general a disregard of fine moral sense among the people. It was, therefore, a source of relief to be able to abolish the system, under the prosperous condition in which the institution had been placed by the liberal endowment of the Legislature.

LOTTERIES.

On the 13th of April, 1819, the Legislature of the State passed a law, authorizing the Mayor of the city of New York to grant licenses to dealers in lottery tickets, and declaring it illegal to carry on the sale of tickets in lotteries, and other similar games of hazard, without such authority. The sum to be paid for licenses was $500 annually, and, in case of violation of the statute, the penalty was fixed at $2,500 in certain cases, and, at the discretion of the court, not to exceed $2,000 for other infractions of the law. The license tax was to be equally divided between the Institution for the Instruction of the Deaf and Dumb, and the Free School Society. The funds of the Society were increased by the revenue thus obtained, the amount received for 1820 being $1,000. The business of vending lottery tickets was, however, much extended subsequently to this period, so that, in 1825, the revenue derived from this source amounted to $2,625, and, in 1826, to $3,625. The following year it reached $3,875. A question having arisen, during the year 1826, as to the constitutionality of the law respecting lotteries, Hon. PETER A. JAY gave his opinion, fully sustaining the law, and the power of the Society to recover penalties. On the reading of this opinion in the meeting of the board, the Executive Committee were directed to take such steps in reference to violations of the statute as they deemed advisable.

In February, 1832, the President of the Institution for the Deaf and Dumb communicated to the Board of Trustees the fact that the directors of that institution had decided to make an application to the Legislature for the appropriation of the whole of the moneys received from the sale of licenses to lottery dealers, and expressing the hope that no opposition to the measure would be made by the Society. The matter was referred to a committee, consisting of J. H. Taylor, W. W. Chester, and James I. Roosevelt, Jr., who had an interview with the officers of the institution. They were directed by the resolution making their appointment, to memorialize the Legislature in opposition to the application, but after a full examination of the question, and after conferences with the directors, the committee reported a resolution declaring it inexpedient to interfere with the application. The matter was thus allowed to go by consent to the Legislature, and the law was amended in compliance with the application of the Institution for the Deaf and Dumb, and so continued until the whole system was overthrown.

A leading motive for this concurrence in the change arose from the fact that there was an apparent inconsistency between the objects of the Society and the revenues from gambling and other vicious pursuits. This feature was always offensive to the Society, and although the money thus raised was appropriated to a noble moral use, the sanction thus given to a demoralizing system by the enjoyment and expenditure of its revenues was felt to be onerous when viewed in a strictly moral aspect. The Society was, therefore, willing to yield that portion of income with little reluctance, and leave the emoluments of vice to be disbursed through other channels. The following language, contained in the twenty-second annual report (1827), expresses these views with distinctness and force, long enough anterior to the relinquishment of the moneys to acquit the Society of any charge of entertaining a sense of morality when it could not control the circumstances:

The subject of lotteries, in which, through the medium of moneys received for licenses to sell tickets, they are directly interested, has engaged much of the serious attention of the trustees. Fully convinced of, and deeply regretting the great and increasing evils incident to, this legalized mode of gambling, they have deemed it their incumbent duty to endeavor to moderate and lessen the mischiefs of this pernicious system, and accordingly directed a committee to prosecute offenders against the provisions of the old law, which prohibited the selling of tickets in foreign lotteries. They also presented a memorial to the Legislature, requesting, if they could not constitutionally abolish the whole system, that such further regulations might be adopted as appeared necessary for the limitation and curtailment of the evil. The board exceedingly regret that an act on this subject, which had passed both branches of the Legislature by large majorities, was negatived by the Executive on the ground of its being unconstitutional. Another bill was, however, subsequently introduced, passed, and has become a law, and which, it is hoped, will prove efficacious in preventing that branch of the evil arising from the sale of tickets in lotteries not authorized by this State.

CORPORAL PUNISHMENT.

To repress every thing which had a tendency to encourage or foster a spirit of violence, was one of the prime objects of the moral government of the schools, and it was believed by the managers that this could be effected in no more efficient manner than in the regulations with regard to corporal punishment. In 1823, a resolution was adopted that teachers dispense entirely with the use of the rod; but should persuasion and admonition fail, then the scholars might be corrected by the use of a small leather strap, applied to the hand, and if this should fail, after suitable trial, the delinquent should be discharged from the school by proclamation.

Several cases of alleged undue severity of punishment having occurred, the teachers were invited to be present at a meeting of the Board of Trustees, in September, 1825, at which time they were admonished that the earnest desire of the Society would be gratified by the entire abolition of bodily punishment, and the exclusive use of moral means. Where, however, delinquents remained insensible to such admonitions, the moderate use of the strap might be resorted to, but only when absolutely necessary.

In 1838, Mr. C. B. Sherman, an assistant teacher in No. 8, applied to the Executive Committee for authority to punish the delinquents in his department—a discretionary exercise not permitted to assistants. The application was referred to a committee, who reported that only principals should be allowed to use corporal punishment, and that assistants ought never to do so, except in the absence of the principal, at which times the assistant was necessarily invested with the powers of the superior teacher. Mr. Brinsmade offered two resolutions—the first, to grant a premium of one hundred dollars to a teacher who should first show that a school can be successfully conducted without corporal punishment; the second resolution was in favor of granting an additional premium of two hundred dollars to the teacher who should conduct a school six months by moral means, without any corporal or degrading punishment. The resolutions and report were recommitted, but the final recommendations confirmed the previous action of the board, in restricting the right to punish to the principals. No premium was ever offered to the teachers as contemplated by the resolutions of Mr. Brinsmade.

A committee was appointed, in 1844, to report on the condition and operations of the schools, and one of the topics which engaged the attention of the committee was that of punishments. The report on this subject recommended the following resolution, which was adopted:

Hereafter no corporal punishment, by blows or otherwise, shall be inflicted on any pupil or pupils in presence of the school, or during school hours, but after the school is dismissed, and then in the presence of the assistant or monitors, or both, with such number of large scholars as may be necessary for witnesses in case of complaint of any aggrieved party; and in no case shall such punishment be inflicted until after proper admonition, parental in its character, be given, with a view of convincing the delinquents of the impropriety of their conduct, and the necessity of reformation; and no stripes or blows to be applied to the head, or any part of the body other than the back near the shoulders.

The resolution granting a pecuniary reward to such teachers as should conduct their schools satisfactorily to the trustees, without the use of corporal punishment, having been rejected, a resolution was adopted that a certificate, signed by the President and Secretary, setting forth the facts, should be given to any teacher who should conduct his or her school twelve months without using the rod or strap.

The predominant idea of the Society was that of PEACE, and any thing that tended to call into exercise the animal passions, either by violence of language, gesture, or discipline, was discountenanced as being peculiarly hostile to the higher moral influence which it was a special object to exert. The sympathy of the moral feelings makes us imitative, and the passional being so impulsive and spontaneous in their exhibitions, the true secret of a teacher's success in moral government was deemed to lie in the power of self-control. Irritation of feeling is quickly betrayed in a teacher, and the frequent resort to bodily chastisement tends to blunt the sensibility of the teacher himself. Hence, all tendency to unnecessary parade or clamor in government, even by the giving of the usual orders of the school in a loud tone of voice, was considered objectionable. One sentence of the manual is worthy of being printed in letters of gold, as a rule for teachers, and should be indelibly written on the mind of every preceptor of youth:

" A SILENT TEACHER MAKES A SILENT SCHOOL."

A paragraph from the manual of the public schools will serve to show the solicitude with which the moral uses of discipline were regarded, as also the suggestions offered for the government of the teachers:

In the regular orders of command, the teacher's voice should seldom, or never, be heard. Approbation and displeasure, too, may very often be as well expressed by looks and gestures as by words; and sometimes better. Such is the language of nature, and the medium of the first moral lessons of infancy—and therefore well understood. In giving orders, signs are always preferable to words. A gentle tap on the desk with the forefinger, a single and slight sound of the bell, or a slight clap of the hands, will sooner command and fix attention than noise or blustering. Gentle sounds act by sympathy on the nervous system, and enforce silence and order when once the school is accustomed to such a mode of discipline. But noise is never effectually prevented by noise; or, if thus repressed, it is only for the moment, and it returns, as a spring recoils on the removal of a weight. "A silent teacher makes a silent school."

Thus, by the proper exercise of firmness and decision, with the constant practice of vigilance and mildness, the alternative of corporal punishment may be very much, if not altogether avoided. Yet every precaution should be taken, lest resort be had to objectionable substitutes for the use of the rod; some of which may be equally painful to the corporeal system—sometimes more injurious, and even dangerous, and not unfrequently hurtful from their moral effects—and, therefore, some of them certainly improper to be used. The sustaining of wearisome burdens, unnatural and long-continued attitudes of restraint, public exposures, and badges of disgrace, are of this class of punishments. Some of these, with judicious modifications of the usual methods by which they are practised, and having due regard to their moral effects on the delinquent, may be used, but only under careful limitations, and with great circumspection and judgment; for it requires a skilful, discreet, and conscientious teacher to use them safely and to advantage. It is ever to be borne in mind that they are best suited to little children, and to boys; and not adapted to the discipline of girls—in whom a nice sense of shame, and a delicate sensibility to reputation, should be carefully cherished. With them, such punishments tend to blunt those feelings which it is the teacher's duty most carefully to cultivate as among the best safeguards to female character. Can punishments of this class, then, be safely ventured upon, without extreme vigilance on the part of the teacher? How hazardous in its moral effects to leave a child publicly exposed, and liable to be neglected by the teacher, till the current of feeling begins to turn! Observe, that this ebbing again of the passions must be nicely watched. It is only by a careful attention to this critical point, that punishment by public exposure can become, as it sometimes does, a powerful means of discipline, especially in the training of little children. But they become worse than useless, if not thus rightly used; for, be it remembered, that, while the teacher may be here and there, the tide of feeling may change, and the first surge of its backward course excite pride, anger, and malevolence. And, though this should be but in a small degree, every moment's continuance of the punishment or exposure beyond the salutary point, inflicts a moral injury that surpasses tenfold any possible good which the teacher can hope to derive from it as a means of discipline. It also renders the punishment altogether ineffectual for another occasion, thereby throwing the teacher into a new perplexity for other substitutes for corporal punishment. It is therefore plain, that, in resorting to such methods of discipline, untiring vigilance alone is to be depended upon to give it any success. Now, there is only one answer to be made to an inquiry that will here arise—*What, then, is to be done?* It is the old, the oft-repeated adage, "An ounce of prevention is worth a pound of cure." Set *vigilance*, then, as the vanguard; send it out far and wide, backed and strengthened by the firm commands of *decision*, while a spirit of *kindness* shall strengthen all the forces brought into the discipline of a school, and how many embarrassments, difficulties, and perplexities will flee away before the faithful and skilful teacher!

MUSIC.

The course of instruction adopted in the schools was for many years rudimentary, and it was only after the increase of means, and the advance in the grade of the schools by long experience, that it was deemed opportune to introduce higher studies. But the progress was steadily onward toward perfection of system and of instruction. In the course of studies, no time was appropriated to musical exercises. The primary or infant schools depended more or less upon singing lively school songs, and moral lessons thus taught were fully appreciated. But this method of refining the taste, as well as of cultivating the mind and heart of the older pupils, had not been recognized as expedient or useful. It was regarded as being merely an accomplishment, and to this consideration was added the conspicuous fact that the time spent in school by a majority of the pupils, before being pressed into industrial employments, was too short to be expended in any other pursuit than the acquisition of knowledge. It is true, moreover, that an influential portion of the trustees, as well as of the members of the Society, was composed of members of the Society of Friends, who do not use music in their public worship, and among whom it is not deemed essential. Whether this fact influenced in any measure the policy of the Society, may be more a matter of surmise than of just conclusion or of evidence.

The example and practice of schools in Europe, particularly those of the continent, at the head of which stood the German institutions, was suggestive of a similar experiment in the schools of New York. Gentlemen of professional ability and zeal in the cause of education, who felt the importance of the introduction of music into the public schools, resolved to take the initiative in the matter, and make an experiment for the purpose of testing its utility.

Mr. Darius E. Jones commenced a course of lessons in School No. 10, and after they had been continued for some time with evident advantage, the "section" or committee for that school reported the case to the board. The subject was referred to a committee, consisting of Messrs. Theodore Dwight, Jr., J. I. Roosevelt, Jr., John Morrison, S. B. Childs, S. F. Mott, J. R. Hurd, and A. R. Lawrence. After the expiration of several months, the committee reported, in August, 1836, as follows:

Your committee, as soon after their appointment as was found convenient, was called together two or three times, at Public School-house No. 10, to hear the performances of the children in the two upper schools, who had been gratuitously taught music by Mr. Jones. It was evident that they had made great progress in an acquaintance with the principles of the science, as well as in the practice of singing, considering the small amount of time they had devoted to that branch. The teachers testified that favorable effects had been produced by its introduction, both in order and study, and that they were very desirous of having it continued.

The lessons in music had, at that time, been suspended about three months, and the whole amount of time ever devoted to them was but twenty hours, chiefly after the close of school, and scattered through a long period of about six months.

Some difference of feeling is believed to exist in this Society in relation to the introduction of vocal music into our schools; and although no facts have come under the knowledge of the committee calculated to show that it has ever produced, or is likely to produce, any bad effects, if conducted on a judicious plan, your committee do not wish to recommend any precipitate measures which may cause disagreement. They feel it, however, to be their duty to recommend that some measures should be resorted to to secure a fair experiment upon this subject in such sections of our schools as are disposed to give it encouragement. It is due to this branch of education to state, that the example of Prussia, Holland, France, Switzerland, and other foreign countries, is in favor of its introduction. In several of them vocal music is taught as an important branch, and with evident and salutary results. In different places in the United States where it has been properly taught on modern principles, it has found numerous advocates and general approbation. In Boston particularly, scientific and practical instruction in music has become highly popular; and, without mentioning other places, in a number of very respectable schools in our city it has been introduced with full success. In some of our own primary schools, music has long been taught by rote, yet, with the disadvantages attending that method, it is approved and continued.

Only two objections have been urged against its introduction into our schools, so far as your committee are informed: 1st. That it would be expensive; and 2d. That it would encroach upon school hours. But music may be taught without exposure to either of these evils. Several teachers have signified a readiness to teach a year or six months gratuitously, one hour in each week (which, experience shows, is sufficient), and the lessons may be restricted to hours not appropriated to the regular school exercises. Several of our teachers are believed to be qualified to instruct their pupils in this branch; and these have expressed their willingness to perform the task.

Your committee would, therefore, report for adoption the following resolution:

Resolved, That the sections shall be at liberty to have vocal music taught in their schools, provided it be done without expense to this Society, and without encroaching on the regular school hours.

All which is respectfully submitted.

The report gave rise to a long and animated debate, which was terminated by a motion to lay the whole subject on the table. The motion prevailed, and the introduction of music into the schools was indefinitely postponed.

In 1840, Mr. A. W. GOFF submitted an application to the Executive Committee for leave to introduce singing into the schools, and for an appointment as instructor. The committee, after consideration of the subject, directed the application to be returned, with the explanation that music was not one of the branches taught in the public schools.

During the year 1843, the teacher of School No. 7 submitted a proposition to the "section" of the trustees to whom the care of that school was committed, for the employment of a teacher of vocal music. The reasons urged were those of an experienced and observant preceptor, who estimated the advantages of such instruction, and the application was fully discussed at a meeting of the section. At the conclusion of the debate, a resolution was unanimously adopted adverse to the suggestion, and a report made to the Board of Trustees, as follows :

On consideration (all the members of the section being present), it was resolved, unanimously, to be inexpedient to adopt the suggestion or proposition of the teacher of No. 7, relative to appointing a teacher of vocal music.

The report of the section was approved by the Board of Trustees, and the subject was thus once more reserved for future action.

No effort was renewed with reference to the introduction of vocal music into the schools for several years. But the advocates of that measure were not satisfied with the position held by the schools of the Society, and it was again deemed expedient to press the question upon the attention of the board. Accordingly, in January, 1847, the ward schools having been in existence five years, a member of the board offered a resolution at a meeting held on the 19th of that month, which reads as follows :

Resolved, That music be taught in the upper schools, and also in the normal schools, and that a competent number of teachers be employed at salaries not exceeding two hundred dollars per annum.

On motion, the resolution was laid on the table, and there remained as long as the table lasted, the proposition not being again renewed during the existence of the Society.

In the minds of many, the action of the board in regard to music will ever be considered as reprehensible, and unworthy of the position held by the institution. But whatever may be the views of others, supported by the very high consideration of moral and intellectual refinement and cultivation, it must not be forgotten that, while the board fully appreciated the services of all who could in any way benefit the schools, they were not desirous of expending considerable portions of a limited income, disproportioned to the demands made upon the institution, in incidentals, and were equally reluctant to accept permanently valuable services for which no compensation could be made. In addition to a sense of justice and honor in this respect, they were, moreover, cautious of adopting measures which promised to make them obnoxious to outside opposition. They had been, for many years, jealously watched by parties ever on the alert to detect weak points, errors in policy, carelessness in system, improvidence in expenditure, or blunders in experiment. The opposition of these parties would be strengthened by measures on which any great diversity of views was entertained, and every false step or premature undertaking would have been only to furnish capital upon which antagonism might feed its spirit of hostility. While other views might have been held, with greater favor to the public sympathy than those which overruled the propositions to introduce vocal music into the schools, the reader of the history should guard against prejudices arising in his mind, because circumstances and considerations of a peculiar character, altogether independent of the merits of the question, interposed a formidable barrier. It is sufficient to know that the decision of the Board of Trustees was founded in conscientious views of rigid adherence to that which, at the time, appeared to be right and true.

MORAL AND RELIGIOUS INSTRUCTION.

Men who regard the present life as being a preparatory stage for an immortality of existence, and are prompted to labor for the elevation of the lowly and the almost friendless classes of society, are, in most cases, influenced by a deep conviction of duty, immeasurably nobler than that of the clamorer for popular favor, who has but his own aggrandizement in view, and looks no higher than the ballot-box, and no lower than the means to secure popular suffrage will require him to descend. The originators of the Free-School Society, and those who continued it to its honorable close, were men of earnest convictions of moral and religious responsibility, and they did not shrink from a constant desire to promote the moral and religious welfare of the objects of their care.

The questions which arose during the career of the Society in regard to the religious character of its system, present, to say the least, some very remarkable exhibitions of reasoning. Its opponents brought conflicting charges against it, which will be found fully presented in the reports of the controversies relative to the school fund. One charge was, that the Society was a religious institution; another, that it was sectarian; another, that it was infidel; and another, that "it was favorable only to the sectarianism of infidelity, and opposed to Christianity." A brief exposition of the practice of the institution is therefore essential in a history of its operations.

The members of the Society, as must be evident from the nature of its organization, represented almost every religious denomination, and, consequently, it would have been impossible to have adopted a system of instruction in religious opinions or creeds which would have been, in the strict meaning of the term, "sectarian." Yet there are certain tenets and articles of faith which are common to all men who have any religious opinions whatever: such as the existence of the Deity, moral responsibility, the immortality of the soul, and the practice of all the moral duties which are elevated above the mere idea of selfish advantage as being more convenient or more to a man's own interests than the indulgence of vice or crime. The maxim that "honesty is the best policy," is good enough as a demonstrable fact, in many cases of human experience, but it is a base and selfish maxim at the best. It requires the higher motive and the higher obligation of spiritual and religious convictions and responsibilities. To denounce the inculcation of such principles in the minds of the youth of our common schools as "sectarian," would argue a strange mental vision on the part of one who holds each and all of these same doctrines and opinions; or, on the other hand, a perversity of opposition which has only selfish ends for its basis. The Society gave religious and moral instruction, but it never descended to the level of "sectarianism."

The importance, however, of devoting a specified portion of time to the religious training of the pupils, led to a demand for some system upon which all denominations could unite, and a regulation was adopted at an early period which afforded the opportunity desired. The afternoon of every Tuesday was appropriated to the instruction of the pupils in the catechisms of the various churches to which they belonged. An association of ladies was formed for the purpose, who met at the schools at the appointed time to conduct these exercises. At the time of the ninth annual report (1814), the number of children educated in the peculiar tenets of the religious denominations represented was as follows :

Presbyterians,	271
Episcopalians,	166
Methodists,	172
Baptists,	119
Dutch Reformed Church,	41
Roman Catholics,	9

The report adds :

In furtherance of the same interesting object, the children have been required to assemble at their respective schools on the morning of every Sabbath, and proceed, under the care of a monitor, to such place of public worship as was designated by their parents or guardians. This requisition has been regularly attended to by many, but the want of suitable clothing has prevented others from complying with it. In cases where an attendance at school previous to going to church is particularly inconvenient, liberty has been given for the children to attend public worship in company with their parents or guardians.

Early in the year 1819, it was deemed proper to print and distribute an address to parents, from which the following extracts are made :

SEC. 8. You know that many evils grow out of idleness, and many more out of the improper use of spirituous liquors ; that they are ruinous and destructive to morals, and debase the human character below the lowest of all created beings ; we therefore earnestly desire you may be watchful and careful in this respect ; otherwise, in vain may we labor to promote the welfare of your children.

SEC. 9. In domestic life, there are many virtues which are requisite in order to promote the comfort and welfare of families. Temperance and economy are indispensable, but without cleanliness your enjoyments as well as your reputation will be impaired ; it is promotive of health and ought not to be neglected. Parents can, perhaps, scarcely give a greater proof of their care for their children than by keeping them clean and decent, especially when they are sent to school, where it is expected they will appear with their hands, faces, and heads perfectly clean, and their clothing clean and in good order. The appearance of children exhibits to every observing mind the character of the mother.

SEC. 10. Among other moral and religious duties, that of a due observance of the first day of the week, commonly called Sunday, we consider of importance to yourselves and to your children. Public worship is a duty we owe to our Creator; it is of universal obligation, and you ought to be good examples thereof. And believing, as we do, that the establishment of what is called Sunday schools has been a blessing to many, and may prove so to many more, we are desirous you may unite in the support of a plan so well calculated to promote the religious duties of that day, which ought to be appropriated to public worship, retirement, and other duties connected with the improvement of the mind.

Sec. 11. Seeing, next to your own souls, your children, and those placed under your care, are, or ought to be, the immediate objects of your constant attention and diligent concern, you ought to omit no opportunity to instruct them early in the principles of the Christian religion, in order to bring them, in their youth, to a sense of the unspeakable love and infinite wisdom and power of their Almighty Creator; for good and early impressions on tender minds often prove a lasting means of preserving them in a religious life even to old age. May you, therefore, watch over them for good, and rule over them in the fear of God, maintaining your authority in love; and as very much depends on the care and exemplary conduct of parents, and the judicious management of children by tutors, we cannot too strongly recommend to their serious consideration the importance of the subject, as one deeply interesting to the welfare of the rising generation, and no less connected with the best interests of civil and religious society.

Sec. 12. As the Holy Scriptures, or Bible, with which you ought all to be furnished, contain a full account of things most surely to be believed, and Divine commands most faithfully to be obeyed, and are said to make "wise unto salvation through faith which is in Jesus Christ," 2 Tim. iii. 15, it is the duty of every Christian to be frequent and diligent in the reading of them in their families, and in privately meditating on those sacred records.

The address from which these passages are taken was signed by De Witt Clinton, President, and the officers and members of the Board of Trustees, among whom were John Murray, Jr., Thomas Eddy, Rensselaer Havens, Jacob Lorillard, Leonard Bleecker, Col. Henry Rutgers, Najah Taylor, Henry Eckford, John Pintard, and George T. Trimble, the last President of the Society.

A committee was appointed to inquire and report upon the state of the schools, and especially with reference to the attendance of the pupils at public service on the Sabbath. In May, the committee reported that there were 480 scholars in No. 1, of whom 397 attended church regularly; of 437 on the register of No. 2, 335 were regular in their Sunday observances; in No. 3, of 333 on the register, 312 attended church. This supervision over the moral and religious habits of their pupils was continued by the Society, although the system of voluntary instruction by catechism once a week was, after a time, discontinued, as well as the special requirements in regard to public worship. The great enlargement of the system of the Society, and its modification, made regulations for the Sabbath unwieldy and inexpedient, if not impracticable.

A resolution was adopted at the time of publishing the address, requiring that the children should commit to memory, each week, passages from tracts on spirituous liquors.; but the resolution was reconsidered and rescinded at the meeting held during the month of June following.

The daily reading of a portion of the Bible at the opening of school had been practised from the organization of No. 1, and was continued till the close of the Society's labors. In 1821, a volume of "Scripture Lessons," which had been adopted in England for the use of schools, was recommended to the board for its adoption. It was referred to a committee, consisting of John E. Hyde, Najah Taylor, Isaac Collins, and Leonard Bleecker. Soon afterward, a catechism, "said to be free from sectarian principles," was also submitted to the board, and referred to the same committee. The report recommended the adoption of both works, and the committee was directed to have the "Scripture Lessons" stereotyped, and an edition of 1,000 copies printed and bound for the use of the schools. Two thousand copies of the catechism were purchased, and distributed among the pupils.

The twenty-second annual report (1827) contains the following passage :

The trustees are aware of the importance of early religious instruction ; and although the nature of their association and its true interests require that none but such as is exclusively general and scriptural in its character should be introduced into the schools under their charge, they require from the teachers stated returns of the number of their scholars who attend a⁴ the various Sunday schools or places of worship on the Sabbath. The last reports from all the schools, except No. 8, show that, on the 1st of April, of 3,925 children on the registers, 2,463 belonged to Sunday schools, and of the remainder, 1,142 were attendants at the various places of worship to which their parents were attached, leaving but 326 unaccounted for, or who are negligent in this important duty.

The thirty-third annual report (1838) alludes to the same topic, in the following language :

The constitution of the Society, and public sentiment, wisely forbid the introduction into these schools of any such religious instruction as shall favor the peculiar views of any sect; and the trustees endeavor so carefully to guard them in this respect, as to give no just cause of complaint, leaving this subject where it rightfully belongs—to the parents and guardians of the children. They wish, however, not to be understood as regarding religious impressions in early youth as unimportant; on the contrary, they desire to do all which may with propriety be done to give a right direction to the minds of the children entrusted to their care. Their schools are uniformly opened with the reading of the Scriptures, and the class-books are such as recognize and enforce the great and generally acknowledged principles of Christianity.

Entertaining views like those expressed in the foregoing extracts, the Executive Committee, during the year 1838, appointed Joseph B. Collins, Samuel R. Childs, and William L. Stone to report upon a manual for moral and religious instruction. In compliance with the directions appointing them, the committee made a report in January, 1839, to which the following resolutions were appended:

Resolved, That the Trustees of the Public School Society hold in high estimation the inculcation of correct elementary education among all classes of children; and, at the same time, they contend that it is of the greater importance as regards their temporal and eternal welfare, that the youthful mind should be imbued with sound moral and religious principles; therefore,

Resolved, That, in their view, it is expedient to introduce into our public and primary schools suitable books setting forth in concise terms the fundamental principles of the Christian religion, free from all sectarian bias, and also those general and special articles of the moral code, upon which the good order and welfare of society are based; the substance of which shall be committed to memory by the pupils.

On the reading of the report and resolutions, some discussion ensued, and the following alteration of the by-laws was proposed:

Special care must be taken to avoid any instruction of a sectarian character; but the teachers shall embrace every favorable opportunity of inculcating the general truths of Christianity, and the primary importance of practical religious and moral duty, as founded on the precepts of the Holy Scriptures.

The whole subject was laid on the table, and the accumulation of other business occasioned a pause in the proceedings, and, in the mean time, the renewal of the controversy in rela-

41

tion to the school fund, which was foreshadowed and opened early in the following year (1840), suspended them altogether.

An illustration of the religious exercises recommended for the use of the teachers at the opening of school will be found in the following passages from the "MANUAL" prepared for the primary departments by SAMUEL W. SETON, and approved and published by order of the Board of Trustees during the year 1830. After the salutation of the teacher to the school, and expressing their dependence upon GOD for sparing them to meet again, the exercise proceeds :

Teacher. How should we feel to our heavenly Father for these mercies ?
Answer. Truly thankful.

T. What example have we for this in the Holy Scriptures ?
A. Psalm c. 4, 5 : " Be thankful unto Him, and bless His name, for the Lord is good. His mercy is everlasting, and His truth endureth to all generations."

T. Children, who is good ?
A. The Lord is good.

T. To whom should we be thankful ?
A. Be thankful unto Him.

T. Whose name should we bless ?
A. Bless His name.

T. What is said, in this Psalm, of God's mercy ?
A. His mercy is everlasting.

T. What is said of God's truth ?
A. His truth endureth to all generations.

T. What is God's truth ?
A. His holy laws.

T. Psalm xxxiv. 11 : " Come, ye children, hearken unto me ; I will teach you the fear of the Lord." My dear children, tell me, who has watched over you, and preserved your lives through the past night ?
A. Psalm iii. 5 : " I laid me down, and slept. I waked, for the Lord sustained me."

T. Does God always see you ?
A. Proverbs xv. 3 : " The eyes of the Lord are in every place."

T. Does God know your very thoughts ?
A. Psalm cxxxix. 1, 2 : " O Lord, thou hast searched me, and known me. Thou knowest my down-sitting and mine uprising ; thou understandest my thoughts afar off."

T. Does God know all you do ?
A. Psalm cxxxix. 3 : " Thou compassest my path and my lying down, and art acquainted with all my ways."

T. Does God hear all you say ?
A. Psalm cxxxix. 4 : " For there is not a word in my tongue, but lo, O Lord, thou knowest it altogether."

T. Does God require the young to serve Him?

A. Ecclesiastes xii. 1: " Remember now thy Creator in the days of thy youth."

To vary the exercises, other lessons were provided, to be used at the discretion of the teacher, one of which is as follows:

T. Is our life uncertain?

A. Proverbs xxvii. 1: " Boast not thyself of to-morrow; for thou knowest not what a day may bring forth."

T. What, then, should you ask of your heavenly Father?

A. Psalm xc. 12: " So teach us to number our days, that we may apply our hearts unto wisdom."

T. How does God encourage you, in the Holy Scriptures, to love and serve Him while you are young?

A. Proverbs viii. 17: " I love them that love me, and those that seek me early shall find me."

These exercises were followed by the repetition of the Lord's Prayer, and the singing or recitation of a hymn suitable for children, commencing with the lines,

> " I thank the goodness and the grace
> Which on my birth have smiled,
> And made me, in these Christian days,
> A highly favored child."

The opening exercise for the youngest children, as they took their places on the gallery in the morning, and also for all the classes when they respectively used the gallery, was the following:

Teacher. My dear children, the intention of this school is to teach you to be good and useful in this world, that you may be happy in the world to come. What is the intention of this school?

T. We therefore first teach you to " remember your Creator in the days of your youth." What do we first teach you?

T. It is our duty to teach you this, because we find it written in the Holy Bible. Why·is it our duty to teach you this?

T. The Holy Bible directs us to " train you up in the way you should go." What good book directs us to train you up in the way you should go?

T. Therefore, my children, you must obey your parents.

Scholar. I must obey my parents.

T. You must obey your teachers.

S. I must obey my teachers.

T. You must never tell a lie.

S. I must never tell a lie.

T. You must never steal the smallest thing.

S. I must never steal the smallest thing.

T. You must never swear.

S. I must never swear.

T. God will not hold him guiltless that taketh His name in vain.

S. God will not hold him guiltless that taketh His name in vain.

T. God always sees you. (*Slowly, and in a soft tone.*)

S. God always sees me.

T. God hears all you say.

S. God hears all I say.

T. God knows all you do.

S. God knows all I do.

T. You should fear to offend Him, for He is most holy.

S. I should fear to offend Him, for He is most holy.

T. You should depart from evil, and learn to do well.

S. I should depart from evil, and learn to do well.

T. May all you, dear children, learn, while attending this school, to be good and useful in this world.

S. May we all, while attending this school, learn to be good and useful in this world.

T. And, with God's blessing, may you be happy in the world to come.

S. And, with God's blessing, may we be happy in the world to come.

The children then sing a hymn by Dr. WATTS, as follows:

> "Let children that would fear the Lord
> Hear what their teachers say,
> With reverence meet their parents' word,
> And with delight obey.
>
> "Have we not heard what dreadful plagues
> Are threatened by the Lord,
> To him who breaks his father's laws,
> And mocks his mother's word?
>
> "But those who worship God, and give
> Their parents honor due,
> Here on this earth they long shall live,
> And live hereafter too."

It is unnecessary to multiply, in this place, quotations from the records of the Society bearing upon the nature and extent of the "religious" instruction sought to be inculcated in the schools. They would present only repetitions of the views already expressed, and these are deemed sufficiently clear and extended to define the position held during the whole career of the institution. For additional information, the reader is referred to the several memorials and papers of the Society which will be found in other pages of this volume, and to the arguments made on its behalf by its advocates and representatives.

CHAPTER XVII.

NORMAL AND HIGH SCHOOLS.

Monitorial Classes Organized—Central School for Advanced Studies—High Schools—
Normal Schools—Classical Institute—Free Academy.

THE experience of all systems of education has shown the necessity of assuring a supply of competent instructors. Where the number of teachers properly qualified for their duties falls below the demand, the deficiency must be supplied by those of indifferent qualifications—which is, at the best, a doubtful expedient, and only a little better than the alternative of temporary suspension in the routine of education until the want can be met. The most perfect machinery of system and the most liberal endowment of means cannot sufficiently compensate for the absence of the skilful and efficient teacher.

The monitorial system in use in the schools of the Public School Society made the training of properly qualified assistants a matter of urgent necessity. The value of expert and well-trained monitors, thoroughly familiarized with the Lancasterian methods, led the Society at an early day to adopt a system of indentures, by which the monitors were apprenticed to learn the art of teaching. As an indispensable part of the means for fully attaining these ends, it was deemed expedient to establish classes for the instruction of the monitors in the schools. This course was adopted in the year 1817, and was the initiative of the normal school system now existing under the Board of Education.

During the year 1826, a committee of three was appointed for the purpose of reporting on a proposition to establish a "CENTRAL SCHOOL" for the instruction of tutors and monitors, and for such advanced pupils of the schools as might deserve the distinction.

The committee promptly reported upon the resolution referred to them, in which the various considerations were strongly urged which should induce the Society to organize such a school. The project of the committee confined the range of studies to the English branches, with natural philosophy, bookkeeping, mercantile education, geology, and chemistry. This course of studies, it was thought, would be more practically valuable for that period, and under the circumstances in which the Society and its schools were then placed, than an institution in which a classical course should be introduced. A liberal and extended view was taken, in the report, of the positive and reflex advantages and influence of such a school in the city, and an appropriation of $25,000 was named as being required to erect suitable buildings, and furnish them with the requisite appointments. A committee was authorized, in accordance with the recommendation of the report, to memorialize the Legislature for a grant of the sum required; but, in consequence of the difference of views entertained in relation to so important a measure, it was finally suffered to rest without decision.

The question was renewed, in 1832, in the report of the Committee on Reorganization, in which it was observed that, as "part of a perfect system," the establishment of a high school, as soon as circumstances would warrant, was to be kept constantly in view.

The growing importance of the common school system of the city and the State at large, had been for some time attracting the attention of prominent citizens and friends of education, and the consultations and correspondence which had been held in reference to the subject, especially in connection with the proper training of a body of efficient teachers, led to the call for a public meeting of the friends of normal schools, to be held in the city of New York. The convention assembled, measures were recommended, and appropriate committees were appointed. A committee of which Gideon Lee was chairman, and Theodore Dwight, Jr., secretary, together with a committee of the Council of the University, laid before the Board of Trustees, in February, 1834, a communication inviting a conference on the subject of their appointment. Messrs. Robert C. Cornell, Gulian C. Verplanck, and James I. Roosevelt, Jr., were appointed on behalf of the Society. The action growing out of these conferences did not come within the administration of the Society, and need not be discussed here.

The Executive Committee, however, sympathizing fully with the movement, and being forced to witness the disadvantages growing out of the non-existence of such a school, directed the Committee on Teachers and Monitors to present a report on a school of the kind contemplated. The report was laid before the board on the 1st of August, in which it was recommended that a school be opened on the last day of every week, except during the usual vacation, in Public School No. 5, in Mott street, for the instruction of assistants and monitors of the primary schools and primary departments. The teachers thus specified, being all females, gave the school the character which it has since maintained, as the "Female Normal School." It was conducted by ELIZA COX and WILLIAM BELDEN, Sr., then and for more than twenty years the principal of Public School No. 2.

The success of the institution was striking and immediate, and its beneficial influence on the day schools was too potent not to be recognized. It was found that teachers practically drilled in the daily routine of school discipline and instruction, and simultaneously taught in those branches which they were expected to teach, were, beyond all comparison, superior in tact, skill, and efficiency to persons educated in high schools or colleges, and placed in the station of assistant teachers without preliminary preparation or apprenticeship.

A branch of this school for the education of the junior teachers of the male departments was established a few months afterward.

In 1841, on the completion of the new edifice called "Trustees' Hall," situated on the corner of Grand and Elm streets, and designed to furnish the trustees of the Public School Society with rooms for their meetings, as well as to provide accommodations for the female normal schools, the institution was removed from its former location in No. 5, and held its sessions in the new building. A large apartment, capable of accommodating four hundred persons, for the general assembling of the school in the morning, and five commodious recitation-rooms were provided, and the school continued to flourish with increased prosperity.

Upon the death of LINDLEY MURRAY, Esq., a member of the committee charged with the care of the several schools, his place was supplied by A. P. HALSEY, Esq.; and on the decease of Mr.

SAMUEL DEMILT, the chairman, Mr. GEORGE T. TRIMBLE, by se-
niority, succeeded him in that station, and the vacant place on
the committee was filled by the appointment of Dr. Charles E.
Pierson. On the resignation of Mr. Halsey, William H. Neilson, Esq., having become a member of the committee, these
three gentlemen—Messrs. Trimble, Pierson, and Neilson—continued the superintendence up to the time of the dissolution of
the Society.

The success and efficiency of the normal schools will be apparent from the fact stated in 1853, in the forty-seventh annual
report, that, out of the 422 teachers of all grades then engaged
in the various departments of the public schools, 386 had been,
or still were, pupils of the normal schools. Nearly 350 were
engaged in ward or other schools, and 460 graduates were engaged in other professions, or in the duties of domestic life. The
whole number, from the time of its establishment in 1834
to 1853, being 1,150 trained in the male and female normal
schools.

In reviewing the history of this institution, it is impossible to
forbear paying a passing tribute to the memory of those noble
and philanthropic men by whose fostering care it was founded
and sustained.

During the last eleven years of his life, SAMUEL DEMILT was
unremitting in his oversight of these schools, attending at each
session; and, during the whole period of five hours, he gave, by
his interest and example, an encouragement and stimulus to the
establishment which, to a great extent, was the means of placing
it on a permanent basis.

During a brief career of usefulness, ISAAC H. CLAPP was also
unwearied in his exertions to promote the interests and welfare
of the institution, devoting all the energies of early manhood to
the cause, with a disinterested zeal and activity rarely seen, and
worthy of the highest admiration.

In addition to those who have ceased from their labors, it
would be unjust not to mention those who were either their coadjutors or successors in this important trust, and who, though
still engaged in similar offices of benevolence and usefulness to
the living, have ceased to be connected with the charge of this
favorite object of their care.

In this connection, George T. Trimble deserves to be remembered and esteemed. During nearly the whole twenty years of the existence of the normal school, he was among the most zealous in his watchful oversight of the female normal school. To him and his associates the city is indebted for the institution which has prepared so large a number of active teachers for their responsible duties.

The trustees of the Public School Society were not behind any of their fellow-citizens in a just appreciation of the advantages and economy of the highest kind of education which could be afforded to the masses. This charge has been made and repeated by men who judged by circumstances, and not by an accurate knowledge of the publications and unsuccessful efforts of the Society to reach the object of their cherished desire. It would argue little for the character of an institution at whose head stood, for forty years, such men as De Witt Clinton, Gulian C. Verplanck, Henry Eckford, Colonel Rutgers, and others of the same class, to suppose that it ever sought to limit the extent of its studies, or to crush out aspirations for the higher walks of literature and science. Its resources were never equal to the calls upon them, and the practical aim was to give to *all* the children of the school age at least some of the advantages of education, rather than to give a higher culture to a limited number who could afford to obtain it through other institutions. It was deemed better to give a good rudimentary education to scores of thousands, than to adopt a course of studies which could be enjoyed only by the minority. It had not the elastic liberty of a board of officers who could call for an almost unlimited amount, but was restricted in its expenditures, so that it was obliged, in order to meet the demand upon it, to mortgage a large portion of its property, that it might erect new buildings for its pupils. The project of a high school, or classical institution, was no novelty with a large portion of the members of the Public School Society.

As early as 1828, at the time of making an appeal to the Legislature for additional means, an address to the public was circulated, in which high schools for advanced English studies, fully up to the standard of the best of the ward schools now in existence, were strongly advocated, and a classical seminary was held before the people as an object of pride, usefulness, and honor. In this address the trustees speak as follows:

We desire to see our public schools so endowed and provided, that they shall be equally desirable for all classes of society. To effect this, the means of instruction which are offered to the poor *should be the very best which can be provided.* They may not all be able to proceed so far in the path of learning as others in happier circumstances; but to the extent of their progress let them have all the helps which the present state of knowledge affords. This is no mere fanciful theory. The advantages of a free intercourse and competition between persons of all ranks and conditions in life, as exhibited in the Edinburgh high school, have been admirably illustrated by one of the first British orators of the age. He regarded such an institution as invaluable in a free State; because, to use his own language, men of the highest and lowest rank in the community sent their children there to be educated together. The practical beneficence of this system is attested by the noble institutions of a sister city. It is by such a union and intercourse that the real worth of outward distinctions is perceived—that the highest rewards of merit are felt to be equally offered to all—that the jealousies which are too apt to arise from differences of condition are melted away—and that the relations which subsist between the different classes of society are felt to be relations of mental advantage and dependence, and not those of hostility.

In connection with this subject, the address urged a scale of higher rewards for the qualifications of teachers, the view held by the trustees being, that the office of teacher, considered as one of grave responsibility and importance, called for high attainments and a proportionate remuneration. In fact, there has been no advance made in the common school system of New York which was not in some form urged repeatedly by the several boards and committees of the Public School Society.

The success and value of the normal school scheme had been illustrated by nine years of experience, and the number of pupils who had progressed to important posts as teachers in New York and other localities, was constantly on the increase. The Board of Education also, under the law of 1842, had sprung into existence, and additional schools were creating an augmented demand for qualified teachers. Under these circumstances, Abraham R. Lawrence introduced, at the meeting of the Board of Trustees on May 16, 1843, the following resolution:

Resolved, That it be referred to a special committee to inquire into and report to this board, at a future meeting, the expediency of making the normal schools day schools, to be open every day in the week, excepting Saturdays and Sundays; that their range of studies be so extended as to instruct male pupils in all the branches of learning necessary to their initiation in any of the colleges of this State, and females in such studies as are taught in the highest grade of seminaries for female instruction in this city; and that the said schools constitute one distinct section.

The resolution was adopted, and referred to a committee, consisting of Abraham R. Lawrence, Lindley Murray, John T. Adams, Burritt Sherwood, and James F. Depeyster.

The committee submitted a report recommending the adoption of the measure, and the name "High Schools" was substituted for that of "Normal Schools." In June, 1844, the subject was renewed, and, after a protracted discussion, a committee, consisting of Messrs. Abraham R. Lawrence, John R. Hurd, Samuel B. Childs, John T. Adams, and Joseph B. Collins, was appointed, to prepare a memorial to the Legislature, asking authority to establish high schools in which Latin and Greek and similar advanced studies should be taught.

The committee submitted their report in January, 1845, in which the necessity of such an institution was earnestly and carefully presented. The memorial was referred back to the committee, to operate in concert with the Executive Committee, who had appointed several of their number to confer with the Board of Education relative to the enterprise.

Several of the teachers in the ward schools of the Fourteenth Ward having been refused admittance to the normal school, the case was laid before the trustees by a committee of the Board of Education. A conference was had, and an explanation of the difficulty having been made, the trustees recognized the claim of the teachers of the ward schools to the privileges of the normal schools, "on their complying with the rules and regulations of the schools."

The measures contemplated by the resolution of Mr. Lawrence were never prosecuted, but they became a stimulus to the movement which resulted in the establishment of the Free Academy, under the care of the Board of Education, which was publicly opened by appropriate exercises on the 5th of February, 1849.

CHAPTER XVIII.

INFANT SCHOOLS AND PRIMARY SCHOOLS.

Female Association—Girls' Schools—The Infant-School Society—Experiment in No. 10 —Junior Department of No. 8—Theory of Infant Schools—The System Approved —Delegation to Visit Boston—Primary Departments Established—Female Teachers Introduced to the Schools—Primary Schools Established.

THE origin of our public system of education antedates the formation of the Free-School Society about three years, and is to be found in the benevolent efforts of a number of ladies, members of the Society of Friends, who were zealously engaged in labors of love and charity among the poor.

In the month of March, 1798, several ladies proposed to organize an "Association for the Relief of the Sick Poor," and a committee was appointed to report rules for the government of the Association. The report was submitted at a meeting held on the 21st of that month, and the ladies entered upon their benevolent labors. The first article excluded all persons *not* members of the Society of Friends from the Association; and, on the other hand, the sixth article provided that "*no relief be afforded to any of the people called Quakers.*" Among the ladies who thus devoted themselves to the wants of the sick, were Catharine Murray, Amy Bowne, Elizabeth Haydock, M. Minturn, Lydia Mott, Agnes Abbatt, Elizabeth W. Underhill, Penelope Hull, Sarah Collins, Hannah Eddy, Deborah Franklin, and others, the names of whose descendants are still found frequent and conspicuous in our public institutions, in the faithful discharge of similar labors. These ladies became intimate with the social condition of the families they visited, and were not long in perceiving the necessity of affording to poor children that kind of instruction best adapted to their condition. In 1801, the proposition to establish a school was fully discussed, and a committee appointed to make the necessary arrangements and employ a teacher. It was opened in June, 1801. The original minute in the record, which appears not to have been used until the close of 1802, is as follows:

The Association of Women Friends for the Relief of the Poor, having concluded that a part of their funds should be appropriated to the education of poor children of the following description, viz., those whose parents belong to no religious society, and who, from some cause or other, cannot be admitted into any of the charity schools of this city, have appointed the following persons as a committee to open a school for that purpose: Lydia P. Mott, Caroline Bowne, Sarah Collins, Mary Minturn, Jr., Hannah Bowne, and Susan Collins; who have, agreeably to permission, rented a room at the rate of £16 per annum, and engaged a widow woman of good education and morals as an instructor, and allow her a salary of £30 a year, to be advanced at the discretion of the committee, which met at the school-room, 28th of 12th month.

The school was attended by children of both sexes, but the committee soon became convinced that the plans they had designed would be more advantageously prosecuted by admitting only girls to the school. The male pupils were discharged, and the institution was restricted to females during the subsequent existence of the schools under its care.

The ladies who organized the Association and were its earliest members, were the following:

Catharine Murray,	Hannah Eddy,
Elizabeth Bowne,	Ann Eddy,
Sarah Robinson,	Agnes Abbatt,
Amy Bowne,	Sarah Collins,
Hannah Pearsall,	Elizabeth Pearsall,
Margaret B. Haydock,	Mary Pearsall Robinson,
Elizabeth Haydock,	Hannah Lawrence,
Sarah Haydock [Mrs. Hicks],	Rebecca Haydock,
Ann Shipley,	Elizabeth W. Underhill,
Mary R. Bowne [Mrs. King],	Esther Robinson Minturn,
Amy Clarke,	Penelope Minturn,
M. Minturn,	Abigail Kenyon,
Lydia Mott,	Penelope Hull,
Martha Stansbury,	E. Hoyland Walker,
Mary Dunbar [Mrs. Slocum],	Sarah Hallet,
Jane Johnston,	Sarah Bowne Minturn,
Harriet Robbins,	Mary Minturn, Jr.,
Sarah Tallman,	Deborah Minturn Abbatt,

Hannah Bowne,
Mary Murray [Mrs. Perkins],
Sarah Robinson,
Mary Wright,
Caroline Bowne,
Elizabeth Burling,

Hannah Bowne,
Ann Underhill,
E. Tallman,
Susan Collins,
Sarah Lyons Kirby,
Hannah Shelton,

Charlotte Leggett.

After the erection of Free School No. 1, in Tryon Row, in 1809, the trustees afforded accommodations to the Association for the school for girls then established, which was continued for many years afterward.

The school-house in Henry street, No. 2, having been erected by the Free-School Society, the trustees delegated a committee to inform the Female Association of the fact, and to tender to that body the use of apartments for a school for girls. On the 16th of December, 1811, John Murray, Jr., attended a meeting of the Association and made the communication, upon the announcement of which a committee was appointed to organize the school, composed of Mary Minturn, Sarah Minturn, Eliza Bowne, Sarah Marshall, Niobe Minturn, Niobe Stanton, Lydia Hathaway, and Sarah Collins. The school was opened February 18th, 1812, with twenty pupils, Mary I. Morgan, teacher.

By the law of 1813, schools not incorporated were excluded from the benefits of the common school fund. The friends of the Female Association, therefore, took immediate measures to secure an act of incorporation for the Association, which was passed by the Legislature on March 26th, 1813. By-laws were adopted, and the officers of the Association were designated as first and second directors, secretary, treasurer, and register. The Board of Trustees consisted of twelve members.

A third school was opened for girls on the 8th of January, 1815. The committee to superintend the opening of No. 3 consisted of Sarah Collins, Rachel Seaman, Elizabeth Clapp, Niobe Minturn, and Mary M. Perkins. At about the same time, the trustees of the Free-School Society granted the use of an additional room in No. 1 to the Association, for one of their schools. During the first three months of the existence of No. 3, 271 pieces of needlework were finished by the girls. The variety and kind of work performed may be seen from the following inventory: 18 shirts, 11 shifts, 21 sheets, 16 samplers, 23 cravats, 4 night-caps, 4 thread cases, 2 pair stockings, 47 diaper towels, 15 pocket kerchiefs, 8 pillow-cases, 7 table-cloths, 33 coarse towels, 9 check aprons, 25 infant shirts, 2 pair neck-gussets, 5 muslin aprons, 5 pair wristbands, 4 muslin borders, 3 window-curtains, 1 pair muslin sleeves, 2 calico ruffles, 6 house-cloths. The following quarter presented an equally flattering report of the industry of the pupils. Susan Morgan, teacher.

On the 9th of May, 1817, a committee was appointed, consisting of Sarah Collins, Sarah Ludlam, Elizabeth W. Lawrence, and Niobe Minturn, to superintend the opening of Girls' School No. 4. The school was opened on the 7th of July, the pupils being transferred from one of the schools of the Free-School Society. Isabella Morgan was appointed teacher.

The provisions of the law which restricted the expenditure of the school money for the payment of teachers' salaries being found inconvenient in practice, the Association petitioned the Legislature for an amendment of the law in favor of the schools under its care. The petition was granted, and a special act passed on the 12th of April, 1819.

The trustees of the African Free School, having erected the new house in Mulberry street, near Grand, offered the use of the lower room to the Association. A committee was appointed to examine the premises and report upon the proposition. The room was rented for $200 a year, and a school commenced for colored girls. The proportion of school moneys received by the Association in 1820, was $1,977.

In May, 1820, the trustees of the Free-School Society requested the Association to appoint a committee to superintend the school for girls in their new building in Rivington street, No. 4, which had just been completed. The committee was accordingly appointed, and consisted of Sarah Collins, Elizabeth Pearsall, Eliza Murray, Mary L. Hartshorne, Sarah Shotwell, Penelope Minturn, and Mary Minturn, Jr. The industrial branches of instruction being considered of great importance, the committee, having examined the school with great satisfaction, reported in favor of appointing an efficient committee for the purpose of aiding the teacher in the sewing department.

The Association having for some time occupied apartments in School No. 2, in Henry street, and the trustees, being desirous of organizing female schools under their own care, notified the

Association, in January, 1823, of their desire to occupy the whole building. Measures were taken to procure other apartments in the neighborhood, which were successful, and the school was removed to the lecture-rooms of the Rutgers Street Church.

The Association for many years held annual public examinations of their pupils, the exercises being held in the large room of Free School No. 1, in Tryon Row. The pupils of the several schools were assembled on these occasions, and, in 1823, about 550 represented the total number present from the schools. The number on register was about 750.

In March, 1828, it was resolved to apply to the Public School Society for the use of a room in one of their buildings for an infant school. The Executive Committee replied affirmatively, granting the gratuitous use of either of the unappropriated basement-rooms of their school-houses for the purpose, during the pleasure of the board. The trustees, however, did not confirm the action of the Executive Committee, and the Association obtained apartments in the Lutheran Church, in Walker street. The school was opened on the 20th of October, 1828, under the care of Anna Harford.

On the 28th of April, the Association closed the school for girls, which had so long been conducted under the original plans. The operation of the law of 1828 deprived this body of the use of the school fund, and it was obliged to contract its sphere of labor. But several bequests and donations having been made to the Association, which yielded about $500 a year, in addition to the contributions and subscriptions of members and friends, it was decided that one or more infant schools be established, as the best mode of appropriating the fund to carry out the objects of the donors.

In February, 1830, a committee was appointed to procure rooms for another school, for which purpose the basement of the Bowery Church was selected. This building was located between Walker and Hester streets. At the same time, however, the Board of Trustees of the Public School Society, having become convinced that the establishment of schools for young children was demanded, adopted a resolution granting the use of the unoccupied basement-rooms of their buildings to the Association for that purpose, and tendering apartments in No. 5, in Mott street. The basement of this house had never been finished, and the trustees proposed that the Association should finish and fit it up, and, whenever possession should be taken by the board, the expense should be repaid to the Association. The proposal was accepted, and the proposed school in the Bowery church was never organized. The rooms in Public School No. 5 were fitted up and furnished, and the school opened in the month of June of the same year (1830), and was sustained until 1845, at which time the trustees notified the Association of their desire to have the infant schools transferred to the jurisdiction of the board, and made a department under the general system which had been adopted by the Public School Society. The school was accordingly transferred, and the Female Association closed its labors for the instruction of poor children.

The character of the schools established by these ladies was always high for the grade. Inspired with the idea that was so predominant in the minds of the trustees of the Public School Society—that of giving the best rudimentary education to the greatest number possible—the range of studies was not advanced as high as it has since been in our public schools, but it was accompanied with a generous and constant supervision by those accomplished and intelligent Christian women, which imparted a moral and elevating influence not gained from splendid and costly appointments or glittering apparatus. The practical instruction in the industrial arts, to which females must mainly look for subsistence at the present time, with the kindness and maternal sympathy which pervaded the school-room, has doubtless exerted a quiet but refining influence over many minds and hearts that will ever remember the attentions and visits of their devoted friends.

The Female Association still exists, but its office is confined to the distribution of the annual income from its funds for charitable uses.

It is worthy of remembrance that Col. Henry Rutgers, who was from an early period a devoted friend of the system of common schools, left a legacy, amounting to $750, for the use of the Female Association. It was committed to the care of the trustees of the Free-School Society, who paid $45 interest annually to the Association—the principal sum to revert to the Society

42

whenever the Association should cease its labors in the cause of education.

INFANT SCHOOLS.

Passing from this brief review of the career of the Female Association, a record must be made of the first efforts to establish a class of schools which were as novel in their design as they were interesting, simply as an educational experiment.

During the year 1826, a great degree of interest and attention was directed to the establishment of "INFANT SCHOOLS," which had recently been introduced in England. Early in 1827, an association of ladies was formed in New York for the purpose of organizing a school upon the same plan, and for children of the same age. The theory of the system may be briefly defined to be this : The mind and heart of the child are susceptible of receiving impressions of a deep and lasting nature, and of forming habits at a very early age. The impressions should be those of virtue, love, gentleness, and piety, all having a tendency to give to the opening moral consciousness of the child a pure and lofty direction. Preoccupy the mind and heart with the seeds of goodness, and they will grow and produce a corresponding character in the after-life. To realize this idea, it was proposed to take children even as young as eighteen months, who, being imitative, could at least begin by learning sounds, motions, and habits of order and stillness. These groups of tender pupils were fittingly denominated "infant schools," and the novelty of the experiment, at least, stimulated the desire to make a fair trial of its value. In addition to these reasons, another was forcibly presented, growing out of the fact that the children of laborers were often left at home, locked up in the absence of parents, and in danger of fire or other accidents, or left to roam in the streets, exposed to casualties and corrupting influences.

The first meeting of ladies was held in the Brick Church Chapel on May 23, 1827, when Mrs. JOANNA BETHUNE was called to the chair, and Mrs. HOLT was appointed secretary.

Two resolutions were adopted : 1st. To organize a society for the care of children from eighteen months to two years of age; and, 2d. Persons contributing one dollar a year, to be members.

The following officers were chosen:

Mrs. BETHUNE, *First Directress.*

Mrs. STRIKER, *Second Directress.*

Mrs. TUTHILL, *Secretary and Treasurer pro tem.*

On the 28th of June, the fourth meeting of the Society was held, at which a constitution was adopted, officers and managers were chosen, and a letter was read from His Excellency DE WITT CLINTON, Governor of the State, who consented to become the patron of the Society, which, in fact, was organized at his suggestion. The officers chosen were the following:

Mrs. JOANNA BETHUNE, *First Directress.*

Miss STRIKER, *Second Directress.*

Mrs. HANNAH L. MURRAY, *Treasurer.*

Mrs. LAURA E. HYDE, *Corresponding Secretary.*

Miss M. A. C. WILLETT, *Recording Secretary.*

A board of thirty managers was also appointed, by-laws adopted, and the Society was fully organized.

As soon as sufficient funds were collected to warrant the commencement of operations, a school was opened, July 16, in the basement-story of the Canal Street Presbyterian Church, corner of Greene street. The school, in a few months, numbered one hundred and seventy pupils on its register, with an average attendance of from sixty to one hundred. Two teachers were employed, with an assistant, who also attended to the fires, keeping the school-room in order, and other general duties.

The age of children was specified, in the constitution, at from eighteen months to *six* years. During the winter, few under three years of age were able to attend.

The school had been in operation less than six months, when Governor CLINTON, who had been the President of the Public School Society from its foundation, made the following allusion to it in his Message to the Legislature:

The institution of infant schools is the pedestal to the pyramid. It embraces those children who are generally too young for common schools; it relieves parents from engrossed attention to their offspring, softens the brow of care, and lightens the hand of labor. More efficacious in reaching the heart than the head, in improving the temper than the intellect, it has been eminently useful in laying the foundation of good feelings, good principles, and good habits.

A communication was sent by Mrs. Bethune to the Public School Society, asking, on behalf of herself and her colleagues, the use of the basement-rooms of No. 8, in Grand street, for school purposes. The Board of Trustees granted the request, and the school was organized. By this means was originated the extensive system known as the "Primary Schools" and "Primary Departments." A few months afterward, Mrs. Bethune, on behalf of "THE INFANT SCHOOL SOCIETY," applied for the use of the rooms in No. 10, in Duane street, which application was referred to the Executive Committee with power, by whom the whole subject was referred to a sub-committee. The report was laid before the Board of Trustees in February, 1828, and was as follows :

The Committee on the Infant School and Junior Department System REPORT :

That they have carefully attended to the duty assigned them, have visited the schools several times, and have had an interview with the first directress of the Infant School Society.

That the infant mind is capable of receiving instruction at the early age of two or three years ; that the inculcation of moral, ideal, and literal knowledge cannot be commenced at too early a period after the faculty of speech is developed ; that the formation of good habits is of immense importance even with children of the age in question ; that the providing a place in which the younger children of the poor may pass the day comfortably, whilst their parents are engaged in their usual avocations, instead of wandering the streets, exposed to the contamination of vice, is an object worthy the regard of the benevolent. These your committee consider as the foundation axioms on which the infant school system is established, and their examination of the subject has led to the conclusion that that foundation standeth sure.

The committee do not consider it necessary to enlarge their report with reasoning, but that facts and the results of their investigation are alone required of them.

The infant school in Canal street has on register one hundred and seventy children of both sexes, and from about two to six years of age, the latter being the limit at which any was received. The number in attendance varies from fifty to one hundred. There are two female teachers, a principal, and one assistant, employed at salaries of $200 each. The children are allowed to come early in the morning, and to remain till near dark, bringing their dinners with them, or to attend during the usual school hours only. The essence of the system pursued in the school appears to be a judicious combination of instruction and amusement, and that both shall be calculated to form and elicit *ideas*, rather than mere literal knowledge, though this is by no means neglected. The children are evidently happy and interested in their employments, and the scene is altogether deeply engaging to the best feelings of humanity. The opinion of the first directress and teachers is, that the same plan may be advantageously adopted in a school of two to three hundred children; and the English Reports inform us of schools of the latter number now in sucessful operation.

In the junior department of No. 8 there are more than three hundred children, giving an average daily attendance of about two hundred and fifty. The system of this school is the same as that of the public schools generally, and therefore well known to the trustees. The children are one degree older than those of the infant school—say from three to seven or eight. The school appeared in as good order as could be reasonably expected.

On a comparison of the mode of instruction adopted in the two schools, your committee are of opinion that the infant school system, as applied to children of such tender years, is decidedly preferable; the one being the mere course of common instruction in the knowledge of letters and words, the other including the first, and extending its views to what is of much greater importance—the knowledge of things and ideas, with moral maxims and scriptural instruction; the whole illustrated by visible objects and verbal explanations calculated to excite the attention and interest the feelings of the infant mind.

From this view of the subject, your committee are led to the conclusion that it is expedient that infant schools be gradually established throughout the city; and the question only remains, whether this shall be done by the already organized Infant School Society of ladies, and to whom the credit and honor are due for having first, and by persevering exertions, introduced this system into this city, or by the Public School Society. As there are thousands of children who would be proper objects for these schools, and many rooms and large funds would be required to carry them on advantageously, it would probably be best that a part of the duty of founding and continuing them be in the hands of a society of men, though their immediate supervision would be better entrusted to the motherly patronage and care of ladies. And as these schools would be introductory to and could be conveniently accommodated in the basements of the public schools, your committee are of the opinion that it is advisable for this Society to undertake the work, and that the Infant School Society, with such other ladies as may hereafter join them, be invited to act as a committee for the visitation and superintendence of the schools.

The committee are aware of the importance of the measure proposed, and believe it will be judicious to embark therein gradually; and, as the final result of their investigations, they with deference propose:

1st. That the junior department school in No. 8 be, for the present, continued without change.

2d. That an infant school be opened by the Public School Society in the basement of No. 10, so soon as competent teachers can be obtained and made acquainted with the peculiarities of the system.

3d. That the Infant School Society be requested to act as a ladies' committee for the management and supervision of said school, and that the school committee of No. 10 be associated with the sub-committee of ladies so far as to act as their advisers and assistants.

4th. That the teachers be appointed by the Executive Committee, on the recommendation of the Infant School Society. That the ladies' committee be requested to adopt such rules and regulations for the schools as they shall deem proper, subject, however, to the advice and control of the trustees.

5th. That the sub-committee of ladies having special charge of the school, make a quarterly report to the Board of Trustees of the state and condition thereof, with the number and progress of the children, &c., &c.,

Robert C. Cornell,
F. Sheldon, } Committee.
Lindley Murray,

The infant school in No. 10 had been in operation about eighteen months, when, in April, 1829, a committee, consisting of Messrs. Samuel F. Mott, Erastus Ellsworth, W. W. Chester, Samuel Demilt, and J. H. Taylor, was appointed to examine it, in connection with the junior department of No. 8, and report upon the adoption of the system, either with or without the aid of the Infant School Society. The committee reported very favorably upon the plan, and recommended it for its superiority over the mixed system of the junior departments. Questions of a financial and legal nature interposed, however, to prevent the immediate extension of the system. The funds were not deemed to be sufficient, and the restrictions of the law relative to the distribution of the school money served to raise a barrier to appropriations for that class of schools ; as the addition of so many children of an age under that specified by the law of the State would give an unequal proportion to the city, by including thousands of pupils who were younger than the school children of the rural and town districts. The report was referred back to the committee, to procure the legal opinion of the law members of the board upon the points suggested by the committee. The opinions of the committee being sustained, it was deemed to be inexpedient at the time to increase the number of infant schools.

In the month of October of the same year, the subject was renewed, the reports of the committee and the legal opinions being read in full. Two of the opinions (those of Messrs. Benjamin Clark and Hiram Ketchum) were adverse to the right of the Society to organize and draw money for those schools ; and four of the opinions (those of Messrs. Robert Sedgwick, James

I. Roosevelt, Jr., Samuel Boyd, and D. Lord) were in favor of the said right. A resolution was offered, declaring it expedient to establish infant schools, which was lost by a vote of fourteen in the affirmative and sixteen in the negative.

Notwithstanding the apparent difficulties and the positive differences of opinion as to the propriety of adopting the infant school as a part of the system of instruction, some of its friends were so convinced of its importance, that they could not long permit the matter to rest. The Executive Committee had the proposition under constant advisement, and in May, 1830, the report of a sub-committee on the junior department of No. 8 was laid before the board. It recommended the alteration of the rooms occupied by the junior department so as to adapt it for the use of an infant school. The subject was referred to a committee, consisting of Messrs. John R. Hurd, Robert C. Cornell, Hiram Ketchum, J. H. Taylor, and Charles Oakley.

The report of this committee, presented to the board in July, recommended the change of the system, and left the details of the arrangements to the several sections, the school-buildings at that time not being equally well adapted for separate departments. The 1st, 2d, 3d, and 4th classes were to be designated as the Third or Junior Department, and to be under the care of female teachers. The important change of teachers thus introduced was alone a great advance, males having been previously almost exclusively employed, and the younger classes of scholars having been usually assigned to the care of male monitors. The advantage of female teachers for these young learners was too evident to the committee, and their introduction was warmly urged in the report. It was referred to a special meeting to be held in September, at which time a preamble and resolutions adopting the infant school system were presented, and adopted by the board. It was resolved to change the junior department of No. 8 into an infant school, and a committee was appointed to examine the school in No. 10, and report such modifications and changes as might be deemed advisable. Messrs. Robert C. Cornell, Myndert Van Schaick, John R. Hurd, Samuel F. Mott, and Lindley Murray were entrusted with this service. Their report was submitted in the month of November, with a code of regulations for the schools, which were designated as " PRIMARY DEPARTMENTS." The school committees, or " sections " of trustees, were to be aided by a sub-committee of ladies, who should be entitled to nominate the teachers and monitors. Female scholars from two years of age and upward were to be admitted, and male scholars from two to six years of age, but no children were to be admitted who were qualified to enter the 4th class of the public schools. Two cents a week was the tuition fee, the pay system being at that time in operation.

The plans and recommendations of the committee were adopted, and the Executive Committee was directed to apply to the Legislature for power to educate and draw school money for all children between two and sixteen years of age. The Manual was also altered and amended to conform to the new system, and copies were printed and distributed to the teachers.

The Society, at the same time, took measures to secure additional means from the Legislature, which were ultimately successful, and a committee was appointed to visit the Boston schools, to examine and report upon the system there in use. The deputation made a report upon the remodelling and improvement of the schools of the Society, a prominent feature of which report was the general plan of primary schools, or schools similar to the primary departments, but located in buildings of a moderate size, and so distributed over the city as to be easy and near of access to young children. These schools were to be exclusively under the care of female teachers, subject to the control of the respective sections to which they might be assigned. The scheme submitted by the committee was adopted in May, 1832, and Messrs. Samuel W. Seton, James B. Brinsmade, George T. Trimble, J. H. Taylor, Mahlon Day, Heman Averill, and Samuel Demilt were selected as the Committee on Primary Schools, to introduce the system under the resolutions adopted, by organizing ten primary schools. The gentlemen thus commissioned held their first meeting on May 22d, 1832, and entered with great zeal upon the discharge of their duties, and a number of schools were soon put into successful operation. They increased in number and importance until about the year 1844, when the questions arose between the Society and the Board of Education as to the power of the former to erect new buildings and acquire additional property for school purposes. At this time the Society had fifty-six primary schools for white children, and five of the same class for colored children, in operation, in which 8,970 pupils were instructed. By the law of 1853, they were transferred to the Board of Education.

CHAPTER XIX.

SCHOOLS FOR COLORED CHILDREN.

The Manumission Society Organized—Objects and Measures—School for Colored Children Proposed—Committee Appointed—Report—Funds—Teachers Employed—School Organized—Purchase of a School Site—Grant of Land from Frederick Jay—Legacy from Estate of John Murray—Evening School—The Lancasterian System Adopted—Manumission Society Incorporated—Change of Location of the School—Grant of Land in William Street by the Corporation—Building Erected—School in Mulberry Street—General La Fayette—C. C. Andrews—School No. 3—School No. 4—School No. 5—School No. 6—Transfer to the Public School Society Proposed—Proceedings of the Societies—Committees Appointed—Authority to Transfer Granted by the Legislature—Transfer Completed—The Schools Reorganized—New School-House in Laurens Street—School for Colored Monitors—Decline of Schools and the Causes—Name Changed—Dissolution of the Manumission Society.

On the 25th of January, 1785, a number of gentlemen of the city of New York, who had witnessed the sufferings of the colored population, and the frequent injustice done to free persons of color, organized " A Society for Promoting the Manumission of Slaves, and Protecting such of them as have been or may be Liberated." The meeting was held at the dwelling-house of John Simmons, innkeeper.

The gentlemen present on that occasion were Robert Bowne, Samuel Franklin, John Murray, Sr., Robert Troup, Lawrence Embree, Melanchthon Smith, William Goforth, Willet Seaman, Elijah Cock, Joseph Lawrence, William Keese, John Murray, Jr., Effingham Embree, Thomas Bowne, Edward Lawrence, James Cogswell, William Shotwell, Ezekiel Robins, and John Keese.

The meeting was called to order by Mr. Troup, who stated the object of the conference, and Melanchthon Smith was chosen chairman. A committee, consisting of Samuel Franklin, Lawrence Embree, Robert Troup, Melanchthon Smith, and John Murray, Sr., was appointed to report a draft of by-laws and regulations for the government of the Society. The meeting then adjourned to the 4th of February.

At the meeting held by adjournment, a number of other gentlemen were present, among whom appear the names of John Jay and Alexander Hamilton, Hon. John Jay being elected chairman.

The Committee on " Rules " submitted their report, which was discussed, amended, and adopted as a constitution of the Society. The preamble is as follows :

The benevolent Creator and Father of men having given to them all an equal right to life, liberty, and property, no sovereign power on earth can justly deprive them of either, but in conformity to impartial government and laws to which they have expressly or tacitly consented.

It is our duty, therefore, both as free citizens and Christians, not only to regard with compassion the injustice done to those among us who are held as slaves, but to endeavor, by lawful ways and means, to enable them to share equally with us in that civil and religious liberty with which an indulgent Providence has blessed these States ; and to which these our brethren are, by nature, as much entitled as ourselves.

The violent attempts lately made to seize and export for sale several free negroes who were peaceably following their respective occupations in this city, must excite the indignation of every friend to humanity, and ought to receive exemplary punishment.

The hope of impunity is, too often, an invincible temptation to transgression ; and as the helpless condition of the persons alluded to doubtless exposed them to the outrages they experienced, so it is probable that the like circumstances may again expose them, and others, to similar violences. Destitute of friends and of knowledge, struggling with poverty, and accustomed to submission, they are under great disadvantages in asserting their rights.

These considerations induce us to form ourselves into a society, to be styled " A Society for Promoting the Manumission of Slaves, and Protecting such of them as have been or may be Liberated."

After the adoption of the constitution, Alexander Hamilton, Robert Troup, and White Matlack were appointed a committee to recommend a course of proceedings to be pursued in the case of persons to be aided by the Society. The meeting then adjourned to the 10th of the same month, for the purpose of effecting a permanent organization under the rules. Accordingly, on that day, the members met, and having balloted for officers, Hon. John Jay was elected president, Samuel Franklin, vice-president, John Murray, Jr., treasurer, and John Keese, secretary. The Standing Committee was composed of six members, as follows: Melanchthon Smith, Lawrence Embree, Dr. James Cogswell, Ezekiel Robins, William Goforth, and Elijah Cock.

The objects of the Society were pursued with great diligence, and it became evident to the friends of the colored race that, in addition to other means of advancing their interests and elevating them in their social and moral condition, a school for the education of children was essential. The Standing Committee, composed at that time (May 11th, 1786) of Jacob Seaman, Lawrence Embree, White Matlack, and Leonard M. Cutting, made a report, in which they recommended the appointment of a committee to report a plan for establishing a free school for negro children. John Murray, Jr., James Cogswell, and John Keese, were appointed as the committee.

At the following meeting, held August 10th, the committee reported their plan, which provided for the raising of money by subscription or donation, the appointment of a teacher at a seasonable time, and the selection and appointment of trustees by the Society. The report was laid on the table until the next meeting, held on November 9th, when the report was amended and adopted, and Melanchthon Smith, John Murray, Jr., Matthew Clarkson, William Goforth, Lawrence Embree, William Backhouse, and Dr. Cogswell were appointed a committee to make collections for the purpose. On the 17th of May, 1787, the fund subscribed amounted to about $5,000, and the committee asked that they be discharged, and that a new committee be appointed. The request was granted, and the new committee consisted of John Murray, Jr., William Backhouse, Abijah Hammond, John Lawrence, White Matlack, Richard Platt, and Ezekiel Robins.

At the meeting held on August 16th, the committee reported that £801 12s. had been subscribed, and urged the adoption of immediate measures for the organization of a school. The report was adopted, and Rev. John Rodgers, D.D., John Murray, Jr., White Matlack, Lawrence Embree, William Backhouse, Dr. James Cogswell, and Ebenezer Harwood, were appointed. The committee reported at the next quarterly meeting, held on November 15th, stating that they had prepared an application to Trinity Church for a donation of a piece of ground for the purpose of a school for colored children, and that they had engaged a schoolmaster to take charge of the school. This gentleman, the committee stated, had dismissed a school of white children in order to take charge of the proposed school, and under such terms as convinced the committee that "gain was not his object," for he would furnish a school-room and fuel, and teach the children for six months, " for sixty pounds." The teacher, Cornelius Davis, having been thus obtained, the next step was to adopt rules for the admission and government of scholars; and, on the 1st of November, a school was opened, which numbered twelve pupils at the time of the report. On the recommendation of the committee, twelve trustees were appointed to have the supervision of the school until the next annual election. The Board of Trustees, at this first organization, consisted of Melanchthon Smith, Lawrence Embree, John Lawrence, Matthew Clarkson, John Bleecker, Thomas Burling, Jacob Seaman, White Matlack, James Cogswell, Willett Seaman, Nathaniel Lawrence, and John Murray, Jr. In February, 1788, the trustees reported 29 pupils in attendance. In November, there were 56 on register.

In May, 1791, a committee of four members—Messrs. James Cogswell, Samuel Franklin, John Lawrence, and Moses Rogers— was appointed to raise funds for the building of a school-house. At the following meeting in November, the President of the Society, Matthew Clarkson, Dr. Cogswell, and William W. Woolsey, were named as a committee to procure a lot from the corporation of Trinity Church. The application was replied to negatively, and the only lot of ground which would answer the wishes of the Society, in the rear of the chapel in Beekman street, was fixed at so high a price, and on such terms, that the Society could not comply with them. The committee was accordingly continued; the Committee on Subscriptions was discharged, and, in February, 1793, a new committee appointed.

In August, 1792, a school for colored girls, taught by Mrs. Davis, was taken under the control of the Society.

The difficulty of procuring a suitable piece of ground presented an obstacle to the operations of the school, and, at the close of 1794 (November 18), a committee of three was appointed to take steps to obtain an act of incorporation for the African Free School, and to apply to the Regents of the University to have the institution recognized by that body. Noah Webster, Jr., Robert Bowne, and William Johnson were named for that duty. The committee reported at the following meeting, and were discharged. At the annual meeting in February, 1795, it was resolved to apply to the Legislature for aid, and a committee of five was appointed to prepare and present a petition, making the wants of the school known to that body. The effort was successful, an appropriation was made, and the committee was discharged, on the reading of their report, in May, 1796.

In May, 1794, Frederick Jay, Esq., had presented the Society a lot of land on Great George street, 25 by 100 feet, for a school-house, and, if deemed not desirable for that purpose, the Society were authorized to sell it, and use the proceeds in the purchase of another site. The committee appointed in November of the same year for the purpose of selecting a location, were continued until February, 1796, when they reported that, in consequence of the high prices at which property was held, they could not make a desirable selection, and they were discharged.

In November, 1795, John Murray, Jr., the treasurer, reported that he had received a legacy of £200 from his father's estate, for the use of the African Free School, the interest on that amount to be a perpetual annuity for the benefit of the school.

In April, 1796, a special meeting of the Society was held, on the call of the trustees of the school, to hear a report on its condition and necessities. The report was discussed, and laid on the table until the regular meeting in May. The trustees reported that they had selected a piece of property in Cliff street, and had taken steps to secure its purchase. The report was accepted and approved, and the trustees directed to proceed with their plans. They were authorized to sell the lot donated by Mr. Jay, and appropriate the proceeds toward the purchase of the property. A large committee was appointed to obtain contributions, viz.: Thomas Eddy, Alexander Hamilton, Matthew Clarkson, Peter Jay Munro, Gabriel Furman, John Campbell, Samuel Boyd, Streatfield Clarkson, Noah Webster, William Johnson, Moses Rogers, Samuel Bowne, Thomas Franklin, William Dunlap, George M. Woolsey, George Gosman, Jacob Mott, John Murray, Jr., and Andrew Cock. The trustees were also directed to employ teachers, whose aggregate salaries should not exceed $700. The treasurer was directed to pay to the trustees £200 on the purchase-money, and £100 for repairs to the premises.

In January, 1797, the trustees reported that they had employed William Pirsson as teacher, at $500 a year, and John Teasman as assistant, with a salary of $120 a year. Abigail Nicolls, the former female teacher, was also continued, with a salary of $200 a year. The branches taught were reading, writing, arithmetic, the elements of geography, with sewing, &c., in the girls' school. The school at that time numbered 122 pupils —63 males and 59 females, with an average attendance of about 80.

The trustees also reported an evening school for colored pupils, taught by the same teachers, having 36 male and 8 female pupils, averaging about 35—the whole number of pupils being 166. The improvement of the school was such that, on the 1st of May, 1797, the salaries were increased, and Mr. Pirsson was paid $625, Miss Nicolls, $250, and Mr. Teasman, $200 a year.

In 1797, the Corporation made a grant of $275 to the school, and the trustees were directed to make inquiries and take all proper steps to secure an apportionment of the public money with the other schools entitled to the use of the fund.

The Corporation made a further donation, in the following year, of $250.

In 1799, Mr. Pirsson was allowed to retire, and John Teasman conducted the school, at a salary of $300, assisted by Miss Nicolls, whose salary was reduced to $200. Want of means occasioned this retrenchment.

In May, 1800, the Corporation made a donation of $517.

In 1801, the Legislature made an apportionment to the school which amounted to $1,565.78, to be loaned on real estate, and the interest only used for the schools. An annual report of its condition was required to be made to the Legislature.

The progress of the school during this time was encouraging to the friends of the depressed people for whose benefit the Society was organized, and the various appropriations made by both the city and State authorities, afforded them very important aid in carrying out their plans. During the year 1807, the Lancasterian system of instruction for poor children, which had been lately introduced into the school of the "Free-School Society," was also adopted in its modified form by the trustees of the African Free School.

The Manumission Society had now been in existence about twenty-three years, and the importance of a more perfect organization and well-defined legal rights induced its members to apply for an act of incorporation, which was granted, and passed on the 19th of February, 1808.

The premises occupied by the school in Cliff street were not as desirable as the trustees wished, and an opportunity for a change was presented at the close of the year 1809. In the month of December, the large school-house on Tryon Row, erected by the Free-School Society, was finished, and opened on the 11th, with public exercises. The school had been previously held in apartments in the old Almshouse building in the Park, and the trustees of the African Free School applied for the privilege of occupying them. It was granted, but, in consequence of inconveniences which arose, the school was soon removed to its former location in Cliff street. Not long afterward, in 1811, its apparatus was enriched by the addition of a library.

The necessity of a better location for the school pressed constantly on the attention of the trustees, and they made an earnest appeal to the Corporation for the donation of a piece of ground for the purpose. In 1812, a site in William street, near Duane, was granted in answer to the appeal. There were leases upon it, a lease of one half being for fourteen years, and the other being a life-lease. The trustees recommended the purchase of these leases, the sale of the Cliff street and other property, and the erection of a new building in William street. The Society accordingly authorized the changes proposed. The Cliff street property was sold for $5,000, and the lease for fourteen years purchased for $400. Before the purchaser took possession of the Cliff street property, the house was destroyed by fire (January 5, 1814), and he refused to close the purchase unless some allowance were made by the trustees. They concluded not to alter the terms, and the sale was not then made.

In October of that year, the trustees were directed to erect a building, 30 by 60 feet, on the William street lots, and to mortgage the Cliff street property for a sufficient sum to pay for the house, which was not to cost over $1,800. The property was mortgaged for $2,500, which was expended in paying for the erection of the house and the purchase of the lease.

In a few months after opening the new school, the room became so crowded with pupils that it was found necessary to engage a separate room next to the school, to accommodate such of the females as were to be taught sewing. This branch had been for some time discontinued, but it was now resumed under a well-qualified young woman, Miss Lucy Turpen, whose amiable disposition, and faithful as well as successful discharge of her duties, made her greatly esteemed both by her pupils and by the trustees. Miss Turpen, after serving the board for some time, removed to Ohio, and her place was supplied by Miss Mary Lincrum, who, with her predecessor, had been a pupil of the Female Association in this city, whose schools were models of the class. Miss Lincrum was succeeded by Eliza J. Cox, and the latter by Mary Ann Cox, under both of whom the female department sustained its character for order and usefulness.

The increase in numbers of the colored people, and the growth and expansion of the city, called for the erection of a new house ; and a location being found in Mulberry street, near Grand, a building was erected, and African School No. 2 was opened in May, 1820. The building was of brick, two stories high, 75 by 35 feet, standing on a lot of ground 50 by 100 feet.

In the year 1824, General LA FAYETTE visited the United States, and, during his stay in the city of New York, he visited the public institutions, and, among others, some of the schools of the Public School Society. General La Fayette had been elected an honorary member of the Manumission Society in the year 1788, in company with Granville Sharpe and Thomas Clarkson, of England, and the members of the Society could not allow the opportunity to pass of presenting so distinguished a guest to the pupils of the school. Accordingly, on the 10th of September, General La Fayette, in company with several of the trustees and officers, visited the school, and witnessed some of their exercises, expressing great satisfaction with the proceedings. One of the pupils addressed him as follows :

GENERAL LA FAYETTE : In behalf of myself and my fellow-schoolmates, may I be permitted to express our sincere and respectful gratitude to you for the condescension you have manifested this day in visiting this institution, which is one of the noblest specimens of New York philanthropy. Here, sir, you behold hundreds of the poor children of Africa, sharing with those of a lighter hue in the blessings of education ; and, while it will be our pleasure to remember the great deeds you have done for America, it will be our delight also to cherish the memory of General La Fayette as a friend to African emancipation, and as a member of this institution.

To which the General replied briefly,

I thank you, my dear child.

The schools continued to prosper under the care given to them, and, in 1829, the pupils in No. 1 numbered 262, while No. 2 had a register of 452 in good attendance. The trustees of the Public School Society at this time were making an appeal to the public for an increased school-tax, in order to afford the means for the necessary extension of the system of public instruction. The trustees of the African Free School united in the effort, which was successful, being generously responded to by the people, and enacted by the Legislature.

In January, 1832, C. C. Andrews, the teacher of No. 2, tendered his resignation, to take effect on the 1st of May, but the time was shortened, and he surrendered his trust on the 10th of April, to James Adams. Mr. Andrews had been employed as a teacher by the Society for twenty-three years, a fact which alone attests his faithfulness and success. But a prejudice against his administration had arisen among the pupils and their friends, and a loss of attendance, showing that his influence was much impaired, led the trustees very reluctantly to accept his resignation. Mr. Andrews wrote a " History of the African Free School," which was published in 1830, containing many interesting productions of pupils of the school. Miss Julia G. Andrews, his daughter, also teacher in the female department of No. 2, resigned at the same time. No. 1 had been changed to a girls' school, of which Caroline Roe was teacher.

About the 1st of November, 1831, a new school, No. 3, was opened in Nineteenth street, near the Sixth avenue, under the care of Benjamin F. Hughes. The attendance was good for some time, the number of pupils being about 80, but it became reduced by reason of its inconvenient location ; and a difficulty having arisen in obtaining suitable premises, owing to the objections urged against a colored school by the people in that vicinity, the trustees chose a building in Amity street, near the Sixth avenue.

The female department of No. 2 was reorganized on the 1st of May, 1832, as School No. 4, and placed under the care of

43

Nancy H. Buckingham. During the summer, No. 5 was opened at 161 Duane street, under the care of Jane A. Parker, and No. 6, at 108 Columbia street, under the care of John Peterson— both of them colored teachers. At this time the number of pupils in the schools was as follows: No. 1, 144; No. 2, 272; No. 3, 385; No. 4, 298; No. 5, 179; No. 6, 161—total, 1,439. At this period, Charles Reason was assistant in No. 2, Eliza D. Richards in No. 3, and Fanny Tompkins in No. 4. In June, 1833, School No. 7 was opened at 38 White street, under Levi Folsom. In September, No. 3 was divided, and the female department was known as Female School No. 3. Soon afterward, a school was opened at 24 Laurens street, as a branch of No 7, under the care of Prince Leveridge.

On the 1st of February, 1834, No. 1 was organized as a boys' school, James Adams, of No. 2, resigned, and Abel Libolt was appointed as his successor. Caroline Roe, of No. 1, was transferred to No. 4, in place of Nancy H. Buckingham, resigned.

While these changes were taking place, and the trustees were adding to the number of schools, a plan of union with the Public School Society had been agitated, and measures taken to consummate it. The law restricted the trustees to the payment of teachers' salaries in the expenditure of their portion of the school moneys, while the Public School Society was authorized to use its revenue for all the purposes of the system. This advantage was obvious, while another consideration was regarded as being of great importance; the original object of the Manumission Society had been secured—the slave-trade had been rendered illegal, the system of slavery had been abolished in the State of New York, and the only practical object of its existence centered in its schools. To place these under a more liberal patronage and a better developed organization, seemed wise as a matter of policy for the Society, and beneficent for the children of the colored schools.

At a meeting of the Board of Trustees of the Public School Society, held November 2, 1832, a communication was received from the trustees of the African Free Schools, informing them that they had appointed a committee to confer with a similar committee on behalf of the Society in relation to a transfer of their schools, and requesting the appointment of such a committee. Messrs. Samuel Demilt, George T. Trimble, John R.

Hurd, Samuel F. Mott, and Lindley Murray were accordingly named for the conference.

On the 14th of December the committee reported progress; the report was referred back, and Hiram Ketchum was added to the number.

The committee met repeatedly, and, on February 1, 1833, a report was laid before the trustees, stating that the proposition was to transfer the schools of the Manumission Society to the Public School Society, on condition that the latter purchase the properties at a fair valuation. The real estate consisted of a house and lots in Mulberry street, near Grand, a house in William street, near Duane, on ground held by a perpetual lease from the city for school purposes, and the furniture and fixtures of the schools.

Beside these there were four smaller schools, kept in hired apartments. The whole number of scholars on register was 1,400, with an average attendance of fifty per cent.

The committee, on a full review of the circumstances, although persuaded that a separate organization was most expedient if it could be maintained without a diversion of the school fund from its special purpose by the Manumission Society, recommended the transfer. The same committee was continued to complete the arrangements, William W. Fox being substituted for John R. Hurd, who resigned.

On the 2d of August, the committee reported that an impediment had been discovered, by which the Manumission Society was incapable of conferring a title to its property until an act to authorize such transfer should be passed by the Legislature, and recommending that the measure be suspended. The report was adopted by the board.

The application of the Manumission Society was laid before the Legislature at the ensuing session, and the act was passed authorizing the transfer of the real and personal property to the Public School Society. On the 2d of May, 1834, the facts were reported to the board, and also that the Common Council had consented to the transfer of the lease for the William street property. Copies of the law, the resolution of the Common Council, and of the agreement between the two Societies were submitted with the report. The committee were directed to proceed and complete the duty assigned them.

On the 1st of August, the committee made a final report. The property had been examined by appraisers chosen by the joint conference committees, and the value fixed at $12,130.32, which had been paid by the Treasurer of the Public School Society.

The Mulberry street property, two lots, 50 by 100 feet, with a two-story brick house thereon, 35 by 75 feet, was valued at $9.500.

The William street school-house, one story high, 35 by 59 feet, $1,000.

The fixtures, apparatus, cabinets of specimens, books, &c., in these houses, and in seven hired rooms, $1,630.22.

The transfer was not actually completed in all its forms until some time in July, but as it had been determined in the early part of the year by the act of the Legislature, the schools were deemed to be under the care of the Public School Society from the 1st of May. The salaries of the teachers, and other expenses, were all commenced, on the part of the Society, at that time, and the teachers' reports for the quarter made to conform to the transfer.

The names of the teachers then on duty are as follows:

No. 1, Ransom F. Wake, of No. 2 (temporary teacher).

No. 2, male, Abel Libolt, teacher; Ransom F. Wake and Charles Reason, assistants.

No. 2, female, Catharine Roe, teacher; Mary Roe and Maria M. De Grass, assistants.

No. 3, male, John Brown, teacher.

No. 3, female, Sarah M. Douglass.

No. 4,　　"　　Eliza D. Richards.

No. 5,　　"　　Fanny Tompkins.

No. 6,　　"　　John Peterson, teacher; Rebecca Peterson, assistant.

No. 7,　　"　　Levi Folsom, teacher; Sarah Freeman, and Sarah M. Freeman, assistants.

No. 7,　　"　　(branch) William Hamilton, teacher; Elizabeth Brady, assistant.

At the meeting of the Manumission Society, held on January 13, 1835, the trustees of the schools presented their final report, asking to be discharged from their duties. The report was accepted, and the labors of the Society in its educational department were terminated.

At the time of sale the Treasurer of the Manumission Society had in his hands an unexpended balance, from the school moneys of 1833, of $1,063.43, to which was added the whole of the apportionment for 1834, amounting to $8,241.21, making a total of $9,304.64, which was paid to the Treasurer of the Public School Society.

The committee submitted several recommendations in regard to the reorganization of the colored schools. They were to be subject to the same by-laws, and conducted on the same system as the other schools. No. 2, in Mulberry street, was to take rank as No. 1, while the original No. 1, in William street, was to be called Primary No. 1, and the other primary schools numbered consecutively.

A special committee was also recommended to examine the schools, and report on such changes in the system of conducting them as might be expedient and proper.

The report was adopted by the board. The following gentlemen, members of the Manumission Society, were balloted for and elected members of the board: Israel Corse, Thomas Bussing, Edmund Willetts, Henry Hinsdale, Charles Walker, Edmund Haviland, Thomas L. Jewett, William L. Stone, and Ira B. Underhill. These gentlemen, together with Samuel Wood and Mahlon Day, were appointed the section for the colored schools.

Messrs. Samuel W. Seton, George T. Trimble, Samuel Demilt, Ira B. Underhill, and Thomas Bussing were appointed a committee on the course of studies and examination.

On the first of May, the number of scholars on register was 1,608, with an average attendance the previous quarter of 757.

On the 7th of November, the Committee on Examination and Change of System laid a report before the board, recommending that the school in William street be reorganized as Primary No. 1, and placed under the care of a female teacher, and made to conform to the other primary schools. The report was adopted.

At the time of the transfer there were five primary schools; No. 2, had been suspended, and No. 1, in William street, had been known as African School No. 1. The others were the following: No. 3, in Amity street; No. 4, at 199 East Broadway;

No. 5, 161 Duane street; No. 6, 108 Columbia street; and No. 7, 38 White and 24 Laurens streets.

On the 6th of February, 1835, the committee submitted a long report in which many recommendations were made, relating to the system of instruction, transfer of schools, and salaries, with other plans, all of which were referred to the Executive Committee, with power.

One of the most important measures recommended was the erection of a new school-house, west of Broadway, for a large school, to which the pupils of No. 7 should be transferred.

On the 7th of August following, the Committee on Locations reported the purchase of lots in Laurens street, near Broome, for the new school-house. The price, $5,250, had been paid for the property. At the same meeting, the Property Committee was empowered to procure plans for the building, subject to the approval of the Executive Committee, and erect the house as soon as possible.

On the 5th of February, 1836, a proposition for a school for colored monitors was made to the board, which, with other measures relative to these schools, was referred to a special committee, consisting of Samuel F. Mott, Lindley Murray, James F. Depeyster, Joseph B. Collins, and Robert Pardow. These gentlemen were to act in connection with the section on African schools.

One of the most important matters taken into consideration by the committee was the great decline in the attendance, and the deterioration in the grade of the schools. They were accounted for, in part, by the fact that the transfer was unpopular among the colored people, who had always regarded the Manumission Society with a grateful esteem, and the members of which they had always loved as their devoted friends. In addition to this, the riots and disorders of the year 1834, by men who had been prompted by violent leaders to attack prominent friends of the emancipation movement, had made the parents very timid about trusting their children at long distances from their homes. The course of studies and books were also novel, and the children were not easily trained to the new discipline. Public meetings were held in order to interest the colored people in their schools, and Prince Leveridge, a colored agent, was employed to visit the families throughout the city, in order to press the importance of education upon their attention personally.

These impediments to the successful operation of the schools gradually wore away, and they have since that time been conducted with the average success of the white schools of the same grade.

At the meeting of the board, held May 4, 1838, a petition from the teachers of these schools was presented, asking that the name be changed. After some discussion on the matter, the petition was responded to affirmatively, and the title of the schools was changed to " Colored," in place of " African."

A proposition was made to the Board of Trustees to open one or more new schools for colored children, but a report on the proposition, on the 1st of March, 1839, determined the board not to entertain it. The Manumission Society, by its committee, offered to contribute $2,500 toward the cost of a new school, but the board felt it necessary to decline the liberal donation.

Soon after this period the Manumission Society, feeling that a new class of agencies, far more extensive than their own, and adapted to a different and vastly larger population, had been called into existence, believing that its work had been practically accomplished, adopted a resolution to terminate its existence. It had nobly filled its place as an agent in protecting the helpless, rescuing such as were unjustly held in bondage, restoring free persons to the liberty of which they had been deprived by kidnappers, or otherwise, and in educating the children of the colored people in the city of New York. It had also witnessed the grand event of emancipation in New York and New Jersey, and the institution whose sorrows and evils had called it into existence had migrated far beyond its sphere of action. In a consciousness of pure and exalted motives, self-sacrificing and laborious action, and hallowed in the sacred memories of lofty philanthropy and Christian benevolence, it ceased its labors, to be remembered as one of the noblest and earliest of American institutions devoted especially to the cause of humanity and freedom.

CHAPTER XX.

HISTORICAL NOTES OF THE SCHOOLS.

PUBLIC SCHOOL NO. 1.

THE first school of the Public School Society was opened in a house in Bancker (now Madison) street, on the 17th of May, 1806, and continued there until removed to the Almshouse building in the Park. The necessity of enlarged accommodations had induced the Society to apply to the Corporation for a grant, and an old building, known as the Arsenal, was accordingly donated for the use of the Society. This, however, proved insufficient, and measures were taken to secure the erection of a commodious structure. The efforts of the trustees were successful, and, on the 11th of December, 1809, the building was publicly opened with appropriate exercises. The President of the Society, De Witt Clinton, delivered an address on the occasion. William Smith, teacher.

On the 18th of December, the committee met to receive applications for admission. A large number of pupils offered themselves, and the registering proceeded rapidly. On the 26th of January, 1810, an arrangement having been made with the Fire Department, a committee, consisting of Robert Wardell, Peter Sharp, and John Caldwell, attended to superintend the admission of pupils from that department. Fifty pupils were to be instructed in the school, the tuition fee being $6 each per annum. Forty-four were admitted on the 26th, and the remainder on the 29th of January.

The school was an object of great interest not only to citizens, but to strangers, and so frequent were their visits as to interfere with the operations of the school. A regulation appointing Thursday morning for visitors was adopted—none being admitted at other hours, except by the special request of a trustee.

On the 22d of January, 1810, John Missing, afterward principal of No. 2, was employed as an assistant in No. 1. In April, 1810, Shepherd Johnston, afterward principal of No. 3, was employed as a monitor, together with William McAlpin, both pupils in the school.

At the end of a year the school numbered 550 pupils.

In 1816, Lloyd D. Windsor was appointed principal, in place of William Smith.

On February 2d, 1813, a committee of twenty-four ladies, of the Presbyterian, Episcopal, Methodist, Associate Reformed, and Reformed Dutch Churches, attended to catechise the children. On the 9th, thirty, and on the 16th, forty ladies attended to give religious instruction. Bishop Hobart opened the exercises with prayer. One afternoon in the week was devoted to these religious services.

In 1820, the managers of the American Bible Society were engaged in selecting a location suitable for their depository, and it was proposed to sell No. 1 for that purpose. A committee of the Public School Society was appointed to present a memorial to the Corporation, asking that a fee-simple of the ground be vested in the Society, to enable it to sell the property and purchase a less public and noisy location. The application was referred to the Finance Committee, who reported adversely, and the proposition failed.

In 1823, the Female Association, which had until that time sustained the girls' school in No. 1, resolved to close it, and the trustees immediately reorganized the female department, so that the girls in that part of the city should not be deprived of instruction.

In 1824, the Corporation made an offer to purchase No. 1, but, after some negotiation, the project was abandoned.

In 1825, John Scudder, the proprietor of the American Museum, proposed to hire the building on a perpetual lease, at a rent of 6 per cent. on $30,000, and an annual admission of the pupils of the schools to the museum, which failed, as the Corporation made a new proposition for the property, and, in 1826, appointed a committee to obtain a release of the ground to the city for the purpose of extending the Park. The trustees adopted a preamble and resolutions, setting forth, that, as the property was held for purposes of public instruction, the Society could not surrender the property without an equivalent, so that the object of the donors, by whose liberality the building was erected, might be secured in another place, and calling for a joint board of five appraisers to make an award. Two appraisers were appointed by the Common Council, and the Committee of Conference were authorized to appoint two on behalf of the Society. Asa Mann and Henry Wyckoff, for the Corporation, and Peter Augustus Jay and E. W. King, for the Society, awarded $26,500 as the value of the lease. The negotiation was not completed. In 1831, a similar movement met with a similar fate.

In 1832, Messrs. W. D. Coit, J. H. Taylor, and others, formed an association for the teaching of apprentices, and other pupils, and applied for the use of No. 1, two evenings in the week, for an evening school. The Executive Committee granted the request, subject to the decision of the section of No. 1, by whom it was deemed inexpedient to grant the building for the purpose.

In 1833, the Board of Assistant Aldermen appointed a Committee of Conference to take measures to obtain absolute possession of the property. The committee renewed the offer on the terms of the joint award previously made, but no result was reached.

In 1837, the long-vexed question was terminated by the order of the Common Council to open Centre street. The commissioners allowed the Society $22,000 damages, and left part of the lot as the property of the Society.

The building in William street, formerly occupied by Colored School No. 1, had been appropriated for a court-house, to which the pupils would have been immediately transferred, but for this occupancy. Until the Society could regain possession of the premises, the pupils were accommodated in other places. The boys' school was held in St. Phillip's Church, in Centre street, and the girls' school in the Brick Church chapel. A new building was erected in William street, and, on October 16, 1838, the pupils were transferred from their temporary quarters to the new house. Appropriate exercises were had, and James I. Roosevelt, Jr., and Samuel W. Seton addressed the audience.

The teachers of No. 1 have been as follows :

William Smith, 1806–1816.

Lloyd D. Windsor, 1816–1836, who was removed from his post by death, August 1.

William Belden, Jr., 1836–1839.

Richard S. Jacobson, 1839–1848.

William W. Smith entered on duty September, 1848, and continued until the transfer of the schools to the Board of Education, in 1853.

The school was reorganized in 1837, and a female department established, under the care of Eliza Harris.

PUBLIC SCHOOL NO. 2.

Col. Henry Rutgers having donated lots of ground to the " Free-School Society," and a new school being demanded by the wants of the eastern portion of the city, it was resolved to erect a building upon the lots so generously granted. A committee was accordingly appointed, consisting of Col. Henry Rutgers, Thomas Collins, and Garrett Van Wagener, to superintend the erection and opening of the building. It was completed during the month of October, and opened for the reception of pupils on the 13th of November, 1811. Forty-seven scholars of both sexes were admitted, and the number was increased in two weeks to 197, under the care of John Missing, teacher.

The boys and girls occupied the same room, all being under the care of one principal. But the number increased so that it became desirable to separate the scholars into two departments. The building was two stories high, with a basement, the school being in the upper story. The first floor was occupied in part as the residence of the teacher, and in part by one of the schools of the Female Association. It was proposed, in 1821, to procure other accommodations for the teacher, extend the schoolroom, and separate the boys and the girls. The alterations were made, and the girls' school was opened on the 1st of November, under the care of Rebecca Leggett, at a salary of $200.

In 1822, the crowded state of the girls' school suggested an exchange of apartments—the boys being transferred to the lower floor, and the girls to the upper, which was accordingly done.

In 1823, the school of the Female Association was removed from the building, and the partitions being taken down, the whole floor was appropriated to the boys' school. Other alterations were made, in 1827, to make the house better fitted for the use of the pupils. The following year (1828), in consequence of widening Henry street, it became necessary to cut off about eight feet from the front of the building, and to make other alterations corresponding to the reduced size of the house, all of which were promptly executed, and the school was reopened on the 15th of September. It continued in that condition until 1834, when it was rebuilt, being larger and more convenient than its predecessor, and finished and furnished for a model school. It was opened on the 1st of November. The primary department was organized at that time.

The succession of teachers in No. 2 was somewhat rapid after Mr. Missing resigned his charge, in 1822. He was followed by Nathaniel C. Hart, who vacated on the 15th of February, 1824, to assume the charge at the House of Refuge, surrendering his place to Henry Hart. He continued in his position only a few months, when he suddenly resigned, in October, much to the regret of the trustees. Jotham Wilson, a monitor in No. 5, and Thomas P. Okie, monitor in No. 3 (and subsequently for many years the principal of No. 6), were placed in charge of the school. Early in 1825, Mr. Thomas Macy entered upon duty as teacher. He held the post until 1832, being followed by A. V. Stout, afterward President of the Shoe and Leather Bank, who found another position in 1833, leaving William Belden, Sr., in his place. Henry Kiddle succeeded Mr. Belden in 1849, and continued to discharge the duties of the principalship until 1856, when he was elected Assistant City Superintendant.

In the female department, Miss Eunice Dean followed Miss Leggett, in 1829. She was removed from her labors during vacation (1831) by death, and Mrs. A. C. Halleck succeeded. Margaret L. Miller, in 1835; in 1837, Miss M. C. Megie; in 1838, Charlotte L. Wykes, who became Mrs. Sammis, in 1841, when Miss Sarah A. Olmsted took the charge until 1844, when Miss Martha Macy succeeded. In 1849, Hannah G. Barnes followed Miss Macy, and, in 1852, resigned her charge to Miss F. A. Westervelt.

It is worthy of remark that James B. Brinsmade entered the

Free School Society, and became a member of the " section " of trustees having charge of No. 2, in 1826, and continued to serve in that capacity until 1853, a period of *twenty-seven* years, and was chosen as one of the trustees under the act of union with the Board of Education, making his whole term of service until his death a period of twenty-nine years.

PUBLIC SCHOOL NO. 3.

At the meeting of the Board of Trustees, held on March 6, 1818, information was communicated that a room in a station-house, owned by the Corporation, at the corner of Hudson and Christopher streets, in what was then known as the village of Greenwhich, could probably be obtained for school purposes, and Thomas C. Taylor, Najah Taylor, and John R. Murray were appointed to make the inquiry. The committee reported, in April, that they had made an application for the room, which had been granted for two years. The same committee was authorized to fit up the premises and propose a teacher. At the meeting in May, a school was directed to be opened at the earliest period possible, and Samuel Boyd, Najah Taylor, and Thomas C. Taylor were appointed a committee of No. 3 to organize and superintend the school. The school was opened on the 25th of May, with 51 children, the number being increased to 196 on the 1st of June. On the 12th of June, the school was so overcrowded with pupils, that a special committee, consisting of William Torrey, Lyman Spalding, and Benjamin Marshall, was appointed to report on the best measures to be adopted. The committee recommended an application to the Corporation for the upper floor of the building, which was obtained and fitted up, and 87 new scholars admitted up to the 7th of August. The large number of pupils made it necessary to relieve the school, and it was proposed to send such of them as resided below Spring street to No. 1 ; but the parents objected so strongly, that it was deemed advisable to obtain separate accommodations for the girls' school. In 1819, " The Eagle Factory " was proposed for a temporary purpose, and William Torrey, Isaac Collins, Ezra Weeks, Leonard Bleecker, and Oliver

H. Hicks were appointed to report in general on the subject. The report recommended the erection of a building on the lots owned by the Society, deeded by Trinity Church, April, 11, 1815, which report was adopted by the board, but reconsidered at the next meeting, and a committee appointed to confer with the vestry of Trinity Church relative to the property, certain conditions of the transfer being an impediment to the plans of the Society. In 1820, the conference resulted in the sale of the property to the Society unconditionally for $1,250.

In April, a committee was appointed to obtain estimates, which were deemed too high, and, at the following meeting of the board, Stephen P. Britton, Whitehead Hicks, and William T. Slocum were appointed for a similar purpose, under instructions. The committee reported a plan, which was adopted, for a house 45 by 80 feet, the whole expense, including fences, &c., not to exceed $6,500. The report was adopted, and William Torrey, Najah Taylor, and Samuel Boyd were named as the Building Committee.

The building was erected, and opened for boys on the 15th of October. The pupils assembled in the old rooms at 9 o'clock, 369 being present, were transferred to the new house, and were all engaged at their usual exercises at 10 o'clock.

On the following Monday, the 22d of the month, the girls, under Sarah Field, the teacher selected for the purpose, were transferred to their apartments in the building. On the 2d of November, 279 female pupils were on the register.

The work having been completed *within* the estimates, and only $217.50 of extra work, the excess over the appropriation amounted to only $109.94.

In September, 1821, a committee, consisting of William Torrey, William T. Slocum, and Edward Kirby, was appointed to have the basement fitted up for school purposes.

On the 10th of September, 1824, General La Fayette visited No. 3, and witnessed the exercises in both departments. The Mayor, some of the Aldermen, and many visitors were present. General La Fayette witnessed a review of all the pupils of the public schools in the Park on the afternoon of the same day. He was unanimously elected a member of the Society at a meeting of the Board of Trustees.

Shepherd Johnston had the charge of the school until March

22, 1825, when he left it, to take the principalship of the junior department of the " New York High School," in Crosby street, between Grand and Broome.

Benjamin F. Hart succeeded Mr. Johnston, and continued in the position until October 18, 1835, when he resigned. Dr. David Patterson assumed the charge of the school, and remained on duty through the whole period of its control by the Society, and passed under the supervision of the new school officers at the time of its transfer to the Board of Education.

Miss Sarah Field, in the girls' school, became Mrs. Bowron, in May, 1821, and resigned on the 15th, giving way to her sister, Maria Field, who had charge until 1825, when Miss Catharine R. Dean succeeded. In 1827, the school was placed under the care of Miss Frances M. Hart, till 1831, when Miss J. F. McCormick followed, and was succeeded, in 1832, by Isabella McCormick, who remained until transferred under the new system.

In November, 1832, Floyd Smith and others applied for permission to use No. 3 for an evening school, to be taught gratuitously, for the benefit of apprentices and others.

Joseph Lancaster visited the school on the 17th of September, 1838, and left the following minute on the visitors' book of the boys' school:

Ninth month, 17.—Joseph Lancaster. Much pleased with the order, obedience, attention, and mental interest displayed in this school. He can only record his general satisfaction, being too much exhausted to enter *now* into particulars; but he truly rejoices in the prosperity which he has seen, and hopes it will go on and increase. It is by the perfection and *example* of such schools as *this* that he hopes knowledge and civilization will extend over the world,

> Far as the ocean waters roll,
> Wide as the heavens are spread.

The entry in the record of the female school is as follows:

Ninth month, 17.—Joseph Lancaster. Highly delighted with the behavior of the excellent pupils in this school. The children and youth in the New York schools may be called the children of attention. Their ears and their hearts seem generally, if not universally, open to instruction, and they eminently distinguish themselves as good listeners. The pupils in this school are so in a most remarkable degree. I find so much to congratulate the public and the friends of these schools respecting their condition, that

I am cautious of repeating the same expressions relative to " the soul's calm sunshine," and the heartfelt joy which I have experienced in every school that I have been in ; yet, on expressing my feelings here, and my satisfaction in other schools, I can truly say, the current of hopes and the brightness of blessings in prospective from the schools, for the people of another day, have flowed on, as the poet expresses himself, repecting other and higher themes, " One tide of glory, one unclouded blaze." I leave my best wishes and cheering approbation for the children, youth, monitors, and teachers of this school, and if I could leave as many blessings as good wishes, they would be abundant indeed.

Mr. Johnston, the original teacher of this school, after an absence of a quarter of a century, returned to visit the scene of his early labors, and left the following minute :

June 12th, 1851.—With feelings of pleasure I enter this room in which I have spent so many delightful days. Things, however, I found much changed ; the whole appearance of the room was altered for the better, and, by the liberality of the present board, the worthy head of this department enjoys advantages which I never had reason to suppose would be extended to the public schools. However, with all of these advantages, I still remain strongly attached to our old system.

S. JOHNSTON.

PUBLIC SCHOOL NO. 4.

In the early part of 1817, Adam Brown, Noah Brown, and Peter Ogilvie addressed a petition to the Society, and a committee was appointed to report the measures necessary to secure the erection of a new school-house in the neighborhood of what was then called " Manhattan Island," Corlear's Hook. Thomas Eddy, James Palmer, Henry Eckford, Noah Brown, and Whitehead Hicks were named for the purpose. They reported that Adam Brown, Noah Brown, Peter Ogilvie, and Henry Eckford would give two lots, and that another could be purchased for about $400. Lots in Columbia street were selected, but afterward rejected, and the committee discharged. In March, 1818, John Murray, Thomas Taylor, Samuel Wood, Whitehead Hicks, and Leonard Bleecker were appointed to select lots in the northeastern part of the city. On the 1st of May, the committee reported the purchase of three lots on the south side of Rivington street, between Pitt and Ridge streets, for $700 each. The report was approved, and the committee directed to close the purchase.

John Murray, Jr., John R. Murray, and Thomas C. Taylor were named as the Building Committee, to report plans and estimates. The report not being satisfactory, John Pintard was added. In September, the report of the committee was submitted and adopted, and the same gentlemen were continued for the superintendence of the new building. An additional committee was subsequently appointed to solicit contributions toward the building, from the residents in the eastern part of the city. The upper room was finished for occupancy, and opened on the 1st of May, 1819, with 133 scholars, under the care of Charles Picton, from England—a gentleman sent by request of the Society, as one specially qualified to illustrate the Lancasterian system as there perfected. Dr. Lyman Spalding, James Palmer, and George T. Trimble composed the School Committee. On the 1st of June, 200 boys and 156 girls had entered the school. On Monday, August 30th, 1819, the girls' school was opened with 182 pupils, under the care of Mrs. Picton.

In 1820, the basement was finished and furnished for school purposes, and occupied by the lower classes of the boys' school, in November. A bell was put up in 1821.

Charles Picton resigned, in 1824, to return to England, being succeeded by E. Wheaton, who remained only until the following year, when he accepted an appointment in the Mechanics' School. In July, he resigned, to be followed by Henry A. Cooper.

On the 31st of October, 1828, Mr. Cooper terminated his services in No. 4, and Mr. S. Hammond took the charge, which he continued until 1834, when Seneca Durand became principal, but he was transferred to another school, and was succeeded by John Patterson, who resigned on the 5th of May, 1852, when Charles W. Feeks succeeded, and remained on duty until after the transfer of the schools to the Board of Education.

In 1820, Mrs. Picton resigned her charge, and Eunice Dean was appointed to the vacancy, which she continued to fill until 1823, when Caroline B. Knapp succeeded, and continued to discharge her duties until 1836, when Mary Doane took charge, and filled the position until 1850. Catharine White succeeded her, under whose care the school passed to the Board of Education.

44

PUBLIC SCHOOL NO. 5.

At a meeting of the Board of Trustees, held on May 11, 1821, a committee, consisting of Leonard Bleecker and Najah Taylor, was appointed to procure lots from Stephen Van Rensselaer, at some point between Broadway and the Bowery, and below Bleecker street. The committee were unable to secure the lots desired. On the 13th of March, 1822, the Bethel Baptist Church having taken measures to secure an extraordinary proportion of the school moneys, the board deemed it advisable to anticipate the proposed school under the care of that church, by appointing a new committee, and Isaac Collins, Rensselaer Havens, William T. Slocum, John L. Bowne, and James Palmer were directed to purchase lots near the Cathedral, and procure estimates for a building. On the 18th of the same month, at a special meeting, the committee reported the purchase of three lots on Mott street, near Prince, for $2,300, which was approved, and the proper authority given to complete the conveyance.

The committee were authorized to erect a school-house, at a cost of $8,000, on these lots, Samuel Boyd being added to the committee. The lots cost $2,295.94. Contracts were made with Rogers & Price, masons, and Woodruff & Thompson, carpenters, for the work, and a loan of $10,000, secured by mortgage on Nos. 4 and 5, was authorized to pay for the structure. The committee were directed to act as temporary School Committee for the organizing and opening of the school, and Joseph Belden was chosen teacher of the boys, and Mary Otis of the girls. The building was erected and completed at a cost of $9,591.09, including the furniture, &c., making the whole cost, including the land, $11,887.03.

The school was opened on the 28th of October, and, on the 1st of December, the number of pupils was 529—328 boys, and 201 girls.

In September, 1832, Joseph Brewster, John H. Smith, Charles Durfee, and others applied for the use of No. 5 for a free evening school, on Friday evenings, for colored persons, which was granted.

In December, 1832, Francis D. Allen and others made application for the use of No. 5, three evenings each week, for a free school for apprentices, &c., which was granted. In October,

1833, the section organized an evening school under their own care, the average attendance weekly being from 75 to 103.

In 1826, at the time of reorganizing the school system, and the appointment of " sections " of the trustees, the section for N. 5 consisted of Isaac Collins, Israel Dean, Dennis McCarthy, J. Smyth Rogers, Knowles Taylor, and James F. Depeyster.

Mr. Joseph Belden, the first teacher, filled his post until September 15, 1828, when he was transferred to No. 11, when Mr. John Tuomy succeeded, and discharged the duties until he surrendered the school to Monmouth B. Hart, in 1832. It passed, in 1836, into the hands of Joseph McKeon, who was afterward City Superintendent, and who, on his resignation as teacher, was followed, on the 2d of November, 1846, by Michael J. O'Donnell. Mr. O'Donnell remained until the transfer.

At the close of 1823, Mary Otis resigned her post, and Miss Eliza Covill succeeded her in the early part of 1824, but remained on duty only a few months, when Catharine Dean took charge of the school. Miss Dean's connection with the school was brief, and, in 1826, Miss Maria M. Field took her place. She became Mrs. Bowron, and remained till 1834, when Sarah A. Olmsted succeeded in the chair till 1841, and was followed by Margaret T. Henratty, who yielded her place to Eliza Ann Field, in 1848. In 1851, Miss Henrietta C. Shepard took charge, but resigned, the following year, to Charlotte A. Purdy.

In March, 1845, the Female Association surrendered the school they conducted in the basement of No. 5, and a primary department was organized, under the care of the section.

No. 5 was used as the depository for some years, until the erection of the Trustees' Hall, now the Hall of the Board of Education. It was also used for the normal school, until it was removed to the Trustees' Hall.

PUBLIC SCHOOL NO. 6.

From a very early period in the history of the Society, the children of the Almshouse department had been educated by the Society, until 1823, at which time that establishment was removed from the City Hall Park to Bellevue, the premises of which were at the time very extensive, but which have since been much reduced by the extension of streets to the river, and the erection of dwellings and other buildings on the new highways. This transfer removed the children from the care of the Society, and it became therefore a matter of anxiety to the trustees to afford instruction to them in their new locality.

At the meeting of the Board of Trustees, June 6th, 1823, a proposition was submitted to make application to the Corporation for permission to establish a school at " Bellevue Hospital " for the benefit of the children in the Almshouse department. The proposition was referred to a committee, consisting of Isaac Collins and Rensselaer Havens. The committee had an interview with the Mayor, and other public officers, and the plan being regarded with approbation, a memorial was reported by the committee for adoption by the board, to be laid before the Corporation. The recommendation was adopted, and the application was made. The Corporation granted the authority, and, at a meeting of the Society, the trustees were directed to establish the said school.

At a meeting of the trustees on the 12th of August, Isaac Collins, William T. Slocum, John R. Hurd, Lindley Murray, and Joseph Grinnell were appointed to select a teacher. Dr. Charles Belden was chosen for the position. Rooms were prepared and furnished with the necessary fixtures and apparatus, and the school was opened on the 27th of October, with 270 boys and girls, under the temporary charge of Shepherd Johnston, of No. 3, and monitors drafted from other schools.

In 1826, when the sections were organized, Samuel Wood, Heman Averill, Samuel F. Mott, Arthur Burtis, and N. C. Everitt were appointed as the first section for No. 6. There were at the time 268 children in the Almshouse, with 13 pupils outside of the institution.

The children were removed from Bellevue to the " Nursery " at the " Long Island Farms," in August, 1842; thence to Blackwell's Island, in April 1847, and were finally removed to Randall's Island, the present location, April 25, 1848.

In August, 1825, Dr. Belden, the principal, was removed by death, and Albert De Montfredy succeeded. Francis Windsor took charge of the school in 1826. In 1829, during the sickness of Mr. Windsor, his brother, Lloyd D. Windsor, had temporary charge, and subsequently William Guest supplied for Mr. Windsor. Thomas P. Okie succeeded Mr. Windsor, May 1, 1831, and continued in charge of the school until the transfer of the system.

The boys and girls were separated into two departments, in 1839, Miss Jane Steel having had charge of the primary school.

Miss Anna Balentine was appointed principal of the primary department, in 1839; she became Mrs. Guest, in 1840, and was followed by Miss Susan Jackson, who remained until the close of the schools under the Society.

In July, 1853, the schools passed to the care of the ward school officers of the Twelfth Ward. On the 17th of August, the school officers held a meeting, at which the "section" of the trustees of the Society were present by invitation. The section consisted of Peter Cooper, Joseph Curtis, Linus W. Stevens, and John Davenport. A consultation was had, the schools were visited, addresses made, and the only section of the trustees of the Public School Society which then remained bade farewell in an official manner to their interesting charge, and surrendered the schools they had so long cherished and sustained to the hands of the new guardians.

By reference to the minute-book, it will be seen that Mr. Lancaster did not omit this school in his examination of the system. His remarks are as follows:

Tenth month [*October*] 3, 1838.—Joseph Lancaster considers this school to be very much like a wire-drawing machine, which can draw out a small quantity of silver or other metal to great fineness and amazing extent.

If a grain of gold be mixed with a pound of silver, it is said that the sign of the gold will be found visible, to all the extent of wire-drawn silver.

Let the wisdom of human knowledge be esteemed as silver; let the knowledge and fear of God be as gold. Oh, may it please the Giver of every good and perfect gift that the pure gold may shine on all the silver in this school, and in every other in New York. The effect of this (figurative) mixture in this school has been very precious and acceptable to my mind. When I do die, I think it will be in more peace for having seen the poor, dear children of this school so happily and usefully provided for in regard to order and learning.

Delighted with the school, and rendered truly happy by the good harvest springing up under the teacher's judicious care. As a father and a friend, I wish him and his very interesting charge "Good speed in the name of the Lord." Peace be with all his exertions, prosperity with all his labors, and the blessing of heaven with all this family of children.

I have been accompanied in this visit by a great-grandson, Charles Gaylor, who seemed as much pleased as myself.

I am truly pleased to see the lively, active attention and diligence of the monitors. They appear to me like the tools of a superior workman, well kept, clean, acute, polished, and in good condition for their work. The monitors of drafts look like men and women, and do their work in a workmanlike style. I am richly rewarded with pleasure and peace for the time given up to visit this school, so highly creditable to all concerned, and so honorable to the city of New York, and its humble, praiseworthy, benevolent institutions and public spirit.

The following noteworthy memorial is found in the minute-book, under date of April 12, 1852:

Eleven years ago to-day seven trustees assembled at the Brick Church, corner of Chatham and Nassau streets, for the purpose of visiting this school, then at Long Island Farms. It was in the midst of one of the severest snow-storms of the season. It had already fallen eight inches. In two carriages we crossed the Grand street ferry to Williamsburgh, thence up East River, crossing the toll-bridge over Newtown Creek, arriving at the school a few minutes after 3 P. M. We found every thing in good order, and had an examination that compensated us for all our toil and expenses.

We returned the same route we came. Storm still continuing and un-abated. We did not arrive at our homes until quite dark. I allude to this circumstance (it being its eleventh anniversary), trusting that some who come after us will read this and be inspired with the zeal that impelled such men as Samuel Demilt and others to pursue and persevere in a cause with an ardor that nothing but duty and public good could have induced to leave their comfortable firesides in such a storm as prevailed on the 12th of April, 1841.

The trustees present on the occassion alluded to, were Samuel Demilt, Heman Averill, Timothy Hedges, Frederic De Peyster, Samuel W. Seton, William Rockwell, M.D., and Burritt Sherwood, M.D.

PUBLIC SCHOOL NO. 7.

The great controversy, growing out of the action of the trustees of the Bethel Baptist Church respecting the school fund, being terminated, the trustees of the Public School Society were prepared to press forward with greater energy and usefulness, the integrity of the common school fund having been secured by

the law of 1825.   At the meeting of the trustees, held May 6th
of that year, a committee of five was appointed to report on the
expediency of hiring, purchasing, or erecting buildings for additional schools, and to select locations.   James I. Roosevelt, Jr.,
J. F. Depeyster, George T. Trimble, R. C. Cornell, and Stephen
Allen were chosen as the committee.   A location was selected
and reported upon in Anthony street, and, on the 16th of September, a location in Chrystie street, between Hester and Pump
streets, the name of the latter being afterward changed to Walker,
and now known as Canal street.   The report was adopted, and
William W. Fox, James Palmer, and Isaac Collins were named
as the Building Committee.   Plans and estimates were submitted
at a special meeting, held on the 23d of the same month, which
were adopted, and the committee authorized to proceed, Stephen
Allen being added to the committee.   On the 6th of January,
1826, Leonard Bleecker, George T. Trimble, and Lindley Murray were appointed a committee to select a teacher for the new
school.   On the 3d of February, Stephen R. Kirby was reported
as the choice of the committee.   Frances C. Coit was subsequently appointed to take charge of the female department.

On the 7th of April, the Building Committee reported that
the house would be ready for early occupancy, and Najah Taylor
and George T. Trimble were assigned to take charge of the
opening and organization of the school.

The school was opened on the 1st of May, 1826, with 87
pupils.   The house was erected by J. & J. Bunting, masons, for
$4,500, and Isaiah Macey, carpenter, for $5,886.62.   The total
cost, including a few items for extra work, was $10,761.20.

In October, Messrs. Joseph Belden and Stephen R. Kirby
applied for permission to use No. 7 for an evening school, to be
under their care.   This appears to be the earliest effort to establish an evening school under the supervision of the Society.
The teachers were to receive compensation from the pupils, as a
private remuneration; but they desired the use of the school-
house on account of their own relations to the Society, as well
as the convenience of the building.

In 1830, Andrew V. Stout, who afterward became principal
of No. 13, in Madison street, was appointed monitor general.
During a period of temporary absence on the part of Mr. Kirby,
he had the charge of the school, and the " section " remark in

the minute-book, " The school has been satisfactorily kept up by Andrew V. Stout, the monitor general of the school." On the 1st of February, he left No. 7 to go to a private school as teacher. Thomas P. Okie, then of No. 12, succeeded him for a short time, when he returned to his former post, and Robert S. Mills took his place.

Mr. Kirby resigned, in 1833, and was succeeded, on the 1st of April, by William P. Lyon, who surrendered his post in May, 1835, and, on the 11th of that month, John W. Ketchum, the present Superintendent of the House of Refuge, took charge of the school. Mr. Lyon gave full satisfaction to the trustees, but he did not like the requisition of the extra service in the evening schools, and preferred resigning his position to a compulsory sacrifice of his evenings to school duties, which conflicted with other arrangements. Mr. Ketchum remained in the school until May, 1846, when he assumed the care of the House of Refuge, and William H. Reuck followed, and filled the post until after the transfer of the schools to the Board of Education.

Frances C. Coit resigned the charge of the girls' school, September 1, 1836, and Mary A. Belden was appointed to the succession. Much to the regret of the Society and to the friends of the school, she was compelled by ill health to resign on the 20th of March, 1839, and was called to rest from earthly labors on the 28th of the same month. The following tribute to her memory appears in the annual report of that year:

When the excellent of the earth are removed from time to eternity, some notice of the fact seems due as a record of the feelings of those who knew and appreciated the worth of the departed; and the trustees cannot close this report without expressing the regret they feel at the loss this institution and the public have sustained in the recent decease of Mrs. MARY ANN BELDEN, late principal of Girls' School No. 7. Her peculiar skill in governing children with mildness, and her success in communicating information to them, were conspicious and gratifying to the trustees through the long course of years she was in their employ. Early imbued with the principles of piety, the moral and religious influences exerted by her over the three hundred girls daily attending her school, cannot but have a lasting effect on many of their susceptible minds; and in reference to the whole character and course of Mary Ann Belden as a public school teacher, the trustees may say, " Many teachers have done well, but thou excellest them all."

Hannah N. Collins succeeded Mrs. Belden, but held the position only till 1842, in the early part of which year she was followed by Miss Sarah Ann Bunker, who remained until the schools were transferred.

On the 7th of September, 1837, N. P. Beers entered on duty as assistant monitor, and, by promotion, became principal of No. 15, in Fifth street, which position he now holds.

On May 6, 1847, Thomas Palmer, first monitor, was transferred to the First Ward school, and Lafayette Olney, present principal of No. 14, succeeded him.

On the 22d of July, 1853, the section of the trustees met officially to bid farewell to their charge. The gentlemen present were William H. Macy, John T. Adams, and George T. Trimble. They distributed sixty-eight certificates in the boys' school, and fifty-four in the girls' school. Mr. Trimble made the following entry in the minute-book:

This act, with some valedictory remarks, closes the official connection of the section with this school. The writer of this minute having been attached to it since it was opened, on the 1st of May, 1826, and made the opening minute on that day. William H. Macy has been in this section since 1837, and John T. Adams since 1840. The other members for shorter periods. Some much respected members of this section only closed their labors with their lives. These recollections, with the reflections arising therefrom, cause the events of this occasion to impress our minds with great seriousness, accompanied by the hope that our labors have not been in vain.

Mr. Lancaster visited this school several times, and it was on his way from No. 7, which he had just left, that he met with the casualty which resulted in his death a day or two afterward. The following are the memoranda he left on the records of the school:

Ninth month, 6.—Joseph Lancaster visited this school, and was most highly pleased with the exemplary behavior and order of the very interesting boys and youth who assemble here for instruction. In this school he has found, felt, and seen abundance to delight a father's eye and gratify the best feeling of a father's heart. If he is to take youth like these as a specimen of American native character, truly he may congratulate the citizens of New York and the American nation, that they possess youth of such high hopes and favorable capacity. May they ever do the same honor to their teachers and parents, and the same credit to these schools, and may the love and peace of God dwell with them, and they all become as diamonds of the purest water, enclosed within the pearl of greatest price.

Ninth month, 6.—Joseph Lancaster. The most delightful conduct and mental attention, good behavior and wise deportment of the highly estimable children and youth in this school, merit from me a tribute of respect which seems almost inexpressible. I have often been highly delighted and gratified with schools, but never more so than in my visits to this school. I congratulate their parents, friends, and teachers on the principles of good conduct, the love of learning, and also rectitude and virtue which I am satisfied are among them. There now are children and youth in this school who do the highest credit to themselves, to their teachers, and to these institutions that the most excellent conduct can do. May they go on and increase and prosper, till heaven shall rejoice and earth be glad for them ; till knowledge shall abound in perfection among them, and they grow up to maturity, like their Reedemer, in favor with God and man.

Ninth month, 25.—Joseph Lancaster. School much increased. We love to see bees in swarms; it is a sure sign there will be more honey. Found the pupils as busy as bees at their writing) with minds intent on working up as much improvement as possible.

PUBLIC SCHOOL NO. 8.

The Committee on Locations for new schools, appointed in 1825, continued their labors, and, in April, 1826, recommended the purchase of lots in Grand street, between Laurens and Wooster streets, 75 by 100 feet. On the 19th, the committee reported that the purchase had been made for $5,000, whereupon Isaac Collins, George T. Trimble, William W. Fox, and Robert C. Cornell were appointed to report plans and estimates for a building to be erected thereon. On the 29th, the report was laid before the board, adopted, and William W. Fox, Isaac Collins, and James Palmer were constituted a Building Committee. On the 6th of October, Messrs. Isaac Collins, Stephen Hasbrouck, Daniel Lord, Eleazar Lord, and Samuel Boyd were appointed section for No. 8. The school was opened on the 1st of November, and during the first quarter there were admitted, in the boys' department, 144 pay and 159 free scholars—total, 303 ; in the girls' department, 132 pay and 44 free scholars—total, 176. The school opened under the care of C. B. Sherman, in the male, and Eunice Dean, in the female department.

On the 4th of April, 1827, the building was considerably injured by fire, but the repairs were promptly made, and the school reopened on the 3d of May following.

Mrs. Joanna Bethune, on behalf of herself and other ladies,

applied, in May, 1827, for the use of the basement for an " infant school," under their care. The application was referred to the Executive Committee. The important improvements in the system growing out of this effort, are detailed in the chapter devoted to that subject. The " junior department " was organized on June 4th, by the section. On the 11th of May, 1829, the section adopted a resolution declaring it expedient to discontinue the " junior department," and establish an " infant school." The organization was found to be inefficient, and, in December, 1830, it was changed into a " primary school," in compliance with the new plans of the board.

In May, 1831, there were on register 236 boys, 270 girls, and 239 in the primary department.

Mr. C. B. Sherman, the first principal, resigned in September, 1841, and was followed by Charles S. Pell, who was succeeded by Cornelius A. Cooper, on the 1st of March, 1852, who remained in the school and passed with it to the jurisdiction of the Board of Education.

Eunice Dean, the first teacher of the girls' school, remained until 1830, when she was followed by Elizabeth Dean, who remained untill 1833, when Elizabeth Winans took the charge of the school. In 1834, Miss Harriet Bartine was appointed to the vacancy occasioned by the resignation of Miss Winans, and continued in her position until the transfer of the school to the ward officers.

PUBLIC SCHOOL NO. 9

This school was organized by the vestry of St. Michael's Church (Episcopal), at Bloomingdale, and was continued under their care until the enactment of the law excluding church schools from participating in the school fund, passed November, 19, 1824, when it was about to be abandoned for want of sufficient income. At the solicitation of the rector, Rev. William Richmond, the situation of the school was laid before the Board of Trustees of the Society, by James F. Depeyster and Stephen Allen, on May 5, 1826, and a committee was appointed, consisting of Stephen Allen, James F. Depeyster, and George T. Trimble, to examine and report on the expediency of establishing schools in the Twelfth Ward. The committee reported, at the meeting on the 12th of the same month, that they found 48 children in school (22 boys and 26 girls), who were taught by Mr. Thomas C. Richmond, son of the rector, who had volunteered his services gratuitously since the withdrawal of the school fund. The committee recommended the employment of a teacher for not more than six months, at a salary of $30 a month, and the adoption of the school as one of the charges of the Public School Society. Jotham Wilson was appointed teacher, and entered on duty on the 22d of May. Stephen Allen and James F. Depeyster were appointed section for No. 9.

The negotiations relative to the other schools in the ward never resulted in any change or transfer, and the action in the case is not important to the reader.

In July, 1827, the committee were directed to ascertain whether a donation of land for a school site could be obtained ; and if not, to purchase a suitable location at a cost of not over $500, and the Building Committee were directed to erect thereon a house not to cost more than $2,600. A plot of ground, 100 feet square, was purchased for $250, on Eighty-second street, between Tenth and Eleventh avenues. A difficulty arising, the Building Committee did not immediately proceed with their work, and new apartments were hired, which afforded better accommodations, until the impediments were removed. In 1830, a committee on the state of No. 9 recommended the erection of the school-house, and the Building Committee were directed to proceed and put up a house not to cost more than $1,500. The instructions were obeyed, and the house was finished and occupied on the 19th of July.

On the 19th of March, 1830, Dr. Abraham V. Williams was elected a trustee of the Public School Society, and being a resident of Bloomingdale, he was able to give the personal supervision required, and which the other members of the section could not give. Dr. Williams was immediately placed on the section of No. 9. Robert Sedgwick was also soon afterward added to the section, so that it consisted of Messrs. Allen, Depeyster, Williams, and Sedgwick.

Mr. Wilson resigned his post as teacher on the 1st of May, 1832, and was succeeded by Seneca Durand. On February 5,

1833, the school had increased to 69, and Dr. Williams, in his minute made that day, remarks the pleasing and unusual circumstance that *every scholar on the register was in attendance.*

In June, 1834, Mr. Durand was transferred to No. 4, and succeeded by Mr. J. P. Hoyt on the 24th of that month. He remained in charge until August, 1844, when Benjamin G. Bruce, who had been his assistant for several years, was promoted to the post of principal.

In 1850, the female department was organized, and Miss Mary Kelly, who had been assistant in the school, was appointed principal.

Under the care of Mr. Bruce and Miss Kelly, the school passed to the jurisdiction of the Board of Education, July, 1853.

PUBLIC SCHOOL NO. 10.

The Committee on New Schools, appointed May 6, 1825, consisted of James I. Roosevelt, Jr., James F. Depeyster, George T. Trimble, R. C. Cornell, and Stephen Allen. Previous to making the report in favor of No. 7, in Chrystie street, they had selected a location in Anthony street, but the negotiations were of a protracted nature. In September, 1826, the same recommendation was repeated, and a conditional resolution, authorizing the erection of a house, was adopted. In November following, a location in Church street, between Duane and Thomas streets, was suggested and approved. In January, 1827, the committee reported that they had not been able to obtain the lots, but that three lots in Duane street, 75 by 100 feet, could be purchased for a site for the new school. The committee were authorized to make the purchase, the price being $8,300, and a right of dower of $50 per annum. The Building Committee was directed to make contracts for the erection of a house on the lots, similar to No. 8, with such improvements as might be deemed expedient. The contracts were made with J. & J. Bunting, masons, and Israel Macy, carpenter, the whole cost, including fixtures, &c., being $12,488.50. On the 13th of October, Benjamin L. Swan, J. Groshon, Thomas R. Mercein, and J. H. Taylor were appointed as the school section; and on the 1st of November, 1827, No. 10 was opened for the reception of pupils, under the care of Albert De Montfredy, in the boys' department, and Eliza J. Cox, in the girls' department.

In 1832, Messrs. W. D. Coit, J. H. Taylor, and others applied for the use of No. 10 two evenings a week, for a free evening school for apprentices and others. The application was referred to the section, with power.

In 1853, the debts of the Society being considerable in amount, and a large school under the care of the ward officers having been erected in the neighborhood, the Board of Trustees were induced to consider the expediency of selling No. 10. This was rendered the more advisable in consequence of the change that had taken place in the vicinity, many of the dwellings having given place to business establishments of various kinds, and the resident population removed to other portions of the city.

At this time, the bill for the union of the two systems of education—the Public School Society and the Board of Education—was pending in the Legislature, and, after a full discussion, it was deemed necessary to sell the property. The Board of Education had failed to appropriate all that the Society required, and the floating debt was on the increase, and the ultimate extinction of the Society was a matter of discussion and anticipation. The Finance Committee were therefore to take steps toward the sale, provided the bill did not become a law. If the bill passed, and received the Executive signature, the property would be transferred to the Board of Education. The bill failed of its final reading, and the committee sold the premises to Thomas Hope for $39,900, on the 31st of May, at auction. At an extra session of the Legislature, held a few weeks after the sale, the school bill became a law, but too late to reverse the sale.

Teachers: Mr. Albert De Montfredy conducted the school until 1836, when N. W. Starr succeeded him; and, in 1852, Charles B. Stout became principal, under whom the school was transferred to the Board of Education.

Miss Eliza J. Cox remained in the girls' department until 1834. She was succeeded by Harriet E. Phelps; and the teachers of this school successively were Angeline Slater, 1837; Maria G. Balsh, 1838; and Maria F. Savage, 1851.

PUBLIC SCHOOL NO. 11.*

The Committee on New Schools recommended, on the 8th of September, 1826, in connection with No. 10, the purchase of lots in Wooster street, between Houston and Bleecker streets. The recommendation was adopted, and the lots purchased.

On the 1st of June, 1827, the Building Committee was instructed to lay the foundation of a house similar to No. 10, on these lots. At the meeting on the 6th of July, the committee reported the work commenced. Contracts were made with the builders of No. 10, and the house completed and occupied on the 15th of September, 1828. The total cost of the house and appointments was $12,400.

On the 1st of August, Robert C. Cornell, Rensselaer Havens, and George T. Trimble were appointed a temporary section for No. 11. The school was organized under the care of Joseph Belden, of No. 5, with 40 boys, and 31 girls in charge of Mary Shourt. On the 1st of November, the number had increased to 82 boys and 92 girls, all " pay scholars."

Mr. Belden died on September 12, 1834, and William H. Brownne became principal, and remained in his post until his death, March 31, 1844, when Michael J. O'Donnell succeeded. During the early part of 1847, Mr. O'Donnell was transferred to No. 5, and George Moore was appointed to fill the vacancy. He served during the remaining period of the existence of the Society.

Miss Shourt, in the girls' school, was succeeded, in 1833, by Caroline Carpenter, who resigned in 1840, when Sophia Carpenter temporarily filled the position, giving way, in a few months, to Anna M. Bussell. Miss Bussell was followed, in 1843, by Sarah Field, who had long been an assistant in the school, and who was on duty until the Society and its schools were merged into the ward school system.

The primary department was organized in the early part of 1832.

The following entry, by Hon. J. S. Buckingham, is on the minute-book :

Friday, December 8, 1837.—I have had the pleasure to visit, to-day, in

* Subsequent to the sale of No. 10, the numbers of the schools were altered— No. 11 became No. 10. No. 18 (the last) became No. 17.

company with my friends, Mr. and Mrs. Mott, the Public School No. 11, and, after examining the four departments of the male and female infant classes, and the two more advanced, my gratification has been of the highest kind. The accuracy of reading and the knowledge of geography were peculiarly striking, as evinced in both boys and girls, and in an equal degree of perfection with each. The specimens of writing were such as surpassed any thing I have ever before seen of the kind; and, on the whole, I think the schools highly creditable to both pupils and teachers, an honor to the city, and a blessing to the nation.   J. S. BUCKINGHAM.

A deputation of clergymen from England to the United States, on a special mission, also visited the school, and left the following note in the minute-book:

April 16, 1834.—Revs. Reed and Mattheson, from England. Much gratified with the examination.

PUBLIC SCHOOL NO. 12.

On the 5th of February, 1830, at a meeting of the Board of Trustees, a communication was received from a committee appointed at a meeting of citizens residing in the vicinity of the Eighth avenue and Twenty-first street, representing the demand for a school in that section of the city. In connection with the communication, a letter was read from Gideon Lee, Esq., Alderman, and afterward Mayor, urging the application, and pledging a contribution of $500 toward building the house. He also recommended the erection of a school in the vicinity of Third avenue and Twenty-eighth street, endorsing his proposition with a subscription of $500 when it should be built. The whole subject was referred to Messrs. Charles Oakley, Ovid P. Wells, R. C. Cornell, and Samuel F. Mott. On the 17th of March, the committee reported in favor of locating a school in that vicinity, and also a new school between Nos. 2 and 4, on the east side of the city. The report was accepted, and the recommendations recommitted, with the addition of Messrs. Underhill, Fox, and Brinsmade to the committee. On the 25th of June, the committee was discharged, and Messrs. Oakley, Cornell, and Mott were appointed as the committee. A report was submitted by these gentlemen at the same meeting in favor of a location in or near Seventeenth or Eighteenth street and the Eighth avenue. A subsequent recommendation, on the 19th of July, of four lots on Seventeenth street, at $675 each, was approved by the board, and the purchase was ordered. The Property Committee was directed to report plans and estimates for a building. A donation of $200 was made by George Rapelye, Esq., on the price of the lots. The plans and estimates were submitted on the 28th of July, and the committee authorized to contract for the building. The contracts were made with J. & J. Bunting, masons, and James Russell, carpenter, and the house built and furnished with books, apparatus, &c., as in the case of other houses, at a total cost of $10,878.85. The school was opened with appropriate exercises on the 17th of January, 1831, in presence of a number of members of the Common Council and other citizens, and daily sessions were held in it until the 22d, when it was destroyed by fire. An insurance had been effected on the building and its fixtures, &c., so that the loss to the Society was only about $3,000. On the 4th of February, the Building Committee reported the completion of their duties, together with the fact of the fire, and recommended the immediate rebuilding of the house. The board approved the report, and temporary accommodations were provided for the schools. Jacob P. Bunting, mason, and James Russell, carpenter, rebuilt the house, which was completed and opened on the 29th of August following.

Mr. George Everett, the first principal, resigned in 1834, and was followed by Benjamin Wightman, who resigned November 1, 1841, Asa Smith being his successor, assisted by William H. Reuck, afterward principal of No. 7, in Chrystie street. Mr. Smith had been in the school several years as an assistant, and held his post until the dissolution of the Society.

Miss Fanny F. Greenoak, principal of the girls' school, was succeeded, in 1836, by Elizabeth Lindon, who resigned in 1849, at which time Miss Susan Wright took the charge of the school, in whose hands it was transferred to the Board of Education, in 1853.

The primary department was organized July 2, 1832, under the care of Caroline Carpenter.

45

PUBLIC SCHOOL NO. 13.

The Committee on Locations (1830) recommended one on the east side of the city, between No. 2, in Henry street, and No. 4, in Rivington street. No further action was had at that time; but in 1832, at the meeting of the trustees held on June 8, a committee was appointed to review the question, and Messrs. James Heard, Swan, Oakley, Mott, Fox, and Cornell were named for that duty. In November, the committee reported the purchase of a location in Madison street, at the cost of $8,000 for four lots of ground. The Property Committee also reported that contracts had been made for the building. In May, 1833, Dr. Samuel R. Childs, W. W. Chester, and S. Haff were appointed section for No. 13, which was opened on the 21st of that month. The school was organized with 143 boys, 58 girls, and 156 boys and girls in the primary department. At the public exercises in the afternoon, Hon. Gideon Lee, the Mayor, a portion of the Common Council, the School Commissioners, a portion of the trustees, and many visitors, were present. The attendance rapidly increased, so that, when the school closed for vacation, there were on register 275 boys and 204 girls.

The school was placed under the care of Andrew V. Stout, who resigned on the 1st of May, 1844, when John H. Fanning entered upon duty, and filled the post until transferred to the ward school officers.

Miss Martha Grier was the first principal of the girls' school, and was followed by Miss Sophia S. Cornell, in 1836, who resigned in 1844, and Mary E. Vail assumed the post. In 1846, Miss A. Harrison was appointed to fill the vacancy occasioned by the withdrawal of Miss Vail, and Mary F. English followed Miss Harrison, in 1848. In 1851, Anna M. Marsh entered upon duty, and in her charge the school was transferred to its new guardians, July 29, 1853.

Miss Catharine King was the first teacher of the primary department.

PUBLIC SCHOOL NO. 14.

The Committee on Lots and Locations, appointed June 8, 1832, reported, on the 14th of December, that they had purchased four lots of ground in North (now Houston) street, near Norfolk, for $6,000. On the 1st of February, 1833, the Property Committee reported that contracts had been made for a building. On November 1, Messrs. Brinsmade, B. S. Collins, and Timothy Hedges were appointed a temporary section for No. 14. The building was opened on November 4, 1833, with appropriate exercises. A large number of citizens were present, and addresses were made by Hon. Peter Augustus Jay, and His Honor Gideon Lee, Mayor, and others. On the 8th of November, the pupils numbered, boys, 180; girls, 125; primary department, 168; the attendance on that day being 171 boys, 96 girls, and 64 boys and 76 girls in the primary school.

Dr. Samuel L. Kennedy, Hiram N. Peck, Matthias O. Halsted, William Beach Lawrence, and Thomas McElrath were appointed permanent section for No. 14. At the annual meeting in May, 1835, Mr. Lawrence was transferred to another section, and Hamilton Fish, afterward Governor of the State and United States Senator, was placed on the section to fill the vacancy.

Mr. Anson Willis was the first principal of the boys' department. He filled the post two years, until 1835, when Leonard Hazeltine succeeded, and continued in charge until the schools passed to the care of the Board of Education.

Miss C. Wynans was appointed to the girls' department at the organization of the school, and discharged her duties until 1837, when she was followed by Mrs. J. M. Wheaton. This lady died in January, 1841, and Sarah A. Bunker succeeded for a few months, when, in July of the same year, Miss Jane W. Miller was placed in the chair. In 1845, Miss Miller resigned, to take charge of Ward School No. 45, in Twenty-fourth street, and Miss Georgiana Watson became principal. The school was in her charge at the time of the transfer to the ward school officers.

The primary department was organized under the care of Miss A. Hanks.

PUBLIC SCHOOL NO. 15.

At a meeting of the Board of Trustees held September 24, 1833, a memorial was presented from about forty residents of that part of the city near the Third avenue and between Fourteenth and Twenty-eighth streets, asking for a school in that district. This was the location which Hon. Gideon Lee had previously indicated, and who also repeated his request in a letter accompanying the memorial. A Committee on Locations was appointed, consisting of Messrs. Charles Oakley, James Heard, B. S. Collins, B. L. Swan, and J. N. Wells; William W. Fox was subsequently added to the committee. The report was laid before the board on October 3, in favor of the measure; the committee was authorized to purchase suitable lots, and the Property Committee was directed to erect a house similar to No. 14, in Houston street. Four lots in Twenty-seventh street, between Second and Third avenues, were purchased for $800 each.

At the annual meeting in May, 1834, the following gentlemen were appointed section for No. 15: Dr. Samuel R. Childs, Anson G. Phelps, Samuel Demilt, Robert C. Cornell, and Samuel F. Mott.

Daniel F. Tieman and Peter Cooper were members of the section for No. 15 for a number of years.

The house was put under contract, finished, and dedicated on the 4th of May, 1835. The following-named members of the board were present on the occasion: Messrs. Oakley, Murray, Demilt, Childs, Collins, Phelps, Baldwin, Whitmore, Day, Halsey, Seton, Depeyster, James Heard, and Peck. Appropriate exercises by pupils of other schools formed the principal feature of the occasion, with an address by Samuel W. Seton.

On the 18th of November, 1848, a fire broke out in the extensive stables corner of Third avenue and Twenty-seventh street, belonging to the omnibus company, when the buildings were all destroyed, together with the Methodist church, the parsonage, and the school-house. The loss of property was almost total, only a portion of the books, furniture, &c., being saved. The building was destroyed. The amount of insurance was $7,500, making a loss of $2,887.81.

Arrangements were immediately made to secure temporary premises, and apartments in the Almshouse buildings, on First avenue and Twenty-sixth street, were secured and fitted up. The schools went into operation on the 4th of December. The new building was erected, and school resumed therein on the 4th of June, 1849.

William A. Walker, afterward School Superintendent, was the first principal of No. 15, and held the office until 1846, when he was succeeded by William H. Wood, who remained in charge of the school until after its transfer to the Board of Education.

Miss Elizabeth Cox organized the girls' school, but remained only a short time, being succeeded, in 1836, by Caroline T. Whiting, who was on duty, and in whose care the school was transferred, in 1853.

The primary department was organized in 1838, under the care of Miss Louisa Lynch.

The autograph of William Cullen Bryant appears in the visitors' book, under date of January 5, 1854.

PUBLIC SCHOOL NO. 16.

At the meeting of the Board of Trustees held September 24, 1833, a committee of five, consisting of Charles Oakley, James Heard, B. S. Collins, B. L. Swan, and J. N. Wells, was appointed to select locations for new schools. At the meeting in October, William W. Fox was added to the number, and they were directed to select a location near the Dry Dock. In 1834, the same committee was continued, and on the 6th of February, 1835, they reported progress, and were authorized to purchase lots in that part of the city. At a special meeting held at School No. 5, at the examination of that school, the committee again reported progress; and on May 1st, a diversity of opinion respecting the location having retarded the action of the committee, the chairman submitted a report in favor of a site in Fifth street, and recommending the purchase of the lots selected, at the price of $1,500 each. The board adopted the resolution so reported.

The negotiations for the purchase were interrupted for some time, and the lots were sold at auction for $1,700 each. The purchaser held them at $2,000 ; and, on the 6th of November, the chairman of the committee reported the facts, requesting final instructions as to the course to be pursued. The board directed the purchase, and on the 6th of May, 1836, it was reported as having been made. On the 5th of August, the Property Committee was authorized to erect a building. On the 4th of August, 1837, the committee reported that contracts had been made with James Russell, carpenter, and Lorenzo Moses, mason, and that the building was commenced. The house was completed, and opened with appropriate exercises on the 27th of April, 1838, Messrs. Charles Oakley, J. B. Collins, H. W. Field, and S. W. Seton being the Committee of Arrangements. The Mayor of the city, Hon. Cornelius W. Lawrence, was present, with Isaac L. Varian, and other citizens, the audience being addressed by the Mayor, and James I. Roosevelt, Jr.

The school was organized on the 7th of May, with 84 boys, 72 girls, and 233 boys and girls in the primary department. During the first quarter, the number rapidly increased, and the first returns made were as follows: 270 boys, 181 girls, and in the primary department, 236 boys and 215 girls. The average attendance was 166 boys, 115 girls, and in the primary school, 264 boys and 223 girls.

The section originally appointed for No. 16 consisted of the following gentlemen: George T. Trimble, Samuel Demilt, William Smith, James H. Blaisdell, Joseph Washburn, Meigs D. Benjamin, and Peter Stuyvesant.

JOSEPH CURTIS was appointed a member of the section in 1839, and so remained until May, 1847, when he was transferred to No. 6 (Randall's Island), and Colored School No. 2. The section adopted the following resolution:

Resolved, That we have heard with regret of the transfer of Mr. Joseph Curtis from this section. His efficient and interesting labors, and his extensive information in affairs of public education, have made him extensively useful, and placed us and the public under lasting obligations to him. Though he will be lost to our section, we are gratified with the fact that his services will not be lost to the Society and the public, and congratulate the section to which he is transferred on the acquisition of his valuable services.

The section for 1844–'45 adopted the following resolution:

In the opinion of the section, the time has arrived that vocal music be taught in our schools, and that this our wish be made known to the Executive Committee, and through them to the board.

Abraham K. Van Vleck organized the boys' school, and conducted it with great fidelity and success, until he was called from his labors by death, in March, 1850. On the 1st of April, Mr. N. P. Beers, assistant in No. 7, Chrystie street, took charge of the school, and passed with it to the supervision of the ward school officers, in 1853, when the change of system took place.

Miss Mary McKay was the first principal of the girls' school, who remained only till 1840, when her successor, Miss Fezzan T. Robbins, followed. Miss Robbins became Mrs. Stiles, and resigned in 1848, when the vacancy was supplied by Miss S. J. Hatfield, who retired in 1851, to be succeeded by Miss Urania Downs, who remained in the school at the time of the dissolution of the Society.

The primary department was organized by Miss Sarah C. Glover at the time of opening the school in 1838.

PUBLIC SCHOOL NO. 17.

The special meeting of the Board of Trustees for the examination of No. 4 was held April 10, 1838. After the exercises were concluded, the board held a meeting to consider a recommendation of the Executive Committee relative to the purchase of lots for a new school in Thirteenth street, near the Sixth avenue, to relieve the pressure upon No. 3, in Hudson street, and No. 12, in Seventeenth street. The Committee on Locations were directed to purchase the lots recommended, but in consequence of a defect in the title, the negotiations were suspended.

In February, 1843, the sections of Nos. 3 and 12 reported that there was an urgent necessity for a new building to relieve their overcrowded condition ; and the board, at the meeting held on the 5th of May, referred the matter to the Executive Committee, with power. A sub-committee was immediately appointed, and after examining a number of locations, the report recommended the purchase of four lots in Thirteenth street, near Seventh avenue, each 25 feet by 103 ft. 3 in. The report was accepted and adopted, and the Property Committee reported plans and estimates for the house, which were also adopted. The committee were authorized to close the contracts with

James Russell, carpenter, and Lorenzo Moses, mason. The Building Committee consisted of Linus W. Stevens, B. R. Winthrop, and Thompson Price.

On the 20th of November, the following gentlemen organized as section No. 17: Floyd Smith, Hamilton Murray, Frederick Havemeyer, Benjamin Ellis, and John R. Hurd. The first three named were elected to the board on the 3d of November, and assigned to that section.

Benjamin Ellis and John R. Hurd were appointed the Committee on Opening, and the arrangements were accordingly made. The house was completed at the close of the year, and the boys' school was organized, and the building appropriately dedicated on the 4th of January, 1844. Col. William L. Stone and Benjamin Ellis made addresses on the occasion. The girls' school was opened for the reception of pupils on the next day, and organized and went into operation on the 8th of the month. On the 1st of February there were in attendance 242 boys and 220 girls.

Mr. Marvin W. Fox organized the boys' school, and sustained it until the time of his resignation, August 1, 1852, when Arthur Murphy succeeded, and continued it until the change of system was made.

Miss Mary C. Kiersted was appointed principal of the girls' department, where she remained till 1845, when she resigned, and was succeeded by Miss H. M. Mackenzie, in whose charge it passed to the care of the ward school officers.

The following entry, by John Inman, appears on the minute-book of the primary department:

January 27, 1845.—Visited the school for the first time, and derived particular gratification from seeing the neatness of appearance and apparent enjoyment of the little ones in their exercises. The school appears to be admirably conducted.   JOHN INMAN.

PUBLIC SCHOOL NO. 18.

The extreme northwestern part of the city, in 1840, was thinly settled, and the wants of the district were supplied by Primary School No. 21, which was provided with accommodations in the basement of the Methodist church in Forty-first street. The population, however, increased with great rapidity, and the necessity for increased facilities, and adapted to a more advanced class of children, became apparent. The section of No. 12, in Seventeenth street, had some discussion on the expediency of opening a new school in the neighborhood of Fortieth street. At a meeting of the Executive Committee of the board, held September 7, 1843, an extract from the minutes of section No. 12 was read, asking for the opening of a school of a higher grade than a primary. The matter was referred to a committee, consisting of Messrs. Murray, Hurd, and Demilt. The committee reported in October, recommending that the basement of the church corner of Eighth avenue and Forty-third street, then building, and which had been hired by the Primary School Committee, be hired by the Executive Committee; that a girls' school be opened therein, under a suitable teacher and assistants; that Primary No. 21, in Forty-first street, be changed to a school for boys, and regularly organized; that they be known as Public School No. 18, and that a special committee be appointed for the purpose.

These recommendations were adopted, and Messrs. John R. Hurd, J. W. Howe, Joseph Curtis, and Linus W. Stevens were appointed said committee. The proper arrangements were made, and the schools were opened for the reception of scholars early in the month of May.

The boys' school was organized on the 14th of May, under James A. Ferguson, in the Methodist church in Forty-first street, near Seventh avenue. The girls' school was organized the same day, in the Baptist church corner of Eighth avenue and Forty-third street, under Amelia Kiersted. Mr. Samuel W. Seton made an address on the occasion.

In the early part of 1845, the demand for increased school accommodations became so urgent, that the section pressed upon the Board of Trustees the inevitable duty of erecting a school-building. At the meeting of the section held on May 12, a resolution was adopted authorizing an application to the board; and one of the section reported that he had secured the refusal of four lots of ground in Forty-seventh street, until the 1st of June following, at the price of $1,900.

The Board of Trustees approved of the measure, but as the state of the funds made it of doubtful expediency to appropriate the money at that time, a committee was appointed, who reported in favor of raising $25,000 by mortgage of property of the Society. This course was adopted, and the means provided. On the 5th of February, 1846, the Executive Committee authorized the Property Committee to issue proposals for estimates, and close contracts for the house as soon as they should be informed by the treasurer that the money had been secured.

The building was opened for the registry of pupils on Monday, November 9, 1846 ; and on the 16th, the public dedicatory exercises were held in the primary department. Addresses were delivered by Samuel W. Seton and William Oland Bourne.

The erection of this edifice gave rise to the question relative to the power of the Public School Society to erect new houses, and it occasioned much anxiety ; for it was a test question which vitally affected its existence as an institution. When its power of expansion ceased and its limits became circumscribed, another and contemporaneous system could not fail to absorb it by its overshadowing growth and patronage. The question was decided in favor of the right of the Society to Public School No. 18, but further expansion was denied. This was, therefore, the last school-building erected by the Society.

On the 5th of October, 1847, the primary department in this school was organized with 117 pupils of both sexes, withdrawn from the upper departments. In October, 1848, the number of pupils had increased to 177, and in October, 1851, there were 436 in attendance.

Mr. James A. Ferguson, the first principal in the boys' school, remained until the 1st of February, 1851, when he was succeeded by William T. Graff, in whose care the school continued until transferred to the Board of Education.

Miss Amelia Kiersted, who organized the girls' department at the original location in the church, continued in uninterrupted service until the change of system took place, by which the Board of Education became the guardian of the schools of the city.

Miss C. C. Cowen was the first principal of the primary department.

[NOTE.—The original numbers of the schools are retained in this chapter. By the sale of No. 10, in Duane Street, the numbers of the remaining schools were changed, and No. 18 became No. 17, under which enumeration the schools passed to the Board of Education. After the transfer the numbers of the Ward Schools were also changed as required by the law, and Ward School No. 1 became No. 18, and others followed in their proper succession.

APPENDIX.

A.

REPORT

Of the Law Committee of the Common Council, to whom were referred the Petitions of Trustees of Church Schools for Participation in the Distribution of the School Fund.

[The law of November 19, 1824, gave to the Common Council the power to appoint ten commissioners of common schools, and to designate the institutions which should be the recipients of the school money. The trustees of St. Patrick's and St. Peter's Roman Catholic schools, the Methodist, and other church schools, submitted their petitions for a continuance of the apportionment to these schools, which were referred to the Law Committee, together with the fourth section of the law. On the 28th of April, 1825, the committee submitted their report.]

The Committee on Laws, to whom were referred the fourth section of the act of the Legislature of this State, relating to common schools in the city of New York, passed the 19th of November, 1824; the memorials of the trustees of the charity schools attached to the Reformed Dutch Church of the city of New York; of the trustees of the First Protestant Episcopal charity school in the city of New York; and of the trustees of the Methodist Episcopal Church, praying respectively for a participation in the common school fund; and also the report of a committee of the trustees of the Free-School Society, on the distribution of the said fund, proposing a change in the constitution of that Society, so as to admit children of all classes to their schools, for a compensation not exceeding fifty cents per quarter, with power to remit in proper cases, REPORT:

That the subject referred to them is one of vital importance to this community, involving, as it does, the high and essential interests of education and of public benevolence in their application to the numerous poor children of our city. The various institutions which have been established for, or have undertaken from the best of motives the relief of this portion of our inhabitants, have been represented before your committee; and their respective claims to a participation respectively in the public bounty have been urged, on the part of their delegates, by all the obligations and motives which could be drawn from the sources of piety and philanthropy, and with all the force and energy of the most persuasive eloquence and the most cogent argument.

These discussions have instructed your committee, and have, at the same time, proved the depth of talent, the eminent virtue, and the laudable public spirit which distinguish those of our fellow-citizens who deservedly take the lead in meliorating the condition of the human race, and especially that of the poor and destitute among the rising generation.

These institutions consist, on the one hand, of the churches and religious societies, many of which maintain charity schools; and, on the other, of societies whose members are of different religious persuasions, and whose exclusive object is the gratuitous instruction of the poor.

On the part of the churches, it has been maintained that the charity schools are of long standing, and have heretofore received the fostering care of the Legislature; that the children are taught in them the branches of a plain, ordinary education, with little or no difference as to efficiency when compared with the other institutions, and in support of this, they offer to submit them to a fair examination; and it is superadded, with much emphasis, that, in these schools, the children receive also the advantages of religious instruction.

On this latter subject it is urged, in the first place, by the advocates of the churches, that for this they receive no compensation; and, in the second, that religion is the best and only foundation of all private happiness, of all sound morality, and of all capacity for public usefulness; and, in answer to the charge of efforts on their part to promote sectarian influence, they deny that such is their intended object; and they further reply and explain, that religion cannot exist but according to some specific form and system; that no religious sentiment can be advanced except of the most general nature, about which professing Christians will not differ; and that the objection would exclude all practical religious instruction whatsoever, since religion must be presented in some definite shape, or it can hardly find access to the heart and become influential on the conduct. And it has, in turn, been argued, " Show me a man of *no sect*, and I will show you a man of *no religion*," and that it is better to have a community of conscientious *sectarians*, than a community of *nothingarians*. And it is further added, that the children attached to the charity schools are habitually instructed in the observance of Sunday, not only by causing them to be kept out of the streets, and to be removed from the temptations and dangers to which they would be there exposed, but by causing them to go to church, and to engage in the duties of that sacred day.

It is further insisted by the churches, that they and the lay corporations together are the only associations for the benevolent purpose of instructing the poor of this city; and that, under the act of the Legislature as it now stands, each will alike be subject to a constant and wholesome supervision on the part of the commissioners appointed by the Common Council. They further contend that there can be no danger of a church establishment growing out of the assistance they wish to receive from this fund, which will fall far short of a *support*, and that the rendering of such *assistance* only is different altogether from endowing or entrusting them with public funds, without a definite and specified object. Under this head, it is maintained that no danger is felt by the General or State Government from the growth of clerical influence, or of its tendency to church establishments, as the employment of chaplains by the House of Representatives, and in the Army and Navy, and also in the State Legislatures, is still continued with the general approbation. The instance of the employment of a chaplain by this board is also mentioned, to prove that no such apprehension is here entertained. It is urged, further, that the State has heretofore directed the division of this fund among the churches maintaining charity schools, and the other lay corporations, as the former wish it still to continue to be divided. That the Legislature of this State has heretofore made to churches considerable grants, and a prominent instance is mentioned of a donation of $4,000 to one of the churches of this city (sec. 37, p. 144) ; and a further and general argument is drawn, favorable to the high literary and intellectual qualifications of the clergy of our country, from the fact that in very many, if not in the large majority of instances, the presidents of colleges and seminaries of learning are chosen from that body by the general consent and approbation of the community at large.

In regard to the argument that children ought to be instructed in catechisms and forms of religion *at home*, as is the case with those taught in the ordinary pay schools, they insist that the situation of poor children, such as are taught in the free and charity schools, does not admit of instruction at home on any subject that is useful, much less that of religion in any form ; and they say that the trustees of the free schools, conscious of this, do teach the children under their care *some* religion, but of that kind and in that degree which is calculated to meet the views of numerous and influential sects of Christians. And on the subject of the prevalence of sectarianism, and the common anxiety to extirpate it, it has been very strenuously insisted that, should either of the lay corporations have the entire benefit of this fund, the so much apprehended effects of sectarian jealousy and animosity would soon be experienced by that body, and that its members would become the subjects, and its place of meeting be transformed into the arena, of their baneful operations. Assuming, therefore, what is predicted of them, the delegates of the churches contend that this sectarian tendency, if it be an evil, is now kept within reasonable limits by encouraging all religious denominations ; whereas, by placing its now divided forces into a more concentrated form, its native intensity would be excited, and the consequences would be fatal to the body or the association which it might infect.

These are some of the most prominent reasons on which the claims of the churches are rested for a participation in this fund.

On the other hand, and in behalf of those institutions not of an ecclesiastical description, but formed out of all religious persuasions indiscriminately, it is insisted that the common school fund will soon become of very large amount, and the annual distribution be consequently greatly increased.

And it is asked, Shall such a portion of the public moneys be placed in any degree under clerical influence? A proposition to tax the people for the support of religion, it is said, would never have been sustained by the Convention of 1777, nor by that of 1821; and the Common Council is now called upon officially to act, as those bodies would have acted had they been called upon to settle this question. The churches, it is alleged, ought not to participate in this fund, because it would be in violation of that rule of civil policy admitted to be prevalent, which forbids all connection between matters of Church and those of State, and upon which the fourth section of the seventh article of the present Constitution, and which is reënacted from the old, is founded, forbidding any minister of the gospel from holding any civil or military office.

It is strongly contended that the trustees of churches are irresponsible to, and independent of, any civil authority, being appointed not by a special law of the Legislature, but by their own act, under the general law for the incorporation of religious societies. That this state of irresponsibility and independence is calculated to produce relaxation in discipline, and an enfeebled attention on their part to the minute and perplexing business of education; and that, as to this branch of their duties, there is no control over them whatsoever.

That part of this fund is raised by tax, and to devote any portion of it, so that by possibility it may be turned into sectarian channels, would be to compel one portion of the community, without their consent, to become the supporters of the religious opinions of others. That to pay teachers of sectarian schools out of this fund, is the same thing, in effect, as to pay the clergymen of the congregations; and that sectarian purposes may be equally promoted by teaching children as by maintaining clergymen.

That, when it is maintained that religion is taught in the charity schools, it must be understood that the catechisms and confessions of the churches are taught, and that, though religious creeds and dogmas are equally tolerated by the law, it by no means follows that all are equally true and equally entitled to support; and that it is impossible they should all be true and equally entitled to support, since some are directly opposed and contradictory to the others. It is further maintained, that one system or the other must be the best, and entitled to a preference; and that, therefore, if a religious education be the best, and entitled to such preference as relates to this fund, the institutions promoting and inculcating it ought to be established, and every other prostrated and condemned.

That churches and religious societies have no common standard, no common principle, and can be subjected to no common superintendence or inspection; and that the school fund, which is founded on taxation and public income, shall be applied indiscriminately to the support of all holding such conflicting and irreconcilable tenets, it will follow, not only that error will be placed on the same ground with truth, and receive at least an equal share of support with it, but that it will produce an unequal, and consequently unjust bearing on different members of the same community, who contribute in the same proportion to this as to the other public burdens.

It is maintained that religious societies do not admit of visitations as such ; and in reply to any proposed discrimination between the churches or their schools, it is said that any provision in favor of one must be founded on a principle which, in its operation, will admit all alike—the long-established with the one of yesterday—the one venerable for its antiquity and its well-acquired reputation for piety and usefulness, with another which may be the offspring of cupidity and speculation, and under the direction of an individual of questionable morality, and set up for the very purpose of depredating on the public charity and munificence, and, consequently, on the hard earnings of the people, which are the sources of that charity and munificence. On the subject of aiding in the support of churches, which, it is contended, results from the late law, and the practice under it, it is strongly urged that true religion requires and admits of no aid from the secular power ; that her only resources are from heaven, and the contributions of willing hearts ; that she seeks only for protection, and not for support ; and that the arm of the State, though strong, has no potency or legitimate control beyond such protection.

These propositions, it is contended, are unanswerable in themselves, and derive great strength from the example of every other county in this State where the common school fund is confined in its application to the purposes of a common or literary education alone, and is not permitted to receive the least share of religious or clerical influence in its distribution ; and also from the examples of some of our sister States, who, in the recent revision of their constitutions, have severally struck from these instruments the provision formerly incorporated in them, favorable to ecclesiastical participation in similar funds in these States.

And it is further contended that, on this very subject, we are admonished and instructed by an act which passed the Assembly (though not the Senate of this State) in the year 1824, founded on the report of a committee of that body, in which the committee state that " the city of New York is the only part of the State where the school fund is at all subject to the control of religious societies. This fund is considered by your committee purely of a civil character, and therefore it ought never, in their opinion, to pass into the hands of any corporation or set of men who are not directly amenable to the constituted civil authorities of the Government, and bound to report their proceedings to the public." And that committee more than intimate that, in their opinion, it would be " a violation of a fundamental principle of legislation to allow the funds of the State, raised by a tax on the citizens, designed for civil purposes, to be subject to the control of any religious corporation."

In regard to religious instruction, it is contended, on the part of the civil or lay corporations, that they cause to be communicated, in imitation of the Bible Society, who publish the Scriptures without note or comment, such precepts, in the form of reading-lessons and catechisms, in the original language of the Bible, on such interesting and familiar subjects of human duty and obligations as children can best comprehend. And as to the specific or sectarian forms of religion, they leave them to be communicated by the parents or guardians at home, or by the churches or Sunday schools, to which it is their constant wish and direction that the children may be sent.

It is further maintained that, if the system which, until lately, was tolerated in this city, should now be revived and perpetuated, the consequence will be a continued and more successful rivalry than heretofore, not on the part of the old, settled, and well-conducted churches, but by others which may be set on foot to discover which can obtain the greatest number of scholars on their registers, and to whose principal object the business of instructing and training up poor children will be altogether subsidiary; and that, while these will be depredating on this fund, which is designed for the most beneficent purposes, the free schools, which have been unparalleled in their useful effects upon the poor, will fall into decay, and become utterly abandoned.

In the conclusion of the argument on this side of the question, it is stated that, before the existence of the common school fund, the charity schools flourished and increased, and, in all probability, will continue to have the same success from the liberality of their friends and patrons. That the free schools will be open for those children who may be left without a charity school, should the churches not be permitted hereafter to participate in this fund; that the instances of such destitution are not likely to be numerous; and that, at all events, a greater number of poor children will be instructed in the free schools alone, than are instructed in all the institutions at present partaking of this fund, in consequence of the more concentrated and successful efforts which they will be enabled to make by the erection of such buildings and the employment of such teachers as may be required, if the common school fund shall be appropriated and expended in the manner proposed by them.

And it is added, that the following are among the further results which may be expected from this mode of distribution :

First, an increased economy in the expenditure and use of the public moneys, arising form the singleness of the object to which they will be devoted, whereby the greatest quantity of good may be expected from the smallest amount of means.

Second, the utmost expedition in the acquirement of useful knowledge by the poor children at large, and in all sections of our city, by reason of the highly-improved methods which are established, and the excellent teachers which are employed in the free schools.

Third, a greater uniformity in the rule, government, and branches of instruction which will be pursued in the public seminaries, than can be expected at present in the diversified and variously conducted schools of the churches and other societies.   •

These are among the reasons urged by the lay, in opposition to the religious societies, why the latter should be excluded, and the former alone receive the benefit of this fund.

Your committee have thus, with the single desire of truth, laid before the Common Council the result of their inquiries, and the substance of the communications that have been made to them.

In the performance of this duty, they have felt all the importance and responsibility of the task assigned to them; and while they would willingly have retired from the appointment, and do each individually wish that the Legislature had passed the necessary law on this subject, on the recent application to them for that purpose, yet your committee cannot permit themselves to hesitate or falter in the course of public duty, when that course is plainly manifest to their understandings. Your committee will not conceal either their own private and personal wishes at the commencement of their duties, that the well-organized churches and religious societies in our city might be permitted to continue in the reception of a part of this fund as heretofore; but the weight of the argument, as urged before them, and which they have endeavored to condense in this report, and the established constitutional and political doctrines which have a bearing on this question, and the habits and modes of thinking of the constituents at large of this board, require, in the opinion of your committee, that the common school fund should be distributed for civil purposes only, as contradistinguished from those of a religious or sectarian description.

As to the existing institutions among which it is now divided, the Common Council will give to the reasons and arguments which have been stated, such weight as they may deserve, on the decision of the question whether they in general ought to participate in the division of a fund drawn in part like the present, from the people, by taxation.

But it would seem to your committee to be a departure from the most ordinary prudence, to permit such religious societies as might hereafter spring up and choose to add to their establishments a charity school, to partake indiscriminately of this fund, since neither the character of their managers and conductors, nor the object which such societies might have in view, could now be foreseen or apprehended. And the arguments and constitutional barriers, and the modes of thinking of our citizens before mentioned, are conclusive, in the opinion of your committee, why any one church or religious society now established, however exemplary or meritorious, equally with all others, should be excluded from a participation in this fund.

In regard to the project contained in the report of a committee of the trustees of the Free-School Society, proposing a change in their constitution, your committee have concluded, as it would require an application to the Legislature before it could be carried into execution, and the present session is probably too far advanced for that purpose, to recommend that it be laid on the table for further consideration.

On the main subject referred to your committee, they beg leave to submit the accompanying draft of an ordinance to the consideration of the Common Council.   Respectfully submitted,

S. COWDREY,
THOMAS BOLTON,
E. W. KING.

46

B.

[At a meeting of the trustees of Roman Catholic churches, held at St. Peter's Church, Barclay street, February 17, 1840 (see page 179), a petition to the Common Council was adopted, which was submitted to the Board of Assistant Aldermen on March 2, when the trustees of the Public School Society submitted a remonstrance. On the 16th of March, the Hebrew congregation in Crosby street, and the Scotch Presbyterian Church, presented a petition for school money. Remonstrances were presented from Lockwood Smith and 209 others; William Holmes and 61 others; the Public School Society, the Methodist Episcopal Church, and Reformed Protestant Dutch churches. On March 30, a remonstrance was presented from the East Broome street Baptist Church, and from S. Devereaux and others. On April 13, the remonstrance from the Reformed Presbyterian Church was presented. These papers were referred to the Committee on Arts, Sciences, and Schools, who reported April 27th.]

DOCUMENT NO. 80.

BOARD OF ASSISTANT ALDERMEN, *April* 27, 1840.

Report of the Committee on Arts and Sciences and Schools, on the petition of the officers and members of the Roman Catholic and other Churches in the city of New York, for an apportionment of school moneys to the schools attached to said churches. Presented by Mr. Dodge. Adopted, and two thousand copies ordered to be printed, with the accompanying petitions and remonstrances, under the direction of the committee.

EDWARD PATTERSON, *Clerk.*

The Committee on Arts and Sciences and Schools of the Board of Assistants, to whom were referred the petitions of the trustees and members of the several Roman Catholic churches in the city of New York, the Scotch Presbyterian Church in said city, and the Hebrew congregation in Crosby street, for an appropriation of a portion of the school moneys to the schools attached to said churches or congregations; and to whom were also referred the resolutions of the Commissioners of School Money, and the remonstrances of the Public School Society, and of other societies and individuals, against making such appropriations, respectfully REPORT:

The subject-matter referred to your committee is one of the highest importance, not only as regards the rights and interests of the petitioners, but as it affects the great cause of public education, the wishes and feelings of the people at large, the intentions of the founders of the existing system of public instruction, and the requirements of the Constitution and laws of the State. Fully impressed with the magnitude of the questions involved, the committee proceeded to the examination of the subject with an anxious desire to render complete justice to all, to advance the interests of the public, and extend the benefits of education to the utmost possible limit. Knowing that many objections were urged by a large and respectable portion of our citizens against the prayer of the petitioners, and that much excitement existed among the petitioners, and in the public mind generally, upon the subject, the committee deemed it their duty to give all parties an opportunity of fully and thoroughly discussing the merits of the question before them. For this purpose, public notice was given that the committee would meet, for the purpose of considering the subject, on the 12th day of March, in the chamber of this board, and all who felt interested were invited to attend. The petitioners on the part of the Roman Catholic churches appeared at the time and place appointed for the meeting, by a committee of three gentlemen appointed for that purpose. The Public School Society, one of the remonstrant parties, also appeared by a committee.

It is unnecessary to detail fully the proceedings of the committee at this meeting. It is sufficient to say, that both the parties who appeared had every opportunity of stating their views to the committee, and that a full discussion of the subject was had. On the part of the petitioners who appeared, it was stated that there were, in the city of New York, seven Roman Catholic churches, each of which maintained a free school, established for the purpose of educating the children of the poor attached to their respective congregations. This, it appears, is the primary object in establishing the schools; though the children of persons attached to other religious denominations are not excluded, and do, in fact, attend them. It was further stated that no religious test or qualification was requisite to admission, and that no means were used to alter the religious views of the child of a person not attached to the Catholic Church. This statement, your committee have no doubt, is correct.

Objection was made, on the part of the Catholic petitioners, to the public schools now existing and supported from the school fund, on the ground that no religious instruction was communicated there; or, if any was given, it was of a character which reflected upon the doctrines of the Catholic Church. The latter branch of this objection was denied on the part of the Public School Society.

The petitioners who appeared also contended that they contributed, in common with all other citizens who were taxed for the purpose, to the accumulation of the common school fund, and that they were therefore entitled to participate in its advantages; that now they received no benefit from the fund, inasmuch as the members of the Catholic churches could not conscientiously send their children to schools in which the religious doctrines of their fathers were exposed to ridicule or censure. The truth and justice of the first branch of this proposition cannot be questioned. The correctness of the latter part of the argument, so far as the same relates to books or exercises of any kind in the public schools reflecting on the Catholic Church, was, as is hereinbefore stated, denied by the School Society.

On the part of the Public School Society, it was contended that any appropriation of the school money to any religious denomination, for the purpose of educating the children of that denomination, was foreign to the design of the common school system as organized by law, hostile to the spirit of the Constitution, and at variance with the nature of our free institutions.

It may be proper here to state that, in the argument, it was admitted, on the part of the Catholic petitioners, that, in the schools attached to their churches, religious instruction in the doctrines of the Church would be given after the usual school hours, with the understanding that no child would be required to attend at that time without the approval of the parents.

The preceding is a brief abstract of the views presented to your committee by the petitioners and remonstrants. It is important that a statement of these views should be presented in this form to the board, that they may fully understand the wishes of the parties, and through them, as far as they can be ascertained in this way, the feelings and opinions of the public.

Upon the facts presented to the committee, two questions have arisen of great moment to the people of this city and State. These questions have received our most attentive examination, and the conclusions to which the committee have arrived are such, they trust, as will meet the concurrence of the board and the approval of the public.

The questions to which the committee have directed their attention are as follows:

First: Have the Common Council of this city, under the existing laws relative to common schools in the city of New York, a legal right to appropriate any portion of the school fund to religious corporations?

Second: Would the exercise of such power be in accordance with the spirit of the Constitution and the nature of our Government?

It is undeniable that the Common Council of the city of New York have, by statute, the power of designating the "institutions and schools" which shall participate in the benefits of the common school fund. Under the statute confirming this power, the question naturally arises, What associations of individuals does the phrase "institutions and schools" include? A brief view of the legislation of the State upon the subject of public instruction in this city will throw much light upon the subject.

The common school system of the State of New York was designed by the people, through whose representatives in the Legislature it was organized, to afford to every child the opportunity of acquiring a plain and practical education of that character which would fit him for the ordinary business of life. To afford to all citizens the privilege of educating their children under the public care and at the public charge, the Legislature perceived the necessity of placing the schools beyond the reach of those influences which might render them obnoxious to the feelings of any citizen. To avoid the introduction of subjects of instruction into the schools that might by possibility lead to the creation of angry and unpleasant feelings in the little neighborhoods which compose the school districts of the State, the entire management and control of the schools, in the first instance, was given by law to commissioners, inspectors, and trustees, elected immediately by the people of the several towns and districts. Private associations and religious corporations were excluded from the management of the funds and the government of the schools. Private interest, under this system, could not appropriate the public treasure to private purposes, and religious zeal could not divert them to the purposes of proselytism. The watchful eye of an interested community guarded the treasure of the schools, and mutual jealousy prevented the introduction of any system of education into the school-room which might by possibility be the means of propagating the doctrines of any denomination at the expense of others. It is evident from the strictly popular character of the system of public instruction as originally established, that the Legislature intended the public school fund to be employed for the purpose of communicating to the children of the State instruction of a strictly secular character, altogether unconnected with either political or religious education. This system for the government of the schools has existed in the State, excepting in the city of New York and some other cities, from the year 1812 to the present time, and has been productive of the happiest results.

The first general act for the establishment of common schools was passed in the year 1812. By that act the common school system was organized in the manner and with the design hereinbefore stated. All the provisions of the act in question did not extend to this city. The officers charged with the expenditure of the school money and the supervision of the schools in the city of New York, were not intended to be elected by the people, nor were the people, through their immediate representatives, to exercise a direct control over the subject. A subsequent act was passed on the 12th of March, 1813, relative to common schools in this city (and supplementary to the act of 1812), by which the Commissioners of School Moneys were directed to pay the moneys received by them to " the trustees of the Free-School Society in the city of New York " (now known as the Public School Society), and to " the trustees or teachers of the Orphan Asylum Society, the Society of the Economical School in the city of New York, the African Free School, and of such incorporated religious societies in said city as now support, or hereafter shall establish, charity schools within the said city, who may apply for the same," &c. Revised Laws, vol. 1, p. 267.

It will be perceived that, by this act, " incorporated religious societies " were expressly named as proper recipients of the public bounty provided for the support of common schools ; and it appears, too, from the language of the act, that the commissioners had no discretion as to the admission or exclusion of religious societies from a participation in the fund. The law was imperative in its character, and the several religious societies of the city possessed a legal right to draw their respective portions of the fund from the public treasury, subject only to the restriction that the money so received should be appropriated to the purposes of free and common education. Under this law many churches of different denominations participated in the benefits of the school fund. At different periods, special acts of the Legislature were passed, conferring portions of the same fund upon several charitable societies other than those of a sectarian character. Another act, which eventually led to the change in the system, which your committee are about to state, was passed in 1822, authorizing the Bethel Baptist Church (then one of the participants in the school fund) " to employ the surplus of school money in their hands in the erection of school-houses and all other needful purposes of a common school education, but for no other purpose whatever." Under this act gross abuses occurred, and the funds received by the church were applied to other purposes than those contemplated by the act. This misapplication of the public money, devoted to the sacred purpose of common education, induced the Legislature, in the session of 1824, not to repeal the act passed for the benefit of the Bethel Church, and under which the abuses in question had occurred, but to repeal that portion of the act of 1813 which included "incorporated religious societies" among the recipients of the school fund. The committee will proceed to state the extent and manner of the repeal in detail.

On the 19th of November, 1824, the Legislature, in consequence of the abuses of the Bethel Church, and evidently with a view to guard against the recurrence of similar or any abuses thereafter, passed a general act, entering fully into details, for the better management of the school fund in the city of New York. By this act many important alterations in the system were effected; and, among others, the whole power of selecting the recipients of the school moneys was delegated to the Common Council. The act to which your committee refer is entitled, "An Act Relating to Common Schools in the City of New York." By the fifth section of this law it is provided as follows: "The institutions or schools which shall be entitled to receive of said school moneys, shall, from time to time, and at least once in three years, be designated by the Corporation of the city of New York, in common council convened, who shall also have power to prescribe the limitations and restrictions under which said moneys shall be received by said institutions or schools, or any of them." Laws of 1824, p. 338. By the ninth section it is provided that the act take effect on the 15th day of May, 1825, and that, from and after that day, the act entitled " An Act Supplementary to the Act, Entitled ' An Act for the Establishment of Common Schools,' " passed the 12th of March, 1813, and all, each and every other act or section and sections of acts heretofore passed, relating to common schools, to moneys arising from the school fund of the State, or to the distribution or apportionment thereof, so far as relates to, or in any wise concerns, the city and county of New York, and societies supporting charity schools therein, and no further, is and are hereby repealed. Laws of 1824, p. 339.

Previous to 1824, the Legislature of the State designated the societies or schools who were entitled to receive a portion of the school fund, but by the act of that year, reënacted in the Revised Statutes, that power is conferred upon the Common Council; and the question now presented to the board is, whether the Common Council have an unlimited discretion in the matter, or whether they are subject to any limitation; and if so, to what?

By the school act of 1812, "incorporated religious societies" supporting or establishing charity schools were expressly named as entitled to receive, with other societies, their ratable proportions of the school fund. One of the "incorporated religious societies" participating in the fund, and authorized by law to employ it for a special purpose, misapplied the money and abused the trust reposed in it. The Legislature immediately thereafter repealed the law of 1813, under which religious societies were then recipients of the money, and authorized the Common Council to designate the "institutions" and "schools" which should be entitled to receive it.

There is something peculiar in the language of the repealing act of 1824, which fully satisfies your committee that the Legislature intended, ever after, to exclude religious corporations from the reception of the school moneys. In the act of 1813 they are named as "incorporated religious societies," and this is the only act under which they ever received any portion of the fund.

By the act of 1824, "institutions" and "schools" are to receive it. It would require much ingenuity to induce any person to believe that the Legislature of the State would, in a solemn legal enactment, describe a church as an "institution" or a "school." The language employed, your committee believe, should be constructed in its plain and familiar meaning; and it must be evident to all, that if the Legislature, in 1824, intended to confer any portion of the school fund upon religious societies, they would have used the words found in the act of 1813, or words of a similar import.

The attention of the board is also called to that part of the ninth section of the act of 1824 which repeals the act of 1813, relative to common schools in this city. This section declares, in the most unequivocal and forcible manner, "that the act of 1813, and all and every other act or sections of acts relating to the distribution and apportionment of the school fund, so far as the same relates to the city of New York, and to societies supporting charity schools therein, are repealed." No language can be more clear and explicit than this, and your committee cannot hesitate in expressing it to be their opinion that the only authority under which religious societies participated in the school fund, was contained in the act of 1813: and that this act was repealed by the Legislature with the full intention that religious societies, as such, should no longer receive any portion of the school money from the public treasury, even for the purpose of supporting common schools. This opinion of your committee is confirmed by the almost universal opinion of the people of this city, from 1824 to the present time.

It is undeniable that the Common Council have a general discretion as to the schools to be supported by the public money; but it appears to your committee that the intentions of the Legislature and the people, although not reduced to the form of a positive legal enactment, should, so far as they can be gathered from the proceedings of the Legislature, be respected by the Common Council. Believing that the act of 1824 was intended to prevent a participation in the school moneys by religious societies, your committee suggest to the board, that their power to apportion the fund among societies of that character, is, at the least, very questionable; and that a prudent regard for the obligations of duty should prevent the exercise of so doubtful a power in any case whatever.

It may be proper here to observe, that the act of 1824, relative to the distribution of school moneys in the city of New York, was reënacted in the Revised Statutes (vol. 1, new ed., p. 483). In the reënactment of this statute, the words "societies or schools" are used in defining the recipients of the fund. It may be urged that the alteration of the language of the act in question indicated an intention on the part of the Legislature to return to the system of distribution established by the act of 1813. But your committee cannot entertain this view of the subject. The revisors of the laws were appointed to digest and codify the then existing statute law of the State. In the performance of this duty, they, in various instances adopted language which they believed to be more clear, explicit, or appropriate than that of the original act. The language of the Revised Statutes, in relation to the subject under consideration, may perhaps be preferable, in some respects, to that of the original act of 1824, but it certainly cannot be construed as intended to alter the legal effect of that law. It relates to the same subject-matter, and is virtually declared to be a reënactment of the former act, by the reference contained in the accompanying note; and the committee can therefore adopt no rule of construction that would defeat the object of that act, which it was evidently the design of the revisors and the Legislature to confirm and perpetuate.

The same remark may be made in relation to the provisions of the Revised Statutes that was made in reference to the act of 1824. If the revisors or the Legislature intended to include religious corporations among the recipients of the school fund, they would have used the words " incorporated religious societies," or words of a similar meaning and import.

There is another important view of the subject to which the committee would call the attention of the board. The Constitution of the State, in the following impressive language, secures to every citizen the utmost liberty of conscience : " The free exercise and enjoyment of religious profession and worship, without discrimination or preference, shall forever be allowed, in this State, to all mankind." Art. 7, sec. 3. There can be no constitutional guarantee more full and general than this; and it was certainly the object of the convention which framed, and of the people who adopted, the Constitution, to prevent the Legislature of the State, and all other branches of the Government, from creating any distinctions between citizens on account of religious faith, or giving to one sect any preference or advantage over another. That this is the object of the constitutional provision referred to, none can deny. The question then arises, How far will the appropriation of the school moneys asked for by the petitioners conflict with the requirements and intentions of the Constitution? This branch of the subject has been attentively considered by your committee, and they offer the following as the results of their deliberations :

The people of the State of New York are divided into almost innumerable religious sects and denominations. These different sects view the progress of each other with watchful jealousy. The natural desire that all men possess, to make converts to the opinions which they have honestly formed and zealously maintain, ever has led, and ever will lead, to exertions and struggles to extend those opinions to the utmost limit. This is true of all opinions; but the history of the world proves that it applies more justly to religious opinion than to any other. The Old World, and even our own country, has witnessed not only religious zeal endeavoring to make proselytes to its own faith by the means of persuasion, argument, and even denunciation; but persecution for opinion's sake is known to the history of every civilized government. Religious zeal, degenerating into fanaticism and bigotry, has covered many battle-fields with its victims; the stake, the gibbet, and the prison have fallen to the lot of countless martyrs; exile from the land of their nativity, expulsion from the seats of civilization to the wilderness of the savage, have been experienced by hundreds of almost every sect, who could not honestly subscribe to the religious opinions of the majority. To prevent, in our day and country, the recurrence of scenes so abhorrent to every principle of justice, humanity, and right, the Constitutions of the United States and of the several States have declared, in some form or other, that there should be no establishment of religion by law; that the affairs of the State should be kept entirely distinct from, and unconnected with, those of the Church; that every human being should worship God according to the dictates of his own conscience; that all churches and religions should be supported by voluntary contribution; and that no tax should ever be imposed for the benefit of any denomination of religion, for any cause or under any pretence whatever. These principles are either expressly declared in the several constitutions, or arise by necessary implication from the nature of our Government and the character of our republican institutions.

In the cases before your committee, the petitioners ask for an appropriation of the public money to the support of schools established by, and conducted under the control of, certain religious corporations; and these schools, in the one case, are established principally for the instruction of the children of indigent members of the Roman Catholic Church. The teachers—if your committee are correctly informed—are appointed by the trustees of those churches, and the plan of instruction pursued is adopted by the same officers. This plan includes religious instruction at stated periods, to be communicated by means of the catechism of the Catholic Church. Your committee are unable to say positively whether any devotional exercises are used or required in the schools; but they regard this as immaterial to be considered in this stage of the question. They are also unable to state whether any religious instruction is given, or intended to be given, in the schools of the other petitioners—the Scotch Presbyterian Church, and the Hebrew congregation. The schools sought to be supported from the public treasury (being controlled by religious corporations) are, to that extent, religious schools.

To a correct understanding of the relation this case bears to the constitutional provisions and principles hereinbefore referred to, it will be necessary to refer briefly to the sources and present extent of the school fund appropriated to the city of New York. This fund arises, in part, from the annual income of the proceeds of lands sold by the State, which belonged to the people of the State in common, the interest of the United States Deposit Fund, and also from annual taxation upon the people of this city.

The amount received from the State Treasury in the
   year 1838 was, ... $34,172.47
Amount of tax raised by the Corporation for common
   schools, under the general law relating to common
   schools, for the same year,   .   .   .   34,172.47
Amount of tax raised in this city for common school
   purposes, under special statutes, in the same year,   73,150.00
                                                        _____
                                                        $141,494.94

The whole amount received from the school fund of the State, the common property of the people, is $34,172.47. The amount raised by tax in the city of New York, for the support of common schools for 1838, was $107,322.47, or nearly the one twelfth part of the whole amount of taxes levied in this city.

It is urged, on the part of the Catholic petitioners, that they, as taxpayers, contribute to the fund thus annually raised, and that they are therefore entitled to participate in its benefits. This is undoubtedly true; but it should be borne in mind that they are taxed not as members of the Roman Catholic Church, but as citizens of the State of New York; and not for the purposes of religion, but for the support of civil government. The Constitution acknowledges no distinctions among men on account of their religious faith; and your committee would call the attention of the petitioners to the fact that our institutions are designed not to create or perpetuate religious distinctions, but to place all mankind upon a common footing of equality. Any legal acknowledgment of any religious denomination, as a dependant upon the public bounty for any kind of pecuniary aid or support, would be an abandonment of the great constitutional principle, that the end and aim of all just government is the equal protection of all men in the free exercise and enjoyment of the rights derived from the written Constitution of the land, or the still higher authority of nature. The appropriation of any portion of the public treasure to the Roman Catholic or any other churches in this city, must be regarded as violative of this great doctrine. Admit the correctness of the claim that the Common Council of the city, or the Legislature of the State, may rightfully appropriate the public money to the purposes of religious instruction of any kind in any school, and the consequence will be, that the people are taxed by law for the support of some one or other of our numerous religious denominations. The amount of one hundred and seven thousand dollars and upward, as hereinbefore stated, has been raised by annual tax in this city, for purposes of a purely civil and secular character. An appropriation of any portion of that sum to the support of schools in which the religious tenets of any sect are taught to any extent, would be a legal establishment of one denomination of religion over another, would conflict with all the principles and purposes of our free institutions, and would violate the very letter of that part of our Constitution which so emphatically declares that "the free exercise and enjoyment of religious profession and worship, without *discrimination or preference*, shall forever be allowed, in this State, to all mankind." By granting a portion of the school fund to one sect, to the exclusion of others, a "*preference*" is at once created, a "*discrimination*" is made, and the object of this great constitutional guarantee is defeated ; taxes are imposed for the support of religion, and freedom of conscience, if not directly trammelled and confined, is not left in the perfect and unshackled state which our systems of government were intended to establish and perpetuate. It requires no argument to prove that taxation of all sects, for the benefit of one, is a violation of the rights of conscience. No difference can be perceived, in principle, between the taxing of the people of England for the support of a church establishment there, and the taxing of the people of New York for the support of schools in which the doctrines of religious denominations are taught here. It is immaterial whether the amount of tax imposed is great or small ; so long as a tax is imposed for the purposes of religious instruction to the slightest possible extent, that tax is unauthorized by the Constitution, violates the rights of conscience, defeats, to some extent, the purposes, and conflicts with the spirit, of our free institutions.

It may be said, in reply to these observations, that all constitutional difficulties will be removed, by admitting all religious denominations to a participation in the fund. This, your committee have no doubt, the petitioners would willingly assent to. The petitioners have no desire of securing a portion of the fund for themselves, and excluding others from the enjoyment of the same advantages. They are willing that other sects should establish schools on similar principles with their own, and that those schools should receive equal encouragement from the public with theirs. These remarks are made with a view to exonerate the petitioners from the suspicion of having been influenced by selfish or illiberal motives. The committee are fully satisfied that they have acted under a conviction of duty, but with an erroneous view of their rights as religious societies, the provisions of the law, and the powers of the Common Council, and not from a desire to advance the interests of the several churches to which they are attached, at the expense of the Constitution.

An extension to all other denominations of the bounty asked for by the petitioners would be not only impracticable, but would be, equally with the grant sought by the Roman Catholic churches, and the Scotch Presbyterian and Hebrew congregations, repugnant to the principles of our Government. If the doctrines of all the religious denominations in the State were taught in the slightest degree at the expense of the people, under the authority of law, there would still be a legal religious establishment, not confined to one or a few sects, it is true, but covering many. Taxes, under such a system, would still be raised for religious purposes ; and those who professed no religion, or belonged to no sect, would be taxed for the benefit of those who did. It is immaterial, in the eye of the law, whether a citizen professes any or no religious faith ; he is still a citizen, and, as such, is entitled to the free enjoyment of whatever opinions he may entertain : and there is no difference, in legal principles, between taxing him for the purpose of educating the young in the doctrines of many churches, to which he does not belong, and taxing the Catholic for the benefit of Protestant schools, or taxing the

Protestant for the support of Catholic seminaries. The rights of conscience are the same in the one case as in the other; and the cases are identical in principle, although, in the one instance, but few may deem themselves injured, and, in the other, thousands may complain of the violation of their rights as free citizens. No government can rightfully deprive any—the humblest being—of the rights which he may derive from nature as a man, or of those which he possesses as a citizen under the Constitution of his country.

There are insuperable objections to dividing the school fund among religious societies for the support of schools. The dependence upon the bounty of .the civil government which it induces, is as foreign to the nature and character of the Christian religion as it is hostile to the theory of our Government. Religion needs not the support of secular power; its appeals are to the judgments and hearts of men. Truth is its only weapon; and the only shield it requires is that of broad and equal protection. Religious liberty is necessary to the free development of religious truth. That liberty all sects possess in the fullest degree, and no sect can rightfully procure more. The purity of the Church and the safety of the State are more surely obtained by a distinct and separate existence of the two than by their union. The opinions of the American people are settled upon this subject, and they will observe with jealous anxiety any approaches to a reëstablishment of the exploded doctrine that it is the duty of the State to protect the religious interests of the people, or propagate, at the public expense, the doctrines of any faith, however true they may be.

The division of the school fund among the different religious denominations of the city would lead to the most unfortunate results. If a division of this character should be made, it would be, doubtless, in proportion to the number of children taught in each school. The schools, although free to all that might desire to enter, would be mainly sectarian in their character. To increase the number of scholars in each school, and thus secure to themselves as large a share of the public bounty as possible, would be the natural desire of each denomination. The main object of the interested parties would be, to make proselytes to their respective faiths, and thus to increase the power and numerical strength of the several churches, and the number and extent of the several schools. The consequence of this state of things it would be difficult to imagine. Jealousies, rivalries, and dissensions would supplant those gentler feelings which should guide and mark the conduct of men toward each other in civil society. Bigotry, fanaticism, and violence might assume the place of charity, meekness, and love; and thus a train of evils be induced, destructive to the true interests of religion, and dangerous to the harmony, the permanency, and the freedom of the State. The history of the world teems with examples of religious excitement degenerating into wild and embittered fanaticism; jealousies converted into open dissensions, and dissensions ripening into wars, and those wars devastating whole nations, until the angry feelings of the partisans were satiated by the blood of their victims.

If the school money should be divided among the religious denominations generally, as some have proposed, there will be nothing left for the support of schools of a purely civil character; and if there should be, in such a state of things, any citizen who could not, according to his opinions of right and wrong, conscientiously send his child to the school of an existing sect, there would be no public school in which he could be educated. This might, and probably would, be the case with hundreds of our citizens. The committee would ask, if any individual could desire to see a fellow-citizen, however humble he might be, deprived of the opportunity of procuring for his child that education which, as a citizen and a taxpayer, he has a right to demand?

An objection is urged by the Roman Catholic petitioners against the schools of the Public School Society, to the effect that no religious instruction is there given; or, if any is given, it is of a character which reflects upon the doctrines of the Catholic Church. The committee are disposed to believe that there is some error in relation to this matter. They have been informed, by the officers of the Public School Society, that no books are used in their schools which reflect in any degree upon the Catholic Church. At the meeting of the committee referred to in the preceding part of this report, several officers of the Public School Society, then present, offered to submit the text-books of the schools to the inspection of the highest clerical officers of that Church for examination, and freely proffered to purge from the exercises and books of the schools every thing (if any could be found) that exposed the Roman Catholic Church, or any thing connected with it, to ridicule or censure.

If any books are used in the public schools relating, in the slightest degree, to the doctrines or ceremonies of the Roman Catholic or any other religious denomination, the directors of the schools, or other proper officers, should cause them to be immediately removed. If religious instruction is communicated, it is foreign to the intentions of the school system, and should be instantly abandoned. Religious instruction is no part of a common school education. The church and the fireside are the proper seminaries, and parents and pastors are the proper teachers of religion. In their hands the cause of religion is safe. Let the public schoolmaster confine his attention to the moral and intellectual education of the young committed to his charge, and he fully performs the duties of his profession, discharges the trust reposed in him as a public agent, and fulfils his obligations as a citizen.

The committee have given the subject referred to them a thorough consideration, and they feel bound to say that, in their opinion, the petitioners, coming before the Common Council in the capacity of religious denominations, have not made out a valid claim to a participation in the common school fund in that capacity. The reasons that have led the committee to this conclusion are hereinbefore stated. The intentions of the Legislature, the will of the people as expressed through their representatives, and the imperative requirements of the Constitution, preclude the Common Council (in the opinion of the committee) from granting their petitions. In arriving at this opinion, the committee have not had reference to one or a few, but to all denominations in religion ; and had such a petition been present ed from the other denominations in this city, all would have received from the committee the answer that is given to these. No desire exists to include one sect in the benefits of the school fund, and exclude others, but the object of the committee has been, to keep that fund sacredly appropriated to the purposes for which it was created—the purposes of free and common secular education. To this purpose all the provisions of our laws and all the requirements of our Constitution invariably tend ; and the committee can do nothing but suggest to the board that the obligations of the laws and the Constitution are such, that the appropriation of the school fund asked for in the several petitions before them, cannot be rightfully granted.

In this opinion, your committee hope, the board, the petitioners, and the public will concur. The question is one of that character which appeals to the liveliest feelings of our nature, and one which is too apt to create excitement and jealousy. That this may not be the case among any portion of our citizens, your committee most earnestly desire. They conclude by expressing the hope that the petitioners, upon a full examination of the question, will perceive that the granting of their petition would be at least of doubtful legality, foreign to the design of the school fund, and at variance with the spirit of our public institutions.

The committee ask to be discharged from the further consideration of the subject.

All which is respectfully submitted.

> CHARLES J. DODGE,
> DAVID GRAHAM, JR.,   } *Committee on Arts*
> THOMAS CONNER,   } *and Sciences, &c.*

C.

DOCUMENT NO. 22.

BOARD OF ALDERMEN, *July* 26, 1841.

Report of the Commissioners of School Moneys for the year ending May 1st, 1841. Laid on the table, and double the usual number of copies ordered to be printed. SAMUEL J. WILLIS, *Clerk.*

To the Corporation of the City of New York, and the Superintendent of Common Schools of the State of New York.

[The report opens with a summary of the condition of the schools for the year, with the moneys received and expended. The commissioners state that *officially* they do not know, or care to know, any differences of religious doctrine, and proceed :—]

*   *   *   *   Their office is one in which their individual convenience and avocations are very often made to yield to their public duty ; which is unconnected with any power of patronage or favor ; which they have always been willing to resign to any who, with their amount of zeal, would surpass their humble ability; which was accepted only because some must perform it, and none who can attend to it faithfully should refuse; and which has rendered no compensating return, but in the feelings awakened by the immense public benefits of which it has made them the witnesses.

It is well known that the education of the youth of this city, by means of the public fund devoted to that purpose, has been placed mainly in the hands of a body of citizens denominated "The Public School Society of the City of New York." So inconsiderable are the exceptions from this control, and so peculiar the circumstances under which each exception is made, that the citizens alluded to may be deemed to have the entire practical execution of the city system of instruction committed to them, subject only to the limitations and government hereafter adverted to. In this broad view we shall consider the Society throughout this report.

As erroneous impressions partially exist in matters which ought to be better understood, it will be proper to prepare the way for their correction by some statements in regard to the fund devoted to public education in this city; to the body by whom the schools are designated which partake of that public fund; to the officers by whom the division of it is made; and to the composition and performance of the Public School Society. These details will swell this report beyond the compass within which we had hoped to confine it; but their importance and necessity seem so manifest, that we must run the hazard of prolixity.

The public fund, then, assigned to the education of youth in this city is derived, to the extent of somewhat more than one fourth part of its amount, from our just proportion of the income of certain funds of the State; an equal sum is raised by taxation on the real and personal estate in the city, by virtue of a general law which places the city, in that respect, under the like ratable burden imposed on the inhabitants of the rest of the State, for purposes of education. In addition to these amounts, however, a tax, peculiar and confined to the city, is raised on the real and personal estate within it, of a sum almost equalling both the proportions of the fund which are before mentioned. The latter tax grew out of the willingness of our citizens to pay this further amount in order to secure to our community the comprehensive, liberal, and efficient system of education adopted by the Public School Society. If this object shall be defeated, wholly or partially, by a discouragement of their schools, and the substitution of establishments of less general benefit, the repeal or the non-assessment of the additional tax would, we presume, follow as a matter of course.

The designation of the schools which participate of the above fund is confided to the Corporation of the city; the members of the Common Council being annually chosen for the several wards by the citizens of the wards possessing the like qualifications as the electors for members of the State Legislature; and the Mayor, or corporate head, who has a veto on their proceedings, being elected by the whole body of citizens authorized to vote for members of the Common Council. The Corporation is required by law to prescribe the rules and regulations under which the public moneys shall be distributed, and provision has accordingly been made for protecting the rights of the people in the schools of the Society, for the due supervision of the schools, both on the part of the public and of the trustees, and for securing from the schools a full performance of all their obligations. A failure in the performance would be followed by the penalty of a withdrawal of the fund appropriated for the support of the schools.

The payment of the school moneys, which is regulated by rules prescribed by law, is committed to a Board of Commissioners chosen by the people of the city through their representatives in the Common Council, in a mode analogous to that by which appointments are made by the State Legislature, to the offices of Secretary of State (who is *ex-officio* the superintendent of all the common schools of the State), State Treasurer, Comptroller, Canal Commissioners, Senators in Congress, &c. One commissioner of school money is thus selected from each ward, for the term of three years, and any vacancy in their board is supplied by the Common Council for the residue of the term. The moneys to be distributed are lodged by the chamberlain of the city, to the credit of the commissioners, in an incorporated bank, from which they are drawn only by checks signed at a meeting of the board, by a majority of the commissioners, and made payable to the Society. The commissioners are bound to make visits half-yearly at least, to all the schools; which duty is performed, as to such of the primary schools as are not held in the same building as the public schools, by committees; and as to the residue, and to all the public schools, by the whole board. The board, before making these general visits, are bound to give three days' notice of the intended visitation to all the members of the Common Council, and to such members of the Legislature as reside in the city; and some of these representatives 'of the people always accompany the board on such occasions. The examinations of the pupils are invariably made at the opening of the book, by any commissioner or visitor named by the chairman, at the instant, without any knowledge until that moment, on the part of the examiner, teacher, or pupil, what book or subject would be selected, or what individual would conduct it. The Board of Commissioners have, beside their stated quarterly meetings, a sufficient number of meetings for the half-yearly visitations, and special meetings whenever occasion requires; and they perform, individually or by committees, any duties which their office may demand, additional to those above enumerated. Of all their proceedings and reports a regular record is kept; and fines are, by a voluntary regulation, exacted from absentees from their meetings, without sufficient excuse, to be judged of by the whole board. Their actual expenses, not exceeding $500 in any year, are reimbursed to them. Reports, annually made according to law, to the Superintendent of Common Schools and to the Corporation of the city, show the division of the school moneys, and the manner in which those allotted the preceding year have been expended. They also show the average number of scholars who have belonged to the schools within each quarter, and the average attendances during the whole year; the year being arbitrarily composed of five hundred half days, and the distribution being determined upon the latter average. In regard to attendances, the law of the State prescribes a different mode of reporting them for this city, as distinguished from the rest of the State; the attendances reported from the district schools in the latter, embracing every pupil who has been at school for even a single day, and the distribution being governed by the whole number of children residing within the respective districts, without regard to the extent or duration of their attendance.

The Public School Society, to whom the daily conduct of the schools is committed, is, in effect, under the laws of the State and of the Corporation of New York, the body of citizens possessing the qualifications prescribed by the Legislature, and the regulations it has authorized, to entitle them to become voters at the election of trustees of the schools which carry out the system of general education in the city. The qualification consists in the payment at any time of the sum of $10, which forever entitles the contributor to this elective franchise; and, as will be seen hereafter, is founded on a more liberal principle than the qualification prescribed for voters for trustees of the common schools of the rest of the State. The Society has the corporate powers often annexed to other franchises, suitable to the accomplishment of its objects; and does not differ in character in this respect from the quasi-corporations which regulate the district schools. No control can be exercised by the Society over the admission of a member; the franchise being obtained as a matter of right, by any citizen, without election, solicitation, or badge of sect or party, by the mere act of the contribution. No one can be excluded from the qualification, who chooses to submit to its requirements; and its essentials are such as every industrious, prudent citizen can attain, by renouncing, for a short time, superfluities or injurious indulgences. The contribution is equal to a perpetuity of only seventy cents per year. Fifty trustees are annually elected by these voters from their own body. The Society has, in practice, generally adopted the wise policy of preferring those who, in a former execution of the same office, had signalized themselves by their assiduous and persevering attention. An abstract, exhibiting the extent of each trustee's visitation and superintendence during the antecedent year, is compiled from the school records, and publicly shown at every election, when inexcusable omission of duty meets its due requital. These fifty, of the very elite of the Society, as regards the love of the labor committed to them, and of its faithful discharge, may choose, if they think proper, an equal number of the whole body entitled to vote, as associate trustees; and in doing so, they elect those whom it is supposed will be most ardent and efficient in the performance of their duty. Such is the formation of the Board of Trustees. For the practical performance of their duty in the supervision of the schools, the weekly examination of the pupils, and the occasional advice necessary for the teachers, the trustees are divided into sections, each embracing one public school-building, and the primary schools attached thereto. Each section meets once in each month, to consider the concerns and interests of its own schools, and to appoint school committees to superintend them during the recess of the section, and discharge the duties of examination and advice before mentioned. In books

47

of minutes, kept at each of the schools, each member of the committee must note his attendances, and write any transactions worthy of record. This book is produced and read at the stated monthly meetings of the section, who make a quarterly report to the whole Board of Trustees, embracing a view of the state of the schools of the section; of its own proceedings, and those of its committees; of the number of times each member of the School Committee has, during the quarter, visited the schools; and of any propositions intended for the consideration of the Board of Trustees at its quarterly meetings. An Executive Committee, of which the chairman of such section is *ex officio* a member, is charged with the general superintending care of the schools during the recess of the Board of Trustees; and meet accordingly once in each month, and oftener, at the request of either of their number. This committee reports annually, on the general state of the schools, to the Board of Trustees; who, from the materials obtained from all the reports presented to them, and their own observation, report to the Society at large. In addition to their quarterly meetings, meetings of all the trustees are annually held in school hours, in each of the schools, for the purpose of general inspection.

The trustees are obliged, annually, to report to the Corporation of the city, and to the Superintendent of Common Schools, " a particular account of the state of their schools, and of the moneys received and expended by them the year preceding, so as to exhibit a full and perfect statement of the property, funds, and affairs of the Society."

The schools of the Society are designated by the names of Primary and Public. The former, of which all the teachers are females, are open to all girls over four years of age, and to boys between four and ten. In these the simplest elements of literary education are taught; and also, among the girls, plain sewing. Perfection in the studies of a lower class is requisite before a child is advanced to a higher. When a pupil has learned to spell correctly and deliberately, read audibly, and write pretty well on the slates, a recommendation is given by the teacher for admission into a public school, and, after satisfactory examination, the child is advanced. It is enjoined as a duty on the teachers of these schools, to make themselves acquainted with the inhabitants of the district in which the school is located, and particularly with those of the poorest classes, in order to induce them to send their children to school. The better to ensure the attention of the teachers to this duty, the amount of their pay is made dependent on the number of children under their tuition.

In the public schools, where due provision is also made for the tuition of boys over the age of ten years, who have not acquired the knowledge imparted by the primary schools, the tuition of the boys and of the girls is conducted in separate rooms of the school-house, under teachers of their own sex. The course of instruction for the boys embraces spelling, reading, including definitions and questions concerning the meaning of the author, writing, making and mending pens, arithmetic, geography, use of the globes and drawing of maps, English grammar, composition and declamation, bookkeeping and the elements of history, astronomy, algebra, geometry, and trigonometry, respectively. The girls are taught in all these branches, except declamation, algebra, geometry, and trigonometry, and with the addition of needlework. Strict rules of the Society secure the punctual attendance of the teachers ; their attention to the comfort, cleanliness, and morals of the scholars, to the ventilation and temperature of the school-rooms, to the causes of the absence of pupils, and to the care of the children, as far as possible, both in and out of the schools. The mildest punishments which can produce reform are alone resorted to, and the teachers can expel a pupil only with the consent of the School Committee or of the section, for habitual disregard of duty or flagrant offence—of which the reason must be communicated to the parent, who may appeal to the Board of Trustees. Registers kept of the names and occupations of the parents, the names of the children, and of the attendance, merits, and deficiences of the latter, are duly exhibited to the trustees. The system of teaching throughout the schools is uniform, so that a child removing from one neighborhood to another is not interrupted in his course by the change of his school. But in order to obtain any advantages that may accrue from the experience of the teachers, or the suggestions of others, stated meetings are held by the teachers for the purpose of considering the means of improving their schools, at which meetings, also, they compare the progress of the schools respectively. Any improvement in the mode of teaching recommended by a majority of them, if formally approved of by the trustees, is adopted in practice.

Each school is provided with a thermometer, in order to regulate the temperature of the school in the cold season ; and in each public school-building a library is contained, of the value of not less than $50, nor more than one $100, consisting of books of voyages, travels, history, &c., to which such pupils as may be selected by the teacher, on account of proficiency and good conduct, are admitted, and may take home from thence one book at a time.

The schools are all divided into classes, pursuing in each the same studies. A mere certificate, properly authenticated, that a child is within the ages of four and sixteen years, entitles him to admission in the schools ; and the tuition and all books and materials necessary for the education of the pupil are furnished without cost to his parents or guardians.

By these regulations, governing the Society and its schools and other auxiliary provisions, a constant supervision is kept over the scholars, the teachers, the Board of Trustees, its sections, committees, and individual members, producing among all the greatest zeal and emulation for the accomplishment of the public aim in view, and resulting in a practical education, offered to the whole youth of the city, carried out in all its bearings with a perfection and efficiency which challenge a comparison of the schools with any others in the world professing the like range of instruction. More than one hundred of these schools are now scattered throughout the city, determined in their location by the wants of the respective neighborhoods, and inviting, by means of agents who patrol the districts for the purpose, every poor and destitute child whose parents are insensible to their duty to their offspring, to come and partake of the benefits within his reach. Nearly forty thousand children have, during the year ending the first day of May last, been enrolled on their registers, and obtained instruction for a greater or lesser period. All this good is effected without the payment of any salary or expenditure, other than the compensation of teachers and agents, the purchase of books and necessaries for the instruction of the pupils, and the erection and repair of the school-houses. No personal or individual advantage results to the trustees from their services, which, springing from the noblest feelings of the human heart, secure gratuitously public benefits of a character and extent that mercenary motives could never accomplish.

Blessings of the magnitude and interest we have described ought to be carefully cherished by all who can exercise any control over them, and the hand of experiment should be stayed from an interference that, with mere partial objects of disputed utility, might impair or destroy the general benefit. Sensible of these truths, the great body of the citizens of New York, and their representatives in their local Legislature, far from asking any alteration in the system, have uniformly approved of and defended it. A number of persons, however, mostly of foreign birth, and belonging to a respectable denomination of Christians—the Roman Catholic—have solicited a change, on the ground that their conscientious scruples require that any schools in which the children of their communion are educated shall, during a certain part of the day, combine the religious instruction of their faith with the literary studies pursued in them. It is proper to add, that by no other denomination has any complaint been made, and that we understand that the sentiment alluded to is not general among the Catholic residents among us from abroad ; a large proportion of them believing that the proposed schools would be, for the most part, composed of the children of foreigners, who might thus lose, in a great measure, the temporal benefits to be derived from an association, at school, with the native children of the republic, and that the fitting place for sectarian culture is the pupil's home, or his church. At the solicitation, however, before referred to, projects have been submitted to the consideration of the Legislature, which, if adopted, would, we believe, violate the received political maxims which have governed our country, and erect, over the ruins of the noble structure we have described, institutions of narrow and partial utility, exclusive in their composition and government, and condemned by former experience.

Vague and general rumors having found their way to the public, affecting the character and efficiency of the schools, and impugning the conduct of the trustees of the Public School Society, several gentlemen of the city, described by the Secretary of State to be "eminently qualified," were selected by him for the purpose of making a personal examination of the schools, who diligently conducted a laborious inquiry, and submitted to that functionary "a mass of valuable information." In his report to the Legislature on the subject of the system of education here, he bears the testimony which will ever be the consequence of such investigations, as long as the schools are conducted as they have hitherto been. "The results of these inquiries" —we copy his language—" show very satisfactorily that commodious houses and good teachers are provided by the Public School Society ; that the sys-

tem of instruction is well devised and faithfully executed; that an efficient
plan of visitation and inspection is prescribed by the trustees; and, although
he has not positive information on the subject, he has no reason to doubt
that such a plan is carried into practical execution." " Certain it is," he
adds, " that the trustees of the Society have exhibited the most praiseworthy zeal and devotion in discharge of the great trust devolved on them;
and many, if not all of them, have spared no exertions to bring into the
schools the destitute children of the city."   But notwithstanding these
favorable results of the efforts of the Public School Society, the Secretary
of State informs the Legislature that the memorials referred to " complain
of the operation of a system which, in fact, devolves upon any private corporation the discharge of one of the most important functions of the Government, without that responsibility to the people which is provided in all
other cases.   They allege," he states, " that, in its administration, the conscientious opinions and feelings of large classes of citizens are disregarded;
that other schools, maintained for the same objects and accomplishing the
same benevolent results, are arbitrarily excluded from a participation of a
common fund, collected by the joint contributions of all; and that a
fearfully large portion of the indigent children are not reached, or in any
way benefited, by the system of public education which now prevails."
After a long examination of the subject, he recommends, nevertheless, the
continuance of the very schools against which such grave objections are
advanced, modifying their powers, however, in such wise as to impart to
them the character of charity schools, in which no children are to be instructed gratuitously but those of parents whose poverty is proved in exemption of payment, and subjecting to charge the children of all whose means
have exposed them to a double taxation for the support of the system, or
who have too much self-respect to claim the privilege of paupers.   He proposes to engraft on the existing system provisions introducing the district
plan in operation in the rest of the State, confining gratuitous instruction in
the schools as before mentioned.   These propositions are combined with
some others which will hereafter be adverted to, in referring to the bill
introduced into the Senate, which, we fear, if adopted, will connect the
schools with the political struggles at the polls; contemplating, as they do,
the creation of offices sufficiently lucrative to tempt the cupidity of the partisan, and thus making institutions intended for the advancement of the
young along the quiet paths of learning, the sport of party management,
contention, and triumph.   Of the district system, it is here, perhaps, the
proper place to say—seeing that the bill in the Senate does not adopt that
part of the recommendation—that we believe it to be wholly unsuited to
the city, whose population is frequently changing residence from one district to another; and that schools teaching by dissimilar books, classes, and
modes of tuition would be of at least doubtful advantage to the children
of the city.   Other objections to this plan exist which it is needless to enumerate, when the fact is before our eyes that the Commissioners of Common
Schools in Brooklyn, a city separated from our own only by the intervening
river, and whose population more resembles ours in its composition and hab-

its than any other in the State, have pronounced the district system to be inefficient and inapplicable there, and lament that they do not possess schools founded on the plan of those of the Public School Society of New York. Of 7,966 children residing in Brooklyn, between the ages of five and sixteen years, only 2,274 appear, by the last schedules presented to the Legislature, to have attended these schools for any period; being about in the ratio, of twenty-three out of eighty. In Williamsburgh, an adjoining community on the same side of the river, where the district system also prevails, only 136 attended out of 943; being in the proportion of one out of seven.

Leaving, then, the further consideration of the results of the district system, which we deem to be virtually abandoned as respects this city, we advert to the objections alleged by the memorials of a portion of the religious sect to which we have before referred. We shall consider them in the order they have been mentioned.

The Catholic memorials complain, first, of the operation of the system which places the education of the youth of the city under the direction of the Public School Society, as "devolving upon a private corporation the discharge of one of the most important functions of the Government, without that responsibility to the people which is provided in all other cases."

Let us look into this allegation.

In the discussion regarding the Public School Society, it has been thought advisable not only to denominate it a private corporation, but, in some of the publications and speeches that have been made on the subject, it has been branded as a close corporation. What attribute it has of a close corporation, no scrutiny has enabled us to discover. That name can be strictly applied only where the trustees, or other governors, constitute the whole corporation, and, in case of vacancy in the board, supply the succession by their own votes. The freest definition could only extend it to institutions who are judges of their own members, and can admit to or exclude from their privileges at the volition of the corporation itself. No such characteristic belongs to the Public School Society. How far it can justly be considered a private corporation, has been seen in the requisites to membership, to which we have adverted. Erected by a law of the State, for the avowed attainment of a momentous public object, in the benefits of which every child of that public to which their sphere of action is confined may participate; open, as to membership, to the whole public who choose to acquire the qualification prescribed by the Legislature of this State, as the only requisite to admission, and which depends alone on the act of the individual, without regard to any wish or objection on the part of the other members; subject to the supervision of officers appointed by the representatives of the whole people of the city; and submitting their accounts to the inspection and scrutiny of those representatives, and, through the publications of the latter, of the whole people—we apprehend that the corporation has been denominated a private one without due reflection. It is not to be regarded in that light, but as the body of voters in the city of New York, on whom the Legislature of the State, representing the sovereignty of the whole people, have thought fit to devolve, through their own enactments, and the powers they have conferred on the Corporation of the city, the selection of the guardians and supervisors of public education within the city. The qualification to constitute a voter is a single payment of a small sum of money, which every man of correct habits may soon lay aside out of his earnings, if he feel any interest in the cause of education. The Legislature, in 1826, when they changed the charity formerly called the Free-School Society of New York, whose tutition was confined to the children of parents unable to pay for their education, into the Public School Society, for the purpose, as the statute expresses it, " so far as their means may extend, for the education of all children in the city of New York not otherwise provided for; whether such children be or be not the proper objects of gratuitous education, and without regard to the religious sect or denomination to which such children or their parents may belong," evidently expected that the education of all the children in the city, whose parents did not prefer to send them to pay schools, would fall under the control of the Public School Society. They therefore defined, by law, the qualification that would be required from any person desirous of being a voter at the election of trustees of the public schools. Proceeding, probably, on the belief that all men are not equally qualified by education and habit to judge of the necessary attainments for the beneficial discharge of a literary duty, they deemed some other qualification than mere residence necessary, and fixed upon one in the nature of a property qualification, which, however temporary in its possession, would, it was supposed, be durable in its results. Each intended voter was required to make a single payment of ten dollars, for which the privilege sought was promised him for life. This qualification is somewhat analogous to that prescribed for voters at elections of- trustees of common schools in the other parts of the State, which is strictly a property qualification, though, if not durable in its possession, is only temporary in its results—every person being subject to a fine of the very same sum of ten dollars for voting at any annual election for trustees of a common school, unless he be a freeholder within the town where he votes; be assessed the same year in which he votes, or the preceding year, to pay taxes in said town; or possess personal property liable to taxation, in the school district, of the value of fifty dollars over and above the list of articles exempted from execution. Between the elective privilege in the city and the country there will be seen this striking difference, that, in the city, the individual who at any time possesses and pays over a ten-dollar bill, which, if of general circulation, may pass hence in a few hours to Plattsburg or Buffalo, obtains a privilege which, whatever be his subsequent fortunes, always accompanies him, and is promised to continue forever; but as regards the country resident, the property qualification is connected with local ownership, and must be continued in its possession; for if, after having been the possessor of real or personal property, in his town or his school district, or paid taxes in his town, he become irretrievably ruined, his privilege sinks with his fortunes, and is lost forever.

That the Society is a private corporation, cannot, therefore, be successfully sustained. Equally untenable, in our opinion, is the allegation that the function discharged by the Society is performed "without that responsibility to the people which is provided in all other cases." The trustees are placed under the direction of the representatives of the people of the very community in which they perform their functions, who, upon any unfaithfulness on the part of the trustees, can deprive them and their constituents of the power conferred on them, and of the funds necessary for its execution. The Society is compelled, by the law of the State, to conform to any rules and restrictions in regard to the receipt of the public moneys which the Corporation of the city may by ordinance prescribe; and the ordinance passed accordingly by the Corporation subjects them to every rule and restriction that has been deemed proper to secure a strict supervision and accountability. The Commissioners of School Moneys, by whom the visitations to the schools are made on behalf of the community, are charged to report to the Common Council any failure or omission of the trustees in regard to the public moneys they receive, in regard to the admission of children to the schools, and to the proper weekly visitation and inspection, on the part of the trustees, of all the schools under their direction. The books of the schools, containing the memoranda of this performance, are at all times subject to the examination of the commissioners, to whom the returns required by law are made under oath or affirmation. In addition to these guards, the Society is obliged to submit, in an annual report to the Superintendent of Common Schools appointed by the State, and to the Common Council of the city, a particular account of the state of their schools, and of the moneys received and expended by them, which may be examined by any citizen disposed to investigate it.

These provisions, if in any manner they differ from those generally governing officers who perform important functions of the Government, certainly secure, in degree, as ample a responsibility to the people. The Society has now exercised the powers confided to them for more than fifteen years, and in that whole period no valid impeachment has been preferred of infidelity to their trust.

It may be added, in connection with this matter, that, in all the plans which have been devised for the alteration of the present system, not a single provision has been suggested that guarantees from the Public School Society, or the proposed additional schools, increased responsibility to the people.

The second charge assumes that, "in the administration of the Society, the conscientious opinions and feelings of large classes of citizens are disregarded; and that other schools, maintained for the same objects and accomplishing the same benevolent results, are arbitrarily excluded from a participation of a common fund collected by the joint contribution of all."

General allegations like the aforegoing give no definite conception of the matter of complaint, and present no tangible point for examination. It were better always, and particularly in cases affecting such momentous interests as are involved in the school question, that the griefs should be distinctly alleged, and specifications offered. It is, however, now generally understood, from newspaper publications of essays and speeches, that the violence imputed against conscientious opinions and feelings is to those of a part of the Catholic communion, who alone constitute the large classes of citizens alluded to ; that the schools attached to their churches, governed by trustees of their own appointment, conducted according to their precepts of religious faith, and ministering, as may well be inferred, to children only of their own denomination, are the schools said to be maintained for the same objects, and accomplishing the same benevolent results, as those of the Public School Society ; and that the arbitrary exclusion from a participation in the common fund collected by the joint contribution of all, which is complained of, is the refusal, by the immediate representatives of the people of this city, to devote a portion of the public moneys toward the support of schools erected and governed by the Catholic denomination, and inculcating their distinguishing forms and creeds.

That the objects and results of institutions founded and acting upon principles so widely different as those which distinguish the schools of the sect and of the Society cannot be very similar, is too apparent to need illustration ; and if the disregard of the conscientious opinions and feelings of large classes of citizens in the administration of the Society consists, as is inferred, in maintaining a perfect impartiality toward the several religious denominations in the schools, not giving reasonable offence, nor yielding submission to any, the Society has done no more than to be faithful to the purposes for which it was created. The motive to its incorporation is stated, in the charter, to be the education of all children, whether or not they be proper objects of gratuitous education, and without regard to the religious sect or denomination to which their parents belong ; and it would have been a plain infraction of their duty to fashion the exercises of the schools according to the requirements of any particular Church.

The allegation remains, that the sect is arbitrarily excluded from a participation of a common fund collected by the joint contribution of all.

In adopting a system of general education at the public expense, the object of the State was to give to its youth such an education as would fit them to discharge the civil obligations of this life, leaving it to their natural and ecclesiastical guardians to prepare them, through a parental and spiritual ministry, to render their account in another world. There ought to be, and there must be, some common platform on which all the children may obtain their secular education, who are destined to act as citizens of the same republic. To that general training all the children are entitled ; but it is the public who are to determine on its particulars and conditions, and not the parents who may claim it for their offspring. That a fund has been raised by the taxation of all for general education, creates no right in the tax-paying sectarian to demand that any portion of it be appropriated to the spread of his particular creed. The tax was imposed on him as a citizen, not as the member of a church. Its object was to provide for a civil purpose exclusively ; not to prepare the path to any designated place of worship. The erection of a church school announces a sectarian object. It has its exclusive rules of system and government ; is superintended by trustees and teachers of a particular faith ; religious conformity is indispensable to a participation in its direction, which is not, and cannot be, attained by means of a civil qualification that any citizen may acquire. It is, in truth, a part of the church establishment, and the sectarian of another denomination justly feels that his privileges are equally violated, whether he be taxed for the support of its religious teacher at the school desk, or for that of its religious teacher in the pulpit. This State has never yet asserted the power to tax its people for ecclesiastical objects; and if its sovereignty comprehends such a power, the rights of conscience require that the religion of the taxpayer be recorded on the assessment-roll, and his contribution be dealt to the encouragement of his own communion.

An obstacle arises, perhaps, out of the provisions of our Constitution, to the establishment and conduct of a sectarian school as a part of the public system, which would be insuperable to some of the claims which have been brought before the public. If the religion of the sect be a necessary part of the education of the children, the choice of a teacher adequate to the accomplishment of that object would seem to be indispensable. Such a teacher would probably be found only in the person of one of the ministers of the religion which the school is to inculcate. If the school which is committed to his direction be adopted as a part of the public system, his office thereafter assumes a civil character; his salary is paid by the whole public out of the proceeds of a general tax. The question immediately arises, whether this would not be inconsistent with the clause of the Constitution which declares that "no minister of the gospel, or priest of any denomination whatsoever, shall at any time, under any pretence or description whatever, be eligible to, or capable of holding, any civil or military office or place within this State."

The commissioners would suggest, that any difficulties in regard to the religious education of the children, which may be desirable, can be accomplished without a violation of the principles or a departure from the objects of the school system, by an application of the rule said to prevail in Holland in regard to the schools controlled by the Government. A time is there set apart when the children of the respective denominations are requested to repair to the appropriate places for their peculiar worship, where they are attended by the proper ministers to their spiritual wants. If the Sabbath and the other day in the week on which the public schools are closed be insufficient for this purpose, some additional portion of the week might be dedicated to it. The arrangement would certainly throw an additional burden on the clergy without additional pecuniary recompense, but their commendable sense of duty in their sacred office would no doubt disregard any considerations of that sort.

The remaining allegation is, that "a fearfully large portion of the indigent children are not reached, or in any way benefited," by the system of education that now prevails in this city. Fortunately, this is a subject that can be brought to the test of mathematical calculation, by which the figures will show that the system of education in this city reaches and benefits the indigent poor far more efficaciously than the system that prevails in the residue of the State.

In order to prove the destitution of the inhabitants of the city in respect to education, the Secretary of State reports to the Legislature that the whole number of white children in New York in 1840, "the year in which the last census of the United States was taken, was 62,952, and that 30,758 only are returned as attending some school, leaving 32,194 who were not in attendance on any school whatever." Of the accuracy of the number of attendances thus returned from the city doubts have been well entertained, but we shall assume that the aggregate is correct. The inference that all would draw from the manner in which the case is stated and the argument deduced by the Secretary, is, that a fraction more than one half of the children of the city are trained up in utter ignorance. "With all the commendable and vigorous efforts of the trustees of the Public School Society," he says, "it cannot be denied that less than one half the children between four and sixteen years of age, in the city of New York, are receiving the benefits of any education whatever." A moment's reflection will correct this error. The schools of the Society receive all children between four and sixteen years of age; let us say, however, in order to make our estimate tally with the figures of the Secretary, between five and sixteen years. At any time within the portion of their lives embracing eleven years, then, they have access to the schools, and in these there is continual change, some retiring, and new scholars succeeding. Now, if one half of this class of population, rejecting fractions, is, on the average, kept at school, it is evident that, on the average, each child would receive five and a half years of tuition, which, in the New York schools, deducting vacations, amounts to somewhat more than sixty months, or five full and complete years without deduction. In imposing on masters the obligation to teach certain children to read and write, the law of the State gives him the alternative of furnishing two years' education, as being sufficient for the purpose; and that, too, while, by another law, the common schools of the country are not required to be open more than four months in the year to entitle them to the benefits of the school fund. If eight months', or even twenty-four months' tuition, in such schools as the inhabitants are obliged to accept in some parts of the State, be recognized by the State as enough to qualify a child to read and write, sixty months' tuition in the schools of the New York Public School Society would not be likely to consign him to hopeless mental destitution. A far less period of education in their youth, and that, in many cases, of an inferior sort, is all that was enjoyed by many of the men who have illustrated the character of our country in the literary and philosophical world. Doctor Franklin seems, from his autobiography, to have been finally taken from school at the age of ten years, to perform the humblest offices in his father's business of a tallow-chandler and soap-boiler, having "failed entirely in arithmetic," though he had "learned to write a good hand," and gained instruction in some other branches.

"A comparison of the results obtained from statistical returns," says the Secretary of State, "between the numbers educated in New York and those instructed in other parts of the State, will exhibit in a more striking manner the lamentable deficiency of the former. It appears," he proceeds,

" from the report of the Superintendent before referred to, that, while there are 592,000 children out of the city of New York between the ages of five and sixteen, there are 549,000 attending the common schools. In the city of New York," he adds, " the proportions were, as above stated, 62,952 children between the same ages, and 30,758 attending all the schools, public as well as private." In another place he states " that, while the Public School Society has registered on its books the names of children who have entered the schools to the number of 22,955, the average actual attendance of pupils amounts only to 13,189."

It was certainly not the intention of the Secretary of State to do injustice to the city in the comparison thus drawn. In making it, however, he seems to have forgotten that the returns from the common schools and the public schools differ altogether in their ingredients, and furnish no proper materials for a comparative estimate in regard to them. In the returns of the common schools, all the children who have attended are indiscriminately numbered as instructed in the schools, whatever be the duration of their attendance, whether for a year, a week, or a day, and whatever be the amount of the tuition they receive. But a different mode of return is prescribed for the city, as distinguished from the rest of the State. From the city it is required that there be two columns of returns, neither of which shows the whole number of children " registered " on the books of the public schools; nor has that number accordingly ever been returned until the present year, when it is done as the voluntary act of the Commissioners of School Money, without requirement by law. It amounts, this year, to nearly 40,000, and could not have been, in the year referred to by the Secretary, less than 38,000.

The returns demanded by law from the city are, firstly, a return of the average quarterly attendance in the schools; the number to be ascertained —to follow the words of the statute—" by adding to the number of children on register at the commencement of each quarter, the number admitted during that quarter, and the total to be considered the average of that quarter." Secondly, a return of the average number that actually attended the school during the whole year, to be ascertained by the teachers keeping an account of the number of scholars present every half day, which, being added together and divided by 500, the number of half school-days of which the year is arbitrarily declared to consist, is considered the average of attending scholars.

That no just contrast can be drawn from numbers representing, as in the country returns, every child as an attending scholar who had visited the school but for a day, and the city returns, whose highest numbers represent only the average quarterly attendance, would not seem to require illustration. As, however, the comparison has been made in a grave public document, let us examine practically its principles, and see how the returns to the Superintendent from a public or city school, and from a common or country school, having an exactly equal number of scholars and attendances throughout the year, would exhibit each to the Legislature in the Superintendent's report.

Suppose the year to begin with 200 scholars; that the 200 old scholars retire before the end of each quarter; that they are succeeded during the quarter by 200 new scholars, who had never before attended; and that each quarter thus begins with 200 scholars;—what is the comparison they would present in the Superintendent's report?

Let us first take the public or city school.

The year begins with scholars, ...	200
New entries during first quarter, ...	200
Retirements during first quarter, 200, leaving for second quarter,	200
New entries during second quarter, ...	200
Retirements during second quarter, 200, leaving for third quarter,	200
New entries during third quarter, ...	200
Retirements during third quarter, 200, leaving for fourth quarter,	200
New entries during fourth quarter, ...	200
	——
	1600

This aggregate of 1600 being divided by 4, gives the quotient for the quarterly average attendance of 400; which is the largest number returned for the city school to the Superintendent of Common Schools.

Take, next, its twin-brother, the country school. What number would it, under circumstances precisely similar, return to the Superintendent?

The year begins with scholars, ...	200
New scholars first quarter, ...	200
" second quarter, ...	200
" third quarter, ...	200
" fourth quarter, ...	200
	——
Number returned, ...	1,000

Thus two schools, not at all distinguishable in their respective numbers of scholars and attendances, would, in the Superintendent's report, exhibit an apparent superiority of one school over another its exact equal in fact, in the ratio of five to two.

Any comparison, therefore, between the *quarterly* attendances at the city school and the attendances as we have explained them at the country school, is evidently misplaced.

That between the average *yearly* attendances at the former and the attendances at the latter is still more objectionable.

The attendances at the country school, of whatever duration, would amount, as we have before seen, to 1,000, at which number they would be returned to the Superintendent, and be reported by him.

The average yearly attendances calculated as prescribed by law for the public school, would stand, in its return (judging from the comparative returns of quarterly and yearly attendances to which the Secretary refers), at two hundred and forty, or nearly, at which number they would be reported by the Superintendent; thus exhibiting an apparent superiority of one school over another its exact equal in fact, in the ratio of more than four to one.

The truth is—and justice to the city, when such comparisons are made, requires, perhaps, it be spoken—that the published returns to the Superintendent give no definite idea of the amount of public education in the State, being deficient in all particulars of the average quarterly or annual attendance of the pupils. They announce the whole number of children returned from each school district; the number that attended the school within the time it was open, and the length of the period it was open; but they afford no means of judging whether a majority, or any other definite proportion, attended for more than a week, or a day. Nor, apparently, is the number of children returned as having at some time been attending, to be depended upon. Owing to a loose or an erroneous method of making up the returns, the number of scholars attending the common schools has been frequently exaggerated beyond the number actually residing within the districts. It would be a matter for wonder if the attendance of every child residing within the districts could be obtained, even for a day, within the periods that the schools are open; but a more extraordinary phenomenon was presented in the returns for a series of years, exhibiting, as they did, the attendance of a much larger number of pupils between the ages of five and sixteen years than there were children in existence between those ages in the whole State. We copy from the schedule F of the last annual report of the Superintendent of Common Schools, giving a " comparative statement of the condition of the common schools from 1815 to 1840," the numbers of children between said ages taught, and the number of children between said ages residing, in all the districts of the State, for the years 1824 to 1829, both inclusive, and have added a column showing the excess of the scholars over the residents.

Year.	No. of children taught in the districts.	No. of children residing in the districts.	Excess of those taught over those in the districts.
1824	402,940	383,500	19,440
1825	425,586	395,586	30,000
1826	431,601	411,256	20,345
1827	441,856	419,216	22,640
1828	468,205	449,113	19,092
1829	480,041	468,257	11,784

Even from the returns for the year 1839, upon which the disparaging comparisons of the Secretary are founded, there appears to be, in twenty-seven counties of the State, an excess of more than 25,000 children between the specified ages taught in their common schools, over the number of the same classes of children residing within those counties, as ascertained by the trustees of the school districts. The Superintendent of Common Schools supposes, in his last report, that the returns from the schools, which give the attendances, are more to be relied upon than the returns from the trustees of the number of children within the districts: but this idea derives no support from the census taken by the Marshal of the United States in the year after, when an increase of the number of the children had taken place. The marshal, in 1840, finds an excess in those twenty-seven counties over the returns of the trustees, in 1839, of less than 4,000, leaving yet an erroneous excess in the returns of scholars attending of more than 21,000. Other errors are detected in the returns to the Superintendent. The returns from the Commissioners of Common Schools make the aggregate number of children, in 1839, in all the districts of the State, excluding the city of New York, to be 592,564; being more, by 14,560, than the whole number of children between five and sixteen years residing in the same parts of the State in 1840; which, by the marshal's returns, are ascertained

to be 578,004

Difference, ... 14,560

The returns of the schools, exclusive of those of New York,
 show scholars attending, ... 549,457

The marshal's returns, exclusive of New York, . . 477,323

Difference, ... 72,134

This difference the Superintendent endeavors to reduce to 42,211, mainly by deducting 26,869 scholars returned by the marshal in another column, as educated at the public charge. The latter number is, however, included in the number of 477,323 above mentioned. In the reports both of the Superintendent and of the Secretary, it is so regarded when referring to New York, to which 10,213 of the 26,869 belong; but are not credited, in either report, to the amount of education in the city.

It is unpleasant thus to dispel flattering illusions by which we, in common with the rest of the State, had been misled, until we were impelled to investigate the subject; but it is manifest that mistakes have existed in the public documents relating to the common schools, which the interests and perhaps the character of the State require should not hereafter occur.

Rejecting comparisons, then, drawn from returns to the Superintendent from the city and the country, having no similitude in their particulars, and widely differing in their accuracy, let us seek for better means to determine the truth. These will be found in additional returns by the marshal, in the census before referred to, which state the number of white persons residing in the city and State, of and over the age of twenty years, who can neither read nor write. The common school system and the public school system have respectively been long enough in existence to test the efficacy of each upon the persons who, under like circumstances, have actually come within the operation of each, and passed to the age last specified. From the census, we find that the whole white population of the State, excluding New York City, of the age of twenty years and upward, is 990,792; and that the like population in the city of New York is 163,920. Thus New York, though possessing an aggregate population comparing with that of the rest of the State, excluding New York, in the ratio of little more than one to seven, has a relative white population, of and over the age of twenty years, of about one to six; or, in other words, it has an excess of more than 17,400 white persons, of the age of twenty years and upward, over its due proportion, as compared with the aggregate population of the other counties. The number of whites of the age of twenty and upward, in the State, who can neither read nor write, is 43,705; of whom there are, in New York, 7,778, and in the rest of the State, 35,927; showing an excess of 1,732 individuals only, in the city, out of a population of 312,932, over its due proportion in the comparison with the counties, if all other circumstances were exactly equal.

But it is to be recollected that, in every year, an immense laboring population is arriving from abroad; many of whom, wholly uninstructed, remain in the city by reason of the labor to be obtained therein, and their capacity for its performance, whilst the mass of the more fortunate class go to the country. The wonder, therefore, is, that the excess before mentioned, of 1,732 persons, is so small. The alien population constituted, in 1835, when the last State census was taken, somewhat more than one fifth of the whole population of the city; and that of the rest of the counties somewhat less than one seventeenth of their whole population. The census taken by the marshal, in 1840, does not furnish the alien population for the city or for the State. If it has kept pace with the ratio for 1835, the number of white aliens, of and over the age of twenty years, in the city, is about 32,500; being more than fourfold the number of the whites of the same age who cannot read or write; while the number of aliens in the counties, of and over the age of twenty years, is about 53,350; being less than one and a half times the number of whites of the same age who cannot read or write.

A large portion of the alien population in the city is poor, or on the verge of poverty, and may be presumed to comprise much ignorance, brought up, as it has been, in countries where the blessings of education are not diffused as in this. Some idea of the extent of the ignorance among adults thus settled among us, may perhaps be gathered from the poverty which appears to exist in their families. A report of the former Secretary of State (Mr. Dix) shows that, in the year ending the 1st of December, 1838, —a year when labor for the poor was very difficult to obtain—the whole number of foreigners relieved or supported by public charity in the State was 64,570; of whom 59,522 were in the city of New York, and only 5,048 in the other counties. He adds, " that, in the county of New York, foreigners appear to constitute more than seventy-three per cent. of the whole number of persons relieved or supported; while, in the other counties, they constitute but little more than twenty per cent. of the whole number."

These explanations fully account for the entire number of white persons in the city, over the age of twenty years, who cannot read nor write—even supposing that the Public School Society and the pay schools had hitherto in due time educated every individual between four and sixteen years within our boundaries, during that interval, or any part of it. Connected with the returns of the marshal, illustrating this matter, they show, contrary to the opinion which the Secretary has pronounced, that the Public School Society has " accomplished the principal object of its organization—the education of the great body of the children of the city." Notwithstanding the very disproportionate influx of foreign population into this city, as compared with the rest of the State, the struggles of the Society have kept down ignorance to an extent which no system, less efficacious and liberal than its own, could have effected; and has enabled the city to make a positive comparison, waiving the consideration of its disadvantages, with many of the counties of the State, some of which are embraced among the twenty-seven which exhibit, in the Superintendent's report, so flourishing a state of education within them.

Of the white persons, of and over the age of twenty years, who cannot read or write, there is, rejecting fractions:

In the city of New York,	.	.	.	.	1 out of every 21
In the County of Montgomery,		.	.	1 " 21
" Rensselaer,	.	.	.	1 " 21
" Wayne,	.	.	.	1 " 22
" Steuben,		.	.	1 " 20
" Delaware,	.	.	.	1 " 20
" Columbia,		.	.	1 " 20
" Essex,	.	.	.	1 " 20
" Dutchess,		.	.	1 " 15
" Franklin,	.	.	.	1 " 14
" Fulton,	.	.	.	1 " 14
" Monroe,	.	.	.	1 " 13
" Chemung,		.	.	1 " 12
" Sullivan,	.	.	.	1 " 12
" Lewis,	.	.	.	1 " 11
" Putnam,	.	.	.	1 " 10
" Tioga,	.	.	.	1 " 9
" Herkimer,	.	.	.	1 " 8
" Clinton,	.	.	.	1 " 5

We have thus sufficiently disposed of the charge that " a fearfully large portion of the indigent children are not reached, or in any way benefited," by the system of education that now prevails in the city. The want of support for the charge will, however, become still more apparent from the comparisons that follow.

The number of paupers, " the indigent " emphatically, in the State, in 1840, as returned by the Secretary of State to the Legislature, is 56,561. Of this number, 27,553 were in New York, and the residue—29,008—in the counties. Looking to the proportion which the population, of twenty years of age and upward, in the city and in the counties respectively, bears to the aggregate population of each, the paupers of the counties would comprise 13,579, of and over the age of twenty years, and the paupers of the city would comprise 14,432 of and over that age; the larger number in the city arising from the fact before mentioned, of its having more than 17,400 persons, of twenty years and upward, beyond its proportion, as compared with

48

the aggregate population of the counties. The paupers, then, of the city, of and over the age of twenty years, bear the proportion to its inhabitants of like age who cannot read or write, of 14,432 to 7,778 ; making the ratio of the paupers to the untaught nearly two to one, and showing that almost one half of the very indigent (throwing altogether out of view the accession of untaught persons from abroad) have been " reached or benefited " by the public schools ; whilst, in the counties, the proportions would be 13,579 paupers to 35,927 untaught ; showing that a number of persons equalling all the paupers, besides about one and two thirds their number, from among those in better circumstances, had not been " reached or benefited " by the common schools. In other words, the untaught in the city would be, in comparison with its poor, as little more than one to two ; while, in the counties, the untaught, in comparison of their poor, would be more than five to two ; thus making a difference in favor of the city, as contrasted with the counties, upon a comparison of their poor and of their untaught respectively, in the ratio of about five to one.

There is no doubt that a commendable anxiety to educate the poor has fearfully exaggerated the number of those who, in this city, obtain no instruction. We had, in some degree, participated of this delusion. It is true that idle children are found in various parts of the city, whose own perverseness, or whose unfeeling parents, prevent them, at times, from coming to school ; but although they may not attend this month, they find their way to school the next ; and, the mode of tuition in all the schools being uniform, thus pick up, from month to month, the elements of learning. An illustration of this is derived from the fact that, during the last year, more than 21,000 children retired, from time to time, from the public schools, their vacant places being refilled by others. In no other way than we have suggested can the results we have presented be accounted for. If no entreaties avail in attracting idle children to school, the poverty of their parents, or their own vicious course, ensures their destiny to the Poor-House or the House of Refuge, whose wholesome discipline imposes the necessity of attending to their books. As fast as the foreign population increases, their children are made the objects of our liberal system. Thus we believe that the portion of the young who, in our city, grow up without education altogether, is very insignificant indeed.

In presenting the statistics contained in this report, some errors may possibly have occurred, drawn, as the materials have in part been, from various columns of the marshal's census and the Superintendent's report, and undergoing, as they necessarily have, after-processes of calculation. We have intended them and believe them to be wholly free from error, and therefore invite all just criticism. If any mistake has accidentally crept in, sure we are that it is not of a character or amount that can affect substantially the general tenor of our statements and conclusions. In making the estimates, we have used the marshal's returns as printed by order of our State Legislature, and have pursued the Superintendent's method of ascertaining therefrom the number of children between the ages of five and sixteen years.

Having thus examined the objections which have been advanced against the public school system, it may be proper to look into the bill reported to the Senate, proposing a substitute. This bill, we understand, received the approbation of the remonstrants (alluded to by the Secretary of State), who sent numerous committees from this city to the Legislature to urge its adoption; and the effort for its passage will probably be renewed at the next session. It may be assumed to have been prepared under the direction of the memorialists; nothing being more common than to introduce a bill into the Legislature framed by the applicants, so that all their propositions may have a fair chance of due legislative discussion and inquiry. We shall therefore regard it as the bill of the remonstrants, and speak of its provisions accordingly. Never, probably, in the history of legislation, were the avowed objects of a bill more at variance with its actual tendency than this.

The remonstrants profess, in substance, a desire that the people shall have a more direct control and administration of the public school system in this city; and for this purpose they commence by taking from the Common Council the immediate and comparatively numerous representatives of the people, and the guardians of their local interests and concerns, all connection with, or control over, the schools whatsoever. In place of the Corporation and the Commissioners of School Money chosen by them, the bill proposes to place the whole government of the system under seventeen commissioners of common schools, one to be elected by the qualified voters of each ward, at the charter election; thus affording the desirable guarantee for a pure and efficacious administration of the system, by connecting its destinies with the political contests of the wards, with the cabals, intrigues, and bargainings of committees, appointed, not at primary meetings of the people, but at partial and interested meetings of partisans, and with the fierce strife of party animosity. In a spirit of hostility to close corporations, and of any abatement of the people's rights, the Commissioners of Common Schools are erected, immediately upon their election, into a close corporation, for their term of service; filling vacancies, whenever they occur in their body, by the votes of the residue; so that, by possibility, it might happen to become a board not one of the members of which had received the popular suffrage; and in no case would the inhabitants of the ward in which the vacancy occurred have any voice, directly or indirectly, in the choice of its new commissioner. Zealous, as the title of the bill purports, "to extend the benefits of common school education in the city of New York," it banishes from the schools all the children, forming so numerous and interesting a class in the primary departments, between the ages of four and five years, by taking away from them all the benefits now enjoyed by them from the school moneys; and it directs the appointment, by the Board of Commissioners, of a superintendent and clerk (offices which would inevitably become political rewards), who are to have the first lien on the school moneys, for the payment of their annual salaries, amounting to three thousand dollars: a sum equivalent to the average tuition, in the public schools, of one thousand scholars, including the average expenses of teachers, school-books, slates, pencils, writing-books and pens, maps, school library, furniture, and room hire. Deprecating grants of power to any private corporation to disburse the public moneys, as wrong in principle and an invasion of popular rights, it contains provisions, compulsory on the commissioners and the public, to admit any number of persons who may choose to associate for the purpose, and such others only as they in their pleasure may choose to adopt as their associates, to the privileges of a district school, and to a participation and expenditure of the school moneys; upon the conditions that the associates will stipulate for the continuance of their school for at least one year; will make it appear that their school will promote the interests of education, and will not interfere with any school already established; and that the persons applying are able to maintain a respectable school for the instruction of children in the branches usually pursued in common schools. Ardent to impart the benefits of education to all, it prescribes no regulation under which all must be admitted, on equal terms, to the contemplated schools. Sensitive to the just rights of the taxpayers in the city, whose contributions to the cause of education are comparatively nearly threefold those of the taxpayers, for the same object, in the counties, the proposed system embraces enactments whose operation would probably drive their children from the schools, and, at best, would leave them but the gleanings, after the harvest had been reaped by those who pay no tax at all. Paying homage to the merits of the schools of the Public School Society, it adopts them as part of the system, but takes from them the means of sustaining their present character and usefulness, and divests them of two of their noblest distinctions—that which forbids the inquiry whether the parent can or cannot pay for the education of his child; and that which, with a just regard to the principles regulating our political institutions, mingles the children of all, without reference to adventitious circumstances of fortune, in a competition for eminence : resembling the struggle in which they are destined to engage, upon terms of like equality, in their future character of men of the nation. Solicitous for the protection of religion, whilst it erects establishments that may be devoted to sectarian objects, it also fashions schools in which infidelity may be taught at the public expense. Professing to pay respect to the feelings inseparable from a due appreciation of the rights of freemen, it humbles the citizen to the proof of pecuniary destitution before he can obtain a gratuitous education for his child, and demands that the name of the latter be then enrolled as the recipient of public relief, on documents open to the inspection of every inquirer; thus carrying down the record of the receipt of public charity as the accompaniment for life of the youth who, under the existing system, obtains a good education as a right, without disclosing the circumstances of the parent to any. Many of our mechanics, and other most useful population, whose struggles enable them to subsist their families, can ill afford the cost of the education of their children; but the just sensibilities belonging to freemen would prompt the indignant refusal of any benefit to their offspring, to be obtained only upon such degrading conditions.

Other objections, not here necessary to enumerate, might be advanced against the project in question, or any other at all resembling it. The fact that a bill containing clauses so odious might possibly have received legislative sanction, without being duly considered by the community on whom its injuries would most immediately fall, admonishes the necessity, before the present system of education for the city shall be changed, of a reference to that community of any proposed substitute, in order that they may pass upon it distinctly by the ballot-box. Of the vast benefits derived from the practical operation of the public schools in this city, there are not, that we are aware, any differences of opinion among those who have visited them and impartially examined into their effect. Advantages of such magnitude, securing, as they do, results of incalculable consequence to the intelligence and morals of the city, should not be hazarded for the sake of untried or exploded systems, that, after inflicting their evils, will cause us to deplore the sacrifice of a healthful state, which, if to be regained at all, will require many years for its restoration. Sensible of their duty to the public, the commissioners have not felt at liberty to avoid that faithful exposition of their views which the occasion demands ; and they pray the Corporation of the city, and the Superintendent of Common Schools, and, through them, the Legislature of the State, to give such a cautious and deliberate consideration of the whole subject as the immense interests involved, and any convictions herein expressed, may respectively appear to deserve.

SAMUEL GILFORD, JR., *Chairman.*

GEORGE W. STRONG, *Secretary.*

INDEX.

A.

Acts Relating to Schools, 5, 12, 24, 25, 26, 36, 48, 74, 101, 120, 137, 521, 573, 583.

Act for Relief of Bethel Baptist Church, 49, 53.

Address—
  of the P. S. Society to the Public, 6.
  of De Witt Clinton, 14.
  to Parents and Guardians, 36.
  by Rev. J. N. Maffit, 43.
  Rev. Thaddeus Osgood, 43.
  of the P. S. Society to the Public, 110.
  Reasons of the P. S. Society, &c., 127.
  of Roman Catholics to Public, 188, 189, 331.

Adelphi Society, Philadelphia, 22.

Administration of the Society, 604.

African Free School, 48, 87, 92, 93, 94, 95, 97, 131, 135, 156, 157, 165, 171, 665–679.

Agent and Visitor, 157, 615.

Aimwell School, Philadelphia, 22.

Albany Lancasterian School, 100.

American Museum, 83.

Americus, Review of Hon. J. C. Spencer, 482–488.

Analysis of Faith, 307.

Aquinas, St. Thomas, 438.

Arcularius, Henry, 145.

Arrowsmith, Edward, 61.

Assembly, House of—
  Report of Committee on Colleges, Academies, and Schools, 70.
  Proceedings on School Law, 352, 497, 521.

Assistant Teachers, see *Teachers*.

Association, Protestant, 302.
  of Women Friends, 2, 653.

Augustine, St., 438.

Authority of the King, 468.
  of the Pope, 247, 303, 305, 468.

B.

Bangs, D.D., Rev. Nathan, 201, 273, 313.

Baptist Tabernacle Church, 43, 69.

Barnes, Erastus, 140.

Barry, Commodore, 302.

Basileopolis, Bishop of, 338.

Beadle, M.D., Edward L., 581.

Beekman, Hon. J. W., 597.

Beggars, 620.

Bell, Dr., 20.

Bellevue Hospital School, see *Public School No. 6.*

Benedict, Hon. Erastus C., 597.

Bethel Baptist Church, 44, 47, 48–75, 78, 100, 124, 726.

Bethune, Mrs. Joanna, 108, 658.

Betting, 211, 257, 300.

Bible, Douay, 236, 237, 246, 258.
  Protestant, 213, 246, 250, 289, **467.**
  Tyndal's, 467.
  Coverdale's, 467.
  Bishop's, 467.
  James I., 467.
  in Schools, 191, 192, 236, **246, 257,** 275, 388, 635–644.

Bloomingdale School, 105, 106.

Board of Education, 521, 526, 528, 534.
  Union of Society with, 576–599.
  and Powers of Public School Society, 535–575.

Bolton, Thomas, 101, 381, 721.

Bond, Rev. Thomas E., 201, 249, 252, 283, 293, 294, 313.

Bonnet, Peter, 70.

Books, School-, Expurgation of, 160–163, 208, 213, 237, 263, 317, 324–349.
  against Catholics, 160–163, 209, 212, 216, 245, 261, 315, 321, 386, 408, 464, 733.

Bossuet, 438.

Boston Schools, 114, 118, 152, 153.

Bosworth, Hon. Joseph L., 560–572.

Bourne, Wm. Oland, 714.

Bradish, Lieut.-Gov. Luther, 426.

British and Foreign School Society, 31, 91, 100.

British Critic, 259, 293, 294, 297.

Brownlee, D.D., Rev. W. C., 241.

Brush, Nehemiah, 140, 142.

Bryant, William Cullen, 709.

Bryson, David, 145.

Buckingham, Hon. James S., 703.

Spencer, Hon. John C., 356.
  review of, 482, 747.
Spring, D.D., Rev. Gardiner, 70, 276.
St. Bartholomew's Day, 214.
St. Michael's Church, 106.
Stafford, Rev. Ward, 70.
State, Duty of the, see *Duty of the State.*
Sterne, Laurence, see *Tristram Shandy.*
Suffern, Thomas, 70.
Summerfield, Rev. George, 43.
Sunday Schools, 27, 40, 108, 111, 248.
Superintendent of Repairs, 167.
Surplus Revenue, 171.
Sweeney, M.D., Hugh, 187, 188, 189, 350.

T.

Tabernacle Baptist Church, 43, 69.
Targee, John, 60, 73.
Taylor, Jacob B., 60.
Taxes for School Money, 45, 116, 117, 183.
Teachers, 29, 30, 32, 33, 62, 158, 606.
Temperance Tales, 252.
Test and Corporation Act, England, 214.
Thompson, Samuel, 70.
Transfer of Property to Corporation, 151,
  165, 398.
  to Board of Education, 576–599.
  of Colored Schools to the Society, 674.
Tribute to Joseph Lancaster, 173.
Trinity Church, 25, 41.
Troy, Rev. Dr. R. C., Archbishop, 258,
  297.
Truancy, see *Vagrancy.*
Trustees, Classification of, 77, 80.
  Hall, 172, 177, 528, 647.
  to be Ward Trustees, 586.
Tuthill, James M., 61.

U.

Union of the Public School Society and
  Board of Education, 574, 576.

Universal Catechism, 44.
Untaught Children, see *Census* and *Vagrancy.*

V.

Vagrancy, 17, 87, 88, 111, 119, 122, 153,
  175, 193, 413, 601, 602, 615.
Van Blarcom, John, Donation, 29.
Van Wyck, William, 140.
Varela, Rev. Felix, 187, 325, 337, 346.
Venice, Republic of, 304.
Verplanck, Hon. Gulian C., see *Personal Index.*
Visit of General La Fayette, 84.
Visit of Common Council to Schools, 82.
  Legislature do., 44, 56.
Visitor Appointed, 119, 157, 615.
Vulté, Charles, 597.

W.

Wainwright, Rev. J. M., DD., 64.
Waldenses, 215.
Washington, George, Address, 288, 435.
  Hall, 350.
Webster, Charles R., 100.
Webster, Daniel, 246.
Wesley, John, 301, 313.
Wheeler, S., 70.
Whig Party, and Schools, 478, 496.
White, James W., 188, 189, 351.
Williams, Rev. John, 69.
Williams, Roger, 470.
Window, the Lighted, 310.
Workshop, 167, 612.

Y.

Yorkville School, 135.

OFFICERS AND TRUSTEES OF THE PUBLIC SCHOOL SOCIETY.

PERSONAL INDEX.

A.

Adams, John, 39, 46.
Adams, John T., 425, 534, 580, 586, 651,
  697.
Allen, Stephen, 60, 75, 85, 104, 105, 179,
  425, 618, 695, 699, 700, 701.
Aspinwall, Gilbert, 5, 6, 8.
Atterbury, Benjamin B., 586.
Averill, Augustin, 425, 587, 664.
Averill, Heman, 118, 153, 692, 694.

B.

Baldwin, Micah, 425, 708.
Barrow, H. H., 580, 586.
Bartlett, Caleb, 425.
Benedict, H. S., 533.
Benjamin, Meigs D., 425, 710.
Betts, George W., 425.
Birdsall, William, 425.
Blackstone, Wyllis, 586.
Blaisdell, James H., 425, 710.

AMERICAN EDUCATION:
ITS MEN, IDEAS, AND INSTITUTIONS
An Arno Press/New York Times Collection

Series I

Culver, Raymond B. **Horace Mann and Religion in the Massachusetts Public Schools.** 1929.

Curoe, Philip R. V. **Educational Attitudes and Policies of Organized Labor in the United States.** 1926.

Dabney, Charles William. **Universal Education in the South.** 1936.

Dearborn, Ned Harland. **The Oswego Movement in American Education.** 1925.

De Lima, Agnes. **Our Enemy the Child.** 1926.

Dewey, John. **The Educational Situation.** 1902.

Dexter, Franklin B., editor. **Documentary History of Yale University.** 1916.

Eliot, Charles William. **Educational Reform: Essays and Addresses.** 1898.

Ensign, Forest Chester. **Compulsory School Attendance and Child Labor.** 1921.

Fitzpatrick, Edward Augustus. **The Educational Views and Influence of De Witt Clinton.** 1911.

Fleming, Sanford. **Children & Puritanism.** 1933.

Flexner, Abraham. **The American College: A Criticism.** 1908.

Foerster, Norman. **The Future of the Liberal College.** 1938.

Gilman, Daniel Coit. **University Problems in the United States.** 1898.

Hall, Samuel R. **Lectures on School-Keeping.** 1829.

Hall, Stanley G. **Adolescence: Its Psychology and Its Relations to Physiology, Anthropology, Sociology, Sex, Crime, Religion, and Education.** 1905. 2 vols.

Hansen, Allen Oscar. **Early Educational Leadership in the Ohio Valley.** 1923.

Harris, William T. **Psychologic Foundations of Education.** 1899.

Harris, William T. **Report of the Committee of Fifteen on the Elementary School.** 1895.

Harveson, Mae Elizabeth. **Catharine Esther Beecher: Pioneer Educator.** 1932.

Jackson, George Leroy. **The Development of School Support in Colonial Massachusetts.** 1909.

Kandel, I. L., editor. **Twenty-five Years of American Education.** 1924.

Kemp, William Webb. **The Support of Schools in Colonial New York by the Society for the Propagation of the Gospel in Foreign Parts.** 1913.

Kilpatrick, William Heard. **The Dutch Schools of New Netherland and Colonial New York.** 1912.

Kilpatrick, William Heard. **The Educational Frontier.** 1933.

Knight, Edgar Wallace. **The Influence of Reconstruction on Education in the South.** 1913.

Le Duc, Thomas. **Piety and Intellect at Amherst College, 1865-1912.** 1946.

Maclean, John. **History of the College of New Jersey from Its Origin in 1746 to the Commencement of 1854.** 1877.

Maddox, William Arthur. **The Free School Idea in Virginia before the Civil War.** 1918.

Mann, Horace. **Lectures on Education.** 1855.

McCadden, Joseph J. **Education in Pennsylvania, 1801-1835, and Its Debt to Roberts Vaux.** 1855.

McCallum, James Dow. **Eleazar Wheelock.** 1939.

McCuskey, Dorothy. **Bronson Alcott, Teacher.** 1940.

Meiklejohn, Alexander. **The Liberal College.** 1920.

Miller, Edward Alanson. **The History of Educational Legislation in Ohio from 1803 to 1850.** 1918.

Miller, George Frederick. **The Academy System of the State of New York.** 1922.

Monroe, Will S. **History of the Pestalozzian Movement in the United States.** 1907.

Mosely Education Commission. **Reports of the Mosely Education Commission to the United States of America October-December, 1903.** 1904.

Mowry, William A. **Recollections of a New England Educator.** 1908.

Mulhern, James. **A History of Secondary Education in Pennsylvania.** 1933.

National Herbart Society. **National Herbart Society Yearbooks 1-5, 1895-1899.** 1895-1899.

Nearing, Scott. **The New Education: A Review of Progressive Educational Movements of the Day.** 1915.

Neef, Joseph. **Sketches of a Plan and Method of Education.** 1808.

Nock, Albert Jay. **The Theory of Education in the United States.** 1932.

Norton, A. O., editor. **The First State Normal School in America: The Journals of Cyrus Pierce and Mary Swift.** 1926.

Oviatt, Edwin. **The Beginnings of Yale, 1701-1726.** 1916.

Packard, Frederic Adolphus. **The Daily Public School in the United States.** 1866.

Page, David P. **Theory and Practice of Teaching.** 1848.

Parker, Francis W. **Talks on Pedagogics: An Outline of the Theory of Concentration.** 1894.

Peabody, Elizabeth Palmer. **Record of a School.** 1835.

Porter, Noah. **The American Colleges and the American Public.** 1870.

Reigart, John Franklin. **The Lancasterian System of Instruction in the Schools of New York City.** 1916.

Reilly, Daniel F. **The School Controversy (1891-1893).** 1943.

Rice, Dr. J. M. **The Public-School System of the United States.** 1893.

Rice, Dr. J. M. **Scientific Management in Education.** 1912.

Ross, Early D. **Democracy's College: The Land-Grant Movement in the Formative Stage.** 1942.

Rugg, Harold, et al. **Curriculum-Making: Past and Present.** 1926.

Rugg, Harold, et al. **The Foundations of Curriculum-Making.** 1926.

Rugg, Harold and Shumaker, Ann. **The Child-Centered School.** 1928.

Seybolt, Robert Francis. **Apprenticeship and Apprenticeship Education in Colonial New England and New York.** 1917.

Seybolt, Robert Francis. **The Private Schools of Colonial Boston.** 1935.

Seybolt, Robert Francis. **The Public Schools of Colonial Boston.** 1935.

Sheldon, Henry D. **Student Life and Customs.** 1901.

Sherrill, Lewis Joseph. **Presbyterian Parochial Schools, 1846-1870.** 1932 .

Siljestrom, P. A. **Educational Institutions of the United States.** 1853.

Small, Walter Herbert. **Early New England Schools.** 1914.

Soltes, Mordecai. **The Yiddish Press: An Americanizing Agency.** 1925.

Stewart, George, Jr. **A History of Religious Education in Connecticut to the Middle of the Nineteenth Century.** 1924.

Storr, Richard J. **The Beginnings of Graduate Education in America.** 1953.

Stout, John Elbert. **The Development of High-School Curricula in the North Central States from 1860 to 1918.** 1921.

Suzzallo, Henry. **The Rise of Local School Supervision in Massachusetts.** 1906.

Swett, John. **Public Education in California.** 1911.

Tappan, Henry P. **University Education.** 1851.

Taylor, Howard Cromwell. **The Educational Significance of the Early Federal Land Ordinances.** 1921.

Taylor, J. Orville. **The District School.** 1834.

Tewksbury, Donald G. **The Founding of American Colleges and Universities before the Civil War.** 1932.

Thorndike, Edward L. **Educational Psychology.** 1913-1914.

True, Alfred Charles. **A History of Agricultural Education in the United States, 1785-1925.** 1929.

True, Alfred Charles. **A History of Agricultural Extension Work in the United States, 1785-1923.** 1928.

Updegraff, Harlan. **The Origin of the Moving School in Massachusetts.** 1908.

Wayland, Francis. **Thoughts on the Present Collegiate System in the United States.** 1842.

Weber, Samuel Edwin. **The Charity School Movement in Colonial Pennsylvania.** 1905.

Wells, Guy Fred. **Parish Education in Colonial Virginia.** 1923.

Wickersham, J. P. **The History of Education in Pennsylvania.** 1885.

Woodward, Calvin M. **The Manual Training School.** 1887.

Woody, Thomas. **Early Quaker Education in Pennsylvania.** 1920.

Woody, Thomas. **Quaker Education in the Colony and State of New Jersey.** 1923.

Wroth, Lawrence C. **An American Bookshelf, 1755.** 1934.

Series II

Adams, Evelyn C. **American Indian Education.** 1946.

Bailey, Joseph Cannon. **Seaman A. Knapp: Schoolmaster of American Agriculture.** 1945.

Beecher, Catharine and Harriet Beecher Stowe. **The American Woman's Home.** 1869.

Benezet, Louis T. **General Education in the Progressive College.** 1943.

Boas, Louise Schutz. **Woman's Education Begins.** 1935.

Bobbitt, Franklin. **The Curriculum.** 1918.

Bode, Boyd H. **Progressive Education at the Crossroads.** 1938.

Bourne, William Oland. **History of the Public School Society of the City of New York.** 1870.

Bronson, Walter C. **The History of Brown University, 1764-1914.** 1914.

Burstall, Sara A. **The Education of Girls in the United States.** 1894.

Butts, R. Freeman. **The College Charts Its Course.** 1939.

Caldwell, Otis W. and Stuart A. Courtis. **Then & Now in Education, 1845-1923.** 1923.

Calverton, V. F. & Samuel D. Schmalhausen, editors. **The New Generation: The Intimate Problems of Modern Parents and Children.** 1930.

Charters, W. W. **Curriculum Construction.** 1923.

Childs, John L. **Education and Morals.** 1950.

Childs, John L. **Education and the Philosophy of Experimentalism.** 1931.

Clapp, Elsie Ripley. **Community Schools in Action.** 1939.

Counts, George S. **The American Road to Culture: A Social Interpretation of Education in the United States.** 1930.

Counts, George S. **School and Society in Chicago.** 1928.

Finegan, Thomas E. **Free Schools.** 1921.

Fletcher, Robert Samuel. **A History of Oberlin College.** 1943.

Grattan, C. Hartley. **In Quest of Knowledge: A Historical Perspective on Adult Education.** 1955.

Hartman, Gertrude & Ann Shumaker, editors. **Creative Expression.** 1932.

Kandel, I. L. **The Cult of Uncertainty.** 1943.

Kandel, I. L. **Examinations and Their Substitutes in the United States.** 1936.

Kilpatrick, William Heard. **Education for a Changing Civilization.** 1926.

Kilpatrick, William Heard. **Foundations of Method.** 1925.

Kilpatrick, William Heard. **The Montessori System Examined.** 1914.

Lang, Ossian H., editor. **Educational Creeds of the Nineteenth Century.** 1898.

Learned, William S. **The Quality of the Educational Process in the United States and in Europe.** 1927.

Meiklejohn, Alexander. **The Experimental College.** 1932.

Middlekauff, Robert. **Ancients and Axioms: Secondary Education in Eighteenth-Century New England.** 1963.

Norwood, William Frederick. **Medical Education in the United States Before the Civil War.** 1944.

Parsons, Elsie W. Clews. **Educational Legislation and Administration of the Colonial Governments.** 1899.

Perry, Charles M. **Henry Philip Tappan: Philosopher and University President.** 1933.

Pierce, Bessie Louise. **Civic Attitudes in American School Textbooks.** 1930.

Rice, Edwin Wilbur. **The Sunday-School Movement (1780-1917) and the American Sunday-School Union (1817-1917).** 1917.

Robinson, James Harvey. **The Humanizing of Knowledge.** 1924.

Ryan, W. Carson. **Studies in Early Graduate Education.** 1939.

Seybolt, Robert Francis. **The Evening School in Colonial America.** 1925.

Seybolt, Robert Francis. **Source Studies in American Colonial Education.** 1925.

Todd, Lewis Paul. **Wartime Relations of the Federal Government and the Public Schools, 1917-1918.** 1945.

Vandewalker, Nina C. **The Kindergarten in American Education.** 1908.

Ward, Florence Elizabeth. **The Montessori Method and the American School.** 1913.

West, Andrew Fleming. **Short Papers on American Liberal Education.** 1907.

Wright, Marion M. Thompson. **The Education of Negroes in New Jersey.** 1941.

Supplement

The Social Frontier (Frontiers of Democracy). Vols. 1-10, 1934-1943.